Neanderthals Among Mammoths

Excavations at Lynford Quarry, Norfolk

Edited by

William A Boismier, Clive Gamble and Fiona Coward

This volume is dedicated to

John Wymer and John Lord

for their contributions to Palaeolithic Archaeology
and the Prehistory of Norfolk

Neanderthals Among Mammoths

Excavations at Lynford Quarry, Norfolk

Edited by

William A Boismier, Clive Gamble and Fiona Coward

with contributions from

Julian Andrews, Stella Blockley, Don Brothwell, Matthew Collins, Russell Coope†,
Francesco d'Errico, Randy Donahue, Laure Dubreuil, Adrian Evans, Michael Field,
Charlie French, Christopher Gleed-Owen, Frances Green, Vaughan Grimes,
David Keen†, Nigel Larkin, Simon Lewis, Adrian Lister, Sonia O'Connor,
Kirsty Penkman, Richard Preece, Edward Rhodes, Michael Richards,
Danielle Schreve, Jean-Luc Schwenninger, Carol Simmonds,
Anthony Stuart, Keith Tovey and Mark White

Published by English Heritage, The Engine House, Fire Fly Avenue,
Swindon SN2 2EH
www.english-heritage.org.uk
English Heritage is the Government's statutory adviser on all aspects of the
historic environment.

© English Heritage 2012

[The views expressed in this book are those of the author[s] and not necessarily those of English Heritage.]

Images (except as otherwise shown) © English Heritage or © Crown copyright. NMR

First published 2012

ISBN 978-1-84802-063-4

Product code 51546

British Library Cataloguing in Publication data
A CIP catalogue record for this book is available from the British Library.

All rights reserved
No part of this publication may be reproduced or transmitted in any form or by any means, electronic or mechanical, including photocopying, recording, or any information storage or retrieval system, without permission in writing from the publisher.

Application for the reproduction of images should be made to the National Monuments Record. Every effort has been made to trace the copyright holders and we apologise in advance for any unintentional omissions, which we would be pleased to correct in any subsequent edition of this book.

The National Monuments Record is the public archive of English Heritage. For more information about English Heritage images, contact Archives Research Services, The Engine House, Fire Fly Avenue, Swindon SN2 2EH; telephone (01793) 414600.

Brought to publication by David M Jones, Publishing, English Heritage

Edited by Louise Wilson
Indexed by Fiona Coward
Page layout by Andrea Rollinson, Ledgard Jepson Ltd
Printed in the UK by 4edge Ltd, 7a Eldon Way, Eldon Way Industrial Estate, Hockley, Essex, SS5 4AD

CONTENTS

Contributors vi
Figures vii
Tables x
Acknowledgements xii
Illustration credits xiv
Summary xv
Résumé xvii
Zusammenfassung xix

1 The Lynford Middle Palaeolithic site

1.1 Background and excavation methods *by W A Boismier* 1
1.2 Faunal conservation *by S O'Connor and N Larkin* 14
1.3 Archive deposition 15

2 Stratigraphy, Association B and dating

2.1 Pleistocene stratigraphy and sedimentology
    by S G Lewis 17
2.2 Association B 32
   2.2.1 Description and stratigraphic succession
        by W A Boismier 32
   2.2.2 Micromorphology *by C French* 47
   2.2.3 Diagenetics *by J Andrews* 53
   2.2.4 Deposit compaction *by N K Tovey* 63
2.3 Dating the deposits and the archaeology 67
   2.3.1 Optically stimulated luminescence
        by J-L Schwenninger and E Rhodes 67
   2.3.2 Radiocarbon dating *by WA Boismier and
        A J Stuart* 70
   2.3.3 Amino-acid racemisation *by K Penkman
        and M Collins* 71
   2.3.4 Discussion *by W A Boismier and F M L Green* 72

3 Environmental evidence

3.1 The insect remains *by G Russell Coope†* 75
3.2 The molluscan assemblages *by D Keen†* 95
3.3 The pollen assemblages *by F M L Green* 101
3.4 Plant macrofossils *by M H Field* 126
3.5 Palaeoenvironmental interpretation of the vertebrate
    assemblage *by A J Stuart* 129

4 Deposit and assemblage formation *by W A Boismier*

4.1 Sedimentary deposits 135
4.2 Size sorting and mixing 138
4.3 Spatial patterning 143
4.4 Conclusions 153

5 The archaeological assemblages of animals and lithics

5.1 The vertebrate assemblage *by D C Schreve* with
    contributions *by D R Brothwell and A J Stuart* 157
5.2 Quantitative analysis of mammoth remains
    by A M Lister 205
5.3 The herpetofaunal remains *by C Gleed-Owen* 214
5.4 Stable isotope analysis (C, N, O) of faunal samples
    by M P Richards, V H Grimes and S M Blockley 216
5.5 The lithic assemblage *by M J White* 219
5.6 Microwear analysis of the flint artefacts: tool use
    by R E Donahue and A A Evans 261
5.7 The sandstone block *by F d'Errico, J Andrews and
    L Dubreuil* 274

6 The Lynford Neanderthals
by C Gamble and W A Boismier 283

Appendix 1: Conservation of the faunal remains 297
Appendix 2: Detailed thin section descriptions 311
Appendix 3: Consolidation booking sheets 313
Appendix 4: Detailed vertebrate assemblage: tables 316
Appendix 5: Concordance list of context numbers 493
Glossary 500
References 506
Index 525

CONTRIBUTORS

Julian E Andrews, School of Environmental Sciences, University of East Anglia, Norwich NR4 7TJ, UK. Email: j.andrews@uea.ac.uk

Stella Blockley, Department of Geography, Royal Holloway University of London, Egham, Surrey TW20 0EX, UK. Email: stella.blockley@googlemail.com

William Boismier, Northamptonshire Archaeology, 2 Bolton House, Wootton Hall Park, Northampton, NN3 8BE, UK. Email: BBoismier@northamptonshire.gov.uk

D Brothwell, Department of Archaeology, The King's Manor, York YO1 7EP, UK.

Matthew Collins, BioArch Biology, S Block, PO Box 373, York YO10 5YW, UK. Email: mc80@york.ac.uk

F Coward, Department of Geography, Royal Holloway University of London, Egham, Surrey TW20 0EX, UK. Email: Fiona.Coward@rhul.ac.uk

G Russell Coope[†], formerly of the School of Geography, Earth and Environmental Sciences, University of Birmingham, Edgbaston, Birmingham B15 2TT, UK.

Francesco d'Errico, CNRS UMR 5199 PACEA, Université Bordeaux 1, avenue des Facultés, F-33405 Talence, France. Email: f.derrico@ipgq.u-bordeaux1.fr

R E Donahue, School of Life Sciences, University of Bradford, Richmond Road, Bradford, West Yorkshire BD7 1DP, UK. Email: r.e.donahue@bradford.ac.uk

L Dubreuil, Department of Anthropology, Trent University, 1600 West Bank Drive, Peterborough K9J 7B8, Ontario, Canada. Email: lauredubreuil@trentu.ca

A A Evans, Archaeological, Geographical and Environmental Sciences, University of Bradford, Bradford, West Yorkshire BD7 1DP, UK. Email: A.A.Evans@bradford.ac.uk

M H Field, Faculty of Archaeology, Leiden University, PO Box 9515, 2300 RA Leiden, The Netherlands. Email: m.h.field@arch.leidenuniv.nl

Charlie French, Department of Archaeology, University of Cambridge, Downing Street, Cambridge CB2 3ER, UK. Email: caif2@cam.ac.uk

Clive Gamble, Faculty of Humanities (Archaeology), Building 65A, Avenue Campus, University of Southampton, Southampton SO17 1BF. Email: Clive.Gamble@soton.ac.uk

C Gleed-Owen, CGO Ecology Ltd, 5 Cranbourne House, 12 Knole Road, Bournemouth BH1 4DQ, UK. Email: chris@cgoecology.com

Frances Green, Sunnyside, Dilham Road, Worstead, North Walsham, Norfolk NR28 9RJ, UK. Email: fran.green@sunbeam.dircon.co.uk

Vaughan Grimes, Department of Archaeology, Memorial University, St. John's, Newfoundland A1C 5S7, Canada. Email: vgrimes@mun.ca

D Keen[†], formerly of the Department of Archaeology, University of Birmingham, Edgbaston, Birmingham B15 2TT, UK

Nigel Larkin, Norfolk Museums and Archaeology Service, Shirehall, Market Avenue, Norwich, Norfolk NR1 3JQ, UK. Email: nrlarkin@easynet.co.uk

Simon G Lewis, Queen Mary University of London, University of London, Mile End Road, London E1 4NS, UK. Email: s.lewis@qmul.ac.uk

Adrian M Lister, Department of Palaeontology, The Natural History Museum, London SW7 5BD, UK. Email: a.lister@nhm.ac.uk

Sonia O'Connor, Archaeological Sciences, University of Bradford, Richmond Road, Bradford, West Yorkshire BD7 1DP, UK. Email: S.Oconnor@Bradford.ac.uk

Kirsty Penkman, BioArCh, Department of Chemistry, University of York, York YO10 5DD, UK. Email: kp9@york.ac.uk

R Preece, University Museum of Zoology, Downing Street, Cambridge CB2 3EJ, UK. Email: rcp1001@cam.ac.uk

E Rhodes, Environmental and Geographical Sciences, Manchester Metropolitan University, Chester Street, Manchester M1 5GD, UK. Email: e.rhodes@mmu.ac.uk

Michael Richards, Department of Human Evolution, Max Planck Institute for Evolutionary Anthropology, Deutscher Platz 6, Leipzig, Germany D-04103. Email: richards@eva.mpg.de

Danielle C Schreve, Department of Geography, Royal Holloway University of London, Egham, Surrey TW20 0EX, UK. Email: Danielle.Schreve@rhul.ac.uk

Jean-Luc Schwenninger, Research Laboratory for Archaeology and the History of Art, Dyson Perrins Building, South Parks Road, Oxford OX1 3QY, UK. Email: jean-luc.schwenninger@rlaha.ox.ac.uk

Carol Simmonds, Northamptonshire Archaeology 2 Bolton House, Wootton Hall Park, Northampton NN3 8BE, UK. Email: CSimmonds@northamptonshire.gov.uk

A J Stuart, Biological and Biomedical Sciences, Durham University, South Road, Durham DH1 3LE, UK. Email: tony.s@megafauna.org.uk

N Keith Tovey, School of Environmental Sciences, University of East Anglia, Norwich NR4 7TJ, UK. Email: k.tovey@uea.ac.uk

Mark J White, Department of Archaeology, Durham University, Durham DH1 3LE, UK. Email: m.j.white@durham.ac.uk

FIGURES

1.1 Lynford quarry in its national and regional setting 2
1.2 The site prior to start of excavation 10
1.3 Mechanical excavation of the site 10
1.4 Site plan of quarry showing excavation area and test pit locations 12
1.5 Plan of excavation area 13
1.6 Mammoth mandible 50287 in its jacket 15
2.1 Location of study site: limits for MIS 12; MIS 2 and Loch Lomond glaciations, regional geology and drainage, Wissey catchment and sites mentioned in text 16
2.2 Long profile of the River Wissey. Top and base of succession at Lynford and Wretton also shown 18
2.3 Generalised N-S geological cross-section through the site, based on BGS geological mapping and boreholes 19
2.4 Schematic diagram showing relationship of major facies (contexts) within Facies Association B, based on field data 24
2.5 Ternary plot of sand, silt and clay content of samples from Facies Association B 26
2.6 Summary of changes in particle size, organic carbon and carbonate content in four profiles through Association B 27
2.7 Stages in the development of the fluvial succession at Lynford 31
2.8 Part of Harris matrix for Association B (northern part of channel) 34
2.9 North-facing central baulk section ....between pp36 & 37
2.10 South-facing central baulk section ....between pp36 & 37
2.11 West-facing central baulk section ......between pp36 & 37
2.12 East-facing central baulk section ......between pp36 & 37
2.13 Schematic type section for Association B 36
2.14 Distribution of sediment gravity flows 37
2.15 Downwarped and diagenetically altered sediments of Association B-ii underlying bounding surface for Association B-iii. West-facing section, central control baulk 38
2.16 Unit B-ii:01 Trough cross-bedded sands (3-D dunes). West-facing section, north-west control baulk 39
2.17 Stony organic sand forming part of Unit B-ii04A. East-facing section, N-S central control baulk 41
2.18 Unit B-ii:04B Sediment gravity flow (debris flow) along north edge of channel. East-facing section, north-west control baulk 41
2.19 Unit B-ii:04C Sediment gravity flow (stony sand) along north edge of channel. East-facing section 42

2.20 Localised slumping of Unit B-ii:04A gravel facies on south side of channel 42
2.21 Unit B-ii:05 Small mid-channel sand bar overlying the organic sediments of B-ii:03. South-facing section, E–W central control baulk 43
2.22 Unit B-ii:05 Lateral infill sediments. East-facing section, south-west control baulk 43
2.23 Photomicrograph of organic fine sandy loam with fine impure clay in B-ii:03 48
2.24 Photomicrograph of laminar, fine sandy, bioturbated organic fabric in B-ii:01 49
2.25 Photomicrograph of amorphous iron-impregnated fine sand with bioturbated organic matter, plant tissue and charcoal fragments in B-ii:03 49
2.26 Photomicrograph of lens of sandy clay at the B-ii:03/01 contact 50
2.27 Photomicrograph of lens of sandy clay with very fine charcoal at the B-ii:03/01 contact 50
2.28 Photomicrograph of bioturbated plant tissue in B-ii:03 (frame width = 2.25mm; plane-polarised light) 51
2.29 Photomicrograph of amorphous iron impregnated sandy clay lens with micro-charcoal in B-ii:01 51
2.30 Photomicrograph of alternating lenses of fine sand, partially humified organic matter and calcium carbonate in B-ii:01 52
2.31 Mean grain size plotted against depth (OD) 57
2.32 Skewness plotted against depth (OD) 58
2.33 Kurtosis plotted against depth (OD) 58
2.34 Wt% organic carbon plotted against depth (OD) 59
2.35 Wt% $CaCO_3$ plotted against depth (OD) 60
2.36 Wt% Corg/Ntot plotted against depth (OD) 60
2.37 Stable carbon isotope ratio of bulk organic matter plotted against depth (OD) 61
2.38 Stable nitrogen isotope ratio of bulk organic matter plotted against depth (OD) 62
2.39 Consolidation curve for sample 1a 65
2.40 Consolidation curve for sample 1b 65
2.41 Consolidation curve for sample 1c 65
2.42 Consolidation data from Lynford compared with samples from elsewhere 66
2.43 Comparison of amino-acid concentrations from *Planorbis* (diamonds) and *Pupilla* (circles) from unbleached and bleached samples 72
2.44 The GISP2 ice-core δ 18O record 73
3.1 Schematic section illustrating pollen sample locations within the palaeochannels 102
3.2 Pollen percentage data (>1%) Lynford Quarry (37095 STD) sample 30168 104

3.3	Pollen percentage data (>1%) Lynford Quarry (37095 STD) sample 30238 112		5.17	Proximal midshaft fragment of left metatarsal (50929) of *Bison priscus*, posterior view 176
3.4	Pollen percentage data (>1%) Lynford Quarry (37095 STD) sample 30257 121		5.18	R and L M3 of *Mammuthus primigenius* (50069 and 50273), buccal view 177
4.1	Tusk partially embedded in the massive sands of Unit B-ii:01 136		5.19	R and L m3 of *Mammuthus primigenius* (51953–51648–51154 and 50656a), lingual view 177
4.2	Lenses and layers of stony organic sand within the organic sediments of Unit B-ii:03 137		5.20	R and L M1 of *Mammuthus primigenius* (51171 and 51201), buccal view 178
4.3	Vertical distribution of materials within the sediments of Association B-ii 139		5.21	Associated R and L second molars of *Mammuthus primigenius* (50002–50003 and 50358–51730), buccal view 178
4.4	Vertical size sorting showing size class means and standard deviations 141		5.22	Tusks of *Mammuthus primigenius* in the main palaeochannel during excavation 179
4.5	Vertical mixing showing size class medians and spreads 142		5.23	Proximal L radius of *Mammuthus primigenius* (51903), posterior view 179
4.6	Distribution of artefacts and vertebrate remains within the sediments of Association B-ii 145		5.24	Proximal R ulna of *Mammuthus primigenius* (51976), anterior view 180
4.7	Cluster 1 146		5.25	Distribution of individual vertebrate finds within the main palaeochannel 183
4.8	Cluster 2 147		5.26	Distribution of refitting and associated vertebrate finds within the main palaeochannel 185
4.9	Cluster 3 149		5.27	Pie chart showing the relative frequency of finds according to size class (1 = 0–30mm diameter; 2 = 30–60mm; 3 = 60–90mm; 4 = 90–120mm; 5 = 120–150mm; 6 >150mm) 186
4.10	Cluster 4 150			
4.11	Cluster 5 152			
4.12	Cluster 6 154			
5.1	Partial right ulna of *Canis lupus* (51860), anterior view 167		5.28	R M1 of *Mammuthus primigenius* (51240), showing polishing along lingual margin, occlusal view 189
5.2	Associated L m1 (51212) and R m1 (51726) of *Ursus arctos*, lingual view 168		5.29	R M1 of *Mammuthus primigenius* (51240), showing polishing along lingual margin, lingual view 189
5.3	L m2 (50558) of *Ursus arctos*, lingual view 168		5.30	Second phalanx of *Mammuthus primigenius* (50733), showing carnivore puncture mark near proximal end, lateral view 190
5.4	Second phalanx of *Crocuta crocuta* (anterior view) ... 169			
5.5	L m3 (50000) of *Mammuthus primigenius*, lingual view 170		5.31	First phalanx of *Rangifer tarandus* (50212), showing carnivore puncture mark near proximal end, lateral view 190
5.6	L M3 (50001) of *Mammuthus primigenius*, lingual view 170			
5.7	Crushed maxilla with R M2 *in situ* (51619) of *Mammuthus primigenius*, lingual view 170		5.32	Tibia diaphysis of juvenile *Coelodonta antiquitatis* (51374), heavily gnawed by spotted hyaena, anterior view 191
5.8	R M1 (51440) of *Mammuthus primigenius*, occlusal view 170		5.33	Digested R dp2 of *Rangifer tarandus* (50795), lingual view 191
5.9	R calcaneum (51869) of *Equus ferus*, proximal view .. 172			
5.10	Distal R femur (51360) of *Equus ferus*, posterior view 172		5.34	Juvenile neural spine (species undetermined, 51392), showing severe pathological deformation at its base .. 192
5.11	Occlusal view of R DP4 (51401) of *Coelodonta antiquitatis* 173			
5.12	Occlusal view of L P3 (50491) of *Coelodonta antiquitatis* 173		5.35	Rib of *Mammuthus primigenius* (51179), showing healed rib fracture, lateral view 193
5.13	Antler beam with two tines (50096) of *Rangifer tarandus*, lateral view 174		5.36	Neural spine of *Mammuthus primigenius* (50853), showing erosive lesion at base, posterior view 194
5.14	L p4 (51322) of *Rangifer tarandus*, buccal view 175			
5.15	L p4 (51322) of *Rangifer tarandus*, occlusal view 175		5.37	Rib fragment (51973), lateral view, showing evidence of infection 194
5.16	Left metacarpal (50869) of *Rangifer tarandus*, anterior view 175			

#	Caption	Page
5.38	Rib fragment (51955), lateral view, showing evidence of infection	194
5.39	Rib fragment (52007), lateral view, showing evidence of infection	194
5.40	Fused caudal vertebrae (51449) showing evidence of massive low-grade infection, dorsal view	195
5.41	Fused caudal vertebrae (51449) showing evidence of massive low-grade infection, lateral view	195
5.42	Long-bone fragments of *Rangifer tarandus* with green bone fractures, external lateral view	198
5.43	Long-bone fragments of *Rangifer tarandus* with green bone fractures, internal lateral view	198
5.44	Fragment of L humerus diaphysis of *Rangifer tarandus* bearing signs of impact fracture to right hand side, external lateral view	199
5.45	R m3 and R lower cheek tooth of *Equus ferus* (51631 and 51612) showing evidence of breakage	200
5.46	Partial thoracic vertebra of *Mammuthus primigenius* (50075) with fragment of central epiphysis of preceding vertebra attached, anterior view	201
5.47	Plate number (excluding talons and platelets) in third molars, upper and lower teeth combined	209
5.48	Width versus lamellar frequency in upper third molars from Lynford (squares), in comparison with last glaciation *Mammuthus primigenius* samples from Předmosti (circles) and the Lea Valley Gravels (triangles)	210
5.49	Age structure of the Lynford mammoth assemblage based on molariform teeth	212
5.50	Growth of the humerus in *Mammuthus primigenius* from the Russian Plain, in comparison with the juvenile specimen from Lynford (51885)	213
5.51	$\delta^{13}C$ and $\delta^{15}N$ isotope ratios of collagen extracted from bone and dentine of mammoth samples from Lynford Quarry	218
5.52	Size distribution of débitage from Lynford plotted against Schick's experimental data	224
5.53	Wenban-Smith's experimental flake data compared to Lynford association B-ii	224
5.54	Orientation plot for plotted artefacts from the main palaeochannel	224
5.55	Distribution of refitted flakes from the Palaeochannel	226
5.56	Handaxe shaping flakes	229
5.57	Comparison of cortex percentage frequency between Lynford Association B-ii and Ashton's experimental series	330
5.58	Size-adjusted scar counts (dorsal scar counts divided by length) for flakes from the main palaeochannel compared to Wenban-Smith's experimental series	233
5.59	Cores	236
5.60	Handaxes: *Bout coupé* (40170); Large pointed cordiforms (40548, 40591)	237
5.61	Allometric length:width relationship for handaxes from B-ii	240
5.62a–i	Tripartite Diagrams for the Lynford handaxes	241
5.63	Handaxes 40018, 40265, 40416 and 40541	243
5.64	Handaxes 40016, 40354 and 40383	244
5.65	Handaxes 40544, 40019, 40481, 40015 and 40100	246
5.66	Edge length and percentage of retouch for handaxes with scraper-type retouch	248
5.67	Mean maximum length of handaxes with and without scraper-type retouch, with 1 SD	248
5.68	Flake tools: 40259, 40278, 40410, 40470, 40498 and 40551	249
5.69	Flake tools: 40401, 40571, 40596 and 40468	250
5.70	Mild particulate polishing	262
5.71	Natural severe wear	267
5.72	Bright spots on artefacts 40265 and 40497	268
5.73	Artefact 40410: a convergent convex side scraper	269
5.74	Artefact 40100: a biface fragment	269
5.75	Mean and standard errors of dorsal ridge rounding for each context	271
5.76	Ideal sequence of wear processes	271
5.77	Different aspects of the sandstone block 40472	275
5.78a–d	Sandstone block: depressions with residues	276
5.79a–c	Microscopic appearance of the sandstone block and depression D1 after cleaning	277
5.80a–b	SEM micrograph of a quartz crystal from depression 1 on face a	278
5.81a–b	Groove longitudinally crossing face a	278
5.82a–c	SEM micrograph of the groove on face a	278
5.83a–f	Micrographs of residues on the Lynford sandstone	279
5.84a–h	Results of the EDS microanalysis	281
6.1	Local site catchment	287
6.2	Regional site catchment	288
6.3	The classical model of socioecology	292
A1.1–A1.5	The mammoth tusks *in situ* during excavations at Lynford	298
A1.6a–b	Mammoth rib 50163	300
A1.7a–c	Antler fragment 51814t	303
A1.8	Rib 51635 after conservation and packing	304
A1.9a–b	Mammoth mandible 50287	307
A1.10	Storage support for rib 50l63	309

TABLES

1.1	Data for sites and localities from the UK with evidence for occupation during MIS 3 6		4.5	Size class summary statistics (non-parametric) 142
1.2	Block number allocations for record types 11		4.6	Cluster descriptions 144
1.3	Summary of record types contained within the excavation archive 12		4.7	Object orientations 146
2.1	Lithostratigraphy of the sedimentary succession at Lynford 19		4.8	Summary of cluster vertebrate data 148
2.2	Particle size, organic carbon and carbonate analyses of Lynford sediments 21		4.9	Summary of artefacts and humanly modified vertebrate remains 151
2.3	Clast lithological analysis of gravel facies from Lynford .. 22		4.10	Summary of condition of artefacts and humanly modified vertebrate remains 153
2.4	Summary of sedimentological characteristics of Association B 23		4.11	Cluster refit data 155
2.5	Summary of textural, organic carbon and carbonate characteristics of selected contexts within Association B .. 26		5.1	Minimum numbers of individuals per taxon 159
2.6	Components of Association B and their subdivisions with constituent context numbers 35		5.2	Abundance and percentage data based on 2091 vertebrate finds with context data 161
2.7	Sediment gravity flows 40		5.3	Measurements of *Spermophilus* sp. 166
2.8	The locations and contexts of the soil micromorphological samples 46		5.4	Measurements of *Microtus gregalis* 167
2.9	Summary of the basal channel fill characteristics by context and facies association/component 47		5.5	Measurements of *Canis lupus* 167
2.10	Samples for environmental characterisation 54		5.6	Measurements of *Ursus arctos* 168
2.11	Grain size analysis 57		5.7	Measurements of *Equus ferus* 171
2.12	Basic data of the geotechnical samples 64		5.8	Measurements of *Coelodonta antiquitatis* 173
2.13	Summary information from consolidation tests on subsamples 1a, 1b and 1c 66		5.9	Measurements of *Rangifer tarandus* 175
2.14	Lynford OSL sample details 68		5.10	Measurements of *Bison priscus* 175
2.15	Lynford final OSL dates 68		5.11	Potential of different bones for dispersal by water according to Voorhies Groups, compared to body-part representation at Lynford 184
2.16	Results of the AMS radiocarbon dating of faunal material 70		5.12	Weathering categories for large mammal bones (after Behrensmeyer 1978) and small mammal bones (after Andrews 1990) and inferred length of exposure in years before burial 188
3.1	The coleoptera from sedimenary Facies Association B .. 78		5.13	Number and distribution of abraded specimens according to context 189
3.2	Mollusca consolidated faunal list 95		5.14	Summary of the Lynford mammoth specimens showing evidence of pathology or pseudopathology, classified under major disease categories 193
3.3	Sample 30198 96			
3.4	Sample 30231 96		5.15	Spirally fractured limb bones of reindeer from Lynford compared with Morrison's marrow utility index 199
3.5	Sample 30228 97		5.16	Identification, measurements and ageing of molariform teeth from Lynford 206
3.6	Samples 63201, 30001, 30081, 61413 and 30083 98			
3.7	Sample 30201 98		5.17	Potential matches or mismatches among all possible combinations of teeth (or tooth pairs) 209
3.8	Sample 30234 98			
3.9	Total pollen and spores from Lynford Quarry, sample 30168 105		5.18	One of several possible combinations of teeth that, based on Table 5.2, constitute the minimum of 11 individuals, with their individual and averaged ages 210
3.10	Total pollen and spore counts from Lynford Quarry, sample 30238 113		5.19	Identifiable mammoth bones for which useful measurements could be taken, in comparison with individuals of known sex from other localities 211
3.11	Total pollen and spore counts from Lynford Quarry, sample 30257 122			
3.12	Plant macrofossil assemblages from profile 37095 127		5.20	Samples taken for isotopic analysis with bone and dentine collagen C and N isotope ratios 217
4.1	Size class data used in the analysis 139			
4.2	Results of the multiple regression 140		5.21	Oxygen isotope results of mammoth enamel and dentine (tusk) 218
4.3	Results of the analysis of variance 140			
4.4	Size class summary statistics (parametric) 141			

5.22	Lithic artefacts from Lynford, by facies association and context	220		
5.23	Basic inventory of artefacts from Lynford by facies association	221		
5.24	Condition of excavated or sieved flint artefacts >20mm, from selected contexts	223		
5.25	Refitting artefacts from Lynford, with stratigraphical association	225		
5.26	Artefact totals from Association B-ii	228		
5.27	Break types on fresh flakes from Association B-ii i	228		
5.28	Summary metrical statistics for fresh flakes >20mm	230		
5.29	Technological attributes of fresh flakes >20mm from Association B-i	231		
5.30	Comparison of cortex percentage for Lynford with experimental datasets	232		
5.31	Dorsal scar counts on soft hammer flakes, compared with Ashton's data	232		
5.32	Size-adjusted dorsal scar counts for Lynford compared to Wenban-Smith's experimental data	233		
5.33	Technological attributes of rolled flakes >20mm from Association B-ii	234		
5.34	Summary metrical statistics for rolled flakes >20mm from Association B-ii	235		
5.35	Technology of the cores from Association B-ii	235		
5.36	Condition of the complete handaxes from the main channel deposits	238		
5.37	Typology of all complete handaxes, by stratigraphical grouping	238		
5.38	Metrical and typological data for complete handaxes from Association B-ii	239		
5.39	Summary metrical data for excavated complete handaxes from B-ii	240		
5.40	Results of two-tailed Students' t-test on selected metrical indices of handaxes from B-ii:01 and B-ii:03	242		
5.41	Selected attributes of complete handaxes from B-ii:01, B-ii:03 and B-ii combined	245		
5.42	Retouch zones on excavated complete handaxes from B-ii	247		
5.43	Flake tools by stratigraphic group for all contexts	250		
5.44	Summary of flake tools from B-ii	250		
5.45	Summary metrical data for scrapers from Association B-ii	250		
5.46	Scrapers with butt removal/thinning, thinned backs or some level of bifacial working	251		
5.47	Catalogue of finds analysed with comments on use, ridge measurements and phases of post-depositional disturbance	263		
5.48	Inter-quartile distance values for all contexts for a given episode	272		
6.1	A comparison of Lynford and the Gravettian locale of Milovice	286		
6.2	Tolerances and preferences for selected climatic parameters among Neanderthals (Mousterian) and Modern humans (Aurignacian and Gravettian) in MIS 3 Europe	295		
A3.1	Consolidation booking sheet for test on Sample 1a	313		
A3.2	Consolidation booking sheet for test on Sample 1b	314		
A3.3	Consolidation booking sheet for test on sample 1c	315		
A4.1	Bulk and environmental samples	316		
A4.2	Wet-sieved residues	321		
A4.3	Dry-sieved residues	343		
A4.4	Individual vertebrate finds	388		
A5.1	Concordance list of context numbers	493		

ACKNOWLEDGEMENTS

The fieldwork described in this volume is the result of the efforts of a large number of people to whom Bill Boismier owes huge debts of gratitude. Particular thanks are due to Ian Findlater and to Mel Williams of Ayton Asphalte for allowing the Norfolk Archaeological Unit to undertake the excavation of the site despite the commercial pressure they were under. Mel and the rest of the staff at Lynford Quarry made the team feel welcome and provided assistance in countless ways throughout the five months of excavation. Forest Enterprise, the owner of the land, is also thanked for its interest and support. The project was funded by English Heritage through the Aggregates Levy Sustainability Fund and particular thanks are due to Kath Buxton, Chris Scull, Catherine Eady, Suzanne Bode, Helen Keeley and Kim Stabler.

Many thanks are owed to Dave Robertson (Site Supervisor), Fran Green (Site Environmentalist) and Sandrine Etienne (Finds Assistant) for their hard work throughout the excavation and post-excavation stages of the project, without which the record for the site would not have been so thorough. Special thanks are also due to John Lord and the late John Wymer for their support and advice, and to Nigel Larkin for his assistance in contacting specialists and undertaking the on-site conservation of faunal remains, assisted by the 'plaster casters' Rebecca Crawford and Laura Stockley. Nigel also carried out the on-site wet sieving with the assistance, later on, of Dennis Payne. The other members of the excavation team who are owed a debt of gratitude include Claire Atton, Michael Boyle, Brian Dean, Maggie Footitt, Aaron Goodie, Rachael Grahame, Jayne Harrison, Richard Jackson, Richard Jennings, Caroline Kemp, Sarah McGourman, Kevin Milner, Imogen Mowday, Felix Riede, Ester Roberts, Kate Russell, Phil Rye, Richard Sims, Amy Thomson, Kerry Tyler, Peter Warsop and Ailsa Westgarth. Kate Russell is also 'mentioned in dispatches' for her commitment and work during the excavation and post-excavation phases of the project. Mark Lewis and Sylvia Warman are also thanked for their work on the wet sieve residues, as is Andy Currant for providing facilities at the Natural History Museum for the work. Sandrine Etienne and Dave Robertson are thanked for initially preparing the line and CAD illustrations and Jeff Wallis for the superb artefact drawings. Amir Bassir helped in stitching together section photos, and the skill of Carol Simmonds in finalising the various line and CAD illustrations and preparing new ones for the volume is much appreciated. Pat Walsh is also thanked for the scanning of a number of illustrations. The work of Theodora Anastasiadou-Leigh in preparing the site archive is acknowledged, as is that of Jonathan Elston and James Ladocha on various archival elements of the project. The post-excavation project would not have proceeded so smoothly without Steve Parry's support, patience and timely advice.

The support and interest of Andrew Hutcheson and David Gurney of Norfolk Landscape Archaeology, the curatorial section of the Norfolk Museums and Archaeology Service is also warmly acknowledged. The students who worked on the lithic and faunal assemblages as part of their research are thanked for the many interesting discussions regarding assemblage patterning: in particular Kate Russell, Geoff Smith, Anita Antoniadou and Tom Cutter. Geoff's work in particular is graciously acknowledged.

Finally Bill would like to thank all the specialists who have contributed to this report.

During the production of this volume Clive Gamble was indebted to the support from Kath Buxton, Helen Keeley, Tim Cromack and Kim Stabler of English Heritage and at Royal Holloway to Martin Kelly and Alice Christie for enterprise and accounting expertise. The time given so generously by so many people to answer queries and test ideas made the task of editing both easier and enjoyable, and special thanks go to Nick Ashton, Scott Elias, Simon Armitage, Fiona Coward, Robert Foley, Robin Dunbar, John Gowlett and Amber Johnson as well as to all the contributors to this volume. The additional research in chapter 6 was supported by the British Academy Centenary Project and the NERC Megafaunal Extinctions Project.

Charlie French thanks Julie Boreham for producing the thin section slides while Julian Andrews thanks Simon Kelly and Sarah Dennis who did the isotopic analyses, and Rick Bryant who did the grain size analyses. Danielle Schreve gratefully acknowledges assistance with processing bulk samples and sorting spit residues from Mark Lewis, Kate Russell and Sylvia Warman. Information on size classes and weathering on much of the material was provided by Sophie Williams as part of an MSc Quaternary Science dissertation undertaken in the Department of Geography at Royal Holloway, University of London in 2003. Pierre Schreve is warmly thanked for his general assistance, help with the databases and curatorial skills, and Andy Currant for staunch support and useful discussion. Finally, thanks must go to Phil Crabb of the Natural History Museum Photographic Unit for providing the images.

Anthony Stuart is grateful to the Natural Environment Research Council for funding research on megafaunal extinctions in northern Eurasia, and to Tom Higham and the staff at the Oxford Radiocarbon Accelerator Unit for the radiocarbon dates on mammoth material from Lynford. Adrian Lister thanks Danielle Schreve for the invitation to study the Lynford mammoths and facilitating the research, and Evgeny Maschenko for discussion of juvenile mammoths. Chris Gleed-Owen thanks Danielle Schreve and sample processing volunteers for their much-appreciated help. Sonia O'Connor would like to thank the conservators Diane Charlton, Leesa Vere-Stevens, Cynthia Lampert and Nigel Larkin; archaeologist Will Higgs helped particularly in the excavation of many of the jacketed pieces, and Kirsten Ward designed the database for the project. She thanks all the members of the conservation team for their comments on the conservation report, and the staff at Archaeological Sciences for their support and for sharing their expertise. The photographs used in this report and held in the project archive were taken by different team members and are used with their permission.

David Keen's death on April 16th 2006 robbed Quaternary studies of one of its leading scientists and we sorely missed the opportunity to draw on his knowledge and advice during the editing of this volume. David's chapter was commented on by Richard Preece, to whom we are very grateful, while the details on amino-acid dating were provided by Kirsty Penkman and Matthew Collins.

ILLUSTRATION CREDITS AND COPYRIGHT

W A Boismier: 1.2–1.3, 2.15–2.22, 4.1–4.2
D Charlton: 1.6, A1.8, A1.9a, A1.9b
P Crabb, Natural History Museum Photographic Unit: 5.1–5.21, 5.23–5.24, 5.28–5.46
C French: 2.23–2.30
N Larkin/Phil Rye: 5.22, A1.1–A1.5
S O'Connor: A1.6a–A1.7c, A1.10
D Payne: back cover image
J Wallis: 5.56, 5.59–5.60, 5.63–5.65, 5.68–5.69
All other illustrations produced by Carol Simmonds from originals and from data supplied by the author(s) of the relevant sections.

SUMMARY

During an archaeological watching brief undertaken in the early spring of 2002 at Lynford Quarry, near the village of Munford in Norfolk, UK, John Lord uncovered the *in situ* remains of mammoth bones and associated Mousterian stone tools. These were contained within a palaeochannel rich in organic sediments. The importance of the site was immediately recognised, and with the support of Ayton Asphalte, the quarry owners, and English Heritage, an excavation took place between April and September of the same year funded through the Aggregates Levy Sustainability Fund.

The excavation recovered exceptionally well-preserved archaeological and palaeoenvironmental information. Such opportunities are extremely rare in the British Middle Palaeolithic when Neanderthals, making distinctive *bout coupé* handaxes (bifaces), intermittently occupied what was then a peninsula of north-west Europe. The association of many woolly mammoth bones, together with a wealth of palaeoenvironmental data, resulted in a unique opportunity to investigate questions of diet, land use and habitat from deposits within a small geological feature and subject the results to rigorous taphonomic and geoarchaeological scrutiny.

The organic silts and sands that fill the palaeochannel contain a cold-stage mammalian assemblage rich in mammoth remains, and an associated Mousterian flint industry. A series of optically stimulated luminescence (OSL) ages places the deposition of the main channel sediments in the interval c 65–57ka, at the transition between Marine Isotope Stages (MIS) 4 and 3. Studies of plant and invertebrate remains indicate open conditions dominated by grasses, sedges and low-growing herbaceous communities, with small stands of birch or scrub, and areas of acid heath or bog. These proxies also indicate a relatively mild climate, with mean July temperatures of up to 14°C and winters of –8° to –15°C. The most likely age of the deposits is therefore early MIS 3, that is, marked by the Dansgaard-Oeschger (D-O) interstadials 14–17. Both beetle and pollen evidence point to many similarities between the interstadial at Lynford and the Upton Warren site in Worcestershire – placing it in one of the most important interstadials in the last cold stage in Britain.

At the time of deposition the channel is interpreted as having been a meander cut-off, or oxbow, with still or very slow-flowing water. Large objects, such as bones, entered the channel periodically from the adjacent land surface by processes such as bank collapse. None of the bank areas were preserved, so reconstructions of hominin behaviour have to be inferred from a detailed study of the faunal and lithic remains, combined with taphonomic assessments derived from an analysis of the sediments.

Most of the archaeological material was excavated from deposits referred to as Association B and divided into three main components. These represent depositional phases in the history of the cut-off: B-i, the lowermost, contains sands and gravels that were deposited before the channel became a cut-off; B-ii is characterised by organic silts and sands representing an inactive phase in the cut-off's history during which most of the mammoth bones and artefacts were deposited by slumping; B-iii is a final phase composed of fine and coarse sands and gravels that mark a return to conditions of flowing water. The palaeoenvironmental indicators from B-ii also point to bioturbation, possibly by megafauna.

The faunal assemblage from Association B consists of 1,365 identified specimens of which 91 per cent are the remains of woolly mammoths. In addition eight other large mammal species and two rodents are represented. The mammoth bones are highly fragmented, but represent at least 11 individuals. These are mostly large males. Cut marks were not evident, while carnivore gnawing is extremely rare. Bone breakage for the extraction of marrow and the lack of limb bones is interpreted, on balance, as evidence for hominin utilisation of the carcasses. It is suggested that the riverine location provided Neanderthals with an opportunity to exploit such large prey.

The lithic assemblage consists of 2,720 pieces, including 41 complete and 6 broken handaxes; 85 per cent of these are cordiform, ovate and subtriangular in form. Association B-ii also produced 20 flake tools. Microwear studies revealed very little evidence for use, although some refitting was possible. The assemblage is made predominantly on local Norfolk flint and conforms to the pattern known from Britain after 67ka, when lithic assemblages show little evidence of the use of the Levallois technique, but contain many handaxes. The technological skill involved in the manufacture of the artefacts indicates anticipation, but not prediction, on the part of the Neanderthals. In addition, a sandstone block was excavated, which bears use traces made by a softer material, possibly wood. While no original residues survive on the block it can be considered the earliest candidate-object for the production of fire using a striker.

The evidence from Lynford can be used to investigate the environmental tolerances and habitat preferences of Neanderthals that resulted in the re-occupation of Britain after a long hiatus during MIS 4 – an extremely harsh phase of the last cold stage. Occupation of the locale occurred well before Modern humans (*Homo sapiens*) reached north-western Europe, and patterns of Neanderthal land use and foraging behaviour are examined by studying a hierarchy of catchments based on the palaeoenvironmental evidence. The volume concludes by considering the socioecology of the Lynford Neanderthals and the relationship between their social structure and the distribution of resources in the landscape. Lynford presents an opportunity to consider a major change in hominin/human social organisation that occurred during the last cold stage.

RÉSUMÉ

Lors d'une mission de surveillance archéologique au début du printemps de l'année 2002 à la carrière de Lynford, près du village de Munford, Norfolk, Royaume Uni, John Lord découvrit les restes *in situ* d'os de mammouths et des outils en pierre Moustériens associés. Ceux-ci étaient présents dans un paléochenal riche en sédiments organiques. L'importance du site fut immédiatement reconnue et, avec le support de Ayton Asphalte, les propriétaires de la carrière, et de English Heritage, des fouilles furent conduites entre avril et septembre de la même année, financées par le Fonds de Soutien de la Taxe sur les Agrégats (Aggregates Levy Sustainability Fund).

Les fouilles ont révélé des informations sur l'archéologie et le paléoenvironnement exceptionnellement bien préservées. De telles opportunités sont extrêmement rares pour le Paléolithique Moyen en Grande Bretagne, une période à laquelle les Néandertaliens, fabricant des bifaces du type *"bout coupé "* très distinct, n'occupaient que de manière intermittente ce qui à l'époque était une péninsule du Nord-Ouest de l'Europe. L'association de nombreux os de mammouths laineux avec des données très riches sur le paléoenvironnement a offert une occasion unique d'étudier des questions d'alimentation, d'usage du terrain et d'habitat à partir de dépôts préservés à l'intérieur d'une petite structure géologique et de soumettre les résultats à un examen taphonomique et géoarchéologique rigoureux.

Les limons et sables organiques remplissant le paléochenal contiennent un assemblage mammifère de période froide riche en restes de mammouths et une industrie de silex Moustérienne associée. Une série de dates obtenues par Luminescence Stimulée Optiquement (OSL) situe le dépôt des sédiments du chenal principal dans l'intervalle env. 65–57ka BP, à la transition entre les Stades Isotopiques Marins (MIS) 4 et 3. Les études des restes de la flore et des invertébrés indiquent un terrain ouvert et dominé par des herbes, des laîches et des communautés herbacées basses, avec de petits bouquets de bouleaux ou de broussailles et des zones de lande acide ou de marais. Ces indicateurs démontrent également un climat relativement doux, avec une température moyenne en Juillet jusqu'à 14°C et des hivers de –8° à –15°C. L'age le plus vraisemblable pour les dépôts est donc le début de MIS3 qui est marqué par les interstades Dansgaard-Oeschger (D-O) 14–17. Les indications des coléoptères et du pollen montrent de nombreuses similarités entre l'interstade à Lynford et le site de Upton Warren dans le Worcestershire qui est un des interstades les plus importants durant la dernière période froide en Grande Bretagne.

Le chenal, à l'époque du dépôt, est interprété comme un méandre coupé, ou bras mort, avec une eau immobile ou au courant très lent. De grands objets tels que des os sont entrés périodiquement dans le chenal depuis la surface du terrain adjacent par des processus tels que l'éboulement de berges. Aucune des zones de berge ne se préserva, en conséquence de quoi les reconstructions du comportement des hominines doivent être déduites d'une étude détaillée de la faune et des restes lithiques, combinée avec des évaluations taphonomiques dérivées d'une analyse des sédiments.

La majorité du matériel archéologique fut excavée de dépôts dénommés Association B qui fut divisée en trois composantes majeures. Celles-ci représentent des phases de dépôt dans l'histoire du bras mort; Bi, la plus basse, contient des sables et graviers qui furent déposés avant que le chenal ne devienne un bras mort; Bii est caractérisée par des limons et sables organiques représentant une phase inactive dans l'histoire du bras mort pendant laquelle la plupart des os de mammouths et objets façonnés furent déposés par effondrement; Biii est une phase finale composée de sables et graviers fins et grossiers qui marque le retour aux conditions d'écoulement de l'eau. Les indicateurs de paléoenvironnement de Bii montrent une bioturbation peut-être causée par la grande faune.

L'assemblage de faune de l'Association B consiste en 1,365 spécimens identifiés dont 91 % sont des restes de mammouth laineux. De plus il y a 8 autres espèces de grands mammifères et 2 rongeurs. Les os de mammouth sont très fragmentés mais représentent au moins 11 individus. Ceux-ci sont principalement des grands males. Les incisions de boucherie ne sont pas présentes et le rongement par carnivore est extrêmement rare. Certaines fractures des os pour la moelle et l'absence d'os des membres sont interprétées, toutes choses prises en compte, comme preuves de l'utilisation des carcasses par les hominines. Nous suggérons que l'emplacement en bord de rivière a fourni aux Néandertaliens une occasion d'exploiter de telles grandes proies.

L'assemblage lithique se compose de 2,720 pièces parmi lesquelles se trouvent 41 bifaces intacts et 6 bifaces cassés; 85 % de ceux-ci sont cordiformes, ovalaires ou sub-triangulaires. L'Association Bii a également produit

20 outils sur éclat. Les analyses tracéologiques ont révélé très peu d'indices d'utilisation et quelques remontages ont été possibles. L'assemblage est aménagé de manière prédominante dans du silex local du Norfolk et se conforme au modèle Britannique où les assemblages lithiques après 67ka BP montrent peu d'utilisation de la technique Levallois mais contiennent de nombreux bifaces. La compétence technologique requise pour la fabrication des objets indique l'anticipation mais non pas la prédiction de la part des Néandertaliens. De plus, un bloc de grès excavé porte des traces d'usure par un matériau plus doux, peut-être du bois. Bien qu'aucun résidu d'origine ne survive sur le bloc, il peut être considéré comme le plus ancien objet candidat pour la production de feu.

L'information provenant de Lynford peut être utilisée pour l'examen des tolérances d'environnement et des préférences d'habitat des Néandertaliens qui résultèrent en la ré-occupation de la Grande Bretagne après une longue interruption durant MIS4, une phase extrêmement sévère de la dernière période froide. L'occupation de la localité prit place bien avant que les humains Modernes (*Homo sapiens*) atteignent le Nord-Ouest de l'Europe et les schémas d'utilisation du terrain et du comportement d'approvisionnement des Néandertaliens sont examinés par l'étude d'une série de territoires à différentes échelles basée sur les données du paléoenvironnement. Le volume se termine par des considérations sur la socioécologie des Néandertaliens de Lynford et la relation entre leur structure sociale et la distribution des ressources du terrain. Lynford offre une occasion d'étudier un changement majeur dans l'organisation sociale hominine/humaine qui prit place durant la dernière période froide.

Traduction: Pierre Schreve

ZUSAMMENFASSUNG

Während eines archäologischen Begehungsauftrags am Lynforder Steinbruch, nahe des Dorfes Munford, Großbritannien, entdeckte John Lord zu Frühlingsbeginn des Jahres 2002 die in-situ liegenden Überreste von Mammutknochen zusammen mit Steinwerkzeugen des Mousterien. Sie befanden sich innerhalb eines ehemaligen Flusslaufes, der reich an organischen Sedimenten war.

Die immense Bedeutung des Fundortes wurde sofort erkannt. Mit der Unterstützung von Ayton Asphalte, den Steinbruchinhabern, und English Heritage fand im April desselben Jahres eine Ausgrabung statt, die vom Aggregates Levy Sustainability Fund finanziert wurde.

Die Ausgrabung erbrachte außergewöhnlich gut erhaltene archäologische und paläoökologische Informationen. Derartige Fundumstände sind im britischen Mittelpaläolitikum, als Neanderthaler die charakteristischen Faustkeile des "bout coupé" Typen herstellten und zeitweilig diesen Raum Nordwesteuropas besiedelten, der zu diesem Zeitpunkt eine Halbinsel war, äußerst selten. Die Assoziation vieler Knochenüberreste des Wollhaarmammuts mit dem Reichtum von Daten zu den damaligen Umweltverhältnissen ergab die einzigartige Gelegenheit, Fragen der Diät, der Flächennutzung und des Lebensraums anhand der Ablagerungen innerhalb eines kleinen geologischen Bereichs nachzugehen und die Ergebnisse einer rigorosen taphonomischen und geoarchäologischen Untersuchung zu unterziehen.

Die organischen Schlicke und Sande, die das ehemalige Flussbett füllen, enthalten eine Sammlung kaltzeitlicher Säugetierreste, die reich an Mammutüberresten, verbunden mit einer Feuersteinindustrie der Tradition des Mousterien, sind. Eine Reihe Optisch Stimulierter Lumineszens (OSL) platziert die Ablagerung der Hauptsedimente in das Interval zwischen c 65–57ka, an den Übergang zwischen den Marinen Isotopenstadien (MIS) 4 und 3. Untersuchungen der pflanzlichen und wirbellosen Überreste deuten auf eine offene Vegetation hin, die von Gräsern, Seggen, niedrigwachsenden, krautigen Arten, vereinzelten Standorten mit kleinen Birken und Büschen, sowie sauren Heiden und Sümpfen beherrscht wurde. Das sind Hinweise auf ein verhältnismäßig mildes Klima mit bis zu 14°C im Juli und zwischen −8° bis −15°C im Winter. Demzufolge ist das wahrscheinliche Alter der Ablagerungen im frühen MIS 3, dass durch die Dansgaard-Oeschger (D-O) Interstadiale 14–17 gekennzeichnet ist, anzusetzen.

Käfer- und Pollenbefunde verweisen auf viele Gemeinsamkeiten zwischen dem Interstadial bei Lynford und dem Fundort Upton Warren in Worcestershire, der eines der wichtigsten Interstadiale des letzten Kaltstadiums in Großbritannien ist. Das Flussbett wird zum Zeitpunkt der Ablagerung als ein abgeschnittener Mäander oder als eine Flussschleife mit stehendem oder sehr langsam fließendem Gewässer interpretiert. Große Objekte, wie zum Beispiel Knochen, gelangten durch gelegentliche Ufereinbrüche von der angrenzenden Landoberfläche in den Urstrom. Keiner der Uferbereiche blieb erhalten. So muss die Rekonstruktion des Verhaltens der Homininen durch die ausführliche Auswertung der faunistischen Überreste und der Steinwerkzeuge mit Hilfe taphonomischer Untersuchungen, abgeleitet von einer Analyse der Sedimente, vorgenommen werden.

Ein Großteil des archäologischen Fundes wurde von Ablagerungen gewonnen, die als Assoziation B gekennzeichnet sind und die in drei Hauptbestandteile unterteilt wurden. Sie repräsentieren folgende Ablagerungsphasen in der Geschichte der Flussschleife: Bi, die unterste Phase: enthält Sande und Kiese, die abgelagert wurden, bevor der Mäander abgetrennt wurde; Bii: ist gekennzeichnet durch organische Schlicke und Sande, die eine inaktive Phase in der Geschichte der Abtrennung des Flusses darstellen, in der die meisten Mammutknochen und Artefakte durch Ufereinbrüche abgelagert wurden; Biii: Endphase, die aus groben und feinen Kiesen und Sanden besteht, die auf eine Rückkehr zu fließenden Wasserbedingungen hindeuten.

Die paläoökologischen Belege von Bii verweisen auch auf Bioturbation, eventuell durch Megafauna.

Die faunistischen Funde von Association B bestehen aus 1,365 identifizierten Exemplaren, von denen 91% Überreste des Wollhaarmammuts sind. Hinzu kommen Funde 8 anderer großer Säugetierarten und 2 Nagetierarten. Die Mammutknochen sind hochgradig zersplittert, gehören jedoch zu mindestens 11 verschiedenen Individuen. Es handelt sich dabei um zumeist ausgewachsene männliche Exemplare. Schnittspuren waren nicht vorhanden und Nagespuren von karnivoren Tieren extrem selten. Einige der Knochenbrüche für die Markgewinnung und der Mangel an Gliederknochen werden weitgehend als Beweis für die Verwendung der Kadaver durch die Homininen gesehen. Das deutet darauf hin, dass die Flusslage den Neanderthalern die Möglichkeit des Erlegens dieser großen Beute einräumte.

Es wurden insgesamt 2,720 Steinartefakte geborgen, unter denen sich 41 komplette und 6 unvollständige Faustkeile befinden. 85% von ihnen sind mandelförmig, oval und annähernd breitdreieckig in ihrer Form. Association Bii beinhaltete auch 20 Abschläge, deren Untersuchung nur geringe Beweise für den Gebrauch der Geräte und einige Anpassungen ergab.

Die Steinartefakte wurden überwiegend aus lokalem Norfolk-Feuerstein hergestellt und stimmen mit dem britischen Muster überein, in dem Artefaktbefunde, die nach 67ka datieren, wenige Belege für den Gebrauch der Levallois-Technik, aber viele Faustkeile enthalten. Die technologischen Fertigkeiten, die bei der Herstellung der Artefakte angewendet wurden, lassen erkennen, dass die Neanderthaler mit einer gewissen Voraussicht arbeiteten, jedoch keine Vorhersage des Ergebnisses treffen konnten.

Zusätzlich wurde ein Sandsteinblock ausgegraben, der Gebrauchsspuren trägt, die durch ein weicheres Material, eventuell Holz, verursacht wurden. Trotz der Tatsche, dass keine ursprünglichen Rückstände auf dem Block erhalten sind, kann er als der früheste Anwärter eines Gegenstandes für die Erzeugung von Feuer unter der Verwendung eines Zündsteines angesehen werden.

Die Fundbelege von Lynford können der Erforschung jener ökologischen Toleranz und der Lebensraumpräferenzen des Neanderthalers dienen, die zur Wiederbesiedlung Großbritanniens nach einer langen Abwesenheit während MIS 4, einer extrem harten Phasedes letzten Kältestadiums, führten. Die Fundstelle wurde, lange bevor der Jetztmensch (Homo sapiens) Nordwesteuropa erreicht hatte, besiedelt. Verhaltensmuster bei der Flächennutzung und der Ernährung des Neanderthalers werden durch die Untersuchung einer Hierarchie von Einzugsgebieten, die auf den paläoökologischen Beweisen basiert, ermittelt.

Die Publikation schließt mit einer Betrachtung der Sozioökologie der Lynforder Neanderthaler und dem Verhältnis zwischen ihrer Sozialstruktur und der Resourcenverteilung in der Landschaft. Lynford bietet eine Gelegenheit, eine bedeutende Veränderung in der homininen/menschlichen Soziorganisation, die während des letzten Kaltstadiums geschah, in Erwägung zu ziehen.

Übersetzung: Dr Farina Sternke

1

The Lynford Middle Palaeolithic site

In late February and early March 2002, an archaeological watching brief at Lynford Quarry, near Mundford in Norfolk, revealed a palaeochannel with a dark, brown-black organic fill. This contained in situ mammoth remains and associated Mousterian stone tools, buried under two to three metres of bedded sands and gravels. Well-preserved, in situ Middle Palaeolithic open-air sites are exceedingly rare in Europe and very unusual within a British context. The site was quickly identified as of national and international importance, and subsequently excavated by the Norfolk Archaeological Unit with funding provided by English Heritage through the Aggregates Levy Sustainability Fund. This chapter sets out the background to the excavation, its research context, and the methods used to record and excavate the site.

1.1 Background, aims and excavation methods

W A Boismier

The site comprised the surviving eastern end of a major palaeochannel feature filled with organic deposits within the current application area of Lynford Quarry, Mundford, Norfolk. The quarry is situated in south-west Norfolk *c* 2km north-east of the village of Mundford and *c* 1km to the south-east of the village of Ickburgh. It lies on the southern side of the floodplain of the River Wissey (centred at NGR TL 825 948) and comprises an overall area of *c* 8.46ha. Soils for this area are predominately sandy and peaty soils of the Isleham 2 Association (Hodge *et al* 1984) overlying glaciofluvial drift of Pleistocene date composed of stratified sand, gravel and stones with rare inclusions of chalky gravel. In relief, the area generally slopes towards the north-west with surface elevations typically ranging between 12m and 15m AOD.

The workings in which the archaeological site was found consisted of a *c* 1.20ha rectangular area located in the north-western part of the application area between the River Wissey to the north and a flooded former pit to the west (Fig 1.1). The palaeochannel was situated in the north-eastern part of these workings (centred at NGR TL 8239 9482) and was preserved for a length of *c* 21.0m with a maximum width of *c* 12.0m. No *in situ* channel deposits survived within the machine-excavated area of the quarry. The feature appears to have been a meander cut-off acting as a small basin or lake, originally orientated in an east/north-east to west/south-west direction.

Context of discovery

An application for an eastern extension to the existing mineral workings at Mundford, Norfolk was submitted to Norfolk County Council by Ayton Asphalte in March 1998 (E/C/3/1998/3010 and 3/98/0509/F). The proposal involved tree clearance, topsoil stripping and the excavation of sand and gravel from an area of *c* 8.46ha situated along the southern floodplain of the River Wissey. Planning permission for the extension was granted by Norfolk County Council in 1998 subject to a programme of archaeological investigation. Specifications for the archaeological work were subsequently issued by Norfolk Landscape Archaeology, the curatorial section of the Archaeology and Environment Division of the Norfolk Museums Service. These specifications also recognised the potential of the application area for Palaeolithic materials, and stipulated that archaeological monitoring of the quarry during extraction was to be undertaken as a watching brief in order to record and recover

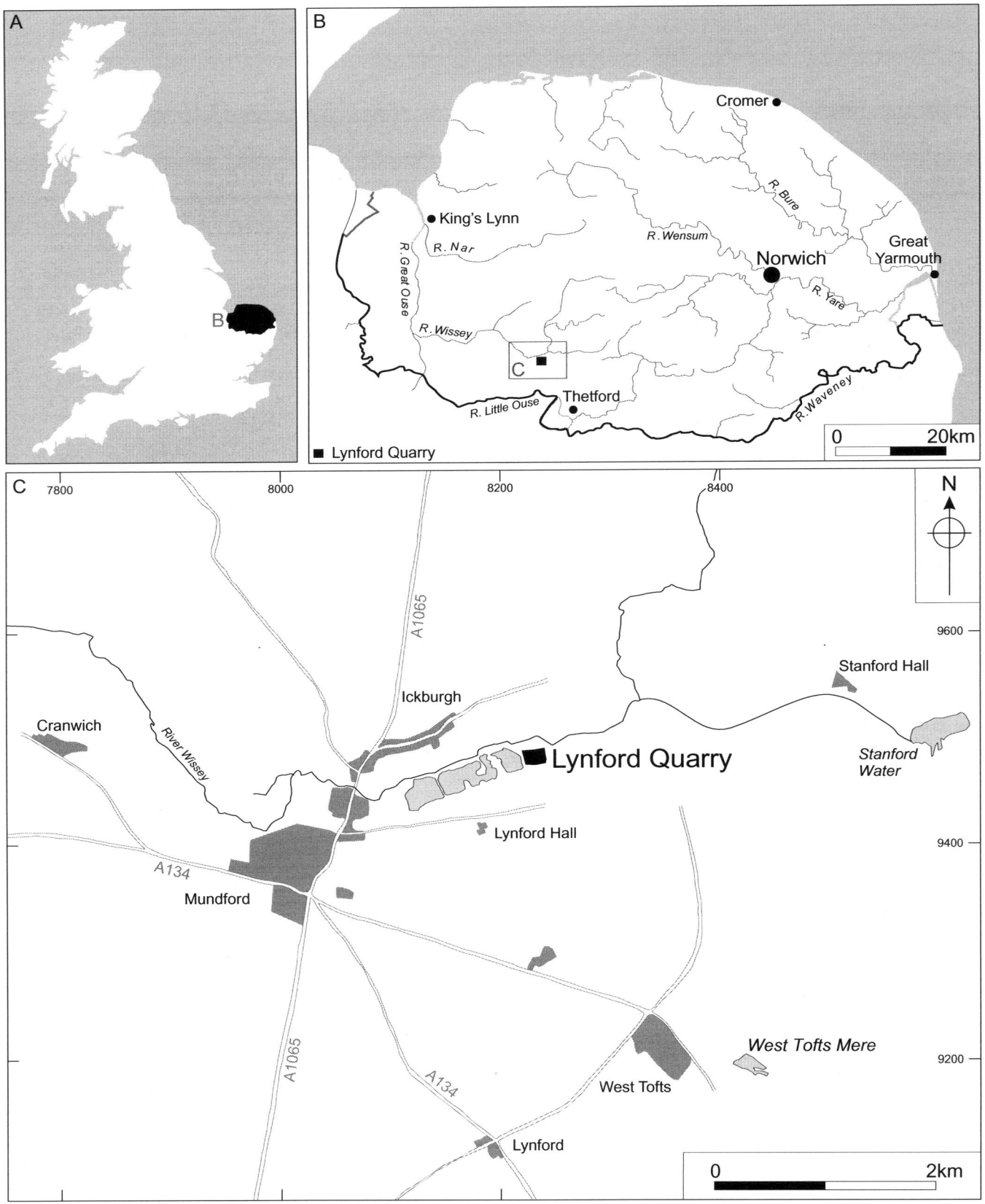

any Palaeolithic remains that might occur within the area of the pit extension (NLA Ref: 1/06/00DG). Trial trenching, small-scale excavation and the monitoring of topsoil stripping operations within the application area were carried out by the Norfolk Archaeological Unit in 2000 and 2001 (Birks 2000, 2001; Birks and Robertson 2005).

On the advice of Palaeolithic specialists a local archaeologist with substantial expertise in lithic technology, John Lord, was directly commissioned by Ayton Asphalte to undertake the monitoring of the extraction area on a monthly basis. Nigel Larkin of the Norfolk Museums and Archaeology Service later joined John Lord at the site after the discovery of some vertebrate remains of Pleistocene age. Further work by both John Lord and Nigel Larkin led to the discovery of apparently *in situ* Middle Palaeolithic artefacts in association with woolly mammoth remains. Nigel Larkin then contacted the Norfolk Archaeological Unit about the importance of the discovery and the possibility of a rescue excavation. The Unit, in turn, contacted English Heritage to request that a grant be made for the site's rescue excavation and English Heritage agreed to fund the excavation through the Aggregates Levy Sustainability Fund. The quarry company was informed of the importance of the site and the need for its rescue excavation, and the Unit, with the support of English Heritage and Ayton Asphalte, was allowed to start work more or less immediately. Excavation was carried out continuously over a five-month period from 8 April to 11 September 2002. Further fieldwork was carried out at the quarry in May and June 2003 to refine knowledge of the site's locality and its position in the local chronological sequence.

Archaeological background

A number of localities with evidence for hominin occupation during the Pleistocene occur within 10km of the site (Wymer 1996, Map LLO-3 Brandon; see also Wymer 1985, figs 13 and 34). Handaxes are recorded at Mundford, Ickburgh and several other localities surrounding the site with large collections of handaxes and other artefacts known from the valley of the Little Ouse River between Little Lodge Farm, Stanton Downham and Brandon, Suffolk (Roe 1968a; Wymer 1985, 102–110, 1996: 99–102). Farther to the south and southeast lie the important and well-researched Lower Palaeolithic archaeological sites of High Lodge (Cook *et al* 1991; Ashton *et al* 1992), Warren Hill (Wymer *et al* 1991), Beeches Pit (Preece *et al* 1991; Gowlett and Hallos 2000), Elvedon (Ashton *et al* 2005) and Barnham (Ashton *et al* 1998). Unlike these sites, with their excavated assemblages and associated stratigraphy and environmental evidence, most of the localities occurring within the 10km area surrounding Lynford are surface findspots in old collections with no or little – and often conflicting – stratigraphic information (Wymer 1985, 103–107). Artefacts typical of the Middle Palaeolithic are uncommon in these collections and limited to two Levallois flakes and a single *bout coupé*-type handaxe from localities within the Little Ouse valley (Wymer 1985, 107; 1999, 99–100; Tyldesley 1987, 22), and to one Levallois flake from Mundford (Wymer 1985, 52; 1999, 102).

Artefacts were initially discovered at Lynford in the 1980s and 1990s by Phil Harding, John and Valerie Lord and John Wymer during earlier phases of gravel extraction (Wymer 1999, 102; Wymer 2008a). The finds included at least 20 handaxes, one Levallois core and an unspecified number of unretouched Levallois and non-Levallois flakes. Some unidentified bones and part of a mammoth tusk were also collected from the site during this period. All of the material appears to have been recovered from reject heaps in stockpile areas or gravel scree along pit faces within a *c* 20ha area some 250m to the west of the current workings. They are considered by both Wymer (1985, 53) and Tydlesley (1987, 37) to have come from the sandy gravel found across the area rather than the coarse gravels lying beneath them. One flat-butted cordate or subtriangular handaxe form and three possible *bout coupé*-type variants have been reported for the collection of handaxes (Wymer 1985, 53; 1996, 112; 1999, 133; Tyldesley 1987, 37). Their crushed edges were considered by Tyldesley (ibid) to indicate transport in torrential waters. These artefacts remain only partially described, with little additional information available for the remaining handaxes other than Tyldesley's brief note (ibid) that one is a handaxe roughout and a few appear to be more ovoid-shaped pieces. Wymer also noted (1996, 112) that the quarry represented one of the few localities in the area with Levallois artefacts and *bout coupé* handaxes, and suggested a Late Pleistocene age for the materials.

Fig 1.1 (opposite) Lynford quarry in its national and regional setting.

In October 2001, John Lord's archaeological monitoring of the current extraction phase at the quarry recovered a woolly rhinoceros humerus fragment from sandy, dark-brown organic sediments infilling a palaeochannel feature buried under two to three metres of bedded sands and gravels (see also Wymer 2008b, 52–5). Other faunal and artefactual materials were also recovered from reject heaps situated within the stockpile areas of the quarry. In February and March 2002 subsequent monitoring of the site by John Lord and Nigel Larkin found the fragmented and partial remains of at least one mammoth with an associated blade within the organic sediments of the palaeochannel. Three flakes were later recovered from the sediments immediately surrounding some mammoth skull fragments and an unrolled *bout coupé* handaxe from an area of sediments a metre or so away from the skull remains. A further four flakes were subsequently found *in situ* in the vicinity of the skull within the organic sediments. Sieving the spoil from areas of the channel already destroyed by quarrying activities also recovered a number of artefacts and mammoth skeletal remains. However, it was not possible to record the dimensions or original length of the channel feature due to quarry working methods.

The artefacts recovered from the channel sediments consisted of three likely *bout coupé*-type handaxes and 38 flakes including axe shaping/thinning and sharpening flakes. All the artefacts retained sharp edges with patination either absent or very light and were variably stained a dark brown-black colour by the surrounding organic sediments. Typologically, the presence of *bout coupé* handaxes was taken as an indication that the assemblage fell within the Mousterian of Acheulian Tradition (MTA) facies of the Middle Palaeolithic as it is known in Britain, and dated to sometime within MIS 3 (Shackley 1977; Roe 1981, 233–52; Tyldesley 1987, 153–7; Coulson 1990, 391–4; Wymer 1988, 1999, 49; White and Jacobi 2002; see also Wymer 1968, 59, 389; Mellars 1974, 62–5). The small assemblage also suggested the manufacture and use of handaxes by Neanderthals at the site, possibly related to butchery activities.

The faunal remains recovered included numerous mammoth skull fragments, pieces of lower jaw, two largish tusk fragments, two molars (one upper and one lower) and fragments of rib and scapula. The material probably represents two mammoths, one younger and smaller than the other, as the epiphyses of a number of the bones recovered were unfused. Other vertebrate material consisted of a fragment of the humerus of a woolly rhinoceros, a couple of undiagnostic limb fragments, the tine of an antler and the tibio-fibula of a frog. The presence of mammoth and woolly rhinoceros in the collection indicated that the vertebrate remains probably belonged within the Pin Hole mammal assemblage-zone spanning the Middle Devensian and associated with the cool, open grassland characteristic of the mammoth steppe biome of MIS 3 age (Currant and Jacobi 2001, 2002). Plant macrofossils, molluscs and insect remains were also collected from the sediments in small quantities and showed that environmental materials were generally well-preserved and moderately abundant within the channel sediments.

The artefactual and faunal materials recovered by the watching brief strongly suggested that the undisturbed sediments in the surviving part of the palaeochannel could contain well-preserved evidence for an *in situ* Middle Palaeolithic kill or scavenging site of MIS 3 age with a range of associated palaeo-ecological proxies. Open-air localities with well-preserved vertebrate remains are relatively rare in Europe (Farizy and David 1989; Gaudzinski 1999a; Gaudzinski and Turner 1999; Conard and Prindiville 2000; Patou-Mathis 2000) and almost unknown in Britain, where most of the evidence for Neanderthal occupation in MIS 3 comes from cave, rockshelter and open-air localities that were largely excavated or collected during the 19th and early 20th centuries (Wymer 1985, 1996, 1999). The quality of the site and its finds make Lynford one of the most important Middle Palaeolithic localities ever discovered in Britain, and of national and international importance in terms of its potential to provide new and more comprehensive data regarding the character of Neanderthal behaviour at the north-western edge of their range.

Research background

The Middle Palaeolithic in Britain is defined by the appearance of prepared core technologies involving the use of Levallois techniques *c* 250,000 years ago (Roe 1981, 213–30, 236; Wymer 1968, 69–76, 1999, 49–50; Bridgland

1994, 26; White *et al* 2006; McNabb 2007, 187–215). In chronological terms, the Middle Palaeolithic spans the period embracing MIS 8 to MIS 3 from *c* 250,000 to 40,000 years ago and is divided into an early phase based on Levallois techniques dated to between *c* 250,000 and 150,000 years ago (MIS 8–7) and a late phase based on a Mousterian biface and flake tool industry dating from *c* 59,000 to 38,000 years ago (MIS 3) (White and Jacobi 2002). These two phases of Middle Palaeolithic settlement are separated by a period of hominin absence lasting between 100,000 and 120,000 years from the MIS 6 cold stage, through the Ipswichian Interglacial (MIS 5e) and into the early cooling stages of the final Devensian glaciation (MIS 5d–5a and MIS 4). Reasons suggested for the abandonment of Britain by hominins at this time have included the harsh climatic conditions of the MIS 6 cold stage, severing of the land bridge with the European mainland during the Ipswichian Interglacial as a result of high sea levels, and changes in climate and habitat preferences by hominin groups (Ashton 2002; Ashton and Lewis 2002; Currant and Jacobi 2002). Whatever the reasons for abandonment, hominins were absent from Britain until recolonisation in terminal MIS 4/early MIS 3 by Neanderthal groups characterised by Mousterian industries.

The Late Middle Palaeolithic embraces the MIS 3 warm phase of the Devensian glaciation and is marked by the presence of a Mousterian of Acheulian (MTA) type industry similar to that in north-western France, although with a distinctive *bout coupé* handaxe type found only in the British Mousterian (Shackley 1977; Roe 1981, 233–52; Tyldesley 1987, 153–157; Coulson 1990, 391–4; Wymer 1988, 1999, 49; White and Jacobi 2002). This period is not well known for the British Palaeolithic, with evidence limited to a small number of cave and rockshelter sites and open-air localities composed largely of findspots of *bout coupé* handaxes (Roe 1981, 254–67, fig 6.6; Tyldesley 1987, 17–103; White and Jacobi 2002). Cave and rockshelter sites with evidence for occupation during MIS 3 comprise Coygan Cave, Carmarthenshire; Robin Hood's Cave, Pin Hole Cave and Church Hole Cave, Derbyshire; Kents Cavern, Devon; the Hyaena Den, Rhinoceros Hole and Picken's Hole, Somerset; Uphill Quarry Cave 8, North Somerset; and Oldbury, Kent. Open-air findspot localities often cited as principal or important sites for the period (Roe 1981, 240–1; Tyldesley 1987, 198–9; Coulson 1990, 391; White and Jacobi 2002; White 2006), include Little Paxton, Cambridgeshire; Bramford Road, Ipswich, Suffolk; Little Cressingham, Norfolk; Fisherton, Wiltshire; and Great Pan Farm, Isle of Wight. Data for these sites and localities are summarised in Table 1.1 (see also White 2006, table 1).

The nature of this record for MIS 3 occupation is highly problematic in terms of the integrity of the data from each site or locality. Most of the principal sites and localities were excavated or collected in the 19th or early 20th centuries, with minimal recording and limited stratigraphic controls. Stratigraphic and contextual information is at best poor by modern standards and at worst, non-existent (Campbell and Sampson 1971; Tratman *et al* 1971; Harrison 1977; Delair and Shackley 1978; Jenkinson 1984; Aldhouse-Green *et al* 1995; White and Jacobi 2002). Artefact and vertebrate samples from these sites and localities are further biased by poor recovery techniques and the dispersal and subsequent loss of individual finds (Dawkins 1874, 295–314; Campbell and Sampson 1971; Jenkinson 1984). No open-air locality has been excavated; most sites are represented by collections of material derived from reject piles and other disturbed contexts (Lawson 1978; Tyldesley 1987, 7; Coulson 1990, 391; Wymer 1999, 33). In addition, artefact assemblages are typically small or represented by single finds, and characterised by a general scarcity of diagnostic artefacts other than *bout coupé* handaxes and poorly documented faunal associations. Many difficulties also exist in identifying artefacts of different ages in mixed collections (Shackley 1973; Wymer 1985, 213–16) or sites lacking extended stratigraphic sequences (Collins and Collins 1970; Cook and Jacobi 1998). The available evidence is thus generally of limited or poor quality and leaves much to be desired when compared to the much richer Continental record.

Sites and localities have been dated by a variety of relative and radiometric methods, and this dating is one area of research where significant advances have been made regarding the study of Neanderthal settlement in Britain. Relative methods are the most prevalent dating techniques for the period and include the use of artefact stylistic or typological criteria (predominately *bout coupé*-type handaxes),

Table 1.1 Data for sites and localities from the UK with evidence for occupation during MIS 3

site	site type	artefact totals[1]	fauna	date	references
Coygan Cave, Laugharne, Carmarthenshire	cave	7	Pin Hole type	14C: 38,684 +2713/−2024 (BM-499)	Hicks 1867, 1884; Grimes and Cowley 1935; Clegg 1970; Aldhouse-Green et al 1995
Robin Hood's Cave, Cresswell Crags, Derbyshire	cave	82	Pin Hole type	14C: >38,500 (OxA 12799); 45,300 ±1000 (OxA 12771); 47,300 ±1200 (OxA 12772); ESR: 55 ±4k	Dawkins 1876, 1877; Mello 1876, 1877; Campbell 1969; Jenkinson 1984; Coulson 1990; Jacobi and Grun 2003; Jacobi et al 2006
Pin Hole Cave, Cresswell Crags, Derbyshire	cave	118	Pin Hole type	14C: 37,760 ±340 (OxA 11980) to 55,900 ±4000 (OxA 14197); ESR: 39 ±2k to 51 ±8k; U-Series: 63.7 ±0.4k, 63.9 ±0.3k	Mello 1875, 1876; Armstrong 1926, 1932, 1939, 1956; Jackson 1966; Jenkinson 1984; Coulson 1990; Jacobi et al 1998; Jacobi et al 2006
Church Hole Cave, Cresswell Crags, Derbyshire	cave	38	Pin Hole type	mammalian biostratigraphy: MIS 3	Mello 1877; Dawkins 1877; Jenkinson 1984; Coulson 1990; Currant and Jacobi 2001
Hyaena Den, Wookey, Somerset	cave	43*	Pin Hole type	14C: 40,400 ±1600 (OxA 4782) to 48,600 ±1000 (OxA 13917)	Dawkins 1862, 1863a, 1863b, 1874; Tratman et al 1971; Coulson 1990; Jacobi and Hawkes 1993; Jacobi et al 2006
Rhinoceros Hole, Wookey, Somerset	cave	6	Pin Hole type	U-series: 45 +5/−4k (M41.9/8a-A), 51 +5/−6k (M41.9/26B)	Procter et al 1996
Picken's Hole, Compton Bishop, Somerset	cave	c 53	Pin Hole type	14C: 34,365 +2600/−1900 (BM-654)	Tratman 1964; ApSimon 1986
Kent's Cavern, Torquay, Devon	cave	45	Pin Hole type	14C: 37,900 ±1000 (OxA 13589) to 45,000 ±2200 (OxA 14761)	Northmore 1868; Pengelly 1869, 1884; Dowie 1928; Benyon et al 1929; Smith 1940; Campbell and Sampson 1971; Coulson 1990; Jacobi et al 2006
Uphill Quarry Cave No. 8, Weston-Super-Mare, North Somerset	cave	47*	Pin Hole type	mammalian biostratigraphy: MIS 3	Harrison 1977; Currant and Jacobi 2001
Oldbury, Ingtham, Kent	collapsed rockshelter	625**	Pin Hole type	typological: Middle Devensian	Harrison 1933; Collins and Collins 1970; Coulson 1990; Cook and Jacobi 1998
Little Paxton, St Neots, Cambridgeshire	open-air findspot	c 210*	Pin Hole type	mammalian biostratigraphy: MIS 3	Paterson and Tebbutt 1947
Little Cressingham, Norfolk	open-air	2		lithostratigraphy: MIS 3; typological: Middle Devensian	Lawson 1978
Fisherton Brick Pit, Salisbury, Wiltshire	open-air findspot	2	Pin Hole type	mammalian biostratigraphy: MIS 3	Delair and Shackley 1978
Bramford Road, Ipswich, Suffolk	open-air findspot	184+***	Pin Hole type	typological: Middle Devensian	Moir 1931; Wymer 1985, 1999
Great Pan Farm, Newport, Isle of Wight	open-air findspot	108**		typological: Middle Devensian	Shackley 1973; White and Jacobi 2002

Key for Table 1.1
[1] Artefact counts represent existing collections.
* mixed assemblage with Late Middle Palaeolithic and Upper Palaeolithic materials (including Early Upper Palaeolithic materials)
** mixed collection with Early and Late Middle Palaeolithic materials

biostratigraphy, river terrace sequences and local stratigraphies to provide chronological constraints for open-air localities (Collins and Collins 1970; Shackley 1973; Delair and Shackley 1978; Lawson 1978; Roe 1981, 236–52; Tyldesley 1987, 116–19; Coulson 1986, 1990, 393; Wymer 1999; Currant and Jacobi 2001, 2002; White and Jacobi 2002). Radiometric methods used include AMS radiocarbon, electron spin resonance (ESR) and uranium-series dating of vertebrate remains and speleothems from a number of cave sites (ApSimon 1986; Aldhouse *et al* 1995; Proctor *et al* 1996; Jacobi *et al* 1998; Jacobi and Grün 2003; Jacobi *et al* 2006). The results of these relative and radiometric dating programmes demonstrate that the whole of the British Late Middle Palaeolithic is confined to MIS 3 and dated to between *c* 59,000 and 38,000 years ago.

Few firm conclusions regarding the further chronological ordering of sites and localities within MIS 3 have been drawn from these results. Reasons for this centre around the lack of resolution for relative dating methods and the fact that the early part of MIS 3 lies at or beyond the background limit of the radiocarbon method of *c* 55 ka. Relative dating methods used to place sites and localities within MIS 3 are simply too coarse-grained in nature to be of much use in providing a chronology for the period. Available AMS radiocarbon dates are typically spread between *c* 40ka and 54ka and tend to cluster close to the background limit of the method. Older ESR and U-series determinations provide only *terminus post quem* dates for Middle Palaeolithic occupations. As a result, the chronology of the period is poorly understood, with many important research questions remaining unanswered regarding the timing of the recolonisation of Britain by Neanderthal groups and the duration of Late Middle Palaeolithic settlement.

A considerable body of palaeoenvironmental and palaeoclimatic evidence for MIS 3 has been assembled over the last 20 years and used to provide an environmental context for Late Middle Palaeolithic settlement (White and Jacobi 2002; Van Andel and Davies 2003; White 2006). In concert, these different proxy records indicate that MIS 3 is characterised by a sharply oscillating sequence of alternating cold and warm episodes of millennial-scale duration with a rich mosaic of grassland and other open habitats (mammoth steppe), and a diverse herbivore community dominated by mammoth, woolly rhinoceros, horse, bison and reindeer (Pin Hole-type fauna) (Stuart 1977, 1982, 147–65; West 2000, 191–215; Currant and Jacobi 2001, 2002; Van Andel 2003). Palaeoclimatic evidence indicates a strongly continental climate for lowland England, characterised by mean July temperatures of *c* 10°–14°C, and winter temperatures as low as −25°C or −27°C, with seasonally frozen ground and the possible presence of discontinuous permafrost (Watson 1977; Ballantyne and Harris 1994, 15; Coope 2002). Mean annual precipitation appears to have been as low as 250–553mm, and highly seasonal in pattern (Lockwood 1979, Guthrie 1984, 1990, 208–25), although in some areas climate modelling results and proxy records provide contrasting pictures of the degree of aridity and seasonal precipitation patterns (Barron *et al* 2003; Guthrie 1982; Jones and Keen 1993, 162–71; see also Guthrie and Van Kolfschoten 2000). Overall, however, the various proxies indicate an open steppic environment with cold winters and dry summers that supported a relatively high biomass of large, mainly migratory, herbivores.

Reconstruction of the palaeoenvironmental settings of Late Middle Palaeolithic sites and findspot localities dating to MIS 3 has been much less successful, largely due to the limited amount of palaeoenvironmental evidence available for cave sites from old excavations, and the use of broad correlations based on lithological evidence and/or terrace sequences to place isolated findspots into some kind of MIS 3 environmental setting (Campbell and Sampson 1971; Tratman *et al* 1971; Campbell 1977, 105; Delair and Shackley 1978; Jenkinson 1984; Aldhouse-Green *et al* 1995; White 2006). Inferences drawn from these data sources have tended to focus on adaptive strategies rather than palaeoecology, and have outlined the physiological, behavioural and technological adaptations required by Neanderthal populations to survive on the mammoth steppe (White 2006; see also Ashton 2002). Few conclusions have been drawn from vertebrate and pollen records regarding the palaeoenvironmental settings of sites and localities, other than that they were situated within cool-cold steppic environments (Jones and Keen 1993, 169; White 2006). These records provide at best only a partial picture of palaeoenviromental settings, and are generally too coarse-grained to be of much use in providing any indications of local habitat conditions. As a result the palaeoecology of sites and localities is poorly understood, with numerous unresolved questions regarding the structure of local habitats making up the mammoth steppe and how this structure might have conditioned Neanderthal land-use behaviour in relation to site location and use (Gamble 1995; Gamble and Roebroeks 1999).

Land-use patterns for the British Late Middle Palaeolithic are also poorly known in comparison to the rich continental record, where vertebrate and artefact records indicate considerable variability and a degree of complexity in Neanderthal subsistence and raw material procurement strategies (Geneste 1989; Patou 1989, 2000; Féblot-Augustins 1993, 1999). Vertebrate assemblages from excavated cave sites are predominately carnivore accumulations (Tratman 1964; Tratman *et al* 1971; Campbell and Sampson 1971; Harrison 1977; Jenkinson 1984; ApSimon 1986; Aldhouse-Green *et al* 1995; Proctor *et al* 1996; Currant and Jacobi 2004), and suggest a pattern of alternating short-term occupations by hominins and carnivores during MIS 3 similar to that recorded across Europe for the Middle Palaeolithic (Straus 1982; Gamble 1983, 1986, 306–21; Stiner 1994; Boyle 1998, 59–60). For a variety of taphonomic and historical reasons few substantive conclusions regarding faunal exploitation patterns have been drawn from these assemblages (Jenkinson 1984; Aldhouse-Green *et al* 1995), with interpretations based on bone condition and skeletal element representation (Campbell and Sampson 1971; Jenkinson 1984, 91) equivocal owing to the general absence of butchery evidence for the period other than a single cut-marked tooth (Jacobi and Hawkes 1993). Raw material sources for the lithic artefacts associated with these assemblages are also only partially known (MacRae and Moloney 1988, 233; Coulson 1990, 324, 329) with the small number of artefacts known from most sites taken as the signature of a highly mobile settlement strategy (Proctor *et al* 1996; White 2006). Consequently, Neanderthal land-use behaviour is poorly understood, with numerous questions about faunal exploitation and raw material transfers and how these relate to subsistence and mobility strategies unresolved.

Intrasite patterns for the Late Middle Palaeolithic are largely unknown due to the poor quality of the record for most sites and localities, and the dispersal and loss of finds from old excavations (Campbell and Sampson 1971; Tratman *et al* 1971; Harrison 1977; Delair and Shackley 1978; Jenkinson 1984; Tyldesley 1987; Aldhouse-Green *et al* 1995). The analysis of spatial data has been limited to the reconstruction of vertical profiles for one site (Jenkinson 1984, 65–6; Jacobi *et al* 1998) with records of hearths poor and often anecdotal (Tratman *et al* 1971; Aldhouse-Green *et al* 1995). Artefact studies have tended to be typological in character and have either applied Bordesian systematics (Bordes 2002) to artefact assemblages (Coulson 1990) or focused on the *bout coupé*-type handaxe to establish a techno-complex for the Late Middle Palaeolithic with cultural affiliations similar to those defined for the Middle Palaeolithic across Europe during MIS 3 (Roe 1981, 236–52; Tyldesley 1987; Mellars 1996; Gamble and Roebroeks 1999; White and Jacobi 2002). Far fewer conclusions have been made regarding site *chaîne opératoires* and tool functions, other than that assemblages are non-laminar and non-Levallois, and that tools such as scrapers and notches were probably used to work different kinds of organic materials (Jenkinson 1984, 75; Coulson 1990; Proctor *et al* 1996; Jacobi 2004; White 2006). Neanderthal site-use behaviour is therefore probably the least understood aspect of Late Middle Palaeolithic settlement in Britain during MIS 3, with numerous unresolved questions regarding site structure and technological organisation and how these relate to land-use and mobility strategies.

It is evident from this brief overview that the archaeological record for the Late Middle Palaeolithic in Britain is reasonably sparse, and that knowledge of the period remains extremely limited. Reasons for this are largely historic and relate to the poor quality of the records made for excavations and collections during the 19th and early 20th centuries and to excavations carried out during the 1950s and early 1960s, when the objectives and levels of recording were very different from those of today (Sackett 1981; Gamble 1986, 5–16). In most cases these data are simply not robust enough to address many of the current research interests regarding Neanderthal ways of life during MIS 3.

Research objectives

Given these significant gaps in archaeological evidence regarding Late Middle Palaeolithic settlement during MIS 3, the excavation of Lynford promised new information that could provide some answers about the character of Neanderthal settlement at the north-western extremes of their range. The locality looked particularly promising in this regard because of the material preservation and the abundance of archaeological remains and palaeoenvironmental materials in the deposits. In addition, the sandy make-up of the sediments also offered the potential for the site to be dated through luminescence methods. Nine key research objectives for the excavation were defined on the basis of national and regional research frameworks for the Palaeolithic (Austin 1997, 2000; English Heritage 1998, 1999) and set out in the Project Design submitted to English Heritage (Boismier 2003). These objectives addressed the nature of Neanderthal behaviour at the site and its place within local, regional and European Late Pleistocene environmental and archaeological contexts, and can be summarised as follows:

- To date the deposit and associated archaeological materials by radiometric and geochronological methods.
- To determine the stratigraphic position of the palaeochannel by recording and interpreting the sequence of deposits at the site and correlating it to known regional and national Pleistocene sequences and the isotope record.
- To identify and characterise the taphonomic processes responsible for deposit and assemblage formation and post-depositional disturbance and modification.
- To characterise the environmental setting of the site during its occupation and/or use.
- To identify the range and the possible spatial organisation of the activities undertaken at the site.
- To provide a characterisation of hominin butchery and carcass utilisation strategies.
- To define the nature of lithic technological organisation at the site, notably raw material selection, reduction sequences, tool use and rejuvenation/reutilisation (*chaîne opératoire*) and its relationship to hominin site use and mobility patterns.
- To place the site within a wider environmental setting in relation to the Middle Devensian environment.
- To place the site within its local, regional and European setting in relation to Middle Palaeolithic hominin behaviour and subsistence adaptations.

The excavation

The palaeochannel and associated deposits containing archaeological remains were excavated and recorded at a detailed level to provide a range of spatial, palaeoenvironmental and taphonomic information with which to address the project's research objectives. Excavation was continuous from April to September 2002. The original twelve-week programme was extended by six weeks owing to the large number of finds exposed by the excavation and to disruptions to the work caused by adverse weather conditions. All palaeochannel deposits with artefacts and vertebrate remains were fully excavated and recorded by 11 September.

An organic channel-fill exposed in the east-facing section on the west side of the active quarry was also investigated in May 2003 to establish its relationship to the excavated organic sediments containing archaeological and palaeontological materials. In the following month (June 2003) a programme of machine-dug test pitting across the unworked areas of the quarry was undertaken to enhance existing stratigraphic data regarding the position of the palaeochannel within the local sequence of deposits.

Excavation methodology

The deposits overlying the surviving part of the site had been removed by mineral extraction before excavation over an area of c 263.60m^2, leaving a c 0.30m to 0.50m thick deposit of sand and gravel covering the palaeochannel deposit (Fig 1.2). Mineral extraction had also removed all deposits covering the palaeochannel for a length of 9.0m (33.92m^2 area) in the north-western part of the site and across a 50.76m^2 area of sand and gravel adjacent to the northern edge of the channel to a depth of c 0.45m below the upper contact surface of the palaeochannel deposit. Vertical sections of more than 2m were left standing on the northern and eastern sides of the area at the end of extraction activities.

Mechanical excavation was used to remove the surviving sand and gravel deposits overlying the palaeochannel and to create a safe working

Fig 1.2
The site prior to start of excavation.

environment for the manual excavation of the area (Figs 1.3 and 1.4). A tracked 9-tonne 360° excavator with a 1.80m wide toothless ditching bucket was employed to step quarry sections on the northern and eastern sides of the excavation area and to remove surviving overburden to the top of the deposits immediately overlying the palaeochannel (in 0.05m–0.10m spits). Stripped surfaces within the excavation area were manually cleaned.

A total station theodolite was used to set out eight survey stations around the quarry to establish the site's position within the National Grid and local OD heights. The excavation area was subdivided into a 2m by 2m grid based on the National Grid and planned/levelled. The 2m by 2m grid in the area of the site containing the palaeochannel and other deposits with *in situ* archaeological materials (199.83m^2 in total) was divided into 1m^2 units composed of

Fig 1.3
Mechanical excavation of the site to remove surviving sand and gravel deposits.

four 0.50m² subunits and excavated manually by trowel using a combination of 0.10m spits and micro-stratigraphy for vertical control. Deposits immediately above the palaeochannel and basal deposits within it containing little or no archaeological material were stratigraphically excavated employing a combination of mattocks and trowels. Baulks of 1.0m width extending north-south and east-west through the excavation area and along the west-facing edge of the quarry were used to record the sequence of deposits in the palaeochannel and for palaeoenvironmental sampling before their excavation. All deposits within the main palaeochannel were fully excavated, with the spoil dumped along the north-western edge of the excavation area back into the quarry.

Recording strategies

Recording strategies were based on the context method of recording where sediments and contacts are assigned unique numbers as they are excavated and recorded (Harris 1979, 1989; Roskams 2001, 239–66). This method of recording was adopted as it provides a highly structured and flexible approach for deposit recording and generates a detailed and well-ordered archive on which the description, analysis and interpretation of the stratigraphic sequence and other categories of data recovered from the site can be based. Blocks of numbers were allocated to each of the seven major record types (Context, Lithic Object, Bone Object, Context Subdivision, Environmental Sample, Graphic, Photographic) used by the excavation before the start of fieldwork. Unique numbers were then assigned to individual records from within their respective block of numbers as required. A listing of block number allocations for record types is set out in Table 1.2.

Contexts were defined on the basis of a range of lithological properties such as general texture, colour and sedimentary structures (Jones *et al* 1999, 38–9), and record sedimentary features ranging in scale from small bedding structures within lithofacies to individual lithofacies and bedding contacts separating depositional units. Deposits, features and layers were assigned individual context numbers and recorded on standard context sheets with a running stratigraphic matrix maintained throughout the excavation to characterise deposit relationships and to guide excavation decisions. Plans and sections were drawn at a scale of 1:10 and tied into the site grid using a total station theodolite. A complete photographic record of the excavation was made in black and white negative and colour slide film. Registers for context, lithic, bone, context subdivision (spit), sample, graphic and photographic records were compiled on-site as the excavation progressed.

Table 1.2 Block number allocations for record types

record type	quantity
context	
cut/contact surface	136
deposit	244
total	380
object	
lithic	487
bone	2,079
total	2,566
graphics	
plan	595
section	299
total drawn record	894
photograph	
colour slide	1,182
b & w negative	973
total photographic record	2,155
spit	3,572
environmental	367
total written record	9,831

Artefacts and faunal remains larger than 0.02m in size were three-dimensionally recorded *in situ* using a total station theodolite. Each object was assigned a unique number, plotted on the relevant spit plan and its context, position (x, y, z coordinates), dip and general orientation within the deposit recorded on the appropriate record (Lithic or Bone Object records). Quantitative orientation data was generated in post-excavation on the basis of the 1:10 plans. Object registers itemising the context number, coordinates, OD height and relevant plan and photograph number for each object were also compiled on-site to provide a summary listing of three-dimensionally recorded materials and for cross-referencing and checking purposes. In total, some 2,566 objects (487 lithic artefacts and 2,079 faunal remains) were recorded utilising these procedures. Fragile objects (bone and tusk) were treated *in situ* with adhesives (Paraloid

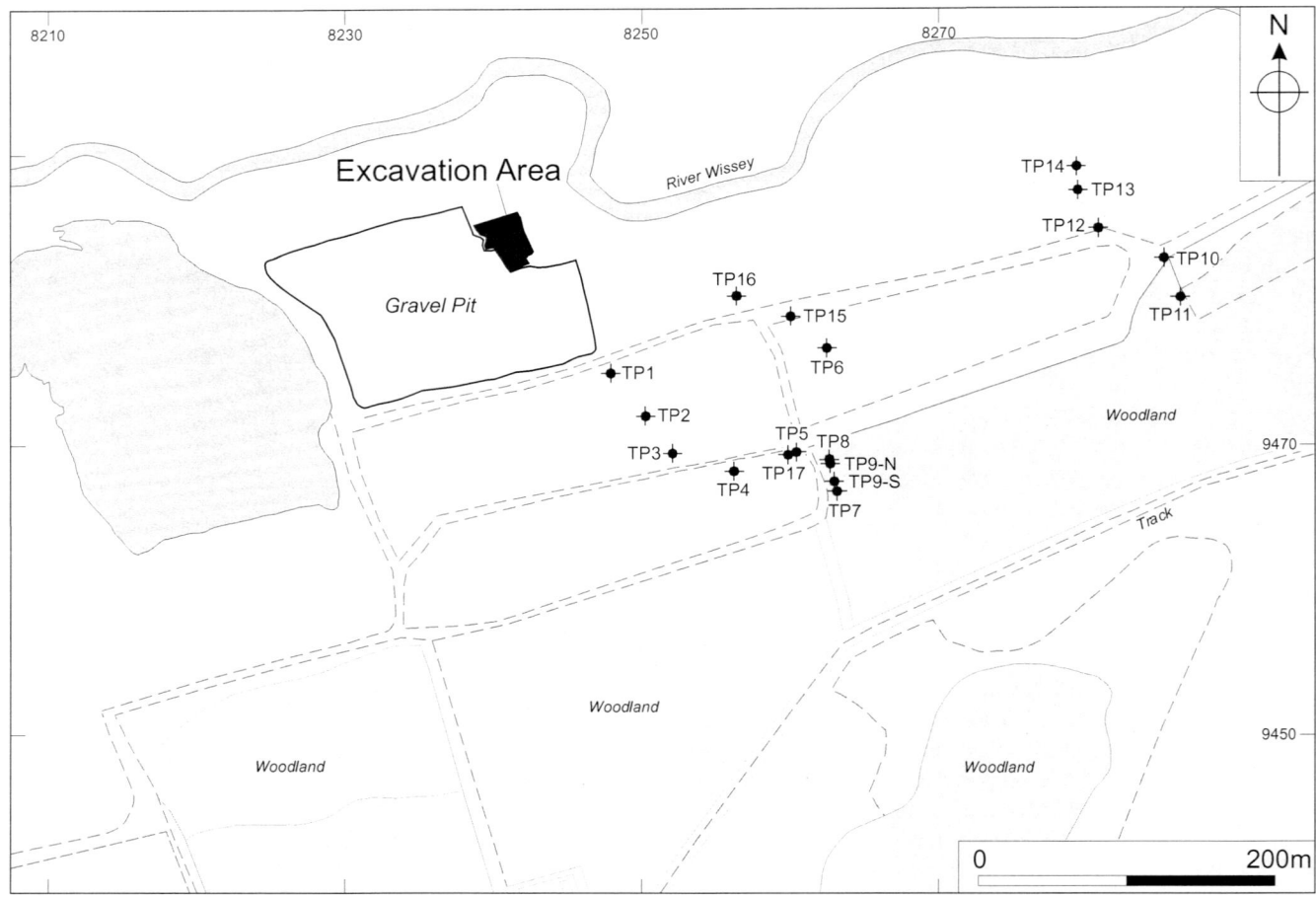

Fig 1.4
Site plan of quarry showing excavation area and test pit location.

B72 with acetone) and, where required, jacketed with plaster of Paris before being lifted and removed from the site. On-site conservation was carried out by Nigel Larkin of the Norfolk Museums and Archaeology Service assisted by two members of the excavation team (R. Crawford and L. Stockley).

Objects less than 0.02m in size were collected and recorded by $0.50m^2$ quadrat and vertical spit or micro-stratigraphy. Three of the four $0.50m^2$ spit quadrats for each $1m^2$ unit were dry-sieved (6mm or 9mm mesh) and one wet-sieved (1mm mesh) to ensure the recovery of small materials. Each spit was assigned a unique number and planned, and data concerning its thickness, sieving method (wet- or dry-sieved), plan number, south-west corner coordinates and OD height were recorded on the context subdivision record. A total of 3,572 spits were recorded utilising this procedure with some 2,872 spits dry-sieved and 700 wet-sieved.

The digitising of plans and the cross-referencing and checking of the written, drawn and photographic elements of the project archive were carried out on-site throughout the excavation and completed in post-excavation. A stratigraphic summary and complete matrix for the sequence of deposits at the site was also completed in the post-excavation stage. A summary of the record types contained within the excavation archive is provided in Table 1.3, and a plan of the final excavation area in Fig 1.5.

Palaeoenvironmental sampling

To meet the objectives of the project design, a targeted non-probabilistic sampling strategy

Table 1.3 Summary of the record types contained within the excavation

record type	number allocations
plans and sections	10000–19999
contexts	20000–29999
environmental samples	30000–39999
artefacts	40000–49999
faunal remains	50000–59999
$0.50m^2$ spit units	60000–69999

1 THE LYNFORD MIDDLE PALAEOLITHIC SITE

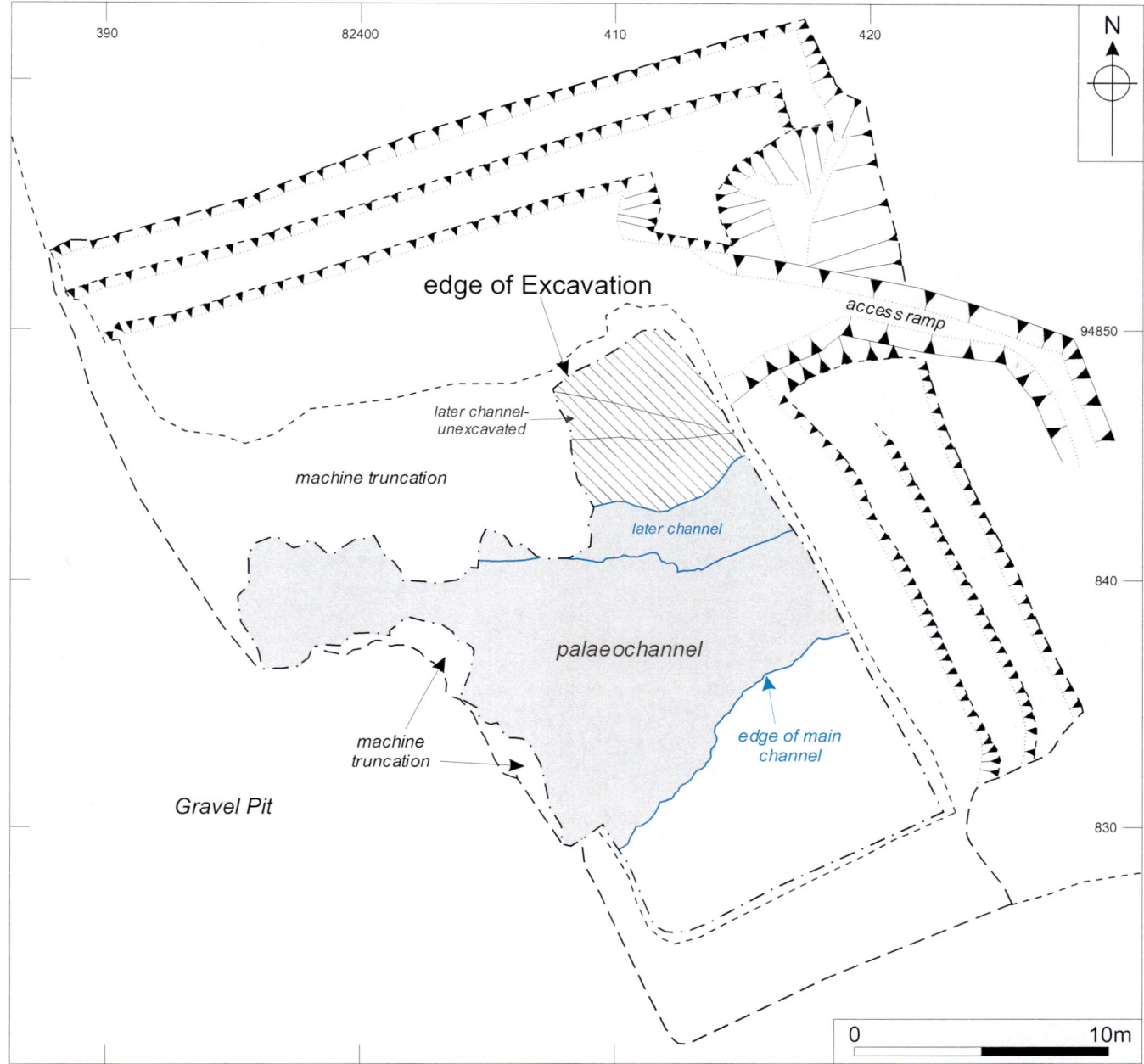

Fig 1.5
Plan of excavation area.

was devised in consultation with external specialists for the recovery of environmental materials from the palaeochannel and associated deposits. The principal aims of this recovery strategy were to retrieve materials for the environmental reconstruction of the site and for the identification and characterisation of the natural processes responsible for deposit and assemblage formation and post-depositional modification. Samples were taken by the relevant specialist or by the Site Environmentalist (F Green) in consultation with the particular specialist. A range of spot samples was also taken by members of the excavation team. Full records were made on-site for each sample.

Standard 5–10-litre bulk samples were taken for microfauna, insects, plant macrofossils and molluscs from baulk sections and other appropriate locations within the excavation area. Marginal (channel-edge) and deep-water palaeochannel deposits were bulk-sampled by serial column samples located on the north-south and east-west baulk sections running through the excavation area. Columns for each category of material were located adjacent to each other, with each column subdivided vertically into 0.10m units and the material from each unit bagged separately. Spot samples of plant macrofossils, molluscs, microfauna and insects were also taken from various locations within the palaeochannel during the excavation as the materials were exposed.

Deposits were sampled for pollen and diatoms employing monolith, column and spot techniques. Monolith and column samples were taken from sections on the north-south and east-west baulks adjacent to the sample locations for microfauna, insects, plant macrofossils and molluscs. Column samples were subdivided vertically into either 0.02m or 0.05m units and the material from each unit bagged separately. Additional monoliths were taken from later Pleistocene and Holocene deposits. A number of spot samples were also taken from Holocene deposits exposed on the south-facing section along the northern edge of the site.

A range of techniques was used to sample deposits for sedimentology, micromorphology, geochemistry and deposit compaction. Deposits were sampled for sedimentology by bulk, spot, monolith and column techniques with columns subdivided vertically into 0.05m–0.10m units or subsamples into 0.05m to 0.15m intervals on the basis of deposit stratigraphy. Spot and monolith samples were taken from deposits and contact surfaces between deposits for examination of the micromorphology, and geochemical samples were taken by spot and column techniques with the column samples subsampled at 0.05 and 0.10m–0.15m intervals on the basis of observable deposit stratification. Small short cores were taken from selected deposits for compaction studies.

Channel fill and test pitting methods

Small trenches were excavated manually across the organic channel-fill exposed on the east-facing section on the west side of the quarry. Sections were cleaned, photographed and the exposed sediments recorded on 1:10 section drawings. Samples were taken for palaeoenvironmental analysis and radiocarbon dating.

Seventeen test pits were excavated by machine at selected locations across the unworked area of the quarry (*see* Fig 1.4). Deposits exposed in section were logged and photographed, and their locations recorded using a total station theodolite. In addition, samples for OSL dating were taken from sediments in test pits 15 and 17.

1.2 Faunal conservation

S O'Connor and N Larkin

The conservation of often very fragile remains formed a significant part of the excavation strategy, full details of which are reported in Appendix A1.

The excavated faunal material is in a subfossil state with no secondary mineralisation (fossilisation). Specimen condition varied considerably, with some material preserved and some forming masses of unidentifiable soft bone splinters, and was largely dependent on the characteristics of the sediments in which the material was embedded. Bones recovered from organic sediments were stained dark brown-black, and were relatively robust and well-preserved. In contrast, bones from the underlying sands and gravels were amber or red-brown in colour, soft when wet, and brittle or crumbly when dry. In particular, bones from the gravels were frequently highly fractured when recovered. Where bones and teeth had lain partly in organic sediments and partly in sands or gravels, their preservation varied between one end or even side and the other, depending on how the specimen had rested in the sediments.

The aim of the conservation strategy was to retain and reveal as much diagnostic data as possible while ensuring the chemical and physical stability of the material. Soft brushes, wooden tools and/or gentle jets of compressed air were used to clean the specimens. Invasive treatments were kept to a minimum, only stable and removable resin adhesives and consolidants were used, and all labelling and storage materials were of archival standard. Each specimen was cleaned, repaired (excavation damage only, ie fresh breaks) and then labelled where appropriate. Specific supportive media were constructed for a number of large, fragile and/or complex bones. Adhesives applied to specimens in the field were reversed to allow cleaning and then rejoined. Jacketed specimens (Fig 1.6) required the removal of the plaster jackets and surrounding sediment before consolidation. Preparation of the jacketed tusks also required the manufacture of a reinforced

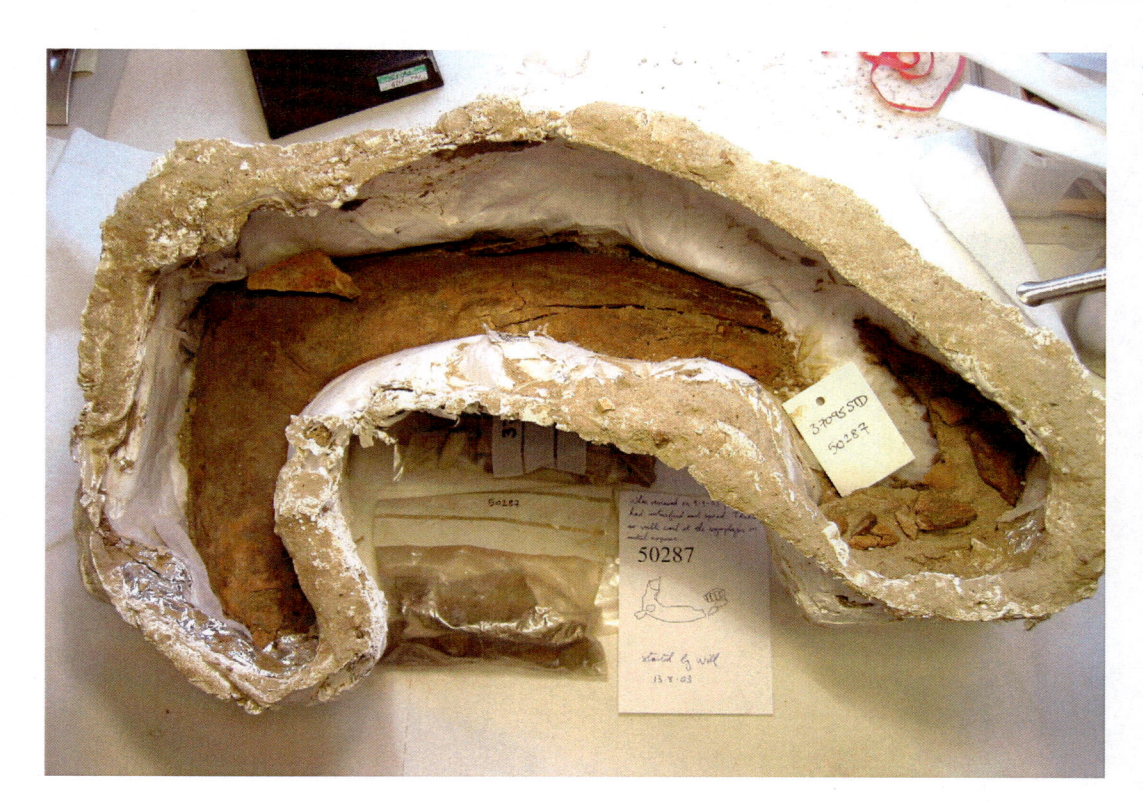

Fig 1.6
Mammoth mandible 50287 in its plaster of Paris jacket (photo courtesy D Charlton).

resin support for the underside of each tusk, onto which they could be turned. The jackets were cut away in stages, the revealed surfaces were cleaned and resin was injected deep into the tusks to consolidate the fragmentary annular laminations. The prepared tusks were then mounted on purpose-built, permanent pallet supports.

1.3 Archive details

The excavation and material archives are stored with the Norfolk Museums and Archaeology Service (NMAS) and access can be arranged by contacting NMAS, The Shirehall, Market Avenue, Norwich, Norfolk NR1 3JQ, website http://www.museums.norfolk.gov.uk. The photographic record is stored by NMAS in the offices of the Norfolk Historic Environment Service (formerly Norfolk Landscape Archaeology) at Gressenhall Farm and Workhouse Museum, Gressenhall, East Dereham, Norfolk NR20 4DR. Microfiche copies of the excavation archive have been deposited with the Norfolk Historic Environment Record in the same facility, as well as with the National Monuments Record, Swindon, Wiltshire. Faunal material is also housed in the NMAS stores at Gressenhall, and lithics in the Archaeology Department of Norwich Castle Museum and Art Gallery where the written and drawn archive is also held.

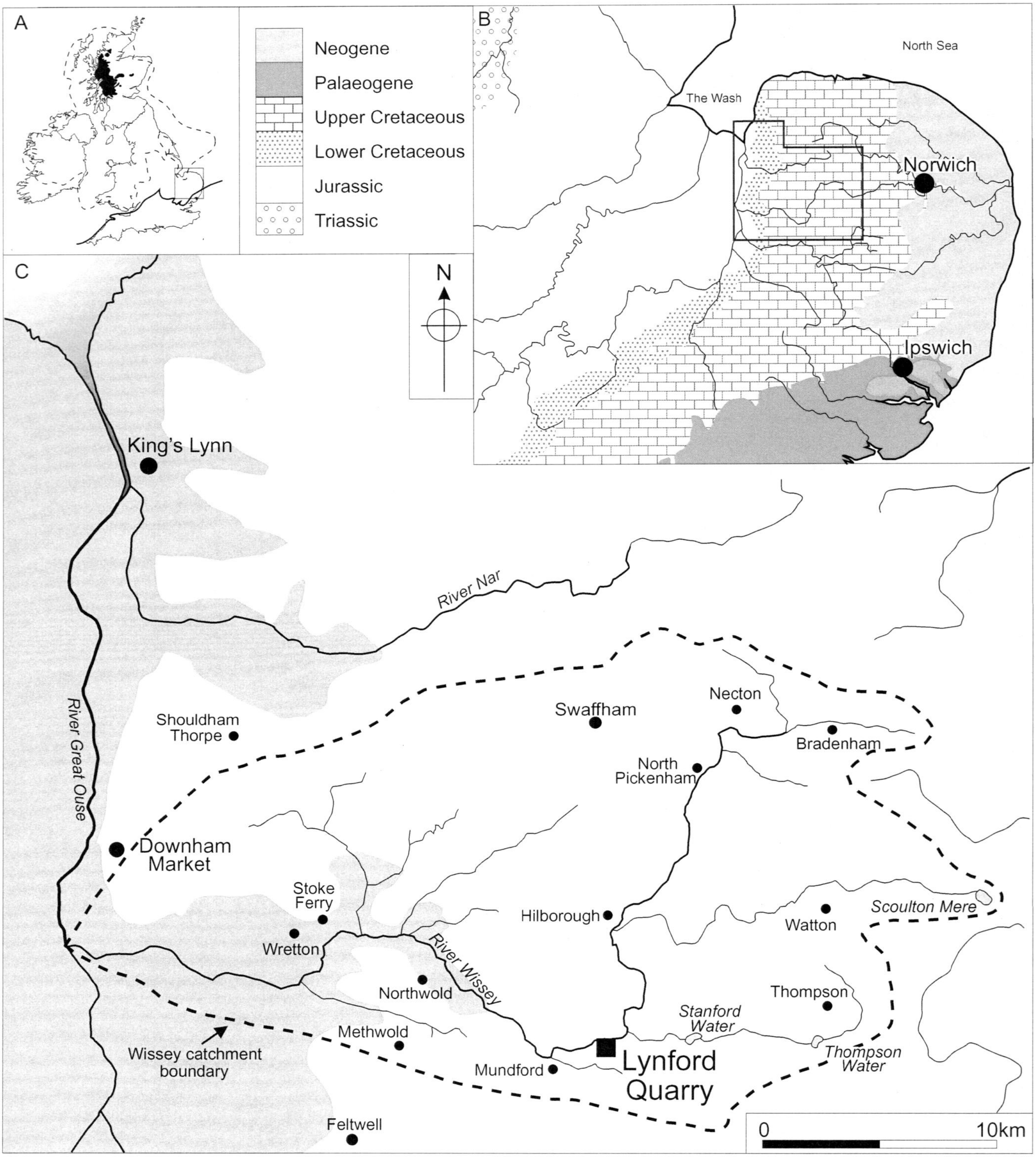
A
Neogene
Palaeogene
Upper Cretaceous
Lower Cretaceous
Jurassic
Triassic
B
North Sea
The Wash
Norwich
Ipswich
C
N
King's Lynn
River Nar
River Great Ouse
Shouldham Thorpe
Swaffham
Necton
Bradenham
North Pickenham
Downham Market
Stoke Ferry
Wretton
Hilborough
Watton
Scoulton Mere
River Wissey
Northwold
Thompson
Stanford Water
Methwold
Wissey catchment boundary
Mundford
Lynford Quarry
Thompson Water
Feltwell
0
10km

2

Stratigraphy, Association B and dating

The exceptional preservation of archaeological material at Lynford is due to a small oxbow lake that formed in the ice age course of the River Wissey. Once this meander was cut off from the river it provided an ideal environment for the preservation of organic evidence and stone artefacts, as the riverbanks where the artefacts had accumulated collapsed, slumping the material into the still waters of the channel. These deposits form a series of geologically distinctive contexts distinguished by their varying sediments and referred to as associations, of which the most archaeologically important is B-ii. These sedimentary envelopes are described here and examined in more detail in chapter 4. The wider stratigraphic framework within which they sit is described, and a place allocated within the last cold stage of the East Anglian Pleistocene sequence.

Three age estimation techniques were applied to the Lynford deposits in order to arrive at a date for the archaeology they contain. These were optically stimulated luminescence (OSL), radiocarbon 14C and amino-acid racemisation. The faunal remains provide a further means of placing the site within Marine Isotope Stage 3 (MIS 3) through biostratigraphic correlations with other assemblages. The oxygen isotope record, contained in cores from both the oceans and ice caps, provides a global framework for observing the repeated climate changes that impacted on hominins such as the Lynford Neanderthals. MIS 3 was a period of variable sea levels and fluctuating climate in the interval 60–24ka. Conditions were cold, but fell short of full glacial. At the beginning of MIS3 was a warmer phase that lasted between 60ka and 44ka during which there were a series of short-lived ameliorations, identified in the Greenland ice cores as Dansgaard–Oeschger events. Between 54ka and 60ka there were four of these milder interstadials, numbered D-O 14–17, and it is on these that the dating of Lynford focuses (chapter 3).

This short phase is of great interest for the re-occupation of northerly latitudes such as Britain after the rigours of MIS4 – a period of severe climate, low sea levels and significant ice advance. Fixing Lynford's position within the MIS framework was the primary task of the dating programme. Once established, the scene is then set for the detailed environmental evidence in chapter 3.

Fig 2.1 (opposite) Location of study site: (A) Ice limits for the Anglian (MIS 12) (solid line), Late Devensian (MIS 2) (dashed line) and Loch Lomond (black) glaciations in the British Isles (after Bowen et al 1986); (B) regional geology and drainage; (C) Wissey catchment and sites mentioned in the text (shaded area = land <8m OD).

2.1 Pleistocene stratigraphy and sedimentology

S G Lewis

Regional geomorphological and geological context

The River Wissey drains an area of some 545km² of central and western Norfolk, and forms a tributary of the River Great Ouse; the latter receives drainage from much of western East Anglia from the Nar valley in the north to the Cam in the south (Fig 2.1). The regional drainage pattern has experienced major adjustment as a result of glaciation during the Pleistocene. The Early and early Middle Pleistocene drainage of eastern England was characterised by major eastward-flowing rivers, including the ancestral Thames in southern Suffolk and Essex and the Bytham River in central Norfolk and Suffolk (Rose 1994; Rose *et al* 2001). These rivers drained into the southern North Sea basin and existed until they were respectively diverted and destroyed by glaciation during the Anglian. The Bytham River traversed the Wissey catchment in a north-south alignment; however, very few deposits associated with this river have been identified within the catchment. Fragmentary remnants of the Bytham River have been identified from gravels rich in quartzite and quartz at Northwold and Methwold (Rose 1987; Lewis 1993) and also at Shouldham Thorpe and Feltwell, just outside the catchment (Lewis 1991; Wymer 2001).

Following deglaciation at the end of the Anglian, a new drainage network formed on the surface of the till-covered East Anglian landscape. The formation of the Fen Basin as a result of erosion by Anglian ice (Perrin *et al* 1979) led to the creation of westward-flowing rivers, including the Nar, Wissey, Little Ouse, Lark and Cam, which drained the higher central part of the region.

The Wissey catchment is characterised by low relative relief, and nowhere exceeds 100m OD in elevation. The northern interfluve, separating the Wissey and Nar valleys, forms a ridge rising to 95m OD at its eastern end at Bradenham Hill. The southern portion of the catchment has less pronounced relief, rising to 56m OD at Frog Hill. The catchment can be divided into two distinct topographic regions; a low plateau in the eastern part – generally above 30m OD, except along the river valleys – and the low-lying Fen region in the west (*see* Fig 2.1). The latter is typically 0–10m OD in elevation, and the natural drainage pattern has been extensively modified.

The River Wissey is approximately 56km in length, measured along the main channel axis from its confluence with the River Great Ouse to its most easterly point 3km east of Bradenham (TF 957084) (*see* Fig 2.1) and has an average gradient of 1.25m km^{-1}. The gradient of the downstream 18km of the river is 0.34m km^{-1}, most of it lying in the Fen basin. The gradient of the middle 18km reach (which includes the site of Lynford) is 0.74m km^{-1} and for the upstream portion it is 2.78m km^{-1}. The river therefore displays a well-developed graded long profile (Fig 2.2).

The pre-Pleistocene geology comprises Upper Cretaceous Chalk over most of the catchment, except for the area west of Stoke Ferry. Here, Lower Cretaceous Gault and Carstone and the Upper Jurassic Kimmeridge/Ampthill Clay underlie the catchment (*see* Fig 2.1b). These rocks display a low-angled eastwards dip across the region. Lynford quarry itself is underlain by Upper Chalk, with Middle and Lower Chalk cropping out to the west. The boundary between the Middle and Upper Chalk lies within 1km of the site. This is significant, as the Brandon Flint Series occurs at the base of the Upper Chalk (Bristow 1990) and is well known as a source of high-quality flint for knapping, continuing to be used almost to the end of the nineteenth century for the manufacture of gun flints (Skertchly 1879). The Crag basin lies to the east of the Wissey and no Early Pleistocene sediments are present within the catchment.

The Pleistocene surface deposits within the catchment form a discontinuous cover and consist of the extensive chalky tills of the Lowestoft Formation and associated glacial gravels, sands, silts and clays. Along the river valley there are spreads of sands and gravels forming fragmentary terrace surfaces. These rise a few metres above the level of the alluvium, which forms a continuous unit along the length of the Wissey and its tributaries. In the Fen basin, alluvium is extensive, with inliers of older Pleistocene and pre-Pleistocene strata occurring as isolated outcrops within the catchment.

Geological mapping of the catchment at 1:50000 or 1:63360 either has yet to be undertaken or dates back to the late nineteenth century. On the basis of the available information it is not possible to identify and differentiate major terrace deposits and/or surfaces, as there are only a small number of

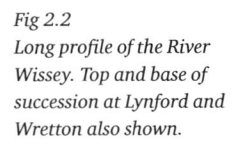

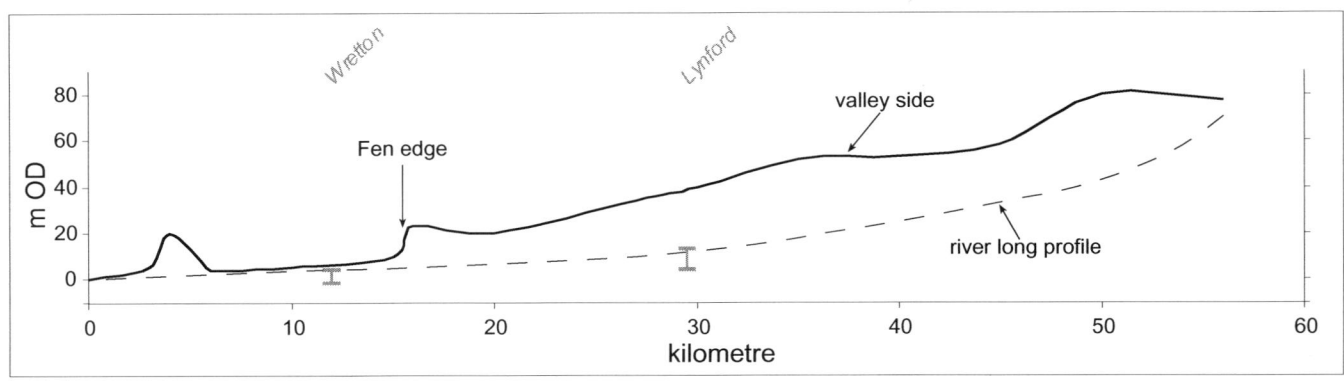

Fig 2.2
Long profile of the River Wissey. Top and base of succession at Lynford and Wretton also shown.

mapped fragments of terrace deposits, for example near Hilborough and North Pickenham. From Stoke Ferry, a large fragment of terrace extends for 5km downstream and includes the important site at Wretton (Sparks and West 1970; West et al 1974). It is also likely that, as at Lynford, substantial bodies of sand and gravel occur beneath the Holocene alluvium, particularly in the lower reaches of the river, downstream of Mundford, where the floodplain is over 1km wide in places.

In addition, several anomalously large patches of terrace deposits are shown on the 1:50000 geological map for Swaffham (British Geological Survey 1999). These include terrace deposits between Necton and Bradenham associated with the upper part of the River Wissey. A similar situation occurs in an unnamed tributary of the Wissey, flowing from a point close to the village of Thompson (TF 922980) via ponds at Thompson Water and Stanford Water to join the Wissey about 1.5km upstream of Lynford Quarry. The 1:50000 geological map (British Geological Survey 1999) also shows an extensive spread of terrace deposits traversing the present watershed, and extending into the upper reaches of the Thet catchment. This geometry suggests that these gravels are of glaciofluvial rather than fluvial origin. Finally a large spread of terrace deposits is mapped between Scoulton Mere (TF9801) and about 2km east of Watton, again following the line of a tributary stream. Mapped terrace deposits are therefore of three types: small fragments along the main Wissey valley above the Holocene alluvium; gravels buried beneath the alluvium; and extensive spreads in the upper reaches of the river and its tributaries, all in the eastern side of the catchment. These deposits record complex drainage development associated with deglaciation probably at the end of the Anglian glaciation and river development since that time.

Formal lithostratigraphic terminology is increasingly being applied to Pleistocene sediments (Bowen 1999), though no deposits in the Wissey valley were formally defined by Lewis (1999). Following the convention established by Bowen (1999), the fluvial deposits associated with the River Wissey may be referred to as the Wissey Valley Formation, with members and/or beds defined as appropriate (Table 2.1).

Table 2.1 Lithostratigraphy of the sedimentary succession at Lynford, Norfolk

unit	facies association	bed	member	formation
peat and alluvium				Fenland Formation
Mundford sands and gravels	E		Mundford Member	Wissey Valley Formation
	D			
	C			
	B	Lynford Bed		
	A			
sands			Plantation Member	
chalky diamicton			Lowestoft Till Member	Lowestoft Formation

Stratigraphic succession at Lynford Quarry

The sediments excavated in detail for archaeological purposes comprise part of an extensive accumulation of sands and gravels that underlie the Holocene alluvium of the River Wissey. Glacial till outcrops on the adjacent valley sides, and the fluvial deposits have incised through these and lie directly on Chalk bedrock (Fig 2.3). In addition to examination of the sections created during the excavations, a series of test pits (TPs) were dug using a

*Fig 2.3
Generalised N–S geological cross section through the site based on BGS geological mapping and boreholes.*

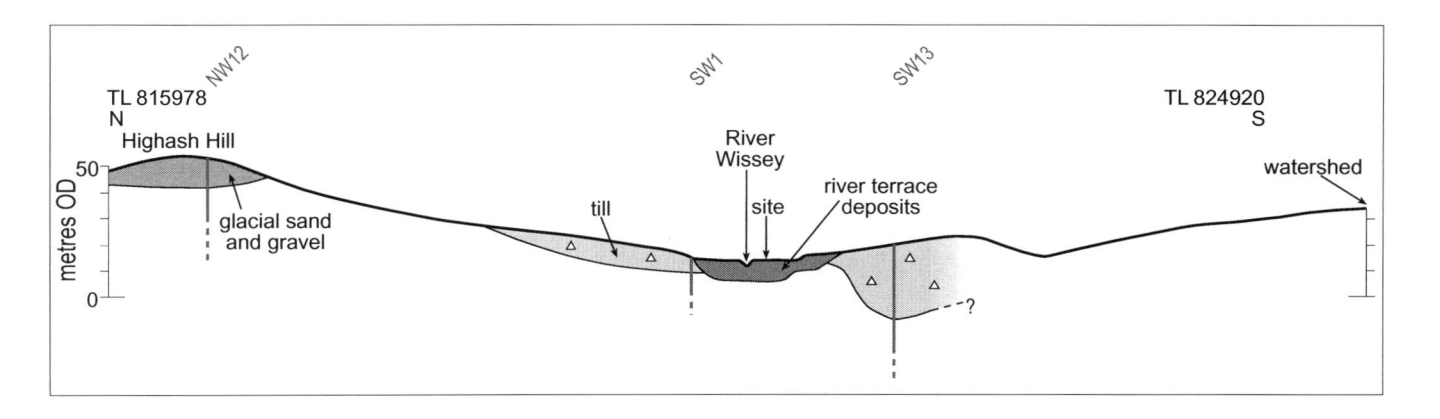

mechanical excavator at a number of points around the quarry in order to establish the sediment body geometry and also the elevation of the Chalk surface. Records of boreholes (BH) sunk in 1995 were made available by the quarry company and provide additional information on the geometry of the sands and gravels. Combining all the available information it is possible to build up a lithostratigraphic succession for the site, described in stratigraphic order below.

Chalk

Cretaceous Chalk is mapped at the surface south of the floodplain (British Geological Survey 1991). To the north of the river, Chalk occurs on the valley sides, either at the surface or beneath a cover of Pleistocene deposits (*see* Fig 2.3).

The entire quarry is underlain by Upper Chalk. It was proved in all the boreholes beneath a variable thickness of Pleistocene sediments. It was also proved in some of the test pits (TPs 1, 3, 7, 9, 10, 12, 13, 15, 16). The Chalk surface was exposed within the active quarry and showed significant variation in altitude. The Chalk surface was lowest at the northern end of the active quarry, at around 4.5–5.5m OD and is at this level beneath the archaeological site. To the south of the site, the Chalk surface rises steeply from 5.9m OD to 8.5m OD and then levels off again to TP 1, which was located on the edge of the active quarry in May 2003, where the Chalk was proved at 8.16m OD. South of this point Chalk was proved in TP 3 at an elevation of 10.2m OD, in TP 9 at 17.6m OD and in TP 7 at 17.4m OD beneath a thin Pleistocene cover.

At the eastern end of the quarry a further transect of test pits was dug. These showed the Chalk surface at 14.4m OD in TP 10 sloping down to the north, to TP 12, where it was proved at 12.7m OD. The Chalk continues to slope down towards the north and was proved at 10.9m OD in BH 6.

Chalky diamicton

This consists of a grey- to white-coloured deposit and contains pebble-sized chalk and flint clasts in a fine-grained, calcareous matrix. This stratigraphic unit was identified in test pits located along the southern margin of the quarry. In TP 7 it rests directly on Chalk bedrock and reaches its maximum observed thickness of 1.3m. It was also observed in test pits 9, 10 and 11. In cross-section, the upper surface of the chalky diamicton dips steeply within TP 9 and is not present in TP 5. Chalky diamicton was also observed resting on Chalk in TP 10. This unit again forms a sloping deposit on the southern flank of the valley, feathering out between TP 10 and 12. The unit is shown to underlie fluvial deposits in the northern end of TP 9.

The limited exposures make interpretation of this unit problematic. Its poorly sorted texture, abundance of chalk and calcareous matrix may indicate that it is part of the chalky Lowestoft till – a glaciogenic sediment that occurs across much of East Anglia. However, it is also possible that this unit is a slope deposit formed by mass movement of material down the valley sides, incorporating weathered chalky debris, glaciogenic sediments and other material to form a diamicton unit. Tills are mapped on the northern flank of the Wissey valley at this locality (British Geological Survey 1999) and recorded in boreholes to the south (*see* Fig 2.3). It is therefore possible that a small remnant of chalky till has survived on the southern side of the valley.

Plantation sands

This unit was revealed during the course of excavation of test pits in the area to the south of the active quarry (*see* Fig 1.4) and is named for the area of plantation forestry that lies immediately to the south of the quarry. A number of test pits proved thick deposits of cross-bedded, fluvially deposited medium-to-fine sands (Table 2.2) up to *c* 6m in thickness. The sands underlie a land surface that slopes up to the south, from the edge of the modern floodplain, reaching a maximum elevation of *c* 20m OD in TP 8, which proved in excess of 6.2m of sand. Sands were encountered in test pits 3, 4, 5, 6, 7 and 17 and also, much thinner, to the east in test pits 10, 11 and 12. Boreholes 4, 6, 7 and 12 also proved a substantial thickness of sands. In all cases the surface elevation of the sands is higher (above 14m OD) than that of the surface of the Mundford sands and gravels. In addition, where proved, the Chalk surface is also higher than that beneath the site. Immediately south of TP 8, the Chalk and overlying chalky diamicton rise steeply to the surface, so that the sands abut against a steeply angled contact. Elsewhere the Chalk surface beneath the sands was proved down to 9.8m OD. However, the stratigraphic relationship between these sands and the Mundford sands and gravels was not seen in the field, as no unconformity between the two units was visible in section. Therefore, the relationship discussed below is conjectural. However the optically stimulated luminescence dating of the sands (Schwenninger, this chapter) indicates that it is probable that the sands form an older and altitudinally higher stratigraphic unit than the sands and gravels exposed in the active quarry.

The sands are interpreted as fluvial sediments laid down by the River Wissey before the deposition of the Mundford sands and gravels, and are separated from the latter by a phase of fluvial incision. The sands now form the remnant of a degraded terrace landform whose topographic and bedrock surfaces are a few metres higher than the Mundford sands and gravels. The sand-dominated sediments would be susceptible to degradation by slope processes and deflation by aeolian mechanisms, and this probably accounts for the lack of a well-defined terrace feature.

Mundford sands and gravels

The Mundford sands and gravels form the main sedimentary unit exposed at Lynford, and comprise fluvial sands and gravels and associated fine-grained and organic facies. They include the fine-grained deposits from which the archaeological and faunal material has been recovered. The Mundford sands and gravels can be divided into five facies associations that are described and discussed in detail below.

The sands and gravels overlie the Chalk, above an erosional lower bounding surface, which is locally subhorizontal, but shows variations in elevation of 2–5m between c 4.5m and 8.5m OD. Localised scour of the Chalk has resulted in greater thickness of sands and gravels in the northern part of the quarry than in the vicinity of BH 6. The upper surface of the sands and gravels is subhorizontal over much of the quarry at an elevation of 12–13m OD in the area of the site.

The Mundford sands and gravels are clearly of fluvial origin and were deposited by the River Wissey. The major changes in the facies identifiable at the site might indicate changes in river behaviour. Interpretation of these sediments and reconstruction of the depositional environment provides the sedimentary context for the archaeological and faunal information discussed elsewhere in this volume.

Peat and alluvium

This stratigraphic unit is usually stripped off before sand and gravel extraction and is therefore not present within the site, but is extensive elsewhere in the quarry. Its relationship to the Mundford sands and gravels is best seen in cross section at the eastern end of the quarry. Here nearly 2m of peat were encountered in TP 14, which was located on the floodplain itself. The peat overlies calcareous sandy silt, to a depth of 2.4m. Fifteen metres to the south, TP 13 proved a thinner succession of peat and alluvial sands and silts resting on a layer of large flint nodules, which in turn overlies the Chalk bedrock. This cross-section indicates that the peat and alluvium thins out against the rising Chalk surface. The stratigraphic unit represents fluvial deposition and peat accumulation on the floodplain during the Holocene.

Laboratory methods

Samples collected during the course of the field excavations were selected for all or some of the following analyses: particle size, carbonate, organic carbon and clast lithological analysis. Particle size analysis of the < 2mm fraction was

Table 2.2 Particle size, organic carbon and carbonate analyses of Lynford sediments

sample	context	facies	quartz	quartzite	Carb chert	flint	chalk	ironstone	igneous	other	total
89/1	–	C?	1	1	0	97.1	0	0.5	0.2	0.2	408
30251	20149, 151, 153	C	0.6	1.8	0	96.9	0	0.6	0	0	327
30249-04	20003	B	0	0	0	100	0	0	0	0	15
30249-08	20254	B	0.8	0	0	99.2	0	0	0	0	125
30243-01	20374	B	0	1.5	0	98.5	0	0	0	0	202
30243-02	20402	B	0.7	3.6	0.7	94.9	0	0	0	0	138
30254	20079	A	0	2.5	0	97.5	0	0	0	0	161
30249-06	20051	A	0.9	0.9	0	98.2	0	0	0	0	331
30243-06	20357	A	0.5	0.7	0	98.3	0	0.5	0	0	411

carried out using sieving for the sand fraction and the SediGraph for the silt and clay fraction, following treatment with hydrogen peroxide and sodium hexametaphosphate to remove organic material and disaggregate clay particles respectively. Analysis of the silt/clay fraction was not done on samples where the total silt and clay fraction was less than 10 per cent. Organic carbon was determined by loss on ignition and carbonate content by dissolution of carbonate with hydrochloric acid and titration with sodium hydroxide. A number of bulk samples were sieved to yield gravel clasts for lithological analysis of the 11.2–16mm fraction. Results of these analyses are shown in Tables 2.2 and 2.3.

Sedimentology of the Mundford sands and gravels

During the excavation, contexts were defined on the basis of field characteristics, such as colour, texture, organic content etc (Boismier, this chapter) and more than 300 contexts have been assigned. This provided the basis for recording the context of artefacts and other finds in the field. Preliminary analysis of the field data resulted in the formulation of 39 context groups. However, following the methodology adopted in studies of Pleistocene fluvial deposits in the Thames valley (Maddy et al 1998, 2003; Lewis and Maddy 1999; Lewis et al 2001), the Mundford sands and gravels

Table 2.3 Clast lithological analysis (11.2–16mm fraction) of gravel facies from Lynford (sample 89/1 from Lewis 1993)

sample	context	facies	$CaCO_3$ (%)	C_{org} (%)	1000µm	500µm	250µm	125µm	63µm	% sand	32µm	16µm	8µm	4µm	2µm	% silt	<2µm
30175	20070	B		1.16	1.28	5.45	29.22	33.71	11.85	81.52	2.59	1.60	1.63	1.77	0.76	8.36	10.13
30179	20003	B	3.25	8.93	0.63	4.93	23.98	37.63	18.96	74.91	2.01	3.27	2.42	1.61	1.76	11.06	14.02
30180	20003	B	2.01	7.80	1.14	5.60	29.91	42.28	19.96	77.59	2.22	2.85	1.96	1.75	1.86	10.64	11.76
30182	20003	B	7.69	7.99	1.28	4.48	20.57	28.54	18.02	63.37	4.51	5.30	3.71	3.48	2.67	19.67	16.96
30184	20003	B	15.64	10.26	1.54	6.36	32.89	41.74	19.43	68.21	2.23	4.72	3.48	2.48	2.67	15.58	16.21
30186	20003	B	7.36	9.39	1.93	5.50	30.45	37.33	17.94	63.01	2.81	4.34	3.98	2.74	3.55	17.42	19.57
30188	20003	B	11.92	17.41	0.60	5.09	27.90	38.46	21.60	59.62							
30189	20004	B	2.25	0.54	7.74	24.36	72.71	50.06	10.96	90.04	0.92	1.69	1.17	0.89	0.71	5.37	4.59
30239/01	20070	B	2.67	8.96	0.53	4.39	27.36	35.31	13.17	75.32	1.70	4.21	3.17	3.11	1.68	13.87	10.81
30239/03	20003	B	2.92	6.68	3.39	8.67	26.60	35.15	19.15	76.42	1.79	2.37	2.46	1.60	1.77	10.00	13.58
30239/05	20003	B	4.80	8.24	4.38	12.50	32.51	26.15	11.09	69.65	2.28	3.34	2.24	2.34	1.79	11.99	18.36
30239/07	20371	B	3.10	4.27	6.53	23.16	49.83	34.24	8.61	83.34	1.82	2.36	1.84	1.15	0.95	8.11	8.55
30239/09	20371	B	19.30	4.04	1.70	5.16	16.29	23.64	16.09	56.31	4.06	6.94	6.30	7.30	5.59	30.19	13.50
30239/11	20371	B	18.18	4.14	5.36	17.92	37.55	38.79	20.57	64.57	2.41	5.24	4.29	4.78	3.47	20.20	15.24
30249/08	20254	B	–	–	1.44	14.18	58.37	44.90	13.81	85.03	2.17	2.81	2.60	1.47	1.06	10.12	4.85
30249/09	20051	A	–	–	31.54	52.05	21.41	3.95	1.43	95.31							
30251		C	–	–	9.12	36.40	41.14	13.20	1.51	95.22							
30252		A	–	–	7.91	30.46	42.79	14.88	1.51	95.89							
30258/01	20012	B	1.31	0.37	0.94	5.46	36.19	48.54	3.99	91.04							
30258/02	20016	B	15.07	4.92	0.04	0.57	13.81	51.65	13.43	78.68	3.50	2.48	2.00	1.26	1.09	10.32	11.00
30258/03	20016	B	16.07	4.38	0.62	4.79	39.03	54.10	9.09	84.98	1.14	1.33	1.40	1.16	0.87	5.90	9.12
30258/04	20016	B	19.37	4.41	0.13	2.61	28.09	47.15	11.90	77.54	2.67	2.87	2.46	2.81	2.16	12.96	9.50
30258/05	20015	B	16.76	0.47	0.09	1.75	34.50	65.26	11.48	86.36	1.35	1.73	1.57	2.06	1.12	7.83	5.81
30278/01	20345	B	12.51	0.87	2.74	5.31	26.74	39.08	13.12	76.78	2.23	4.24	3.72	2.67	2.02	14.88	8.34
30278/02	20116	B	13.32	0.93	0.49	5.28	31.27	45.20	18.72	81.82	2.73	3.23	2.51	2.82	1.31	12.60	5.58
30278/03	20003	B	13.11	15.43	0.23	1.47	8.17	21.18	18.22	54.91	4.96	4.13	3.17	3.02	2.48	17.77	27.32
30278/05	20003	B	13.92	13.23	4.46	20.86	59.43	54.60	24.97	75.53	1.93	3.52	2.06	2.89	1.88	12.29	12.19
30278/07	20003	B	13.58	10.55	2.51	9.13	32.72	35.40	17.97	77.45	2.39	3.48	2.52	1.65	1.40	11.43	11.12
30278/09	20003	B	12.54	2.23	6.53	18.54	47.40	39.69	13.13	90.47	2.08	1.84	1.25	1.28	0.69	7.14	2.39
30278/10	20255	B	14.51	0.57	1.23	6.61	28.25	47.78	17.68	98.49							
30379	TP2 (108–112cm)		–	–	0.04	0.45	8.76	55.81	20.85	85.91							
30380	TP2 (142–147cm)		–	–	0.13	0.44	20.75	74.44	4.16	99.91							
30386	Plantation sands (TP15)		–	–	0.08	1.61	52.29	44.70	0.96	99.65							
30388	Plantation sands (TP17)		–	–	0.63	3.24	34.07	56.89	4.31	99.13							

can be divided into five facies associations. A facies association is a grouping of genetically related lithofacies (Reading 1986) and provides an appropriate scale at which to consider sedimentology and river behaviour over 10^3–10^5 (ice age) year timescales (Maddy *et al* 2003). The characteristics of the facies associations recognised at Lynford are summarised in Table 2.4 and Fig 2.4 and discussed below. Following this, the evidence for river behaviour and changing fluvial regime will be considered.

Association A

Facies Association A is characterised by dominance of coarse gravel lithofacies, consisting of angular flint clasts, up to cobble size. It overlies Chalk bedrock in the northern part of the active quarry, above a 6th order bounding surface, where the Chalk is locally scoured to greater depths and is cut out against the rising Chalk surface to the south of the site. The gravels form massive to crudely bedded, laterally persistent facies, with some minor sandy facies also present (*see* Table 2.4).

Clast lithological analysis of samples from this association (*see* Table 2.3) indicates that this association is dominated by flint, which comprises over 95 per cent flint of all samples. Minor quantities of quartz, quartzite, Carboniferous chert and ironstone are also present. Particle-size analysis of the < 2mm fraction of samples 30252 and 30249-09 indicates that the sand proportion is in excess of 95 per cent, with modes in the medium sand and coarse sand categories respectively (*see* Table 2.2).

The sedimentology of Association A indicates deposition in a high-energy fluvial environment, in which coarse gravel-bed load is transported, probably in a multiple-channel river system. The coarse calibre of the gravels might result from rapid incision into Chalk bedrock and incorporation of flint into the fluvial system. The clast lithology of the gravels is almost exclusively flint, indicating that the material is

Table 2.4 Summary of sedimentological characteristics of Association B

association	dominant facies (architectural element)	lower bounding surface (and order)	geometry	depositional environment
E	Gp, Gt, Fl, Fm, peat (CH)	concave-up, erosional (5th order)	stratified gravels, sands and fines, overlie channelled lower bounding surface, some reworked peat blocks	moderate-high energy fluvial, single channel, sinuous planform system
D	Sh, Sp, St, (SB)	planar, sub-horizontal or concave-up (5th order)	tabular sediment body, typically 2m thick, over 3m thick in places	sandy bedload, multiple-channel fluvial system
C		planar, sub-horizontal, locally concave-up, erosional (5th order)	tabular sediment body, up to 2m thick	in-channel bars and bedforms, mixed sand and gravel bedload; high-energy, multiple-channel fluvial system
B	Fl, Fm, Sm, Sh, Gms, Gm (CH)	concave-up, erosional (5th order)	channel-shaped geometry, lateral extent c 20m up to c 2m in thickness; consists predominantly of massive organic silty sands, some sandy and gravelly facies	channel complex; avulsion and abandonment, occasional inundation, reactivation, bank collapse and post-depositional disturbance; still- to slow-flowing water body
A	Gm (GB)	planar, sub-horizontal, locally concave-up, erosional (6th order)	tabular sediment body geometry, up to c 4m in thickness; consists of massive, poorly stratified gravel facies; overlies Chalk bedrock in northern part of the active quarry; cut out to the south against the rising Chalk surface	in-channel longitudinal bars; high-energy, multi-channel fluvial

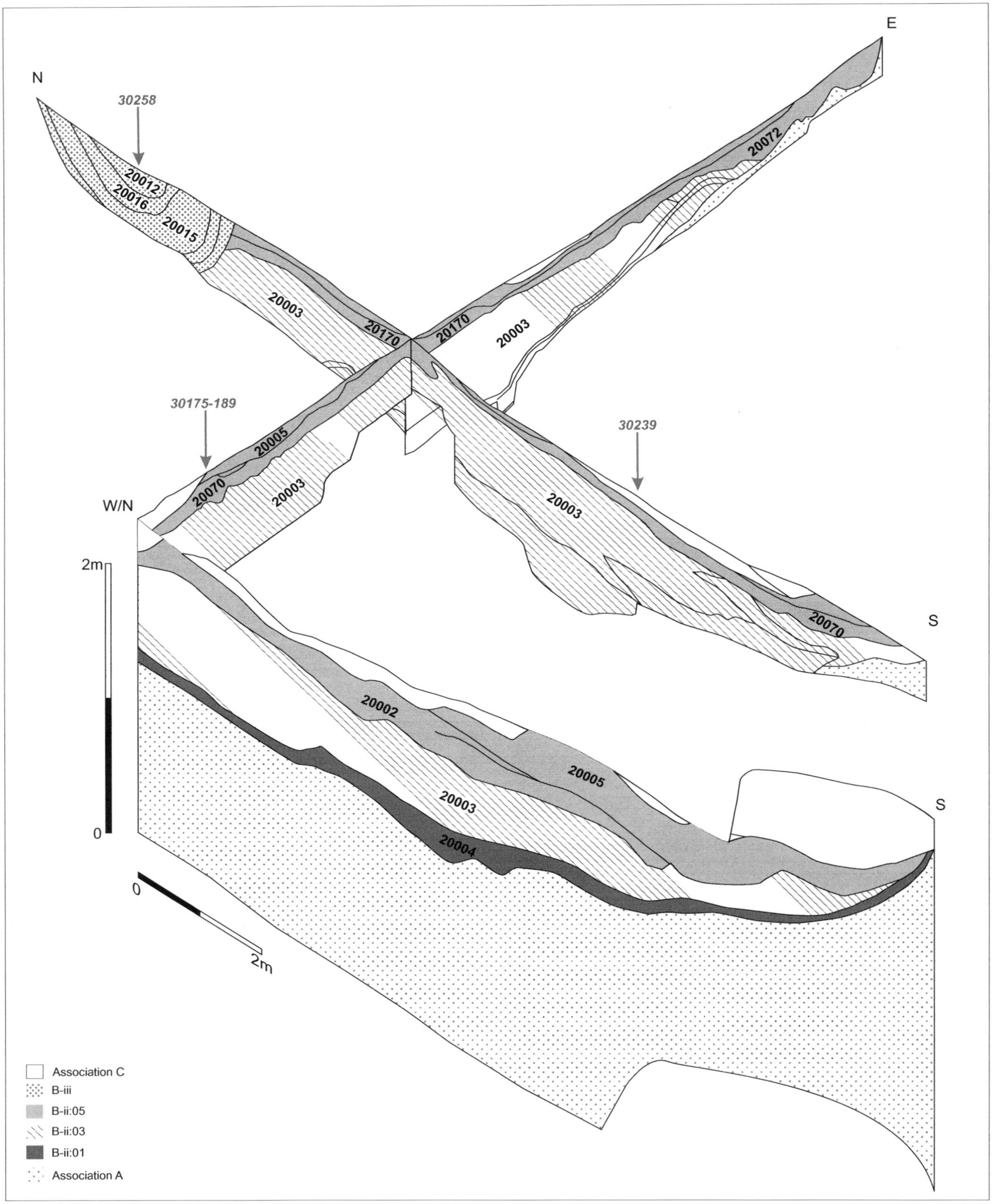
N
E
30258
20012
20016
20015
20003
20170
20170
20003
20072
30175-189
20005
20070
20003
W/N
30239
20003
20070
S
2m
0
20002
20005
20003
20004
S
0
2m
Association C
B-iii
B-ii:05
B-ii:03
B-ii:01
Association A

locally derived from the underlying bedrock; any clasts reworked from older gravels containing a more diverse lithological suite have been heavily diluted by flint. Non-durable lithologies such as chalk have either not survived the high-energy transport and depositional environment, or have been removed by solution.

Association B

The sediments in this facies association and their contained fauna, flora and archaeological material were the focus of the excavations undertaken during 2002. This association was exposed in a number of sections, in particular the cruciform N-S and E-W baulk sections across the excavated area (Boismier, this chapter). In addition, the geometry of the basal bounding surface is well exposed in the section forming the western extremity of the site. The upper contact of this association is not well exposed, due to the removal of overlying sediments during sand and gravel extraction. Within this association the internal geometry of the constituent facies and their bounding surfaces is complex and laterally variable.

Facies Association B overlies a concave-up, 5th order lower bounding surface and forms a prominent channel feature. The channel base is best seen in the section at the western edge of the site. The channel cuts into the underlying gravels of Association A. In the centre of the channel feature, gravels immediately overlie the lower bounding surface, while towards the edges sandy facies directly overlie the channel base.

The dominant facies consists of organic silty sands, which are in places finely laminated, but elsewhere are massive and/or display evidence of post-depositional disturbance. Coarse flint clasts occur in varying proportions in these deposits, with some of the organic units displaying a significant proportion of flint material, including humanly struck flakes.

Association B can be further subdivided into three main components: B-i comprises coarse gravels immediately overlying the basal bounding surface; B-ii comprises the majority of the organic silty sand facies within the channel-fill; B-iii consists of a final series of deposits separated from B-ii by a 4th order bounding surface and forming a discrete channel-fill.

Association B-ii overlies another concave-up bounding surface (20032) which in places cuts the gravels of B-i, but elsewhere cuts the gravels of Association A. The channel geometry is clearly seen in the N-S sections and in the western edge section. Although the northern extent of the channel is difficult to establish, it is at least 12m wide and approximately 1m in depth. The sediments infilling the channel are laterally and vertically variable, though most are characterised by having an organic content and a silty sand texture. There is a marked lateral variation from the centre to the edge of the channel. The major facies present within the channel are basal sands (20004 and equivalents), organic silty sands (20003/20021/20258) and the overlying laminated organic sands (20002/20070/20170/20116 and 20005/20345). Large stones also occur within these sediments, some of which are associated with vertical deformation of the adjacent sediments. Towards the margins of the channel, a more complex assemblage of facies is present, particularly along the SE edge where there is a series of stony organic sands (including contexts 20374/20376 and 20055). The stones in these sediments are in places matrix-supported and show no evidence of sorting. These facies are replaced laterally by the organic silty sand filling the central part of the channel. Similar deposits containing abundant flint clasts are present along the NW margin of the channel. These units occur both below (contexts 20374, 20376) and also within (20055) the organic sediments. The upper part of the channel-fill succession (20002/20070/20170/20116 and 20005/20345) forms a laterally persistent tabular unit across much of the channel-fill sediments.

Association B-iii overlies a concave-up bounding surface (20121) and represents the uppermost phase of infilling of the channel. These facies overlie a concave-up bounding surface (20121), which cuts the uppermost facies of B-ii (20345). The channel containing B-iii is approximately 3m wide and up to 0.5m thick and runs in an E-W direction across the northern part of the site. It is infilled by a series of predominantly sandy organic facies, with minor gravel facies in the base of the channel.

The clast lithological composition of Association B (*see* Table 2.3) is dominated by flint (in excess of 95 per cent), with very minor amounts of quartz, quartzite and chert present. This assemblage is similar to all the other samples from Lynford.

Fig 2.4 (opposite) Schematic diagram showing relationship of major facies (contexts) within Facies Association B, based on field data.

Table 2.5 Summary of textural, organic carbon and carbonate characteristics of selected contexts within Association B

context	no. samples	sand (%)	silt (%)	clay (%)	$CaCO_3$ (%)	C_{org} (%)
20016	3	77.5–84.9	5.9–13.0	9.5–11.0	15.1–19.4	4.4–4.9
20015	1	86.4	7.8	5.8	16.8	0.5
20345	1	76.8	14.9	8.3	12.5	0.9
20116/20070	3	75.3–81.8	8.4–13.9	5.6–10.8	2.7–13.3	0.9–9.0
20003	11	90.5–54.9	7.1–19.7	2.4–27.3	2.0–15.6	6.7–17.4
20004	1	90.0	5.4	4.6	2.3	0.5
20371	3	83.3–56.3	8.1–30.2	8.6–15.3	3.1–19.3	4.0–4.3

The texture, $CaCO_3$ and organic carbon content of these deposits are summarised in Table 2.5. The proportions of sand, silt and clay in all the samples analysed are generally quite similar, consisting predominantly of sand, with lesser quantities of silt and clay (Fig 2.5, Table 2.5). In the centre of the channel, sandy facies immediately overlie the lower bounding surface of B-ii (20004, 20255), and are overlain by the organic silty sands of 20003. There is no consistent upward trend in texture in this facies (Fig 2.6); a coarsening upward trend is shown in sample column 30175–189, while a fining upward pattern is apparent in column 30278. This facies is overlain by the laminated sands of 20116/20070 and 20345. In sample column 30239 beneath 20003 there is a further organic silty sand facies (20371). This facies contains more silt than the overlying 20003 and has a higher $CaCO_3$ content. The Corg values are

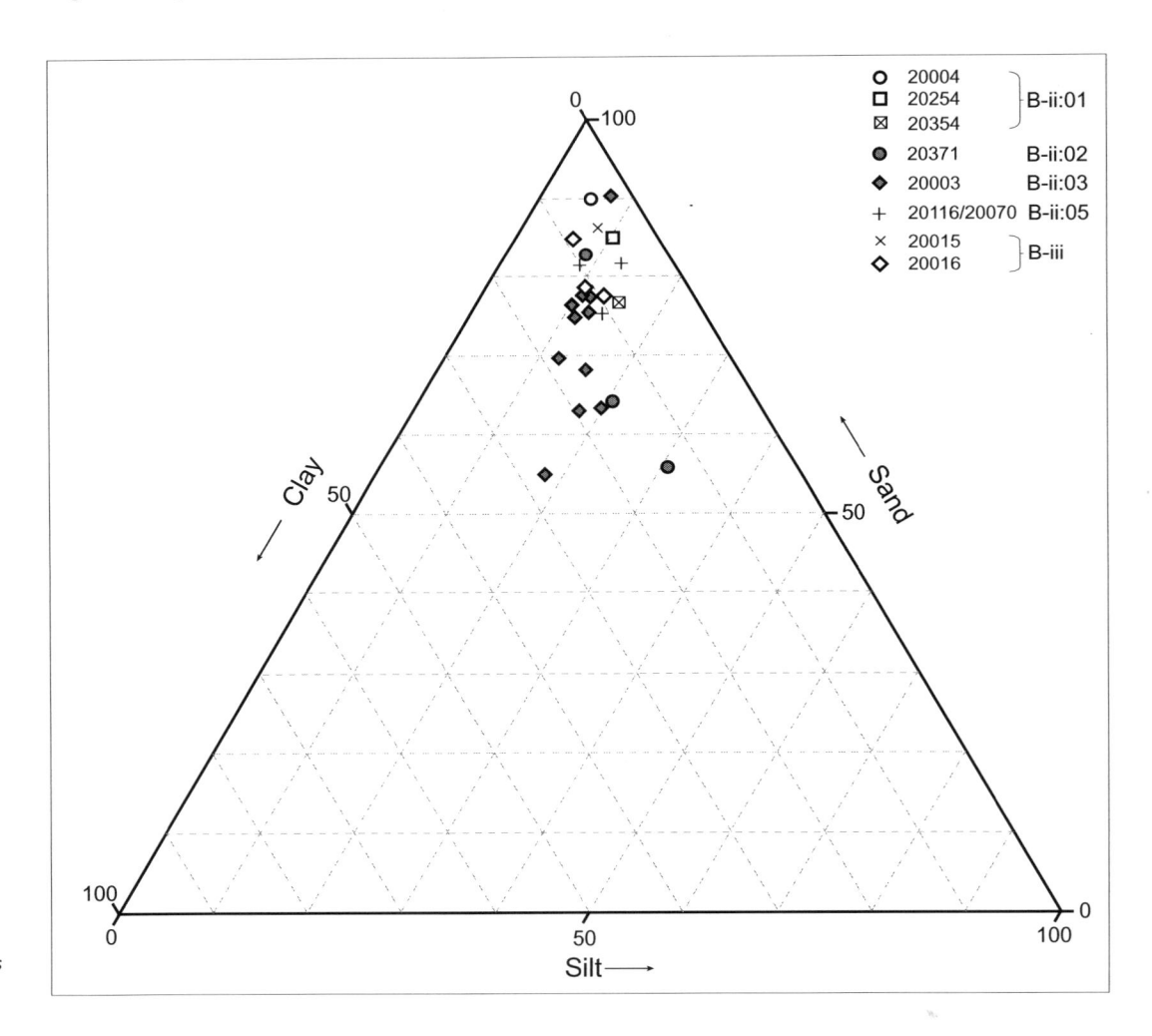

Fig 2.5
Ternary plot of sand, silt and clay content of samples from Facies Association B.

nowhere in excess of 20 per cent. The basal deposits have the lowest organic content, with highest Corg values in 20003, particularly in the central part of the channel-fill.

Association B-iii consists of basal inorganic sands (20015) overlain by organic sands (20016), which are in turn overlain by inorganic sands (20012). There is little textural variation through this profile, though Corg and CaCO$_3$ content decrease towards the top of the profile (*see* Fig 2.6).

The lower bounding surface of Association B indicates channel avulsion, followed by deposition of a sequence of sediments within the channel feature. Following avulsion, this channel carried flowing water, resulting in the deposition of coarse gravels of B-i. However, the change to finer-grained organic sediment deposition indicates that the channel was abandoned soon after its formation, probably as the main channel belt migrated to another part of the floodplain.

Following channel abandonment, deposition occurred under dominantly still to slow-flowing water conditions, depositing the sediments of Association B-ii. Influx of coarser sediments into the channel-fill is apparent, particularly at the margins. This might result from periodic inundation by floodwater. However, the distribution of the gravelly deposits and the matrix-supported character suggests an origin related to slope processes operating on the margins of the channel. The influx of gravel material is probably the result either of debris flow or bank collapse. This might account for many of the large clasts within the organic sands and silts. However, towards the centre of the channel many of the large flint clasts are associated with structures indicative of deformation of sediment as a result of impact of the clast into the sediment, and might suggest an alternative mechanism; possibly the melting of ice formed on the water surface during the winter, and the release of any stones accumulated on the frozen surface. In common with the underlying gravels of Association A, gravel clasts within Association B are dominantly composed of flint, indicating that there has been no change in the sources of gravel supplied to these deposits. The laminated sediments in the upper part of Association B-ii suggest a return to flowing water conditions, possibly indicating a reoccupation of this part of the floodplain by the river. The final phase of

Fig 2.6
Summary of changes in particle size, organic carbon and carbonate content in four profiles through Association B.

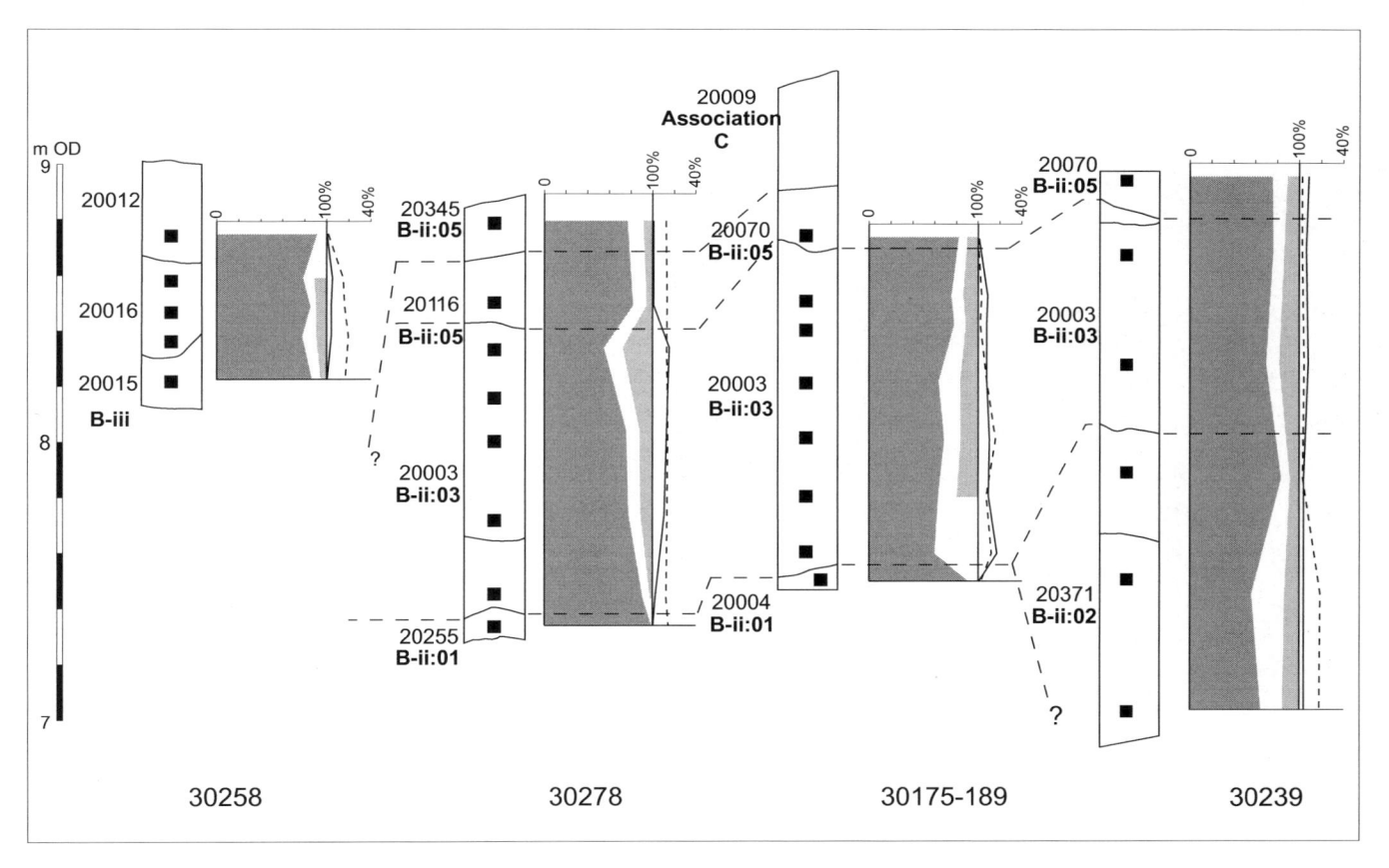

deposition of Association B-iii follows a small-scale channel scour, of much smaller size than the main channel feature. This again is partly in-filled with organic silty sands.

Association C

This association overlies Association B above an erosional, subhorizontal, locally concave-upwards lower bounding surface. Unfortunately the contact with the underlying deposits over the excavation area had been largely removed during sand and gravel extraction. However it can be recognised in sections along the eastern edge of the site, and in places the basal deposits of Association C are preserved in the top of the N–S and W–E sections within the site. Association C comprises predominantly sand and gravel lithofacies, with few fine-grained facies. It is *c* 2–2.5m in thickness.

The sedimentology of this association is characterised by superimposed channels with high width-to-depth ratios, typically 2–5m in width, but rarely reaching 1m in maximum depth. These channels are particularly clearly seen in the west-facing sections along the eastern edge of the site. These sections are presumably aligned approximately normal to the flow direction of the river. Sections elsewhere in the quarry that are aligned parallel to flow direction do not show such clearly defined channel geometry. The infill of these channels varies from sands and silty sands to medium gravels. However, the calibre of the gravel facies is generally finer than seen in Association A.

A return to a higher-energy fluvial depositional environment is indicated by the transition to Association C, which suggests a mixed bed-load river system, transporting and depositing gravels and sands. Once again the clast lithological suite is almost entirely of flint, and is indistinguishable from the underlying gravels. The uniformity of the gravel lithology indicates that no major influx of sediment into the catchment has taken place during deposition, such as might have occurred if glacier ice impinged upon the catchment.

Association D

Sections along the eastern edge of the site and elsewhere in the active quarry show that the predominantly gravelly texture of Association C passes upwards into dominantly sandy lithofacies. These sand-dominated facies form Association D (*see* Table 2.4). The contact between associations C and D is difficult to define as sandy facies occur throughout the sediments overlying Association B, though they become more significant in the upper part of the succession. Similarly, a few gravel facies are present in the upper part of the sequence. The boundary is therefore placed at point where substantial, laterally extensive sandy facies become dominant.

The lower bounding surface of Association D is erosional and subhorizontal to concave-up. In the sections on the eastern edge of the site the lower bounding surface falls to lower elevations towards the northern end of the section. The facies within Association D include horizontal and cross-stratified sands. Gravelly lithofacies are also present within Association D, either as tabular to lenticular bodies of gravel several metres wide and up to 1m thick, or as thin layers or stringers of gravel on reactivation surfaces within predominantly sandy sediments.

This association indicates continued fluvial deposition, but probably resulting from lower peak discharges than the underlying gravel-dominated sediments. The sedimentology suggests a multiple-channel system, with flow in broad, shallow channels and deposition of sandy bedforms. The significance of the transition from Association C to D is discussed further below.

Association E

This association is present in the sections along the eastern and northern edges of the site. It overlies an erosional lower bounding surface. The south-facing section along the northern edge of the site was recorded in order to provide sufficient sedimentological information to interpret the sediments. However, during the investigation of these sediments, a number of struck flint flakes were found. These are clearly of later prehistoric type and indicate that the sediments are probably mainly of Holocene age. A sample of material from the basal part of one of the organic sequences was sampled for radiocarbon dating to establish the age of the sediments above the association D-E boundary. Other than this, these sediments were not investigated in detail.

The lower bounding surface is planar to locally concave-upwards. The sedimentology of this association is variable, with a range of facies present (*see* Table 2.4), including stratified gravels and sands as well as massive silts, containing abundant visible plant remains and blocks of reworked peat.

Association E indicates a major change in river behaviour. This association forms a complex series of channel-fills, which contain a variety of sediments, including organic silts and reworked peat blocks. The geometry and sedimentology of the channel-fills suggest that deposition took place in a more sinuous channel system, with cohesive banks formed of peat, which is eroded and redeposited as blocks within the channel-fill. Elsewhere in the quarry extensive peat deposits have formed over the floodplain of the river, helping to stabilise the river channel and minimise channel migration. It is probable that Association E represents deposition by the River Wissey during the Holocene.

The east-facing section

Before the excavations in 2002, a watching brief at Lynford had identified an organic deposit exposed in the east-facing section on the west side of the active quarry. The relationship of this organic unit to that on the eastern side of the active quarry, which became the focus of the 2002 excavations, was difficult to establish in the field as the intervening sediments had been removed during sand and gravel extraction. Nonetheless, the 'working hypothesis' was that the two organic units were part of the same channel-fill and that the palaeochannel could therefore be reconstructed as running NE-SW across the quarry (compare Lord 2002, fig 9).

However, closer inspection of the sedimentology of this channel-fill indicated that the facies were markedly different from those on the eastern side of the pit, and required a more detailed assessment of its significance. To this end a further phase of fieldwork was undertaken in May 2003 to record the sedimentology of this channel-fill and sample it for palaeoenvironmental analysis and radiocarbon dating.

The resulting section revealed yellowish-brown (10YR 5/8) to olive-brown (2.5Y 5/6) sands at the base, overlain by black-coloured (5Y 2.5/2), laminated, organic silts, exposed over a width of 10m. The lower bounding surface of the laminated organic silts is concave-upwards, forming a broad- shallow channel feature. These silts are overlain by olive-grey coloured (5Y 4/2) sandier sediments, in places displaying cross-bedding. This is in turn overlain by a series of alternating yellow sands and grey-black organic silts. Above this was a gravel facies approximately 0.2m thick. This is overlain by further laminated sands and silts, with prominent organic layers in the basal part, but becoming less so in the upper two metres of the section. Lateral variation in the facies was also observed; the upper series of laminated sand and silts were observed to cut out a thin peat layer, which was formed on top of the gravel unit and consisted of a basal 200mm of laminated sands with some peat material, overlain by a poorly humified peat 100–150mm in thickness. The peat was succeeded and cut out by laminated sands and silts, which overlie a concave-upwards lower bounding surface forming a channel feature.

The sedimentology indicates the infilling of a fluvial channel feature under slow to moderately high energy conditions, resulting in laminated silts and sands, with at least one high-energy event resulting in the deposition of medium to coarse gravels. The formation of a peat unit indicates that the channel became either dry, or significantly reduced in size to enable limited peat formation. This was followed by reactivation of the channel and renewed deposition of laminated sands and organic silts, with progressive reduction in the organic component.

The channel-fill sediments exposed in this section therefore display a somewhat different sedimentology to that of Association B in the archaeological excavations 150m to the east. This could reflect differences in the depositional environment within the abandoned palaeochannel, resulting in the formation of different sedimentary facies. Alternatively, the sedimentological differences indicate that the two deposits are not part of the same channel feature and represent channels formed and filled at different times and possibly under differing environmental conditions. Also noteworthy are the observations of sandy sediments immediately underneath the laminated organic silts and the dominance of sands within the upper part of the channel-fill. The observed sequence is also similar to that in BH 9, which is located 30m to the NE of the section (*see* Fig 1.4). This borehole proved predominantly sandy facies beneath 1.5m of gravel, resting on Chalk bedrock at 4.8m OD and with a *c* 1m-thick grey silt between 6.2m and 7.3m OD. These data might suggest that this channel-fill sequence should be equated with Association D on the eastern side of the active quarry. This correlation would place it later in the succession than the channel-fill of Association B and, if correct, would preclude any reconstruction of the channel containing the artefacts and faunal remains between the east and west sides of the active quarry.

Results of palaeoenvironmental analysis and radiocarbon dating of the organic facies are reported elsewhere (Field, Coope, Green and Keen, chapter 3), and provide additional information to place these sediments within the overall succession at Lynford. The significance of these data in reconstructing fluvial system development is considered further below.

Geochronology

Geochronological investigations of the Lynford deposits are reported in detail elsewhere in this chapter. These data can be used to establish the timing of fluvial deposition and in particular the changes in depositional style indicated by the transitions between facies association. Optically stimulated luminescence (OSL) and radiocarbon-dating methods have been applied to these deposits. The results provide limiting dates on each of the facies associations and are summarised below.

Association E: A basal OSL age estimate of 1008 ± 120 years BP and a radiocarbon age estimate of 1310 ± 80 years BP constrain the age of this association.

Association D: Sands from this association yielded OSL age estimates of 34750 ± 2870 years BP and 32360 ± 2210 years BP. In addition, radiocarbon dating of organic facies exposed in the east-facing section on the opposite site of the active quarry yielded a basal age estimate of $35800 + 1200/-1050$ years BP.

Association C: No age estimates are available from these deposits.

Association B: A range of OSL age estimates from this association have a lower limit of 71670 ± 6450 years BP and an upper limit of 47200 ± 3370 years BP.

Association A: This association yielded an OSL age estimate from sand facies within Association A of 78640 ± 8800 years BP.

Plantation sands: The sands forming the higher terrace to the south of the active quarry yielded an OSL age estimate of $179,500 \pm 28,900$ years BP

Fluvial activity at Lynford

The sedimentological and geochronological information from Lynford allows a model for the formation of the site to be developed (Fig 2.7).

The sands forming the degraded higher terrace to the south of the site represent the oldest fluvial sediments at Lynford (Fig 2.7A). These reach a maximum observed elevation of c 20m OD. As these sands were only seen in deep test pits, little detailed sedimentological information is available, though they are clearly of fluvial origin. The absence of significant gravel facies might reflect local variation or basin-wide characteristics; this cannot be evaluated further at the present time. The OSL age estimate suggests that these sediments were deposited before the last (Ipswichian) interglacial (MIS 5e), probably during MIS 6.

Following deposition of these sands, incision into Chalk bedrock occurred to around 4m OD, down to the base of the Mundford sands and gravels. The precise timing of incision cannot be established at this site. This was followed by deposition of Association A, to a maximum height of 7.82m–7.92m OD, during the Early Devensian (late MIS 5 or MIS 4) (Fig 2.7B).

The incision event forming the channel that contains Association B occurred sometime around 71.7ka, close to the MIS 5/4 boundary. The infill of this channel took place some time during MIS 4 and/or 3 (Fig 2.7C). This was initially of coarse gravels, though abandonment of the channel resulted in a switch to deposition of silty sands with a significant organic component. The channel continued to in-fill with fine-grained organic sediments until around 47.2ka.

The transition to Association C is not well constrained but occurred some time after 47.2ka. At this time there is a change to coarse gravel deposition and the channel-fill deposits of Association B are overlain by coarse sands and gravels deposited in a multiple-channel, braided river depositional environment (Fig 2.7D).

The transition to deposition of the sands of Association D occurred before 35.8kyr BP. This change is associated with incision into the underlying gravels. Following this incision, fluvial deposition of predominantly sandy facies took place (Fig 2.7E). Deposition of Association D probably continued into the Late Devensian, although there are no dated fluvial sediments attributable to the Last Glacial Maximum (MIS 2) as the youngest OSL age estimate from Association D falls within MIS 3.

The transition from gravel-dominated to sand-dominated sediments from Association C to D might indicate either a reduction in peak discharge and therefore in the energy available to transport gravel-sized clasts, or the exhaustion of gravel-sized material from the catchment. Exhaustion seems unlikely as the Chalk bedrock source for the flint is ubiquitous, making a change in the discharge regime more likely. A reduction in peak discharge could be the result of less precipitation falling on the catchment, possibly as a result of regional aridity. However, there is little supporting evidence for aridity during deposition of Association D. Neither is there evidence for aeolian sedimentation at Lynford, which might be associated with increased aridity, nor any cryogenic structures that might also lend support to such an interpretation. Therefore the hypothesis of regional aridity causing reduced discharge remains speculative. However, in the rivers Nene and Welland, a pattern of channel abandonment resulting from reduced discharge has been identified during much of MIS 3–2, and attributed to regional aridity (Briant 2002). Aeolian input into fluvial systems in southern England has also been recognised at this time (van Huissteden *et al* 2001). A regional climatic phenomenon affecting these rivers draining into the western Fen basin might also have influenced the behaviour of the Wissey.

Association E was deposited over the site above a locally channelled lower bounding surface. The presence of later prehistoric lithic material in Association E points to an early to mid Holocene age for Association E. However, it is dated to the late Holocene by both OSL and radiocarbon dating methods, suggesting that the lithic material might be reworked from older alluvial sediments. The lower bounding surface of Association E therefore represents a significant hiatus in the fluvial sequence. The sedimentology suggests that the river continued to transport and deposit coarse clastic sediments and exhibit a mobile planform throughout much of the Holocene.

Conclusions

The sedimentological information presented above indicates that the archaeological material and faunal remains are associated with an abandoned channel feature that was infilled under predominantly still- to slow-flowing water conditions. Influx of coarser sediments also occurs under high-energy conditions and as a result of mass movement of sediment from adjacent slopes.

This abandoned channel represents one small component in the history of the River Wissey during the last glacial cycle. During this time the river incised to the level of the base of the Mundford Member. Following this incision the coarse gravels of Association A were

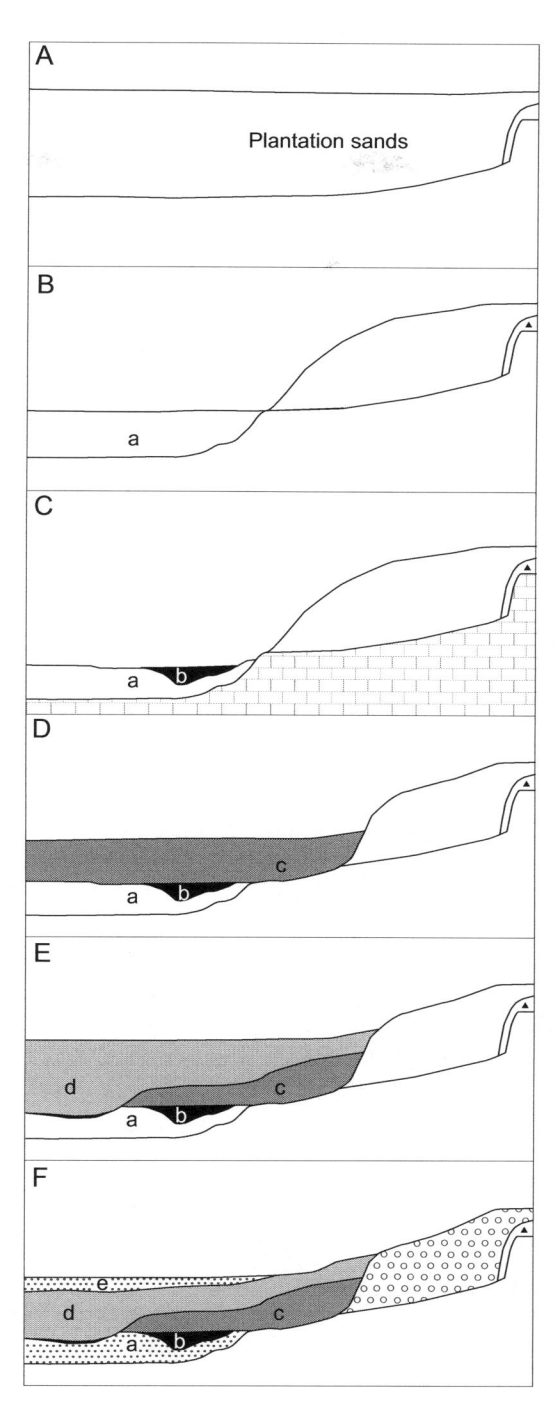

Fig 2.7
Stages in the development of the fluvial succession at Lynford.

deposited. Avulsion and abandonment of a channel resulted in the accumulation of the fine-grained, organic deposits of Association B. Association C indicates a return to high-energy fluvial deposition, with a reduction in peak discharge possibly suggested by the transition to a sandy bedload river and deposition of Association D. Association E represents fluvial deposition during the present Holocene warm period.

The human activity recorded at Lynford can therefore be placed in a local landscape that is essentially fluvial in character, consisting of a low-relief floodplain, with minimal topographic differentiation and with an active channel belt, bounded by semi-active or inactive areas of the floodplain including abandoned channels such as the one represented by Association B. Land surfaces in such a dynamic landscape are ephemeral in nature and susceptible to burial by later sediments, erosion by encroachment of the active channel belt, or degradation by collapse of unconsolidated channel edges.

One final consideration is the availability of raw material for tool manufacture. The gravels deposited by the river include a significant coarse component, which might provide flint of suitable quality for knapping. However it is also likely that exposed Chalk would be present on slopes adjacent to the floodplain, which might also yield *in situ* nodular flint of much higher quality. It is possible that high-quality Brandon Series Flint was in close proximity as the site lies close to the Middle-Upper Chalk boundary. The Brandon Series flint is found at the base of the Upper Chalk (Bristow, 1990) and was exploited at Grimes Graves some 5km to the south of the site, during the Neolithic. The issue of raw material will be considered in greater detail in subsequent chapters (White, chapter 5).

2.2 Association B

2.2.1 Description and strategraphic succession

W A Boismier

The sediments of Association B represent the remains of a probable east–west-orientated palaeochannel feature that had been heavily truncated and largely removed by sand and gravel extraction before the start of excavation in 2002. This association comprises a complex succession of inorganic sands and gravels and organic sediments forming three component facies associations – B-i, B-ii and B-iii – representing distinct depositional phases in the sedimentary history of the channel (Lewis, this chapter). Most of the artefactual, faunal and palaeoenvironmental materials recovered by the excavation occurred in the sediments of Association B, with the majority within the sediments of one component – B-ii.

This section deals primarily with a description of the sediments comprising the three component facies associations and their stratigraphic relationships. Attributes of these deposits are presented in detail because of their importance for understanding the contexts in which the vertebrate remains and artefactual materials occurred and the likely agencies responsible for their deposition in the channel. The sedimentology, micromorphology and geochemistry of the sediments, and the stratigraphic position of the association within the succession of deposits at the site, are dealt with by Lewis, French and Andrews (this chapter).

Methods

The analysis was carried out using a method of facies analysis known as architectural-element analysis (Miall 1985, 2006; Jones 1999; see also Brown 1996; Lewis and Maddy 1999; Lewis this volume). In this approach, a hierarchy of bedforms and bounding surfaces representing different depositional timescales is used to group bedforms into depositional units, or architectural elements, on the basis of facies associations, internal geometries, external form and upper and lower bounding surfaces (Miall 2006, 91; Jones *et al* 1999, 38–9). The approach standardises facies description into a number of lithofacies types, and defines nine basic architectural elements characteristic of fluvial depositional systems that can be recognised in modern and ancient settings: channels, gravel bars and bedforms, sandy bedforms, downstream-accretion macroform, lateral-accretion macroform, scour hollows, sediment gravity flows, laminated sand sheet and overbank fines (Miall 2006, 89–94). Each of these architectural elements is characterised by a distinctive set of facies associations and bounding surfaces with the horizontal and vertical stacking of different elements, forming complex three-dimensional sequences of channel-fill sediments. The approach provides a scheme for the description, grouping and stratigraphical ordering of lithofacies and an interpretative framework for considering deposit formation and depositional phasing over timescales of up to a thousand years.

Facies and bounding surface grouping and stratigraphic ordering was carried out with a Harris matrix (Harris 1979, 1989; Roskams 2001, 239–66; Goldberg and Macphail 2006, 40–1): a sequence diagram that is used to organise complex, three-dimensional stratigraphic data in a two-dimensional format (Orton 1980, 66–73). Like architectural-element analysis, the diagram is based on the partition of sediment bodies into discrete deposits and surfaces or interfaces and the grouping of these units into higher-level entities and stratigraphic sequences. It simplifies grouping and ordering by reducing the level of detail down to basic stratigraphic relationships with units represented by either numbers or codes enclosed within boxes and arranged hierarchically in a lattice according to their stratigraphic relationships. Stratigraphic succession is represented by the vertical axis, while groups of contemporary units forming periods or phases within the depositional sequence are represented by the horizontal axis. The diagram provides a method for representing complex sequences of bedforms and bounding surfaces in an abstract and interpretable form and the definition of depositional units and phases within sequences of channel-fill sediments. Part of the Harris matrix for Association B is shown in Fig 2.8.

The single-context recording and excavation procedures carried out on site partitioned the sediments of Association B into 106 separate contexts. These contexts were defined on the basis of a range of lithological properties such as general texture, colour and sedimentary structures (Jones *et al* 1999, 38–9). They record sedimentary features ranging in scale from small bedding structures within lithofacies to individual lithofacies and bedding contacts separating depositional units. Contexts were grouped in a sequence diagram by order of scale, with units representing small-scale sedimentary features grouped into larger facies units on the basis of lithological properties, followed by the grouping of higher-order units composed of individual facies and bedding contacts into facies associations. These context groups were then arranged vertically and horizontally in the diagram to form the stratigraphic sequence for the channel, and divided into the three component associations defined by Lewis for Association B. The facies comprising these associations were further subdivided into separate units on the basis of lithological characteristics and stratigraphic relationships to characterise the depositional environments of the channel and the agencies responsible for the occurrence of vertebrate remains and artefactual materials in the sediments of the channel. These units are summarised in Table 2.6, and Figs 2.9 to 2.12 show the succession of sediments recorded in the cruciform N-S and E-W baulk sections across the excavation area.

Association B-i

Association B-i comprises a sequence of gravel, sand and silt facies indicative of a succession of in-channel longitudinal bars or bedforms formed along channel margins during high-energy, waning flow and low-stage or low-flow periods of discharge prior to channel abandonment. This association was visible only in the north-western section at the edge of the site, with upper elements of it partially exposed along segments of the northern edge of Association B-ii and on the lower west-facing section on the eastern edge of the excavation area, as well as in the eastern corner of the north- and south-facing sections of the central E-W baulk. These exposures suggest that Association B-i extends from the north-western section east-south-east across the area of surviving channel deposits and beyond the eastern edge of the excavation. The gravel and sand facies that make up B-i are similar in texture and bedding structures, and have been subdivided into three separate units on the basis of the sequence visible in the north-western section along the edge of the site (Fig 2.13). Elements of B-i exposed elsewhere on site were assigned to the upper part of this sequence on the basis of their relative OD height positions and facies similarities.

Unit B-i:01: Unit B-i:01 is the lowermost unit in the sequence and directly overlies the base of the channel cut into the underlying gravels of Association A. It consists of a 0.15–0.40m thick bed of medium to coarse flint gravel and pale-brown coarse sand, overlain by a layer of light grey-green sandy silt with a thickness of between 0.04m and 0.12m. The gravel is typically subrounded and subangular, poorly sorted and displays a crude horizontal stratification with coarse sand dispersed throughout the gravel and in lenses 0.05m–0.10m thick.

Fig 2.8
Part of Harris matrix for Association B (northern part of channel).

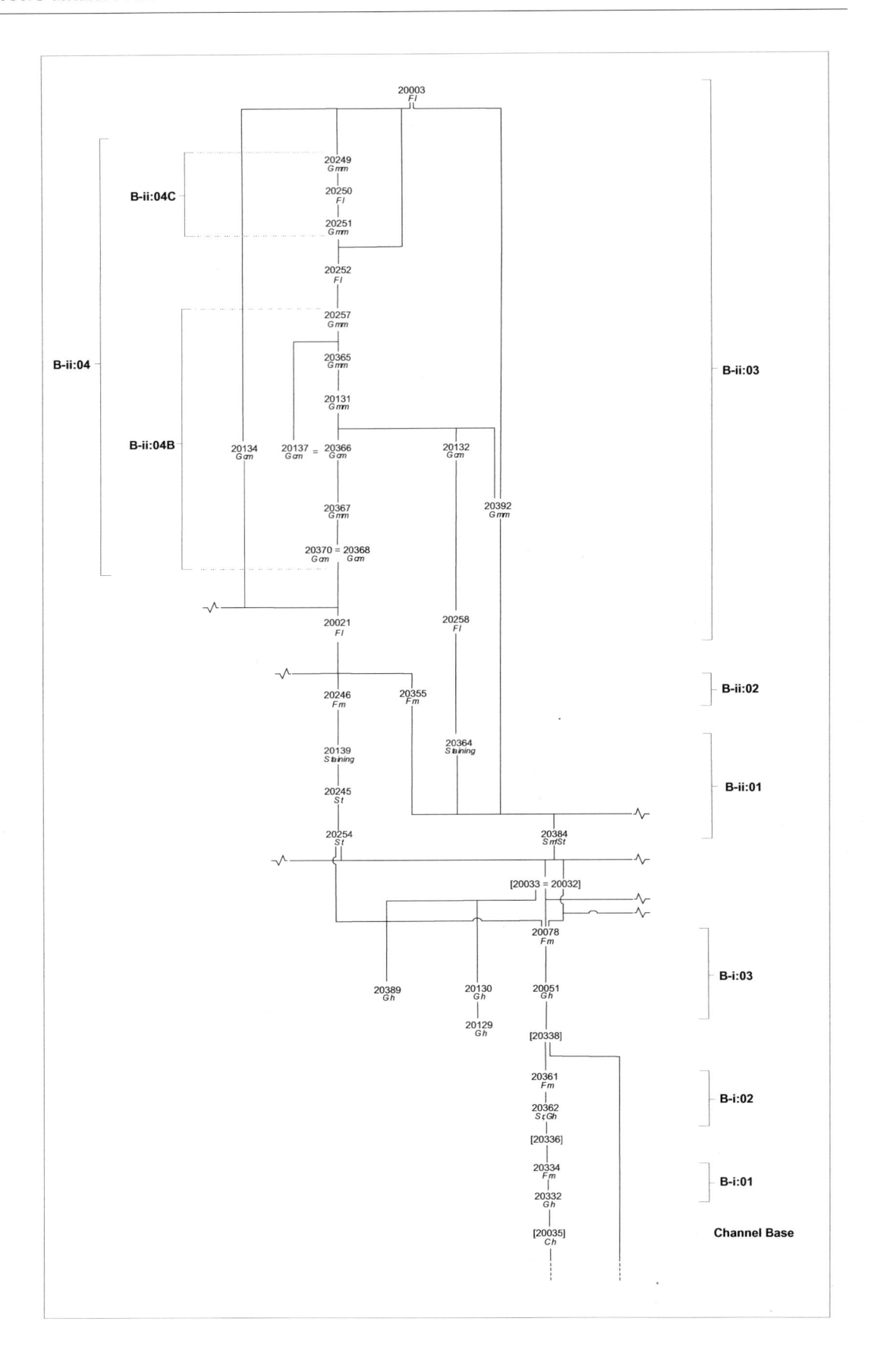

Table 2.6 Components of Association B and their subdivisions with constituent context numbers

component	subdivision	facies[1]	description	interpretation
B-iii		Sp, Gh, Fm	fine to coarse sand, silty sand, organic sediment and small to coarse flint gravel arranged in a lateral succession of lenticular beds of laminated sand and gravel with a final depositional phase composed of fine laminated sand, organic sediment, coarse sand and gravel, infilling a narrow u-shaped channel-type scour	point bar and stream infill sediments; slow-flowing water alternating with periods of high-energy flow and/or flood events
B-ii	B-ii:05	Sr, Ss, Gm, Fm, Flr	fine sand, silty organic sand, clasts of reworked organic sediment and fine to medium-coarse gravel and cobbles arranged in a graded succession of subhorizontal-inclined layers	small mid-channel bar and lateral infill sediments; return to flowing water conditions with high-energy events followed by waning and standing or tranquil flow
	B-ii:04	Gmm, Sm	medium to coarse sands and small to medium-coarse gravel and cobbles, laterally and vertically variable from clast-supported gravel to discrete lenses and layers of unsorted stony sand; laterally discontinuous and forming discrete deposits; partially interbedded with the organic sediments of B-ii:03	sediment gravity flows
	B-ii:03	Fl	detrial fine-grained organic silty sand (organic 'mud'), predominately massive with fine alternating discontinuous parallel-subparallel laminae of sand and organic matter in upper 0.20m, laterally variable densities of medium to coarse gravel and cobbles and lenses of stony organic sand; partially interbedded with the sediment gravity flow deposits of B-ii:04	organic 'mud' and small, localised bank collapses; standing or tranquil flow conditions; likely periods of subaerial exposure
	B-ii:02	Fm	organic clayey silt with variable densities of unsorted medium to coarse sand and gravel, laterally discontinuous	organic silt; standing or tranquil flow conditions with episodes of higher-flow regimes
	B-ii:01	St, Sm	medium to fine sand, laterally variable ranging from cross-bedded pebbly sand with undulating upper contact surfaces to massive sands with unsorted medium to coarse gravel	linguoid or sinuous-crested (3-D) dunes and sediment gravity flows; slow-moving but variable-flow conditions; likely periods of subaerial exposure
B-i	B-i:03	Gh, Fm	small to medium coarse gravel and coarse sand, laterally and vertically variable ranging from clast supported to lenses and layers of coarse sand with fining-upward normal grading or crude horizontal-subhorizontal bedding; capped by discontinuous sandy silt	longitudinal bar; high-energy, waning flow and low-stage or low-flow conditions
	B-i:02	Gh, Sr/Sh, Fm	small to medium-coarse gravel and coarse to fine sand, well sorted with fining-upward normal grading; capped by sandy silt drape with eroded upper contact	longitudinal bar; high energy, waning flow and low-stage or low-flow conditions
	B-i:01	Gh, Fm	medium to coarse gravel and coarse sand with crude horizontal stratification, poorly sorted; capped by sandy silt drape with eroded upper contact; lower contact concave-up channel base.	longitudinal bar; high-energy, waning flow and low-stage or low-flow conditions

[1] lithofacies coding after Miall 1985, 2006, 79, table 4.1; see also Lewis and Maddy 1999, 114, table 5.1

These sedimentary structures indicate fluvial deposition under high-energy flow conditions in which gravel and coarser sediment fractions are transported as bedload. The overlying sandy silt has an abrupt wavy eroded upper contact with fine discontinuous and non-parallel dark grey-green ripple laminae present in places within the sediment body that indicate deposition under low-stage or slow-flowing water conditions.

Unit B-i:02: This unit overlies the erosion surface of Unit B-i:01 and is composed of a 0.11m–0.58m thick deposit of small to medium-coarse flint gravel and pale-brown coarse to fine sand, and an upper 0.02m–0.08m thick layer of calcareous light to medium grey silty sand. The gravel is typically subrounded and subangular, well sorted, and displays a fining-upward normal grading of clasts intermixed with coarse sand that indicates fluvial deposition in a waning flow environment. A 0.09m–0.35m thick wedge-shaped body of pale-brown fine sand with internal dark-grey silty clay ripple laminae, representing possible bar-top sediments deposited under low-stage conditions, occurs within the gravel on the north edge of the section. The silty sand overlying the gravel has an abrupt, wavy, slightly concave-up, eroded upper contact. Fine discontinuous dark-grey ripple laminae are present within this layer in places, indicating that deposition largely took place during low-stage conditions of standing or gently flowing water.

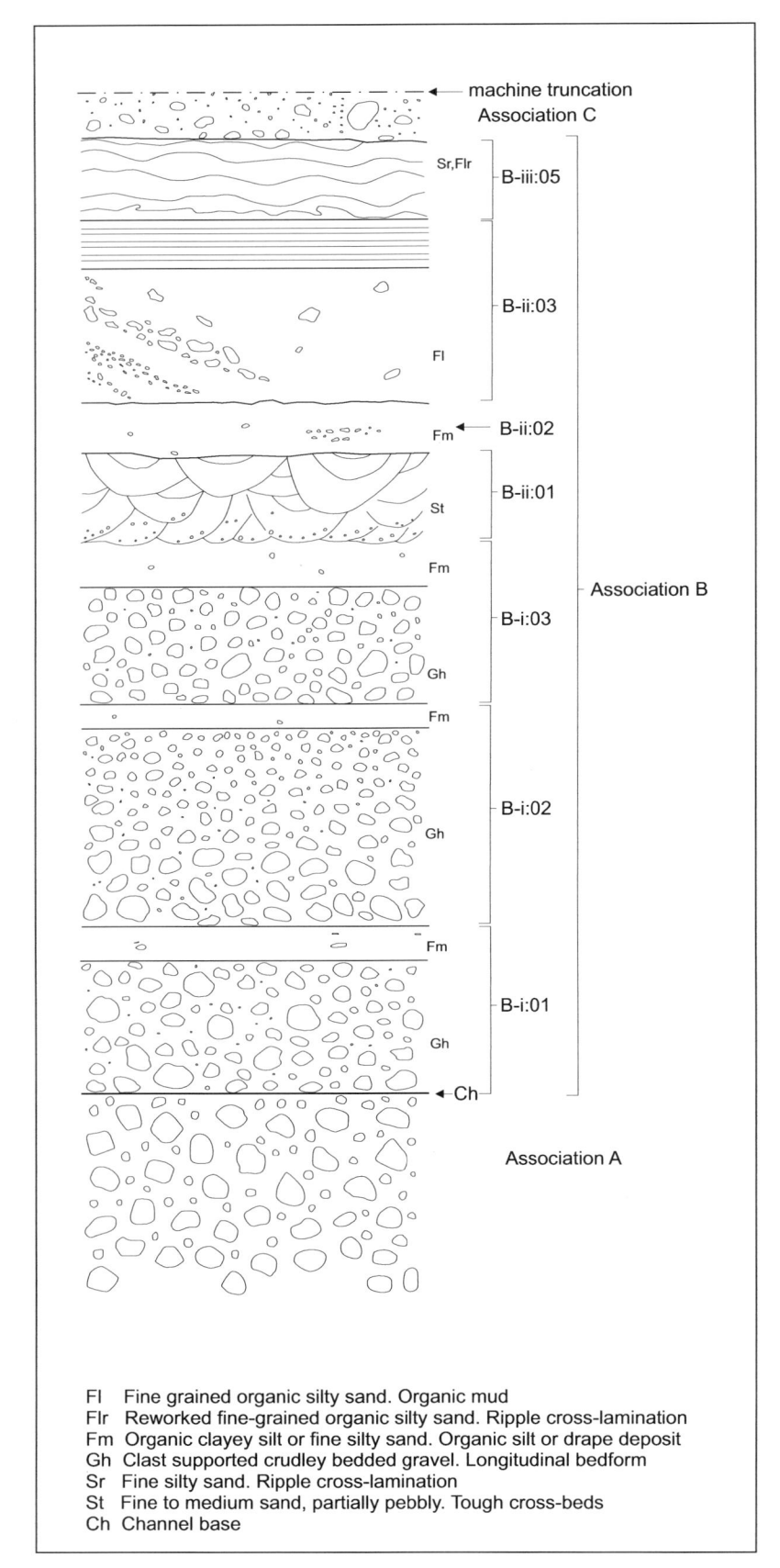

Unit B-i:03: Unit B-i:03 is the uppermost deposit in the sequence of gravel bedforms and was exposed in a number of sections and areas within the excavation. This unit exhibits a degree of lateral and vertical variation in sedimentary structures, and is composed of a set of tabular-lenticular beds of small to medium-coarse flint gravel and pale brown-yellow to light grey-white predominately coarse sand partially overlain by a discontinuous deposit of grey-pale-brown sandy silt. The gravel for this unit is typically rounded, subrounded and/or subangular, variably sorted with a matrix ranging from predominately clast-supported to discrete lenses and layers of coarse sand, and displaying either a fining-upward normal grading of clasts or crude horizontal or subhorizontal bedding. Deposition during high-energy and waning-flow periods of channel discharge is indicated by these sedimentary structures. Upper contacts for the gravel vary laterally on exposures, and range from convex-up to concave-up surfaces with a minor erosion surface separating two possible bar-top assemblages in the east corner of the north-facing central E–W baulk (*see* Fig 2.9). This evidence indicates a degree of lateral variation in the erosion and deposition of sediment on gravel bedform surfaces. Its lower contact remains incompletely defined as it is only exposed on the north-western section at the edge of the site where it rests on the erosion surface of Unit B-i:02. Upper contacts are partially overlain by sandy silt drapes or sheets and by the sands of Association B-ii.

The sandy silt overlying the gravel comprises two irregular areas in the north-eastern and central parts of the channel, separated by a slightly raised and eroded area of gravel where it survives in two small patches (Fig 2.14). It is

Facies C
B-iii
B-ii:05
B-ii:04 SGF
B-ii:03
B-ii:02
B-ii:01
B-i:03

Fig 2.9 (top two)
North-facing central baulk section.

Fig 2.10 (bottom two)
South-facing central baulk section.

Facies C

B-iii

B-ii:05

B-ii:04 SGF

B-ii:03

B-ii:02

B-ii:01

B-i:03

0   5m

S

9.13m aOD N

bones and tusks

N

8.80m aOD S

Fig 2.11 (top two)
West-facing central baulk section.

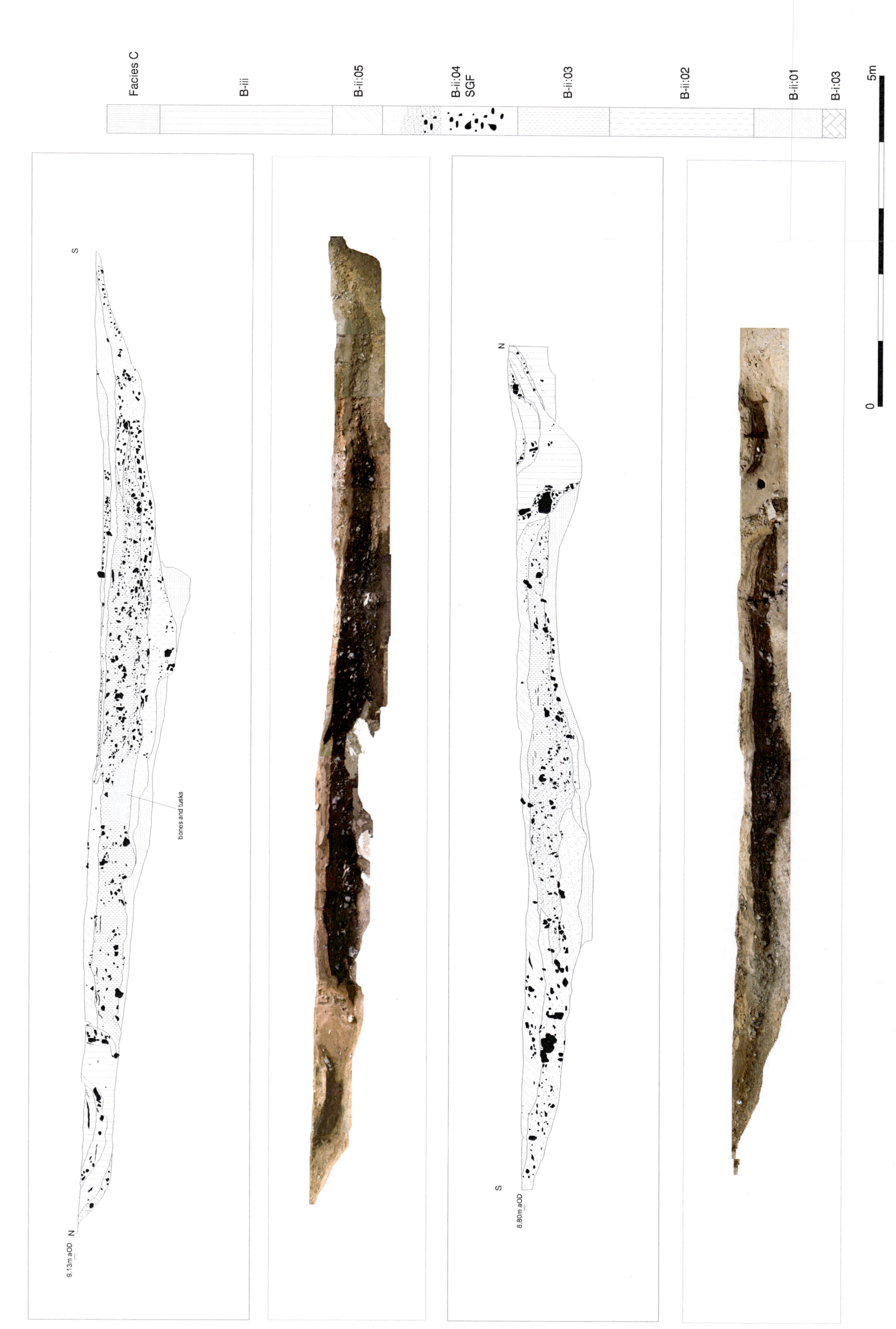

Fig 2.12 (bottom two)
East-facing central baulk section.

typically between 0.05m and 0.14m thick, with a wavy-irregular, concave-up upper contact. Internally, the sediment is massive with sparse to moderate densities (5–10 per cent) of medium to coarse gravels present within it in the north-western part of the channel. Deposition under low-stage conditions of standing or slow-flowing water is indicated by sediment characteristics.

Association B-ii

Association B-ii comprises a set of sand, gravel, silt and organic silty sand facies indicative of fluvial deposition under still to slow-flowing water conditions and the incorporation of bank sediments and materials into the channel after its abandonment. Periods of subaerial exposure during low- water stages are also indicated by the micromorphology of the sediments (French, this chapter). It is typically between 0.20m and 1.50m in thickness, fills the entire area of the channel, and exhibits substantial lateral and vertical variation in sedimentary structures. This association overlies a concave-up bounding surface, which partially cuts the upper gravels and silt of Association B-i and merges into the contact for the channel cut into the gravels of Association A along the edges of the channel (Lewis, this chapter). Along its northern edge the association is partially cut and overlain by the concave-up channel contact for Association B-iii. The sediments underlying this contact are down-warped, compacted and diagenetically altered by the weight of the overlying facies (Fig 2.15). Elsewhere the upper sediments of B-ii have been truncated by their partial

Fig 2.13 (page 36)
Schematic type section for Association B.

Fig 2.14
Distribution of sediment gravity flows.

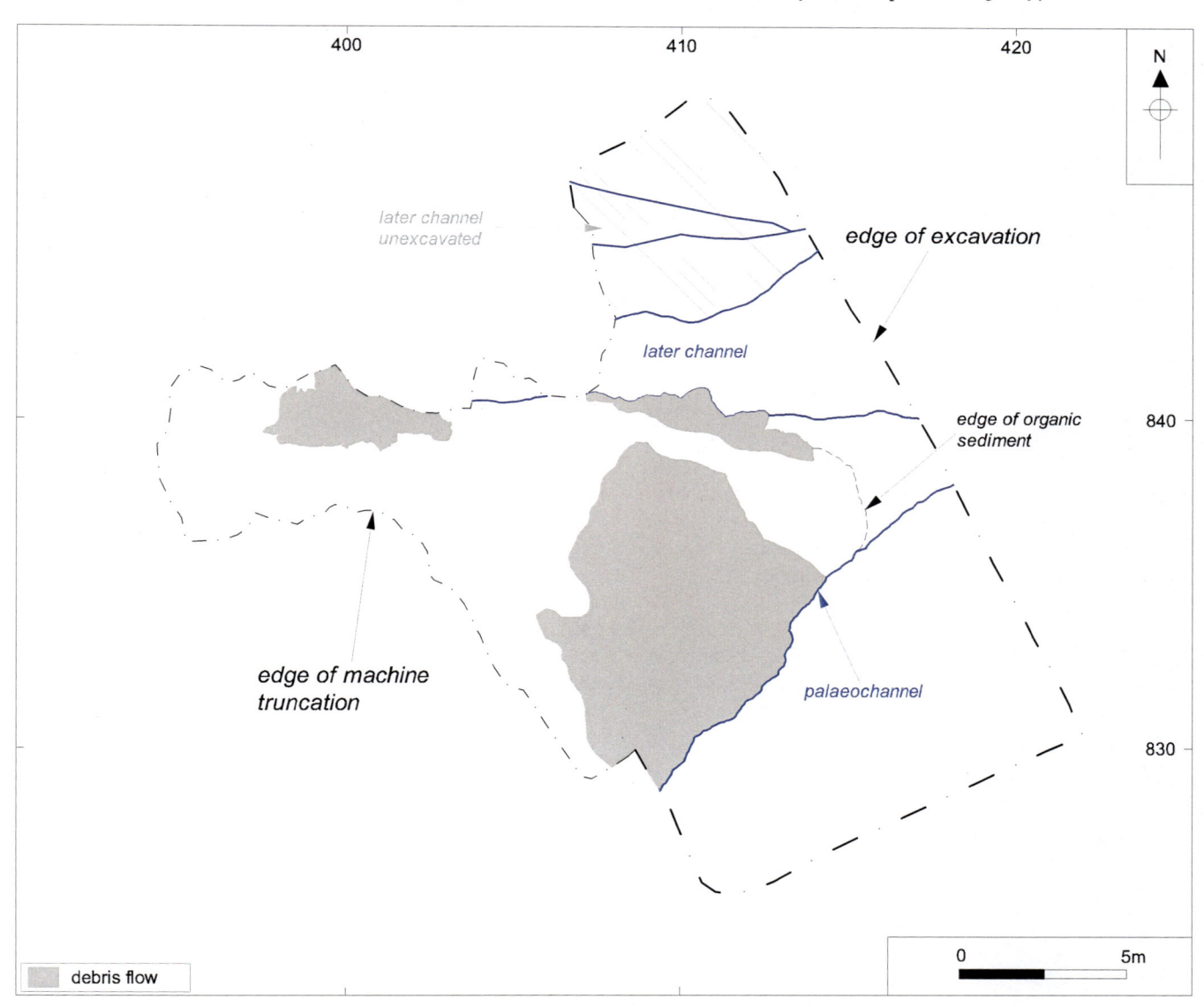

*Fig 2.15
Downwarped and diagenetically altered sediments of Association B-ii underlying bounding surface for Association B-iii. West-facing section, central control baulk..*

removal during sand and gravel extraction, and are cut locally by scour features of Association C. Most of the artefactual, faunal and palaeobiological materials retrieved by the excavation were recovered from the sediments making up Association B-ii.

The facies that comprise this association have been subdivided into five separate units on the basis of sediment characteristics and stratigraphic relationships, to characterise the depositional environment of the channel and the agencies responsible for the occurrence of archaeological materials in the sediments. These are distinguished by a separate number after the unit number.

Unit B-ii:01: Unit B-ii:01 is the lowest deposit in the sequence of sediments for Association B-ii and rests directly on the lower bounding surface separating Association B-ii from the underlying gravel and silt of Association B-i. It is overlain by units B-ii:02 and B-ii:03. These basal sands comprise a bed of trough cross-bedded sand and massive sand 0.07m–0.26m thick, sloping in a west-south-west direction. The sand is typically light grey-pale brown to medium-grey in colour, fine- to medium-grained in texture, and exhibits a pale-brown to medium-brown staining on upper contacts where it occurs below organic sediment.

Trough cross-beds are situated in the east and north-west parts of the channel with small-scale bedding structures present within the north-west area and indistinct in the eastern part of the excavation area. These small-scale structures (Fig 2.16) comprise a pebbly, light-grey fine to medium sand, overlain in places by a fine, light-grey to pale-brown sand. Upper contact surfaces are typically wavy and undulating. Bedform structure indicates linguoid or sinuous-crested dunes and hence the deposition of the sand under variable but generally slow-moving water, with periods of subaerial exposure during low-water stages.

Massive sand occurs between the two areas of cross-bedding. It is sheet-like in character along the northern edge of the channel and contains varying densities of unsorted medium to coarse flint gravel and buried or partially buried artefacts and faunal remains. Unsorted medium to coarse flint gravel and cobbles also occur elsewhere in the deposit underneath or along the margins of later sedimentary structures immediately overlying it. Its upper contact ranges from an inclined surface along the north margins of the channel to a wavy-irregular one elsewhere. Sediment characteristics also suggest post-depositional modification of the sand by sediment gravity flow from bank slumping and disturbance by later sedimentary (debris flow) and possibly biological (bioturbation) processes.

Unit B-ii:02: This unit comprises a horizontally discontinuous deposit of dark-grey/green-brown, organic clayey silt overlying the sands of Unit B-ii:01 in the north-west and central parts of the surviving channel. The unit is typically between 0.02m and 0.23m thick, with wavy or diffuse upper contacts that grade into the overlying organic silty sand. Varying densities of unsorted medium to coarse flint gravel and cobbles also occur on and immediately below the upper contact for areas of the deposit, lying underneath a later debris flow deposit in the central part of the channel and along its south edge. Elsewhere flint gravel is relatively rare.

Deposition of finer sediments and organic matter in shallows along the north edge of the channel or during periods of still to slow-flowing water conditions is indicated by the fine-grained texture of the sediment. Episodes of higher energy-flow regimes causing influxes of coarser sediments are suggested by the presence of coarse sand laminae interbedded with fine-grained sediment in the central part of the channel.

Unit B-ii:03: Unit B-ii:03 comprises a 0.20m–0.54m thick bed of detrital, fine-grained, dark-brown organic silty sand that overlies both units B-ii:01 and B-ii:02, and is partially interbedded with the debris flow and bank sediment deposits making up Unit B-ii:04. The deposit has a predominately massive lower unit and an upper 0.10m–0.30m thick laminated unit composed of fine alternating discontinuous parallel-subparallel laminae of pale-brown sand and organic matter. Small to medium-coarse flint gravel and cobbles occur in varying densities throughout the deposit with lenses of stony organic sand present within the sediments along the north and south sides of the channel. Its upper contact is marked by the occurrence of wavy ripple laminae of reworked organic sediment and by a graduated change to the predominately inorganic sand of Unit B-ii:05. Small sand diapirs also occur in places along the upper contact and include flame structures, sand pillows and possible small load cast ripples. Mudballs are also present within the organic sediments.

Sediment texture and structures for this facies suggest fine-grained sediment and organic matter deposition within a predominately still to slow-flowing body of water with micromorphology (French, this chapter)

Fig 2.16
Unit B-ii:01 Trough cross-bedded sands (3-D dunes). West-facing section, north-west control baulk (scale 1.0m).

indicating periods of lower water levels that exposed sediments along the margins of the channel to episodes of wetting and drying. Suspension sedimentation is clearly indicated by the fine alternating inorganic and organic laminae of the upper unit with the ripple bedforms along the upper contact documenting a return to flowing water conditions within the channel in Unit B-ii:05. Post-depositional disturbance by sediment gravity flow and/or bioturbation is also indicated by the massive lower unit and the lenses of stony organic sand representing small, localised episodes of bank collapse.

Unit B-ii:04: This unit comprises the sediment gravity flow and disturbed organic deposits indicative of bank erosion that occur within the south-south-east and central parts of the channnel and along its northern edge (*see* Fig 2.14). These deposits are highly variable and comprise gravel, stony sand and stony organic sand facies composed of a mixture of bank and channel sediments (Table 2.7). They are partially interbedded with the organic silty sand of Unit B-ii:03 and form a complex succession of sediments representing multiple episodes of debris flow, small localised bank collapses and the washing-in of sediments and materials over a period of time (Figs 2.17 to 2.19). Gravel facies of this unit overlie organic sediments along the north side of the channel and form new channel edges against which further organic and redeposited bank sediments built up. Localised slumping of these facies on the south side of the channel is also indicated by a u-shaped feature of gravel, embedded into an underlying deposit of predominately organic sediment filling a small depression on the surface of the gravels of Association A (Fig 2.20).

Unit B-ii:05: Unit B-ii:05 overlies the organic sediment of Unit B-ii:03 and marks a return to flowing water conditions within the channel. It comprises a deposit of sand, silt, organic and gravel sediments 0.11m–0.43m thick, which has been truncated by the partial removal of its upper sediments during sand and gravel extraction and locally cut by scour features of Association C. These sediments are laterally and vertically variable, and exhibit sedimentary structures indicative of a minor mid-channel

Table 2.7 **Sediment gravity flows**

units	facies[1]	description	external form	upper contact	lower contact	interpretation
B-ii:04A	Gmm, Sm	succession of interdigitated medium to coarse-grained pale grey-brown sands, dark grey stony organic sands and small to medium-coarse flint gravel and cobbles, unsorted and largely matrix supported	wedge	inclined convex-up	inclined	multiple episodes of debris flow and bank collapse; localised slumping of gravel facies
B-ii:04B	Gmm	small to medium-coarse flint gravel and cobbles and pale-grey-brown to yellow-orange coarse sand, well sorted, matrix supported and partially imbricated	wedge	inclined convex-up	undulating	debris flow; lowermost of two sediment gravity-flow deposits situated on the same stretch of the north side of the channel; severely truncated by gravel extraction
B-ii:04C	Sm	light grey-pale brown to medium-grey coarse sand and small to medium flint gravel and cobbles arranged in a succession of thin, inclined beds of sand and unsorted gravel (stony sands); separated into upper and lower units by small eroded lens of organic sediment	wedge	inclined convex-up	inclined concave-up	multiple episodes of small bank collapse and washing-in of sediments and materials; uppermost of two sediment gravity flow deposits situated on the same stretch of the north side of the channel
B-ii:04D	Gmm	small to medium-coarse flint gravel and cobbles, and pale-grey to yellow-orange medium- to coarse-grained sand, poorly sorted and predominantly matrix supported	wedge	inclined convex-up	inclined concave-up	debris flow; truncated by the channel contact for Association B-iii

[1] lithofacies coding after Miall 1985, 2006, 79, table 4.1; see also Lewis and Maddy 1999, 114, table 5.1

sand bar and associated lateral infill sediments that suggest deposition under variable but predominately slow-flowing water conditions.

The small mid-channel bar was observed mainly in section within the central area of the channel (Fig 2.21; and *see* Figs 2.9, 2.10). This feature is composed of pale grey-brown fine sand with dark grey-brown silt and organic laminae and clasts of reworked organic sediment. Internally this feature is arranged

Fig 2.17
Stony organic sand forming part of Unit B-ii:04A. East-facing section, N–S central control baulk (scale 1.0m).

Fig 2.18
Unit B-ii:04B Sediment gravity flow (debris flow) along north edge of channel. East-facing section, north-west control baulk.

Fig 2.19
Unit B-ii:04C Sediment gravity flow (stony sand) along north edge of channel. East-facing section (scale 0.30m).

Fig 2.20
Localised slumping of Unit B-ii:04A gravel facies on south side of channel.

in a sequence of west or downstream-orientated sediments with a convex-up upper contact that exhibits an undulating east-west profile indicating the downstream accretion of sediment. A wedge-shaped bed of matrix-supported small to medium-coarse flint gravel rests on this feature and is overlain by a graded succession of subhorizontal-inclined beds of fine pale grey-brown to mid grey-brown and yellow-orange sands, silty sand and organic sediment, which suggest deposition under predominately waning and standing or

2 STRATIGRAPHY, ASSOCIATION B AND DATING

tranquil-flow water conditions (Fig 2.22). Elsewhere, the sediments for this unit comprise parallel-subparallel beds of sand and silty sand with fine, wavy ripple laminae and small shallow scours filled with coarse sand and fine- to-coarse flint gravel. Dropstones surrounded by impact deformation structures occur throughout the deposit, with possible water escape structures and small-scale convolute laminations present within the bar feature.

Bedding structures for this unit suggest a flowing body of water with a variable flow regime composed of high-energy flow events followed by periods of waning and standing or tranquil flowing water. Deposition predominately occurred under waning and still-tranquil flow water conditions, with episodes of higher-energy flow regimes eroding the bed of the channel and depositing coarse-grained sediments, indicated by the occurrence of scour features filled with gravel and coarse sand. Episodes of higher-energy flow regimes that tore chunks of sediment away from the underlying deposit (Unit B-ii:03) are also indicated by the occurrence of clasts of reworked organic sediment within the bar feature. Influxes of water from seasonal rainfall, floods and the break-up of winter ice are some of the likely agencies responsible for increased water velocities and bed erosion. The presence of winter ice in the channel is also suggested by the dropstones in the deposit (Lewis, this chapter).

Association B-iii

Association B-iii is the uppermost phase of channel infilling and comprises a set of sand, gravel and organic facies indicative of a succession of point bar sediments formed along a meander in the channel. It is typically between 0.42m and 0.53m thick, with its upper sediments truncated by their partial removal during sand and gravel extraction. This association overlies a concave-up basal channel contact that cuts and partially overlies the upper sediments of Association B-ii and that is cut by the lower contact for Association C (Lewis, this chapter). Its northern limit was not fully established, as the deposit extended under the north baulk of the excavation area, nor was it fully excavated.

The deposit is made up of fine-grained to coarse-grained pale grey-brown to dark grey-brown sands, silty sand, organic sediment and small to coarse flint gravel and cobbles. It is arranged in a north to south succession of lenticular beds of laminated sand and gravel, with a final depositional phase composed of fine laminated sands and organic sediment and/or coarse sand and gravel infilling a narrow east-west orientated u-shaped channel-type scour in the southern part of the deposit (see Fig 2.12, 2.13). Individual beds in the succession contain either inclined wavy-irregular dark-grey, silty sand laminae or unsorted and matrix-supported gravel, with

Fig 2.21
Unit B-ii:05 Small mid-channel sand bar overlying the organic sediments of B-ii:03. South-facing section, E–W central control baulk.

Fig 2.22
Unit B-ii:05 Lateral infill sediments. East-facing section, south-west control baulk.

the gravel unit along the south side of the channel post-depositionally folded into a near-vertical orientation by the downward deformation of the underlying sediments of Association B-ii (*see* Fig 2.16). The channel-type feature is filled with beds of unsorted matrix- and clast-supported flint gravel and pale-grey, fine-grained sand with dark-grey silty sand laminae and a small deposit of laminated organic sediment, partly interbedded with and overlain by coarse sand and gravel. Elsewhere a shallow scour feature cut into the sand contains a succession of medium-coarse sand and gravel.

Sedimentary structures for this association suggest periods of slow-flowing water alternating with periods of higher-energy water flow and/or flood events. Deposition was initially on bar surfaces that accreted laterally across the channel with episodes of higher-energy flow regimes eroding the bed of the channel and depositing gravel and coarse-grained sediment on bar surfaces during waning flow stages. One or more of these high-energy flow episodes scoured a narrow u-shaped channel in the accreting bar sediments and left lag deposits of gravel along both sides of the feature. The infill of this feature occurred under variable but predominately slow-flowing water conditions, with fluctuations in current velocity eroding the bed and leaving shallow scours filled with coarse sand and gravel. A small stream with varying discharge levels is suggested by these deposits.

Discussion

The three components of Association B are interpreted as representing distinct depositional phases in the sedimentary history of the channel that all occurred under cool climatic conditions (Coope, Green and Keen, chapter 3). Association B-i represents a pre-abandonment phase of flowing water, where bar structures composed of relatively coarse sediments were formed along channel margins while the channel was still part of the larger river system. An inactive phase after channel abandonment is represented by the sediments of Association B-ii. These sediments indicate a still to slow-flowing body of water cut off from the river, with fluctuating water levels where fine-grained sands and organic matter settled out of suspension and sediment gravity flows deposited bank sediments and materials into the channel. The upper sediments of this association (Unit B-ii:05) also indicate a return to flowing water conditions in the channel where it might have functioned as a minor secondary tributary that perhaps only contained flowing water when the river was at a high stage of flow. Association B-iii represents the final phase of flowing water where the channel shifted slightly to the north and cut into and partially overlaid the sediments of Association B-ii. Bar structures, formed of coarse sand and gravel, laterally filled the channel with the infilling of a small channel-type scour representing the final phases of deposition. OSL dates (Schwenninger and Rhodes, this chapter) suggest a possible gap of at least 1,200 years between the deposition of the upper sediments of Association B-ii and the incision of the channel containing the sediments of Association B-iii.

Artefacts and vertebrate remains are present in the upper sediments of Association B-i (B-i:03), in all of the units comprising Association B-ii, and in the sediments of the small channel marking the final depositional phases of Association B-iii (Schreve, White, chapter 5). This succession raises fundamental questions as to whether the occurrence of materials in each of the three associations represents stratigraphically distinct assemblages or simply mixed accumulations of vertically reworked materials. Resolving this question is of some importance for understanding hominin use of the site through time, as refitting studies carried out at Palaeolithic sites elsewhere have demonstrated substantial vertical displacement and mixing of materials within soft sediment deposits (Bunn *et al* 1980; Villa 1983, 65–75; Delanges and Ropars 1996, 154–7; Street 2002, 15).

Lithic and bone conjoins (*see* Tables 4.11 and 5.25 and Figs 5.26 and 5.55) occur in the basal sands, sediment gravity flows and organic sediments of Association B-ii and in the channel infill sediments of Association B-iii. No refits were found within Association B-i or between any of the three facies associations. In Association B-ii, refit vertical distances are all less than 0.60m with surprisingly few conjoins crossing sediment boundaries, and none crossing the contact separating the sediments of this association from those of Association B-i. This absence of conjoins suggests little or no mixing of materials between the two facies associations and the possibility that the small assemblage from Association B-i might represent a stratigraphically distinct group rather than just an accumulation of materials reworked from overlying sediments. The position of the channel containing Association B-iii, adjacent to Association B-ii, makes the vertical migration of materials between these two associations highly unlikely, and the small assemblage from Association B-iii stratigraphically distinct from that of Association B-ii. The evidence for the mixing of materials is thus very limited, and indicates that at least two, and possibly three, stratigraphically distinct assemblages of archaeological materials are present at the site and represent different periods of hominin activity around the channel. In addition, the small size of the assemblages from associations B-i and B-iii also suggest that hominin activity and/or deposition during these periods was much lower or more intermittent than for the period represented by Association B-ii.

The upper sediments of B-i:03, marking the final active stages of the pre-abandonment phase, are composed of coarse sand and sandy silt facies and are interpreted as sediments deposited on bar tops and edges during waning and low-stage flow conditions, and possibly subjected to periods of subaerial exposure. The artefacts from these sediments are typically in good condition with most unrolled or lightly rolled, unstained and unpatinated (White, chapter 5; Donahue, chapter 5). Their condition indicates that surface exposure could not have been long, and suggests that fluvial reworking was relatively minimal (Schick 1986, 162; Harding *et al* 1987). The few remaining artefacts are severely rolled, stained and patinated, suggesting extensive fluvial transport and likely deposition as bedload materials on bar surfaces (Knighton 1998, 126–50; Miall 2006, 99–105; see also Morton 2004).

Most of the artefacts and vertebrate remains recovered from the site accumulated in the channel during its inactive phase after abandonment. The sediments for this phase are composed of sand, silt and silty organic sand facies interbedded with sediment gravity-flow deposits, and are interpreted as representing the infill succession of a small lake or pond deposited under predominately still to slow-flowing water conditions. Sediment gravity flow deposits and other structures indicative of bank erosion dominate this facies association, and are represented by the various facies comprising Unit B-ii:04 (Table 2.10; *see* Figs 2.3.7 and 2.3.10–2.3.12), and by the lenses of stony organic sand in B-ii:03 and the massive sands of B-ii:01 (Thorne 1982; Innes 1983; Costa 1984; Fritz and Moore 1988, 256–74; Miall 2006, 105, 123). Vertebrate remains and artefactual materials are concentrated within these deposits and around their margins, and suggest that the subaerial erosion of channel banks was one of the major agencies responsible for the transport and deposition of archaeological and palaeontological materials into the channel during this depositional phase. Coleopteran (dung beetles) and pollen (coprophilous fungal spores) data also suggest substantial animal activity in the environs of the channel, probably related to its use as a water source. This activity would also have resulted in the erosion and transport of bank sediments and materials into the channel and their subsequent post-depositional mixing (Buckhouse *et al* 1981; Trimble 1994).

The sediments of the final depositional stages of Association B-iii are composed of a succession of partially interbedded gravel, fine sand and silty organic sand facies that are interpreted as sediments deposited within a small stream channel under variable but predominately waning to still or tranquil-flow conditions. Artefacts from these sediments are unrolled or lightly rolled, unstained and unpatinated (White, chapter 5), indicating brief periods of surface exposure (Schick 1986, 162; Harding *et al* 1987). The bone from these sediments, on the other hand, is heavily weathered (Schreve, chapter 5) and indicates prolonged periods of surface exposure prior to burial. Bone conjoins for one mammoth long-bone fragment (*see* Table 4.11, Fig 5.26) have horizontal refit distances under 0.45m and suggest that some limited fluvial transport and rearrangement of archaeological materials has occurred within the deposit (Morton 2004, 54–74).

These sedimentary contexts have some important implications for the interpretation of the archaeological evidence contained within them. Bedform and lithological properties document deposition under high-energy, waning and low-stage or tranquil-flow fluvial conditions and the incorporation of terrestrial sediments into the channel through bank slumping and the washing-in of fine particles by surface run-off. Archaeological evidence within these sediments is unlikely to represent the residues of *in situ* hominin activities carried out within the channel. Rather, such evidence represents secondary accumulations of material derived from the surrounding banks, which was subjected to further fluvial rearrangement and probable bioturbation by megafauna. This is most apparent for Association B-ii, where sediment gravity flows appear to be the major depositional agency, and to a slightly lesser extent in Association B-iii, where limited fluvial rearrangement of a small palimpsest assemblage appears to have taken place. It is less clear for the bar-top sediments of Association B-i, which contain a largely unabraided artefact assemblage. It is likely that some fluvial reworking of this assemblage did occur given the nature of the depositional environment of the sediments. The origins of the unabraided artefacts and associated faunal remains, however, remain more ambiguous, and suggest three possible alternative explanations: that they represent materials derived from channel banks; that they are a mixed accumulation derived from overlying sediments, or that they are the residues of *in situ* hominin activities carried out on bar surfaces during low-stage periods. The sedimentary evidence by itself is unable to distinguish between these alternative explanations.

Conclusions

On the basis of the stratigraphic analysis and associated sedimentological evidence from Lynford a number of conclusions can be made:

1. Three distinct depositional phases are represented by the facies associations: a pre-abandonment phase composed of in-channel longitudinal bar structures; an inactive phase after channel abandonment represented by predominately fine and organic sediments interbedded with sediment gravity flows; and an upper succession of fluvial infill sediments indicating a return to flowing water conditions; and a post-abandonment phase made up of point bar and probable stream sediments, which might have been deposited at least 1.2ka after the end of the previous phase.

2. Artefacts and vertebrate remains were contained in sediments deposited under predominately low-energy waning, standing or tranquil-flow fluvial conditions and bank collapse by sediment gravity flow.

3. The succession of sediments containing archaeological materials indicates that at least two, and possibly three stratigraphically distinct assemblages are present and represent different periods of hominin activity around the channel.

4. Sediment gravity flows indicate that the subaerial erosion of terrestrial sediments was one of the major agencies responsible for the occurrence of archaeological materials in the sediments of Association B-ii, with coleopteran and pollen data suggesting probable bioturbation of the sediments by megafauna.

5. Some fluvial rearrangement of archaeological materials appears to have

Table 2.8 The locations and contexts of the soil micromorphological samples

sample	context	facies	description
30151/1	20170/20171/20003	B-ii:05 B-ii:03	southern edge basal contact of detrital organic sandy channel fill and channel bar sands
30151/2	20118 20003	B-ii:05 B-ii:03	as above, taken from opposing section
30152	20003 20004	B-ii:03 B-ii:01	central/northern edge contact between finely laminated organic sandy channel fill and basal sands
30153	20003 20139/20245	B-ii:03 B-ii:01	contact between the first organic fills of the channel and the basal sands
30261	20118 20003	B-ii:05 B-ii:03	contact of detrital organic sandy channel fill and basal sands
30246 (monolith)	20120 20003 20139/20245	B-ii:05 B-ii:03 B-ii:01	sequence at base of channel of finely bedded/laminated sands over dark brown organic, fine sand/silt over laminated, organic, fine sands/silt over basal sands/gravel

occurred in Association B-iii and possibly Association B-i, with the origins of most of the assemblage from this association open to several interpretations.

2.2.2 Micromorphological analysis of selected channel sediments

C French

Introduction and aims

The basal channel-fills of Facies Association B-ii contained most of the artefactual, faunal and palaeobiological materials investigated in this excavation. These were sampled in six locations (Table 2.8) for micromorphological analysis using the methodology of Murphy (1986) and described using the terminology of Bullock *et al* (1985).

The aims of the micromorphological analysis were to:

1. Characterise the primary inorganic/organic fills of the channel.
2. Provide information on the depositional processes involved in the accumulation of these primary channel-fill sediments.
3. Contribute to the interpretations of the stratigraphic and palaeobiological data.

The samples selected for further analysis are briefly described by sample and context (Table 2.9) with more detailed descriptions provided

Table 2.9 Summary of the basal channel fill characteristics by context and facies association/component

context	facies association lower unit	facies association upper unit	interpretation
20170, 20171, 20003	B-ii:03: iron impregnated organic fine sand with common impure clay; once laminated	B-ii:05: fine to medium sand with minor impure clay; once laminated	bed scour, organic and overbank accumulation in still to slowly moving water; subject to groundwater fluctuation, oxidation and bioturbation
20118, 20003	B-ii:03: laminated fine sand with impure clay	B-ii:05: amorphous iron impregnated, organic fine sand; bioturbated	slow to still water; organic accumulation and oxidation; bioturbation
20003, 20245	B-ii:01: organic, laminated, fine to medium sand; oxidised; bioturbated; very fine charcoal	B-ii:03: very fine to medium sand with minor impure clay; once laminated; bioturbated	as for above
20003, 20139/20245	B-ii:01: laminated fine sand with minor impure clay, very fine charcoal and calcium carbonate; bioturbated	B-ii:03: alternating laminae of greater/lesser amorphous iron impregnated, organic, fine to medium sand	alternating slow/still water conditions and variable bioturbation, waterlogging and oxidation
20118, 20003	B-ii:03: laminated, amorphous iron, organic fine sand below once laminated fine to medium sand	B-ii:05: once laminated, bioturbated, amorphous iron impregnated, fine sand	still/organic to slow/inorganic to still/organic water conditions
(base) 20245	B-ii:01: bioturbated fine to medium sand and fine flint gravel	B-ii:01: amorphous iron, calcium carbonate, organic fine to medium sand	slow to still water and oxidation
20139	B-ii:01: laminated, organic, very fine to medium sand with oxidised organics, plant tissue and calcium carbonate	B-ii:01: as for lower unit	repeated episodes of organic deposition in slow to still water with partial oxidation
20139	B-ii:01: iron impregnated organic fine to medium sand	B-ii:01: alternating fine sand, sand and impure clay and calcium carbonate, and iron impregnated organic fine to medium sand	still to slow water with overbank flooding episodes and drying out/oxidation
(top) 20003	B-ii:03: iron impregnated organic fine to medium and with fine flint pebbles	B-ii:03: once laminated, fine sand with discontinuous organic/impure clay lenses	still to slow water with overbank flooding episodes and drying out/oxidation

in Appendix 2 and as selected photomicrographs (Figs 2.23–2.30).

The micromorphological analyses

Samples 30151/1 and 30151/2 Two samples, 30151/1 and 30151/2, were taken from opposing sections of contexts 20170/20171 and 20003. In sample 30151/1, two main fabric units are present. The lower unit (B-ii:03) is predominantly a fine quartz sand with common impure or dusty clay (that is, containing micro-contrasted silt and very fine organic/carbonised matter) strongly impregnated with amorphous sesquioxides (iron oxides and hydroxides). This merges over a diffuse contact with the upper unit (B-ii:05), which is composed of a fine and medium-sized quartz sand with very minor amounts of dusty clay coating the grains, and the occasional fine flint-gravel pebble. Both fine fabrics are highly bioturbated. These units might once have been finely laminated and also much more organic, but the combination of oxidation and bioturbation has significantly altered and largely destroyed the laminar aspect and organic component.

The primary organic fine sand unit (B-ii:03) suggests the first erosion/accumulation in the base of the channel, followed by a slight increase in water volume and velocity leading to the deposition of a medium sand. The greater and lesser amounts of dusty clay are indicative of overbank flooding and the deposition of a fine component of eroded soil. Since these alternating standing to slow-flowing sediments were deposited in the channel, subsequent and intermittent lowering of the groundwater table has caused oxidation and iron impregnation of the fine groundmass.

In sample 30151/2 (B-ii:05/03), the deposit sequence is very similar in composition to that observed in the lower Unit 2 present in sample 30152 (B-ii:01). In this case, there are four formerly micro-laminated horizons, each 10–20mm thick, all composed of variable quantities of a similar fabric. The fabric is a strongly amorphous sesquioxide-impregnated, organic, fine-to-medium quartz sand, with a minor calcium carbonate component. The horizonation results from greater or lesser amounts of sesquioxide-impregnated organic matter present in relation to the sand component. These organic deposits overlie a once laminated but now thoroughly mixed very fine to medium quartz sand containing minor amounts of dusty clay with micro-charcoal inclusions. It is possible that the charcoal present hints at fire in the immediate catchment due either to the action of hominins or of lightning strikes, but this requires further corroboration from other data sources.

Sample 30152 Two main units are present in both samples, which derive from contexts 20003 and 20004. The upper unit 1 (B-ii:03) is a very fine to medium quartz sand with a ubiquitous but minor fine groundmass component of dusty clay (Fig 2.23). This fabric was once finely laminated, but has subsequently been subject to much bioturbation. The lower unit 2 (B-ii:01) is a laminated, fine-to-medium quartz sand with abundant organic remains, all of which are bioturbated and strongly impregnated with amorphous sesquioxides (Fig 2.24). The organic component is present either as oxidised plant tissue or as small subrounded pellets, essentially former plant tissue, which has passed through an active soil fauna and fine irregular fragments of plant tissue. Within the fine groundmass there is also a minor occurrence of very fine, subrounded charcoal fragments.

This sequence is suggestive of an organic fine sand accumulating under alternating wetting and drying, oxidation/reduction conditions. This is succeeded by an increase in water flow to a slow but variable flow that is transporting and depositing finer sand sediments derived from either channel bed and/or edge scouring. The dusty clay component is indicative of a certain amount of eroded fine soil material

Fig 2.23 Photomicrograph of organic fine sandy loam with fine impure clay in B-ii: 03 (frame width = 2.25mm; cross polarised light).

*Fig 2.24
Photomicrograph of laminar, fine sandy, bioturbated organic fabric in B-ii: 01 (frame width = 2.25mm; plane polarised light).*

being included, most probably derived from fine overbank sediments settling out of suspension in still or standing water. It is tempting to view the minor presence of a 'dusting' of very fine charcoal as evidence of local fire, but as with the dusty clay, this is most probably derived and included.

Sample 30153: This sample, taken from contexts 20003 and 20139/20245 exhibits the same sequence and very similar composition to sample 30152. It is composed of an upper unit (B-ii:03) of amorphous iron-impregnated, bioturbated, organic fine quartz sand (Fig 2.25), essentially equivalent to the upper three horizons evident in sample 30152 (above), over a once laminated but now well-mixed, fine quartz sand with occasional flint pebbles (B-ii:01).

In addition, there is a thin lens (<2mm) of fine sandy clay present on the upper surface of the basal sands at the B-ii:03/01 contact. It is characterised by about 40 per cent impure or dusty clay (Fig 2.26) and a very fine dust of charcoal (Fig 2.27). This silty clay exhibits weak reticulate striations and moderate birefringence, which, at this stage in the history of the channel, is suggestive of some structural development in this deposit. This probably represents the redeposition in still/standing water conditions of some overbank, eroded, brown-earth type of soil prior to a rise in water table and organic accumulation, rather than a very brief period of stabilisation and incipient soil growth.

Sample 30261: This sample across the B-ii:05/03 boundary from contexts 20003 and 20118 exhibits three units: a once-laminated, amorphous iron-replaced, organic fine quartz sand (B-ii:05) overlying a once laminated fine-to-medium quartz sand (B-ii:03), which in turn

*Fig 2.25
Photomicrograph of amorphous iron impregnated fine sand with bioturbated organic matter, plant tissue and charcoal fragments in B-ii: 03 (frame width = 4.5mm; plane polarised light).*

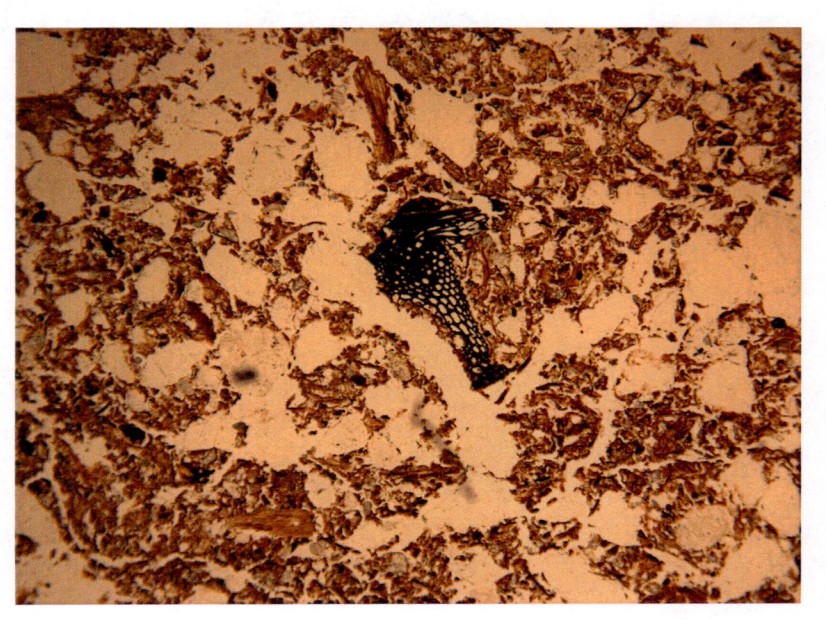

*Fig 2.26
Photomicrograph of lens of sandy clay at the B-ii: 03/01 contact (frame width = 4.5mm; cross polarised light).*

*Fig 2.27
Photomicrograph of lens of sandy clay with very fine charcoal at the B-ii: 03/01 contact (frame width = 4.5mm; plane polarised light).*

has accumulated on a laminated, amorphous iron-replaced, organic fine-to-medium quartz sand (also B-ii:03) (Fig 2.28). Again, this is indicative of *in situ* organic accumulation, drying out and oxidation, then the deposition of fine minerogenic sands in slow but intermittently flowing water, followed by renewed organic accumulation in shallow standing water with subsequent drying-out and oxidation.

Sample 30246: This sequence of samples was taken through the lowest part of B-ii:03 and into the basal channel-fill B-ii:01, from contexts 20120, 20003, 20139 and 20245. The basal sample (0–120mm) is essentially similar to the other profiles examined, with a strongly amorphous, iron-impregnated, organic, fine-to-medium quartz sand overlying a fine-to-medium quartz sand with a few subangular to subrounded, fine flint pebbles. But in this case, no silty clay component was present in the minerogenic sand.

The overlying sample (120–230mm), and the lower half of the overlying sample (230–290mm), were composed of amorphous iron; impregnated and oxidised organic matter; and plant tissue material. This contained a minor presence of amorphous calcium carbonate and micro-sparite crystals and a 30–50 per cent very fine to medium quartz sand component.

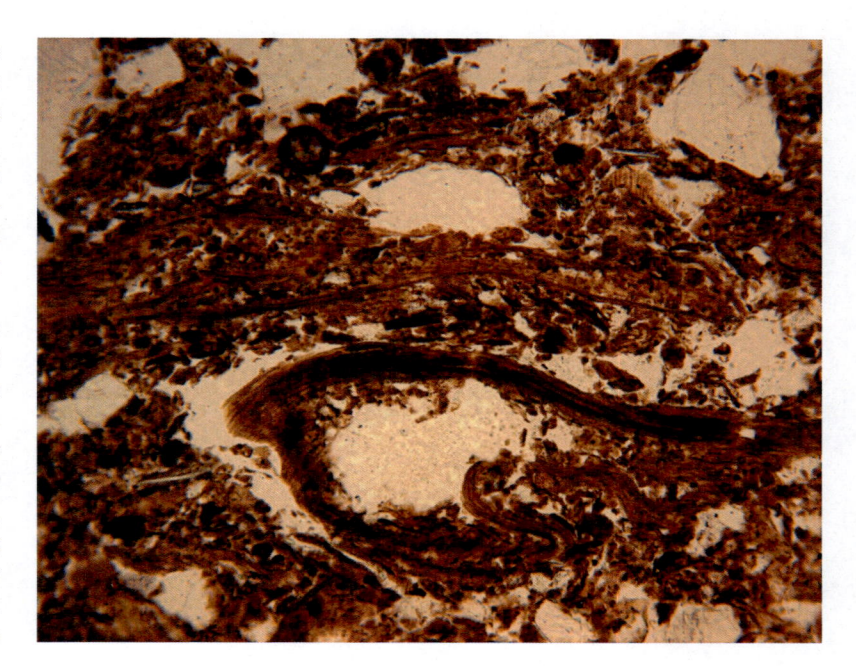

The upper half of the overlying sample (290–365mm) was comprised of four lenses, each of less than 20mm thick, comprising two different or alternating fabrics: a fine-medium quartz sand (*c* 60–80 per cent) with irregular areas of amorphous iron-impregnated organics and dusty clay (*c* 20–40 per cent) (Fig 2.29), and alternating and discontinuous lenses/ laminations of fine quartz sand and amorphous

*Fig 2.28
Photomicrograph of bioturbated plant tissue in B-ii: 03 (frame width = Fig 2.25mm; plane polarised light).*

*Fig 2.29
Photomicrograph of amorphous iron impregnated sandy clay lens with micro-charcoal in B-ii: 01 (frame width = 2.25mm; plane polarised light).*

iron-impregnated organics with occasional micro-sparite calcium carbonate present.

The lower two-thirds of the uppermost sample (365–500mm) was composed of amorphous iron-impregnated and oxidised organic matter and plant tissue material with a minor presence of amorphous calcium carbonate and micro-sparite crystals and a 30–50 per cent very fine to medium quartz sand component (Fig 2.30), with the addition of common flint gravel pebbles. This was overlain by once finely laminated, fine sandy material with dusty clay, and included micro-charcoal (B-ii:03).

It appears that there were frequent variations in the flow and organic content regime in this part of the channel, including brief periods when the surface dried out and other periods of still or standing and slow-flowing water. These contrasting regimes largely appear to account for the variations in microfabric observed in this infilling sequence.

Conclusions

The micromorphological results (summarised in Table 2.9) both complement and corroborate the sedimentary analyses presented in chapter 2 and the environmental conditions set out in chapter 3. All of the thin sections of the primary sediments sampled essentially tell the same story, with only minor variations evident.

The basal fill of the channel was composed of fine sandy sediments and/or organic accumulations, generally with a fine laminar aspect. The sandy sediments were deposited in slow-moving, but variable-flow water conditions, probably representing channel scour and slow bedload transport. The organic accumulation occurred in shallow, standing water, which has subsequently become partially dried out and strongly oxidised and subject to considerable bioturbation. This latter deposit probably represents intermittent organic accumulation alternating with periods of lowered groundwater table conditions, surface drying and strong oxidation, and faunal mixing of the organic matrix, situated in a cut-off channel or small pool.

There also appears to be a minor amount of eroded fine soil material in the system, presumably transported via overbank flooding. This is seen as a fine groundmass of silty clay with variable quantities of included micro-charcoal. This sandy clay type of fabric would be typical of any brown-earth soil fabric found today, or in prehistory, on a terrace gravel

Fig 2.30 Photomicrograph of alternating lenses of fine sand, partially humified organic matter and calcium carbonate in B-ii: 01 (frame width = 4.5mm; plane polarised light).

subsoil in any of the river valleys draining the fenland region (French 2003). This fabric appears in this intermittently waterlogged channel as fine overbank sediment, associated with periods of still/standing water. At first glance this might seem at odds with the other palaeoenviromental evidence that is suggestive of open, unshaded ground, calcareous grassland, immature soils and somewhat cooler temperatures (*see* chapter 3). However, this soil type might be either a relict of earlier interglacial times or, more probably, be associated with calcareous grassland.

Intriguingly, the dusty or impure clay component contains minor amounts of very fine included charcoal. This charcoal dust was probably in the air and water system of the catchment and does not necessarily imply local fires associated with human activity.

2.2.3 Palaeoenvironmental and diagenetic considerations

J Andrews

Introduction

This chapter describes field and laboratory data collected from the organic sediments (Unit B-ii) of the excavated channel. One of the key goals of the post-excavation analysis of the sediments and materials recovered from the site was to accurately reconstruct the environmental conditions prevailing at the time of deposition. To this end, grain-size analysis and organic carbon content of the deposit were required to constrain the energy of deposition. It was also highly desirable as part of this analysis to assess the relative importance of post-depositional effects on the deposit and on the archaeological and palaeontological materials recovered from it. To assess this, basic measurements and observations of geochemical conditions and other diagenetic changes (such as cementation/leaching) were made.

Fieldwork, sampling and storage

Fieldwork entailed on-site observations, sampling and measurement of pH and redox potential. Samples for environmental characterisation (Table 2.10) were taken as a set of discrete but related samples in vertical sequence through the organic palaeochannel deposits for organic carbon and grain-size analysis. A number of other discrete samples were taken for pH determinations. A further discrete sample of cemented sand below the main organic palaeochannel deposit was taken for thin-section analysis.

Contamination is only likely to be an issue for organic carbon (C_{org}) determinations. Common problems centre around young/active root material-penetrating deposits. In this case the organic palaeochannel deposit was buried under 3–3.5m of overburden (too deep for shallow-rooted plant contamination). There was no evidence of larger root penetration/disturbance from bigger trees at the sampled section.

It is possible that organic carbon (and pyrite sulphur) content in these samples has been affected by post-depositional oxidation. This is only likely to have occurred when the sediments were drained prior to excavation. Since site drainage occurred only one year before sampling, there was no time for extensive carbon oxidation, and at the time of sampling, the reduced nature of the organics was indicated by black coloration. Surface oxidation/alteration was observed on the exposed sample face over the course of three months exposure, but the sampled material has retained its black coloration indicating minimal post-sample oxidation.

The samples were stored dry, except for the organic-rich samples, which were refrigerated until the organic geochemistry was completed.

Methods

Percentage weight of organic carbon (wt% C_{org}) was determined by weight loss following overnight combustion at 500°C in a muffle furnace (Brimblecombe *et al* 1982) and cross-compared with elemental analysis data (see below). Owing to sample inhomogeneity, the 500°C combustions on large samples were deemed the most reproducible measure of organic carbon content. The total percentage weights of carbon, nitrogen and sulphur were determined using a Carlo Erba 1108 elemental analyser with combustion at 1020°C (Andrews *et al* 1998). Determination of percentage weight calcium carbonate was done by weight loss after leaching with 10 per cent (vol) HCl.

Stable carbon and oxygen isotope analyses of carbonate cements were performed as described in Andrews *et al* (1993), while stable carbon and nitrogen isotopes in organic matter were measured using a continuous flow isotope ratio mass spectrometer (CF-IRMS; PDZ Europa 20–20) coupled to an elemental analyser.

Table 2.10 Samples for environmental characterisation

sample	context	OD	description	quantity (g)	purpose	wt%Corg	wt%Ntot	wt%Stot	Wt%CaCO$_3$	Corg/Stot	Corg/Ntot	d_{13}Corg	d^{15}Norg
west-facing section exposed by machine													
sample series 30014–30026 for organic Carbon, Nitrogen and Sulphur (CNS) determinations													
(plus 30010)													
30026	20002	8.62	laminae (mm-scale) of grey and white medium sands with some laminae of organic dark brown silt	20	CNS	1.18	0.05	0	1.58		23.60	−29.1	−0.1
30025	20002	8.52	laminae (mm-scale) of grey and white medium sands with some laminae of organic dark brown silt	20	CNS	0.53	0.02	0	1.02		26.50		
30024	20002	8.52	laminae (mm-scale) of grey-yellow medium sands and laminae of organic dark brown silt, rare medium sub rounded/subangular gravel and flint cobbles	20	CNS	1.65	0.09	0	1.51		18.33	−29.4	0.9
30023	20002	8.47	laminae (mm-scale) of grey-yellow medium sands and laminae of organic dark brown silt, rare medium sub rounded/subangular gravel and flint cobbles	20	CNS	0.70	0.03	0	1.45		23.33		
30022	20003	8.41	dark brown-black organic deposit, some laminae/lenses of coarse light grey sand and sparse (5%) flint cobbles	20	CNS	6.83	0.43	0.69	3.80	9.90	15.88	−27.3	2.2
30021	20003	8.36	dark brown-black organic deposit, some laminae/lenses of coarse light grey sand and sparse (5%) flint cobbles	20	CNS	6.49	0.37	0.72	4.69	9.01	17.54	−28.0	2.0
30020	20003	8.31	dark brown-black organic deposit, some laminae/lenses of coarse light grey sand and sparse (5%) flint cobbles	20	CNS	8.63	0.43	0.42	3.25	20.55	20.07		
30019	20003	8.26	dark brown-black organic deposit, some laminae/lenses of coarse light grey sand and sparse (5%) flint cobbles	20	CNS	6.92	0.42	0.45	3.11	15.38	16.48	−28.3	2.8
30018	20003	8.21	dark brown-black organic deposit, some laminae/lenses of coarse light grey sand and sparse (5%) flint cobbles	20	CNS	8.53	0.42	0.36	3.18	23.69	20.31		
30017	20003	8.16	dark brown-black organic deposit, some laminae/lenses of coarse light grey sand and sparse (5%) flint cobbles	20	CNS	7.81	0.48	0.69	4.38	11.32	16.27	−25.3	2.7
30016	20003	8.11	dark brown-black organic deposit, some laminae/lenses of coarse light grey sand and sparse (5%) flint cobbles	20	CNS	6.30	0.4	0.7	6.75	9.00	15.75	−25.6	2.9
30015	20003	8.06	dark brown-black organic deposit, some laminae/lenses of coarse light grey sand and sparse (5%) flint cobbles	20	CNS	4.50	0.34	0.35	6.24	12.86	13.24	−25.6	2.2

continued ▶

Table 2.10 Samples for environmental characterisation – continued

sample	context	OD	description	quantity (g)	purpose	wt%Corg	wt%Ntot	wt%Stot	Wt%CaCO$_3$	Corg/Stot	Corg/Ntot	d13Corg	d15Norg
\multicolumn{14}{l}{*west-facing section exposed by machine – continued*}													
\multicolumn{14}{l}{*sample series 30014–30026 for organic Carbon, Nitrogen and Sulphur (CNS) determinations*}													
\multicolumn{14}{l}{*(plus 30010)*}													
30014	20004	7.96	light yellow-brown silty medium sand with abundant flint cobbles and common flint gravel; Calcium-carbonate cementation	20	organic C (combustion)	0.31			1.58				
30010	20004		light yellow-brown silty medium sand with abundant flint cobbles and common flint gravel; Calcium-carbonate cementation	20	thin section and isotope determination							d^{13}C CaCO$_3$ −3.1	d^{18}O CaCO$_3$ −5.8
			mean values			7.00	0.41	0.55	4.43	13.96	16.94		
\multicolumn{14}{l}{*west-facing section (west edge) exposed by machine*}													
\multicolumn{14}{l}{*samples series 30037–3003*}													
30038	20031	7.97	clayey silt, greenish-grown, rare sand lenses	20g	PSA-matrix	(see below)							
30037	20031	7.97	clayey silt, greenish-grown, rare sand lenses	20g	CNS	2.83	0.54	0	29.93	5.24			
\multicolumn{14}{l}{*west-facing section exposed by machine*}													
30009	20003		dark brown-black organic deposit, some laminae/lenses of coarse light grey sand and sparse (5%) flint cobbles	10g	laboratory pH	nd							
30008	20003		dark brown-black organic deposit, some laminae/lenses of coarse light grey sand and sparse (5%) flint cobbles	10g	laboratory pH	7.11 (pH)							
30007	20003		dark brown-black organic deposit, some laminae/lenses of coarse light grey sand and sparse (5%) flint cobbles	10g	laboratory pH	6.83 (pH)							
\multicolumn{14}{l}{*sample series 30027–30036 for matrix particle size analysis (PSA)*}													
30036	20002	8.64	laminae (mm-scale) of grey and white medium sands with some laminae of organic dark brown silt	20g	PSA-matrix								
30035	20002	8.55	laminae (mm-scale) of grey and white medium sands with some laminae of organic dark brown silt, rare medium sub rounded/subangular gravel and flint cobbles	20g	PSA-matrix								
30034	20002	8.48	laminae (mm-scale) of grey and white medium sands with some laminae of organic dark brown silt, rare medium sub rounded/subangular gravel and flint cobbles	20g	PSA-matrix								
30033	20003	8.4	dark brown-black organic deposit, some laminae/lenses of coarse light grey sand and sparse (5%) flint cobbles	20g	PSA-matrix								

continued ▶

Table 2.10 Samples for environmental characterisation – *continued*

sample	context	OD	description	quantity (g)	purpose	wt%Corg	wt%Ntot	wt%Stot	Wt%CaCO$_3$	Corg/Stot	Corg/Ntot	d13Corg	d15Norg
sample series 30027–30036 for matrix particle size analysis (PSA) – continued													
30032	20003	8.34	dark brown-black organic deposit, some laminae/lenses of coarse light grey sand and sparse (5%) flint cobbles	20g	PSA-matrix								
30031	20003	8.24	dark brown-black organic deposit, some laminae/lenses of coarse light grey sand and sparse (5%) flint cobbles	20g	PSA-matrix								
30030	20003	8.14	dark brown-black organic deposit, some laminae/lenses of coarse light grey sand and sparse (5%) flint cobbles	20g	PSA-matrix								
30029	20003	8.09	dark brown-black organic deposit, some laminae/lenses of coarse light grey sand and sparse (5%) flint cobbles	20g	PSA-matrix								
30028	20003	8.03	dark brown-black organic deposit, some laminae/lenses of coarse light grey sand and sparse (5%) flint cobbles	20g	PSA-matrix								
30027	20004	7.95	light brown silty clay with diffuse base (?staining from humics leached from 20003)	20g	PSA-matrix								
west-facing section (west edge) exposed by machine samples series 30037–30038													
30038	20031	7.97	clayey silt, greenish-grown, rare sand lenses	20g	PSA-matrix								
30037	20031	7.97	clayey silt, greenish-grown, rare sand lenses	20g	CHNS	2.83	0.54	0	29.93		5.24		

Grain-size measurements were made on the bulk sediment and matrix samples by standard sieving (see McManus 1988; Folk 1974) of the coarser than 63μ fraction and laser granulometry (laser coulter) of the finer than 63μ fraction. Before grain-size analysis, organic matter was removed by oxidation in 10 per cent (vol) hydrogen peroxide. The laser coulter analyses were converted to notional sieve fractions, and combined with the sieve data for full moment statistical analysis of grain size, sorting, skewness, kurtosis and sand/mud ratio (see Folk 1974; McManus 1988). Standard resin-impregnated thin sections were used for fabric study of cemented carbonate sands.

Results

Most of the samples selected for detailed study came from gravelly muddy sands (gmS of Folk 1974) of an organic channel-fill (Units B-ii:03 and B-ii:05; contexts 20003 and 20002).

pH determinations: Although *in situ* field pH measurements were taken in the organic deposits (20003 of B-ii:03), the results were not reliable due to the low water content of the deposit. Instead, pH was measured in the laboratory using standard soil pH methods (Brimblecombe *et al* 1982). The middle to upper part of the deposit has a pH of 7.11, while the base of the deposit is slightly more acidic (pH 6.83). These near-neutral pH values are typical of pH values in humid region mineral sediments and soils (Brady and Weil 1999). The local supply of Chalk in the sediments (and dissolved in deeper groundwater) would buffer the pH to near-neutral values. Semi-quantitative, *in situ* Eh (oxidation/

Table 2.11 Grain size data. Organic unit (20003): mean grain size is 125–150 microns (fine sand). Sorting generally classifies as very poorly sorted. Skewness is very positively skewed (*strongly fine skewed*). Kurtosis is extremely leptokutic (ie strong sorting in the centre of the distribution). Streaky unit (20002) basically the same as above, ?slightly finer (100–125μm). Flint pebble/cobble content in these units is about 8–10 per cent (5 per cent according to Green based on field measurements).

context code	sample code	folk desc.	mean phi	sorting	skewness	kurtosis	sand/mud	OD (m)
20002	30036	gmS	3.89	2.32	2.41	3.14	2.33	8.64
20002	30035	gmS	3.02	2.15	2.38	3.28	4.85	8.55
20002	30004	gmS	2.56	2.12	2.47	3.32	5.48	8.48
20003	30033	gmS	3.33	2.5	2.31	3.51	3.03	8.395
20003	30032	gmS	3.23	2.47	2.49	3.49	3.33	8.335
20003	30031	gmS	2.25	2.73	2.02	3.75	3.52	8.235
20003	30030	gmS	3.02	2.59	2.47	3.61	3.17	8.135
20003	30029	gmS	2.89	2.4	2.32	3.46	3.62	8.085
20003	30028	gmS	2.36	2.01	1.97	3.14	7.64	8.025
20004	30027	msG	−1.42	3.18	3.16	4.32	7.15	7.945
	30038	sM	4.74	2.98	−1.15	3.74	0.75	7.97
mean (20002) streaky lam unit			3.16	2.20	2.42	3.25	4.22	
mean (20003) organic unit			2.85	2.45	2.26	3.49	4.05	

reduction or redox potential) values were around 145–65mV, typical of low oxygen conditions in soils and sediments restricted from the atmosphere. These types of Eh are consistent with nitrate, Mn and Fe reduction in mineral soils (Brady and Weil 1999). It is, however, possible that Eh values were lower (less oxidising and possibly anoxic) before drainage of the deposit. Green (this volume) reports locally high concentrations of pyrite framboids in pollen preparations, which indicate anoxia, possibly in the sediment as a whole, or in microenvironments.

Overall, the near-neutral pH and low-oxic Eh values are consistent with the organic carbon and nitrogen data (see below). Low-oxic conditions in particular would have been favourable to good preservation of organic materials (bone and wood), but also organic walled microfossils and palynomorphs.

Sedimentological data: grain size: The gravel component of these sediments is generally between 5 and 10 per cent, and is dominated by flint cobbles and pebbles.

Grain-size analysis of the $< -2\varphi$ (< 4mm) fraction shows that sediments from both the organic sediment Unit B-ii:03 (20003), and the overlying sandy laminated channel-fill, Unit B-ii:05 (20002), have mean grain sizes in the fine sand fraction, that is, between 2.85 and 3.16φ (100–150 microns; Table 2.11). Overall, these bulk sediments have mean σ1 (sorting) values of 2.2–2.45 (*see* Table 2.11) indicative of poor sorting. However, the mean kurtosis values (K_G), are between 4.05 and 4.22 (*see* Table 2.11), indicating very strong sorting in the centre of the particle distribution: in essence the fine sand fraction is very well sorted. These sediments have mean SK1 values between 2.26 and 2.42, indicating a very positive skew to the fine fraction, although the sand/mud ratios (2.00–0.063mm/< 0.063mm fraction) are typically around 3–4 (*see* Table 2.11).

Grain size shows a slight overall upward-fining trend (2.3–3.9φ) from fine-sand to very-fine-sand/coarse silt (Fig 2.31), accompanied by a general increase in < 0.063mm fraction and increase in skewness toward the fine fraction (Fig 2.32). Sorting in the fine-sand fraction decreases slightly up-sequence (Fig 2.33).

The exception to these trends is from a pale brown-yellow msG (muddy sandy gravel; Folk 1974) of Unit B-ii:01 (20004), which underlies the organic palaeochannel. Although the sample from this unit has a mean grain size in the medium sand fraction (−1.42φ; 360

Fig 2.31
Mean grain size plotted against depth (OD). Note gradual fining up. Basal sample is from unit 20004. Other samples are from the organic unit 20003, except the upper three, which are from the sandy laminated channel fill unit 20002.

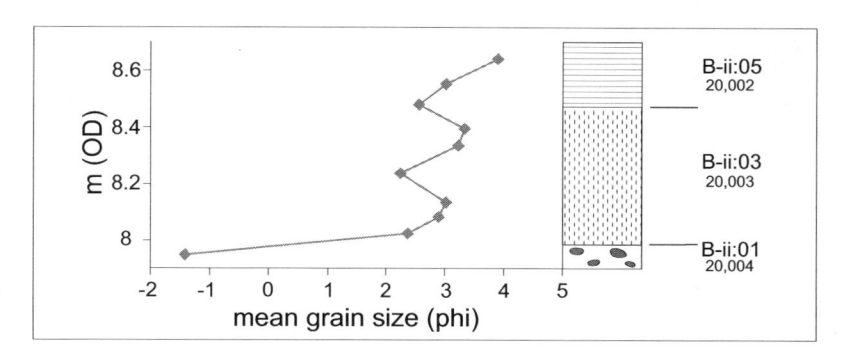

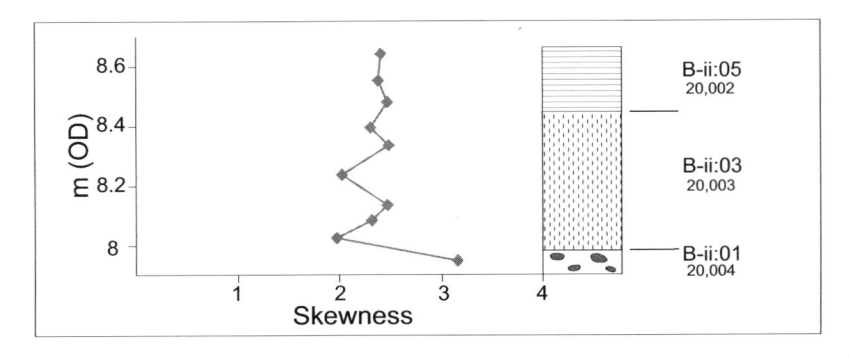

Fig 2.32
Skewness plotted against depth (OD). Basal sample is from unit 20004. Other samples are from the organic unit 20003, except the upper three, which are from the sandy laminated channel fill unit 20002.

Fig 2.33
Kurtosis plotted against depth (OD). Basal sample is from unit 20004. Other samples are from the organic unit 20003, except the upper three, which are from the sandy laminated channel fill unit 20002.

microns; *see* Table 2.11) the distribution is strongly bimodal, with 58 per cent gravel content, and a second mode in the medium sand fraction at 1.25φ. The sand/mud ratio is 7.15, reflecting the increased sand content (*see* Table 2.11).

The grain-size data are most significant in showing that there is no clear sedimentological break in the transition from the organic palaeo-channel, Unit B-ii:03 (20003), into the overlying sandy laminated channel-fill unit, B-ii:05 (20002). Rather, the overall characteristics of the sediment suggest upward fining with a gradual increase in the silt and clay content up-sequence.

During the course of fieldwork, and in subsequent thin-section preparation, it was noted that many of the sand grains in the sediment sequence (typically the 0.3–0.5mm size range) are subrounded to well-rounded, and in some cases highly spherical. These grains demonstrate a source of aeolian-derived grains in the area – either older aeolian material eroded and reworked by the stream that deposited the sediments, or a local input of contemporary wind-blown sand.

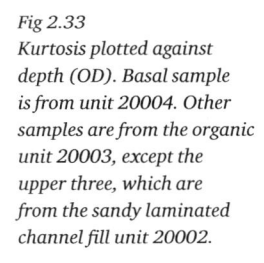

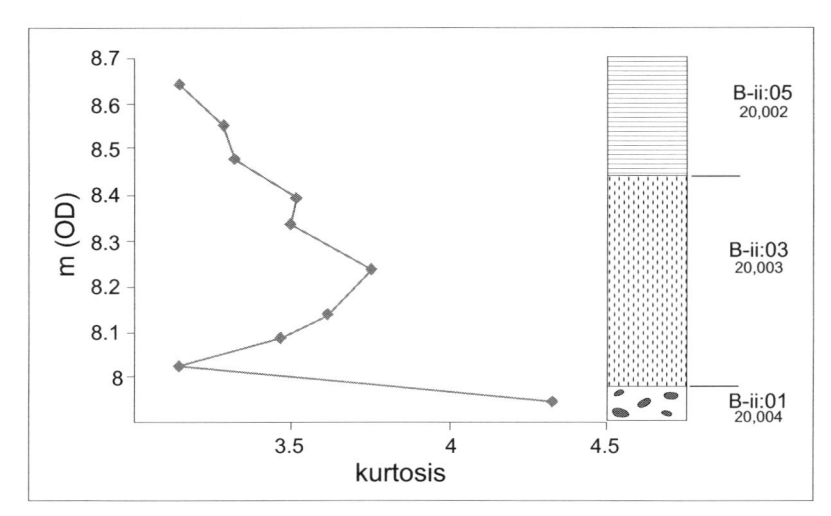

It was noted in the field that Unit B-ii:01 (20004: pale brown-yellow muddy sandy gravel), underlying the organic sediment, was lightly cemented. Resin-impregnated thin sections showed this cement to be a very fine-grained micritic calcite with abundant spherical carbonate components (?foraminifera) and rare ostracod shells. Many of these biogenic carbonates contained secondary cement growths as rinds. The source of these carbonates is not clear, but they are probably derived from erosion of the local Chalk bedrock: indeed, they are also found in the organic Unit B-ii:03 (20003) itself (Green, chapter 3.4). Whatever the origin, these biogenic carbonates acted as a nucleus for subsequent microspar and micritic carbonate cement formation.

Stable isotope data from the cemented matrix gave the following compositions ($\delta^{18}O$ –5.8 per mille VPDB, $\delta^{13}C$ –3.1 per mille VPDB). The oxygen isotope composition is consistent with precipitation from meteoric water at temperatures between 8 and 10°C (depending on assumptions about the isotopic composition of meteoric water, but assuming $\delta^{18}O$ values of recharge were close to those of the present day – see Andrews *et al* 1994). The carbon isotope compositions are not strongly negative; input of large amounts of soil-zone carbon would tend to drive equilibrium $\delta^{13}C$ values toward strongly negative values (–10 per mille VPDB) as seen in, for example, tufa deposits (Andrews *et al* 1993, 1997). The less negative Lynford values suggest a strong input of isotopically heavy carbon. This could be from the biogenic material but could equally be derived from dissolution of chalk bedrock ($\delta^{13}C$ composition around 0 per mille) in groundwater. Assuming open-system geochemical conditions, values of about –3.1 per mille suggest that roughly 50 per cent of the carbon comes from Chalk dissolution and 50 per cent from a soil-zone source. These data are consistent with the interpretation that cementation of the sand occurred in a groundwater setting (meteoric phreatic), removed from the pedogenic zone (where stronger soil-carbon influence would be expected).

Thin-section evidence also shows that in places the sandy unit of B-ii:01 (20004) has pyrite cements that post-date calcite cementation. This pyrite almost certainly formed when sulphate was leached from the overlying organic deposit, probably through oxidation of pyrite in the organic deposit

(Green, chapter 3.4, has also noted pyrite framboids), or leaching of organic sulphur. Whichever it was, local leaching of sulphate and organic matter resulted in small-scale pyrite cementation of 20004. These findings are consistent with field observations of pale-brown sand found in 20004 that appeared to be humic-stained from the overlying organic deposits.

Organic carbon and calcium carbonate geochemistry: Organic matter in these deposits will reflect the original deposition of organic materials, mostly plant- or soil-derived matter, while calcium carbonate ($CaCO_3$) content will reflect material from shelly fossils such as molluscs, ostracods and reworked detrital material, particularly ground-up chalk bedrock (*see above*).

The organic sediment unit (20003) has organic carbon values ranging from 4.5 to 8.6 percentage weight C (mean 7.0 percentage weight Corg; *see* Table 2.10 and Fig 2.34). The sandy laminated channel-fill unit (20002), on top of the organic deposit, has lower organic carbon contents, in the range 0.5 to 1.6 percentage weight Corg, depending on whether sand-rich or organic-rich laminae were sampled (*see* Fig 2.34). These much lower values suggest either that the depositional environment of Unit 20002 was less organic-matter-rich, or that this part of the deposit was originally more organic-matter-rich and that it has been partially decomposed by post-depositional processes, for example by groundwater flow.

In addition to the marked difference in organic carbon content between Units 20003 and 20002, these units also have markedly different calcium carbonate ($CaCO_3$) contents (*see* Table 2.10 and Fig 2.35). The organic sediment unit (20003) contains between 3.1 and 6.2 percentage weight $CaCO_3$ (mean 4.4 percentage weight $CaCO_3$), whereas the overlying sandy laminated channel-fill unit (20002) contains only 1.0–1.58 percentage weight $CaCO_3$.

The data above (markedly lower Corg and $CaCO_3$ content in context 20002 relative to 20003) can be simply interpreted as partial, post-depositional removal of both organic matter and $CaCO_3$ (decalcification), presumably due to groundwater interaction. This interpretation is supported by data from other specialists who report: (1) entire removal of aragonitic molluscan shells in both Unit 20002 and in the upper 200mm and lower 100mm parts of Unit 20003 (ie the upper 400mm and lower 100mm of the channel-fill deposit sampled at 30198 (Keen, chapter 3.3); (2) complete lack of insect fossils in the upper 100mm of context 20002 and decomposed/weathered insect fossils in the uppermost 150mm of Unit 20003 (Coope, chapter 3.2); and (3) a slight increase in corrosion of spores and pollen in Unit 20002 (Green, chapter 3.4). Alteration to the tops of organic units by groundwater leaching is known elsewhere in the British Pleistocene (Bottrell *et al*, 1998).

The ratio of organic carbon to total nitrogen (Corg/N) is a useful indicator of the type – and in some cases, quality – of organic material preserved (Andrews *et al* 1998, 2000). The quality of the preserved organic matter is essentially an index of the amount of microbial degradation that has affected the organic matter. Corg/N is thus a potentially powerful indicator of early diagenetic microbial alteration that typically removes labile nitrogenous organic matter, leaving a residue of more refractory carbon-rich material.

Corg/N weight ratios from the organic deposit (20003) are between 13 and 20 (mean

*Fig 2.34
Per cent by weight organic carbon plotted against depth (OD). Basal sample is from unit 20004. Other samples are from the organic unit 20003, except the upper four, which are from the sandy laminated channel fill unit 20002.*

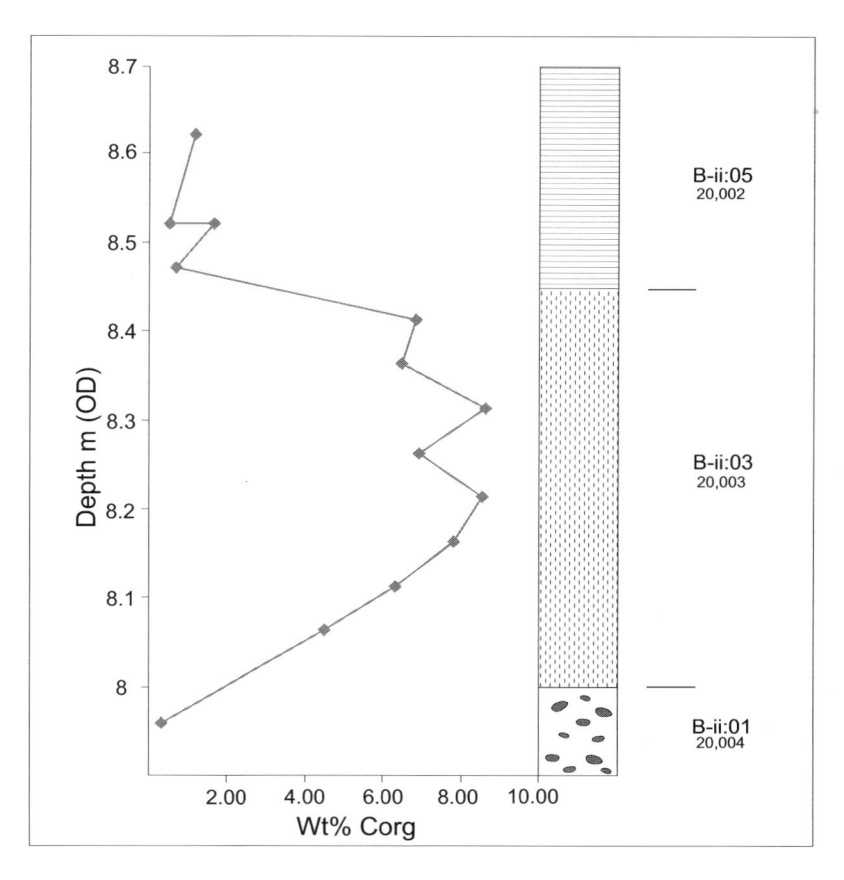

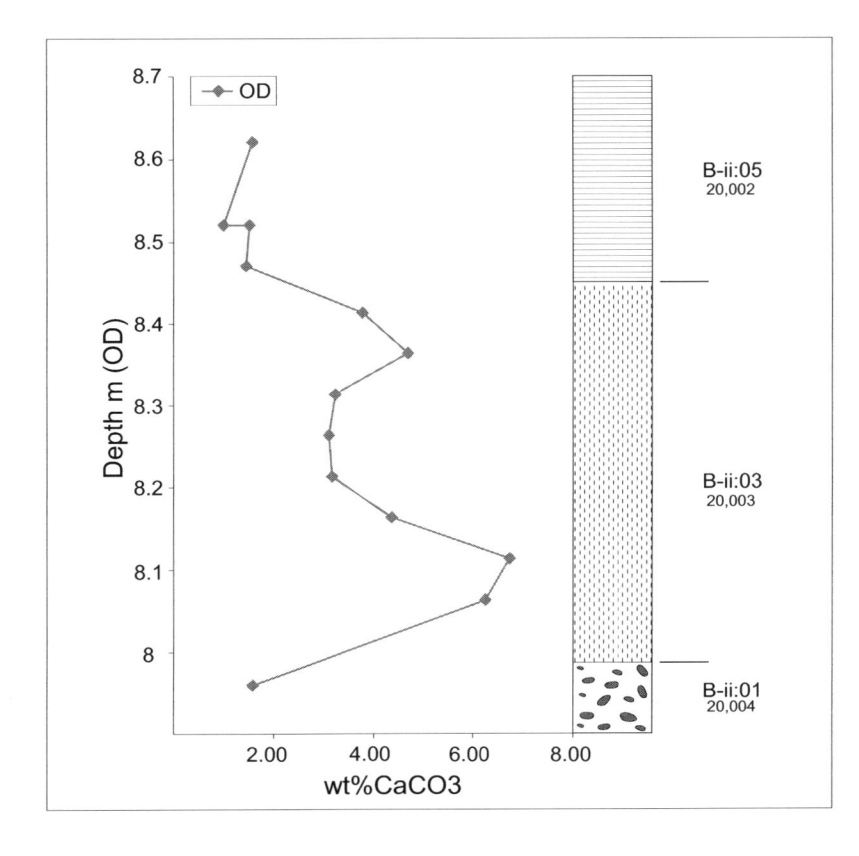

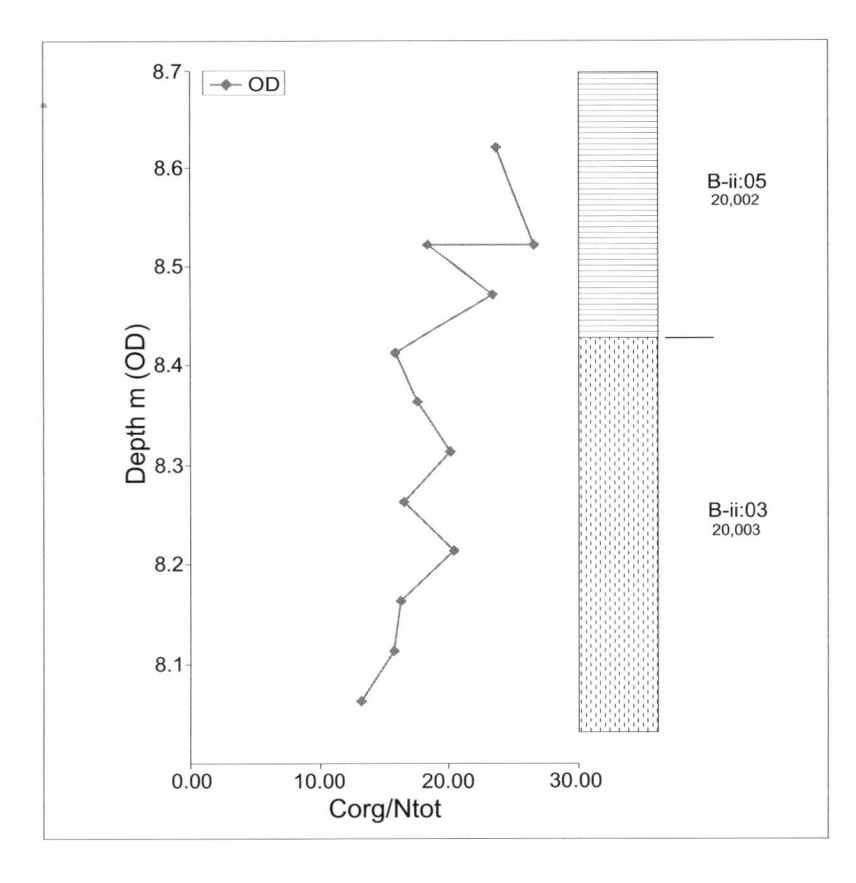

16.9), which are fairly typical of degraded terrestrial organic matter (Bordovsky 1965; Thornton and McManus 1994). It is also clear that the Corg/N ratio progressively increases from around 13 at the base of the unit to higher values (*see* Table 2.10 and Fig 2.36), a trend that continues into the overlying sandy laminated channel-fill unit (20002). In this deposit (20002) Corg/N ratios are between 18 and 26, reflecting the more carbon-rich nature of the organic matter. The progressive increase in Corg/N up-sequence implies that either: 1) the deposited organic matter type changed over time; or 2) the upper part of the deposit has undergone more extensive microbial decomposition. There is no evidence that, or clear reason why, organic matter input type changed up-sequence, given that the organic matter is probably derived from local terrestrial biomass. This suggests that variation in Corg/N ratio is primarily controlled by the degree of post-depositional microbial diagenesis, which became more important up-sequence, and was most marked in Unit 20002.

The validity of the interpretation of the Corg and Corg/N profiles given above was further tested by examining the carbon and nitrogen isotopic compositions of the preserved organic matter. The results (*see* Table 2.10) show a progressive decrease in $\delta^{13}C_{org}$ from –25 per mille at the base of the organic unit (20003) to –29 per mille into the sandy laminated channel-fill unit (20002; Fig 2.37), concomitant with decreasing $\delta^{15}N_{org}$ values from +2.9 to –0.1 per mille (Fig 2.38).

The decreasing isotopic values are clearly strongly related to both the lower amount, and the more carbonaceous nature of, the organic material preserved up-sequence (*see* Figs 2.35 and 2.36). The $\delta^{13}C_{org}$ data are entirely consistent with bacterially-mediated diagenesis, which is well known to selectively remove labile components of organic matter such as proteins and carbohydrates (Harvey *et al* 1995; Hedges *et al* 1998). Selective removal of these compounds leaves behind more refractory components such as lignin, which is isotopically more negative than the starting bulk organic matter (Benner *et al* 1987; Spiker and Hatcher 1987; Lehmann *et al* 2002).

The changes in $\delta^{15}N_{org}$ are, on the face of it, more problematic because $\delta^{15}N$ transformation as bacterial decomposition usually results in an isotopically enriched (more positive) organic residue (see Turner et al 1983; Thornton and McManus 1994; Lehmann et al 2002), probably due to kinetic isotope fractionation during protein hydrolysis (Bada et al 1989; Silfer et al 1992). One exception to this has been documented in experimental work and fieldwork on organic matter alteration in alpine lake sediments (Lehmann et al 2002). This study showed that although oxic degradation of algal organic matter resulted in enrichment of δ^{15}Norg in the residue, the same material, degraded under anoxic conditions, resulted in depletion of δ^{15}Norg in the residue. The changed δ^{15}N profile under anoxic conditions was attributed to accumulation of isotopically light bacterial cell material that formed *in situ*, using the soluble organic compounds that had been released during organic matter decomposition (see also Macko and Estep 1984). However, the lowering of the bulk Corg/N ratio, usually associated with accumulation of bacterial cell material, is not in evidence in the Lynford samples.

If the presence of isotopically light bacterial cells is not the explanation for the unusual δ^{15}Norg isotopic profile, then another nitrogen source must have impacted the upper part of the profile. Since all the other evidence shows that groundwater has interacted with this part of the profile, it is logical to assume that groundwater nitrogen is a likely source. As it is also likely that this part of the deposit reacted with groundwater recharged from above by local rainfall (*see below*), it is thus logical to examine the isotopic composition of nitrogen in the recharging rainwater. Unfortunately, present-day nitrogen sources in the rainfall of both rural and urban eastern England are polluted by numerous anthropogenic sources, resulting in isotopically positive δ^{15}N values of around +9 per mille (Yeatman et al 2001), which propagates into surface and shallow groundwater (Rivers et al 1996). However, pre-industrial/pre-anthropogenic, pristine, unpolluted rainfall from westerly oceanic sources, would almost certainly have had much lower δ^{15}N values (likely total aerosol NO_3^- δ^{15}N around –1 per mille, and aerosol NH_4^+ δ^{15}N around –15 per mille; Yeatman et al 2001). This isotopically light nitrogen source would have translated to the shallow groundwater, where it seems to have been involved (possibly exchanged with soluble organic nitrogen species) during the diagenesis and mineralisation of organic matter in the sandy laminated channel-fill unit (20002). This interpretation is supported by evidence that nitrogen species in modern oceanic rainfall can lower the δ^{15}N of soil nitrogen and associated biomass significantly (Vitousek et al 1989), such that soil nitrogen δ^{15}N is dependent on relative input/output of nitrogen species with time (Brenner et al 2001). If correct, this interpretation implies that organic matter diagenesis in the Lynford deposit occurred early in the burial history, long before major anthropogenic contamination of the terrestrial atmosphere.

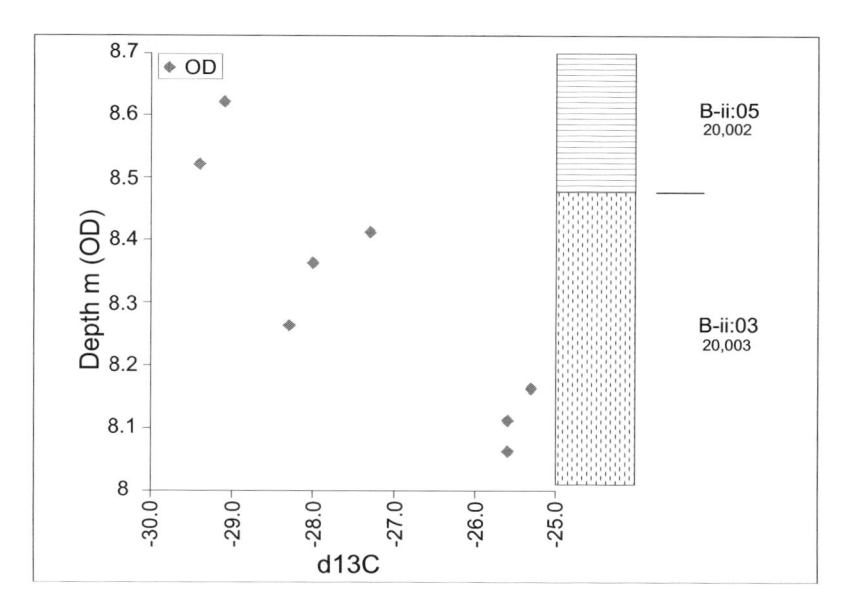

It is worth emphasising that Keen (chapter 3.3) also reports decalcification of the lower 100mm of the channel-fill unit (20003), although Coope (chapter 3.2) does not detect insect fossil alteration in this zone. Samples from this horizon had very low organic matter content (0.3 percentage weight Corg) and low $CaCO_3$ content (1.58 percentage weight $CaCO_3$), partly of reworked Chalk material and early diagenetic cement (see above). The loss of aragonite implies dissolution associated with partial calcite re-cementation, while the low organic matter content is consistent with either microbial degradation, or originally low values during deposition. Organic matter alteration in this horizon could be consistent with humic-staining from the overlying organic deposits and pyrite cementation (see above); alternatively, good insect preservation could support the notion that organic matter content was originally low in this unit and organic diagenesis negligible.

Total percentage weight sulphur (S) in the organic unit (20003) is very low – 0.3 to 0.7

Fig 2.37 (above)
Stable carbon isotope ratio of bulk organic matter plotted against depth (OD). Samples are from the organic unit 20003, except the upper two, which are from the sandy laminated channel fill unit 20002.

Fig 2.35 (top left)
Per cent by weight $CaCO_3$ plotted against depth (OD). Basal sample is from unit 20004. Other samples are from the organic unit 20003, except the upper four, which are from the sandy laminated channel fill unit 20002.

Fig 2.36 (bottom left)
Per cent by weight Corg/Ntot plotted against depth (OD). Samples are from the organic 20003, except the upper four, which are from the sandy laminated channel fill unit 20002.

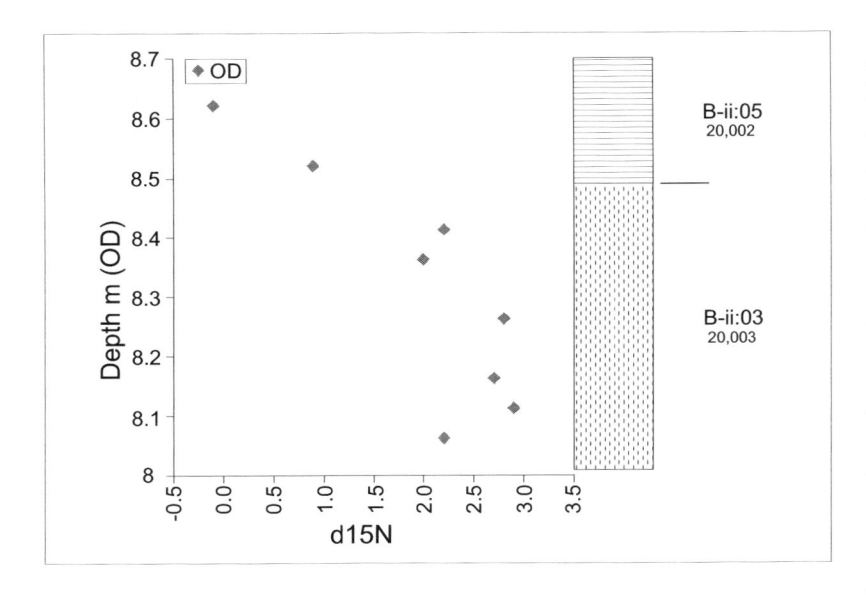

Fig 2.38
Stable nitrogen isotope ratio of bulk organic matter plotted against depth (OD). Samples are from the organic unit 20003, except the upper two, which are from the sandy laminated channel fill unit 20002.

percentage weight S (mean 0.5 percentage weight S) – as expected for freshwater deposits where pyrite sulphur is low or absent. Corg/S ratios are thus consistent with other East Anglian Quaternary organic freshwater sediments (Bottrell *et al* 1998). The low but detectable sulphur content probably derives from the organic material (organic sulphur). It might be significant that some of the lowest S values are in the base of the deposit, immediately overlying carbonate-cemented sands with some pyrite cements (*see above*). It is likely that sulphur was oxidised and leached from this basal horizon, proving a sulphate supply for pyrite formation in the sand below.

The sandy laminated channel-fill unit (20002) contains no detectable sulphur, consistent with leaching and complete removal by groundwater.

Chemistry of Lynford groundwaters

The combined information above shows, beyond doubt, that groundwater interaction in the upper part of the organic unit was with waters slightly undersaturated with respect to aragonite (causing dissolution of aragonite molluscs) but close to saturation with calcite (allowing preservation of some calcium carbonate, probably ground-up Chalk and other calcitic elements such as the plates of Limacid slugs; Keen, chapter 3.3). Moreover, groundwater at the base of the deposit was capable not only of aragonite dissolution, but also precipitation of calcite cements (*see above*).

These observations are consistent with likely hydrogeological scenarios for the deposit. Water that interacted with the top of the deposit was almost certainly more aggressive and capable of both organic matter and calcium carbonate diagenesis. It is well established that rainwater recharge through glacial deposits in Norfolk results in waters with pH of around 6.6–7.4 (consistent with the pH ranges measured) and undersaturated with respect to calcite and aragonite (Hiscock 1993, table 6, saturation index for calcite (SIC) –0.03 to –2.47). This suggests that recharging water formed a perched aquifer on top of the organic deposits, acting as a local aquiclude. This aggressive water was capable of aragonite dissolution, and prompted bacterial degradation of organic matter. As the water reacted with the deposit it became gradually buffered with respect to calcite and was then less able to cause further dissolution.

By contrast, the base of the organic unit probably reacted mainly with up-flowing chalk groundwater. In this part of west Norfolk, geochemical analyses for unconfined chalk groundwater (Hiscock, pers comm) have a pH of around 7.2, Eh 190mV (oxic), but SIC values of around 0.17. These types of water are thus close to saturation with aragonite and calcite, less able to alter calcium carbonate, and perhaps less able to alter organic components of the sediment. Oxidation of organic sulphur (see above) might have generated enough acidity for some aragonite dissolution at the base of the deposit.

Overview and implications for preservation of artefacts and environmental indicators

Overall, the grain-size data show that there is no clear sedimentological break in the transition from the organic palaeochannel Unit B-ii:03 (20003) into the overlying sandy laminated channel-fill Unit B-ii:05 (20002). Rather, the overall characteristics of the sediment suggest upward-fining and a gradual increase in the silt and clay content up-sequence. These results are consistent with an overall environmental interpretation of still- to slow-flowing water in a silting-up river channel.

The geochemical data are most useful in showing that early diagenesis by groundwater has most severely affected the upper and lower parts of Unit B-ii. This early diagenesis will have had no material impact on the preservation of stone or bone artefacts or large animal-bone fragments (except staining by humic acids as reported by Schreve, chapter 5.1). However, early diagenesis will have compromised some of the environmental record indicators in such a way that absence of calcium carbonate fossils or organic components cannot be simply assumed to represent environmental change. The combined geochemical (this chapter) and mollusc preservation data (Keen, chapter 3.3) show clearly that only the middle 400mm of Unit B-ii:03 (20003) can be considered the most pristine, unaltered sediment. This is where the most reliable indicators (geochemical or fossils) of environmental conditions will be found. Further geochemical work on stable isotopes in bone collagen (*see* Richards *et al*, chapter 5.4) should pay particular attention to the archaeological context of the samples specifically, material from Unit B-ii should only be selected from contexts where well-preserved organic matter is found. Oxygen isotopes in bone phosphate will be particularly vulnerable to exchange with groundwater at the base of Unit B-ii:03 (20003) and in Unit B-ii:05 (20002) and this probably explains the wide range of preliminary values presented by Richards *et al* in chapter 5.

In the context of preserved organic matter, the best-preserved palaeochannel sediments contain ~7–8 per cent by weight of organic matter with a C_{org}/N ratio of around 17, consistent with a source from degraded terrestrial organic matter (see above). The carbon isotope compositions between –25 and –28 per mille are indicative of terrestrial C3 vegetation (Deines 1980), and agree with the similar values found in Mammoth bone collagen (Richards *et al*, this volume). The nitrogen isotope values of around +2 per mille are entirely consistent with data from modern soils (Kendall 1998) and modern 'lacustrine peats' or their humic acid extracts (Kaplan 1983, tables 2–23). These combined data are thus all consistent with the riverine/lacustrine palaeoenvironmental interpretations for the Lynford deposit.

2.2.4 Deposit compaction studies

N K Tovey

Introduction

The purpose of this investigation was to determine whether it is possible to estimate the amount of compaction of the organic sediments comprising Unit B-ii and to assess any effect this might have on the archaeological material. The analysis was undertaken by assessing the bulk density of samples and by subjecting the silt clay to standard one-dimensional consolidation tests.

Method

Three core samples of the silty organic clay and three samples from the overburden were taken from the site. The three sand samples were used for bulk density measurements obtained by successive weighing of the core sample, both in its *in situ* condition, and after drying in the oven. The relevant information relating to the six samples is summarised in Table 2.12. Samples 2 and 3 were also originally intended for consolidation testing. Unfortunately, by the time Sample 1 had been fully tested, samples 2 and 3 revealed evidence of minor additional desiccation, while one sample also contained significant particles of up to 5mm, making it impossible to trim satisfactorily. Both samples were thus rendered unsuitable for testing.

The water content (sometimes known as moisture content) can be defined in two ways: (a) the percentage obtained by dividing the weight of the water by the weight of solid matter, and (b) the percentage obtained by dividing the weight of the water by the total weight of solid matter plus water. Though the latter definition is perhaps the more scientifically correct, it is more difficult to determine directly because the denominator also includes the weight of the water. This analysis thus uses the first definition, which is also convenient in that it leads directly to the convention needed for the consolidation analysis. As can be seen, the water content is low in samples 4 and 5, but moderate in Sample 6.

From a knowledge of the total weight of the sample and its volume (estimated from the volume of the core tube), the *in situ* density can be determined.

The void ratio is an estimate of the volume of voids to the volume of solids, and this is a measure of the amount of compaction. The values obtained suggest a moderately dense to loose sand, with Sample 6 more consistent for a sample with more clay.

The porosity is also quoted, as it is often used as an alternative to void ratio, to which it is uniquely related.

The degree of saturation (usually expressed as a percentage) is a measure of the proportion

Table 2.12 Basic data of the geotechnical samples

		sample no.					
		1	2	3	4	5	6
	reference	(30058)	(30059)	(30060)	(30061)	(30062)	(30063)
	easting	582398.898	582403.743	582403.242	582407.073	582401.715	582399.629
	northing	294838.283	294839.235	294839.337	294844.614	294855.595	294855.1
	OD	8.027	8.382	8.442	8.526	10.753	11.277
shear vane tests	peak (kPa)	785	630	770			300
	residual (kPa) units	300	200	370			120
moisture content		35.2%			2.8%	2.9%	25.9%
dry bulk density	kg m-3	962.46	samples damaged and unsuitable for consolidation testing		1653.93	1479.93	1098.33
in situ void ratio		1.75			0.60	0.79	1.41
in situ porosity		0.64			0.38	0.44	0.59
degree of saturation		53.2%			12.2%	9.6%	48.5%
in situ bulk density	kg m-3	1301.4			1699.9	1522.3	1382.3
saturated bulk density	kg m-3	1599.3			2029.8	1921.5	1683.9
submerged bulk density	kg m-3	599.3			1029.8	921.5	683.9

of the voids filled with water. The values in Table 2.12 are consistent with a well-draining sand.

The saturated bulk density and the submerged bulk density are the densities applicable to the samples if (1) the voids became fully saturated with water, or (2) the sample was below the water table. A sample below the water table is obviously saturated, but differs from those above the water table in that the full effects of its buoyancy due to water must be taken into account. That samples are saturated does not necessarily mean that they are below the water table, particularly if a perched water table existed.

Consolidation tests

The samples taken were not of the standard diameter used for consolidation tests, as normally such sampling requires sophisticated sampling rigs. Nevertheless the results obtained should give a good approximation of the likely consolidation behaviour of the samples. Some experimentation was necessary to obtain adequate samples for testing, and it is possible that the initial loading of the samples might not be exactly representative of the true nature of the soil. However, it is the behaviour of the material under virgin consolidation conditions that is most important.

Three separate samples were obtained from the core of Sample 1, and are referred to as 1a, 1b and 1c respectively. Of the three samples, most difficulty was experienced with Sample 1c, and the reloading line for this sample is likely to be the least accurate.

Consolidation tests follow three distinct phases. First there will usually be a loading line in which the variation of void ratio with stress is linear when plotted against the logarithm of the loading stress. Second, when the site was excavated, there will have been some rebound of the sample, and this loading will represent the reloading of the sample back to its previous maximum level. If the overburden has lain undisturbed since deposition, then this loading line should proceed to the load expected from the *in situ* overburden. At that point the rate of consolidation with increasing load will be greater, as the sample has never previously been loaded in this region. This steeper line represents the virgin (or normal) consolidation line.

Finally, at the end of the test the sample is unloaded, and this will show a third linear relationship in logarithmic space. The maximum load on the samples during the test was 1340kPa, which is likely to be well beyond the maximum stress encountered and would represent an overburden of around 100m.

Full details of the test on the samples are shown in Appendices A2.1–A2.3.

The point at which the two parts of the loading sequence intersect represents the previous maximum load that the samples have experienced, as shown in Fig 2.39.

In Fig 2.39, the previous maximum stress appears to be around 169kPa. If this stress level is consistent with the overburden pressure prevailing before excavation, then this would indicate that the sample had not experienced any additional loading other than the weight of sediment above. On the other hand, if this figure is greater than the *in situ* stress immediately prior to excavation, this would suggest one of three possible causes: (a) the area has been glaciated, and the weight of ice accounted for the extra stress; (b) additional sediment was deposited only to be eroded some time later; and (c) the water table was lowered sometime in the past either naturally or by human activity. Clearly, since the precise conditions prevailing before excavation are not known, only approximate inferences can be made in this respect.

The consolidation behaviour of the second subsample is shown in Fig 2.40. The maximum previous consolidation pressure is 155kPa, giving a mean value between the two tests of 162kPa. The third sample (Fig 2.41) shows a very similar virgin consolidation line, although the change between the two curves is a little higher at just over 200kPa. It should be noted that the experimental notes did suggest some sample disturbance during preparation for this sample, and thus this higher figure is unlikely to be representative.

The three subsamples all have virgin consolidation lines that are close to being linear in logarithmic space. The equation of this line is given by:

$$e = e_1 - C_c \log \sigma \qquad (1)$$

where: e is the void ratio; e_1 is the void ratio at unity stress (ie intercept on Y-axis in log plot); σ is the stress; and C_c is the gradient of the line, and is known as the compression index.

The parameters e_1 and C_c are required for analysis of previous compaction, and the results from the tests on the three subsamples from Sample 1 are shown in Table 2.13.

Assuming that the sample was normally consolidated before extraction – that is, that the previous maximum consolidation stress was compatible with the *in situ* stress before excavation – it is possible to make a first estimation of how much compaction has taken place. To do this it is necessary to assume that the layer was originally sampled at the surface, and that it was deposited at around the same time as any artefacts contained in the layer. It is also necessary to assume a layer thickness in the analysis. For the purpose of the analysis, a layer thickness of 100mm has been assumed, which is sufficiently small to resolve subtle differences, and yet sufficiently large to make computation manageable. For the purpose of

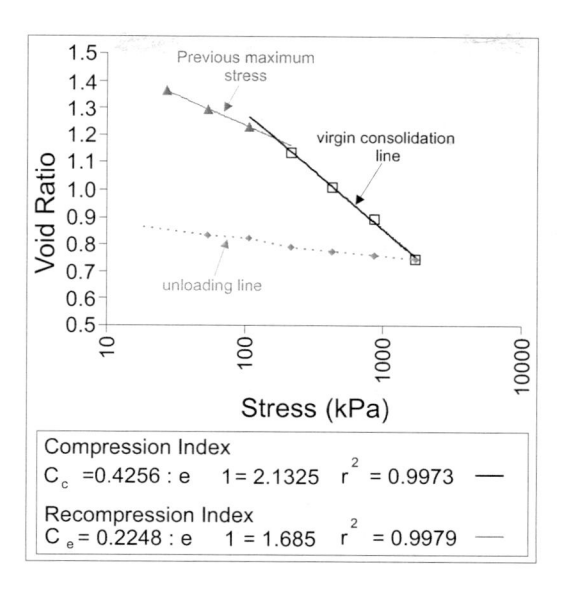

Fig 2.39
Consolidation curve for Sample 1a. Parameters of virgin consolidation line (equation 1) are: $e_1 = 2.1325$ and $C_c = 0.4256$.

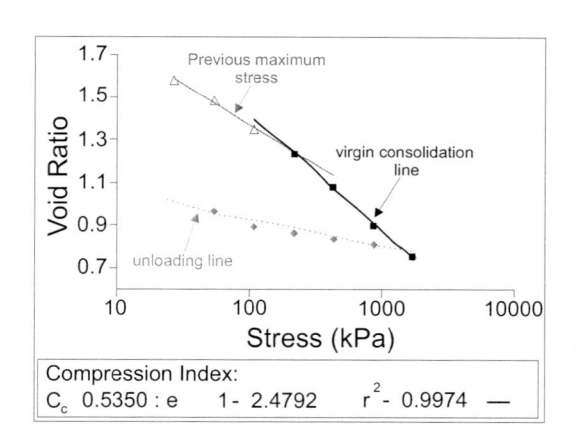

Fig 2.40
Consolidation curve for Sample 1b. Parameters of virgin consolidation line (equation 1) are: $e_1 = 2.4792$ and $C_c = 0.5350$.

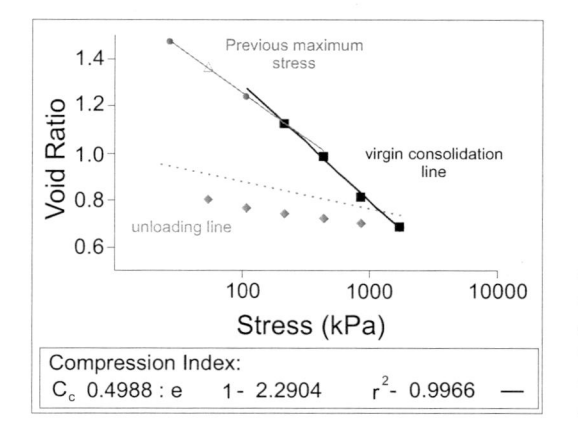

Fig 2.41
Consolidation curve for Sample 1c. Parameters of virgin consolidation line (equation 1) are: $e_1 = 2.2904$ and $C_c = 0.0.4988$.

Table 2.13 Summary information from consolidation tests on sub-samples 1a, 1b and 1c.
Mean values: $C_c = 0.4865$ and $e_1 = 2.2974$

sample	virgin consolidation			recompression			preconsolidation pressure
	C_c	e_1	r^2	C_e	e_e	r^2	
1a	0.4256	2.1325	0.9973	0.2248	1.6850	0.9979	169
1b	0.5350	2.4692	0.9974	0.3775	2.1241	0.9916	155
1c	0.4988	2.2904	0.9966	0.3858	2.0263	0.9967	217
averages	0.4865	2.2974		0.3293	1.9451		180

the preliminary analysis, a layer thickness of 100mm has been assumed at a stress level consistent with the kink in the consolidation curve. The analysis procedure needs iterative numeric modelling of successive layers to achieve an equilibrium stress level consistent with the kink point. Though the consolidation relationship is known from Equation 1 and the parameters given in Table 2.13, it is not possible to solve the full sequence, because the stress level is dependent on the bulk density, which is in turn dependent on the void ratio. To overcome this problem, an initial value of void ratio of unity was assumed throughout the depth, giving a profile that was then successively iterated until convergence was achieved. During each iteration a revised value for the bulk density in each layer was computed, and the procedure repeated many times until the difference between the bulk density assumed before and after an iteration was negligible. This procedure follows that outlined in Tovey and Paul (2002).

Once an equilibrium profile is evaluated, it is a simple matter to compare the void ratio agreeing with the kink point and the surface, and thus estimate the compaction of the layer.

The depth corresponding to the kink point is approximately 9.5m, which is slightly more than the physically surveyed depth, suggesting a small amount of compaction before the artefacts were deposited. This was investigated in the following analysis.

During the consolidation process, a given amount of solid material remains constant throughout time, while it is the voids that reduce the thickness of the layer during consolidation. If the amount of solid material in any layer is known, it is then possible to calculate the total thickness of the layer before consolidation. At the stress level corresponding to the kink point (ie an implied depth of 9.5m), the void ratio is 1.22, leading to a reduced thickness (ie the thickness of the solid material in the 100mm section) of 45mm. It is this equivalent thickness of 450mm that remains constant, and with the voids ratio in the topmost layer at 2.36 (Fig 2.42), leads to a total thickness of 151mm. This implies that over time, the 100mm-thick layer from which the samples were taken was originally 151mm thick and reduced by 51mm: a 33 per cent reduction in overall thickness.

As indicated above, the 9.5m of implied overburden at the present time is a little larger than expected. However, the minimum overburden at the site might be 6m. Therefore, a layer measuring 100mm at this 6m depth would originally have been 145mm. Consequently, any error in resolving the precise position of the stress at the kink point, with respect to present overburden, is not great. On the other hand, if the discrepancy in the kink

Fig 2.42
Consolidation data from Lynford compared with samples from elsewhere.

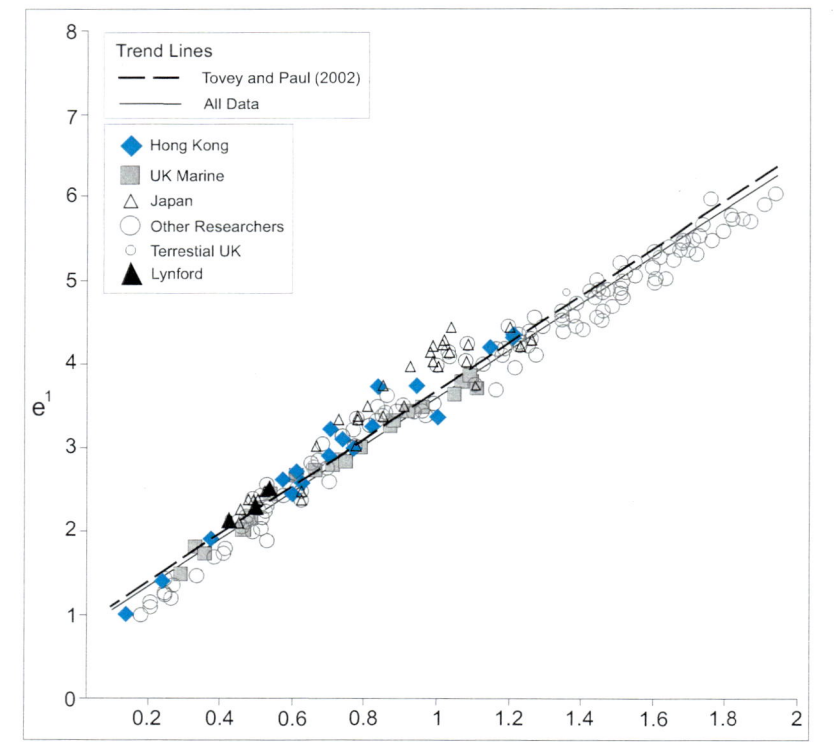

point values were attributed to pre-compaction of the surface layer prior to deposition of the artefacts, perhaps by ground water lowering of around 1m, the degree of subsequent compaction after the deposition of the artefacts would be less. It was not possible in this study to complete further work in this area, but the total amount of compaction since the artefacts were deposited would appear to be in the range of 31–33 per cent.

Comparisons with other samples

The modelling and decompaction routines used here are similar to those used for modelling Holocene marine sediments (Tovey and Paul 2002). This previous study showed an unexpected but strong empirical relationship (coefficient of correlation 0.97) linking the parameters of e1 and Cc:

$$e_1 = 2.874C_c + 0.8154 \qquad (2)$$

This relationship tends to reinforce the concept of an omega point first suggested by Schofield and Wroth (1968), indicating that the virgin consolidation relationship can be fully defined from a knowledge of C_c only. Subsequent to the work reported in Tovey and Paul (2002), those authors have extended their study with a much larger range of samples from across the world (*see* Fig 2.42). To date, few terrestrial deposits have been examined in a similar way, but the samples from Lynford appear to plot precisely on the line predicted from the other samples tested, and this would give some confidence that the parameters derived for the virgin consolidation line for the Lynford samples are indeed reasonable.

Conclusions

Although significant compaction has taken place in the deposits at Lynford, the stress levels are unlikely to have caused damage to the artefacts as the pressure is one-dimensional and particularly lateral. By contrast, it is largely differential forces that cause fracture of solid materials. What is more likely to happen during compaction is a flow of sediment around artefacts as the new pressure is accommodated, and such effects have been observed by the author in scanning electron micrographs of marine sediments. In the case of hollow objects such as bone, these stress levels are unlikely to cause fracture, as bone structure tends to be strong. However, it is possible that some distortion might take place and cause an initially circular cross-section to become slightly elliptical (long axis in the horizontal direction). However, that would depend on the physical properties, and in particular the modulus of elasticity of the objects themselves.

Prior to this work on samples from Lynford, there was little information relating to terrestrial samples, as almost all other data had come from marine sediments. Testing samples in consolidation is time-consuming, requiring specialist equipment, and it is difficult to ensure that the samples are completely undisturbed unless sophisticated sampling equipment is used. However, it is possible to obtain an estimate of Cc from simple tests such as liquid limit tests, and the advantage of these is that the samples can be disturbed. Tovey and Paul (2002) showed that there was a reasonable relationship relating Cc to the liquid limit, such that:

$$Cc = 0.02818.LL - 0.7513 \qquad (3)$$

where LL is the liquid limit expressed as a percentage.

However, the actual consolidation relationship as required in equation (1) still remains unknown unless e1 can be measured. As has been shown above (equation 2), there is indeed a relationship between e_1 and C_c, and this suggests that in future work it would be possible to assess the amount of compaction from an accurate profile of the site and relatively simple liquid limit tests.

2.3 Dating the deposits and the archaeology

2.3.1 Optically stimulated luminescence

J-L Schwenninger and E Rhodes

In total, seventeen samples were collected for luminescence dating. Fifteen samples were collected from selected deposits throughout the stratigraphic sequence by staff of the Luminescence Dating Laboratory, University of Oxford (J-L Schwenninger) and a further two were collected from sandy sediments exposed in the machine-excavated test pits. *In situ* radioactivity measurements were made with an EG&G Ortec MicroNomad NaI gamma-ray spectrometer for the fifteen samples collected by laboratory staff. No *in situ* measures were made for the two test-pit samples. All samples

Table 2.14 Lynford OSL sample details

field code	lab. code	excavation code	context	height (m OD)	comments on sedimentary units
LYN03-01	X1098	30126	20327	6.102	yellow sand lens in lower gravel
LYN03-02	X1099	30125	20003	8.362	dark brown organic sandy silt
LYN03-03	X1100	30124	20003	8.532	dark brown organic sandy silt
LYN03-04	X1101	30123	20002	8.655	greenish-grey sand
LYN03-05	X1102	30122	20005	8.752	greenish-grey sand
LYN03-06	X1103	30127	20015	8.723	light grey sand
LYN03-07	X1104	30128	20002/20003	9.107	orange sand
LYN03-08	X1160	30265	20357	7.750	greyish-brown silty sand overlying gravel
LYN03-09	X1161	302066	20390/20403	7.700	dark brown organic stony sand
LYN03-10	X1162	30267	20371	8.000	greenish-brown organic stony sand
LYN03-11	X1163	30264	20254	7.614	white silty sand below organic sand
LYN03-12	X1164	30263	20205	9.908	yellow sand between sandy gravel
LYN03-13	X1165	30262	20317	11.04	brownish-grey stony sand
LYN03-14	X1166	30268	20285	11.481	brownish-grey sand overlying upper gravel
LYN03-15	X1167	30269	20305	10.656	pale yellow sand between gravel
LYN03-16	X1837	30385	Test pit 15	~12.56	yellow sand
LYN03-17	X1838	30387	Test pit 17	~17.30	yellow sand

were collected in opaque PVC tubes hammered into vertical sections. Sample details are set out in Table 2.14.

The age estimates discussed in this section include the preliminary results reported for four samples (X1098, X1100, X1103 and X1104) in an interim Optically Stimulated Luminescence (OSL) report (Schwenninger and Rhodes 2005). Adjustments for the correct burial depth and true water content, which were not available at the time, subsequently resulted in minor changes to the preliminary dates reported in the pilot study.

Results

The OSL dating results including age estimates, palaeodose and environmental dose rate measurements are summarised in Table 2.15. Age estimates are based on luminescence measurements of sand-sized quartz grains (180–255µm) extracted from each sample. All samples were measured using a Single Aliquot Regenerative-Dose (SAR) post-infrared blue OSL protocol (Murray and Wintle 2000; Banerjee et al 2001). Gamma dose rates are based on *in situ* gamma-ray spectroscopy measurement. Beta dose rate values were calculated using concentrations of uranium, thorium and potassium as determined by neutron activation analysis. However, the presence of large flint clasts in the sediments, coupled with the lack of sufficiently deep sections across the excavation area, occasionally prevented making *in situ* measurements. In

Table 2.15 Lynford final OSL dates

field code	lab. code	palaeodose(Gy)	total dose rate (mGy/a)	in situ γ-ray spectrometry	code ± 1 sigma	age (ka BP)
LYN03-01	X1098	47.90 ±2.80	0.61 ±0.04	yes but poor geometry	OxL-1337	78.6 ±6.7
LYN03-02	X1099	56.55 ±2.51	0.87 ±0.06	yes	OxL-1490	64.8 ±5.5
LYN03-03	X1100	60.86 ±3.83	1.04 ±0.07	yes	OxL-1338	58.3 ±5.6
LYN03-04	X1101	66.84 ±2.93	1.20 ±0.06	no	OxL-1491	55.9 ±3.9
LYN03-05	X1102	67.64 ±2.65	1.27 ±0.05	yes	OxL-1492	53.4 ±3.3
LYN03-06	X1103	41.30 ±1.83	0.86 ±0.04	yes	OxL-1339	48.0 ±3.2
LYN03-07	X1104	72.50 ±3.10	1.19 ±0.06	yes	OxL-1340	60.7 ±4.3
LYN03-08	X1160	60.00 ±3.38	0.92 ±0.08	yes	OxL-1493	65.0 ±6.9
LYN03-09	X1161	47.88 ±2.20	0.69 ±0.05	no	OxL-1494	69.9 ±6.1
LYN03-10	X1162	45.86 ±1.61	0.77 ±0.05	yes	OxL-1495	59.5 ±4.9
LYN03-11	X1163	45.82 ±2.25	0.80 ±0.04	yes but poor geometry	OxL-1496	57.4 ±4.2
LYN03-12	X1164	15.23 ±0.98	0.44 ±0.02	yes	OxL-1497	34.7 ±2.9
LYN03-13	X1165	0.68 ±0.04	0.70 ±0.03	yes	OxL-1498	0.97 ±0.08
LYN03-14	X1166	0.90 ±0.09	0.83 ±0.04	yes	OxL-1499	1.08 ±0.12
LYN03-15	X1167	23.12 ±0.78	0.71 ±0.04	yes	OxL-1500	32.4 ±2.2
LYN03-16	X1837	115.93 ±9.20	0.65 ±0.09	no	OxL-1501	175.6 ±27.7
LYN03-17	X1838	131.35 ±14.20	0.78 ±0.09	no	OxL-1502	169.2 ±26.9

these instances, the gamma dose rate was calculated either from the concentrations of radioactive elements as determined by neutron activation analysis (X1168 and X1169), or from interpolated gamma dose rate values of neighbouring samples (X1101 and X1161). Corrections were made in the age calculations for the water content of the sediment samples using the correction factors of Aitken (1998). The contribution of cosmic radiation was calculated as a function of latitude, altitude, burial depth and average overburden density according to the formulae of Prescott and Hutton (1994). Further details regarding individual samples are available in the project archive.

All samples displayed well-defined luminescence signals, and other OSL characteristics were also found to be well-suited for SAR age determination. Moreover, saturation did not provide a limitation to the dating of the samples. A moderate degree of inter-aliquot variability was observed with standard deviations of 8–15 per cent, typical of Pleistocene fluvial samples. Most samples showed excellent recycling ratios, with mean sample recycling ratios of less than 1 per cent from unity. The size of the mean thermal transfer signal was generally below 2 per cent and only rarely as high as 5 per cent for individual aliquots.

Overall, the observed luminescence characteristics (low variability, good sensitivity, good recycling and low thermal transfer values) strongly suggest that the calculated age estimates are reliable. Occasionally, one or two aliquots gave higher palaeodose values, and these were rejected from the age analysis. They are interpreted as aliquots containing grains that suffer from incomplete bleaching. In all cases, this made very little difference to the calculated ages. The results appear to be broadly consistent with archaeological expectations, suggesting that the measured OSL signals were sufficiently stable: a large majority of mineral grains had been well bleached and had generally undergone complete zeroing at the time of deposition.

For the two test-pit samples, X1837 and X1838, no on-site radioactivity measurements are available, and the environmental dose rate is based entirely on the concentrations of radioactive elements as determined by neutron activation analysis. For this reason, these age estimates should be considered with some degree of caution. Both samples provided age estimates that are substantially older than those directly associated with deposits from the palaeochannel at the archaeological site. Although no gamma dose rate measurements are available, it is unlikely that any difference between the true dose rate and the one derived from neutron activation analysis could account for this substantial gap in age. Indeed, the samples were collected from thick, relatively homogenous deposits of sand and away from major sedimentary boundaries, a situation where relatively good agreement between *in situ* and laboratory-based dose rate measurements is expected.

Discussion

The OSL age estimates obtained from samples in various sections appear to be in good stratigraphic order. Sample LYN03-01 provided the oldest date for the base of the stratigraphic sequence and was collected from a thick bed of sand within the fluvial gravels of Association A underlying the palaeochannel. The dates for the organic sediments of Association B suggest that these accumulated between c 65ka and 57ka. Two series, each of four (LYN03-02 to LYN03-05 and LYN06 to LYN09) and three (LYN03-08 to LYN03-10) samples were collected at two sampling localities with an additional single sample (LYN03-11) collected elsewhere. No *in situ* gamma dose rate measurements could be made for samples LYN03-04 and LYN03-09, due to closely spaced sampling. In these two instances a linear interpolation of gamma dose rate was used between overlying and underlying measurement locations with augmented errors. Although this approach seems justified, some degree of over- or under-estimation is possible. This might explain the apparent age inversion noticed between sample LYN03-09, dated to 69.9ka, and the underlying sample LYN03-08, dated to 65.0ka. Both samples, however, have overlapping error ranges.

OSL dates from the beds of laminated sands (Unit B-ii:05) immediately overlying the organic sediments (Unit B-ii:03) provided dates from 53.4ka to 60.7ka (LYN03-04, LYN03-05, LYN03-07). The basal sand of the final infilling of Association B-iii, represented by the channel-type scour along the north edge of Association B-ii, was dated to 48.0ka (LYN03-04). No samples were taken from the sediments comprising Association C. Samples LYN03-12 and LYN03-15 obtained from contexts 20205 and 20305 provided age estimates for Association D of respectively 34.7ka and 32.3ka. Radiocarbon dates obtained from contexts 20415 and 29423 of the organic channel sediments exposed in the east-facing section on the western edge of the quarry have provided similar age estimates of c 36ka and 30ka and show this channel to be younger than the excavated channel containing archaeological materials on the other side of the pit, and part of Association D.

Two samples (LYN03-13 and LYN03-14) were taken from the Holocene sediments of Association E in order to complete the geochronological framework for the site and to assess the reliability of OSL dating. Sample LYN03-13 was collected from context 20317 in the south-facing section along the northern edge of the excavation area. Here it is possible to compare the OSL age estimate with the radiocarbon date obtained from plant debris in the lowest monolith of sample 30085. The OSL age estimate of 970±80 years is in good agreement with the calibrated 14C date of 1050±110; 1310±80 years BP. OSL sample LYN03-14 gave a very similar date of 1080±120 years.

2.3.2 Radiocarbon dating

W A Boismier and A J Stuart

A total of five samples were submitted for radiocarbon dating. Two samples of faunal material were submitted to the Oxford Radiocarbon Accelerator Unit for high precision AMS dating as part of the Megafaunal Extinctions in Europe and Northern Asia Project (A J Stuart and A M Lister, University College London) funded by the Natural Environment Research Council (NERC). These samples comprise a mammoth molar fragment (50137) and a mammoth mandible fragment attached to a molar (50000) recovered from the organic sediments (20003, 20021) of Association B-ii (Unit B-ii:03). Three samples of sediment were submitted to the Centre for Isotope Research at Gröningen University through English Heritage as part of the Aggregates Levy Sustainability Fund (ALSF) programme. The samples comprise organic sediment taken from the lower (20415) and upper (20423) fills of the channel exposed on the east-facing section on the western edge of the quarry. In addition, a subsample of plant debris from a pollen monolith (30085) was taken from the basal Holocene deposits (20317) of Association E on the south-facing section along the northern edge of the excavation area.

The samples were processed and measured according to methods outlined in Mook and Streurman (1983), Aitken (1990), and Hedges and van Klinken (1992). A programme of quality assurance procedures is maintained by the laboratories in addition to participation in international comparisons (Rozanski *et al* 1992; Gulliksen and Scott 1995).

Results

The 14C dating results are summarised in Table 2.16. They are presented as conventional radiocarbon ages (Stuiver and Polach 1977) and are quoted in accordance with the international standard known as the Trondheim Convention (Stuiver and Kra 1986).

Discussion

The 14C dating of the faunal remains was undertaken while the excavation was underway in order to obtain a preliminary assessment of the age of the faunal and archaeological assemblage at the site. However, it was anticipated that the true age might well lie beyond the limits of the method, in which case the dates would indicate a minimum age. The finite date provided by one sample (OxA-11571) was regarded as beyond the reliable limit of the radiocarbon method, and the date for the other sample (OxA-11572) was a minimum estimate of its true age. The two dates indicated that the true age of the faunal material was probably in excess of 50,000 years.

The plant debris from the pollen monolith subsample (GrN-28399 and GrN-28400) has provided dates for the basal unit of the Holocene deposits of Association E that agree with the sequence of OSL age estimates obtained for the deposits at the site (see OSL section). The

Table 2.16 Results of the AMS radiocarbon dating of faunal material

laboratory number	sample reference	radiocarbon age (BP)	$d^{13}C$ ($^0/_{00}$)	material
OxA-11571	50137	53,700 ±3,100	−21.2	*Mammuthus primigenius*: anterior fragment of molar DM_3 or M_1
OxA-11572	50000	>49,700	−21.1	*Mammuthus primigenius*: part of mandible attached to molar M_3

calibrated 14C date of 1310±80 years BP (AD 660–980) is in agreement with the OSL age estimate of 1080±120 years BP, and indicates a significant hiatus in the fluvial sequence between the Holocene deposits of Association E and the underlying braided river deposits of Association D, dated by OSL to c 34.7ka and 32.3ka. Dating of the organic sediments exposed in section on the western edge of the quarry has established that this channel is c 25–30ka younger than the organic deposits containing the archaeological material within the excavated channel on the eastern side of the quarry. It is also found to be in general agreement with the OSL age estimates obtained for the sequence of braided river deposits of Association D exposed on the west-facing section on the eastern edge of the quarry. These dates suggest that it probably forms part of this association. In addition, the dates (GrN-28395, GrN-29396, GRN-29397 and GRN-28398) also indicate that both the start and end of the succession of organic deposits for this channel are also in broad agreement with those obtained by OSL for the eastern half of the site.

2.3.3 Amino-acid racemisation

K Penkman and M Collins

A new technique of amino-acid analysis has been developed for geochronological purposes (Penkman et al 2007, 2008; Penkman 2005) combining a recent reverse-phase, high-pressure liquid chromatography (RP-HPLC) method of analysis (Kaufman and Manley 1998) with the isolation of an 'intra-crystalline' fraction of amino acids by bleach treatment (Sykes *et al* 1995). This combination of techniques results in the analysis of D/L values of multiple amino acids from the chemically protected protein within the biomineral, thereby enabling both decreased sample sizes and increased reliability of the analysis.

The acidity of the organic sands, which entirely removed the shell content at some levels (Keen this volume), limited the shell material available for amino-acid analysis. Two species of molluscs were selected for analysis, *Planorbis planorbis* and *Pupilla muscorum*, although unfortunately neither had been fully tested for this new technique of amino-acid dating. These shell samples were recovered from context number 20003 – the organic sediment grouped within Unit B-ii:03. The *P. planorbis* samples comprised two shells from 30198 (400–500mm) (NEaar 466–8) and three from 30228 (10) (NEaar 469–71). The sample of *P. muscorum* comprised three shells from 30331 (10) (NEaar 472–4).

All samples were prepared using the procedures of Penkman *et al* (2008). Shell samples were cleaned, sonicated and rinsed in High Performance Liquid Chromatography (HPLC) grade water (that is, water with low organic carbon content). The shells were then crushed to < 100µm, and split into two portions, one of which was bleached to isolate the intra-crystalline fraction of protein. Two subsamples were then taken from each of the 'unbleached' and 'bleached' fractions: one subsample was directly demineralised and the free amino acids (FAA) analysed; and the second was treated to release the peptide-bound amino acids (7M HCl, heated 110°C for six hours), thus yielding the 'total' amino-acid concentration, referred to as the 'Total Hydrolysable Amino Acid' fraction (THAA). Samples were analysed in duplicate by RP-HPLC. During preparative hydrolysis, both asparagine and glutamine undergo rapid irreversible deamination to aspartic acid and glutamic acid respectively (Hill 1965). It is therefore not possible to distinguish between the acidic amino acids and their derivatives and they are reported together as Asx and Glx respectively.

Results

In total, 75 analyses were conducted, most of which (70 per cent, 60 runs) were on unbleached samples: anticipated bleaching reduces the yields of amino acids and also increases reproducibility. The key findings were as follows:

1 Amino-acid yields were reduced following bleaching, as expected. However the extent of reduction was greater for *Planorbis* than for *Pupilla* (Fig 2.43).

2 Reproducibility was greater for bleached than for unbleached shells.

3 Amino-acid concentrations in the bleached fraction from *Pupilla* were higher than in *Planorbis*.

4 Most shells failed to provide a series of D/L ratios that are consistent with the normal protein degradation (eg Preece and Penkman 2005), even with a generous 20 per cent allowance for the standard

deviation – that is, all those with a standard deviation of predicted versus observed values of less than 20 per cent were considered acceptable.

From these values the level of protein degradation observed in the same shell for the THAA and FAA fractions gives very different age estimates for the different amino acids. The differences might be the result of different patterns of racemisation in these species, or alternatively might be due to the dissolution of the shells.

Discussion

The lack of consistency in the results can be explained by an examination of the free and total amino-acid fractions isolated from the same shell. Most shells failed to provide a series of D/L values that are consistent with expected protein degradation. In some cases the FAA gave much older values than the THAA from the same shell, while in others, the relative extent of racemisation between the amino acids was inconsistent. By bleaching to isolate the intra-crystalline protein, it has been shown that the fraction of protein retained within gastropod shells behaves as a 'closed system', with consistent patterns of breakdown independent of the environment (Penkman *et al* 2008). This is not the case with the samples from Lynford; one possible reason for this divergence from normal behaviour is the extent of corrosion observed on the shells caused by the low pH of the sediments at the site (Keen, chapter 3). Low pH has two opposing effects on an amino-acid age estimate. Firstly, dissolution destroys the closed system, increasing the rate of leaching of the most highly racemised and mobile free amino acids, which depresses the extent of racemisation in the total fraction. This results in underestimation of the age. Secondly, the low pH conditions, which can now infiltrate the intra-crystalline fraction, accelerate protein decomposition, increasing the extent of racemisation and leading to an over-estimation of age. The very low D/L values of the THAA in some shells also suggest that some of this corrosion has occurred in the recent past. We therefore conclude that it is not possible to provide reliable age estimates for the Lynford site based on amino-acid ratios.

2.3.4 Discussion

W A Boismier and F M L Green

Dating MIS3 sites presents particular problems, and the results from Lynford are no exception. The AMS dates for faunal material from the channel proved to be beyond the reliable limit of the radiocarbon method (see Schreve and Stuart, chapter 5, for discussion of the biostratigraphy), while the results of the amino-acid racemisation analysis are unreliable due to the diagenetic corrosion of shell from the organic sediments of Unit B-ii:03. As a result, OSL age estimates provide the basis for the dating of the channel sediments containing the archaeological and palaeobiological materials. These, together with the 14C dates obtained from the Holocene deposits overlying the channel, and the channel sediments exposed on the western side of the quarry, provide the framework for the chronology of the deposits at the site.

The OSL and 14C dates have established an absolute chronology for the site in terms of the timing of fluvial deposition and, in particular, the changes in depositional style indicated by the facies associations established for the stratigraphic sequence. The calibrated 14C and the OSL dates are in good agreement with each other and have identified a significant hiatus in the fluvial sequence at the site between the

Fig 2.43 Comparison of amino acid concentration from Planorbis *(diamonds) and* Pupilla *(circles) from unbleached and bleached samples. Note the decrease in concentration following bleaching due to isolation of the intra-crystalline fraction.*

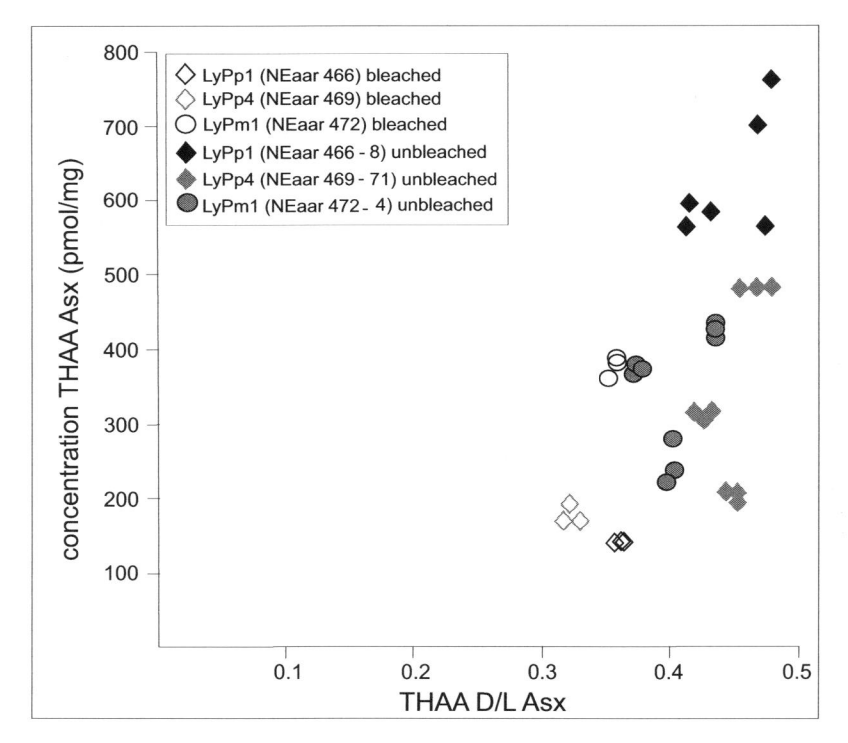

Holocene deposits and the underlying Devensian deposits at the site. The succession of deposits and their age is discussed in detail by Lewis in this chapter.

Insect and pollen data bear a close similarity to that from Upton Warren and strongly indicate that Lynford is more or less contemporary with this non-archaeological site (Coope and Green, chapter 3). The OSL dates for Association B-ii range from 53.4±3.3ka to 64.8±5.5ka and typically fall around 59ka with substantial overlap in errors. The age of Association B-iii is estimated to be around 48.0±3.2ka, but by a single date. These dates clearly indicate that the published radiocarbon dates obtained from Upton Warren – around 40ka – must now be viewed as minimum values only, and should no longer be used as acceptable ages for this site. The OSL dates obtained for Lynford suggest that the Upton Warren Interstadial might fall within the beginning of MIS 3 and be possibly correlated with one or both of the two early D/O warm events (16, 17) for MIS 3 identified by ice core studies (Fig 2.44; van Andel 2003; van Andel and Tzedakis 1996). It is possible on the basis of the OSL dates to suggest correlations with two early Stage 3 interstadials noted in the European terrestrial record. At La Grande Pile these interstadials were recognised as Coulotte and Pile (Woillard and Mook 1982), and in Germany the same interstadials were identified as Oerel and Glinde (Behre and van der Plicht 1992). Oerel is the earlier of the two and is dated 58–54ka, with Glinde dated at 51–48ka. During the Oerel Interstadial the vegetation in northern Germany was open, treeless shrub tundra with abundant dwarf birch. The lack of trees has suggested temperatures significantly lower than the present day (–8°C), which would have resulted in continuous permafrost (Walkling 1997). The absence of any evidence of permafrost in these deposits (Caspers and Freund 2001) indicates temperatures greater than this and, as such, could be correlated with the Lynford deposits.

Recent research has indicated a complete occupational hiatus in hominin settlement in the British Isles for around 90,000 years from latter MIS 6 to the end of MIS 4, followed by a small-scale re-colonisation sometime around the beginning of MIS 3 (Wymer 1988; Ashton and Lewis 2002; Currant and Jacobi 2002, 2001; White and Jacobi 2002). The OSL age-estimates for the palaeochannel (Association B-ii) indicate that the faunal and artefactual material dates to around the end of MIS 4 and the early part of MIS 3 and provide the earliest securely dated occurrence of Late Middle Palaeolithic archaeological materials in Britain after MIS 6. Early dates for the Late Middle Palaeolithic have also been obtained from three sites by the recent AMS dating of bone, using ultrafiltration and AMS technical developments (Jacobi *et al* 2006).

Radiocarbon determinations from Pin Hole and Robin Hood Cave, Derbyshire, and from the Hyaena Den, Somerset, indicate an age range for the Late Middle Palaeolithic at these sites of between 40ka and 54ka (Jacobi *et al* 2006, tables 1 to 3) with an apparent overlap of the older uncalibrated 14C dates with the younger OSL age estimates for Lynford. The remaining OSL dates for Association B at Lynford appear to be older by some 5,000 years, but this might be an artefact of current calibration methods for dates greater than

Fig 2.44
The GISP2 ice-core δ 18O record from the last interglacial (MIS 5d) with selected Dansgaard-Oeschger warm events labelled (modified from Huntley and Allen 2003, fig 6.1).

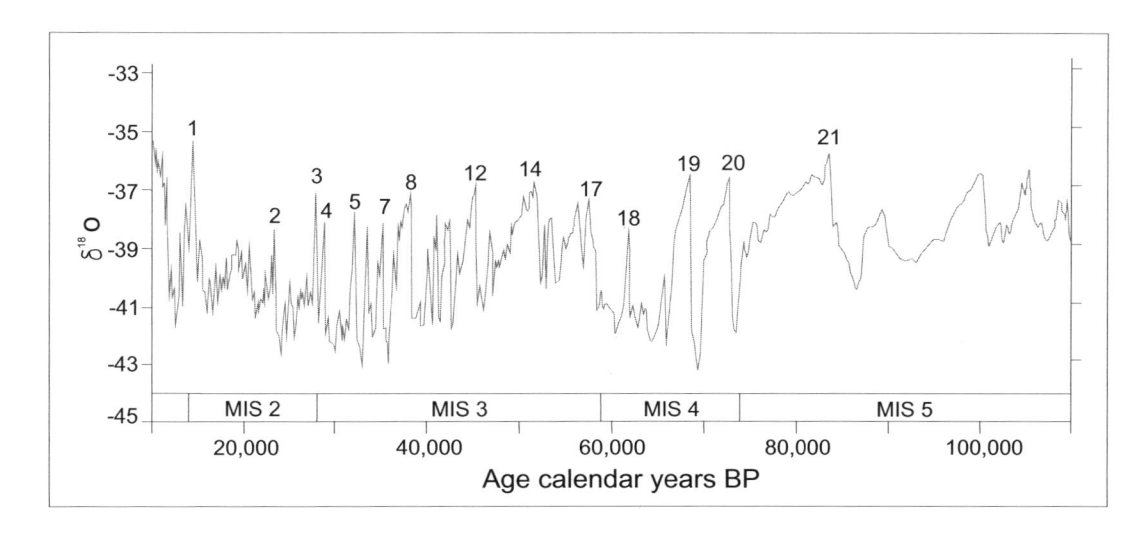

26ka (Jacobi *et al* 2006; Reimer *et al* 2004). The OSL dates for Lynford indicate that the Neanderthal recolonisation of Britain occurred sometime around the end of MIS 4 and the beginning of MIS 3. These age estimates, when taken with those obtained for Pin Hole, Robin Hood Cave and the Hyena Den, suggest the possibility that the Late Middle Palaeolithic settlement of Britain might have been more extensive and prolonged than previously anticipated (Jacobi *et al* 2006; White and Jacobi 2002).

3

Environmental evidence

The Lynford deposits were rich in a range of environmental evidence. Preservation was excellent for insects and pollen, and good for mollusca and plant macrofossils. In addition, the large mammal remains, dominated by the remains of woolly mammoths, were also both abundant and well preserved. Such multi-proxy environmental evidence is rare. When available it allows cross-checking of interpretations such as summer and winter temperatures, as well as reconstruction of the immediate environment and the regional habitat. In addition, the environmental evidence provides further information on the history of the channel and its contents, a topic more fully investigated in chapter 4 where the taphonomy of the site is explored.

Here the primary evidence for the environment comes from the large assemblage of insect remains. The lack of many more extreme cold-adapted species is significant, and although temperature estimates are limited by gaps in our knowledge about the tolerances of well-represented species, when combined with the pollen indicators, a consistent picture does emerge. Lynford enjoyed summer temperatures of between 12°C and 14°C, while in winter these dropped to at least –8°C or even –15°C. Comparable temperatures for today's interglacial climate in eastern England are 13–22°C for July and 2–6°C for January. These temperatures, along with increased snow cover and frosts, resulted in a vegetation very different to that of today. Although the temperatures should have permitted trees to colonise the landscape, all the evidence indicates that they did not. The climate and environment were not precisely those of a full glacial or a temperate interglacial. The closest parallel in Britain is the site of Upton Warren in Worcestershire, identified fifty years ago (Coope, Shotton and Strachan 1961), though it is a locale with no archaeology. Were these the conditions that Neanderthals preferred, or were they living at the extreme of what they could tolerate?

But the Lynford evidence also presents an ecological conundrum of a more down-to-earth nature. With the remains of so many mammoths present in the channel, why are there so few of the beetle species that feed on dried-out carcasses? Dung beetles are common, but their carnivorous counterparts are largely absent. The integration of this wide variety of evidence and of scales ranging from the channel to the region, and from a tiny beetle or pollen grain to a woolly mammoth make the Lynford archive of environmental evidence extremely valuable.

3.1 The insect remains from the mammoth channel at Lynford, Norfolk

G Russell Coope[†]

Introduction

Insect remains are abundant in terrestrial and freshwater sediments that have remained waterlogged since their deposition and thus in reducing conditions. Insect fossils rarely survive in oxidised sediment. At Lynford, the organic silts filling the main channel from which most of the bones and implements were recovered (Sedimentary Facies Association B), fulfil these criteria for the preservation of insect fossils, and these sediments yielded an abundant and diverse fauna, most of which were of Coleoptera (beetles). Many can be recognised as species that are still living today, though some are now found thousands of kilometres away from present-day Norfolk. Since each species has precise habitat preferences, it is possible to build up a detailed mosaic picture of the local environmental conditions in the area when it was occupied by the Neanderthal group that exploited the mammoths and other large mammals.

Sampling procedure

Numerous bulk samples were taken from the exposures in Facies Association B (the channel deposits) at various stages of the excavation. Altogether, 52 samples were analysed for insect remains, though not all of them yielded fossils. Thus, in Table 3.1 only 34 samples are listed; the others, yielding insignificant numbers of insect remains, have been omitted. In this table only beetle species are listed, following the nomenclature and the taxonomic order of Lucht (1987). The numbers in each sample column indicate the minimum number of individuals of each beetle taxon in that sample. Samples are arranged in the order of their field sample numbers with the lowest samples on the left-hand side. Where the exposures of sediments were sufficiently thick, a vertical series of subsamples were collected in order to detect any possible faunal changes during the period of deposition. Series of samples are separated by double vertical lines.

Two groups of samples were subjected to rather different laboratory procedures. The first group was processed specifically for the recovery of insect remains, indicated in Table 3.1 by 'i' at the top of each sample column. The second group was processed primarily for mollusc remains, and the insect fossils picked out from the residues after the molluscs had been removed. These are indicated by 'm' at the top of each sample column.

The laboratory procedures for the recovery of insect fossils from unconsolidated sediment has been well documented (eg Coope 1986) and are only briefly summarised here. As far as possible, the sediment sample should be kept in 'field damp' condition, and in a cool store, before processing. In the laboratory, the sample was initially disaggregated under water in a large polythene bowl either by means of a gentle stream of water from a hose or by being gently broken up by hand. The resultant slurry was then washed over a sieve with a mesh aperture of 0.3mm. The residue held in the sieve was then thoroughly mixed with paraffin (kerosene) and returned to a polythene bowl fitted with a pouring spout. Enough water was introduced to ensure a clear separation between the floating and sinking fractions. The floating fraction was then decanted into a sieve and washed in a detergent solution to remove the oil and then with alcohol to remove the detergent. The float can then be stored in 30 per cent alcohol until it is convenient to sort it in the laboratory. This is undertaken using a binocular microscope. The selected insect remains are stored in tubes of no more than 30 per cent alcohol, as a higher concentration can lead to bleaching of the insect cuticle, rendering it unidentifiable.

The laboratory procedure for the recovery of mollusc shells is described in section 3.2 below. In brief, it involves drying of the sample in a furnace at 40°C, which facilitates the disaggregation of the sediment without destroying the fossils. The dried sediment is then wet-sieved over a mesh aperture of 0.5mm – a coarse mesh size that lets through many of the smaller specimens. The repeated drying and wetting leads to further fragmentation of the insect fossils and results in a distortion of the insect fossil record by loss of the small, frail and inconspicuous species. This can be seen in Table 3.1 where the faunas from the series of samples 30004 and 30232, which were processed specifically for insect remains, yielded relatively large numbers of the minute, cryptic beetle *Ochthebius*, compared with those from the series of samples 30198, 30226 and 30234, which had been processed for mollusc analysis but yielded none. In spite of these drawbacks, the fossils recovered from the samples rigorously treated for mollusc extraction provided valuable corroborative environmental evidence derived from both molluscs and insects obtained from exactly the same samples.

The insect fauna

By far the majority of identifiable insect fossils from these deposits are of Coleoptera (beetles), because their robust exoskeletons are the most readily preserved as fossils. In this account only the beetle fauna will be considered in detail. Other orders of insect were also found, but have not been extensively investigated here. These include Hemiptera-heteroptera, Saldidae, *Salda litoralis* (L); Hemiptera-homoptera, Jassidae, *Aphrodes bifasciatus* (L); Megaloptera, Sialidae, *Sialis* sp. (represented by large numbers of larval mandibles); Trichoptera (larval sclerites), Hydropsychidae, *Hydropsyche* sp., Phryganidae, *Phrygania* sp., Linnephilidae, *Anabolia nervosa* (Curtis); Hymenoptera, (many undetermined adult heads and body parts), Formicidae (a few heads); and Diptera, Tipulidae (larval head capsules), Chironomidae (larval heads), Bibionidae, *Dilophus* sp. Apart from insects, there were also abundant Arachnida in the form of mites and the rare cephalothoraxes of spiders.

The coleopteran assemblage

Table 3.1 lists the beetle species and their occurrences in those samples from which a significant number of fossils were obtained. Altogether 224 beetle taxa have been recognised from the Lynford deposits, of which 178 could be determined to the species level; 34 species are no longer living in the British Isles: these are indicated by *. Ten of these species are no longer found in Europe either, and are indicated by **. The numbers opposite each species, and in each sample column, indicate the minimum numbers of individuals of that species in the sample and are estimated on the basis of the maximum number of any identifiable skeletal element present in each sample. In Table 3.1 the samples are arranged in numerical order according to the Environmental Sample Register for the site. Vertical lines have been used to separate the various sampling sites. The lowest samples are on the left of each series.

Taphonomy of the insect assemblage

Many of the skeletal elements of the larger species were fragmentary, and this would seem to be a property of the original samples – that is, not the result of laboratory processing. No matter how gentle the treatment, these fossils were almost always found disarticulated, and frequently broken. However, the preservation of the fragments themselves was remarkably fine, suggesting that the fragmentation might have occurred while the fossils were actually embedded within the sediment, perhaps caused by bioturbation by large vertebrates. Although the species composition of the faunas from all the samples is essentially the same, there are considerable differences in the productivity of the samples. The uppermost samples were less rich in insect remains than the ones towards the base of the sequence. Also, the specimens from the top of the sequence were more rotted, appearing frail and pale-brown in colour, which might have been due to the channel deposits being exposed to a period of weathering prior to the emplacement of the overlying gravel beds. Had the rotting effect been due to leaching by percolation of ground water, it would have been expected to attack the fossils in the layers both at the top and at the bottom of the sequences where the organic sediment of Association B-ii (Unit B-ii:03) was in contact with the permeable sands and gravels.

No fossil insects were found in the upper sediments of association B-ii (B-ii:05); that is, from layered organic horizons directly overlying the main channel sequence. The organic matter in these layers would appear to represent re-deposited plant debris eroded from the underlying deposit of organic sediment (B-ii:03).

The local environment interpreted from the coleopteran assemblage

Since there is no significant difference in the species composition of the insect faunas obtained from any of the samples, the insect assemblage will be referred to here as a single unit. The variety of insect species in this assemblage includes a wide spectrum of different ecological types. Some of them must have actually lived in the immediate vicinity, while others were probably brought together from farther afield more or less adventitiously either by floodwater or in wind drift. The local habitats will be grouped into four main categories: (a) aquatic habitats, (b) transitional (marshy) habitats, (c) dry ground habitats and (d) the dung and carcass community. These groupings are to some extent artificial and grade into one another so that some species could easily have been included in more than one category.

Aquatic habitats

Exclusively aquatic species in this assemblage include members of the following families; Haliplidae, Dytiscidae, Gyrinidae, Hydraenidae and Hydrophilidae as well as some Chrysomelidae and Curculionidae. These aquatic species include active predators as well as phytophages, feeding on various water plants.

Very few species in this assemblage indicate running water, and they occur only as isolated individuals. *Oreodytes rivalis* is found in streams and rivers where the bottom is sandy and firm. It is also found on exposed lake shores (Nilsson and Holmen 1995). Similarly *Potamonectes depressus* is often found in lakes or larger bodies of running water and sometimes in smaller streams. Both these species live in habitats with little or no vegetation. The haliplid *Brychius elevatus* usually lives in streams and rivers with gravelly bottoms, where it feeds on filamentous

Table 3.1 The Coleoptera from Sedimentary Facies Association B (the mammoth channel) at Lynford, arranged where possible according to the nomenclature and in the taxonomic order of Lucht (1987). The sample numbers are those adopted at the time of the excavation. The lowest samples are on the left hand side of the table. The numbers in each column indicate the minimum numbers of individuals of each species in the sample. Non-British species are indicated by *. Non-European species are indicated by **. The letters at the top of each column indicate which samples were specifically processed for insect remains (indicated by 'i') and which were initially processed for molluscs (indicated by 'm').

facies	B-ii:01	B-ii:03													
context	20004	20003													
sample number	30000	30002	30004				30198						30201			30202
top of profile (metres OD)	7.778	8.39	8.287				8.764						8.963			8.938
subsample / sample interval			45–60	30–45	15–30	0–15	70–80	60–70	50–60	40–50	30–40	20–30	60–70	50–60	40–50	60–70
	m	m	i	i	i	i	m	m	m	m	m	m	m	m	m	i
Carabidae																
Carabus problematicus Hbst.	1		1	1												1
Carabus granulatus L.			1													
**Carabus maeander Fisch.	1		1	1												
*Carabus cancellatus Illiger				1												
Carabus arvensis Hbst.	1	1	1	2	1					1						1
Carabus monilis F.	1			1												
*Carabus hortensis L.				1												
**Carabus sp.	1		4	1	1											1
Carabus sp.			1	1	1		1	2	1							
Leistus rufescens (F.)													1			
Pelophila borealis (Payk.)			2													1
Notiophilus pusillus Wtrh.			3	4	2											
Notiophilus aquaticus (L.)	1	3	9	6	5		2	4	3	2			1	2	2	4
Blethisa multipunctata (L.)	1		3	3					1					1		1
*Diacheila polita (Fald.)		1	1	3	1		2		1							1
Elaphrus cupreus Duft.		2	5	1			2	2	1	1				2		1
Elaphrus riparius (L.)		1	1	2			1									1
Loricera pilicornis (F.)		2	5	9	2			2	2	1			1			2
Dyschirius tristis Steph. = luedersi Wag.		1	9	1		1										
Dyschirius globosus (Hbst.)		1	10	10	5	1	2	2	2	2	3	2	3	4	5	2
Dyschirius obscurus (Gyll.)		1		1												
Bembidion properans (Steph.)																
Bembidion bipunctatum (L.)	1	1	4	6	3		1	1	3	3	1		1	1		1
Bembidion obliquum Sturm.	1	2	1	2			2	1	1							1
Bembidion gilvipes Sturm.																
*Bembidion transparens (Gebl.)		1	2	2			1			2	1		2			1
Bembidion aeneum Germ.		1	2	2	1		1									
Bembidion guttula (F.)				1												
Patrobus septentrionis Dej.	2	2	2	4	1			1	2	1						2
Patrobus assimilis Chaud.																
Harpalus aeneus (F.)																
Poecilus lepidus (Leske)			2	4	1		1	1								1
Poecilus versicolor (Sturm.)			2								1					
Pterostichus diligens (Sturm.)			1	1												
Pterostichus nigrita (Payk.)			1	1									1			1
*Pterostichus kokeili Mill. (? = tundrae Tsch.)	4	10	15	7	4	1	7	11	9	5	3	2	2	2	1	5
Pterostichus aethiops (Panz.)		1														
Pterostichus adstrictus Esch.																
Calathus melanocephalus (L.)			2	2					2				1			1
Agonum sexpunctatum (L.)			1													1
Agonum ericeti (Panz.)																
*Agonum sahlbergi (Chaud.)			1	3												
Agonum cf viduum (Panz.)		2	2	2	1			1	1	5			1	1		1
*Agonum consimile (Gyll.)			1	1												

continued ▶

Table 3.1 – continued

facies	B-ii:01	B-ii:03												
context	20004	20003												
sample number	30000	30002	30004				30198						30201		30202
top of profile (metres OD)	7.778	8.39	8.287				8.764						8.963		8.938
subsample / sample interval			45–60	30–45	15–30	0–15	70–80	60–70	50–60	40–50	30–40	20–30	60–70	50–60	40–50	60–70
	m	m	i	i	i	i	m	m	m	m	m	m	m	m	m	i
Agonum scitulum Dej.			1													
Agonum gracile (Gyll.)			2	4	1			1					1			
Agonum fuliginosum (Panz.)							1		1							
Amara quenseli (Schonh.)		1	1	2												
*Amara municipalis (Duft.)			3				1									1
*Amara torrida (Panz.)	2	7	8	6	1		4	3	7	2	1			1		2
Amara sp.			1	2	1		1									
Chlaenius nigricornis (F.)				1												
*Chlaenius costulatus Motsch.				1									1			
*Cymindis angularis Gyll.				1												

Haliplidae
Brychius elevatus (Panz.)																
Haliplus sp.			1	1												1

Dytiscidae
Coelambus impressopunctatus (Schall.)			1													
Hygrotus inaequalis (Schall.)			1													
Hygrotus quinquilineatus (Zett.)																
Hydroporus spp.	1		23	18	2		1	1	1				1			9
Potamonectes griseostriatus (Geer)																
Potamonectes depressus (F.)																
Potamonectes assimilis (Payk.)																
Oreodytes rivalis (Gyll.)				1												
Agabus bipustulatus (L.)				2												
Agabus arcticus (Payk.)																
Agabus sturmi (Gyll.)	1		2													
Agabus cf unguicularis Thoms.																
Agabus congener (Thunb.) group		1	3	4	1	2	1		1							
Ilybius subaeneus Er.	1	2	6	8	2	1	1	1	3	1						2
Rhantus sp.			1	1		1										1
Colymbetes fuscus (L.)			1	2	1											1
*Colymbetes paykulli Er.	1		1		1		1									
Graphoderus sp.																1
Dytiscus marginalis L.				1												
Dytiscus lapponicus Gyll.			1					2	1							1

Gyrinidae
Gyrinus minutus F.			1	1	1											1
Gyrinus aeratus Steph.			1		1		1									1
Gyrinus sp.																

Hydraenidae
Ochthebius lenensis Popp.			14	7	1											4
Ochthebius sp.																
Helophorus grandis Illiger		1	12	25	6	1	1		1	1			1			5
Helophorus 'aquaticus' (L.) = aequalis Thomps	1	1	4	5	5	2	1						1			9
*Helophorus glacialis Villa																
**Helophorus aspericollis Angus			3	5	2											1
Helophorus misc. small spp.	2	1	126	47	33	3	1									47

continued ▶

Table 3.1 – continued

facies	B-ii:01	B-ii:03											
context	20004	20003											
sample number	30000	30002	30004				30198					30201		30202
top of profile (metres OD)	7.778	8.39	8.287				8.764					8.963		8.938
subsample / sample interval			45–60	30–45	15–30	0–15	70–80	60–70	50–60	40–50	30–40	20–30	60–70	50–60	40–50	60–70
	m	m	i	i	i	i	m	m	m	m	m	m	m	m	m	i
Hydrophilidae																
Sphaeridium scarabaeoides (L.)						1										
Cercyon haemorrhoidalis (F.)					2	1										
Cercyon melanocephalus (L.)			3	2		1	1	1			1		1			1
Cercyon marinus Thoms.	1		16	7	2	2	2	1			2					1
Cercyon unipunctatus (L.)			1													
Cercyon pygmaeus (Illiger)		1	1	1												
Cercyon tristis (Illiger)	2	1	8	5	1				2	1	1		1			3
Cercyon convexiusculus Steph.	1		2	2		1	2			2	1			1		
Cercyon sternalis Shp.			6	4	1	1										2
Cercyon analis (Payk.)		1	1					1	1	1			1	1		2
Cryptopleurum minutum (F.)			1	1										1		
Hydrobius fuscipes (L.)	3	3	16	13	4	1	2	5	4	1	1		1	1		3
Laccobius sp.			1													
Enochrus melanocephalus (Ol.)		1	1	1	1											
Silphidae																
Necrophorus sp.																
Thanatophilus dispar (Hbst.)	2	6	14	20	15	4	2	10	8	2	3	1	1			4
Blitophaga opaca (L.)			1	1					1							
Silpha tyrolensis Laich			1				1									
Catopidae																
Choleva sp.			1													
Liodidae																
Liodes sp.			4													1
Agathidium marginatum Sturm.		1	1				1									
Staphylinidae																
Eusphalerum sp.																
*Pycnoglypta lurida (Gyll.)			4	1	2											4
Omalium sp.																
Deliphrum tectum (Payk.)																
Olophrum fuscum (Grav.)		1	3	7	1		1	2								2
Olophrum assimile (Payk.)						1										
Eucnecosum brachypterum (Grav.)		1	14	14	4	1	1			1						8
Acidota crenata (F.)		1	2	2	1				1	1						2
*Acidota quadrata Zett.																1
Geodromicus nigrita (Müll.)			7	5	1	1		2		2			1			3
*Boreaphilus henningianus Sahlb.			1													
Aploderus caelatus (Grav.)			4	1												1
Trogophloeus sp.			5	4	1											5
Oxytelus rugosus (F.)		1	5	3	1		1	1								3
Oxytelus laqueatus (Marsh.)			2	2				1	1	1			1			2
**Oxytelus gibbulus Epp.			5	3	1											2
Oxytelus nitidulus Grav.			3	2	1											
Platystethus arenarius (Fourcr.)			2													
Platystethus cornutus (Grav.)			12	6	1				2							4
Platystethus nodifrons Mannh.		1	34	20	6											22
Platystethus nitens (Sahlb.)																1

continued ▶

3 ENVIRONMENTAL EVIDENCE

Table 3.1 – *continued*

facies		B-ii:01		B-ii:03													
context		20004		20003													
sample number		30000	30002	30004				30198						30201			30202
top of profile (metres OD)		7.778	8.39	8.287				8.764						8.963			8.938
subsample sample interval				45–60	30–45	15–30	0–15	70–80	60–70	50–60	40–50	30–40	20–30	60–70	50–60	40–50	60–70
		m	m	i	i	i	i	m	m	m	m	m	m	m	m	m	i
Bledius sp.				2	2	1											1
Stenus juno (Payk.)																	1
Stenus spp.			2	16	14	7		1			2						7
Euaesthetus laeviusculus Mannh.						1											
Lathrobium cf *terminatum* Grav.																	
Xantholinus sp.		1	1	6	2	1		1	2	1	3						1
**Philonthus linki Solski			2					2	1	1	1						2
Philonthus spp.		1		3	2	1		1	2	2	1	1		1			2
Staphylinus erythropterus L.																	
Ocypus aeneocephalus (Geer)/ *cupreus* (Rossi)		1	3	6	4	2		1	2		3	1					
Quedius spp.		1		3	2	1		1	1					1			
Boletobiinae Gen. et sp. indet.																	
Tachyporus chrysomelinus (L.)				2	2												1
Tachyporus sp.						1											
***Tachinus glacialis* Ullrich and Campbell						1											
***Tachinus jacuticus* Popp.		3	1	8	7	3	1	1	1		3	3		1	1		5
Tachinus fimetarius Grav.																	
Tachinus corticinus Grav.				1													3
Gymnusa variegata Kiesw.				1													
Alaeocharinae Gen. et sp. indet.				103	50	12	2	1									30
Elateridae																	
Ctenicera cuprea (F.)				2	1	1					1						2
Hypnoidus riparius (F.)				3	2	1											
*Hypnoidus rivularis (Gyll.)																	3
Helodidae																	
Gen. et sp. indet.				1													
Dryopidae																	
Dryops sp.		2	2	3	2	1	1				1				1		
Heteroceridae																	
Heterocerus cf *hispidulus* Kiesw.																	
Heterocerus sp.				1													1
Byrrhidae																	
Simplocaria semistriata (F.)				1	1	1											1
Cytilus sericeus (Forst.)				1													
Byrrhus fasciatus (Forst.)		1	2	7	10	7	2			3	1				1		2
Byrrhus pilula (L.)																	
Byrrhus pustulatus (Forst.)							1	1			1		1				
Curimopsis sp.																	
Nitidulidae																	
Cateretes rufilabris (Latr.)				1													
Cryptophagidae																	
Atomaria sp.				1													

continued ▶

Table 3.1 – *continued*

facies	B-ii:01	B-ii:03												
context	20004	20003												
sample number	30000	30002	30004				30198						30201			30202
top of profile (metres OD)	7.778	8.39	8.287				8.764						8.963			8.938
subsample / sample interval			45–60	30–45	15–30	0–15	70–80	60–70	50–60	40–50	30–40	20–30	60–70	50–60	40–50	60–70
	m	m	i	i	i	i	m	m	m	m	m	m	m	m	m	i
Lathridiidae																
Corticarina fuscula (Gyll.)			1		1											
Coccinellidae																
Scymnus redtenbacheri Muls.																
**Scymnus bipunctatus* Kug.			1	1	1											
Scymnus sp.																1
**Hippodamia septemmaculata* (Geer)			3	1												
Coccinella sp.								1								
Tenebrionidae																
Crypticus quisquilius (L.)			2	1	2	1		1	1							1
Scarabaeidae																
Aegialia sabuleti (Panz.)	1	2	5	10	5	1	2	2	3	1	1	1		1	1	4
***Aphodius (Teuchestes)* sp.			1	1												1
Aphodius rufipes (L.)		5	1	12	7	4	3	4	4	1			1			2
***Aphodius holdereri* Reitt.		5	8	15	9	2	2	5		1						4
Aphodius fimetarius (L.)	1	1	2	3	4		1		2							3
***Aphodius* sp.	1	2	10	3	4	3										4
Aphodius spp.	6	33	153	165	79	31	22	26	15	12	9	1	6	5	1	53
Chrysomelidae																
Donacia dentata Hoppe.		1														
Donacia semicuprea Panz.								1								
Donacia sparganii Ahr.			1													
Donacia aquatica (L.)	2	1	4	6	2	1	1	2								1
Donacia obscura Gyll.			1													
Donacia cinerea Hbst.																
**Donacia* sp.			4	10	6	1										
Plateumaris sericea (L.)	1	2	22	16	10	1	2	5	2	3			1			6
Chrysomela staphylea L.																
Chrysomela marginata L.			2		1											
Gastroidea viridula (Geer)			2	1												
**Phaedon pyritosus* (Rossi)		1	2	2	1		1	1	1							2
Phaedon spp.			4	3	1											
Prasocuris phellandrii (L.)			1													
**Melasoma collaris* (L.)			1													
Phytodecta sp.																
Phyllodecta vitellinae (L.)/ polaris Schneid.			1	1												
Timarcha sp.			1													
Galeruca tanaceti (L.)			2	2	1											
Phyllotreta flexuosa (Illiger)																
Aphthona sp.			1													
Haltica sp.			1											2		
Chaetocnema concinna (Marsh.) group	2	1	27	18	2			1	1							2
Chaetocnema sp.									1							1
Psylliodes sp.			1	4	1								1	1		

continued ▶

3 ENVIRONMENTAL EVIDENCE

Table 3.1 – continued

facies	B-ii:01	B-ii:03												
context	20004	20003												
sample number top of profile (metres OD)	30000 7.778	30002 8.39	30004 8.287				30198 8.764						30201 8.963			30202 8.938
subsample																
sample interval			45–60	30–45	15–30	0–15	70–80	60–70	50–60	40–50	30–40	20–30	60–70	50–60	40–50	60–70
	m	m	i	i	i	i	m	m	m	m	m	m	m	m	m	i
Curculionidae																
Apion spp.		1	2	1	2		2	1		1				1		2
Otiorhynchus arcticus (F.)	4	18	26	20	8		8	17	13	12	15	2	4	6	4	12
Otiorhynchus dubius (Ström.)												1				
Otiorhynchus rugifrons (Gyll.)	1	1	3	2	1	2	1	2	2	1	3					
Otiorhynchus ovatus (L.)	50079.778	1	5	3	1		1	1	3		1	1	1	3	1	3
Phyllobius sp. and/or Polydrusus sp.	1	1	20	17	1	1	1	1	1		1					5
Strophosomus faber (Hbst.)	48		1													
Barynotus obscurus (F.)		1	29													
Sitona flavescens (Marsh.)		1	3	2	1							1	1		1	1
Sitona sp.		3														1
Bagous spp.			4	2	2	1	1									
Notaris bimaculatus (F.)		1	1	3	1	1	1	1	1	1		1		1		1
Notaris aethiops (F.)	4	8	12	21	8	3	5	12	15	9	10	2	4	5	7	7
Thryogenes sp.													1			
Grypus equiseti (F.)							1								1	
Alophus triguttatus (F.)	1	2	11	5	1	2		1	1	1	4					2
Hypera sp.		1							1	1					1	
Eubrychius velutus (Beck)			2	1									1			1
Litodactylus leucogaster (Marsh.)			13	4	2				1							1
Phytobius sp.			1			1		1								
Gymnetron sp.														1	1	
Miarus cf campanulae (L.)								1								

facies	B-ii:02	B-ii:01	B-ii:03				B-ii:02					B-ii:03	B-ii:02	B-ii:03			
context	20371	20371	20139	20003			20390	20371				20003	20355	20021			
sample number top of profile (metres OD)	30212 7.86	30213 7.86		30228 8.749				30232 8.684						30234 7.974			
subsample			5	4	3	2	1	12	11	10	9	8	4	5	4	3	2	1
sample interval			34–36	31–34	22–31	12–22	0–12	95–99	87–95	80–87	69–80	61–69	20–30	40–50	30–40	20–30	20–10	0–10
	i	m	m	m	m	m	m	i	i	i	i	i	i	m	m	m	m	m
Carabidae																		
Carabus problematicus Hbst.															1			
Carabus granulatus L.		1																
**Carabus maeander Fisch.																		
*Carabus cancellatus Illiger																		
Carabus arvensis Hbst.						1		1										
Carabus monilis F.																		
*Carabus hortensis L.																		
**Carabus sp.												1						

continued ▶

Table 3.1 – *continued*

	B-ii:02	B-ii:02	B-ii:01	B-ii:03					B-ii:02	B-ii:02						B-ii:03	B-ii:02	B-ii:03				
facies																						
context	20371	20371	20139	20003					20390	20371						20003	20355	20021				
sample number	30212	30213		30228						30232								30234				
top of profile (metres OD)	7.86	7.86		8.749						8.684								7.974				
subsample				5	4	3	2	1	12	11	10	9	8	4				5	4	3	2	1
sample interval				34–36	31–34	22–31	12–22	0–12	95–99	87–95	80–87	69–80	61–69	20–30				40–50	30–40	20–30	20–10	0–10
	i	m	m	m	m	m	m	m	i	i	i	i	i	i				m	m	m	m	m
Carabus sp.				1																2	1	
Leistus rufescens (F.)																						
Pelophila borealis (Payk.)														1				1	1	2		
Notiophilus pusillus Wtrh.																						
Notiophilus aquaticus (L.)	1	3		6	3	2	1		1			1		4				1	5	6	8	2
Blethisa multipunctata (L.)				1	2	1	1											1	2	1		
**Diacheila polita* (Fald.)	1		1	1														1		1	1	
Elaphrus cupreus Duft.	1			2	3	1			1	2									1	1	3	1
Elaphrus riparius (L.)																						
Loricera pilicornis (F.)	1		1	2	3	1			1										3	3	3	
Dyschirius tristis Steph. = *luedersi* Wag.	1				1								1									
Dyschirius globosus (Hbst.)	2	1		3	3				3			1	1							2	1	
Dyschirius obscurus (Gyll.)																		1				
Bembidion properans (Steph.)	1			1	1																	
Bembidion bipunctatum (L.)	1			2	2	2	2		1	1								2	1	3	3	1
Bembidion obliquum Sturm.										1												
Bembidion gilvipes Sturm.		1																				
**Bembidion transparens* (Gebl.)	1	1		1	1	1			1									1	1	2	1	
Bembidion aeneum Germ.	2	1										1										
Bembidionguttula (F.)																						
Patrobus septentrionis Dej.		1		1	1			3	1	1								2	1	1	1	
Patrobus assimilis Chaud.		1																				
Harpalus aeneus (F.)									1													
Poecilus lepidus (Leske)													1									1
Poecilus versicolor (Sturm.)		1				1													1			
Pterostichus diligens (Sturm.)																						
Pterostichus nigrita (Payk.)																						
**Pterostichus kokeili* Mill. (? = *tundrae* Tsch.)	11	12	1	4	4		2		5	16	3	2	1					2	6	13	10	2
Pterostichus aethiops (Panz.)																						
Pterostichus adstrictus Esch.																						1
Calathus melanocephalus (L.)	1								3	1												
Agonum sexpunctatum (L.)		1			1														1			
Agonum ericeti (Panz.)									1													
**Agonum sahlbergi* (Chaud.)																						
Agonum cf *viduum* (Panz.)		1		1		1				1				1				1	1	1	1	1
**Agonum consimile* (Gyll.)																						
Agonum scitulum Dej.																						
Agonum gracile (Gyll.)																						
Agonum fuliginosum (Panz.)	1								1												1	
Amara quenseli (Schonh.)																						
**Amara municipalis* (Duft.)				1		1			1				1	1								1
**Amara torrida* (Panz.)		2		7	6	2			1	1				1				2	5	8	10	3
Amara sp.																						
Chlaenius nigricornis (F.)																						
**Chlaenius costulatus* Motsch.				1	1														1	1		
**Cymindis angularis* Gyll.																						

continued ▶

3 ENVIRONMENTAL EVIDENCE

Table 3.1 – *continued*

facies	B-ii:02	B-ii:01	B-ii:03				B-ii:02					B-ii:03	B-ii:02	B-ii:03			
context	20371	20371	20139	20003			20390	20371				20003	20355	20021			
sample number	30212	30213		30228				30232						30234			
top of profile (metres OD)	7.86	7.86		8.749				8.684						7.974			
subsample			5	4	3	2	1	12	11	10	9	8	4	5	4	3	2	1
sample interval			34–36	31–34	22–31	12–22	0–12	95–99	87–95	80–87	69–80	61–69	20–30	40–50	30–40	20–30	20–10	0–10
	i	m	m	m	m	m	m	i	i	i	i	i	i	m	m	m	m	m
Haliplidae																		
Brychius elevatus (Panz.)	1							3	1									
Haliplus sp.	6							3	2	1		1						
Dytiscidae																		
Coelambus impressopunctatus (Schall.)																		
Hygrotus inaequalis (Schall.)									1									
Hygrotus quinquilineatus (Zett.)	1							2										
Hydroporus spp.	1	1		1	1	1		4			1	2		1		1		3
Potamonectes griseostriatus (Geer)	1																	
Potamonectes depressus (F.)								2	1									
Potamonectes assimilis (Payk.)								2										
Oreodytes rivalis (Gyll.)																		
Agabus bipustulatus (L.)								2										
Agabus arcticus (Payk.)								1	1	1	1							
Agabus sturmi (Gyll.)				1														
Agabus cf *unguicularis* Thoms.								1	1									
Agabus congener (Thunb.) group			1	1										1	3			1
Ilybius subaeneus Er.		1		1	1	1	1	1			1			3	1	2		1
Rhantus sp.								1		1	1	1						
Colymbetes fuscus (L.)				1				1										
Colymbetes paykulli Er.														1	1			
Graphoderus sp.																		
Dytiscus marginalis L.																		
Dytiscus lapponicus Gyll.								1	1			1			1			
Gyrinidae																		
Gyrinus minutus F.								1			1			1	1			
Gyrinus aeratus Steph.	1	1						1						1				
Gyrinus sp.															1			
Hydraenidae																		
Ochthebius lenensis Popp.	4							4	2	2	3	4						
Ochthebius sp.	3								1	3								
Helophorus grandis Illiger	1			2	1	1		2			1			1	1	3	2	
Helophorus 'aquaticus' (L.) = *aequalis* Thomps	2						1		1	1	1	2			1	1		
Helophorus glacialis Villa								2										
**Helophorus aspericollis* Angus	4	1						5	7	3	5	4			1	1		
Helophorus misc small spp.	13	1				1		4	9	2	3	11	3					
Hydrophilidae																		
Sphaeridium scarabaeoides (L.)																		
Cercyon haemorrhoidalis (F.)		1																
Cercyon melanocephalus (L.)	2				1			2							1			
Cercyon marinus Thoms.	1			6				1	1			1		1	5	4		1
Cercyon unipunctatus (L.)															1			
Cercyon pygmaeus (Illiger)																		

continued ▶

Table 3.1 – *continued*

facies	B-ii:02	B-ii:02	B-ii:01	B-ii:03	B-ii:03	B-ii:03	B-ii:03	B-ii:03	B-ii:02	B-ii:02	B-ii:02	B-ii:02	B-ii:02	B-ii:03	B-ii:02	B-ii:03	B-ii:03	B-ii:03	B-ii:03
context	20371	20371	20139	20003	20003	20003	20003	20390	20371	20371	20371	20371	20371	20003	20355	20021	20021	20021	20021
sample number	30212	30213		30228					30232							30234			
top of profile (metres OD)	7.86	7.86		8.749					8.684							7.974			
subsample				5	4	3	2	1	12	11	10	9	8	4		5	4	3	2	1
sample interval				34–36	31–34	22–31	12–22	0–12	95–99	87–95	80–87	69–80	61–69	20–30		40–50	30–40	20–30	20–10	0–10
	i	m	m	m	m	m	m	i	i	i	i	i	i		m	m	m	m	m
Cercyon tristis (Illiger)	1	1			1	1		1								1	1	3	
Cercyon convexiusculus Steph.		1	1	3		1						1			2	4	1		1
Cercyon sternalis Shp.								1				1				1	1		
Cercyon analis (Payk.)					1	1										1	1		
Cryptopleurum minutum (F.)	1	1		1	1				1						1				1
Hydrobius fuscipes (L.)	2	1		2		1		5	1	1		1				3	4	7	1
Laccobius sp.	5							1	3		1								
Enochrus melanocephalus (Ol.)								1	1										
Silphidae																			
Necrophorus sp.																1			
Thanatophilus dispar (Hbst.)	1	1	1	9	5	10	3	1				1				9	6	11	7
Blitophaga opaca (L.)																			
Silpha tyrolensis Laich		1		1		1										1			1
Catopidae																			
Choleva sp.		2																	
Liodidae																			
Liodes sp.	1			1				2											
Agathidium marginatum Sturm.		1				1													
Staphylinidae																			
Eusphalerum sp.									1	1	1	1							
Pycnoglypta lurida (Gyll.)	9							13	2	1	3								
Omalium sp.	1							1	1										
Deliphrum tectum (Payk.)											1								
Olophrum fuscum (Grav.)	2	1	1	1				4	3	1		1					1	1	
Olophrum assimile (Payk.)	1							1	1							2			1
Eucnecosum brachypterum (Grav.)	11	2						11	6	2	6	1						2	
Acidota crenata (F.)		1		1			1		1									1	1
Acidota quadrata Zett.									1										
Geodromicus nigrita (Müll.)	4	2				1		7	3	2	2	1				1			
Boreaphilus henningianus Sahlb.								1	1		1								
Aploderus caelatus (Grav.)								3											
Trogophloeus sp.	1	4						1			1								
Oxytelus rugosus (F.)	4			1				2			1								
Oxytelus laqueatus (Marsh.)		2																	
**Oxytelus gibbulus* Epp.	1								1		1	1							
Oxytelus nitidulus Grav.	2								2	1									
Platystethus arenarius (Fourcr.)																			
Platystethus cornutus (Grav.)	1								1	1									
Platystethus nodifrons Mannh.	3								1	2	2	2							1
Platystethus nitens (Sahlb.)		1							1	1									
Bledius sp.	3								2	2									
Stenus juno (Payk.)	1								2	1									
Stenus spp.	7	2		1		2			7	4		3	2				1		1
Euaesthetus laeviusculus Mannh.																			
Lathrobium cf terminatum Grav.																1			1
Xantholinus sp.	6	4						3	1	1	1					1			

continued ▶

Table 3.1 – *continued*

facies	B-ii:02		B-ii:01	B-ii:03					B-ii:02					B-ii:03	B-ii:02	B-ii:03			
context	20371	20371	20139	20003					20390	20371					20003	20355	20021			
sample number	30212	30213		30228						30232							30234			
top of profile (metres OD)	7.86	7.86		8.749						8.684							7.974			
subsample				5	4	3	2	1	12	11	10	9	8	4	5	4	3	2	1
sample interval				34–36	31–34	22–31	12–22	0–12	95–99	87–95	80–87	69–80	61–69	20–30	40–50	30–40	20–30	20–10	0–10
	i	m	m	m	m	m	m	m	i	i	i	i	i	i	m	m	m	m	m
**Philonthus linki* Solski				1											3	1	5		
Philonthus spp.	1	2		1	2	1			3		1	1			2	2	2	1	
Staphylinus erythropterus L.																	2	1	
Ocypus aeneocephalus (Geer)/ *cupreus* (Rossi)				1	1														
Quedius spp.	3								3	3	2	3			2		2		
Boletobiinae Gen. et sp. indet.	3								2	1									
Tachyporus chrysomelinus (L.)	2								2										
Tachyporus sp.		1							1		1								
***Tachinus glacialis* Ullrich and Campbell	1																		
***Tachinus jacuticus* Popp.	1			1	1			1	1		1				3	3	2	1	
**Tachinus fimetarius* Grav.	2																		
Tachinus corticinus Grav.	4								3	1	1	1							
Gymnusa variegata Kiesw.																			
Alaeocharinae Gen. et sp. indet.	24								20	17	3	9	5						
Elateridae																			
Ctenicera cuprea (F.)	1	1							2	2	1	1	1		1			1	
Hypnoidus riparius (F.)	1	1		1					2	1								1	
**Hypnoidus rivularis* (Gyll.)																			
Helodidae																			
Gen. et sp. indet.									1	1									
Dryopidae																			
Dryops sp.				1								1				1			
Heteroceridae																			
Heterocerus cf *hispidulus* Kiesw.									1						1				
Heterocerus sp.	1									1	1								
Byrrhidae																			
Simplocaria semistriata (F.)		1							1			1			1				
Cytilus sericeus (Forst.)																			
Byrrhus fasciatus (Forst.)		2		2	2	1			1			1		1		1	1	1	
Byrrhus pilula (L.)															1				
Byrrhus pustulatus (Forst.)																			
Curimopsis sp.						1										1			
Nitidulidae																			
Cateretes rufilabris (Latr.)	1								1	2	1	1							
Cryptophagidae																			
Atomaria sp.	1																		
Lathridiidae																			
Corticarina fuscula (Gyll.)	3								1	2	3	3	1						

continued ▶

Table 3.1 – *continued*

facies	B-ii:02		B-ii:01	B-ii:03				B-ii:02					B-ii:03	B-ii:02	B-ii:03			
context	20371	20371	20139	20003				20390	20371				20003	20355	20021			
sample number	30212	30213		30228					30232						30234			
top of profile (metres OD)	7.86	7.86		8.749					8.684						7.974			
subsample				5	4	3	2	1	12	11	10	9	8	4	5	4	3	2	1
sample interval				34–36	31–34	22–31	12–22	0–12	95–99	87–95	80–87	69–80	61–69	20–30	40–50	30–40	20–30	20–10	0–10
	i	m	m	m	m	m	m	i	i	i	i	i	i	m	m	m	m
Coccinellidae																			
Scymnus redtenbacheri Muls.									3	1									
**Scymnus bipunctatus* Kug.		2																	
Scymnus sp.	1								1	1	1								
**Hippodamia septemmaculata* (Geer)																			
Coccinella sp.																1			
Tenebrionidae																			
Cryptichus quisquilius (L.)		1									1					1			
Scarabaeidae																			
Aegialia sabuleti (Panz.)	8	11		5	2	2	1		3	3	1		1		1	3	5	6	1
***Aphodius* (*Teuchestes*) sp.																			
Aphodius rufipes (L.)	1	1		4	5	4	1									3	2	5	2
***Aphodius holdereri* Reitt.				4	1	2	1					3					3	1	
Aphodius fimetarius (L.)	2				2	1				1			1			2	2	4	
***Aphodius* sp.	6								1	3	2	1	1						
Aphodius spp.	124	19		12	7	5	3		44	65	30	24	14	3		13	19	15	10
Chrysomelidae																			
Donacia dentata Hoppe.																			
Donacia semicuprea Panz.																			
Donacia sparganii Ahr.																			
Donacia aquatica (L.)				1	1				1	1						2	2		1
Donacia obscura Gyll.									1										
Donacia cinerea Hbst.																			
**Donacia* sp.									1										
Plateumaris sericea (L.)	1	1	1	4	4	1			3	1		1	2			6	13	12	4
Chrysomela staphylea L.	1								1										
Chrysomela marginata L.		1				1			1		1					1			
Gastroidea viridula (Geer)																			
**Phaedon pyritosus* (Rossi)		1		1					2	2	1	1	1			1	1		
Phaedon spp.									1										
Prasocuris phellandrii (L.)																			
**Melasoma collaris* (L.)																			
Phytodecta sp.																1			
Phyllodecta vitellinae (L.)/ *polaris* Schneid.	1																		
Timarcha sp.																			
Galeruca tanaceti (L.)	1	1														1			
Phyllotreta flexuosa (Illiger)									1										
Aphthona sp.																			
Haltica sp.																			
Chaetocnema concinna (Marsh.) group	2								1	1	1	1	13		1	1	3		
Chaetocnema sp.													4						
Psylliodes sp.	1								1			1							

continued ▶

Table 3.1 – *continued*

facies	B-ii:02	B-ii:02	B-ii:01	B-ii:03	B-ii:03	B-ii:03	B-ii:03	B-ii:03	B-ii:02	B-ii:02	B-ii:02	B-ii:02	B-ii:02	B-ii:02	B-ii:03	B-ii:02	B-ii:03	B-ii:03	B-ii:03	B-ii:03	B-ii:03
context	20371	20371	20139	20003	20003	20003	20003	20003	20390	20371	20371	20371	20371	20371	20003	20355	20021	20021	20021	20021	20021
sample number	30212	30213		30228	30228	30228	30228	30228		30232	30232	30232	30232	30232			30234	30234	30234	30234	30234
top of profile (metres OD)	7.86	7.86		8.749	8.749	8.749	8.749	8.749		8.684	8.684	8.684	8.684	8.684			7.974	7.974	7.974	7.974	7.974
subsample				5	4	3	2	1		12	11	10	9	8	4		5	4	3	2	1
sample interval				34–36	31–34	22–31	12–22	0–12		95–99	87–95	80–87	69–80	61–69	20–30		40–50	30–40	20–30	10–20	0–10
	i	m	m	m	m	m	m	m	i	i	i	i	i	i	i	m	m	m	m	m	m
Curculionidae																					
Apion spp.	2	1		1		1				2									1		
Otiorhynchus arcticus (F.)	1	2		13	16	22	10		2	2				4			9	6	15	18	13
Otiorhynchus dubius (Ström.)																					
Otiorhynchus rugifrons (Gyll.)	1		1	1	1	3	1		2								1	2	5	4	3
Otiorhynchus ovatus (L.)		2		1	1	1		2		1			1	1			2	4	2	1	
Phyllobius sp. and/ or *Polydrusus* sp.	2	1		1					1	2		1		2			1		1		
Strophosomus faber (Hbst.)	1																		1		
Barynotus obscurus (F.)																					
Sitona flavescens (Marsh.)																					
Sitona sp.	1									1	1										
Bagous spp.	2										1		1						1		
Notaris bimaculatus (F.)		1		1	2	1	1										2	1	1	1	
Notaris aethiops (F.)	3	3	1	10	6	9	5		2	1	2	1	1	1		3	5	9	15	7	
Thryogenes sp.																					
Grypus equiseti (F.)																					
Alophus triguttatus (F.)		1		3	1	2			1								1	3	4	5	
Hypera sp.		1		2	2												1	2	1	1	
Eubrychius velutus (Beck)	1									1	1										
Litodactylus leucogaster (Marsh.)		1		1					1	1		1						1	1		
Phytobius sp.																					
Gymnetron sp.																	1			1	
Miarus cf *campanulae* (L.)																					

algae, though again the species can also be found occasionally in lakes (Holmen 1987). In this context it is interesting to note the presence of larval sclerites of various Trichoptera (caddis flies) that inhabit rivers. Species of *Hydropsyche* are predaceous, building capture nets across slow currents. *Anobolia nervosa* feeds on diatoms and filamentous algae in slow-moving clear water with a current speed of 0.05–0.2m^{-s} (Lepneva 1971). These species were also relatively rare compared with the numbers expected if the deposit had been truly riverine, and it is likely that these rare running-water insects were animals accidentally washed into the deposit at times of flood from some adjacent river.

The rest of the aquatic Coleoptera indicate stationary, eutrophic, well-vegetated water, suggesting that the hollow in which the sediment accumulated was normally separated from the main course of the river, possibly representing an abandoned channel. All the dytiscid species are active predators, feeding on a wide variety of pondlife. The Gyrinids are the familiar whirligig beetles that hunt on the surface for other insects accidentally trapped by the surface tension. Most of the hydraenid and hydrophilid species have voracious predatory larvae, but the adults feed on decomposing plant matter (Hansen 1987). They are for the most part characteristic of the margins of ponds choked with waterweed. Species of *Haliplus* are chiefly found in alkaline ponds where many of the larvae feed on characeans. Because of the frailty of haliplid exoskeletons, they are always poorly preserved as fossils and no doubt were more common than their representation here might suggest. Some hydrophilid species inhabit accumulations of decomposing vegetation in damp places (including dung) and their occurrence in this fauna will be discussed later.

Among the aquatic phytophagous beetles, species of *Donacia* have adult beetles that feed on a variety of water plants, while their larvae respire by tapping the air channels of their host plants. *Donacia dentata* is found on various species of Alismataceae. *Donacia semicuprea* feeds chiefly on the aquatic grass *Glyceria* (Koch 1992). The subaquatic weevils *Eubrychius velutus* and *Litodactylus leucogaster* feed principally on species of *Myriophyllum*. *Bagous* sp. is another subaquatic weevil that feeds on a wide variety of pondweeds.

Transitional habitats

Species indicating marshy environments with rich vegetation are by far the most numerous in this fossil assemblage. Their environmental requirements range from exclusively waterside habitats to more or less damp grassland.

One of the most important families in this assemblage, whose species indicate marshy habitats, is the Carabidae – carnivorous or scavenging ground beetles. The following is a selection of stenotopic species (species with fairly restricted habitat requirements) in this category. Their ecological significance is derived mainly from Lindroth (1992). *Pelophila borealis* lives in wet places beside still or slow-moving water, where there is a patchy vegetation cover of *Carex* species. *Blethisa multipunctata* is usually found in unshaded, intensely sun-exposed, very wet places, sometimes at a distance from the water's edge such as in swampy meadows, and often where there is a more or less continuous surface cover of mosses. *Elaphrus cupreus* is found in very damp habitats near stagnant water shaded by tall reedy plants, but where there are also patches of bare soil. It is also found in places where the surface is covered with moss. *Loricera pilicornis* is also typical of wet habitats beside stagnant water, which is often foul-smelling, and where the vegetation occurs in patches and the soil contains much decomposing organic debris. *Dyschirius tristis* is a fossorial species that excavates burrows in damp clayish soil such as those occurring in marshy meadows where the vegetation is moderately tall and consists of *Carex*, *Glyceria* and grasses. The beetle actually lives on the bare patches between the plants, where it is probably a predator on burrowing species such as *Trogophloeus* and *Platystethus*. Species of *Bledius* and *Heterocerus* burrow in wet sand, feeding on algae and, in turn, were probably preyed on by *Dyschirius obscurus*, a species that lives in totally barren places where it burrows in very fine damp sand. According to Lindroth (1992, 398) it is a stenotopic quicksand species. *Bembidion obliquum* occurs beside both stagnant and flowing water where the soil is wet and soft, and is exposed in places among the vegetation, made up of *Carex*, *Juncus* and *Equisetum*. *Patrobus septentrionis* is eurytopic in the extreme north of its range, but farther south it is confined to wet clay-banks overgrown with sedges, where it occurs with *Pelophila borealis*. Though rare in this assemblage, *Pterostichus nigrita* is today a common species beside fresh water where there is a growth of *Carex* with a more or less clayish soil. It is more common than *Pterostichus diligens*, as it is here, when the water is eutrophic. *Agonum viduum/moestum* inhabits well-vegetated margins of all types of fresh water. *Chlaenius nigricornis* is found on clayish or sandy-clay soils that are firm and well vegetated with larger species of *Carex*, but with bare patches between the plants. It is usually found beside stagnant or slow-flowing water but also at times in swampy meadows at some distance from the water's edge. *Chlaenius costulatus* is also a swamp species, found on the borders of lakes and ponds. In summary, the ground beetle species provide a consistent picture of a sedge-rich marsh growing beside a pool, with occasional patches of bare soil consisting of clay or muddy sand that was at times covered with moss.

Two other well-represented families also include many species characteristic of marshy habitats. Thus the species of Staphylinidae in this assemblage are mostly predators that feed on other small soil arthropods and worms in heaps of damp, decomposing plant debris. Some of the Hydrophilidae also inhabit accumulations of decaying vegetation beside water.

Among the phytophagous species there are also abundant indications of the local presence of sedge swamps. The data on the food preferences for these species is derived chiefly from Koch (1992). Thus *Donacia dentata*, *Donacia aquatica*, *Donacia obscura*, *Donacia cinerea* and *Plateumaris sericea* all feed principally on reedy vegetation, notably species of *Carex*. The weevils *Notaris aethiops* (the only species present in all samples) and *Notaris bimaculatus* feed chiefly on the leaves of sedges; their larvae eat the roots and stems of similar plants. The larvae of *Chrysomela staphylea* feed on *Plantago maritima*. *Gastroidea viridula* feeds chiefly on species of *Polygonum* and *Rumex*. *Chaetocnema concinna* is also usually found feeding on the leaves of species of *Polygonum*. *Prasocuris phelandrii* feeds exclusively on aquatic species of Umbelliferae. *Phaedon pyritosus* lives in damp meadows where it feeds on *Ranunculus repens*. *Alophus triguttatus* is polyphagous on various herbs in damp sandy habitats. *Grypus equiseti* lives principally on *Equisetum arvense* and *Equisetum palustre*. Species of Byrrhidae, both as larvae and as adults, are exclusively moss-feeders. *Blitophaga opaca* feeds on fleshy leaves of various large plants such as large Cruciferae. *Phyllotreta flexuosa* also feeds on various species of Cruciferae. The rare occurrences of *Salix sp.* is indicated by the occasional presence of *Melasoma collaris*, *Phytodecta* sp. and *Phyllodecta* sp., though these might have been have been feeding on dwarf willows.

Many carabid species live in damp habitats that were probably farther away from the water where the soil is rich in humus. This group resembles communities that today are encouraged by human agricultural practices. Thus *Carabus granulatus* and *Carabus cancellatus* are found together in open, damp, cultivated areas where the soil is clayish with an admixture of humus, and the vegetation is rather tall. *Carabus monilis* lives today in wet meadows or weedy pastures. *Bembidion properans* lives in open, sun- exposed places on clayish or fine sandy soil, usually close to water and where the vegetation is sparse. *Bembidion bipunctatum* is also found in open country on sand, or on clay mixed with sand, where there is a dense but short turf of grasses or sedges. Lindroth (1992, 175) points out that its most important requirement is for hard ground. *Amara torrida* inhabits moderately humid meadow-like habitats with rich but not tall vegetation. Although *Calathus melanocephalus* lives in both moist and fairly dry meadow-like habitats, the most important environmental factor is that it must be exposed to adequate sunlight. Both of these species are encouraged today by old-fashioned agricultural practices. The scarabaeid species *Aegialia sabuleti* lives at the roots of grass in damp sandy places. The elaterids *Hypnoidus riparius* and *Hypnoidus rivularis* live in damp detritus where the larvae develop in the soil. *Ctenicera cuprea* is characteristic of damp sandy meadows where the larvae (the familiar wireworms) feed on grass roots, sometimes causing sufficient damage for bare patches to develop.

Several carabid species in this fauna are pronounced heliophiles – that is, they are active in the bright sunlight. Thus *Elaphrus riparius* lives on the borders of standing water usually where there is little or no vegetation. *Agonum sexpunctatus* is likewise found in sun-exposed places where it lives on humid sandy or gravelly soils but where there is a dense but short vegetation of grasses and sedges.

Dry ground habitats

Considering that the channel was filled with water-laid sediment, it is surprising that so many of the beetles present in this assemblage are xerophilous, living in dry habitats. These include both carnivores and phytophagous species. Since some of them are wingless or otherwise unable to fly, they must represent members of rather more distant communities that were passively incorporated into the sediment.

Several carabid species are decidedly xerophilous. *Carabus problematicus* and *Carabus arvensis* live in dry open heathland where the soil is gravelly with little vegetation cover. *Carabus hortensis* is usually considered to be a species typical of open woodland fringes although it is also found in gardens where the soil is rich in humus and preferably gravelly. Similarly *Agonum ericeti* is also often found on heathland, though it can also live on moist acid soils with *Sphagnum*. *Cymindis angularis* inhabits firm, dry gravel or sand where there is low vegetation. *Notiophilus aquaticus*, in spite of its specific name, is typically found on dry gravelly soils that have an admixture of clay, and where the vegetation is sparse or sometimes totally absent. *Diacheila polita* is a species of the drier parts of the tundra in the north, and of the forest steppes farther south in central Asia. *Amara municipalis* also prefers dry sandy or gravelly soils where the vegetation is sparse. *Harpalus aeneus* and *Pterostichus lepidus* live on dry gravelly or sandy soils exposed to the sun, and both species are highly heliophilous.

One of the most abundant carabid species in this assemblage is *Pterostichus kokeili* (probably the same species as *Pterostichus tundrae* Tsch. (see Holdhaus and Lindroth 1939). The ecological preferences of this species are poorly known, but it is reported in the Carpathian Mountains and the High Alps to live especially in relatively dry grassy places.

Among the phytophagous species in this assemblage, the flightless species *Otiorhynchus arcticus*, *Otiorhynchus rugifrons* and *Otiorhynchus ovatus* are particularly common. They are polyphagous, the adult beetles feeding on a wide variety of low herbs and the larvae feeding underground on their roots. Species of *Sitona* feed on various species of Papilionaceae (legumes), and again the larvae feed on the roots (the young larvae eating the bacterial nodules). *Chrysomela marginata* lives in dry sandy places where it feeds on various Compositae including *Artemisia*. *Galeruca tanaceti* is xerophilous, living in open country and feeding on various species of Compositae.

The dung and carcass community

Dung and carcass beetles are of particular importance in archaeological contexts because they are often intimately associated with hominin exploitation of large vertebrates. Their profusion in a fossil assemblage implies the close proximity of these activities and, conversely, their rarity implies that such activities were carried out some distance away.

At Lynford the dung community is especially well represented. Species of the scarabaeid *Aphodius* are by far the most abundant beetle fossils in this assemblage. For the most part these species feed on the dung of large mammals, though some can live in rotting accumulations of plant debris. Among them are a wide variety of species, including some species not found in Europe today. For instance *Aphodius holdereri* is today largely confined to the high plateau of Tibet (Coope 1973). Another species belonging to the sub-genus *Teuchestes* is similar, but not identical to *Aphodius brachysomus* Solski – a species from eastern Siberia and Japan. It looks like a foreshortened version of the familiar *Aphodius fossor* but with a large red spot on the apical half of each elytron. Other species of *Aphodius* are also present, but are difficult to name in this enormous genus. They do not seem to match any present day European species. The extraordinary abundance and diversity of dung beetles here would appear to be a reflection of the rich and exotic vertebrate fauna of the times.

Some of the hydrophilid species – *Sphaeridium scarabaeoides*, *Cercyon haemorhoidalis*, *Cercyon melanocephalus* and *Cercyon pygmaeus* – are also coprophages. Among the staphylinids, *Aploderus caelatus*, *Platystethus arenarius* and *Tachinus jacuticus* are also found in dung.

The abundance of dung beetles in this assemblage is significant because they are terrestrial species. Their presence here in such numbers indicates that the dung of large mammals must have been locally abundant on land at this time. The occurrence of their remains in water-lain deposits suggests that had been washed off the nearby land surface and into the channel sediment. They support the view that the abundant bones at this site were local in origin, and had not been washed into the deposit from farther afield.

Many beetle species are today associated with carcasses, either directly as a source of food or else as predators feeding on the insects associated with them. Curiously, in spite of the abundant evidence of bones at the Lynford site, remains of carcass beetles were remarkably rare in the fossil insect assemblage. Only *Thanatophilus dispar* was at all abundant. This is a medium-sized species, usually found under rotting carcasses where it predates on dipterous larvae (maggots). Other groups of carrion beetles were rare or totally absent. Thus *Necrophorus* sp. (the familiar Sexton Beetle), was represented by a single specimen only. There were none of the expected species that predate other necrophilous dipterans (eg Histeridae or some Cleridae). Furthermore, there were few fly puparia present in the deposit in spite of the fact that they are robust and usually survive well as fossils.

The Lynford beetle assemblage also lacked the species associated with dried-out carcasses, where they feed directly on the meat and skin (eg Dermestidae and some Anobiidae). Nor were there any species that feed on the dry periosteum on old bones (eg *Omosita*). These curious absences are difficult to reconcile with the evidence for the immediate presence of living, large mammals, and with abundant bones representing their dead and exploited carcasses. Several hypotheses can be advanced to explain this anomaly. One might be cold climatic conditions – however, the species concerned can live today in the Arctic. A second reason could be that the mammalian remains had become rapidly submerged in the pool, where they would have been inaccessible to these wholly terrestrial insect species. Thirdly, much of the mammalian exploitation could have been carried out elsewhere; too far away for the beetle species associated with this activity to be incorporated in the deposit. Their absence, however, remains puzzling.

Summary of the local environment interpreted from the coleopteran assemblage

A consistent mosaic picture of the local environment can be put together from the habitat preferences of the beetle species in this assemblage. The deposit accumulated in a pool of standing, eutrophic water, probably representing an abandoned channel of a fairly large river. Various aquatic plants grew in the pool, such as *Myriophyllum* and species of Alismataceae. From time to time during periods of flood, sediment was washed into the channel from the nearby river. Along the water's edge was a rich growth of reedy vegetation, at times extending down into the water itself. Other plants, for example tall Umbelliferae such as *Equisetum*, grew in the marsh. The soil was a mixture of sand and clay, exposed to the sun in places between the patches of vegetation. It is likely that some of the soil surface was covered with mosses. Farther away from the water the ground was sandy and better drained, producing drier habitats with thin grassy vegetation and abundant weedy plants. There is no evidence for the local presence of any trees at this time. The abundance of dung beetles indicates the local presence of large herbivorous mammals, but the rarity of beetles that feed on dried-out carcasses remains an intriguing enigma.

Climatic interpretation of the coleopteran assemblage

The coleopteran assemblage as a whole is dominated by species with present-day boreal or boreo-montane distributions, indicating that the thermal climate at the time when the deposit was laid down was much colder than it is in Norfolk at the present time. Significant cold-adapted species include *Diacheila polita, Pterostichus kokeli, Agonum sahlbergi, Agonum consimile, Amara torrida, Colymbetes dolabratus, Helophorus glacialis, Pycnoglypta lurida, Acidota quadrata* and *Boreaphilus henningianus*. This fauna also includes a number of species that are no longer found living anywhere in Europe, but that are widespread today in Siberia. These species are often relatively abundant and include *Carabus maeander, Helophorus aspericollis, Philonthus linki, Tachinus glacialis, Tachinus jacuticus* and *Aphodius holdereri* (Coope 1973). Together they indicate that the climate at the time was both cold and very continental. The present-day geographical distributions of many other predominantly northern species in this assemblage are more widespread, but they also extend across Siberia and some into northern North America.

In contrast to these northern and eastern species, there are a few species in the assemblage that do not fit into this general picture. They are today wholly European in their distributions, though most of their ranges extend into eastern Russia. Thus *Carabus hortensis* is predominantly eastern European, extending from Norway to the River Volga. *Carabus monilis* ranges as far east as Kharkov. But while this is a relatively southern species at the present day, it has also been recorded from glacial deposits in Poland (Lindroth 1992, 318). It has also been found as a fossil in a full glacial context in association with numerous obligate high northern species at Whitemore Haye (Coope, unpublished data). Thus its thermal tolerance might have been greater in the past than it is today, or its known present-day range might appear to be smaller than its actual climatic tolerances, either because of inadequate knowledge or because a species has not managed to occupy its full geographical potential.

Although it is always problematic to argue from negative evidence, the large and comprehensive fauna from Lynford has some notable absentees. The beetle fauna from the continental (cold) phase of the full glacial phase of the 'Last Glaciation' is now well known for Britain, and includes many obligate northern species. These include *Nebria nivalis, Bembidion fellmanni, Bembidion dauricum, Amara alpina. Pterostichus (Cryobius)* spp. *Helophorus obscurellus, Helophorus jacutus* and *Holoboreaphilus nordenskioeldi*, none of which were found at Lynford. The absence of so many cold-adapted species from the Lynford assemblage is surely climatically significant. It suggests that the palaeoclimate at Lynford was not quite as cold as it was during much of the full glacial period.

In this particular case a problem arises in the application of The Mutual Climatic Range (MCR) of calculating the mean monthly temperatures (Atkinson *et al* 1987). This is because the assemblage includes exclusively Asiatic species whose geographical ranges are difficult to plot adequately and whose thermal tolerances might not be precisely determined. Furthermore, since the assemblage includes a number of European species with ranges that are distinct from those of the Siberian species. Hence their climatic envelopes do not quite overlap, and there is no area of climate space in which the 90 per cent of the 87 species in this fauna that are also on the MCR database overlap – the conventional limit of acceptability adopted for the method. As a result, it has not been possible to provide an MCR estimate of the mean monthly temperatures in this particular case. However, a likely estimate, based on the geographical limits of most of the species in this assemblage, suggests that the mean temperature of the warmest month (July) lay somewhere between 14°C and 12°C, with the mean temperature of the coldest months (January/February) at or below –15°C.

It is difficult to quantify precipitation levels at this time on the basis of the fossil insect fauna. However, during the summer months there must have been adequate moisture to maintain the marsh and pool in which the fauna flourished. The presence of larvae of the riverine caddis flies suggest that the nearby river continued running during the summer months, indicating that precipitation must have been available to maintain a continuous flow at this time. Furthermore, the evidence that at times the river overflowed its banks, washing sediment into the abandoned channel, might hint at occasional spring floods, perhaps during the melting of the accumulated winter snow.

Stratigraphical implications of the coleopteran assemblage

In Britain there are two main types of fossil beetle faunas that date from the full-glacial phase of the Last (Weichselian, Würm, Devensian) Glaciation. Firstly, many assemblages are characterised by numerous cold-adapted species indicative of tundra conditions. They are also rich in exclusively Asiatic species (eg Coope 1968). Secondly, there are rich beetle assemblages made up of western European species with temperate geographical distributions (eg Coope and Angus, 1975; Coope 2000). Both these very different beetle faunas lived in a landscape that was completely treeless, and inhabited by a similar mammalian megafauna. This habitat has been broadly referred to as 'mammoth steppe' but it is evident that different episodes of 'mammoth steppe' were characterised by contrasting climatic regimes, some entirely temperate and some wholly arctic-continental. These full-glacial coleopteran assemblages are usually attributed to one or other of the numerous Devensian interstadials. Although these have in the past been extensively dated by radiocarbon (Coope 2002), many of the original dates that are older than 35,000 yrs BP are now considered unreliable. Thus the precise age of many of these deposits and their respective chronological positions are now uncertain.

The Lynford fauna does not fit neatly into either of the arctic-continent or the temperate faunal groupings. It lacks many of the more *extreme* Arctic and Asiatic species that characterise the beetle faunas of the cold, climatically continental interstadials. On the other hand, it does include many boreal and Asiatic species, clearly excluding it from the group of temperate, more oceanic, interstadial assemblages.

The only coleopteran assemblage bearing a close resemblance to that from Lynford is that described from Upton Warren (Coope *et al* 1961). The similarity between these two faunal assemblages is remarkable. Both these faunas include the abundant presence of numerous Asiatic species (eg *Amara torrid*, *Tachinus jacuticus* and *Aphodius holdereri*), but lack many of the more extreme high Arctic elements of the cold-continental faunas. In common with the Lynford assemblage, the Upton Warren fauna also includes occasional temperate species. This similarity suggests that the deposits at Lynford and Upton Warren might be of approximately the same age; namely dating from one of the middle Devensian interstadials.

There are, however, differences between the Lynford assemblage and that from Upton Warren, the most noticeable of which is the abundance at Lynford of *Pterostichus kokeil*, and the somewhat less common *Diacheila polita*, both of which were totally absent from the Upton Warren fauna. These species can hardly have been overlooked at Upton Warren because they are large and distinctive species. Since the local environments were very similar at the two sites, it is likely that these differences indicate that the sites are slightly different in age, in climate, or in both. Furthermore, the presence of cold-adapted species at Lynford that were absent at Upton Warren indicates that the climate at Lynford was somewhat colder than that at Upton Warren. However, it is not possible, on the basis of their beetle assemblages, to say which of these sites was the earlier.

The general stratigraphical context of the Upton Warren site is also similar to that of Lynford. The fossiliferous deposits at both localities occur in channel-like depressions near to the base of the gravels of a low river terrace, close to the level of the present-day floodplain of a river. The vertebrate fauna is also similar, including large numbers of mammoths, woolly rhinoceros, reindeer, bison and horses, but no evidence of any hominin presence at Upton Warren. The published radiocarbon dates obtained from Upton Warren of around 40ka BP must now be viewed as minimum values only and should not be used as acceptable ages for this site. Thus, the stratigraphy, the vertebrae fauna and the radiocarbon dating do not permit any finer resolution of the relative ages of the two sites.

3.2 The molluscan assemblages

D Keen†

Sampling and taxonomic nomenclature

The material collected for molluscan analysis consists of 53 samples, of which eight are recorded as being from Holocene channels and are not yet examined. A consolidated molluscan faunal list for the Lynford Pleistocene sequence can be seen in Table 3.2. The remaining 45 Pleistocene samples consist of five sets of serial samples (30198, Table 3.3; 30231, Table 3.4; 30228, Table 3.5; 30201, Table 3.7; 30234, Table 3.8; and a number of single, point samples Table 3.6) taken through the organic sands of Association B-ii. The former three samples yielded good numbers of Mollusca, while the latter two were mostly unfossiliferous. In addition to these stratified samples, further spot samples were taken from those silts that were seen to be mollusc-rich during excavation. All sediment collected was in the form of bulk samples of *c* 5kg in field condition, which was wet-sieved to 500µm, oven-dried at 400°C and sorted under a 40–60× binocular microscope. A *c* 0.5kg subsample was taken from each sample before sieving and put aside for plant macrofossil analysis. Any vertebrate or insect material was removed for further study by the relevant specialist.

The fauna is made up of existing British species, so taxonomic conventions follow Kerney (1999) and Anderson (2005).

Shell preservation and identification

The Mollusca present are moderately well to well preserved. The only particular problem relating to preservation has been caused by the acidity of the organic sands, which has entirely removed the shell content at some levels. The most abundant Mollusca were found in 30198 (*see* Table 3.3) where levels between 300mm and 600mm produced up to 715 individuals. Above 300mm there was no shell, and below 600mm shell content was sparse or absent. In

Table 3.2 Mollusca consolidated faunal list

Mollusca
Valvata cristata (Müller, 1774)
Valvata piscinalis (Müller, 1774)
Bithynia tentaculata (Linnaeus, 1758)
Stagnicola palustris (Müller, 1774)
Lymnaea truncatula (Müller, 1774)
Lymnaea stagnalis (Linnaeus, 1758)
Radix balthica (Linnaeus, 1758)
Planorbis planorbis (Linnaeus, 1758)
Anisus leucostoma (Millet, 1813)
Anisus vortex (Linnaeus, 1758)
Bathyomphalus contortus (Linnaeus, 1758)
Gyraulus laevis (Alder, 1838)
Gyraulus crista (Linnaeus, 1758)
Sphaerium corneum (Linnaeus, 1758)
Pisidium casertanum (Poli, 1791)
Pisidium personatum (Malm, 1855)
Pisidium obtusale (Lamarck, 1818)
Pisidium obtusale lapponicum (Clessin, 1877)
Pisidium milium (Held, 1836)
Pisidium subtruncatum (Malm, 1855)
Pisidium henslowanum (Sheppard, 1823)
Pisidium lilljeborgii (Clessin, 1886)
Pisidium hibernicum (Westerlund, 1894)
Pisidium nitidum (Jenyns, 1832)
Succineidae undet.
Vertigo spp.
Pupilla muscorum (Linnaeus, 1758)
Vallonia spp.
Limax spp.
Trochulus hispidus (Linnaeus, 1758)
total 30 species (24 freshwater, 6 land)

Table 3.3 Sample 30198

sample 30198 context top of profile 8.764m OD	Unit B-ii:05 20070 0–10	 10–20	UnitB-ii:03 20003 20–30	 30–40	 40–50	 50–60	 60–70	 70–80
Valvata cristata (Müller, 1774)				1				
Valvata piscinalis (Müller, 1774)				2		1		
Bithynia tentaculata (Linnaeus, 1758)					1			
Galba truncatula (Müller, 1774)				18	35	13	2	
Lymnaea stagnalis (Linnaeus, 1758)				1	6			
Radix balthia (Linnaeus, 1758)				7	23	5		
Lymnaeidae				32	36	17	3	
Planorbis planorbis (Linnaeus, 1758)				11	30	5		
Anisus leucostoma (Millet, 1813)				39	56	2		
Bathyomphalus contortus (Linnaeus, 1758)				5	6	1		
Gyraulus laevis (Alder, 1838)					3			
Gyraulus crista (Linnaeus, 1758)				9	10	1		
Gyraulus undet.				1				
Planorbidae undet.				59	113	15		
Pisidium obtusale lapponicum (Clessin, 1877)				118	160	22	1	
Pisidium subtruncatum Malm, 1855						1		
Pisidium henslowanum (Sheppard, 1823)				1				
Pisidium lilljeborgii (Clessin, 1886)				2	3			
Pisidium hibernicum (Westerlund, 1894)					3	2		
Pisidium spp.				91	207	32	4	
Succineidae undet.				1	12	2	1	
Vertigo spp.					1			
Pupilla muscorum (Linnaeus, 1758)				3	7	3	2	
Limax spp.				1	3		2	
total 20 species (16 freshwater, 4 land)				402	715	122	15	

Table 3.4 Sample 30231

sample 30231 context subsample top of profile 8.691m OD	B-ii:05 20070 01 0–5	 02 5–10	B-ii:03 20003 03 10–20	 04 20–30	 05 30–40	 06 40–50	 07 50–60	B-ii:02 20371 08 60–70	 09 70–80	 10 80–88	 11 88–96	 12 96–102	20390 13 102–110
Valvata piscinalis (Müller, 1774)										46		2	
Galbatruncatula (Müller, 1774)										6			
Radix balthica (Linnaeus, 1784)										23			
Lymnaiedae										2			
Anisus leucostoma (Millet, 1813)										2			
Planorbidae undet.			1							2			
Sphaerium corneum (Linnaeus, 1758)										2			
Pisidium casertanum (Poli, 1791)										1			
Pisidium personatum Malm, 1855										1			
Pisidium obtusale (Lamarck, 1818)										1			
Pisidium obtusale lapponicum (Clessin, 1877)										1			
Pisidium milium (Held, 1836)													
Pisidium subtruncatum (Malm, 1855)										38			
Pisidium henslowanum (Sheppard, 1823)										4	1		
Pisidium hibernicum (Westerlund, 1894)											1		
Pisidium nitidum (Jenyns, 1832)										3			
Pisidium spp.										90	3		1
Succineidae undet.										15			
Pupilla muscorum (Linnaeus, 1758)										193	4		1
Vallonia spp.										1			
Limax spp.										3			
Trochulus hispidus (Linnaeus, 1758)										2			
total 19 species (15 freshwater, 4 land)			1							436	11		2

the other serial samples abundant shell is restricted to one or two levels. In 30231 and 30228 (*see* Tables 3.4 and 3.5) significant shell is found only in a single sample. Other single, point samples (*see* Table 3.6) are also rich in Mollusca.

In a number of samples (see 30234 – Table 3.8) partial dissolution has primarily preserved the calcite plates of limacid slugs, but only vestigial remnants of the aragonite shells of gastropods and bivalves, the latter sometimes preserved only as internal casts. There are, however, enough samples in which acid attack has been sufficiently restricted to allow considerable shell content to remain (*see* Tables 3.3, 3.4 and 3.5). As with all freshwater molluscan assemblages, large numbers of juvenile shells occurred that could only be identified to generic level (see particularly the Planorbidae and *Pisidium* spp. in Tables 3.3, 3.4 and 3.5).

However, even where the shells present seemed only lightly damaged by acid attack, evidence from amino acid racemisation data suggested that sufficient corrosion had occurred to render them impossible to date by this method (Penkman and Collins, chapter 2).

Thus, although many shells were sufficiently well preserved to allow specific identification, all had suffered some degree of acid attack.

The only family that gave particular problems in identification was the Succineidae. The species in this family have a moderately wide range of shell morphology even within species, which preclude identification beyond family level. The identity of living Succineidae is usually confirmed by dissection of the soft parts (Kerney and Cameron 1979), an option not available for fossil material, and therefore the Succineidae in the Lynford samples are identified to family level only.

Local environment as indicated by the molluscan assemblage

The molluscan assemblage consists of 30 taxa, 24 from freshwater and six from land environments. The fauna is predominantly of aquatic origin, but there are also marsh and terrestrial taxa present. In some samples the latter dominate in terms of numbers of shells (compare *Pupilla muscorum* in 30231, *see* Table 3.4), although species of aquatic Mollusca are

Table 3.5 Sample 30228

sample 30228	B-ii:03				B-ii:01		
context	20003				20139	20245	20254
subsample	01	02	03	04	05	06	07
top of profile 8.759m OD	0–12	12–22	22–31	31–34	34–36	36–43	43–58
Valvata piscinalis (Müller, 1774)	7	2	1				
Galba truncatula (Müller, 1774)	70	27					
Lymnaea stagnalis (Linnaeus, 1758)	17	5					
Radix balthica (Müller, 1774)	30	2					
Lymnaeidae	41	28	5				
Planorbis planorbis (Linnaeus, 1758)	118	8					
Anisus leucostoma (Millet, 1813)	99	6					
Anisus vortex (Linnaeus, 1758)	6						
Bathyomphalus contortus (Linnaeus, 1758)	17						
Gyraulus laevis (Alder, 1838)	14						
Gyraulus crista (Linnaeus, 1758)	34	5		1			
Planorbidae undet.	120	34	1				
Pisidium casertanum (Poli, 1791)		2					
Pisidium personatum (Malm, 1855)		2					
Pisidium obtusale lapponicum (Clessin, 1877)	600	63					
Pisidium milium (Held, 1836)	1						
Pisidium subtruncatum (Malm, 1855)		1					
Pisidium hibernicum (Westerlund, 1894)	25						
Pisidium spp.	261	150	2	1			1
Succineidae undet	15	8	1				
Pupilla muscorum (Linnaeus, 1758)	13	5					
Deroceras/Limax spp.	3	5	1		1		5
total 19 species (16 freshwater, 3 land)	1491	353	11	2	1		6

Table 3.6 Samples 63201, 30001, 30081, 61413 and 30083

facies context	B-ii:02 20371 (63201)	B-ii:03 20003			
sample top of profile (metres OD)	30213 7.86	30001 8.362	30081 8.591	61473 8.51	30083 8.495
Valvata piscinalis (Müller, 1774)	11				
Bithynia tentaculata (Linnaeus, 1758) opercula		1			
Galba truncatula (Müller, 1774)			25	2	
Stagnicola palustris (Müller, 1774)				1	
Lymnaea stagnalis (Linnaeus, 1758)			9		
Radix balthica (Linnaeus, 1758)			28	1	
Lymnaeidae	14		18	36	
Planorbis planorbis (Linnaeus, 1758)			45	13	
Anisus leucostoma (Millet, 1813)	1		49	16	1
Bathyomphalus contortus (Linnaeus, 1758)			4		
Gyraulus laevis (Alder, 1838)			4	2	
Gyraulus crista (Linnaeus, 1758)			6	1	
Planorbidae undet.			63	13	
Pisidium casertanum (Poli, 1791)				1	
Pisidium obtusale lapponicum (Clessin, 1877)			191	86	1
Pisidium hibernicum (Westerlund, 1894)			13		
Pisidium spp.	13	2	194	63	
Succineidae undet.	5		9	1	
Vertigo spp.	1				
Pupilla muscorum (Linnaeus, 1758)	159	1	4	3	
Vallonia spp.	1				
Limax spp.			1	2	
Trichia spp.	2				
total 20 species (14 freshwater, 6 land)	198	4	653	240	2

Table 3.7 Sample 30201

sample 30201	B-ii:05			B-ii:03			B-ii:01
context	20005		20002	20003			20004
top of profile 8.963m OD	0–10	10–20	20–30	30–40	40–50	50–60	60–70
Valvata piscinalis (Müller, 1774)					1		
Planorbis planorbis (Linnaeus, 1758)							1
Pisidium spp.			1				
total 3 freshwater species			1		1		1

Table 3.8 Sample 30234

sample 30234 context		B-ii:03 20021			B-ii:02 20355
subsample top of profile 7.974m OD	1 0–10	2 10–20	3 20–30	4 30–40	5 40–50
Valvata piscinalis (Müller, 1774)				1	
Bithynia tentaculata (Linnaeus, 1758)				1	
Lymnaeidae		1			
Pisidium lilljeborgii (Clessin, 1886)				1	
Desoceres/Limax spp.		2	1	2	
total 5 species (4 freshwater, 1 land)		3	1	5	

most numerous in all samples examined. The serial samples show little environmental change through the sequence, with the assemblage as a whole being one of a shallow, well-vegetated body of standing water. Because of the lack of change in the fauna, the sediment was probably deposited in a short time-span over tens, rather than hundreds or thousands, of years.

At certain levels within Unit B-ii:02 (20371) there is evidence of flowing water gaining access to the water body. In Sample 30231 (Table 3.4) the two most abundant freshwater taxa are *Valvata piscinalis* and *Pisidium subtruncatum*. Both of these species prefer moving to still water (Kerney 1999) and are also found at greater water depths (2–5m for *V. piscinalis*) than the other aquatic species in the sequence. The impression of a flood event allowing the river access to the pool is reinforced by the high counts for the land snail *Pupilla muscorum* in 30231. Pools without an inflowing stream or connection to an active river channel seldom contain any land shells unless there are significant water level changes to drown the land fauna and wash them into the pool. Without water-level changes of this type land snails do not occur in such water bodies except for individuals that fall in by chance (Jones *et al* 2000). In the case of rivers, floods wash land shells from the flood plain to be deposited in the fluvial sediments with the aquatic fauna of the river. The high totals for *P. muscorum*, along with those for *V. piscinalis* and *P. subtruncatum*, probably therefore indicate a flood into the pool, which was the site of deposition. It is also significant that four specimens of the river bivalve *Pisidium henslowanum*, which is unusual in closed pools (Kerney 1999), also occur in 30231.

The occurrence of six species of planorbid (*Planorbis planorbis*, *Anisus leucostoma*, *Anisus vortex*, *Bathyomphalus contortus*, *Gyraulus laevis*, *Gyraulus crista*) suggest that the water body had considerable stands of aquatic macrophytes growing in it, as these gastropods primarily live on waterweed. The sporadic occurrence of *Valvata cristata* and the bivalve *Pisidium milium*, both inhabitants of weed-rich water, also reinforce this environmental indicator.

The high numbers of the bivalve species *Pisidium obtusale lapponicum* suggest cool water, as this species, although recorded living in Britain at depth in large, deep lakes (Lough Neagh, N. Ireland; Ellis 1978), is only found in shallow water in subarctic and Arctic areas (Kuiper *et al* 1989). *Pisidium lilljeborgii* and *Pisidium hibernicum* are also regarded as northern species by Kerney (1999) and are found most commonly in Scotland, although both have ranges that in Britain at present sporadically extend into the lowlands of the south.

Although a number of the samples from Lynford have high values for *Anisus leucostoma*, a species capable of living in ephemeral pools (the aquatic slums of Sparks 1961), the sparse representation of *Pisidium casertanum* and *Pisidium personatum*, two other typical slum species, together with the abundance of shells of species that avoid slum conditions, indicate that the pool in which deposition took place was a permanent one not subject to complete drying-up at any season.

The number of terrestrial species is very limited. Only six taxa are recorded in all of the samples. The most abundant by far are shells of Succineidae and *Pupilla muscorum*. The Succineidae are a family of marsh snails that live on emergent aquatic vegetation and in swampy river and lake marginal areas. They were probably washed into the Lynford pool at times of river flood, as discussed above.

Pupilla muscorum is generally regarded as a species typical of dry grassland and scree (Kerney and Cameron 1979). However, it has been known since the 1960s that the tall, cylindrical, morphotype of *P. muscorum* found in cold stage deposits, and at Lynford, is a common associate of the Succineidae, despite their seemingly contrasting ecological requirements (Kerney 1963, 1971). There are two possible explanations for this ecological paradox: that one or other of the two species has changed its ecological requirements since Pleistocene times, or that the two species have been washed together from their contrasting habitats. Of these two possiblilities, the distinctive morphotype of *P. muscorum* seems to give a clue to the true state of affairs. This form, given subspecific rank by some authors as *Pupilla muscorum pratensis* Clessin 1871 (see Turner *et al* 1998; Gedda, 2001), is unlike the small grassland form of the species of modern Britain, but similar to the form of *P. muscorum* which today inhabits wet meadows in Scandinavia (Gedda 2001). Thus it seems most likely that the Lynford examples lived in similar swampy conditions to the Succineidae.

The other land taxa are *Trichia hispida*, *Vallonia*, *Vertigo* spp. and *Limax* spp. The first of these lives in areas of sparse vegetation and disturbed ground, and is often found as an associate of *P. muscorum* in cool environment deposits (Kerney 1963, 1971). The *Vallonia* species present was represented by a single, broken and juvenile shell (Sample 30231; *see* Table 3.4). Species of this genus inhabit grassland and swamp in modern Europe, environments not inconsistent with the indications of land habitats from the other terrestrial molluscs.

The *Vertigo* spp. are represented only as the apices of the shells. With this genus, the diagnostic characteristics of the species are found in the shell aperture, so it is impossible to identify the species present from the apex alone. There are several species of *Vertigo*, which today inhabit subarctic or montane areas of Europe (Kerney and Cameron, 1979), and which might be identified from these shells.

The plates of limacid slugs are relatively common in the deposits at Lynford, due, in part, to their resistance to corrosion in acid environments. The molluscan totals of the heavily leached sample 30234 (*see* Table 3.8) are actually dominated by slug plates. However, most species of limacidae are poor indicators of local environment as they live in any damp habitat.

Regional environment indicated by the Mollusca

The regional environment is more difficult to determine from the Mollusca than that of the pond and its surrounding area. The terrestrial fauna is more sensitive to climate than the aquatic Mollusca, which are buffered from the atmosphere by their watery habitat, but their limited numbers do not allow precise climatic inferences to be determined. However, aspects of the fauna do give some indications of the climate during deposition.

One of these indications is the number of species present in the fauna. In modern Europe molluscan species numbers decrease steadily in more northerly latitudes with increasingly cold and open, unvegetated landscapes restricting land taxa, and with freshwater taxa limited by the length of time ice cover persists into the summer (Kerney and Cameron 1979; Økland 1990). Thus assemblages with more than 50 species present are invariably interglacial in type (Keen *et al* 1999; Schreve *et al* 2002). Faunas with fewer than ten species are usually of full cold stage type (Holyoak 1982; Keen 1987). Faunas with species counts intermediate between these extremes are the product of climates neither of full glacial nor fully temperate character. The Lynford assemblage of 30 taxa would therefore indicate a climate colder than Norfolk today, but not one of glacial intensity.

A second indicator of regional climate is the modern geographical ranges of species. All of the species in the Lynford fauna are found in the British Isles at present, although *P. muscorum* is only represented by the large form of this species (see above), and *Pisidium obtusale lapponicum* is only found living in the cold depths of Lough Neagh, Northern Ireland (Ellis 1978), and lives in shallow water only in subarctic and Arctic latitudes (Kuiper *et al* 1989). However, the 30 species at Lynford are exclusively those tolerant of diverse climates and that today range up to, and in some cases beyond, the Arctic Circle. That the climate was not fully Arctic, is however suggested by the presence of limacid slugs in almost all of the samples that have produced Mollusca, as only two species of this family occur north of the Arctic Circle in modern Europe (Kerney and Cameron 1979). The presence of *T. hispida* also supports such conditions, since this species is only found north of the Arctic Circle at the Norwegian coast where the moderating effects of the Atlantic maintain higher temperatures. The occurrence of *Pisidium henslowanum* might also indicate cool rather than truly cold conditions as this species is not currently found north of the Arctic Circle in Europe, although it does live in Siberia where cold winters are moderated by hot summers (Kuiper *et al* 1989; Kerney 1999).

Summary of the environment according to the molluscan evidence

A summary of the local depositional environment as indicated by the Mollusca suggests that the site of deposition was for most of the time a permanent, shallow body of water with considerable aquatic vegetation and a silty or fine sand substrate. The river still had access to this floodplain pool and the land surface around the water body was a muddy swamp. However, there were also times when water flow and depth were increased, probably due to floods from the nearby river channel or seasonal fluctuations in water intake. The limited land mollusc fauna suggests that areas of wet grassland and swamp were predominant around the water body.

Climatic interpretation based on the molluscan evidence

Although Mollusca have been recorded from numbers of cold stage sites across southern Britain (see Holyoak 1982 and Keen 1987 for summaries), most of the faunas described are from fluvial contexts in the Thames catchment (Gibbard et al 1982; Kerney et al 1982; Coope et al 1997; Maddy et al 1998) or from small ephemeral streams, often on Chalk or Jurassic Limestone bedrock (Briggs and Gilbertson 1973; Keen, unpublished data from Swalecliffe, Kent, and 2001). The former, because of their origin in large rivers, exhibit a slightly different molluscan fauna from that at Lynford. In these contexts, taxa living in moving water, such as *Ancylus fluviatilis* (Müller 1774), are common. However, many of the other species present, such as the Lymnaeidae and Planorbidae, are also found at Lynford. The small chalkland streams commonly have very large numbers of Succineidae and *Pupilla muscorum*, which totally dominate the molluscan assemblage being swept from nearby land surfaces in the spring thaw.

There also appears to be an element of climatic control over these faunal types, in that the large river assemblages are predominantly those dating to the relatively warm Upton Warren Interstadial, according to associated insect faunas and radiocarbon dates (see Coope et al 1997 for a discussion). In contrast, the Succineidae/*Pupilla muscorum* assemblages derive from Arctic conditions and often include the Arctic/Alpine gastropod species *Columella columella* (von Martens 1830) as a significant minority constituent.

The molluscan assemblage from Lynford is differentiated palaeoecologically from the faunas of both large rivers and cold stages noted above. In terms of local environment, the Lynford deposits accumulated in a pond rather than a large river, or a stream that flowed only intermittently, perhaps in the Arctic spring flood. Regional conditions were also intermediate between the warmth of the Upton Warren Interstadial and the true Arctic climate of the ephemeral stream sediments previously described. Although all of these types of assemblage are largely made up of tolerant molluscan taxa found in a wide range of habitats, the slight differences between them in species composition allows the identification of the Lynford environment as distinct in both local and regional palaeoenvironment from most other sites described in the literature.

Stratigraphic implications of the Mollusca

The molluscan assemblage from Lynford gives no direct indicators of age. Molluscan biostratigraphy is only possible using the large numbers of taxa found in interglacial assemblages (Keen 2001), as cold stage faunas are invariably made up of the same climatically tolerant species irrespective of age (Briggs and Gilbertson 1973; Kerney 1977; Holyoak 1982; Keen 1987). Although the Lynford assemblage is environmentally distinct from most other sites of similar aspect, this might not be significant in terms of age, as the cool rather than cold Lynford sequence might represent either an episode in its own right separate from the Upton Warren or other named stages, or a short-lived episode in the warming or cooling phase of some other climatically distinct phase. The potential during the last cold stage for episodes of cold, cool or warm type, repeated on a number of occasions, has been indicated by the identification of numerous short-lived climatic-change events in the oceanographic record of the North Atlantic and in the Greenland ice cores (Bond et al 1993). It is therefore difficult to associate any individual molluscan assemblage with a named interstadial or any other phase. Furthermore, due to the extent of corrosion of the shells caused by the low pH of the sediments at the site, it is not possible to provide reliable age estimates for Lynford based on amino acid ratios.

3.3 The pollen assemblages

F M L Green

Sampling and laboratory procedures

The study of pollen preserved in the Lynford deposits allows the reconstruction of environmental conditions at the site during the period of channel abandonment, as represented by Association B. With this aim, a total of 46

*Fig 3.1
Schematic section illustrating pollen sample locations within the palaeochannels.*

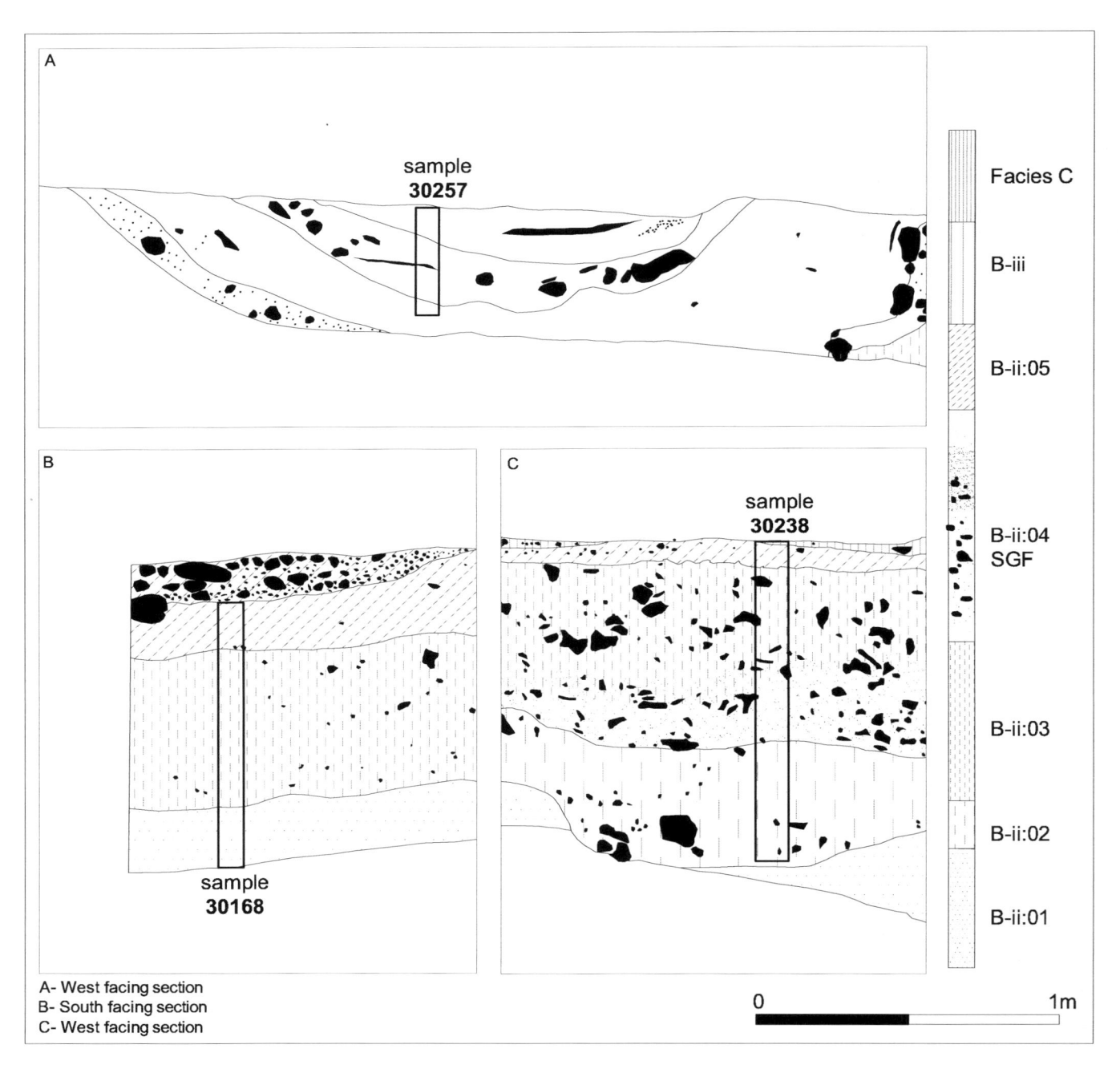

samples from three separate sampling locations within the channel were prepared for pollen analysis. Sediments were sampled from the main palaeochannel (20032) (Association B-ii) and smaller palaeochannel (20121) (Association B-iii) incised into the upper sediments of the main palaeochannel. These comprise sample numbers 30168 (monolith and bagged samples) and 30238 (monolith and bagged samples) from the sand and organic sediments of Association B-ii and 30257 (monolith) composed of sand and organic sediments from Association B-iii. A summary of the lithology and the relevant context numbers are given in Figs 3.1 to 3.4. A schematic section illustrating pollen sample locations within the palaeochannels is shown in Fig 3.1.

Subsamples of 10–20mm³ were cut from the cleaned faces of the monoliths, and similar volumes were obtained from the bagged samples. The sediment was disaggregated by boiling in 5 per cent sodium hydroxide, with silicates removed by heating at 80°C in hyrodrofluoric acid and cellulose by acetolysis

(Faegri and Iverson 1975). The remaining material was stained and mounted on slides. Slides were viewed under magnifications of x400 and x1000 and a minimum count of 200 non-tree pollen grains attempted for each sample. Pollen identifications were assisted by reference to Moore *et al* (1991) and Andrew (1984). Fungal spores referred to Van Hoeve and Hendrikse (1998). Diagrams were drawn using TILIA (Grimm 2005) with most data expressed as a percentage of total land pollen (tlp), ie trees, shrubs and terrestrial herbs. Note that aquatics, spores and unidentified are expressed as a percentage of tlp plus aquatics, and algae and fungi are expressed independently as a percentage of tlp (ie not including algae or fungi in the final sum). It is acknowledged that some of the plant nomenclature might need to be updated to Stace (1997) but an older nomenclature (Fitter *et al* 1985) has been used for ease of comparison with other published sites. The diagram has been divided into local pollen zones (LPZs) using the constrained incremental sum of squares (CONISS) in the TILIA program (Grimm 1987).

The pollen assemblages

Pollen and spores were obtained in good condition from most samples, but at relatively low concentrations. Several coverslips were counted in some samples and in all cases two were counted. Despite this, many samples did not contain 200 land pollen types. A slight increase in corroded pollen was observed in the upper samples from 30168 and pollen was sparse and of poor quality in the upper three samples of 30257. Although not noted in the figures and tables, high concentrations of framboids (spherules of iron pyrite) were found in many deposits. The pollen results are shown in Figs 3.2 to 3.4 and the pollen and spore counts in Tables 3.9 to 3.11. The common names for the taxa identified are referred to in the tables but not in the text. The samples are referred to by their depth from the top of the monolith or section and not by their sample numbers.

Profile 1: 30168 (Fig 3.2 and Table 3.9)

Profile 1 was from the centre of the main palaeochannel (20032) (Association B-ii) (*see* Fig 3.1). In total, 17 samples were analysed from this location. A thin (20–40mm) deposit of whitish carbonate-rich, silty sand (20004) (Association B-ii) (Unit B-ii:01) formed the lowest deposit in the palaeochannel, and above this 560mm of organic sands (20,003) (Association B-ii) (Unit B-ii:03) were observed. Overlying the organic sands was a grey sand with silt lamina (20070) (Association B-ii) (Unit B-ii:05), which in places was highly deformed. The top of the sequence (20070) was truncated by coarse, orange flint gravel (20009) (Association C).

The entire sequence is dominated by non-tree pollen (90–100 per cent tlp) with tree pollen contributing generally less than 5 per cent of tlp. Tree pollen included *Betula*, *Pinus* and *Alnus*, with lesser quantities of *Abies* and *Picea*. With the exception of the uppermost sample, Cyperaceae was the most abundant pollen type (60–85 per cent) with lesser, although significant, amounts of Poaceae (25–30 per cent). Shrubs were almost totally absent, with the exception of rare *Corylus*, occasional *Salix* and a small peak in *Calluna* and *Vaccinium* at 240mm and 280mm.

Throughout the sequence there was a wide range of terrestrial plants suggesting a variety of local habitats. The herbs include a wide range of heliophytes, specifically *Armeria maritima*, *Artemisia*, *Helianthemum*, *Linum anglicum*, *Thalictrum* and *Selaginella selaginoides*. All of these are widespread in Devensian deposits with many having a modern northern and Alpine distribution (such as *Armeria maritima*, *Thalictrum* and *Selaginella selaginoides*). Poaceae (20 per cent tlp) indicates the presence either of grassland or *Phragmites* (reed). Various types of grassland can be described, based on the pollen from other herbs. Relatively tall, dry grassy areas with a calcareous soil are suggested by the presence of *Centaurea nigra*, *Campanula*, *Helianthemum*, *Gentianella*, *Linum anglicum* (an isolated grain was identified at 240mm), *Sanguisorba* cf. *officinalis* and possibly Umbelliferae. *Helianthemum* pollen might be from one of several species (probably *H. canum*), most of which grow on very open, dry, well-drained calcareous soils. The pollen of *Helianthemum* is frequently identified in Devensian deposits; however, today this species has a particularly southern range (not occurring north of 62°C in Scandinavia) (Godwin 1975). *Linum anglicum* also appears regularly in Mid-Late Devensian deposits (Bell 1970; Godwin 1975). It is a short–medium plant of dry calcareous

Fig 3.2
Pollen percentage data (>1%) Lynford Quarry (37095 STD) sample 30168.

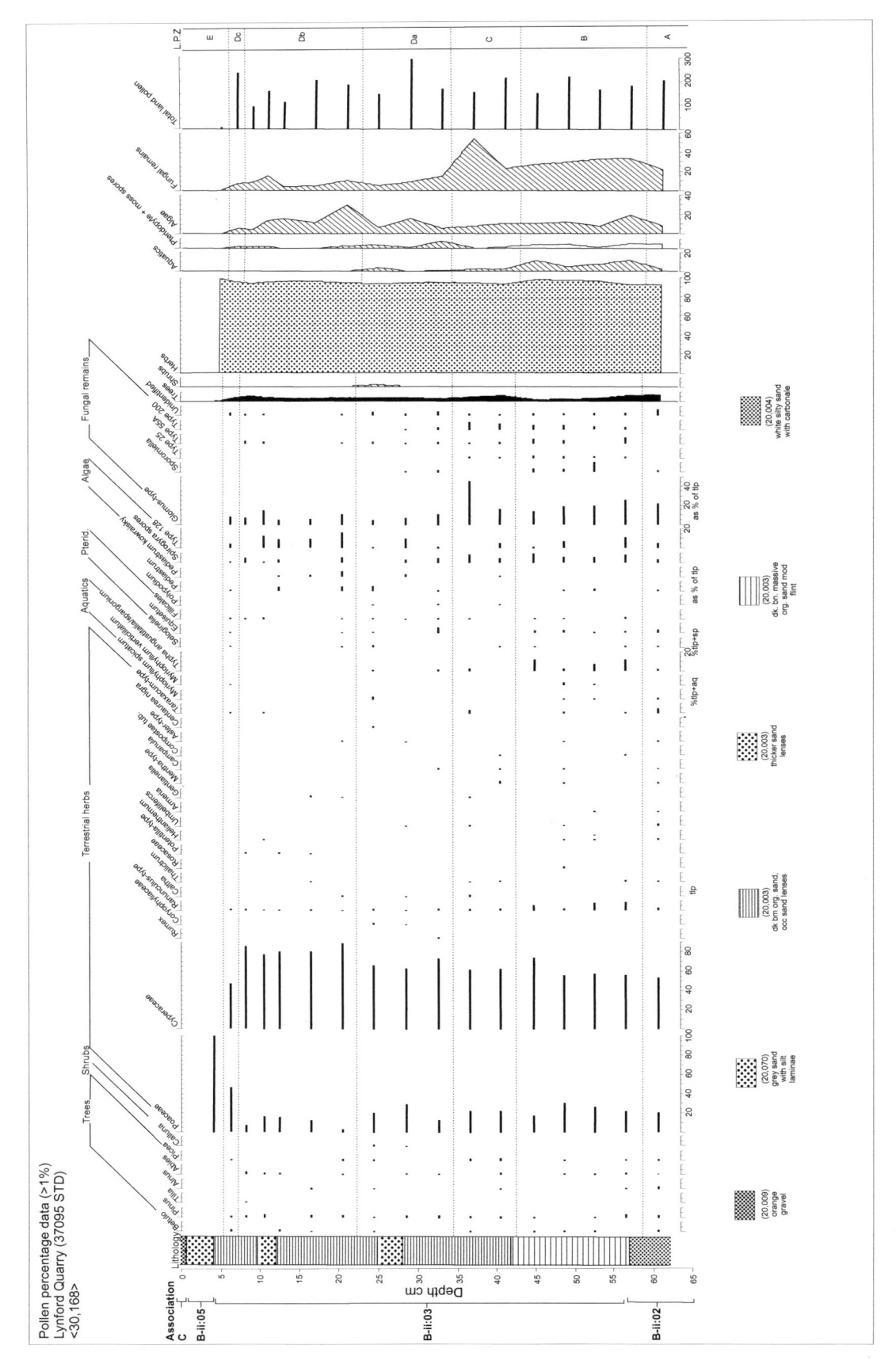

Table 3.9 Total pollen and spores from Lynford Quarry, sample 30168

facies context	B-ii:05 20070			B-ii:03 20003					
depth (cm) from top of section	4.0	6.0	8.0	10.0	12.0	16.0	20.0	24.0	28.0
trees									
Betula (birch)		4			2	1		2	
Pinus (pine)		4	2	5		4	4	1	7
Tilia (lime)			1						
Alnus (alder)						1		1	
Abies (fir)			2	1	1		1		3
Picea (spruce)		1					2	1	
shrubs									
Corylus/Myrica (hazel, bog myrtle)						1			
Salix (willow)									
Calluna (heather)								2	1
Vaccinium (bilberry/crowberry)									2
terrestrial herbs									
Poaceae (grasses)	6	108	6		16	24	5	30	85
Cyperaceae (sedges)		112	80		88	165	167	99	186
Polygonum (bistort)									
Oxyria type (eg mountain sorrel, curled, clustered, wood dock)									
Rumex (dock)									
Chenopodiaceae (goosefoot family)									
Caryophyllaceae (pink family)					1	3		1	6
Spergula type (eg corn spurrey)									
Ranunculus-type (incl buttercup/crowfoot)		2	1		1	1	1	3	1
Caltha (marsh marigold)							1		1
Thalictrum (meadow rue)						1			
cf. *Anemone*-type (eg wood, yellow, blue anemone)						1			
cf. *Papaver* sp. (poppy)									
Cruciferae (cabbage family)									
Drosera (sundew)								1	
Rosaceae (rose family)									
Filipendula (meadowsweet)									
Sanguisorba (eg great burnet)									
Potentilla-type (cinquefoils/tormentil)			1		1	1		1	
Linum (flax)									
Helianthemum (rock roses)				1					
Umbelliferae (carrot family)									1
Armeria (thrift)									
Menyanthes (bogbean)								1	
Gentianella (eg field gentian)						3	1		
Galium-type (bedstraw)								1	
Labiatae (eg mint, woundwort, hemp-nettle)						1			
Mentha-type (mint)									
Scrophulariaceae (figwort family, eg mullein, toadflax, foxglove, speedwell)									
Plantago major/media (greater, hoary plantain)									1
Plantago maritime (sea plantain)									
Succisa (devilsbit scabious)									
Campanula (campanula)									
Compositae tub. (daisy family)									
Aster-type (eg daisy, aster, cudweed, coltsfoot, ragwort)							1		1
Artemisia (mugwort/wormwood)									1
Centaurea nigra (black knapweed)								2	

continued ▶

Table 3.9 – *continued*

facies *context*	B-ii:05 20070			B-ii:03 20003					
depth (cm) from top of section	4.0	6.0	8.0	10.0	12.0	16.0	20.0	24.0	28.0
Compositae *lig.* (incl dandelion, hawkweed, hawsbeard, hawkbit, sow thistle)									
Taraxacum-type (eg dandelion)		2		1					
Anthemis-type (incl chamomile, yarrow, ox-eye daisy, tansy, feverfew)									
aquatics									
Myriophyllum spicatum (spiked water milfoil)								4	
Myriophyllum verticillatum (whorled water milfoil)		1							
Potamogeton (pond weed)									
Typha latifolia (bulrush)				1				1	
Typha angustifolia/Sparganium (lesser bulrush, bur-reed)								1	
fern spores									
Selaginella selaginoides (lesser clubmoss)		1					1	3	
Equisetum (horsetail)		1					1	1	
Filicales (undifferentiated ferns)		1	1	2				1	1
Polypodium (polypody)								1	
moss spores									
Sphagnum									
algae									
Pediastrum		1			4		8	8	
Pediastrum kawraiskyi					1	4	10		7
Mougeotia									2
Zygnema				1					
Spirogyra spores		2	4	1	3		10		9
Type 128		10		20	10	20	30	2	31
fungal remains									
Glomus-type		17	6	23	5	10	20	7	21
Sporomiella									2
Type 20									
Type 25									
Type 90									1
Type 55A			2				1	2	3
Type 200									1
foraminifera									
foram test linings				2					
planktonic forams									1
unidentified									
unidentified		5	1				1	5	5
total land pollen	6	233	93	155	109	204	187	147	296

facies *context*				B-ii:03 20003				B-ii:01 20004
depth (cm) from top of section	32.0	36.0	40.0	44.0	48.0	52.0	56.0	60.0
trees								
Betula (birch)		2		1	2	1		3

continued ▶

Table 3.9 – continued

facies context			B-ii:03 20003					B-ii:01 20004
depth (cm) from top of section	32.0	36.0	40.0	44.0	48.0	52.0	56.0	60.0
Pinus (pine)	3	2	3	1		1	5	4
Tilia (lime)								
Alnus (alder)			2				1	5
Abies (fir)	2		3		2	2	3	1
Picea (spruce)		3	4		1		1	1
shrubs								
Corylus/Myrica (hazel, bog myrtle)			1			1	1	
Salix (willow)							1	
Calluna (heather)								
Vaccinium (bilberry/crowberry)								
terrestrial herbs								
Poaceae (grasses)	22	34	49	26	66	43	39	42
Cyperaceae (sedges)	125	97	137		123	93	103	111
Polygonum (bistort)				1				
Oxyria type (eg mountain sorrel, curled, clustered, wood dock)						1		
Rumex (dock)	2							
Chenopodiaceae (goosefoot family)					1			
Caryophyllaceae (pink family)	8		2	110	4		2	4
Spergula type (eg corn spurrey)				1		1		
Ranunculus-type (incl buttercup/crowfoot)	3	3	4	8	4	13	16	5
Caltha (marsh marigold)		2						
Thalictrum (meadow rue)		1	3				3	3
cf. *Anemone*-type (eg wood, yellow, blue anemone)								
cf. *Papaver* sp. (poppy)								1
Cruciferae (cabbage family)		1					1	1
Drosera (sundew)								
Rosaceae (rose family)					3			
Filipendula (meadowsweet)					1			
Sanguisorba (eg great burnet)				1				
Potentilla-type (cinquefoils/tormentil)								
Linum (flax)								
Helianthemum (rock roses)					1	1		3
Umbelliferae (carrot family)		2			1			6
Armeria (thrift)						1		2
Menyanthes (bogbean)								
Gentianella (eg field gentian)		2						
Galium-type (bedstraw)								
Labiatae (eg mint, woundwort, hemp-nettle)								
Mentha-type (mint)				4	1			1
Scrophulariaceae (figwort family, eg mullein, toadflax, foxglove, speedwell)	1		1		1			
Plantago major/media (greater, hoary plantain)					1			
Plantago maritime (sea plantain)			1					
Succisa (devilsbit scabious)		1						
Campanula (campanula)	2		1		1			1
Compositae tub. (daisy family)			1				2	
Aster-type (eg daisy, aster, cudweed, coltsfoot, ragwort)					1			2
Artemisia (mugwort/wormwood)			1		1			1
Centaurea nigra (black knapweed)								
Compositae lig. (incl dandelion, hawkweed, hawsbeard, hawkbit, sow thistle)						1	1	
Taraxacum-type (eg dandelion)		5		4		1		10

continued ▶

Table 3.9 – *continued*

facies	B-ii:03							B-ii:01
context	20003							20004
depth (cm) from top of section	32.0	36.0	40.0	44.0	48.0	52.0	56.0	60.0
Anthemis-type (incl chamomile, yarrow, ox-eye daisy, tansy, feverfew)						1		
aquatics								
Myriophyllum spicatum (spiked water milfoil)					1	1		2
Myriophyllum verticillatum (whorled water milfoil)					5	1		
Potamogeton (pond weed)		1						
Typha latifolia (bulrush)								
Typha angustifolia/Sparganium (lesser bulrush, bur-reed)	2	3	5	20	5	12	23	3
fern spores								
Selaginella selaginoides (lesser clubmoss)			1	1			1	2
Equisetum (horsetail)	10			4	6	1	3	7
Filicales (undifferentiated ferns)	1	1		1	2		3	
Polypodium (polypody)	2		1					
moss spores								
Sphagnum							1	
algae								
Pediastrum	1				1	3		1
Pediastrum kawraiskyi			3					
Mougeotia						1		
Zygnema								
Spirogyra spores	7	13	10	14	11	8	14	6
Type 128	2		10	2	15		20	10
fungal remains								
Glomus-type	18	70	34	20	40	31	46	44
Sporomiella	3			6	7	16		3
Type 20						1		
Type 25		2	1	3	3	2	1	
Type 90								
Type 55A	3	1	4	7	7		11	
Type 200	3	12	12	6	10	4	3	
foraminifera								
foram test linings								
planktonic forams								
unidentified								
unidentified	5	3	1	2	3	3	3	13
total land pollen	169	155	216	148	219	161	180	207

grassland and considered to be a coloniser of open habitats. A single grain of *Sanguisorba* cf. *officinalis* was identified in the sample at 440mm. It is a relatively tall plant of open, damp, calcareous grassland which today has a southern modern distribution, not extending north of 60°N in Scandinavia, but with a distinctively continental, rather maritime distribution (West 1979). The pollen of *Sanguisorba* cf. *officinalis* is found frequently in Middle-Late Glacial deposits but is less common in the Flandrian (Godwin 1975).

Also present are taxa characteristic of bare disturbed ground or short turf, including *Armeria maritima* (a facultative halophyte that tolerates but does not require saline conditions), *Artemisia*, Aster-type, Caryophyllacaea, Compositae tub, *Plantago major/*

media, Taraxacum (*c* 5 per cent tlp) and *Thalictrum* (if *T. alpinum*). The climatic inferences that can be made based on this group of plants are limited, but the presence of *Armeria maritima* (possibly B type) might suggest winter snow cover, though it will not grow in winter temperatures below −8°C (Iversen 1954).

Damp and/or mossy grassland environments were indicated by the presence of *Succisa* (single grain at 360mm) and by low but consistent occurrences of *Selaginella selaginoides*. The latter is a species with a restricted modern distribution in Britain, occurring locally in northerly hill habitats. It is most abundant in extreme northern areas, particularly northern Fennoscandia.

There was a consistent presence of *Ranunculus* type in all samples, increasing to about 10 per cent tlp in association with the most aquatic phase of the profile. Although the pollen of *Ranunculus* type includes plants of widely diverse habitats, and the pollen is difficult to distinguish, comparison with a pollen-type slide suggests the *Ranunculus* identified is *Ranunculus aquatilis* (common water crowfoot). This plant is typical of still or slow-flowing water up to 1m in depth.

Cyperaceae was the most abundant pollen type. The Cyperaceae are not exclusively aquatic but it is probable, given the level of abundance, that they represent one or many species of aquatic and semi-aquatic sedges. Although *Phragmites* (reed) is not easily distinguishable from the Poaceae, the overall environmental conditions suggest the possibility of its presence as part of the semi-aquatic flora. Therefore the local vegetation was probably one of reed and sedge swamp.

There were a few identifiable taxa associated with fen or marsh conditions, and these included isolated grains of acidophilous *Menyanthes* (suggesting localised areas of raised bog), Mentha type, *Filipendula*, and possibly *Potentilla* type (if *P. palustris*).

Emergent aquatic vegetation was represented by *Typha latifolia* and by the more abundant *Typha angustifolia/Sparganium* type that would have grown within a shallow water body and on its wet margins. True aquatics include *Myriophyllum spicatum*, characteristic of calcareous water, and the more abundant acidophile *Myriophyllum alterniflorum*. This implies that the water was more acid than the surrounding grasslands.

Also present were algae of shallow pools or slow-flowing water: *Spirogyra* and *Pediastrum* spp., *Pediastrum kawraiskyi* and Type 128. *Spirogyra* suggests algal blooms probably in temporary, shallow water. It is probable that *Spirogyra* sporulates either in pools isolated from the main river and containing fresh to slightly brackish, stagnant sun-warmed water, or in slow-moving shallow water surrounded by sedge fen (Van Geel 1976). *Pediastrum kawraiskyi* is a colonial green algae reported from Europe and North America, occurring in small ponds and lakes with clean, nutrient-poor waters. It is rare in the British Isles today, but has been recorded from Ormesby Broad (Griffiths 1927), and Loch Sharrey, Caithness (John *et al* 2002). Its presence suggests at least a small body of open water. Type 128 is considered indicative of shallow meso-eutrophic fresh water (Pals *et al* 1980). *Pediastrum* has been recorded as an indicator of increasing water depth (Stewart *et al* 1984), and is not regarded as typical of ephemeral water bodies in the same way as *Spirogyra*.

Other non-pollen types identified in this sequence include *Glomus*-type bodies (mycorrhizal fungi), which are only found within aerobic bioactive soils (Bagyaraj and Varma 1995). Since such fungi do not grow under anaerobic/aquatic conditions and are not dispersed far by wind, they are probably derived from the erosion of surrounding soils. Spores of the fungi *Sporormiella* were identified in several samples with a distinct peak in LPZB. *Sporormiella* is a dung fungus and is strongly associated with dense populations of herbivores. In particular its abundance has been related to Pleistocene megafaunas (Davis 1987), and might indicate the presence of grazing animals such as mammoths on the adjacent grasslands. Other fungal spores identified include Type 25 (compare *Clasterospoirium caricinum*) (Van Hoeve and Hendrikse 1998), which occurs most frequently in LPZB and C. Interestingly *Clasterospoirium caricinum* is a fungus found on the leaves of sedges in marshes subjected to periodic flooding (Van Hoeve and Hendrikse 1998). Type 55A (Van Geel 1978) was found in almost all samples. This fungal spore is part of the Sordariaceae and is associated with eu-meso eutrophic environments and might indicate wet stands of helophytes (marsh plants) and can also be associated with animal dung. Type 200 (Van Geel *et al* 1989) occurs frequently at low abundances in the lower deposits of 30168. It is a fungal microfossil, found in association with *Equisetum fluviatile*, *Phragmites* and *Carex rostrata* (all of which are consistent with the pollen identified). Type 200 is characteristic of the first stages following the drying-out of temporary pools.

Iron pyrite framboids occurred in several samples, principally those of mid LPZB and from LPZDa and Db. Framboids are indicative of stagnant, anaerobic water rich in organic elements (Wiltshire *et al* 1994). Their presence in only a proportion of samples suggests the possibility of differential post-depositional preservation that affected either the development of framboids, or indicates that environmental conditions were not constant during the accumulation of the deposit.

Foraminifera were rare in the pollen preparations, with a single test noted in sample 280mm. The foraminifera were derived from the underlying chalk, and suggest an input of clastic material from the chalk in the sequence. The single foraminifera suggests there was a minimal input of such sediments, but calcite tests could have been removed by post-depositional dissolution in the acidic organic deposits.

Local pollen zones

Despite the overall similarity of the sequence in profile 1, it was possible to identify five local pollen zones (LPZ) A-E, with three further subdivisions of zone D. The data are described below, zone by zone (*see* Fig 3.1)

LPZ A (600–570mm): This single sample was from white, silty sand with carbonate (20004) of Association B-ii (Unit B-ii:01). Tree pollen was found at low frequencies (c 5 per cent) and includes *Betula*, *Pinus* and *Alnus* with lesser quantities of *Abies* and *Picea*. Of the non-tree pollen, Cyperaceae was the most abundant (60 per cent tlp) with Poaceae contributing about 20 per cent. There was a wide range of terrestrial herbs including those of open and disturbed habitats (*Aster* and *Taraxacum*) and calcareous grassland eg *Armeria maritima Campanula*, *Thalictrum* and *Helianthemum*. *Glomus* (soil fungi) was moderately abundant, suggesting inclusion of surrounding soils into the deposit.

Low levels of aquatic pollen and spores such as *Myriophyllum spicatum* and *Typha angustitifolia/Sparganium* type and the algae *Pediastrum*, suggest at least localised open water of moderate water depth (c 1m), and spores of *Spyirogyra* indicate limited areas of probably shallower water. Marginal marsh would have supported *Carex*, *Equisetum* and algae Type 128. Occasional spores of the dung fungus *Sporormiella* indicate herbivores grazing in the locality.

LPZ B (570–420mm): This zone was defined by the massive unlaminated organic sands (20003) of B-ii (Unit B-ii:03) and contained a similar pollen assemblage to LPZA. The principal difference was an increase in both aquatic pollen and fungal spores of all types, in particular *Sporormiella*.

Myriophyllum spicatum and *Myriophyllum verticillatum* and probably *Ranunculus* Type (*R*. cf. *aquatilis*, indicate still or very slow-flowing water of up to 1m in depth. Stagnant water conditions at this time are indicated by the presence of iron pyrite framboids. Associated with open water, *Spirogyra* perhaps grew in the more temporary pools. Fungal spore Type 200 also reflects the drying-out of temporary pools and Type 25 indicates periodic flooding. *Typha angustitifolia/Sparganium*, *Carex* and *Equisetum* indicate marginal marsh. Fungal spore Type 55A was identified in most samples and is associated with both marsh plants and dung.

Glomus was also relatively important, 20 per cent of tlp excluding fungal spores reflecting moderate input of soils from the catchment. There is a strong peak in the dung fungus *Sporormiella* that probably entered the deposits with soil eroded from the grazed valley sides.

LPZ C (420–340mm): At 420mm the nature of the deposit changes to a laminated organic sand (20003) with occasional two- to three-centimetre-deep lenses of clean sands. The palynology of this zone reflects this change in sedimentology. There was a sudden decline in aquatic pollen, in particular *Myriophyllum*, *Typha* and *Ranunculus* Type. Aquatic algae (*Pediastrum*) and algal spores (*Spirogyra*) were still present and are indicative of a continued aquatic environment. Other indicators of marsh and sedge fen include an unchanged curve of *Carex* pollen, and the presence of fungal spores of Type 25 and Type 55A, possibly indicating the presence of animal dung, and Type 200.

Pollen from extra-local sources include *Thalictrum*, *Gentianella* and *Campanula* derived from calcareous grassland, together with Compositae tub. and *Taraxacum* from drier, more disturbed ground. A strong peak in *Glomus* indicates increased erosion of soils from the valley sides. Unlike LPZB, there were no dung fungal spores associated with the soil erosion, and *Sporomiella* was not identified.

The overall pattern in this zone suggests the end of a still water body and the initiation of increased water flow, albeit potentially more seasonal in nature.

LPZ D (340–50mm): The upper deposits of (20003) are included within LPZD. The zone was further divided into three subzones, LPZDa-c. Throughout LPZD there was a gradual removal of aquatic pollen. Within LPZ Da, *Ranunculus*, *Typha* and *Myriophyllum* declined further and are not found at all in LPZ Db. Framboids in the sediments of LPZ Da indicate at least localised areas of stagnant water. As in LPZC, strong curves of aquatic algae (*Pediastrum*) and algal spores (*Spirogyra*) show that an aquatic environment still existed. At the base of LPZD, slightly higher abundances of marsh plants were identified. These include *Carex*, *Equisetum*, a single grain of *Menyanthes*, frequent algal spores of Type 128, together with fungal spores of Type 55A, possibly also indicating the presence of animal dung and Type 200. The frequency of *Glomus* declined, suggesting a reduction of soil input from the catchment. There was an overall reduction in Poaceae and pollen from plants growing on all types of grassland. This indicates a reduction in the influence of non-local vegetation within the pollen assemblage. Such a change might be caused either by a decline in soil erosion and inclusion of grassland pollen derived from the soils, or by an expansion of the area of *Carex* surrounding the pool/stream that formed a barrier to pollen drifting in from surrounding grasslands. The former seems a more likely explanation.

LPZ E (50–0mm): This zone comprised a single sample from a grey sand with silt lamina (20070) of Association B-ii (Unit B-ii:05) and contained extremely sparse pollen (six grains) all of which were Poaceae. The very low pollen abundance might result from the post-depositional corrosion of pollen that could originally have been within the deposit. The more likely explanation is that the highly inorganic deposits were pollen-poor when deposited.

Profile 2: 30238 (Fig 3.3 and Table 3.10)

Profile 2 was located towards the southern margin of the main palaeochannel (20032) (Association B-ii) *see* Fig 3.1. At this location, 21 samples were processed to include all the deposits observed in this section. The sequence was more complex than that in the centre of the channel and included a greater proportion of coarse sediments in the lower sediments, mostly eroding from the channel margins. A sequence of silty and stony organic deposits (20371 and 20390) (Association B-ii) (Unit B-ii:02) were observed below the organic sands (20003) of palaeochannel (20032) (Association B-ii) (Unit B-ii:03). At this location the organic sands (20003) showed a distinct change through the sequence. The lower part of the 0.7m-deep deposit (20003) was an organic dark grey, poorly sorted stony sand, with sand lenses in which animal bone was frequently identified. This deposit had a gradational boundary with *c* 250mm of massive, dark-brown organic stony sand (20003). This deposit gradually gave way to the upper 250mm of (20003), which was less stony but highly laminated organic and inorganic sand. Above these organic laminated deposits was a pale-grey sand with silt lamina (20070) (Association B-ii) (Unit B-ii-05).

All samples were dominated (>90 per cent) by non-tree pollen; in particular by Poaceae (10–70 per cent tlp) and to a lesser extent by Cyperaceae (20–80 per cent tlp). Trees were only identified at low frequencies, reaching a maximum of 8 per cent but generally less than 5 per cent. These included *Betula*, *Pinus*, *Abies*, *Picea* and *Alnus*. Shrubs such as *Corylus* were rarely encountered.

Terrestrial herbs included a similar range of species to those identified in 30168. The majority of the species are those of open sites (heliophytes) and include those of calcareous grassland eg *Helianthemum* and *Thalictrum*. *Armeria maritima*, *Artemisia*, Caryophyllaceae Compositae tub, *Plantago major/media*, *Rumex acetosa* and *Taraxacum* indicate short turf and disturbed soils. The spores of *Selaginella selaginoides* indicate damp and/or mossy grassland. The presence of tall fen assemblages is suggested by *Filipendula*, *Galium* and *Mentha*.

Pollen from aquatic species included *Myriophyllum spicatum*, *M. verticillatum*, *Typha latifolia*, *Typha angustifolia/Sparganium* type together with *Ranunculus* cf. *aquatilis*

Fig 3.3
Pollen percentage data (>1%) Lynford Quarry (37095 STD) sample 30238.

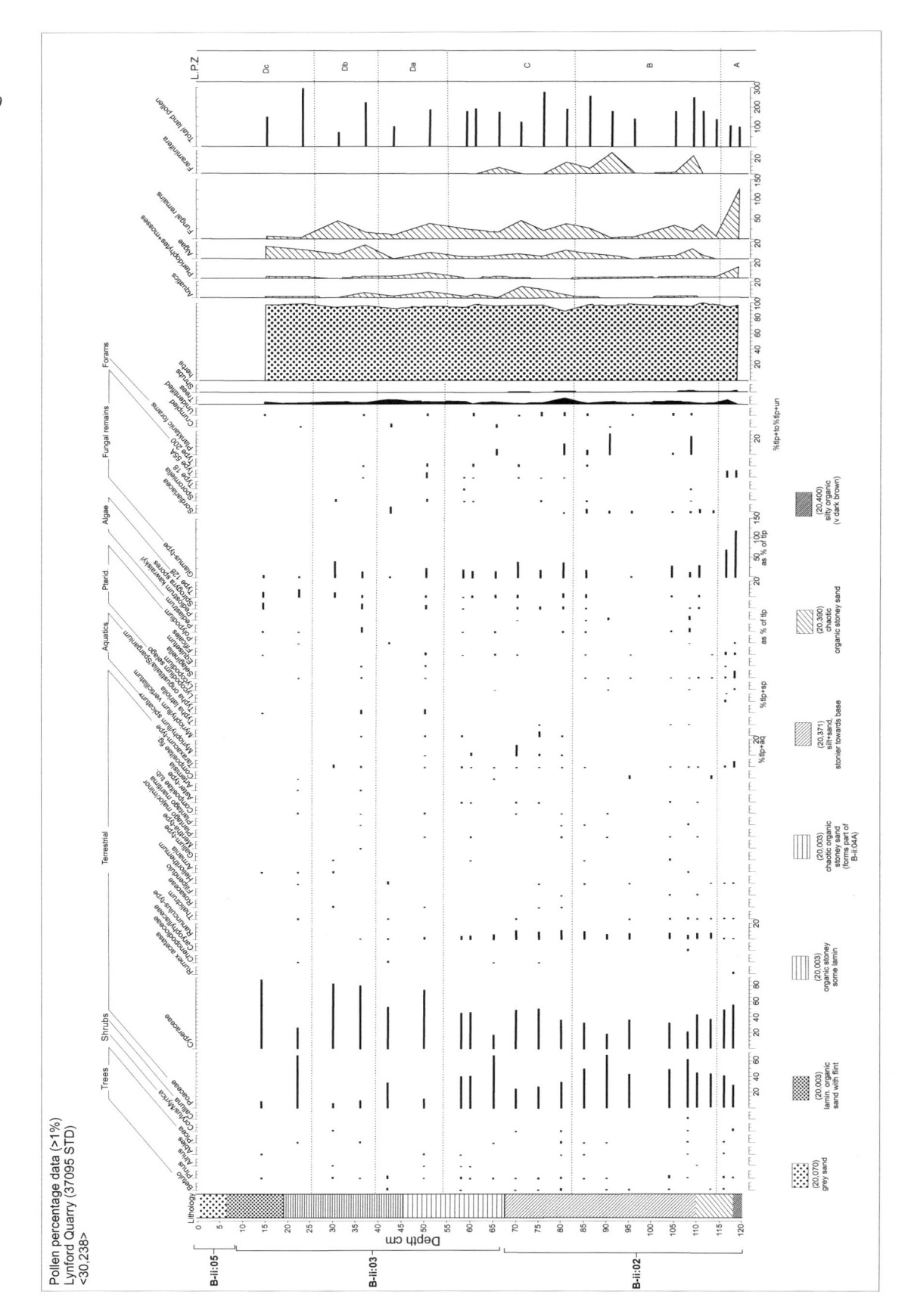

Table 3.10 Total pollen and spore counts from Lynford Quarry, sample 30238

facies	B-ii:05	B-ii:03					
context	20070	20003				20408	
depth (cm) from top of section	14.00	22.00	60.0	36.00	42.00	50.00	60.0
trees							
Betula (birch)					3		
Pinus (pine)	1		1	2	3	2	1
Ulmus (elm)							
Alnus (alder)			1			1	1
Abies (fir)	2					3	
Picea (spruce)		3		4			
shrubs							
Corylus/Myrica			1				
Salix						1	
Calluna							
terrestrial herbs							
Poaceae	13	195	4	20	32	22	79
Cyperaceae	130	80	58	179	53	140	90
Polygonum							
Rumex				1			
Rumex acetosa							
Chenopodiaceae		1			2		
Caryophyllaceae				3	1	3	1
Spergula type							
Stellaria-type							
Scleranthus							
Ranunculus-type				2	1	5	10
Thalictrum		3			1		
cf. Papaver sp.							
Cruciferae							
Rosaceae			1			1	
Filipendula							
Potentilla-type							
Leguminosae							
Hypericum cf. elodes							
Helianthemum		1			3		
Epilobium						1	
Umbelliferae				1			
Armeria	1	1	1				
Gentianella							1
Galium-type			1				1
Labiatae				1			1
Mentha-type				1			
Scrophulariaceae							
Rhinathus type							
Plantago major/media						1	3
Plantago lanceolata							
Plantago maritima				1			
Succisa						1	
Compositae tub.		4		1		4	
Aster-type							1
Artemisia		4		2			
Cirsium							
Centaurea nigra							1
Compositae lig.		1					
Taraxacum-type			2	3		2	1
aquatics							
Myriophyllum spicatum						1	8
Myriophyllum verticillatum				1		2	
Myriophyllum alterniflorum			1				

continued ▶

Table 3.10 – *continued*

facies	B-ii:05	B-ii:03					
context	20070	20003				20408	
depth (cm) from top of section	14.00	22.00	60.0	36.00	42.00	50.00	60.0
Potamogeton							
Typha latifolia							
Typha angustifolia/Sparganium	1			11		11	
fern spores							
Lycopodium selago							
Lycopodium						0.00	
Selaginella		3		3		1	
Isoetes	1						
Equisetum				3		5	
Filicales	1					7	1
Polypodium		1			2		
algae							
Pediastrum	2	2		15			
Pediastrum kawraiskyi							
Spirogyra spores	11			16		10	
Type 128	10	30	4	6		4	4
fungal remains							
Glomus-type	10	10	29	35	3	47	32
Sordiariacea					8		
Sporomiella						7	1
Type 18							
Type 55A				1		13	1
Type 200				1		6	7
Type 201							1
foraminifera							
planktonic forams							
crumpled		3			5		
unidentified							
unidentified	2			3		5	7
total land pollen	147	293	70	221	99	187	192

facies	B-ii:03			B-ii:02			
context	20408			20371			
depth (cm) from top	65.0	70.0	75.0	80.0	85.0	90.0	95.0
trees							
Betula (birch)		1	2	5		1	2
Pinus (pine)	3	1	4	5	1	2	
Ulmus (elm)				1			
Alnus (alder)							
Abies (fir)				1	1		
Picea (spruce)	2			4	1	2	
shrubs							
Corylus/Myrica		1		2			
Salix							
Calluna							
terrestrial herbs							
Poaceae	117	32	77	64	130	121	62
Cyperaceae	32	65	145	72	87	34	53

continued ▶

Table 3.10 – *continued*

facies context	B-ii:03 20408			B-ii:02 20371			
depth (cm) from top	65.0	70.0	75.0	80.0	85.0	90.0	95.0
Polygonum						1	
Rumex							
Rumex acetosa							
Chenopodiaceae	1		1				
Caryophyllaceae	2	2	3	1	2		4
Spergula type	1						
Stellaria-type							
Scleranthus	1						
Ranunculus-type	12	15	28	23	25	12	11
Thalictrum		2					1
cf. *Papaver* sp.		1			1		
Cruciferae			1				
Rosaceae			1	1			
Filipendula				1			
Potentilla-type				1		1	
Leguminosae							
Hypericum cf. *elodes*					1		
Helianthemum			3		1		1
Epilobium							
Umbelliferae			2				
Armeria			1				
Gentianella				1			
Galium-type			2		1		
Labiatae			1				
Mentha-type		3					
Scrophulariaceae			1				
Rhinathus type			1				
Plantago major/media		1	4	3		1	
Plantago lanceolata				1			
Plantago maritima				1	3		
Succisa							
Compositae tub.		1		1		1	
Aster-type		2	1				
Artemisia							
Cirsium					1		
Centaurea nigra							
Compositae lig.	2						6
Taraxacum-type	1	1	2	2	1		
aquatics							
Myriophyllum spicatum		22	10	2			
Myriophyllum verticillatum			20	3			
Myriophyllum alterniflorum							
Potamogeton					1		
Typha latifolia			4				
Typha angustifolia/Sparganium							
fern spores							
Lycopodium selago							
Lycopodium	1					1	
Selaginella					2	1	1
Isoetes							
Equisetum							
Filicales	3	1			2		1
Polypodium							
algae							
Pediastrum	3	1		5	2		
Pediastrum kawraiskyi					1	7	
Spirogyra spores		4	10	6	3		
Type 128	6	4		10	10		

continued ▶

Table 3.10 – continued

facies	B-ii:03			B-ii:02			
context	20408			20371			
depth (cm) from top	65.0	70.0	75.0	80.0	85.0	90.0	95.0
fungal remains							
Glomus-type	30	54	56	74	48		2
Sordiariacea				2	14	5	4
Sporomiella			4		2		
Type 18							
Type 55A		2	1	1			
Type 200		3			5		
Type 201		1			1		
foraminifera							
planktonic forams	15			33	16	65	
crumpled	6					2	
unidentified							
unidentified		1	12	9	7		3
total land pollen	174	128	280	190	255	177	140

facies	B-ii:02					
context	20371			20390		
depth (cm) from top	104.0	108.0	110.0	113.0	116.0	118.0
trees						
Betula (birch)	1			2	1	
Pinus (pine)	6	1			2	1
Ulmus (elm)						
Alnus (alder)			1			
Abies (fir)		1			1	
Picea (spruce)		1			1	
shrubs						
Corylus/Myrica		1				2
Salix		1				
Calluna		4				
terrestrial herbs						
Poaceae	86	155	80	62	44	29
Cyperaceae	58	55	78	53	54	57
Polygonum						
Rumex						
Rumex acetosa						2
Chenopodiaceae						
Caryophyllaceae		2		3		
Spergula type			1			
Stellaria-type				1		
Scleranthus						
Ranunculus-type	13	13	12	11	1	1
Thalictrum	1	3	1	1	1	1
cf. Papaver sp.						
Cruciferae				1		
Rosaceae						
Filipendula	1			2		
Potentilla-type				1		
Leguminosae			1			
Hypericum cf. elodes						
Helianthemum				1	1	1
Epilobium						
Umbelliferae						

continued ▶

Table 3.10 – *continued*

facies	B-ii:02					
context	20371			20390		
depth (cm) from top	104.0	108.0	110.0	113.0	116.0	118.0
Armeria		1				
Gentianella						
Galium-type	3					
Labiatae		1				
Mentha-type						
Scrophulariaceae						
Rhinathus type						
Plantago major/media	1	6	1			
Plantago lanceolata						
Plantago maritima						
Succisa						
Compositae tub.						
Aster-type	3		1			
Artemisia						
Cirsium						
Centaurea nigra		1				
Compositae lig.				6		
Taraxacum-type	1	1	1		2	8
aquatics						
Myriophyllum spicatum						
Myriophyllum verticillatum						
Myriophyllum alterniflorum						
Potamogeton						
Typha latifolia	1	1				
Typha angustifolia/Sparganium						
fern spores						
Lycopodium selago					3	
Lycopodium		1				2
Selaginella	1	1	3	1	2	11
Isoetes						
Equisetum					1	
Filicales				1	4	3
Polypodium						1
algae						
Pediastrum	3	13				
Pediastrum kawraiskyi		14				
Spirogyra spores		3	3			
Type 128	3		4			
fungal remains						
Glomus-type	52	35	56	2	76	122
Sordariacea	3	5	8	4		
Sporomiella		1				
Type 18		1				
Type 55A					10	9
Type 200						
Type 201	1					
foraminifera						
planktonic forams	2	75				
crumpled						
unidentified						
unidentified	4	6				
total land pollen	175	249	180	140	108	102

and were found in moderate frequencies in the upper deposits of 20071 and the lower deposits of 20003.

Algae indicative of aquatic conditions (*Pediastrum* undif. and *Pediastrum kawraiskyi*) were also identified, particularly in the upper deposits of 20003. In addition, fungal spores/bodies were observed at several levels and included those typically associated with animal dung, Sordiariacea, *Sporomiella*, possibly type 55A, together with those from soils (*Glomus*-type). Planktonic foraminifera derived from the underlying chalk were found in relatively high proportions in 20371 and indicate the inclusion of eroded chalk within these deposits.

Iron pyrite framboids were sporadically present, rarely below 1.1m (20371), in moderate abundance between 1.1m and 0.58m (20371 and 20003) but not at all in the deposits above 0.58m. The distribution suggests that 20371 and the lower deposits of 20003 accumulated within stagnant, organic-rich conditions (Wiltshire *et al* 1994).

Local pollen zones

Four local pollen zones (LPZA-D) were identified in profile 2 using CONISS (*see* Fig 3.2).

LPZ A (1.2–1.14m): This zone consists of two samples from 20390 of Association B-ii (Unit B-ii:02). Cyperaceae was the dominant pollen type (50–60 per cent tlp) with an important contribution made by the Poaceae (30–40 per cent). The presence of such high frequencies of Cyperaceae implies a local damp-wet sedge sward and grassland beyond.

Tree pollen was found at low frequencies, 5 per cent tlp, principally comprising *Pinus* with occasional grains of *Betula*, *Abies* and *Picea* with *Corylus/Myrica* forming the shrub component. This low level of tree pollen suggests trees were not growing on the site. It is uncertain whether the tree pollen was derived from reworking of earlier sediments, or if there were limited stands of these trees at some distance from the site. It is worth noting that small clasts of reworked peat were observed in the deposits of 20390, which could account for at least some of the tree pollen as being recycled from earlier, possibly Ispwichian, deposits.

Pollen and spores of disturbed, open and damp sites include: *Taraxacum*, *Selaginalla selaginoides*, *Lycopodium* and *Filicales*. The presence of Poaceae, *Selaginella*, *Lycopdium*, *Helianthemum* and *Thalictrum* are indicative of damp and calcareous grasslands. These grasslands probably developed within a temperate, but probably more continental, climate than today.

The deposit was full of fungal hyphae but contained no forams or framboids. There was a peak of sordariaceaeous fungal spores (Type 55A), which live frequently, but not exclusively, on animal dung and a possibly related peak of the soil fungus *Glomus*.

This mix of resistant spores and pollen types, and absence of aquatics and algae, suggest that this sediment is probably partially derived from a soil where many less resistant pollen types have been differentially removed. The high concentration (75–124 per cent tlp) of *Glomus*, a soil fungi and fungal hyphae, reinforces this interpretation. It should be noted that the appearance of percentages greater than 100 reflect the fact that, following routine practice, fungal spores were not included in the tlp calculations in order to prevent these figures from being swamped by large proportions of spores or aquatic pollen. When calculating the number of fungal spores, therefore, the count is divided by the tlp, thus resulting in counts that might exceed 100 per cent. Cyperaceae is not a resistant pollen type and it must represent the local vegetation into which the eroding soils were deposited. This suggests that 20390 is a redeposited soil from the margin of the channel.

LPZ B (1.14–0.87m): Six samples formed this zone within Association B-ii (Unit B-ii:02) and included the upper sample from 20390 and the lower 220mm of 20371. LPZB was dominated by non-tree pollen at 95 per cent, of which Poaceae was the most significant at 45–70 per cent tlp, together with Cyperaceae at 20–45 per cent tlp. The Poaceae might be derived from both regional grassland and from local reedswamp (*Phragmites*). Unfortunately it has not been possible to distinguish the different grasses. Given the predominance of Cyperaceae in 30168, which was located almost in the centre of the observable palaeochannel, it seems more likely that the high levels of Poacaea in 30238 were largely derived from the regional grassland rather than from *Phragmites*. The presence of fungal spore type 18 (van Hoeve and Hendrikse 1998), which develops on cotton grass (*Eripohorum vaginatum*), suggests at least limited areas of wet acid soils on moorland, heath or bog. The pollen of

Eripohorum vaginatum itself is included within the undifferentiated Cyperaceae. Tree pollen was found at very low concentrations, less than 5 per cent, and includes *Betula*, *Pinus*, isolated *Alnus* grains, *Abies* and *Picea*. This very low frequency, as in LPZA, suggests limited stands of *Betula* and *Pinus* at some distance from the site, together with the reworking of earlier sediments.

Herbaceous pollen was moderately diverse, and together with Poacaea, indicates the following: open grassland, *Thalictrum* and *Helianthemum*; fen and damp habitats: Cyperaceae, *Filipendula* and *Selaginella*; low turf and disturbed soils *Armeria*, *Artemisia*, Compositae Lig., *Plantago media/major, P. maritima* and *Taraxcum*.

Aquatic pollen was rare, but included occasional grains of *Typha latifolia* and 5–10 per cent *Ranunculus* cf. *aquatilis* pollen in all samples. Algae indicating aquatic conditions were more common and included low levels of *Pediastrum, Pediastrum kawraiskyi, Spirogyra* and Type 128. Framboids suggest stagnant water and the development of anaerobic mud.

Glomus was found at moderate frequencies in the lower part of LPZB but was not present in the upper three samples. Fungal spores of the Sordiariacae, probably dung fungi, were found in low frequencies in all samples. In two samples (1.08m and 0.90m) there were abundant planktonic foraminifera, indicating the incorporation of chalk from the valley.

The deposit probably accumulated in semi-aquatic conditions with at least periodic areas of slow-flowing or still water. The input of eroding soils appears to have declined in the upper sediments but there was a continued presence of grazing herbivores on the surrounding grassland.

LPZ C (0.87–0.54m): This zone includes the upper 200mm of 20371 in Unit B-ii:02, and the lower 200mm of chaotic stony sand deposits (20408) forming part of Association B-ii:03. Non-tree pollen remains dominant, forming 90–95 per cent tlp. However, Cyperaceae was more important than in the underlying deposits. This might suggest an increase of locally sourced pollen from the sedge marsh on the fringes of the palaeochannel. The presence of Type 18 fungal spores indicates that some of the Cyperaceae is cotton grass, illustrating the acidity of soils within the palaeochannel at this time. The proportion of tree pollen is slightly elevated reaching 8 per cent tlp at 0.8m. There was an almost consistent presence of *Betula* and *Pinus*, with more sporadic occurrences of *Picea*, *Abies* and *Alnus*.

Calcareous grassland and areas of disturbed soils are indicated by the same taxa identified in LPZB, eg *Thalictrum*, *Helianthemum*, *Armeria*, Caryophyllaceae, Compositae Tub and *Taraxacum*.

The main feature of this zone is the increased proportion of aquatic pollen. The aquatic pollen include plants of open water; *Myriophyllum spicatum, M. verticillatum* and *Ranunculus* cf. *aquatilis*. The latter contributed about 10 per cent tlp, and indicates the presence of stable water conditions in which the plant could flourish. Such conditions would be still or slow-flowing water up to 1m in depth, with areas of stagnant water being suggested by the presence of framboids. Also indicating an aquatic environment in all samples were the algae *Spirogyra*, Type 128, *Pediastrum* and *Pediastrum kawraiskyi*.

Relatively high levels of soil erosion from channel banks are implied by a continuous curve of *Glomus* and the presence of planktonic foraminifera derived from the underlying chalk. Related to the input of soil from the surrounding grassland are the constant low levels of fungal spores commonly associated with animal dung. These fungal spores included *Sporomiella*, Sordariacea and Type 55A.

LPZ D (0.54–0.14m): This zone includes the upper 50–100mm of chaotic stony sand deposits of 20408 and 220mm of organic stony sand with rare laminations and the upper highly laminated organic sands (20003) forming part of Association B-ii:03. Three subdivisions of this zone have been made: LPZDa-c.

Cyperaceae was dominant throughout, and apart from a slight reduction in tree pollen there was no overall change in the non-tree pollen to tree-pollen ratio compared with the previous zone. Although the same spectra of trees were identified in LPZD, as well as the rest of the diagram, *Pinus* was the only tree identified in virtually every sample. *Betula* was no longer identified routinely. This suggests that trees were no longer growing in the locality, even to a limited extent. The ability of *Pinus* to travel significant distances could account for its presence, with other tree and shrub pollen such as *Abies, Picea, Alnus* and *Corylus* being derived from the reworking of earlier deposits.

Herbs were similar to those noted in all deposits within 30238, and include plants of grassland and open disturbed areas, *Thalictrum*, *Helianthemum*, *Armeria*, and *Plantago maritima*, Compositae Tub, Compositae lig. *Artemisia* and *Taraxacum*.

Once again it was the aquatic flora that defined the environmental changes noted in this zone. By LPZDa, *Myriophyllum* had disappeared from the spectra, and *Ranunculus* cf. *aquatilis* had sharply declined. Associated with this apparent decline of open stable water conditions was a small peak in the marginal aquatics *Typha angustifolia/Sparganium*. Although by LPZDc, *Typha angustifolia/Sparganium* had virtually disappeared, aquatic algae such as *Pediastrum*, Type 128 and *Spirogyra* showed a minor increase in abundance. These taxa, together with an isolated grain of *Isoetes* (quillwort), indicate the presence of at least seasonal slow-flowing or standing water. However, such an assemblage would not preclude the possibility of occasional faster-flowing water, perhaps as the result of seasonal snowmelt.

The remains of fungi associated with soil and dung (*Glomus*, *Sordiariacea*, *Sporomiella* and Type 55A) were present in the lower part of LPZD but disappeared in LPZDc, ie in the increasingly laminated sand deposits of 20003. It is notable that no foraminifera were identified in the sediments of LPZD. This change implies a reduction in the input of eroded soils from the margins of the palaeochannel within the increasingly laminated sands.

Profile 3: 30257 (Fig 3.4 and Table 3.11)

This profile was taken from sediments infilling a small channel (3m wide and 0.45m deep) (20121) (Association B-iii), which incised into the upper sediments at the northern margin of the palaeochannel (20032) Association B-ii. The location of this profile is shown in Fig 3.1. All the deposits within this channel belong to Association B-iii. Above the base of the channel was 0.15m of clean fine white sand (20015) overlain by 0.10m of massive silty organic brown sand (20066). It is notable that 20066 was the only deposit identified in the profiles analysed that provided evidence of *in situ* plant growth. A thin layer of flint gravel (20065) (not observed in the monolith) separated 20066 from 0.18m of laminated, dark-brown organic sand with occasional flint gravel (20016).

Above these organic deposits were orange, slightly laminated sands (20012).

The organic sand (20066) contained evidence of plant roots, and was the only deposit identified on site with evidence of *in situ* plant growth.

All samples were dominated by non-tree pollen (85 to almost 100 per cent). Poaceae was the most abundant throughout the sequence (30–100 per cent tlp) although Cyperaceae were also important in most samples (20–50 per cent). Tree pollen contributed 15 per cent tlp at the base of 20066, but declined to about 5 per cent in all samples above this lowest sample. No thermophilous trees were identified, and the tree pollen consisted principally of *Betula* with lesser amounts of *Pinus*. It seems likely that *Betula* grew not far from the site in limited areas of scrub. It is possible that the *Betula* pollen was derived from *Betula nana* (dwarf birch). Unfortunately it was not possible to differentiate between *Betula* pollen of tree or shrub in the small count obtained. It is unlikely that the *Betula* is reworked from earlier deposits, as when the results of this location are compared to the proportions of tree pollen in Association B-ii, *Betula* occurs in a higher proportion in this later channel. It therefore seems unlikely there could have been any differential reworking of this taxa. *Pinus* might also have been growing locally, but could feasibly have blown in from farther distances. Single grains of *Picea* and *Abies* were also found in the lowest deposits of 20066, which might be derived from the reworking of earlier deposits. It is notable that these trees are not inconsistent with the rest of the vegetation and it is possible the pollen is derived from a few isolated trees in the locality.

Shrubs were represented by occasional grains of *Corylus* and *Salix* in the lowest sample, and an isolated identification of *Salix* at 230mm. *Vaccinium* was found in two samples within 20066. The presence of *Vaccinium* indicates the presence of acid heath or bog close to the site, since this pollen type does not travel very far.

Herbs were only found in the deposits of 20066 and the less laminated deposits of 20016, and include those of open disturbed ground – Chenopodiaceae, Caryophyllaceae, Compositae Tub, *Aster* type, *Cirsium*, *Plantago major/media*, *Artemisia* and *Anthemis*-type; those of wet grassland and fen – *Filipendula*, compare *Parnassia palustris*, compare *Viola*

3 ENVIRONMENTAL EVIDENCE

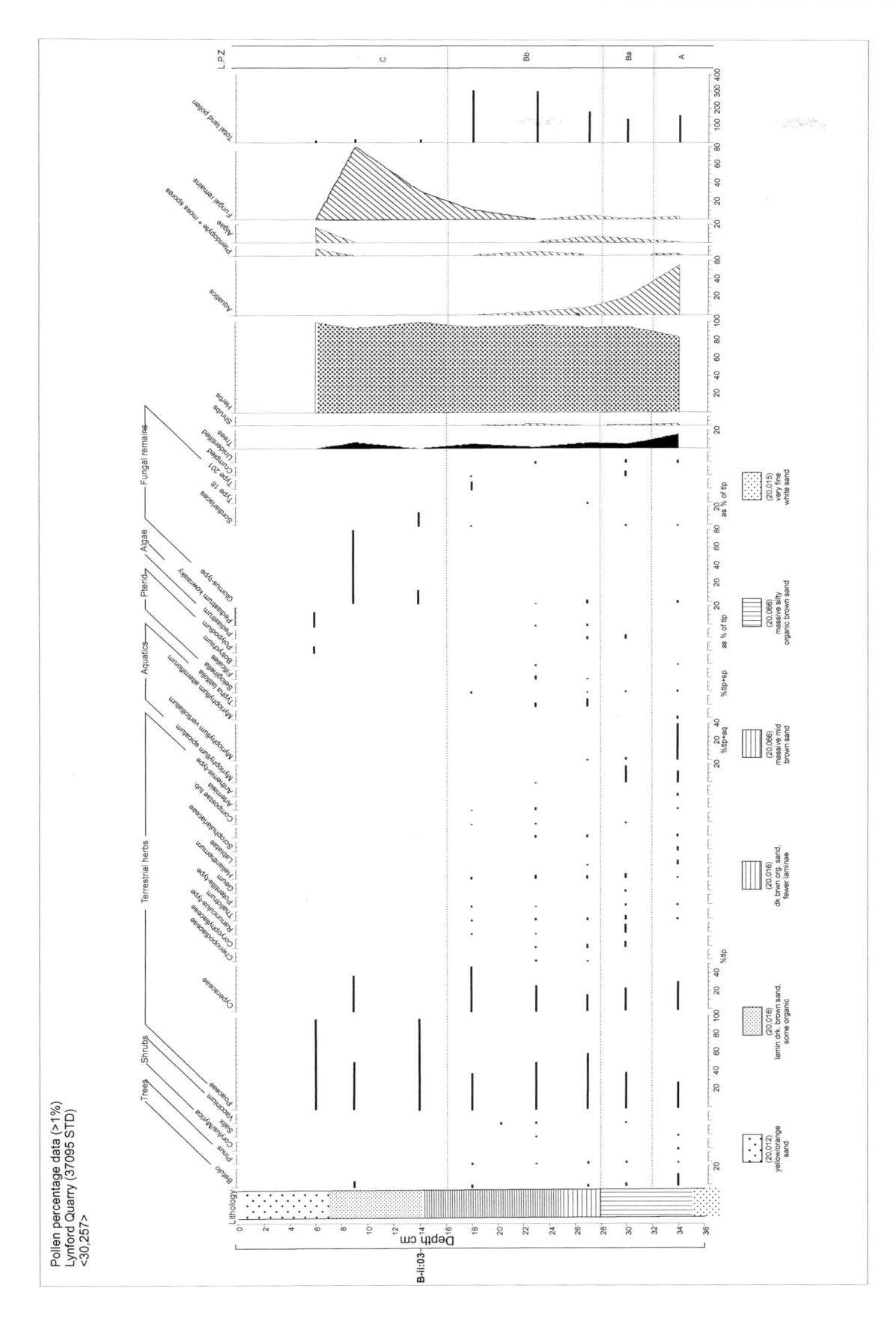

*Fig 3.4
Total pollen percentage data (>1%) Lynford Quarry (37095 STD), sample 30257.*

Table 3.11 Total pollen and spore counts from Lynford Quarry, sample 30257

facies	B-iii							
context	20012		20016				20066	
depth (cm) from top of section	6.0	9.0	14.0	18.0	23.0	27.0	30.0	34.0
trees								
Betula (birch)		1		9		4	4	20
Pinus (pine)				6	3	5	2	2
Abies (fir)								1
Picea (spruce)						1		
Corylus/Myrica (hazel, bog myrtle)								2
Salix (willow)					3			1
shrubs								
Vaccinium (bilberry/crowberry)					3		1	
terrestrial herbs								
Poaceae (grasses)	12	8	13	125	155	106	52	45
Cyperaceae (sedges)		6		155	83	31	32	49
Urtica (nettle)					1			
Polygonum (bistort)						1		
Oxyria type (eg mountain sorrel, curled, clustered, wood dock)						1		
Chenopodiaceae (goosefoot family)					6	1		
Caryophyllaceae (pink family)					3	6	8	
Ranunculus-type (incl buttercup/crowfoot)				2	1		12	
Thalictrum (meadow rue)				2	7	3	6	2
cf. *Anemone*-type (eg wood, yellow, blue anemone)								1
cf. *Papaver* sp. (poppy)								1
cf. *Parnassia palustris* (grass of parnassus)								1
Filipendula (meadowsweet)						1		
Potentilla-type (cinquefoils/tormentil)				3	1		2	2
Geum (herb bennet)							3	
Trifolium-type (clover)								1
cf. *Viola palustris* (marsh violet)								1
Helianthemum (rock rose)				7	11	5	6	1
Gentiana								1
Labiatae (eg mint, woundwort, hemp-nettle)						1		7
Scrophulariaceae (figwort family, eg mullein, toadflax, foxglove, speedwell)								6
Melampyrum (cow-wheat)						1		
Plantago major/media (greater, hoary plantain)					8	5		4
Plantago maritime (seaplantain)								1
Valeriana (valerian)					1			
Compositae tub. (daisy family)				1	3		1	
Aster-type (eg daisy, aster, cudweed, coltsfoot, ragwort)						1		1
Artemisia (mugwort/wormwood)				1	7			2
Cirsium (thistle)							1	
Anthemis-type (eg yarrow, corn marigold, ox-eye daisy)								3
aquatics								
Myriophyllum spicatum (spiked water milfoil)					1		29	39
Myriophyllum verticillatum (whorled water milfoil)						1	3	135
Myriophyllum alterniflorum (alternate water milfoil)								10
Typha latifolia (bulrush)					10	15		

continued ▶

Table 3.11 – *continued*

facies	B-iii							
context	20012		20016				20066	
depth (cm) from top of section	6.0	9.0	14.0	18.0	23.0	27.0	30.0	34.0
fern spores								
Selaginella selaginoides (lesser clubmoss)				4		1	1	2
Equisetum (horsetail)					2			
Filicales (undifferentiated ferns)					10	1		
Botrychium (moonwort)					3			1
Polypodium (polypody)		1						
algae								
Pediastrum						5	6	
Pediastrum kawraiskyi		2			3	5		
fungal remains								
Glomus-type		12	2		1	7		4
Sordiariacea			2	4		2	1	1
Type 18						2		
Type 201				30				
unidentified								
crumpled				3			8	
unidentified						5	4	4
total land pollen	12	15	13	311	296	173	130	155

palustris and *Polygonum* and those of grassy places – *Geum, Helianthemum, Thalictrum, Melampyrum* and *Valeriana*. Of interest is the presence of *Parnassia palustris* (Grass of Parnassus). This is a plant with a relatively northern distribution, with a modern range extending into the north of Scandinavia. It is typical of marshes and damp, grassy sites and is recorded from several Mid-Late Devensian sites (Godwin 1975). The pollen of *Melampyrum* is indicative of a fen community if derived from *M. pratense* or *M. sylvaticum*. *Ranunculus*-type, perhaps the aquatic species *Ranunculus aquatilis*, was found in most samples and was relatively abundant at 300mm (20066) contributing almost 10 per cent tlp.

Aquatic pollen was most abundant in the lower deposits of 20066, and consisted of *Myriophyllum spicatum*, indicative of base-rich, still or slow-flowing water, together with lesser quantities of *Myriophyllum verticillatum* and *M alterniflorum*. Emergent and marginal plants include Cyperaceae and *Typha latifolia*. The presence of cotton grass in 20066 is suggested by the presence of fungal spore Type 18, which grows on *Eriophorum vaginatum*. Therefore, an acidic bog or wet, moor-type environment must have also existed either within or on the margins of this small palaeochannel. The aquatic algae *Pediastrum* was also present at low frequencies. Occasional fungal spores of the Sordiariaceae, indicators of animal dung, were present in most samples, with an increase in relative abundance in the laminated sands of 20016. Evidence for a drying-out of the pool/slow-flowing stream is provided by an increase in fungal debris and spores of Type 201 in the upper deposits of the partially laminated organic sands of 20016.

Limited *Glomus* (soil) fungi were found within 20066, but an increase in this fungal type occurred in the pollen-poor deposits of the laminated sands of 20016. In contrast to the deposits of Association B-ii, no iron pyrite framboids were noted in any of the deposits.

Local pollen zones

Three local pollen zones have been identified in Profile 3.

LPZ A (340–320mm): This zone consists of a single sample from the lowest deposits of 20066. The distinguishing feature of this zone was the elevated quantity of tree pollen – 15 per cent tlp. *Betula* was the main tree identified, with lesser amounts of Pinus, and a single grain of *Abies*. There was a significant quantity of aquatic pollen, 50 per cent tlp+aquatics, in this zone, which is accounted for by *Myriophyllum verticillatum* and *M. spicatum*. This high level of aquatics indicates the presence of base-rich, still or slow-flowing water up to 1m in depth. Other pollen types include those from plants of calcareous grassland (*Thalictrum, Helianthemum, Trifolium*), wet marshland (compare *Parnassia palustris*, compare *Viola palustris*) and in particular open disturbed areas (*Artemisia, Anthemis, Aster, Plantago major/media* and compare *Papaver*). Fungi derived from soils were rare, suggesting a limited input of soil into the deposit.

LPZ B (320–160mm): This zone comes from the deposits of 20066 and 20016, which overlie those of LPZA. Two further subdivisions, LPZBa and LPZBb, have been made.

LPZBa is a single sample from context 20066, and is in many ways similar to LPZA, although it contains reduced tree and aquatic pollen. *Myriophyllum verticillatum* in particular declines, which might suggest a reduced volume of water, for when compared with *M. spicatum* this species appears to be abundant in larger bodies of water (Stace 1997). *Pediastrum* was identified at low frequencies in this deposit, but was absent in the lower sample. The reason for this change is not readily explained but might be related to areas of still water being present only seasonally. An increase in *Ranunculus* cf. *aquatilis* was also noted, together with an increase in pollen from plants of grassland rather than disturbed soils such as *Helianthemum, Thalictrum, Geum* and *Potentilla* type.

The upper sample from 20066 and two samples from the partially laminated organic sand of 20016 make up LPZBb. In these deposits, aquatic pollen declined further, in particular *Myriophyllum* and *Ranunculus* cf. *aquatilis*, while *Pediastrum* persisted at low levels. This might reflect the gradual removal of a stable body of water and its replacement by a more seasonal regime in which water bodies suitable for the growth of aquatic plants declined. A range of terrestrial herbs from both disturbed open areas and grassland were identified.

LPZ C (160–60mm): The increasingly laminated organic sands of the upper part of 20016 and the orange-brown sands of 20012 constitute LPZC. These three samples showed a marked decrease in pollen content, less than 20 grains in any sample, an increase in fungal hyphae, and, in the lower two samples, greatly increased volumes of the soil fungus, *Glomus*. Poaceae dominated the assemblage in this zone and it contained little tree pollen and no terrestrial herb pollen.

The upper deposits of 20066 suggest increased water flow within the channel and sedges with cotton grass forming the marginal vegetation. The landscape surrounding the palaeochannel was one of open grassland, perhaps with limited stands of birch and possibly pine.

Summary of the environmental conditions as indicated by the pollen assemblages

The lower organic sediments of Association B-ii (Unit B-ii:03) infilled the channel under conditions of shallow, permanent or semi-permanent, still, stagnant or possibly very slow-flowing water up to 1m in depth. A very similar environment is indicated by all faunal and pollen evidence reported in this chapter. Interestingly, the Molluscan evidence supports the presence of a permanent rather than semi-permanent water body (Keen, this chapter). The open water supported several rooted aquatic plants including *Myriophyllum* and probably *Ranunculus* cf. *aquatilis*. Plant macrofossils of the latter were identified in large numbers, suggesting that the water surface might have been covered in water buttercup/Crowsfoot (Field, this chapter). Marginal to the open water was a sedge and possibly reed swamp with limited areas of fen marsh. There is also evidence to support periodic, probably seasonal flooding of the marginal swamp. The presence of framboids suggest at least localised areas of still and stagnant water conditions and the development of anaerobic muds due to the decay of a large volume of organic material, which supported acidophiles such as *Menyanthes* and *Vaccinium* in these areas. Plant macrofossil evidence also indicates areas of organic-rich soils. Bank erosion during this period appears to have been at times dramatic with the slumping of bank sediments into the standing water in the form of mud flows. The presence of areas of bare soil consistent with disturbed ground is also supported by the presence of *Aphanes arvensis* (Field, this chapter).

The range of terrestrial herbs indicates that predominantly open calcareous grassland landscape surrounded the site. This included patches of bare, disturbed and wet ground with small stands of birch trees or scrub, and areas of acid heath or bog. The influence of grazing mammals in this landscape cannot be underestimated. The incorporation of moderate quantities of dung fungus in the initial phase of organic accumulation indicates the presence of herbivores in the local environment. Such fungi do not develop on dung in an aquatic environment, and it seems most likely that the dung fungal spores were derived from surrounding grazed grasslands, which then became incorporated into the deposit along with the eroded soils.

A significant observation from the pollen evidence is that the surrounding landscape was not entirely treeless. Although no significant quantities of thermophilous tree pollen were identified, birch and pine pollen were consistently identified in almost all samples. It is possible the *Betula* pollen was derived from *Betula nana* (dwarf birch), a prostrate form of birch that grows at high latitudes, but it was not possible to differentiate between the *Betula* pollen in the small count obtained. It seems likely that *Betula* grew not far from the site in limited areas of scrub. The overall image of the regional landscape was one of calcareous grassland supporting stands of birch or dwarf birch scrub together with limited growth of pine trees.

The upper deposits of Association B-ii (Units B-ii:03 and B-ii:05) are marked by a significant reduction in aquatic pollen (including *Ranunculus* type), which suggests that a change in hydrological regime had occurred. Algal remains indicate that these deposits continued to accumulate in an aquatic environment of still or slow-flowing water, but it is most likely to have only been seasonal, and their presence suggests that faster-flowing water reoccupied the channel on a more regular basis. Perhaps this was a result of an increase in the volume of spring thaw water and the higher discharge being redirected down a secondary channel. Alternatively, seasonal ice on the surface of the water body that melted during the warmer months would have produced similar deposits.

The pollen profiles from the centre and edge of the palaeochannel (Association B-ii) were similar, suggesting that they were connected as the palaeochannel infilled, and were affected by the same conditions and processes. The principal difference was a higher proportion of grasses at the marginal site that reflected the proximity of grassland at this location.

The later palaeochannel, Association B-iii, contained a remarkably similar assemblage of aquatic and terrestrial plants. The lower deposits indicate the presence of a permanent or semi-permanent small stream or pond surrounded by a sedge-rich marsh in a moderately temperate climate. The regional landscape was one of grassland supporting stands of birch or dwarf birch and isolated pine trees, perhaps with more woodland present at this time compared with the earlier palaeochannel. The pool or stream appears to have been replaced in the upper deposits by faster-running water and periods of drying-out. Such changes could have been brought about in a similar way to those identified in the earlier palaeochannel, for example, an increase in seasonal water flow resulting from increased rainfall or snowmelt. It might equally have been caused by channel-switching in a multi-channel river system.

Climatic interpretation of the pollen assemblage

The flora identified exhibits a mixture of both northern and southern plants together with those of both continental and oceanic affinities. One of the overriding characteristics of the flora is that they are almost all heliophytes. The presence of a large number of species indicative of calcareous grassland is typical of Devensian grassland where soil immaturity, rather than temperature, seems to determine the assemblage. Northern taxa include *Thalictrum* and *Selaginella selaginoides*, while southern taxa include *Helianthemum*, which does not occur north of 62° in Scandinavia (Godwin 1975). The presence of facultative halophytes such as *Armeria maritima* and *Plantago maritima* might suggest saline soils that can develop under very dry conditions such as those of the high Arctic. They are also typical of glacial floras and generally associated with aridity rather than salinity, (Bell 1969). The mixture of northern and steppe floras including halophytes, with more southern plants has previously been described by Bell (1969, 1970) and Coope (2000).

The general lack of trees in the flora identified at Lynford is typical of Middle

Devensian floras. The climate was perfectly suitable for tree growth: several factors, some of which have been much debated (Kolstrup 1990; Coope 2000), could be responsible.

For example, the lack of trees might reflect the level of grazing by large herbivores such as mammoths and horses; the remains of both are present at Lynford. Constant grazing of the seedling trees by these species prevents trees from becoming established (Coope *et al* 1961, 2000).

Estimates of temperature are difficult to make, but a few of the identified taxa provide some indication of minimum winter and summer temperatures. Winter temperatures might not have dropped below $-8°C$, since *Armeria maritima* will not grow when winter temperatures are lower than this (Iversen 1954). Relatively warm summers are indicated by *Typha angustifolia* and *Typha latifolia*, which require mean summer temperatures of $14°C$ (Kolstrop 1980) and $13°C$ (Isarin and Bohncke 1998). These temperatures suggest a climate not dissimilar to that of northern Britain today, with moderately warm summers, perhaps cooler winters, and conditions slightly more continental in nature.

A change in hydrological regime was observed in Profiles 1 and 2 from the main palaeochannel. The upper deposits indicate a breakdown in the stable aquatic environment, which had created a permanent shallow body of water, to one where there was likely to have been seasonal fast-flowing water alternating with shallow pools supporting algae in the warmer, drier months. A wide range of factors could have caused the changes in hydrological pattern. Climatic considerations include increased rainfall, heavier winter snowfall followed by spring thaw, and drier summers or much colder winters.

Stratigraphic implications of the pollen assemblage

There are numerous Middle Devensian sites in southern Britain with a similar flora to that identified at Lynford. There is a strong affinity between the flora identified at Lynford and at other sites of Upton Warren Interstadial age including Upton Warren itself (Coope *et al* 1961), Sidgwick Avenue (Lambert *et al* 1963), Earith (Bell 1970) and Isleworth (Kerney *et al* 1982). There are also affinities with other Devensian deposits not specifically identified as belonging to the Upton Warren Interstadial in date. For example, the flora identified at Lynford is comparable with that from an organic mud (WU/WUB) identified at Wretton, also in the Wissey valley (Sparks and West 1970). These muds remain undated but stratigraphically post-date organic deposits with probable Chelford Interstadial affinities (Rendell *et al* 1991). Other comparable Devensian deposits are those of Zone E from Wing in Rutland (Hall 1980).

3.4 Plant macrofossils

M H Field

Sampling, preparation and analysis

Thirteen bulk samples, all taken from one sediment profile, 37095, were chosen for analysis. Sample 1 was taken from the top of the profile and its uppermost elevation was measured at 8.691m OD. The samples were collected at irregular intervals to avoid sampling across stratigraphical boundaries. Analysis began with a subsample of $0.1m^3$ being taken from each bulk sample and then disaggregated in cold water. Each subsample was then washed through a nest of sieves, with the smallest sieve mesh being 150μm. Macroscopic plant remains were picked from the resulting residues using tweezers and, when necessary, a paintbrush under a low-power binocular microscope. Identification of the fossils was accomplished by comparison with modern reference material. The nomenclature follows Stace (1997).

Presentation of data

The assemblages are displayed in Table 3.12 where the number of each taxon's remains per $0.1m^3$ of sediment is recorded. The taxa are sorted into habitat classifications in order to aid the reconstruction of past vegetation and palaeoenvironment. The categories are deliberately kept broad to reduce the possibility of taxa falling into a number of the habitat classifications. The aquatic category contains taxa that can only be described as obligate aquatic plants. The bare ground component of the grassland, open, bare and disturbed ground category describes areas where soil is exposed and plant densities are very low. An unclassified category exists for taxa that were identified only to too high a taxonomic level to allow classification into a habitat category, or for taxa that might survive in a number of habitat types.

3 ENVIRONMENTAL EVIDENCE

Table 3.12 Plant macrofossil assemblages from profile 37095 at the Lynford Quarry, Norfolk

sample 30231		B-ii:05		B-ii:03					B-ii:02					
context		20070		20003					20371					20390
subsample		1	2	3	4	5	6	7	8	9	10	11	12	13
top of profile 8.691m OD		0–5	5–10	10–20	20–30	30–40	40–52	52–62	62–67	67–78	78–86	86–91	91–96	96–106
woodland														
Betula sp(p).	fr	0	0	1	0	0	0	0	0	0	0	0	0	0
grassland, open, bare and disturbed ground														
Arenaria serpyllifolia	s	0	0	0	0	0	0	0	0	0	1	0	0	0
Bellis perennis	a	0	0	0	0	0	0	0	0	0	1	0	0	0
Linum perenne	s	0	0	0	0	0	0	0	0	1	0	0	0	0
Potentilla anserina	a	0	0	0	2	2	0	0	1	0	0	2	0	0
Rumex acetosella	n	0	0	0	0	0	0	1	0	1	2	0	0	0
Scabiosa cf. columbaria	fr	0	0	0	0	0	0	0	2	1	0	0	0	0
Selaginella selaginoides	mg	0	0	5	0	0	4	1	17	6	6	16	0	22
waterside and damp ground														
Caltha palustris	s	0	0	0	0	0	0	0	0	1	0	1	0	0
Eleocharis palustris	n	0	0	0	0	0	1	0	1	0	0	0	0	0
Rorippa palustris	s	0	0	0	0	0	2	0	0	0	0	1	0	0
aquatic														
Characeae sp(p).	oo	0	0	0	0	1	3	19	11	7	8	4	0	11
Groenlandia densa	fr	0	0	0	0	0	1	0	0	2	2	0	0	0
Myriophyllum spicatum	fr	0	0	0	0	1	19	4	28	1	0	5	0	1
Potamogeton sp(p).	fr	0	0	0	1	1	2	0	0	2	1	3	0	1
Potamogeton cf. pusillus	fr	0	0	0	0	0	0	0	0	1	0	0	0	0
Potamogeton pusillus	fr	0	0	0	0	0	0	0	0	0	0	3	0	0
Ranunculus subgenus Batrachian sp(p).	a	0	0	0	5	15	18	13	34	26	11	17	0	8
unclassified														
Carex sp(p).	bin	0	0	0	1	0	7	5	3	3	3	8	0	2
	trn	0	0	6	15	10	19	2	3	10	6	11	0	14
Caryophyllaceae sp(p).	s	0	0	0	0	0	2	0	2	6	1	3	0	3
Cenococcum geopilum	sc	0	0	0	0	1	2	2	0	5	2	5	0	0
Luzula sp(p).	s	0	0	0	0	0	0	0	0	1	0	0	0	0
Musci sp(p).	ps	0	0	0	6	9	9	8	11	10	7	13	0	10
Potentilla sp(p).	a	0	0	1	0	0	1	0	0	0	0	0	0	0
Ranunculus subgenus Ranunculus sp(p).	a	0	0	0	0	0	0	2	1	3	0	3	0	1
Rumex sp(p).	n	0	0	0	0	0	0	0	1	0	1	0	0	0
	pif	0	0	0	0	0	0	0	1	1	0	1	0	0
Viola sp(p).	sf	0	0	0	0	0	0	0	0	0	0	0	0	1
total number of taxa		0	0	4	5	8	13	9	12	18	13	15	0	10
total number of species		0	0	1	1	3	6	4	4	7	6	7	0	2
total number of remains		0	0	13	30	40	90	57	116	88	52	96	0	74

a – achene, bin – biconvex nutlet, fr – fruit, mg – megaspore, n – nutlet, oo – oospore, pif – perianth fragment, ps – piece of stem, s – seed, sc – scelotium, sf – seed fragment, trn – trigonous nutlet)

Note: All samples originate from profile 37095 STD, context 30231. 100cm^3 of each sample analysed. Top of profile was 8.691m OD.

Reconstruction of the vegetation and environment and the time of deposition

Concentrations of plant macrofossils from the samples analysed are generally low, with three sandy samples (1, 2 and 12) yielding no plant macrofossils. The highest concentration of plant macrofossils is found in sample 8 (116 fossils per $0.1m^3$). The assemblages are relatively diverse, with 27 taxa identified. Preservation has allowed 13 of these taxa to be determined to species level. The subsample that exhibits greatest diversity is 9, with 18 taxa of which seven can be identified to species.

The plant macrofossil assemblages indicate that a variety of habitats existed in the vicinity of the site where deposition took place, but the only tree or shade-tolerant taxon represented is Betula. This finding indicates that any cover created by tree canopies was very limited in the local landscape.

A grassland habitat with open, bare and disturbed ground is evident from the presence of seven taxa in the subsamples from profile 37095. *Bellis perennis*, *Linum perenne* and *Scabiosa* cf.*columbaria* are recorded and suggest that conditions near to the site of deposition were relatively dry with a calcareous substrate. Some of the taxa placed in the unclassified habitat category might also have grown in this grassland (eg *Ranunculus* subgenus *Ranunculus* and Viola). *Arenaria serphyllifolia* and *Potentilla anserina* often inhabit areas where disturbance has exposed bare soil. Their presence, together with that of *Aphanes arvensis*, which was recorded while examining other residues extracted from the fossiliferous sediments, points to some sort of activity near to the site such as animal trampling or bank collapse that resulted in the exposure of bare earth. The existence of damp grassland, possibly located next to the water body, is indicated by *Selaginella selaginoides*. It is probable that some of the waterside and damp ground taxa recovered grew on the banks of the body of water and also among the damp grassland.

Remains of *Eleocharis palusris* and *Hippuris vulgaris* indicate that fine grained sediments possibly with a high organic content occurred in the shallows at the margins of the water body. Certain areas at the edge of the water body might have been occupied by pure stands of *Eleocharis palustris*. Moreover, *Hippuris vulgaris* was identified while examining other residues extracted from the fossiliferous sediments. *Rorippa palustris* probably grew in moist areas where there was intermittent standing water, while *Caltha palustris* occupied damp grassland or marshy areas at the water body margin.

The aquatic taxa are well represented in the assemblages recovered. For example, in Samples 7 and 8 over 60 per cent of the fossils recovered originate from aquatic plants. The aquatic taxa present suggest that deposition took place in relatively shallow water, probably less than 1.5m deep, with still or slow-flowing water. *Potamogeton pusillus* can tolerate a range of pH and nutrient status (Preston 1995) and, therefore, its presence helps little in reconstructing the conditions in the water body. However, the occurrence of *Myriophyllum spicatum* and *Groenlandia densa* would suggest slightly alkaline to neutral water conditions with a mesotrophic to eutrophic nutrient status. The large number of achenes of *Ranunculus* subgenus *Batrachium* recovered suggests that the surface of the water body was covered in a carpet of Water Buttercup. However, the difficulty in identifying these achenes to species level does not allow any further comment on the nature of the water body. The surface of the submerged substrate was occupied by members of the aquatic algae family, the Characeae.

The climatic conditions at the time of deposition are difficult to reconstruct with any accuracy because of the relatively limited plant macrofossil data available. Conditions were not Arctic in nature, but the under-representation of trees or shade-tolerant taxa, and the absence of any very thermophilous taxa might suggest climatic conditions similar to that of the northern part of Britain or southern Scandinavia today. All of the species recorded are found in these areas today (Hultén and Fries 1986; Jalas and Suominen 1972; Meusel and Jäger 1965, 1978).

Age of the sediments, correlation with other sites and duration of deposition

The relatively limited plant macrofossil data does not allow a relative age determination of the sediments, making it impossible to correlate with assemblages from other British sites. The similarity of the assemblages from the fossiliferous subsamples would suggest that deposition was rapid. There might have been pulses of relatively rapid sedimentation over a relatively short period of time – tens of years. Some of these periods of sedimentation may have been relatively energetic, leading to the deposition of sand. At other times, low energy conditions prevailed, possibly when the body of water became detached from the main channel.

3.5 Palaeoenvironmental interpretation of the Lynford vertebrate assemblage

A J Stuart

Introduction

The large mammal remains from Lynford provide another source of palaeoenvironmental information. Interpretation requires the use of modern species as analogues, supplemented by data drawn from past distributions and well-preserved specimens from across the mammoth steppe (Guthrie 2001) of Eurasia and Alaska.

As described by Schreve (chapter 5), the Lynford mammalian assemblage exhibits a wide range of preservation types, due to differing times and degrees of exposure on the land surface before burial in the channel sediments. However, in addition to a preponderance of more weathered material (Behrensmeyer 1978, Classes 3–5), nearly all of the mammalian taxa occurring at Lynford are also represented by material in Classes 1 and 2 and thus showing minimal weathering, indicating that they were buried relatively quickly. In the absence of detailed data on weathering of bone in cold environments, it is difficult to rule out the possibility that this part of the assemblage is significantly older than the channel sediments and the plant and invertebrate fossils contained therein, but a reasonable estimate of the time difference would be only tens and at most a few hundred years. The good preservation of the fish and some of the amphibians does not indicate significant subaerial exposure, and this part of the fauna probably accumulated at the same time as the channel sediments. With the important exception of *Bison priscus*, only represented by material in Class 4, the Lynford fauna will be treated here as essentially representing a living community, more or less contemporaneous with the other palaeontological data.

The mammalian assemblage from Lynford includes three species that are entirely extinct: woolly mammoths, woolly rhinoceros and 'steppe' bison, together with spotted hyaenas, which now survive only outside northern Eurasia. The other species represented in the assemblages still occur today in northern Eurasia and North America.

Large herbivores

Our knowledge of the Late Quaternary history of woolly mammoth *Mammuthus primigenius*, the best-represented taxon at Lynford, is much better than for any other extinct European megafaunal species. It is known not only from relatively abundant bones, tusks and teeth, but also from rare frozen soft tissues, including entire carcasses, and from depictions in Upper Palaeolithic art.

In the late Pleistocene, woolly mammoths appear to occur mostly or exclusively in association with open herb-dominated vegetational conditions. From frozen carcasses preserved in the Siberian permafrost and Upper Palaeolithic paintings and carvings from south-western France to northern Siberia, we know that during the Last Cold Stage woolly mammoths possessed a long shaggy coat and underwool, a thick layer of subcutaneous fat, a short tail and very small ears – all adaptations to cold climatic conditions (Kubiak 1982; Lister and Bahn 2007). The high-crowned molar teeth and densely packed enamel ridges indicate adaptation to a diet of grasses, sedges and other low-growing vegetation, in which the teeth have to cope not only with the abrasive silica content of the grasses but also with gritty soil ingested incidentally with its food. Preserved stomach contents recovered from the Berosovka and Shandrin carcasses from north-eastern Siberia confirm that the woolly mammoth diet comprised mostly grasses with additional other herbs (Ukraintseva 1993; Lister and Bahn 2007). The Shandrin mammoth gut contained 90 per cent grasses, with a few twigs of willow, birch, larch and alder, indicating that shrubs and trees were also browsed where available. Clearly such a large animal as a mammoth would have required large quantities of plant food all year round. Although mammoths might have been able to uncover grasses and other vegetation in winter by digging through snow with their feet or tusks, heavy snow cover is likely to have been a limiting factor in their distribution.

Mammuthus primigenius probably evolved from *Mammuthus trogontherii* in north-east Siberia c 800,000 years ago, but did not enter Europe until c 200,000 years ago (Lister and Sher 2001; Lister *et al* 2005). During the Last Cold Stage (the interval c 115–10ka BP, corresponding to MIS 5d – 2), the woolly mammoth was very widely distributed, ranging throughout most of Europe, across northern Asia – including the far north and several islands in the Arctic Ocean, and into the northern half of North America (Stuart 1991; Kahlke 1999). However, it should be appreciated that the reconstructed Pleistocene range of this and other taxa (Kahlke 1999) is time-averaged over a period of tens of millennia, and does not represent its distribution at any given time. Recent work using finds directly dated by radiocarbon has shown that mammoths occurred from before 36ka to 20ka (uncalibrated radiocarbon chronology) over most of northern Asia and Europe, including Britain and Ireland (Stuart *et al* 2002; Stuart 2004). After c 20ka they were absent from Iberia, Italy and Ireland, and at c 12ka there was a sudden and rather dramatic withdrawal from most of the former range, except the far north of Siberia. This event can be correlated with the major spread of trees at the expense of open 'steppe-tundra' over most of northern Eurasia at the onset of the Allerød Interstadial, demonstrating that forested habitats were generally unsuitable for woolly mammoths. Significantly, the Taymyr Peninsula (north central Siberia), where mammoth are known to have survived post 12ka, continued to support open 'steppe-tundra' vegetation (Sher 1997; Sulerzhitsky 1997; Vasil'chuk *et al* 1997; Stuart *et al* 2002; Stuart 2004). Similarly, the survival of woolly mammoth as late as 3.7ka on Wrangel Island off north-eastern Siberia was due, at least in part, to the probable persistence of open herb-rich vegetation through the Holocene (Vartanyan *et al* 1993, 1995; Sher 1997).

The woolly rhinoceros *Coelodonta antiquitatis* has been widely regarded as having been a 'fellow traveller' of the woolly mammoth, as their remains commonly occur together in Last Cold Stage deposits, and both subsequently went extinct. However, the overall Pleistocene range of woolly rhinoceros was significantly less extensive, excluding Ireland, nearly all of Fennoscandia, north-west and north-central Siberia and all of North America (Kahlke 1999). The high-crowned cheek teeth with thick enamel and the low-slung carriage of the head indicate an animal adapted to grazing on grasses and other low-growing vegetation, resembling the living African white rhinoceros *Ceratotherium simum* Burchell, which is a grass eater (Halternorth and Diller 1980). Depictions in Palaeolithic art, rare finds of frozen soft tissues from Siberian permafrost, and above all the entire carcasses preserved in salt and hydrocarbons from Starunia in the Ukraine, indicate a large animal with a long woolly coat, small ears and short tail – all adaptations to cold – and two (keratin) horns, known from several Siberian permafrost finds. The larger anterior horn, reaching more than a metre in length, was laterally flattened, unlike the horn of any living rhinoceros. Wear facets suggest that the horns were used in a side-to-side motion to clear thin snow to expose plant food. The large bulk and short legs, lacking spreading hooves or pads, indicate an animal unable to traverse deep snowfalls (Kahlke 1999). Curiously, woolly rhinoceros were absent from Britain after c 20ka, although it survived much later elsewhere in Europe. However, it disappeared entirely from Europe in around 12ka, as steppe-tundra gave way to forest, but unlike mammoths did not find a post 12ka refugium in northern Siberia (Stuart and Lister 2007).

The extinct 'steppe' bison, *Bison priscus*, only represented at Lynford by weathered material, occurred widely in northern Eurasia, including the far north of Siberia, and North America in the Late Pleistocene, but is unknown from Ireland and Fennoscandia, and occurred only in the northern part of Iberia (Kahlke 1999). The taxonomy and phylogeny of *Bison* are difficult to interpret, but if *B. priscus* is regarded as a valid species, it can be distinguished from both of the living species – the North American *Bison bison* and European *Bison bonasus* – by its larger size and larger horns, and there were also significant differences in the spinal column (Guthrie 1990). From its dentition and by analogy with extant *Bison* species, *Bison priscus* primarily fed on grasses, and probably required more productive herbage than most other species of the so-called 'mammoth steppe'. Its abundance in many fossil assemblages is consistent with congregating in large herds, like the living plains bison (*Bison bison*). The short legs and rather small hooves indicate that, unlike reindeer, it was intolerant of deep snow cover, which would have impeded locomotion and restricted access to food. In Europe it probably disappeared by 20ka at the onset of the Last Glacial maximum, suggesting that it was not adapted to the coldest phases, but it apparently survived much later in Siberia and Alaska (Guthrie 1990; Kahlke 1999).

The taxonomy of Pleistocene horses is confused, and several species of caballine horse have been recognised by various authors in Eurasia and North America, but most or all of these can be regarded as a single species – *Equus ferus*. In the Last Cold Stage the range of *E. ferus* extended from most of Europe across northern Eurasia, even to the far north of Siberia (Kahlke 1999), and into North America. Remarkably, all North American horses became extinct at the end of the Pleistocene, but survived in Eurasia and Africa (zebra). *Equus ferus* occurs widely in Pleistocene faunas, and very probably occupied open grassland habitats in cold stages, and also open woodlands in north-west Europe in interglacials. It occurs abundantly in many Last Cold Stage assemblages and very probably formed large herds. The single hooves of horses are unsuited to deep snow or soft ground (Guthrie 1990), so that widespread firm substrates are necessary. In north-west Europe it survived through the Last Glacial Maximum into the early Holocene.

Today, the reindeer or caribou, *Rangifer tarandus*, has a circumpolar distribution in the tundra and taiga (boreal forest) biomes from Fennoscandia across Siberia into Alaska, Yukon and northern Canada. The present-day Fennoscandian populations comprise domesticated animals, other than some wild reindeer that still occur in Norway (MacDonald and Barrett 1993), but their range approximates to that of their wild ancestors. They never occur in mixed or deciduous woodland. During the Last Cold Stage the overall range of *Rangifer tarandus* was even more extensive, including Britain and Ireland, and at times reaching as far south as southern France, northern Spain, northern Italy and the Crimea (Kahlke 1999). Reindeer are the only deer in which both males and females have antlers – they are more highly developed in the male – and the antlers are grown and shed annually. Reindeer appear to have evolved in high latitudes and are highly adapted to Arctic and sub-Arctic environments, with long legs and large spreading hooves enabling them to cope with moderate snowfalls, and feeding on lichens, grasses and sedges, scraping away snow to feed on the vegetation beneath (Kahlke 1999). Reindeer can congregate in herds of tens of thousands of individuals and some populations undertake extensive migrations from summer tundra to winter boreal forest, in which they can cover 150km to 200km in a day. It is likely that Pleistocene herds made similarly long migrations within the steppe-tundra in response to seasonal climatic extremes and availability of food.

Carnivores

At first sight the presence of spotted hyaenas (*Crocuta crocuta*) in the Lynford assemblage suggests a warm climate, as today this animal is found only in sub-Saharan Africa. However, it occurs very widely in both Last Interglacial and Last Cold Stage assemblages from northern Eurasia (but not North America), and its absence from Europe and Asia today should be viewed as part of the phenomenon of Late Quaternary megafaunal extinction, which for some reason did not affect the African part of its range (Stuart 1991). In Africa today it is typical of open grasslands and savannahs, avoiding dense forest. Similarly, in the Pleistocene it occurred in association with open steppe-tundra in cold stages and probably open woodland during interglacials. Modern spotted hyaenas not only scavenge the kills of other predators or the carcasses of animals that have died of accident or disease, but are also themselves active predators, hunting in packs to bring down prey as large as zebra (Halternorth and Diller 1980). Likely prey at Lynford would have included reindeer, horse and young bison, and perhaps occasionally calves of woolly mammoth and woolly rhinoceros. Together with the other large carnivores at Lynford, they very probably would have competed with Neanderthals for both live prey and carcasses. The powerful jaws and massive cheek teeth of spotted hyaenas are superbly adapted for carcass destruction, including crushing and eating bones to extract the collagen. Pleistocene spotted hyaenas from Europe were significantly larger than those in Africa today, so they might have been able to take larger prey, and chew larger bones. Hyaena coprolites, comprising the remains of crushed and digested bone, are commonly found in Pleistocene assemblages, including at Lynford.

The overall Late Pleistocene range of spotted hyaenas was much more restricted than mammoths, not reaching farther north than 55–58° Latitude (Kahlke 1999), suggesting that it was significantly less tolerant of low temperatures. Moreover, its probable disappearance from Europe c 20–18ka (Stuart and Lister 2007), during the Last Glacial Maximum, also suggests that it could not cope with the harshest conditions of the Last Cold Stage.

The natural Holocene range of the brown bear (*Ursus arctos*), including the American grizzly, which extended from Europe across northern Asia and into North America, has been much reduced and fragmented in the last two centuries by human persecution and habitat destruction (MacDonald and Barrett 1993). It occupies a wide range of habitats, including temperate and mixed woodlands, boreal forests and open pasture in mountains, and extends north just into the tundra. However, in open habitats it requires some dense cover and shelter. It was also very widely distributed in the Late Pleistocene, occurring both in interglacial and cold stage faunas. Brown bears are able to walk over encrusted snow (Guthrie 1990) and are omnivorous, exploiting a diverse range of plant and animal foods according the habitat and seasonal availability. Thus the diet can include roots, fungi, herbs, some grasses, berries, rodents, carrion, insects and fish – especially salmon (MacDonald and Barrett 1993). These bears are also capable of killing large prey, such as moose and reindeer and in summer and autumn they accumulate fat reserves to sustain them through winter hibernation in caves or dens excavated in a bank or under a tree. At Lynford many of these foods might have been available in the warmer months, including abundant carcasses of large mammals, grasses and herbs, perhaps some berries, insects, possibly salmon, and voles and ground squirrels. Interestingly, in view of the occurrence of *Spermophilus* at Lynford, modern brown bears also feed on ground squirrels, which they dig from their burrows. Very probably, at Lynford, these large and formidable bears disputed 'kills' with hyaenas, wolves and lions. Considering their diverse dietary requirements, it seems likely that brown bears would have been unsuited to the coldest phases of the Last Cold Stage.

In the Late Pleistocene and Holocene, wolves lived throughout Europe, northern Eurasia (including the far north of Siberia), parts of southern Asia and throughout almost all of North America (Kahlke 1999; Corbet 1978).

In the Holocene they occurred in almost all biomes from semi-desert to temperate forest, boreal forest and Arctic tundra. In the late Pleistocene they are recorded in association with a similar wide range of biomes, including temperate forests in interglacials, and steppe-tundra in cold stages. However, today their range has been drastically reduced due to active persecution and they have been exterminated from many areas, including the British Isles and most other parts of Europe (MacDonald and Barrett 1993). Wolves are opportunistic feeders, taking rodents and lagomorphs, birds and carrion, and hunting in packs to kill large mammals from roe deer to reindeer, moose and bison (Banfield 1974). Likely prey at Lynford would have included voles, ground squirrels, birds, reindeer and horses. In the absence of suitable locations under rocks or trees, as must have been the case at Lynford, they excavate dens in soil where there is local vegetational cover.

The red fox (*Vulpes vulpes*) has a Holarctic distribution, including almost all of northern Eurasia and most of North America, from steppe and prairie to temperate broadleaf forest, boreal forest and tundra except some parts of the far north of Siberia and Canada (Banfield 1974; Corbet 1978; MacDonald and Barrett 1993). Red foxes are opportunistic feeders, with a diet including: berries, fruits and other plant food, invertebrates, birds, rodents and carrion. The last three are likely to have been important at Lynford.

Small mammals

The tundra vole (*Microtus gregalis*) does not occur in Europe today, even in northern Fennoscandia, but ranges across northern Asia into Arctic North America. Its Asian distribution is curiously disjunct, occurring in distinct regions of tundra in northern Siberia and steppe in central Asia, separated by a vast zone of taiga from which it is absent (Corbet 1978; Stuart 1982 fig 5.18). In the Last Cold Stage its range extended much farther west to include Britain. In common with other *Microtus* species it lives in burrows and feeds on grasses, herbs and other plants, together with some invertebrate food.

Today ground squirrels (or susliks), genus *Spermophilus*, are absent from western Europe, but range from south-eastern Europe across central Asia to north-eastern Siberia and into North America. They occur in steppe, semi-desert and open woodland in association with dry continental climates, and at times during the Last Cold Stage extended their range as far west as Britain. The Siberian or long-tailed ground squirrel (*Spermophilus undulates* (Pallas)), usually regarded as con-specific with the North American *S. parryi* (Richardson), is the most northerly species of *Spermophilus*, occurring across a large area from the Tian Shan and Altai region of central Asia through Mongolia to eastern Siberia, including Kamchatka, Amur and Chukotka, and into Alaska and Arctic Canada (Ellerman and Morrison-Scott 1966; Banfield 1974). In North America, *S. parryi* is found in tundra and forest clearings, and is restricted to areas of sand and gravel where the absence of permafrost allows it to make extensive burrows (Banfield 1974). The food includes grasses and other green plants, seeds, green plants, roots, berries, insects and meat from carcasses of reindeer or other animals. In late summer Siberian ground squirrels cache food in their burrows for consumption in the spring when they awake from hibernation.

Fishes and amphibians

The modern distribution of perch (*Perca fluviatilis*) includes most of northern Eurasia, except the extreme north of Fennoscandia and Siberia (Muus and Dahlstrøm 1971). It requires permanent freshwater or brackish lakes, ponds or rivers where it eats aquatic invertebrates and smaller fish, including other perch. Spawning occurs only when water temperatures reach 7–8°C. In north-west Europe, including Britain and southern Scandinavia, the three-spined stickleback *Gasterosteus aculeatus* occurs principally in freshwater rivers, lakes and ponds, but in northern Europe it occurs exclusively in brackish and marine habitats (Muus and Dahlstrøm 1971). It requires aquatic invertebrate food. The pike (*Esox lucius*) occurs throughout Europe, except in the extreme south and extreme north (Muus and Dahlstrøm 1971). It ranges across a wide belt of central Asia, but avoiding the tundra and northern taiga biomes, and into North America. Pike are found in ponds, lakes and slow-flowing rivers, generally in well-weeded habitat, and also tolerate brackish water. Spawning takes place when water temperatures reach 2–12°C. Pike prey mainly on various other fish, including other pike, as well as frogs, ducklings and invertebrates.

Frogs (*Rana* spp.) are largely terrestrial but favour moist habitats and are tied to freshwater ponds for breeding (Arnold and Burton 1978). They occur almost everywhere in northern Eurasia today except in permanently frozen areas. They feed on terrestrial invertebrates and overwinter as tadpoles or by hibernating as adults.

Birds

Crakes are strong indicators of freshwater wetland habitats such as swamps and fens, preferring shallow fresh waters with good ground cover and possibly floating vegetation or debris. They have a widespread continental distribution but are at present relatively scarce throughout Britain and Ireland. They are also migratory but still tend to utilise wetlands while on passage. Pleistocene remains of *Porzana* species are widespread throughout the Palaearctic from the Middle Pleistocene onwards. In the UK, specimens have been identified from Late Glacial caves in Derbyshire and a Late Pleistocene-Holocene fissure fill at Ightham in Kent (Tyrberg 1998; Cooper pers comm).

Conclusions

The limited diversity of the Lynford vertebrate fauna is usual in both cold stage assemblages and modern sub-Arctic and Arctic faunas.

The fishes and amphibians provide very limited information, except to confirm other sources of evidence that there was a permanent body of freshwater at Lynford, and that there were sources of aquatic and terrestrial invertebrate food.

The much richer mammalian fauna includes no obligate forest species or obligate thermophiles, and is a typical 'mammoth steppe' assemblage (Guthrie 2001), indicating a predominantly open vegetation of grasses and low-growing herbaceous vegetation in a cool continental climate. Similar faunas occurred across much of northern Eurasia during the Last Cold Stage. The vertebrate evidence is therefore consistent with the picture of predominantly open grassland 'steppe-tundra' or 'cold steppe' vegetation, indicated by the pollen, plant macrofossil and beetle evidence (Green, Field, Coope, this chapter).

The very presence of a range of large herbivores implies a productive environment with abundant plant food, with much greater productivity than modern Arctic tundra. It is likely that the grazing activities of herbivores helped to maintain a diverse mosaic vegetation, and perhaps inhibited colonisation by trees. The presence of reindeer indicates a cold, Arctic or sub-Arctic climate, while ground squirrel, and probably also tundra vole, imply a cold continental climate with low precipitation and a large seasonal temperature range – paralleling the beetle evidence (Coope, this chapter). The extinct woolly mammoth and woolly rhinoceros also indicate a cold, dry continental environment, while the presence of bison, brown bears and hyaenas suggests that the assemblage represents a milder phase of the Last Cold Stage. Perhaps significantly, the Arctic lemming (*Dicrostonyx torquatus*), was not found in the small vertebrate assemblage, although this is commonly recorded from the colder phases of the Last Cold Stage. Similarly red fox (*Vulpes vulpes*) is present, rather than Arctic fox (*Alopex lagopus*), which today has a circumpolar distribution in tundra and the northern part of the boreal forest (taiga) biomes (Banfield 1974; Corbet 1978; MacDonald and Barrett 1993). The occurrence of mammoth, woolly rhinoceros, horse and bison implies an absence of deep snow cover. Some of the large herbivores might have migrated in response to large seasonal changes in the availability of food. We can speculate, for example, that if they occurred at the site within the same time period, bison was only present in the summer, migrating from the south east across the exposed North Sea floor, and reindeer only in the winter, migrating from Scotland or northern England, but alternatively both may have occurred at the site all year round. The find of a male shed antler shows that reindeer certainly were present at Lynford in the winter, but does not imply that they were necessarily absent at other seasons. Ground squirrel and brown bear responded to seasonal changes by hibernating. In the winter months the other carnivores probably found plentiful carrion as well as live prey.

Large mammals might have been attracted to the floodplain because of the availability of aquatic and waterside vegetation (Field, Green, Coope, this chapter), and their presence in the vicinity of the depositional site is attested not only by their skeletal remains but also by abundant dung beetles, and spores of the dung fungus *Sporormiella* (Coope, Green, this chapter).

It is interesting to speculate how Neanderthals at Lynford might have interacted with the other formidable large predators, which very probably included lion as well as spotted hyaena, brown bear and wolf. On the one hand there must have been competition for prey and for carcasses, but on the other the 'kills' of each predator would have provided scavenging opportunities for the others.

4

Deposit and assemblage formation

W A BOISMIER

One of the most important questions at Lynford concerns the integrity of the deposits containing the archaeological materials. The previous chapters have shown that most of the artefacts and vertebrate remains recovered from the site accumulated in the channel during its inactive phase after abandonment. The sediments representing this phase are dominated by sediment gravity-flow deposits and other structures indicative of bank erosion, and suggest that most of these materials were transported downslope and deposited into the channel as the bank eroded. They were probably further disturbed after deposition by bioturbation (trampling by animals) and other sedimentary processes. Given these depositional and post-depositional agencies, a key concern is how the three-dimensional spatial patterning of the materials in the channel were impacted on by these processes and what, if anything, the deposits can tell us about human behaviour around the channel margins.

This chapter sets out to investigate the formation of the deposit and the assemblages it contains. It begins with an overview of the various sedimentary contexts in which the archaeological materials occurred, which will provide an interpretative baseline for the analyses in the following sections. This is followed by analysis of the vertical arrangement of objects, undertaken to assess the likely extent of vertical reworking within the channel sediments. The results of a quantitative spatial analysis carried out to investigate pattern and assemblage formation are then considered, and an interpretation offered regarding the integrity of the three-dimensional arrangement of artefacts and vertebrate remains within the sediments of Association B-ii and their potential for the reconstruction of Neanderthal behaviour at the site before the study of the archaeological assemblages in chapter 5.

4.1 Sedimentary deposits

The sediments enclosing the artefact and vertebrate assemblages recovered from the site were laid down by distinctive sets of sedimentary processes associated with the incorporation of terrestrial sediments into the channel through bank slumping and the washing-in of fine particles by surface run-off. Multiple debris-flow episodes, small localised bank collapses, and the washing in of sediments and materials over a period of time are represented by the various facies comprising unit B-ii:04 (*see* Table 2.6 and Figs 2.17–2.20), as well as by the lenses of stony organic sand in the organic sediments of unit B-ii:03 and the massive sand of unit B-ii:01 (*see* Fig 2.16). Bedform and lithological properties of these deposits record local differences in the scale and mode of bank erosion and indicate that deposit formation at Lynford was a complex multi-dimensional affair. Understanding how these sedimentary processes contributed to the three-dimensional arrangement of artefacts and vertebrate remains in the sediments of Association B-ii is fundamental to answering questions as to whether the accumulations of material remains simply represent signatures of sedimentary processes or more complex arrangements reflecting hominin behavioural as well as sedimentary processes (Callow 1986a; Dibble 1995; Street 2002, 5–7; Schild 2005, 61). A key concern for the interpretation of the archaeological evidence from the site is thus an understanding of the sedimentary contexts in which the vertebrate remains and artefactual materials occurred. These contexts are summarised below and provide an interpretative framework for the quantitative analyses in the following sections.

Mass-movement deposits

Facies B-ii:04A, B-ii:04B and B-ii:04D show textural and structural properties typical of the mass movement of water-saturated sediments by debris or mud flow (Innes 1983; Costa 1984; Fritz and Moore 1988, 265–74) with those for the massive sand of unit B-ii:01 characteristic of the mass movement of sediments by bank collapse (Thorne 1982; Miall 2006, 123). Gravel facies B-ii:04B and B-ii:04D are poorly sorted, matrix- to clast-supported, and in B-ii:04B, partially imbricated, with the undulating lower contact of B-ii:04B also indicating the progressive deposition of sediment lobes from the bank into the channel (see Fig 2.18). These fabrics are characteristic of highly viscous laminar pseudoplastic flows initiated by the oversaturation of sediments from heavy rainfalls and/or snowmelt (Caine 1980). Facies B-ii:04A comprises a succession of interdigitated stony organic sands and sandy gravels that are unsorted and matrix-supported with fabrics characteristic of high-velocity slurry-like mud flows (Benedict 1970; Van Steijn *et al* 1988a). Multiple depositional episodes are indicated by this succession, with overbank flood events, sheet wash and the saturation of sediment by torrential or seasonal rainfall, three of the most likely mechanisms responsible for the transport of bank sediments and materials. The massive sand of unit B-ii:01 is sheet-like in character and contains varying densities of unsorted gravel, and buried or partially buried artefacts and vertebrate remains (Fig 4.1). Sediment characteristics suggest multiple shallow slips of bank material, possibly due to rainfall, snowmelt and/or trampling (Buckhouse *et al* 1981; Knighton 1998, 113–18).

Studies of debris and other forms of sediment gravity flows in a variety of modern situations have indicated a number of recurrent patterns in the arrangement of constituent objects. Elongated objects such as stones, artefacts and vertebrate remains within and below the flowing sediment of the main body are typically orientated parallel to flow (Collcutt 1986; Van Steijn and Coutard 1989). The extent of this alignment varies according to type of flow, with objects in highly viscous flows more strongly aligned parallel to flow than those in high-velocity slurry-like flows, which show more variation in orientation but still retain a marked central tendency parallel to flow (Kluskens 1995). Elongated objects also tend to be aligned parallel to flow direction along the boundaries of the flow (Larsson 1982; Van Steijn *et al* 1988a) with objects rafted on the surface either transported and deposited with little change in arrangement or incorporated into the body of the flow as the sediment at the front rolls over (Benedict 1970; Enos 1977; Collcutt 1984). Within or along the lobe at the front of the flow, however, elongated objects tend to be aligned perpendicular to the direction of flow (Larsson 1982; Van Steijn *et al* 1988a), and where the lobe fans out as it slows to a stop, their arrangement becomes more variable as they follow the flow directions of the sediment lobe (Innes 1983; Owen 1991). Object size classes are typically poorly sorted vertically (Kluskens 1995) although field and experimental studies have documented the sorting of large objects towards flow boundaries (base and sides) and a gradual decrease in the size and amount of the coarsest materials downslope (Benedict 1970; Pierson 1981; Collcutt 1984, 1986).

Colluvial deposits

Facies B-ii:04C and the layers and lenses of stony organic sand in unit B-ii:03 show textural and structural properties typical of colluvial

Fig 4.1
Tusk partially embedded in the massive sands of Unit B-ii:01.

deposits produced by slopewash and small-scale slips of bank material (Limbrey 1975, 205–8; French 1976, 141–3; Ballantyne and Harris 1994, 120–5; Goldberg and Macphail 2006, 76–84). The stony sands of Facies B-ii:04C are arranged in a succession of thin, inclined beds of sand and unsorted gravel, vertically separated in places by small eroded lenses of organic sediment with elongated clasts, typically aligned downslope and partially imbricated (see Fig 2.19). These bedding structures are characteristic of colluvial sediments deposited largely by slopewash and small-scale sediment slips, and indicate multiple depositional episodes of bank materials (Gil and Slupik 1972; Limbrey 1975, 91–3; Allen 1991). Periodic interruptions in sedimentation are also suggested by the lenses of eroded organic sediment embedded within the deposit. The stony organic sands of unit B-ii:03 comprise lenses and layers of unsorted gravel and coarse sand of variable thickness and area (Fig 4.2). These sediments are interpreted as rapid, small-scale depositional episodes of bank sediment and materials by slopewash, sediment slips and bank collapse (Reineck and Singh 1980, 145–6; Ballantyne and Harris 1994, 120). The last of these is possibly also related to the movements of large animals in and around the channel (Trimble 1994).

Studies of slope processes have shown a number of characteristic features in the arrangement of objects by slopewash and small-scale sediment slips. Elongated objects tend to be orientated predominantly downslope, parallel or near-parallel to the direction of sediment flow (Frostrick and Reid 1983; Petraglia 1993; Kluskens 1995; Morton 2004, table 2.4). Alignments perpendicular or transverse to direction of flow also occur, but in lower frequencies, and appear largely to be the result of objects sliding or rolling downslope with sediment slips (Rick 1976; Butzer 1982, 101–3; Kluskens 1995). Sorting is much more variable and dependent on factors such as slope gradient, length of slope and flow velocity as well as the weight and size of objects (Rick 1976; Kluskens 1995; Morton 2004, table 2.4). Overall, small size classes tend to be transported farther downslope than large or heavy objects, while longitudinal sorting is characterised by the coarse-tail grading of objects in a downslope direction (Allen 1991; Kluskens 1995). In sediment slips objects are poorly sorted longitudinally as they are largely transported as part of the sediment body (Rick 1976; Thorne 1982). Object size classes also tend to be poorly sorted vertically with colluvial sediments characteristically composed of a mixture of different size classes (Butzer 1982, 56–7, table 4.2; Bell 1983; Allen 1991; Goldberg and Macphail 2006, 86, table 5.1).

Discussion

The deposits indicate that sedimentation occurred over a reasonable time period though probably less than 100 years. Facies B-ii:04B partially buries the organic sediments of unit B-ii:03 and forms a new channel edge against which the sediments of Facies B-ii:04C built up.

Fig 4.2
Lenses and layers of stony organic sand within the organic sediments of Unit B-ii:03.

The succession of sediments for B-ii:04A reflect at least two, and probably more, depositional episodes with multiple shallow slips of bank material suggested by the massive sand of unit B-ii:01. More discrete episodes of bank erosion are also indicated by Facies B-ii:04B and B-ii:04D and the isolated lenses and layers of stony, organic sand. Thus it is likely that the three-dimensional arrangement of archaeological materials in the sediments of Association B-ii is largely the result of a variety of sedimentary processes, and that deposition was intermittent and took place over variable periods of time. These processes have been shown to produce a number of characteristic signatures in the arrangement of materials, and suggest that the artefacts and vertebrate remains at Lynford have probably been subjected to a substantial degree of reworking through the downslope transport and deposition of bank sediments and materials into the channel. This would have been a cumulative process, suggesting that the three-dimensional arrangement of materials at the site is more likely to reflect local differences in the mode and scale of bank erosion than hominin behaviour. Fluvial reworking and the effects of other post-depositional processes such as trampling on the condition and arrangement of vertebrate remains and artefacts have been discussed elsewhere by Schreve, White and Donahue and Evans (chapter 5).

4.2 Size sorting and mixing

Lithic and bone conjoins (*see* Tables 4.11 and 5.25, and Figs 5.26 and 5.55) occur in the basal sands, sediment gravity flows and organic sediments of Association B-ii and in the channel infill sediments of Association B-iii. In Association B-ii the vertical distances of refits are all under 0.60m and document the displacement and differential sinking of at least some of the artefacts and bones within the sediments of this association.

The small number of these conjoins raises a number of fundamental questions concerning the extent of vertical reworking within the sediments of Association B-ii. In particular, we need to ask whether the distribution of materials in the sediments represents significant depositional patterning reflective of hominin behaviour, or simply the mixed accumulations of vertically reworked materials with little interpretive value for the archaeologist. Resolving this question is of some importance, as a number of palaeobiological and archaeological studies have shown that the bioturbation and other sedimentary disturbance processes identified for Association B-ii have a substantial impact on the vertical arrangement of materials within soft sediments (Gifford and Behrensmeyer 1977; Wood and Johnson 1978; Bunn *et al* 1980; Shipman 1981, 95–6; Villa 1982; Haynes 1988a; Lyman 1994a, 410–11; Monnier 2003, 45–57; Morton 2004, 48–9; see also Behrensmeyer 1982; Rigaud and Simek 1987; Gaudzinski and Turner 1999). To address this question, the vertical reworking of materials hinted at by the refitting was further investigated by a quantitative analysis of object size and position within the sediments of Association B-ii.

Methods

Multiple regression (Blalock 1979, 451–504; Shennan 1985, 33–44, 1988, 166–87; Baxter 2003, 55–9) was used to assess the effects of channel geometry (slope of channel base and sides) on object position with OD height as the dependent variable and grid coordinates (x: easting; y: northing) as the independent variables. The residuals from this analysis represent the amount of variation in OD height unexplained by channel geometry, and provide the data for examining size-sorting and mixing effects produced by the post-depositional vertical movement of objects. Analysis of variance (Blalock 1979, 335–75; Drennan 1996, 171–7) was used to examine vertical size-sorting effects with residual OD height from the multiple regression as the dependent variable, and six size classes as the independent variables. Mixing effects were assessed using box-and-whisker plots (Tukey 1977, 39–41; Hartwig and Dearing 1979, 23–5; see also Drennan 1996, 39–44) of residual OD height values for the six size classes. Object size class data for the sediments of Association B-ii (units B-ii:01; B-ii:02 and B-ii:03) used in the analysis are set out in Table 4.1.

Channel geometry

The channel is orientated west-north-west and slopes gently from c 8.68m OD in the east to c 7.42m OD in the west at an angle of approximately 3° to 4°. Fig 4.3 shows the longitudinal and transverse profiles of the vertical

4 DEPOSIT AND ASSEMBLAGE FORMATION

Table 4.1 Size class data used in the analysis

	Sc01 <3cm	Sc02 3–6cm	Sc03 6–9cm	Sc04 9–12cm	Sc05 12–15cm	Sc06 >15cm
mammoth	41	269	273	129	87	171
woolly rhinoceros		8	2	1		1
reindeer	8	25	21	5	5	7
horse		1	3	1		1
bison					1	3
indeterminate and unidentified	125	320	135	30	4	4
carnivores	3	8	4			
lithics	35	138	77	39	12	5
total	212	769	515	206	108	192

distribution of faunal and lithic material in the channel. Along the longitudinal east-west axis the material is distributed in a thin almond-shaped lens, dipping to the west in accordance with the slope of the channel. On the transverse north–south axis this distribution is also lens-shaped and displays a broad shallow convex-up profile following the shape of the channel. The transverse distribution is also partially separated into upper and lower elements by the sediment gravity flow deposits along the north edge of the channel. These patterns clearly suggest that the vertical position of an object in terms of its OD height is related to the geometry of the channel.

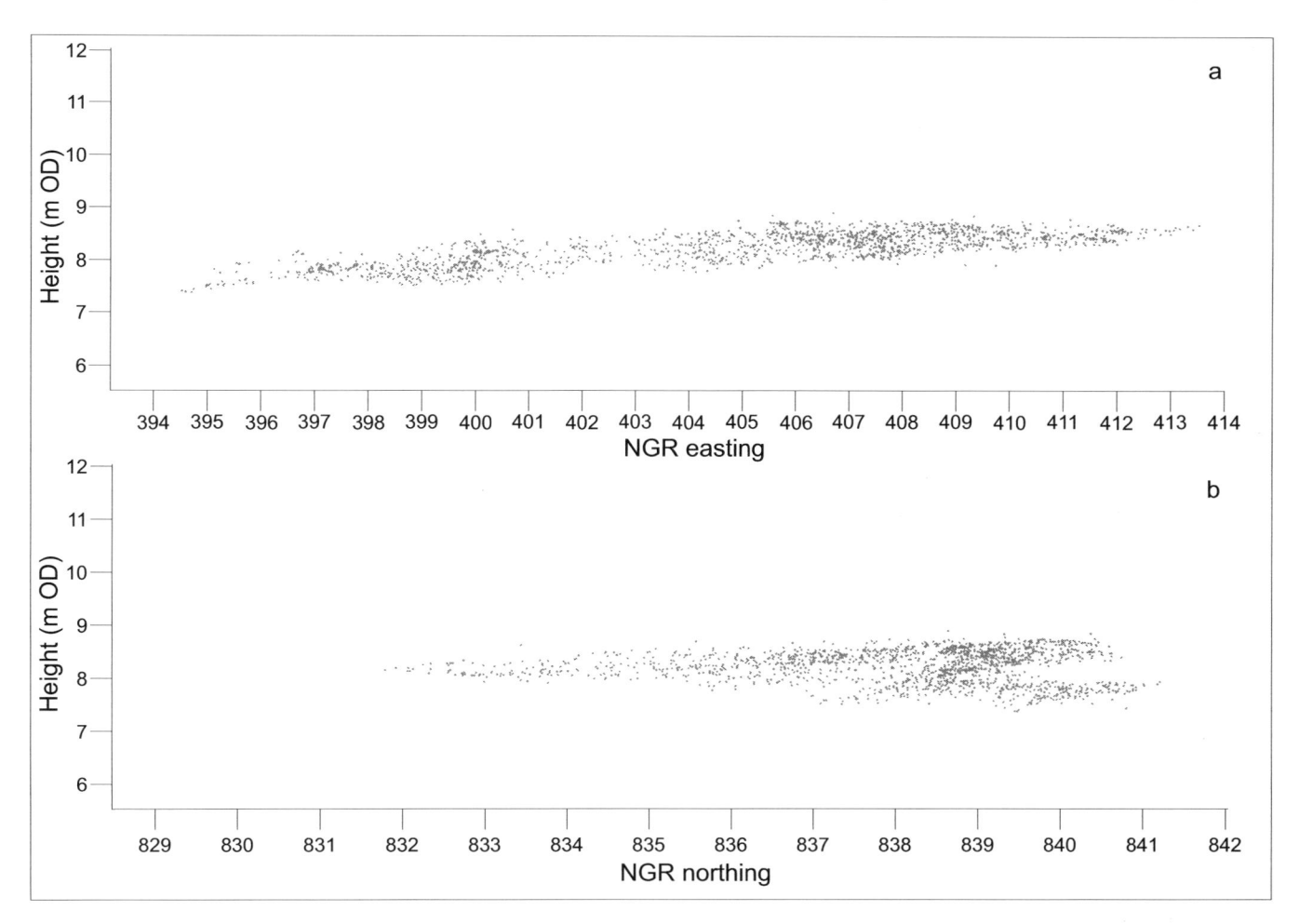

The results of the multiple regression analysis used to assess the effects of channel geometry on object vertical position are

Fig 4.3
Vertical distribution of materials within the sediments of Association B-ii: (A) longitudinal (east–west) profile; (B) Transverse (north–south) profile.

Table 4.2 Results of the multiple regression

faunal remains

zero-order correlations

	OD height	X coord	Y coord
OD height			
X coord	0.812		
Y coord	0.394	−0.434	

coefficients

constant (A)	−51.319	multiple R	0.812
X coord	0.058	R^2	0.659
Y coord	0.043	adj R^2	0.658

lithic artefacts

zero-order correlations

	OD height	X coord	Y coord
OD height			
X coord	0.85		
Y coord	0.296	−0.424	

coefficients

constant (A)	−39.124	multiple R	0.858
X coord	0.065	R^2	0.736
Y coord	0.025	adj R^2	0.734

presented in Table 4.2. Zero-order correlations for both classes of material show OD height to be highly positively correlated with the x coordinate along the longitudinal east-west axis, and weakly correlated with the y coordinate on the transverse north–south axis. The two coordinate variables are also negatively correlated with each other, and reflect the shape of the surviving channel deposits. Values for R^2 in the table show that 65.84 per cent ($R^2 \times 100$) of the variation in OD heights for faunal remains, and 73.55 per cent of the variation in OD heights for lithics is accounted for or 'explained' by the least-squares surface of the x and y coordinates, that is, by the geometry of the channel. The results also indicate that a given increase/decrease in longitudinal (x) position has a greater effect on object OD height than a given increase/decrease in transverse (y) position and show that the slope of the channel to the west-north-west partly determines object OD height within the sediments making up its fill. That is, where the channel is deeper, objects have lower OD heights, and where the channel is shallower, objects have higher OD heights. Only 34.16 per cent and 24.45 per cent of the variation in faunal and lithic OD heights remains unexplained by channel geometry.

Size sorting

The results of the analysis of variance carried out to identify the possible size sorting of objects after the effects of channel geometry (that is, variation in object OD height accounted for by its location in the channel) had been removed are presented in Table 4.3. Values of F for both categories of material are significant at the .05 level of probability, and indicate that when channel geometry is controlled for, the remaining variance in object OD height is largely accounted for by size.

Residual OD height means for faunal and lithic size classes appear to be differentially distributed vertically and fall into three principal size class groupings (Fig 4.4, Table 4.4). The first group is composed of objects such as handaxe finishing flakes and small bone fragments less than 60mm in size (size classes Sc01 and Sc02), which have positive residual OD height means, suggesting that smaller sized objects typically tend to occur higher up in channel sediments. The second group is made up of a similar set of vertebrate fragments, débitage and façonnage products, and retouched tools between 60mm and 150mm in size (size classes Sc03, Sc04 and Sc05) that have negative residual OD height means. These values suggest that objects in this size range have a tendency to occur lower in channel sediments than the materials comprising the first group. The third group is

Table 4.3 Results of the analysis of variance

	sums of squares	degrees of freedom	estimate of v (Variance)	F
faunal remains				
total	52.652	1696		
between	2.135	5	0.4269	14.29
within	50.517	1691	0.2988	
lithic artefacts				
total	8.934	302		
between	0.419	5	0.0839	2.93
within	8.516	297	0.0287	

4 DEPOSIT AND ASSEMBLAGE FORMATION

Table 4.4 Size class summary statistics (parametric)

size class	no.	mean	standard deviation	minimum	maximum	range
faunal size classes						
Sc01 <3cm	177	0.036	0.180	−0.350	0.459	0.809
Sc02 3cm–6cm	637	0.033	0.179	−0.410	0.516	0.927
Sc03 6cm–9cm	431	−0.018	0.176	−0.543	0.534	1.077
Sc04 9cm–12cm	172	−0.029	0.156	−0.353	0.409	0.763
Sc05 12cm–15cm	95	−0.022	0.154	−0.319	0.518	0.837
Sc06 >15cm	185	−0.069	0.155	−0.604	0.417	1.022
lithic size classes						
Sc01 <3cm	35	0.049	0.157	−0.233	0.397	0.629
Sc02 3cm–6cm	138	0.021	0.187	−0.410	0.570	0.980
Sc03 6cm–9cm	75	−0.019	0.142	−0.313	0.329	0.643
Sc04 9cm–12cm	39	−0.049	0.179	−0.499	0.337	0.837
Sc05 12cm–15cm	11	−0.048	0.129	−0.247	0.148	0.396
Sc06 >15cm	5	−0.157	0.069	−0.239	−0.079	0.160

composed of objects greater than 150mm in size (size class Sc06) and includes complete and/or large fragments of mammoth bone, tusk and teeth, reindeer antler and a small number of large unretouched flakes and handaxes. This group possesses the largest negative mean residual OD height values, and clearly suggests that these large objects typically occur at lower sediment depths than the other two groups of material. Therefore, residual OD height means values appear to reflect the effects of vertical size sorting on object positions.

Mixing

Box-and-whisker plots, used to identify the possible mixing of objects after the effects of channel geometry on object position had been removed, are presented in Fig 4.5 and the data summarised in Table 4.5. Plots for both categories of material show the spread of residual OD heights around their respective medians, and appear to reflect the vertical mixing and sorting of objects within the sediments of Association B-ii. Residual OD height medians for faunal and lithic size classes fall into the same three size class groupings identified previously, suggesting that the different size classes tend, on average, to be differentially distributed vertically. The spread of residual OD heights around these medians is reasonably wide for most size classes and indicates that objects appear to be dispersed vertically throughout channel sediments with the overlap of residual OD height values for individual size-class spreads, suggesting the

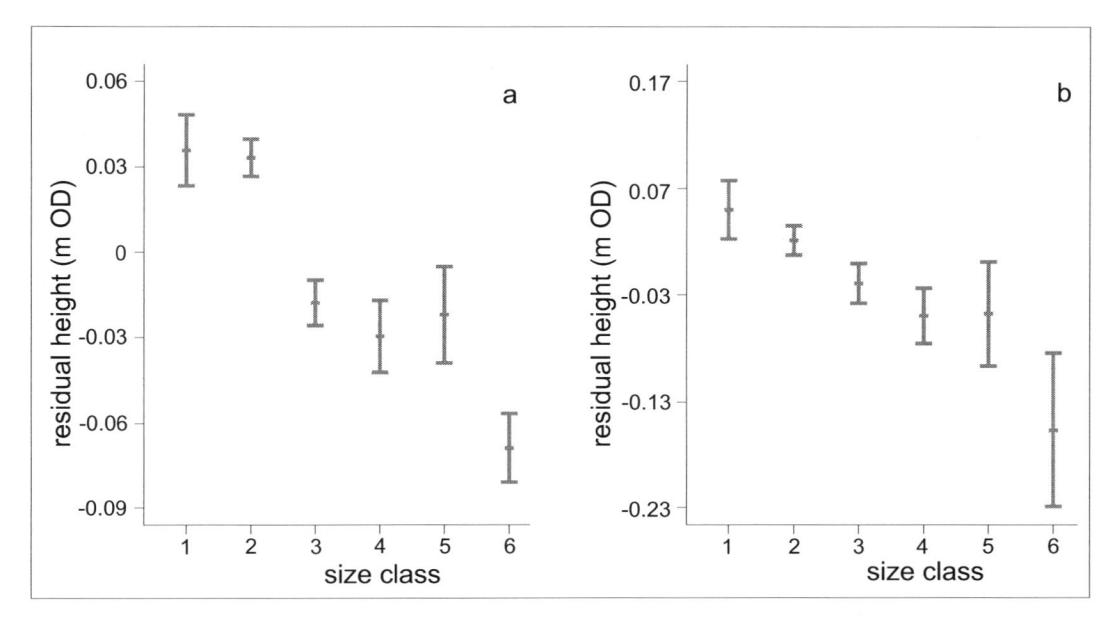

Fig 4.4 Vertical size sorting showing size class means and standard deviations: (A) faunal remains; (B) lithic artefacts. Note: bar equal to one standard deviation.

Table 4.5 Size class summary statistics (non-parametric)

size class	no.	median	lower quartile	upper quartile	interquartile range
faunal size classes					
Sc01 <3cm	177	0.027	−0.101	0.143	0.244
Sc02 3cm–6cm	637	0.019	−0.099	0.161	0.261
Sc03 6cm–9cm	431	−0.023	−0.147	0.109	0.257
Sc04 9cm–12cm	172	−0.035	−0.139	0.083	0.223
Sc05 12cm–15cm	95	−0.048	−0.135	0.068	0.203
Sc06 >15cm	185	−0.089	−0.158	0.016	0.174
lithic size classes					
Sc01 <3cm	35	0.068	−0.096	0.173	0.539
Sc02 3cm–6cm	138	−0.004	−0.117	0.148	0.529
Sc03 6cm–9cm	75	−0.018	−0.116	0.054	0.339
Sc04 9cm–12cm	39	−0.050	−0.179	0.090	0.538
Sc05 12cm–15cm	11	−0.049	−0.126	0.045	0.341
Sc06 >15cm	5	−0.141	−0.215	−0.109	0.211

Fig 4.5
Vertical mixing showing size class medians and spreads: (a) faunal remains; (b) lithic artefacts. Note: box equal to upper and lower quartiles around median, whiskers – the spread of values and isolated dots outliers. (1) Sc01 <30mm; (2) Sc02 30mm–60mm; (3) Sc03 60mm–90mm; (4) Sc04 90mm–120mm; (5) Sc05 120mm–150mm; (6) Sc06 >150mm.

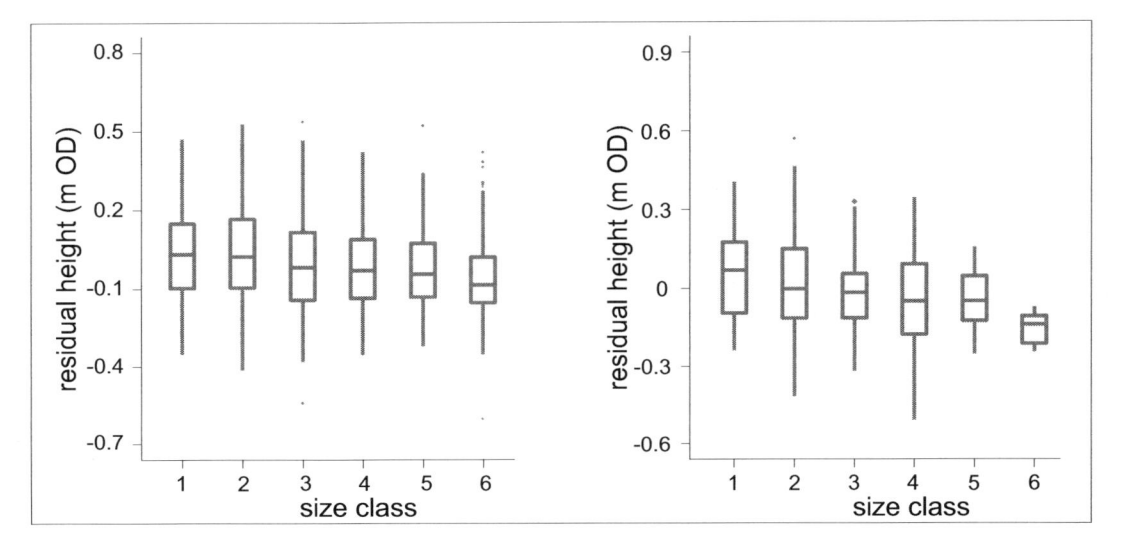

vertical mixing of different-sized objects. Outliers are also present in three faunal and two lithic size classes and indicate that median and, by implication, mean values, are marginally biased and tend to slightly over- or under-estimate residual OD heights. These outliers, however, do provide further evidence for the vertical mixing of objects within channel sediments suggested by the residual OD height values for size-class spreads. Residual OD height patterning displayed by the plots thus appears to reflect the effects of both vertical mixing and sorting processes on object positions.

Discussion

The results of these analyses indicate that, when channel geometry is controlled for, the remaining variance in object OD height can largely be interpreted or 'explained' as reflecting the joint mixing and sorting actions of sedimentary processes on the vertical positions of objects. Sedimentary processes identified for Association B-ii include the deposition of artefacts and vertebrate remains by sediment gravity flow, surface run-off and other forms of bank erosion; limited fluvial rearrangement by oscillating wave or water levels; and the reworking of sediments and objects by animals moving in and around the margins of the channel. These processes would have acted cumulatively on the three-dimensional arrangement of artefacts and bones and therefore it is not possible to separate the effects of one set of processes from those of another using object vertical positions. However, it is reasonable to assume that these depositional processes would have produced vertically mixed accumulations of faunal and lithic size classes as a result of their episodic nature and the differential sinking of different-sized objects in soft sediments. Moreover, the massive character and micromorphology of the organic sediments, together with the *in situ* trampling breakage suggested by the close conjoins of some bone and antler refits strongly hint that trampling and other post-depositional disturbance processes were reasonably extensive and would have further rearranged these accumulations of material. The actions of these depositional and post-depositional processes thus appear to largely account for the patterns identified by the analysis, and indicate that a degree of vertical reworking of material has occurred in the sediments of Association B-ii.

How serious were the effects of this vertical reworking on the three-dimensional arrangement of artefacts and vertebrate remains? Data presented in Tables 4.3 and 4.4 show the vertical spread of faunal and lithic size classes to be highly variable with individual ranges extending from 0.16m to 1.07m and generally greater than 0.50m. Size classes appear to be widely dispersed vertically, with their variable ranges indicating that the different size classes are reasonably well mixed vertically. These patterns suggest that for Association B-ii as a whole, the vertical reworking of objects within sediments has been extensive. The three-dimensional arrangement of artefacts and vertebrate remains in the sediments of Association B-ii thus appears to represent, at least in part, mixed distributions of vertically reworked materials.

4.3 Spatial patterning

Taphonomic, refitting and quantitative analyses of the artefact and vertebrate remains from the sediments of Association B-ii indicate minimal fluvial rearrangement, horizontal refit distances under 5.95m and the vertical mixing of objects by depositional and post-depositional processes (see also Schreve, White, chapter 5). These patterns pose a number of questions concerning the preservation of information regarding hominin behaviour within Association B-ii sediments. Do the accumulations of artefacts and vertebrate remains simply represent signatures of sedimentary depositional and post-depositional processes, or more complex spatial arrangements reflecting behavioural as well as sedimentary processes? If the latter is even partially true, then at what scale or level of resolution do these arrangements of material provide reliable information on which to base inferences regarding the character of Neanderthal behaviour at the site? How the material accumulated in the channel is thus of some importance for understanding both wider mobility strategies (Duchadeau-Kervazo 1986; Geneste 1989; Turq 1989; Burke 2000; Conard and Prindiville 2000; Patou-Mathis 2000) and the organisation of Neanderthal activities around and in the channel (Farizy 1994; Conard and Adler 1997; Pettitt 1997; Alder and Conard 2005; Vaquero 2005). Spatial analysis of the three-dimensional arrangement of artefacts and vertebrate remains within the sediments of Association B-ii was undertaken to investigate these issues.

Methods

K-means pure locational clustering (Kintigh and Ammerman 1982; Kintigh 1990; see also Simek 1984; Koetje 1987; Vaquero 1999) was employed to identify spatial patterning within channel sediments and followed the procedures set out by Koetje (1991) for the analysis of three-dimensional distributions. Artefacts and vertebrate remains from the sediments of Association B-ii (units B-ii:01, B-ii:02 and B-ii:03) were pooled together for the analysis, and a first-order trend surface fitted to the three-dimensional distribution. The residuals from this surface were then weighted by a factor of 11 to ensure the vertical separation by the cluster analysis of objects with grid coordinates converted into z-scores. The k-means cluster analysis was performed on the converted coordinate data using the KMEANS programme of the TOOL KIT package (Kintigh 1992) with the maximum number of clusters set to 16. Significant decreases in the sum-squared-error statistic showed an optimal clustering solution at six clusters, which was considered an appropriate level of detail for an initial investigation into the three-dimensional arrangement of artefacts and vertebrate remains in channel sediments. Characteristics such as shape, density and assemblage composition were tabulated for each of these clusters, and the data examined for interpretable patterning. Clusters defined by the analysis are shown in Figs 4.6 to 4.12 with data summarising individual cluster characteristics presented in Table 4.6. Specific details of individual clusters are also available in digital archive.

Table 4.6 Cluster descriptions

	Cluster 1	Cluster 2	Cluster 3	Cluster 4	Cluster 5	Cluster 6
area m^2	42.10	8.83	57.96	45.83	10.02	22.74
volume m^3	33.26	6.36	47.53	42.16	5.21	18.42
density per m^2	11.05	20.16	9.40	10.71	9.18	5.19
density per m^3	13.98	27.99	11.47	11.65	17.66	6.41

Location and context

Figs 4.6 to 4.12 show that the clusters identified by the analysis are located in the north-west (clusters 1 and 2) and central (clusters 4, 5 and 6) parts of the channel and along its northern edge (Cluster 3). Cluster 1 is composed of objects occurring largely in the stony organic sands of unit B-ii:03 and within the upper 0.05m to 0.10m of the underlying sands of B-ii:01. Cluster 2 occurs within the organic sediments of B-ii:03 and is situated above Cluster 1, which is also partially underneath sediment gravity flows B-ii:04B (debris flow) and B-ii:04C (stony sands), with Cluster 2 distributed along their leading edges and the large mammoth tusk in it partly embedded in B-ii:04B. The extent to which sediment gravity-flow deposits originally covered Cluster 1 is unknown, as the deposits overlying the organic sediments in this area were removed by mineral extraction prior to the start of excavation. Cluster 3 is spread along the sloping north side of the channel and is partially situated underneath sediment gravity-flow B-ii:04D (debris flow) and above Cluster 5, with the objects making up this cluster occurring in both the stony organic sands of B-ii:03 and the underlying massive sand of unit B-ii:01. Clusters 5 and 6 are also largely composed of objects in or on the surface of the massive sand of B-ii:01, and appear to form parts of a larger distribution, separated by the analysis on the basis of OD height differences. Cluster 4 is situated within the stony organic sands of sediment gravity flow B-ii:04A.

Data presented in Table 4.6 suggest that cluster area and object density varies in accordance with the different sediments recorded for Association B-ii. The stony organic sands found within the organic sediments of unit B-ii:03 are concentrated in one part of Cluster 1 and represented in other parts by isolated layers and lenses, whereas in Cluster 3 they are more uniformly distributed. Objects tend to be distributed within these sediments, with cluster areas and densities appearing to represent depositional zones reflecting local variations in the slumping and washing-in of bank sediments along the north side of the channel, rather than differences in the mode of deposition. Cluster 3 is further distinguished by the occurrence of objects within the underlying massive sand of unit B-ii:01, which also contains clusters 5 and 6; together these clusters form a much larger depositional zone that is associated with multiple sediment gravity flow episodes. Objects making up Cluster 2 are distributed along, and occasionally in, the leading edges of sediment gravity flows B-ii:04B (debris flow) and B-ii:04C (stony sands), and suggest that Cluster 2 represents a depositional zone reflecting the outcome of a succession of different modes and scales of bank erosion. The objects comprising Cluster 4 all occur within the spread of stony organic sands, making up sediment gravity flow B-ii:04A (mud flows) and indicate that this cluster represents a depositional zone associated with the succession of sediment gravity flows along the south side of the channel.

Internal arrangement

Internally, the spatial arrangement of objects within clusters tends to comprise spreads of material. These form either one or more localised concentrations, or discrete concentrations largely separated from the rest of the distribution (Figs 4.4–4.10). Localised concentrations of material within larger distributions are apparent for clusters 1, 3 and 4, and less so for the remaining clusters, although the distribution of material in clusters 5 and 6 suggests a degree of small-scale object clustering around mammoth tusks. Discrete concentrations of material forming part of larger cluster distributions are also present in clusters 3 and 4, and suggest that these clusters are made up of more than one depositional area grouped together by the analysis on the basis

Fig 4.6 (opposite) Distribution of artefacts and vertebrate remains within the sediments of Association B-ii.

4 DEPOSIT AND ASSEMBLAGE FORMATION

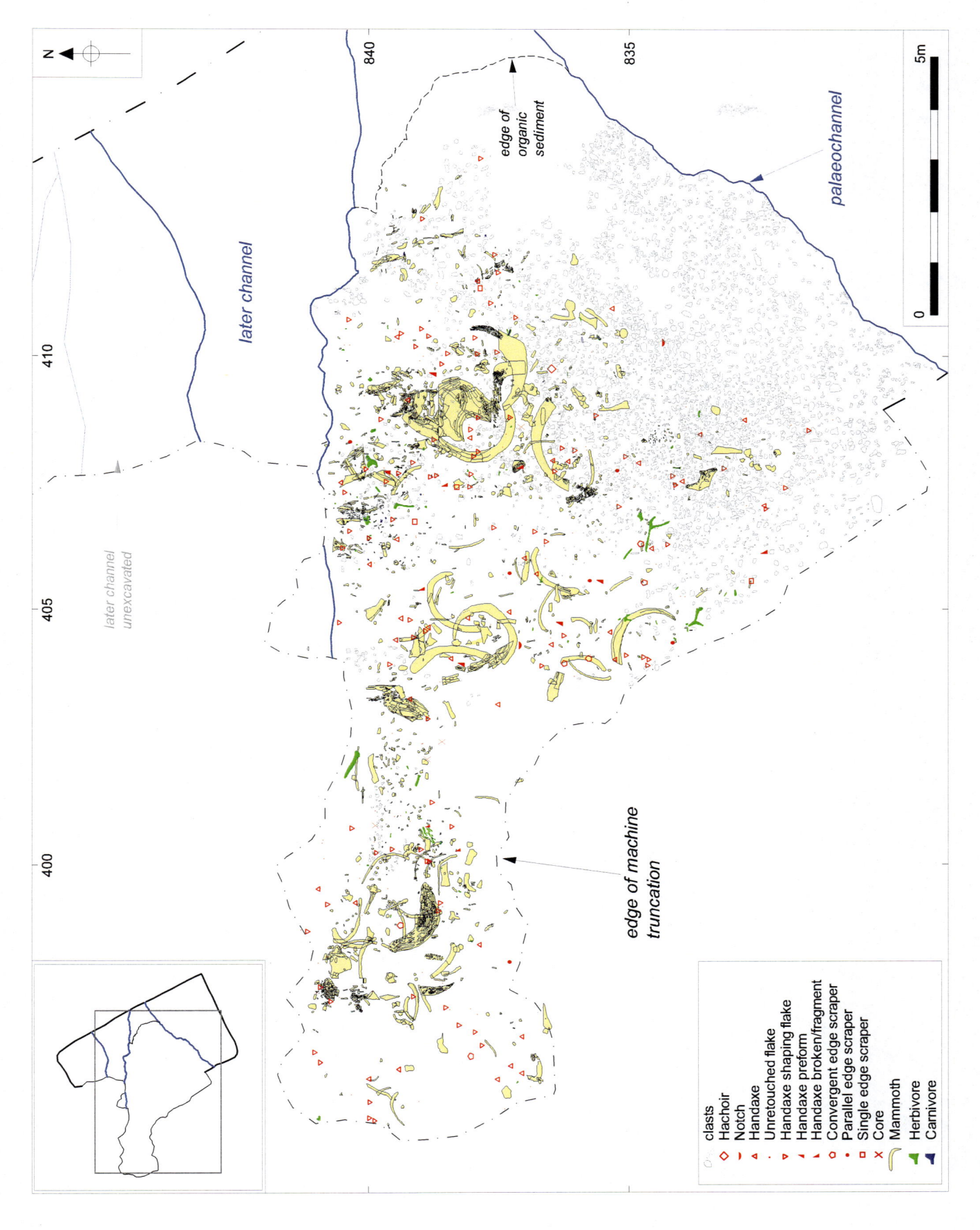

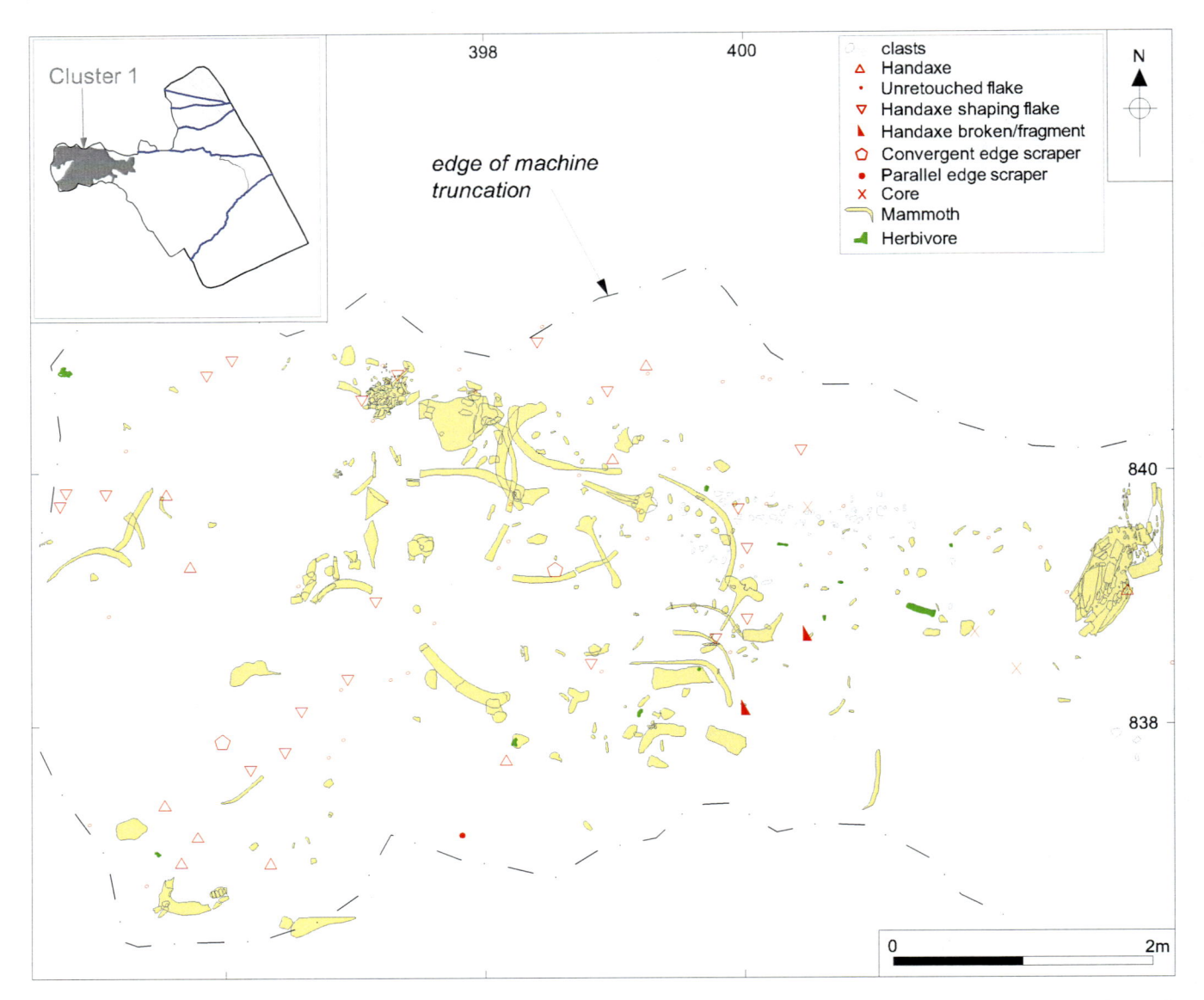

Fig 4.7
Cluster 1.

of OD height similarities. They do occur, however, within the same sediments as the rest of the cluster and provide a further indication that the clusters defined by the analysis represent accumulations of material derived from multiple depositional episodes and not discrete depositional episodes associated with specific sedimentary or behavioural processes. These patterns support those identified for cluster locations noted previously, and clearly indicate that the clusters represent depositional zones rather than depositional episodes.

Data summarised in Table 4.7 suggest that object orientations are related to local variations in depositional environments. Clusters 1 and 3 form a near-contiguous distribution of objects along the north edge of the channel with some 616 (70.48 per cent) of the total number orientated north–south and either at right or near-right angles to the channel edge and 258 (29.52 per cent) orientated parallel-near-parallel to it. Parallel-near-parallel orientations (east–west axis) are dominated in Cluster 1 by elongated objects

Table 4.7 Object orientations: north–south orientations 315° to 45° and 225° to 135°; east–west orientations 315° to 225° and 45° to 135°

	north–south		east–west	
	no.	%	no.	%
Cluster 1	254	67.73	121	32.27
Cluster 2	57	39.58	87	60.42
Cluster 3	362	72.55	137	27.45
Cluster 4	274	63.28	159	36.72
Cluster 5	40	53.33	35	46.67
Cluster 6	58	57.43	45	42.57

Fig 4.8 Cluster 2.

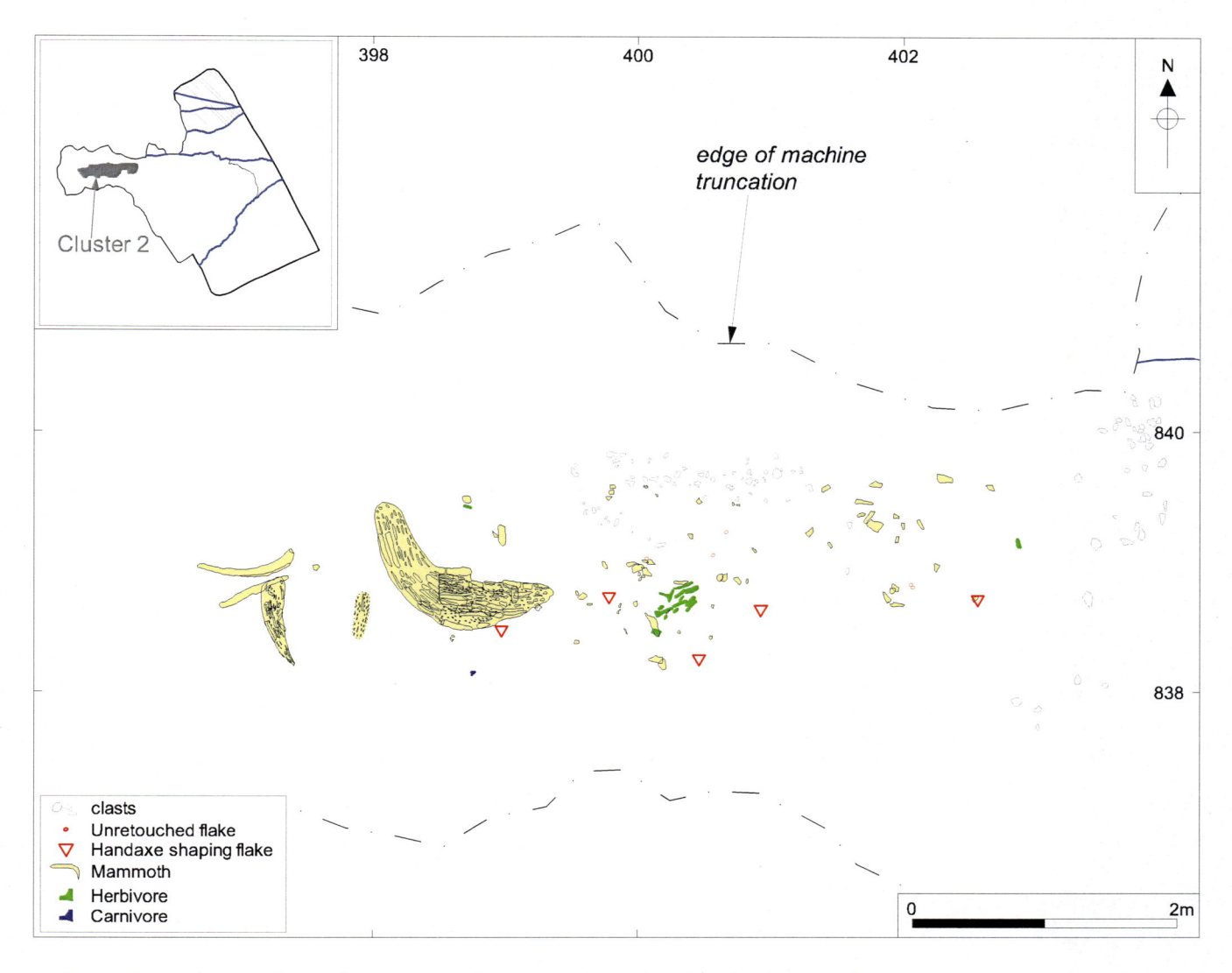

such as ribs and other bone fragments and suggest a degree of fluvial rearrangement for materials deposited along the margins of the channel by bank erosion (Behrensmeyer 1975; Shipman 1981, 69–76; Morton 2004, 34–7). In Cluster 3 a similar set of objects dominates perpendicular orientations (north-south axis) and indicates that alignment largely follows the downslope flow of sediments deposited by small-scale slips and slopewash (Frostrick and Reid 1983; Petraglia 1993; Kluskens 1995). Objects in clusters 5 and 6 do not display any preferred orientation and are very similar in appearance to those for sediment gravity flows, where elongated objects tend to fan out with the sediment lobe at the front of the flow and give object orientation a random appearance (Benedict 1970; Innes 1983; Owen 1991). Object orientation for clusters 2 and 4 also appears to represent sediment gravity-flow patterning with the dominance of east-west orientations in Cluster 2 typical of the perpendicular alignment of elongated objects along the fronts of debris flows (Larsson 1982; Van Steijn *et al* 1988b), and the predominantly north-south orientations in Cluster 4 characteristic of the tendency for objects within debris and mud flows to align parallel to the flow (Collcutt 1986; Van Steijn and Coutard 1989; Kluskens 1995).

Assemblage composition

Data for vertebrates summarised in Table 4.8 show that cluster assemblages are dominated by mammoth, with woolly rhinoceros, reindeer, horse and bison less abundant, and often absent or represented by single specimens in some of the assemblages. Mammoth cranial and post-cranial skeletal elements are numerically

Table 4.8 Summary of cluster vertebrate data

	Cluster 1	Cluster 2	Cluster 3	Cluster 4	Cluster 5	Cluster 6
vertebrate representation						
mammoth	222	79	279	295	54	42
woolly Rhinoceros	1	1	6	2		
reindeer	10	12	12	10	2	13
horse	1			2		
bison	1		1	2		
indeterminate & unidentified	141	74	167	183	20	29
carnivores		1	9	3		
total	376	167	474	497	76	84
size class summary						
Sc01 <3cm		45	33	47	43	36
Sc02 3cm-6cm	122	81	188	166	13	22
Sc03 6cm-9cm	101	32	108	150	17	33
Sc04 9cm-12cm	34	11	55	50	16	9
Sc05 12cm-15cm	23	6	25	33	12	2
Sc06 >15cm	51	4	51	55	15	12
total	376	167	474	497	76	84
weathering summary						
Stage 1	8	1	8	4		
Stage 2	86	23	67	56	10	9
Stage 3	211	110	270	307	41	56
Stage 4	46	22	84	99	16	13
Stage 5	25	11	45	31	9	6
total	376	167	474	497	76	84
bone modification summary						
carnivore gnawing	11	1	18	23	1	7
rodent gnawing	2			2		
root etching		1	2	2		
abrasion	5	4	6	6	3	1
total	18	6	26	33	4	8

abundant in all cluster assemblages, and together with indeterminate bone fragments account for between 84 per cent and 98 per cent of the total number of vertebrate remains in individual assemblages. Reindeer remains are also present in all six clusters and represented by low frequencies of antler, teeth and leg bones. Horse and woolly rhinoceros are represented primarily by teeth and leg bones in four clusters, with bison present in three. The remains of three carnivore species (bear, fox and wolf) are also present in three clusters and comprise a small number of teeth and bones. No complete or partial skeletons are present in any cluster assemblage (see also Schreve, chapter 5). Cluster assemblages are thus composed of different skeletal elements from a number of species, suggesting that skeletal material was largely disarticulated and widely dispersed prior to deposition (Hill 1979; Behrensmeyer 1991; Haynes 1985, 1988a).

Vertebrate remains in these clusters are typically fragmentary, are in varying states of preservation and are characterised by a wide range of bone sizes (*see* Table 4.8). Most specimens are highly fragmented, with cluster assemblages composed predominately of fragments less than 150mm in size regardless of species, with the majority of fragments smaller than 90mm in overall dimensions. Vertebrate remains larger than 150mm in size represented in cluster assemblages tend to be mammoth skeletal elements such as tusks, ribs, vertebrae and scapula or pelvis fragments and fragments or splinters of tusk and leg bones. Weathering stages 2 to 5 (see Schreve, chapter 5)

4 DEPOSIT AND ASSEMBLAGE FORMATION

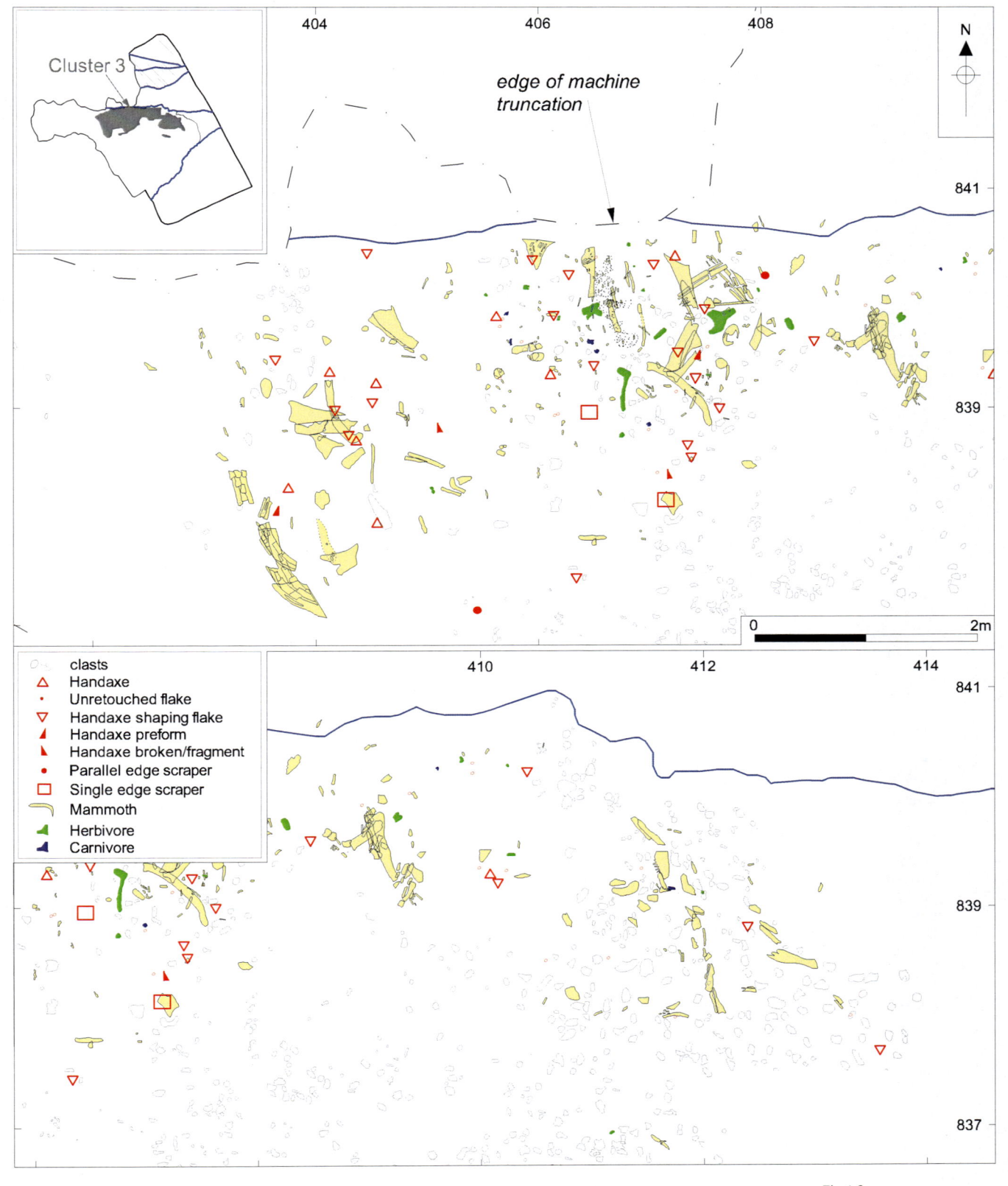

edge of machine truncation

clasts
△ Handaxe
· Unretouched flake
▽ Handaxe shaping flake
◣ Handaxe preform
◣ Handaxe broken/fragment
● Parallel edge scraper
☐ Single edge scraper
⌒ Mammoth
◣ Herbivore
◣ Carnivore

Fig 4.9
Cluster 3.

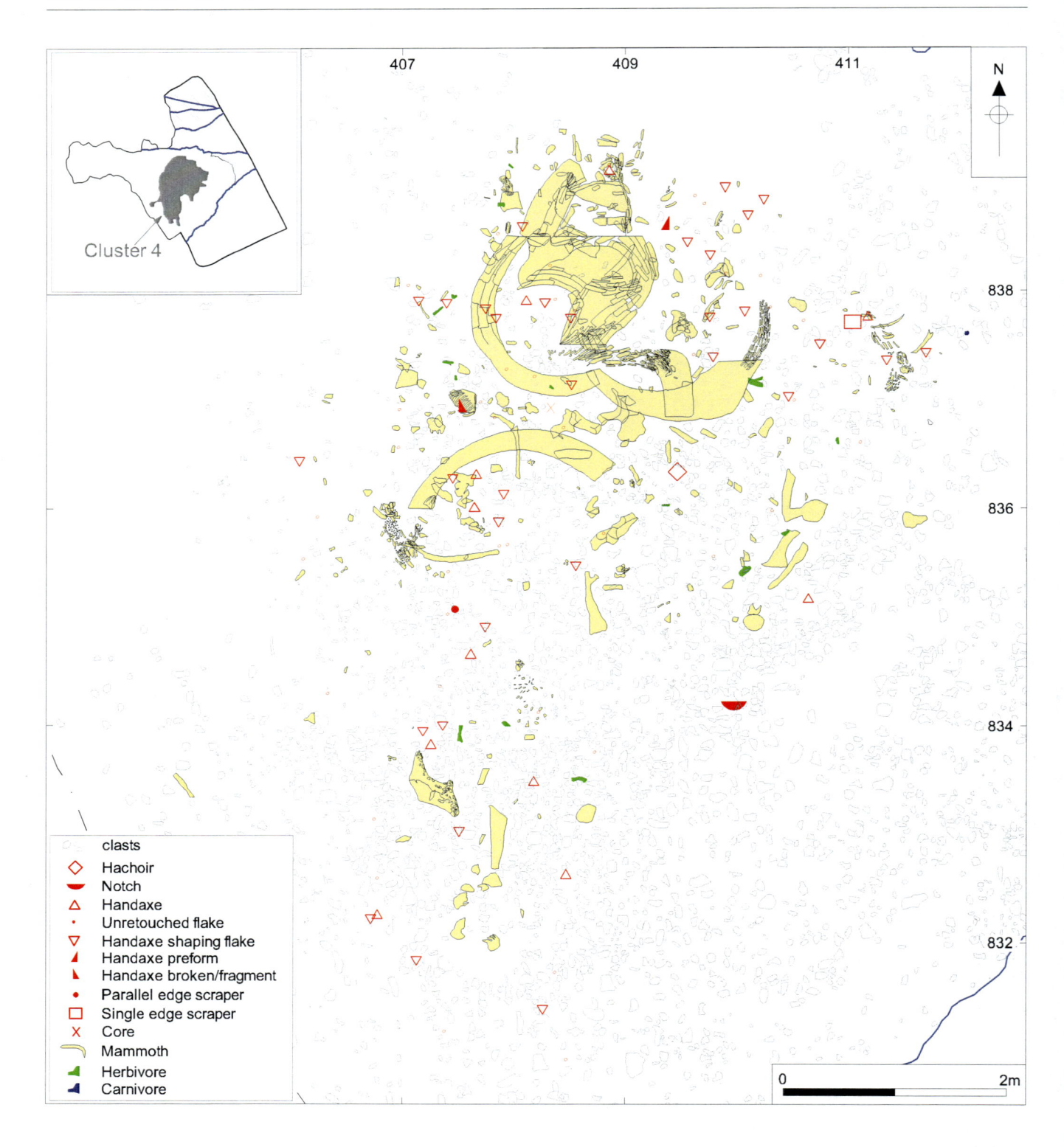

Fig 4.10
Cluster 4.

dominate assemblage composition and appear to indicate substantial and/or variable periods of surface exposure for vertebrate remains prior to final burial. Root damage and other forms of bone modification such as scratches and incisions largely attributable to trampling, as well as carnivore gnawing damage, are also present on bones in all six cluster assemblages. These patterns indicate that cluster assemblages are composed of highly fragmented and variably weathered vertebrate remains subjected to a substantial degree of breakage, attrition and subaerial exposure prior to their final burial in the channel (Hill 1980; Haynes 1988a and b, 1993, 141–58; Lyman 1994a, 354–84).

Lithic materials also display a degree of variation in assemblage representation between clusters (Tables 4.9 and 4.10). Handaxes and scrapers are present in five clusters and absent from one (Cluster 2) while cores, handaxe preforms and other flake tools are variably represented in the same five assemblages. Unretouched flakes, handaxe shaping flakes and reindeer bone cracked open for marrow are more widespread and present in varying frequencies in all six cluster assemblages. Bones and teeth of horse, woolly rhinoceros and indeterminate species which have been modified by hominins are also present in a further four assemblages. Non-cultural edge-damage occurs on most artefacts and a number are broken (White, Donahue and Evans, chapter 5). Moreover, the presence of a small number of rolled artefacts in four clusters indicates the reworking of older material from within former bank sediments. Faunal condition is dominated by weathering Stage 2 with low frequencies for stages 1, 3 and 4, and suggests variable periods of surface exposure for individual specimens. Carnivore gnawing damage is also present on reindeer and horse bones in two assemblages. These patterns show that the clusters are comprised of a mixture of different types and kinds of artefacts and faunal remains with varying degrees of edge-damage, abrasion and other non-cultural modification, and suggest that archaeological materials were widely dispersed and subject to a degree of breakage, attrition and exposure prior to their deposition in channel sediments (Stapert 1976, 1979; Keeley 1980, 24–5; Callow 1986b, 306; Harding et al 1987; Behrensmeyer 1987).

The assemblages defined by the analysis thus represent collections of different types and kinds of material remains derived from a variety of events and the actions of both Neanderthals and animals, which probably occurred within a circumscribed area surrounding the channel (see also Schreve, White, chapter 5).

Table 4.9 Summary of artefacts and humanly modified vertebrate remains

	Cluster 1	Cluster 2	Cluster 3	Cluster 4	Cluster 5	Cluster 6
lithic artefacts						
unretouched flake	42	4	24	45	6	10
core	3			1		
handaxe shaping flake	23	6	26	35	2	10
handaxe	12		11	14	4	4
handaxe preform			2	1	1	1
scrapers*	4		4	2	1	6
notch, hachoir				2	1	
total	83	10	67	100	15	31
artefacts and humanly modified bone and teeth						
woolly rhinoceros			2			
reindeer	1	2	3	4	1	1
horse	2					1
indeterminate	1			2		
total	4	2	5	6	1	2
size class†						
Sc01 <3cm	8	5	6	15		1
Sc02 3cm–6cm	44	4	28	44	4	14
Sc03 6cm–9cm	20	1	15	25	7	9
Sc04 9cm–12cm	6		11	15	3	4
Sc05 12cm–15cm	5		3	1		3
Sc06 >15cm			4		1	
total	83	10	67	100	15	31

* Includes single edge, parallel edge and convergent edge types. † Includes humanly modified bones and teeth.

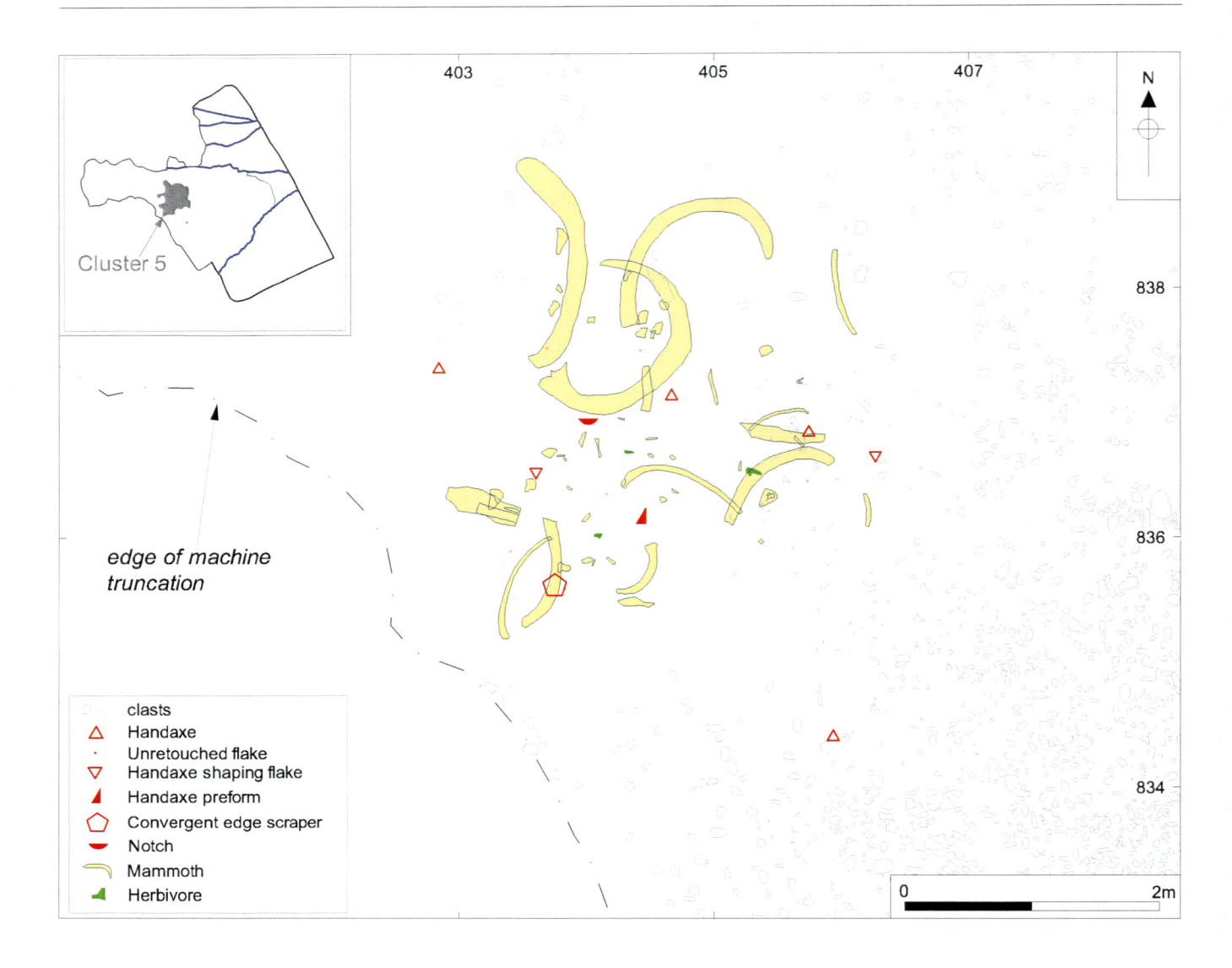

Fig 4.11
Cluster 5.

Variations in the condition and preservation of cluster contents appear to suggest that these materials were formerly lying on, or within, bank sediments over variable periods of time, and were subjected to varying degrees of breakage, edge-damage, attrition and weathering prior to their final burial in the channel. The sedimentary evidence summarised earlier also indicates that assemblage formation was probably largely accretional in character, with accumulations of material building up from multiple depositional episodes and relating to local variations in the scale and mode of bank erosion. Cluster assemblages thus appear to represent 'time-averaged' accumulations of artefacts and vertebrate remains derived from former banks, with assemblage composition largely the outcome of multiple depositional episodes that probably occurred over timescales of less than 100 years (Behrensmeyer 1982; Haynes 1985, 1988a; Lyman 1994a, 164; Miall 2006, 60–8).

Refits

Data summarised in Table 4.11 (*see also* Figs 5.26 and 5.55) show that bone and lithic conjoins occur within and among four clusters and largely reflect local variations in depositional environments. Two lithic refit pairs (40463–40481 and 40565–40265) occur between clusters 1 and 3, and indicate that the two clusters form a larger distribution of materials along the north edge of the channel. One of these refit pairs (40463–40481) also documents the vertical migration of objects through the organic sediments of Unit B-ii:03 (White, chapter 5). A molar refit group

Table 4.10 Summary of condition for artefacts and humanly modified vertebrate remains

	Cluster 1	Cluster 2	Cluster 3	Cluster 4	Cluster 5	Cluster 6
lithic artifact condition						
unabraded						
complete: no edge-damage	2					
complete: edge-damage	49	3	37	41	10	12
broken: edge-damage	24	7	23	25	4	12
slightly rolled						
complete: edge-damage	4		2	13		2
broken: edge-damage	1		1	2	1	1
rolled						
complete: edge-damage	2		1	8		2
broken: edge-damage	1			2		2
total	83	10	64	91	15	31
weathering summary						
Stage 1			2	1		
Stage 2	3	2	2	2	1	1
Stage 3	1			3		1
Stage 4			1			
Stage 5						
total	4	2	5	6	1	2
bone modification summary						
carnivore gnawing	1				2	

(51154–51648–61953) and a long-bone refit pair (50369–50373) in Cluster 2 also link the small concentration on the north-east edge of the channel with the rest of the distribution forming the cluster, and provide a further indication that the clusters represent depositional zones rather than depositional episodes. Object condition and associated sedimentary contexts suggest that these lithic and bone refit groups were probably spatially distinct prior to deposition and were introduced into the channel at different locations and possibly different times (small north-east concentration) as a result of local variations in bank erosion. Close conjoins of antler in Cluster 2 and some bone refit pairs in other clusters also indicate a degree of *in situ* breakage, suggesting that these vertebrate remains could have been broken by large animals stepping on them (Shipman 1981, 173; Behrensmeyer 1987; Haynes 1988a; Olson and Shipman 1988).

Bone refit pairs for Cluster 4 display a degree of variability in orientation, and show no preferred alignment indicative of possible flow directions for sediment gravity flow B-ii:04A. They are separated by distances ranging from 0.01m to 1.06m, with the close conjoins for three pairs suggesting possible *in situ* breakage. Object condition for the remaining two pairs suggests that they were either originally separated on the surface prior to deposition, or were broken and separated during transport as part of the sediment mass of sediment gravity flow B-ii:04A. A single bone refit pair (51031–51032) also occurs within sediment gravity-flow B-ii:04D situated in the north-east part of the channel along its northern edge (*see* Fig 5.26). The close conjoins for this pair also suggest the possibility of breakage during the mass movement of bank sediments into the channel.

4.4 Conclusions

The arrangement and composition of the clusters defined in this analysis appear to be related to local variations in the mode and scale of bank erosion processes. So what does the spatial distribution of materials in the Lynford channel tell us about hominin behaviour at the site? Overall, the simplest conclusion is that the concentrations of vertebrate and artefactual materials do not represent the

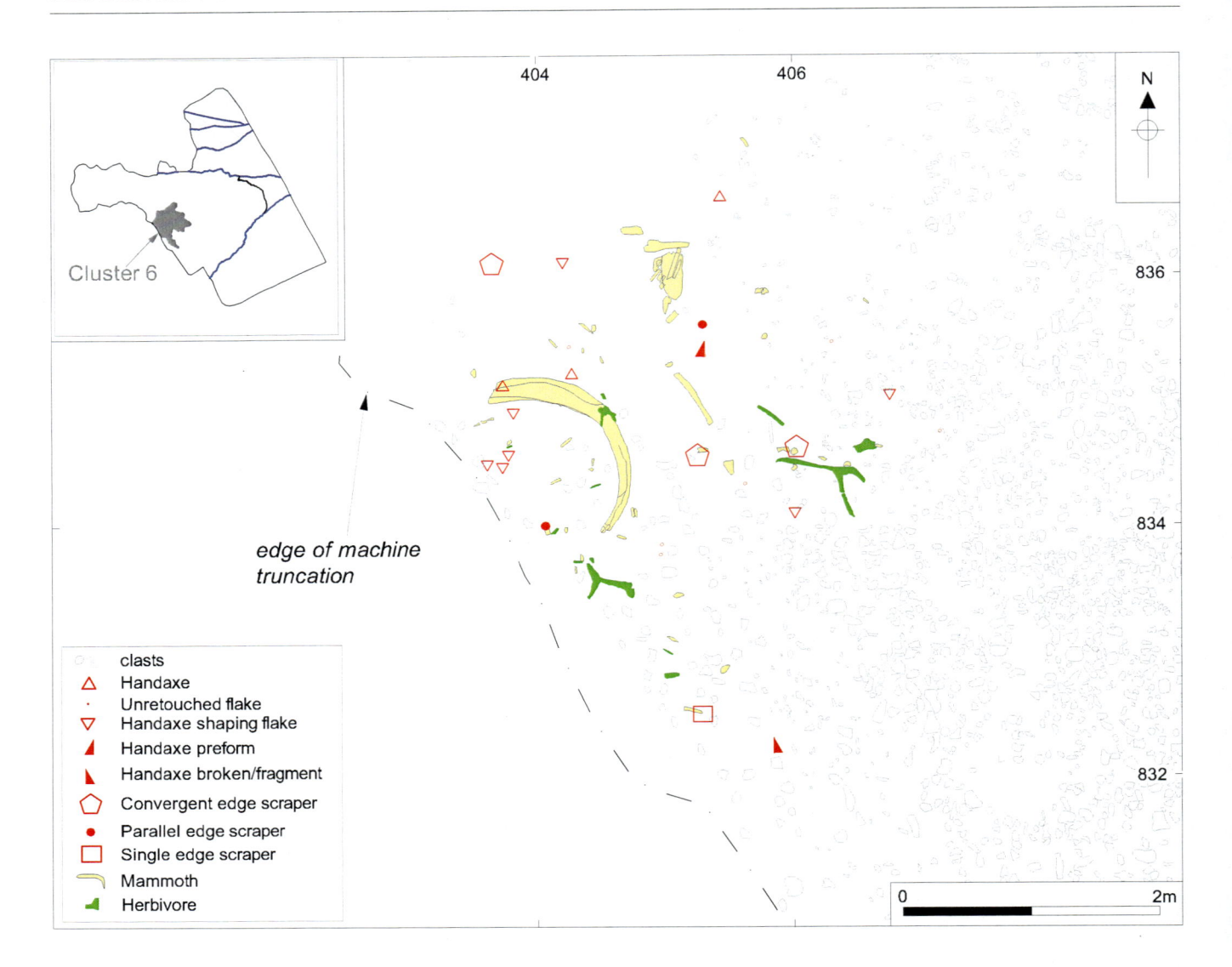

Fig 4.12
Cluster 6.

residues of *in situ* behaviour carried out within the channel during its abandonment phase. Instead they represent secondary accumulations of materials derived from the surrounding banks and deposited in the channel by a variety of sedimentary processes associated with bank erosion, and the movement of large animals in and around the channel. The clusters thus represent palimpsest or 'time-averaged' accumulations of material built up from multiple depositional episodes that occurred over a period of time.

Given this conclusion, what is the potential of the artefact and vertebrate assemblages from the site for archaeological interpretation? It appears that their deposition into the channel did not alter either the basic technological or typological characteristics of the lithic assemblage, or the overall patterns of species and skeletal element representation among the vertebrate assemblage. In other words, despite being reworked, the archaeological assemblages have maintained their basic compositional integrity across the whole site. Thus, while Lynford is far from a 'pristine' site, the archaeological materials are appropriate for further behaviourally orientated analyses and interpretation at the site or locale level (White and Schreve, chapter 5).

The deposits at Lynford clearly document the complexity of the sedimentary processes involved in their formation. Bedform and lithological properties record local differences in the mode and scale of bank erosion, and indicate that mass-movement sediment gravity flows, sheetwash and small sediment slips were the major agencies responsible for the transport and deposition of terrestrial sediments and

Table 4.11 Cluster refit data

cluster	refits	description	horizontal distance	vertical distance
lithic refits				
Cluster 1	40088-40015	handaxe-handaxe shaping flake	2.16	0.24
	40458-40438	handaxe frags	0.75	0.10
	40463-40481	handaxe-handaxe shaping flake	5.26	0.51
	40565-40265	handaxe-handaxe shaping flake	5.95	0.59
Cluster 2				
Cluster 3	40463-40481	refit to Cluster 1 see above		
	40565-40265	refit to Cluster 1 see above		
	40115-40116	handaxe shaping flake frags	0.26	0.07
Cluster 4				
bone refits				
Cluster 1	51228-51229	mammoth rib frags	0.90	0.01
	52010-52011-52012	ind rib frags	0.78	0.01
	50981-50980	mammoth vertebrae frags	0.05	0.02
	51228-51229	mammoth rib frags	0.90	0.01
	51378-51377	mammoth vertebrae frags	0.25	0.05
	51448-51451	mammoth rib frags	0.13	0.02
	52011-52010-52012	ind rib frags	0.78	0.04
Cluster 2	50622-50625-50626-50627-50629-50630-50631-50628	antler frags	0.08–0.34	0.01
Cluster 3	51038-51619	mammoth skull frags	0.15	0.04
	51154-51648-51953	mammoth molar frags	2.05	0.05
	50755-50756	mammoth rib frags	0.11	0.02
	51299-51300	unid frags	0.09	0.01
	50373-50369	mammoth long bone frags	4.49	0.10
	51218-51223	wolf mandible frags	0.04	0.02
	*51031-51032	mammoth long bone frags	0.06	0.04
Cluster 4	51259-51262	mammoth rib frags	0.01	0.02
	50233-51860	wolf ulna frags	1.04	0.07
	50649-50650	mammoth vertebrae frags	0.01	0.00
	51831-51869	horse astragalus-calcaneum	0.39	0.19
	50184-50151	mammoth rib fragments	0.10	0.07

archaeological materials into the channel. In addition, the massive character and micromorphology of the organic sediments of unit B-ii:03 also indicate the post-depositional disturbance of the materials deposited in the channel by fluvial, bioturbation and other sedimentary processes.

The quantitative analyses undertaken here have shown that the artefacts and vertebrate remains were subjected to a substantial degree of reworking. In particular, the three-dimensional arrangement of materials displays a number of signatures characteristic of depositional and post-depositional sedimentary processes. More specifically:

1. Artefacts and vertebrate remains are reasonably well mixed together vertically, suggesting that, for Association B-ii as a whole, the vertical reworking of objects within sediments has been extensive.

2. The clusters defined by the analysis appear to represent a series of depositional zones associated with differences in the mode and scale of local deposition by sedimentary processes. Internally, each cluster is composed of an accumulation of material derived from multiple depositional episodes and not the result of discrete depositional events associated with specific sedimentary or behavioural processes.

3 Object orientations and refit data appear to reflect local variations in depositional environments and post-depositional disturbance processes. Variations in the condition and preservation of cluster contents indicate that the artefacts and vertebrate remains making up individual assemblages were formerly lying on or within bank sediments for variable periods of time prior to their final burial in the channel.

4 The assemblages in each cluster are reasonably homogeneous judged by their overall content, and comprise collections of different artefacts and vertebrate remains derived from a variety of events and actions by both Neanderthals and animals, which probably occurred within the immediate environs of the channel. They appear to be 'time-averaged' accumulations, with assemblage composition largely the outcome of multiple depositional episodes.

These results demonstrate that the arrangement of artefacts and vertebrate remains in the sediments of Association B-ii represent secondary accumulations of material derived from the surrounding banks and not the residues of *in situ* behaviour carried out within the channel. No discernible behavioural patterning thus appears to have survived in the spatial arrangement of the archaeological materials within channel sediments. However, the archaeological materials do remain amenable to interpretations of Neanderthal behaviour at the site level.

5

The archaeological assemblages of animals and lithics

Besides a rich array of environmental evidence (chapter 3), the Lynford channel contained two large assemblages of stone tools and animal bones. It was this archaeological association, apparent to John Lord when he discovered the site, that marked it out as especially important and worthy of detailed excavation. Furthermore, the preponderance of mammoth bones and the occurrence of distinctive bout coupé handaxes raised the prospect of investigating whether Neanderthals exploited such large animals, and if so how?

Chapter 4 examined where the archaeological material originated and how it had slumped into the channel. This chapter gives further information from observations of the preservation of the bones and the degree of abrasion on the artefacts. The question then arises: is Lynford the site, much sought after by Palaeolithic archaeologists, where 'smoking gun' evidence in the form of a stone spear-point embedded in a rib cage demonstrates deliberate hunting of such large animals? Such easy solutions are rarely encountered in Palaeolithic research, and Lynford is no exception. What might at first seem a simple relationship between the faunal assemblages and the Neanderthals who created them turns out to be more complicated, but also more interesting, for our understandings of the capabilities of these hominins. Indeed, the Lynford evidence challenges what we understand by hunting and what we will accept as evidence that it took place.

The Lynford animal bones are dominated by the remains of at least 11 mammoths, mostly large males. Not all the anatomical elements are represented and it is this observation that drives the analysis of how the accumulations of stones and bones built up. There are just under 3000 lithics, including 85 retouched tools. Attention focuses on the patterns of knapping as much as on the varied shapes of the 41 complete handaxes that were excavated. What emerges is a picture of skilled flint-knappers who carefully selected raw material from that available in their local environment, worked to a plan, and frequently recycled the products. Their goal was to make a handaxe with a range of functions that would be adaptable to a variety of circumstances in these open, cold landscapes, which were well stocked with large herbivores. A further glimpse of Neanderthal survival skills is also provided by a small sandstone block that could possibly be one of the earliest examples of a fire-making technology. Such capacity is not unexpected, but until now has proved elusive.

5.1 The vertebrate assemblage from Lynford: taphonomy, biostratigraphy and implications for Middle Palaeolithic subsistence strategies

D C Schreve with contributions by D R Brothwell and A J Stuart

Materials and methodology

The larger vertebrate material was excavated by hand, with the majority of specimens assigned an individual finds number and context and recorded in three dimensions (see Appendix 4). Seventy-seven specimens were collected from spoil dumps in various parts of the quarry, but could still be related to their original contexts. These are included in the following discussion where stated, but have been excluded from the majority of the analyses described later. Objects smaller than 20mm were allocated a spit number, with the exception of some from contexts that were excavated without using a spit system. Tusks extending into control sections left standing until towards the end of the excavation were excavated in two parts, each of which was given an individual object number. The complete tusk was then assigned a master number in post-excavation; these cases, where more than one individual number was superseded by a master number, are shown in Appendix 4. Specimens were normally bagged in field-damp condition, unless particularly fragile or complex, in which case they were conserved and jacketed in plaster before being lifted (see Appendix 4 for further details). Of the individually numbered finds, 432 were initially sent to the Department of Archaeological Sciences at the University of Bradford for cleaning, exposure of material in plaster jackets where required, and basic conservation work. The remainder were removed directly to the Department of Geography, Royal Holloway, for identification and analysis. A total of 2014 individually numbered finds was excavated, of which 1362 were identified to species, genus or family level. Thirty-seven specimens, mostly cranial, rib and small long bone fragments, were identified as 'large mammal' (size of *Mammuthus* or *Coelodonta*), but lacked sufficient diagnostic characters for further identification. A further 652 specimens (32 per cent of the assemblage) were unidentifiable.

In addition to the recovery of large vertebrate material, bulk sampling for microvertebrate remains was undertaken on site. Thirty-seven bulk samples weighing a combined total of 450.694kg were extracted in five serial column samples from the 1m-wide baulks and other appropriate exposures. The serial samples were taken in spits of approximately 100mm depth, or down to the nearest stratigraphical junction, and were located in such a way as to ensure that both marginal (channel-edge) and deeper water contexts were evaluated and that the columns were directly relatable to both the pollen profile and to column samples taken for other biological data sets. As well as serial bulk samples, a further 38 spot samples were taken from the most calcareous sediments, either from around features such as mammoth tusks, or where patches of small vertebrate material were discovered, as and when they became exposed during the course of the excavations. Specimens considered to be possible coprolites were also bagged on site as spot samples. All of the samples taken are listed in Appendix 3, Table 1. All bagged samples from the site were transported in field-damp condition to the Department of Geography, Royal Holloway (University of London), where they were first weighed and air-dried before being wet-sieved through a 500μm mesh. The sieved residues were then dried, scanned under a low-power binocular microscope and vertebrate remains extracted where present. The material was subdivided into fish, herpetofaunal, birds and mammals and assigned to appropriate specialists where necessary. Additional vertebrate material was obtained from 21 bulk sample residues taken for malacological analysis (Keen, chapter 3).

All sediment from principal deposits was sieved on site through 6mm and 9mm meshes, with one spit unit per 1.0m2 wet-sieved (total 700 spits) and three dry-sieved (2,872 spits), and the residues scanned by eye for microvertebrates and other small bone fragments. Finds recovered from wet- and dry-sieved spits are presented in Appendix 4, Tables A4.2 and A4.3).

Systematic taxonomic determinations of the Lynford mammalian material were established using modern and comparative skeletal material in the Departments of Zoology and Palaeontology at the Natural History Museum and in the Department of Geography at Royal Holloway. Small vertebrate remains were measured using a low-powered stereo zoom microscope with a Pixera Pro 600ES Colour camera. Images were captured and measured using Image Pro-Express with in-built measuring software. Standard measurements on large mammal specimens were made using Vernier callipers (to 0.02mm), according to Von den Driesch (1976).

Secondary data: NISP and MNIs

Numbers of Identified Specimens (NISP) and Minimum Numbers of Individuals (MNIs) are shown in Table 5.1. Calculations of NISP are based on the presence of individual identifiable elements. MNIs have been calculated by dividing the NISP according to the most commonly represented anatomical parts (taking the side into consideration) for each species – that is, calculating the smallest number of individuals required to account for all of the skeletal elements of a particular species at the site. The degree of wear in the dental elements, as well as the overall size of the element, the inferred age of the animal and its sex, where determinable, were also taken into consideration in order to maximise the potential number of individuals recorded. For the purposes of the analysis, each individual

5 THE ARCHAEOLOGICAL ASSEMBLAGES OF ANIMALS AND LITHICS

Table 5.1 Minimum numbers of individuals (MNI) per taxon, based on 1401 identified specimens (excluding material from the bulk and sieved spit residues and all undetermined material). The distribution of body part fragments per taxon for all individually numbered finds is shown in bold type and the percentage of each element of the total for that taxon in italics: 'a' denotes an adult animal and 'j' a juvenile. Figures are based on counts of one element per finds number as individual bags may contain tens or hundreds of fragments. Actual numbers of fragments per individual find may therefore be higher (see Appendix 4, Table A4.4 for details). Where an individual finds bag contained more than a single body element (eg cranial and rib fragments), a score of 1 has been given to each category.

	B. priscus	Cervidae	R. tarandus	C. antiquitatis	E. ferus	M. primigenius	C. crocuta	U. arctos	V. cf. vulpes	C. lupus
antler		**5** *83.3*	**40** *54.8*							
tusk						**392** *31.4*				
cranial fragments						**352** *28.4*				
jugal						**7** *0.6*				
tusk alveolus						**12** *1*				
tooth			**4** *6.8*	**10** *71.4*	**3** *50*	**30*** *2.4*	**1** *100*	**7** *87.5*	**1** *100*	
Mammuthus molar fragments						**92** *7.4*				
mandible		**1** *8.4*	**2** *2.7*			**16** *1.3*		**1** *12.5*		**3** *50*
maxilla and palate						**8** *0.6*				
vertebra			**3** *4.1*			**27** *2.2*				
rib			**1** *1.4*			**130** *10.4*				**1** *17*
sternum						**4** *0.3*				
scapula						**4** *0.3*				
humerus	**3** *74*		**3** *4.1*	**2** *14.4*		**4** *0.3*				
ulna			**1** *1.4*			**2** *0.2*				**2** *33*
radius			**1** *1.4*			**1** *0.1*				
pelvis			**2** *2.7*	**1** *7.1*		**10** *0.8*				
femur		**1** *8.4*	**4** *5.5*		**1** *17*	**7** *0.6*				

continued ▶

Table 5.1 – continued

	B. priscus	Cervidae	R. tarandus	C. antiquitatis	E. ferus	M. primigenius	C. crocuta	U. arctos	V. cf. vulpes	C. lupus
tibia			5 6.8	1 7.1		3 0.2				
indet long bones and bone frags			1 1.4			138 11.1				
podials					2 33	4 0.3				
metapodials	1 25		3 4.1							
phalanges			2 2.7			2 0.2				
% of assemblage	0.3	0.4	5.4	1	0.4	91.3	0.07	0.6	0.07	0.4
MNI	2a	1a	7a 1j	2a 2j	2a	10a 1j	1a	1a	1a	1a

find was treated as a single specimen, although in the case of more fragile elements, such as cranium or mammoth tusk, there might be tens or even hundreds of small fragments in each finds bag.

It was not possible to calculate Minimum Numbers of Elements – the number of complete skeletal elements required to account for all the fragments of that skeletal part for each taxon – because the comminuted nature of the assemblage has resulted in a lack of usable counting portions. In particular, the predominance of multiple small fragments of mammoth tusk, cranium, rib midshaft and shards of long bone diaphyses made it impossible to ascertain how many fragments would make up a single complete element.

It is apparent that taphonomic processes have resulted in very different depositional histories for the vertebrate fossils (*see below*), although the supposed accumulation of the main palaeochannel sediments occurred over only a short space of time, perhaps just tens of years (Keen, Field, chapter 3). The NISP and MNIs are therefore not intended to demonstrate changing relative frequencies over time, but simply to provide a broad indication of the relative abundances of bones of different species in the vicinity at the time of the main channel infilling. The assumptions inherent in using these simple calculations are fully acknowledged (see Ringrose 1993; Lyman 1994b) and the taphonomic biases that potentially influence them are discussed fully in the section on taphonomy.

The stratigraphical distribution of the vertebrate remains

With the exception of three specimens recovered unstratified from the high-energy sands and gravels of Association C, all vertebrate remains were collected from the different units within the underlying palaeo-channel deposits that make up Association B (Boismier, Lewis, chapter 2). The distribution of the finds according to context is shown in Table 5.2. Eleven specimens were recovered from deposits attributed to Association B-i:03, comprising a series of coarse flint gravels of fluvial origin below the organic-rich sediments of the palaeochannel, and one from B-i, although no further provenance was recorded. One specimen with a double context number (20003+20384) was found spanning the contact between the sands of B-ii:01 and the organic sediment of B-ii:03. The principal source of the fossils was Association B-ii, which forms the main palaeochannel context (20032). 141 individually-numbered specimens were recorded from unit B-ii:01, which consists of grey-pale-brown sands at the base of B-ii, and

5 THE ARCHAEOLOGICAL ASSEMBLAGES OF ANIMALS AND LITHICS

Table 5.2 Abundance and percentage data based on 2091 vertebrate finds with context data, arranged according to context and stating the percentage for each context of the total assemblage

			NISP per large mammal taxon											
facies association	context	sediment field description	C. lupus	V. cf. vulpes	U. arctos	C. crocuta	M. primigenius	E. ferus	C. antiquitatis	R. tarandus	Cervidae	B. priscus	total no. of individual finds	% of individual finds per context
B-ii:01	20004	basal sands and clay, fill of channel 20032					3			1			7	0.33
	20133	brown sand, fill of channel 20032					1						2	0.10
	20139	brown grey sand, fill of channel 20032					2						3	0.14
	20245	brown sand, fill of channel 20032					5			1			9	0.43
	20254	grey brown sand, fill of channel 20032					21						39	1.87
	20255	brown silty sand, fill of channel 20032					1						1	0.05
	20363	brown gravelly sand, fill of channel 20032											1	0.05
	20364	brown silty sand, fill of channel 20032					9						14	0.67
	20369	yellow brown silty sand, fill of channel 20032					20		1	1			30	1.43
	20375	grey sand, fill of channel 20032					1						1	0.05
	20384	grey brown sand, fill of channel 20032					25			2		1	33	1.58
B-ii:02	20371	green grey clayey silt, fill of channel 20032					2						4	0.19
	20246	organic clayey silt with medium–coarse gravel										1	1	0.05
B-i:03	20051	orange gravel					1			1			2	0.10
	20078	pale brown sandy clay, fill of channel 20032					3						6	0.29
	20129	grey, yellow and orange laminated sand, fill of channel 20027					1						2	0.10
	20130	orange gravel, fill of channel 20024											1	0.05

continued ▶

Table 5.2 – continued

facies association	context	sediment field description					NISP per large mammal taxon						total no. of individual finds	% of individual finds per context
			C. lupus	V. cf. vuples	U. arctos	C. crocuta	M. primigenius	E. ferus	C. antiquitatis	R. tarandus	Cervidae	B. priscus		
B-ii:03	20003	dark brown/black organic sand, fill of channel 20032	6	1	7	1	852	3	11	51	6	2	1422	68.01
	20003 and 20252	dark brown/black organic sands, fill of 20032					1							0.05
	20021	black organic sand (W. end of site), fill of channel 20032					164	3		3	1		267	12.77
	20135	part of organic silty sand											1	0.05
	20248	brown black sandy organic, fill of channel 20032			1		16			2			25	1.20
	20250	brown silty sand, fill of channel 20032					1						1	0.05
	20252	brown black sandy organic, fill of channel 20032				(1)	38			2			59	2.82
	20258	brown organic sand, fill of channel 20032					9			3			16	0.77
B-ii:03 and 01	20003 and 20364	dark brown/black organic sand and brown silty sand, fill of channel 20032											1	0.05
B-ii:03 and 01	20003 and 20369	dark brown/black organic sand and yellow brown silty sand, fill of channel 20032					1						1	0.05
B-ii:03 and 01	20003 and 20371	dark brown/black organic sand and green grey clayey silt, fill of channel 20030											1	0.05
B-ii:03 and 01	20003 and 20384	dark brown/black organic sand and grey brown sand, fill of channel 20032											1	0.05
B-ii:03 and 04	20003 and 20140	dark brown/black organic sand and yellow brown silty sand, fill of channel 20032					6						14	0.67
B-ii:04	20053	medium to coarse sands and gravels											1	0.05
	20131	pale grey sand and gravel, fill of channel 20032					8	1					9	0.43

continued ▶

Table 5.2 – continued

			NISP per large mammal taxon											
facies association	context	sediment field description	C. lupus	V. cf. vuples	U. arctos	C. crocuta	M. primigenius	E. ferus	C. antiquitatis	R. tarandus	Cervidae	B. priscus	total no. of individual finds	% of individual finds per context
	20132	orange gravel, fill of channel 20032					3			1			5	0.24
	20134	orange yellow sand and gravel, fill of cut 20138					1						1	0.05
	20140	yellow brown silty sand, fill of channel 20032											1	0.05
	20247	grey sand, fill of channel 20032					7						12	0.57
	20249	grey gravelly sand, fill of channel 20032					2						2	0.10
	20251	grey and orange sandy gravel, fill of channel 20032					1						2	0.10
	20365	medium–coarse sands, small–medium gravels											1	0.05
	20366	orange yellow sand, fill of channel 20032					3						3	0.14
	20367	yellow white sand, fill of channel 20032					3						4	0.19
	20374	yellow gravel, fill of channel 20.032											1	0.05
	20389	yellow sand and gravel, fill of channel 20032					1						1	0.05
B-ii:04 and 02	20374 and 20371	see above					1						1	0.05
B-ii:05	20002	laminated sands and organic material, fill of 20032											2	0.10
	20005	laminated sand deposit, fill of scour 20006											1	0.05
	20116	brown and orange laminated sand, fill of 20117					1			1			3	0.14
	20119	orange brown silty sand					1						1	0.05
	20136	grey and orange laminated sand											1	0.05

continued ▶

Table 5.2 – continued

facies association	context	sediment field description	C. lupus	V. cf. vuples	U. arctos	C. crocuta	M. primigenius	E. ferus	C. antiquitatis	R. tarandus	Cervidae	B. priscus	total no. of individual finds	% of individual finds per context
B-iii	20018	grey sand, fill of channel 20019					1						1	0.05
	20028	orange yellow sand and gravel, fill of channel 20121					5						5	0.24
C	20009	blue-black and orange gravel and sand, fill of scour								1			2	0.10
–	20011	yellow brown sand, fill of channel 20045						1					1	0.05
–	20022	number not used/unstratified											1	0.05
–	20044	no data					5						6	0.29
–	20048	unstratified, from spoil in centre of quarry					27			2			29	1.39
–	20049	unstratified, from spoil in west of quarry								1			1	0.05
–	20050	unstratified					20						20	0.96
–	20052	destroyed/disturbed sediment					4						6	0.29
–	20356	redeposited on W. edge of site during quarrying					1						1	0.05
–	20385	unstratified					1						1	0.05

five from the overlying B-ii:02, a discontinuous dark grey-greenish-brown organic clayey silt. However, by far the richest unit was B-ii:03, with 1804 specimens comprising 90 per cent of the individually numbered mammalian assemblage. Material from this unit comes from seven separate contexts (20003, 20021, 20135, 20248, 20250, 20252 and 20258), all of which have been attributed to Facies B-ii:03, an *in situ* detrital fine-grained, dark-brown organic silty sand found between apparent phases of debris flow and bank collapse. Most significant among these richly fossiliferous contexts were a dark brown-black organic sand (20003) and a black organic sand (20021), which contributed 1422 and 266 specimens respectively (70 per cent and 13 per cent of the assemblage). Fourteen specimens bearing double context numbers (20003+20140) appear to come from the contact between *in situ* organic silty sands and a coarse, orange sand reflecting a subsequent period of debris flow.

The deposits of the main palaeochannel overlap to a certain degree, and the different contexts recorded above might thus form parts of a single laterally variable surface. This is highlighted by the presence of refitting artefacts within the different palaeochannel facies, which indicates that there has been vertical movement (White, this chapter). Nevertheless, the predominance of a single context (20003) as the source of the material further suggests that, as with the archaeological record, the vertebrate assemblage from the main palaeochannel could possibly be considered as a coherent single unit, even though it is clearly time-averaged (see below). In this respect, the observation that 90 per cent of the assemblage is from the dark-brown organic silty sands, and not from other facies within B-ii:03 that have been attributed to debris flows, is also significant. However, unlike the archaeology from the main palaeochannel, the vertebrate remains individually show different degrees of weathering and other evidence of exposure prior to burial. Therefore, although some specimens might be contemporary with the infilling of the main palaeochannel, others have clearly lain on the adjacent land surface for varying numbers of years before being incorporated through over-bank flooding or bank collapse. This presents certain difficulties in analysis, for although apparently entering the palaeochannel more or less synchronously the bones probably accumulated over a somewhat wider time range than the inferred tens of years during which the channel became filled in.

A small number of specimens were recovered from contexts post-dating B-ii:03. Forty-seven specimens were recorded from unit B-ii:04 and six from B-ii:05, a series of mixed deposits of sands and gravels reflecting a period of more energetic fluvial conditions. Nine specimens were recovered from predominantly sandy organic deposits of Association B-iii, which cuts into the deposits of Association B-ii and represents the uppermost infill of the palaeochannel. As reported above, three specimens are known from Association C.

Systematic palaeontology

Twelve mammalian taxa have been identified at Lynford, in addition to four fish taxa and a single avian taxon. The genus *Homo* (presumably *Homo neanderthalensis*) is included on the basis of artefactual material, although no skeletal remains were present. A single herpetofaunal species, the common frog, is also recorded (see Gleed-Owen, this chapter).

Pisces
Esociformes
Esocidae
Esox lucius Linné, 1758, pike

Gasterosteiformes
Gasterosteidae
Gasterosteus aculeatus Linné, 1758, three-spined stickleback

Cypriniformes
Cyprinidae undet., cyprinid

Perciformes
Percidae
Perca fluviatilis Linné, 1758, perch

Amphibia
Anura
Ranidae
Rana temporaria Linné, 1758, common or grass frog

Aves
Gruiformes
Rallidae
Porzana sp(p)., crake(s)

Mammalia
Rodentia
Sciuridae
Spermophilus sp., ground squirrel

Cricetidae
Microtus gregalis (Pallas 1779), narrow-skulled vole

Microtus sp., indeterminate vole

Primates
Homininae
Homo sp. (artefacts and modified bone)

Carnivora
Canidae
Canis lupus Linné, 1758, wolf
Vulpes cf. vulpes Linné,.75 1758, red fox

Ursidae

Ursus arctos Linné, 1758, brown bear

Hyaenidae

Crocuta crocuta Erxleben, 1777, spotted hyaena

Proboscidea
Elephantidae

Mammuthus primigenius (Blumenbach 1803), woolly mammoth

Perissodactyla
Equidae

Equus ferus Boddaert, 1785, horse

Rhinocerotidae

Coelodonta antiquitatis (Blumenbach 1807), woolly rhinoceros

Artiodactlya

Cervidae

Rangifer tarandus Linné, 1758, reindeer

Bovidae

Bison priscus Bojanus, 1827, bison

The following systematic descriptions relate only to the mammalian material in the assemblage. Full details of the specimens are given in Appendix 4.

Rodentia Bowdich, 1821
  Sciuridae Gray, 1821
  Spermophilus **sp., ground squirrel**

The ground squirrel is represented at Lynford by two molars (L m2 and L M1) from the wet-sieved spit residues (61883 and 61610 respectively). Two individuals are indicated, as the specimens present markedly different stages of wear (the L m2 is extremely worn but the L M1 is only in mid-wear). Measurements are given in Table 5.3. The dentition of *Spermophilus* is characterised by a single pair of continuously growing incisor teeth in both the upper and lower jaws. The cheek teeth are rooted and low-crowned with low, rounded cusps on the margins, connected to each other by weak transverse ridges (Matthews 1960). Characters for the identification of *Spermophilus* and its separation from *Sciurus* are given by Chaline (1966). Of note are the relatively larger size of the upper anterior premolars and the greater height of the tubercles and principal ridges in the cheek teeth in *Spermophilus*. The crowns of the upper molars are a conspicuous 'U' shape in occlusal view when moderately worn. The lower molariform teeth are similar to Sciurus, although the crowns are higher and more compressed, the cusps much more prominent and the central depression deeper and narrower. The skull is considered to be more massive than in the arboreal squirrels, and the postcranial skeleton is modified to cope with a strictly terrestrial existence in the form of less elongated feet and short, flattened dorsal vertebrae (Miller 1912). The taxonomic classification of modern Palaearctic species of *Spermophilus* is extremely unstable, although nine species are currently recognised (Corbet 1978). On the basis of the limited material from Lynford, including an extremely worn specimen, specific determination has not been attempted. The earliest records of ground squirrel are from the Arctic Freshwater Beds, deposits that pre-date Anglian till at Mundesley, Norfolk (Newton 1882), but the greatest abundance occurs in the deposits of the lower Middle Terrace of the Thames, at sites such as Crayford, Kent (Kennard 1944).

Cricetidae Rochebrune 1883
  Microtus gregalis **(Pallas 1779), tundra or narrow-skulled vole**

The tundra vole is represented by five specimens, indicating five individuals, all from wet-sieved spit residues (60152 L dentary with broken m1; 61096 anterior L m1; 61497 L dentary with m1; 63646 L m1 and 608?? [sample number partially erased] L m1). Measurements are given in Table 5.4. The first lower molar in *M. gregalis* is readily identifiable, possessing three inner and two outer closed triangles with a distinctive 'mitten-shaped' anterior loop. An ancestral morphotype of this species, *Microtus gregaloides* (Hinton 1923), is known from early Middle Pleistocene temperate episodes at West Runton (Stuart 1996) and Westbury-sub-Mendip (Currant 1999). A single occurrence in the late Middle Pleistocene is recorded at Pontnewydd Cave (Schreve 1997), but the majority of finds are known from the Devensian (Sutcliffe and Kowalski 1976), where populations display a high degree of intra-specific morphological variation. The specimen from spit sample 61497 at Lynford reflects this variability since it does not present the classic anterior loop, but does have the strong enamel differentiation that is also characteristic of this species.

A further 30 remains extracted from the bulk samples and wet-sieved spit residues, comprising incisor fragments, molars other than m1 and molar fragments, could be attributed to Microtus sp. or Microtinae but lacked sufficient diagnostic characters for further determination (30.200 600–700mm molar fragment; 30.226 190–290mm R M1 and

Table 5.3 Measurements of *Spermophilus* sp.: all measurements in mm (L = maximum length; B = maximum breadth)

Spermophilus sp.	L	B
61883 L m2	3.16	2.18
61610 L M1	2.67	2.25

5 THE ARCHAEOLOGICAL ASSEMBLAGES OF ANIMALS AND LITHICS

Table 5.4 Measurements of *Microtus gregalis*: all measurements in mm (L = maximum length)

Microtus gregalis	L
607?? L m1	2.61
61497 L m1	2.83
63646 L m1	2.66

I fragment; 30.228 01 juvenile molar fragment; 30.234 02 R I, 30.235 0–100mm L m2; 30.235 100–200mm I fragment; 60297 L I; 60379 i fragment; 60523 i fragment; 60992 R I; 60996 R m1 fragment; 61280 I fragment; 61482 I fragment; 61540 R M3; 61606 anterior L m2 fragment; 61640b L I; 61642 R I; 61723 R m1 fragment; 61906 i fragment; 62218 R M3; 62422 I fragment; 62429 R I; 62504 L i and i fragment; 62976 i fragment; 63125 L I; 63214 L I; 63808 R m2 and 64764 i fragments).

Carnivora Bowdich, 1821
Canidae Gray, 1821
Canis lupus Linné, 1758, wolf

Wolf is represented by the articular condyle of a left dentary, two conjoining right mandible fragments (one with a fragment of second lower molar *in situ*), a proximal rib fragment and two conjoining fragments of a right ulna (Fig 5.1). A solitary R p2 was also recovered from the wet-sieved residue of spit 61235. Measurements are given in Table 5.5. Kurtén and Poulianos (1977) have suggested that *C. lupus* originated from one of the small Villafranchian canids, either *C. etruscus* Major or *C. arnensis* Del Campana. Wolves of the early Middle Pleistocene have been attributed to a small-bodied species or subspecies, *Canis mosbachensis* or *Canis lupus mosbachensis*. According to Bonifay (1971), the first known occurrence of the true wolf is in the Holsteinian, and the species increases progressively in size throughout the Middle and Late Pleistocene until it reaches a maximum in the Devensian (Schreve 1997). These results are paralleled by findings on the continent by Bonifay (1966, 1971).

Vulpes cf. *vulpes* L., 1758, red fox

A small canid, attributed to *V.* cf. *vulpes*, is represented by a single find of a right upper canine. The specimen is of smaller size and more slender form that the equivalent tooth in *C. lupus*, and compares most closely with modern red fox from Britain. The red fox can be differentiated from the Arctic fox, (*Alopex lagopus* L. 1758), on the basis of its larger size, greater robustness, more elongated dentary and more widely-spaced premolars, but on the basis of only a single canine from Lynford the specific attribution can remain only tentative at present. *V. vulpes* probably evolved from the ancestral *V. alopecoides* during the Middle Villafranchian (Kurtén 1968). The earliest record to date of *V. vulpes* in Britain is from the early Middle Pleistocene site of Westbury-sub-Mendip (Bishop 1982).

Fig 5.1
Partial right ulna of Canis lupus *(51860), anterior view (scale in mm).*

Table 5.5 Measurements of *Canis lupus*: all measurements in mm (L = maximum length; B = maximum breadth; BPC = greatest breadth across coronoid process)

Canis lupus	L	B	BPC
61235 R p2	14.86	8.04	
51860 R ulna			16.42

167

Fig 5.2 (top right) Associated L m1 (51212) and R m1 (51726) of Ursus arctos, lingual view (scale in mm).

Ursidae Gray, 1825
Ursus arctos L., brown bear

Remains of brown bear from Lynford comprise a fragment of right dentary with p1 alveolus, found in association with a R c, a basal canine fragment including the root, an associated L and R m1 (Fig 5.2), a L m2 (Fig 5.3), a R m3, a broken C tip and a partial root and enamel fragment of a R C. Measurements are given in Table 5.6. The canines of brown bear are long and robust and lack the pronounced median ridge on the lingual side that is seen in large felids. The cheek teeth are bunodont with large occlusal expansions adapted for crushing. In contrast to the cave bear, *Ursus spelaeus* (Rosenmüller and Heinroth 1794), *U. arctos* nearly always retains two small anterior premolars in the upper jaw and at least one in the lower jaw (Reynolds 1906) and has generally higher-crowned teeth than those of the cave bear. The postcranial remains are normally more robust than in large felids of equivalent size but are smaller than those of the cave bear. The brown bears have their origins in China, where they have a continuous record from the early Middle Pleistocene to the present day (Kurtén 1968). According to Kurtén (1959), they share a common ancestor with U. spelaeus in the small Early Pleistocene bear, U. etruscus Cuvier. The brown bear appears in Europe for the first time during the Holsteinian interglacial at sites such as Lunel-Viel, France, where it

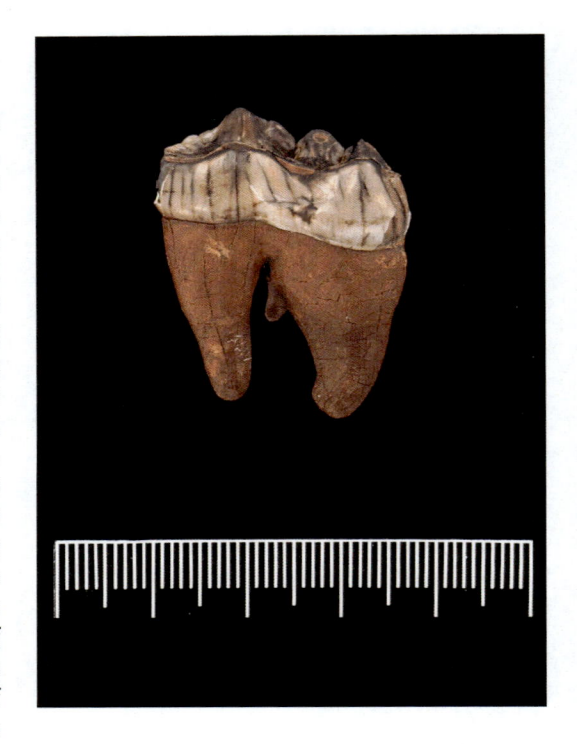

Table 5.6 Measurements of *Ursus arctos*: all measurements in mm (L = maximum length; B = maximum breadth)

Ursus arctos	L	B	max height (from crown to root tip)
51212 L m1	26.30	13.74	31.00
51726 E m1	25.92	13.38	31.10
50558 L m2	27.46	17.92	32.06

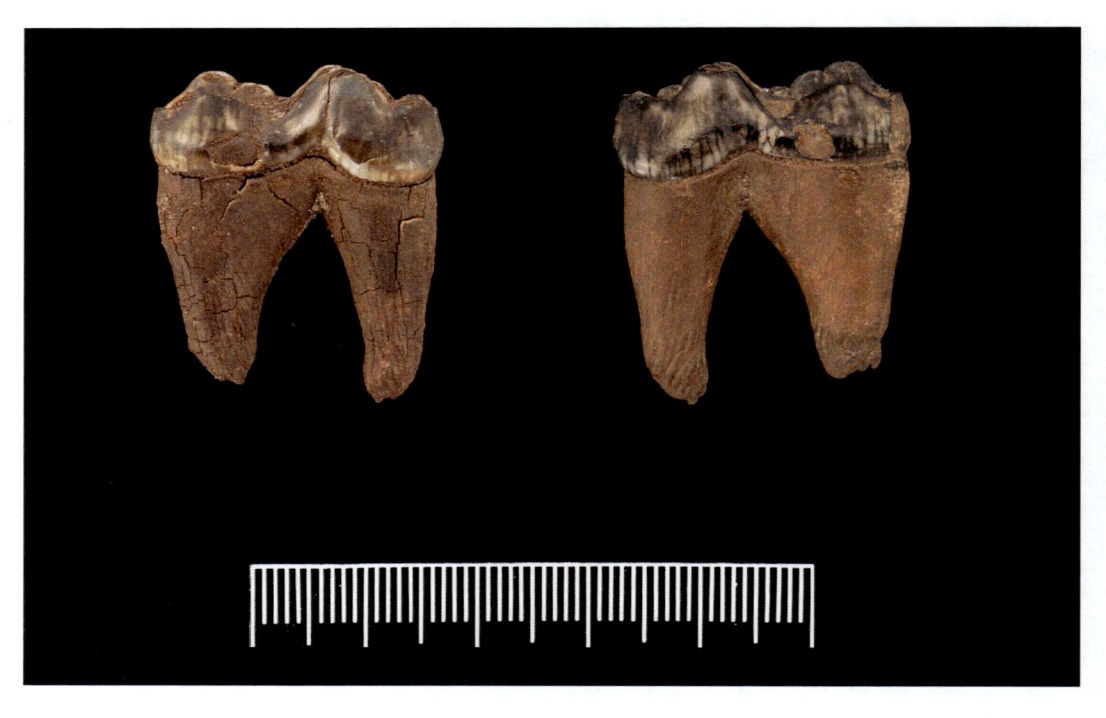

Fig 5.3 L m2 (50558) of Ursus arctos, lingual view (scale in mm).

co-existed with the cave bear (Kurtén 1968) but did not enter Britain until MIS 9, when it completely supplanted U. spelaeus (Schreve 2001a; Schreve and Currant 2003).

Hyaenidae Gray, 1869
Crocuta crocuta Erxleben, 1777, spotted hyaena

Although amply represented at Lynford by characteristic gnawed bones, the digested teeth of prey species and occasional coprolites, actual fossil remains of the spotted hyaena at the site consist only of a single posterior fragment of a well-worn L p4 and a second phalanx from dry-sieved spit 60726, the latter showing clear signs of digestion (Fig 5.4). The dentition of *C. crocuta* is highly specialised. The post-carnassial molars are either vestigial or have been lost completely, and the m1 is bicuspid, as in felids. The canines are rather small, whereas the premolars have been modified into massive conical structures, adapted for crushing bones (Stuart 1982). Turner (1981) has demonstrated that from the Ipswichian to the Devensian, there was a decrease in the tooth size of p1–3 and an increase in the size of p4-m1 in *C. crocuta*. This indicates an overall shift in power and chewing efficiency towards the more posterior cheek teeth during the Devensian. The ancestor of *C. crocuta* is thought to be the Villafranchian *C. sivalensis* (Falconer and Cautley), which spread out from its origins in India in the early Middle Pleistocene (Kurtén 1968). *C. crocuta* first appeared in Britain in the early Cromerian Complex at West Runton, Norfolk (Stuart 1996) and went on to be the only species of hyaena present in Britain during the later Middle Pleistocene. Later Cromerian Complex finds of *C. crocuta* include remains from Westbury-sub-Mendip (Bishop 1982). The species is apparently absent from the Hoxnian in Britain (Schreve 2001a) and indeed from contemporary deposits across NW Europe (Schreve and Bridgland 2002), although it reappears during the subsequent MIS 9 interglacial at sites such as Purfleet and Grays in Essex (Schreve 2001a) and is a regular component of all later interglacials. It is absent from Britain during the Early Devensian, but reappears during the middle part of the last cold stage (Currant and Jacobi 2001), where it is present as a particularly robust morphotype (Kurtén 1968). A coprolite (30,161) from Lynford was sampled for ancient DNA.

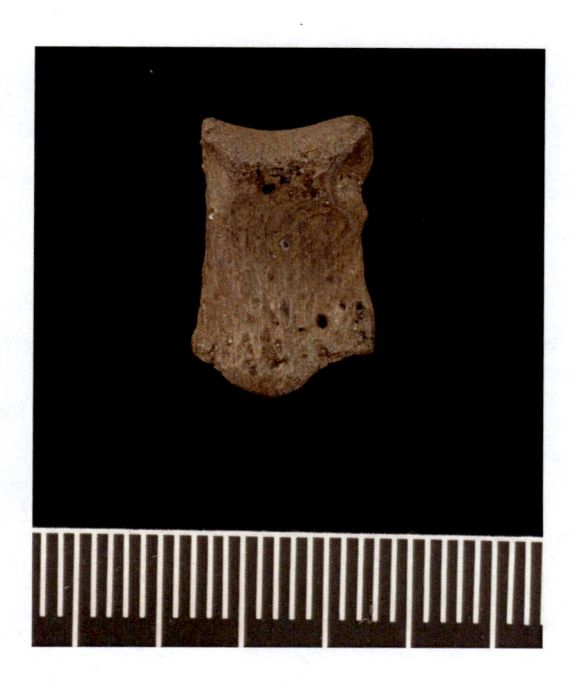

Fig 5.4
Second phalanx of *Crocuta crocuta* (anterior view).

Proboscidea Illiger, 1811
Elephantidae Gray, 1821
Mammuthus primigenius (Blumenbach, 1803), woolly mammoth

The mammoth assemblage from Lynford includes many thousands of tusk fragments (391 finds), cranial fragments (353 finds) and ribs and rib fragments (130 finds). In addition to a mandible with L and R m3 *in situ* (51046 and 51047), and a crushed maxilla with R M2 *in situ* (Fig 5.5) (51619 + 51038), twenty-seven isolated molars or partial fragments were noted. These comprise a R dp4 or m1 (50137), L m2 (51730), L m2 or m3 (51252), 2 R m2s (51710, 50358), partial R ?m2 (52038), 3 L m3s (Fig 5.6), 50656, 50000, 51997), R m3 (51953 + 51648 + 51154), fragmentary R m3 (51820), 2 L M1s (51171, 51234), 3 R M1s (51201, 51440, 51240), 2 L M2s (51966, 50002), R M2 (50003), 2 L M3s (Fig 5.7), 50273, 50001), partial L M3 (51965), R M3 (50069, 52063) and a fragmentary R M3 (51887). Many hundreds of individual molar plate and root fragments were also recovered. Postcranial material is poorly represented (see later). Measurements are given in Lister (this chapter).

The tusks of *M. primigenius* possess a distinctive spiral twist. The molars are also very diagnostic, with broad crowns and narrow, closely spaced plates with very thin, finely wrinkled enamel. A thick layer of cement is often present, particularly around the edges

Fig 5.5 (top left)
Crushed maxilla with R M2 in situ (51619) of Mammuthus primigenius, *lingual view (scale in cm).*

Fig 5.6 (top right)
L M3 (50000) of Mammuthus primigenius, *lingual view (scale in cm).*

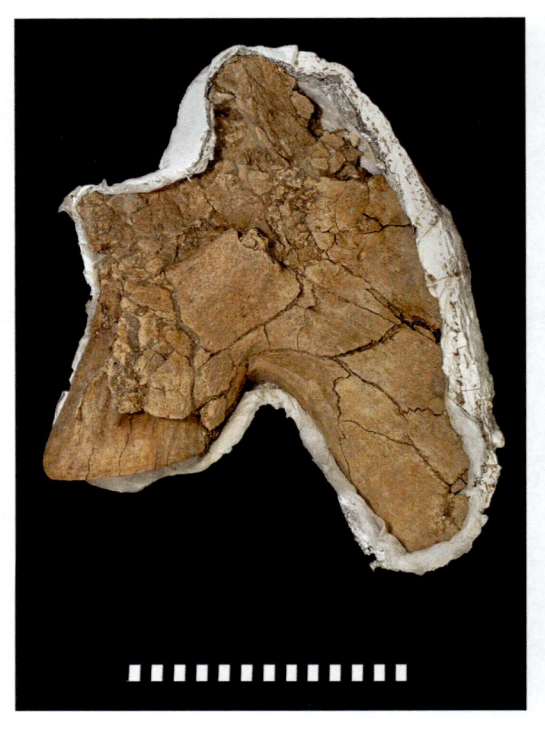

Fig 5.7 (bottom left)
L m3 (50001) of Mammuthus primigenius, *lingual view (scale in mm).*

Fig 5.8 (bottom right)
R M1 (51440) of Mammuthus primigenius, *occlusal view (scale in cm).*

of the occlusal surface. The plates wear to narrow ribbons with no median expansion, forming thin bands on the occlusal surface (Fig 5.8). Criteria for the identification of the postcranial skeleton are given by Adams (1877–1881), Osborn (1942), Garrutt (1964) and Olsen (1972).

The mammoth lineage shows significant morphological change from the Late Pliocene through to the Late Pleistocene. Although important changes in the cranium and postcranial skeleton occur during this period, the most commonly available and diagnostic elements are the molar teeth. Three main trends are discernible in the molars over time, which are particularly well expressed in the M3. The crowns double in height, the number of enamel plates (lamellae) in the teeth more than doubles and the thickness of the enamel becomes reduced by around two-thirds (Lister 1993). The increased 'tooth-life' resulting from these changes is thought to reflect an adaptation to the coarse vegetation of the 'steppe-tundra' biome, corresponding to a shift in the distribution of the genus from warmer, forested habitats to cold, open regions during the Pleistocene (Lister 1993). On the basis of these trends, four chronospecies have been defined, with the following known time ranges in Europe: *Mammuthus rumanus* (Stefanescu), from 3.5Ma to 2.6Ma, *Mammuthus meridionalis* (Nesti) from 2.6Ma to 0.8Ma, *Mammuthus trogontherii* (Pohlig) from 1.0Ma to 0.2Ma and *M. primigenius* from 0.2Ma to 0.01Ma. Their chronological replacement and the lack of alternative ancestors imply that they represent an approximate evolutionary line of descent, although some of the transitions occurred earlier in Asia (Lister *et al* 2005), and overlap between the morphological ranges can be seen at successive stages in the sequence.

The steppe mammoth, *M. trogontherii*, of the type Cromerian interglacial deposits at West Runton (Norfolk) is typically of very large size, with high crowned molars and a relatively low plate count of 19 to 22 plates in the M3 compared to the standard Devensian *M. primigenius*, which has between 20 and 28 plates in the M3. During successively later Middle Pleistocene interglacials, while plate number and hypsodonty index in the molars remain similar to *M. trogontherii*, there is a broad trend towards reduced size. In the late Middle Pleistocene, at sites such as Ilford (Essex), attributed to MIS 7 (Sutcliffe 1995; Schreve 2001a), the same plate count is retained, although size reduction in the tooth continues still further (Lister and Joysey 1992; Lister *et al* 2005). Traditionally, it was thought that intermediate forms between M. trogontherii and M. primigenius began to occur as early as the Elsterian, that forms closer to *M. primigenius* than to *M. trogontherii* appeared during the Saalian and that the fully-evolved *M. primigenius* was restricted to the Late Pleistocene, particularly in Devensian/Weichselian assemblages (Adam 1961; Kurtén 1968). However, it is now apparent that during the Late Middle Pleistocene (c 400–200ka BP), mammoths essentially similar to *M. trogontherii* but of reduced body size persisted in Europe, to be replaced by *M. primigenius* only in MIS 6 (Lister and Sher 2001; Lister *et al* 2005). The Lynford mammoths have a relatively low plate count of 20–22 in the M3, overlapping both *M. primigenius* populations from the last cold stage and *M.* cf. *trogontherii* of the late Middle Pleistocene (see Fig 5.47, Lister, this chapter) although this is a known feature among European samples (Lister and Sher 2001; Lister *et al* 2005) and is entirely consistent with the Devensian age inferred from other lines of evidence at the site.

Perissodactyla Owen, 1848
Equidae Gray, 1821
Equus ferus Boddaert, 1785, horse

The horse is represented at Lynford by three teeth (L I1, a R lower cheek tooth (p3-m2) and a R m3) and three postcranial elements, a complete R astragalus, articulating with a complete R calcaneum (Fig 5.9), and a distal right femur (Fig 5.10), possibly from the same individual. The dry-sieved spit residues yielded one additional specimen (64246 L i3) and the wet-sieved spit residues another 3 (64202 R dp germ, 1.2 M fragment and 64001 M fragment). Measurements are given in Table 5.7.

The taxonomy of the Pleistocene equids is extremely complicated, with a plethora of different subspecific names assigned to the various forms. '*Equus caballus*' has been used by certain authors to describe Pleistocene caballine horses (Prat 1966), although this term is only really appropriate for domesticated animals (Gentry *et al* 1996). Consequently, the name *Equus ferus* has been applied here, as to all British later Middle Pleistocene and Late Pleistocene caballine equids. The first caballine horses appeared during the early Middle Pleistocene and have most frequently been assigned to *E. mosbachensis* Reichenau (Prat 1966). The early caballines were of large size and possessed relatively derived dentitions compared to stenonid forms. The cheek teeth of the Equidae are hypsodont with a complex pattern of enamel folds. The upper cheek teeth are characterised by elongated 'caballine' protocones and the inner valley

Table 5.7 Measurements of *Equus ferus*: all measurements in mm, figures in brackets are minimum measurements because of breakage

Equus ferus	L	B	L double knot	max height of tooth	Bd
51612 R lower cheek tooth	31.08	15.80	15.66	(76)	
51631 R m3	32.08	12.16	14.02	(66.88)	
51360 distal R femur					92.92

L = maximum length; B = maximum breadth; Bd = greatest breadth of distal end

Fig 5.9
R calcaneum (51869) of Equus ferus, *proximal view (scale in cm).*

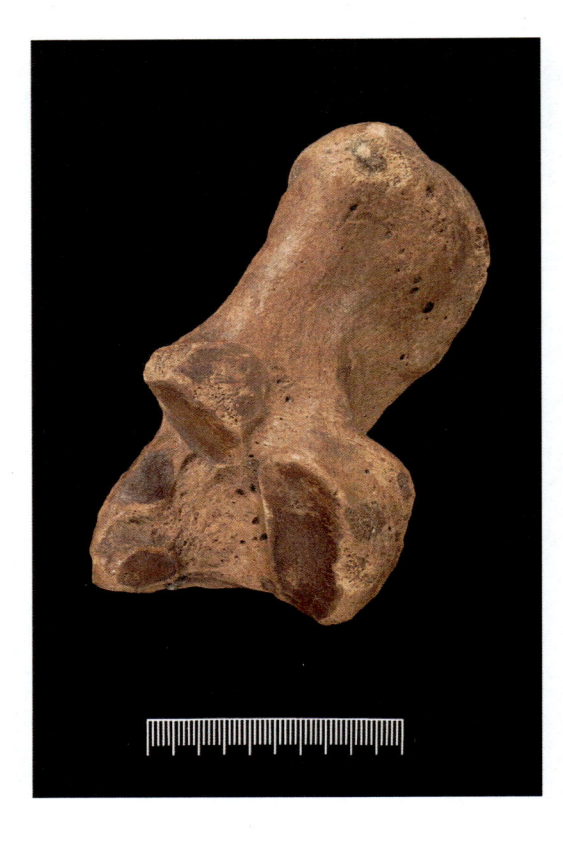

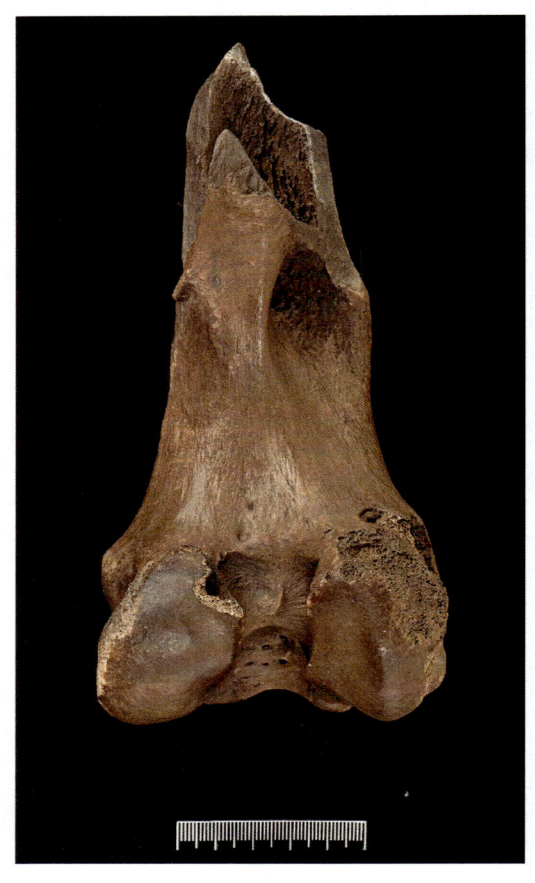

Fig 5.10
Distal R femur (51360) of Equus ferus, *posterior view (scale in cm).*

usually terminates in a simple caballine fold. The buccal infoldings are concave, and both the parastyle and mesostyle have outer vertical grooves, although these might not be present in the upper dentition. The lower cheek teeth have a 'U'-shaped lingual fold and the buccal fold does not extend beyond the isthmus (Turner 1990).

The postcranial bones of the horse are relatively slender for a large animal, and the third metapodials, with their single distal articulation, are particularly diagnostic (Schmid 1972). The calcaneum (*see* Fig 5.9) and astragalus are of typical perissodactyl form, the latter possessing two characteristic diagonally oriented articular facets. In the femur, the *fossa plantaris* is particularly deep (*see* Fig 5.10) and a third trochanter is present. From the later Middle Pleistocene onwards, a general reduction in size can be seen in both the dentition and the overall body size of the caballine horses, although the variation is unfortunately not so great that specimens can always be referred with any certainty to one of the many named species. Furthermore, the age resolution of many older sites is too poor to establish any meaningful succession (Forstén 1991).

Rhinocerotidae Owen 1845
Coelodonta antiquitatis (Blumenbach, 1807), woolly rhinoceros

The woolly rhinoceros is represented by an unworn R DP3, a R DP4 (Fig 5.11), two L P3s (Fig 5.12), three conjoining fragments of a LM, a fragmentary R dp2, L p3, L m1, incomplete R m2, an extremely comminuted lower molar, two medial distal articular fragments of a left and right humerus respectively, a R acetabulum and a juvenile tibia diaphysis. Measurements are given in Table 5.8.

Basic characters for the identification of this species are given by Bouchud (1966a) and Guérin (1980). The massive, low-slung skull is very diagnostic, since the nasal septum is usually completely ossified, and the occiput is large and squarish, with a heavy occipital crest. The teeth, which are the best-represented elements at Lynford, are large in size, plagiolophodont and hypsodont, with extremely rugose enamel and layers of cement layers between the enamel folds on the occlusal surface and on the external walls. The upper dentition is highly distinctive since the crista and crochet fuse to form an isolated enamel islet (medifossette) on the occlusal surface of the upper teeth in both the deciduous and permanent sets (see Figs 5.11 and 5.12). The permanent lower cheek teeth are formed of two lobes, which, when viewed from the lingual side, have 'V'-shaped anterior valleys and 'U'-shaped posterior valleys, and pronounced external synclines (Turner 1990). With wear, the anterior lobe of the lower teeth assumes an angular form and the posterior lobe a crescent form on the occlusal surface. The postcranial skeleton, particularly the extremities of the bones, is relatively large and robust.

The earliest appearance of *Coelodonta* in Europe is a matter of contention, with both Anglian and Saalian occurrences cited. *C. antiquitatis* has been identified in Britain from three sites of reportedly Anglian age (Homersfield [Stuart 1982; Lister 1989], King's Newnham/Lawford Pit, Warwickshire and Lillington, Warwickshire [Shotton 1953; Lister 1989]), from four sites in Romania of approximate Elsterian age (Araci-Carieră, Araci-Fintina Fagului, Ghidfalău-1 and Sfintu Gheorghe/Cariere Sud [Rădulescu and Samson 1985]), and from three sites in Germany of Elsterian age (Bad Frankhausen, Bornhausen and Neuekrug [Bouchud 1966a]). Support for an Elsterian (MIS 12) entrance into Europe has recently come from a reappraisal of the Bad Frankenhausen material by Kahlke and Lacombat (2008), although these authors reassign the specimens to *Coelodonta tologoijensis* Belyaeva, an archaic continental Asian woolly rhinoceros first noted from the early Middle Pleistocene onwards. Guérin (1980), on the other hand, limits the first occurrence of the species to the Saalian, regarding the Saalian woolly rhinoceroses as a more primitive subspecies, *C. antiquitatis praecursor*, and recognising a second subspecies, the more evolved and robustly built *C. antiquitatis antiquitatis*, as the Weichselian representative. According to Guérin, the M3s of the Saalian subspecies display a rectangular form, while those of the Weichselian animals possess a triangular form, although this biostratigraphical character has since been dismissed by van Kolfschoten (in van Kolfschoten and Roebroeks 1985). Guérin (1980) also considers the third metatarsal of *C. antiquitatis* to be shorter and stockier in the Weichselian than in the Saalian, and the radius to be longer and stouter but again, little supporting evidence

Fig 5.11
Occlusal view of R DP4 (51401) of Coelodonta antiquitatis (scale in mm).

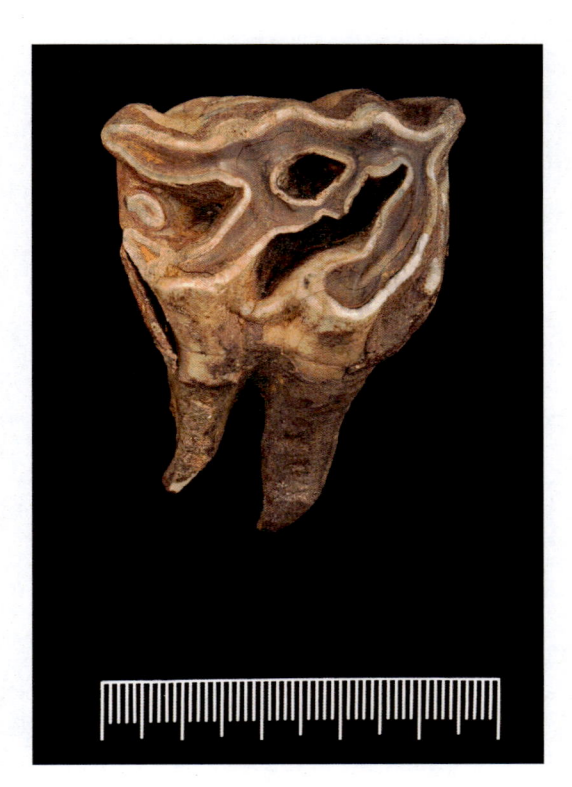

Table 5.8 Measurements of *Coelodonta antiquitatis*: all measurements in mm

Coelodonta antiquitatis	L	B
51324 R DP3	34.60	40.62
51401 R DP4	46.26	42.10
50491 L P3	36.02	39.00

L = maximum length; B = maximum breadth

Fig 5.12
Occlusal view of L P3 (50491) of Coelodonta antiquitatis (scale in mm).

was found for this by Turner (1990), since fossils of *C. antiquitatis* tend to be extremely robust whatever the age of their deposit.

However, although there appears to be little basis for Guérin's proposed subspecific division of *C. antiquitatis*, recent investigation by van Kolfschoten (1990) and Turner (1990) into the later Middle Pleistocene mammalian biostratigraphy of the Netherlands and Germany respectively also places the first appearance of the species within the Saalian. Re-examination of the British evidence has drawn similar conclusions (Schreve 1997), since the provenance of the *C. antiquitatis* material at Lillington and the attribution of the remaining aforementioned British localities to the Anglian glaciation are questionable. The first verifiable appearance of *Coelodonta* in Britain is therefore considered to occur within the Saalian *sensu lato*, more precisely in cold-climate sediments attributed to MIS 8 such as Northfleet in Kent and Stoke Newington in London (Schreve 1997). Although *C. antiquitatis* is usually associated with cold-stage faunas and is a typical element of the open steppe (*see* Stuart, this chapter), it is nevertheless recorded from interglacial deposits attributed to the later part of MIS 7, where its presence more probably confirms the opening-up of the environment and the development of steppic grassland, as opposed to a cold climate (Schreve 2001b). The species is a common component of Middle Devensian assemblages but was apparently absent from the early Devensian in Britain (Currant and Jacobi 2001).

Artiodactyla Owen, 1848
Cervidae Gray, 1821
Rangifer tarandus, L., 1758, reindeer

Remains of *R. tarandus* from Lynford include 40 antlers or antler fragments. Reindeer antlers are especially diagnostic and are carried by both sexes. The beam is long, slender and medio-laterally flattened, either sharply angled halfway along or sweeping upwards in a pronounced forward-directed curve (Fig 5.13). Two basal tines are present, placed low down near the brow and usually with palmated ends. The beam and tines are relatively thick-walled and have a smooth outer surface with broad, shallow gutters. Five isolated teeth were also identified among the excavated finds (R dp2, R p3, L p4 and L m3), one tooth was recovered from the dry-sieved spit residues (61354 L M2) and a further four, from the wet-sieved spit residues (61093 R p4, 62106 lingual fragment of ?R p4, 61648 L m1 and 64764 very worn m1 or m2 fragment). The teeth are smaller than in red deer, being both relatively rounded and very low-crowned with smooth enamel and more pronounced folding of the enamel on the buccal and lingual faces (Turner 1990). Molarisation of the p3 and p4 (Figs 5.14 and 5.15) is typical for this species. Criteria for the identification of the postcranial elements are given in Bouchud (1966b) and Lister (1981). The metapodials of *R. tarandus* differ from those of other cervids in possessing an extremely pronounced posterior groove with splayed distal epiphyses (Fig 5.16). Following an early appearance in probable Anglian levels at Westbury-sub-Mendip (Stringer *et al* 1996), no further unequivocal records of *R. tarandus* are known from Britain until the Devensian, with the sole exception of Balderton, Lincolnshire, attributed to MIS 6 by Lister and Brandon (1991). Measurements are given in Table 5.9.

Bovidae Gray, 1821
cf *Bison priscus* Bojanus, 1827, bison

Only four postcranial fragments of a large bovid have been recovered from Lynford. These are a fragment of proximal end and medial diaphysis of a left radius, two fragmentary

Fig 5.13
Antler beam with two tines (50096) of Rangifer tarandus, *lateral view (scale in cm).*

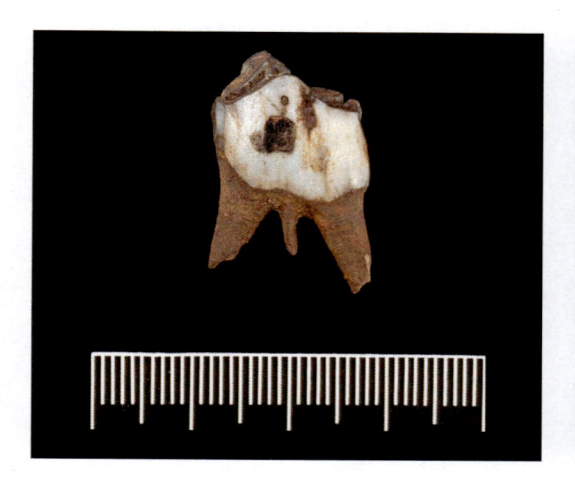

Fig 5.14 (top left) L p4 (51322) *of* Rangifer tarandus, *buccal view (scale in mm).*

Fig 5.15 (top right) L p4 (51322) *of* Rangifer tarandus, *occlusal view (scale in mm).*

Table 5.9 Measurements of *Rangifer tarandus*.: all measurements in mm

Rangifer tarandus	L	B	LAR	Bp	Dp	SD	Bd	B distal condyle
61354 L M2	17.90	12.00						
51322 L p4	15.70	10.78						
61093 R p4	14.20	10.30						
61648 L m1	15.62	9.44						
50906 L m3	21.30	8.50						
50823 R femoral head		25.30						
51023 L acetabulum			38.86					
50869 L metacarpal	169			33.64	23.70	23.72	41.68	19.82

L = maximum length; B = maximum breadth; Bp = greatest breadth of proximal end; Dp = greatest depth of proximal end; SD = smallest breadth of diaphysis; Bd = greatest breadth of distal end; LAR = length of the acetabulum on the rim

distal left humeri and a proximal posterior fragment of a left metatarsal midshaft (Fig 5.17). Measurements are given in Table 5.10. The remains are in poor condition, showing clear evidence of rolling and breakage, and have been tentatively attributed to Bison (*Bos primigenius* not being recorded from any part of the Devensian except the Late Glacial Interstadial; see Currant and Jacobi 2001). Remains of large bovids are notoriously difficult to identify to species level, and various attempts to define diagnostic characters based on postcranial bones or teeth have been made by a number of authors, for example Schertz (1936), Reynolds (1939), Olsen (1960), Browne (1983) and Gee (1993). Further difficulties are presented by pronounced sexual dimorphism and by wide morphological

Table 5.10 Measurements of *Bison priscus*: all measurements in mm

Bison priscus	BT
51889 distal L humerus	108.64

BT = greatest breadth of trochlea

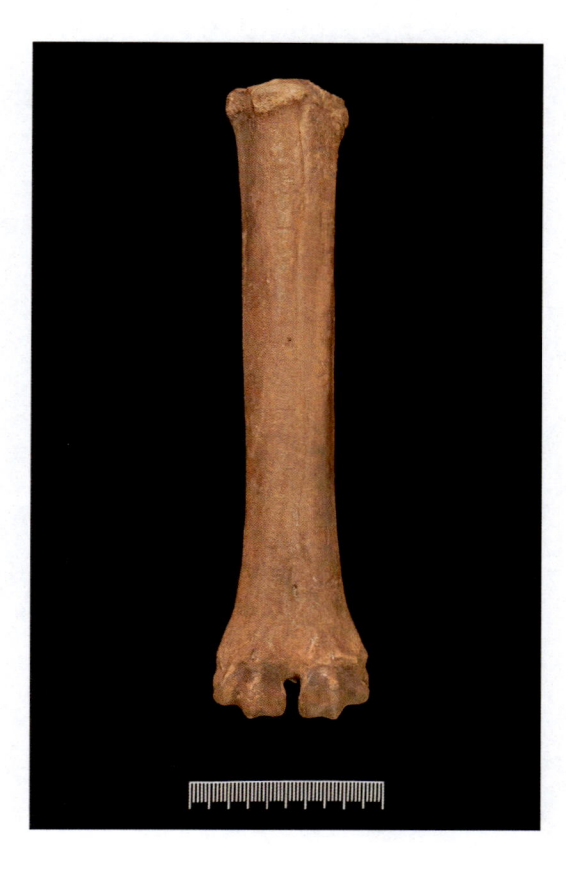

Fig 5.16 Left metacarpal (50869) *of* Rangifer tarandus, *anterior view (scale in mm).*

Fig 5.17
Proximal midshaft fragment of left metatarsal (50929) of Bison priscus, *posterior view (scale in mm).*

variability within this group. The skull and horn cores of bison are, however, easily distinguishable, since the horns are angled upwards only, whereas in *Bos primigenius* Bojanus 1827 (aurochs), the horns are twisted in two planes, both forwards and upwards.

The metapodials (particularly the metacarpals) are also widely cited as displaying useful diagnostic features (Schertz 1936; Olsen 1960; Browne 1983; Gee 1993). Those of *B. primigenius* taper gently outwards from diaphysis to distal epiphysis, while those of *B. priscus* diverge outwards above the distal epiphysis, resulting in a 'shouldered' appearance. The applicability of other discriminant characters in the postcranial elements is discussed by Gee (1993). Attempts have also been made to identify *Bos* or *Bison* on the morphology of the upper and lower cheek teeth (Delpech 1983), but the problem of separating the fossil remains of *Bos* and *Bison* has been compounded by questions as to the taxonomic validity of the two genera, since captive populations have been shown to be capable of interbreeding (Krasinska 1971). The two living species, the Eurasian wisent, *Bison bonasus* L., and the North American *Bison bison* L., differ from each other in general body form and colour, but the Pleistocene steppe bison, as portrayed in Upper Palaeolithic cave paintings, was apparently unlike either extant species. Reconstruction of a mummified *B. priscus* carcass from Alaska has revealed that in addition to differences in pelage colour and length, the dorsal hump in the Pleistocene bison was higher, more convex and placed in a more posterior position along the spine than in any living bison (Guthrie 1990).

Although *B. priscus* is known from early Middle Pleistocene sites in Germany, such as Mauer and Mosbach (Turner 1990), the steppe bison does not seem to have entered Britain until after the Anglian, apparently replacing the small, gracile *Bison schoetensacki* Freudenberg, which was present in Europe during the Cromerian and has been tentatively identified at Waverley Wood (Shotton *et al* 1993), and at Westbury-sub-Mendip (Gentry 1999). *B. priscus* is a common element of the early part of the Devensian (MIS 5a; Currant and Jacobi 2001; Gilmour *et al* 2007).

Composition of the large vertebrate assemblage

The presence of differentially weathered bones within the main channel assemblage precludes the possibility of attributing significance to any apparent mammalian faunal change upward through the sequence. All species recorded at the site are present within the dark brown-black organic sands of the main palaeochannel contexts, 20003 and 20021 (*see* Table 5.2), and all carnivore taxa and *E. ferus* are restricted to these two contexts alone. By contrast, *M. primigenius* is more evenly distributed, occurring above, below and within the organic deposits of the main palaeochannel, in all but 15 of the fossiliferous contexts. As with the other species, the greatest concentrations of mammoths are in the organic sands of the main palaeochannel (Association B-ii), but five finds have come from the gravels and sands below the organic sands (B-i:03) and six from the sands and gravels above (B-iii) (*see* Table 5.2). A single specimen of *R tarandus* is also found in each of the coarser sands and gravels above (Association C) and below the main organic sandy silts (Bi:03), and a single find of *C. antiquitatis* was also recovered from Association C. Thus, only mammoths and reindeer occur in sediments pre-dating the deposition of the main organic channel deposits and only these two species, with the addition of woolly rhinoceros, post-date the main channel infilling.

M. primigenius is by far the most abundant species, comprising over 90 per cent of the assemblage of 1401 identified individually-numbered and unstratified finds. At least 11 individuals are represented, including one juvenile. The mammoth remains are dominated by tusk fragments at 31.4 per cent of the mammoth assemblage, cranial fragments (28.4 per cent of the assemblage) and rib fragments (10.4 per cent of the assemblage). The high frequency of these friable elements is considered to be a direct reflection of the taphonomic processes that have affected the assemblage, most noticeably trampling by large mammals (see later). Eight pairs of molars have been found within the assemblage (see Lister, Tables 5.47–5.49, this chapter): 50002 and 50003; 50069 and 50273 (Fig 5.18); 50358 and 51730; 50656a and 51953/51648/51154 (Fig 5.19); 51171 and 51201 (Fig 5.20); 51234 and 51140; 51820 and 51997; and 51965 and 52063), and a possible further association has been noted between an upper and lower pair of second molars (50002–50003 and 50358–51730 respectively, Fig 5.21). The presence of these paired teeth, in addition to the occurrence of fragments of mandibular or maxillary bone between the roots of the molars, indicates that whole jaws and/or crania were initially present on site but have since been destroyed. Only three molars were found to be still *in situ* within jaws: a pair of lower third molars (51046 and 51047) in a mandible, and a right upper second molar in a maxilla (51619). Fifteen complete or partially complete tusks were also excavated and photographed *in situ* within the main palaeochannel deposits (Fig 5.22). Four of these were considered to be sufficiently robust to warrant jacketing in plaster for further conservation, but the remainder proved too fragile to recover.

In sharp contrast, mammoth postcranial elements other than ribs are very poorly represented in the assemblage and are highly variable in terms of their preservation when encountered. In total, 206 individually numbered finds could be attributed to non-rib postcranial elements, comprising only 16 per cent of the total number of mammoth remains (*see* Table 5.1). Of these, more than

Fig 5.18
R and L M3 of Mammuthus primigenius *(50069 and 50273), buccal view (scale in mm).*

Fig 5.19
R and L m3 of Mammuthus primigenius *(51953–51648–51154 and 50656a), lingual view (scale in mm).*

Fig 5.20
R and L M1 of Mammuthus primigenius *(51171 and 51201), buccal view (scale in mm).*

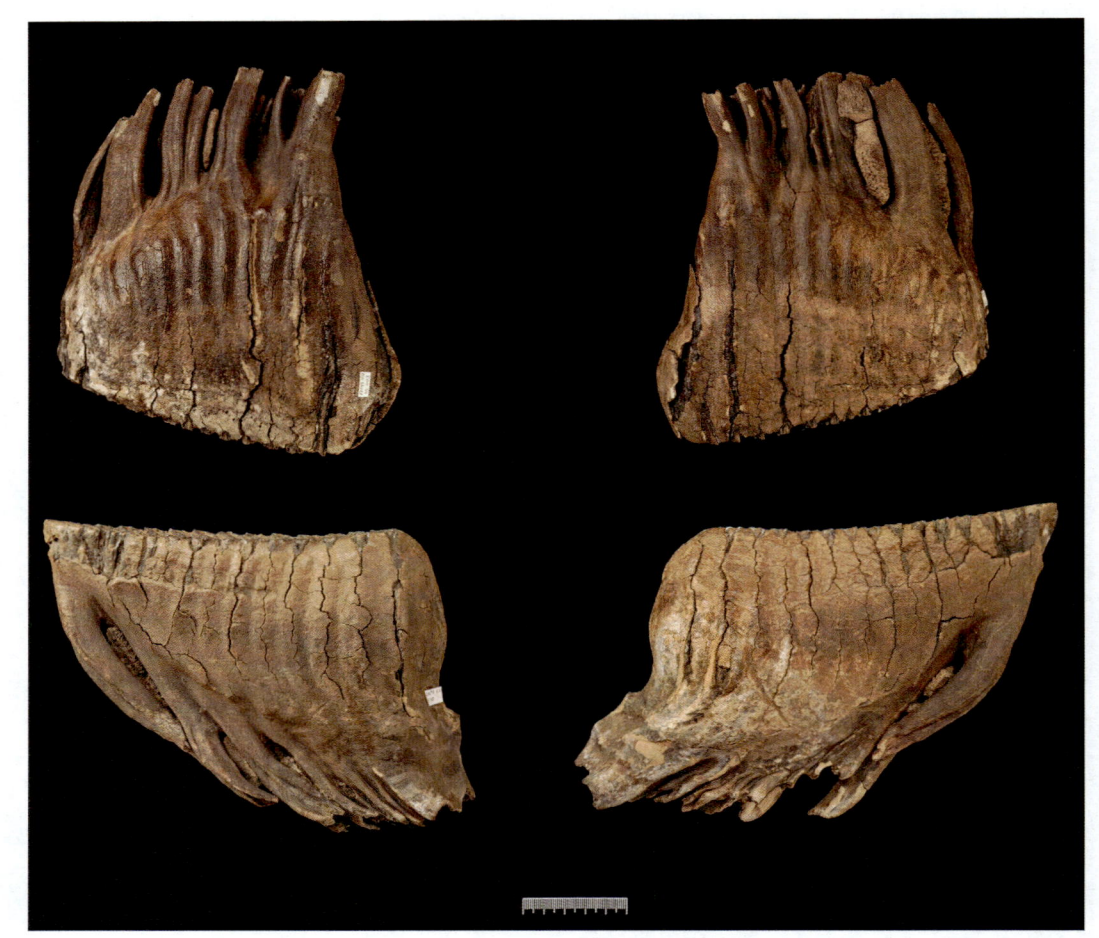

Fig 5.21
Associated R and L second molars of Mammuthus primigenius *(50002–50003 and 50358–51730), buccal view (scale in mm).*

half are fragments of long-bone and other indeterminate postcranial fragments. These rarely exceed 150mm in length and have been reduced in the majority of cases to bone 'shards', which are roughly twice as long as they are wide. Of the remaining non-rib specimens, the most abundant are vertebrae (27 specimens), with smaller numbers of specimens distributed fairly evenly among the major limb elements – never comprising more than 10 finds of each. Four podials were recovered, but no metapodials are present and only two phalanges. This is surprising given the relative robustness of these small, compact elements, although feet are often one of the areas preferentially targeted by carnivores. Only 11 of the vertebrae and 12 ribs approach any degree of completeness and no complete mammoth limb bones are present in the assemblage; the two best-preserved major elements are a proximal left radius (51903) (Fig 5.23) and a proximal right ulna (51976) (Fig 5.24). Where present, limb bones are generally reduced to diaphyseal fragments and, more rarely, epiphyseal elements. Even allowing for the high degree of breakage in the bones, it is clear that long-bones and long-bone fragments are very under-represented within the assemblage. With a minimum number of 11 individuals in an unmodified assemblage, one would expect to encounter 165 major limb bone elements (scapulae, humeri, radii, ulnae, pelvises, femora, tibiae and fibulae) as well as at least 275 vertebrae (not including sacral or caudal vertebrae) and 220 ribs. The paucity of postcranial elements other than ribs and vertebrae must therefore be attributable to *post mortem* differential destruction and removal.

Remains of *R. tarandus* are the next most abundant in the assemblage with 73 specimens, 40 of which (approximately 55 per cent) consist of antlers or antler fragments. At least seven adult animals are present and two juveniles (*see* Table 5.2). Preservation is similarly variable, ranging from large and fairly complete (although often crushed) sections of antler beam to detached tines and small beam fragments. Antler bases, the most robust part of the element, are most frequently encountered. Five isolated reindeer teeth were excavated as individual finds from the palaeochannel deposits, together with 26 postcranial elements. Only two of the latter were complete, a well-preserved left metacarpal (50869) and a gnawed second phalanx (50212). *C. antiquitatis* is the next most common taxon, with

*Fig 5.22 (above)
Tusks of* Mammuthus primigenius *in the main palaeochannel during excavation.*

*Fig 5.23
Proximal L radius of* Mammuthus primigenius *(51903), posterior view (scale in mm).*

*Fig 5.24
Proximal R ulna of
Mammuthus primigenius
(51976), anterior view
(scale in cm).*

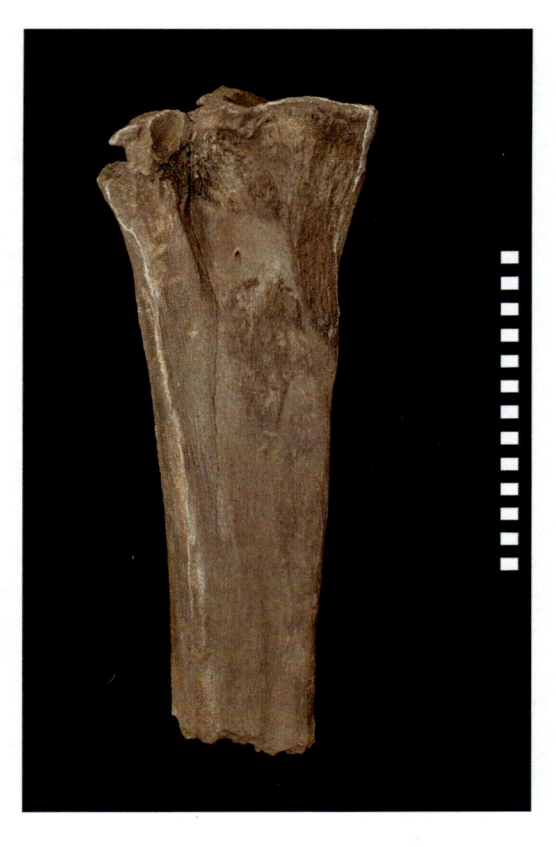

14 remains representing two adults and two juveniles (1 per cent of the assemblage). Again, the more durable elements such as teeth and robust postcranial elements like distal humeri are best represented. Numbers of *E. ferus* are also low, and with the exception of three elements from the hind limb, consist exclusively of teeth. Two adults are represented by the excavated finds, although a juvenile animal is recorded in the wet-sieved spit residues on the basis of a deciduous lower second tooth. Bison is the least abundant taxon with only three postcranial elements represented, two of which are durable distal humerus fragments. A minimum number of two adults is implied (*see* Table 5.2). Carnivores, although usually scarce in assemblages from open sites, are comparatively well represented at Lynford, with predominantly dental elements preserved. Four taxa have been recorded, each represented by a minimum of one individual.

Results from the bulk samples and sieved spit residues

Remains extracted from the bulk sample residues are shown in Appendix 3, Table 1. In addition to the serial samples taken for microvertebrates, bones and teeth were also recovered from 21 bulk samples taken for molluscan remains (Keen, chapter 3). In total, 2040 fragments were recorded, ranging from large tusk or cranial fragments of *M. primigenius* to small vertebrate remains, including fish, herpetofauna and occasional small mammal remains. In the large bone fraction, the samples were dominated by mammoth tusk fragments (345 specimens), followed by indeterminate bone fragments, most probably also of mammoth (284 specimens), and mammoth cranial fragments (131 specimens). Three fragments of molar plate of *M. primigenius* were also noted.

In the smaller fraction, indeterminate bone fragments were most commonly encountered (710 specimens, 35 per cent of the smaller fraction). These were generally less than 5mm in diameter and consisted mainly of very comminuted fragments of larger bones. In the identifiable small vertebrate fraction (468 specimens), remains of fish dominated (376 specimens), particularly spines and vertebrae of three-spined stickleback (*Gasterosteus aculeatus*), with smaller numbers of perch (*Perca fluviatilis*), rare remains of pike (*Esox lucius*) and a single find of a cyprinid. The fish remains are uniformly well preserved and include particularly fragile elements such as perch scales and a cyprinid pharyngeal bone with the teeth still *in situ*, attesting to the gentle depositional environment. Herpetofaunal remains are the next most common elements (Gleed-Owen, this chapter), with 82 specimens from one species, but mammalian remains are comparatively rare. Only eight molars or molar fragments and incisors can be attributed to *Microtus* sp. or to Microtinae, and no other identifiable small mammal remains were recorded. Ninety-nine small vertebrate long-bone fragments lacking articular ends were also extracted from the samples. These do not have the distinctive hollow diaphyses and flaring morphology of herpetofaunal long-bones and are therefore most probably the postcranial remains of small mammals. However, the state of degradation in these long-bone fragments makes them impossible to identify further. Without exception, the bones are crushed and longitudinally split, suggesting that they have been subject to weathering or pressure, probably from trampling, prior to their incorporation in the deposits.

The herpetofaunal remains are similarly poorly preserved, even though they are a relatively more autochthonous component of the deposits than the mammalian remains (Gleed-Owen, this chapter).

In terms of faunal representation relative to sampling position within the channel, no discernible difference could be detected between the various column series. This would suggest that in such a shallow-water environment, distance from the channel margin has not been a significant factor in influencing either preservation or the relative abundance of the different taxa. Mammalian remains, which one would expect to find in greater abundance near the channel edge, are rare in all cases. Similarly, the column samples provide no clear indication of faunal change up through the sequence. Indications of periods of overbank flooding are present in the molluscan assemblage (Keen, chapter 5), illustrated by the influx of higher numbers of terrestrial taxa, but no such patterns are discernible in the vertebrate record. Only the decrease in fish remains in the highest samples of series 30.198, 30.225, 30.226 and 30.234 hints at a period of drying-out, although the paucity of vertebrate remains in general in these samples might equally point to weathering of the uppermost deposits.

Remains extracted from the wet- and dry-sieved spit residues are shown in Appendix 3, Tables 2 and 3. The dry-sieved fraction yielded 26423 fragments (combined weight 28.04kg after sieving), predominantly of tusk and cranium of *M. primigenius* (Appendix 3, Table 2). The yield of the samples varied from single finds to over 500 small fragments in a single bag. Indeterminate bone fragments are well represented and only a single sample (64236) yielded remains of any large mammal species other than mammoths, in this instance a left lower third incisor of *E. ferus*. The dry-sieved residues were very poor in the remains of small vertebrates. No small mammal remains were recovered, and the only specimens recorded were six herpetofaunal bones (62278, 62280, 62406, 62425, 62667 and 64504), three fish bones (61959, 62410, 62667) and a single find of a bird bone (61276, a proximal left tarsometatarsus of a crake [*Porzana* sp.], identified by Dr Joanne Cooper, Natural History Museum, London).

The wet-sieved spit residues (Appendix 3, Table 3) yielded 17660 specimens (combined weight 10.36kg after sieving) from a much wider range of taxa than were observed in the dry-sieved material. Both dry- and wet-sieved spits were sieved through the same mesh sizes on site but the greater range of material extracted from the latter implies that the cleaned residues were easier to scan, resulting in a higher yield of fragments and a concomitantly greater species diversity. As with the dry-sieved residues, the samples were dominated by indeterminate bone fragments, mammoth cranial fragments and tusk. However, in contrast to the dry-sieved residues, a much wider range of other large mammals was encountered (cf *C. lupus*, *E. ferus*, *C. antiquitatis*, *R. tarandus* and Bovidae sp.). These mammals were represented by teeth and tooth fragments, and small vertebrates were also recovered, although in substantially fewer numbers than in the wet-sieved bulk samples; again, a likely reflection of processing methods as the bulk samples were sieved to 500µm under laboratory conditions, and the spit residues sieved to 6mm on site. Of the identified fish material, spines of *G. aculeatus* were most abundant (nine specimens), followed by teeth of *E. lucius* (six specimens) and scales of *P. fluviatilis* (two specimens). Undetermined fish bone fragments numbered 42. In the small mammal assemblage, five molars of *M. gregalis* and two teeth of *Spermophilus* sp. were noted, together with 24 specimens, molar fragments and incisors, of *Microtus* sp. and indeterminate Microtinae. As in the other spit and bulk residues, the small vertebrate long-bones were uniformly split, crushed and lacking epiphyseal ends. One bird bone was present, a distal right tarsometatarsus (61634), also of crake (J. Cooper, pers comm). Although the morphology of both crake specimens reliably allows classification to genus, they are too fragmentary to be confidently referred to a species as the remains fall into the overlapping size range of several small crakes; the spotted crake *Porzana porzana* (L.), the little crake *Porzana parva* (Scopoli) and Baillon's crake *Porzana pusilla* (Pallas).

Taphonomy

A comprehensive study of the taphonomy of the Lynford vertebrate assemblage was undertaken, involving the integration of the sedimentary history at the site with the vertebrate evidence

Fig 5.25 (opposite) Distribution of individual vertebrate finds within the main palaeochannel.

in order to understand how the assemblage was formed. The preservation potential of bone is dependent on a number of characteristics including size, shape, composition and other physical attributes. Large bones are less susceptible to transportation by normal current velocities and less vulnerable to complete destruction by predators or by weathering or trampling. The composition of individual elements is also significant, in particular the ratio of spongy to compact bone (S/C ratio). The spongy bone present in the epiphyseal ends of long-bones is particularly attractive to carnivores such as *C. crocuta* (Haynes 1980) and will therefore be preferentially destroyed, leaving only the diaphyses. The spongy epiphyseal bone is also more friable than the compact bone of the midshafts, and is therefore less likely to be preserved. Teeth, in contrast, tend to preserve well because of their small size, low S/C ratio and dense enamel and dentine composition. The surface area to volume ratio (SA/V) also has a bearing on the survivability and transportation potential of different skeletal elements. Bones with a high SA/V, such as scapulae and innominates, tend to be thin and flat and are therefore more susceptible to general breakage and to carnivore damage (because the marrow cavity can be readily accessed) (Shipman 1981). These elements are also more prone to hydrodynamic dispersal as their greater surface area enhances the potential for drag and suspension by a water body. All of the above factors have potentially influenced the formation process of the Lynford assemblage.

For each species it was therefore established which skeletal elements were present at the site, their degree of completeness and their distribution within the channel. The condition of the material was also assessed in detail, involving (1) examination of the bone surface for evidence of rolling and abrasion in order to determine whether parts of the assemblage have been transported by water action, (2) inspection for root etching, weathering or polishing that might indicate prolonged exposure prior to burial, (3) examination for signs of trampling or crushing by large mammals, and (4) assessment of evidence for accumulation or modification by hominins, carnivores or other agents (eg cutmarks, deliberate bone breakage, carnivore or rodent gnawmarks or digestion).

Orientation of the bones within the palaeochannel and the nature of the depositional environment from the vertebrate assemblage

The vertebrate material is aligned in a broad east-north-east to west-south-west direction, according to the course of the palaeochannel (Boismier, chapter 4), but the bones themselves show no discernible preferred orientation within the deposits from examination of the plans (long-axis orientation and the angle of dip of the bones were not measured during the excavation, although all excavated elements were drawn in plan view). The distribution of the vertebrate remains is shown in Fig 5.25. This would initially suggest that very little dispersal or sorting of the bones had occurred once they had been deposited in the channel, although no articulated remains were recovered. However, in order to further assess whether fluvial activity had played any part in sorting the material, the assemblage was compared with the three groups of skeletal elements defined by Voorhies (1969). These groupings indicate which skeletal elements are most likely to be transported and deposited together by hydraulic action, thereby allowing the degree of preferential sorting to be calculated (Table 5.11). Elements that are likely to be removed immediately by water action (Group I), even by low-velocity currents, include ribs, vertebrae, sacrum and sternum. These elements are generally long and thin or have a relatively complex structure, giving them a high SA/V ratio. They are also comparatively fragile, with a high S/C ratio, and are thus more vulnerable to transportation. At the other end of the spectrum (Group III) are those compact and/or massive elements that can only be transported by high-velocity currents. These include crania and mandibles, both of which have a low SA/V ratio and a low S/C ratio (Voorhies 1969; Shipman 1981). The major limb bones occupy intermediate positions between these two groups. An assemblage containing all three Voorhies groups is probably underived or transported and is therefore considered to be an appropriate subject for palaeoecological reconstruction (Shipman 1981).

Of the individually numbered finds from Lynford, 624 can be categorised according to the Voorhies groups. Examination of the distribution of the different elements reveals that 30 per cent of the 624 finds can be assigned to Group I and 62 per cent to Group III.

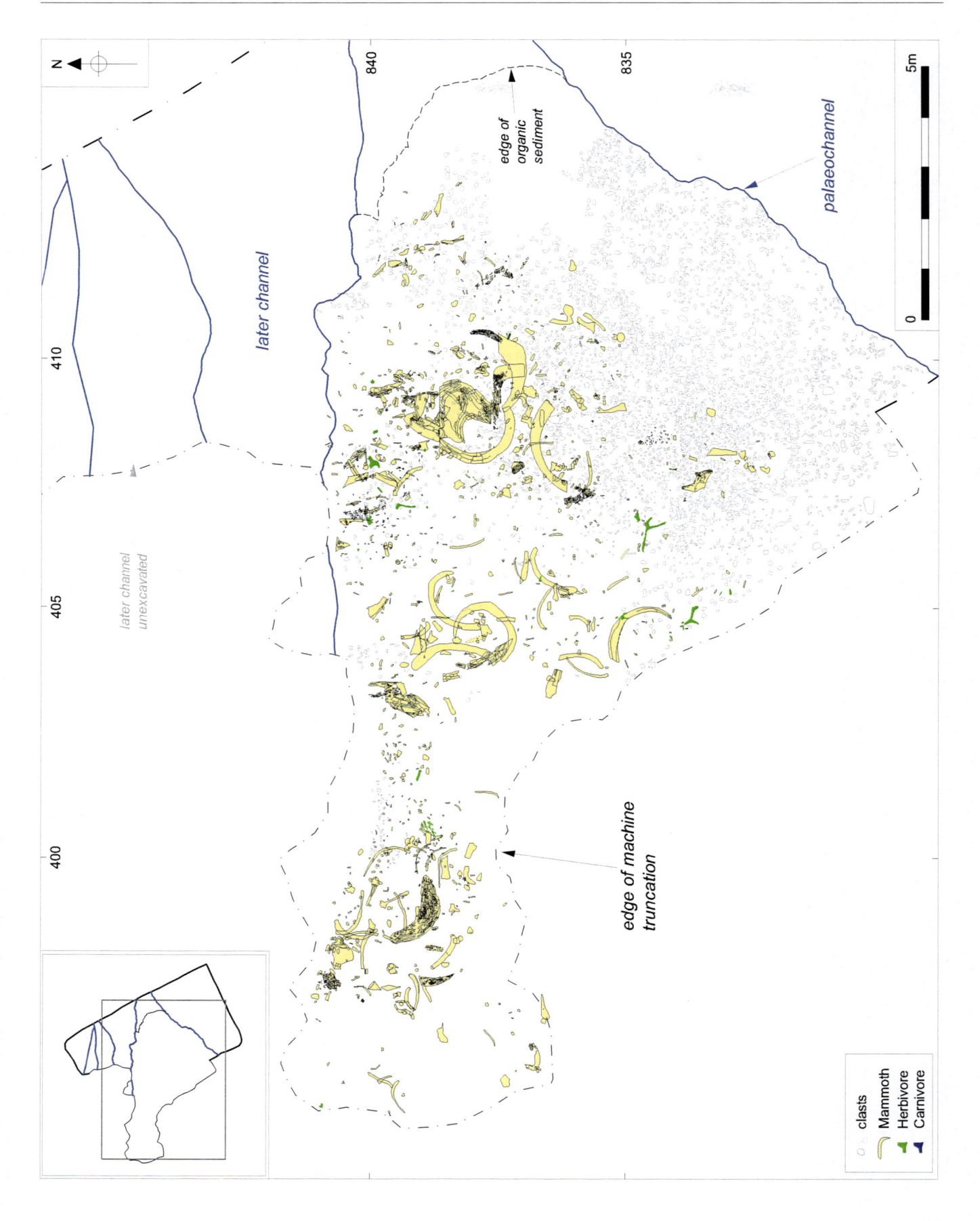

Fig 5.26 (opposite) Distribution of refitting and associated vertebrate finds within the main palaeochannel.

Table 5.11 Potential of different bones for dispersal by water according to Voorhies Groups, compared to body part representation at Lynford

Voorhies Group I: bones immediately removed by low velocity currents; high SAV ratio; high S/C ratio

element	count
ribs	132
vertebrae	30
sacrum	0
sternum	4

intermediate between I and II

element	count
scapula	4
phalanges	4
ulna	5

Voorhies Group II: bones removed gradually by moderate currents; low SA/V ratio; intermediate S/C ratio

element	count
femur	13
tibia	9
humerus	12
metapodials	–
pelvis	–
radius	–

intermediate between II and III

element	count
mand. ramus	23

Voorhies Group III: lag deposit moved only by high-velocity currents; low SA/V ratio; low S/C ratio

element	count
skull	380
mandible	8

Even taking into account the higher proportion of friable cranial fragments, this would imply that there has been little disturbance of the assemblage by fluvial activity following its deposition. This is supported by the presence of elements such as complete vertebrae with intact neural spines in the large mammal fraction, and by elements such as delicate fish scales in the microvertebrate assemblage.

However, a number of refitting bone and tooth fragments with old breaks and rearticulating elements have been noted in the assemblage. Specimens with fresh breaks caused by excavation damage are excluded, as are specimens apparently from the same element with consecutive finds numbers and conjoining fragments within the same finds bag. These refits occur across all parts of the site and are not concentrated in a single area, as is the case with the refitting lithics (White, this chapter). The refitting elements include mammoth rib fragments (50184 and 50151; 51259 and 51262; 51448 and 51451; 51972 and 51999), mammoth cranial and maxillary fragments (51038 and 51619), a mammoth R m3 (51154, 51648 and 51953), a mammoth atlas vertebra (51515 and 51537) two fragments of a wolf ulna (50233 and 51860) and wolf dentary (51218 and 51223) and an astragalus and calcaneum of horse (51831 and 51869). The greatest distance between refitting elements is 4.49m (Fig 5.26). All the refits noted occur in the organic sediments of Unit B-ii:03, with the exception of the mammoth cranial fragments and maxilla, which were found in the sands of Unit B-ii:01 (20364 and 20384 respectively). Carcasses lying on the adjacent land surface prior to incorporation in the channel would have been disarticulated, dispersed and broken by various agents, including large herbivores, carnivores and, possibly, Neanderthals. It is therefore not possible to determine whether the remains were broken on the land surface or once they had been deposited in the channel sediments. Either way, bioturbation from the trampling activities of large mammals around the edge of the channel or in the water body itself are likely to be the primary cause of these breakages and dispersals. Parallels have been noted within the insect assemblage from Lynford, where a high proportion of remains in the palaeochannel are fragmented (Coope, chapter 3).

The absence of evidence of transportation or winnowing of the assemblage means that palaeoecological reconstructions based on the mammalian remains can be undertaken with a good degree of certainty that the animals represented at the site inhabited the local area, a point highlighted by the abundance of dung beetles in the channel deposits (Coope, chapter 3). The spatial distribution of the finds within the channel gives no clue as to hominin activities within the channel itself, since there are no apparent concentrations of particular body elements in certain areas. The edge of the

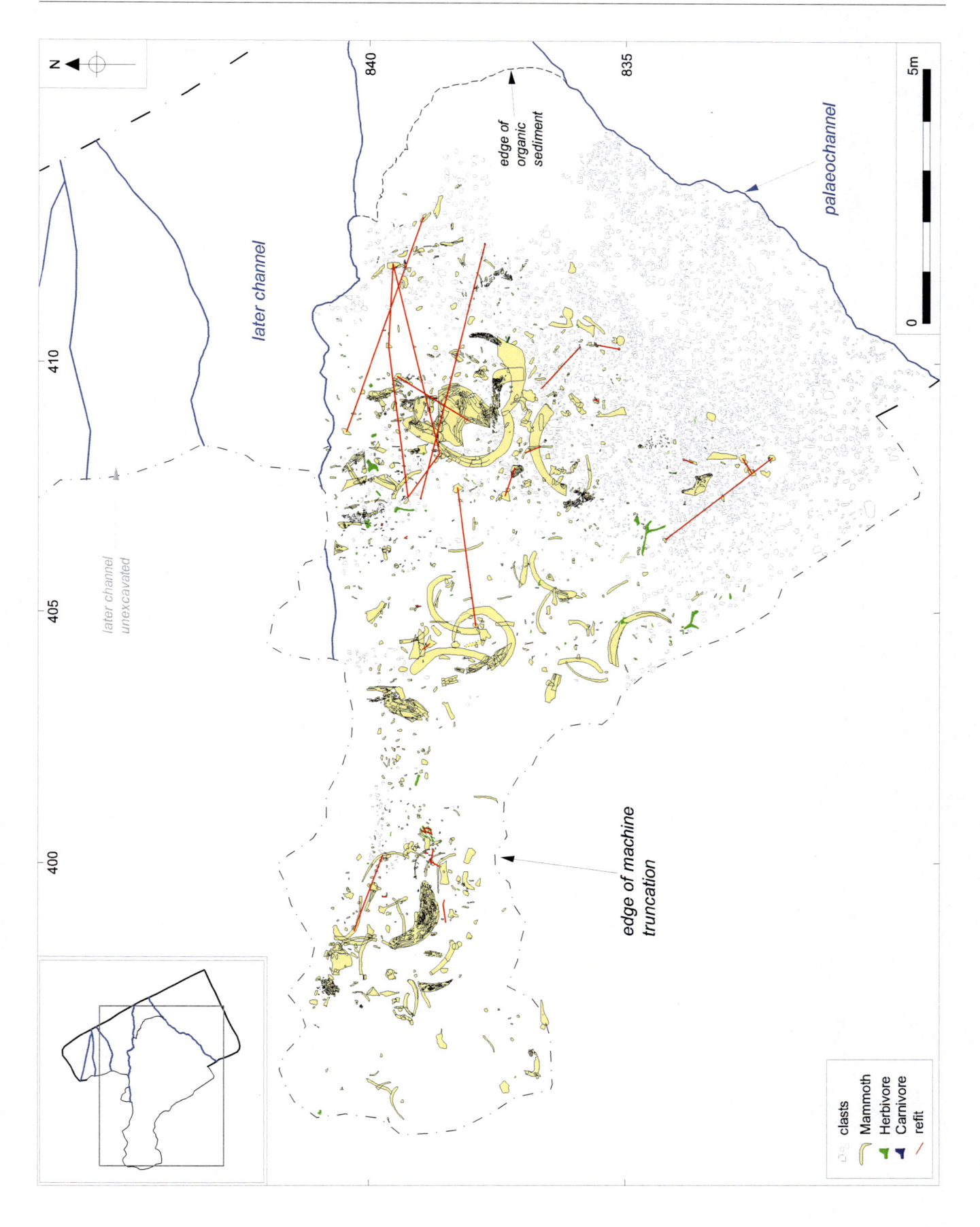

5 THE ARCHAEOLOGICAL ASSEMBLAGES OF ANIMALS AND LITHICS

channel, where butchering and consumption activities might have left a noticeable pattern, is unfortunately not preserved.

Size of the individual finds

It was apparent from the outset that extraordinarily little complete material was present in the assemblage. The majority of the 55 isolated teeth recovered during the excavation were in a perfect or near-perfect state but, as stated above, the cranial and postcranial specimens were almost all fragmentary. Robust elements, such as the large limb bones of mammoths, are generally considered to be less susceptible to breakage than those with a long slender form such as ribs. However, this is not the case at Lynford where more complete mammoth ribs than long-bones survive. Crania characteristically fracture along the sutral lines (Kos 2003), but while the abundance of cranial fragments in the assemblage is not particularly surprising, the degree of further fragmentation in these cranial elements is noteworthy. Analysis of the degree of fragmentation in the assemblage might provide some measure of the destructive forces to which the Lynford assemblage was exposed, both before and after burial. In the majority of cases, bones will be broken by the natural processes of decay, weathering, the actions of predators, fluvial transportation, trampling and diagenesis, including compaction by the overlying sediments.

The broken and irregular nature of the Lynford material dictated the methods chosen to analyse the size of the individual specimens and a system of six concentric circles, drawn on card, was accordingly devised, against which each find was measured. The diameters of the circles increased in 30mm stages (Class 1: 0–30mm; Class 2: 30–60mm; Class 3: 60–90mm; Class 4: 90–120mm; Class 5: 120–150mm and Class 6: > 150mm). A total of 2022 specimens were measured. In cases where more than one fragment was present in the finds bag, the measurement was taken on the largest fragment present in order to gauge the minimum amount of breakage that the specimen had been subjected to. This also allowed for further post-excavation damage to be discounted. The following results were obtained: Class 1: 212 specimens (approximately 11 per cent of the measured assemblage); Class 2: 748 specimens (37 per cent); Class 3: 506 specimens (25 per cent); Class 4: 208 specimens (10 per cent); Class 5: 119 specimens (6 per cent) and Class 6: 229 specimens (11 per cent). The relative abundances of each size class are shown in Fig 5.27. Since so few elements are complete, the high degree of fragmentation in the assemblage is immediately obvious. Over 72 per cent of the measurable specimens are under 90mm in diameter, and only 11 per cent fall within the largest size category of 150mm and above.

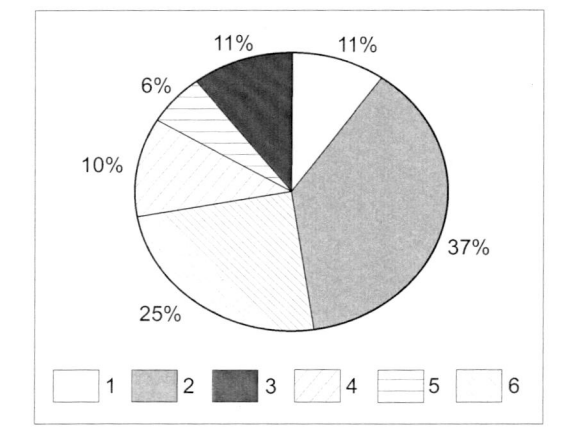

Given the apparent lack of fluvial transportation, the extreme fragmentation of the material must be attributed to other agents. The activities of predators are likely to have played a significant role in disarticulating and dispersing carcasses in the vicinity of the channel and then in the selective destruction of some skeletal elements. Carnivore gnawing tends to reduce long bones first to cylindrical shafts, and then to bone splinters (Binford 1983). This might account for some of the shards of mammoth long bone observed in the assemblage. However, it is the trampling activities of large mammals that are considered here to have amplified the degree of bone breakage. The trampling of bones near a water source is a common occurrence, particularly by herds of ungulates coming to drink – a scenario that seems likely to have occurred around the channel at Lynford. The effects of trampling on large mammal bones have been documented in detail by Andrews and Cook (1985) and Behrensmeyer et al (1986). These include not only fragmentation of the bones, but also a wide range of surface modifications such as scratches, gouges, scrapes and cuts, some of which might superficially resemble the butchery marks left by flint tools. The greater the degree of weathering of the material, the more fragmentation is likely to occur, and

Fig 5.27
Pie chart showing the relative frequency of finds according to size class (1 = 0–30mm diameter; 2 = 30–60mm; 3 = 60–90mm; 4 = 90–120mm; 5 = 120–150mm; 6 = >150mm).

only the smallest and most dense elements will survive. The inferred post-depositional compaction of the main channel sediments by 33 per cent (Tovey, chapter 3) is also likely to have contributed to the further fragmentation of the material and to the crushing that is apparent on many of the larger specimens, which were recovered using plaster jackets. In addition, the subsequent quarrying activities and pressure from heavy machinery could have further deformed the bones and sediments.

Experiments carried out on trampling of small mammal bones (Andrews 1990) revealed patterns of breakage on all elements, resulting in a complete absence of crania, a reduction in the number of maxillae, a high proportion of isolated teeth, the considerable breakage of larger postcranial elements and some degree of loss, but no loss or breakage in the smaller elements. The allochthonous component of the Lynford small vertebrate assemblage (the mammalian and avian remains) are very few in number, but their generally poor condition, typified by split and broken long-bones, potentially reflects trampling and/or weathering action on the land surface adjacent to the channel.

Condition of the vertebrate assemblage

The condition of the vertebrate assemblage was examined in detail, including the degree of weathering, and evidence of abrasion and root damage, in order to assess the depositional history of the material, particularly relating to questions of hydraulic transportation and rapidity of burial. Bones from the main channel infill (B-ii:03) are generally stained mid- to dark-brown in colour, and a pale grey-white 'bloom' occurs on some specimens, possibly a post-excavation microbial growth. Teeth from B-ii:03 are stained dark grey-blue in colour. Bone stained to varying intensities of orange, the result of iron oxides in the depositional environment, is also common. Occasionally, specimens have been only partially stained, for example on one surface only, or along half their length.

The degree of weathering observed in a bone can reveal information about the rapidity of burial. Weathering is the consequence of exposure to the elements prior to deposition, the result of the physical agents of wind, sun, rain and temperature change that will ultimately destroy the skeletal elements if they are not buried. Six categories of weathering were identified for large mammal bones under tropical climatic conditions by Behrensmeyer (1978) and four categories for small mammal bones under wet temperate climatic conditions by Andrews (1990). These are shown in Table 5.12. The surface of all individually numbered bones in the Lynford assemblage was examined, and each assigned to one of the weathering categories established by Behrensmeyer (1978). The small vertebrate bones from the bulk samples and sieved spit residues were not considered individually but by Class (Mammalia, Amphibia etc).

A total of 2090 specimens were analysed, including all unstratified and un-numbered finds. Of these, no specimens were found for Class 0, 24 specimens (1 per cent) were attributed to Behrensmeyer's Class 1, 299 (14 per cent) to Class 2, 1192 (57 per cent) to Class 3, 419 (20 per cent) to Class 4 and 156 (8 per cent) to Class 5. The predominant category is therefore that of bones that are estimated to have been exposed on the surface for between 4 and 15 years or more before burial (Class 3), followed by material exposed for between 6 and 15 years or more (Class 4). Seriously weathered material with a characteristic flaking 'onion peel' texture, and occasionally exposed cancellous bone, accounts for 8 per cent (Class 5). Only 1 per cent of the material was considered to be sufficiently well preserved to have been buried less than four years after the death of the animal, the majority of which is dental remains, and therefore less susceptible to degradation in any case. A greater number, 14 per cent (Class 2), however, indicate exposure of material for between two and seven years before burial. Material from the different classes is evenly distributed in the sediments of the main palaeochannel, although the most weathered specimens come from the sands overlying the black organic sediments. It is important to bear in mind, however, that the figures given for years of exposure are an indication only, since bones that are exposed in hot or humid climates, as in Behrensmeyer's original study, will be destroyed through weathering more rapidly than in cool climates. Under the climatic regime inferred for Lynford (mean July temperature 12–14°C and mean January/February temperatures at or below −10°C), bones might have remained relatively well preserved for longer. The inferred exposure rates prior to burial should therefore be viewed as minimum estimates only.

Table 5.12 Weathering categories for large mammal bones (after Behrensmeyer 1978) and small mammal bones (after Andrews 1990) and inferred length of exposure in years before burial

stage	large mammal bone weathering categories (after Behrensmeyer 1978)	years since death	small mammal bone weathering categories (after Andrews 1990)	years since death
0	no cracking or flaking; greasy; soft tissue still present; marrow contains tissue	0–1	no modification	0–2
1	longitudinal cracking parallel to fibre structure in long bones; shiny and smooth surface; fat, skin and other tissues may or may not be present	0–4	slight splitting of bone parallel to fibre structure; chipping of teeth and splitting of dentine	1–5
2	flaking of outer surface usually associated with cracks; flakes long and thin with one end attached to bone; edges of cracks angular on cross-section; exfoliation begins; remnants of soft tissue may still be present	2–7	more extensive splitting but little flaking; chipping and splitting of teeth leading to loss of parts of crown	3–5+
3	bone surface rough with fibrous texture; weathering penetrates 1–1.5mm; tissue rarely present	4–15+	deep splitting and some loss of deep segments or 'flakes' between splits; extensive splitting of teeth	4–5+
4	bone surface rough and coarsely fibrous; splinters of bone loose on surface; weathering penetrates inner cavities; cracks open with splintered or rounded edges	6–15+		
5	bone very fragile and mechanically falling apart; large splinters present; cancellous bone exposed	6–15+		

The evidence of prolonged exposure of most of the skeletal material on the surface prior to burial might account for the paucity of beetle species normally associated with dried carcasses, such as the Dermestidae (Coope chapter 3). These beetles would have utilised the carcasses and departed from the scene long before the bones became incorporated in the main palaeochannel. Therefore, although the coleopteran assemblage (notably the high proportion of dung beetles) provides a clear indication of the presence of large mammals in the vicinity of the channel at the time of its infilling, it does not reveal evidence of the presence of dried carcasses. The absence of species feeding on the dried periosteum of old bones is therefore puzzling, since the degree of weathering of the bones clearly indicates that such material was available in abundance. In the case of the better-preserved bones, the selective removal of limb bones, and the covering of the carcasses by water, would likely have prevented the colonisation of the flesh by fly larvae, thereby accounting for the absence of puparia.

Signs of abrasion were noted on 44 specimens (2.15 per cent of the assemblage). Abrasion, which can be generated either by hydraulic or aeolian activity, is manifested by the rounding of normally distinct anatomical features such as ridges or muscle scars, by the wearing of broken edges, by pitting of the bone surface and occasionally by polishing of the surface. Severe abrasion can also ultimately remove the bone surface (Shipman 1981). Three broad categories of abrasion have been identified by Shipman (1977): (1) little or no abrasion – fresh, sharp edges or breaks; (2) moderate abrasion – some rounding of edges or breaks, and (3) heavy abrasion – edges obscured, breaks well rounded, surface bone possibly missing. Although the classification is coarse and the observations subjective, only three specimens within the Lynford abraded fraction were deemed to show heavy abrasion (Category 3), whereas the remainder are only moderately abraded (Category 2). With the exception of five specimens, two unstratified finds, a single find from context 20051 (unit B-i:03) – an orange gravel immediately below the main palaeochannel – a single find from an unspecified context and a single find from 20005 (unit B-ii:05) – a laminated sand deposit filling a scour feature above the main palaeochannel – all of the abraded material is from the infill of the channel itself. The number and distribution of abraded specimens are shown in Table 5.13.

Within the channel infill, ten abraded specimens come from sand and gravel contexts, where a degree of abrasion would be anticipated, but a further 29 come from the dark brown-black organic sands of contexts 20003 and 20021 (B-ii:03). The presence of abraded remains within these finer-grained contexts indicates that a small amount of material has most probably been transported into the channel by fluvial activity, although abrasion by wind cannot be ruled out. This would appear to confirm the minimal fluvial influence inferred from the orientation and body-part representation studies. Two specimens show an unusual degree of polishing. Specimen 50162 (a diaphyseal fragment of reindeer humerus) has a highly polished surface although the cause of this has not been determined. Specimen 51240, a R M1 of *M. primigenius*, also displays unusual polishing on parts of the occlusal surface and posterior lingual margin, with apparent resorption of the dentine (Figs 5.28 and 5.29). This is considered to be the natural result of the animal rubbing the tooth and the gum area, as opposed to the result of aeolian or other action (AP Currant, pers comm).

Root damage, in the form of an acid-etched tracery of fine lines on the surface of the bone, was noted on 11 specimens (0.05 per cent of the assemblage). The presence of root etching indicates that the bones were not buried immediately after death, but were exposed on a land surface long enough for the bone surface to be exploited by the root systems of local plants. This also has implications for the inferred palaeoenvironment, since it indicates the development of terrestrial vegetation in the vicinity. Of the affected material, ten specimens come from the main fill of the palaeochannel (eight from 20003 and two from 20248 [both B-ii:03]), and one was unstratified (20048). Although the presence of root damage indicates delayed burial, it does not correspond directly to the degree of weathering observed, presumably because in some cases the vegetation cover might offer protection from the elements. Of the root-damaged specimens, one specimen was classified as Condition Group 2, six as Condition Group 3, two as Condition Group 4 and two as Condition Group 5.

Fig 5.28
R M1 of Mammuthus primigenius *(51240), showing polishing along lingual margin, occlusal view (scale in mm).*

Fig 5.29
R M1 of Mammuthus primigenius *(51240), showing polishing along lingual margin, lingual view (scale in mm).*

Table 5.13 Number and distribution of abraded specimens according to context

facies	context	no. of abraded specimens
B-i:03	20051	1
B-ii:01	20254	2
B-ii:01	20369	3
B-ii:01	20384	1
B-ii:03	20003	27
B-ii:03	20021	2
B-ii:03	20022	1
B-ii:04	20132	1
B-ii:04	20247	1
B-ii:04	20367	1
B-ii:04	20374	1
B-ii:05	20005	1

Modification of the bones by carnivores, rodents and non-mammalian predators

All bones within the assemblage were scrutinised for evidence of modification by non-hominin agents, most notably carnivores, cervids, rodents, avian predators and insects. The occurrence of gnawmarks indicates not only indicates that bones have been exposed prior to burial, but can also shed light on the modifying species in terms of preferred prey or population density. Bones that have been gnawed by carnivores, in particular by the spotted hyaena, are frequent finds in Pleistocene sediments in caves, often where the animals have been denning. Carnivore gnawing is manifested by a number of features, most commonly pitting puncture marks from canines, striations of the internal and external bone surfaces, 'scalloping' of the broken edges and the cracking open of bones to extract marrow. Certain skeletal elements, for example the neural spines of vertebrae and the foot bones of non-ungulate mammals, may be preferentially destroyed (Shipman 1981), as might the epiphyseal ends of long-bones. In the most extreme cases, bone-chewing specialists such as *C. crocuta* will swallow and partially digest bones, rendering even large bones unrecognisable in a few days (Kruuk 1972).

Within the Lynford mammalian assemblage, 67 specimens (0.03 per cent of the assemblage) show evidence of carnivore modification. These remains are predominantly of *M. primigenius* (43 specimens), with smaller numbers of *R. tarandus* (eight specimens), *C. antiquitatis* (two specimens) and *E. ferus* (one specimen). The remaining 21 specimens are of undetermined taxa. Large long-bones, ribs, cranial elements and phalanges are most commonly affected. In cases where the modifying agent has been identified, the spotted hyaena appears to be the most likely culprit. This is particularly interesting, since only a single tooth fragment and a second phalanx of this species have been recovered from the site, together with two putative coprolites. A number of bones show clear puncture marks and depression fractures created by the piercing action of canine teeth, for example a second phalanx of *M. primigenius* (50733, Fig 5.30) and a second phalanx of *R. tarandus* (50212, Fig 5.31). In several cases, large limb elements of mammoths, including femora, humeri and tibiae, have had their epiphyses completely destroyed and the surviving diaphyses display characteristic scalloped edges and scratches. In others, the bones have been split longitudinally and the greasy interior cancellous bone attacked (eg 50004, a right humerus midshaft of *M. primigenius* that has deep grooves and gouges on its internal surface).

Although it cannot be ascertained what percentage of the gnawed bones came from animals killed by spotted hyaenas, scavenged from the kills of other predators or dead of natural causes, it is interesting to note that two specimens, a distal diaphyseal portion of a left humerus of *M. primigenius* (51885) and a tibia midshaft of *C. antiquitatis* (51372,

Fig 5.30
Second phalanx of Mammuthus primigenius *(50733), showing carnivore puncture mark near proximal end, lateral view (scale in mm).*

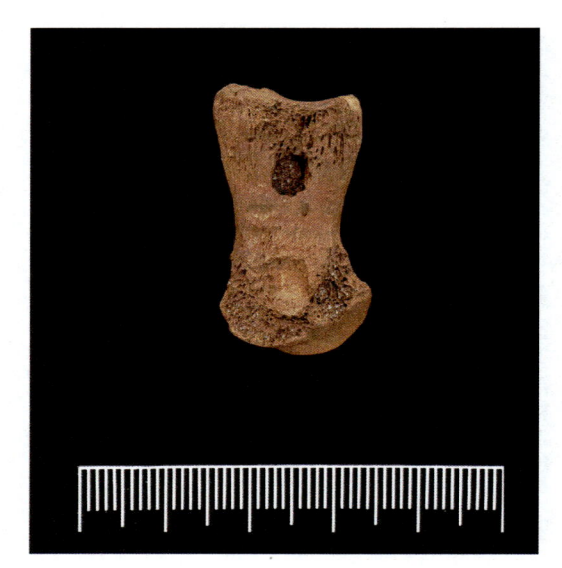

Fig 5.31
First phalanx of Rangifer tarandus *(50212), showing carnivore puncture mark near proximal end, lateral view (scale in mm).*

5 THE ARCHAEOLOGICAL ASSEMBLAGES OF ANIMALS AND LITHICS

vertebrate material from the bulk and sieved spit samples was also examined for signs of digestion, in the form of pitting or corrosion, by avian predators. Two first lower molars of *Microtus gregalis* (61096 and 63646) possess slightly rounded salient angles and are partially eroded, suggesting light digestion. Although it is sometimes possible to identify the agent of accumulation from the degree of corrosion and breakage observed (Andrews 1990), the assemblage is too small to establish this at Lynford.

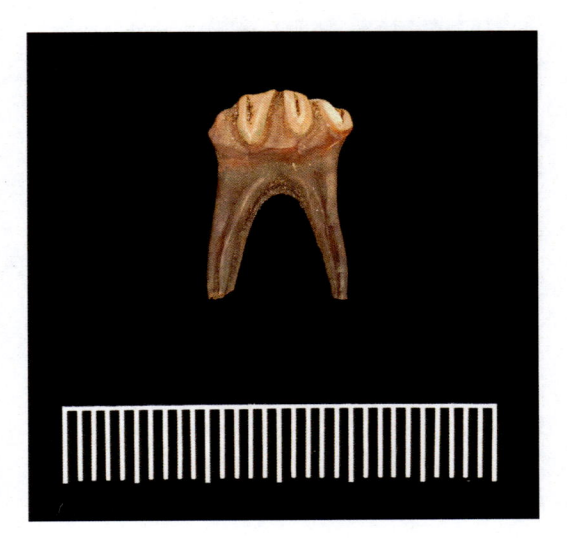

Fig 5.32 (top left)
Tibia diaphysis of juvenile Coelodonta antiquitatis *(51374), heavily gnawed by spotted hyaena, anterior view (scale in mm).*

Fig 5.32), both belong to juvenile animals that would have been more vulnerable to predation than the adults. In the latter case, both epiphyseal ends are missing, and the specimen has been reduced to little more than a ring of diaphyseal bone. Similar finds of gnawed and partially digested woolly rhinoceros material are known from the Middle Devensian cave deposits of Kent's Cavern, near Torquay, Devon. A R dp2 of *R. tarandus*, (50795, Fig 5.33) also from a juvenile animal, and a second phalanx of *C. crocuta* (spit sample 60726, *see* Fig 5.4) have been partially digested, almost certainly the result of being swallowed by a spotted hyaena. Cases of hyaenas consuming their own kind have been noted at other British Pleistocene sites, for example Tornewton Cave in Devon (Currant in Roberts 1996). Although remains of two other large carnivores – wolf and brown bear – are also present in the assemblage, neither of these species have the ability to crack open bones and to consume them in the manner of spotted hyaenas. The evidence from the gnawed fraction of the assemblage highlights the fact that these elements were not buried immediately, but remained exposed on the surface for some time, perhaps weeks or even years in the case of the most heavily-gnawed specimens.

Four specimens – two rib fragments and two indeterminate bone fragments – show evidence of gnawing by rodents, in the form of small, slanting, parallel grooves. The small

Pathologies in the Lynford mammoth assemblage

D Brothwell and D C Schreve

Very little is known of the health status of any fossil Proboscidea, and it is therefore appropriate to consider the pathologies associated with the Lynford mammoths. In the assemblage of mammoth bones, which include 108 large (> 150mm diameter) postcranial specimens, it would normally be unlikely that more than one or two instances of pathology would be present. In domestic species, there is some apparent variation in the prevalence of disease, with domestic dog (*Canis familiaris* L.) perhaps showing the most evidence of abnormality. However, in wild species there is usually a scarcity of pathology, although occasional instances have been noted, even in Pleistocene species (Brothwell 1983). Moreover, even when there is pathology, there can be problems in establishing a differential diagnosis (Brothwell 2008).

Fig 5.33
Digested R dp2 of Rangifer tarandus *(50795), lingual view (scale in mm).*

It is pertinent in a consideration of fossil elephants to establish the range and prevalence of disease in recent elephants, especially those that are likely to leave physical indications in the skeleton. Unfortunately, there are as yet few good epidemiological studies available for any of the megaherbivores, but there is a growing body of data concerning elephant health and mortality, mainly being assembled by ecologists and conservationists (Laws *et al* 1975; Eltringham 1979; Owen-Smith 1992; Sukumar 1992; Fowler and Mikota 2006). In the case of these modern populations (excluding mortality from hunting and culling), elephants seem to survive well, although in some areas and at certain times, the most common pathologies appear to be from fatal injuries caused by humans, or the result of infected wounds that finally result in death. Except in very young animals, wounds or death are unlikely to be the result of carnivore attack. However, other causes of death and sickness in elephants can leave their mark on the skeleton.

Environmental stress, in the form of inadequate nutrition, drought or heat stress, may kill or reduce the overall health of the animal, rendering the individual more susceptible to other diseases. Accidents, including falls, are uncommon, although instances of animals becoming mired and dying as a result of being unable to free themselves have been observed in straight-tusked elephant specimens from Aveley, Essex (Sutcliffe 1995) and Condover, Shropshire (Lister 2009). Other proboscidean remains, for example the frozen carcasses of woolly mammoths from the Siberian permafrost, appear to represent animals that became mired in saturated mud (Guthrie 1990). Although aggression between males is not uncommon, it rarely results in fatality. Death can occur from gastrointestinal disorders, and pulmonary and cardiovascular disease (in older animals), but it is not known whether the contagious diseases that can affect elephants today, such as anthrax, rinderpest, rabies, foot and mouth disease, tuberculosis, pneumonia, dysentery and trypanosomiasis, have a long history of association with the genera. The less destructive nematodes are probably prehistoric in their association with elephants, as indeed they are in humans and other mammals. The Lynford mammoths possibly experienced environmental stress from low winter temperatures of $-10°C$ or lower (Coope, chapter 3), which might have resulted in the death of poorly nourished individuals. However, neither nematode activity nor climatic stress is likely to result in changes to the skeleton, and if the evidence of the impact of specific diseases today can be projected into the past, they are unlikely to have caused significant mortality. Although information concerning recent elephant morbidity and mortality do not provide the precision needed for good demographic analysis, there is nevertheless a strong case that hunting and maiming (leading to infected wounds) by hominins, rather than epidemic disease, might have been one of the principal causes of death.

Of the larger bone fragments examined for pathology in the Lynford sample, 34 required detailed examination. One specimen was a distal femur of a horse (see below), two were undetermined and 31 were of mammoth. One of the undetermined specimens, a juvenile neural spine (51392, Fig 5.34) has a noticeable expansion of bone towards its base which nearly doubles the surface dimensions in that area. While the external bone surface is generally smooth, there are multiple

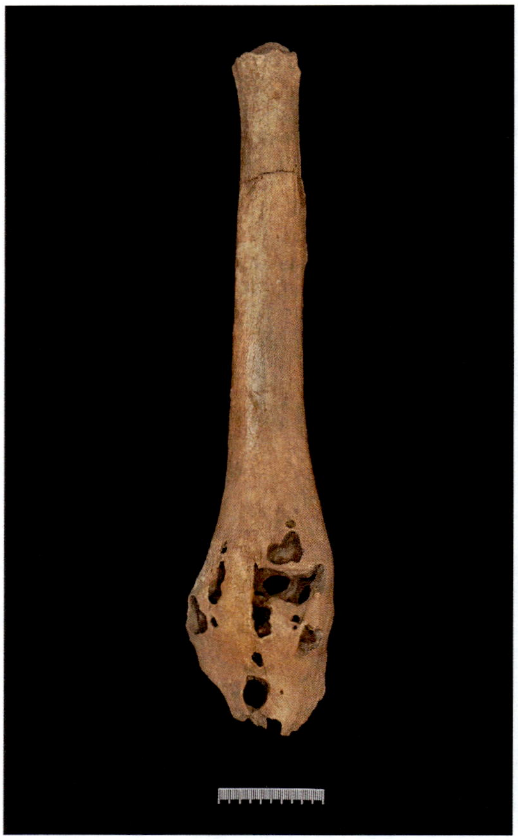

Fig 5.34
Juvenile neural spine (species undetermined, 51392), showing severe pathological deformation at its base (scale in mm).

Fig 5.35 (opposite bottom)
Rib of Mammuthus primigenius *(51179), showing healed rib fracture, lateral view (scale in mm).*

perforations extending from the interior, at least partly of ante-mortem origin. This does not suggest an osteomyelitis but in terms of a differential diagnosis, neoplasm, actinomycosis, a complex cyst or even polyostotic fibrous dysplasia must all be considered. Further studies on this and other pathology cases are planned with a view to narrowing down certain alternative diagnoses. In the mammoth sample, 34 separate items of pathology, and four cases considered to be pseudopathology were observed. Mammoth pathology has not been commonly reported in the past, with the exception of the individual from Condover (Lister 2009), and is thus deserving of detailed description and analysis.

A summary of the mammoth pathologies is given in Table 5.14 and shows that the anomalies can tentatively be placed into five categories. This classification takes into account the most obvious pathology, although in the case of infections the initial abnormality might have been trauma which was then followed by wound infection. Congenital conditions were observed in seven specimens and are all minor features, mainly concerned with asymmetry at the joint surfaces. At least one mature and one immature animal are involved. There are five possible instances of changes to ribs as the result of trauma, although the bone changes are very minor in four cases. However, there is a well-healed rib fracture (51179, Fig 5.35) and a fragment of right ulna (51976, see Fig 5.24) with a fragment of radius united with it proximally, and concomitant reaction in the ulna surface. In both of these cases, the injuries might be explained by a fall rather than hominin intervention. Eight specimens show evidence of arthropathies. In five cases, the changes to the joints are slight and could have occurred as a result of natural 'wear and tear', but in one

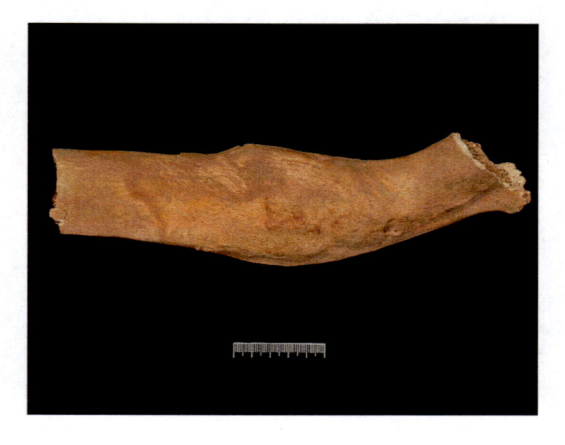

Table 5.14 Summary of the Lynford mammoth specimens showing evidence of pathology or pseudopathology, classified under major disease categories

specimen no.	diagnosis
congenital	
50075	spinous process with central defect and asymmetrical posterior facets
50853	thoracic vertebra. Spinous process facets asymmetrical
50914	thoracic vertebra. Spinous process facets asymmetrical (anterior and posterior)
51279	thoracic vertebra (immature). Spinous process facets asymmetrical (anterior and posterior)
51495	thoracic vertebra. Slight asymmetry of anterior and posterior facets at base of spinous process
51525	thoracic vertebra (immature). Spinous process facets asymmetrical
51923	thoracic vertebra. Spinous process facets asymmetrical
trauma	
50290	possible old minor rib damage
51179	well-healed rib fracture
51512	three rib fragments, each with possible evidence of old trauma
51976	right ulna with probable fused proximal fragment of radius (sequel to trauma?)
arthropathies	
50075	thoracic vertebra fragment with minor rib facet changes
50551	right ulna with spicular bone near joint; stress?
50853	base of neural spine with erosive lesion (?) near spinous process facets
51279	thoracic vertebra with left and right minor rib facet defects
51495	thoracic vertebra with left and right minor rib facet defects
51525	thoracic vertebra (immature). Rib facets grooved (but not from osteoarthritis)
51903	Proximal L radius. Probable joint stress with minor irregularity (osteochondritis)
52062	Caudal vertebra. 'Osteophyte' development, possibly associated with infection
infection	
50551	right ulna with irregular plaques of new bone (healing?)
50684	immature rib with periostitis
51448	immature rib with small plaques of new bone
51449	caudal vertebrae with at least 2 united and osteomyelitic
51512	rib with possible infection following trauma
51634	rib midshaft with possible healed bone infection
51635	rib with active infection and considerable remodeling
51955	rib with swelling and infection
51973	rib with periostitis
52007	rib with swollen and still active infection
abnormalities of as yet uncertain aetiology	
50755	expanded external cortical bone (?small ossified haematoma/healed infection-trauma)
50853	concave lesion, possibly similar to 51525, at base of spinous process
50914	Thoracic vertebra. Spinous process deviates noticeably to the left (congenital or muscle trauma?)
51451	immature rib with local irregularity (minor trauma?)
51525	immature thoracic vertebra. Deep concavity at base of spinous process, possibly associated with abnormal insertion of interspinous ligament
51944	restricted rib protuberance (?old minor trauma)

Fig 5.36 (top left)
Neural spine of Mammuthus primigenius *(50853), showing erosive lesion at base, posterior view (scale in mm).*

Fig 5.37 (middle)
Rib fragment (51973), lateral view, showing evidence of infection (scale in mm).

Fig 5.38 (bottom left)
Rib fragment (51955), lateral view, showing evidence of infection (scale in mm).

Fig 5.39 (bottom right)
Rib fragment (52007), lateral view, showing evidence of infection (scale in mm).

specimen (50853, the base of a neural spine, Fig 5.36), an erosive lesion is apparent, and in two others minor infection could be involved. Similar erosive lesions have been noted in the neural spines of an individual of *Mammuthus primigenius* from Condover, Shropshire (Lister 2009).

Evidence for inflammatory changes, indicative of infection, is especially significant, and affects ten mammoth specimens. Although taphonomic factors obscure the full extent of their potential distribution over the whole skeleton, it could be argued that the eight instances of rib infection (eg 50684, 51973, Fig 5.37; 51955 Fig 5.38 and 52007, Fig 5.39) represented in such a small sample of proboscideans strongly suggests that the wounds were inflicted by humans, although in older animals some might be the consequence of combat injuries. At least two caudal vertebrae (51449) show a massive low-grade infection (Figs 5.40 and 5.41) and an ulna displays subperiosteal new bone which appears to reflect remodelling and healing. In the six other cases, three or four anomalies might be of minor traumatic origin. The others are of less certain aetiology.

In summary, this is a surprising amount of pathology in a small sample of bones and a small assemblage of mammoths (or indeed any mammalian assemblage of this size). Congenital factors in this group, in the form of recurring joint asymmetry, might suggest possible relatedness between two or even more of the animals. The trauma observed could be natural, although there is no evidence that modern elephants are particularly accident-prone. Equally, it is not thought to be primarily a reflection of fighting between individuals, since modern-day combatants usually back off before inflicting major injury. The arthropathies have resulted from minor joint stress, but an inflammatory response could explain three cases. The evidence of bone infection at multiple sites in at least one mature and one immature animal, together with some trauma, is a plausible result of human influence. Thus, the trauma might have been caused by Neanderthals actively engaging with the animals, for example herding them into marshy areas where they could fall and injure themselves (see below), or it might relate to previous failed hunting attempts. Of the 15 instances of trauma, all but four occur in the thoracic region (ribs), and of the 14 cases of joint anomalies, all but one occur in the vertebrae. Both of these are prime target areas for hunters. It is significant to note that even today, the culling of elephants by shooting regularly leads to trauma and infection. In one African study, wounding rather than immediate death occurred in *c* 37 per cent of targeted animals, and that appears to be a minimum estimate (Laws *et al* 1975). Therefore, at least a similar, if not higher, level of hunting-related trauma might reasonably be expected in the Lynford assemblage, given the harder task of killing an elephant outright with a spear. The high proportion of pathology at the site thus offers support to the contention that the animals were being hunted, wounded and, at times, clearly surviving for variable periods after these episodes.

Modification of the mammal bones by Neanderthals and implications for subsistence strategies

The contemporary mammalian fauna would have provided the Neanderthals with a wide range of resources. Under cold climatic conditions, with limited access to carbohydrates, it is likely that the acquisition of bone marrow and fat (both subcutaneous and located around the major organs) would have been even more important than meat for Neanderthals, on account of their higher calorific content by weight. Even in modern hunter-gatherer societies living in a wide range of environments, fat and marrow are especially sought-after because most wild animals have only lean meat on their bodies (Speth 1983, 1987). As well as hides, the bones themselves might have been valuable for their grease content, both as a dietary component and as a fuel resource in an open, treeless landscape. The bones could further have provided raw material either for the construction of shelters or in the production of artefacts. Again, the paucity of wood available for making spears or other hunting weapons might have encouraged the use of alternatives such as bone to make implements, as for example the sharpened mammoth rib projectiles observed at Salzgitter-Lebenstedt in Germany (Gaudzinski 1999a). Intentionally worked elephant-bone artefacts are known from a range of Pleistocene European sites, including handaxes and other tools from Fontana Ranuccio (Segre and Ascenzi 1984), Castel di Guido (Campetti *et al* 1989),

Fig 5.40
Fused caudal vertebrae (51449) showing evidence of massive low-grade infection, dorsal view (scale in mm).

Fig 5.41
Fused caudal vertebrae (51449) showing evidence of massive low-grade infection, lateral view (scale in mm).

La Polledrara (Anzidei et al 1989) and Rebbibia Casal de Pazzi (Anzidei and Ruffo 1985) in Italy, and from Bilzingsleben in Germany (Mania 1995). Putative mammoth bone 'cores', from which thick flakes could be detached, have also been noted at Lange-Ferguson, Old Crow and other sites in the USA (Haynes 2002), although the availability of flint in the vicinity of Lynford might have precluded the need to produce such organic artefacts.

All mammalian remains from Lynford were therefore examined for cutmarks or other indications of use or modification by hominins. Cutmarks left by flint tools are characterised by sharp, parallel incisions that are V-shaped in cross-section under a high-power microscope. They are frequently clustered around the major articulations as a consequence of carcass dismemberment, but are often confused with a myriad of cuts, scratches and other marks produced by non-cultural causes. Particular attention was paid to the articular ends of the various elements, to the areas where the major muscle blocks occurred and to points of attachment for sinews or tendons. In addition, teeth, hyoid and dentary fragments were scrutinised for signs of detachment of the tongue or the fracturing of the mandible to access the marrow cavity.

Although the surfaces of many of the bones and tusk fragments from Lynford display scratches, no unequivocal cutmarks were identified on any element of any species (Schreve 2006). Fine parallel or deeply incised marks were sometimes noted, but in every case these proved to be structural, of recent or indeterminate origin, or indistinguishable from the overall 'background noise' of random marks on the specimens. It is likely that the majority of these marks are the result of trampling of the bones by large mammals near the water source. Such activities can produce scratches that closely mimic butchery marks, often appearing either as single, sharply incised scratches or as sets of marks that can be preferentially oriented. Haynes (1993) reported that at modern die-off locales in Africa, the bones of dead elephants are systematically investigated by living elephants that kick and push the bones with their feet, resulting in the creation of localised trample marks. Under a scanning electron microscope, the marks possess parallel longitudinal striations within the single marks, and a notably raised edge on one side of each mark (Haynes 1993). At Lynford, the presence of bones of dead mammoths might have proved an equal curiosity to the living animals, thus creating the patterns of breakage and occasional parallel incisions seen in the material.

The absence of cutmarks is not, however, unexpected, given the variable weathering on some of the bones, which possibly obscured significant features. In addition, in the case of mammoths, the hide and flesh is so thick that accidental contact made with the surface of the bone by a flint tool would rarely have been made. Even in modern butchery experiments, the presence of cutmarks and chopping damage is highly variable, depending on the haste of the butchering process, the types of tools used in the butchering and the skill of the butchers themselves. Haynes, who has made a comprehensive study of contemporary and past elephant butchery, concluded that in modern experiments '...*the expert butchers never left a mark on post-cranial bones that they completely stripped of meat or disarticulated*' (Haynes 2002, 151). Haynes acknowledged that while inexpert butchers, who are unaccustomed to processing large carcasses or have no knowledge of anatomy, might misjudge where to cut and thus make contact with the bone surface, an experienced butcher will know precisely the right moves to make in order to process the carcass as efficiently as possible and minimise damage to the edges of his tools. Haynes observed that modern elephant femora from carcasses that had been comprehensively filleted and disarticulated showed no evidence of cutmarks on the bone surface at all (Haynes 2002, figs 3.24 and 3.25). In addition, aspects of elephant anatomy are considered by Hannus (1990) to further inhibit the degree of direct contact between bone and artefact during butchery. For example, the particular structure of the joint capsules in the limb bones allows them to be disarticulated without damaging the epiphyses. It is not possible to know precisely the butchering accomplishments of the group of Neanderthals at Lynford, but the apparent position of Neanderthals as top carnivores (Bocherens et al 1999), and the balance of evidence from numerous sites across Europe, points to the fact that they were skilled hunters with detailed knowledge of animal anatomy and behaviour. It thus seems entirely feasible that they were experienced in the butchery of a wide range of species, both large and small. The fact that we do not see evidence of cutmarks on the mammoth bones might be testament to their proficiency in dismembering these carcasses. The butchery of even a single mammoth would have required a reasonable degree of skill, co-operation and time, most likely involving repeated re-sharpening of tools, and possibly the production of new implements to replace terminally blunted or broken ones. Although some of the damage observed on the handaxe tips could be from use (White, this chapter) – perhaps in prising apart joints – use-wear analyses (Donahue, this chapter) and the high incidence of recycling of the lithic material support the notion that tools were being resharpened on site after having been used for butchery (White, this chapter).

In common with other wild animals, elephants have relatively little body fat, and their limb bones might therefore have been rich sources of necessary nutrients (Haynes 1993). Although carnivore damage is apparent on the longitudinally broken shafts of some of the mammoth long-bones, Klein (1975) maintained that hominins are more likely than carnivores to have broken into large bones to extract marrow. Nevertheless, in the case of such large material, this task would have required a substantial application of force and skill. Replication butchery experiments by Stanford *et al* (1981) suggested that a hard impactor, such as a boulder weighing at least 9–10kg, would have been necessary in order to break the bones apart, and also that the force of the impact should be concentrated in a small but optimal area of the bone to propagate the fracture. However, most elephant limb bones do not possess a large medullary cavity full of marrow, but instead have the marrow contained within the hollows of the trabecular bone. Accessing this valuable resource might therefore have resulted in a greater degree of fragmentation than observed in the bones of other species at Lynford, and this might account for some of the 'shards' of long-bone present in the assemblage. Unfortunately, given the overall high degree of breakage at the site, extraction of marrow extraction from elephant bones cannot be firmly established.

The subject of elephant exploitation during the Middle and Late Pleistocene of Europe has received a substantial amount of attention from past researchers, but the precise nature of potential interactions remains shrouded in controversy (Gaudzinski 1999a). Most recently, Bocherens *et al* (2005) have suggested that an under-representation of mammoth bones in Middle Palaeolithic sites might mask the true importance of these animals in the Neanderthal diet. They suggested that the substantially higher proportion of ^{15}N observed in Neanderthal bones from Saint-Césaire (France), when compared to those of spotted hyaena from the same site, is a reflection of different hunting strategies and the consumption of prey with different ^{15}N enrichment. In the case of the hyaenas, the dominant prey appears to be large and medium-sized ungulates, particularly horses, large bovids and deer, with only low proportions of woolly rhinoceros and woolly mammoths in their diet. In contrast, the Saint-Césaire Neanderthals appear to have consumed substantially more rhinoceros and mammoth. Since hyaenas would undoubtedly have taken advantage of any large herbivore carcasses available, Bocherens *et al* (2005) conclude that rhinoceros and mammoth were relatively rare in the landscape at that time and were therefore obtained by Neanderthals through active hunting. The authors acknowledge that at most Neanderthal sites, mammoths and rhinoceros are under-represented within the bone assemblages (clearly not the case at Lynford) and attribute this to difficulties transporting carcass parts from the exploitation area to the occupation site.

The juxtaposition of artefacts and elephant bone led to claims of hunting at sites such as Torralba and Ambrona in Spain, yet reassessment of the evidence in the light of modern taphonomic analyses has proved inconclusive (Santonja and Villa 1990; Villa 1990). Only at a few select sites, such as Lehringen (Adam 1951) and Neumark-Gröbern (Mania *et al* 1990) in Germany, La Cotte de St Brelade on Jersey (Scott 1980) and Aridos in Spain (Villa 1990), can the relationship between the hominins and the elephants be explored with greater certainty. Critically, at all four sites, the hominins appear to have had early access to elephant carcasses. However, even in cases where there is evidence of such interaction, it cannot be unequivocally established whether the Neanderthals were actually hunting these animals, scavenging the kills of other carnivores or had simply chanced upon animals dead of natural causes. There is not a single site where a 'smoking gun', such as a projectile point in a vital area, points to unambiguous hunting, although the presence at Lehringen of a wooden spear implies that the

Fig 5.42
Long-bone fragments of Rangifer tarandus *with green bone fractures, external lateral view (scale in mm).*

Neanderthals might have played a role in the animal's demise there. There is no denying that a healthy adult mammoth would have been difficult prey to tackle, but a range of procurement behaviours is plausible, from driving them into a mire to finish them off, to herding them over cliffs or bluffs, as appears to be the case at La Cotte (Scott 1980). The precise nature of the encounter would therefore have been dependent on the features of the local landscape. If, as seems likely, Neanderthals had intimate knowledge of their environment, they would have been well acquainted with places in which to ambush prey or to find mired animals.

Fig 5.43
Long-bone fragments of Rangifer tarandus *with green bone fractures, internal lateral view (scale in mm).*

Given the high frequency of pathological mammoth specimens at Lynford, it is tempting to speculate that the Neanderthals might have been selectively targeting these more vulnerable individuals. Almost all of the pathologies observed cluster in key vital areas of the body, particularly around the ribs and the vertebrae, and it is hoped that further analysis will determine whether some of them result from previous (failed) hunting attempts. Hannus (1990) has noted that wounded elephants frequently seek out water to soothe their injuries, and the cut-off meander at Lynford might have served as a location where weakened individuals could then be despatched. The marshy edges of the shallow channel might also have acted as a natural trap in which animals could become mired after coming to drink. For this reason, Neanderthals might have actively 'shepherded' animals towards it (see White, this chapter), in the hope of killing them at close quarters once the animals became exhausted. The channel would thus have acted as a focal point for predators and prey alike, offering Neanderthals the possibility of actively hunting animals that came down to the water or became mired, or the chance to scavenge from the kills of other carnivores.

The most convincing *direct* evidence for hominin interaction occurs on the bones of species other than mammoth, most notably reindeer and horse. Fourteen reindeer bones and three postcranial bones of undetermined species show spiral fractures created when the bone was still fresh or green (Figs 5.42 and 5.43). One specimen (51786), a midshaft fragment of a left humerus of *R. tarandus*, also bears a possible impact mark (Fig 5.44) with evidence of chipping and flaking of the surrounding bone. These are interpreted as evidence of bones being deliberately split open for the purposes of marrow extraction. Where the skeletal element has been identified, it is most frequently of an element that has high marrow 'utility' (after Binford 1981). A simplified marrow index has been established by Morrison (1997) by measuring the marrow cavity volume in millilitres, assigning a value of 1 to elements without a marrow cavity, and collapsing proximal and distal values for long-bones, previously considered separately by Binford (1978). Thus, in reindeer, elements such as the skull and vertebrae will have a value of 1, whereas the tibia has the highest marrow utility, with a value of 64 (Morrison 1997).

Fig 5.44
Fragment of L humerus diaphysis of Rangifer tarandus *bearing signs of impact fracture to right hand side, external lateral view (scale in mm).*

Without exception, the 13 spirally-fractured specimens of *R. tarandus* and cf *R. tarandus* that could be identified to body part were elements identified as having the highest marrow indices (Table 5.15). Thus, although the data set is admittedly small, there does appear to be a positive correlation between the evidence of breakage on these bones and their marrow

Table 5.15 Spirally fractured limb bones of reindeer from Lynford compared with Morrison's marrow utility index

element	marrow index (after Morrison 1997)	no. of reindeer bones with spiral fractures
skull	1	–
mandible	11	1
atlas vertebra	1	–
axis vertebra	1	–
cervical vertebra	1	–
thoracic vertebra	1	–
lumbar vertebra	1	–
pelvis	6	–
rib	1	–
sternum	1	–
scapula	5	–
humerus	38	3
radio-ulna	36	1
metacarpal	21	–
femur	52	4
tibia	64	3
calcaneum	3	–
metatarsal	51	1
1st phalanges	4	–
2nd phalanges	2	–

utility. The actions of carnivores, trampling by large herbivores, and even modern pressure from quarry machinery can create spiral fractures, but the fact that the breakage occurs in only two taxa, both of which are known food resources for Middle Palaeolithic hominins (see for example Gaudzinski and Roebroeks 1999; Conard and Prindiville 2000), is considered to be significant. It is possible that some of the breakage noted in the mammoth crania could have resulted from the extraction of brain for consumption, but this cannot be verified.

Two other species show evidence of possible Neanderthal interaction. Specimens 50599 (L p3) and 50522 (R m2) of *C. antiquitatis*, have been fractured lengthways in such a way as to expose the pulp cavity. It is difficult to envisage how such an unusual breakage might occur naturally and it is therefore suggested that the teeth were damaged when the mandibular cavity was split open for marrow extraction. Similar patterns of breakage can be seen in two teeth of *E. ferus*, possibly from the same individual: 51612 (R lower cheek tooth) and 51631 (R m3) (Fig 5.45). In the case of the R m3, the roots and basal part of the molar have been snapped off (an unusual breakage in such a robust element) and this is likewise attributed to the extraction of marrow from the lower jaw. Comparable broken horse teeth have been noted in the late Middle Pleistocene interglacial assemblage at Grays in Essex (Schreve pers ob) and at the Late Glacial Interstadial site of Gough's Cave in Somerset (Parkin *et al* 1986). A distal femur of an adult horse (51360, *see* Fig 5.10) also bears a sharp, green bone spiral fracture to the diaphysis, suggestive of marrow extraction, together with an enigmatic puncture mark in the upper part of the medial condyle. Although carnivore gnawing is also apparent on the lateral condyle of the same specimen, and there is some recent damage around the margin of the hole, the interior of the puncture mark is entirely smooth, suggesting that the bone had healed while the animal was still alive. It is equally clear that the hole cannot have been caused during the excavation process, for example by the point of a grid square nail, since site archive photographs demonstrate that the condyles were buried downwards in the sediment and were the last part of the bone to be uncovered. A latex mould of the interior of the hole revealed a tapering bevelled tip, approximately 10mm in length, 6mm wide at the top and 7.86mm wide at the base. The origin of the puncture mark remains unclear, but it is possible that it was created deliberately by the impact from a projectile point. In this respect, in a predominantly treeless landscape, the sharpened mammoth bone projectiles from mid Last Cold Stage sites in Germany (Gaudzinski 1999a) offer a possible parallel.

As explained above, evidence of elephant exploitation has been notoriously difficult to establish at any Pleistocene site, and in this respect, Lynford is no different. There are apparently no cutmarks on any of the elephant bones, although this is to be expected, and the degree of fragmentation in the assemblage makes it difficult to separate out possible evidence of elephant marrow extraction. Only a single thoracic vertebra of a mammoth (50075), with a fragment of the central epiphysis of the preceding vertebra still attached, might provide an indication of forcible disarticulation (Fig 5.46). However, the absence from the site of almost all major meat-bearing limb bones hints at the possibility that there has been selective removal of these elements. The presence of all three Voorhies Groups of bones at the site, and the lack of evidence for fluvial transportation, indicate that hydraulic activity is not responsible for the absence of these elements. Although carnivore activity is a possible explanation for the destruction or removal of some of the

Fig 5.45
R m3 and R lower cheek tooth of Equus ferus *(51631 and 51612) showing evidence of breakage (scale in mm).*

mammoth bones, it seems unlikely that the Lynford Neanderthals would have shunned a readily available resource, particularly when they clearly possessed the capabilities and the technology to deal with it.

What is clear is that Lynford does not represent a single major hunting and/or exploitation event. Even taking into consideration the problems associated with time-averaging, the vertebrate assemblage does not reflect the totality of the contemporary biocoenose. If one takes the mammoth remains as an example, it is clear from the ages of the individuals present (Lister, this chapter) that they do not reflect the natural range of ages found in a matriarchal elephant herd at the present day, where adult females and juveniles predominate. The age structure of the mammoth dental and postcranial sample from Lynford shows a very marked predominance (nearly 90 per cent) of young to middle-aged prime adults (approximately 18 to 45 years). Although the presence of female animals cannot be ruled out, where sex has been established, the individuals are all male. A comparison of the Lynford age-range data with other elephant assemblages is provided by Lister elsewhere in this chapter, but in summary, the age profile at Lynford differs substantially that observed at sites where there is evidence of non-selective or catastrophic mortality, as evidenced by a full age range of animals. It also differs from sites where there is highly selective mortality, as highlighted, for example, by abundant juveniles. The closest comparison is with sites where a predominance of middle age classes and a paucity of juvenile and old animals appear to indicate selective mortality over an extended period. The taking of prime animals has been repeatedly interpreted as a feature of human hunting in a range of medium to large animals (for example, Stiner 1994; Steele 2003) and is extrapolated here to include the very largest mammals. Given the intensive excavation and sampling methods in operation at the site, it seems unlikely that there has been a collecting bias against the remains of young and old individuals, although taphonomic processes might have played a part in influencing their preservation. Thus, the age profile in the Lynford mammoths can be taken to be a reasonably accurate reflection of the pattern of mortality at the site.

If Neanderthals were involved in any way with the deaths of the animals or the exploitation of their carcasses, this could quite plausibly have occurred over a number of years, with elephants encountered alive or dead, either deliberately or opportunistically. The age profile of the mammoths is consistent with a picture of young and adult animals, particularly males who would be alone or in small groups, entering the catchment of the site. Young males are more prone to get into difficulties, as they are innately curious, but lack the experience of older animals and the 'safety net' of the better-defended matriarchal herd to guide them. At the site of Hot Springs (USA), the mammoth assemblage is dominated by male animals that had become trapped around the former lake margin (Lister and Agenbroad 1994). Evidence from other European sites, such as Salzgitter-Lebenstedt and Taubach in Germany (Bratlund 1999a), and Mauran (Farizy *et al* 1994) and La Borde (Jaubert *et al* 1990) in France, indicates planned behaviour by Neanderthals in the form of selective monospecific hunting (of reindeer, Merck's rhinoceros, bison and aurochs) often involving particular age classes (for example, adult reindeer at Salzgitter-Lebenstedt, female and young bison at Mauran) at predicted points in the year, and especially during seasonal migrations. However, encounters with mammoths are more likely to have occurred on an *ad hoc* basis, necessitating a flexible approach to provisioning and associated tool manufacture and use (White, this chapter).

Fig 5.46
Partial thoracic vertebra of Mammuthus primigenius *(50075) with fragment of central epiphysis of preceding vertebra attached, anterior view (scale in mm).*

This does not, however, mean that there was no element of foresight in Neanderthal interactions with proboscideans (since focal points in the landscape for ambushing animals or finding carcasses would undoubtedly have been favoured places to visit), but rather that Neanderthals could not predict exactly when such encounters might occur and what form they might take (Schreve 2006). This conforms to the widespread observation that Neanderthals were able to modify their provisioning strategies at will, by hunting either opportunistically or selectively, or by a combination of the two (Burke 2000).

Summary

Due to the presence at the site of so many handaxes in fresh condition and showing evidence of use and resharpening, it seems reasonable to posit some form of interaction between the Neanderthals and the mammal fauna. This is readily identified in reindeer, horse and woolly rhinoceros, but is harder to pinpoint in the case of the mammoths. However, although *direct* evidence of exploitation cannot be unequivocally identified in the mammoth assemblage, perhaps unsurprisingly, given the unlikelihood of cutmarks being present on the bones, the *indirect* evidence for hunting is more persuasive. In particular, the combination of (1) a mortality profile that does not indicate a natural or carnivore accumulation, (2) pathologies in key vital areas of the body and (3) the clear paucity of major meat-bearing long-bones, which hints at selective removal, is considered convincing (Schreve 2006). Neanderthals might furthermore have made use of the landscape itself in order to shepherd animals towards, or ambush them at, the meander cut-off and might have targeted either individual young males that lacked the guidance of the matriarchal herd, or more vulnerable wounded animals. The Lynford site might record several such episodes occurring over a number of years. These encounters were possibly on an *ad hoc* basis, but it is clear from the planned behaviour evident in the lithic assemblage that the Neanderthals were prepared for the task in hand. In the face of the harsh climatic conditions and environmental challenges of the Middle Devensian in Britain, such flexibility in terms of resource acquisition and subsistence strategies was an absolute necessity.

Seasonality

Because of the time-averaged nature of the mammal assemblage, it is not possible to give any indication of the season of deposition of the channel sediments. However, the occurrence of both shed and unshed antlers of *R. tarandus* indicates that these animals were present in the vicinity of the river at more than one season. Unusually among the Cervidae, both male and female reindeer have antlers, and there is little difference between the sexes, apart from a 'shovel' that acts as an eye guard in the male, although even some females have these. In the adult male, the antlers grow in March and April. The velvet is shed between August and September and the antlers are shed after the rut, in late October to November, although young males can carry their antlers until February or March. Females shed their antlers about one week after calving in spring.

On the basis of their large size, two antlers were attributed to male animals. Of these, one (51437) was shed naturally, indicating that the animal was present at Lynford in the late autumn or early winter, and the other (50376) is unshed, indicating that the animal died at the site in a different season. A further four antler bases that could not be confidently sexed are shed, indicating the presence of animals between late autumn and spring, and two are unshed, indicating the presence of animals at other times of year. Thus, the evidence from the antlers indicates that reindeer were present at the site in more than one season, and either shed their antlers naturally or died at other times of year.

The dating of the Lynford mammalian assemblage

D C Schreve and A J Stuart

The biostratigraphical ranges of mammal taxa

The First and Last Appearance Datum (FAD, LAD) for each taxon present at Lynford can only give a broad guide to the age range of the site, although species composition (see below) gives a much clearer indication. *M. primigenius* was present in central and western Europe from around 200ka to approximately 13.6 Cal ka (12 14C ka), although it survived into the Holocene in northern Siberia (Stuart *et al* 2002, Stuart 2004). *Coelodonta* first appeared in Britain in the late Middle Pleistocene and disappeared from there *c* 41 Cal ka (35 14C ka) (Stuart and Lister 2007), although it persisted in western Europe until *c* 13.6 Cal ka (c 12 14C ka). *Crocuta crocuta* probably abandoned Europe *c* 30 Cal ka (c 26 14C ka) (Stuart and Lister 2007). Thus, on this basis, it can be stated that the Lynford assemblage is almost certainly older than 30 Cal ka, and very probably older than *c* 41 Cal ka.

Direct ages in the form of AMS 14C dates have been obtained on two samples of woolly mammoth (one mandibular fragment and one molar tooth fragment) from the main channel deposits in an attempt to refine the dating of the assemblage. The samples were submitted to the Oxford Radiocarbon Accelerator Unit as part of a programme of 14C dating of extinct megafauna in Europe and Northern Asia by A J Stuart and A M Lister, funded by the Natural Environment Research Council (NERC). The two samples yielded age estimates of 53,700 ± 3,100 (δ 13C = –21.2) (OxA-11571) and > 49,700 (δ 13C = –21.1) (OxA-11572). These are consistent with other lines of dating evidence from the site (see below, also Schwenninger, chapter 2), suggesting that the true age of the site is likely to be in excess of 50,000 years.

Comparison with British sites

In terms of its species composition, the Lynford assemblage compares closely with the Pin Hole Mammal Assemblage-Zone (MAZ) of Currant and Jacobi (2001), which these authors correlate with the Middle Devensian (MIS 3 of the marine oxygen isotope record) on the basis of radiocarbon dating of key faunal elements.

At the onset of the Early Devensian, there was an apparent reduction in the diversity of thermophilous mammals in Britain during MIS 5c, although the overall aspect of the fauna remains clearly temperate (Currant and Jacobi 2001). In contrast, mammalian assemblages attributed to the final temperate substage of MIS 5 (5a) are noticeably of cold-climate affinity. These assemblages, assigned to the Banwell Bone Cave MAZ of Currant and Jacobi (2001), were initially placed within MIS 4 by those authors but have since been pushed back into MIS 5a on the basis of new TIMS Uranium-series age-estimates (Gilmour *et al* 2007). To date, no assemblages can be confidently attributed to MIS 4 in Britain – a period of extremely cold conditions. The composition of the early Devensian Banwell Bone Cave MAZ differs considerably from that seen at Lynford. The early Devensian assemblages are uniformly of low species diversity and consistent composition, being dominated by exceptional numbers of reindeer and bison, with wolf, wolverine (*Gulo gulo* [L.]), mountain hare (*Lepus timidus* L.) and an extremely large-bodied brown bear also regularly represented. The small mammal assemblages from the Banwell Bone Cave MAZ are also of low species diversity and are composed entirely of remains of northern vole (*Microtus oeconomus* [Pallas]). These species are tolerant of cold maritime conditions with high snow cover, and appear to reflect a biozone of relative stability and longevity, albeit one punctuated by several interstadials (Currant and Jacobi 2001). At this time, open tundra or cold steppe had replaced most or all of the boreal woodland and taiga in NW Europe (van Andel and Tzedakis, 1996).

The Middle Devensian marks a significant period of faunal change within the last cold stage in Britain. In contrast to the assemblages of the Early Devensian, the Middle Devensian mammalian faunas bear more resemblance to interglacial assemblages in terms of their relative high species diversity. Important characteristics of this period include the return to Britain after a protracted absence (more than 100ka) of Neanderthals, together with horses, woolly mammoths, woolly rhinoceros and spotted hyaenas. These assemblages are correlated by Currant and Jacobi (2001) with MIS 3, and have been assigned to the Pin Hole MAZ, after the cave site of Pin Hole at Creswell Crags, Derbyshire. These authors consider the Pin Hole-type faunas to represent a western extension of central Asian faunas, indicating the spread of extreme continental conditions and the open environments that characterise the 'mammoth steppe' of Guthrie (1982) as far as the Atlantic seaboard. The age of the mammal fauna is well constrained by a combination of Uranium-series, Electron Spin Resonance and radiocarbon dates, indicating deposition during the interval 50–38ka (Hedges *et al* 1988, 1989, 1996, 1998; Jacobi *et al* 1998, 2006). In terms of species composition, the Lynford mammalian assemblage almost exactly mirrors that from the Lower Cave Earth at Pin Hole. The latter assemblage is marginally more diverse in terms of its carnivore component, as one might expect for a cave site, containing two extra mustelid species, stoat (*Mustela erminea* L. 1758) and polecat (*M. putorius* L.), as well as lion (*Panthera leo* [L.]). Mountain hare (*Lepus timidus* L.) and giant deer (*Megaloceros giganteus* [Blumenbach]) are also present (Currant and Jacobi 2001). Although red deer (*Cervus elaphus* L.) has not been recorded from Pin Hole, this species is a consistent component of Middle Devensian faunas in southern Britain, where it occurs as an exceptionally large 'strongylocerine' form. Aside from Pin Hole itself, significant MIS 3 assemblages have also been recorded in Britain from Ash Tree Cave (Derbyshire), Brean Down, Limekiln Hill Quarry, Picken's Hole and the Hyaena Den at Wookey Hole (Somerset) and Cassington (Oxfordshire), where they occur in clear stratigraphic superposition above faunas of the Banwell Bone Cave MAZ (Currant and Jacobi 2001). Other Middle Devensian assemblages are known from Robin Hood Cave and Church Hole, also in Creswell Crags, Kent's Cavern (Devon), Coygan Cave (Carmarthenshire) and Paviland (Gower).

The duration of MIS 3 was approximately 30ka, encompassing multiple periods of climatic instability, as demonstrated by the Greenland ice-core data (Bond *et al* 1993; Grootes *et al* 1993). Towards the end of MIS, the D/O oscillations became progressively less frequent as the Fennoscandian ice sheet grew and the glacial maximum approached. Understanding how the mammalian faunas, including hominins, responded to these millennial scale climatic oscillations still presents a great challenge to vertebrate palaeontologists. One might expect to see changes in the climate equally reflected in the mammals, with periods of cold represented by the bison-reindeer faunas typical of MIS 5a, interspersed with more temperate continental episodes characterised by the mammoth-woolly rhinoceros fauna seen at Lynford. However, the resolution in the terrestrial record has thus far been too poor to enable detection of any biostratigraphical patterning within this complex stage, added to which are the problems associated with the limits of radiocarbon dating. Nevertheless, the fact that the bison remains from Lynford are low in number and uniformly of very weathered and/or rolled aspect indicates that they can reasonably be considered as separate from the main assemblage. The problems of time-averaging notwithstanding, Lynford thus offers an opportunity to characterise in detail the mammalian fauna of a reasonably discrete time period within this stage, bounded by a multiproxy chronological framework.

Comparison with continental sites

The considerable problems of dating for the relevant time range, misidentifications of vertebrate material, and past poor standards of excavation and recording at many sites, mean that there are rather few assemblages from Continental Europe that can be used to reconstruct the history of the vertebrate fauna during MIS 4, and during MIS 3 beyond the range of 14C dating, or that can be meaningfully compared with Lynford. Interestingly in the Last Cold Stage Continental assemblages, there is no discernable pattern of earlier assemblages with bison and reindeer, and later assemblages with mammoths and woolly rhinoceros as described for southern Britain (Currant and Jacobi 2001).

Tönchesberg in the German Rhineland, excavated to modern standards, is a volcanic crater-fill that preserves a series of Palaeolithic archaeological horizons with mammalian faunal assemblages (Conard 1992; Conard and Prindiville 2000). Horizon 2B, thought to date from an early Weichselian post-Eemian warm phase, yielded a fauna with temperate woodland elements such as *Dama dama* (L.) fallow deer, red deer *Cervus elaphus* and the interglacial rhinoceros *Stephanorhinus hemitoechus* (Falconer), but lacking cold steppe-tundra elements such as mammoth, woolly rhinoceros and reindeer. In contrast the overlying Layer 1B, has a cold fauna and a TL date of 65 kyr that invite comparison with Lynford (Frechen 1991, 1994). The Tönchesberg 1B assemblage includes woolly rhinoceros, reindeer and horses as at Lynford, but also includes the extinct ass *Equus hydruntinus* Regalia, not recorded anywhere from Britain at this time. Surprisingly, mammoth is not noted, although it seems very probable that it occurred in the region at this time. The record of abundant red deer, also unknown from Lynford, suggests the presence of shrubs and even some trees, perhaps indicating that Tönchesberg represents a warmer phase than Lynford and thus implying an age difference. Alternatively, it might reflect the more southerly location of the German site.

Several cave sites of broadly similar age from southern Germany have comparable faunas. Hohlenstein Stadel in the Lonetal Valley, Baden-Württemberg, has yielded an assemblage attributed to MIS 4 and again comparable with Lynford, including wolf

(*Canis lupus*), fox (*Vulpes*) or (*Alopex*), lion (*Panthera leo*), spotted hyaena (*Crocuta crocuta*), woolly mammoth, woolly rhinoceros and horse (Gamble 1979; Hahn *et al* 1985; Niven 2006). The presence of red deer, giant deer (*Megaloceros giganteus*) and cave bear (*Ursus spelaeus*), again suggests a milder climate than at Lynford. The extinct cave bear, so abundant at many sites in Continental Europe, is absent from most or all Last Cold Stage faunas in Britain. Its dentition indicates that it was more herbivorous than the brown bear, and that it was entirely unsuited to the steppe-tundra (Kahlke 1999). The Mousterian levels (probably pre 40ka) of Vogelherd Cave, also in the Lonetal, have yielded a very similar fauna, with the important addition of reindeer (Hahn *et al* 1985; Niven 2006).

There are several cave sites in Belgium with Mousterian artefacts, but stratigraphic interpretation is difficult and the provenance of many faunal remains is uncertain. Layer 1A of Scladina Cave, Sclayn, near Namur, is attributed to an interstadial ca 40ka and has yielded a fauna including brown bear, cave bear, spotted hyaena, woolly mammoth, woolly rhinoceros, horse, giant deer and large bovid (Simonet 1992). The Scladina fauna is likely to be composite, probably covering several climatic phases, and given the geographical proximity to southern Britain, the cave bear and giant deer remains are likely to record a warmer episode or episodes than at Lynford.

It is therefore clear that the Lynford vertebrate assemblage, with its secure stratigraphical context, dated by OSL and with a wealth of associated palaeontological data, is of exceptional importance for reconstructing the faunal history of the Last Cold Stage beyond the range of radiocarbon dating.

5.2 Quantitative analysis of mammoth remains from Lynford, Norfolk, England

A M Lister

In this contribution the Lynford mammoths are examined in terms of their morphology, taxonomy, body size, number of individuals represented, age structure and gender. The Lynford sample, and especially molariform teeth, provides an opportunity to study the morphology and taxonomy of mammoths from the early part of the last glaciation in north-west Europe, and highly relevant to the reconstruction of mammoth evolution. The age and sex structure of the sample are also of significance for interpreting the taphonomy and likely human involvement in the Lynford assemblage.

Materials and methods

Specimen selection and identification

This study encompasses all mammoth remains yielding information pertinent to the aims discussed above. It does not, therefore, represent an exhaustive description of all mammoth fossils from the site. Specifically, the study focuses on all molariform teeth, skull fragments and postcranial bone elements for which meaningful measurements could be taken and for which comparison with other samples is possible. Thus, the numerous small fragments of bone or tooth, and most vertebrae and ribs, are not discussed here. The latter, although well-preserved in several instances, cannot with certainty be allocated to their precise position in their respective series, and comparative data on accurately-positioned mammoth vertebrae and ribs are scarce, although it is likely that further progress will be made in this area in the future. Schreve (this chapter) provides images of many of the specimens, and discusses the mammoth assemblage as a whole.

Post-cranial measurements are based on Melentis (1963) and Roth (1982), and will be described individually. Identification of postcranial elements was based on comparative material and illustrations in Olsen (1972).

The six sets of molariform teeth are numbered dP2–4 and M1–3. The teeth were identified to position based on size and plate number (Maglio 1973; Roth 1982); in only one or two cases was there any uncertainty between two adjacent possibilities. It was also evident that in a number of cases, left-right matching pairs from the same individual were present in the collection. These were all easily recognisable on the basis of size, shape, degree of wear and morphological idiosyncrasies, and there were no uncertain or ambiguous cases. All the studied molariform teeth are listed in Table 5.16, with matching left-right pairs indicated.

Table 5.16 Identification, measurements and ageing of molariform teeth from Lynford: symbols explained in text

no.	label	tooth	L	W	H	e	PF	PF est	LF	worn	Laws'	AEY
50273	1L	**LM³**	(246) **250**	**95 (5)**	**161 (14)**	1.7-2.1-2.2	−22p	x22p	8.53	−13	**XXII+**	41
50069	1R											
51965	2L	**LM³**	(156)	**90 (7)**	**187 (4–6)**	−	x12−	x12−	10.52	none	**XVIII**	30
52063	2R											
50001	3	**LM³**	272	**105 (4)**	**203 (13)**	1.9-2.2-2.7	x22p	x22p	8.33	x12	**XXII**	39
51887	4	**RM³ (M²)**	−	**100 (4)**	≥167 (2)	−	x6−	x6−	−	none	**XVI+**	25
50656	5L	**LM₃**	(282) **285**	**81 (8)**	**116 (16)**	2.0-2.1-2.2	−22p	x22p	7.69b	−15	**XXIII**	43
51953+51648+51154	5R											
50000	6	**LM₃**	(285) **290**	**84 (7)**	**126 (16)**	2.4-2.7-3.4	−20 (−19p)	x20 (x19p)	5.57b	−15	**XXIII**	43
51047	7R	**RM₃**	(300) **310**	**97 (9)**		1.7-2.1-2.2	∞21p	x21p	6.99b	∞18	**XXIV**	45
51046	7L											
51820	8R	**RM₃ (M₂)**	(67)	(≥85) (3)	≥134 (3)	−	x3−	x3−	6.82b	none	**XVIII**	30
51997	8L											
51966	9	**LM²**	(159) **162**	**80 (5)**	≥105(14)	1.6-1.6-1.6	−14x	x14x	9.14	−14x	**XVIII**	30
51619+51038	10	**RM² (M¹)**	(~160)	**74 (III)**	>116 (II)	1.5-1.9-2.1	−12x	−12x	−	−12x	**XVIII**	30
50002	11L	**LM²**	(168) **170**	**84 (7)**	>125(14)	1.3-1.4-1.6	x13x	x13x	9.43	x13x	**XVI**	24
50003	11R											
52038	12	**RM₂ (M²)**	(73)	(≥78)(II)	−	~2.1-2.3-2.5	−4xˣ	−4xˣ	8.57b	−4xˣ	**XXII**	39
51730	13L	**LM₂**	(203) **205**	**82 (11)**	>102(15)	1.6-1.7-1.9	−15x	x15x	6.91b	x15	**XVII**	26
50358	13R											
51710	14	**RM₂**	(193) **195**	**85 (II)**	**125 (13)**	1.4-1.8-2.2	x15x (ˣx14x)	x15x (ˣx14x)	7.67b	x12	**XV**	22
51252	15	**LM₂/₃**	(73)	**82 (5)**	>74 (5)	1.5-1.7-2.0	−5−	x5−	8.23b	−5	−	−
51171	16L	**LM¹**	(170) **172**	**68 (9)**	**135 (9)**	1.2-1.3-1.4	x14x (x13xˣ)	x14x (x13xˣ)	10.27	x9	**IX**	10
51201	16R											
51440	17R	**RM¹**	(90)	**66 (III)**	−	1.1-1.2-1.3	∞8x	∞8x	11.11	∞8x	**XV**	22
51234	17L											
51240	18	**RM¹**	(122)	**73 (II)**	>55 (I)	1.4-1.6-1.8	∞10xx	∞10xx	9.32	∞10xx	**XIII**	18
50137	19	**RdP₄/M₁**	(55)	(56) (2)	**92 (2)**	−	ˣx3−	ˣx3−	9.30b	none	**III or VI+**	1 or 5

Tooth data

Dental measurements are modified after Maglio (1973) and Lister (1996a) and are in millimetres (*see* Table 5.16). In the case of matched pairs, only one of the pair (the most complete) has been measured. Data not in bold in Table 5.16 are either incomplete measurements, because of specimen breakage, or, in the case of tooth position or plate formula, less likely identifications. Column headings in Table 5.16, and the codes used in the table entries, are as follows:

No.: the catalogue number of the specimen. Multiple numbers indicate that the tooth was re-fitted from two or three separate finds.

Label: Numbers given to the specimens for the purposes of this study. Left-right pairs share a single number.

Tooth: L = left, R = right, superscript = upper tooth, subscript = lower tooth. Less likely identifications are in brackets. In two cases (labels 15 and 19), the identity of the tooth is uncertain.

L: length of tooth, measured perpendicularly to the average orientation of the plates, seen from the side. Figures in brackets are actual specimen lengths; figures in bold are estimated original lengths.

W: width of tooth, measured at the widest plate, parallel to the plate itself, and including cover cement. The number of the plate is given in brackets after the width value. Where the front of the tooth is missing, the plate number is counted from the back and indicated in Roman capitals. If cement is unformed or abraded, a correction of up to 5mm has been added, based on other regions of the same specimen or similar specimens in the sample.

H: Height of tooth, measured from crown base to apex at the highest preserved plate. Where all plates are worn, only a minimum height can be given, indicated by '>'. The number of the plate measured is indicated in brackets, as for width. Sher and Garutt (1987) showed that there is a 'zone of maximum crown height', extending approximately between plates 6 and 12 in *Mammuthus primigenius* M3s of total plate number 20–23, as in the Lynford sample, so that an unworn crown height measured in this region is likely to be the maximum for the tooth, falling off gradually in plates farther back in the crown.

e: enamel thickness, measured parallel to the vertical orientation of the enamel itself (often oblique to the occlusal surface). The measurement is taken at up to 10 points on the occlusal surface. The three values given are minimum, mode and maximum.

PF: Plate Formula. This gives the number of full enamel plates – lamellae – in the tooth. The symbol 'x' represents a talon, a small plate at the front or back of a tooth that does not extend fully to the crown base but instead attaches, at least in part, to the adjacent plate. A superscript 'x' indicates a small talon attached to the main one. The symbol 'p' indicates a platelet – a terminal plate that does extend to the crown base, but that is much smaller than the adjacent plates (Lister and van Essen 2003). A dash indicates breakage; an 'infinity' sign indicates natural anterior wear.

PF est.: This is an estimate of the original plate formula prior to breakage or anterior wear. Mammoth teeth have a very particular morphology at the anterior end, enabling reliable reconstruction of missing plates or talons (Sher and Garutt 1987) In particular, the front of the tooth is supported by a large, single anterior root, separated by a clear space from those behind, which are distinguished by being arranged in pairs. If the anterior root is intact, no more than the anterior talon can have been lost by wear.

LF: Lamellar frequency, the number of enamel plates plus cement intervals occupying a 100mm length of tooth crown. In practice, as many plates as possible are measured, preferably in the central region of the tooth, and divided by their total length, Because of lateral curvature of the tooth, LF is measured on both medial and lateral sides and the result averaged. For upper teeth, this is performed at the top and base of the crown on both sides, and the four estimates averaged (Maglio 1973). For lowers, only measurements at the base of the crown on each side have been taken, because of the tendency of the plates to converge to the top of the crown, rendering LF measurements at the occlusal surface highly dependent on state of tooth wear. The LFs of lower molars are suffixed 'b' ('basal') to indicate this fact.

Ageing

Several of the parameters listed in Table 5.16 relate to the age determination of the tooth, as follows:

Worn: This indicates which plates were in wear at the time of death, starting from the anterior end of the tooth.

Laws': This is the dental replacement and wear category according to the criteria of Laws (1966), based on the tooth or teeth erupted at time of death, plus the number of plates in wear and/or lost anteriorly. Laws' (1966) criteria were based on African elephants (*Loxodonta africana*) and have been modified for use with mammoths (Lister 1999), essentially by correcting for the difference in the total number of plates per molar. For example, *L. africana* typically has 12 plates in its M3, whereas Lynford *M. primigenius* typically has 22. Therefore, a wear stage for *L. africana* with six plates in wear is taken to be equivalent to a *M. primigenius* with 6 × (22/12) = 11 plates in wear. Laws (1966) based his criteria on lower teeth only; here they have been applied directly to both lowers and uppers, even though there might be a slight offset between their respective wear stages in a given animal (Debruyne 2003).

AEY: African Equivalent Years is the age at death found by Laws (1966) to correspond to each of his wear stage categories for *L. africana*. AEY probably overestimates or underestimates true age for smaller or larger elephantid species, respectively, but as *L. africana* and *M. primigenius* were of similar body size, it is likely that AEY is a reasonable estimate of true age in woolly mammoth (Lister 1994). Jachmann (1988) showed that the absolute ages for some of Laws' (1966) categories were slightly exaggerated in the age range 10–30 years; Jachmann's corrections have been incorporated in the AEY estimates in Tables 5.16 and 5.18.

Minimum number of individuals

Minimum Number of Individuals (MNI) was first estimated using the conventional method of seeking the element (single midline or one side of a pair) most commonly represented in the assemblage. However, the assemblage of 19 molariform teeth or paired teeth (Table 5.16) allowed further exploration of MNI, by seeking possible matches or mismatches in terms of position in the series, dimensions and degree of wear. Elephantid dentitions lend themselves particularly well to this enterprise, due to their sequential mode of eruption. For example, a P4 in mid-wear and an M2 in mid-wear of a horse or bovid could plausibly belong to the same individual, whereas in an elephantid they could not possibly do so, as they erupt at quite different times in the animal's growth. For the Lynford mammoth sample, every tooth was compared with all others in the sample, and a decision made as to whether they might plausibly belong to the same individual, or could not possibly do so. To fulfil the requirements of an MNI estimate, a conservative approach was adopted whereby teeth were taken to be plausibly associated if there was any possibility that they might belong to the same individual. A table was drawn up summarising the results of this survey (Table 5.17). From this table, plausible groupings of teeth were drawn up, and swapped among groupings in an iterative process until a minimum number of groupings (MNI) was reached; in other words, until no possible move of a tooth or teeth among groupings reduced the MNI.

Results

The dental sample comprised 27 useable molariform teeth, including eight left-right pairs, resulting in 19 units of analysis (*see* Table 5.16). Measurements and ageing data were used for only one side of a left-right pair.

Taxonomy

The evolution of the mammoth lineage in Eurasia presents a complex picture of population differentiation and replacement, which conventional taxonomic divisions are not well suited to represent (Lister 1996a; Lister and Sher 2001; Lister et al 2005). Mammoth remains from the 'last glaciation' (approximately MIS 4–2) are universally regarded as representing *M. primigenius* – the woolly mammoth. Late Middle Pleistocene mammoths in Europe show somewhat more 'primitive' dental morphology and have been regarded either as early *M. primigenius* or as late representatives of *M. trogontherii*, a species best known from the early Middle Pleistocene (for discussion, see Lister 1996a; Lister *et al* 2005).

Plate number of the molars is an important taxonomic indicator within *Mammuthus* as a

Table 5.17 Potential matches or mismatches among all possible combinations of teeth (or tooth pairs), labelled as in Table 5.16. 'Zero' indicates that the specimens could not belong to the same individual; 'one' indicates that they could plausibly do so.

label	tooth	1	2	3	4	5	6	7	8	9	10	11	12	13	14	15	16	17	18	19
1	L&RM³																			
2	L&RM³	0																		
3	LM³	0	0																	
4	RM3 (M²)	0	0	0																
5	L&RM₃	1	0	1	0															
6	LM₃	0	0	0	0	0														
7	RM₃	0	0	1	0	0	0													
8	L&RM₃ (M²)	0	1	0	1	0	0	0												
9	LM²	0	1	0	1	0	0	0	1											
10	RM² (M¹)	0	1	0	1	0	0	0	1	0										
11	L&RM²	0	1	0	1	0	0	0	1	0	0									
12	RM₂ (M²)	1	0	1	0	0	0	0	0	0	0	0								
13	L&RM₂	0	1	0	1	0	0	0	1	1	0	1	0							
14	RM₂	0	1	0	1	0	0	0	1	1	0	1	0	0						
15	LM₂/₃	1	1	1	1	0	0	1	0	1	1	1	0	0	0					
16	L&RM¹	0	0	0	0	0	0	0	1	0	0	0	0	0	0	0				
17	L&RM¹	0	0	0	0	0	0	0	0	0	0	1	0	1	1	1	0			
18	RM¹	0	0	0	0	0	0	0	0	0	0	0	0	0	0	1	0	0		
19	RdP₄ (M₁)	0	0	0	0	0	0	0	0	0	0	0	0	0	0	0	0	0	0	

whole, and is plotted for Lynford M3 in Fig 5.47, together with some comparative samples. In this graph, upper and lower molars are combined to increase sample size, as they do not differ significantly in this parameter. The Lynford sample shows a relatively low plate count for *M. primigenius* in the range 20–22, which overlaps both with other last-glacial samples such as those from Předmosti in the Czech Republic and Lea Valley, UK, as well as with those of the Late Middle Pleistocene including finds from Steinheim, Germany and Ilford, UK. The persistence, in the last glaciation, of a substantial proportion of mammoth molars with relatively low plate counts in the range 20–22, alongside more 'advanced' specimens with up to 28 plates, is a consistent feature of European samples (Lister and Sher 2001, Lister et al 2005), and given the small sample size at Lynford, the observed range is consistent with a last-glacial age. Regarding the M2, the Lynford plate count corresponds exactly to that of Předmosti, the largest available sample of European *M. primigenius*, which dated to c 26ka. For Lynford (n = 4), mean M2 plate number is 14.25±0.48 (range 13–15); for Předmosti (n = 33), mean is 14.21±0.18, range 12–16. In a plot of lamellar frequency versus crown width (Fig 5.48), a further useful taxonomic indicator among elephantids (Lister and Joysey 1992), Lynford M3s fall within the middle range of the Předmosti and Lea Valley samples. Nonetheless, among the lower molars, specimen 50000, with only 20 plates, has a remarkably low basal lamellar frequency of 5.57, outside the range of the Předmosti sample (6.17–9.13, n = 31), and more similar to Middle Pleistocene *M. trogontherii*; unless

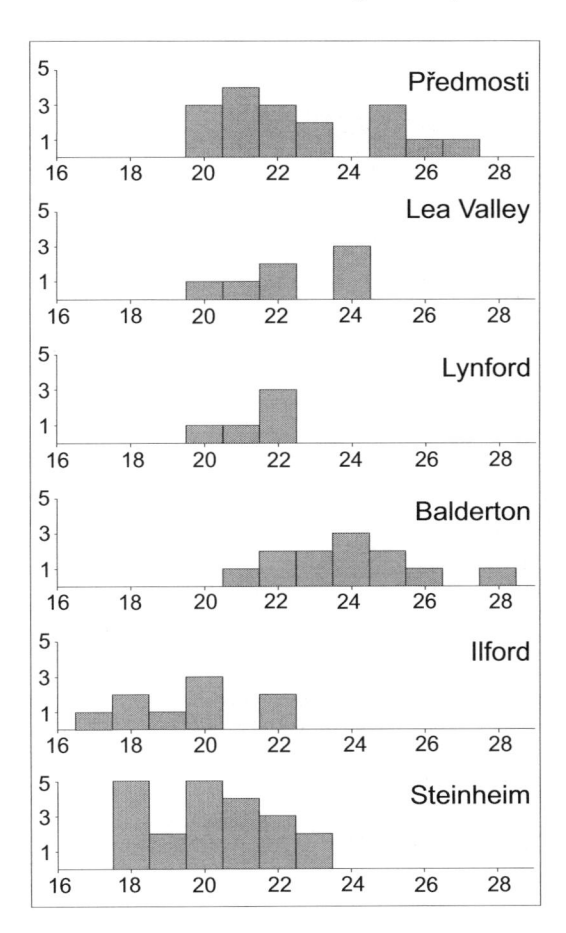

Fig 5.47 (left) Plate number (excluding talons and platelets) in third molars, upper and lower teeth combined. Approximate dates of the comparative samples are as follows: Předmosti, 26ka; Lea Valley Gravels, 28ka; Balderton, 130ka; Ilford, 200ka; Steinheim, 350ka. For details of the stratigraphy and dating of these samples, see Lister and Sher (2001, supplementary information).

Fig 5.48
Width versus lamellar frequency in upper third molars from Lynford (squares), in comparison with last glaciation Mammuthus primigenius *samples from Předmosti (circles) and the Lea Valley Gravels (triangles). The Lynford molars are consistent with* M. primigenius *in both size (represented by width) and LF/W proportion.*

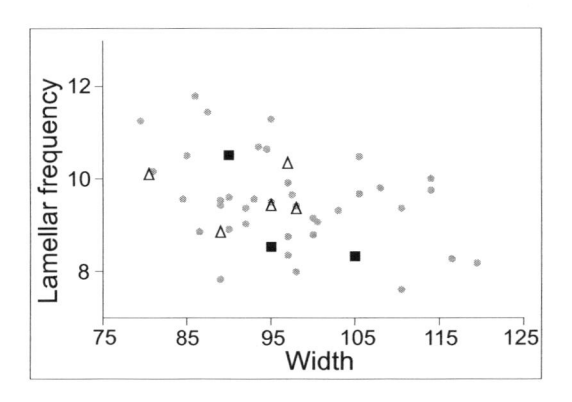

derived from an older deposit, this presumably represents an extreme of individual variation within *M. primigenius*.

Minimum number of individuals (MNI)

The conventional method of estimating MNI gives a value of three individual animals (based on left M3, or right M3, or right M1; *see* Table 5.16). Taking into account wear and dimensions, however, a higher MNI can be obtained, as described above. The process of comparing every tooth with every other, to determine possible matches or mismatches, resulted in the matrix shown in Table 5.17. This manual iterative process results in an MNI of 11 individuals. An example combination is shown in Table 5.18, where specimens or specimen pairs are indicated by their label (in brackets) as in Table 5.16, and the groupings by Roman capitals.

Two of the specimens (labels 6 and 19; groups II and XI above) cannot be matched with any other specimen under any combination; others can be swapped among groupings but with no reduction in MNI. Specimen 15 (51252), which may be either an LM2 or LM3, was excluded from the analysis, but can be added to existing groupings under either identification. For example, as an LM2, it can join with groups VIII or IX; as an LM3 it can join group IV. It therefore does not alter MNI under either identification.

Among the limb bones (Table 5.19), there are two right proximal ulnae and two femur heads, representing at least two individuals. However, it is impossible to allocate these, or any of the other adult or subadult bones, to absolute ages with sufficient confidence to combine them with the dental remains for MNI purposes. The two juvenile bones (Table 5.19) last two rows) have rough age estimates of 2–4 and 6–9 years (see below), suggestive of two individuals additional to those identified from tooth remains, since the only two juvenile teeth are one at one or five years, and another at 10 years. However, given the uncertainties inherent in these estimates, and the need for conservatism in ensuring that MNI is truly a minimum, they have not been formally added to the dental MNI count of 11.

Age structure

The age structure of the dental sample (*see* Table 5.16, AEY) shows a very marked predominance of young to middle-aged adults. Modern elephants are conventionally taken to have reached adulthood at about 15 years (Sukumar 2003), and the same can be applied to mammoths as a working hypothesis. Using the entire dental sample, 17 of the 19 individuals are adult; one left-right M1 pair in early wear (no. 16) is a subadult about 10 years old, and another (no. 19) is a juvenile animal. The latter specimen comprises the anterior end of an unworn lower tooth, and it is uncertain if it is a dP4 (implying an age of 1 AEY) or an M1 (5 AEY). Its maximum preserved width, 56mm,

Table 5.18 One of several possible combinations of teeth that, based on Table 5.17, constitute the minimum of 11 individuals, with their individual and averaged ages

grouping	teeth included	AEYs (Table 1)	average age AEY
I	RM$_3$ (7)	45	45
II	LM$_3$ (6)	43	43
III	LM^3 (3) + L&RM$_3$ (5)	39, 43	41
IV	L&RM^3 (1) + RM2 (12)	41, 39	40
V	RM^3 (4) + RM$_2$ (14) + LM^2 (9)	25, 22, 30	38.5
VI	L&RM^3 (2) + L&RM$_3$ (8) + RM^2 (10)	30, 30, 30	30
VII	L&RM^2 (11) + L& RM$_2$ (13)	24, 26	25
VIII	L&RM^1 (17)	22	22
IX	RM^1 (18)	18	18
X	L&RM^1 (16)	10	10
XI	RdP$_4$/M$_1$ (19)	1 or 5	1 or 5

Table 5.19 Identifiable mammoth bones for which useful measurements could be taken, in comparison with individuals of known sex from other localities. Males are from Condover (UK), Ahlen, Borna and Pfannerhall (Germany) and Lena and Mamontovaya Rivers (Russia); females are from Aa River (France), and Sanga-Jurjach and Oyosh (Russia) (data from Baigusheva and Garutt 1987, Siegfried 1959, Felix 1912, Toepfer 1957 and Lister 2009): all measurements in mm; A = adult, SA = subsadult, J = juvenile. Details of sexing in Lister 1996 and Averianov 1996. Measurements marked in bold provide meaningful comparison of Lynford with other sites because (a) Lynford measurement complete, (b) Lynford age evident and (c) comparative measurements available.

number	age	element	dimension	Lynford	males	females
51666	A	occipital condyle of skull	max dimension	99	92 (n=1)	80 (n=1)
51515+ 51537	A	atlas vertebra	medio-lateral diameter of posterior condyles	**240**	**233–255 (n=3)**	
51999	A	axis vertebra	medio-lateral diameter of anterior condyle	270	222–275 (n=3)	
	A		posterior medio-lateral diameter of centrum	160	140 (n=1)	
51976	A	R prox ulna	prox antero-posterior diameter	≥ 250	283–315 (n=3)	300
50551	A	R prox ulna	prox antero-posterior diameter	≥ 220	283–315 (n=3)	300
	A		prox medio-lateral diameter	≥ 210	211–242 (n=4)	175
	A		min medio-lateral diaphysis diameter	**123**	**100–114 (n=3)**	**75 (n=1)**
51903	A	L prox radius	prox medio-lateral diameter	≥ 110	118–122 (n=2)	120
	A		min medio-lateral diaphysis diameter	**59**	**51 (n=1)**	
51628	A	R magnum	max medio-lateral diameter	**110**	**93–111 (n=5)**	**75 (n=1)**
	A		max antero-posterior diameter	125	131–141 (n=3)	
50733	A	2nd phalanx of 3rd digit	max length	56		
	A		prox medio-lateral diameter	57		
51024	SA-A	prox femur head (unfused)	max diameter	**190**	**150–183 (n=4)**	
51832b	SA-A	prox femur head (unfused)	max diameter	155	150–183 (n=4)	
51575	SA-A	femur diaphysis	min medio-lateral diameter	113	128	
51967	SA-A	femur diaphysis	min medio-lateral diameter	104	128	
51885	J	L humerus diaphysis	min medio-lateral diameter	44	37 (1 yo), 49-50 (3–6 yo)	
50404	J	L first rib	lateral contour length minus epiphyses	385	240 (3–6 yo), 600–640 (adult, n=3)	

is within the range of a sample of *M. primigenius* dP4s from Předmosti (range 44–61, n = 13), and below that of the M1s from the same locality (58.5–73.0, n = 27), but these are maximum widths measured toward the posterior end of the tooth. The position of the Lynford tooth, and therefore its precise age, are thus indeterminate, but it still represents the only juvenile tooth (one to five years) in the assemblage. The age distribution of the whole sample is plotted in Fig 5.49a.

An arguably more rigorous approach to estimating the age distribution would be to restrict the sample to the minimum number of individuals. Taking the 11 groupings listed above, each can be assigned an age because, being groups of teeth plausibly from the same individual, the teeth in a group have similar or identical age estimates. Where a slight difference was found, an average was taken for purposes of analysis (*see* Table 5.18). By the same token, other combinations of teeth into 11 groupings would give a very similar age distribution. The results based on the groupings in Table 5.18 are plotted in Fig 5.49b. The age range is unchanged from the full data set, but the peak at 30 AEY has been flattened because it was based on a number of specimens plausibly from the same individual.

Limb bones can also provide some indication of individual age because elephantid bones continue growth well into adult life, and their epiphyses thus fuse late. Roth (1984) showed that for living elephants the epiphyses fuse in a defined order, and Lister (1999) extended the method to mammoths and related it to dental age.

Table 5.19 lists all limb bone elements for which at least one useful measurement could be taken, and compares them with a sample of European and Siberian *M. primigenius* skeletons. Although comparative sample sizes are small, Table 5.19 shows that for nine of the 11 Lynford specimens for which meaningful comparison can be made, the Lynford dimensions are of large size, corresponding to largely- or fully-grown adult individuals. In several cases the Lynford specimens are large even in comparison to the reference sample, indicating individuals at or close to the termination of growth, which occurred at around 40–45 years in males and 20–25 years in females (Lister 1999).

Two specimens (51024 and 51832b) are isolated ball joints from femurs, with the surfaces of unfused epiphyses visible, indicating that the animal had not completed growth. The proximal femur is, however, one of the last epiphyses to fuse in elephantids – in the mid-40s in male *M. primigenius* (Lister 1999). One of the Lynford femurs is among those specimens that are larger than the male comparative sample, indicating a more or less fully-grown adult; the other is somewhat smaller and hence either a (not quite fully-grown) subadult-to-adult male or a (probably fully-grown) adult female. A similar conclusion applies to two femur diaphysis fragments (51575 and 51967).

Only two of the analysed postcranial bones are of juvenile animals. The first, the central part of the diaphysis of a left humerus (51885), has a minimum shaft diameter (medio-lateral) of 44mm, allowing for a little surface bone loss. In Fig 5.50, this specimen is plotted against a series of juvenile humeri from Russian Plain sites, for which age (in AEY) is approximately known from associated dentitions (Mashchenko 2002). Based on linear estimation from the Russian sample, this predicts a most likely age of *c* 34 months for the Lynford humerus, although in view of the scatter around the line, an age of *c* 2–4 years is a suitably cautious estimate. The second specimen is a left first rib, complete except for the proximal and distal

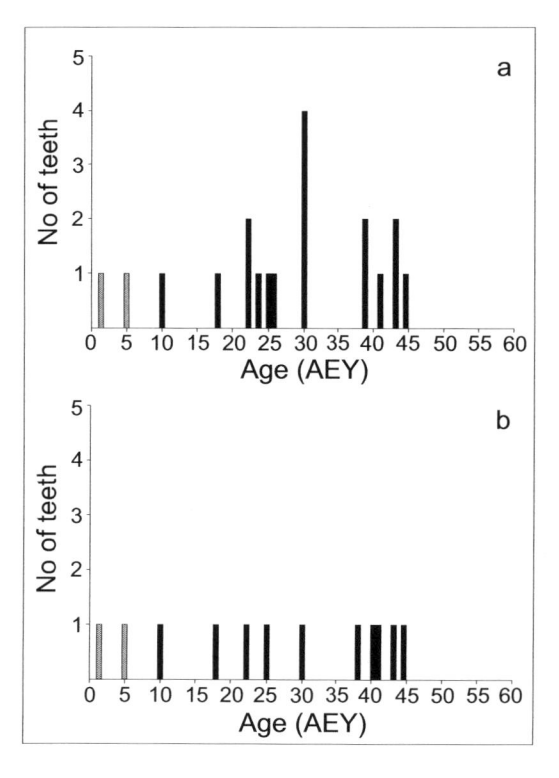

Fig 5.49
Age structure of the Lynford mammoth assemblage based on molariform teeth. Ages plotted in African Equivalent Years: (a) all 19 specimens or pairs, from Table 5.16; (b) one of the combinations of 11 specimens comprising the MNI. Two alternative positions are marked for specimen 19 (group XI), as its age is indeterminate at either 1 or 5 AEY.

epiphyses. This specimen has a contour length of 385mm along the centre of the lateral face. There are limited published data for ribs of juvenile mammoths of known age. A personal communication by Maschchenko (2004) indicates that an individual from Sevsk (Russian Plain) of dental age c 2.5–3 years, has a first rib contour length of 235mm. This is similar to a measurement of 240mm on a juvenile mammoth from Condover, Shropshire (Lister 2009) associated with a mandible of dental age 3–6 years. The Lynford specimen is from a considerably larger animal; Mashchenko (pers comm) suggests an age of c 6–9 years.

Sex determination

Mammoth remains can be sexed on the basis of tusk size, skull morphology, pelvic morphology, and, with caution, postcranial size (Averianov 1996; Lister 1996b). Dental size is very weakly, if at all, sexually dimorphic in elephantids (Debruyne 2003).

Little information on the gender of the Lynford mammoths can be gleaned from pelvic elements, crania or tusks, due to lack of sufficiently well-preserved material. Nonetheless, some indications are available.

First, specimen 51134 is a partial premaxilla (tusk socket) of a mammoth, preserving about a third of the circumference of the lip where the tusk emerged. Since mammoth tusks at their emergence are approximately circular in section, the preserved arc was traced onto paper and, by simple geometry, the complete circumference reconstructed, giving a circle of diameter approximately 208mm. This represents a large tusk that is almost certainly that of an adult male. Based on a large sample of adult woolly mammoth tusks from Siberia, Vereshchagin and Tichonov (1986) indicated diameters of 89–180mm near the base for males, and 47–90mm for females.

Second, the dimensions of most of the measurable bones are suggestive of males. Mammoths, like other elephantids, were significantly sexually dimorphic in body size (Averianov, 1996). In Table 5.19, comparative samples were restricted to skeletons for which gender has been ascertained (Lister 1996b). Although comparative sample sizes are small, Table 5.19 shows that for all seven adult or subadult Lynford specimens for which meaningful comparison can be made, the Lynford dimensions correspond to likely males.

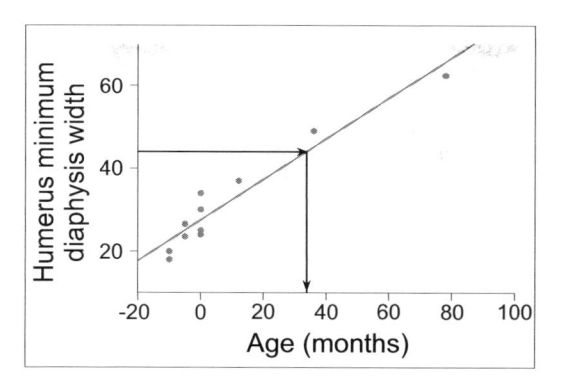

Fig 5.50 Growth of the humerus in Mammuthus primigenius from the Russian Plain (data from Mashchenko 2002, table 13), in comparison with the juvenile specimen from Lynford, No. 51885. Age of Russian specimens (in months), based on associated dentitions, includes foetal specimens plotted as negative values. A linear regression line has been fitted to the Russian data, from which the epiphysis diameter of the Lynford specimen predicts an age of c 34 months.

With the exception of the very large, unfused femur head (51024), which was probably that of a male, sex determination of the subadult and juvenile individuals is not possible from their size.

Discussion

The taxonomic and evolutionary significance of the assemblage lies in the fact that the Lynford mammoths provide valuable additional evidence for relatively low molar plate counts among European last-glaciation mammoths, which Lister and Sher (2001) suggested might result from introgression in the late Middle Pleistocene between native European *Mammuthus trogontherii* and incoming *M. primigenius* from eastern Asia.

In terms of the light the assemblage sheds on mammoth and Neanderthal behaviour, dental and postcranial material both indicate an age-structure in the preserved assemblage that is dominated by prime adult animals, with relatively few juveniles, subadults or aged individuals. Haynes (1991) and Lister (2001) have discussed differing age profiles of fossil proboscidean assemblages, and their possible interpretation. The Lynford age profile clearly differs from Haynes' type A, in which all age classes are represented, increasing in abundance toward the juvenile classes. This reflects a typical living population and suggests non-selective mortality (that is, all ages have an equal chance of dying), either as a sudden event or over a period of time. The age profile of mammoths at La Cotte, Jersey (Scott 1986) is similar to type A but lacks animals over the age of 36, suggesting an element of selectivity, and also differs from that at Lynford in its high proportion of juveniles and subadults. Lynford also differs from Haynes' type B, where a very strong preponderance of juvenile animals represents highly selective mortality, as found, for example, in the hyaena-accumalated assemblage at Kent's Cavern, UK (Lister 2001), or in modern elephant populations stressed by drought (Haynes 1991). Lynford differs again from the human-accumulated assemblage at Předmosti, where all age categories are represented, but with a high proportion of subadults (Musil 1968; author's unpublished data).

The Lynford assemblage is most similar to Haynes' type C, where the middle age classes predominate, and juvenile and old animals are rare. Haynes suggests that such profiles might result from selective death over an extended period, although this would require a causal agent resulting in preferential survival of the very young and very old. Such a profile could also result from taphonomic or collecting bias against young individuals whose fossils are smaller and less robust. The molars of very old individuals, having lost most of their bulk by wear, are also relatively small and inconspicuous. Haynes notes that a 'type C' assemblage is found in the mammoth sample from the fluviatile sands of Mosbach (Germany), and it occurs also in UK gravel assemblages such as those from Balderton, Lincolnshire. (Lister and Brandon 1991) and Tattershall Thorpe, Lincolnshire (author's unpublished data). However, the combination of fluviatile accumulation and opportunistic collecting at these sites predisposes them to taphonomic bias of this kind, whereas at Lynford the lack of pre-depositional transport and the preservation and recovery of large numbers of small and fragile fossils indicate that a different explanation for the lack of juveniles is required.

Mammoths, like living elephants, almost certainly had a matriarchal social structure in which females lived in tight-knit groups with their young, while adult males wandered singly or in temporary small groups (Lister and Bahn 2007). The presence of adult males at Lynford indicates that the assemblage does not represent the sudden death of one or more matriarchal groups, as has been suggested for mammoth assemblages such as Sevsk (Russia) or Dent (Colorado, USA), where adult females and young are predominant (Lister and Bahn 2007). Nor does it represent the accretion of all age/sex classes by a random or opportunistic process (Schreve, this chapter). The Lynford assemblage, dominated by prime-age males, most closely resembles the Hot Springs site, South Dakota, a natural trap where adult males predominantly mired (Lister 1994). This interpretation of the Lynford sample has the proviso that the gender profile is based on only eight specimens (seven postcrania plus one tusk socket), with a possible MNI as low as two in this subsample (Table 5.19; see above). Thus, the presence of adult females in the Lynford assemblage is by no means excluded, even if it cannot be positively demonstrated.

The question of whether Neanderthals, at Lynford or elsewhere, hunted or scavenged large mammals such as mammoths, is unresolved (White, this chapter; Schreve 2006, this chapter). The selective age and sex structure of the assemblage cannot be used to determine between these alternatives, but provides an interesting perspective on each. If the Lynford mammoths were hunted, selection for adult males might reflect a strategy targeting those individuals that led more solitary lives in preference to matriarchal groups of females and young, whose co-operative defensive behaviour, and protection of injured or dead individuals (Sukumar 2003), could have made both attack and recovery more problematic for Neanderthal hunters. Attracted to the channel by water and/or food, mammoths could have been ambushed *in situ*. Conversely, if the Lynford site presented a danger of miring, the greater propensity of lone adult male elephants to become trapped in these situations, compared to the more cautious and co-operative female and young groups, could account for the age/sex distribution at Lynford as it does at Hot Springs (Lister 1994). White (this chapter) and Schreve (this chapter) suggest a possible combination of these factors if Neanderthals shepherded individual mammoths into the boggy environs of the Lynford channel before dispatching them.

5.3 The herpetofaunal remains

C Gleed-Owen

Amphibian remains from the Late Pleistocene channel at Lynford, Norfolk, were examined and are reported on in this contribution. Only one species – *Rana temporaria*, the common frog – was identified, but this species was present in numerous samples. The absence of other amphibian and reptile species is consistent with sites of broadly similar age in Britain, and probably reflects the cool climatic conditions that prevailed at the time.

Methodology

Small vertebrate remains were recovered manually from several hundred bulk samples of sandy organic channel-fill. The herpetofaunal component was largely separated by D Schreve and placed in gelatine tubes (151 samples). The remainder was identified by the author (amphibians in 19 extra samples, but not separated from other small vertebrate remains). All remains were examined by low-power binocular microscope, and identified to the highest taxonomic level possible. Most remains were determinable to genus; some to species. Specific identification was generally possible from ilia, male humeri and some metacarpals. Sex and species was determined by presence of humeral crests and metacarpal tubers in males, and absence of same in females. Humeral crests are evident even in juvenile males. Results were tabulated and totals of each element and MNI values calculated.

Results

Two hundred and seventy-eight recognisable amphibian remains were identified from 166 samples, and one bone was recovered as a find. Sixty specimens were specifically identifiable but they only represented one species of amphibian, the common frog (*Rana temporaria*). Nearly all other elements were referred to Rana sp., and one to *Anura* indet., but all were consistent with *R. temporaria* and it is likely that all belonged to that species. No reptiles were present. The skeletal make-up of the assemblage is typical for high-energy environments, largely comprising ilia, tibiofibulae, radioulnae, humeri and vertebrae, with lesser quantities of a few other bones. Most of the remains are from juvenile and immature animals. Most of the bones are incomplete, and many are fragmentary and seem to be disintegrating. The formation of grey salt crystals in many bone interiors appears to have contributed to the disintegration. The cracking and curling of bone surfaces might also suggest they have been dried too quickly. Some also have an appearance similar to that seen in burnt bone or frost cracking. One partial tibio-fibula bears a series of fine parallel scratches in it that look like fine tooth marks but that could be modern. One or two bones have a crunched, splayed end, which could be due to predation at or just before death. No signs of digestive damage were observed. The minimum number of individuals represented is 31 from the most numerous element, the right ilia. The corpus of the ilium in anurans is usually preserved when the ala/vexillum are broken, and the partial ilia counts represent survival of a corpus which can be used in an MNI count. A larger MNI value might have been possible using tibiofibulae (74 including fragments), but possession of the distinctive feature – the mid-shaft foramen nutrimen – was not counted in fragments. The humeri counts (17 male, 13 female) indicate an MNI value of at least nine males and nine females.

Systematic palaeontology

Rana temporaria:

17 left ilia, 4 partial left ilia, 20 right ilia, 8 partial right ilia, 6 male left humeri, 1 partial male left humerus, 6 male right humeri, 2 partial male right humeri, 1 male right 2nd-digit metacarpal.

Rana sp.:
4 partial left ilia, 3 partial right ilia, 2 partial left or right ilia, 2 male left humeri, 1 partial male right humerus, 6 female left humeri, 3 partial female left humeri, 3 female right humeri, 1 partial female right humerus, 12 femora, 3 partial femora, 14 tibiofibulae, 60 partial tibiofibulae, 5 tibiales, 3 fibulares, 1 partial fibulare, 25 radiulnae, 4 partial radioulnae, 4 left and 2 right scapulae, 17 trunk vertebrae, 1 partial trunk vertebrae, 3 sacra, 8 left and 3 right angulosplenials, 1 metatarsal, 2 partial metatarsals, 3 metapodials or phalanges, 1 male right 2nd digit metacarpal, 1 partial phalanx, 5 urostyles, 5 partial urostyles, 1 left and 1 right pterygoid, 1 right exoccipital, 2 left and 1 right coracoid, 1 partial right coracoid.

Anura indet:
1 partial urostyle. Probably also a few other indeterminate fragments not extracted from some samples.

Discussion

Only the most robust anuran (frog/toad) skeletal elements tend to survive in high-energy environments, in contrast to caves and archaeological deposits where they are often well preserved. Therefore the poor preservation and unrepresentative skeletal composition of the assemblage is not surprising, and perhaps typical of Pleistocene fluvial deposits. Most of the elements are from juveniles and immature animals, but some whole elements and many fragments are from subadult and adult frogs. It is likely that attrition in the fluvial environment has reduced larger bones into smaller fragments, and a degree of sorting might have taken place. There is no suggestion that all the animals died in one season as is sometimes apparent with juveniles in pitfall situations (for example, Gleed-Owen 2003).

There are very few recorded instances of herpetofaunal remains from Middle Devensian contexts in Britain, and almost none with dating control. MIS 3 deposits at Sutton Courtenay, Oxfordshire, produced a single bone of natterjack toad (*Bufo calamita*) (Gleed-Owen 1998) suggesting a temperate episode with 2 AMS dates around 33,000 BP. Stuart (1982) reported *R. temporaria* of probably similar age from Upton Warren. Amphibian remains expected to be of MIS 3 age from Wookey Hole, Somerset, were AMS dated to MIS 2 (Gleed-Owen 1998). Other fluvial, cave and fissure site assemblages might include amphibian remains of MIS 3 age, but this author is not aware of any specific data. It is certainly a period that would merit further investigation.

It is highly unlikely that any amphibian or reptile species survived in Britain during the worst climatic extremes of the Devensian. However, it is possible that with extremely cold winters, but summers similar to Arctic Scandinavia today, common frogs could have survived in places. Temporal resolution of MIS 3 and MIS 4 climate change in Britain is too poor to define short warmer/colder episodes, but thermal stability (of summers) lasting hundreds of years would be required to allowcolonisation by frogs from a refuge perhaps 1,000km to the south. The Upton Warren Interstadial was evidently longer than this and allowed distinct thermophiles to enter the British Isles. As the interstadial appears to have 'tailed off' over the subsequent millennia, probably with a certain degree of climatic fluctuation, there is plenty of scope for these remains to fit into this chronology.

5.4 Stable isotope analysis (C, N, O) of faunal samples

M P Richards, V H Grimes and S M Blockley

We report here on the measurement of the stable isotopes of carbon, nitrogen and oxygen from mammoth bone and teeth from the site. These analyses were undertaken for a range of reasons. First, to explore the preservation of the bone and teeth and see if the samples were suitable for isotope research. Second, to measure the carbon and nitrogen isotopes of any extracted bone and tooth protein (collagen) to get some measure of the diet of the mammoths, and especially how they relate to other published mammoth isotope values. Thirdly, we wanted to explore the use of bone and teeth from the site as climatic indicators through the measurement of oxygen isotopes in phosphate in hydroxyapatite. Some of the samples were quite well preserved, and were suitable for isotopic analysis: the findings are reported below.

Carbon and nitrogen isotopes

Bone and tooth dentine collagen carbon and nitrogen isotope ratios are indicative of the sources of dietary protein exploited by the animal concerned (Ambrose 1993; Ambrose and Norr 1993). In the context of European Pleistocene herbivores, collagen carbon-isotope ratios (expressed as $\delta 13C$ values) can be used to estimate the percentage of C3 and C4 plants in diets, and also as fairly insensitive proxy indicators of climate values. Collagen nitrogen isotope values (expressed as $\delta 15N$ values) indicate the main protein sources, as they are 3–5 per mil more enriched over dietary protein, and these can also be indirect indicators of climate.

Extraction procedures

The goal of the bone and tooth dentine pre-treatment is to remove the inorganic mineral phase, which is a source of carbon, and isolate the protein fraction, which is overwhelmingly composed of collagen. In the Bradford Stable Isotope Laboratory, this was accomplished through the demineralisation of bone in 0.5 M HCl at 5°C, then the gelatinisation and filtration of the remaining proteins, followed by ultra-filtration to further purify the extract (Brown *et al* 1988). In modern bone the amount of collagen is approximately 20 per cent by weight, and therefore the measurement of the amount of collagen remaining in a fossil bone is an indicator of the preservation state of that bone. Additionally, the ratio of carbon and nitrogen in the 'collagen' extract is an indicator of collagen preservation (DeNiro 1985), as is the actual percentage of carbon and nitrogen.

Table 5.20 presents the δ 13C, δ 15N, %C, %N and collagen yield data for the samples used in the analysis. Relatively well-preserved collagen (often defined as having a C:N ratio between 2.9 and 3.6, as well as a collagen yield of over one per cent) was extracted from roughly half of the samples, which is somewhat surprising for samples of this age. Sample extraction was undertaken at the Stable Isotope Laboratory at the Department of Archaeological Sciences, University of Bradford, and the isotope ratios were produced though continuous-flow isotope ratio mass spectrometry, using a ThermoFinnigan Flash EA coupled to a Delta Plus XL.

Mammoth δ 13C and δ 15N data

The isotope ratios of the samples yielding 'good' collagen are plotted in Fig 5.51. As can be seen, values cluster fairly tightly. Unsurprisingly, the δ 13C values indicate an entirely C3 plant diet and are consistent with values from cold climates observed by other researchers (Iacumin *et al* 2000). The δ 15N values are often elevated in mammoths compared to other herbivores from the same contexts, and the reason for this is not well known. In a pioneering early study, Heaton *et al* (1986) plotted the δ 15N values of African elephants from a variety of geographical locations in South Africa, and found a close correlation between increased aridity and elevated δ 15N values. Using similar criteria, these δ 15N values are probably indicative of an arid environment, and would correspond to a value of approximately 500mm of rainfall per year, but it is unlikely that the data from modern elephants is directly applicable to mammoths. Taking both the δ 13C

Table 5.20 Samples taken for isotopic analysis, with bone and dentine collagen C and N isotope ratios, as well as weight % collagen, %C and %N in the collagen extract, and site context data. All reported isotope results are the average of duplicate collagen measurements. Measurement errors (1σ) are ± 0.1 ‰ for δ ^{13}C and ± 0.2 ± for δ ^{15}N. δ ^{13}C values are measured relative to the vPDB standard, and the δ ^{15}N values relative to the AIR standard.

sample no.	element	species	δ^{13}C	δ^{15}N	%C	%N	C:N	% coll	comments	object no.
LQ2	tusk	mammoth						0.0	no collagen	50076
LQ3	bone	mammoth	−22.1	7.4	41.4	13.6	3.5	1.4		51143
LQ4	bone	mammoth	−22.3	6.9	45.2	15.0	3.5	1.5		50368
LQ5	bone	mammoth	−21.9	6.0	43.6	15.3	3.3	5.5		50289
LQ6	bone	mammoth						0.0	no collagen	51120
LQ 7	dentine	mammoth	−23.2	6.7	40.5	11.6	4.1		poor C:N	51009
LQ10	bone	mammoth	−23.4	6.5	39.6	9.5	4.8	0.3	poor C:N	51670
LQ11	bone	mammoth	−21.8	7.6	44.2	15.2	3.4	4.4		51530
LQ12	tusk	mammoth	−22.4	7.8	40.2	13.6	3.4	2.6		51615
LQ13	?	mammoth						0.2		51366
LQ14	bone	mammoth	−22.0	6.0	40.9	14.1	3.4	3.5		51348
LQ15		mammoth	−24.9	6.0	20.7	4.0	6.1	0.4	poor C:N	51660
LQ 16	bone	mammoth	−24.2	7.7	36.4	8.9	4.8	0.2	poor C:N	51818
LQ17	tusk	mammoth	−22.2	7.2	36.4	11.8	3.6	1.4		51706
LQ18	tusk	mammoth	−22.1	8.1	32.3	10.1	3.7	1.1	poor C:N	51756
LQ19	bone	mammoth	−23.5	6.6	3.0	0.8	4.2	0.3	poor C:N	51721
LQ20	tusk	mammoth	−23.1	6.4	18.3	5.3	4.1	0.5	poor C:N	51778
LQ21	?	mammoth						0.0	no collagen	52009
LQ22	bone	mammoth	−21.9	6.9	44.5	15.0	3.4	0.2		51928
LQ23	bone	mammoth	−22.4	7.2	39.0	13.4	3.4	1.6		51971
LQ24	bone	mammoth	−22.6	5.5	39.6	11.8	3.9	0.1	poor C:N	51975
LQ25	tusk	mammoth	−21.1	8.6	44.2	15.4	3.3	6.3		51952
LQ26	skull bone unstratified	mammoth	−22.2	6.7	36.3	11.9	3.6	1.6		
LQ27	tusk	mammoth	−22.0	7.8	42.9	14.7	3.4	2.7		51303
LQ28	tusk	mammoth	−22.3	9.3	44.0	14.6	3.5	2.3		51303
LQ29	tusk	mammoth	−22.1	7.6	44.7	15.6	3.3	5.8		51979
LQ30	?	mammoth						0.0	no collagen	50076
LQ31	antler frag	reindeer						0.0	no collagen	20051
LQ32	bone	?						0.0	no collagen	52065
LQ33	tusk	mammoth	−21.7	8.6	40.8	13.2	3.6	0.6		51775

Fig 5.51
δ 13C and δ 15N isotope ratios of collagen extracted from bone and dentine of mammoth samples from Lynford Quarry. Only those samples with acceptable collagen criteria (defined by % yield, C:N ratio and %C and %N) are plotted here.

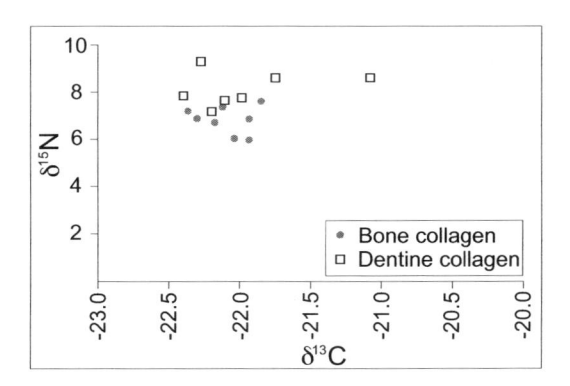

and δ 15N data together, a picture emerges of these mammoths living in a cold and arid landscape, which is entirely as expected.

Oxygen isotopes

The analyses of phosphate oxygen isotope ratios (expressed as δ 18Op) from the hydroxyapatite of animal bone and teeth (enamel and dentine) are typically used as a proxy for determining continental palaeoclimates (Longinelli 1984; Fricke *et al* 1998; Iacumin *et al* 2004). The δ 18Op signal has been shown to be directly related to the oxygen isotope values of ingested (meteoric) water, which are in turn influenced by climatic parameters such as air temperature, humidity and amount of precipitation (Dansgaard 1964; Longinelli 1984; Luz *et al* 1990). Although oxygen is stored in both the carbonate (CO3) and phosphate (PO4) sites within hydroxyapatite, it has been suggested that the phosphate site is more resistant to potential diagenetic processes that could alter the original *in vivo* oxygen isotope signature (Luz and Kolodny 1989). Therefore, phosphate oxygen was chosen as the target site for isotopic analysis here.

Oxygen extraction procedures

The phosphate oxygen extraction procedure at the Bradford Stable Isotope Laboratory follows established methods described by Stephan (2000), which are a modification of those of O'Neil *et al* (1994) and Crowson *et al* (1991). In an inversion of the method of collagen extraction described above, accurate isotopic analysis of phosphate oxygen in hydroxyapatite requires the complete removal of the organic fraction of bone and teeth, including any humic acids originating from the burial environment. This was achieved by pre-treating powdered samples with sodium hypochlorite (2.5 per cent NaOCl) followed by sodium hydroxide (0.125 M NaOH). Phosphate (PO4) in the sample was then isolated through acid digestion in hydrofluoric acid (2 M HF), neutralised with potassium hydroxide (2 M KOH), and precipitated as silver phosphate (Ag_3PO4) with the addition of a silver ammine solution. The Ag3PO4 crystals were collected through filtration, dried and weighed. Analysis of oxygen isotope ratios of Ag_3PO4 was conducted through high-temperature pyrolysis (Gehre 2001) and continuous-flow isotope ratio mass spectrometry using the ThermoFinnigan TC/EA and Delta Plus XL, respectively.

Mammoth δ ^{18}O data

Only a small subset of the mammoth samples taken for isotopic analyses have been measured for their phosphate oxygen isotope ratios. The data from the four sample analyses are presented in Table 5.21 and indicate wide variation in oxygen isotope values. Although this could be interpreted as major shifts in environmental oxygen, and thus represent changes in climate or possible migratory behaviour, it is more likely indicative of an alteration of the original oxygen isotope signature. This is particularly evident in samples LQ2 and LQ9, whose δ 18Op of dentine material are much higher than would be expected. The probability that several of the samples analysed for phosphate oxygen have been diagenetically altered is supported by the lack of collagen present in the same material (*see* Table 5.20). Until more of the samples from the remaining mammoths as well as other fauna from the Lyford Quarry site are analysed, it will be difficult to draw specific conclusions about the environment in which they lived from these oxygen isotope data.

Table 5.21 Oxygen isotope results of mammoth enamel and dentine (tusk) from Lynford Quarry: presented δ ^{18}Op values are averages of raw (non-normalized) data of at least two replicate measurements relative to the vSMOW oxygen standard; analytical errors on in-house standard material (synthetic Ag^3PO^4, Alfa Aesar) are ± 0.5‰ (1σ)

sample no.	element	δ^{18}Op (‰)	object no.
LQ2	tusk	28.8	50076
LQ9	tusk	29.0	51667
LQ30	tusk	14.2	50367
LQ51887	enamel	21.1	51887

Summary

The extraction of intact and well-preserved bone and dentine collagen from samples of the antiquity of those from Lynford is unusual. The measured δ 13C and δ 15N collagen values are consistent with the expected values for arid and cold conditions, and are in line with those observed by other researchers for Eurasian mammoths (Bocherens *et al* 1994, 1996; Iacumin *et al* 2000, Jones *et al* 2001). Further work on the other species recovered from the site is underway to explore trophic relationships within this ecosystem, as well as to better understand the climatic conditions that prevailed.

5.5 The lithic assemblage from Lynford Quarry and its bearing on Neanderthal behaviour in Late Pleistocene Britain

M J White

Introduction

Despite nearly two centuries of investigation, the archaeological record of the Neanderthal occupation of Britain remains remarkably slight, especially when compared to many of its western European neighbours (compare Roe 1981, 233ff). Britain notably lacks the deep, archaeologically rich cave sequences found in Spain, Italy and, most famously, SW France – a pattern that cannot purely be explained by the paucity of suitable localities – and even open-air occurrences are few in number and often comprise just a handful of artefacts. This pattern has led many to argue that, at most, Britain was host to low-density, intermittent settlement during the Late Middle Palaeolithic, with several workers now postulating a complete occupational hiatus between *c* 150,000 and 60,000 years ago (MIS 6 to 4/3) followed by a small-scale recolonisation sometime around the beginning of MIS 3 (Wymer 1988; Currant and Jacobi 2001, 2002; Ashton 2002; White and Jacobi 2002).

To make matters worse, many of the potentially important sites that Britain has produced are poorly understood. Most were investigated during the 19th and early 20th centuries, using different methods and asking different questions than modern excavations, and often in less than ideal circumstances. Consequently much evidence has gone, and given that many sites have long since ceased to exist, this situation is unlikely to be remedied. In the worst cases – for example Bramford Road, Ipswich (Moir 1931) and Oldbury, Kent (Harrison 1892) – we lack even a meaningful geological context. Given this historical and archaeological background, the recent findings from Lynford Quarry are clearly of national and international importance, providing a rare opportunity to study the lithic technologies and inferred activities of Neanderthals in the most north-westerly corner of their world. This discovery is made all the more important by a combination of other factors. First, the assemblage is relatively large and, while in secondary context, has merely slipped from the channel edge where it was discarded. Second, despite a rescue dig, the site was excavated using modern methods to a well-planned research design (Boismier, chapter 1). Third, it is associated with a range of environmental proxies that provides a vivid picture of the landscapes in which these peoples lived and the animals they lived alongside.

This chapter presents an analysis of the stone tools from Lynford. It takes an explicitly techno-typological approach, and is particularly concerned with exploring the chaîne opératoire of lithic manufacture and use. Taking inspiration from several recent studies (eg Geneste 1985; Turq 1988; Boëda *et al* 1990; Pelegrin 1990; Conard and Adler 1997; papers in Cliquet 2001; Soressi and Hays 2003) it hopes to unlock the potential of the Lynford lithics, moving beyond the classification of types towards an understanding of the organisation of technology at Lynford as spatially and temporally dispersed practices, which can be interrogated for the insights they offer into Neanderthal behaviour and social practices.

Context and content

The excavation produced a total of 2,720 lithic artefacts, recovered *in situ* from nine Facies Associations and subdivisions, of which 1,982 were chips and spalls, and 738 were flakes, cores and tools (Table 5.22). In addition, 21 artefacts were found in previously disturbed palaeochannel deposits. Of these, the most important, numerically and archaeologically, are those from Facies Associations B-ii (subdivisons B-ii:01 to B-ii:05), representing the finds from a 1m to a 1.5m-deep sequence of low-energy silts and sands filling a palaeochannel. This has produced a total of 2579 artefacts (94 per cent of the total), with subdivision B-ii:03 alone (the principle organic fill of the palaeochannel) yielding 83 per cent of the total artefact assemblage (see Table 2). Spatially, the artefacts from the palaeochannel deposits were found in a diffuse and fairly low-density spread throughout the ~199m^2 of surviving palaeochannel deposits, with an average of ~12.9 per m^2 or ~8.6 per m^3.

A further 72 artefacts were recovered from the sand and gravels of association B-i underlying the organic sediments of unit B-ii. The deep sequence of deposits above Facies Association B-ii (B-iii and C) produced a combined total of just 48 artefacts. The majority of these were chips or unretouched flakes, but two handaxes and a handaxe roughout were recovered. These are typologically and technologically indistinguishable from those in the main palaeochannel, and, with the exception of one rolled handaxe, were in the same fresh, unpatinated and unstained condition. The basic counts and inventory of artefact types for all these units are provided in Tables 5.22 and 5.23, but they are not considered further in this report. Finally, 21 artefacts were found during initial prospecting or cleaning prior to excavation. While some of these probably belong to the main palaeochannel, the circumstances of their recovery raised question marks over their precise context. Including them within the B-ii palaeochannel assemblage offered no analytical advantages, and they are therefore excluded from the present sample.

This study thus concentrates on the materials from the main palaeochannel deposits of Facies Association B-ii. Although these comprise five subdivisions and ostensibly five stratigraphically discrete assemblages, the refitting analysis (see below) demonstrates that vertical mixing has occurred. Moreover, much of the lithic assemblage is likely to have been incorporated into the channel by periodic bank collapse and mass movement, thus introducing, at different times, artefacts that might originally have lain together on the channel edge (Lewis, chapter 2). There is also a degree of overlap of the various deposits of the palaeochannel, which in places might have formed contemporaneous parts of a single laterally variable surface. All of these observations mean that the material from Facies Assocation B-ii cannot be meaningfully separated into distinct sub-assemblages. As a result of this apparent admixture, and given the small sample sizes from most palaeochannel contexts, it was decided to treat the material from Facies Association B-ii as a single time-averaged assemblage, although separate data for B-ii:03, the largest single assemblage, is also presented.

The main palaeochannel assemblage is characterised by handaxes (generally ovate, cordiform and subtriangular forms) and handaxe manufacturing debris, with an important flake tool element that includes scrapers, notches and bifacial pieces. Apart from one probable recurrent centripetal Levallois core in rolled condition, Levallois material is absent from the B-ii assemblage. Other Levallois material – all in very rolled condition – has previously been recovered from the basal Wissey Gravel during earlier phases of gravel extraction at Lynford Quarry (John Lord, pers comm 2003; personal observation).

Chips and spalls of less than 20mm in dimension are well represented in B-ii (n = 1941), the recovery of these objects made possible by an intensive sieving program. Only fresh chips and spalls showing firm evidence of percussion flaking have been included, all rolled pieces being excluded as natural or

Table 5.22 Lithic artefacts from Lynford, by facies association and context

facies	archaeological contexts	no. artefacts
C	20007, 20009	2
B-iii	20015, 20016, 20023, 20028, 20065, 20066	46
B-ii:05	20002, 20005, 20070, 20116	15
B-ii:04	20053, 20055, 20131, 20137, 20251, 20366, 20367, 20374, 20376	51
B-ii:03	20003, 20021, 20135, 20248, 20250, 20252, 20253, 20258	2,269
B-ii:02	20246, 20355, 20371, 20378, 20403	86
B-ii:01	20004, 20133, 20139, 20245, 20254, 20255, 20346, 20347, 20363, 20364, 20369, 20375, 20383, 20384	158
B-i:03	20051, 20078, 20129	20
B-i:02	20361	52

Table 5.23 Basic inventory of artefacts from Lynford by facies association

facies	chips and spalls	flakes	scrapers	flake tools	cores	handaxes (parenthesis = incomplete)	handaxe roughouts	misc	total
C		1				1			2
B-iii	33	11				1	1		46
B-ii:05	10	5							15
B-ii:04	30	18	1			2			51
B-ii:03	1,760	456	11	2	2	31 (5)	2	5*	2,269
B-ii:02	63	21	1			1			86
B-ii:01	78	59	4	2	2	13 (1)	1		158
B-i:03	8	12							20
B-i:02	0	50	1	1					52
disturbed palaeo-channel deposits	–	13	1			5		2	21
totals	1,982	646	18	5	4	54	4	7	2,720

*1 conjoinable shattered tip fragment, 1 sandstone block, 2 chunks, 2 handaxe preforms, 1 quartzite hammerstone

unrelated to the main occupation of the palaeochannel. When assessing the chip and spall data, however, it should be remembered that positive identification of human modification on such objects can often be quite difficult, and some might be naturally produced by collision, subsurface pressure flaking and other post-depositional processes (compare Warren 1920, 1923; Harding et al 1991; Bridgland and Harding 1993). Many workers prefer to exclude such items, but, as a key aim of this study was the assessment of the coherence and integrity of the Lynford lithic assemblage, they have been retained.

Taphonomy of the lithic artefacts

An appreciation of the types of geological disturbance or other post-depositional factors that might have operated on the Lynford lithics is vital to our understanding of the integrity of the assemblage, and is an essential prerequisite of any technological or behavioural interpretation, including the nature of the association between the stone tools and the animal remains. The range of processes that could potentially disturb and re-arrange a lithic assemblage, and the various effects these have on pristine assemblages, have been the focus of a number of experimental and site-based studies (eg Isaac 1967; Shackley 1974; Villa 1982; Schick 1986; Harding et al 1987; Dibble et al 1997; Ashton 1998a). In this section, the integrity of the lithics from the main palaeochannel is examined through a consideration of the following lines of evidence: geological context, macroscopic artefact condition, refitting studies, artefact size distribution and artefact orientation. The spatial patterning of the lithic artefacts (Boismier, chapter 4) and microscopic evidence of wear (Donahue and Evans, this chapter) are considered elsewhere in this volume.

Geological context

The deposits comprising Facies Association B-ii consist of sand, silt and organic silty sands deposited under still to slow-flowing water conditions, with localised incorporation of coarser bank sediments and materials (Lewis, chapter 2). It has been interpreted as representing a body of water cut-off from the main river, with fluctuating water levels. Given the basic premise that the level of fluvial transport is mainly controlled by flow velocity and artefact density, it seems highly improbable that such gentle conditions would have subjected the present Lynford assemblage to significant fluvial winnowing or re-arrangement; energy levels were certainly too low to have displaced objects of handaxe size.

However, periodic and localised disturbance is documented by sediment bodies indicative of mass movement, bank erosion and surface run-off, suggesting that part or much of the lithic assemblage was incorporated into the inactive channel via these means (Lewis, chapter 2). Significant bioturbation by the large herbivores whose remains were found within the channel have also played a significant role in trampling and rearranging lithic artefacts. Further 'foot-traffic' dispersal might also be expected if parts of the palaeochannel dried up seasonally (French, chapter 2), or if artefacts were randomly dispersed onto winter ice cover, becoming incorporated into the sediments during a thaw.

The biggest geological obstacle to interpretation, however, is the fact that the proximate channel margins have been destroyed by quarrying activity and later fluvial channels. This means that Lynford only preserves evidence of those activities that took place close to the channel edge.

Artefact condition

An artefact's preservational state is routinely used as a measure of hydrological and geological transport, the macroscopic signs being surface abrasion, edge damage, surface polishing and battering. Levels of abrasion and edge damage are believed to increase with the duration and violence of fluvial transport, although it is also widely appreciated that the extent of this process is context-specific and likely to vary according to bedload. As well as testifying to transport in a bedload, localised battering and abrasion can also form where an object has become partially buried or trapped, but is still susceptible to collision and attrition. Similarly, the degree of surface polish is also believed to vary according to the time and intensity of transport (Ashton 1998a). While abrasion and edge damage are usually taken as markers of the same processes, here they are regarded as separate phenomena because, while edge damage can be formed in transit, it can also be caused *in situ* via such processes as animal trampling, incorporation into a bank collapse and post-depositional crushing.

Table 5.24 presents the preservational state of flint artefacts of more than 20mm from selected contexts. Data are presented for the degree of abrasion, edge damage and surface polishing, patina and staining. The vast majority of artefacts from B-ii are in fresh condition with virtually no evidence of surface polishing. However, practically all the artefacts showed some evidence of edge damage, although in the majority of cases this was graded as minor, and in some instances might be use-related rather than post-depositional. There is a strong correlation between these variables, with 82 per cent of the artefacts displaying a combination of fresh condition, no polish and minor edge-damage. On the whole, this implies that most of the material from B-ii has undergone minimal fluvial transport or abrasion. The high incidence of edge damage is consistent with the crushing seen on the faunal remains (Schreve, this chapter), and probably relates to post-depositional sediment pressure, gravitational mass movement and animal trampling.

A small proportion of the artefacts from B-ii are rolled or heavily rolled, and show greater evidence of surface polishing and edge damage. Again, there is a high level of correspondence between these variables. Of the 32 rolled or heavily rolled artefacts, 26 (81 per cent) show some degree of surface polishing and 29 (91 per cent) moderate to severe edge damage. Similarly, of the 42 slightly rolled artefacts, 29 (69 per cent) show surface polishing and 24 (57 per cent) moderate to severe edge damage. Clearly, edge damage and polishing do increase with the level of abrasion.

These data suggest that two basic elements are present within the B-ii assemblage – a numerically large fresh assemblage and a numerically small rolled assemblage. As these assemblages were both excavated from the same very low-energy contexts but occur in contrasting condition, they are considered to be discrete entities with different histories rather than as falling along a continuum of damage demonstrated by a single assemblage, although it is less certain where the slightly abraded material fits within them. The fresh assemblage is postulated to be in primary context, although with evidence of limited fluvial transport (or winnowing), having been originally discarded within, or close to, the palaeochannel deposits in which it was finally buried. The rolled element, however, is believed to be in secondary context, with the majority of the pieces derived from elsewhere. The most likely source of the latter is the basal Wissey Gravels into which the palaeochannel is incised, which are a known source of rolled artefacts including handaxes and Levallois cores (Lord 2002 and pers comm; compare Wymer 1985, 52–3). These artefacts probably found their way into the fine silty sands through the combined effects of bank collapse, periodic flood and mass-movement events, animal dispersal and human agency.

The level of chemical alteration to artefact surfaces is also minimal (*see* Table 5.24). Only 64 artefacts showed evidence of patination, and of these 49 (76.6 per cent) were also in an abraded condition. This indicates that most of the artefacts did not undergo long periods of subsurface weathering and/or subaerial

Table 5.24 Condition of excavated or sieved flint artefacts >20mm, from selected contexts

	B-ii:03 (n=509)	B-ii:02 (n=23)	B-ii:01 (n=80)	B-i (n=53)	B-ii combined subdivisions (n=638)
abrasion					
fresh	454 (89.2%)	18 (78.3%)	74 (92.5%)	47 (88.7%)	564 (88.4%)
slightly rolled	33 (6.5%)	4 (17.4%)	2 (2.5%)	3 (5.7%)	42 (6.6%)
rolled	20 (3.9%)	1 (4.3%)	4 (5%)	2 (3.8%)	30 (4.7%)
heavily rolled	2 (0.4%)	0	0	1 (1.9%)	2 (0.3%)
surface polish					
matt	455 (89.4%)	19 (82.6%)	70 (87.5%)	44 (83%)	559 (87.6%)
silky	45 (8.8%)	4 (17.4%)	10 (17.5%)	8 (15.1%)	68 (10.7%)
glossy	9 (1.8%)	0	0	1 (1.9%)	11 (1.7%)
patina					
unpatinated	463 (91%)	22 (95.7%)	74 (92.5%)	48 (90.6%)	574 (90%)
mildly patinated	43 (8.4%)	1 (4.3%)	6 (7.5%)	5 (9.4%)	61 (9.6%)
heavily patinated	3 (0.6%)	0	0	0	3 (0.5%)
edge damage					
minimal	442 (86.8%)	22 (95.7%)	70 (87.5%)	48 (90.6%)	550 (86.2%)
moderate	51 (10%)	1 (4.3%)	10 (17.5%)	3 (5.7%)	69 (10.8%)
severe	16 (3.1%)	0	0	2 (3%)	19 (3%)
staining					
unstained	250 (49.1%)	19 (82.6%)	67 (83.75%)	44 (83%)	354 (55.4%)
mildly stained	8 (1.6%)	0	7 (8.75%)	4 (7.5%)	21 (3.3%)
heavily stained	1 (0.2%)	0	0	1 (1.9%)	2 (0.3%)
black	250 (49.1%)	4 (17.4)	6 (7.5%)	4 (7.5%)	261 (41%)

exposure sufficient for the formation of a patina, and that the small patinated element is largely in secondary context. Similarly, the level of surface staining is negligible: only 23 artefacts showed any macroscopically visible signs, and 11 of these also showed evidence of fluvial abrasion. The data for both patina and staining therefore support the idea that two basic assemblages with different histories are present.

Some of the material from the palaeochannel, however, shows a black mineral coating. This is a particular characteristic of B-ii:03 finds, where it is displayed by 49.1 per cent of the artefacts. In fact, this mineral coating is so characteristic of the material from this stratigraphical subdivision that its presence in other groups, albeit in small numbers, suggests not only that post-depositional displacement occurred between layers, but also that this movement occurred after the coating developed (see refitting study below).

Table 5.24 also shows the condition of artefacts from Association B-i, underlying the main palaeochannel. Again the majority are fresh, unpolished, unpatinated, unstained and minimally edge-damaged. The overall good preservational state of these artefacts is somewhat unexpected, given the large amount of rolled and heavily rolled material previously collected from the basal Wissey gravel. Presumably, the artefacts from the Association B-i relate to earlier primary occupation at this terrace level, while the material within the basal Wissey gravel belongs to a much older period of occupation, and might even pre-date the gravels within which they occur.

Débitage size distribution

Knapping experiments by Schick (1986) and Wenban-Smith *et al* (2000) have generated data sets that replicate the size-frequency distribution of complete lithic reduction episodes. Under experimental conditions, the vast majority (~70 per cent) of lithic débitage is less than 20mm in maximum dimensions, with an exponential fall-off in the percentage of artefacts of greater size. For the present taphonomic study, these data are particularly useful for assessing the potential impact of fluvial winnowing of the smaller-sized elements away from the site, once they were incorporated into the channel.

Fig 5.52
Size frequency distribution of débitage from Lynford plotted against Schick's experimental data.

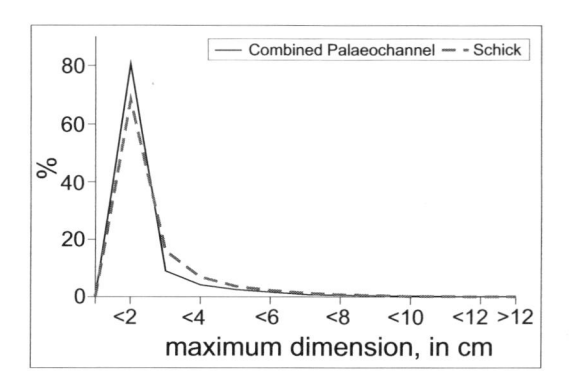

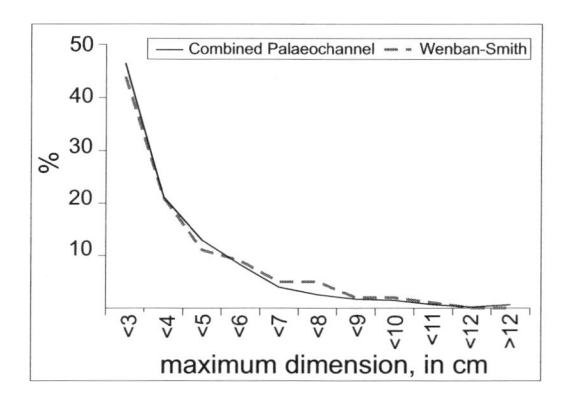

Fig 5.53
Wenban-Smith's experimental flake size data compared to Lynford Association B-ii.

Fig 5.52 shows the size-class distribution of fresh unretouched débitage from B-ii, compared with Schick's experimental data. The débitage for the combined palaeochannel débitage shows the same distribution as Schick's experimental series, with a strong skew to the right and leptokurtic tail, suggesting that an essentially unwinnowed assemblage is present. However, the archaeological series shows some 10 per cent more chips and spalls (of < 20mm) than Schick's data set. While Schick's series is an experimental heuristic with which one should not necessarily expect complete parity, this difference is statistically significant (KS Test, $n = 2420$, $D = 0.12$, $D\sqrt{n} = 5.9$, $p < 1$ per cent). The difference can probably be explained by a combination of factors: the selective introduction of smaller elements within the slow-flowing channel; the inclusion of geofacts in the sample; raw material differences generating different numbers of chips (the Lynford assemblage is made on flint, the artefacts in Schick's series on igneous and metamorphic rocks); and the effects of the technological activities that Neanderthals were actually performing at the site (*see below*). Some of these factors can be partly controlled for by comparing Lynford with Wenban-Smith's experimental data, which was produced on flint, excludes objects less than 20mm, and was generated solely through handaxe manufacture, the inferred dominant activity at Lynford. As shown in Fig 5.53, Lynford closely matches Wenban-Smith's data, and while the Lynford assemblage includes more flakes of less than 30mm, the difference is not statistically significant (KS Test, $n = 470$, $D = 0.04$, $D\sqrt{n} = 0.978$, $p > 10$ per cent).

In conclusion, while the flake sample is not identical to experimental expectations, fluvial winnowing and sorting size has had a minimal effect on the Lynford flake assemblage. The differences seen between the experimental and archaeological samples might relate to taphonomic factors (preferential introduction of smaller elements), analyst error (the unwitting inclusion of geofacts) or Neanderthal behaviour (extensive retouching to tool edges).

Artefact orientation

The study of artefact orientation is based on the premise that an assemblage that has suffered little fluvial disturbance will show no preferred alignment, whereas an assemblage that has been fluvially re-arranged will show directional patterning, with laminar artefacts tending to become orientated with their long-axis either parallel or transverse to the direction of flow (Isaac 1967; Schick 1986). Orientation data for the B-ii assemblage was collated from a 1:10 plan. The orientation of all artefacts shown on the plan as having a clear long axis (length:width ratio > 2:1) was measured and plotted on a rose diagram (Fig 5.54). The data were then processed using Georient, which showed a

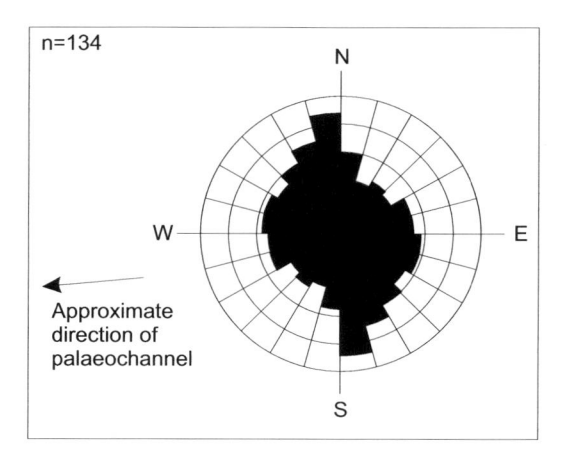

Fig 5.54
Orientation plot for plotted artefacts from the main palaeochannel.

mean orientation of 154° but found no clear patterning indicative of sorting by linear flow. As expected from the size distribution and geological context, fluvial alignment is limited. It should be noted, however, that the effects of artefact size were not controlled for, and some re-orientation of the smaller element might exist. On a purely visual and subjective basis, there is a hint of a north-south bias, perhaps conforming to the interpretation derived from the geology that objects were randomly incorporated by bank erosional processes and disturbances generated by megafaunal activity.

Refitting and site formation processes

Refitting studies are a standard tool in Palaeolithic research (eg Cziesla et al 1990; Roberts and Parfitt 1999). In terms of site formation, the presence of conjoinable artefacts is one of the best measures of assemblage integrity, with the degree of spatial clustering also helping to identify the level and direction of any disturbance that has occurred (eg Villa 1982).

All artefacts from the palaeochannel, including those from the spit samples, were laid out in their original positions. It was immediately clear that no complete knapping scatters were present, and that generally the finds represented a diffuse spread of mostly technologically unrelated objects (Fig 5.55). Refitting was hindered by the black coating on many of the pieces, and by the general lack of cortex, both of which made the initial identification of individual pieces of raw material difficult. Nevertheless, a small number of refits could be made, showing that the assemblage has some level of integrity, although no refitting group contained more than two pieces. The relative paucity of refitting in such an assemblage is probably related to the levels of lateral and horizontal re-arrangement by the processes proposed above, combined with the fact that only a very small part of the palaeochannel remained to be excavated and that time was extremely limited. Given more time, more refits would probably have been found.

Table 5.25 and Fig 5.55 present the refitting data, detailing the type of refit and vertical and horizontal distances between conjoinable pieces. Horizontally, conjoins were found between 70mm and 5.33m apart. These distances might simply relate to the nature of emplacement, but might equally have been caused by humans or herbivores. Vertically, refit distances ranged from 70mm to 510mm, and in the most extreme case the conjoinable artefacts were separated by two facies subdivisions (B-ii:03 – B-ii:01). These observations unequivocally show that vertical displacement of related objects has occurred. This might have taken place during emplacement, or might show differential sinking of heavier objects into the soft substrate (chapter 4): in two cases the handaxes are 240mm and 500mm lower than their conjoining flakes.

Overall, the refitting data suggest that while the lithic assemblage is not *in situ*, it has not moved far from its primary context. The distribution of the refits also supports the decision to treat the B-ii assemblage as a single entity.

Summary of the site formation study

Interpreting the above data is not straightforward. The Lynford assemblage was discarded in and around a still or very slow-moving abandoned channel incapable of moving anything but the very smallest artefacts. The vast majority of the material is in fresh condition, with preservational state, size distribution and orientation showing that it has not been subject to major fluvial transport, size sorting or linear flow alignment. A major fluvial influence can therefore be largely eliminated.

However, this does not automatically imply that the assemblage is undisturbed. The few refits do testify to some parts of the assemblage having a high level of integrity, but also show

Table 5.25 Refitting artefacts from Lynford, with stratigraphical association

artefact numbers	type of refit	horizontal distance (m)	vertical distance (m)	facies association
40565 → 40265	production: cortical flake to handaxe	5.95	0.59	B-ii:03 + B-ii:03
40463 → 40481	modification: flake to re-cycled handaxe	5.33	0.51	B-ii:03 + B-ii:01
40458 → 40383	break: tip fragment to broken handaxe	0.76	0.10	B-ii:03 + B-ii:03
40088 → 40015	modification: notch spall to handaxe	2.27	0.24	B-ii:03 + B-ii:03
40115 → 40116	break: flake fragments	0.27	0.07	B-ii:03 + B-ii:03
40402 → 40431	break: flake fragments	0.06	0.12	B-i:03 + B-i:03

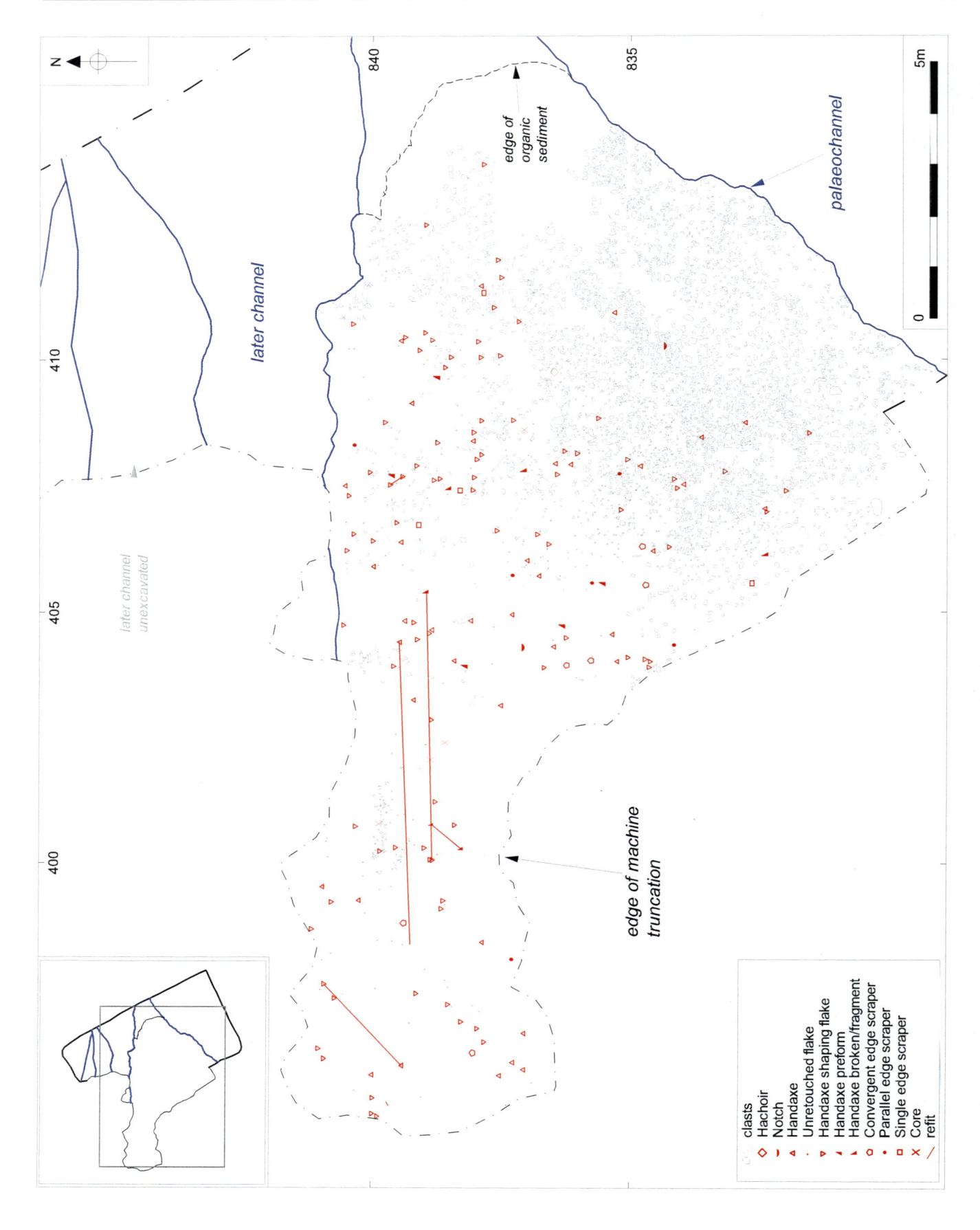

vertical displacement. Furthermore, while behavioural factors must also be considered, the lack of longer sequences and diffuse distribution shows that horizontal movement has also occurred. The orientation plot hints at some alignment with the edges of the channel, pieces sliding or rolling down the sloping margins under gravitational or hydraulic impetus. Periodic bank collapses and mass movements certainly disturbed and destroyed parts of the channel margins, locally re-arranging the fresh assemblage and introducing abraded stone tools and occasional larger clasts from older gravel deposits. It is also possible that parts of the assemblage slid from the riverbank onto winter ice, and subsequently became incorporated into the channel sediments during a thaw. Last, but certainly not least, assuming that the some of the large mammals whose remains were found in the channel deposits were active in the channel while alive, it seems inconceivable that animal-generated disturbance would not have re-arranged the original lithic discards at the channel edges.

In sum, the fresh assemblage is probably not *in situ*, but is spatially proximate to its original primary context. Some of the handaxes and related flakes might even lie where they were dropped during use and modification. Part of the assemblage, though, most likely consists of spatially and temporally disparate material that was discarded close to the channel edge, and that subsequently moved a very short distance into the palaeochannel deposits by the bank erosion processes discussed above. To conclude, the lithic assemblage probably offers a representative sample of the artefacts originally discarded and used in the immediate environs, and is thus capable of elucidating aspects of Neanderthal behaviour both in and around the palaeochannel, even if fine-scale spatial patterns have been obliterated.

The artefact assemblage from Facies Association B-ii

This section provides a techno-typological analysis of the fresh artefacts from B-ii. For the reasons stated above, these are treated as a single assemblage. Data for B-ii:03, the only individually statistically meaningful group, are also presented separately, but as these make up 83 per cent of the combined palaeochannel assemblage, the patterns are almost identical.

Raw materials

All of the chipped stone artefacts from Lynford are made of flint. There is a clear selection for good quality flint of local Norfolk origin, which is generally matt black and homogenous in texture, with few inclusions. Atomic absorption spectrophotometric analysis of 13 artefacts collected during earlier phases of gravel extraction, showed that the Lynford materials had been manufactured on local flints from the Brandon Series, although it was not possible to say whether this was obtained from one or more flint layers (Lord, unpublished manuscript). Such material was undoubtedly available from Chalk outcrops, and comprises the majority of the local river gravels within a short distance of the site. Judging from the size of some artefacts, the raw material selected by Neanderthals was generally very large.

A single handaxe is made on a white-banded flint – commonly referred to as Lincolnshire flint – which is ultimately of glacial derivation in this area but which occurs in small quantities within the local Wissey gravel. This flint type is generally of large size and good quality and can be found in much higher proportions in the glaciofluvial gravel deposits at Crimplesham, 18km to the north-west (John Lord, pers comm, 2003). The Wissey gravels at Lynford also contain a high proportion of a dark brown flint, which occurs as occasional large nodules, and which has a strongly weathered surface and frequent frost damage. Not a single artefact recovered during the recent excavations was made on this material, showing that Neanderthals were selecting flint carefully according to size *and* quality. Most of their needs were probably met by the gravel and other outcrops along the Wissey Valley.

Residual cortex on the fresh artefact collection shows a continuum of preservational states, ranging from very abraded to very fresh, with a dominance of the worn states (74 per cent of artefacts retaining cortex). During the excavation phase, a similar diversity of preservational states was observed in the Wissey gravels into which the palaeochannel was incised; the main river here flowed east–west over the relict margins of the East Anglian till plain, reworking its earlier aggradations and incising locally into Chalk. The range of types seen on the artefacts thus matches what is expected to have been accessible from the valley environs, much of it available from the

Fig 5.55 (opposite) Distribution of refitting flakes from the Palaeochannel deposits.

Table 5.26 Artefact totals from Association B-ii

artefact class	fresh assemblage			rolled assemblage		total
	count	percent	percent (>20mm)	count	percent (>20cm)	
chips and spalls	1,941	77.5		not retained		1,941
flakes	489	19.5	86.5	70	95.9	559
scrapers	17	0.7	3	0		17
flake tools	3	0.1	0.5	0		3
cores	3	0.1	0.5	1	1.4	4
handaxes (broken)	45 (6)	1.8	8	2	2.7	47
handaxe roughouts	3	0.1	0.5	0		3
misc	5	0.2	0.9	0		5
total	2,506	100%	100%	73	100%	2,579

river itself, leading to the conclusion that most of the flint was probably obtained locally (within 5km).

Flakes

A total of 646 complete and broken flakes measuring 20mm or more were recovered from the excavation, of which 559 (86.5 per cent) came from the palaeochannel fill of Association B-ii. In general, the number of flakes per stratigraphical unit is low, with the notable exception of B-ii:03, which yielded 456 (70.5 per cent of the entire flake sample).

The flakes were examined using a technological attribute analysis broadly following that devised by Ashton and McNabb (Ashton and McNabb 1996b; Ashton 1998c), with some modifications to facilitate comparison with the experimental data generated by Wenban-Smith (for example, Wenban-Smith *et al* 2000). Each flake was measured, and the following technological attributes recorded: hammer mode, cortex percentage, butt type, scar count, scar pattern, whole/broken. The purpose of this study was to examine the nature of the flaking activities evident within the palaeochannel deposits, with the wider aim of determining the organisation of lithic technology at the Lynford site. As the taphonomic study (*above*) had already highlighted the possible presence of two assemblages within the palaeochannel – one fresh, the other rolled – these were treated separately in order to establish whether they could also be regarded as technologically distinct or part of the same basic activity set. The results are summarised in Tables 5.26 to 5.34.

The fresh assemblage

The fresh assemblage (Table 5.26–5.34) comprises 489 flakes (Table 5.26). Of these, 258 are soft-hammer flakes from handaxe thinning and finishing, identified on the basis of their general thinness, curved profile and relatively complex dorsal morphology, showing earlier flat skimming flakes, minimal cortex and marginal butts with frequent crushing and lipping (compare Newcomer 1971; Bradley and Sampson 1986, Wenban-Smith 1999). Over half of the soft-hammer flakes are broken to some degree (54.2 per cent), mostly due to flexion and shattering during knapping, although their thinness also makes them susceptible to post-depositional breakage (Table 5.27). Thirteen flakes can be categorised as handaxe modification pieces that removed part of an earlier handaxe edge. Several of these resemble tranchet flakes and were presumably used to sharpen the tip, but others are thicker lateral removals aimed at notching or recycling the lateral margins.

Of the remaining flakes, 137 are clearly hard-hammer struck showing pronounced bulbs, cones and points of percussion and thick butts. However, 94 (19.2 per cent of the total flake population) could not be assigned to a hammer mode, being either too fragmentary or possessing ambiguous features.

Experimental replication has traditionally divided handaxe manufacture into three phases: roughing-out, shaping and thinning, and finishing (Newcomer 1971; Bradley and Sampson 1986; Ashton 1998b; Wenban-Smith 1999, Wenban-Smith *et al* 2000). Both experimentally and archaeologically, the first phase is generally carried out using a hard hammer, the other two phases with a soft hammer, although of course the knapper might resort to either type as necessary. Although often presented as discrete steps, these phases in fact occur

Table 5.27 Break types on fresh flakes from Association B-ii

break type	count	% of total assemblage (n=489)
proximal piece	45	9.2%
distal piece	88	18.0%
medial piece	28	5.7%
lateral piece/Siret	7	1.4%
butt shatter	45	9.2%
total	213	43.6%
total broken hard hammer	26 (19% of hard hammer flakes)	
total broken soft hammer	140 (54.2% of soft hammer flakes)	

along a continuum and distinguishing among them is not always possible in practice; this is particularly true of phases two and three, which are usually divided on the basis of size and cortex coverage. In the present study only two divisions are recognised – roughing-out and thinning/finishing – although some attempt is made to refine the latter division below.

While hard-hammer roughing-out flakes are generally indistinguishable from those generated during basic core reduction/flake production (compare Ashton 1998b; Roberts and Parfitt 1999), the low number of cores, and high frequency of handaxes and other bifaces, leads to the conclusion, even in the absence of complete refitting groups, that the hard-hammer flakes from Lynford mostly result from the production of bifacial tools (see Roberts and Parfitt 1999 and Sampson 1978 for similar conclusions; Fig 5.56). In fact, the technological character of a number of hard-hammer flakes conforms to those produced during fairly advanced biface reduction, even if struck with a hard hammer, while some of the handaxes show hard-hammer removals as part of the final working.

Of the flakes that could be confidently assigned a hammer mode (excluding indeterminate pieces), Lynford shows 65.3 per cent flakes made by a soft hammer and 34.7 per cent hard-hammer flakes. Newcomer's work produced a ratio of 72 per cent soft-hammer and 28 per cent hard-hammer flakes. The higher percentage of soft-hammer flakes generated in Newcomer's experiments probably relates to a number of factors such as personal knapping style and the fact that he had the luxury of knowing precisely which hammer mode had been employed in every case (whereas 19.2 per cent of the total flake sample was deemed indeterminate). Moreover, as suggested above, hard-hammer percussion appears to have been used at a fairly advanced stage of handaxe reduction at Lynford. Taken at face value, these data seem to show that a fairly full range of handaxe reduction was conducted on the site.

Having said that, it should be emphasised that there is a marked deficit of flakes at Lynford. The combined results from Newcomer's and Wenban-Smith's experiments suggest a 'normal' flake ($\geq$ 20mm) to handaxe ratio of 60:1 (Wenban-Smith *et al* 2000). As Lynford produced 50 fresh handaxes (complete and broken), we would therefore expect to find around 3000 flakes. The 45 handaxes themselves show a minimum of 2343 scars, yet the observed number of fresh flakes measuring 20mm or more is just 470 (Table 5.28). There is

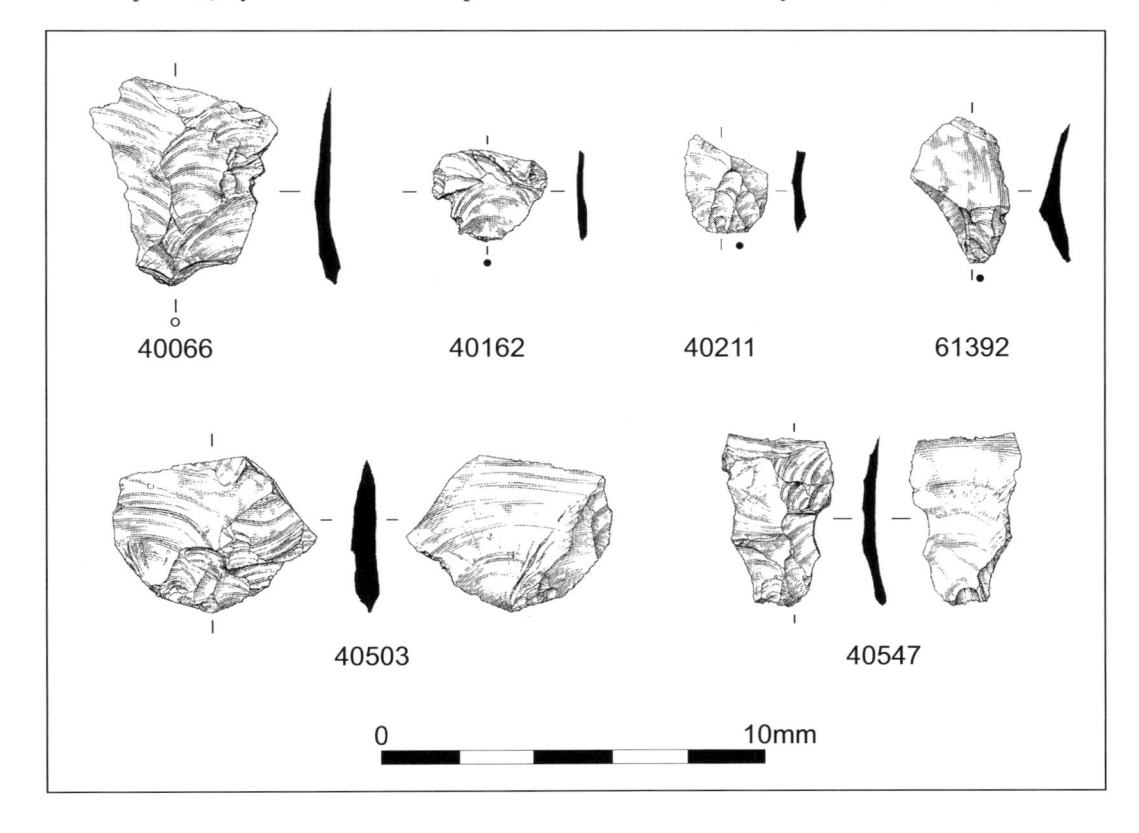

Fig 5.56
Handaxe shaping flakes.

Table 5.28 Summary metrical statistics for fresh flakes >20mm, in mm

	B-ii:03 whole flakes (n=228)	B-ii:03 all flakes (n=404)	B-ii whole flakes (n=276)	B-ii all flakes (n=489)
length				
mean	36.1 ±21.5	34.7 ±19.5	37.0 ±22.6	35.3 ±20.3
range	2.1–142	2.1–142	2.1–172.5	2.1–172.5
width				
mean	32.3 ±21.2	31.1 ±18.4	32.7 ±21.6	31.6 ±18.8
range	3.4–168.5	3.4–168.5	3.4–168.5	3.2–168.5
thickness				
mean	7.2 ±6.3	6.2 ±5.3	7.3 ±6.6	6.4 ±5.5
range	1.4–42.6	1.4–42.6	1.4–49.1	1.4–49.1

also a potential problem of broken flakes being counted more than once and artificially inflating the apparent number of flakes. Taking this into account reduces the overall figure, to just 318 (= minimum number of flakes, calculated as whole flakes + proximal fragments + essentially whole flakes with butt shatter (*see* Tables 5.26 and 5.29). Proximal fragments are used instead of the more numerous distal fragments because each proximal end unequivocally represents a separate flake, whereas the distal fragments can feasibly comprise several pieces of the same flake. Clearly, Lynford contains evidence for only partial on-site manufacture.

Other attributes allow us to investigate the flaking technology further. Residual dorsal cortex (Tables 5.29 and 5.30) shows that 69.6 per cent of the total flake sample (63.6 per cent of all the whole pieces) comprise 'tertiary' flakes retaining no cortex. 'Secondary' flakes with partially cortical dorsal surfaces account for a further 25.5 per cent, and only 24 flakes among the whole population (4.9 per cent) or just 20 complete flakes (7.2 per cent) are 'primary' pieces retaining 100 per cent cortex. Most of the latter, unsurprisingly, are hard-hammer struck and, judging by the cortex and flint surfaces, belong to a small number of raw material units/knapping episodes. The earlier stages of reduction are thus poorly represented and there is a strong bias towards the latter end of the knapping process. To take these data beyond impressionistic interpretations and fully understand their implications, it is necessary to compare them with experimentally generated flake populations.

Table 5.30 and Fig 5.57 compare the residual cortex percentages at Lynford with experimental handaxe manufacture data sets published by Wenban-Smith *et al* (2000) and Ashton (1998b). Two things are immediately apparent. First, the two experiments produced different results, although the combined percentage of flakes with 0–50 per cent and 50–100 per cent cortex is similar in both cases. As the same person (F F Wenban-Smith) conducted both sets of experiments, and both were aimed purely at producing handaxes (not specifically Middle Palaeolithic forms), these contrasts presumably relate to the precise knapping trajectory followed, as well as factors such as the size and shape of the initial raw materials. This clearly shows the dangers of uncritically using single experimental data sets for interpreting archaeological assemblages, reminding us that such experiments provide analogies rather than actualities, rendering formal statistical comparisons redundant.

The second point is that the cortex percentages from Lynford differ from the experimental data sets in terms of complete

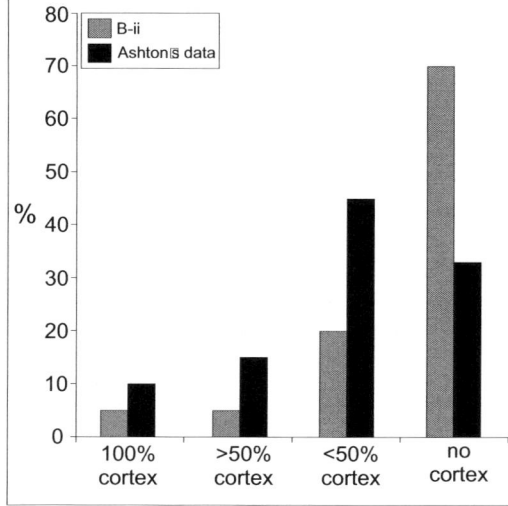

Fig 5.57 Comparison of Cortex Percentage Frequency between Lynford Association B-ii and Ashton's Experimental Series. NB: remainder = indeterminate hammer mode.

Table 5.29 Technological attributes of fresh flakes >20mm from Association B-ii (figures in parentheses = percentages)

	B-ii:03 (n=404)		B-ii combined (n=489)	
whole	228 (56.4%)		276 (56.4%)	
broken	176 (43.6%)		213 (43.6%)	
hammer mode				
soft	221 (54.7%)		258 (52.8%)	
hard	106 (26.2%)		137 (28%)	
indeterminate	77 (19.1%)		94 (19.2%)	
cortex %	whole flakes	all flakes	whole flakes	all flakes
0	145 (63.6%)	281 (69.6%)	168 (60.9%)	334 (68.3%)
≤ 20	28 (12.3%)	50 (12.4%)	39 (14.1%)	65 (13.3%)
≤ 40	8 (3.5%)	26 (6.4%)	15 (5.4%)	21 (4.3%)
≤ 60	18 (7.9%)	14 (3.5%)	22 (8%)	32 (6.5%)
≤ 80	7 (3.1%)	7 (1.7%)	7 (2.5%)	8 (1.6%)
≤ 100	22 (9.6%)	26 (6.4%)	25 (9.1%)	29 (5.9%)
(100%)	18 (7.9%)	22 (5.4%)	20 (7.2%)	2 (4.9%)
butt type				
broken/missing	139 (34.4%)	169 (34.6%)		
cortical/natural	29 (7.2%)	34 (7%)		
plain	62 (15.3%)	75 (15.3%)		
dihedral	9 (2.2%)	10 (2%)		
polyhedral	7 (1.7%)	8 (1.6%)		
marginal	141 (2.5%)	166 (33.9%)		
facetted	7 (8.7%)	10 (2%)		
mixed	10 (2.5%)	17 (3.5%)		
% flakes hammer with crushing or lipping (excluding missing butts)	35%	31.8%		
handaxe related	238	267		
handaxe modification	13	13		
scar pattern (whole flakes only)				
1	83 (36.4%)		102 (37%)	
2	43 (18.9%)		54 (19.6%)	
3	14 (6.1%)		17 (6.2%)	
4	13 (5.7%)		17 (6.2%)	
5	6 (2.6%)		9 (3.3%)	
6	4 (1.8%)		4 (1.4%)	
7	20 (8.8%)		20 (7.2%)	
8	3 (1.3%)		4 (1.4%)	
9	1 (0.4%)		1 (0.4%)	
10	37 (16.2%)		43 (15.9%)	
11	0	0		
12	4 (1.8%)		4 (1.4%)	
scar count (whole flakes only)				
0	38 (16.7%)		45 (16.3%)	
1	26 (11.4%)		35 (12.7%)	
2	32 (14%)		39 (14.1%)	
3	36 (15.8%)		46 (16.7%)	
4	20 (8.8%)		27 (9.8%)	
5	30 (13.2%)		31 (11.2%)	
6	15 (6.6%)		17 (6.2%)	
7	12 (5.3%)		15 (5.4%)	
8	5 (2.2%)		7 (2.5%)	
9	6 (2.6%)		6 (2.2%)	
10+	8 (3.5%)		8 (2.9%)	

Key to dorsal scar patterns

Table 5.30 Comparison of cortex percentage for Lynford with experimental datasets, in percent

Wenban-Smith's experimental data (only % data available)

	0%	1–20	21–40	41–60	61–80	81–100
Lynford Bii (n=489)	68.3	13.3	4.3	6.5	1.6	5.9
exp handaxe complete	53.5	14.5	9.0	9.0	5.0	9.0
exp handaxe early	8.0	20.5	16.0	16.0	16.0	23.5
exp handaxe middle	57.0	18.5	7.5	11.0	–	6.0
exp handaxe late	85.0	7.5	5.0	2.5	–	–

Ashton's experimental data

	0%	<50	>50	100
Lynford Bii (n=489)	68.3	20.7	6.1	4.9
Lynford hard hammer (n=137)	38.9	37.2	13.1	10.9
Lynford soft hammer (n=258)	89.1	8.9	0.4	1.5
exp handaxe complete (n=323)	32.8	44.3	14.9	8.0
exp hard hammer (n=147)	10.9	49.7	22.4	17
exp soft hammer (n=176)	51.1	39.8	8.5	0.6

reduction episodes; Ashton's individual hammer modes and Wenban-Smith's knapping stages (see Table 5.30). Lynford shows far more flakes with 0 per cent cortex and fewer flakes with 50–100 per cent cortex than the experimental sets. This supports the above contention that the initial stages of reduction are under-represented at the site. On the basis of the cortex data, Lynford seems to contain an assemblage comprised of the middle and late stages of Wenban-Smith's model. Part of this almost certainly relates to the fact that some 31 per cent of the Lynford handaxes have been manufactured on flake blanks (see below), which would automatically act to reduce the frequency of cortical flakes and inflate the non-cortical element. However, it is clear from several other attributes that this alone cannot fully explain the nature of the Lynford flake assemblage (see dorsal scar counts below). Moreover, many Lower Palaeolithic assemblages with which these data sets would be compared without hesitation – including those for which they were originally generated to study – show variable frequencies of flake blanks; in a study of 22 British sites these frequencies varied between 7 and 41 per cent (White, unpublished data). As nodules of different shapes and sizes will be expected to produce different ratios of cortical and non-cortical flakes, the experimental data must again be treated as guides not rules. Replication experiments using a variety of flake and nodule blanks are needed to make such comparisons more meaningful, preferably using raw material from the site under study. Unfortunately such a procedure was outside the scope of the present work. In sum, while there are a number of significant difficulties in comparing Lynford with the experimental assemblages, the flakes at the site predominantly preserve evidence for the later stages of working to minimally cortical blanks and/or tools.

These data are complimented by the dorsal scar counts, which have been argued to provide another rough guide to reduction stage, the frequency of higher scar counts increasing as knapping proceeds (Wenban-Smith et al 2000). At Lynford, 42.2 per cent of whole flakes show four or more dorsal scars (Tables 5.29 and 5.31), again indicating that the later stages of fairly intensively worked tools are preferentially represented. This is particularly true of the soft-hammer flakes, which show elevated frequencies of high scar counts when compared to experimental data sets (see Table 5.31). Given the frequency of flake blanks, if the early stages of handaxe manufacture were present, then a high proportion of flakes bearing a relict ventral surface on the dorsal would be expected

Table 5.31 Dorsal scar counts on soft hammer flakes, compared with Ashton's data, in per cent

scar count	Lynford (n=258)	Ashton (n=176)
0	2.0	0.6
1	5.3	5.1
2	12.1	34.7
3	20.2	34.7
4	14.6	19.3
5	15.9	4
6	8.0	1.1
7	8.9	0.6
8	3.7	0
9+	9.8	0

5 THE ARCHAEOLOGICAL ASSEMBLAGES OF ANIMALS AND LITHICS

Table 5.32 Size-adjusted dorsal scar counts for Lynford compared to Wenban-Smith's experimental data, in per cent (original experimental data available only in percentages)

DSC/L	exp complete (n=210)	exp early	exp middle	exp late	Lynford (n=489)
0–0.2	9.5	30.0	1.5	0.0	12.5
0.2–0.4	11.5	27.0	11.0	0.0	8.0
0.4–0.6	13.5	23.5	17.0	2.5	9.8
0.6–0.8	13.0	9.5	20.0	10.0	9.9
0.8–1	12.0	3.0	21.5	11.0	13.7
1–1.2	10.5	1.0	15.5	13.5	6.5
1.2–1.4	9.5	3.0	6.0	17.0	9.1
1.4–1.6	5.0	1.5	3.0	10.0	6.5
1.6–1.8	5.0		0.0	12.0	7.2
1.8–2	4.0		1.5	8.5	3.3
2–2.2	5.0		1.5	8.5	2.8
2.2–2.4	2.0		1.5	3.5	2.8
2.4–2.6	0.5			1.0	1.9
2.6–2.8	0.0			0.0	1.3
2.8–3	0.5			1.0	4.5

(in lieu of cortex). This is not true of the Lynford assemblage, where only six flakes (1.2 per cent) show this dorsal characteristic, supporting the inference made above that only the later stages of finishing and modification are present.

According to Wenban-Smith, scar count is a more sensitive measure of reduction stage when adjusted for size (dorsal scar count/maximum flake length). Table 5.32 presents size-adjusted scar counts for all Lynford flakes compared to Wenban-Smith's experimental series. Lynford is different from all these experimental sets, with the closest similarity being with the complete reduction sequence (Fig 5.58). However, there are still a number of differences here, with Lynford showing fewer flakes in the lower size-adjusted scar-count range and more in the higher range, again suggesting an assemblage skewed towards the later stages of reduction.

Dorsal scar patterns (DSP; see Table 5.29), while very tricky to interpret, are not inconsistent with these conclusions. To aid comparison with other published data sets, the 12 DSP listed in Table 5.29 have been combined into three groups: unidirectional (DSP 1, 5 and 6), bidirectional (DSP 2,7,8,and 12) and multi-directional (DSP 3, 4, 9 and 11). At Lynford, whole flakes show 49.6 per cent unidirectional scars, 35.3 per cent bi-directional scars and 15.1 per cent multi-directional scars (excludes flakes with 0 scars). As shown by recent work

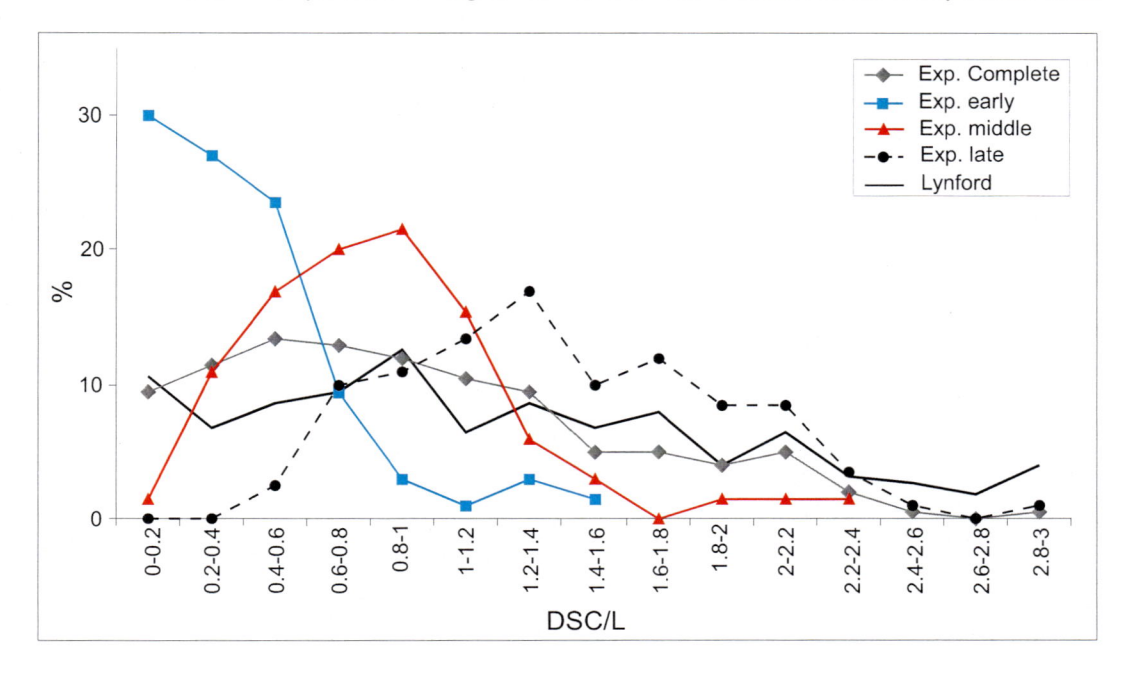

Fig 5.58
Size-adjusted scar counts (dorsal scar counts divided by length) for flakes from the main palaeochannel compared to Wenban-Smith's experimental series.

at Boxgrove (Roberts and Parfitt 1999, 358), bidirectional and multidirectional scarring are preferentially generated during thinning, when large areas of an already complex bifacial surface are removed by flaking. Moreover, somewhat counter-intuitively, it is during finishing that the percentage of unidirectional scar patterns reaches its greatest proportion, as at this point flakes tend to be shorter and less invasive, only showing the working from the parent edge. While the percentages from Lynford are in no way as exaggerated as those so far published from Boxgrove, they are nonetheless consistent with an assemblage in which handaxe thinning and finishing form the dominant technological acts. Indeed, although no formal distinction has been recognised in this study, flake size alone might suggest that finishing is highly represented; 56.5 per cent of the complete soft-hammer flakes are less than 30mm in length, 19.5 per cent between 30mm and 40mm, and 23.7 per cent greater than 40mm, with few of these possessing any cortex.

In summary, the fresh assemblage from Lynford is dominated by diminutive soft-hammer flakes, with an arithmetically smaller hard-hammer component. Numerically there are too few flakes to account for all the handaxes found. Cortex data show that the vast majority of flakes retain cortex, with very few showing more than 50 per cent cortex, suggesting a bias towards the later stages of the knapping spectrum, a pattern exaggerated by the use of flake blanks for some of the handaxes. However, dorsal scar counts and scar patterns also seem to be skewed towards the later phases of handaxe reduction.

The rolled assemblage

The rolled assemblage comprises just 70 flakes in slightly rolled to very rolled condition, as well as one core and two handaxes (Tables 5.26, 5.33 and 5.34). The core is a small radial form, worked on both sides with a clear plane of intersection, and possibly representing a centripetal recurrent Levallois core. It is in a rolled condition with clear abrasion to the arêtes and shows a developing patina. The two handaxes however (numbers 40288 and 40532), are only very slightly rolled, and are technologically and typologically indistinguishable from the rest of the B-ii materials. For this reason they have been included in the main section on handaxes below.

Of the flakes, 53 are hard-hammer and just five are soft-hammer (the remainder are indeterminate), a pattern that is reflected in the

Table 5.33 Technological attributes of rolled flakes >20mm from Association B-ii

Association B-ii (n=70)		
whole	57	(81.4%)
broken	13	(18.6%)
hammer mode		
soft	5	(7.1%)
hard	53	(75.7%)
indeterminate	12	(17.1%)
cortex % (whole flakes only)		
0	14	(24.6%)
≤ 20	12	(21.1%)
≤ 40	9	(15.8%)
≤ 60	5	(8.8%)
≤ 80	3	(5.3%)
≤ 100	14	(24.6%)
(100%)	11	(19.3%)
butt type		
broken/missing	9	(12.9%)
cortical/natural	14	(20.0%)
plain	25	(35.7%)
dihedral	0	
polyhedral	3	(4.3%)
marginal	9	(12.9%)
facetted	1	(1.4%)
mixed	9	(12.9%)
handaxe related	3	
handaxe modification	0	
dorsal scar pattern (whole flakes only)		
1	23	(40.4%)
2	7	(12.3%)
3	1	(1.8%)
4	1	(1.8%)
5	2	(3.5%)
6	1	(1.8%)
7	0	
8	2	(3.5%)
9	0	
10	20	(35.1%)
11	0	
12	0	
dorsal scar count (whole flakes only)		
0	20	(35.1%)
1	14	(24.6%)
2	7	(12.3%)
3	11	(19.3%)
4	3	(5.3%)
5	0	
6	1	(1.8%)
7	0	
8	0	
9	0	
10+	1	(1.8%)

Table 5.34 Summary metrical statistics for rolled flakes >20mm from Association B-ii, in mm

Association B-ii (n=70)	
length	
mean	42.2 ±22.8
range	14–110.6
width	
mean	39.7 ±20.4
range	17.5–109.4
thickness	
mean	10.6 ±6.4
range	3.2–25.5

low breakage rates (81.4 per cent are whole, 18.6 per cent broken). Cortex percentages show that many are heavily cortical, with only 24 per cent of the whole flakes being devoid of cortex and 43 per cent showing 50–100 per cent cortex. This is mirrored in the dorsal scar counts and dorsal scar patterns. Only five flakes show four or more scars, 35 per cent have cortical or natural dorsal surfaces, and the more complex bi-directional and multi-directional patterns combined represent just 19.4 per cent of the total assemblage (30 per cent if excluding those with entirely cortical/natural dorsal surfaces). Similarly, simple butt types (plain, cortical or mixed) are most common (71 per cent), with few marginal, facetted or other types (18.6 per cent combined total).

These data demonstrate clear technological contrasts between the rolled and the fresh assemblage. The rolled assemblage shows limited knapping intensity and is biased towards the early stages of nodule reduction.

As stated above, it is generally impossible to distinguish between flakes generated during simple core reduction and those generated during initial handaxe manufacture, and the rolled assemblage might therefore relate to either of these activities. Given the nature of the fresh assemblage, one might argue that the rolled assemblage represents the 'missing' elements of the latter, being the initial phases of handaxe roughing-out from the eroded margins of the channel. However, given that the channel edge is presumed to have been just a few metres away, it seems improbable that the flakes would have arrived in the channel deposits in such an abraded state. It seems most likely that much of the rolled flake assemblage, as well as the radial core from older accumulations, derived from the Wissey Gravels.

Cores (Fig 5.59)

The excavation produced only three fresh cores: one from B-ii:03 and two from B-ii:01 (Table 5.35). Technologically, the fresh cores fit within the broad repertoire of Mousterian technology, although none show any evidence of the Levallois method or any other technological unity. They are best described as migrating platform cores exploited in a fairly *ad hoc* fashion to produce medium-large flakes (see Ashton 1998b and c, Ashton and McNabb 1996a and b, White and Ashton 2003). They consist of unrelated sequences of flaking from different platforms (core episodes), each involving single, parallel or alternate flaking techniques. Knapping proceeded in a varied and organic fashion, with the evolving morphology of the core, as well as the location

Table 5.35 Technology of the cores from Association B-ii

			core episodes						
artefact	no episodes	no. of removals	A (single)	B (parallel)	C (alternate)	D	% cortex	weight (gm)	block type
40242 (B-ii:03)	3	3	3	0	0	0	10	215	small orthogonal block with multiple thermally fractured surfaces and abraded cortex
40318 (Bii:01)	5	17	1	1	2	1	<5%	121	?
40594	2	10	0	1	1	0	50	1,061	large nodule with thick white cortex and a thermally fractured surface

Fig 5.59
Cores.

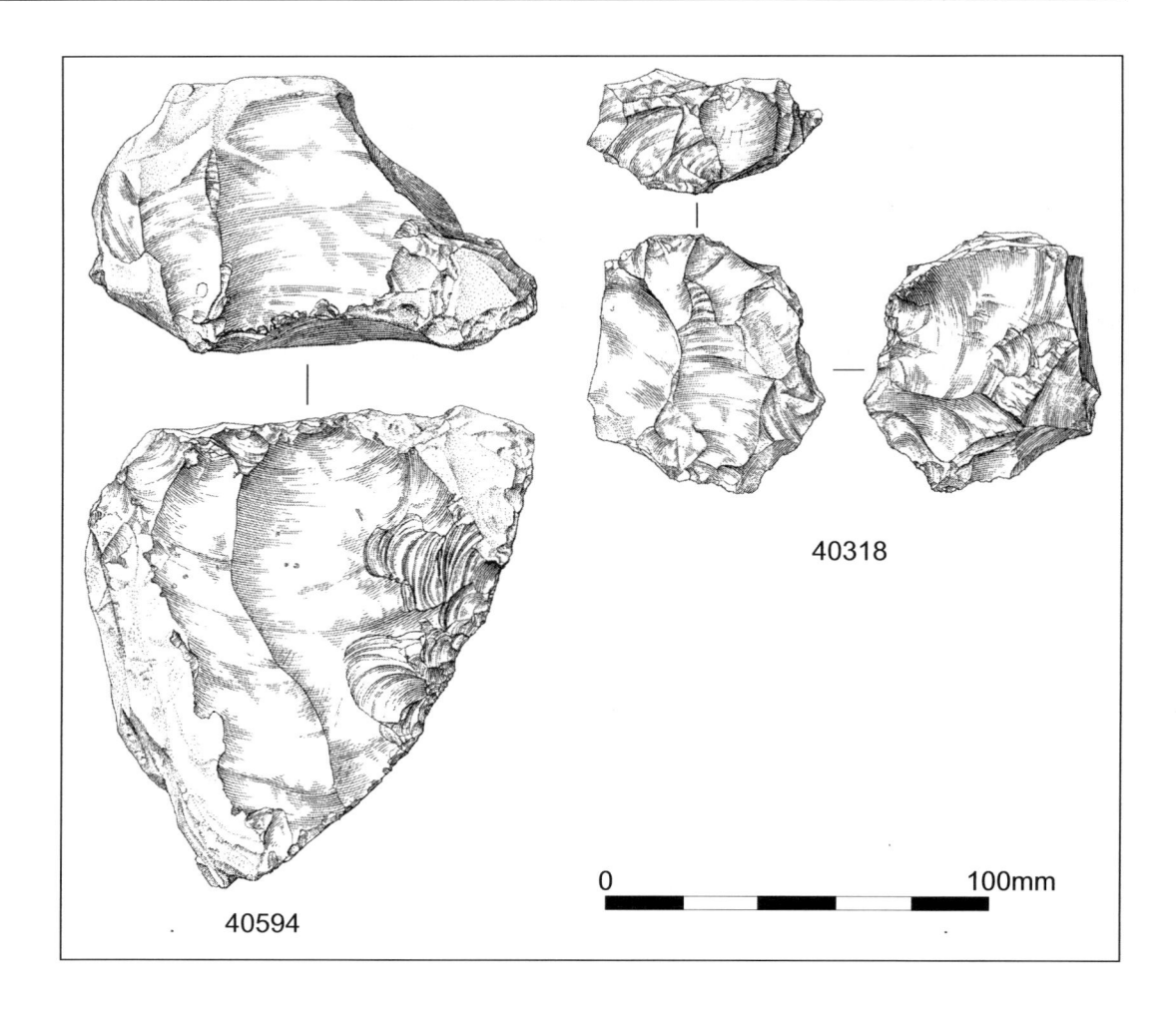

and character of each episode, dependant on the relatively uncontrolled effects of earlier flaking. The final shape of the piece is thus of little consequence, relating most to the shape of the starting block and the actual methods of flaking used.

The technological details of the three cores are presented in Table 5.35. Two (40242 and 40594; Fig 5.59) have seen only limited flaking and retain much of the form of the parent block. The third core (40318; Fig 5.59) is more intensively utilised, presumably to exhaustion, and has been worked in a more or less radial fashion. Attempts to further reduce the largest core (40594) are clearly evidenced by several strong incipient cones of percussion. Another interesting feature of this core is that the short parallel sequence (*see* Table 5.35) appears to be soft-hammer. It is located along an acute edge formed by a thermal fracture and the distal end of scars belonging to the separate alternate flaking sequence. Opposite this edge is a rounded cortical face, and the parallel 'retouch' might have been intended to transform this core into a heavy-duty chopper. It certainly shows moderate macroscopic edge damage in this area.

What is most remarkable about the Lynford cores is their very low numbers. Given that the flake analysis shows the dominant technological activity at Lynford to be handaxe reduction and modification, one might justifiably conclude that core reduction was relatively unimportant to Neanderthal needs there, as also seems to have been the case at the much older (MIS 13) site at Boxgrove (Roberts and Parfitt 1999). One should remember, however, that a number of handaxes and flake tools were manufactured on large flakes that must have come from the breaking-up of large nodules. Yet, of the three cores found at Lynford, only one (40594; *see* Fig 5.59) is large enough to have produced suitable blanks for even the smallest of the various flake implements. The implications of this are discussed below.

5 THE ARCHAEOLOGICAL ASSEMBLAGES OF ANIMALS AND LITHICS

Handaxes (Fig 5.60)

Forty-one complete or almost complete handaxes, six severely broken ones (four butt ends, one reworked fragment and a heavily reworked broken handaxe), and three handaxe roughouts were recovered from the excavation (Table 5.36).

As noted above, several of the handaxes have clearly been made on flakes. Some retain extensive evidence of the original ventral surface, and under Bordes' definition (1961) might be classed as partial bifaces. In addition, the site also yielded a number of flake tools with minimal bifacial working. After consultation with Roger Jacobi and Nick Ashton, these have been classified as scrapers. These pieces actually form something of a continuum of variation with the handaxes, and in the recent literature on neighbouring areas of northern France, very similar pieces have been termed partial bifaces or bifacial scrapers (eg Cliquet *et al* 2001a and b; Molines *et al* 2001; Turq 2001). Their significance is discussed below.

Some 95 per cent of the handaxes from the palaeochannel are in fresh, unpatinated condition and only two show signs of abrasion (these have been included in the present sample, as the level of abrasion is extremely minor (Table 5.36). Those from B-ii:03 show a high incidence (61.5 per cent) of a characteristic black staining. This is also evident on three pieces from B-ii:01, probably indicating

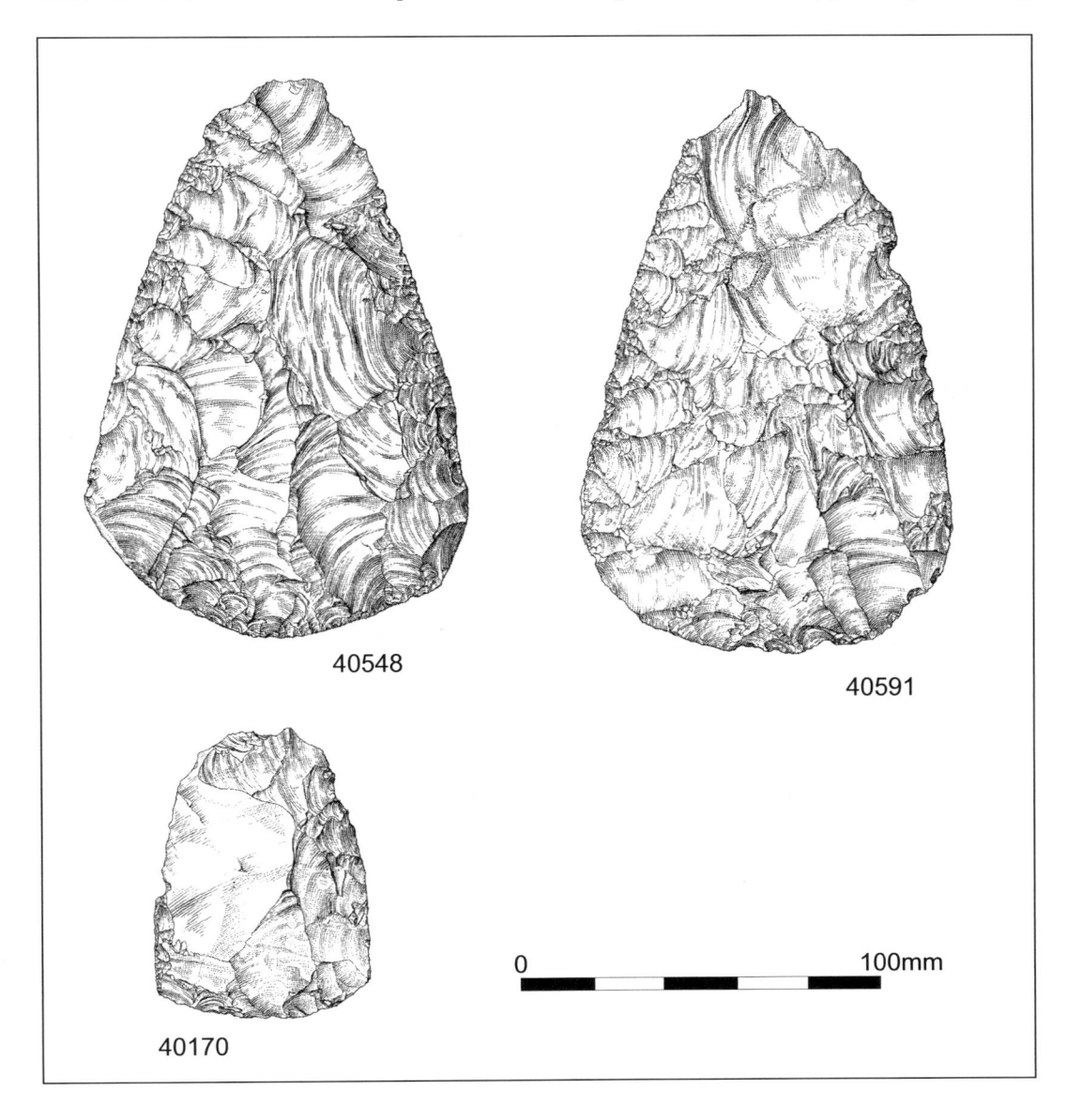

Fig 5.60
Handaxes: Bout coupé *(40170); Large pointed cordiforms (40548, 40591).*

Table 5.36 Condition of the complete handaxes from the main channel deposits

	B-ii:03 (n=26)		B-ii:01 (n=12)		B-ii combined (n=41)	
rolling						
fresh	25	(96.2)	11	(91.7%)	39	(95.1%)
slightly rolled	1	(3.8%)	1	(8.3%)	2	(4.9%)
rolled+	0				0	
edge damage						
minor	22	(84.6%)	9	(75%)	34	(82.9%)
moderate	4	(15.4%)	3	(25%)	7	(17.1%)
severe	0		0		0	
surface lustre						
matt	24	(92.3%)	11	(91.7%)	38	(92.7%)
slight sheen	2	(7.7%)	1	(8.3%)	3	(7.3%)
glossy	0		0		0	
patina						
none	26	(100%)	10	(83.3%)	39	(95.1%)
slight	0		2	(16.7%)	2	(4.9%)
moderate	0		0		0	
heavy	0		0		0	
staining						
none	9	(34.6%)	7	(58.3%)	18	(43.9%)
slight	1	(3.8%)	2	(16.7%)	3	(7.3%)
heavy	0		0		0	
black mineral	16	(61.5%)	3	(25%)	20	(48.8%)

vertical displacement from above. Two pieces were recovered during inspection of previously disturbed organic sediments, which, although not included in this report, almost certainly belong with the B-ii sample. Macroscopic edge damage is generally very minor.

The handaxes were analysed techno-typologically using the methods devised by Roe (1964, 1968b), White (1996, 1998) and Wymer (1968, 1985), and with reference to recent French work on the form and function of Middle Palaeolithic handaxes (eg Soressi and Hays 2003, Boëda 2001; Depaepe 2001). Wymer's typology is preferred to Bordes's (1961) to facilitate the comparison of Lynford with the data published in Wymer's magisterial surveys of British Lower and Middle Palaeolithic assemblages (Wymer 1968, 1985, 1999).

Typology

Typologically, the majority (85 per cent) of the handaxes from the Association B-ii are cordiform, ovate and subtriangular (Tables 5.37 and 5.38), including a number of flat-butted cordiforms and/or 'true' *bout coupés* (eg 40170; *see* Fig 5.60) (Wymer Type N, see Tyldesley 1987). The latter type has been argued to be a characteristic of the Late British Middle Palaeolithic, representing a distinctive form associated with the Neanderthal recolonisation of Britain during the Middle Devensian (White and Jacobi 2002), an assertion that fits well with the proposed dates for the Lynford assemblage (chapter 2). Other types are present in very limited numbers, including two crude hard-hammer examples, two small irregular pieces and an elongated point. One has been

Table 5.37 Typology of all complete handaxes, by stratigraphical grouping

	C	B-iii	B-ii:04	B-ii:03	B-ii:02	B-ii:01	disturbed palaeochannel	total
type D (crude, hard-hammer)				2				2
type E (small, irregular)				1		1		2
type F (pointed)						1	1	2
type G (sub-cordate)	1		1	8	2	1		13
type H (cleaver)				1				1
type J (cordiform)				1	3			4
type K, including JK (ovate)			1	10	4	2		17
type N (flat butted cordiform)		1		3	1	1	1	7

Table 5.38 Metrical and typological data for complete handaxes from Association B-ii

	L	W	Th	L1	B1	B2	T1	T2	Wymer type	Roe type
B-ii:04										
303	118.4	83.2	33.1	45.0	56.5	78.8	16.8	26.5	JK e/v	ovate
307	94.5	72.7	26.0	38.9	54.7	67.5	17.0	26.1	G	ovate
B-ii:03										
015	129.3	94.4	24.6	58.3	69.5	84.4	16.2	24.7	K e/v	ovate
054	112.6	77.8	22.7	46.4	49.0	66.2	11.2	22.7	G	ovate
101	70.6	48.4	23.4	28.0	29.3	44.3	15.6	19.2	E	ovate
180	77.3	60.5	15.7	30.1	43.5	59.3	13.3	14.0	K e/v	ovate
182	103.0	76.9	27.3	24.2	55.2	71.3	12.0	19.2	JK e/v	point
218	116.7	82.7	32.2	32.6	53.3	76.5	18.8	32.3	G	point
219	79.0	65.8	17.4	19.0	35.7	53.0	6.3	16.4	G	point
223	77.7	67.2	15.0	23.0	31.7	56.0	8.6	14.2	J e/v	point
265	125.0	67.3	50.8	48.0	57.7	58.1	16.4	45.8	D	ovate
288	76.4	61.1	19.0	30.0	48.1	54.9	11.0	20.8	K e/v	ovate
290	81.3	68.8	17.7	16.5	44.0	66.7	15.2	15.8	N e/v	point
295	97.7	63.2	22.6	26.5	36.2	62.1	11.0	25.1	J e/v	point
309	93.9	76.6	27.8	34.3	52.4	65.9	15.7	26.5	G	ovate
311	69.7	49.7	21.0	29.0	39.2	42.3	8.7	12.0	K e/v	ovate
353	120.0	83.6	24.5	43.0	62.0	77.7	15.1	22.2	K e/vi	ovate
354	184.3	114.3	30.5	72.0	88.2	106.0	16.2	29.2	K e/v	ovate
416	146.5	95.6	26.0	53.1	64.3	87.7	19.2	21.8	K e/v	ovate
499	84.8	65.3	22.1	26.0	35.1	64.2	12.3	22.0	G	point
509	77.0	66.5	26.8	24.0	25.5	54.7	62.8	14.8	GK e/v	point
523	105.5	80.2	27.3	40.0	59.0	72.7	12.5	20.0	N e/vi	ovate
541	101.0	65.3	29.3	42.8	45.9	51.4	15.2	27.5	G	ovate
544	71.0	52.4	17.8	35.8	42.0	39.8	10.2	13.8	K e/v	ovate
556	93.1	72.8	27.8	57.7	64.2	64.8	13.6	23.5	HK e/v	cleaver
558	90.0	64.3	27.3	32.0	41.2	60.3	13.8	27.3	G	ovate
563	65.6	45.0	20.5	31.0	33.0	41.5	12.7	13.4	K e/v	ovate
564	92.2	70.0	28.7	40.0	58.1	65.7	17.6	26.1	N e/v	ovate
B-ii:02										
170	82.3	59.2	17.9	12.8	45.0	58.8	13.5	15.5	N e/v	point
B-ii:01										
195	126.9	83.0	26.5	44.9	56.2	80.7	15.0	23.5	JK e/v	ovate
199	80.5	61.9	24.8	25.8	40.5	58.5	127.0	18.8	G	point
245	95.8	67.5	25.5	34.8	41.0	61.0	16.1	23.0	J e/v	ovate
297	81.1	57.5	23.8	29.3	41.8	48.2	10.9	20.6	G	ovate
328	116.8	87.7	27.7	36.8	59.2	83.8	14.0	26.8	N e/v	point
412	109.5	84.0	26.2	48.7	67.3	75.8	14.8	23.5	K e/v	ovate
496	113.2	94.8	25.0	43.3	65.5	88.7	17.8	24.8	JK e/v	ovate
532	98.3	63.5	21.5	21.7	37.5	60.5	11.7	21.5	F b/i	point
545	52.4	39.4	22.5	9.0	27.8	39.5	13.2	22.2	E	point
548	153.0	105.4	24.0	38.0	57.1	101.8	13.5	23.8	J e/vi	point
550	141.0	94.7	26.1	50.0	64.2	90.5	16.5	22.0	JK e/v	ovate
591	158.0	102.4	27.5	50.5	58.5	101.7	17.0	23.3	J e/vi	point
disturbed palaeochannel deposits										
016	146.0	108.0	31.3	51.7	89.0	101.0	13.1	32.0	K e/v	ovate
017	136.2	102.7	28.2	32.1	70.0	95.8	17.3	23.0	N e/vi	point
018	100.0	60.1	21.0	26.1	27.0	56.3	10.7	17.4	F a/i	point
019	85.4	62.0	17.0	35.2	46.1	61.8	14.0	12.2	K e/v	ovate
444	96.4	74.0	28.7	33.8	48.9	66.5	15.3	22.0	G	ovate

classified as a cleaver, although the tip of this handaxe is damaged, possibly through use, and it is largely this that produces the transverse cleaver-type edge.

Metrical data, including shape indices

Basic measurements of the complete handaxes are given in Table 5.38, with summary data presented in Table 5.39. These data show that

Table 5.39 Summary metrical data for excavated complete handaxes from B-ii

		B-ii:03	B-ii:01	all B-ii
length	mean	97.7 ±27.3	110.5 ±31.4	101.5 ±28.1
	range	65.6–184.3	52.4–158	52.4–184.3
width	mean	70.6 ±15.5	78.5 ±20.3	73.0 ±16.8
	range	45–114.5	39.4–105.4	39.4–114.5
thickness	mean	24.8 ±7.1	25.1 ±1.9	25.0 ±6
	range	15–50.8	21.5–27.7	15–50.8
elongation (B/L)	mean	0.734 ±0.079	0.717 ±0.059	0.729 ±0.071
refinement (Th/B)	mean	0.360 ±0.108	0.340 ±0.092	0.354 ±0.099
edge shape (B1/B2)	mean	0.784 ±0.132	0.702 ±0.098	0.759 ±0.123
profile shape (T1/T2)	mean	0.640 ±0.164	0.633 ±0.082	0.643 ±0.141

slight differences exist between the handaxes from Group B-ii:01 and those from B-ii:03. However, with the exception of B1/B2, these differences are statistically insignificant, justifying the conclusion drawn from the refits and staining that a single assemblage is present, but one that nevertheless represents a palimpsest that built up over several visits to the site. It must be noted, though, that the small sample size for B-ii:01 render these comparisons weaker than would be ideal, illustrated by the fact that simply omitting the two large pointed cordiforms (40548 and 40591; Fig 5.60) from the B-ii:01 sample eliminates the difference in the B1/B2 index.

Variation in size is considerable, with lengths ranging from 52.4mm to 184.3mm, and widths from 39.4mm to 114.5mm (see Table 5.39). Indeed, many of the handaxes are larger than one might expect from traditional descriptions of Middle Palaeolithic handaxes from the classic region of south-west France, which are generally characterised as being small (eg Mellars 1996). There is also a near-perfect allometric relationship between length and width ($r = 0.93$, $R2 = 0.85$, $p = 0$), indicating that shape was adjusted for size to maintain the necessary weight, balance and prehensive qualities of the implement (Gowlett and Crompton 1994; Fig 5.61). As this seems to be a feature of handaxes from at least one million years ago onwards, these relationships were probably tacitly worked out 'in hand' during manufacture, relating to the biomechanics of the human body, rather than being a deliberately imposed formula. Thickness is less variable, with all but one handaxe (an outlier made on a cobble with a thick butt) being less than 33mm, and 74 per cent of them measuring between 20mm and 30mm in thickness.

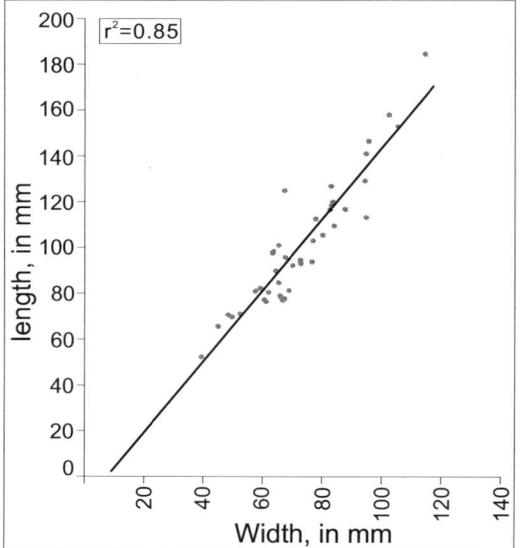

The other values on the summary table are indices designed to express various elements of handaxe shape (Roe 1964, 1968b). These show that the 'average' Lynford handaxe is broad and highly refined, with a moderately lenticular profile and rounder/squarer edge shape. This average type is of course an abstraction, but when the data are plotted on tripartite-shape diagrams to examine the range of variation within the assemblage, the Lynford handaxes do form a tight group (Fig 5.62a-i). Some are typologically and technologically so similar that one is tempted to infer that they are the work of the same hand.

Fig 5.61
Allometric length:width relationship for handaxes from B-ii.

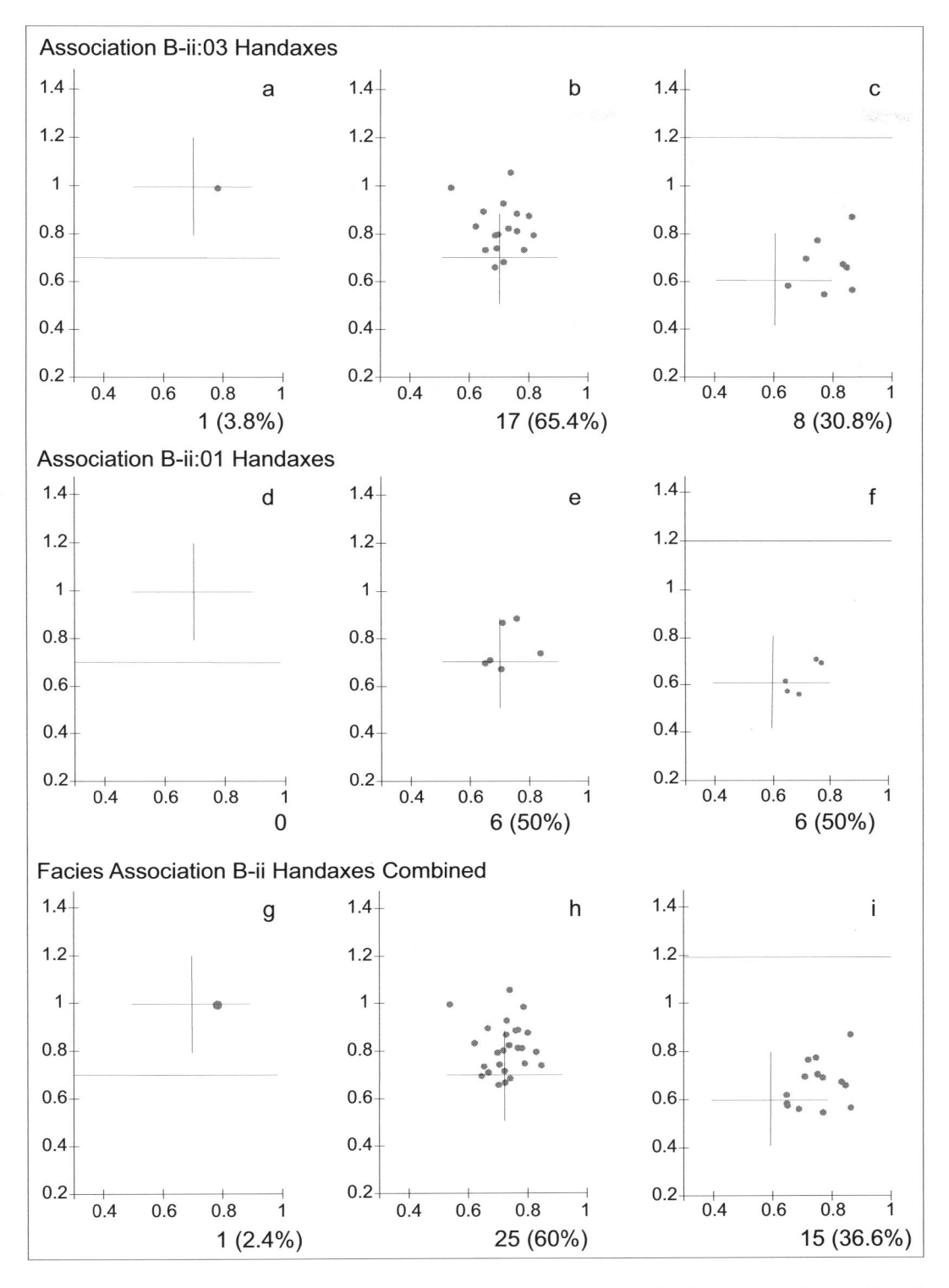

Fig 5.62
Tripartite Diagrams for the Lynford handaxes: (a) Association B-ii:03 Handaxes 1 (3.8%); (b) Association B-ii:03 Handaxes 17 (65.4%); (c) Association B-ii:03 Handaxes 8 (30.8%); (d) Association B-ii:01 Handaxes 0; (e) Association B-ii:01 Handaxes 6 (50%); (f) Association B-ii:01 Handaxes 6 (50%); (g) Facies Association B-ii Handaxes combined 1 (2.4%); (h) Facies Association B-ii Handaxes combined 25 (60%); (i) Facies Association B-ii Handaxes combined 15 (36.6%).

Taken as a single assemblage, the Lynford handaxes are dominated by metrically defined ovate types, with 60 per cent showing this form. Individually B-ii:03 is still dominated by ovates, showing 65.4 per cent ovates, but B-ii:01 is non-committed, with 50 per cent ovates and 50 per cent points. The latter is again considered to be due to sample size, and many of those pieces classed as metrical points are in fact very well-made cordiforms on which the position of maximum width relative to length just happens to be lower than on others of the same type.

Notably, the handaxes cluster in terms of edge shape and elongation, a pattern that transcends the point-ovate divide. While 36.6 per cent of the handaxes are metrically pointed, an examination of Roe's shape key diagram (*see* Fig 5.62) shows that these generally fall into the rounder/squarer sector, being mostly cordiform or pointed ovates. Similarly, the ovates cluster into the rounder and less elongated quadrant of the diagram. Comparison of this diagram with those published by Roe (1968b) shows that Lynford has a similar range of forms to those seen in the two Middle Palaeolithic sites in his sample – Oldbury Rock Shelter in Kent (which is admittedly a very mixed and confused sample; see Cook and Jacobi 1998) and Great Pan Farm on the Isle of Wight. In general, the Lower Palaeolithic sites, regardless of sample size, show far greater variation between and within samples (see Roe 1968b, 33–53), perhaps indicating that Middle Palaeolithic handaxes exhibit greater standardisation than their Lower Palaeolithic counterparts at both the site and regional levels (compare Mellars 1996, White and Jacobi 2002).

Technology
The majority of the handaxes from the B-ii assemblage are well-worked, refined pieces showing high levels of symmetry (Table 5.40). At least 13 have been manufactured on flakes, three on river cobbles and one on a thin plaquette of tabular flint; the remaining 24 bear insufficient evidence to determine the original blank type.

As a group, the handaxes show a strong technological unity. In terms of basic knapping patterns 31 (75.6 per cent) show that at least the finishing stage was essentially hierarchically organised (Boëda *et al* 1990), the negative flake scars demonstrating that the handaxes had been completely or almost completely finished on one side before being flipped over and worked on the other. In most cases, the ventral or flatter surface was worked first, before being used as a platform to work the dorsal or more convex surface. However, the prevalence of this pattern is somewhat exaggerated by the high incidence of edge retouch (see below), which tends to be on the more convex surface. Six show a different pattern, having been worked along one margin on one face before being flipped over and worked on the opposite margin on the other face (alternate edge working). One piece is completely unifacial and the remainder show no strong overall pattern, the knapper apparently responding to events as they unfolded.

The majority of the handaxes are completely or almost completely bifacial (those identified as being made on flakes obviously retaining part of a relict ventral surface) and very well worked (but see bifacial pieces below). Only five handaxes deviate far from the pattern (40018, 40265, 40416, 40541 and 40545; Figs 5.63 and 5.64). Three of these have been manufactured on cobbles or pebbles, the forms of which have clearly been a major consideration in the fashioning of the final tools; the other is a crude piece made on a thermally affected blank. The most extreme example is 40416, a unifacial ovate handaxe with absolutely no ventral working. It is classed as a handaxe rather than a scraper because it shows no evidence of scraper retouch, but rather intensive dorsal thinning and shaping. Donahue and Evans (chapter 5) identified tentative meat and hide polish on this piece, suggesting that it also served as a handaxe.

Even handaxes produced on flakes have been subject to a high level of thinning and shaping, as demonstrated by the summary technological data presented in Table 5.41. The minimum number of flakes scars per handaxe is high, with 80.4 per cent showing more than 40 visible scars. Sixty-five per cent show working around the entire circumference, and only five pieces are entirely unworked at the butt end (three of these are on cobbles, one on a flake, and the other has a naturally fractured, yet sharp, butt). The handaxes with partial working to the butt tend to be on flakes (8 of the 11), with the limited knapping in this area simply geared towards reducing the bulb and striking platform of the original blank. Concomitantly, cortex retention is very low, with 24 (58.5 per cent) showing no residual cortex and only seven (17 per cent) having more than 10 per

Table 5.40 Results of two-tailed Student's t-test on selected metrical indices of handaxes from B-ii:01 and B-ii:03

index	DF	t-statistic	p=
B/L	36	0.691	0.49
Th/B	36	0.559	0.58
B1/B2	36	1.930	0.06
T1/T2	36	0.126	0.90

cent cortex. Furthermore, with the exceptions of those made on cobbles and a flake handaxe with a rind of cortex around the entire circumference, residual cortex is more or less restricted to isolated patches on the faces, or close to the butt. This intensive working around the entire circumference is directly reflected in the number of pieces with all-round sharp edges (65.9 per cent). Those showing only partial cutting edges include the three pieces on cobbles mentioned above and handaxes on flakes with partial butt working, the blunt area being adjacent to the original striking platform.

These data allow us to infer that the Lynford handaxes were manufactured in a process of intensive, uncompromised knapping of large flakes and nodules. The overall morphology of all but a handful conformed not to any external restrictions, but to the choices made by the Neanderthal makers. So, even though the Lynford assemblage was, in all probability, largely made on flint from a gravel source, the careful selection of blanks from exposures found in the wider landscape has transcended the type of restrictions that the use of essentially immediate sources seem to have imposed during the Lower Palaeolithic (compare White 1998).

Other techno-functional features provide further insights into the organisation of

Fig 5.63
Handaxes 40018, 400265, 40416 and 40541.

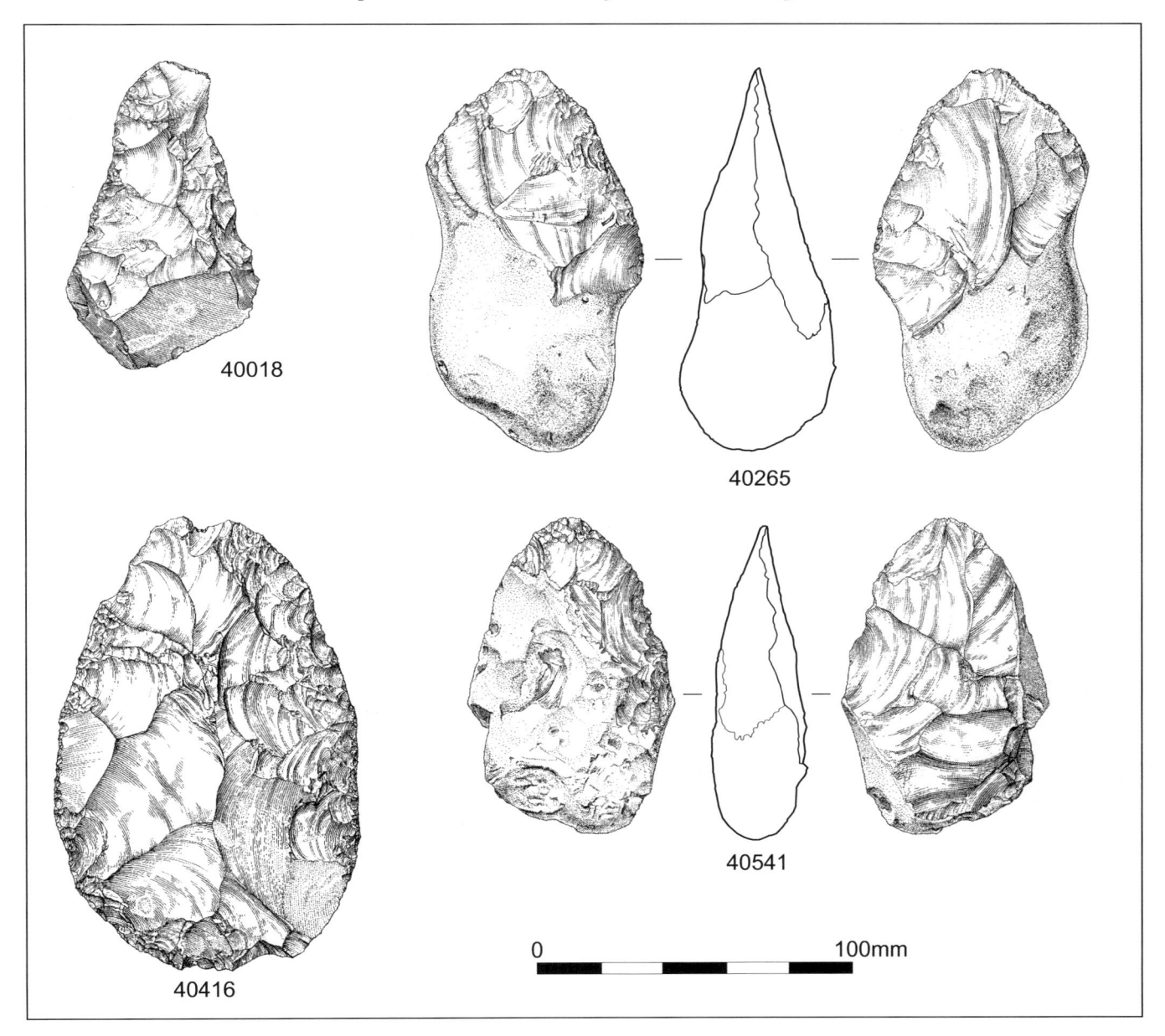

Fig 5.64
Handaxes 40016, 40354 and 40383.

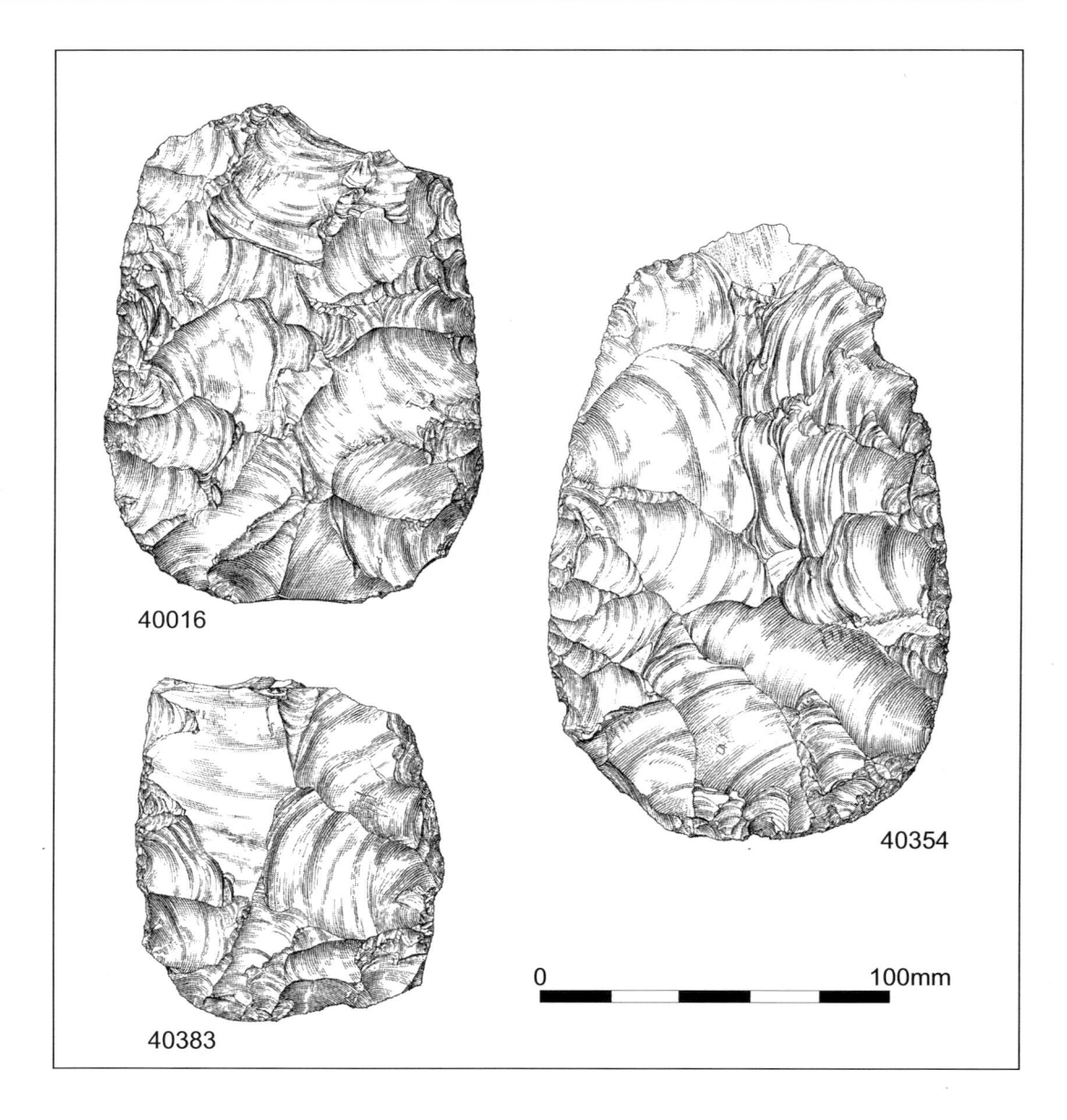

technology and behaviour at the site. At least 19 complete handaxes and four of the more severely damaged handaxes show varying levels of macroscopic tip damage (some of which could be post-depositional – see Donahue and Evans, this chapter – but much of which is interpreted here to be use-related). This generally takes the form of snaps rather than crushing, and in several cases is quite severe, with evidence of several large snaps. The large ovate 40016 (*see* Fig 5.64) shows two snaps ~40–50mm long, which originate in opposite directions and which were produced either by a twisting motion or by repeated levering back and forth; another example of the same type of damage can be seen on the morphologically similar ovate handaxe 40354 (*see* Fig 5.64). The snapping on the broken handaxe 40383 (*see* Fig 5.64) is even more severe, and it is estimated that a full third of the object is missing. The presence of a refitting fragment separated from the handaxe by 100mm horizontally and 760mm vertically clearly shows that the damage is not post-depositional and occurred in the context of use at the site. This recurrent pattern of breakage suggests that one of the major uses to which the handaxes were being put involved a levering motion, the tip being in active contact with whatever was being prised apart. In two cases the break surface shows evidence of fine regular 'retouch', which might indicate that the tip spalled as it

Table 5.41 Selected attributes of complete handaxes from B-ii:01, B-ii:03 and B-ii combined

	Association B-ii:03 (n=26)		Group 33 (n=12)		all palaeochannel (n=41)	
cortex %						
mean		6.15%		4.17%		5.24%
mode		0%		0%		0%
0%	16	(61.5%)	6	(50%)	24	(58.5%)
<5	5	(19.2%)	4	(33.3%)	10	(24.4%)
~10%	1	(3.8%)	1	(8.3%)	2	(4.9%)
~20%	2	(7.7%)	1	(8.3%)	3	(7.3%)
~30%	1	(3.8%)	0		1	(2.4%)
~40%	0		0		0	
50%+	1	(3.8%)	0		1	(2.4%)
cortex position						
butt	7	(26.9%)	5	(41.7%)	12	(29.3%)
isolated on face	1	(3.8%)	1	(8.3%)	3	(7.3%)
lateral margin	1	(3.8%)	0		1	(2.4%)
combination	1	(3.8%)	0		1	(2.4%)
none	16	(61.5%)	6	(50%)	24	(58.5%)
butt working						
full	16	(61.5%)	8	(66.7%)	26	(63.4%)
partial	7	(26.9%)	3	(25%)	11	(26.8%)
unworked	3	(11.5%)	1	(8.3%)	4	(9.8%)
edge position						
all round	16	(61.5%)	9	(75%)	27	(65.9%)
dull butt sharp tip and margins	6	(23.1%)	1	(8.3%)	8	(19.5%)
cortex/meplat on one butt margin	2	(7.7%)	1	(8.3%)	3	(7.3%)
tip only	2	(7.7%)	1	(8.3%)	3	(7.3%)
blank type						
flake	6	(23.1%)	4	(33.3%)	13	(31.7%)
cobble/pebble	2	(7.7%)	1	(8.3%)	3	(7.3%)
plaquette	1	(3.8%)	0		1	(2.4%)
indeterminate	17	(65.4%)	7	(58.3%)	24	(58.5%)
scar count						
mean	54		67		57	
10–19	1	(3.8%)	1	(8.3%)	2	(4.9%)
20–29	2	(7.7%)	0		2	(4.9%)
30–39	2	(7.7%)	1	(8.3%)	4	(9.8%)
40–49	7	(26.9%)	1	(8.3%)	9	(22%)
50–59	5	(19.2%)	0		6	(14.6%)
60–69	5	(19.2%)	3	(25%)	8	(19.5%)
70–79	1	(3.8%)	2	(16.7%)	3	(7.3%)
80–89	2	(7.7%)	2	(16.7%)	4	(9.8%)
90–99	1	(3.8%)	1	(8.3%)	2	(4.9%)
100+	0		1	(8.3%)	1	(2.4%)
tranchet tip						
present	5	(19.2%)	4	(33.3%)	9	(22%)
absent	21	(80.8%)	8	(66.7%)	32	(78%)
scraper-type retouch						
present	12	(46.2%)	7	(58.3%)	19	(46.3%)
absent	14	(53.8%)	5	(41.7%)	22	(53.7%)

broke, or could alternatively represent an attempt by the user to repair the break and make the edge thicker and more robust.

Nine handaxes also show a tranchet removal at the tip, and the flake sample contains 13 pieces interpreted as tranchet flakes or 'long resharpening flakes' (compare Callow and Cornford 1986). Given the levels of breakage and reworking that apparently took place at Lynford, and the absence of complete reduction episodes, these probably represent the resharpening of broken or blunted tips rather than the final phase of manufacture.

Other evidence for repair or recycling is widespread. The small ovate handaxe 40544 (made on a flint plaquette) has a flat oval area along one margin formed by a break surface, and the 'finished' piece is the recycled butt of a larger handaxe that either end-shocked during manufacture or lost its tip during use. Following this, a series of short hard-hammer flakes have been removed using the break surface as a platform, reshaping the piece and converting one of the original lateral margins into a new tip; the orientation of the handaxe was thus rotated around 90°. In an almost identical case, handaxe 40019 (*see* Fig 5.65) shows semi-invasive scaly retouch along the entirety of one edge; this again appears to be the butt of a larger handaxe that has been reworked following a break. Similarly, the asymmetrical broken handaxe 40531, which is somewhat 'micoquian' in form, appears to have taken on this shape only after extensive reworking to one edge following the loss of its tip.

The most extreme example of recycling is the broken handaxe 40481 (Fig 5.65). This was originally a well-made ovate or cordiform handaxe over 127mm long, which at some point in its history lost its tip. The treatment of the piece subsequent to this event suggests that it occurred at the site in the context of use. Following the loss of the tip, the break surface was used as a platform for the removal of two blade-like, hard-hammer flakes directed along the entire length of the lateral margins, completely removing the sharp edges and leaving two flat surfaces in their place. Although

Fig 5.65
Handaxes 40383, 40019, 40481, 40523 and 40100.

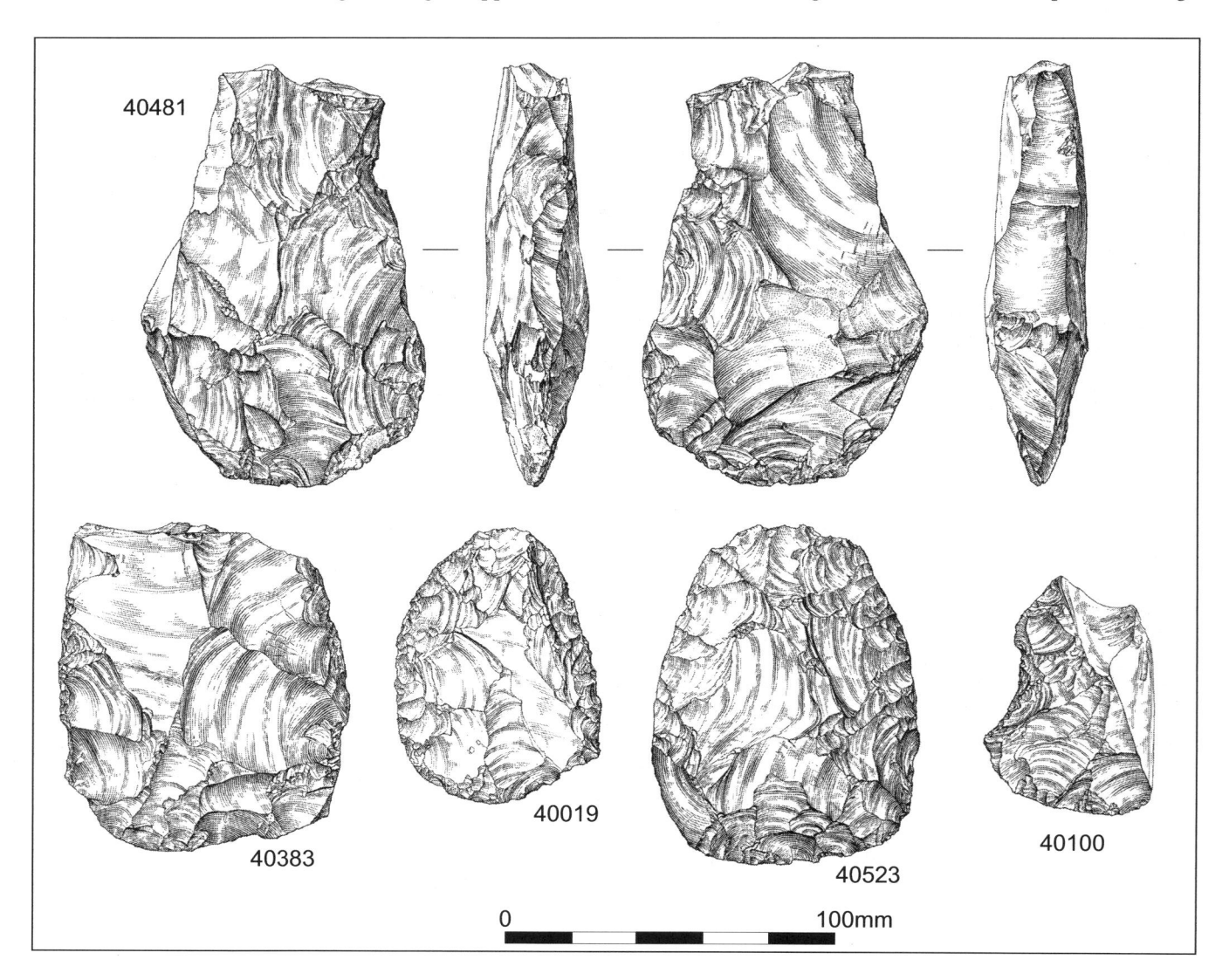

not in the present collection, these flakes would have resembled crested blades. A further blade-like removal, which hinged and failed to travel the length of the piece, has then been detached from one side. Finally, a squat hard-hammer flake has been removed from one of the now flat edges, forming a notch. The presence of a conjoinable flake (the third described above) shows that at least part of this sequence of events happened within the Lynford palaeochannel. It is difficult to interpret the significance of these actions. It might represent a failed attempt to resharpen the handaxe following the loss of the tip, or the re-use of a broken handaxe as a core. A more emotive interpretation is that it was caused by wanton destruction, the result of an over-heated Neanderthal temper, and probably the first recorded case of 'flint-rage'.

Five complete handaxes also show evidence of notching to the edges similar to that described for 40481. Some of these might be the result of natural damage or use-damage, but the 30–40mm concavity (notch) seen on the edge of handaxe 40015, was certainly created by a deliberate hard-hammer blow. The refitting notch spall 40088 removed during this act was found separated from its parent handaxe by 2.72m horizontally and 240mm vertically.

Whether the blow was actually intended to form a notch or to more delicately modify the edge is debatable, but another instance (40100; see Fig 5.65) is far less equivocal. This is a fragment of a broken handaxe with a large retouched concavity ~50mm long, though it is impossible to tell whether this was done prior to the break or was an attempt to recycle the handaxe subsequently. In its final state it might be classed as a concave side-scraper.

In such a context it is particularly noteworthy that 20 of the complete handaxes show 'scraper-like' retouch to the edges (compare Depaepe 2001; Soressi and Hays 2003; see Table 5.42). This retouch can be continuous or discontinuous, on one or both margins (and sometimes also on the butt), and on one or both faces. The number of retouch zones ranges from 1 to 4, with the length of retouch varying from 40mm to 300mm, representing from 16 per cent up to 71 per cent of the total edge length (Fig 5.66). Unsurprisingly there is a strong correlation between handaxe size and retouch length ($r = 0.88$, $r2 = 0.77$, $p = 0$), but the percentage of retouch is more variable, suggesting that this procedure operated on a pragmatic basis depending on the need for edge modification or repair. Eight of those with retouch also show tranchet removals at the tip. Although Donahue and Evans (this chapter) identified severe micro-fracturing, usually 0.1–1mm in diameter, the retouch identified here is much larger, more regular and more directed than would be expected from post-depositional modification. The handaxes with retouch are also significantly larger than those without (two-tailed t-test, $df = 44$, $t = 2.59$, $p = 0.0$; Fig 5.67). This might indicate that some of the larger and better-made handaxes were curated items that saw several episodes of use and resharpening, both at Lynford and elsewhere. Such an interpretation would certainly help explain some aspects of the flake data, such as the paucity of primary flaking débitage and abundance of microdébitage.

Given the high incidence of recycling at Lynford, it is tempting to infer that this retouch represents resharpening, repair or edge modification rather than original edge finishing or regularisation. There is little to suggest that it was imposed to perfect the original symmetry. A number of handaxes also show what might be deliberate backing to the margins, some of which might be post-depositional damage, but much of which appears to exceed the size of the microfractures identified by Donahue and Evans (this chapter). In at least one case this 'backing' is found on the opposite margin to

Table 5.42 Retouch zones on excavated complete handaxes from B-ii (n=19)

number of retouch zones	count
1	4
2	6
3	4
4	5
distribution	
continuous	13
discontinuous	6
localisation	
one margins	5
two margins	14
one face	10
both faces	9
no. with associated tranchet blow	8
mean retouch length	157mm
mean edge length	317mm

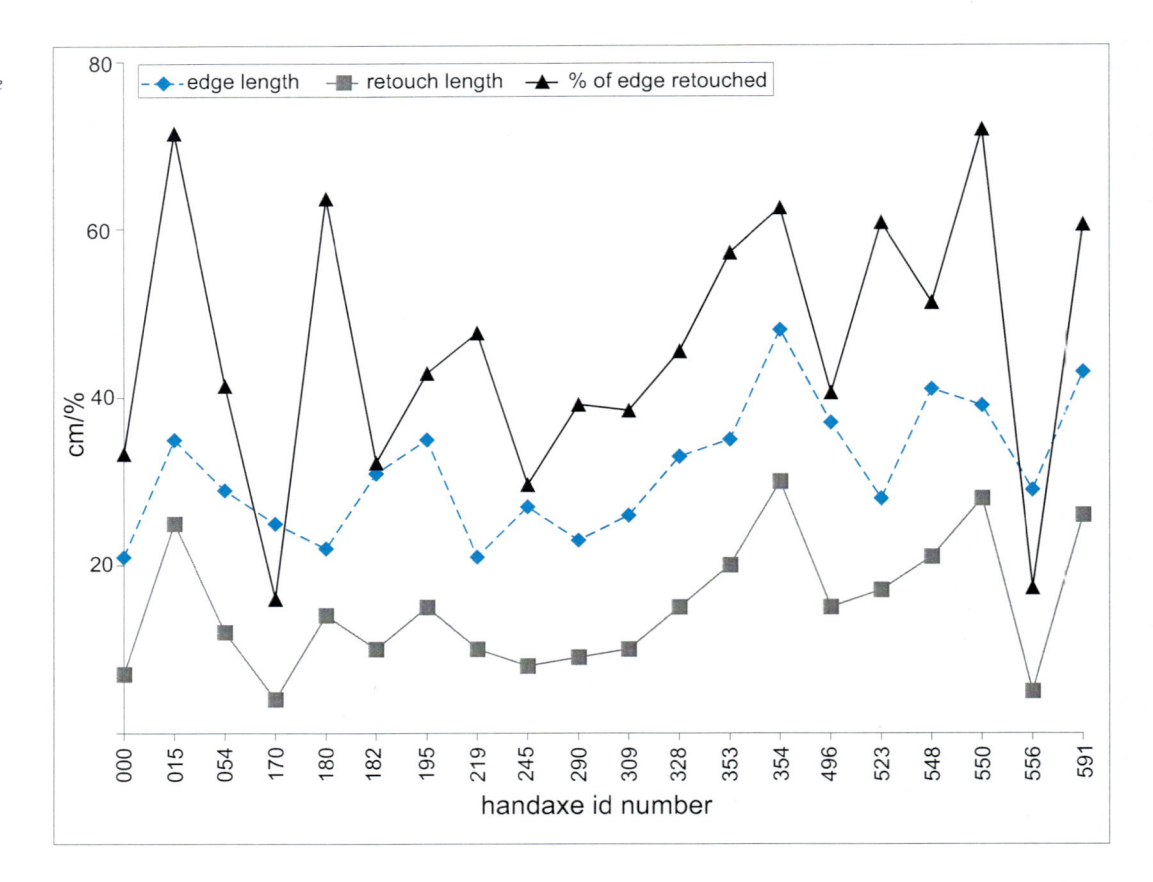

Fig 5.66
Edge length and percentage of retouch for handaxes with scraper-type retouch.

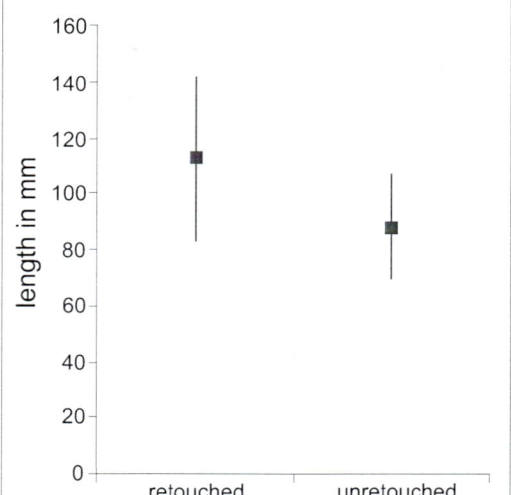

Fig 5.67
Mean maximum length of handaxes with and without scraper-type retouch, with 1 SD.

an area of scraper retouch. Other pieces retain areas of cortex or original striking platforms opposite sharp edges. This conforms to suggestions that Middle Palaeolithic handaxes possessed prehensive and active edges, the role and location of which might have changed during the life of the tool (Boëda 2001; Soressi and Hays 2003).

There is, however, limited evidence that some more complete handaxe manufacturing sequences were conducted or attempted on site. One of the minimally worked handaxes made on a cobble (40265; *see* Fig 5.63) has a refitting cortical hard-hammer flake, showing that it was made, used and abandoned in the immediate area. Three other pieces are interpreted as rough-outs. All of these are on medium- to large-sized flakes, and two have been abandoned due to knapping errors or flaws; the other could conceivably be regarded as a crude handaxe or partial biface. Two very large flakes (~150mm) are interpreted as handaxe pre-forms. The most convincing of these has seen fewer than 15 removals, originating from both the ventral and dorsal surfaces (two of which appear to be soft-hammer) and was abandoned when the flaking exposed a large thermal flaw running through the entire length of the piece. There are three incipient cones of percussion immediately adjacent to the flaw, which might be an attempt by the knapper to break the piece before deciding to discard it.

Overall, the observed patterns conform to the widely accepted notion that Middle

Palaeolithic handaxes were highly flexible implements with vari-functional edges that formed tools and supports for other 'tools' such as scrapers and notches, and which were subject to extensive resharpening throughout an extended use-life (eg Boëda *et al* 1990; Turq 2000; Soressi and Hays 2003).

Flake tools (Fig 5.68 and 5.69)

Association B-ii produced 20 flake tools, comprising 17 scrapers, two notches and a hachoir (Tables 5.43 and 5.44). Notable by their absence are simple worked flakes (Ashton *et al* 1991), otherwise the most common flake tool of the British Lower Palaeolithic. All but two of the flake tools are complete, and all are in fresh unpatinated condition, although eight have the characteristic black coating associated with the organic deposits of B-ii:03.

Scrapers

Table 5.43 presents the typological classification of the Lynford scrapers. Eight different types are present, with convergent-convex

Fig 5.68
Flake tools: 40259 déjeté scraper; 40278 double convex scraper; 40410 convergent convex side scraper; 40470 double straight-convex side scraper; 40498 single convex side scraper; 40551 convergent convex side scraper.

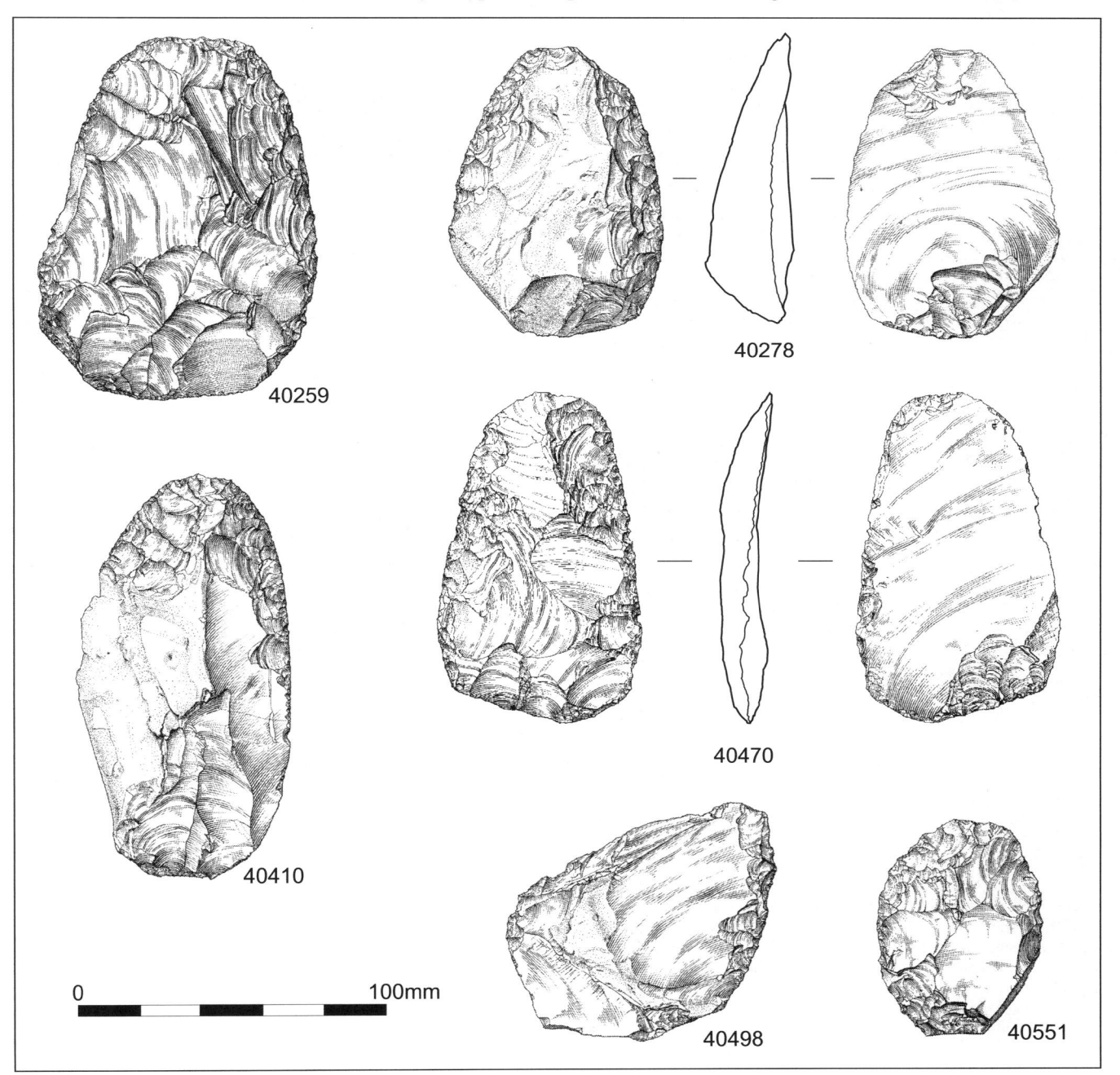

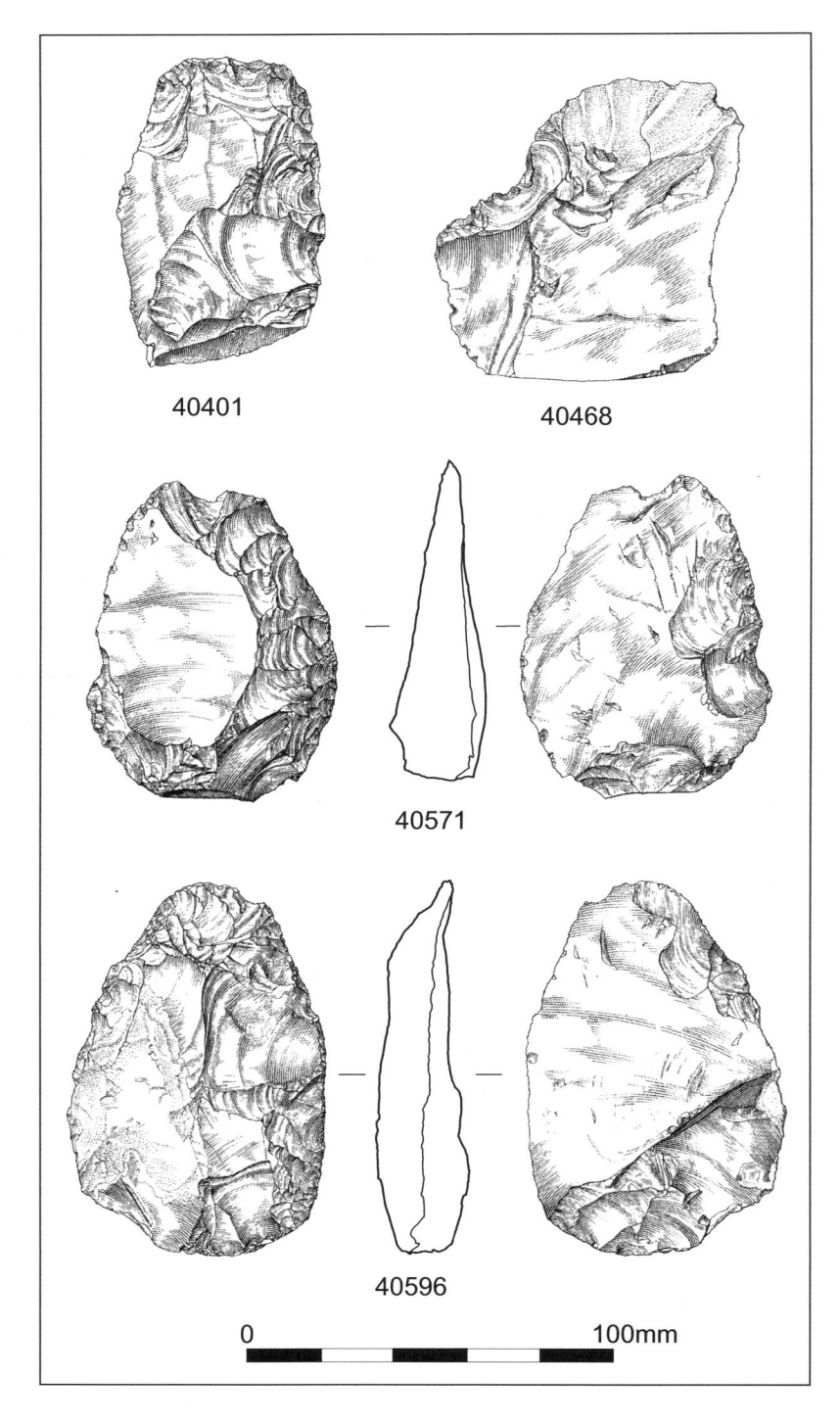

Fig 5.69

Flake tools: 40401 single convex side scraper; 40571 double scraper with alternative retouch; 40596 convergent convex side scraper; 40468 notch.

scrapers being the most common. Scraper length ranges from 64mm to 133.4mm, showing that flakes from the larger end of the size range had been preferentially selected (Table 5.45). Retouch tends to be situated along the longest or most convenient edge, and is mostly continuous in distribution (70 per cent), invasive or semi-invasive in extent (35 per cent and 47 per cent respectively), and scale subparallel to scaly in form. The edges are exclusively convex, although verging on being straight on two examples. One piece (40410; Fig 5.68) is of Quina type, showing steep, stepped retouch on the dorsal with some thinning to the ventral.

Table 5.43 Flake tools by stratigraphic group by context; numbers in parentheses are Bordes' (1961) types

facies	type	count
B-ii:04	convergent convex side-scraper (19)	1
B-ii:03	single convex side-scraper (10)	2
	double convex side-scraper (15)	1
	convergent convex side-scraper (19)	3
	déjeté scraper (21)	2
	side-scraper on the ventral face (25)	2
	side-scraper with thinned back (27)	1
	notch (42)	1
	hachoir (55)	1
B-ii:02	double straight-convex side-scraper (13)	1
B-ii:01	convergent convex side-scraper (19)	1
	déjeté scraper (21)	1
	side scraper on the ventral face (25)	1
	double side-scraper with alternate retouch (29)	1
	notch (42)	1
B-i:03	convergent convex side-scraper (19)	
	notch (42)	

Table 5.44 Summary of flake tools from B-ii; numbers in parentheses are Bordes' (1961) types

type	frequency
single convex side-scraper (10)	2
double straight-convex side scraper (13)	1
double convex side-scraper (15)	1
convergent convex side-scraper (19)	5
déjeté scraper (21)	3
side-scraper on the ventral face (25)	3
side-scraper with thinned back (27)	1
double side-scraper with alternate retouch (29)	1
notch (42)	2
hachoir (55)	1
total	20

Table 5.45 Summary metrical data for scrapers from Association B-ii

	mean and SD (mm)	range (mm)
length	92.4 ±18.1	64–133.4
width	68.2 ±11.5	47.5–90
thickness	22.1 ±5.6	14.8–35.6
retouch length	109.2 ±42.2	59.6–189

Notches

One of the notches (40468; *see* Fig 5.69) is a simple 'clactonian notch' with a single hard-hammer removal forming a concavity, the other (40525) is a retouched notch with fine parallel working to a 22mm concavity.

Hachoir

One flake tool has been classified as a hachoir. This is a flat rectilinear flake 86 × 68mm, showing irregular bifacial retouch to a straight distal end, with some irregular retouch to both faces of both margins.

A marked feature of the Lynford flake tools is the high frequency of working to both faces (Table 5.46), with 12 of the scrapers plus the hachoir showing some level of bifacial working. In eight cases this has been directed towards thinning or removing the butt, with further working occasionally found elsewhere on the ventral surface to regularise edges. Such modification might have served to facilitate hafting but in fact, rather than forming a discrete category, many of the Lynford scrapers seem to form a technological continuum with the handaxes from the site, from which they are separated rather arbitrarily by the intensity of bifacial working. In terms of shape and general morphology, most could actually be subsumed within the handaxe assemblage. Recent studies of Middle Palaeolithic biface assemblages in northern France have begun to emphasise a number of similarly blending categories: true bifaces, partial bifaces and bifacial scrapers (see papers in Cliquet 2001), with the artefacts from each class serving as either tools in themselves or as supports for other tools (ie the scraper edges and notches to handaxes described above). Depaepe (2001) has suggested that at a number of sites in the Vanne Valley, scrapers and tools with convergent edges compensated for the absence of handaxes.

Non-flint artefacts

A possible quartzite hammerstone (41021) was recovered from disturbed deposits prior to the excavation, but the only non-flint object recovered directly from B-ii is 40474, a block of coarse sandstone, predominantly quartz with some feldspar in a cemented siliceous matrix. This material occurs infrequently within the local gravels. The object measures 133 × 97 × 70mm, and has a roughly L-shaped profile. The flat surface of the longer limb of the object shows two shallow depressions, and a smooth U-shaped groove occurs between the two 'limbs'. Microscopic analysis has led to the conclusion that these features are anthropogenic (d'Errico and Dubreuil, this chapter), the groove being produced by a repetitive back-and-forth motion, possibly related to the polishing or sharpening of organic artefacts.

Behavioural inferences from refitting

As well as applications in site formation studies, refitting studies are also a powerful tool in understanding technological and wider behavioural practices (eg Roebroeks and Hennekens, 1990; de Loecker 1994; Conard and Adler 1997; Roebroeks *et al* 1997; Roberts and Parfitt 1999; L'homme and Connet 2001). The refits from Lynford have already been detailed in Table 5.25.

For present purposes it is important to note that the presence of technological and modification refits shows that the material found at Lynford was used and in some cases even manufactured there, in whole or in part. The horizontal and vertical distances between the refits are probably post-depositional, resulting from their mode of incorporation into the channel, rather than Neanderthals moving around in the water while using and (re)working artefacts. The absence of reduction sequences longer than two pieces limits their interpretative value in technological terms, but is important in other respects, as possibly reflecting the combined results of taphonomic and behavioural factors.

The following sections are aimed at synthesising the results of the lithic analysis, and will concentrate on two areas. First, Lynford is examined in terms of the settlement history of Britain in comparison with neighbouring areas of western Europe. Second, an attempt is made to distil the behavioural information provided by the stone tools, especially concentrating on the organisation of technology in the landscape in relation to resource availability, mobility and planning.

Table 5.46 Scrapers with butt removal/thinning, thinned backs or some level of bifacial working

acies	count	
Bii:03 (n=11)	8	(73%)
B-ii:02 (n=1)	1	(100%)
B-ii:01 (n=4)	3	(75%)
combined (n=17)	12	(70.5)

Settlement history and cultural signatures

The OSL dates on the organic sediments of B-ii suggest that the channel was infilled c 65,000–57,000 years ago (chapter 2). The Lynford assemblage therefore currently represents the earliest evidence for Neanderthal recolonisation of Britain, sometime towards the end of MIS 4 or the beginning of MIS 3 (compare Currant and Jacobi 2001, 2002; White and Jacobi 2002). This was a climatically unstable and relatively cold period, a 'failed interglacial' marked by dramatic fluctuations in temperature on millennial time-scales known as Dansgaard-Oescher events, but mild compared to the previous MIS 4 glacial (Van Andel and Davies 2003). Sea levels were depressed by up to 80m, leaving Britain as a westerly 'upland' peninsula of mainland Europe. Access would still have been restricted by the large river systems that flowed through the Channel and North Sea basins (see Pettitt 2008), but a terrestrial route from Europe remained open. Attempting to pinpoint the source of Neanderthal dispersal is an interesting exercise, but one fraught with difficulties, as while lithic technology and typology provide one means of doing this, chronological and spatial patterns are currently still too poorly defined to make many unqualified statements. Across Europe, many sites, and indeed regions, show a cyclical pattern, with different technological systems and tool types fluctuating over time and area in response to a number of potential social, environmental and economic factors (eg Geneste 1985; Rolland and Dibble 1990; Dibble and Rolland 1992; White and Pettitt 1995; Mellars 1996; Roebroeks *et al* 1988, 1997; Conard and Fischer 2000). The absence of Neanderthal remains also currently precludes the use of isotopic signatures (eg Richards *et al* 2008).

In a British context, Lynford is typologically and technologically similar to the only other significant middle Devensian open-air site, at Little Paxton in Cambridgeshire (Paterson and Tebbutt 1947), as well as to a number of other smaller assemblages and isolated finds. It also bears typological affinities to the assemblages from Middle Devensian caves sites at Kent's Cavern, Creswell Crags and Coygan Cave, among others. Assemblages of this type and period – defined archaeologically as the British Late Middle Palaeolithic (White and Jacobi 2002) – are generally characterised by industries with cordiform handaxes and a low Levallois index. *Bout coupé* and other flat-butted cordiforms form a small but important component at many of these sites, and are often found as isolated discards or as parts of very small assemblages. Two finds, from Little Cressingham and Saham Toney, deserve special mention. These mint-condition *bout coupé* handaxes were found on opposite sides of the Blackwater, a tributary of the Wissey, in deposits assigned to the Middle Devensian (Lawson 1978; Wymer 1985; Tyldesley 1987; White and Jacobi 2002). Typologically and technologically they are astonishingly similar to a number of the Lynford handaxes, and given they come from only 10km to the north-east, one cannot help but speculate that they represent the wider foraging behaviour of a related Neanderthal group in and around the Wissey Valley.

As for Lynford, the Middle Palaeolithic assemblages from these Devensian sites have been dated on radiometric, biostratigraphic and sedimentological grounds to between 60kyr and 34kyr, suggesting a probably intermittent Neanderthal presence throughout at least the warmer parts of early MIS3 (Campbell and Sampson 1971; Coulson 1990; Aldhouse Green *et al* 1995; Hedges *et al* 1996; White and Jacobi 2002; Jacobi *et al* 2006; Van Andel and Davies 2003). Despite new and intensive dating programmes (ie Jacobi *et al* 2006), the lack of stratigraphic sequences and the uncertainties involved in correlating radiocarbon determinations leaves us a long way from identifying the number and duration of Neanderthal occupations of Britain, which may have been very few and at times used only as a summer hunting ground (White 2006).

Throughout the rest of Europe, Lynford has closest affinities with localities in northern France normally assigned to the Mousterian of Acheulean Tradition (MTA), although a number of French authors (see Cliquet *et al* 2001b) have recently proposed that an MTA designation should be reserved only for those assemblages with triangular handaxes. Other assemblages containing cordiform handaxes, but lacking triangulates, are simply referred to as 'Mousterian facies with bifaces'. Many such sites exist close to the modern coastlines of Normandy and Brittany, including the important and recently re-investigated localities at Saint-Brice-sous-Rânes 'la Bruyére',

Saint Nichols-D'Attez 'la Madeleine', Le Bois-du-Rocher and Kervouster, which date to between MIS 5 and MIS 3, and which are dominated by a range of ovate/cordiform handaxes, partial bifaces and bifacial scrapers, along with a variable frequency of Levallois (Cliquet *et al* 2001a and b; Molines *et al* 2001; Locht and Antoine 2001; compare Bordes 1984). Lynford also shares features with the classic open-air and cave MTA sites of SW France, many of which also date to around MIS 3 (Mellars 1996). There are, however, certain typological differences in handaxe shape between Britain and France, with Lynford and other British sites containing *bout coupés*/flat butted cordiforms but lacking the exaggerated triangular forms seen in France (and vice versa). Such contrasts might show that local or regional socio-cultural significance does reside in the shape of some Late Middle Palaeolithic handaxes (White and Jacobi 2002).

Bifaces are also a key feature of central European Middle Palaeolithic sites of this period. During the last glacial, this area was host to several Middle Palaeolithic facies including the Micoquian/Keilmessergruppe, the Blattspitzengruppe and a range of more diverse biface assemblages (Bosinski 1967; Conard and Fischer 2000; Jöris 2006). These assemblage types seem to have a rather wide chronological range (Conard and Fisher 2000, fig 2) but all can be found within MIS 3. Indeed, almost the whole Neanderthal lithic repertoire, including Levallois, leafpoints, Micoquian bifaces and most other handaxe forms, are broadly contemporary within this period in central Europe. Moreover, although the Lynford handaxes are qualitatively different from Keilmesser (see Jöris 2006), one or two of the recycled pieces do approach the Micoquian type. This might lend some credibility to Richter's suggestion that Micoquian forms represent a more heavily reduced variant of other Mousterian tools (1997, cited in Conard and Fischer 2000). In contrast, neither Lynford nor any other British Late Middle Palaeolithic assemblage contains evidence of dedicated laminar technology, which is a feature of some last glacial sites in central Europe, such as Tönchesburg 2B (Conard 1992) and Wallertheim D (Conard and Adler 1997), as well as a number of other diachronous sites throughout France and Britain, for example the MIS 7–6 site at Crayford, Kent, the MIS 6 site at Pucheuil, Seine Maritime (Series B, Cliquet *et al* 2001b) and the MIS 5 site at Seclin (Tufrreau *et al* 1994).

It is also important to note that Lynford, like the rest of the British Late Middle Palaeolithic, exhibits a very low Levallois index. In fact, while assemblage composition is generally highly variable, there seems to be a chronologically meaningful negative correlation between Levallois technology and handaxes in the British Middle Palaeolithic. Sites dated to the Early Middle Palaeolithic (*c* 300–160ka) are generally dominated by Levallois technology, with unequivocally associated handaxes being rare or absent, while Late Middle Palaeolithic sites (after 67ka) are dominated by bifaces, with Levallois technology being rare or absent (White and Jacobi 2002; Ashton *et al* 2003; White *et al* 2006).

This binary division stands in contrast to the rest of Middle Palaeolithic Europe, where a temporally and geographically diverse range of technological signatures is found. The classic Mousterian region of south-west France famously shows chronological fluctuation in the frequency of Levallois products and various tool types throughout MIS 5–3 (Mellars 1996; Pettitt 2003), although Bordes (1972) did observe that the handaxe-rich MTA had a low Levallois index, although this is highly variable, while handaxes were rare in other variants. Yet in Germany handaxes seem to be absent prior to the advent of prepared core technology during the Saalian (MIS 8: compare Conard and Fischer 2000; Conard and Prindiville 2000), after which both elements are often found in association: for example at the MIS8 site at Markkleeberg (Baumann and Mania 1983) and the MIS3 site of Salzgitter-Lebenstedt (Gaudzinski and Roebroeks 2000). In northern France the picture is highly varied, with almost every conceivable permutation of handaxes and Levallois evident within the MIS 3 and earlier contexts, although the stratigraphy and dating of many sites must be refined before any meaningful patterning can be established (eg Antoine *et al* 1998; Depaepe 2001; Locht and Antoine 2001; Cliquet *et al* 2001b). Conversely, both elements are absent from many open-air sites, including Mauran and La Borde in France (Farizy and David 1992; Farizy *et al* 1994; Jaubert *et al* 1990) and Site J at Maastricht-Belvédère, The Netherlands (Roebroeks *et al* 1997). These sites are believed to date to an early part of the last glacial (?MIS 5a), a period during which Levallois dominates many assemblages in south-west France (Pettitt 2003). At Maastricht-Belvédère, the authors interpret this as an *ad hoc* response to an unplanned foraging opportunity.

Several workers have suggested that typological and technological contrasts in the Middle Palaeolithic relate to different mobility and raw material economising strategies. Roebroeks *et al* (1988, 1997) have argued that prepared cores and blanks, handaxes and other retouched forms were flexible technologies transported from place to place in anticipation of a future need for cutting edges, and that the items that were 'moved around' were different from those that 'stayed at home'. Similarly, Geneste (1985) showed that Levallois products, handaxes and Mousterian points were often associated with non-local raw materials, while Turq (2001) and Soressi and Hays (2003), among others, see Middle Palaeolithic handaxes as functionally fluid tools that metamorphosed in both form and purpose throughout their use-life as they were moved, albeit not necessarily very far, through the landscape. The British data do not contradict these suggestions.

In the British Early Middle Palaeolithic, we find a suite of highly prolific 'extraction' sites adjacent to abundant local raw materials at which Neanderthals manufactured and probably exported Levallois technologies; for example Bakers Hole (Smith 1911; Wenban-Smith 1995), Purfleet (Wymer 1985; White and Ashton 2003), Crayford (Spurrell 1880a, 1880b; Kennard 1944) and West Thurrock (Schreve *et al* 2006). These exist alongside a smaller number of 'episodic' sites (Turq 1988) some distance from raw-material sources, which contain small transported assemblages comprising a few Levallois cores and products, for example Stoke Tunnel/Maidenhall, Ipswich (Layard 1912, 1920; Wymer 1985) and Aveley, Essex (Schreve *et al* in prep). Critically, however, none of these sites contain many, if any, truly associated handaxes or evidence of handaxe manufacture (Scott 2006). In contrast, in the Late Middle Palaeolithic, what little evidence exists reveals no prolific manufacturing sites, the few sites and the much larger number of isolated discards rather conforming to the patterns expected of the residue from a transported technology. As well as highlighting complexity in landscape use and general organisational strategies, these patterns might also genuinely show large-scale chronocultural variation in the lithic repertoires of Neanderthals in Britain, with Levallois and handaxes representing different solutions used at different times to meet the need for a flexible, transportable technology.

As dating and our understanding of the context of human action improves, these technological and typological observations might ultimately aid us in mapping the increasingly complex cultural geography and behavioural repertoires of the Late Middle Palaeolithic in Europe (Gamble and Roebroeks 1999).

Neanderthal behaviour and the organisation of technology

The lithic assemblage was discarded around the margins of a low-energy abandoned channel situated in an open grassland landscape. Various proxies reveal a rich herbaceous vegetation, with patches of bare, disturbed and wet ground, small stands of dwarf birch or scrub, and areas of acid heath or bog (chapter 3). A cool climate with mean July temperatures of c 12°C and January/Feburary temperatures of c −10°C is revealed by the coleopteran fauna (Coope, chapter 3). Periods of low water level and possible stagnation are also evident (French, chapter 2; Keen, chapter 3).

Over 35,000 bones of large mammals were associated with the lithic artefacts, including at least 11 individual mammoths, along with reindeer, woolly rhinoceros, horses and bison (Schreve 2006, and this chapter). The presence of manufacturing refits and fragments conjoinable to broken and recycled tools demonstrates that Neanderthals were actually using, modifying and in some cases producing stone tools here, making the association between the animal bones and lithic artefacts more than coincidental. That the association is causal is supported by spiral fractures on horse and reindeer remains indicating that fresh bones were being broken open to extract marrow (Boismier *et al* 2003; Schreve 2006, and this chapter). No cutmarks were found on the mammoth bones, but this is perhaps not surprising given the size of these animals and the state of preservation of the bone surfaces. Nevertheless, the results of the faunal analysis, which shows that the meaty hind limbs are mostly absent, suggests that Neanderthals were at least exploiting some of the mammoth carcasses, even if is not possible to demonstrate how they procured them (Schreve 2006, and this chapter).

The geological resolution is insufficient to determine whether the main palaeochannel assemblage was deposited in one or many episodes, although strict contemporaneity (Conard and Adler 1997) between some objects can be demonstrated through refitting. The fact that vertical displacement has occurred throughout the palaeochannel deposits, with some conjoinable artefacts cutting across stratigraphical units, led to the conclusion that only a single assemblage should be recognised, but this does not mean that it was deposited in a single event. Indeed, it seems most unlikely that over 100kg of flint and dozens of animal carcasses would have been exploited in a single visit (compare Jaubert and Brugal 1990), suggesting that the site contains a palimpsest of several episodes. The amount of time-averaging involved could be weeks, months or decades.

However, the biggest obstacle to offering a definitive interpretation of Neanderthal behaviour at Lynford is not the establishment of the precise length of time involved in the site's formation – as the patterning in the lithic assemblage present is arguably clear enough to provide an indication of Neanderthal technological strategies – but the subsequent destruction of the wider channel setting and other potential taphonomic issues. Any interpretation can only be based on what happened directly adjacent to, or perhaps sometimes actually in the palaeochannel, and as usual we must work within the opportunities provided by excavation rather than speculate about what might or might not have occurred outside it. Nevertheless, some attempt at interpretation is desirable, and while acknowledging the problems associated with temporal resolution, sedimentation rates (see Roebroeks and Tuffreau 1999) and the unresolved taphonomic issues, the following account takes the optimist's approach to the interpretative potential of Lynford.

Stone tools and Neanderthal behaviour at Lynford

Lynford is most plausibly an ephemeral (Marks 1988) or episodic (Turq 1988) open-air location that Neanderthals visited on a number of occasions in the anticipation of gaining access to a range of animals by various means. It probably formed a focal point on the open mammoth steppe, where the combination of water and other resources attracted large herbivores, which in turn attracted Neanderthals and non-human carnivores. While never entirely predictable, the presence of prey or carcasses at such locations could be anticipated on an encounter basis.

The lithic industry Neanderthals employed there can be can be summarised as follows:

1. The tool assemblage is dominated by handaxes, partial bifaces and bifacial scrapers, but evidence of the Levallois method is absent.
2. The débitage is dominated by evidence of handaxe manufacture. However, there is a flake deficit and a lack of complete knapping signatures, with the débitage present being characterised by later-stage handaxe thinning and finishing, and a paucity of heavily cortical primary flakes.
3. Handaxe rejuvenation flakes are present and several of the handaxes show evidence of recycling or reworking in the form of edge modification and scraper retouch.
4. Cores are rare.

The cortex patterns can be explained at least in part by the fact that a third of the handaxes were made on flake blanks that would automatically produce fewer cortical flakes, both hard- and soft-hammer. Yet the overall assemblage is dominated by finer soft-hammer working from the final phases of biface reduction, with minimal evidence of the initial phases of flake-blank working. As stated above, even though the original flake blanks must have come from the breaking up of very large nodules, suitable cores are absent from the site. This might be explained in the following ways:

1. Core reduction and roughing-out (possibly using local flints) took place on the eroded and quarried-away banks of the channel outside the excavated area. This would also help explain the paucity of primary flaking débitage and low flake numbers.
2. Sufficient large flakes were produced during the early roughing-out stages of complete handaxe production sequences from large nodules, which again took place outside the excavated area.
3. Flake blanks and finished artefacts were imported from primary manufacturing sites farther afield, the primary working never

actually being present. As shown for example at Maastrict-Belvédère (Roebroeks *et al* 1992), Neanderthals used the landscape in many different ways and spread their activities across it, with different localities variously acting as places of lithic manufacture, maintenance, use or discard (and numerous combinations of these), depending on context.

None of these can be entirely eliminated, and given the time-averaging involved, all might correctly describe the situation at different times. Lord's (2003) evaluation favours the first two options. He proposes that the evidence for primary flaking of large nodules and cores has already been found in the shape of the rolled material collected during earlier phases of extraction at Lynford. Presumably this argument could be expanded to include the rolled material recovered in the palaeochannel during the recent work. If true, then the nature of the present flake population is largely a preservational construct, an illusion created by the preferential incorporation of smaller and lighter elements from later handaxe manufacture into the channel sediments, while the cores and primary débitage remained on the wider floodplain and were later swept away completely. However, the condition and technology of the rolled material previously and recently recovered from Lynford does not support the idea that it belongs with the palaeochannel assemblage, but suggests that it pertains instead to a much older phase of activity captured within the gravels of the Wissey as the terrace formed. It is also important to note here that during the excavation, large flint nodules were occasionally found scattered throughout the palaeochannel deposits, but none showed any evidence of human working. If they were manuports they were not tested prior to introduction and were never used. Furthermore, given the conclusion that much of the assemblage – including the handaxes – was incorporated into the channel by bank collapse and mass-movement debris flows, with little fluvial influence, there is no reason why cortical flakes and cores would be preferentially excluded from these processes. It is possible that the initial stages of manufacture were conducted outside the catchment of these geological processes, but this is of course impossible either to prove or disprove. The most parsimonious explanation, then, is that what was found in the channel is a representative sample of the types of activities that took place at Lynford.

The presence of very large flakes interpreted as partly decorticated preforms and more advanced rough-outs also suggests that the Neanderthals were physically introducing 'dressed' blanks to the palaeochannel and working them there, a secondary point in the chaîne opératoire. The thickness and size of these preforms, and the workmanship of the resulting handaxes, shows that a level of shaping and thinning and some hard-hammer work was still required, both of which are represented in the range of flakes present. Refitting evidence also demonstrates that some of the bifaces were manufactured entirely on the spot from cobble blanks, again producing a range of flakes. The characteristics of the majority of handaxes and the few associated refits also lead to the conclusion that they were actually used, broken and reworked in several different ways around, and perhaps within, the channel. A number of different activities can therefore be recognised, again showing that the nature of the assemblage is not entirely the result of taphonomic processes.

The handaxes themselves can contribute to our understanding. There are basically three types of biface at Lynford:

1. Very well-made and generally large handaxes bearing extensive evidence of resharpening, retouching and recycling.
2. Cruder handaxes made on cobbles or flakes, with less intensive working and generally lacking evidence of reworking.
3. Minimally bifacial pieces/bifacial scrapers made on flakes.

The first category is here interpreted as representing tools that were mostly produced elsewhere, moved around in anticipation of future need, and potentially saw several periods of use. At Lynford these pieces were subject only to modification and rejuvenation. Several were broken and repaired, lost or discarded at the site, while others were probably taken away again. The repair, retouching and rejuvenation of finished handaxes in and around the channel would contribute to the pattern of small 'finishing' flakes, chips, spalls and rejuvenation flakes found in the Lynford assemblage, even if these have subsequently been moved from their original positions.

The way in which Neanderthals at Lynford worked and maintained these handaxes shows that they embodied a number of critical properties, being versatile (multifunctional), flexible (adaptable to purposes other than that originally envisaged) and maintainable (if they broke down they could be quickly repaired) (Bleed 1986; Ohel 1987). Thus, unlike their rather functionally and technologically 'monolithic' Lower Palaeolithic counterparts, Middle Palaeolithic handaxes provided Neanderthals with considerable 'room for manoeuvre' and left them prepared for a number of contingencies in the course of their daily routines. They might also have invested these objects with personal and social import (Gamble 1999; White and Jacobi 2002).

If this interpretation is correct, then these handaxes conform to Binford's (1973, 1979) original definition of a curated tool, however abused and bloated this concept has since become (Nelson 1991; Odell 1996, Nash 1996; Bamforth 1986). Specifically, they were made in advance of use, were carried around in anticipation of that use, and the duration of use was prolonged via reworking – although for how long or how far remains unknown. The transport and curation of Middle Palaeolithic bifaces has been commented upon many times and, in contrast to Binford's oft-cited assertion that deficiencies in strategic forward planning were a major difference between archaic and modern humans (eg Binford 1985, 1989), a growing number of recent studies have emphasised the importance of planning in Neanderthal life, be it in the form of long-distance raw material transfers or of the movement of particular objects in time and space (Geneste 1985; Roebroeks *et al* 1988; Marks 1988; Henry 1992; Féblot-Augustins 1997, 1999; Conard and Adler 1997; Soressi and Hays 2003; papers in Gamble and Roebroeks 1999).

The curation of valued tools around the landscape also helps explain why so many British Middle Palaeolithic handaxes have been found as isolated discards, a pattern also encountered in the surface scatters in neighbouring regions of the Netherlands (Kolen *et al* 1999). There is of course the problem of differentiating between curation and economising on raw material, especially when it comes to recycling (Bamforth 1986; Odell 1996), but in the context of Lynford, raw material was unlikely to have been a limiting resource.

Here, 'being prepared' and the conservation of tools and tool edges during use were probably more important considerations than raw material economising, an element of behaviour that in any case shows some degree of forethought.

The majority of the other two categories of biface, however, were probably made on-site in response to proximate needs – that is, they were more 'expedient' variations on the same theme. This might have represented an unexpected encounter for which some members of a group were poorly equipped, or retooling to replenish those items irretrievably broken or lost during use (such as 40481). In other cases they were fashioned from 'dressed' blanks specially taken to the channel, objects that were perhaps carried around in advance of manufacture that provided a range of options when the time came to use them. Some might have been bifaces at the beginning of an intended longer use-life, but that for some reason were abandoned at Lynford.

In the foregoing description, Lynford shows a range of organisational strategies all based around the handaxe: the importation and modification of well-made handaxes; the manufacture of handaxes from preformed flake blanks brought to the channel edge (from earlier core working that might have taken place metres or miles from Lynford); the use of local cobbles for cruder handaxes and the rapid manufacture of minimally bifacial tools from smaller flakes. These different activities might not all have been undertaken at the same time or during the same visit, but they nonetheless show the implementation of a range of curated and more expedient technologies, these representing different planning options used by Neanderthals, not mutually exclusive patterns of behaviour (Nelson 1991).

This interpretation also leads to some interesting typological tensions. While the various classes of biface outlined above remain useful descriptors, the data can be interpreted as highlighting a more unified bifacial phenomenon, in which varying degrees of working, modification, retouch and recycling are related to the flexible organisation of technology in different situations. In other words, are the categories of true biface/handaxe, partial biface and bifacial scraper all in fact inseparable parts of an underlying chaîne opératoire of biface manufacture, the results of which vary according to the precise social and economic circumstances of each technical act?

These variables might include duration of use; the nature of the social and economic encounter; mobility; the level of curation and spatial organisation of people and things in the landscape; and the need for quickly replacing irreparable objects. Similar questions emerge from recent studies of biface assemblages in France (eg Turq 2001, Cliquet *et al* 2001a), where the Middle Palaeolithic biface is seen as a flexible and metamorphic category, shifting between tools, supports for other tools and cores, and between partially and fully bifacial, throughout an extended use-life. Unfortunately, the inconclusive results of the microwear analysis (Donahue and Evans, this chapter) provides no evidence to determine whether these different classes were used for similar or different purposes.

Neanderthals and mammoths at Lynford

The interpretation offered here, based on the lithics and fauna, is that Neanderthals went to Lynford fully geared-up for encountering animals and killing and butchering them: mammoths or otherwise, dead or alive. It posits highly mobile, anticipatory planning, logistically organised around a versatile curated toolkit, all focused on the exploitation of large animals that were known to be available on the mammoth steppe of MIS 3 Britain, but whose precise distribution, location and accessibility was difficult to predict completely (see also Ashton 1998c; Conard and Adler 1997; contra Binford 1989; Stringer and Gamble 1993; Kuhn 1995). The curation of this type of toolkit thus mitigated the relative unpredictability of mobile resources and the spatial differentiation between the sources of stone and the locations in which stone tools would be needed (Torrence 1986, 1989; Nelson 1991; Ashton 1998c). The open environment of Britain at this time no doubt played a role in Neanderthal decision-making and technological organisation. If the Lynford Neanderthals were hoping to ambush animals or run sick or wounded animals into the ground they still could not predict the location of their ultimate demise, but the boggy environment at Lynford might have tempted them to try to shepherd animals there and could thus explain the apparent repeated use of the locality. If just scavenging dead animals or actively seeking out sick ones, a mobile tool kit would have been vital to be able to respond quickly to visual cues such as carrion birds circling overhead. This type of behaviour would indicate thoughtful, well-prepared Neanderthals reading the signs available in their environment. Handaxes were eventually discarded there in a broken state or were left behind in favour of more valuable food resources. It seems almost inevitable that such important resource locations would become focal points for human litter.

Broadly similar organisational strategies to those seen at Lynford can also be detected at other open-air human/elephant sites. The level and nature of human-elephant interaction during the earlier Palaeolithic is still hotly contested (Gaudzinski 1999a), and at many relevant sites it has not been possible to unequivocally demonstrate a real link between humans and elephants, as for example at Torralba/Ambrona (Santonja and Villa 1990; Villa 1990) and Bollschweil (Conard and Niven 2001). In only a few open-air sites is the claim for direct human involvement particularly compelling (see below). Even at these places, and in spite of the evidence that Neanderthals were not only highly successful hunters of medium-large game but actually top carnivores (eg Gaudzinski 1996, 1999; Gaudzinski and Roebroeks 2000; Bratlund 1999b; Conard and Prindiville 2000; Adler *et al* 2006; Stiner *et al* 2009), who probably did eat mammoth meat (Bocherens *et al* 1999, 2001; 2005), it is often not clear whether Neanderthals were hunting or just scavenging mammoths and other elephants. These questions cannot easily be answered by the Lynford data. Where this site can contribute, though, is to the bigger picture of how Neanderthals organised themselves in order to take advantage of different opportunities to exploit the contemporary Pleistocene megafauna. Even though the data are often medium-grained and certainly not unambiguous, and only tiny fragments of previous landscapes are preserved, interesting patterns nevertheless emerge.

At the Eemian (MIS 5e) site of Lehringen, Germany, the carcass of a straight-tusked elephant was found in fully interglacial lakeside deposits, overlying a wooden spear and associated with a small lithic assemblage (n is ~25) of good Baltic flint. A reassessment of the old excavation by Thieme and Veil (1985) identified two raw material units forming closed technological sets, part of a larger imported toolkit of prepared cores and blanks, and possibly a biface. The spear suggests that Neanderthals had some role in the final despatching of the elephant. A practically identical situation, minus the spear, was found at another German Eemian site at Neumark-Gröbern (Mania et al 1990), where an almost complete elephant carcass was found in lake sediments, associated with 27 flint artefacts structurally very similar to those at Lehringen, some bearing traces of use. Yet another strikingly similar site was described at Pagnano d'Asolo, Italy, discovered in the nineteenth century but only poorly documented (Mussi 1999).

A Middle Pleistocene (MIS 9) example from Aridos, Spain, shows two butchery events, both following the natural deaths of elephants to which humans had early access (Villa 1990). There is good evidence of tool manufacture and use at the site, with 16 cores and three choppers fully flaked at Aridos 1, and seven partly flaked nodules at Aridos 2. Bifaces were found at the latter but not the former, although the presence of handaxe manufacturing and resharpening flakes at Aridos 1 suggests that they had once been present and then removed. Villa proposed that raw materials were introduced from several kilometres away in a variety of forms at both sites. The movement of lithics again shows some degree of planning, and Villa concluded that humans had gone to Aridos anticipating access to elephant carcasses. The La Cotte de St Brelade mammoth-rhino bone heaps are another obvious example of possible mammoth hunting (Scott 1986), but sadly, decent lithic associations are lacking from the key contexts (Callow and Cornford 1986).

For a different view of Neanderthal technical organisation, it is instructive to contrast these sites with other open-air death sites, particularly the multiple-kill locations at, for example, Mauran (Farizy and David 1992; Farizy et al 1994) and La Borde (Jaubert et al 1990). These sites represent natural traps where a large number of animals of the same species (bovids) were brought down, possibly transported a short distance (Mellars 1996) and then intensively processed. The mortality profiles suggest that these were not mass culls, but represent the selective hunting of specific animals during the rutting season (Gaudzinski 1996, 1999). The lithic assemblages are dominated by simple flakes, denticulates and chopper tools, worked on the spot using quartzite obtained a few hundred metres from the sites (Farizy and David 1992; Jaubert et al 1990; Mellars 1996). Unused manuports were also present, as well as some exotic flint. According to one interpretation, these probably seasonally important and repeatedly used places (ie kill sites along migration routes or seasonal rutting grounds) where Neanderthals had predictable access to large numbers of individuals (Farizy and David 1992). The presence of hearths and levels of processing, suggest that the activities involved minimal mobility, were fairly long-term and certainly unhurried. At Mauran, Farizy et al (1994, 241) speculate that Neanderthals made a base for an extended period possibly involving weeks or months with groups of 30 or more. The dating of both sites is unclear. Geological indicators suggest that they belong to a cold, dry phase early in the last glacial cycle (MIS 5a-d), although ESR dates on bison teeth from Mauran gave an age of c 35,000–45,000 before present (Grün 1994).

The lithic assemblages at these sites appear simple and *ad hoc*, but the overall nature of the Neanderthal engagement shows strategic hunting behaviour. In contrast to the human/elephant sites described above, the location of the resource encounter was almost entirely predictable in advance and mobility was accordingly low. Access to abundant, if not exactly ideal, local raw materials was also guaranteed. The technology is simple and expedient because Neanderthals knew that everything they would need to successfully complete the task at hand was available. It did not need to be elaborate or particularly flexible, maintainable or reliable, because if it broke down it could easily be replaced with stockpiled or quickly gathered material. Thus, the technology can again be interpreted as catering to a particular set of conditions in a world that Neanderthals knew and understood intimately.

These two different open-air animal encounters thus reveal subtle but important differences between resource acquisition that could be anticipated, and situations that could be more or less fully predicted, with critical logistical differences in the technological and organisational strategies designed to deal with each situation. The context of lithic use is paramount, and brings into sharp focus the dangers of concentrating on individual proxies in isolation when trying to reconstruct hominin behaviour. Without the faunal remains, the latter set of sites would probably be interpreted as evidence for unplanned *ad hoc* behaviour – entirely the wrong impression. The danger lies not in misconstruing simple behaviour as more complex forms, but vice versa. If we really want to understand the Neanderthals, perhaps we should spend less time comparing them with modern humans, and more time comparing them with each other.

Stiner and Kuhn's work at the Pontinian Cave sites of the Latium Coast of Italy (Stiner and Kuhn 1992; Stiner 1994; Kuhn 1995) produced similar results. They noted a transition in technological and subsistence patterns around 55ka. Before this date, cores were worked in a centripetal fashion and scavenging apparently formed the basis of ungulate procurement (but see Mussi 1999), while after this date a more economical parallel method of flaking was used, accompanied by a shift to ambush hunting. A high incidence of transported exotic materials and retouching prior to 55ka was interpreted as a system of high mobility of diffuse resources in which people were provisioned, whereas the greater use of local materials after 55000 BP was seen as the result of prolonged and more substantial occupations in which places were provisioned with flint and hunted animals. In other words, the lithic technology varied in accordance with mobility and the predictability of faunal resources in terms of place and time of access.

A different combination is evident at the MIS 3 site of Salzgitter-Lebenstedt, where a high-investment biface and Levallois-based assemblage, alongside evidence for whittled bone tools, including possible projectiles, is associated with the mass killing of reindeer during the autumn migration (Gaudzinski and Roebroeks 2000). Like Lynford, the environment has been reconstructed as open tundra, but here the topography of the site was ideal for ambushing prey. The reindeer assemblage showed a selective mortality profile, suggesting well-planned and targeted hunting of seasonally predictable prey, but in this case it was accompanied by a high-investment, probably curated toolkit. Given the high insulation value of reindeer hides (Stenton 1991) and the sheer numbers of animals taken, it is possible that the need to gear up for winter clothing might have been a crucial factor in instigating this hunting episode, with a reliable and maintainable toolkit imported to complete the task.

At the root of all of this is a complex and sophisticated foraging repertoire, not a monotonous opportunistic one. What is more, these different occurrences also seem to represent different social contexts. The ephemeral death sites were possibly host only to task groups – small foraging parties with a particular social make-up and role within a wider group, whereas some of the mass death sites saw much longer use (perhaps semi-residential) by larger communities who must have engaged in a wider range of economic and social activities. Each situation had its own social dynamic, and this is reflected in the activities Neanderthals were engaging in there.

Of equal importance to understanding the subsistence and technological organisation of Neanderthals in MIS 3 Britain is the inferred paucity or absence of trees from which to make wooden hunting weapons and which also provided other affordances such as shelter and fire. Given inferred Neanderthal activity levels, metabolic rates and daily caloric requirements of c 5500 kcal (Sorensen and Leonard 2001; see also Aiello and Wheeler 2003; Steegmann *et al* 2002), a purely scavenging lifestyle would appear unsustainable in Britain, making their presence in the absence of critical resources needed to feed and protect themselves even more baffling. White (2006) has recently highlighted the problems of reconciling current behavioural, anatomical and palaeoenvironmental reconstructions in the British Middle Palaeolithic. The crux of this argument is that if the environment really was completely treeless, and Neanderthals culturally and physically (compare Aiello and Wheeler 2003) ill-equipped to deal with the climates and environments of MIS 3 Britain, then it is hard to understand how they were able to colonise and survive in the first place (White 2006).

Alternative materials such as bone, as used to make pointed implements at least 0.8m long at Salzgitter-Lebenstedt (Gaudzinski 1999a, 1999b), would presumably have been plentiful, and could have been used as a substitute for fuel and raw materials. However, while sharpened mammoth ribs could have serviced the close-encounter, ambush hunting strategies inferred from other Neanderthal hunting sites and traumas seen on Neanderthal skeletons (Berger and Trinkhaus 1995), Gaudzinski casts doubt on the efficiency of the mammoth rib points for thrusting, given their curvature. The use of bone as fuel is also problematic, as it requires another source of fuel to generate sufficient heat for it to ignite (White 2006). Although evidence of trees is often found in MIS 3 contexts, it is usually dismissed as far-travelled or reworked. Clearly, the data are not straightforward, and more well-excavated sites are required to unravel the complex tapestry of MIS 3 Britain beyond bones and stones.

The task of understanding Neanderthal behaviour at the most north-westerly extent of the Neanderthal world is really just beginning, and must await more discoveries like Lynford, and renewed targeted excavations of surviving sites such as Creswell Crags and Kent's Cavern. While at present Neanderthals in Britain seem to be organising technology and subsistence in similar ways to their European counterparts, the nature of the British landscape, its particular resource issues and scarcity of natural shelters, might yet reveal a different pattern of occupation and behaviour to that seen in the Neanderthal heartlands.

5.6 Microwear analysis of the flint artefacts: tool use

R E Donahue and A A Evans

The analysis of the microwear displayed by the lithics aims to identify the varied uses of lithic artefacts and record the natural processes that affected them. This chapter describes the methods of analysis that allow the identification and characterisation of the taphonomic processes recorded on the surfaces of the flint artefacts, including post-depositional disturbance and modification, as well as the identification of the range of activities involving tool use that occurred at the site.

Method

A sample of 109 artefacts was examined, including virtually all bifaces and retouched flakes, and a sample of the unmodified flakes from various contexts. Six artefacts were selected from unstratified contexts for comparison with artefacts recovered from known contexts. At Bradford's Lithic Microwear Research Laboratory the artefacts were photographed and experiments were performed on some small waste flakes to assess the most appropriate cleaning method. The artefacts selected for microwear analysis were immersed in water for 10 minutes, cleaned under running water with a soft bristle brush where sediment was obdurate, soaked in 10 per cent hydrochloric acid for 10 minutes, and then immersed in water again for a further 10 minutes. They were then rinsed with acetone and aired to dry.

Microscopic examination of the artefacts was performed with an Olympus BH2 microscope using incident light. Observations were made primarily at 200× with long working-distance objectives. Occasionally, supplementary observations were made at 50×, 100× and 500× magnifications. The larger bifaces did not fit under the objectives on the microscope stage, so the microscope stand and stage-mounting system were modified to extend the maximum distance between stage and objectives from approximately 80mm to 160mm.

The amount of ridge-rounding on each artefact was recorded as a proxy for the amount of post-depositional modification. The technique is a modified version of a technique first described by Shackley (1974) and later used by Keeley (1980). The degree of rounding is calculated by averaging the breadth of intense reflected light observed at a magnification of 200x from a series of ten measurements taken along one or more ridgelines. Where there is no rounding, the intersecting surfaces that form the ridge produce an almost invisible, and immeasurable, ridgeline (< 1 μm). Experimental research (ongoing; Burroni *et al* 2002) indicates that natural wear causing dorsal ridge rounding of just 4.2μm begins to impair the inference of use from microwear. Most kinds of use-wear will be obliterated when natural wear has rounded ridges of approximately 14μm. Estimation of ridge-rounding is performed independently of use-wear analysis and thus provides an independent check on inferences about tool use.

Many surface and fracture scar characteristics were recorded during the microscopic examination of the artefacts. Among the most important attributes in this study were: the size, depth, initiation, termination, angle and facial distribution of fracture scars; the length, depth, width, location and direction of striations and furrows; the texture, microtopography, brightness or reflectivity and location of surface polishing; the size, shape and location of surface pitting, and the amount of edge and arris rounding – arrises being the scars at the very edges of tools produced by use, retouch and post-depositional processes. These attributes are defined elsewhere (Donahue 1994, 1986) and are consistent with terminology used by many microwear and use-wear analysts (eg Hayden 1979; van Gijn 1990).

Data were recorded on an Excel spreadsheet. Digital photomicrographs were taken using an Olympus C5060 Wide Zoom camera attached to the microscope using an adapter designed by the authors.

Results

Post-depositional modification was observed on all artefacts, and in most cases proved to obliterate or significantly alter most evidence of tool use, seriously limiting the amount that can be confidently said about the activities conducted at the site and their spatial patterning. Here we review the kinds of post-depositional modifications that have affected the artefacts, and their contribution to an improved understanding of the site and of the limitations on the use-wear analysis. Table 5.47 presents the catalogue of finds that were analysed, with comments on use, ridge measurements and phases of post-depositional disturbance as explained below.

Post-depositional modifications

Numerous kinds of post-depositional modifications were observed among the Lynford Quarry lithic artefacts. Most noticeable among these were mild particulate wear, severe wear, 'bright spots' primarily caused by plastic deformation, fracture scarring and metal residues.

Mild particulate polishing

This form of wear was observed in varying degrees on all the artefacts examined. It consisted of a brightly polished surface that tends to be extremely localised to protruding surfaces, and is often observed as a bright line of surface polishing located directly on the edges, dorsal ridges or arrises of an artefact (Fig 5.70). The wear is very smooth and is occasionally associated with narrow striations that are most evident when running perpendicular to the edge or ridge. When limited in extent it is difficult to discern from wear produced by bone. It develops as a result of rubbing either by sediments or by particles of flint derived from the surface of the flint itself. Problematically, this kind of wear is often observed on the extreme edges of tools used for cutting meat. While it is possible that the wear on meat-cutting tools is the result of incidental contact with bone, it is also possible that it is caused by contact with flint particulates that have come off the edge during use. In all these cases the principal mechanism is the same: mild rubbing with small silica particulates causing adhesive and abrasive wear.

As indicated, the polishing agent might be debris from the flint artefact itself, incorporated into the surrounding matrix. Controlled rolling and sliding sediment experiments by Burroni *et al* (2002) indicate that all the sharp corners, mainly edges and ridges, act as local stress raisers. Micro-cracks soon grow and coalesce to produce flint wear debris often smaller than 1.0μm in length. The process continues until the sharpness of the edges and ridges is reduced and a more stable profile is reached. Much wear debris remains on the tool's surface and is ground to a fine powder by continued rubbing. Sophisticated tribological experiments with glasses and ceramics show that this debris powder not only tends to stay at the interface filling the surface irregularity, but might also react with water vapour to form a film. Localised high temperatures that develop during sliding further promote these reactions (Blomberg *et al* 1993; Fischer *et al* 2000). While all artefacts in the Lynford assemblage display various degrees of this mild form of wear, it does vary in intensity according to its position on an edge or ridge. However, while it is often observed on

Fig 5.70
Mild particulate polishing.

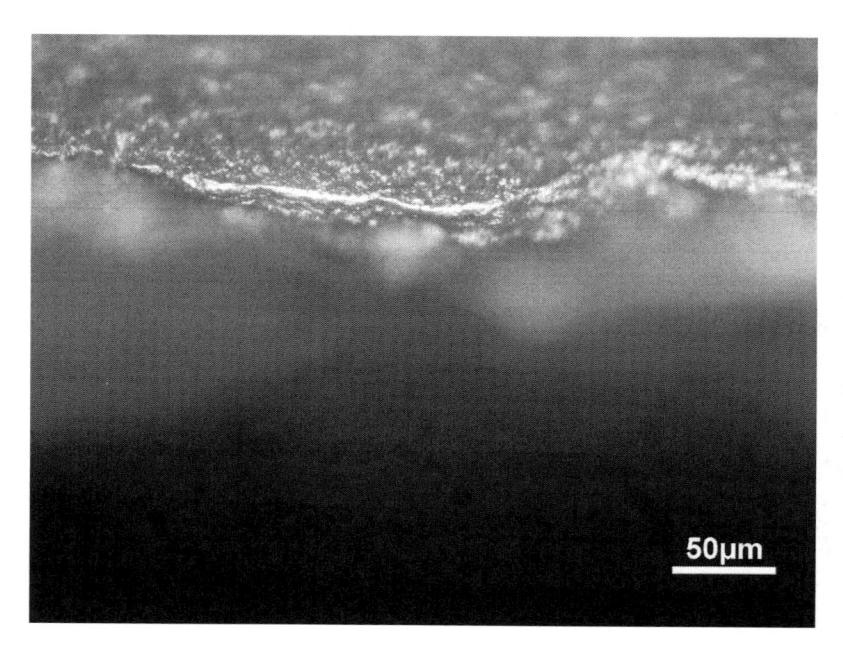

5 THE ARCHAEOLOGICAL ASSEMBLAGES OF ANIMALS AND LITHICS

Table 5.47 Catalogue of finds analysed with comments on use, ridge measurements and phases of post-depositional disturbance, results of the microwear analysis

facies unit	artefact	context	type	use	mean ridge width (um)	phases of post-depositional modification					comment
						PDE1	PDE2	PDE3	PDE4	PDE5	
C	40465	20009	biface	undetermined	32.7	VF	HR/SW	LF	MW/PD		facies association C
B-iii	40000	20015	uniface	impact	7.1	SF	MR/SW	LF	SW		
B-ii:04	40105	20131	scraper	undetermined	8.3	SF	HR/SW	VF	MW		
B-ii:04	40303	20366	biface	undetermined	21.2	SF	MR/SW	SF	MW		
B-ii:04	40307	20367	biface (small)	undetermined	8.9	VF	HR/SW/MW	VF	MW		
B-ii:03	40015	20021	biface	undetermined	6.1	VF	MR/SW	VF	NR		
B-ii:03	40054	20003	biface	undetermined	27.1	VF	MR/SW	VF	MW		
B-ii:03	40055	20003	blade	undetermined	8.0	LF	MR/SW/MW	LF	MW	LF	phase shift?
B-ii:03	40080	20003	retouched flake	undetermined	19.0	LF	HR/SW	SF	MW		
B-ii:03	40088	20021	flake	undetermined		VF	VR/SW/MW	VF	MW		
B-ii:03	40100	20003	notched flake	soft scraping	3.8	SF	SW		MW		
B-ii:03	40101	20003	small biface	undetermined	7.6		HR/SW	VF			
B-ii:03	40102	20003	flake	undetermined	5.2	MF	MR/SW	MF	MW		
B-ii:03	40131	20003	cortical flake	undetermined	31.3	LF	HR/SW/MW	SF	MW	SF	no fresh rounding
B-ii:03	40164	20003	large blade	undetermined	7.1	SF	HR/SW	VF	MR/SW/MW		
B-ii:03	40180	20003	small biface	undetermined		MF	MR/SW	MF	MW		
B-ii:03	40182	20003	biface	undetermined	9.7	VF	MR/SW/MW	VF	MW	VF	
B-ii:03	40218	20003	small biface	undetermined	6.2	SF	MR/SW	MF	SF	SF	multiple recent episodes
B-ii:03	40219	20003	small biface	undetermined	3.7	SF	MR/SW	LF	MW/PD		
B-ii:03	40278	20003	biface	undetermined	3.5	LF	MR/SW	VF	MW		
B-ii:03	40288	20003	biface	undetermined	11.4	VF	HR/SW	VF	MW		
B-ii:03	40290	20003	small biface	undetermined		SF	MR/SW/MW	SF	MW		
B-ii:03	40295	20003	small biface	undetermined	3.1	SF	MR/SW/MW	SF			
B-ii:03	40309	20003	biface	undetermined	3.5	VF	MR/SW	VF	MW		
B-ii:03	40311	20003	small biface	undetermined	6.6	MF	MR/SW/MW	SF	MW		
B-ii:03	40322	20003	flake	undetermined		VF	MR/SW	VF	MW		

continued ▶

Table 5.47 – continued

facies unit	artefact	context	type	use	mean ridge width (um)	PDE1	PDE2	PDE3	PDE4	PDE5	comment
						\multicolumn{5}{c}{phases of post-depositional modification}	
B-ii:03	40330	20003	flake fragment	undetermined		SF		VF	NR/MW		
B-ii:03	40348	20003	Tortoise core?	undetermined		VF	HR/SW		HR/SW?		
B-ii:03	40353	20021	biface	undetermined	20.9	SF	MR/SW/MW	VF	MW/PD		
B-ii:03	40354	20003	biface	undetermined		SF	MR/SW	MF	MW		
B-ii:03	40365	20003	biface	undetermined		SF	MR/SW	SF	MW/PD		
B-ii:03	40381	20021	snapped flake	undetermined	5.9	SF	NR	SF	MW		
B-ii:03	40383	20021	biface	undetermined	5.4	VF	MR/SW	LF	MW		
B-ii:03	40401	20003	scraper	undetermined	3.7	MF	MR/SW	LF			
B-ii:03	40407	20021	biface thinning flake	undetermined		LF	NR	LF	MW		
B-ii:03	40409	20003	scraper	undetermined	3.7	LF	HR/SW/PD	LF	MW		
B-ii:03	40410	20003	scraper	soft cutting	2.7	VF	VR/SW/MW	LF	MW	SF	
B-ii:03	40416	20021	uniface	undetermined	8.0	VF	VR/SW	VF	MW		
B-ii:03	40458	20021	flake	unused	5.4	VF	MR/SW	VF	MW		
B-ii:03	40463	20021	burin spall	unused	2.3	SF	NR/MW		NR/MW		
B-ii:03	40464	20021	biface thinning flake	unused		SF	NR/SW	SF	MW		
B-ii:03	40468	20003	notched flake	undetermined	3.9	VF	MR	MF	MW		
B-ii:03	40469	20003	flake	undetermined	3.8	SF	MR/SW	VF	MW		
B-ii:03	40476	20003	flake	unused	3.5	SF	MR/SW	SF	NR/MW		
B-ii:03	40485	20003	scraper	undetermined	5.9	SF	MR/SW	SF	MW		
B-ii:03	40494	20003	refresher flake	undetermined	7.8	SF	HR/SW	LF	MW		
B-ii:03	40498	20003	scraper	undetermined	12.4	VF	HR/SW	VF			
B-ii:03 shift?	40499	20003	small biface	undetermined	3.7	SF	NR/SW	SF	NR/MW	SF	phase
B-ii:03	40508	20003	flake	undetermined	19.9	LF	HR/SW/MW	MF	MW	MF	phase shift?
B-ii:03	40509	20003	biface	undetermined	6.3	SF	MR/SW	SF	MW	LF	
B-ii:03	40514	20003	biface (small)	undetermined	4.5	VF	MR/SW	MF	MW		

continued ▶

Table 5.47 – *continued*

facies unit	artefact	context	type	use	mean ridge width (um)	phases of post-depositional modification					comment
						PDE1	PDE2	PDE3	PDE4	PDE5	
B-ii:03	40518	20003	thinning flake	undetermined	23.5	LF	MR/SW	SF	MR/SW		
B-ii:03	40520	20003	flake	undetermined	7.5	VF	MR/SW				
B-ii:03	40523	20003	biface	undetermined	6.5	SF	NR/MW	LF	MW	SF	no fresh rounding
B-ii:03	40530	20003	flake fragment	undetermined	14.7	MF	HR/SW	VF	MW/PD		
B-ii:03	40531	20003	small biface	undetermined	17.6	VF	SW	VF	MW		
B-ii:03	40541	20003	biface preform	undetermined	22.3	SF	MR/SW/MW	VF			
B-ii:03	40542	20003	flake	undetermined		MF	MR/SW/MW	SF	MW		
B-ii:03	40544	20003	small biface	undetermined				VF	MR	VF	ancient damage obliterated
B-ii:03	40551	20003	scraper	undetermined		MF	MR/SW/MW	LF	MW	SF	
B-ii:03	40555	20003	'burin'	undetermined	5.5	VF	VR/SW	LF	MW		
B-ii:03	40556	20003	small biface	undetermined	26.6	VF	HR/SW	VF	MW/PD		
B-ii:03	40558	20003	small biface	undetermined	4.4	VF	NR	VF	MW/PD		
B-ii:03	40563	20003	small biface	undetermined	8.2		MR/SW/MW	SF	MW	MF	no fresh rounding; phase shift
B-ii:03	40564	20003	biface	undetermined	7.2	SF	MR/SW	LF	MW		
B-ii:03	40580	20003	retouched flake	undetermined	6.9	SF	NR/SW	LF	MW		
B-ii:02	40170	20246	biface	undetermined	10.6	VF	MR/SW/MW	LF	MW		notch is fresh
B-ii:02	40173	20246	thinning flake	undetermined	4.2		MR/SW	LF	MW		
B-ii:02	40176	20246	blade	unused	4.9	SF	NR/SW	LF	MW		
B-ii:02	40178	20246	flake	undetermined		LF		LF	MW		
B-ii:02	40470	20371	scraper	undetermined	15.5	SF	HR/SW	SF	MW/PD		
B-ii:01	40195	20254	biface	undetermined		VF	MR/SW/MW	SF	MW		scars: cutting soft mat.
B-ii:01	40199	20254	small biface	undetermined	3.9	SF	MR/SW/MW	VF			
B-ii:01	40297	20254	small biface	undetermined	3.7	SF	MR/SW/MW	LF	MW		
B-ii:01	40328	20369	biface	undetermined	4.9	SF	HR/SW	SF	MW		

continued ▶

Table 5.47 – continued

facies unit	artefact	context	type	use	mean ridge width (um)	PDE1	PDE2	PDE3	PDE4	PDE5	comment
						\multicolumn{5}{c}{phases of post-depositional modification}	
B-ii:01	40412	20363	biface	undetermined	19.7	SF	HR/SW	LF			
B-ii:01	40443	20254	scraper	undetermined	6.3	SF	MR/SW	LF	MW	VF	
B-ii:01	40481	20384	'burin'	undetermined	4.4	SF	MR/SW	MF	MW		
B-ii:01	40496	20384	biface	undetermined	17.3	MF	MR/SW	MF	MW		
B-ii:01	40497	20384	flake	undetermined	12.4	VF	HR/SW	VF	MW/PD		
B-ii:01	40525	20384	notched flake	undetermined	5.5	SF	MR	SF	MW		
B-ii:01	40532	20004	biface	undetermined	11.1	MF	HR/SW	LF	MW	LF	notches are fresh
B-ii:01	40545	20384	small biface	undetermined	14.1	SF	MR/SW/MW	VF			patina
B-ii:01	40548	20004	biface	undetermined	37.6	SF	HR/SW/MW	LF	MW		
B-ii:01	40550	20384	biface	undetermined		LF	HR/SW/MW	VF	MW		
B-ii:01	40570	20139	thinning flake	undetermined	3.7	VF	NR/SW	VF	MW		
B-ii:01	40571	20254	scraper	undetermined	5.9	VF	MR/SW/MW/PD	VF			
B-ii:01	40590	20369	flake	undetermined	6.6	SF	VR/SW	VF	MW/PD		
B-ii:01	40591	20369	biface	undetermined	11.3	VF	MR/SW/MW	LF	MW/PD		
B-ii:01	40593	20369	blade	undetermined		SF	HR/SW	SF	MW		
B-ii:01	40596	20254	scraper	undetermined	3.4	VF	MR/SW	SF	MW		
B-i :03	40193	20078	notched flake	undetermined	9.4	SF	MR/SW	SF	NR		
B-i :03	40349	20078	flake fragment	undetermined	473.8	LF	HR/SW				no record of fresh damage
B-i :03	40374	20078	flake	undetermined	28.2	SF		LF			
B-i :03	40389	20078	biface fragment	undetermined	7.1			LF	MW	LF	very fresh severe damage
B-i :03	40418	20051	convergent scraper?	undetermined	3.7	VF	MR/SW	VF	MW	SF	
B-i :03	40427	20051	broken flake	unused	2.5	VF	NR	SF	NR/MW		
B-i :03	40428	20051	flake	undetermined	3.8	SF	MR/SW	MF	MW		
B-i :03	40435	20051	cortical flake	unused	3.1	SF	NR	SF	NR/SW		no ancient rounding
–	40016	20048	biface	undetermined	11.4	LF	HR/SW/MW	VF	MW		unstratified

continued ▶

Table 5.47 – *continued*

facies unit	artefact	context	type	use	mean ridge width (um)	phases of post-depositional modification					comment
						PDE1	PDE2	PDE3	PDE4	PDE5	
–	40017	20048	bout coupe	undetermined	6.1	SF	HR/SW	SF	MW	SF	unstratified biface
–	40018	20048	small biface	undetermined	11.7	VF/MR/SW	SF/MR/SW	VF	MW		multiple ancient episode unstratified
–	40019	20049	biface	undetermined	7.1	SF	HR/SW		MW		unstratified
–	40058	20048	notched flake	undetermined	11.0	LF	HR/SW	SF	MW		unstratified
–	40444	20048	small biface	undetermined	19.6	VF	HR/SW	SF	MW/PD		unstratified

Key to post-depositional codes: SF, small fracture scars; MF, medium fracture scars; LF, large fracture scars; VF, variable fracture scars; NR, no or little edge rounding; MR, medium edge rounding; HR, heavy edge rounding; VR, variable edge rounding; PD, plastic deformation; MW, mild wear; SW, severe wear

heavily rounded edges and ridges, there is no evidence that such rounding was the result of mild wear. In these cases it is clear that the mild wear occurred after discard. It should be noted that fracture scars referred to as 'very fresh' have no rounding either of their arrises or along their edges, and no evidence of mild wear. In other words a 'fresh' fracture scar displays no surface wear whatsoever.

Natural severe wear

This form of modification abrades, rather than polishes, the surface. It occurs frequently and often extensively in the Lynford assemblage and is makes interpretation of tool use at the site highly problematic. In its milder forms it can mimic wear produced by working dry hide but produces a mild sheen and a very rough, rather than a matt, texture (Fig 5.71). In its more severe form the surfaces are very rough, with much pitting. Severe wear is differentiated from mild wear by the larger particulates of wear debris produced. Furthermore, instead of remaining on the surface, these particles mostly become loose, as observed experimentally for ceramic and glasses (Blomberg *et al* 1993). Unlike the wear on edges used to work dry hide, this form of wear lacks wide striations and linear depressions. It can occur either as a few striations or as a multitude of narrow, multiple-direction striations. Other mechanisms as well as mild wear are involved in this process, and among these, brittle fracture is clearly predominant. Because the artefact edges are the most vulnerable part of the flake, they become rounded relatively quickly, and the aggressive nature of brittle fracture is thought to be able to rapidly remove virtually all traces of any form of wear caused by tool use. Like mild wear, severe wear is observed on almost all the tools from Lynford, but varies in intensity among artefacts and among contexts.

Bright spots

'Bright spot' is a term often used to describe large patches of unusually highly reflective surfaces that do not appear to result from use. However, this is no longer an appropriate explanation as there are a variety of ways that

Fig 5.71 Natural severe wear.

'bright spots' can occur, including through use and hafting. Usually this form of surface modification is the result of plastic deformation, where the surface has been reshaped and indented by a very hard object. It is characterised by a relatively flat and bright surface, demonstrated by artefacts 40265 and 40497 (Fig 5.72) that often features shallow and wide striations across its surface. The striations could have occurred either at the time of the deformation or at a later time. When plastic deformation occurs near an edge, such as on artefacts 40591 (*see* Fig 5.60) and 40219, at low or no magnification it can resemble 'sickle gloss', the name given to wear resulting from the cutting of opal-rich or siliceous soft plant fibre.

'Bright spots' can also be caused by other phenomena. Among the 'bright spots' observed in this assemblage were those on artefact 40563. Examined at higher magnifications in a scanning electron microscope (SEM) these were found to be remnant fossil fragments, probably of sponge, within the flint.

Thermal shock and its effects

Thermal shock is caused by significant, rapid changes in temperature. It is often the result of fire, but thermal shock can be caused by shifts to cold temperatures, particularly under cycles of temperature change such as extreme daily temperature changes. It causes heat spalls (potlids), crazing and surface cracking. It can also produce indirect effects, such as the promotion of more rapid formation of white patina on an artefact's surface. While thermal alteration might not obliterate use-wear patterns, the early-stage development of white patina clouds the artefact surface, making it difficult to identify use-wear characteristics. In later stages, it results in complete loss of the original surface characteristics. Evidence of thermal shock which might be missed by macroscopic observation, such as very fine hairline fractures, can be observed microscopically.

Only artefact 40542 displays characteristics suggestive of thermal alteration. The left and distal edges of this flake have been discoloured to a light grey. In addition, some non-conchoidal fracture scars display a somewhat crazed surface, which would be typical of the effects of thermal shock. There is no evidence, however, that this was caused by fire.

Metal residue

The protruding surfaces of some artefacts show very small, extremely bright, silvery patches that correspond to contact with metal, most likely steel. The metal residue, a form of adhesive wear, was probably caused during excavation when contact with trowels or other field equipment occurs. It can also occur in the laboratory as a result of contact with metal callipers or other instruments.

Numerous artefacts show very small patches of metal residue. These patches are very distinctive but are too limited in distribution to affect the visibility and identification of use-wear, and were therefore not recorded in detail.

Other post-depositional traces

Many artefacts have fracture scars along their edges that may mimic fracture scars produced by tool use and even mimic retouch. In addition, and rather surprisingly, large snap fractures occur on relatively large, thick flakes such as 40531, as well as on the thin edges of artefacts. In a few cases virtually all edges were snapped, for example, 40374. Large snap fractures result from high load-forces applied to the artefacts approximately perpendicular to the ventral surface plane. Many examples at Lynford Quarry probably result from post-depositional processes given the lack of wear on their edges and arrises. The snapped surfaces also display much less wear than retouched or flaked surfaces of the artefact. Some snap fracture scars, however, have ancient severe wear on

Fig 5.72
Bright spots on artefacts 40265 and 40497.

their edges, indicating that the artefacts were snapped during manufacture, use or soon after being discarded. The timing of these modifications is considered below.

Tool use

Only two artefacts display wear and fracture characteristics that permit tentative interpretations regarding past tool use. Artefact 40410 (*see* Fig 5.68) is a convergent convex side scraper with long lateral edges and a wide convex distal end. Much of the dorsal face and left edge retain cortex. The right lateral edge displays both ancient and recent fracture scars. The ancient scars tend to vary in size and form, except along the mid-section where the flake scars are consistently small and shallow with feather terminations and point initiations. Edge rounding is quite pronounced and affects the edge and the arrises. The surfaces along the edge display a mild sheen (Fig 5.73). A bright line of surface polishing occurs directly on the edge about midway along the lateral edge and increases in intensity distally. However, it always stays very fine and is interrupted only by later (recent) fracture scarring. These brightly polished localities are likely to have been caused by the mild rubbing of sediments, as they also occur on dorsal ridges. Although all of the ancient edge-wear characteristics could be the result of natural processes, the systematic fracture scarring along the mid-section strongly supports the proposition that the edge was used to cut soft organic material, most likely meat and hide. Dorsal ridge-rounding averages only 2.8 µm, well within the range for the survival of most forms of use wear, but not necessarily that from cutting meat.

Artefact 40100 (*see* Fig 5.65) is a biface fragment with an ancient break at its proximal end. A wide but shallow retouched notch occurs at the distal end. Within the notch are small fracture scars on both faces with point initiations and predominantly feather terminations (Fig 5.74). The edge within the notch is moderately rounded with wear that is slightly contrasting and often rough, although brightly polished areas also occur. This wear is most evident on the ventral surface, while the dorsal surface appears very fresh except directly on the edge. There is a distinct directionality to the wear indicative of motion perpendicular to the edge. The lateral edge beyond the notch displays less wear. The wear characteristics are similar to those produced by working fresh hide but are generally too intense and could also be the result of severe wear caused by post-depositional processes including soil movement. However, the variation along the edge suggests that the concavity was used in a scraping or whittling motion on relatively soft material and the notch was further modified by post-depositional processes after discard. The convex left lateral edge also displays numerous small fracture scars and wear that might relate to use, but it appears to be heavily modified by post-depositional processes. The dorsal ridge is moderately rounded (averaging 3.8µm). The fracture scar

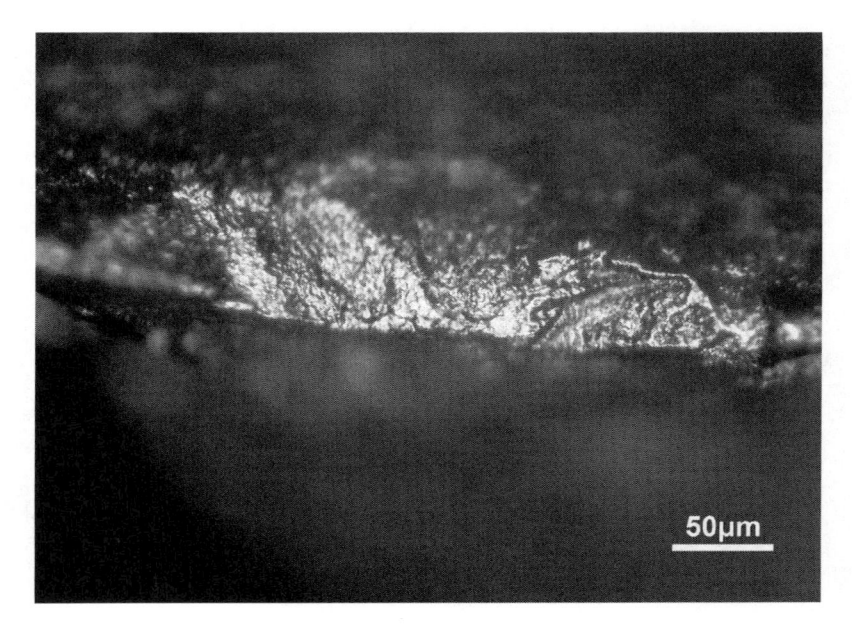

Fig 5.73
Artefact 40410: a convergent convex side scraper with long lateral edges and a wide convex distal end. The right lateral edge displays both ancient and recent fracture scars.

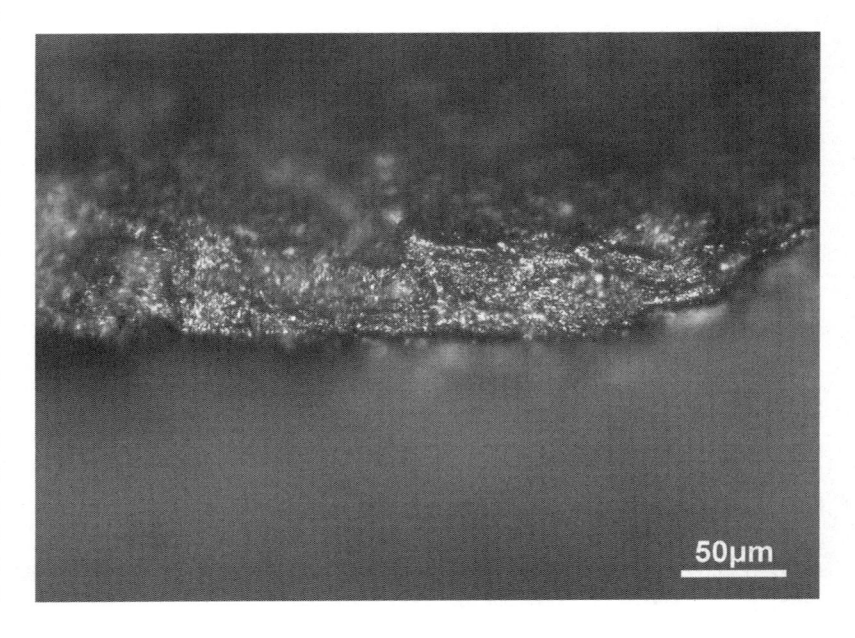

Fig 5.74
Artefact 40100: a biface fragment with an ancient break at its proximal end and a wide but shallow retouched notch.

and wear characteristics of this tool would seem to indicate that it had been used, but later post-depositional processes have modified working edges and make clear inferences about its past use impossible.

Impact damage

Numerous artefacts display scarring resulting from ancient impacts. Impact scarring is an important attribute for discerning tool use and it is particularly important for the Middle Palaeolithic because of the controversies surrounding the use of stone-tipped spears (Holdoway 1989; Plisson and Beyries 1998; Shea 1988; Churchill *et al* 2009; Donahue *et al* 2002, 2004). Impact damage is exactly that – evidence of impact – and is produced when applied force is directed into the approximate centre of the stone. Impact might result from uses such as those associated with projectiles, or from chopping and wedging. Such damage can also result from the technological attempt to thin a tool, but such a thinning technique using bipolar flaking generally lacks the control of other flaking techniques.

Among the artefacts with impact damage is a small triangular, unifacially retouched flake, 40000. This piece has fracture scars that could be interpreted as indicative of its use as a point. On the ventral surface of the tip of this unifacial flake there are long ancient fracture scars, with one ending in a step termination. However, the large fracture scar at the tip on the dorsal face is fresh, as are virtually all of the fine scars and nibbling at the tip. Although the tip also shows evidence of ancient impact, it is possible that these impact fracture scars are the result of manufacture and not use. Similar, but even less convincing examples include artefacts 40468 (*see* Fig 5.69) and 40170. The most severe examples of impact damage, artefacts 40548 (*see* Fig 5.60) and 40353, have been confirmed as the product of post-depositional processes. In addition, perhaps the largest biface in the collection, 40016 (*see* Fig 5.64), also displays the largest ancient impact fracture scars. However, it is impossible to determine whether this damage relates to its use or to post-depositional processes.

Unused artefacts

Seven of the 109 sampled artefacts, principally unmodified flakes, exhibited little edge modification, and were considered unused. These include a biface thinning flake, 40176; an unmodified flake, 40458; a 'burin spall', 40463; a broken flake, 40427; and a cortical flake, 40435. Five of these artefacts derive from just two contexts, 20021 (Unit B-ii:03) and 20051 (B-i:03). There are other artefacts that have a single good edge with no evidence of use, but post-depositional processes have modified the other edges too heavily to be certain that they also were unused.

Ridge-rounding

Analysis of dorsal ridge rounding followed the same procedures as for the microscopic analysis of tool edges to detect use and therefore acted as a means evaluating the accuracy and consistency of the use-wear interpretations. Of the 109 artefacts in the sample, 92 were measured for dorsal ridge rounding. This includes artefact 40349, which was deliberately included because it had visible rounding of edges and ridges. Its ridge measured 475µm, more than a magnitude greater than the next most rounded dorsal ridge, and it is therefore excluded from the following summary statistics as an outlier.

Ridge rounding ranges from 2.3µm to 37.7µm with a mean of 9.61µm and a standard deviation of 7.67µm. The distribution is strongly skewed with a value of 1.7Q. In general, many artefacts displayed characteristics suggestive of limited post-depositional modification, and so were potentially capable of retaining some evidence of tool use on their edges. However, it needs to be remembered that some uses, particularly cutting meat, are extremely sensitive to such post-depositional modification. Comparison of the means of dorsal ridge rounding of artefacts with identifiable use or classified as unused (mean = 3.53µm) with the mean dorsal ridge rounding of artefacts considered undetermined (mean = 10.20µm) demonstrates a significant difference between the two ($t = 2.411$, $df = 88$, $p = 0.018$).

Dorsal ridge rounding varies quite substantially among contexts, although artefact frequencies in many contexts are too low to be very meaningful. Fig 5.75 displays the mean and standard errors of dorsal ridge rounding for each context. Mean values tend to be relatively low with only a few specimens tending to have extremely high values and some contexts; for example, 20003 (Unit B-ii:03), 20051 (B-i:03), and 20254 (B-ii:01), show extremely low standard errors. The artefacts identified as unused all come from contexts 20021 (B-ii:03) and 20051 (B-i:03), which contain only 11 of the 109 artefacts in the sample. Both contexts also have low means. It is not clear whether these low means and standard errors for these contexts result from sample bias, with a high proportion of unretouched flakes, or if they reflect the post-depositional environment of these contexts.

Discussion

Constructing temporal records

At the time of detachment, the ventral faces of flakes and the fracture scar faces on nuclei display clean and unmodified surfaces. Modifications to these surfaces resulting from wear are records of the processes and events that have affected that particular artefact. Identification of the kinds of wear on these fracture scar surfaces makes it possible to identify the kinds of processes that affected the artefact, but not necessarily the history or sequence of those processes or events. This, however, can also be achieved by studying the association of fracture scars and wear features on artefact surfaces. The relationship between wear and fracture scarring is based on the law of superposition and principles, which have proved valuable for modelling temporal relationships among these static morphological features (Donahue and Burroni 2004).

The first principle is that if wear exists on the surfaces forming an edge or ridge, then that edge and its defining surfaces existed before the processes that produced the wear (Fig 5.76a). According to the second principle, if wear exists on a surface, but does not extend onto the surface of an adjoining fracture scar, then the processes that produced the wear preceded the formation of the fracture scar (Fig 5.76b). Using these two principles one can construct a sequence of events or processes that led to the formation of the microwear characteristics of the flake. These relationships, of course, apply not just to retouch but also to natural fracture scars.

Episodes of wear formation

It is possible to measure and compare the degree of homogeneity or dispersion within each context during each episode of post-depositional modification. This can be done by examining the frequency of fracture scar sizes resulting from episodes 1, 3 and 5, and the

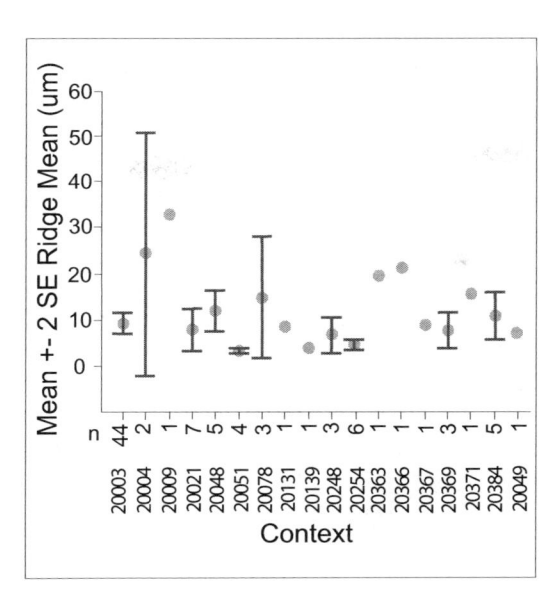

Fig 5.75
Mean and standard errors of dorsal ridge rounding for each context.

amount of edge rounding resulting from episodes 2 and 4. The inter-quartile distance (Qd) provides a measure of dispersion for ordinal scale data. Qd equals the difference between the first quartile and fourth quartile in a set of ordinal values:

$$Qd = (Q3-Q1).$$

To produce a single inter-quartile distance value for all contexts for a given episode, the contexts were weighted according to the proportion of artefacts that they contribute to

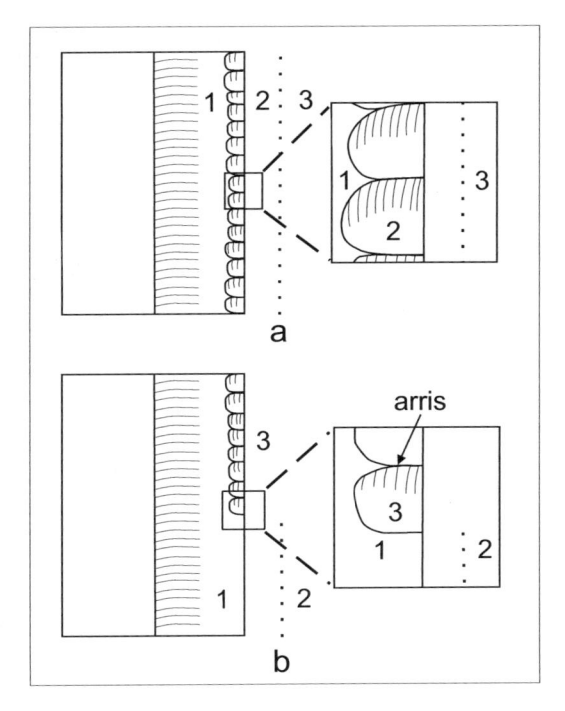

Fig 5.76
Ideal sequence of wear progression.

the study, and the weighted Qd is averaged. The result of this approach is that each artefact contributes equally to the overall distance measure, irrespective of its context. Thus:

$$Qd \text{ (weighted)} = m_i/n \sum (Q_{i,3} - Q_{i,1})$$

Where m_i is the sample size for the i-th context, and n is the total sample size. The weighted inter-quartile distance does not measure differences among contexts, but measures the internal homogeneity observed within all contexts for a given episode.

The results are presented in Table 5.48. Note that there is less dispersion in Episodes 2 and 4 than in Episodes 1, 3 and 5. This probably results from different variables being measured in the sets of episodes. Fracture-scar ranks are based on flake sizes that increase exponentially, while ridge rounding ranks are quasi-arithmetical in scale.

For most contexts, episode 1 displays a predominance of small fracture scars and an inter-quartile distance of 0.937. Only the small sample from context 20048 (unstratified) differs from this pattern, with a prevalence of large fracture scars.

Episode 2 is characterised by the prevalence of moderate edge rounding in all but one context, 20048, which is dominated by heavy rounding. There is relatively little dispersion across contexts with the inter-quartile distance measuring 0.793. The Qd for context 20048 is 0.0, as four of five artefacts studied have predominantly large fracture scars.

Episode 3 yields an inter-quartile distance measuring 1.607. The data show that many contexts have bimodal distributions, and thus that artefacts with large fracture scars and those with small scars occur in the same context. This is also the episode with the greatest proportion of artefacts recorded as having fracture scars of various sizes, further supporting these results. It is hypothesised that the damage that occurred during this episode resulted from highly variable, unsystematic forces acting on the deposits, such as those represented by quarry excavation equipment. At one end of the spectrum these forces are capable of being highly destructive if artefacts are positioned at certain angles, in contact with other artefacts, or lying in a context with gravels and other materials that will tend to focus applied pressures in discrete locations along an artefact edge. At the other end, with artefacts lying flat in soft fine sediments, there is likely to be little if any damage to the edge. Finally, it is noted that contexts 20048 (unstratified) and 20051 (B-i:03) contain no artefacts with large fracture scarring.

Episode 4 shows the greatest intra-context consistency (inter-quartile distance measurement of 0.0) with little or no rounding characterising the edges modified at this time. Mild wear is prevalent on the edges, suggesting that whatever caused the serious fracture damage during Episode 3, there were few severe forces applied during Episode 4. This episode seems to confirm that the artefacts were relatively stable within their contexts during this episode.

Episode 5 seems primarily related to the artefacts in context 20003 (B-ii:03) and the numbers are quite low, partly due to this episode not having been clearly identified previously. Small fracture scars are prevalent, but the context displays little homogeneity (.273). Fracture scars of Episode 5 were apparently produced quite recently as there has been no development of surface wear from rubbing on any of the scar ridges or surfaces. The high inter-quartile distance (Qd) of 2.0 displayed by the sample indicates that the processes that produced this damage are probably associated with recent quarrying or the archaeological excavation activities themselves.

Artefacts from Lynford Quarry consistently showed characteristics of multiple episodes of post-depositional modification. This involved at least two and possibly three or more cycles of post-depositional modification. Each cycle usually consisted of an episode of fracture scarring along the edges, which was then followed by various kinds and amounts of surface wear that rounded and polished primarily edges and ridges. As expected, the first cycle appears to have been very ancient for almost all artefacts. Ancient fracture scar damage varied substantially among the

Table 5.48 Inter-quartile distance values for all contexts for a given episode

episode	weighted Q_d	% Variable
PDE1	0.937	32.04
PDE2	0.793	28.69
PDE3	1.607	34.95
PDE4	0.000	22.62
PDE5	2.000	15.38

artefacts, although small fracture scars (under 0.1mm) predominated. However, very large fracture scars and breaks were also common (such as on artefact 40100; see Fig 5.65), indicating that some artefacts underwent severe applied forces, assuming these scars were not related to use or manufacture. Edge rounding caused by severe wear usually followed this earliest episode of fracture scarring. Edges and ridges varied in the amount of rounding, but they usually displayed similar wear characteristics including very rough and usually dull surfaces, which would show little contrast with unmodified surfaces. Non-fractured edge segments often showed greater rounding than edges within these ancient fracture scars. This could be because such edges protruded the furthest, or because initial rounding resulted from use and was then enhanced by post-depositional processes. Occasionally, the polishing of edges from mild wear was evident. However, it was often difficult to ascertain if this occurred during the first cycle of post-depositional modification or during the next. A few artefacts showed little or no ancient post-depositional modification, as described here (for example, the small biface 40544). Because a high proportion of the artefacts that showed little ancient post-depositional modification were unretouched flakes, it must be emphasised that some of the fracture scarring and wear observed on the retouched tools probably resulted from tool use, although the ways in which the tools were used could not be inferred. Finally, a few artefacts seemed to display multiple episodes of ancient post-depositional modification (such as artefact 40018; see Fig 5.63).

Most artefacts showed a second cycle of modifications that was quite distinct from the earlier cycle. The second cycle is characterised by an episode of medium and large fracture-scar damage (scars measuring 0.1 to 1.0mm wide and greater than 1.0mm wide, respectively). Again there was the occasional extremely large break or fracture scar. Unlike the previous cycle, however, the following episode of edge wear was characterised primarily by mild and not severe wear. This produced a brightly polished surface, generally observed as a linear feature along the immediate edge or ridge. There was very little rounding of these edges and ridges.

Finally, some artefacts appeared to show a third cycle of post-depositional modification. This included either small or large fracture scarring, which is not followed by surface polishing or edge rounding. Originally it was thought that this cycle was the same as the previous, but without further sediment movement. However, during the analysis of the data it became evident that such patterns occurred on edges that also bore clear evidence of the second cycle and thus could only be explained by recognising the possibility of a third cycle of post-depositional modification. As a result, it is possible that some third-cycle modifications might have been misinterpreted as second-cycle modification.

The analysis of the sequencing of post-depositional modifications to the lithic artefacts has allowed evaluation of various models for site formation. The first cycle of modification appears to encompass the systemic role of the artefacts and their original discard and *in situ* post-depositional modification, probably on the banks of the fluvial channel. Breaks and fracture scarring might have occurred from manufacture, tool use, or trampling. At the same time, the surface of the artefacts would have also undergone severe and mild wear processes, which would have continued during early burial. As the depth of burial increased, the amount of severe wear would have lessened and allowed for the formation of mild wear. The second cycle of post-depositional modification consisted of the slumping of bank deposits into the basin. It is thought that this would have occurred as one or more high-energy events and that it could be associated with large mammal trampling. Once redeposited within the sediments of the basin, the artefacts could have been affected by trampling, but soon would be buried and then affected primarily by mild sediment rubbing across their surfaces to produce mild wear. This process would also imply that the basin stratigraphy would have little bearing on the relative ages of the artefacts. The third cycle encompasses episodes of impact or, more probably, severe forces bearing down on the artefacts. This could include heavy (quarry) equipment rolling over the deposits as well as archaeological recovery and transport. No wear processes follow this episode of edge fracturing.

Technomorphological attributes resulting from natural processes

The results of the analysis demonstrates that there were multiple episodes of post-depositional modification to the artefacts and confirms that some artefacts are neither technologically nor typologically tool forms. While careful typological study might differentiate naturally modified flakes from retouched flakes, microwear analysis of this assemblage provided further clarification. Among retouch characteristics mimicked by natural processes are 'abrupt retouch' or backing, burinations, and notches formed by a series of fracture scars (for example, 40433 and 40555). Impact fracture scars are also demonstrated to have resulted from post-depositional processes (for example, 40548; *see* Fig 5.60).

Influence of the sediments on wear and fracturing

Characteristics of the sediments were examined following analyses of the association of contexts with the microwear results. Most of the seriously damaged artefacts in PDM episode 3 come from organic sediment contexts with varying densities of gravel clasts (Unit B-ii:03), suggesting that the damage was derived from contact with the gravel matrix. Interestingly, all four artefacts from context 20246 (B-ii:02), described as mud, display predominantly large fracture scars, but occur within a localised area of gravel clasts derived from the former north bank of the channel. The varying inter-quartile measurements (Qd) appear to reflect in part the varying densities of gravels within individual contexts. Context 20048, which seems to buck the trends seen in Episodes 1, 2 and 3, is identified as consisting of unstratified material from spoil in the centre of the gravel quarry. While it is interesting that this context of unstratified material is uncharacteristic of other contexts during these episodes, it is certainly surprising that it displays low inter-quartile measurements within each of these episodes.

Conclusion

The lithic microwear analysis examined a sample of 109 artefacts from Lynford Quarry in order to identify possible tool uses and to characterise post-depositional modifications. The results of this study show that post-depositional modification to the artefacts has erased virtually all evidence of past tool use. One tool (40410; *see* Fig 5.68) possibly shows evidence of having been used for butchery, while a second (40100; *see* Fig 5.65) shows less convincing evidence of having been used for scraping a moderately soft material, perhaps fresh hide. Although impact damage was observed on some artefacts, in most cases this was the result of post-depositional processes, and at other times was probably the result of technological modification of the artefact. There was no clear evidence that it was ever the result of use as a projectile or as a wedge. Five artefacts were identified as unused, and many others had at least one edge unused. This is significant primarily because it shows that post-depositional modifications were often limited, such that if tool use had occurred it could have been detected and interpreted.

Post-depositional modification was distinguished across five episodes. The results tend to show that the artefacts were not found in their original discarded locations but have undergone transport from this primary context to the palaeochannel context. This was probably a result of bank erosion processes. The artefacts suffered much fracture scarring along their edges between their discard and their arrival in the secondary context of deposition. However, it is uncertain when the damage principally occurred. The second episode of post-depositional modification, consisting primarily of severe wear along edges and ridges, probably occurred prior to burial of the artefacts within their secondary contexts. The third phase of post-depositional modification occurred much later and comprised a short episode of severe pressure that caused much of the large-fracture scar damage observed on the artefacts. It is thought that this might relate to quarrying activities and particularly the movement of heavy machinery over the deposits. Episode 4 consisted of a long period of mild sediment movement around the artefacts. Episode 5, not extensively represented, appears to be the result of very recent damage, possibly from archaeological excavation and processing.

5.7 The sandstone block

F d'Errico, J E Andrews and L Dubreuil

A sandstone block (40472) recovered from the channel sediments of Association B-ii (Unit B-ii:03), and bearing possible traces of residues associated with its use was submitted to detailed analysis in order to verify the possible anthropogenic origin of the wear pattern and propose a functional interpretation.

5 THE ARCHAEOLOGICAL ASSEMBLAGES OF ANIMALS AND LITHICS

Description

The block (dimensions: 134 × 94 × 71mm) has a peculiar L-shaped section with a broad horizontal and a squat vertical 'limb' (Fig 5.77). This aspect will be known in this chapter as Face a. The block presents an elongated flat area with two localised depressions (D1 at the top and D2 at the bottom), partially covered with a thin layer of black and, in places, reddish sediment (Fig 5.78a–b). The same type of residue (D3) is present on the middle of the slightly convex area that constitutes the top of the squat vertical limb (Fig 5.78d). A U-shaped worn groove with no residues is present at the junction between the vertical and the horizontal limbs of the object. Additional areas bearing possible traces of utilisation are observed on the adjacent Face e, showing a circular depression (Fig 5.78c), and on Face d, which presents two parallel shallow grooves (Fig 5.78d).

Methodology

A low-power reflected light microscope equipped with a digital camera was used to conduct a microscopic survey of the entire surface of the object and document morphological differences between clearly natural and

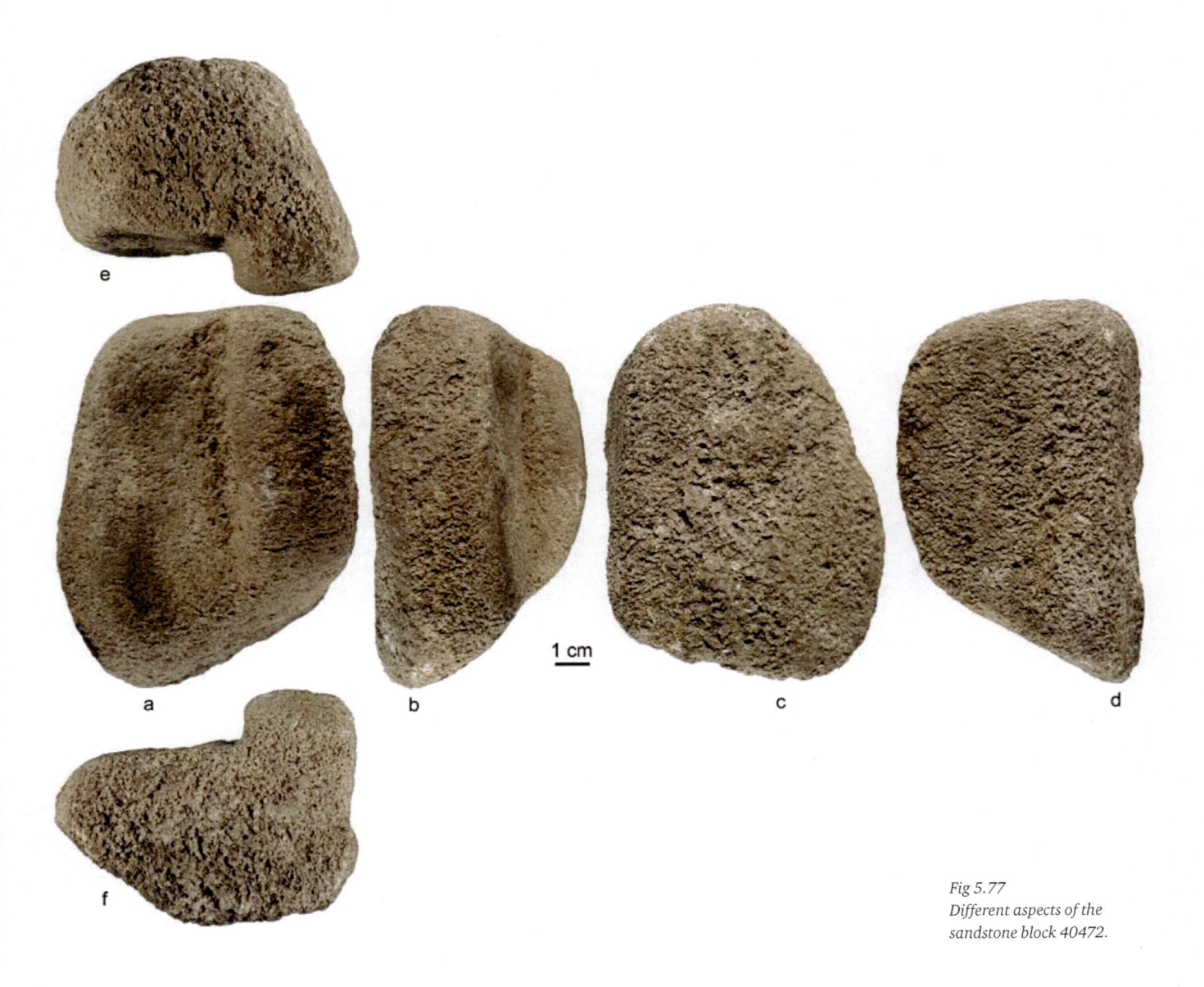

Fig 5.77
Different aspects of the sandstone block 40472.

Fig 5.78
Sandstone block:
(a) and (b) depressions with residues;
(c) subcircular depression on Face e;
(d) patches of residues on D3. Scale = 10mm.

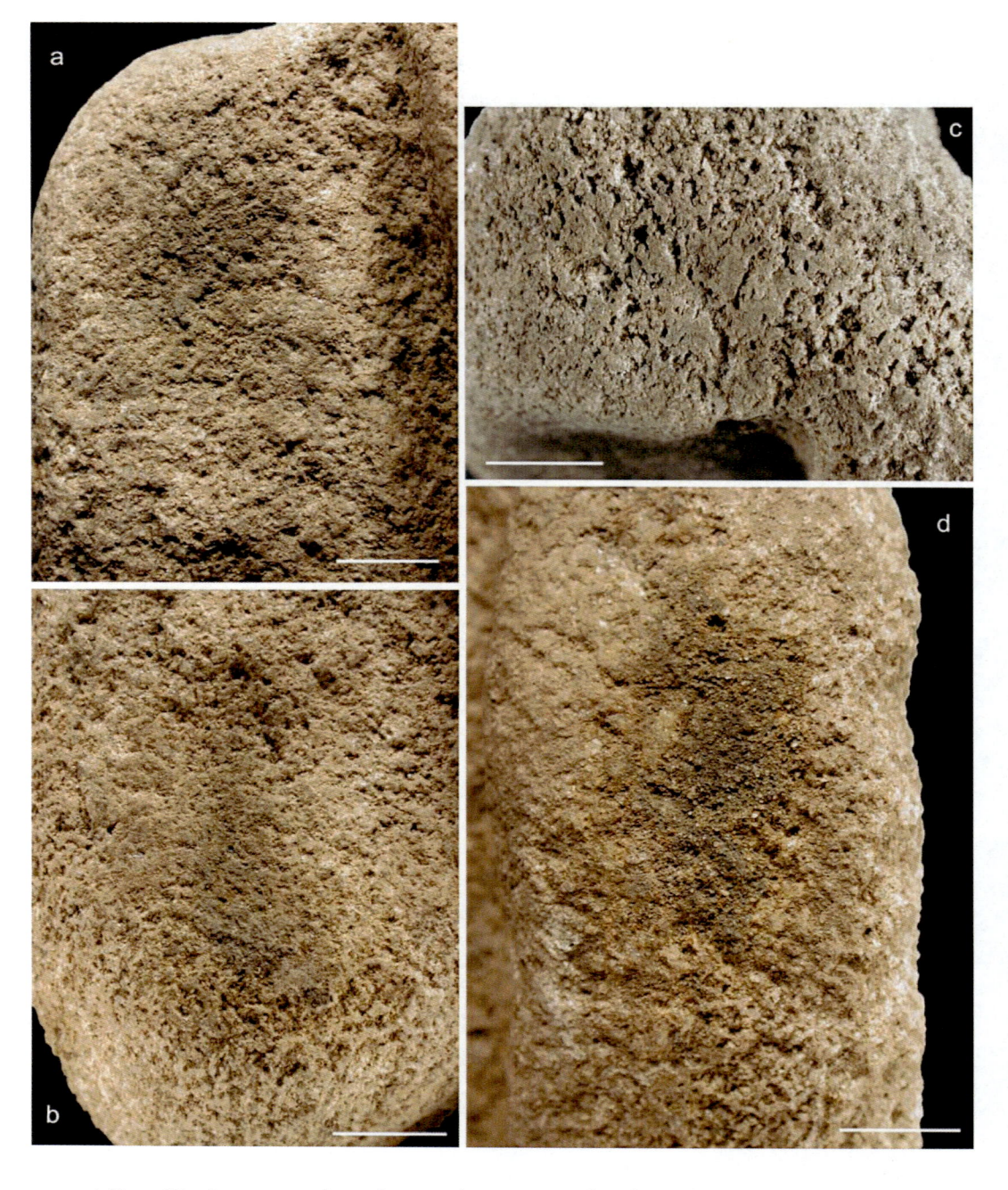

Fig 5.79 (opposite) Microscopic appearance of the sandstone block and depression D1 after cleaning: (a) microscopic appearance on Face c after cleaning; (b) and (c) surface depression D1. Scale = 1mm.

potentially utilised areas, and to characterise the wear pattern present on each. The microscopic appearance of the residues on D1–3 was recorded and compared to the sediment infilling the remainder of the object surface, in particular on Face c, where residue was more abundant. Three small areas of the objects were cleaned with acetone and a soft brush before being replicated with Cutter Perform Light Vinyl Polysiloxane impression material (Miles Inc. USA). The areas were: 1) an area of D2 located at the right of the zone covered with residues, 2) a short portion of the groove on Face a close to D2, and 3) a natural area on Face c.

The first replica covered a surface of 5mm², the others of ~10mm². Positive casts, made in RBS resin (CIBA T2L Chimie, France), were observed with a scanning electron microscope (SEM) Jeol 840A. Transparent casts obtained with the same replica technique were also observed and photographed in transmitted light. Eight samples were collected for microanalysis from six areas of the sandstone block.

Sampling was conducted under the microscope in order to select particles of sediment representative of each type of residue, while causing no visual modification of the object appearance. Particles of black and red residues were sampled from D1 and D3, along with particles of black residue from D2, a crust of beige sediment adhering in places on the bottom of the main groove on Face *a*, dark-brown sediment infilling the quartz grains on Face *c*, and the white cement of the sandstone on this same face. Samples were mounted on stubs and analysed with an EDS microprobe attached to the SEM. A small amount of sediment from patch D3, and from bone fragments found at similar depth in the deposit (samples 50811a and 50811b) was also studied by SEM (Jeol 5900LV at the University of East Anglia (UEA)). These samples were carbon-coated to allow element mapping in backscattered electron (BSE) mode and EDS analysis.

Results

Use-wear analysis

A remarkable difference was observed at microscopic scale between the unworn areas of the block and the surface of depressions and groove on Face *a*. The natural surface of the object on Faces *b–d* presented a highly irregular appearance. This was due to the 'open nature' of the sandstone matrix, made of coarse quartz grains (Fig 5.79a). The gradual erosion of these grains, and of the enclosing cement, had produced deep gaps. The tip of prominent grains still in place showed some smoothing, which was probably the result of a light abrasion produced by fine abrasive particles.

In contrast, the surface of depressions 1–3 on Face *a* was almost completely flat, with few residual shallow gaps. Quartz grains were also levelled and only appear in section (Fig 5.79b). At higher magnification (Figs 5.79c and 5.80) their surface was covered with micro-breaks resulting from repeated impacts. The freshness of the scar edges indicated that the depressions were not submitted to any significant post-depositional alteration.

The groove that crosses Face *a* longitudinally bore features that differed both from those recorded on the depressions and those on the natural surface of the object (Figs 5.81 and 5.82). Although more irregular than those of

Fig 5.80
SEM micrograph of a quartz crystal from depression 1 on Face a. (a) Scale = 1mm; (b) Scale = 100μm.

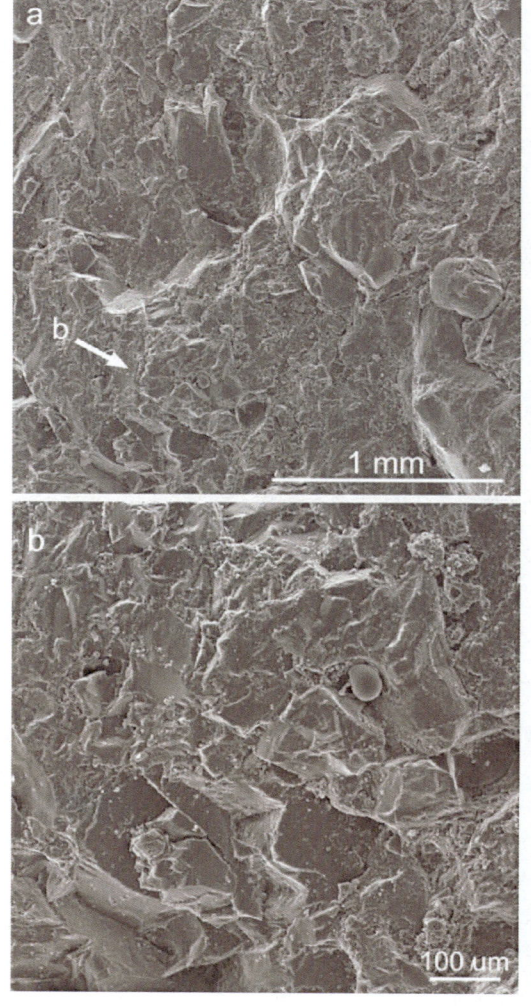

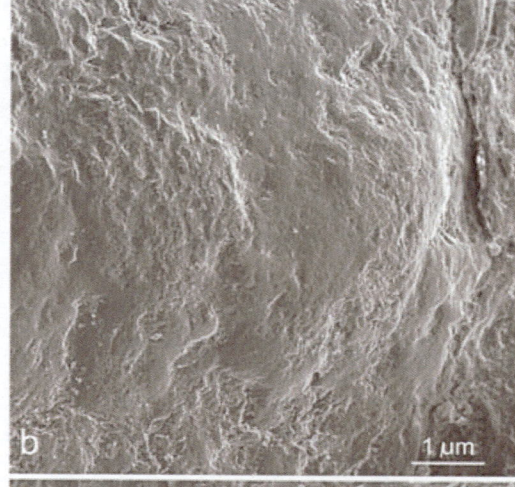

Fig 5.81 (below)
Groove longitudinally crossing Face a: (a) general; (b) close-up view illustrating the smoothing affecting quartz grains on prominent areas and in particular on the groove walls.

Fig 5.82 (above)
SEM micrograph of the groove on Face a: (a) general; (b) and (c) close-up views of the smoothing on quartz grains located on the groove walls.

the depressions, the surface of the groove lacked the gaps seen on the natural surface. Quartz grains on prominent areas showed no breaks, were slightly convex in section and highly smoothed, and had a characteristic opaque appearance. The wear was more developed on the wall of the groove than on its bottom.

The centre of the depression on Face *e* (*see* Fig 5.78c) also showed a localised smoothing. This smoothing, however, did not seem to differ significantly from that observed on the top of individual quartz grains close to this area. The same applied to the shallow grooves on Face *d* that, in addition, presented an even lower degree of smoothing of the quartz grains.

Residue analysis

The three spots of residue on Face *a* consisted of thin layers of black material surrounded by a reddish staining. Microscopic analysis revealed that the latter was due to the presence of tiny residues of fine, red powder, infilling residual gaps (Fig 5.83a). Small patches of the same red powder were also present within the black spots (Fig 5.83b). Both the red and the black powder were mixed with quartz grains deriving from the sandstone matrix. These grains were particularly abundant on the spot D3 (Fig 5.83e–f). In addition, the black was mixed, in places, with white particles between 50µm and 100µm in diameter (Fig 5.83d).

Fig 5.83
Micrographs of residues on the Lynford sandstone: (a) red infilling on D1; (b) black residues obliterating red staining on D2; (c) red powder mixed with quartz grains from the sandstone matrix on D2; (d) black powder mixed with white particles infilling a gap; (e) and (f) spots of red and black powder mixed to quartz grain on D3.

Microscopic rootlets trapped in the gaps between quartz grains were frequently observed on Face c, where the case of a 1mm-long seed was also recovered. A similar rootlet was also recovered from D2 during the sampling for microanalysis.

The EDS microanalysis demonstrates (Fig 5.84a–c and 5.84e–f) that both the black and the red residues were mainly composed of sulphur (S) and iron (Fe). These elements, which account for between 75 per cent and 95 per cent of the weight of the residues, were virtually absent in the cement of the sandstone and in the sediment composing the archaeological layer where the block was found (Figs 5.84g–h). The proportion of these two elements, however, differed significantly in the residues of the two colours. While the black powder was composed, in weight, of roughly the same amount of iron and sulphur, the red powder contained four to six times more iron than sulphur. The variable amount of silicon (Si) and calcium (Ca) in the residues was mainly due to the presence of quartz grains and calcite cement in the sandstone matrix (Figs 5.84g–h). The detection of carbon (C) in the red residues indicated the presence of an organic component. However, the very low amount of this element in the black residues, which were thicker, and which should have better preserved any traces of organic material, suggest that carbon in the red residue might be due to contamination from the enclosing archaeological layer. This is very likely considering the high values of organic carbon that characterised the sediment recovered from Face c (Fig 5.84h). The composition of the crust from the groove (Fig 5.84d) did not differ from that of the cement of the sandstone matrix (Fig 5.84g), indicating that the groove did not seem to preserve any detectable trace of the material that had worn its wall.

A tentative technological and functional interpretation

Analysis demonstrated that the Lynford sandstone block preserved clear traces of anthropogenic modification and use. The perfect state of preservation of the broken quartz grains on D1 and D2 suggested that the light polishing visible on the tip of quartz grains on Face c, and the intense smoothing of those inside the groove on Face a, could not be post-depositional. The first phenomenon is the probable outcome of a slight abrasion which the block was submitted to before its collection by Neanderthals. The second must be interpreted as the result of an intense use-wear produced by the to-and-fro movement of an elongated object inside the groove. The section and length of the groove indicate that this object had a diameter of ~10–15mm. The absence of fractures and striations indicates that it was made on a material softer than the sandstone matrix, but hard enough to wear portions of prominent quartz grains. Hard wood, bone or a soft mineral might be likely candidates. However, only experimental reproduction of this wear on a similar sandstone will identify the more probable worked material.

The surface of the horizontal limb of this L-shaped object has been intensively hammered, probably using a hard-stone pebble. This could have been made to shape the two depressions found therein, to increase the natural concavity of these two areas, or to grind a mineral. Two reasons suggest that the first two are more likely. Firstly, the pecking was applied with the same intensity to a surface larger than that stained by the residues, covering zones close to the edge of object where the grinding of the mineral would have been difficult to perform. No detectable hammering was observed on D3, where a consistent amount of residue is found.

Secondly, the EDS microanalysis provides only the elemental composition of the residues and does not identify the mineral, or minerals in these residues. However, the presence of both iron and sulphur suggests the presence of either iron sulphide such as the pyrites (FeS_2), and marcassite (FeS_2), or pyrrhotite ($Fe1-xS$), or iron sulphate such as melanterite ($FeSO_4.7H_2O$). The sediment from patch D3 contained no obvious framboidal pyrite, though isolated pyrite crystals, about 1μm across, were quite common, showing up as bright spots in BSE mode and confirmed by EDS. The sediment also contained frequent patches of micronscale (typically crystals with 10μm long axis) cementation by euhedral cements, which, under EDS, proved to be composed of calcium sulphate, clearly the mineral gypsum ($CaSO_4.2H_2O$). Similarly, sediment scraped from bone fragments found at a similar depth in the deposit (37095STD samples 50811a and 50811b) contained tiny pyrite crystals and gypsum cements.

Fig 5.84 (opposite) Results of the EDS microanalysis: (a) black residue from D1; (b) black residue from D3; (c) black residue from D2; (d) crust from the bottom of the groove on Face a; (e) red residue from D1; (f) red residue from D3; (g) cementum of the sandstone; (h) sediment infilling gaps between quartz grains on Face f.

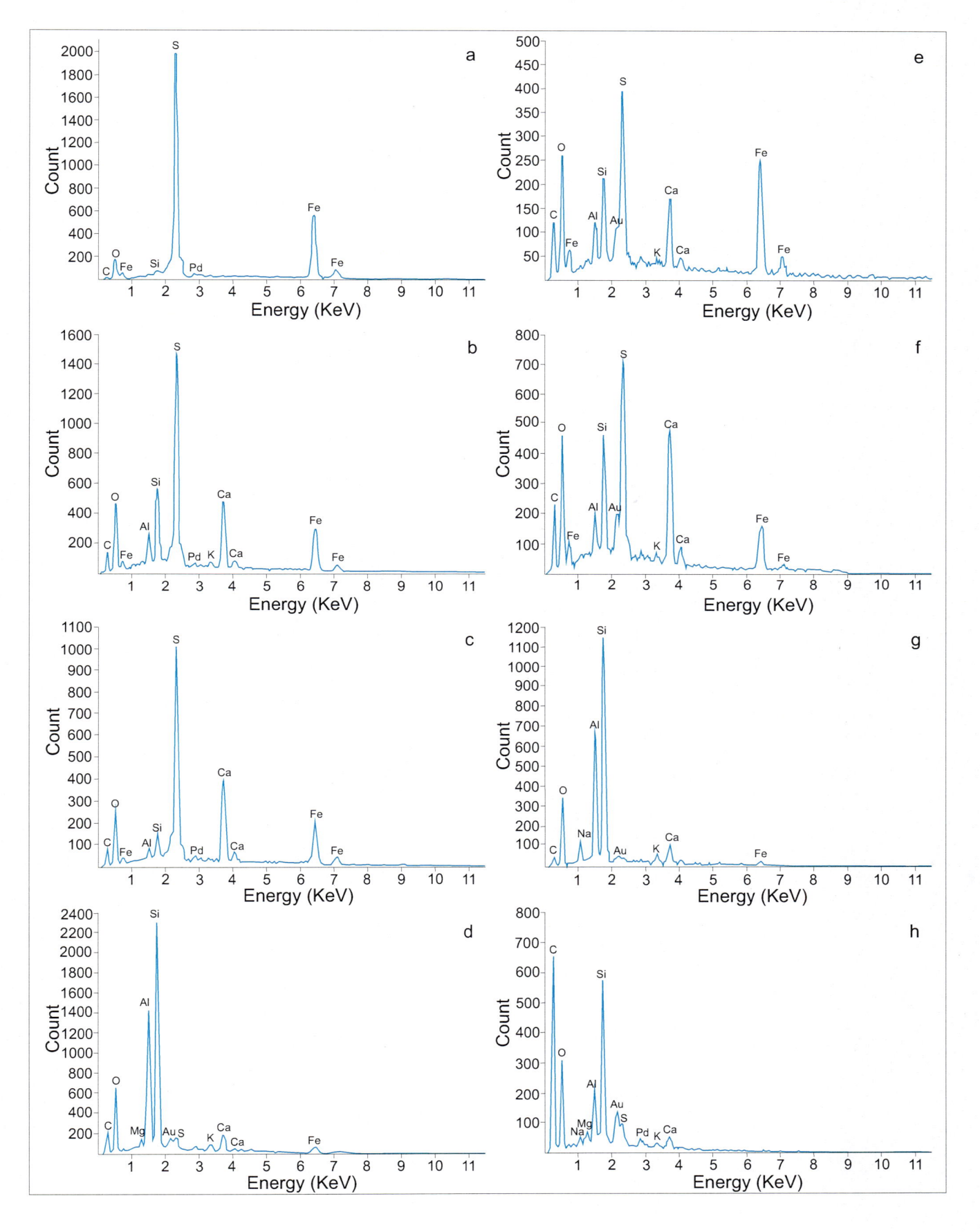

Although bacterial framboidal pyrite was not seen in any of the samples analysed, it was seen in pollen separations from the same horizons in the bulk sediment (Green, this chapter). The lack of framboidal pyrite suggests post-depositional oxidation of original framboidal pyrite, releasing small amounts of sulphate, which prompted renewed, localised, bacterial sulphate reduction in microenvironments (compare Bottrell *et al* 1998). This caused slow nucleation of tiny pyrite crystals in a relatively closed geochemical microenvironment. Oxidation of pyrite also generated acidity (Bottrell *et al* 1998), causing micro-scale dissolution of calcium carbonate in the sediment and the subsequent reprecipitation of gypsum and possibly also melanterite crusts on some surfaces. As this mineralogical association was seen in sediment patches on both the sandstone block and bone fragments, it suggests a natural process of formation during sediment diagenesis, rather than one directly associated with use of the block itself.

The interpretation that the residues are natural seems reasonable, although the association of some residues with the humanly modified depressions means that an anthropogenic origin of the residues should also be considered. The use of pyrite and marcassite to make fire is well attested historically and ethnographically (see references in Perlès 1977; Collina-Girard 1998). The most common technique is that of striking a fragment of marcassite tangentially several times with a flint or quartz crystal. This produces sparks that start to smoulder when directed onto dry plant fibres or, traditionally, on a crumbled dried mushroom tinder (*Polyporus fomentarius*). Pyrite is known from the Mousterian layers of the Grotte de la Hyène at Arcy-sur-Cure, (Yonne, France) and the Upper Palaeolithic layers of the Trou-de-la-Mère-Clochette (Jura, France), Vogelherd (Germany), as well as Pincevent (Seine-et-Marne, France). These fragments, however, do not seem to bear clear traces of use. The oldest fragments of pyrite with clear marks of impacts were recovered from the Magdalenian levels of the Trou-de-Chaleux (Belgium) and Laussel (France). These objects become common at Mesolithic, such as at Star Carr (UK) and more recent sites. The oldest known fragments of tinder are from the Mousterian site of Salzgitter-Lebensted (Germany). However, they show no traces of burning to suggest they were used to make fire.

The association of what are possibly residues related to iron sulphate, and the modification recorded on the Lynford block, make this a *candidate* object for the oldest known evidence for the production of fire using a striker. Interestingly, however, ethnographic studies to date suggest that a residue is not normally left behind on the artefact. This is consistent with the Lynford evidence, as there is no positive proof that the residues are anything other than the natural products of sediment diagenesis. Despite this, further experiments are being conducted to test whether the production of iron-sulphide powder, scraped or ground onto a striker surface, would be an effective way of improving ignition. If so, this might suggest that a new, currently ethnographically unknown, technique was at least possible.

6

The Lynford Neanderthals

C GAMBLE AND W A BOISMIER

*Buttercups are not the first flower that comes to mind when thinking about Neanderthals. But when a small group of these distinctive hominins walked into the Lynford locale on a mild, early summer's day 60,000 years ago, their first sight would have been a dazzling carpet of water crowsfoot (*Ranunculus cf aquatilis*, a close relative of the terrestrial buttercup), its distinctive white flowers with yellow centres covering the surface of the still water.*

The going would have been soft, slippery and squelchy. The nearby river, swollen by the spring melt and topped up by seasonal rains, had inundated the surrounding flood plain, making walking difficult and keeping to the tracks essential. The tracks were made by animals that had traversed this local swamp before the hominins arrived, to graze on the rich seasonal abundance of grass in the drier areas, and browse the diverse aquatic flora that fringed the banks and pools. These tracks do not survive, but would have formed an obvious route for the Neanderthals, who, although they travelled light, were nonetheless encumbered with carrying the smaller children and the few materials with which they made a living.

The hominins would have been aware of the locale long before they saw it: the smell of decomposing carcasses thawing out; residues from their previous visits added to by carnivore kills and the seasonal deaths of animals in poor condition. Their distinctively large noses told them exactly where they were, summoning up olfactory memories of the place, who had been there and what they had done. Soon after the familiar smells reached them, so did the blizzard of flies and biting midges, which, although a feature of these people's lives in landscapes where standing water was widespread and mammoth dung ubiquitous, was still something of note.

Their attention would also have been drawn to changes; how much the bank had collapsed, the depth of the water, the opportunities for finding stone and brush for firewood, and the availability of immediate foods to snack on – stranded fish or birds perhaps? Someone might recall a previous visit, when a horse had been drawn to the locale by a desperate need to forage and had slid into the water and been trapped by the steep bank. This initial source of food would have affected decisions about how long to stay and what to do while they were there. On most occasions the hominins were probably not lucky enough to find anything in the oxbow. However, they have been alert, on their arrival, to any opportunities for shepherding animals towards this watery trap.

A visit in winter would have been very different from the summer arrival: hominins would have encountered a white, treeless landscape, its few topographic features rendered undifferentiated, as snowdrifts covered frozen lakes, pools and rivers. No colours, smells, midges or circling carrion would have indicated the particular features of the area in this season. However, as long as the ice was thick, movement was easier, and with temperatures dropping sometimes as low as −15°C this was generally the case. Reindeer were present, but only in years when the snow cover was less than 600mm – for they cannot dig for food if snow cover is more than 600mm. The problem for all the predators who visited the locale – wolves and hyaenas as well as Neanderthals – was the same every winter; the need to find prey, dead or alive, in sufficient quantities to stave off hunger. Neanderthals had some flexibility in how far they were prepared to move, and in adjusting the size of the groups that travelled together. However, 60,000 years ago, living at 52°N on a windswept peninsula of north-west Europe, there would always have been two clearly contrasting seasons of plenty and scarcity.

This reconstruction of some of the evidence from Lynford brings to the fore the stark fact of life for any hominin living in northern latitudes – how the Neanderthals responded to the annual challenge of plenty and scarcity is of particular importance to understanding what kind of hominins they were. To examine this issue we will summarise evidence presented in the earlier chapters, place it in a broader context of Neanderthal studies and ask four questions:

1. Why do we think the Lynford people were Neanderthals?
2. Were they hunters?
3. How did they use the land?
4. Can we call them human?

We will conclude by examining a key issue in human evolution – the emergence of male control over resources and female reproduction – and ask if the Lynford data provide a pointer to when our unique human socioecology appeared.

Why do we think the Lynford people were Neanderthals?

There are no fossil hominin remains at Lynford. Instead there are distinctive bifaces (White, chapter 5), that for over a century have been regarded as the Middle Palaeolithic signature of the Neanderthals. However, the plethora of new fossil species uncovered worldwide in the last 30 years has led to a questioning of the old certainties about the relationships between fossil grade and technological competence. As a result, stone technology and typology are now less sure guides to the identity of the hominins responsible for their manufacture. For example, recent research has demonstrated long-term continuity in lithic traditions between the sites of Mata Menge (880–800ka) and Liang Bua Cave (95–12ka) on Flores, Indonesia (Moore and Brumm 2007). Such continuity from the Middle to the Upper Pleistocene encompasses at least two very different hominin species, *Homo erectus* and *Homo floresiensis*, and major changes in hominin brain size (Rightmire 2004). At a wider scale, Clark's (1969) Mode 3 technologies, represented by the flake and Prepared Core Technology of the Eurasian Middle Palaeolithic, the African Middle Stone Age and the Pleistocene technology of Australia, were made in different places by both Neanderthals and modern humans (*H. sapiens*), and possibly other species as well (Foley and Lahr 1997).

In the case of Lynford, the assumption that the hominins were Neanderthals is based on chronology. All the palaeoenvironmental indicators, and especially the beetles, point to milder conditions in an otherwise cold climate regime (Richards *et al*, chapter 3). The programme of OSL dating identifies these periods as corresponding to the Dansgaard-Oeschger (D-O) events at the beginning of MIS 3 (Schwenninger and Rhodes, chapter 2; *see* Fig 2.44). D-O events 14–17 are four brief and weakly developed interstadials that occurred in rapid succession between 53ka and 60ka, and collectively form the early part of the stable warm stage used in modelling MIS 3 environments in Europe (Van Andel and Davies 2003, table 4.3). Further corroboration is currently lacking from other dating methods. The assemblage lies beyond the range of radiocarbon (Boismier and Stuart, chapter 2) and the shells were too corroded to establish Lynford's position in the amino-acid sequence (Penkman and Collins, chapter 2).

The impact of the D-O interstadials on tree cover and temperature varied according to the effect of the orbital parameters of precession and obliquity. For example, D-O 16–17 saw stronger expansion of forest cover in the western Mediterranean than in more northerly latitudes, which experienced substantial tree growth both earlier and later in D-O 19 and 11 (Sánchez-Goñi *et al* 2008). The pollen evidence from Lynford (Green, chapter 3) shows a general scarcity of trees in the catchment, and none were growing at the site. These data suggest a D-O 14–17 age for the interstadial.

Lynford is not a unique environmental locale, as demonstrated by the close similarity in the beetle assemblages of Lynford and Upton Warren, Worcestershire (Coope, chapter 3), long recognised as an important interstadial during the last cold stage in Britain (Coope *et al* 1961). Field (chapter 3) draws attention to the similarities in the pollen assemblage between Lynford and several other interstadial last cold stage assemblages, also including Upton Warren. Furthermore, as Coope points out (chapter 3), the similarities between Lynford and Upton Warren extends to their stratigraphic contexts in channel-like depressions as well as to the composition of their large mammal assemblages. Upton Warren, however, has yielded no archaeological evidence and its radiocarbon estimation of *c* 40ka can no longer be regarded as indicating its true age.

An early MIS 3 age rules out *Homo sapiens* as the Lynford hominin. Currently the earliest human fossil in Europe is the Peştera cu Oase 1 find from Romania ~40ka (Trinkaus 2003), while the earliest modern human in Britain comes from Kent's Cavern and is probably less than 40ka old (Stringer 2006, 197). The age of the Earliest Upper Palaeolithic in Europe is still under debate (Mellars 2005; Adler and Jöris 2009; Soares *et al* 2010), but even on the most optimistic reading of the evidence dates to no later than 50ka.

It therefore seems unlikely that the Lynford Neanderthals either met or otherwise engaged with modern humans, as the latter appear in north-western Europe in significant numbers only after the climatically extreme cold event (Heinrich 5) that occurred between 47ka and 49ka (Adler and Jöris 2009).

Were they hunters?

The excavations and research undertaken at Lynford serve as a timely reminder of the advances that have been made in the way we assess hominin skills and capacities, particularly hunting, from archaeological evidence. For example, when excavations were undertaken at Torralba and Ambrona, Spain, in the 1960s (Howell 1965, 1966) the association of elephant bones and Lower Palaeolithic stone tools led to interpretations of big-game hunting. However, such a view was subsequently challenged on taphonomic grounds, and the assemblages re-interpreted as the result of mixing by fluvial processes (Santonja 2005). If Lynford had been excavated 40 years earlier it might well have entered the literature as an unproblematic Neanderthal mammoth-hunting site. As it was, the reassessment of Torralba and Ambrona and many other big-game hunting sites in the 1980s produced a view of early hominins, including Neanderthals, as merely opportunistic scavengers of meat and marrow (Binford 1981, 1985; Stiner 1994).

Such speculative excavation history emphasises the importance of the taphonomic debates during the 1980s and 1990s that brought a much-needed caution and rigour to the interpretation of hominin ways of life. This was achieved, as research at Lynford shows, by fully integrating the archaeological and palaeoenvironmental evidence to weave a stronger cable of inference.

The last decade has seen major advances in obtaining direct measures of hominin diets, and these, combined with traditional archaeological proxies such as animal bones, present a convincing picture of sophisticated Neanderthal hunting abilities. Stable isotopes now reveal that Neanderthals were top carnivores (Richards and Trinkaus 2009). Furthermore, their exploitation of prime-aged animals from herds of reindeer (Gaudzinski and Roebroeks 2000), bison (Gaudzinski 1992), *Bos primigenius* (Jaubert *et al* 1990), thar (Adler *et al* 2006) and ibex (Blasco Sancho 1995) in a range of mountain, upland and lowland settings underscores their dominant position in the carnivore guild. However, Neanderthals showed less interest in the potentially high yields from smaller packages of resources such as fish, shellfish, small mammals, birds and amphibians. Nevertheless, instances of the utilisation of these resources still occur, even though the calorific yields from these resources were small when measured against those of the terrestrial herbivores. In a study of predator pressure, Stiner *et al* (2000) argue that while Neanderthals at several Italian sites exploited tortoises and hares, predation pressure appears to have been slight in comparison with the same use of such foods by later modern humans. The exploitation of shellfish at Vanguard's Cave upper area, Gibraltar (Barton 2000) is a further case in point. Here a small assemblage of shells documents a modest dinner-time encampment, contrasting sharply with the middens composed of many millions of shellfish from modern human sites in South Africa such as Klasies River Mouth (Singer and Wymer 1982) and Pinnacle Point (Marean *et al* 2007).

Top carnivores do not have to prove themselves to us by also being unequivocal mammoth hunters. Questions about how the mammoths were procured, and how often, are not easily answered by the Lynford data, as Schreve (chapter 5) shows. But this is also the case in other archaeological instances. It seems that hard-line sceptics will only accept the evidence of spear points proven by experiment to penetrate elephant hide (Frison 1989), or found in the rib cages of mammoths, as occurs occasionally at a few North American Palaeoindian sites (Frison 1991). But apart from the wooden spear from Lehringen (Thieme and Veil 1985), its killing efficacy untested experimentally, the European record lacks such data. Instead, arguments must be based on the bone material itself, but – in this case – without the benefit of cut-marks. This makes the burden of proof even heavier.

What we can say is that the archaeological evidence for Neanderthal technology (a lack of bows and spear-throwers and a dependence on hand-thrown spears) points to a Neanderthal strategy of disadvantaging prey in order to kill it (Binford 2007). In his study of contemporary northern hunters using hand-thrown and thrusting spears, Churchill (1993, 19) argued that the killing of prey animals 'may have been restricted to places in the environment where the technology was most effective for the hunting of medium to large size terrestrial game'. In other words, if disadvantaging contributes substantially to hunting success, then natural or man-made traps, such as swamps, snow-drifts or bodies of water (Churchill 1993, 18) are essential for the technology to be deployed effectively.

Lynford is not the only site where these interpretive difficulties arise. At the Upper Palaeolithic Gravettian locale of Milovice, Czech Republic, dated to between 22ka and 26ka, almost 99 per cent of an excavated assemblage of 63,000 bones are from mammoths, representing at least 86 animals (Brugère et al 2009). Here the excavated material comes from discrete clusters rather than channel-fill deposits (Table 6.1). The ages at death of the calves points to spring as the season when the locale was visited, with hunters targeting the largest females from matriarch-led herds. As at Lynford, cut-marks and carnivore gnawing are rare. The breaking of bones for marrow did occur, but was a minor activity; fragmentation rates, which at Lynford are extremely high, are low at Milovice. However, in contrast to Lynford, all post-cranial anatomical elements are well represented and any oddities in the representation of individual elements can be ascribed to the effect of bone density on survival rates. A few hearths were found and are interpreted as meat-smoking fires.

The principal interest at Milovice, however, lies in the use of ivory. Far fewer tusks were recovered than expected (up to 89 per cent fewer) given the age profile of the animals that were exploited. This has led the zooarchaeologists to conclude that obtaining ivory rather than meat was the most important activity at the locale. Situated as it was at the border of several geographical and cultural territories, the importance of Milovice lay in its supply of ivory that was then transported away.

The simple fact is that even at Milovice there is no better evidence for how, how often, or indeed exactly where these animals were killed or scavenged than that seen at Lynford. The association of the two locales with modern humans and Neanderthals respectively, makes no difference when it comes to lessening the burden of proof set by those opposed to the idea of Neanderthals hunting mammoths. But it is clear from a comparison of the representation of elements and patterns of bone breakages that the mammoth resources acquired by the hominins from the two locales met rather different needs – a point we return to below.

How did they use the land?

Neanderthals were top carnivores with a rich animal protein diet coded into the isotopes of their bones. Interest in Neanderthals as hunters now shifts to an investigation of how the locale of Lynford contributed to their strategy of disadvantaging prey by shepherding mammoths, and other prey, to their deaths (White and Schreve, chapter 5), and to the question of what these resources represented in terms of a seasonal model of plenty and scarcity?

Table 6.1 A comparison of Lynford and the Gravettian locale of Milovice (Schreve chapter 5; in Brugère et al 2009)

	Lynford	Milovice
area excavated m²	200	500
all taxa		
herbivores	5	6
carnivores	4	3
rodents & lagomorphs	2	1
season of use	more than one	spring
mammoth		
% of total NISP	91.3	98.7
NISP	1246	63000
MNI	11	86
MNI:NISP	113.3	732.5
pathology (%NISP)	3	no data
carnivore gnawing (%NISP)	0.03	0.08
cut marks/bone breaking	very rare	very rare
limb bones	rare	common
tusks	common	rare

Local and regional catchments

The potential of the locale for Neanderthals' strategy can be analysed through two nested catchments. The first (Fig 6.1) uses the multi-proxy environmental data to reconstruct a 10km catchment around the locale, representing a walking catchment for Neanderthals of approximately a day's journey. The palaeoenvironmental evidence presented in chapter 3 indicates an essentially open, treeless landscape composed of a mosaic of different plant communities and habitats, situated on a low-relief flood plain with minimal topographic differentiation and subject to episodes of inundation by overbank flooding from the active river channel. These elements added up to fen-like habitats in abandoned channels cut off from the river. A mosaic of vegetation was found on the sand dunes and bare stony soils, which supported shrub and scrub communities, while abundant herbs and heath-like elements characterised the damp sedge-grass meadows and calcareous grasslands. The vegetation in the walking catchment was dominated by these last two habitats; damp or wet meadows and dry calcareous grassland. Furthermore, the co-occurrence of short turf or sedge and tall taxa point to a patchwork of plant communities extending from wet lake- or riverside areas to drier valley sides. Crucially, these habitats would have supported a high biomass of large, mainly migratory, herbivores on a seasonal basis. The abundance of coprophilous fungal spores and dung beetles in the pollen and coleopteran assemblages indicates that they were extensively utilised by herbivores, and allows a reconstruction of a heavily grazed landscape with areas of eroded and trampled vegetation. The seasonal abundance of large herds of herbivores would have acted as a magnet to top carnivores such as the Neanderthals, with flood-plain habitats such as cut-off lakes and ponds offering potential ambush or drive localities for the hunting of large mammals, and opportunities for scavenging from natural mortalities and carnivore kills. The presence of shrubs with edible berries, such as crowberry or bilberry, would have also provided some opportunities for the harvesting of plant resources.

The scale of the walking catchment is emphasised by the raw materials used to make the stone tools. These are overwhelmingly local in origin (White, chapter 5), and the Lynford locale lies only nine kilometres from the boundary between the Middle and Upper Chalk where high-quality Brandon flint was available in outcrops and from the local river gravels. However, a single handaxe was manufactured on a white-banded flint present in small quantities in the local gravels, but more common in glaciofluvial gravel deposits 18km to the north-west at Crimplesham (outside the local catchment). Other local raw materials do not appear to have been selected for tool manufacture. The Neanderthals thus appear to have been carefully selecting flint according to size and quality from outcrops and river gravels along the Wissey Valley, with the single white-banded flint handaxe possibly suggesting the movement of raw materials and people across the larger regional landscape.

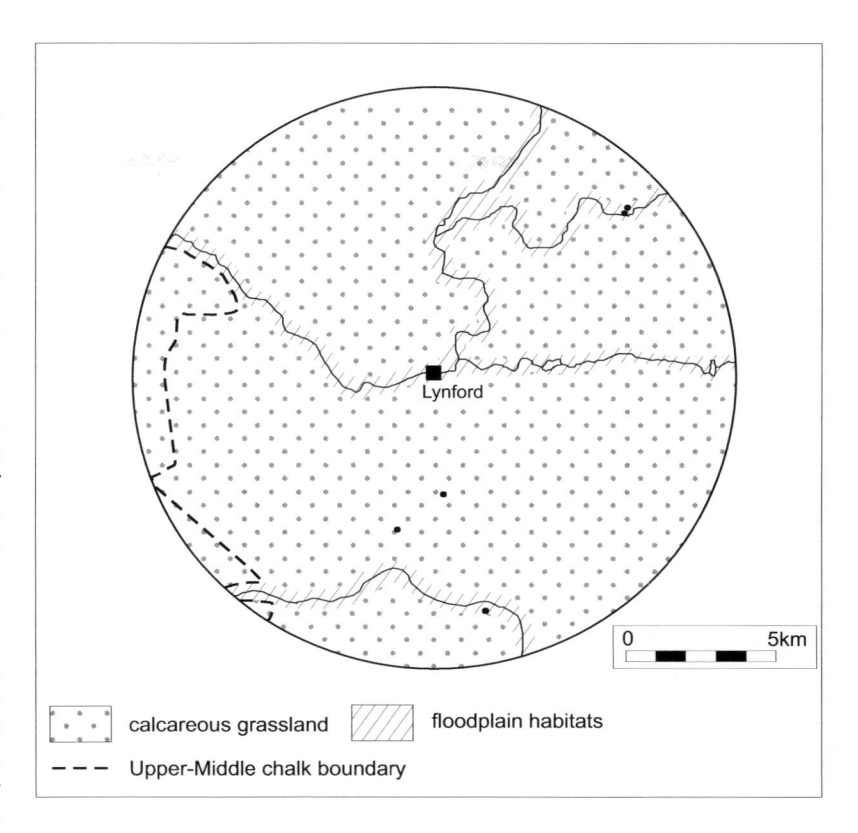

The second catchment is regional in scale (Fig 6.2). The limits are necessarily arbitrary, but do include other findspots of *bout coupé* artefacts (White and Jacobi 2002). These are most likely of MIS 3 age, though none are associated with the diverse fauna recovered from Lynford.

At this regional scale, the landscape is composed of upland areas dissected by river valleys such as those of the Wissey and Nar, and lowlands comprising the Fen Basin to the west

Fig 6.1
A reconstruction of the local, 10km walking catchment around the Lynford archaeological site.

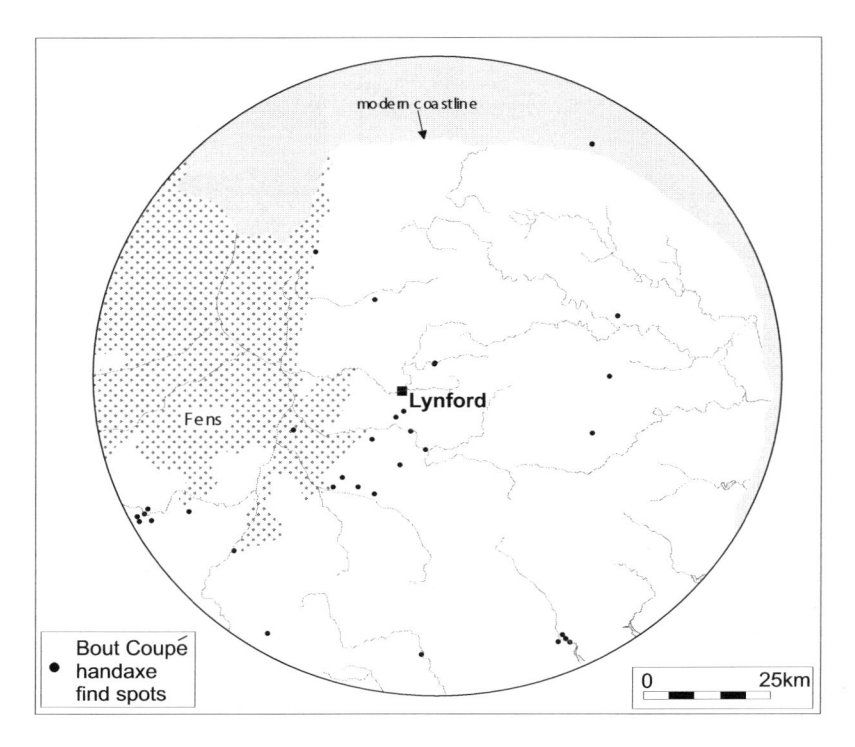

Fig 6.2
A reconstruction of a regional catchment around the Lynford archaeological site.

and south-west, with large braided rivers like the Great Ouse. Added to this were the areas now submerged by the North Sea around the coasts of Norfolk and Suffolk. The better-drained uplands would have supported a calcareous-type grassland made up of a patchwork of short turf and long-stemmed grasses and herbs. Based on evidence summarised by Guthrie (1982, see also Vereschagin and Baryshnikov 1982) and Kahlke (1999), it is likely that this patchwork was used differently by a herbivores, with short turf areas exploited by woolly rhinoceros, bison and reindeer, and long-stemmed areas of more coarse grasses and herbs favoured by mammoths and horses. River valleys, with their richer and more diverse mosaic of different plant communities and habitats, would have provided areas of high-quality forage for herbivores and abundant prey for predator-scavengers, including Neanderthals. Lowlands such as the Fen Basin would have also contained a complex mosaic of open plant communities and habitats according to local edaphic and microclimatic factors, possibly including trees such as pine in sheltered locations. The prevalence of *bout coupé*-type handaxes in river valleys suggests that these areas of the MIS 3 landscape were preferred foraging areas for Neanderthals. This was due to the seasonal abundance and predictability of a range of large herbivores both alive and as carcasses, and potential opportunities for the harvesting of edible plant resources.

Settlement system

Lynford stands out as an exceptional locale at the regional scale due to the quantity of material found at the site. However, because material slumped from the bank and into the channel, it is difficult to determine its significance in the wider settlement system. With imagination, Lynford might fit the criteria of a home base in Isaac's (1989) central-place foraging model, a place to which food is brought back daily. At the moment, however, such seasonal home bases are rare in northern Europe. The most convincing evidence comes from the substantial open-air camp site of Schöningen, Germany, attributed to *Homo heidelbergensis*. But Schöningen is Middle Pleistocene in age (Thieme 2005), as is Maastricht-Belvédère, Netherlands (Roebroeks 1988), which also has impressive quantities of flint work but little further evidence for features and purposeful structures, including hearths. This is common for Middle Palaeolithic sites, leading Kolen (1999) to describe the hominins responsible for them as 'hominins without homes'. Caves and rockshelters could have provided an alternative kind of home, but with the exception of La Cotte de St Brelade on Jersey (Callow and Cornford 1986), the evidence from north-west Europe is much poorer in terms of quantities of artefacts than Southern and Mediterranean regions (Gamble 1999).

An alternative to central-place foraging is Binford's (1984) model of routed foraging, in which Neanderthal groups were thought to follow the availability of resources through the seasonal cycle. This pattern established a regular itinerary, or route, so that over time materials accumulated at well-favoured locales. The frequency of movement was determined by the abundance of the resources and the size of the group, and the distance between moves depended on the size and quality of the food patch. Neither model implies any storage of food, relying instead on immediate consumption.

The Lynford data do not allow us to choose between the two models of land-use, but suggest instead that they have more in common than has often been supposed. Both models are variants on a strategy for obtaining essential resources that does not practice artificial storage, and both predict a large number of annual moves but within a relatively modest annual range. Where they differ is that the model of routed foraging best describes repeated visits to a locale, as indicated by the Lynford data., Either way, we can assume that MIS 3 Neanderthals were dependent upon the local distribution of resources under a cold climate, with no recourse to inter-regional solutions to mitigate the problems of seasonal scarcity (Gamble 1999).

Growth and subsistence foods

The limited geographical scale of the Neanderthals' strategy raises issues when considering their behaviour from the perspective of evolutionary ecology. Of particular interest is the role of cooperation in obtaining high-quality foods which are distributed unevenly in patches at different seasons, a topic explored by Wrangham (1980) for a wide variety of primate species. His focus is on female-bonded species such as vervets, gelada baboons and macaques, for whom the amount and quality of the food they absorb is of paramount importance (Wrangham 1980, 264). From this observation stems the proposition that the social relationships these animals form will reflect the strategies, including cooperations that they use for obtaining these resources.

Wrangham (1980, 269) distinguishes between a *growth* diet and a *subsistence* diet. The former is eaten when food is abundant, the latter in times of scarcity. It is the distribution of resources in the seasons of growth diet that matter most, since access to such abundance improves reproductive success. These foods in particular are unlikely to be continuous across a landscape. Among primates, such localised patches of resources such as fruit and plant foods can also be defended if animals cooperate – thus social relationships and the creation of social bonds result in reproductive benefits.

The situation facing Neanderthals would have been different, due to their reliance on animal protein, providing highly mobile food staples. However, the distinction between growth and subsistence diets still holds. Cooperation, both to obtain and to defend resources, would provide an advantage when such resources were sufficiently concentrated. Therefore the Neanderthals' best strategy was not simply to follow food as it became available, but rather to position themselves within a region in which they could exploit the seasonal opportunities presented by resource patches that allowed a growth diet.

Our suggestion is that the Lynford locale represents one such opportunity to obtain a growth diet. Cooperation between the sexes was essential if Neanderthals were to find, concentrate and kill animals and then defend them against other Neanderthal groups as well as other social carnivores. Such *consumption* and *defence* probably took place within a short distance from the archaeological site. The cooperative effort to *concentrate* resources focussed on the walking catchment, within which there were undoubtedly other opportunities comparable to the Lynford oxbow to disadvantage animals and so tap into a growth diet. And finally, it was at the regional scale that movements among an already rich animal biomass determined where the concentration would take place; in effect, Neanderthals created a growth diet patch by means of the landscape activity of shepherding (White and Schreve, chapter 5).

The growth diet model we present here has two principal settlement types; locales such as Lynford, created by the concentration of resources, and nearby sites where defence and consumption occurred. When preservation is favourable, sites that result from the concentration of resources will be more visible archaeologically, as is the case for the prime aged hunting locales described in the previous section. Lynford should not be regarded as a unique locale, and within its catchment (*see* Figure 6.1) other similar concentrations may await discovery. Consumption and defence locales will be less visible, forming scatters and occasionally denser patches of material in the vicinity.

The principle that cooperation benefitted the reproductive fitness of Neanderthal group members by making the concentration, consumption and defence of resources possible is indicated by further regional data. Stuart (chapter 3) argues that bison would have been at the locale in summer, moving east onto the North Sea plain in winter where the snow depths were less. In contrast, the shed reindeer antler indicate the presence of some animals in winter, and Stuart believes they would have spent the summer farther north, perhaps in Scotland. Therefore, a double migration is to be expected, determined by such factors as gaining access to winter forage, and mammoth would have been critical in this regional arrangement. No precise seasonality data is available for the Lynford mammoths but we would suggest, following Soffer (1985), that mammoths were more sedentary during the summer, due to the local abundance of the prodigious quantities of plant foods they required. The summer attraction of the energy-rich aquatic and riverside flora in the Wissey catchment (see Figure 6.1) began the process of concentrating animal resources that the Neanderthals then intensified. At the same time, the presence of reindeer during the winter season, when the subsistence diet prevailed, suggests that Neanderthals could still have been present in the region, albeit dispersed into smaller groups because of the less abundant and more widely dispersed patches that did not require cooperation. However, should concentration be possible during the winter, then there would have been occasions when the parameters of the growth diet were achieved, and the settlement system reflected this.

Can we call them human?

Almost twenty years ago Stringer and Gamble (1993, 219) argued from the archaeological evidence then available, that while Neanderthals 'were as human as us...they represented a different brand of humanity, one with a distinctive blend of primitive and advanced characteristics'. The authors also urged that since no impenetrable curtain separates Neanderthals from modern humans we should direct our efforts to examining the curtain itself rather than continuing to force the evidence into a model of two distinct and opposed types of hominin or human.

At first sight, however, the Lynford evidence appears to support a hypothesis of major differences between Neanderthals and modern humans. The artefact assemblage contains no tools other than those of stone. Evidence for composite, hafted tools is also lacking (White, chapter 5). None of the bone bears cut-marks, let alone engraving (Schreve, chapter 5). There are no hearths, although this is unsurprising given the character and history of the deposit (Boismier, chapter 4). Therefore, it would be easy to draw a picture of difference between the Lynford Neanderthals and, say, the modern humans at Paviland Cave, South Wales, who 29ka ago buried their dead with both honours and objects (Aldhouse-Green and Pettitt 1998; Jacobi and Higham 2008). Casting the net wider, it would also be possible to make the same argument for a significant difference between hominins by comparing the Lynford assemblage with the 80ka-year-old assemblage of engraved ochre, bone points, hafted Still Bay projectile points and *Nassarius* shell necklaces from Blombos Cave, South Africa (Henshilwood et al 2002; d'Errico et al 2005). Therefore, looking both forward and back in time, as well as outside the Eurasian world of Neanderthal hominins, the Lynford evidence initially contains little to challenge a paradigm of difference and otherness. However, the sandstone block analysed by d'Errico et al (chapter 5) is a possible candidate for the intentional production of fire, and adds further texture to White's (chapter 5) assessment of the Lynford Neanderthals as anticipating though not predicting their needs in the environment. However, possessing the skill to make and control fire would not tip these people into a new category of hominin, as fire and hearths are well attested at much older Middle Pleistocene locales such as Schöningen, Germany (Thieme 2005) and Beeches Pit, Suffolk (Gowlett 2010). Moreover, the evidence from MIS 3 cave sites shows that some Neanderthal locales had complex hearths, patterned activity areas and even a few ornaments (Balter 2009; Zilhão et al 2010).

Therefore the texture of the curtain that separates Neanderthals from modern humans is highly porous. This is hardly surprising given their similar degrees of encephalisation, and it is now axiomatic that large-brained hominins such as Neanderthals were highly intelligent and behaviourally flexible. Comparative studies of the relationship between brain size and community size among primates reveals a highly significant correlation between the two (Aiello and Dunbar 1993), suggesting that the cognitive demands of living in larger groups drove hominin encephalisation. The sizes of their brains predicts community sizes of around 150 individuals for both Neanderthals and modern humans, meaning that both species shared the social complexity involved in monitoring and maintaining social information on almost double the number of individuals that any non-human primate can achieve. New mechanisms were needed to reduce the cognitive load of such multiple interactions, and language has been proposed as one outcome. Neanderthals may have had the anatomical apparatus to produce speech (Arensburg *et al* 1989), and early results from the Neanderthal genome project indicate that they shared the modern human form of the so-called 'language gene' FOXP2 (Krause *et al* 2007). In addition, and using the same comparative data, it is clear that Neanderthals possessed advanced Theory of Mind (ToM) and were able to grasp multiple levels of intentionality, and so recognise that another individual's point of view differed from their own (Dunbar 2003); the implications of this for our understanding of Middle Pleistocene stone tools have been explored by McNabb (2007).

As a result it is now very possible to consider Neanderthal hominins human, albeit ones different to ourselves. However, one element of difference remains to be understood in terms other than simply those of a simpler technology and the rarity of ornaments. For example, how does the Lynford evidence look when considered within a general model of hunters and gatherers using ecology to understand factors such as diet choice and settlement pattern (Binford 2001; Kelly 1995)?

The growing season

The measure of Effective Temperature has been used by Binford (2001) to examine the environmental distribution of contemporary hunters and gatherers, and in particular the extent to which groups are reliant on fishing, hunting or gathering. Effective Temperature ranges between 8°C and 26°C for the world's habitats, and reflects the length of the warm growing season between the equator and the Arctic. It is calculated as follows: $ET = 18W - 10C/W - C + 8$, where W is the warmest month (July) and C the coldest (January). For a full description see Binford (2001) and Kelly (1995).

When population densities are low (< 9.098 persons per 100km^2) a threshold appears at ET values of 12.75°C: below this, no contemporary foraging society depends on plant foods for the majority of its diet. Furthermore, the majority of economies that depend on fishing – either riverine or marine – occur between ET values of 11.75°C and 9.5°C. Moreover, they share this environmental space with cold-climate terrestrial and marine mammal hunting. Contemporary foragers living in the lowest ET environments between 9.5°C and 8°C acquire their subsistence almost exclusively by fishing (Binford 2001, table 5.01; Binford 2007, figure 2).

How do the Lynford Neanderthals compare to the contemporary sample? Current temperature values for East Anglia give an ET value of 13.82°C (July = 21°C:Jan = 6°C), well within the environmental zone of plant subsistence that might be expected for an agriculturally rich region. The Lynford archaeological site produced two cold-season temperature estimates: –15°C as indicated by the climatic tolerances of beetles (Coope, chapter 3), and –8°C from pollen (Green, chapter 3), while both lines of proxy temperature evidence give estimated warm-season temperatures at 14°C. These figures produce ET values for MIS 3 Lynford of between 11.06°C and 10.86°C.

Both the Lynford values fall well below the plant diet threshold (ET 12.75°C), but above the temperatures (ET <9.5°C) at which, in modern cases, only fishing is found. Given that Binford's sample is based exclusively on contemporary hunters and gatherers, the question that needs to be considered is how the Lynford Neanderthals managed to survive at such low values of ET without modern technology such as spear-throwers and bows, and without fishing, as the stable isotope evidence shows (Richards and Trinkaus 2009). The answer must lie in the levels of biomass among the large mammals where megafauna such as mammoths and woolly rhinoceros are a significant addition.

Moreover, while contemporary foragers can exist in very cold environments with the shortest growing seasons (ET <9.5°C) by fishing, it seems that Neanderthals could not. When summer temperatures only reach 9°C and winter temperatures are at or below 0°C, then ET values are always less than the 9.5°C threshold. If MIS 4 environments were characterised by such short growing seasons (R Coope pers comm) then this might have marked an important environmental threshold, and explains the absence of Neanderthal occupation in Britain and north-west Europe during this stage (White, chapter 5). Higher ET values at the start of MIS 3 therefore produced resource patches at sufficient density, boosted by the presence of megafauna to meet the growth diet model, and resettlement subsequently occurred. A lack of interest in fish does not exclude Neanderthals from being human, but it does make them different.

Explaining the differences: a model of human socioecology

Therefore, the question 'what kind of hominins were Neanderthals?' now receives the answer that they were socially complex, behaviourally sophisticated and adaptively accomplished. But if Neanderthals generally, and those responsible for the Lynford assemblage in particular, are now classified as less of a hominin 'other' and more like another kind of human, then a major issue still remains: what explains the differences? These were large-brained, potentially language-capable people with high levels of ToM and able to deal cognitively with multiple levels of intentionality. They were top carnivores, their behaviour characterised by anticipation and foresight, planning for the future both literally and metaphorically by burying their dead in caves and accumulating significant objects such as the Lynford bifaces (White, chapter 5). But why do their material inventories demonstrate comparatively little interest in the accumulation and consumption of aesthetic objects? The discovery of four perforated and pigment-stained shells from the Middle Palaeolithic of Cueva de los Aviones and Cueva Antón, Iberia, dated to 50ka (Zilhão et al 2010), while significant, does not challenge the volume or diversity of Wobst's (1990) aptly named 'Arctic hysteria' of art and ornament in the European Upper Palaeolithic. And while other areas of the modern human diaspora, notably Australia, are similarly impoverished in aesthetic materials during initial colonisation (Brumm and Moore 2005), the archaeology of global dispersal shows that only *Homo sapiens* made such sea journeys, relatively late in hominin evolution, and assisted by a variety of technologies that allowed social separation. Aesthetic display was just one element in this development (Gamble 2010).

These are two of the differences between the archaeology of Neanderthals and modern humans that need explaining. Aesthetic display is not exclusive to modern humans, and its variable expression by quantity and diversity of forms is a prime example of the nuanced texture of the interpretative curtain that separates them from Neanderthals. However, their different dispersal histories are fundamental, as shown by the restricted Old World distribution of Neanderthals, and the global diaspora of modern humans.

What light can the Lynford data shed on these issues? In this final section we adopt a socioecological perspective that builds on the interdisciplinary investigations conducted at the locale. A socioecological approach takes as its premise the notion that social structure is shaped by resources, and asks how ecology and social behaviour interact to optimise reproductive advantage. Foley and Gamble (2009) have drawn attention to Wrangham's (1980, fig 2) socioecological model for primates, in which the distribution of resources controls the

Fig 6.3
The classical model of socioecology, in which owing to the different costs of male and female reproduction, females are more strongly influenced by the distribution of resources, and males by the distribution of females. During the course of human social evolution, the increased ability of males to control resources has led to closure of the cascade model, with males exerting control over female distribution through their control over resources.

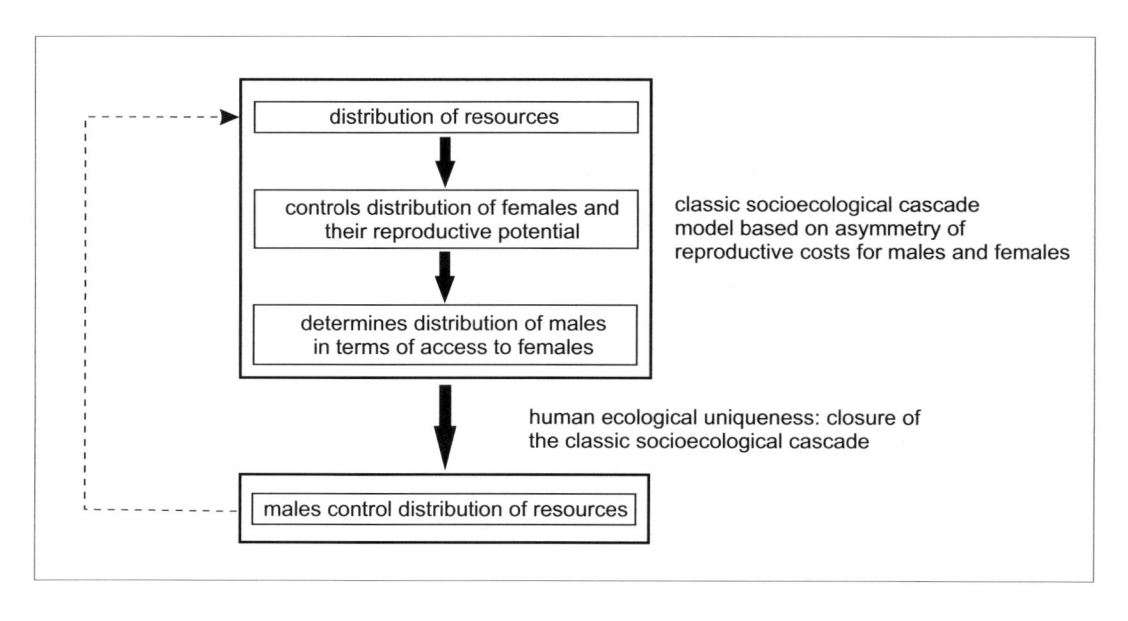

distribution of females and their offspring, which in turn determines the locations of the males (Fig 6.3), whose main role is to defend those high-quality patches of foods for the growth diet.

What is unique in human socioecology is that this cascade of resources and social structure has been fundamentally altered. In the human system, males have come to control resources directly and therefore, through a variety of geographical mechanisms such as storage and their defence of static food resources, the distribution of females and their young as well. This novel situation can most clearly be seen in agricultural and pastoralist societies with male control of social capital, in the form of fields of crops, herds of animals and female reproduction. Clearly the question of when this pattern of human socioecology first appeared is a major question for human evolution, and the Lynford evidence is highly relevant to establishing the form that Neanderthal socioecology might have taken. At issue is the use of resources not just to provide food and meet other adaptive needs, but to sustain the complex relationships that underpin social reproduction. If social reproduction depends upon male control over access to resources, then this will set up a different socio-ecological pattern than those that exist when females have autonomy. The male strategy can take two forms:

1. The accumulation of food resources as a store so that access can be controlled and, if necessary, defended.

2. The investment in, and accumulation of, aesthetic materials and artefacts that enable males to control access to the ceremonies and rituals of social reproduction where they are used, and from which they derive their significance.

The availability of food resources often results in accumulation at particular seasons. For example, nuts and 'underground storage organs' (tubers such as the potato) are highly suitable for storage (Ingold 1983). What distinguishes human storage is the harvesting of resources at one time and place, and their transport and disbursement at another: the classic *granary* model of stored foods where a surplus in one season is accumulated and controlled for future use. Storage is therefore constituted by social relations of production and consumption, and not simply by the capacity of the resources to resist decay. In the same way, the social storage of aesthetic items and tokens is also determined by social relationships, and expressed in patterns of exchange: the familiar model of the *treasury*, or hoard, which then feeds back into those very relationships and chains of connection between individuals.

These strategies were examined by Woodburn (1980), who drew the distinction between delayed and immediate systems of return among contemporary hunters and gatherers. In particular, Woodburn recognised the importance of rights over valued assets (1991, 32), which include technology (boats and nets, for example) as well as stored food, wild foods and female kin. The delayed system, often found in continents and regions (such as the Arctic) where encapsulation by agriculturalists had not taken place, depends to some extent on the ability to store, and for the most part the societies in Woodburn's sample were associated with temperate and cold climates. The immediate return system, characterised by low-latitude foragers in southern Africa and Australia, did involve some access to naturally stored foods, such as underground storage organs (Barham and Mitchell 2008, 91), but this was not common. If defence of territory or resources took place, it was conditioned by the local abundance of resources; for example along the fertile corridor of the Murray/Darling (Pardoe 1990) and in the Queensland rainforests of Australia (Best 2003).

But what characterises both return systems is the capacity to create material capital as the basis for social relations, using a wide variety of aesthetic means. The exchange of shell, stone, narcotics, artefacts, songs and ceremonies is a well-known feature among the extensive *hxaro* partnerships of the Kalahari (Wiessner 1982) and the continent-wide chains of connection in Australia (McBryde 1988). Moreover, Woodburn also points to the control over ritual knowledge by fully initiated Australian men, and the control of the distribution of women this makes possible in an otherwise largely immediate but unencapsulated return system: what he terms 'farming (and farming out) the women' (1980, 108–9). Woodburn's phrase captures the major change in the socioecological cascade that led to the unique human pattern (*see* Figure 6.3). In other words, once systems of storage were applied to social goods such as items of aesthetic display and ritual knowledge, then males could assert control over the right to use them.

Towards a socioecology of the Lynford Neanderthals

How does Lynford contribute to this model? Its geographical position on a north-western peninsula of Europe during an amelioration of the last cold stage provides important information about Neanderthal dispersal history. This peninsula formed part of the wider biotidal zone (Gamble 2009) that saw the repeated ebb and flow of fauna, flora and hominins as a result of climate cycling. For example, the settlement history of Britain and northern France (Roebroeks et al 2010) reveals there was no occupation during the severe climate regimes of MIS 4, when ice accumulation was strongly marked, permafrost extensive and temperatures low and highly seasonal; a point confirmed by the paucity of mammal assemblages between 80ka and 60ka (Schreve and Stuart, chapter 2). However, the Lynford evidence indicates the speed of the population flow into the biotidal zone following warming during D-O interstadials 14–16 at the beginning of MIS 3, a dispersal by both hominins and herbivores including horses, reindeer, bison, woolly mammoths and woolly rhinoceros.

The speed of dispersal was clearly controlled by the sudden availability of resources that could support a top carnivore in a previously uninhabited landscape. As mentioned above, the density of resources would have varied in the Lynford catchment and across the wider region; a factor amplified by the potential mobility of many of the prey species. The size of some of these prey species, and the suggestion that animals might have been shepherded to the locale, all point to cooperative effort by the community. So could the mammoth carcasses have been used as a form of storage, not only allowing Neanderthals to reduce the distances the group had to move during the year, but also giving males the opportunity to control a key resource?

The rarity of limb bones leads Schreve (chapter 5) to conclude that meat was being processed and transported off-site, but any further suggestion of storage is not supported by the evidence. Instead the contents of the oxbow are an indication of local abundance in an ecologically rich riverine setting (chapter 3); a pattern that would have been repeated throughout the Lynford region in comparable settings and with other prey species. The locations of these opportunities could be exploited by routed foraging as discussed earlier. Moreover, the local and regional distribution of these growth diet resources was what determined the location of females and offspring, and this ancient pattern of hominin socioecology then established the cooperative role of the males in defending these foods. The high incidence of trauma on Neanderthal skeletons, comparable to the injuries suffered by rodeo riders (Trinkaus 1983), might in part arise from this form of socioecology.

The lack of aesthetic objects found at Lynford and their extreme rarity on other early MIS 3 Neanderthal sites provides another line of evidence. Such objects, when found, can perhaps be regarded as 'symbolic'. But perhaps more significantly, their production is indicative of other ways of accumulating, and potentially controlling access to, the resources of social and sexual reproduction.

Lynford provides no evidence for the use of exotic raw materials. The flint sources are all local, as is the provenance of the sandstone block. In the European Middle Palaeolithic most raw materials were obtained less than 20km from the archaeological locale (Gamble 1999, figure 6.13) and nearly all from within 100km of the source. Larger distances are known (Slimak and Giraud 2007), but only a few retouched pieces, as opposed to blocks of raw material, made the longer journey. A case could perhaps be made that the accumulation of so many bifaces at Lynford (White, chapter 5) represents a form of social storage, but the local character of the raw material and the absence of any other aesthetic objects shows that this was not a strong feature. Therefore, the data do not suggest that the ancestral hominin socioecology had changed at the time the assemblages found at Lynford were deposited.

But what evidence exists that this pattern changed at all prior to the granaries of the Neolithic? Here the role of climate modelling and the comparison of Neanderthal and modern human niches proves illuminating. Davies and Gollop (2003) compared the tolerances and preferences of the two types of hominins, based on chronological distribution and climate reconstruction. Their findings suggest that while Neanderthals' and modern humans' tolerances are comparable, modern humans tolerated harsher conditions with respect to temperature, wind chill and snow cover (Table 6.2); a finding that agrees with the ET data presented above, and explains why Neanderthals are not found in the coldest environments such as those of MIS 4. Greater snow depth and more days of snow cover limit the ability of many herbivores to search for food, and the preferences estimated for modern humans could therefore be interpreted in terms of the differences in the density and predictability of food resources between Neanderthals and their ways of life. In this view, modern humans were adapted to their harsher environmental regimes by virtue of the social medium of storage, both of food and the materials of social reproduction in a system of delayed returns.

An analysis of competitive exclusion between Neanderthals and modern humans provides a further perspective (Banks *et al* 2008). Geographic projections of their varied eco-cultural niches show that replacement of Neanderthals by modern humans occurred during D-O 8 (38.6–36.5ka), rather than during an earlier severe climatic downturn such as Heinrich event 4 (40.2–38.6ka). Neanderthals might perhaps have been expected to thrive in the milder conditions of D-O 8 (Banks *et al* 2008, figure 3), but it is during this time that they became restricted to a southern refuge. Competitive exclusion provides a compelling explanation for these observations, but what form did it take?

Increased calorific yields through the innovation of a composite hunting technology, as found in the European Upper Palaeolithic, is a possibility. But such innovations need to be placed in a broader context. As Woodburn (1991) states in his model of return systems, it is rights over valued assets that matter. Male control over hunting equipment, and hence the means of production, is one such facet of a changing socioecology. The creation of stores over which males also exert control is another. However, demonstrating storage in the European Upper Palaeolithic is also problematic (Soffer 1991), despite exhaustive ethnoarchaeological studies (Binford 1978). Less contentious, however, are the 'treasuries' of accumulated aesthetic objects that have received so much attention in studies of the Upper Palaeolithic Revolution in Eurasia (Bar-Yosef 2002; Mellars *et al* 2007). The interpretation of Upper Palaeolithic activities at Milovice (*see* Table 6.1) as focused primarily on ivory rather than mammoth meat, is of considerable interest in this regard. The attention paid to a raw material that can be traded and made into items of aesthetic display represents the production of social capital that can be easily controlled. What eventually excluded the Neanderthals from their Eurasian homeland and led to their extinction could well have been a difference in the way their social behaviour was structured by the ecology of resources relating to the all-important growth diets, and which was radically different among the modern human groups that now arrived. Using anatomical and archaeological evidence, Soffer (1992, 254) has also forcefully argued that the difference between the Neanderthals and incoming modern humans was a dramatic change in economic and social relationships; in short, the gender-based separation and division of labour. Such a change would be expected as a result of a redirection of the evolutionary pressures on cooperation that occurred (*see* Fig 6.3) in the human, rather than hominin, socioecological cascade.

Table 6.2 Tolerances and preferences for selected climatic parameters among Neanderthals (Mousterian) and Modern humans (Aurignacian and Gravettian) in Europe during the variable conditions of MIS3 (59–26ka); based on archaeological site maps plotted on simulations of temperature, wind-chill and snow cover (Davies and Gollop 2003, table 8.3)

	Neanderthals	Modern humans
tolerance (range)		
temperature, wind-chill, snow cover and depth	similar	similar
preference (habitat)		
winter temperature and wind chill	milder	colder
days of snow cover	<60	<120
depth of snow cover	<50mm	<20mm

Therefore, the Lynford evidence lends itself to interpretation not as a place where mammoths were hunted (although this might well have occurred), or even where Neanderthals lived (although taphonomic factors render impossible an assessment of this either way). Rather, the density of resources in early MIS 3 in this part of the Neanderthal world was sufficient to allow the dispersal of people into this uninhabited part of the European bio-tidal zone. What controlled the pattern of dispersal and the establishment of a regional population were the opportunities for growth diets that supported females and their offspring according to the ancestral pattern of hominid and hominin socioecology. Males were secondary to this process, although their cooperation was undoubtedly necessary to secure those same resources. In short, the Neanderthals at Lynford were not the 'farmed' women James Woodburn identified in his work on modern humans, but instead 'tethered' men.

APPENDIX 1

Conservation of the faunal remains

S O'CONNOR AND N LARKIN

Conservation Strategy

The aim of the conservation strategy for the faunal remains from Lynford was to retain and reveal as much diagnostic data as possible, while ensuring the integrity and chemical and physical stability of the material. The general principles of the strategy were: that invasive treatments were to be kept to a minimum; only stable and removable resins and adhesives were to be used; all the labelling and storage materials were to be of archival standard and a record would be kept of the conservation materials and techniques applied to each specimen.

To make most efficient use of the limited time and budget available for conservation, the work was targeted to address the needs of the other specialists involved in the post-excavation project. This close liaison ensured that the conservation treatments for specific objects did not conflict with proposed chemical analyses or dating procedures, and enabled the drawing-up of a priority list and staged completion dates that allowed the faunal identification and taphonomic studies to be run in parallel with the later stages of the conservation work. Figures A1.1–5 illustrate both the condition of the bone material and the working conditions faced by the team in the field.

The conservation work is reported in full and in detail here, in part because of its importance in ensuring that the faunal material was in a satisfactory condition for further study, and in part to inform and guide similar work in future field projects.

The conservation team

The conservation of osseous material is a specialist area, overlapping both the fields of natural history and archaeology, and requiring a knowledge of appropriate conservation techniques and ethics; bone chemistry, structure and decay; site formation, taphonomy and the analytical and dating techniques currently applied to this class of material. During the excavation, Nigel Larkin, then Curator of Geology for Norfolk Museums and Archaeology Service, carried out treatments in the field assisted by Rebecca Crawford and Laura Stockley, and undertook initial conservation assessments. The subsequent conservation work was carried out in the Conservation Laboratories of the Department of Archaeological Sciences at the University of Bradford. Sonia O'Connor was the project leader, and the team included conservators Diane Charlton, Leesa Vere-Stevens and Cynthia Lampert, who were assisted by archaeologist Will Higgs. Kirsten Ward provided IT support. Nigel Larkin acted as conservation consultant, in particular providing details of the conservation work carried out on site.

Recovery of the faunal material

As the site conservator, Larkin's role was to ensure the recovery of all evidential material in the best condition possible. However, the weather pattern for the duration of the excavation was one of extremes. Exposed material was in danger of being washed away in sudden thunderous downpours, rapidly dried in high temperatures and bleached by the sun, all within the same day. With no shelter available, these were difficult conditions in which to record and retrieve such sensitive and often ephemeral material. In addition, the necessary pace of the excavation meant that there was great pressure to lift objects with the minimum of delay. The approach to the conservation of material on site was therefore very pragmatic. Work was occasionally carried out in less than ideal conditions or at great speed by a number of the site staff, for instance if a

Figs A1.1-A1.5
The mammoth tusks in situ during excavations at Lynford.

violent thunderstorm was approaching, and was sometimes done without the supervision of Larkin who could not always be on site.

Once exposed, material was often sprayed with a small amount of water or covered with damp cloth and a layer of clean sieved sediment to reduce the rate of drying. This prevented damage, but those finds that were exposed during the hot, dry weather, sometimes suffered extensively from warping and cracking, especially the ivory. The majority of the objects were lifted by hand, or on supporting boards, and bagged or boxed as appropriate. Where necessary, consolidation of very friable areas and adhesion of fresh breaks was undertaken before lifting. Some 30 objects were lifted in the field using plaster jackets. These included spreads of apparently related material, where it was felt important to retain the exact relationships between the fragments and fragmented or fragile whole bones, especially those that were very large and might no longer be capable of supporting their own weight.

The plaster jackets were applied in the standard manner for faunal remains. After excavation to reveal the surface of the bone, or the extent of the spread, each object was isolated on a supporting pillar of deposit while the excavation was continued around it. Once the depth of the object had been established, often by slightly undercutting the sides, the top and sides were covered with acid-free tissue and then a layer of aluminium foil, to act as a separating layer between the bone or ivory and the plaster jacket. Over this, the jacket was built up from layers of Plaster of Paris applied at the moment the plaster began to set, so that its flow could be controlled and it could be spread evenly using a trowel. Embedded within the jacket were layers of coarse hessian scrim, which, when the plaster had hardened, added strength to the jacket. The scrim reduced the risk of the plaster cracking when the object was finally undercut, inverted and carried from the site on a suitably padded wooden stretcher. The longer and heavier jackets also had lengths of wood or metal rods incorporated into them to improve their rigidity.

Some objects, including both jacketed and non-jacketed specimens, were either stuck together with adhesive, or consolidated in the field. In both cases the resin employed was the ethyl methacrylate co-polymer, Paraloid B72, diluted to different extents with acetone to suit the purpose.

After excavation, the material was moved to temporary storage at Gressenhall, the Norfolk Museums and Archaeology Service's large object conservation laboratory, where as much as possible of the material was unpacked and allowed to dry slowly in this largely unheated accommodation over several weeks. Finally, the material was repacked for transportation to Bradford in polyethylene bags, card skeleton boxes or boxes custom-made from corrugated polypropylene board (Correx) supported on wood frames and padded with bubblewrap, acid-free tissue, polyethylene foam sheets (Jiffy Foam) or blocks (Plastazote), as appropriate.

Condition of the material

The bones from Lynford were 'subfossil', which means that their preservation was not primarily influenced by secondary mineralisation (fossilisation). On site it was immediately clear that the bones from different deposits were very differently preserved. Bones from the black, organic-rich deposits were stained dark brown-black, and were relatively robust, with good preservation of surface features and often a lustrous look when clean and dry. These characteristics indicated good preservation of the organic component of the bone and very little net loss of the mineral component. In contrast, bones from the underlying sands and gravels were amber or red-brown in colour, soft when wet, and brittle or crumbly when dry.

Bones from the gravels in particular were frequently highly fractured when recovered (Fig A1.6). This additional mechanical damage was probably caused shortly after deposition by trampling. Bones pushed into these deposits by the feet of passing animals would be crushed against the stones, while those in the organic deposits would be cushioned by the soft, wet, bulky rotting vegetation and rapidly incorporated into the protecting sediment. A small number of individually numbered specimens did not survive excavation in these extreme weather conditions and eventually arrived at Bradford as bags of ginger-coloured bone frass. This fragility when wet, and loss of cohesion when dry, indicated that very little of the organic structure of this bone survived. Some of the larger bones and tusks, and one or two of the mammoth teeth, lay partly in the organic deposits and partly in the sands and gravels, and their preservation varied accordingly, from end to end or side to side.

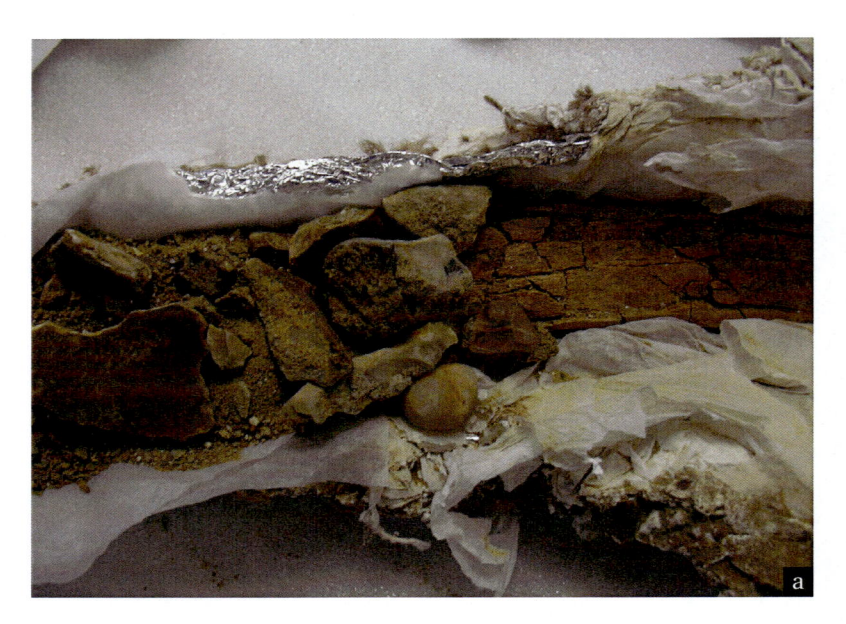

*Fig A1.6
Mammoth rib 50163:
(a) during removal from its plaster jacket; and (b) detail of the surface of the bone.*

this is reflected in the way that it breaks during degradation. The ivory was stained to the same range of colours as the bone, but had shattered into layer upon layer of roughly cuboidal fragments. Four of the tusks were lifted in individual plaster jackets but the others were so shattered and scattered that they had completely lost their shape, and lifting as discrete objects was not attempted. The molars, which consist of dentine interleaved with darkly stained enamel, had fared much better and were largely intact, with good preservation even of the thin-walled roots.

Although there were only about 2100 individually numbered osseous finds, each find could consist of one to fifty or more pieces packed together. Some groups of fragments were from single bones but others clearly were not. Sizes varied from a few centimetres in length to over a metre for individual bones such as ribs. The largest plaster jackets required several people to move them. At the other end of the scale there were thousands of fragments a few millimetres across, recovered from the sieving of each spit of the deposits. In addition there were 32 sacks of ivory fragments weighing several kilogrammes each.

The surfaces of the bone and ivory were obscured to a greater or lesser extent by deposits from the site. However, the skeletal material preserved a palimpsest of information such as evidence of pathologies, trauma, abrasion from use of the tusks *in vivo* and taphonomic information (Schreve, chapter 5). Fresh breaks and other damage sustained by the material during excavation were easily distinguishable from old damage, as they revealed the lighter colouration of the material beneath the surface.

During excavation, some of the exposed bones developed areas of whitened surface as a result of several distinctly different processes. In some instances, over a period of days, an efflorescence of crystals formed a crust on a bone or tusk, just above the surface of the ground. This was a result of salt-laden ground water being drawn up into the porous bone. Some of these salts might have originated from the degraded bone itself. Evaporation concentrated the salts at the surface until the solution became saturated, and then the salts precipitated and formed a white tide-line. There could also have been a reaction between the salt solution and the atmosphere, as, once the tide-line formed, it could not be removed

The very few identifiable fragments of antler were similarly stained by the different deposits. The fractures in the beams and tines were both transverse and longitudinal, often producing wedge-shaped slivers running through the compact bony cortex into the spongy medulla beneath (Fig A1.7a). The bigger antler finds were therefore fragile, and branched in several directions, making them quite difficult to lift in the field and to conserve.

Mammoth teeth, including tusks, molars and milk teeth were also recovered (Schreve and Lister, chapter 5). Ivory tusks are composed of dentine, which, although chemically very similar to bone, is structured differently, and

with water. FT-Raman spectroscopy of samples of the ivory identified surface deposits of gypsum, anhydrite, limonite and lepidocrocite (Edwards et al 2005).

A second type of surface whitening seemed to be due to an alteration of the bone itself. This occurred where bone or ivory was exposed to the bright summer sunshine for a few days. Although the actual processes involved are not known, the phenomenon was referred to as 'bleaching'. This colour change could not be reduced by brushing or by the application of water or organic solvents.

The third form of white deposit only occurred on bone and ivory fragments that were consolidated on site, and was due to application of Paraloid B72 to objects that were too wet. It is often very difficult to determine when an object is dry enough to consolidate successfully at depth, especially when the object is still partially buried. Some resins can be used as an emulsion, and these will penetrate damp material but set only when the water evaporates. Unfortunately emulsions take much longer to dry than solvent-based resins and if the object is in damp ground, the emulsion will not set until the object is lifted and dried. Furthermore, where an object is particularly wet, the emulsion will become diluted and, when dry, might not consolidate the material sufficiently. When a resin consolidant dissolved in an organic solvent, such as acetone, is mixed with water, the resin comes out of solution and forms a sticky, viscous, translucent mass, which becomes more opaque and whiter as it dries. On site, if the surface of the bone or ivory is dry but the core of the object is damp, the penetration of the consolidant is limited to the dry region only. If the object is wet to its surface, the resin does not penetrate at all, but forms a milky skin over the surface of the bone. Fortunately, this resin skin can be redissolved and removed using acetone once the object is dry, but the limited penetration might give the dangerous impression that the object is more robust than is actually the case.

Post-excavation conservation project

The post-excavation conservation of the faunal remains consisted of a number of stages. The conservation of any particular object was determined by its condition, what treatment it had received on site, the information revealed during its conservation, and how it related to the post-excavation research agenda. Generally, the work undertaken closely followed that outlined in the conservation assessment. However, there were many more fragments than originally estimated and these, combined with the pathologies encountered and the unforeseen hardening of the sandy deposits (see below), resulted in the need to reassess the conservation strategy and particular procedures, to ensure that the conservation was completed to a satisfactory level within time and budget.

Database and recording

To reduce the time spent in recording the conservation of so many thousands of fragments, a computer database was designed specially for the project by Kirsten Ward.

As well as describing the condition of individual finds and the conservation procedures applied, the database also contains notes of interest to other specialists working with the assemblage. These might include observations of unusual patterns of damage or decay; surface marks; pathologies; possible signs of butchery; records of the removal and retention of samples; and references to X-radiographs, photographs or additional reports. Copies of this conservation record, and digitised X-ray films were forwarded with the objects and have been placed in the site archive. The original records and X-radiographs were retained at Bradford.

Conservation process

Depending on the condition of each find, different degrees of conservation intervention were required to reveal the surviving information, and ensure its future preservation. Each process is described below.

Cleaning trials

To ascertain the best treatment options, a series of tests was performed by Leesa Vere-Stevens based on some of the cleaning methods described in the conservation literature, particularly Turner-Walker (1998). The aim of these tests was to explore cost-effective ways of removing the adhering sediments without degrading the surface information surviving on the bone and tusk material. After discussions with Bill Boismier and Danielle Schreve, the fragments used in these tests were selected from context 20048, which consisted of a large group of disassociated, unstratified samples

Fig A1.7 (opposite) Antler fragment 51814: (a) as consolidated and recovered from site; (b) detail of consolidated fragments; (c) after conservation.

showing a range of preservation characteristics. Sediment removal using an airbrasive, brushes and compressed air and solvents, were all evaluated and compared.

In summary, the results were much as expected. Airbrasive cleaning, using compressed air and a range of abrasive powders with different particle shape and hardness, was too aggressive, visibly changing the surface texture of the material. Aluminium oxide and sodium bicarbonate powders produced a matt surface, and glass beads produced a shiny (buffed) finish. Manual, mechanical cleaning using a range of soft brushes and compressed air, and solvent cleaning using cotton wool swabs moistened with acetone, industrial methylated spirits or de-ionised water, both produced good results. When examined by eye and under ×40 magnification, neither technique caused any visible degradation of the surface detail compared with uncleaned areas on the same fragments.

Although both the manual, mechanical cleaning and solvent cleaning tests produced equally good results, the mechanical techniques were preferred over solvent cleaning. This is because the former are easier to control allowing local and continuous variation in technique and tools, as conditions vary over the surface of a specimen. Also solvent cleaning, depending on the solvent or solvent mixture used, and the state of preservation of the bone, can potentially cause stresses in the material by dehydrating or rehydrating the organic components, or cause disassociation of very degraded inorganic components. Therefore, in every instance during this project, solvent cleaning techniques were only applied where manual cleaning or mechanical techniques proved to be unsuitable or inadequate.

Cleaning the surfaces

Upon drying, the organic deposits became quite loose and friable, resembling fibrous potting compost. Some of the sandy deposits remained loosely bound when dry, although a crisp crust often formed at the exposed surface. In places, the sand hardened throughout its thickness, binding the stones within it to form a hard concretion. This was very tenaciously attached to the underlying bone, which itself was often very degraded. It is possible that solutes from the bone could have contributed to the compounds that bound the sand as it dried. Edwards (above) noted the formation of gypsum, which suggests that these concretions were literally plastered onto the bones.

The only tools used in the mechanical cleaning of surfaces were wooden cocktail and barbecue sticks, and a range of paintbrushes of different widths, length and stiffness of bristle. To avoid sand and grit abrading the surface detail, brushing was kept to a minimum and loose material was blown from the surface using a variable-pressure, compressed air jet. This compressed air was delivered through a nozzle of about 2mm in diameter, which made it very useful for blowing out deposits trapped in convoluted structures such as the sinuses of the mammoth skull.

The dark organic deposits were relatively easy to remove, but were occasionally left in place, for example as supports for fragments whose position was thought to be in some way significant. Where the sandy deposits were very hard, dampening them with drops of acetone often helped soften them so that they could be broken up with the point of a cocktail stick. Although water did soften these concreted deposits, it could not be used close to the bone. Absorption of water into the bone caused softening of the surface and potential cracking, by swelling the surviving organic component. With the most degraded material, the results of wetting the bone were more spectacular. In these cases the structure was so weakened that, probably due to a combination of increased weight and surface tension forces, a single drop of water could cause the collapse of exposed cancellous tissue, and soaking could lead to the complete disintegration of a bone. The acetone also had the advantage that it evaporated much faster than water and was compatible with the adhesive and consolidant resin, which could then be applied with little delay if necessary. Even so, the removal of these hardened deposits was a very meticulous and slow procedure. The sticks quickly blunted and frequently had to be reshaped, but the use of metal tools carried too great a risk of damaging the surface of the bones, which were often degraded to the point that they could be marked by drawing a fingernail across the surface.

As there had been a fairly comprehensive sampling strategy on site, the sediment removed during cleaning was only retained in exceptional circumstances, such as where the colour or texture seemed atypical of the surrounding deposit. Insect, plant remains and lithic material were also collected for further examination by other specialists.

APPENDIX 1 CONSERVATION OF THE FAUNAL REMAINS

Conservation of the finds consolidated on site

Many of the finds consolidated on site would clearly not have been successfully recovered without the application of the resin consolidant, but this first-aid treatment was not without its problems. Sometimes the concentration of consolidant at the surface gave a false sense of robustness to an object. This was especially true for bones such as the centra of the vertebrae, which had only thin layers of compact tissue over a very degraded cancellous core. Occasionally, although fractured, the bone exterior seemed complete, but the interior had entirely collapsed upon drying.

As discussed earlier, it is very difficult to ensure deep penetration of organic solvent-based resins during excavation if the core of the bone is damp. Many of the bones consolidated in haste, and probably in difficult working conditions, had dribbles or a sheen of excess resin, the white bloom that resulted when resin was applied to wet bone, or sediment bound to the surface. These deposits had to be removed with acetone to reveal the surface detail and morphology of the bone before re-consolidation in the laboratory. In other cases, although the resin held the fragments of an object together, they were not lying in their proper positions, having been displaced by trampling shortly after deposition.

The fragments of the broken antler 51814 were so displaced before they were consolidated on site that it was difficult to determine how much of the antler was represented or, indeed, whether all of the fragments belonged together (Fig A1.7a and b). Because the antler was wet, the solvent-diluted consolidating resin formed the white skin at the surface and did not penetrate to any depth, merely sticking the fragments and surrounding matrix together. To prepare this object for study, it first had to be disassembled using acetone vapour, and cleaned of resin and encrusting sediment, before it could be reconstructed (Fig A1.7c). The specimen might have been quite soft when wet, but once dry, the antler fragments proved quite robust. If, instead of consolidation, the antler had been lifted and carefully packed or given a plaster jacket, most of this work, and the risk to the object, could have been avoided. This is easy to see with hindsight, but in the field the most appropriate approach is not always clear-cut and often has to be the lesser of several evils.

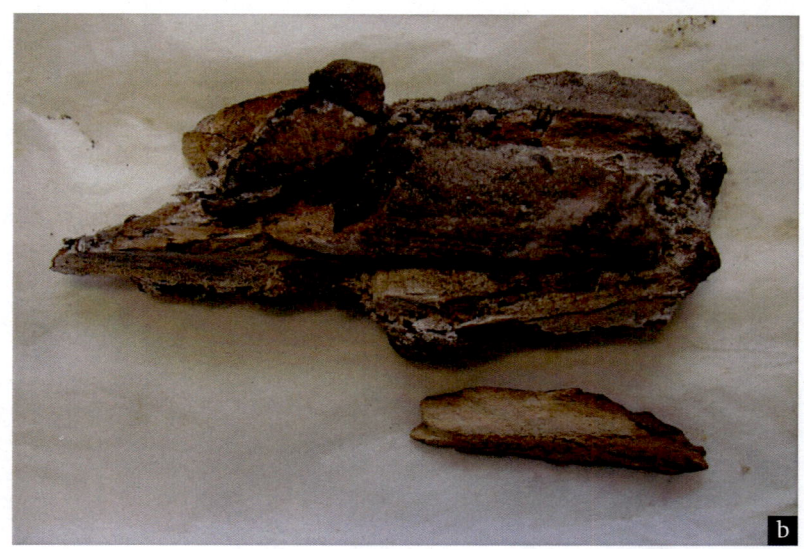

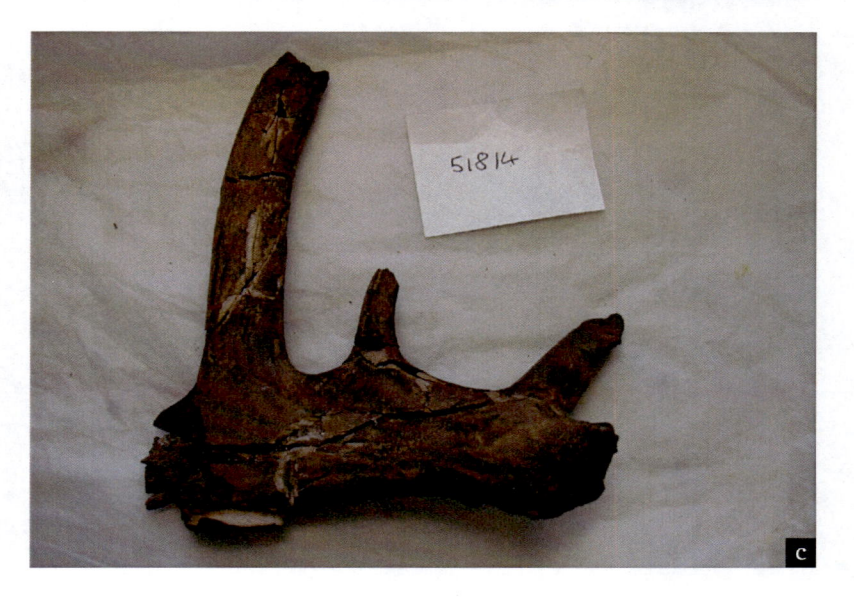

Joining, consolidation and gap-filling

With the faunal studies and the possibility of future biochemical analysis in mind, the use of adhesives and further consolidation was avoided wherever possible. Only fresh breaks were re-attached, and then only where this seemed necessary to aid the interpretation of the object or to prevent further physical damage occurring. To keep consolidation to a minimum, packaging was designed to improve the physical support of the objects and reduce the need for handling. Similarly, gap-filling was done only where this was necessary to ensure the physical integrity of a piece. In all cases Paraloid B72 was used as the resin base for these procedures. In some instances even fresh breaks were not rejoined, as in the case of the rib 51635 (Figs A1.8a and b). This bone had extensive pathology and the decision was taken to only partially reassemble the fragments so that both the internal and external features could be examined.

Application of adhesives: For ease of application, the adhesive used was bought ready-made (HMG B72). Although water and organic solvents such as acetone are readily drawn into dry, decayed bone, the more viscous adhesive might not penetrate far into the surface. The result is a weak join, which, when it fails, can pull away the surface of the bone, reducing the closeness of the fit. Wetting the surfaces of the break with acetone, prior to applying the adhesive, ensured that this penetrated a little way into the bone and formed a stronger join. Sealing the edges with a dilute solution of Paraloid B72 before sticking a break both hardened and strengthened the degraded bone, and acted as a key for the adhesive layer. In either case the bone was not flooded with the solvent or solution as this could produce a tide-mark stain in the bone either side of the join.

Consolidation: For consolidation, pearls of Paraloid B72 resin were dissolved in acetone and used at 10 to 20 per cent (w/v), depending on the fragility and porosity of the material to which it was being applied.

One class of material in particular, the mammoth molars, did require consolidation. These molars are formed of alternating layers of dentine and enamel. The dentine is a bony, porous material with an appreciable amount of organic content *in vivo*, mostly the protein collagen. The enamel is a largely mineral, crystalline material. These materials decay differentially during burial, the enamel generally being more persistent. When the

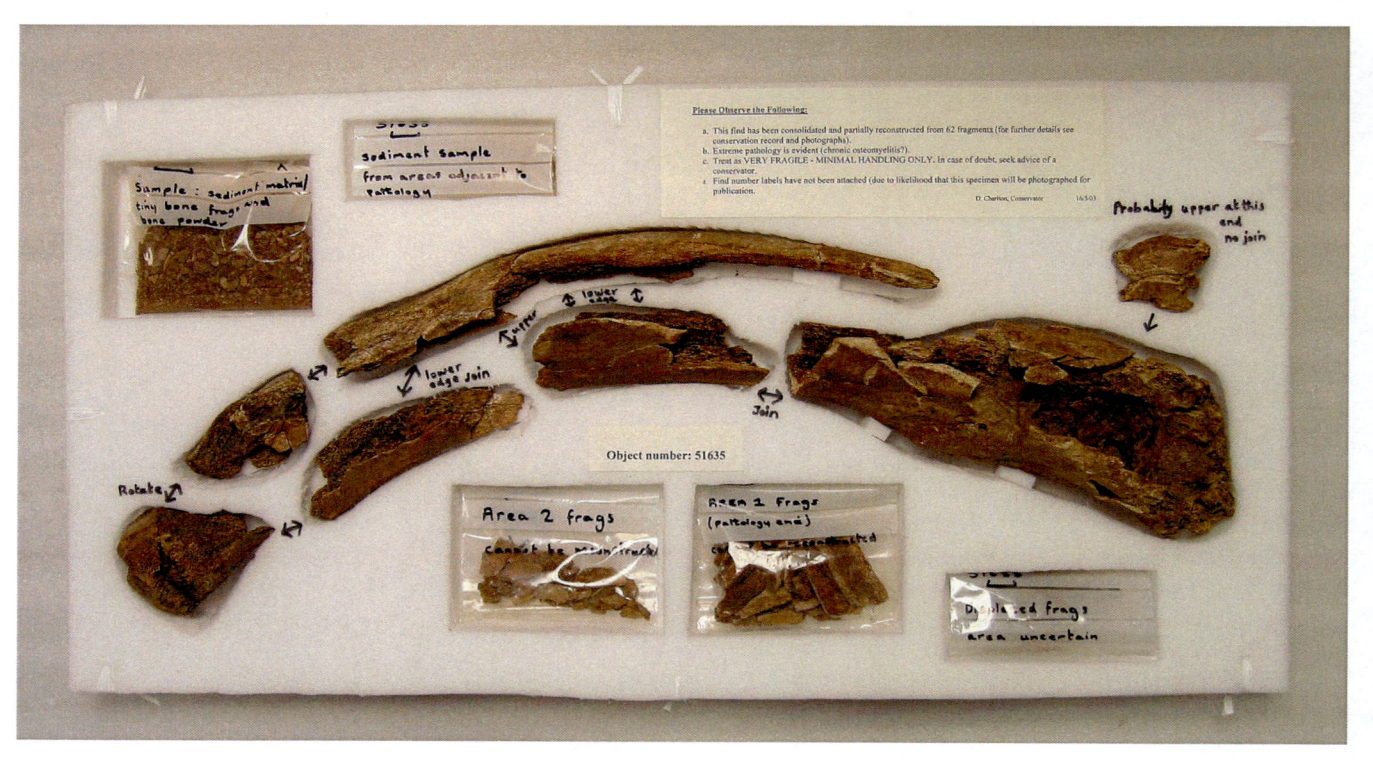

Fig A1.8
Rib 51635 after conservation and packing.

tooth dries out, the organic component shrinks and collapses, producing stresses in the dentine that lead to cracking along weaknesses in the structure, and causing surface layers to curl and lift. As the enamel does not move in the same way, this leads to a loss of cohesion between the layers of dentine and enamel. Once dry, changes in relative humidity in the storage environment will continue to produce minute dimensional changes in the dentine that, with time, can lead to the complete break-up of the tooth. Apparently stable teeth can later be discovered looking as if they have been shattered by the blow of a hammer.

Many of the mammoth molars from Lynford began to form cracks within days of being uncovered. On arrival at Gressenhall, any mammoth molar showing evidence of cracking or flaking was treated by immersion in Paraloid B72 as a matter of priority. To reduce the risk of further damage to the teeth, the environment of the conservation laboratory and finds store at the University of Bradford was stabilised at 50 per cent RH (relative humidity) and a temperature of 21°C. However, many cracks in the teeth widened and some surface flakes became even more distorted, showing that the teeth, and possibly the bones, were still drying out some nine to fifteen months after excavation.

As it is not possible to guarantee that in future the relative humidity in which the teeth are to be studied or stored will be as stringently controlled as it was Bradford, it was decided that the teeth needed some further consolidation. Following the principle of minimising intervention, the option of consolidation by total immersion of the teeth in a resin/solvent mixture was rejected in favour of a more limited, local application. The idea of this approach was not to prevent all dimensional changes, by filling entirely the pores of the tissue with an impermeable resin, but to minimise these movements, and reinforce the weak areas, by replacing the decayed organic framework of the dentine with a relatively strong and slightly flexible resin. Using fine brushes and syringes, Paraloid B72 in acetone was introduced into the cracks and behind the surface flakes until an excess of resin was observed at the surface. Several applications were made, with a pause between each to allow the resin to be absorbed. Starting with dilute solutions to maximise penetration of the dentine and enamel in the immediate environment, consolidation was completed with a more concentrated solution (c 20 per cent) to help adhesion between the surfaces of the cracks.

Compared with the teeth, few of the bones required consolidation. Exceptions were usually bones lifted in plaster jackets from the gravel layers, which were either highly crushed, such as the rib 50163 (see Figs A1.6a and b), or which had lost so much of their organic framework that the slightest mechanical abrasion would powder the bone. The most fragile areas were those with the thinnest covering of compact bone tissue, such as the epiphyseal surfaces of the mammoth vertebrae 51923, and areas of pathology that had lead to the production of areas of very porous bone including specimen 51449.

Consolidation was usually done in stages as each area of the bone was revealed. Once cleared of deposits, consolidant was introduced to the under-surface of the bone or into the interior through cracks and breaks, using brushes, pipettes and syringes. This avoided a build-up of consolidant on the surface, which could have given the material a permanently wet-looking, shiny finish. Excess resin was removed with swabs moistened with acetone before the resin could set. When the consolidant had set, the more viscous adhesive was introduced into cracks and breaks as required.

With some of the very poorly preserved pieces, however, even the application of the consolidant could prove damaging. These pieces had very little organic material surviving to bind their structure together, and upon drying they appeared chalky and became very fragile. Where the cancellous tissue of the interior was exposed, this would break into a pile of bone spicules at the touch of a brush. Although the compact bone exterior could respond well to consolidation, too-rapid wetting of the cancellous tissue with acetone or resin resulted in total collapse of this structure into a soggy mush. In areas where the outer layer of bone was very thin, such as the surfaces of the centra of the mammoth vertebrae, this internal disruption could pull with it the remains of the compact bone surface and precipitate the break-up of the whole bone.

Gap-filling: Even after all fragments were relocated in their correct positions, many specimens had substantial gaps that threatened to compromise their stability. These gaps were not necessarily the result of missing material, but were often the result of distortion by over-burden (Tovey, chapter 2). Most of these problems could be dealt with by providing appropriately designed packaging or an external, custom-made support, but a few pieces required gap-filling. These were generally large bones with complex 3D shapes, such as thoracic vertebra or the mammoth mandible 51047 and reindeer antler 37095, both of which were conserved by Nigel Larkin. A robust but lightweight gap-filler was produced by combining Paraloid B72 (20 per cent in acetone, weight:volume) with glass beads, in a ratio of 1 part to 3. These 44 micron beads, commonly used for airbrasive work, are inert, and produce a spreadable paste that adheres well to the bone (Larkin and Makridou 1999).

Extraction of the plaster-jacketed objects

Although fewer than 0.5 per cent of the finds were jacketed on site, the conservation of these finds possibly accounted for over 80 per cent of the time spent on conservation. They were generally medium to large-sized, complex specimens, often very fragile or fragmented. The majority were from the sand and gravel deposits where bone preservation was at its poorest and the dried matrix at its hardest and most difficult to remove. These had to be excavated, retrieved from their plaster jackets and cleaned and stuck together. Many also needed consolidation, gap-filling or supports fabricating. Most had been consolidated on site before lifting, and required removal of extraneous consolidated deposits and realignment of fragments, before further consolidation or reconstruction could be done.

Photographs were available of the upper surfaces of many of these finds, but these photographs were of limited use for inferring either the shape of the underside of the bones or the depth at which they would be encountered during the excavation of the inverted jackets. Wooden tools were used to remove the dark organic deposits relatively quickly, but the sand and gravels were slow and often very much more resilient than the underlying bone. Acetone was applied, in drops, to a couple of cubic centimetres at a time in order to soften the deposits before they were removed mechanically. Using acetone ensured that areas of the matrix that had become inadvertently consolidated with resin could also be softened and removed in the same action. The loose sediment was then removed using small hand shovels, spoons or spatulas. An industrial, variable-suction vacuum cleaner also proved very useful for removing deposits from awkward corners. 1mm plastic mesh fabric attached over the vacuum pipe prevented loose fragments of bone from being lost and the pipe from becoming blocked by stones and gravel.

As the project progressed, it became apparent that this cautious approach was proving very time-consuming. Objects could take hours or days to fully expose, and the wooden tools required frequent replacement or reshaping. The rate of removal was improved by employing metal tools to excavate the jackets, reverting to the wooden tools only once the surface of the object was located. The black organic layers and the softer sands were excavated by trowel and, after wetting with acetone, the most recalcitrant sands and gravels were removed using a range of dental tools. With metal tools the risk of marking the object when it was first exposed, was slightly greater, but this was minimised by good lighting and the increasing experience of the staff.

The rate of retrieval of the jacketed objects was further improved by using an experienced excavator, Will Higgs, to undertake the initial excavation of the remaining jackets, freeing the conservators to concentrate on the tasks requiring their particular skills.

As the excavation of the objects progressed, craft knives and a rotary mortuary saw were used to cut down the jackets to aid the removal of the loosened matrix, and to improve the visibility and accessibility of the specimen. Once the level of the matrix was reduced, the excess jacket was cut vertically and horizontally and removed as a series of small blocks. The removal of the sediment and reduction of the jacket was repeated until the level of the bone was reached. In most cases this left the object accessible but still supported on the remains of the jacket, and attention could turn to the needs of the object itself.

However, some of the objects still remained trapped in their jackets, either because the jacket followed the form of the object too closely where it was undercut, or because it had been formed around complex details, which had become trapped (Fig A1.9, *see also* Fig 1.4). In both cases the jacket had to be cut away from the object, with no protection between the object and the saw blade, except the separating

APPENDIX 1 CONSERVATION OF THE FAUNAL REMAINS

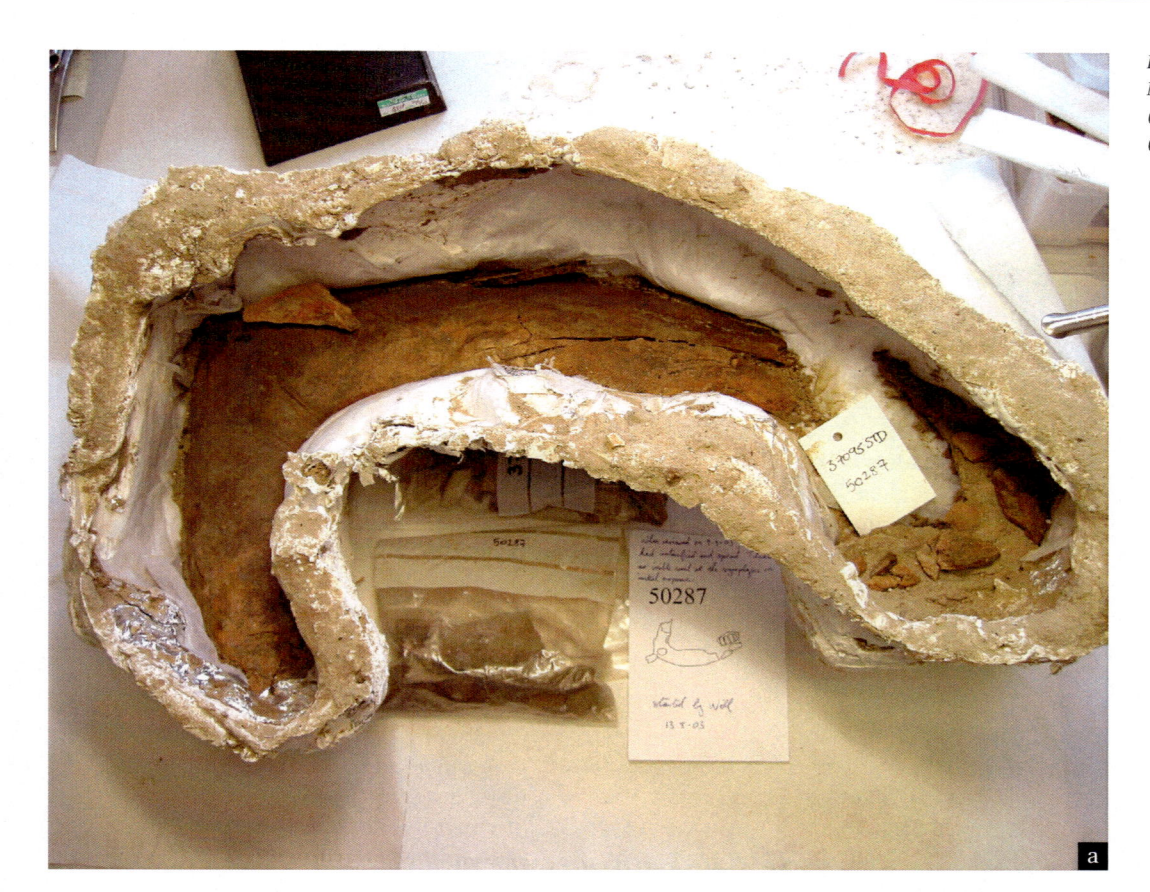

Fig A1.9
*Mammoth mandible 50287:
(a) still trapped in the jacket;
(b) after successful removal.*

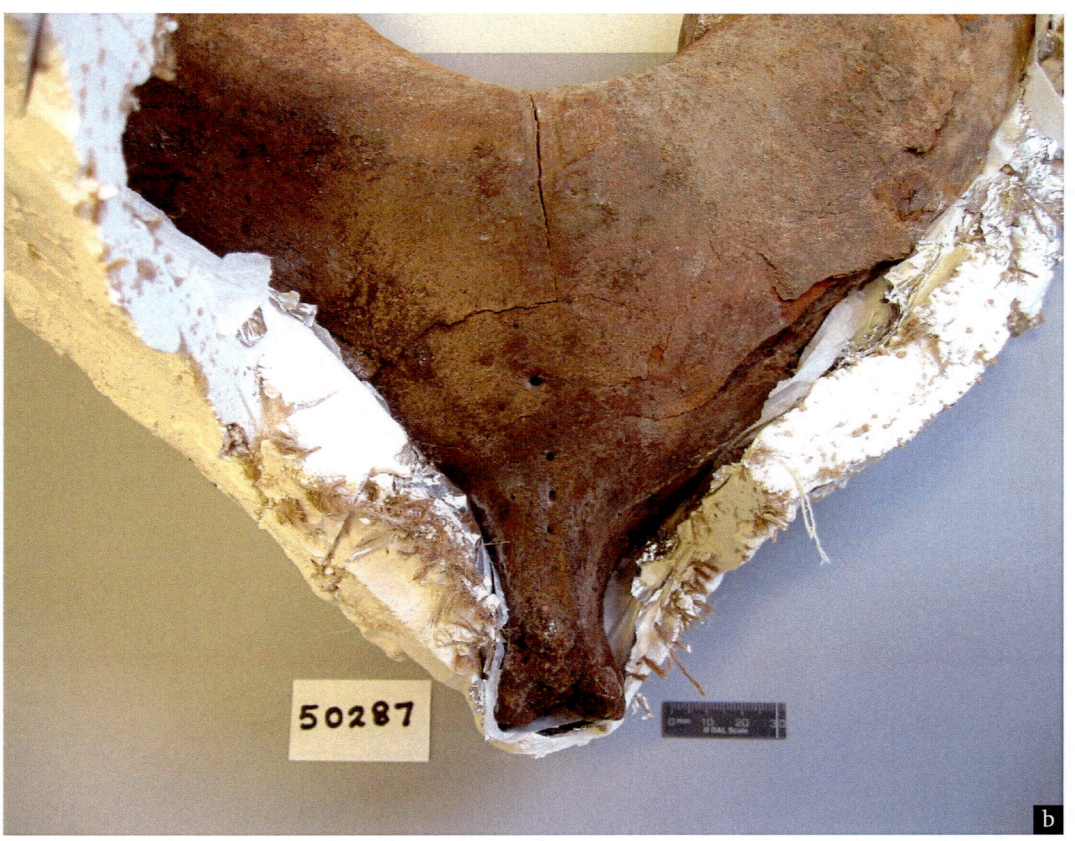

layer of foil and paper. The technique adopted in these situations was to only partially cut through the plaster and then to lever the sections of the jacket apart. This cracked the plaster through its thickness and allowed access to the strands of the hemp scrim, which could then be cut with a blade or scissors to free the section completely. This was, however, a risky procedure as the thickness of the plaster varied considerably and unpredictably, and the shape of the underlying object was not always obvious. These problems can be avoided by leaving a layer of sediment on the objects but this is not always possible where the shape of the specimen has to be determined by partial excavation before the jacket is applied. Packing material can be used to protect details and fill undercuts, provided that the jacket is tight enough to prevent movement during transportation.

Despite the time-constraints on the project, all the jacketed specimens were investigated. As the purpose of the conservation was not display, full cleaning and complete removal of a specimen from its plaster jacket could not always be justified. The upper surfaces of all the finds had been photographed on site, so once sufficient sediment was removed to allow detailed study of the lower surface, work was halted on a few of the specimens, leaving them supported on the remaining sediment. The preliminary excavation of some jackets revealed often large groups of loosely associated fragments, referred to, on site, as 'taphonomic spreads'. Where these fragments did not readily seem to be adjacent parts of the same bone, or did not appear to fit together, no further excavation was undertaken. This, at least, maintained the relative positions of the fragments.

Supports and packaging

The majority of the finds arrived at Bradford packed in perforated polythene bags grouped in card boxes lined with plastic bubble sheeting. Upgrading consisted of cleaning or replacing the resealable polythene bags, and replacing stained or mould-spotted, acid-free tissue paper. Sheets of polythene foam 4mm thick were inserted into the bags to improve the support of the object and to prevent damage among objects in adjacent bags. Where more support was required, a shallow tray or sheet of rigid corrugated plastic board (Correx) might also be introduced into the bag, which was then stored flat. These improvements in the padding and support increased the space required for storage and the finds had to be spread among more buffered card boxes.

Many of the mammoth ribs and vertebrae had been packed together, at Gressenhall, into shallow, purpose-built boxes, fabricated from corrugated plastic board and supported on a marine ply base. These boxes were lined with plastic bubble sheeting and acid-free tissue, and each bone was packed round with crushed wads of acid-free tissue to prevent movement during transportation. As these were mostly complete and intact bones, their overall shape changed little during conservation, and the packaging could be re-used in its entirety.

Other specimens, especially the plaster-jacketed finds, did change considerably during conservation, both in their shape and their need for support. The emphasis in repacking these finds was in providing simple, chemically inert, lightweight solutions that minimised the need for handling (see Fig A1.8). If the final destination of the finds had been known, the requirements of that storage environment (shelving dimensions, environmental control, etc) would also have been taken into account. Where standard-sized, buffered card boxes were not suitable for adaptation for individual specimens, boxes were fabricated from corrugated plastic board using plastic cable ties, plastic-coated wire or cotton twill tape to secure the joins. These were lined and padded with acid-free tissue, bubble sheeting, Jiffy foam or more substantial polyethylene sheet (Plastazote) of various thicknesses, as the needs of the specimen dictated.

Despite consolidation and even gap-filling, some objects were still not capable of safely supporting their own weight if inappropriately handled. For these, close-fitting, custom-made supports were formed using either glass-fibre matting and the acrylic resin Jesmonite or Modrock (a fine plaster bandage), or Plaster of Paris for the smaller items. To produce a perfect fit, these supports were built up directly over the specimen, with only a layer of acid free tissue and then a separating layer of barrier foil, aluminium foil or plastic, between the support and the bone. In the case of the decayed and crushed rib 50163 (see Fig A1.6), a support was made for each side, allowing the bone to be examined from both sides without the need for handling it directly (Fig A1.10).

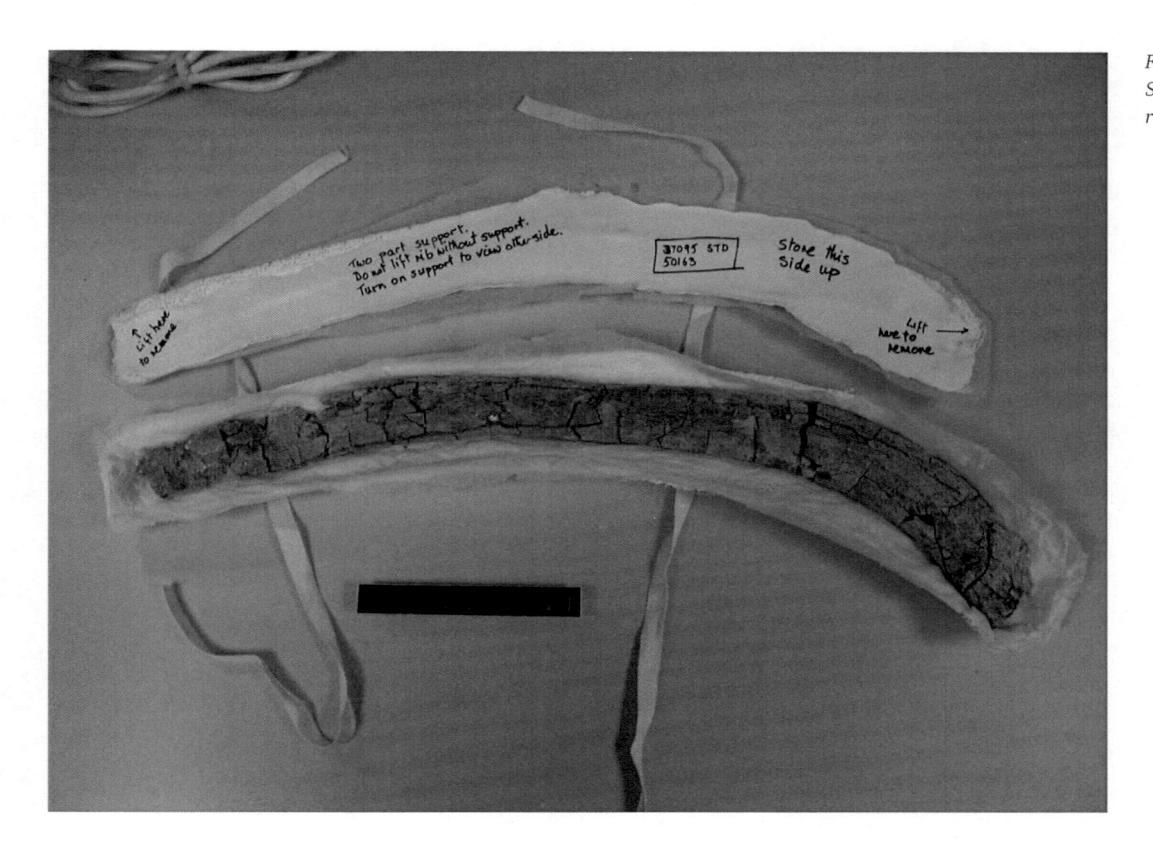

Fig A1.10
Storage support for rib 50l63.

Labelling

All bags and boxes were labelled, using permanent black ink markers. Wherever possible, a small label giving the site and find numbers was also attached directly to the surface of the bone. However, time, and the sheer number of fragments often constituting an individual find, made it impractical to number each individual piece of bone. In addition, many of the fragments were too small to label and often only a couple of the largest fragments in a group were individually labelled. The location of the label was determined by factors such as the presence of a large enough area of relatively flat bone to which to attach it, and finding an area where the label would not obscure diagnostic details or feature too prominently in photographs.

Originally the intention was to produce computer-printed labels on Resistall archival paper using an archivally stable printer ink. Unfortunately the recommended ink was no longer available and as no printer-compatible substitute was available, the labels were instead hand-written on the archival paper using technical or mapping pens and Indian ink. The labels were attached to the surface of the bone first by sealing the back of the label and a similar sized area at an appropriate place on the object, with 10 per cent Paraloid B72. When this coating was dry, the label was stuck to the prepared surface using the preparatory adhesive. Without this surface preparation, it is not uncommon for a label to become detached during storage or handling of the specimen.

Health and safety

Diane Charlton carried out risk assessments for all the chemicals and procedures required to execute the proposed conservation strategy, and safe working practices were put in place. None of the work was particularly hazardous or unusual, but the previous storage of the material did present some problems. Under current COSHH legislation it is now required that biological hazards are also assessed. As we began to unpack the finds from Lynford, it became apparent that there had been a considerable amount of fungal growth on the damp material, particularly within the matrix and on the paper-based packaging materials. Dr Hilary Dodson, Biomedial Sciences, University of Bradford, carried out a survey of the problem and recommended the safe working practices that were subsequently adopted.

Conclusions

The conservation of the Lynford bone assemblage was a complex and pressured project. The range of specimens and their varied states of preservation, combined with the extremes of weather experienced, made their recovery in the field very challenging. The schedule for the post-excavation project brought its own challenges, but the multi-disciplinary conservation team proved its worth in its flexibility and in the individual skills that each member contributed.

The frequency of pathological specimens discovered during this work was unexpected (Schreve and Brothwell, chapter 5) and meant there was not enough time to attend to every recovered fragment of bone. However, the potentially deleterious results of this were minimised by the reassessment of priorities through discussion with other members of the post-excavation project. Some shortcomings of the project might have been avoided had there been an opportunity for all the specialists to meet and explain their roles and research aims at the beginning. Where liaison did pay off was in the integration of the conservation programme with sampling for dating and analysis. This enabled, for instance, OSL dating of sediments immediately adjacent to bone by cutting an access hole through the side of the plaster jacket in which samples were lifted.

APPENDIX 2

The detailed thin section descriptions

C FRENCH

Sample profile 30151/1

Two units with distinct boundary: unit 1 (B-ii: 05; upper 75mm): <95% fine-to-medium quartz sand, 100–750µm, subrounded, with <5% dusty clay coating grains, pale yellow (CPL), moderate birefringence; with 10% small flint pebbles, <10mm, subrounded to subangular; pale grey (CPL), pale greyish-brown (PPL); 10% complex/irregular packing voids; possibly once laminated, now thoroughly bioturbated; unit 2 (B-ii: 03; lower 35mm): sandy loam fabric, c 70–85% medium-to-fine quartz sand, 100–750µm, subrounded, with amorphous sesquioxide-impregnated dusty clay (c 15–30%) coating/between grains; 10% complex/irregular packing voids; pale reddish-brown (CPL/PPL).

Sample profile 30151/2

Upper unit (1; B-ii: 05) of 30mm of amorphous sesquioxide-impregnated organic fine sand over 70mm of unit 2 (B-ii: 03) of once laminated fine quartz sand with 10% small, subangular flint pebbles.

Sample profile 30152

Sample 2/1

Two units with distinct boundary; unit 1 (B-ii: 03; upper 75mm): 25% very fine, 30% fine and 15–30% medium quartz sand, 50–750µm, subrounded, 15–30% dusty clay, moderate birefringence, pale yellow (CPL) of grains, groundmass and in small aggregates (<50µm); grey (CPL), pale yellowish-brown (PPL), pale yellow (RL); once micro-laminated, now much mixed; 10% porosity composed of discontinuous horizontal and irregular voids, <750µm wide; unit 2 (B-ii: 01; lower 60mm): 60% amorphous sesquioxide replaced organic matter and plant tissue, 5% medium, 15% fine and 20% very fine quartz sand, subrounded, 50–750µm; reddish-brown (CPL), organgey/reddish-brown (PPL), very dark reddish-brown (RL); <20% complex packing voids; very rare (<1%) charcoal fragment, subrounded, <100µm; once micro-laminated, now bioturbated.

Sample 2/2

Similar to sample 1/2 above (B-ii: 01).

Sample profile 30153

Two units with a lens of different fabric at the contact; unit 1 (B-ii: 03; upper 70mm): composed of 4 horizons; upper horizons 1–3 similar to horizon 4, but greater amorphous iron-impregnated organics, up to 50%, and less fine-to-medium sand, down to 50%, and occasional micro-sparite calcium carbonate (<5%); horizon 4: similar to unit 2 of sample 2/1, except less amorphous sesquioxide-impregnated organics and greater amounts of fine-to-medium sand; unit 2 (B-ii: 01; lower 25mm): 35% medium, 45% fine and c 13% very fine quartz sand, <5% dusty clay with <2% very fine including charcoal and <2% sparite calcium carbonate; 20–30% complex packing voids; once laminated, now well mixed; transitional fabric between units 1 and 2: fine sandy clay loam with 40% very fine-to-medium quartz sand and 60% dusty clay with weak reticulate striations, golden brown (CPL), brown (PPL), and commonly including very fine charcoal.

Sample profile 30261

Upper unit (1; B-ii: 05) of 20mm of once laminated, amorphous sesquioxide-impregnated, organic fine sand over 70mm of middle unit (2; B-ii: 03) of once laminated fine-to-medium quartz sand over 20mm of a lower unit (3; B-ii: 03) of laminated amorphous sesquioxide-impregnated organic fine quartz sand.

Sample profile 30246

Sample 1 (top; B-ii: 03)

Two units present with merging boundary over 5mm; unit 1 (upper 45mm): up to 90% fine and medium quartz sand, 100–750µm, subrounded, <10% amorphous sesquioxide-impregnated dusty clay coating grains and in hoizontal lenses, <1mm thick; once laminated, now partially mixed; pale grey (CPL/PPL); unit 2 (lower 75mm): c 20–30% very fine and fine quartz sand, 50–250µm within amorphous sesquioxide-impregnated, amorphous organic and plant tissue material with 5–10% micro-sparite and common (c 30%) flint pebbles, <20mm, subangular to subrounded; pale reddish-brown (CPL/PPL).

Sample 2 (B-ii: 01)

Five units, all units with distinct to 1mm merging boundaries: unit 1 (0–10mm): alternating lenses/laminae of fine quartz sand and amorphous sesquioxide-impregnated organic material with 5% micro-sparite in discontinuous laminae, reddish-brown to black (CPL), dark grey (PPL); unit 2 (1–25mm): fine-to-medium quartz sand (<60%) with irregular zones (c 30–40%) of fine groundmass of amorphous organic matter and dusty clay, and amorphous calcium carbonate, with some amorphous sesquioxide impregnation; reddish-brown (CPL), pale greyish-brown (PPL); unit 3 (35–45mm): same as unit 1; unit 4 (45–70mm): same as unit 2; unit 5 (70–125mm): amorphous sesquioxide- impregnated organic and plant tissue material with c 30–40% fine-to-medium quartz sand, 100–750µm, subrounded.

Sample 3 (B-ii: 01)

All one fabric: c 40–70% oxidised, amorphous sesquioxide organic matter and plant tissues (= peat) with c 30–40% included very fine to medium quartz sand, 50–750µm, subrounded, which increases from 30% to 50% down profile, 5% micro-sparite and 5% amorphous calcium carbonate; exhibits laminations, but organic remains partially bioturbated; very dark reddish- brown (CPL) to dark greyish-brown (PPL); one subrounded zone of micro-sparitic fine sand with included amorphous plant matter, <10mm.

Sample 4 (base; B-ii: 01))

Two units; unit 1 (upper 40mm): amorphous sesquioxide-impregnated organic fine-to-medium sand with minor (<5%) amorphous calcium carbonate with included fine charcoal punctuations; over unit 2 (lower 90mm) of very mixed, fine-to-medium quartz sand in all orientations with no fine groundmass component present.

APPENDIX 3

Table A3.1 Consolidation Booking Sheet for test on Sample 1a

	School of Environmental Sciences				
Basic Data		Lynford Sample 1a			
Rig Number (1–3):	1				
Date of Experiment	25/07/2002			38.89	108.89
Weight of dish:	107.78 gms	Final Voids Ratio		0.946	
Weight of dish + wet sample:	255.56 gms				
Weight of dish + dry sample:	216.67 gms	Reduced Thickness		9.034	mm
Specific gravity of soil: (use 2.65 if uncertain)	2.65				
Diameter of consolidometer (mm)	76.1 mm	0.00454841			

Enter data in White Boxes below: Enter END in Load column when finished

Load on hanger (lbs)	Dial Gauge (raw)	Pressure (kPa)	Voids Ratio	Total Thickness (mm)
0.0	0000	0.0	2.041	27.470
2.5	3050	26.9	1.366	21.370
5.0	3380	53.9	1.292	20.710
10.0	3661	107.7	1.230	20.148
20.0	4085	215.4	1.136	19.300
40.0	4652	430.8	1.011	18.166
80.0	5172	861.7	0.896	17.126
160.0	5840	1723.4	0.748	15.790
80.0	5782	861.7	0.761	15.906
40.0	5724	430.8	0.774	16.022
20.0	5641	215.4	0.792	16.188
10.0	5493	107.7	0.825	16.484
5.0	5443	53.9	0.836	16.584
0.0	4943	0.0	0.946	17.584
END				

Table A3.2 Consolidation Booking Sheet for test on Sample 1b

School of Environmental Sciences

Basic Data   Lynford Sample 1b

Rig Number (1–3):	2				
Date of Experiment	25/07/2002				
Weight of dish:	107.78	gms	Final Voids Ratio	0.998	
Weight of dish + wet sample:	232.50	gms			
Weight of dish + dry sample:	198.39	gms	Reduced Thickness	7.517	mm
Specific gravity of soil:	2.65				
(use 2.65 if uncertain)					
Diameter of consolidometer (mm)	76.1	mm	0.00454841		

Enter data in White Boxes below: Enter END in Load column when finished

Load on hanger	Dial Gauge	Pressure	Voids Ratio	Total Thickness
(lbs)	(raw)	(kPa)		(mm)
0.0	0000	0.0	1.765	20.787
2.5	0702	26.9	1.578	19.383
5.0	1061	53.9	1.483	18.665
10.0	1556	107.7	1.351	17.675
20.0	2013	215.4	1.230	16.761
40.0	2578	430.8	1.079	15.631
80.0	3273	861.7	0.894	14.241
160.0	3799	1723.4	0.754	13.189
80.0	3592	861.7	0.809	13.603
40.0	3498	430.8	0.835	13.791
20.0	3388	215.4	0.864	14.011
10.0	3285	107.7	0.891	14.217
5.0	3023	53.9	0.961	14.741
0.0	2885	0.0	0.998	15.017
END				

Table A3.3 Consolidation Booking Sheet for test on Sample 1c

School of Environmental Sciences

Basic Data   Lynford Sample 1c

Rig Number (1–3):	3				
Date of Experiment	25/07/2002				
Weight of dish:	107.78	gms	Final Voids Ratio	0.905	
Weight of dish + wet sample:	224.73	gms			
Weight of dish + dry sample:	194.97	gms	Reduced Thickness	7.234	mm
Specific gravity of soil: (use 2.65 if uncertain)	2.65				
Diameter of consolidometer (mm)	76.1	mm			

Enter data in White Boxes below: Enter END in Load column when finished

Load on hanger (lbs)	Dial Gauge (raw)	Pressure (kPa)	Voids Ratio	Total Thickness (mm)
0.0	0000	0.0	1.732	19.763
2.5	0945	26.9	1.471	17.873
5.0	1323	53.9	1.366	17.117
10.0	1785	107.7	1.238	16.193
20.0	2199	215.4	1.124	15.365
40.0	2693	430.8	0.987	14.377
80.0	3330	861.7	0.811	13.103
160.0	3797	1723.4	0.682	12.169
80.0	3736	861.7	0.699	12.291
40.0	3668	430.8	0.718	12.427
20.0	3581	215.4	0.742	12.601
10.0	3493	107.7	0.766	12.777
5.0	3363	53.9	0.802	13.037
0.0	2993	0.0	0.905	13.777
END				

APPENDIX 4

Table A4.1 Bulk and environmental samples

sample	context	serial no. or depth in cm, where applicable	cranial	tusk	mammuthus molar fragment	indet. large bone fragments	E. lucius teeth	G. aculeatus spines	G. aculeatus vertebrae	P. fluviatilis scale	fish bone	fish teeth	herpetofauna	Microtus sp. and Microtinae	indet. small mammal	split long bone fragments	indet. small bone fragments	notes
30000	20030							3								3	1	DHK mollusc sample
30001	20030					2												
30042	20070																4	
30043	20066																	
30046	20066																	
30050	20015																	
30073	20003																	
30077	20003																	
30078	20003																	
30081	20003							1		1						2	5	
30086	20003																	registered as a coprolite – missing
30110	20003			8		44											147	
30130	20252																	registered as a coprolite – missing
30157	20021														2			
30159	20021										1							
30161	20021																	coprolite
30164	20005			1														
30166	20021			3														registered as a coprolite – missing
30198	20003	20–30									1							DHK mollusc sample

continued ▶

Table A4.1 Bulk and environmental samples – *continued*

sample	context	serial no. or depth in cm, where applicable	cranial	tusk	mammuthus molar fragment	indet. large bone fragments	E. lucius teeth	G. aculeatus spines	G. aculeatus vertebrae	P. fluviatilis scale	fish bone	fish teeth	herpetofauna	Microtus sp. and Microtinae	indet. small mammal	split long bone fragments	indet. small bone fragments	notes
30198	20003	30–40			1	1												DHK mollusc sample
30198	20003	40–50				9		1					3				7	DHK mollusc sample
30198	20003	50–60		15		19				6			10			5	8	DHK mollusc sample
30198	20003	60–70				15		6		2			2			7	4	DHK mollusc sample
30198	20003–4	70–80				3		1	2								1	DHK mollusc sample
30200	20070	0–10																	
30200	20070	10–20				3													
30200	20003	20–30	14	83		28										1	15		
30200	20003	30–40	5	18	1	31											148		
30200	20003	40–50																	
30200	20003	50–60																	
30200	20003	60–70	18	25		73		4					3	1*		11	51	* molar fragment, Microtinae
30200	20003–4	70–80	1	6													37		
30201	20002–3	40–50											1						DHK mollusc sample
30203	20005	0–10																	
30203	20005	10–20																	
30203	20005	20–30																	
30203	20002–3	30–40																	
30203	20002–3	40–50																	
30203	20002–3	50–60																	

continued ▶

Table A4.1 Bulk and environmental samples – continued

sample	context	serial no. or depth in cm, where applicable	cranial	tusk	mammuthus molar fragment	indet. large bone fragments	E. lucius teeth	G. aculeatus spines	G. aculeatus vertebrae	P. fluviatilis scale	fish bone	fish teeth	herpetofauna	Microtus sp. and Microtinae	indet. small mammal	split long bone fragments	indet. small bone fragments	notes
30207	20021																	registered as a coprolite – missing
30209	20371									1								
30211	20371					1			1	6	32*	1**	7				12	* includes 17 large fish vertebral fragments; ** abraded undetermined tooth
30213										7	3					1	6	DHK mollusc sample
30215	20371									2								
30217	20371									2								
30218	20371									1								
30225	20070	0–7		4														
30255	20003	7–11																
30225	20003	11–23															1	
30225	20003	23–34															–	
30225	20003	34–44				18											3	
30225	20003	44–54	1	3		3											18	
30225	20003	54–65	2	1														
30225	20371	65–74	1										1			1	7	
30225	20371	74–84									2		2				6	
30225	20371	84–94																
30225	20371	94–104																
30226	20003	0–10	2	18		3					1		2				19	
30226	20003	10–19		200		17												
30226	20003	19–29							2		4		10	2*		4	70	*R M1, Microtus sp. and 1 fragment, Microtinae sp.
30226	20003	29–33	15	47		56		2					2		1*	2	15	* vertebra fragment
30226	20139	33–36	5			3							1				70	
30226	20245	36–45	2	7		7											60	
30226	20245	45–61															44	

continued ▶

Table A4.1 Bulk and environmental samples – *continued*

sample	context	serial no. or depth in cm, where applicable	cranial	tusk	mammuthus molar fragment	indet. large bone fragments	E. lucius teeth	G. aculeatus spines	G. aculeatus vertebrae	P. fluviatilis scale	fish bone	fish teeth	herpetofauna	Microtus sp. and Microtinae	indet. small mammal	split long bone fragments	indet. small bone fragments	notes
30228		01					1	12	1		9	1		1*		14	4	DHK mollusc sample. * juvenile molar fragment, *Microtus* sp.
30228		03						22	4		9*		2		1**	6		DHK mollusc sample. * includes 1 large fish vertebra; ** vertebral centrum fragment
30228		04						18			2		8				6	DHK mollusc sample
30228		05						1	1							5		DHK mollusc sample
30231		08						1	1		2		2				1	DHK mollusc sample
30231		10						1			4		2				1	DHK mollusc sample
30231		13									1						1	DHK mollusc sample
30234		01						8			4					3	1	DHK mollusc sample
30234		02						21	3		13	1*	7	1**		10	8	DHK mollusc sample. *pharyngeal bone of Cyprinidae with 5 teeth *in situ*; ** R 1, Microtinae sp.
30234		03						23			30		2			6	2	DHK mollusc sample
30234		04	3					13	1		9		2			8		DHK mollusc sample
30235	20021	0–10						3	1		1		9	1*		2	42	* L m2, *Microtus* sp.
30235	20021	10–20	15	3		6		1	2		5		5	1*		3	111	* 1 fragment, Microtinae sp.
30235	20021/139	20–30	3	1		41		1	1		15		5			3	16	
30235	20021/139	30–42	20								6		3			5	65	
30235	20078	42–51															5	
30237	20003																	
30240	20003				153	1	17											
30241	20137					63	1											
30242	20021		50	3		7					1		2	1*			221	* 1 fragment, Microtinae sp.
30249					1	4							1					
30253	20390–430																	
30328	20003																	

continued ▶

Table A4.1 Bulk and environmental samples – *continued*

sample	context	serial no. or depth in cm, where applicable	cranial	tusk	mammuthus molar fragment	indet. large bone fragments	E. lucius teeth	G. aculeatus spines	G. aculeatus vertebrae	P. fluviatilis scale	fish bone	fish teeth	herpetofauna	Microtus sp. and Microtinae	indet. small mammal	split long bone fragments	indet. small bone fragments	notes
30331																		
30340																		bag contained mud pellet – discarded
30342	20371						1											
30358	20003											1						
30361	20003															16		
30364	20044										14							
30365	20048											1						
30366	20003									1								
31165	20003				6													
No number	20004						14	3		8	2							DHK mollusc sample

Table A4.2 Wet sieved residues

spit no.	weight (g)	ccanial	tusk	mammuthus molar fragment	other large mammal tooth fragment	indet. large bone fragments	E. lucius teeth	G. aculeatus spines	P. fluviatilis scale	fish bone	fish teeth	herpetofauna	bird bone	M. gregalis	Microtus sp. and Microtinae	Spermophilus sp.	indet. small mammal	split long bone fragments	indet. small bone fragments	notes
1.1	1.2	3				1														
1.2	19.7	10	6		1*	43	1		1									1	12	* small M fragment, *E. ferus*
1.3	15.1	16				36														
1.4	25.2	17	4	1	1*	8														* L dp2, *C. antiquitatis*
1.5	8.6	11				10														
1.6	12.0	8	8	1		10														
1.7	2.9	3	8			4												2		
1.8	20.3	21	1			20						1						2		
1.9	10.3	8	7	1		13						3							3	
1.10	39.2	15	27	1		17						2							2	
2.2	2.2	3				4														
2.3	22.0	31				9														
2.5	0.8					7														
2.7	4.2		2			24	1													
2.8	31.5	5	1			39														
2.9	16.1	2	2			10														
2.11	7.5	15				14														
2.13	1.7	2				2														
3.1	6.3		2	1		11														
3.3	10.2	11				3		1		6										
3.4	7.2	9	4	1		6														
3.5	10.7	–	20	3		5														
3.6	14.0	8	3	1		6														
3.7	3.1	–	2	2		5														
3.9	17.6	6	–	1		1														
3.10	3.6	6	1	–		5						1						1		
4.1	125.0	42	7	–		125														

continued ▶

Table A4.2 Wet sieved residues – *continued*

spit no.	weight (g)	ccanial	tusk	mammuthus molar fragment	other large mammal tooth fragment	indet. large bone fragments	E. lucius teeth	G. aculeatus spines	P. fluviatilis scale	fish bone	fish teeth	herpetofauna	bird bone	M. gregalis	Microtus sp. and Microtinae	Spermophilus sp.	indet. small mammal	split long bone fragments	indet. small bone fragments	notes
4.2	6.2	13	–		1	7														
4.3	15.0	41	1	–		7														
4.4	6.1	8	2	–		6														
60006	1.0	–	–	–		1														
60022	3.4	–	–	–		13														
60026	2.9	–	–	–		2													1	
60035	<1.0	–	–	–																
60040	1.6	–	–	–		6														
60053	<1.0	–	–	4																
60076	3.5	–	–	1		12														
60082	5.1	–	7	–		11														
60086	1.3	2	1	1		3														
60090	0.8	–	–	1																
60093	25.1	3	8	2		26														
60096	8.6	3	–	–		19														
60152	<1.0	–	–	–		–									1*					* L dentary with i and broken L m1
60169	5.0	–	–	–		4														
60210	68.7	4	44	–		29													1	
60213	36.3	11	45	–		9					1								1	
60218	50.3	20	16	–		13														
60222	13.3	6	18	–		3													1	
60228	56.2	13	86	1		7														
60231																				bag missing
60233	4.6	8				1				2									3	
60241	5.2	15	3			4													1	
60258	17.8	4	9			2														

continued ▶

Table A4.2 Wet sieved residues – continued

spit no.	weight (g)	ccanial	tusk	mammuthus molar fragment	other large mammal tooth fragment	indet. large bone fragments	E. lucius teeth	G. aculeatus spines	P. fluviatilis scale	fish bone	fish teeth	herpetofauna	bird bone	M. gregalis	Microtus sp. and Microtinae	Spermophilus sp.	indet. small mammal	split long bone fragments	indet. small bone fragments	notes
60262	5.7	2			1	6														
60263	0.8					3														
60265	6.2		1	2		11														
60269	6.3	1	3	1		13														
60273	31.4	18	16	2		47														
60278	25.5	17	49	4		12														
60281	21.8	2	26			2												2	1	
60284	26.3	24	39	2		27						2						4		
60288	6.9	2				4														
60292	5.7	7		1		3													2	
60297	12.7	9	4	1		1									1*					* L 1, Microtinae
60298	74.4	10	26	2		7														
60306	36.5	6	3	3		7														
60310	19.6	1	3	1		12														
60315	2.2					2														
60319	44.8	15	1			17												2	3	
60322	30.4	3				19					1							4		
60325	9.2		15			38														
60326	25.1	1	2	3		14					1							4	1	
60333	26.0	13				2												1		
60338	6.1	1		1		5														
60341	12.5	10	1			9														
60345	15.0	10	2			10												1		
60348	100.7	58	8	1		53					4							2	4	
60369	70.6		3			155														
60376	2.2	6				3														
60379	12.2	2	2			8									1*					* i fragment, Microtinae

continued ▶

Table A4.2 Wet sieved residues – *continued*

spit no.	weight (g)	ccanial	tusk	mammuthus molar fragment	other large mammal tooth fragment	indet. large bone fragments	E. lucius teeth	G. aculeatus spines	P. fluviatilis scale	fish bone	fish teeth	herpetofauna	bird bone	M. gregalis	Microtus sp. and Microtinae	Spermophilus sp.	indet. small mammal	split long bone fragments	indet. small bone fragments	notes
60384	29.0	19	12			15						1								
60394	2.1	3	1			3														
60455	0.8	1																		
60458	48.9	18	5			25				1										
60467	1.2					1														
60475	9.4	15	2			8														
60479	3.7	2				5														
60485	13.9	14	1			15														
60507	29.4	4	6			3														
60508	25.4	3	6	1		9														
60509	5.4	2	4			3												2	1	
60511	3.1	4	2									2							1	
60517	1.3	1	1																	
60523	5.1	5				9									1*		3			* 1 fragment, Microtinae
60526	10.2	9	6			10						2						2	1	
60531	7.6	11				6	1					2							1	
60533	2.6	5				3											1			
60536	4.1	5	4			1						2						6		
60544	5.1	4	1			2						3						3	1	
60546	5.4	2	2			5														
60550	21.9	11	10	1		6														
60613	3.3	1				9												3		
60619	2.5					5														
60623	2.4	1				11														
60626	6.4	4	5			11														
60630	23.0	6	56			21												2		
60635	68.7	59	8	1		45				1		3						5		

continued ▶

Table A4.2 Wet sieved residues – *continued*

spit no.	weight (g)	ccanial	tusk	mammuthus molar fragment	other large mammal tooth fragment	indet. large bone fragments	E. lucius teeth	G. aculeatus spines	P. fluviatilis scale	fish bone	fish teeth	herpetofauna	bird bone	M. gregalis	Microtus sp. and Microtinae	Spermophilus sp.	indet. small mammal	split long bone fragments	indet. small bone fragments	notes
60702	3.2	3	1	2																
60707	11.9	16	3			2													1	
60708	31.7	22	8	2		32						1						1		
60715	34.3	12	1	2		16													1	
60718	35.1	15	9			19														
60727	45.4	42	8			39												2	2	
60729	21.5	38	4			13						1							2	
60734	45.8	9	1	2		30														
60803	18.4	23	5	1		11						1						5	1	
60813	3.0		1			8														
60818	1.6		2			3														
60822	3.9					5														
60827	5.3	3	3			18														
60832	2.6	1				2												1		
60836	2.6	3	3			3														
60839	42.5	32	16			101													5	
60841	18.6	20	2	1		10						1							1	
60844	10.3	3	1			9														
60846	2.9		8			9														
60919	10.9					126														
60932	0.8					1														
60936	2.9			1		5														
60946a	4.4		1	1		5														
60946b	4.9					2														
60949	0.7					1														
60958	4.0		2																	
60960	4.3					6													1	

continued ▶

Table A4.2 Wet sieved residues – *continued*

spit no.	weight (g)	cranial	tusk	mammuthus molar fragment	other large mammal tooth fragment	indet. large bone fragments	E. lucius teeth	G. aculeatus spines	P. fluviatilis scale	fish bone	fish teeth	herpetofauna	bird bone	M. gregalis	Microtus sp. and Microtinae	Spermophilus sp.	indet. small mammal	split long bone fragments	indet. small bone fragments	notes
60964	7.6					8														
60966	0.8					3														
60971	7.4			4		7													1	
60975	39.5		53	6		75					1									
60978	12.2			5		23													13	
60985	22.2		2	2		4		1										1		
60988	52.9		42			2														
60992	20.9	1	68	1		37					1				1*				1	* R i, Microtinae
60996	101.2	7	28	2		128									1*			2	3	* central fragment of R m1, Microtus sp.
61000	119.8	14	180	3		23												1	1	
61007	<1.0				1*	1						·								* enamel fragment, ?Cervidae
61010	15.5	17	14			11												3	2	
61053	13.9	15	3			3												1	1	
61055	2.3	2				4			1											
61059	10.8	11	4			10						2							1	
61063	12.4	8	8			3		·				2								
61065	<1.0										1								1	
61078	16.9	21	2	1		16					1								6	
61081	6.4	3	6	1		15														
61084	3.7		1			7					1								1	
61088	3.9	1	1	2		6					1									
61093	16.7	7			1*	6					1								1	* R p4, R. tarandus
61096	16.3	7		4		6					1				1*				2	* anterior L m1, digested
61104	10.5	1	5														1		1	
61116	24.8	38	12	1		35	2		1		4							2		
61118	18.9	7	4			19					2							7	11	

continued ▶

APPENDIX 4

Table A4.2 Wet sieved residues – *continued*

spit no.	weight (g)	ccanial	tusk	mammuthus molar fragment	other large mammal tooth fragment	indet. large bone fragments	E. lucius teeth	G. aculeatus spines	P. fluviatilis scale	fish bone	fish teeth	herpetofauna	bird bone	M. gregalis	Microtus sp. and Microtinae	Spermophilus sp.	indet. small mammal	split long bone fragments	indet. small bone fragments	notes
61124	9.8	11	6			3												1	7	
61128	2.5	2	2			1			1									1		
61136	4.3	6				1			1											
61154	17.4		3			15													2	
61158	4.2	9	2			5	1		1									4	1	
61163	23.6	6	6			14						3					1*	2	3	* fragment of atlas vertebra (size of medium mustelid)
61169	39.8	21	14	2		13						3					1	2	3	
61170	25.4	15	4	2		15						1						1	1	
61173	13.6	7	1	1		6												4	1	
61176	24.6	8	1	2		10						3								
61180	7.0	8	5			6						1							1	
61181	48.1	28	2	3		24						2						2	2	
61187	18.2	20	6	1		36											1	4	1	
61190	9.2	1	3			10												3	1	
61195a	6.9	8	1	1		10						2						3	3	
61195b	4.0	4				4														
61198	21.1	25	2			22												5	4	
61200	13.1	22	1	1		18						1						2		
61208	22.4					14													2	
61211	14.2		2			35													1	
61212	8.8					14														
61216	8.3					12														
61218	30.5					31														
61221	1.0		3																3	
61225	15.3					40														
61231	40.8					23														

continued ▶

Table A4.2 Wet sieved residues – continued

spit no.	weight (g)	ccanial	tusk	mammuthus molar fragment	other large mammal tooth fragment	indet. large bone fragments	E. lucius teeth	G. aculeatus spines	P. fluviatilis scale	fish bone	fish teeth	herpetofauna	bird bone	M. gregalis	Microtus sp. and Microtinae	Spermophilus sp.	indet. small mammal	split long bone fragments	indet. small bone fragments	notes
61235	29.05		2	3	1*	11						1							2	*R p2, C. lupus
61240	9.2					5														
61254	0.2					1														
61258	4.6	2				18													3	
61262	40.4	1	116			38														
61263	10.3	3	1			6													1	
61267	4.5	4	1	1?		1														
61269	41.3		2			39														
61279	5.2	2	1			3														
61280	44.9	50	4			53						1			1*					*1 fragment, Microtinae
61283	49.5		2			67														
61285	46.2	23	4			28												1		
61289	4.2			1		5														
61291	9.8	5				9														
61292	16.4					16														
61294	21.6	20				8												2		
61297	3.0	1	1	1							1									
61299	<1.0							1												
61304	10.5		2			10														
61311	6.6		7			20						1							7	
61314	<1.0					4														
61318	12.8	1	8	1?		35												1	3	
61323	25.5		3	7		26													3	
61326	2.8		1			3													2	
61334	127.9	1	163	1		87														
61338	54.0	1	16	2		13														
61342	34.2	3	19	8		34						1								

continued ▶

Table A4.2 Wet sieved residues – *continued*

spit no.	weight (g)	ccanial	tusk	mammuthus molar fragment	other large mammal tooth fragment	indet. large bone fragments	E. lucius teeth	G. aculeatus spines	P. fluviatilis scale	fish bone	fish teeth	herpetofauna	bird bone	M. gregalis	Microtus sp. and Microtinae	Spermophilus sp.	indet. small mammal	split long bone fragments	indet. small bone fragments	notes
61346a	18.5		22			8												1	2	
61346b	26.9		33			9														
61351	24.5	17	14			52						1						2		
61360	10.2	12				4														
61366	21.6	5	3	1		13												2		
61370	34.5	7	3			24						1							1	
61375	5.1	3				4		2										2	2	
61379a	20.0	14	3			12		2		2								2	3	
61379b	96.2	30	2			51														
61379c	<1.0																			
61383	39.9	14	2			6														
61386	2.7	4				4														
61388	25.4	20	2	1		14						3								
61394	36.4	63	1	1		22						1						2	1	
61397	23.6	33	1			30				3		6						2	1	
61442	18.5	1		2		10														
61451	21.9	2	1	2	1*	17												1	1	*dp germ, C. *antiquitatis*
61456	16.75	2	11			16														
61462	14.3	8	3			10									1*			2	4	*1 fragment, Microtinae
61466	18.7		9	1		34						1?							7	
61470	48.2	10		2		9													2	
61474	16.7	12	4	2		17												3	9	
61476	7.4	10	6			24													2	
61477	34.0	5	1			6													8	
61479	12.8	5	5	2		24														
61483	66.2	12	14	2		40												1	1	
61487	25.55	26	3	1		34												3		

continued ▶

Table A4.2 Wet sieved residues – continued

spit no.	weight (g)	ccanial	tusk	mammuthus molar fragment	other large mammal tooth fragment	indet. large bone fragments	E. lucius teeth	G. aculeatus spines	P. fluviatilis scale	fish bone	fish teeth	herpetofauna	bird bone	M. gregalis	Microtus sp. and Microtinae	Spermophilus sp.	indet. small mammal	split long bone fragments	indet. small bone fragments	notes
61491	8.7	2				2														
61495	19.9	6	1	1		7														
61497	19.2	18	2	1		9								1*					2	* L dentary with L m1, cf. M. gregalis
61501	1.0					1														
61503	5.1	3	5			41														
61504	9.1					11					1								1	
61508	25.6	7	3			12				1								1		
61518	3.7	8	2	1		8														
61523	1.7					11														
61526	20.9	1				6														
61531	28.0	18	7	2		11		2												
61533	56.6	31	2			40												3	1	
61535	12.4	15		2		4				1								1		
61540	69.6	42	13			73				1					1*		1	9	1	*R M3, Microtus sp.
61543	44.9	40	36			5														
61549	9.8	16	2			6				1										
61566	3.6					1														
61606	21.6	16	3			18				1					1*			9	1	* anterior L m2 fragment, Microtus sp.
61610	31.0	13	10			13		3		4					1*			5	3	*LM1
61619	5.5	3	1			13														
61623	22.6	9	16			26														
61626	26.4	25	6	2		35				1								2	3	
61630	34.9	20	4			22				2								2		
61634	18.0	31	2	2		30				2	1*							3	1	* distal tarsometatarsus
61635	42.2	16	14	2		21	1											2		
61640a	20.1	21	2			1				1										

continued ▶

Table A4.2 Wet sieved residues – *continued*

split no.	weight (g)	ccanial	tusk	mammuthus molar fragment	other large mammal tooth fragment	indet. large bone fragments	E. lucius teeth	G. aculeatus spines	P. fluviatilis scale	fish bone	fish teeth	herpetofauna	bird bone	M. gregalis	Microtus sp. and Microtinae	Spermophilus sp.	indet. small mammal	split long bone fragments	indet. small bone fragments	notes
61640b	14.0	16	1			23						1			1*			1	1	* L I, Microtinae
61642	31.1	38	5			11						2			1*			1	1	* R I, Microtinae
61646	21.7	30	3	2		17												2	2	
61648	34.9	10	31		1*	14													2	* L m1, R. *tarandus*
61649	4.9	3	7																	
61652	2.2		3																	
61654	8.8				1	8														
61664	54.6	22	3	3		20						1							1	
61666	13.6					10														
61702	27.5					2														
61718	1.1					6													10	
61723	1.1					7										1*				* R m1 fragment, Microtinae
61725	1.8					5														
61731	6.1	3	1			33														
61736	<1.0		1			7													3	
61741	<1.0					1														
61750	1.7		3			11														
61765	2.2					17														
61853	18.5	18	4			12	1					2						1		
61854	31.6	31	18	1		46						1						3		
61858a	11.1	17				15														
61858b	16.4	6		1		10														
61866	6.4	13				10						2						1		
61869	50.2	25	3	1		30														
61873	6.0	4	1			16														
61882	28.2	16				27														
61883	14.7	32				12										1*				* L m2

continued ▶

Table A4.2 Wet sieved residues – *continued*

spit no.	weight (g)	ccanial	tusk	mammuthus molar fragment	other large mammal tooth fragment	indet. large bone fragments	E. lucius teeth	G. aculeatus spines	P. fluviatilis scale	fish bone	fish teeth	herpetofauna	bird bone	M. gregalis	Microtus sp. and Microtinae	Spermophilus sp.	indet. small mammal	split long bone fragments	indet. small bone fragments	notes
61906	277.8	17	505			30	1								1*			2	2	* 1 fragment, Microtinae
61913	36.9	3	46	2	1*	22														* buccal enamel fragment of M, cf. Bovidae
61917	6.4	1	5	1		2														
61958	<1.0																	1		
62006	1.5		1			1														
62010	3.4		1			1														
62017	0.8					1														
62034	9.8					4														
62042	0.8		4			1														
62046	1.2					12														
62102	3.2	2	1	1		7														
62106	2.7		1		1*	3													1	* small lingual fragment of ?R p4, R. tarandus
62110	13.7	1	2			14														
62114	21.0	3	13			22													3	
62118	42.1	5	7	6		23					1								2	
62122a	18.0		15			7														
62122b	71.6	1	168	3		16														
62126	26.5	22	5			20												3		
62131	14.7	5	19			3												1		
62134	24.7	12	7	1		10					1							1	1	
62142	6.3	4				2												3	1	
62201a	14.0	2	6	1		9					1							1	1	
62201b	7.8	2	5			6					1							1		
62204	22.6	3	1	1		11					1								1	
62209a	13.1	7	2			9					1							3	1	
62209b	49.6		59			9														

continued ▶

Table A4.2 Wet sieved residues – *continued*

spit no.	weight (g)	ccanial	tusk	mammuthus molar fragment	other large mammal tooth fragment	indet. large bone fragments	E. lucius teeth	G. aculeatus spines	P. fluviatilis scale	fish bone	fish teeth	herpetofauna	bird bone	M. gregalis	Microtus sp. and Microtinae	Spermophilus sp.	indet. small mammal	split long bone fragments	indet. small bone fragments	notes
62210	<1.0																			
62211a	5.3	2	2	2		6						1								
62211b	9.7	11	6			3														
62218	29.65	4	47			7						2			1*				3	*RM3
62221a	7.6	4	13	1		3												1		
62221b	59.5	4	85			2														
62225	43.7	12	45	1		4												2	2	
62226	33.0	27	40	1		9														
62233	11.4		6	1		9														
62252	24.8	9	1			27													1	
62256	26.6	18				15														
62260a	18.1	18	4			2													2	
62260b	18.3	18				2														
62263	41.5	19	3	1		17														
62267	8.3	11		1		6														
62273	34.6	33	5	1		15	1		1			2								
62275	28.9	15	3	1		4														
62281	22.9	13	3			4						1						1		
62282	8.6	8				5						2								
62289	16.2	13	3			2														
62292	4.0	7	3			4														
62299	26.8	30	3			5	1					3							1	
62317	1.5					1														
62330	<1.0	1																		
62409	21.1	43	11			26			1			1						1	4	
62412	14.6	26				8						2						1		
62415	29.9	63	3			29						1						1		

continued ▶

Table A4.2 Wet sieved residues – continued

spit no.	weight (g)	ccanial	tusk	mammuthus molar fragment	other large mammal tooth fragment	indet. large bone fragments	E. lucius teeth	G. aculeatus spines	P. fluviatilis scale	fish bone	fish teeth	herpetofauna	bird bone	M. gregalis	Microtus sp. and Microtinae	Spermophilus sp.	indet. small mammal	split long bone fragments	indet. small bone fragments	notes
62419	<1.0				1*	1														* canine tip, ?C. lupus
62422	3.4	12	1			1				1		1			1*					* 1 fragment, Microtinae
62429	20.0	41	6			16	1	1							1*			2	3	* R 1, Microtinae
62435	3.3	1	2			3				1		3						1	2	
62443	10.5	18	2			6													4	
62449	9.5	13				6			3			1						1	2	
62453	16.0	1	5			12						1						1		
62455	21.1	8	2			6						1						1		
62459	2.7	2				7				1		3							5	
62461	3.3	6	1			1														
62464a	5.9	4	5			4						1							3	
62464b	30.2	9	22			9														
62468	16.1	26	2			4												1		
62472	29.7	32	4			9												2		
62475	4.7		1			2						1								
62477	4.5	4	1			1												2		
62480	2.7	6				5						1							1	
62481a	29.2	13				9												2		
62481b	5.5	9				2														
62484	6.2	8	1			1						1								
62491	21.4	5	1			1														
62504	3.7					1									2*					*1 L i and 1 i frag., Microtinae
62513	22.4					11													4	
62517	25.7					32												2	6	
62524	<1.0					1														
62535	2.5					2														
62546	3.9	8	6			4						1								

continued ▶

Table A4.2 Wet sieved residues – *continued*

spit no.	weight (g)	ccanial	tusk	mammuthus molar fragment	other large mammal tooth fragment	indet. large bone fragments	E. lucius teeth	G. aculeatus spines	P. fluviatilis scale	fish bone	fish teeth	herpetofauna	bird bone	M. gregalis	Microtus sp. and Microtinae	Spermophilus sp.	indet. small mammal	split long bone fragments	indet. small bone fragments	notes
62550	2.6	6	2			6						4								
62563	<1.0					1														
62592	1.1		2			1														
62598	3.05	1			1?	7														
62606	2.4	9				3												1	1	
62608	5.2	8	1			6						2							4	
62655	25.6	28	3	1		18														
62662	6.6	17				5						4								
62669	22.6	12				10						2						1	4	
62670	1.0	1				3														
62674	9.9	9	1			5						4						1	1	
62679	1.9	6				5		1			2								2	
62708	3.0	1	1			1														
62724	2.7					1														
62735	15.4	9	5	1		11						2						1		
62746	0.7	2																		
62852																				sample missing
62859	20.6		1	1		11												1	1	
62862	20.3		4			8													3	
62867	10.0					2														
62869	50.4	10	12	1		61														
62871	84.5		30	7		20													1	
62878	56.1		23	6		9														
62883a	21.2	9	3	2		19													1	
62883b	26.4	1	2			10						2								
62884	124.7	4	8	4		16	1					1								
62887	29.3	2	58			32														

continued ▶

Table A4.2 Wet sieved residues – continued

spit no.	weight (g)	ccanial	tusk	mammuthus molar fragment	other large mammal tooth fragment	indet. large bone fragments	E. lucius teeth	G. aculeatus spines	P. fluviatilis scale	fish bone	fish teeth	herpetofauna	bird bone	M. gregalis	Microtus sp. and Microtinae	Spermophilus sp.	indet. small mammal	split long bone fragments	indet. small bone fragments	notes
62888	20.3	3	2	1		5														
62889	48.75	4	20			14												3	1	
62893	68.55	7	20	3		30												1	1	
62952	2.9			1		6														
62958	N/A				1*															*L p4 fragment & R p4, R. tarandus
62962	3.7					7														
62976	30.2	13	43			14		1	1		1				1*			2	3	* 1 fragment, Microtinae
62979	51.2	52	29			20												1	1	
62986	11.3	7	2			1						3					1*	1		* metapodial
62996	24.4	37				25													2	
63000	12.6	7	1			30														
63052	10.3					23														
63056	8.8	13	3			8														
63061	2.5	4				5	1		2		1									
63103	1.6					1														
63108	3.1			1		4			1		2									
63112	2.6	5	1			4														
63116	4.7	3				2														
63120	1.1		1															1	2	
63125	1.6					2					1				1*			1	1	*L I, Microtinae
63128												1								sample missing
63132	6.85					5					1							1	1	
63136	12.2			1?		5	1												3	
63140	<1.0									1*										*broken
63148	<1.0				1*															* buccal enamel fragment of M, cf. Bovidae
63153	16.2		53			16														

continued ▶

Table A4.2 Wet sieved residues – *continued*

spit no.	weight (g)	ccanial	tusk	mammuthus molar fragment	other large mammal tooth fragment	indet. large bone fragments	E. lucius teeth	G. aculeatus spines	P. fluviatilis scale	fish bone	fish teeth	herpetofauna	bird bone	M. gregalis	Microtus sp. and Microtinae	Spermophilus sp.	indet. small mammal	split long bone fragments	indet. small bone fragments	notes
63154	6.5		1			2												1		
63162	5.25		1			7														
63171	1.15																			
63173	2.35																			
63176	8.7																			
63180	5.6		4			1				4									1	
63182	8.4		1			5				2									2	
63186	6.25					4				1									1	
63195	<1.0																		3	
63202	1.75																			
63214	<1.0															1*				*L 1, Microtinae
63216	21.0		2			3				4									1	
63218	3.5	2																		
63234	<1.0										1									
63268	2.5			3		5														
63311	7.7	9	1			3				3									1	
63317	4.4		1			1				2								1	1	
63319	11.1	2								1								1	3	
63321–2	3.7	4				1														
63353	<1.0																		3	
63369	<1.0										2									
63556	23.9		3			11													3	
63562	57.7	10	2	3		15														
63563	<1.0																	1	3	
63567	30.5	2	5	1		7														
63570	26.6	3	2	1		6														
63577	52.0	32	16	3		36					1									

continued ▶

Table A4.2 Wet sieved residues – *continued*

spit no.	weight (g)	ccanial	tusk	mammuthus molar fragment	other large mammal tooth fragment	indet. large bone fragments	E. lucius teeth	G. aculeatus spines	P. fluviatilis scale	fish bone	fish teeth	herpetofauna	bird bone	M. gregalis	Microtus sp. and Microtinae	Spermophilus sp.	indet. small mammal	split long bone fragments	indet. small bone fragments	notes
63582	14.7	11	2	1													1*		1	* vertebral centrum fragment?
63585	70.5	35	40	4		39						1							2	
63595	25.9	8	2	2		9													3	
63608	5.5					22														
63631	10.8			2		6													3	
63633	11.4					41													1	
63638	10.6					5														
63646	32.3	2	2	1		30									1*					* damaged L m1, ?digested
63648	43.0	1		2		29														
63724	4.2	1*	1			1						1								
63734	24.3	1	63			2														
63739	9.5					2														
63756	12.5	3				12													1	
63759	6.1	2				9														
63763	3.0	1		2		2													1	
63774	2.4					1														
63782	12.5			1		6														
63804	<1.0									4									1	
63808	23.8	10	7			7						1			1*				2	* R m2, *Microtus* sp.
63813	16.3	29	3			9						1					1*	5	3	* metapodial
63818	19.2	30		4		7												1	1	
63851	<1.0								1											
63953	29.4	2	1	4		7														
63957	3.2	1				2														
63967	16.7	14	3			1												1		
63971	81.8	30	3	5		23														
63974	60.4	23	2	4		40						1								

continued ▶

Table A4.2 Wet sieved residues – *continued*

spit no.	weight (g)	ccanial	tusk	mammuthus molar fragment	other large mammal tooth fragment	indet. large bone fragments	E. lucius teeth	G. aculeatus spines	P. fluviatilis scale	fish bone	fish teeth	herpetofauna	bird bone	M. gregalis	Microtus sp. and Microtinae	Spermophilus sp.	indet. small mammal	split long bone fragments	indet. small bone fragments	notes
63975	43.3	15				38											1*		1	* small vertebral fragment
63980	17.6	18	2			2						1								
63985	3.9	8				2						1								
63988	2.7	8				1														
64001	30.2	16	12	1*		41														* M fragment, *E. ferus*
64004	37.1	1	10	1		25												4		
64005	41.7	15	6	1		17	1					2								
64008	29.9	11	3			8														
64009	13.6	8	2	1?		6						1							1	
64014	18.4	7	1	1		22													1	
64051	3.0					1														
64071	<1.0					1														
64103	7.6	4	1			17														
64110	6.0	13				5														
64110–133	15.3	23	13	1		1												2		
64114	14.6	14	3			15						3					1*		3	* proximal ulna
64117	21.6	22				19						2					3	4	5	
64120	14.9	11				4						1							1	
64125	9.0	12	5	1		6			1											
64126	9.0	9	2	1?		7	1					4						1	1	
64133	24.5	32	3	2		25						4						2	3	
64135	22.4	12				17						4						3		
64140	3.8		1		1*	4														* undetermined
64144	29.6	26	3	3		37						8								
64147	31.4	20	2	1		9						4								
64174	2.4					1														
64179	6.2					4														

continued ▶

Table A4.2 Wet sieved residues – continued

split no.	weight (g)	cranial	tusk	mammuthus molar fragment	other large mammal tooth fragment	indet. large bone fragments	E. lucius teeth	G. aculeatus spines	P. fluviatilis scale	fish bone	fish teeth	herpetofauna	bird bone	M. gregalis	Microtus sp. and Microtinae	Spermophilus sp.	indet. small mammal	split long bone fragments	indet. small bone fragments	notes
64185	0.9					3														
64197	7.9	11				8						1								
64202	17.9	19	1		1*	7						2								* germ of R dp2, E. ferus
64206	19.4	9	1			4						3							1	
64209	33.05	4	5			8													1	
64213	5.8	2				2												1		
64217	20.2	50	1			32						2						1	3	
62419	1.0				1*	1														* canine fragment
64223	24.6	14	4			9														
64228	20.1	6	2			11														
64231	42.5	27	1	3		14														
64234	33.3	49	12			22		1		1									1	
64236	60.1	36	3	1		26						1					1*	2	4	*vertebra
64244	17.7	12	2			6						1							1	
64256	32.4	16	10			16						2							2	
64258	19.1	33				21						1							1	
64260	58	26				69													2	
64265a	97.4	75	4			66						6					1*			*vertebra
64265b	3.3	6	2			3														
64274	1.1					4						1								
64300	1.1					4														
64303	0.7			1																
64305	<1.0					1														
64309	8.1			1		12														
64314	43.1			2	6	14						1							1	
64320	14.6			3	1	10														
64331	5.3	14				20														

continued ▶

APPENDIX 4

Table A4.2 Wet sieved residues – *continued*

spit no.	weight (g)	ccanial	tusk	mammuthus molar fragment	other large mammal tooth fragment	indet. large bone fragments	E. lucius teeth	G. aculeatus spines	P. fluviatilis scale	fish bone	fish teeth	herpetofauna	bird bone	M. gregalis	Microtus sp. and Microtinae	Spermophilus sp.	indet. small mammal	split long bone fragments	indet. small bone fragments	notes
64332	17.5	1	5	2		21												3	1	
64333	30.9	2	11	2		13						1								
64344	5.5		3			35												2		
64350	21.7		31			5														
64405	2.3			1		4														
64410	1.9	3	1			2														
64417	3.1					8														
64457	22.5	9	1			23		1											1	
64502	1.0	3	1																	
64503	1.5	4	1			2						2						1	1	
64554	0.8					2						1								
64715	28.9	2	38	1		32														
64721a	22.8	1	10	1		18														
64751b	5.2					10														
64764	9.8	2	4		1*	36									2**					* very worn m1/m2 fragment, R. tarandus; ** i fragments, Microtinae
64803	2.7	2																		
65654	27.7	4	14	1		2												4		
65655	18.1	6	3			6						1						2	1	
65660	2.2	1	2			2												1		
65665	10.7	1				6														
65672	<1.0																	1		
65675	<1.0					1												1		
65677	18.7	6	23	1		8						4						5		
65678	3.3		2			1												1	3	
65679	8.1	5	7			2						2								
65681	1.5		1			1												1	1	

continued ▶

Table A4.2 Wet sieved residues – continued

spit no.	weight (g)	ccanial	tusk	mammuthus molar fragment	other large mammal tooth fragment	indet. large bone fragments	E. lucius teeth	G. aculeatus spines	P. fluviatilis scale	fish bone	fish teeth	herpetofauna	bird bone	M. gregalis	Microtus sp. and Microtinae	Spermophilus sp.	indet. small mammal	split long bone fragments	indet. small bone fragments	notes
65682	6.6	5	1			3														
65684	1.1	1				1														
65685	9.0	6	1			9														
65686	5.5					4														
65688	60.6	18	5			100														
65689	28.9	8	2	1		43												1		
65692	1.1	2																		
65693	22.0	18	37			21														
65694	5.0					5														
65697	53.7	21	1			19														
sediment	184.5	372							4									1	1	'near mammoth skull'
608xx						10								1*				1		*L m 1
no number				4		12														uncertain location. 20.028 from 408E/840N

APPENDIX 4

Table A4.3 Dry sieved residues: ü denotes presence of multiple comminuted fragments. 61810 omitted as débitage only; 63135 omitted as no vertebrate material

spit no.	weight (g)	cranial	tusk	mammuthus molar fragment	other large mammal tooth fragment	indet. large bone fragments	other large vertebrate remains	fish bone	herpetofauna	bird bone	notes
60047	32.4		20			5					
60058	0.8					6					
60066	2.7		1			3					
60067	5.0				1	6					
60071	1.4					3					
60073	0.7					1					
60074	17.4		5	13		2					
60078	2.4		1	2							
60079	1.8			2		1					
60080	10.0					4					
60081	1.4				1	3					
60092	6.9		1			1					
60094	16.6		3	1		4					
60095	3.0	2	1			2					
60211	83.2		16			10					
60212	99	19	76			11					
60213	49.2		17								
60214	46.5	4	28			18					
60215	89.65	1	37	1		45					
60216	360	63	551			68					
60217	151	20	196			3					
60218	66.5	6	29			7					
60219	5.7		3			4					
60220	60.2	14	60			18					
60221	63.0	22	39			12					
60224	90.1	5	200			5					

continued ▶

Table A4.3 Dry sieved residues: ü denotes presence of multiple comminuted fragments. 61810 omitted as débitage only; 63135 omitted as no vertebrate material – *continued*

spit no.	weight (g)	cranial	tusk	mammuthus molar fragment	other large mammal tooth fragment	indet. large bone fragments	other large vertebrate remains	fish bone	herpetofauna	bird bone	notes
60225	7.0		26								
60226	26.8		21								
60227	14.8		11								
60228	13.2		17								
60229	27.65	2	55			1					
60230	73.4	2	6			10					
60231	52.15	30	29	8		22					
60232	3.25	4	2			2					
60237	3.25	1			1	1					
60240	11.1		1			1					
60243	20.5		24	1							
60245	2.2		1			1					
60247	1.9	2				1					
60248	1.3		1								
60249	5.8		13			1					
60255	80.0		31			2					
60256	4.0					1					
60259	2.1	2				1					
60266	5.3	1	3			3					
60267	5.7	2	4			3					
60276	10.7		8								
60282	6.5	1	1			3					
60285	3.8		2								
60287	14.8	4				8					
60291	95.6	17	8			28					
60293	10.2	4				2					

continued ▶

Table A4.3 Dry sieved residues: ü denotes presence of multiple comminuted fragments.
61810 omitted as débitage only; 63135 omitted as no vertebrate material – *continued*

spit no.	weight (g)	cranial	tusk	mammuthus molar fragment	other large mammal tooth fragment	indet. large bone fragments	other large vertebrate remains	fish bone	herpetofauna	bird bone	notes
60294	3.3	1	1			1					
60295	20.1	1	4			1					
60296	1.4		1								
60299	1.6	1									
60300	26.6	1	7			3					
60301	8.5			1		1					
60305	24.7	1	3	2		15					
60307	28.2	1	4	1		10					
60309	3.8			1		1					
60313	2.1			1		1					
60314	6.8					2					
60316	27.2		32			1					
60318	4.9					4					
60320	21.8	3	1			7					
60321	8.7	4				5					
60323	18.7	2	2			6					
60325	11.9	1	5	1		6					
60326	3.2					2					
60329	6.5		1			2					
60331	7.9	4	1			3					
60332	9.2	7	1			9					
60335	87.4	23	4			43					
60336	17.1	7				2					
60337	1.6	2									
60339	43.7	2		1		17					
60340	9.6	2	8			4					

continued ▶

Table A4.3 Dry sieved residues: ü denotes presence of multiple comminuted fragments. 61810 omitted as débitage only; 63135 omitted as no vertebrate material – *continued*

spit no.	weight (g)	cranial	tusk	mammuthus molar fragment	other large mammal tooth fragment	indet. large bone fragments	other large vertebrate remains	fish bone	herpetofauna	bird bone	notes
60342	11.2	2	1			4					
60344	5.7	1				2					
60346	32.9	13	2			4					
60347	50.5	16	9			8					
60349	22.7	7	8			3					
60350	21.4	11				12					
60368	1.4		2			1					
60371	4.2	6	6								
60375	27.7					12					
60384a	18.7	2				2					
60384b	3.5	11				3					
60385a	8.8	3				13					
60385b	8.7	7				10					
60386a	5.6					6					
60386b	6.9	5				4					
60391	6.2	3									
60392	24.4	16				33					
60393	16.5	7				40					
60395	12.4	5				23					
60398	<1					12					
60399	4.5					40					
60455	7.9	4				2					
60469	5.7		1			7					
60471	1.3					2					
60477	1.0					1					
60479	<1.0					2					

continued ▶

**Table A4.3 Dry sieved residues: ü denotes presence of multiple comminuted fragments.
61810 omitted as débitage only; 63135 omitted as no vertebrate material** – *continued*

spit no.	weight (g)	cranial	tusk	mammuthus molar fragment	other large mammal tooth fragment	indet. large bone fragments	other large vertebrate remains	fish bone	herpetofauna	bird bone	notes
60480	1.3					1					
60483	11.1	3				9					
60485	1.0					2					
60501a	13.1		2								
60501b	6.9		4								
60503	18.5		2			9					
60504	6.4	1	2								
60505	4.4		10			1					
60506	4.8					4					
60506	3.9		5								
60510	3.1		6								
60512	2.3		2								
60514	11.3		18			1					
60520	3.5	1	2			1					
60522	1.1					2					
60523	13.8					8					
60524	1.6					1					
60525	12.6		3			4					
60527	21.4	3	14			3					
60529	4.1		1								
60530	6.2	1	4								
60532	5.2	6				2					
60537	1.9		2			2					
60539	13.1	7	3								
60540	5.4	2	1			3					
60541	8.8					5					

continued ▶

Table A4.3 Dry sieved residues: ü denotes presence of multiple comminuted fragments. 61810 omitted as débitage only; 63135 omitted as no vertebrate material – *continued*

spit no.	weight (g)	cranial	tusk	mammuthus molar fragment	other large mammal tooth fragment	indet. large bone fragments	other large vertebrate remains	fish bone	herpetofauna	bird bone	notes
60543	6.8	5	1			1					
60544	2.9					2					
60547	8.4	3									
60549	19.6			22	1	2					
60588	1.0					5					
60621	1.0					1					
60622	2.6					1					
60624	4.8					2					
60625	7.8					2					
60626	1.5				1						
60628	1.9			4							
60629	2.3					1					
60631	7.1	2				1					
60632	6.6					2					
60633a	1.8					2					
60633b	47.4	19	6			31					
60636	24.0	9				7					
60660	1.8					3					
60668	6.1					2					
60701	5.2		1			3					
60703	29.6		11	5		3					
60705	33.7	6				10					
60706	74.1	12	3			21					
60710	24.7	4				5					
60711	38.5	9	4			11					
60712	1.6			2	1	1					

continued ▶

Table A4.3 Dry sieved residues: ü denotes presence of multiple comminuted fragments. 61810 omitted as débitage only; 63135 omitted as no vertebrate material – *continued*

spit no.	weight (g)	cranial	tusk	mammuthus molar fragment	other large mammal tooth fragment	indet. large bone fragments	other large vertebrate remains	fish bone	herpetofauna	bird bone	notes
60713	6.1	1	1			1					
60714	16.7	1	1	1		8					
60716	15.6	1	6			2					
60717	1.6	2	1								
60721	65.3	7	1			18					
60722	51.0	8				8					
60723	19.6	7				3					
60725	21.4	6			2	7					
60726	18.4	10	3			2	1*				* 2nd phalanx of C. crocuta
60728	52.9	23	6			6					
60730	13.4	2									
60731	47.8	16	3			2					
60735	22.7	5				3					
60801	20.5	14				7					
60802a	10.1	1	3			1					
60802b	51.25	13	3			13					
60804	2.1	1	3								
60811	5.5					2					
60815	2.1					2					
60816	3.8	1	1			1					
60820	1.1					2					
60830	8.9	6	33			13					
60831	6.8	6				6					
60837	75.4	6	30			9					
60838	22.6	10	3			8					
60840	55.9	10	35			46					

continued ▶

Table A4.3 Dry sieved residues: ü denotes presence of multiple comminuted fragments. 61810 omitted as débitage only; 63135 omitted as no vertebrate material – *continued*

spit no.	weight (g)	cranial	tusk	mammuthus molar fragment	other large mammal tooth fragment	indet. large bone fragments	other large vertebrate remains	fish bone	herpetofauna	bird bone	notes
60842	2.3	2									
60843	1.1	1									
60845	8.3					1					
60867	16.9					3					
60936	5.4	2	1			1					
60937	17.2	1	3			3					
60938	1.8		17								
60943	0.7					2					
60945	10.5			2		7					
60946a	0.9					1					
60946b	4.0	1	3			8					
60948	10.6	2	2			3					
60949	3.4					4					
60960	28.5					4					
60962	41.6		33	1		15					
60963	0.7					1					
60965	28.5		17			3					
60967	2.2					1					
60969	11.0		1			5					
60970	48.6					13					
60971	33.6		1			12					
60972	43.9		157								
60973a	90.1		126			3					
60973a	26.3		29			3					
60974b	83.7		62			1					
60974b	64.1		99								

continued ▶

Table A4.3 Dry sieved residues: ü denotes presence of multiple comminuted fragments. 61810 omitted as débitage only; 63135 omitted as no vertebrate material – *continued*

spit no.	weight (g)	cranial	tusk	mammuthus molar fragment	other large mammal tooth fragment	indet. large bone fragments	other large vertebrate remains	fish bone	herpetofauna	bird bone	notes
60975a	137.5		60								
60975b	50.6		47			9					
60976	95.6	1	22	6		24					
60977	108.1		10			26					
60978	11.9					3					
60979	100.5		2	1		45					
60980	47.4		3			19					
60981	45.5	1	1	1		28					
60983	590.5	1	269	2		8					
60984	891.0		416			7					
60987	51.4		96			22					
60988	53.2		46			2					
60990	1,039.0		532			7					
60991	304.8		178			26					
60992	29.9		6			11					
60993	47.7		21								
60994	13.0		1			1					
60995	145.4	1	75	1		1					
60997	62.7	1	14	4		28					
60998	9.4		8	2		5					
61051	20.0	3	4			3					
61052	5.7	5	2			1					
61057	2.3	1	1								
61058	22.7		1			1					
61060	15.0	11	4			3					
61061	11.0	4	7			4					

continued ▶

Table A4.3 Dry sieved residues: ü denotes presence of multiple comminuted fragments. 61810 omitted as débitage only; 63135 omitted as no vertebrate material – *continued*

spit no.	weight (g)	cranial	tusk	mammuthus molar fragment	other large mammal tooth fragment	indet. large bone fragments	other large vertebrate remains	fish bone	herpetofauna	bird bone	notes
61062	31.6	9	11			2					
61063	5.7	1	1								
61064	8.7	5	4			2					
61065	2.0	1	1			1					
61068	49.5	5			1	20					
61069	27.1	12	5			2					
61070	7.5	8				2					
61073	5.7					1					
61075	12.7					2					
61079	3.5					2					
61084	15.2	1				1					
61085	5.1	5	1			1					
61086	17.2		9			2					
61087	4.4	2				1					
61089	2.4	2									
61090	38.7	1				35					
61094	13.7	2	5								
61095	12.8	7	1			4					
61097	8.8		11								
61101	62.6		56			9					
61102	11.4		9			4					
61112	12.6	2	9								
61113	9.5	7	10			1					
61115	0.9					9					
61116	9.4		4			8					
61117a	6.5	3	14			3					

continued ▶

Table A4.3 Dry sieved residues: ü denotes presence of multiple comminuted fragments. 61810 omitted as débitage only; 63135 omitted as no vertebrate material – *continued*

spit no.	weight (g)	cranial	tusk	mammuthus molar fragment	other large mammal tooth fragment	indet. large bone fragments	other large vertebrate remains	fish bone	herpetofauna	bird bone	notes
61117b	4.5	2	2			1					
61117c	80.6	20	19			48					
61118	26.2	6	10			4					
61120	11.8		8								
61121	54.0	26	19			40					
61122a	64.4	13	34	1		23					
61122b	7.6	2	1								
61123a	3.0	5	8								
61123b	11.5		5								
61123c	3.2	2	1								
61124a	1.3	2	1								
61124b	1.8	2	3			1					
61125	2.4	3	3			3					
61126	<1.0	2									
61128	5.2	1	5			1					
61129	9.5	10				15					
61130a	2.5	3	3			2					
61130b	9.5	4	6			7					
61130c	3.0	4	5			1					
61131a	10.8	4	3			6					
61131b	32.5	14	35	1		22					
61131c	2.1	1				1					
61131d	3.1	1	11			4					
61131e	2.6					2					
61131f	13.9	4	16			10					
61132a	11.9	15		1		28					

continued ▶

Table A4.3 Dry sieved residues: ü denotes presence of multiple comminuted fragments. 61810 omitted as débitage only; 63135 omitted as no vertebrate material – *continued*

spit no.	weight (g)	cranial	tusk	mammuthus molar fragment	other large mammal tooth fragment	indet. large bone fragments	other large vertebrate remains	fish bone	herpetofauna	bird bone	notes
61132b	7.35	3	6			2					
61133a	8.4	17	6			19					
61133b	5.2	5	6			2					
61133c	20.2	5	5			11					
61134a	1.0					2					
61134b	91.5	58	35			122					
61136	8.5	9	4			4					
61151	18.0	1	1	2		12					
61152	15.5	1	3			6					
61153	2.5					8					
61154	3.5		1			7					
61157	5.6	1	2			1					
61159	10.8	2	10			3					
61160	36.3	3	69			14					
61161	6.4					1					
61162	13.4	2	9								
61164	22.6		2	2		6					
61165	7.2	6				5					
61166	12.0		4			5					
61167	12.4		3			9					
61168	10.5	4	5			3					
61169	2.3		2								
61170	1.7					2					
61171	31.3	15	22			12					
61172	18.2	10	11			7					
61173	6.3	1				1					

continued ▶

Table A4.3 Dry sieved residues: ü denotes presence of multiple comminuted fragments. 61810 omitted as débitage only; 63135 omitted as no vertebrate material – *continued*

spit no.	weight (g)	cranial	tusk	mammuthus molar fragment	other large mammal tooth fragment	indet. large bone fragments	other large vertebrate remains	fish bone	herpetofauna	bird bone	notes
61174	11.9	2				7					
61175	15.0	5	7			2					
61176	12.0	4				2					
61177	17.2	9	1			8					
61178	30.3	19	3			15					
61179	13.6	7				9					
61180	8.0		17								
61181	8.4	3				8					
61182	32.9	14	13	2		11					
61183	34.1		25			5					
61184	48.1	16	33			12					
61185	55.9	34	3	1		46					
61186	6.7	3	2			8					
61187	7.5	1	3			1					
61188	16.8	5				12					
61189	6.7	2	1			5					
61190	7.1		6			2					
61191	22.2	6	6			8					
61192	4.1	1	3			13					
61193	33.2	1	31			32					
61194	10.4	1	7			9					
61195	10.0					14					
61196	28.1	6	7	1		17					
61197	16.5	11	1			14					
61198	3.2					5					
61199	50.4	25	4			44					

continued ▶

Table A4.3 Dry sieved residues: ü denotes presence of multiple comminuted fragments. 61810 omitted as débitage only; 63135 omitted as no vertebrate material – *continued*

spit no.	weight (g)	cranial	tusk	mammuthus molar fragment	other large mammal tooth fragment	indet. large bone fragments	other large vertebrate remains	fish bone	herpetofauna	bird bone	notes
61200	4.4	8	2			1					
61202	0.7					1					
61208	1.9		2								
61211a	6.3					10					
61211b	1.7					1					
61212	8.7					4					
61213	3.5.					2					
61214	<1.0		1								
61216	23.6					2					
61217	24.8					7					
61218	2.1					1					
61219	2.2		3								
61220	11.4					2					
61223	17.8					5					
61224	2.3					3					
61231	3.7	2	6			11					
61233	9.1		1			4					
61235	18.4					3					
61236	7.2					2					
61239	3.6					1					
61241	2.1		1								
61243	1.9	6	1								
61244a	8.1					3					
61244b	68.9					11					
61247	18.2					4					
61249	14.8					2					

continued ▶

APPENDIX 4

Table A4.3 Dry sieved residues: ü denotes presence of multiple comminuted fragments. 61810 omitted as débitage only; 63135 omitted as no vertebrate material – *continued*

spit no.	weight (g)	cranial	tusk	mammuthus molar fragment	other large mammal tooth fragment	indet. large bone fragments	other large vertebrate remains	fish bone	herpetofauna	bird bone	notes
61250	6.7		2								
61251	9.9	4				2					
61264	1.3		1			4					
61265	8.2		1			1					
61266	1.9					3					
61269	22.0	1				6					
61270	21.6					4					
61272	31.5	1				3					
61274	1.0	5									
61275	7.2	1	2								
61276	27.2	12	1			2				1	
61277	8.6	7	3			2					
61278	79.5	20				24					
61281	32.3	4	3	1		3					
61282a	20.0	13	1			3					
61282b	21.0	9				3					
61283	18.6	5	1			2					
61284	96.9	21	1			9					
61285a	31.1	9									
61285b	15.0	9	1			2					
61285a	7.2	4				2					
61285d	11.8	21	2			7					
61291	1.6	3									
61292	26.2	26	2			17					
61293	23.1	25	1			10					
61294	31.5	20	6			2					

continued ▶

Table A4.3 Dry sieved residues: ü denotes presence of multiple comminuted fragments. 61810 omitted as débitage only; 63135 omitted as no vertebrate material – *continued*

spit no.	weight (g)	cranial	tusk	mammuthus molar fragment	other large mammal tooth fragment	indet. large bone fragments	other large vertebrate remains	fish bone	herpetofauna	bird bone	notes
61296	9.7	9	1			3					
61297	15.6	3	12			3					
61300	15.4	12				6					
61305	3.2		1			6					
61312	5.6			1		17					
61316	8.2	1	5			9					
61317	16.6	1	5			13					
61319	32.9	2	2	1		15					
61320	3.3					3					
61321	2.7	1				7					
61322	13.7			4		6					
61324	12.0	2	5	4		9					
61325	7.6		2								
61327	2.2		7	4		7					
61328	30.0		13	3		19					
61329	4.0		4			10					
61331	89.3	6	9	4		75					
61332	163.9	1	297			33					
61333	205.3	2	228			22					
61335a	28.6		31			3					
61335b	37.95		15			15					
61335c	28.0		43			11					
61337	44.8	2	35	4		23					
61338	195.2	1	122	5		23					
61339	22.3	1	23			12					
61340	235.1		180			10					

continued ▶

APPENDIX 4

Table A4.3 Dry sieved residues: ü denotes presence of multiple comminuted fragments.
61810 omitted as débitage only; 63135 omitted as no vertebrate material – *continued*

spit no.	weight (g)	cranial	tusk	mammuthus molar fragment	other large mammal tooth fragment	indet. large bone fragments	other large vertebrate remains	fish bone	herpetofauna	bird bone	notes
61341	38.7		15	1		56					
61343	95.05	2	84	1		65					
61344	144.4		136	1		114					
61346	86.75		156			3					
61347	182.3	2	332	3		40					
61348	15.1	2	4			13					
61349	20.0		20	3		16					
61353	1.3	1									
61354	4.8	12			1*	2					* very worn L M2, R. tarandus
61355	<1.0	1									
61356	2.0					1					
61361	8.5	4				2					
61364	7.6	2	2			3					
61365	9.9	3									
61367a	8.1	3				6					
61367b	1.6	1									
61369	6.9	8	2			7					
61371	34.2	13	3			5					
61378	20.2	17	6			8					
61380	30.9	12	11			3					
61381	37.8	10	1			10					
61382	29.1	20	3			4					
61384	19.5	13	2			16					
61385	21.1	26	3			12					
61386	6.3	4				1					
61387	50.3	48	7			39					

continued ▶

Table A4.3 Dry sieved residues: ü denotes presence of multiple comminuted fragments. 61810 omitted as débitage only; 63135 omitted as no vertebrate material – *continued*

spit no.	weight (g)	cranial	tusk	mammuthus molar fragment	other large mammal tooth fragment	indet. large bone fragments	other large vertebrate remains	fish bone	herpetofauna	bird bone	notes
61388	3.0	4	2			1					
61389	22.4	28		1		14					
61390	46.1	21	18			37					
61391	28.6	8	11			7					
61392	33.8	14	35			8					
61393	7.4	16				4					
61395	17.5	22	10			6					
61396	16.9	27	2	1		11					
61398	13.8	9				4					
61399	33.4	23				7					
61400	10.1	11		2		2					
61452	6.6	1	5								
61454	4.6		1			9					
61455	7.9		1			3					
61456	14.6		1	1		6					
61457	25.3	2	9			26					
61460	20.0	7	7	1		11					
61461	20.1	2	7	10		38					
61462	29.1	2	5	1		15					
61463	34.6		9	1		16					
61464	16.2	3	13	1		15					
61465	26.0	1	28			31					
61466	4.4		1			1					
61467	20.5		14			14					
61468	15.5					8					
61469	12.4	5				8					

continued ▶

APPENDIX 4

Table A4.3 Dry sieved residues: ü denotes presence of multiple comminuted fragments.
61810 omitted as débitage only; 63135 omitted as no vertebrate material – *continued*

spit no.	weight (g)	cranial	tusk	mammuthus molar fragment	other large mammal tooth fragment	indet. large bone fragments	other large vertebrate remains	fish bone	herpetofauna	bird bone	notes
61470	2.8	1				1					
61471	7.9	1	2			8					
61472	22.3	4				13					
61473	87.9	6	10	1		47					
61474	0.7	2				1					
61475	93.4	9	13	1		58					
61476	29.7	3	17			27					
61478	29.9	8	2			12					
61479	8.1		3			4					
61480	40.7	3	19	1		49					
61481a	51.6	8	9	1		26					
61481b	2.0					1					
61481	5.5	3	1	1							
61482	94.7	3	13	1		67					
61483	34.6		1			6					
61484	31.9	12	15	4		11					
61485	55.7	14	2			23					
61486	129.7	30	15	2		44					
61487	16.5	1	2	1		10					
61488a	51.3	15	7			28					
61488b	56.5	5	1			33					
61488b	16.4	1				15					
61489	30.5	11	8			16					
61490	20.0	17				13					
61493a	2.1	3									
61493b	2.6		3								

continued ▶

Table A4.3 Dry sieved residues: ü denotes presence of multiple comminuted fragments. 61810 omitted as débitage only; 63135 omitted as no vertebrate material – *continued*

spit no.	weight (g)	cranial	tusk	mammuthus molar fragment	other large mammal tooth fragment	indet. large bone fragments	other large vertebrate remains	fish bone	herpetofauna	bird bone	notes
61494	3.5	4	2								
61495	16.0					7					
61498	72.1	11	3	1		24					
61509	36.9	10				9					
61519	2.0					2					
61520	2.4		2			2					
61522	4.8		2			5					
61525	<1.0					5					
61527	5.5	1	2								
61528	<1.0	1									
61530	6.4	2				7					
61532	21.3	10	10			4					
61534	23.5	14	4	2		6					
61536	22.9	13	4	1		8					
61537	6.8	4				5					
61538	31.7	11	1	1		2					
61539a	27.0	16	1			5					
61539b	59.2	22	9			4					
61540	17.4					1					
61543	1.7		4								
61544a	29.6	22	2			2					
61544b	6.3	6				1					
61545	13.6	13				6					
61546	12.6	9				2					
61547	10.4	8				2					
61548	2.5	5				1					

continued ▶

APPENDIX 4

Table A4.3 Dry sieved residues: ü denotes presence of multiple comminuted fragments. 61810 omitted as débitage only; 63135 omitted as no vertebrate material – *continued*

spit no.	weight (g)	cranial	tusk	mammuthus molar fragment	other large mammal tooth fragment	indet. large bone fragments	other large vertebrate remains	fish bone	herpetofauna	bird bone	notes
61601	14.0	7	2			14					
61602	27.4	6	7	1		22					
61603	10.1	4	3			7					
61604	5.5	7	2			7					
61605	74.85	27	1			53					
61607	6.9	10				2					
61608	56.95	43	5			37					
61609	33.3	17	8			15					
61611	27.4	16	2			31					
61614	6.4	7	3			1					
61615	107.0	22	26			121					
61616	20.8	7	1			18					
61617	20.8	8	4			20					
61618	4.35	5				1					
61620	6.0	2	5			9					
61621	10.0	10				1					
61624	56.2	35	22	1		43					
61625a	31.8	30	1			16					
61625b	11.75	5				6					
61627	38.55	36	2			30					
61628	17.65	20				16					
61629	22.4	24	2			9					
61631	46.3	28	5	2		33					
61632	5.7	2	4	1		9					
61633	24.6	16	18			12					
61634	8.0	2	4			5					

continued ▶

Table A4.3 Dry sieved residues: ü denotes presence of multiple comminuted fragments. 61810 omitted as débitage only; 63135 omitted as no vertebrate material – *continued*

spit no.	weight (g)	cranial	tusk	mammuthus molar fragment	other large mammal tooth fragment	indet. large bone fragments	other large vertebrate remains	fish bone	herpetofauna	bird bone	notes
61636	34.1	25	15	1		21					
61637	42.15	13	1	1		16					
61638	21.9	24	6	1		18					
61639	15.4	13	1			9					
61641a	<1.0					1					
61641b	7.3	4				9					
61643	34.1	42	7			30					
61645	35.6	33	2			49					
61647	6.5	3	10			2					
61650	23.65	28	2			15					
61651	24.6		10								
61653	5.4		1			3					
61655	20.9		28			2					
61656	24.5		33			3					
61658	41.4		28			4					
61659	<1.0		3								
61660	12.3	1				6					
61664	0.9					3					
61665	2.8					1					
61666	12.0					6					
61667	12.2		2	2		6					
61669	1.9					7					
61689	13.9		32			2					
61693	21.8		65								
61699	<1.0		1								
61708	1.0					1					

continued ▶

Table A4.3 Dry sieved residues: ü denotes presence of multiple comminuted fragments. 61810 omitted as débitage only; 63135 omitted as no vertebrate material – *continued*

spit no.	weight (g)	cranial	tusk	mammuthus molar fragment	other large mammal tooth fragment	indet. large bone fragments	other large vertebrate remains	fish bone	herpetofauna	bird bone	notes
61719	2.3	3				2					
61724	11.1			2		8					
61730a	4.6	6		1							
61730b	8.2	1		2		9					
61731	9.6										
61731	44.4	4	21			20					
61732	14.5		2			28					
61750	<1.0		1			1					
61767	1.6					6					
61779	3.3					3					
61801a	1.1					9					
61801b	6.4					4					
61802	2.0					7					
61803	3.0			1		2					
61806	2.4					2					
61806	2.4					4					
61851	39.7	2	4	15		6					
61852	90.4	31	6			31					
61853	15.5	3	10			2					
61854	7.5	7				2					
61854	33.6	11	7			5					
61855	6.8	1	2			9					
61856	55.4	15	16			18					
61857	24.2	7	2	1		3					
61859	15.0	5	2			7					
61859	8.1	5				3					

continued ▶

Table A4.3 Dry sieved residues: ü denotes presence of multiple comminuted fragments. 61810 omitted as débitage only; 63135 omitted as no vertebrate material – *continued*

spit no.	weight (g)	cranial	tusk	mammuthus molar fragment	other large mammal tooth fragment	indet. large bone fragments	other large vertebrate remains	fish bone	herpetofauna	bird bone	notes
61860	34.9	12				5					
61861	19.4	7	1			7					
61862	37.2	19	7			13					
61865	46.6	17	2			7					
61866	18.6	10				8					
61867	9.5	5				4					
61868	8.2	12									
61869	26.9	17	4			8					
61871	39.0	28				12					
61872	50.8	57				13					
61874	70.7	86		1		29					
61876	9.7	1				1					
61884	3.3	1				2					
61901	10.6		1			6					
61903	67.3	1	26			4					
61905	110.9		115	5		14					
61906	79.7		41								
61907	37.3	1	5			19					
61908	10.0		9			2					
61909	3.1		1								
61910	131.2	1	107			10					
61911	152.0	2	86			12					
61912	48.6		16			15					
61913	21.3		2			5					
61915	35.2		14								
61916	22.5	3	8	1		2					

continued ▶

Table A4.3 Dry sieved residues: ü denotes presence of multiple comminuted fragments. 61810 omitted as débitage only; 63135 omitted as no vertebrate material – *continued*

spit no.	weight (g)	cranial	tusk	mammuthus molar fragment	other large mammal tooth fragment	indet. large bone fragments	other large vertebrate remains	fish bone	herpetofauna	bird bone	notes
61951	99.5	7	75			31					
61952	26.9	6	2			9					
61955	19.9	20				7					
61956	3.0	3				1					
61957	10.2	6	3			1					
61959	3.9					3		1			
61960	~0.4					2					
61961	~0.4					1					
61962	1.2					1					
62002	2.3	1				3					
62021	6.8					9					
62103	13.9		2			18					
62104	6.2		3			7					
62105	21.0		45	1		10					
62106	15.2	1	9			17					
62106	9.0		6			22					
62107	13.7		6			30					
62108	21.0		6			23					
62113	30.8		27	2		23					
62115	44.6	2	41	1		29					
62116	24.8	1	21			23					
62117	36.1		12			21					
62119	31.3		8			25					
62120	40.8		7	1		17					
62121	77.5	1	156	2		13					
62123	47.5	6	26			50					

continued ▶

Table A4.3 Dry sieved residues: ü denotes presence of multiple comminuted fragments. 61810 omitted as débitage only; 63135 omitted as no vertebrate material – *continued*

spit no.	weight (g)	cranial	tusk	mammuthus molar fragment	other large mammal tooth fragment	indet. large bone fragments	other large vertebrate remains	fish bone	herpetofauna	bird bone	notes
62124	38.1	4	13			31					
62125	24.0	3	10			25					
62127	10.3	6	4			7					
62128	28.3		13			19					
62129	18.7	2	43			20					
62130	31.3	10	124	1		6					
62132	37.4	17	24	5		40					
62133	22.4	6	13	2		11					
62135	12.4	8	12	1		14					
62136	4.6	1	3			3					
62137	<1.0	1	1								
62139	8.6		1			8					
62140	7.7	3	2	1		2					
62141	16.6	5	10			4					
62144	4.4	1				1					
62152	4.5		10			1					
62153	0.9		2			1					
62160	3.0					2					
62162	9.5		11								
62166	3.8		2			5					
62167	2.9					2					
62168	4.8					4					
62170	2.9					3					
62171	6.5		6			1					
62173	4.2		4			2					
62176	3.7	1				5					

continued ▶

Table A4.3 Dry sieved residues: ü denotes presence of multiple comminuted fragments.
61810 omitted as débitage only; 63135 omitted as no vertebrate material – *continued*

spit no.	weight (g)	cranial	tusk	mammuthus molar fragment	other large mammal tooth fragment	indet. large bone fragments	other large vertebrate remains	fish bone	herpetofauna	bird bone	notes
62180	8.6		1			2					
62180	1.0		2								
62182	17.4	8									
62183	10.1					4					
62184	9.9		1			7					
62185	33.3					12					
62187	71.4					38					
62190	9.9					1					
62192	8.3					3					
62198	6.7		11								
62202	87.8	7	126			6					
62203	37.95	7	14	2		16					
62204	18.5		23			4					
62205	12.6	2	12			3					
62206	50.6	4	20			47					
62207	38.3	5	21	3		16					
62208	85.7	3	79	3		38					
62210	23.4		43			12					
62212	33.0	6	8			14					
62213	21.3		45	1		13					
62214	9.5	4	152			1					
62215	20.4	5	12			14					
62216	20.3	7	6	1		13					
62217	11.95	6	14			4					
62219	34.7	5	22	2		20					
62220	10.2		9			5					

continued ▶

Table A4.3 Dry sieved residues: ü denotes presence of multiple comminuted fragments. 61810 omitted as débitage only; 63135 omitted as no vertebrate material – *continued*

spit no.	weight (g)	cranial	tusk	mammuthus molar fragment	other large mammal tooth fragment	indet. large bone fragments	other large vertebrate remains	fish bone	herpetofauna	bird bone	notes
62222	10.3	1	23			5					
62223	14.0	8	1			4					
62224	7.9	3	2	1		6					
62227	7.6	4	5								
62228	19.8	3	4			7					
62229	24.1		34	1		4					
62230	6.2		14			1					
62232	4.8		1			5					
62251	59.3	10	9			11					
62253	8.6	10	1			4					
62254	9.7	4				1					
62255	35.9	9		4		10					
62257	7.5	8									
62258	17.5	8	1			8					
62259	39.0	50	4	1		4					
62261a	11.4	2				8					
62261b+A694	12.4	5	2			9					
62262	10.4	2	1			4					
62264	4.8	4				4					
62266	22.3	11				7					
62270	15.8	8				7					
62271	29.2	26	2	1		6	1				
62272	6.1	5				4					
62274	31.1	13				10					
62277	49.0	14	16	1		10					
62278	40.2	16	12			7			1		

continued ▶

**Table A4.3 Dry sieved residues: ü denotes presence of multiple comminuted fragments.
61810 omitted as débitage only; 63135 omitted as no vertebrate material** – *continued*

spit no.	weight (g)	cranial	tusk	mammuthus molar fragment	other large mammal tooth fragment	indet. large bone fragments	other large vertebrate remains	fish bone	herpetofauna	bird bone	notes
62279	31.9	17		1		12					
62280	34.7	23	1	1		5			1		
62284	13.0	3		1		2					
62285	0.8					2					
62286	26.7	14	2			7					
62287	16.2	26				6					
62288	39.1	1				11					
62290	23.5	10				2					
62291	8.5	1		1							
62293	16.9	3				3					
62295	12.9			1		7					
62298	16.1	7				5					
62301	10.1	9				7					
62301	6.2					1					
62302	5.6					6					
62302	8.5	11				6					
62304	3.4					5					
62316	5.4	6									
62319	10.8	4	1			9					
62322	2.9	1				7					
62331	<1.0					3					
62354	6.3					1					
62370	23.3		21								
62385	2.9					2					
62401	10.4	5	4			2					
62402	18.2	6	7			1					

continued ▶

Table A4.3 Dry sieved residues: ü denotes presence of multiple comminuted fragments. 61810 omitted as débitage only; 63135 omitted as no vertebrate material – *continued*

spit no.	weight (g)	cranial	tusk	mammuthus molar fragment	other large mammal tooth fragment	indet. large bone fragments	other large vertebrate remains	fish bone	herpetofauna	bird bone	notes
62403	23.8	7	6			3					
62404	6.2	3	1			7					
62405	23.8	6	3			6					
62406	15.6	18				11			1		
62407	5.9	1				3					
62408	39.5	12	3			5					
62409	31.8	7				12					
62410	8.2	21				1			1		
62411	25.8	24	1	1		5					
62413	21.7	16				7					
62414	20.6	17	3			5					
62416	24.9	26	3			10					
62417	25.7	26				11					
62418	19.4	8	5			19					
62420	8.7	15									
62423	18.4	16				14					
62424	39.7	64	2			7					
62425	8.9	7	1			7			1		
62426	2.9	1	2			1					
62427	15.6	10	1								
62428	11.1	3				3					
62428	16.6	6	4			1					
62428	7.5	5									
62430	6.4	2	1			3					
62432	19.6	15	2			1					
62433	11.0	8									

continued ▶

APPENDIX 4

**Table A4.3 Dry sieved residues: ü denotes presence of multiple comminuted fragments.
61810 omitted as débitage only; 63135 omitted as no vertebrate material** – *continued*

spit no.	weight (g)	cranial	tusk	mammuthus molar fragment	other large mammal tooth fragment	indet. large bone fragments	other large vertebrate remains	fish bone	herpetofauna	bird bone	notes
62434	7.0					1					
62437	13.7	4				5					
62439	7.9					1					
62439	6.4	2	6								
62444	14.8	2				1					
62448	1.8	3									
62449	3.7	1	3								
62452	47.8	41	8	1		16					
62453	6.2					1					
62454	5.2		3			1					
62457	15.3		16			2					
62460	8.1		1			2					
62462	37.3	4	62			7					
62465	25.2	18	35			8					
62466	17.2	11	10			11					
62467	1.6					6					
62469	8.1	3	14			4					
62470	17.3	15				6					
62472	53.1	25	20			12					
62474	39.8	26	6			16					
62475	9.9	4	1	1		2					
62476	25.6	16	3			8					
62478	50.7	3	4			19					
62479	51.2	23	4	2		19					
62481	52.3	4		1		2					
62486	19.1	10	1			8					

continued ▶

Table A4.3 Dry sieved residues: ü denotes presence of multiple comminuted fragments. 61810 omitted as débitage only; 63135 omitted as no vertebrate material – *continued*

spit no.	weight (g)	cranial	tusk	mammuthus molar fragment	other large mammal tooth fragment	indet. large bone fragments	other large vertebrate remains	fish bone	herpetofauna	bird bone	notes
62489	3.8	2	5								
62490	1.4		1			1					
62493	13.4	11	3			7					
62494	10.0	3				2					
62497	1.7	1	3								
62498	8.7	8	3			1					
62499	13.7	18	1	1		5					
62512	6.6					2					
62516	23.7					2					
62518	4.3					2					
62521	15.8					1					
62534	7.2					2					
62539	26.2					7					
62545	6.9					3					
62547	2.3		2			1					
62548	1.0			1							
62602	17.5	1	56			1					
62608	26.1	28				7					
62609	12.3	20	1			19					
62651	5.8	4	3			2					
62652	7.8	3	3			2					
62653	37.0	5	2			5					
62654	34.3	43	7			30					
62656	5.5	6	1			1					
62657	4.2					6					
62658	41.9	37		1		26					

continued ▶

APPENDIX 4

**Table A4.3 Dry sieved residues: ü denotes presence of multiple comminuted fragments.
61810 omitted as débitage only; 63135 omitted as no vertebrate material – *continued***

spit no.	weight (g)	cranial	tusk	mammuthus molar fragment	other large mammal tooth fragment	indet. large bone fragments	other large vertebrate remains	fish bone	herpetofauna	bird bone	notes
62660	9.0	3	1			3					
62663	1.1	3									
62664	9.8	8	1			2					
62665	24.2	53				22					
62666	1.8	4									
62667	40.8	22				12		1	1		
62668	7.8	14				14					
62669	20.2	12				3					
62671	0.6	2				1					
62672	22.8	26	1			17					
62673	15.4	21				3					
62675	25.8	39	1			28					
62676	4.7	5				4					
62677	13.3	19				17					
62680	14.7	18				5					
62681	5.8	5	1			4					
62701	5.2					3					
62702	0.6			2							
62703	1.0					1					
62707	2.7					1					
62712	5.8					1					
62713	2.2					1					
62714	4.0			1		1					
62718	13.5					2					
62729	3.7					1					
62734	9.8	4									

continued ▶

Table A4.3 Dry sieved residues: ü denotes presence of multiple comminuted fragments. 61810 omitted as débitage only; 63135 omitted as no vertebrate material – *continued*

spit no.	weight (g)	cranial	tusk	mammuthus molar fragment	other large mammal tooth fragment	indet. large bone fragments	other large vertebrate remains	fish bone	herpetofauna	bird bone	notes
62736	15.3	1	1	2		1					
62737	2.4		2								
62743	14.7	2	5								
62747	10.0	3	2								
62801	3.8					2					
62855	3.6					1					
62857	4.0					1					
62859	16.8	1	13			5					
62860	16.0					9					
62861	<1.0					1					
62862	3.0		1								
62863	17.2		13	1		29					
62864	31.0		4			12					
62865	46.8		11	2		6					
62866	36.6		9	1		5					
62867	6.3		6	1		1					
62868	7.5		2			4					
62870	50.0	1	3	1		11					
62872	111.6	1	24	4		39					
62874	30.0		15			16					
62875	50.6	2	8	3		14					
62880	14.7		3			1					
62881	46.5	2	12	2		12					
62882	52.0		2	3		32					
62883	35.1		2			6					
62885	21.3	7	8	1		14					

continued ▶

**Table A4.3 Dry sieved residues: ü denotes presence of multiple comminuted fragments.
61810 omitted as débitage only; 63135 omitted as no vertebrate material** – *continued*

spit no.	weight (g)	cranial	tusk	mammuthus molar fragment	other large mammal tooth fragment	indet. large bone fragments	other large vertebrate remains	fish bone	herpetofauna	bird bone	notes
62886	22.9		14	1		9					
62887	92.9	1	1	1		6					
62888	41.5	3	9	2		4					
62889	12.2					1					
62890	77.5	4	6	4		11					
62891	14.6		2	1							
62891	19.2	1	2			12					
62892	67.6	3	1	4		9					
62893	21.3	1	4			3					
62895	15.4	1	2			6					
62899	49.6	8	7	3		14					
62980	2.7	2									
63051	16.0	11				2					
63052	6.3	1	1								
63053	6.3	8	2								
63054	41.2	15	2			6					
63057	3.3	2									
63059	0.9	1				2					
63101	9.7					4					
63111	10.8	1				1					
63121	12.0	1									
63123											discarded – twig
63129	0.7					1					
63139	11.6	2		2		1					
63141	5.0					1					
63157	1.9					1					

continued ▶

Table A4.3 Dry sieved residues: ü denotes presence of multiple comminuted fragments. 61810 omitted as débitage only; 63135 omitted as no vertebrate material – *continued*

spit no.	weight (g)	cranial	tusk	mammuthus molar fragment	other large mammal tooth fragment	indet. large bone fragments	other large vertebrate remains	fish bone	herpetofauna	bird bone	notes
63158	0.8					2					
63172	1.0					1					
63174	7.1.0					8					
63178	9.4	1	2			3					
63181	5.4	1	2								
63184	3.3		1								
63189	6.3	3	1								
63221	2.9		1								
63309	4.1	1									
63310	11.6	1									
63417	3.2					1					
63421	9.5		12	1							
63423	7.6			4							
63429	8.2		10								
63431	1.5		5								
63551	1.7		1								
63561	35.5		1			14					
63564	46.8					8					
63565	11.9			1							
63570	13.3		1			3					
63575	10.0	4	2			4					
63575	33.5	8	7			3					
63576	78.6	5	2			10					
63578	29.3	17	1			11					
63579	20.5	6	1			6					
63580	6.0	6	2	1							

continued ▶

**Table A4.3 Dry sieved residues: ü denotes presence of multiple comminuted fragments.
61810 omitted as débitage only; 63135 omitted as no vertebrate material** – *continued*

spit no.	weight (g)	cranial	tusk	mammuthus molar fragment	other large mammal tooth fragment	indet. large bone fragments	other large vertebrate remains	fish bone	herpetofauna	bird bone	notes
63581	14.9	3	5			2					
63583	7.3	3				2					
63584	31.0	9	6			3					
63586	15.5	2				3					
63587	45.3	13	24			1					
63588	59.9		41			3					
63589	6.6		3								
63591	22.9	6				2					
63592	12.7	6	3			1					
63593	29.1		1	1		1					
63594	2.1	2	1								
63594	48.1	5	8			3					
63595	57.9	11	8			10					
63597	17.3	14	1			1					
63598	55.5	27	3			6					
63599	37.0	7	1			16					
63600	37.3	1				13					
63603	7.7					3					
63609	8.3					6					
63617	13.5					1					
63622	47.7					25					
63626	3.0					1					
63629	7.2				1	3					
63630	6.1					2					
63631	17.5					5					
63634	2.8					2					

continued ▶

Table A4.3 Dry sieved residues: ü denotes presence of multiple comminuted fragments. 61810 omitted as débitage only; 63135 omitted as no vertebrate material – *continued*

spit no.	weight (g)	cranial	tusk	mammuthus molar fragment	other large mammal tooth fragment	indet. large bone fragments	other large vertebrate remains	fish bone	herpetofauna	bird bone	notes
63643	53.1		1			27					
63644	29.3					10					
63645	18.0	2	1	1		10					
63646	17.6					5					
63646	1.5					3					
63647	3.6					12					
63731	50.4		67								
63732	24.2		8			3					
63733	11.9		5	1							
63735	7.2		1			1					
63736	7.0			1		1					
63736	28.8					5					
63749	2.0					1					
63750	23.9		17			6					
63755	44.5	2		1		25					
63757	5.5	1	1			5					
63758	3.9					7					
63760	14.2					1					
63766	4.2	1	1			3					
63769	41.5					10					
63951	2.5		6			1					
63952	1.8					2					
63960	3.6	1				1					
63961	118.9	1									
63964	17.5	17	4			2					
63965	24.6	1	18								

continued ▶

APPENDIX 4

Table A4.3 Dry sieved residues: ü denotes presence of multiple comminuted fragments. 61810 omitted as débitage only; 63135 omitted as no vertebrate material – *continued*

spit no.	weight (g)	cranial	tusk	mammuthus molar fragment	other large mammal tooth fragment	indet. large bone fragments	other large vertebrate remains	fish bone	herpetofauna	bird bone	notes
63966	31.9	11	3			5					
63968	76.9	20				5					
63969	42.1	6	3	1		4					
63970	25.1	2									
63972	25.9	1				2					
63972	15.3	7				1					
63979	13.5					2					
63981	6.1	1									
63984	16.7	17	48			1					
64001	2.6	1				7					
64003	36.5	4	9								
64006	24.3	2	7								
64008	18.3	5	2			1					
64015	19.2		36								
64016a	63.1	5	34			6					
64016b	36.8	2	10			2					
64016	13.7	3	5			7					
64017	41.1	11	13			8					
64018	1.7	2				3					
64019a	53.7	23	11								
64019b	138.0	10	46	2							
64020	8.3	3	11								
64073	9.0					1					
64101	2.6					2					
64105	12.2	1			1	3					
64107	4.4	3				1					

continued ▶

Table A4.3 Dry sieved residues: ü denotes presence of multiple comminuted fragments.
61810 omitted as débitage only; 63135 omitted as no vertebrate material – *continued*

spit no.	weight (g)	cranial	tusk	mammuthus molar fragment	other large mammal tooth fragment	indet. large bone fragments	other large vertebrate remains	fish bone	herpetofauna	bird bone	notes
64107	5.4	7									
64111	13.6	3	1								
64112	8.9	1	3								
64115	1.5	1	2			1					
64116	1.0	1									
64118	2.0	1									
64119	24.1	7									
64120	33.7	3									
64122	13.0	3				1					
64123	6.2	1				2					
64125	37.9	8				3					
64128	17.9	3									
64129	25.2	8	2			2					
64130	2.3		1			1					
64130	19.2	8	3			5					
64134	55.3	6		1		4					
64141	15.5	2				5					
64142	6.8	3									
64143	22.1	9	3			7					
64146	11.0	4	2			1					
64147	3.7	1									
64148	11.5	2				2					
64149	8.3					1					
64150	66.3	16				13					
64176				ü							
64181	12.0				1	1					
64201	14.9	2	1			1					
64203	88.3	12	4								
64204	11.4	5	3								

continued ▶

Table A4.3 Dry sieved residues: ü denotes presence of multiple comminuted fragments.
61810 omitted as débitage only; 63135 omitted as no vertebrate material – *continued*

spit no.	weight (g)	cranial	tusk	mammuthus molar fragment	other large mammal tooth fragment	indet. large bone fragments	other large vertebrate remains	fish bone	herpetofauna	bird bone	notes
64205	2.1	1	1								
64210a	4.7	1	3			2					
64210b	3.5	6									
64211	32.6	3				4					
64212	6.9	2									
64214	12.0	1	1	1							
64215	37.3	7	3			3					
64216	21.7	9	12			5					
64218	38.1	2	3			8					
64219	45.4	9	5			4					
64220	7.5	3	1			4					
64221	30.7	6	3	1		5					
64222	38.7	5	4			8					
64224	25.1	2	2	1		7					
64226	15.5	1	1			2					
64229	11.0	1	2								
64229	13.9		2			8					
64233	23.9	4	3			7					
64234	26.2	3				2					
64235	65.5	9	1	1		8					
64237	47.9	17	2	1		11					
64238	30.2	6	13			1					
64240	4.2	3				1					
64241	9.9		7								
64245	100.0	2	1	1		6					
64246	22.6				2	1*					*L i3, E. ferus

continued ▶

Table A4.3 Dry sieved residues: ü denotes presence of multiple comminuted fragments. 61810 omitted as débitage only; 63135 omitted as no vertebrate material – *continued*

spit no.	weight (g)	cranial	tusk	mammuthus molar fragment	other large mammal tooth fragment	indet. large bone fragments	other large vertebrate remains	fish bone	herpetofauna	bird bone	notes
64247	42.0	13	19	1		5					
64251	18.2	5	1			3					
64252	4.9	8									
64253	<1.0	1									
64254a	15.9	10				3					
64254b	4.6		19								
64255	6.5	3	18			2					
64259	125.9	104	3			34					
64262	17.0	7	12								
64263	14.6	13	7			6					
64264	8.6	1				3					
64266	20.8	23				3					
64268	1.1	4									
64272	3.9	5				7					
64274a	2.3	3									
64274b	63.5	11	1								
64277	3.6					7					
64278	5.6	1				5					
64280	2.1	5				1					
64281	4.2					5						3 fragments of ?coprolite
64285	1.4	1				4					
64299	1.7					2					
64300	28.3					30					
64308	1.1	1				3					
64313	8.75		2			1					
64315	10.6					3					

continued ▶

Table A4.3 Dry sieved residues: ü denotes presence of multiple comminuted fragments.
61810 omitted as débitage only; 63135 omitted as no vertebrate material – *continued*

spit no.	weight (g)	cranial	tusk	mammuthus molar fragment	other large mammal tooth fragment	indet. large bone fragments	other large vertebrate remains	fish bone	herpetofauna	bird bone	notes
64316	26.2		21	1		10					
64317	17.3		3	1		14					
64318	26.8	1	2			24					
64319	17.6	3	19								
64321	11.9	3	4			10					
64322	6.0		3	1							
64326	8.6		3			3					
64327	4.1					6					
64328	52.85		8	2		15					
64329a	20.25		16			6					
64329b	48.9	2	3	5		36					
64330	13.5	2	3	2		4					
64332	14.75		9	2		4					
64334	13.15		6			1					
64335	26.45	1	16			5					
64336	24.65	1	45			1					
64339	8.05					3					
64340	5.45					3					
64341	16.75		2			4					
64343	13.85		10			3					
64345	6.05		3			4					
64346	3.35					1					
64347	7.25					5					
64351	17.2	2	16								
64353	6.85		8			1					
64404	78.85					102					

continued ▶

Table A4.3 Dry sieved residues: ü denotes presence of multiple comminuted fragments. 61810 omitted as débitage only; 63135 omitted as no vertebrate material – *continued*

spit no.	weight (g)	cranial	tusk	mammuthus molar fragment	other large mammal tooth fragment	indet. large bone fragments	other large vertebrate remains	fish bone	herpetofauna	bird bone	notes
64504	<1.0								1		
64526	1.0	1									
64602	9.0			2		4					
64703	5.3		5								
64705	0.5					1					
64710a	31.25	1	1	1		18					
64710b	3.4		5								
64711	60.8	1	14	1		23					
64712	3.8			1		8					
64713	23.7		2	3		13					
64714	197.7	5	20	4		47					
64717	1.4		1	1		1					
64718	15.6		25			7					
64719	28.4			1		29					
64720	72.0	3	10	4		21					
64722	18.9	2		1		16					
64723	121.1	3	56	5		52					
64724	183.4	5	106	2		47					
64725	11.5	1	1			5					
64726	27.7	4	23			8					
64727	21.7	2	40	2		12					
64730	21.8	1	5	4		5					
64731a	12.9	2	1	1		5					
64731b	2.2	2				1					
64732	24.4		24	1		6					
64733	29.2	6	6	1		9			1		

continued ▶

Table A4.3 Dry sieved residues: ü denotes presence of multiple comminuted fragments.
61810 omitted as débitage only; 63135 omitted as no vertebrate material – *continued*

spit no.	weight (g)	cranial	tusk	mammuthus molar fragment	other large mammal tooth fragment	indet. large bone fragments	other large vertebrate remains	fish bone	herpetofauna	bird bone	notes
64734	23.6	6	10	1		8					
64735	11.5		7	1		6					
64756	18.3					19					
64758	1.2					1					
64763	1.0					1					
64771	13.8					4					
64775	0.8					1					
64778	2.4					1					
64806	3.6		1								
64808	5.0					1					
65006	4.4	3									
65007	5.1	1	1								
65013	9.1	4				3					
65019	5.0	6				1					
65036	8.7					2					
65037	2.5					2					
65652	14.3	1	1	1							
65657	5.5	1	2								
65659	8.5					1					
65661	15.6					8					
65663	12.5		3			1					
65683	2.5					4					
65696	1.0					2					
65698	2.2	1									
65699	3.7					6					

Table A4.4 Individual vertebrate finds: boxes 1–19 provided directly from Gressenhall; boxes with 'B' after the number came from Bradford; 'Spec.' denotes 'Special Box' built by Bradford; 'pj' = plaster jacket; 'C' = Crate. Note 1: not in a numbered box, brought in by Nigel Larkin

object no.	box	split no.	context no.	facies	size	weathering	iron staining	abrasion	root damage	carnivore gnawing	rodent gnawing	deliberate fracturing	taxon	element
50000	26B	unstratified	20050	destroyed/disturbed channel sediments	6	3							Mammuthus	L m3, see also 50.030
50001	25B	unstratified	20050	destroyed/disturbed channel sediments	6	3							Mammuthus	L M3
50002	24B	unstratified	20048	destroyed/disturbed channel sediments	6	3							Mammuthus	L M2 with fragments of maxilla between roots, pair of 50003
50003	23B	unstratified	20048	destroyed/disturbed channel sediments	6	3							Mammuthus	R M2 with fragments of maxilla between roots, pair of 50002
50004	C6	unstratified	20048	destroyed/disturbed channel sediments	6	3				ü			Mammuthus	R midshaft fragment of humerus, showing deltoid tuberosity
50005	1	unstratified	20048	destroyed/disturbed channel sediments	6	2				ü			Mammuthus	L jugal
50006	21B	unstratified	20048	destroyed/disturbed channel sediments	6	5							Mammuthus	2 limb bones (possibly femoral) midshaft fragments, do not conjoin destroyed/disturbed channel sediments
50007	12B	unstratified	20049		5	5							Rangifer	antler beam fragment
50008	1	unstratified	20003	B-iii03	1	1							Rana temporaria	tibio-fibula
50009	1	unstratified	20009	C	3	2							Rangifer	proximal L radius fragment
50010	1	unstratified	20009	C	3	5	ü						large mammal	indeterminate bone fragment (3 fragments stuck together plus 3 small bits)
50011	1	unstratified	20015		X	X							XXXXXXXX	not bone fragment (limestone with encrustation)
50012	1	unstratified	20003	B-iii03	6	3							cf. Mammuthus	distal neural spine
50013	1	unstratified	20021	B-iii03	6	3							Mammuthus	proximal R scapula fragment (glenoid, part of neck); sampled for isotopes.
50014	1	unstratified	20003	B-iii03	4	4		ü					undetermined	indeterminate bone fragment
50015	1	unstratified	20003	B-iii03	2	2							cf. Ursus	fragment of canine root and basal part of tooth

Table A4.4 Individual vertebrate finds: boxes 1–19 provided directly from Gressenhall; boxes with 'B' after the number came from Bradford; 'Spec.' denotes 'Special Box' built by Bradford; 'pj' = plaster jacket; 'C' = Crate. Note 1: not in a numbered box, brought in by Nigel Larkin – continued

object no.	box	spit no.	facies	context no.	size	weathering	iron staining	abrasion	root damage	carnivore gnawing	rodent gnawing	deliberate fracturing	taxon	element
50016	1	unstratified	B-iii:03	20003	2	3							*Mammuthus*	tusk fragment
50017	1	unstratified	B-iii:03	20003	2	3							large mammal	rib fragment
50018	1	unstratified	B-iii:03	20003	2	3							large mammal	small rib fragment
50019	1	unstratified	B-iii:03	20003	3	3							cf. *Mammuthus*	cranial fragment
50020	1	unstratified	B-iii:03	20021	1	3							*Mammuthus*	small tusk fragment, broken in 2 pieces
50021	1	unstratified	B-iii:03	20003	4	3							large mammal	indeterminate bone fragment
50022	6B	unstratified	B-iii:04	20131	5	4							*Coelodonta*	medial distal articular fragment of L humerus
50023	27B	unstratified	B-iii:04	20131	6	3							*Mammuthus*	distal end of anterior rib (missing distal epiphysis)
50024	22B	unstratified	B-iii:03	20021	6	3							*Mammuthus*	large fragment of tusk alveolus
50025	1	unstratified	B-iii:03	20003	3	3							*Mammuthus*	proximal epiphysis of rib
50026	15B	unstratified	B-iii:01	20004	5	4							*Mammuthus*	conjoining rib midshaft fragments
50027	1	unstratified	destroyed/disturbed channel sediments	20048	3	3				ü	ü		cf. *Rangifer*	broken tine
50028	2	unstratified	destroyed/disturbed channel sediments	20050	3	3							*Mammuthus*?	15 cranial fragments
50029	2	unstratified	destroyed/disturbed channel sediments	20050	6	3							*Mammuthus*	large fragment of L dentary
50030	2	unstratified	destroyed/disturbed channel sediments	20050	6	3							*Mammuthus*	large fragment of R mandibular ramus (showing impression of molar plates, ?m3) attaches to 50000
50031	2	unstratified	destroyed/disturbed channel sediments	20050	6	3							*Mammuthus*	tusk alveolus fragment
50032	2	unstratified	destroyed/disturbed channel sediments	20050	6	3							*Mammuthus*	L palatal fragment

continued ▲

Table A4.4 Individual vertebrate finds: boxes 1–19 provided directly from Gressenhall; boxes with 'B' after the number came from Bradford; 'Spec.' denotes 'Special Box' built by Bradford; 'pj' = plaster jacket; 'C' = Crate. Note 1: not in a numbered box, brought in by Nigel Larkin – continued

object no.	box	spit no.	context no.	facies	size	weathering	iron staining	abrasion	root damage	carnivore gnawing	rodent gnawing	deliberate fracturing	taxon	element
50033	2	unstratified	20050	destroyed/disturbed channel sediments	6	3							Mammuthus	part of R ascending ramus?
50034	2	unstratified	20050	destroyed/disturbed channel sediments	4	3							Mammuthus	cranial fragment
50035	2	unstratified	20050	destroyed/disturbed channel sediments	4	3							Mammuthus	probable palatal fragment
50036	2	unstratified	20050	destroyed/disturbed channel sediments	4	3				ü			Mammuthus	L occipital condyle
50037	2	unstratified	20050	destroyed/disturbed channel sediments	6	3							Mammuthus	large tusk fragment
50038	spec 1	unstratified	20050	destroyed/disturbed channel sediments	6	3							Mammuthus	anterior rib, missing proximal and distal ends
50039	2	unstratified	20050	destroyed/disturbed channel sediments	4	3							Mammuthus	basicranial fragment
50040	2	unstratified	20050	destroyed/disturbed channel sediments	6	3							Mammuthus	cranial fragment, near anterior end of right jugal?
50041	2	unstratified	20050	destroyed/disturbed channel sediments	6	3							Mammuthus	large fragment of L dentary
50042	2	unstratified	20050	destroyed/disturbed channel sediments	6	3							Mammuthus	part of R ascending ramus
50043	2	unstratified	20050	destroyed/disturbed channel sediments	5	3							Mammuthus	R mandibular condyle
50044	2	unstratified	20050	destroyed/disturbed channel sediments	6	3							Mammuthus	large fragment of ?L mandibular ramus
50045	2	unstratified	20050	destroyed/disturbed channel sediments	6	3							Mammuthus	L mandibular condyle
50046	note 1	unstratified	20003	B-iii03	5	3							Mammuthus	7 large cranial fragments
50047	3	unstratified	20052	destroyed/disturbed channel sediments	1	3							undetermined	indeterminate bone fragment

Table A4.4 Individual vertebrate finds: boxes 1–19 provided directly from Gressenhall; boxes with 'B' after the number came from Bradford; 'Spec.' denotes 'Special Box' built by Bradford; 'pj' = plaster jacket; 'C' = Crate. Note 1: not in a numbered box, brought in by Nigel Larkin – continued

object no.	box	split no.	context no.	facies	size	weathering	iron staining	abrasion	root damage	carnivore gnawing	rodent gnawing	deliberate fracturing	taxon	element
50048	3	unstratified	20003	B-iii:03	2	2							Coelodonta	comminuted lower molar (>30 fragments); sampled for isotopes.
50049	3	unstratified	20005	B-iii:05	2	5		ü					undetermined	multiple small indeterminate bone fragments
50050	3	unstratified	20021	B-iii:03	5	3							undetermined	cranial fragment
50051	3	unstratified	20022	unstratified	1	3		ü					undetermined	3 small indeterminate bone fragments
50052	3	unstratified	20002	B-iii:05	1	3							undetermined	4 small indeterminate bone fragments and 1 small tusk fragment
50053	3	unstratified	20003	B-iii:03	3	4							large mammal	indeterminate bone fragment
50054	3	unstratified	20003	B-iii:03	2	3							large mammal	indeterminate bone fragment
50055	3	unstratified	20003	B-iii:03	3	3							Mammuthus	multiple small tusk fragments
50056	3	unstratified	20003	B-iii:03	1	2							undetermined	small indeterminate bone fragment
50057	3	unstratified	20003	B-iii:03	4	4		ü					large mammal	rib fragment
50058	3	unstratified	20003	B-iii:03	4	4							large mammal	4 indeterminate long bone fragments
50059	3	unstratified	20003	B-iii:03	3	3							large mammal	2 cranial fragments
50060	3	unstratified	20018	B-iii	3	4							Mammuthus	molar plate fragment; sampled for isotopes.
50061	3	unstratified	20021	B-iii:03	1	3							undetermined	small indeterminate bone fragment
50062	3	unstratified	20021	B-iii:03	1	3							undetermined	4 small indeterminate bone fragments
50063	3	unstratified	20021	B-iii:03	1	3							undetermined	small indeterminate cranial fragment
50064	3	unstratified	20021	B-iii:03	1	3							undetermined	2 small indeterminate bone fragments
50065	3	unstratified	20021	B-iii:03	1	3							Mammuthus	small tusk fragment
50066	3	unstratified	20021	B-iii:03	2	3		ü					Mammuthus	small tusk fragment
50067	3	unstratified	20021	B-iii:03	1	3		ü					Mammuthus	small tusk fragment

continued

Table A4.4 Individual vertebrate finds: boxes 1–19 provided directly from Gressenhall; boxes with 'B' after the number came from Bradford; 'Spec.' denotes 'Special Box' built by Bradford; 'pj' = plaster jacket; 'C' = Crate. Note 1: not in a numbered box, brought in by Nigel Larkin – continued

object no.	box	spit no.	context no.	facies	size	weathering	iron staining	abrasion	root damage	carnivore gnawing	rodent gnawing	deliberate fracturing	taxon	element
50068	3	unstratified	20021	B-iii03	1	3							Mammuthus	small tusk fragment
50069	26B	unstratified	20003	B-iii03	6	3							Mammuthus	R M3, pair of 50273
50070	3	60208	20021	B-iii03	2	3							Mammuthus	multiple small tusk fragments
50071	pj	unstratified	20003	B-iii03	6	3							Mammuthus	large portion of crushed tusk
50072	3	60208-10	20021	B-iii03	2	3							Mammuthus	tusk fragment
50073	C6	unstratified	20003	B-iii03	6	3							Mammuthus	proximal rib articulation
50074	3	unstratified	20385	unstratified from scree	3	4							Mammuthus	large indeterminate bone fragment
50075	80B	unstratified	20004	B-iii01	6	1							Mammuthus	fragmented thoracic vertebra, comprising partial centrum and fragment of central epiphysis from preceding vertebra attached, neural spine and small fragments
50076a	1B	62361	20131	B-iii04	3	4							Mammuthus	multiple tusk fragments 'found during cleaning'
50076b	3	?	20003	B-iii03	3	2							Mammuthus	multiple small tusk fragments
50077	3	unstratified	20003	B-iii03	2	3							Mammuthus	small tusk and indeterminate bone fragments
50078	3	60066	20003	B-iii03	2	3							undetermined	3 small indeterminate bone fragments
50079	3	60208	20021	B-iii03	5	3							Mammuthus	cranial fragment
50080	3	60208	20021	B-iii03	5	3							Mammuthus	cranial fragment
50081	3	60210	20021	B-iii03	3	3							Mammuthus	tusk fragment
50082	3	60210	20021	B-iii03	4	3							Mammuthus	small tusk fragments
50083	3	60211	20021	B-iii03	3	3							Mammuthus	small tusk fragments
50084	3	60215	20021	B-iii03	3	3							large mammal	3 cranial fragments
50085	3	60213	20021	B-iii03	3	3							Mammuthus	tusk fragment

APPENDIX 4

Table A4.4 Individual vertebrate finds: boxes 1–19 provided directly from Gressenhall; boxes with 'B' after the number came from Bradford; 'Spec.' denotes 'Special Box' built by Bradford; 'pj' = plaster jacket; 'C' = Crate. Note 1: not in a numbered box, brought in by Nigel Larkin – continued

object no.	box	split no.	context no.	facies	size	weathering	iron staining	abrasion	root damage	carnivore gnawing	rodent gnawing	deliberate fracturing	taxon	element
50086	3	60218	20021	B-iii:03	4	4							Mammuthus	tusk fragment
50088	3	60216	20021	B-iii:03	3	3							large mammal	3 cranial fragments (see 50238)
50089	3	60216	20021	B-iii:03	3	3							Mammuthus	multiple small tusk and indeterminate bone fragments
50090	3	60216	20021	B-iii:03	2	2							Mammuthus	small tusk fragments
50091	3	60217–8	20021	B-iii:03	4	3							Mammuthus	multiple small tusk fragments
50092	3	60218	20021	B-iii:03	6	3							undetermined	?fragment of ascending ramus (compares most closely to Equus)
50093	3	60218	20021	B-iii:03	4	3							undetermined	multiple small bone fragments, probably cranial
50094	11B	60224	20021	B-iii:03	1	5							Mammuthus	multiple tusk fragments
50096	pj	60022	20116	B-iii:05	6	4							Rangifer	flattened and crushed antler beam with two tines
50097	3	60316	20003	B-iii:03	4	3							Mammuthus	multiple tusk fragments
50098-50100	3	60221+60236	20021	B-iii:03	2	3							Mammuthus	multiple tusk fragments
50101	3	60236	20021	B-iii:03	6	4							Mammuthus	tusk fragment
50102	3	60236	20021	B-iii:03	4	4							Mammuthus	tusk fragment
50103	3	60217	20021	B-iii:03	4	4							Mammuthus	tusk fragment
50104	3	60217	20021	B-iii:03	3	4							Mammuthus	tusk fragment
50105	3	60217	20021	B-iii:03	5	4							Mammuthus	tusk fragment
50106	3	60217	20021	B-iii:03	3	4							Mammuthus	tusk fragment
50107	3	60217	20021	B-iii:03	3	4							Mammuthus	tusk fragment
50108	3	60272	20003	B-iii:03	2	3							Mammuthus	small tusk fragment

continued ▲

Table A4.4 Individual vertebrate finds: boxes 1–19 provided directly from Gressenhall; boxes with 'B' after the number came from Bradford; 'Spec.' denotes 'Special Box' built by Bradford; 'pj' = plaster jacket; 'C' = Crate. Note 1: not in a numbered box, brought in by Nigel Larkin – continued

object no.	box	spit no.	context no.	facies	size	weathering	iron staining	abrasion	root damage	carnivore gnawing	rodent gnawing	deliberate fracturing	taxon	element
50109	3	60272	20003	B-iii03	3	4							undetermined	2 cranial fragments
50110	3	60272	20003	B-iii03	3	4							undetermined	cranial fragment
50111	3	60272	20003	B-iii03	3	3							Mammuthus?	cancellous bone, cranial
50112	3	60272	20003	B-iii03	1	3							undetermined	cranial fragment
50113	3	60272	20003	B-iii03	1	3							Mammuthus	small molar root fragment
50114	3	60272	20003	B-iii03	3	3							Mammuthus	large fragment of cranial cancellous bone and 1 small fragment
50115	3	60272	20003	B-iii03	5	3							Mammuthus?	large fragment of cranial cancellous bone and 2 small fragments
50116	3	60220	20021	B-iii03	6	2							Mammuthus	large tusk fragment
50117	3	60220	20021	B-iii03	2	2							Mammuthus	multiple small tusk and indeterminate bone fragments
50118	3	60220	20021	B-iii03	2	4							undetermined	small cranial fragment
50119	3	60220	20021	B-iii03	2	3							undetermined	small cranial fragment
50120	3	60220	20021	B-iii03	2	3							undetermined	small cranial fragment
50121	3	60220	20021	B-iii03	2	4							undetermined	small cranial fragment
50122	3	60310	20003	B-iii03	1	3							undetermined	2 small cranial fragments
50123	3	60273	20003	B-iii03	1	4							undetermined	small cranial fragment
50124	3	60265	20003	B-iii03	2	3							Mammuthus	small molar plate fragment
50125	3	60320	20003	B-iii03	3	4							undetermined	cranial fragment
50127	3	60277	20003	B-iii03	2	3							Mammuthus	small tusk fragments, from interior of tusk
50128a	pj	60370	20003	B-iii03	6	4							Mammuthus	extremely fragmented large bone, ?lateral view of humerus

Table A4.4 Individual vertebrate finds: boxes 1–19 provided directly from Gressenhall; boxes with 'B' after the number came from Bradford; 'Spec.' denotes 'Special Box' built by Bradford; 'pj' = plaster jacket; 'C' = Crate. Note 1: not in a numbered box, brought in by Nigel Larkin – continued

object no.	box	spit no.	context no.	facies	size	weathering	iron staining	abrasion	root damage	carnivore gnawing	rodent gnawing	deliberate fracturing	taxon	element
50128b	3	60370	20003	B-iii:O3	2	4							undetermined	multiple small indeterminate bone fragments
50129	3	60321	20003	B-iii:O3	1	3							undetermined	small cranial fragments
50130	3	60276	20003	B-iii:O3	2	3							undetermined	cranial fragment
50131	3	60278	20003	B-iii:O3	2	4							undetermined	2 small cranial fragments
50132	3	60279	20003	B-iii:O3	2	3							undetermined	multiple small cranial fragments
50133	3	60322	20003	B-iii:O3	3	3							large mammal	2 indeterminate bone fragments
50137	24B	60231	20021	B-iii:O3	4	3							Mammuthus	R dp4 or m1, anterior frag.
50138	3	60243	20021	B-iii:O3	2	2							Mammuthus	5 small tusk fragments
50139	3	60232	20021	B-iii:O3	3	3							undetermined	cranial fragment
50140	4	60236	20021	B-iii:O3	3	3							Mammuthus	tusk fragment
50141	4	60244	20021	B-iii:O3	3	3							Mammuthus	4 tusk fragments
50143	4	60244	20021	B-iii:O3	4	3							Mammuthus	5 tusk fragments
50144	4	60244	20021	B-iii:O3	3	3							Mammuthus	multiple tusk fragments
50145a	31–32B	60281	20003	B-iii:O3	6	3							Mammuthus	tusk fragments
50145b	4	60281	20003	B-iii:O3	2	2							Mammuthus	small molar plate fragment
50146	4	60282	20003	B-iii:O3	3	4							undetermined	indeterminate bone fragment
50147	4	60282	20003	B-iii:O3	1	3							undetermined	small cranial fragment
50148	4	60282	20003	B-iii:O3	2	3							Mammuthus	molar root
50149	4	60231	20021	B-iii:O3	2	3							Mammuthus	multiple small tusk fragments
50150	4	60323	20003	B-iii:O3	2	3							undetermined	cranial fragment
50151	4	60372	20003	B-iii:O3	2	3							Mammuthus	4 rib fragments (2 large ones refit), attaching to 50184

continued

Table A4.4 Individual vertebrate finds: boxes 1–19 provided directly from Gressenhall; boxes with 'B' after the number came from Bradford; 'Spec.' denotes 'Special Box' built by Bradford; 'pj' = plaster jacket; 'C' = Crate. Note 1: not in a numbered box, brought in by Nigel Larkin – continued

object no.	box	spit no.	context no.	facies	size	weathering	iron staining	abrasion	root damage	carnivore gnawing	rodent gnawing	deliberate fracturing	taxon	element
50152	4	60323	20003	B-iii:03	2	3							Mammuthus?	small cranial fragment
50153	4	60322	20003	B-iii:03	3	3			ü				Mammuthus	cranial fragment
50154	4	unstratified	20116	B-iii	5	4							Mammuthus	indeterminate long bone fragment
50155	4	unstratified	20116	B-iii	2	4							undetermined	small indeterminate bone fragment
50156	4	unstratified	20119	B-iii:05	3	4							Mammuthus	2 small fragments of long bone
50157	4	60284	20.003	B-iii:03	2	3							Mammuthus?	cranial fragment
50158	4	60284	20003	B-iii:03	1	3							undetermined	cranial fragment
50159	4	60284	20003	B-iii:03	2	4							Mammuthus	molar talon fragment
50160	4	60286	20003	B-iii:03	2	3							undetermined	small indeterminate bone fragment (2 bits)
50161	4	unstratified	20048	destroyed/disturbed channel sediments	6	3							Mammuthus	large chunk of tusk + bone fragments
50162	4	unstratified	20048	destroyed/disturbed channel sediments	2	1						ü	Rangifer	diaphyseal fragment of R humerus
50163	33B	60239	20021	B-iii:03	6	5							Mammuthus?	very fragmentary and crushed rib midshaft
50164	4	60287	20003	B-iii:03	1	3							undetermined	small indeterminate bone fragment
50165	4	60287	20003	B-iii:03	2	3							Mammuthus?	cranial fragment
50166	4	60287	20003	B-iii:03	2	3							undetermined	cranial fragment
50167	4	60287	20003	B-iii:03	2	3							undetermined	multiple small cranial fragments
50168	4	60287	20003	B-iii:03	3	3							Mammuthus	cranial fragment
50169	4	60290	20003	B-iii:03	3	3						ü	cf. Rangifer	internal fragment of ?tibia midshaft
50170	4	60290	20003	B-iii:03	2	3							Mammuthus	molar talon fragment
50171	4	60290	20003	B-iii:03	2	3							Mammuthus	cranial fragment
50172	4	60291	20003	B-iii:03	3	3							undetermined	multiple cranial fragments

APPENDIX 4

Table A.4.4 Individual vertebrate finds: boxes 1–19 provided directly from Gressenhall; boxes with 'B' after the number came from Bradford; 'Spec.' denotes 'Special Box' built by Bradford; 'pj' = plaster jacket; 'C' = Crate. Note 1: not in a numbered box, brought in by Nigel Larkin – continued

object no.	box	spit no.	context no.	facies	size	weathering	iron staining	abrasion	root damage	carnivore gnawing	rodent gnawing	deliberate fracturing	taxon	element
50173	4	60291	20003	B-iii:03	2	3							Mammuthus	cranial fragment
50174	4	60291	20003	B-iii:03	2	3							Mammuthus	2 small cranial fragments
50175	4	60291	20003	B-iii:03	2	3							undetermined	small cranial fragment
50176	4	60291	20003	B-iii:03	2	3							undetermined	5 small bone fragments, ?rib
50177	4	60291	20003	B-iii:03	2	3							Mammuthus	small cranial fragment
50178	4	60419	20003	B-iii:03	2	2							Mammuthus	small tusk fragments
50179	4	unstratified	20028	B-iii	6	4							Mammuthus	long bone midshaft fragment
50180a	40B	unstratified	20028	B-iii	6	4							Mammuthus	large tusk fragments, multiple small tusk fragments and 3 small cranial fragments
50180b	4	unstratified	20028	B-iii	4	4							Mammuthus	long bone fragment, probably same bone as 50179
50181	4	unstratified	20028	B-iii	3	4							Mammuthus	long bone fragment, probably same bone as 50179
50182	4	unstratified	20028	B-iii	4	4							Mammuthus	long bone fragment, probably same bone as 50179
50183	4	unstratified	20003	B-iii:03	3	3							Mammuthus	small tusk fragment
50184	27B	unstratified	20003	B-iii:03	6	4							Mammuthus	2 rib midshaft fragments, conjoin with 50151
50185	4	60507	20003	B-iii:03	5	3							Mammuthus	tusk fragment
50186	4	60285	20003	B-iii:03	4	3							Mammuthus	cranial fragments, ?alveolus
50187	4	60285	20003	B-iii:03	2	3				ü			undetermined	indeterminate small bone fragment
50188	4	60331	20003	B-iii:03	2	3							Mammuthus	cranial fragment
50189	4	60340	20003	B-iii:03	3	3				ü			undetermined	indeterminate bone fragment
50190	4	60298	20003	B-iii:03	2	1						ü	Rangifer ?	tibia diaphyseal fragment

continued ▶

Table A4.4 Individual vertebrate finds: boxes 1–19 provided directly from Gressenhall; boxes with 'B' after the number came from Bradford; 'Spec.' denotes 'Special Box' built by Bradford; 'pj' = plaster jacket; 'C' = Crate. Note 1: not in a numbered box, brought in by Nigel Larkin – continued

object no.	box	split no.	context no.	facies	size	weathering	iron staining	abrasion	root damage	carnivore gnawing	rodent gnawing	deliberate fracturing	taxon	element
50191	4	60319	20003	B-iii03	2	3							Mammuthus	small cranial fragments
50192	4	60333	20003	B-iii03	3	3							Mammuthus	cranial fragment
50193	4	60298	20003	B-iii03	4	3							Mammuthus	large cranial fragment
50194	4	60703	20003	B-iii03	3	2							Mammuthus	tusk fragments
50195	4	603??	20003	B-iii03	3	3							Mammuthus?	2 conjoining flat bone fragments, ?cranial
50196	4	60702	20003	B-iii03	3	2						ü	cf. Rangifer	humerus midshaft
50197	4	60520	20003	B-iii03	3	4							Mammuthus	tusk fragment
50198	4	60523	20003	B-iii03	3	3							Mammuthus	midshaft of rib fragment
50199	4	60523	20003	B-iii03	2	3							undetermined	?rib fragments
50200	4	60704	20003	B-iii03	3	2							undetermined	cranial fragment
50201	5	60704	20003	B-iii03	2	3							Mammuthus	molar plate fragments
50202	5	60337	20003	B-iii03	1	3							undetermined	small cranial fragment
50203	5	60337	20003	B-iii03	2	3							Mammuthus	small tusk fragment
50204	5	60337	20003	B-iii03	2	3							undetermined	small cranial fragment
50205	5	60337	20003	B-iii03	2	3							Mammuthus?	indeterminate bone fragment
50206	5	60335	20003	B-iii03	2	2							Mammuthus	small tusk fragment
50207	5	60335	20003	B-iii03	2	4							undetermined	cranial fragment
50208	5	60335	20003	B-iii03	3	3							undetermined	multiple small cranial fragments
50209	5	60335	20003	B-iii03	2	3							undetermined	2 cranial fragments
50210	5	60706	20003	B-iii03	2	3							undetermined	cranial fragment
50211	5	60706	20003	B-iii03	3	3							undetermined	2 cranial fragments
50212	5	60706	20003	B-iii03	1	3						ü	Rangifer	2nd phalanx

APPENDIX 4

Table A4.4 Individual vertebrate finds: boxes 1–19 provided directly from Gressenhall; boxes with 'B' after the number came from Bradford; 'Spec.' denotes 'Special Box' built by Bradford; 'pj' = plaster jacket; 'C' = Crate. Note 1: not in a numbered box, brought in by Nigel Larkin – continued

object no.	box	split no.	context no.	facies	size	weathering	iron staining	abrasion	root damage	carnivore gnawing	rodent gnawing	deliberate fracturing	taxon	element
50213	5	unstratified	20003	B-iii03	4	3							Mammuthus	posterior plate of molar
50214	5	unstratified	20003	B-iii03	3	3							Mammuthus	multiple small tusk fragments, 2 bags: 1 large, 1 small
50215	5	60346	20003	B-iii03	2	3							undetermined	indeterminate bone fragment
50216	5	60346	20003	B-iii03	2	2							undetermined	cranial fragment
50217	5	60706	20003	B-iii03	2	2							undetermined	2 small cranial fragments
50218	5	60706	20003	B-iii03	2	3							undetermined	cranial fragment
50219	5	60706	20003	B-iii03	3	3							Mammuthus	cranial fragment
50220	5	unstratified	20136	B-iii05	2	3							undetermined	small indeterminate bone fragment
50221	5	60621	20003	B-iii03	3	3							Mammuthus	molar plate
50222	5	60621	20003	B-iii03	2	1						ü	undetermined	thin shard of long bone
50223	5	60716	20003	B-iii03	3	3							large mammal	rib fragment
50224	5	60716	20003	B-iii03	1	3							Mammuthus	very small molar plate fragment
50225	5	60716	20003	B-iii03	3	2							Mammuthus	multiple small tusk fragments
50226	5	60716	20003	B-iii03	3	3			ü				large mammal	rib fragment
50227	5	60621	20003	B-iii03	1	3							Mammuthus	very small molar plate fragments
50228	5	60714	20003	B-iii03	3	3							Mammuthus	small cranial fragments
50229	5	60475	20003	B-iii03	1	3							undetermined	small cranial fragments
50230	5	60623	20003	B-iii03	1	3							undetermined	very small fragment, ?cranial
50231	5	60716	20003	B-iii03	2	3							undetermined	2 small cranial fragments
50232	5	60718	20003	B-iii03	3	3							large mammal	rib fragment
50233	5	60717	20003	B-iii03	2	2							Canis lupus	distal R ulna, conjoins with 51860

continued ▶

Table A4.4 Individual vertebrate finds: boxes 1–19 provided directly from Gressenhall; boxes with 'B' after the number came from Bradford; 'Spec.' denotes 'Special Box' built by Bradford; 'pj' = plaster jacket; 'C' = Crate. Note 1: not in a numbered box, brought in by Nigel Larkin – continued

object no.	box	spit no.	context no.	facies	size	weathering	iron staining	abrasion	root damage	carnivore gnawing	rodent gnawing	deliberate fracturing	taxon	element
50234	5	60718	20003	B-iii03	5	4							*Mammuthus*	tusk fragment
50235	21B	unstratified	20048	destroyed/disturbed channel sediments	6	5			ü				*Mammuthus*	2 conjoining fragments of ?tibia midshaft, split longitudinally
50236	5	unstratified	20048	destroyed/disturbed channel sediments	6	3							*Mammuthus*	midshaft of rib
50237	5	61477	20003	B-iii03	1	5							undetermined	small indeterminate bone fragment
50238	73B, 5		20021	B-iii03	6	3							*Mammuthus*	large cranial fragment, multiple small fragments and posterior rib fragment found in association with large tusk (jacketed)
50239	5B	6170?	20003	B-iii03	5	3							*Mammuthus*	one large and multiple small cranial fragments
50240a	67B	607??	20003	B-iii03	5	3							*Mammuthus*	complex of tusk alveolus fragment and multiple shattered small cranial fragments, lifted in jacket
50240b	5	607??	20003	B-iii03	2	3							*Mammuthus* fragments	multiple small indeterminate bone and tusk
50241	5	60721	20003	B-iii03	3	4							undetermined	indeterminate bone fragment
50242	5	60721	20003	B-iii03	2	3							undetermined	indeterminate cranial fragment
50243	5	60722	20003	B-iii03	5	3							undetermined	2 large cranial fragments
50244	5	60215	20021	B-iii03	3	3							*Mammuthus*	cranial fragment
50245	5	60479	20003	B-iii03	2	3						ü	undetermined	small indeterminate bone fragment, ?humerus midshaft
50246	5	60479	20003	B-iii03	1	2							*Mammuthus*	minute tusk fragment
50247	5	60349	20003	B-iii03	3	2							*Mammuthus*	tusk fragment
50248	5	60348	20003	B-iii03	3	3							undetermined	cranial fragment
50249	5	60348	20003	B-iii03	2	4							undetermined	cranial fragment

APPENDIX 4

Table A4.4 Individual vertebrate finds: boxes 1–19 provided directly from Gressenhall; boxes with 'B' after the number came from Bradford; 'Spec.' denotes 'Special Box' built by Bradford; 'pj' = plaster jacket; 'C' = Crate. Note 1: not in a numbered box, brought in by Nigel Larkin – continued

object no.	box	split no.	context no.	facies	size	weathering	iron staining	abrasion	root damage	carnivore gnawing	rodent gnawing	deliberate fracturing	taxon	element
50250	5	unstratified	20129	B-i:03	5	4							undetermined	large bone fragment
50251	5	unstratified	20129	B-i:03	2	2							Mammuthus	small tusk fragments
50252	5	60724	20003	B-ii:03	4	3							Mammuthus	cranial fragment
50253	5	60724	20003	B-ii:03	3	3							undetermined	cranial fragment
50254	5	60725	20003	B-ii:03	4	3							Mammuthus	cranial fragment
50255	5	60725	20003	B-ii:03	3	3							Mammuthus	cranial fragment
50256	5	60350	20003	B-ii:03	3	4							Mammuthus	tusk fragment
50257	27B	unstratified	20134	B-ii:04	6	4							cf. Mammuthus	multiple conjoining rib midshaft fragments
50258	5	60350	20003	B-ii:03	2	3							undetermined	indeterminate bone fragments
50259	5	60722	20003	B-ii:03	3	3							Mammuthus	cranial fragment
50260	5	60722	20003	B-ii:03	3	3							Mammuthus	2 cranial fragments
50261	5	60722	20003	B-ii:03	2	3							undetermined	cranial fragment
50262	5	unstratified	20130.000	B-i:03	6	5							large mammal	large long bone fragment
50263	5	60630	20003	B-ii:03	2	3		ü					Mammuthus	tusk fragments
50264	5	60348	20003	B-ii:03	3	3							Mammuthus	tusk fragment
50265	5	60348	20003	B-ii:03	2	2							Mammuthus	2 small cranial fragments
50266	5	60801	20003	B-ii:03	2	3							Mammuthus	2 cranial fragments
50267	5	60729	20003	B-ii:03	3	4							Mammuthus	2 cranial fragments
50268	5	60731	20003	B-ii:03	3	3							Mammuthus	multiple small cranial fragments
50269	5	60726	20003	B-ii:03	2	3							Mammuthus	small cranial fragments
50270	5	60569	20003	B-ii:03	2	3		ü					undetermined	small indeterminate bone fragment

continued ▶

401

Table A4.4 Individual vertebrate finds: boxes 1–19 provided directly from Gressenhall; boxes with 'B' after the number came from Bradford; 'Spec.' denotes 'Special Box' built by Bradford; 'pj' = plaster jacket; 'C' = Crate. Note I: not in a numbered box, brought in by Nigel Larkin – continued

object no.	box	spit no.	context no.	facies	size	weathering	iron staining	abrasion	root damage	carnivore gnawing	rodent gnawing	deliberate fracturing	taxon	element
50271	5	60541	20003	B-iii03	2	3							Mammuthus	2 small cranial fragments
50272	5	60541	20003	B-iii03	3	3							Mammuthus	2 small cranial fragments
50273	25B	60271+60274	20003	B-iii03	6	3							Mammuthus	L M3, pair of 50069
50274	6	60735	20003	B-iii03	4	3							Mammuthus	molar plate fragments
50275	70B	60816	20003	B-iii03	6	4							Mammuthus	tusk fragments
50276	6	60546	20003	B-iii03	4	3							large mammal	rib fragment
50277	6	60546	20003	B-iii03	3	3							Mammuthus	cranial fragment?
50278	6	60549–50	20003	B-iii03	6	2							Mammuthus	tusk fragments
50279	6	60548	20003	B-iii03	3	3					ü		large mammal	rib fragments
50280	6	61151	20003	B-iii03	3	3							Mammuthus	molar plate fragment
50282	6	61204	20003	B-iii03	2	3		ü					undetermined	indeterminate bone fragment
50283	6	61204	20003	B-iii03	2	3		ü		ü			undetermined	small indeterminate bone fragment
50284	6	60964	20003	B-iii03	2	3							undetermined	rib fragment
50285	6	60592	20003	B-iii03	3	3							undetermined	indeterminate small bone fragments
50286	6	61102	20003	B-iii03	2	2							Mammuthus	2 small tusk fragments
50287	77B	61068+61724	20003	B-iii03	6	3							Mammuthus	symphyseal portion of adult mandible
50288	6	60588	20003	B-iii03	2	3							undetermined	small indeterminate bone fragment
50289a	1B	61062	20003	B-iii03	6	3							Mammuthus	fragment of ilium
50289b	6	61062	20003	B-iii03	3	4							undetermined	multiple indeterminate bone fragments
50290	spec 1	61061	20003	B-iii03	6	3							Mammuthus	proximal part of anterior rib (proximal epiphysis missing)

APPENDIX 4

Table A4.4 Individual vertebrate finds: boxes 1–19 provided directly from Gressenhall; boxes with 'B' after the number came from Bradford; 'Spec.' denotes 'Special Box' built by Bradford; 'pj' = plaster jacket; 'C' = Crate. Note 1: not in a numbered box, brought in by Nigel Larkin – continued

object no.	box	spit no.	context no.	facies	size	weathering	iron staining	abrasion	root damage	carnivore gnawing	rodent gnawing	deliberate fracturing	taxon	element
50291	6	61060	20003	B-iii03	2	3							undetermined	cranial fragment
50292	6	60059	20003	B-iii03	3	3							undetermined	rib midshaft fragment
50293	6	60969	20003	B-iii03	2	3				ü			large mammal	rib fragment
50294	6	60830	20003	B-iii03	3	3							Mammuthus	small tusk fragment
50295	6	61162	20003	B-iii03	2	3							undetermined	small indeterminate bone fragment, possibly cranial
50296	6	61164	20003	B-iii03	2	1							Mammuthus	small tusk fragment
50297	6	61167	20003	B-iii03	2	3							Mammuthus	small fragment of large long bone
50298	6	61211	20003	B-iii03	1	3							Mammuthus	small tusk fragment
50300	6	61211	20003	B-iii03	4	3							Mammuthus	long bone fragment
50301	6	61211	20003	B-iii03	4	4							Mammuthus	long bone fragment
50302	6	61211	20003	B-iii03	4	5							Mammuthus	long bone fragment
50304	6	61212	20003	B-iii03	3	3							large mammal	indeterminate long bone fragment
50306	6	61212	20003	B-iii03	2	5							large mammal	indeterminate bone fragments
50307	1B	61212+61218	20003	B-iii03	2	5				ü			undetermined	multiple small fragments of cancellous bone
50308	6	61223+61218	20003	B-iii03	6	4							Mammuthus	large long bone fragment
50309	6	61217	20003	B-iii03	3	3							large mammal	small fragment of large long bone
50310	6	60971	20003	B-iii03	2	3							large mammal	small fragment of large long bone
50313	6	61213	20003	B-iii03	3	2							Mammuthus	rib fragment
50314	6	61216	20003	B-iii03	3	5							large mammal	small fragment of large long bone
50315	6	61216	20003	B-iii03	5	4							Mammuthus	2 large long bone fragments

continued ▶

Table A4.4 Individual vertebrate finds: boxes 1–19 provided directly from Gressenhall; boxes with 'B' after the number came from Bradford; 'Spec.' denotes 'Special Box' built by Bradford; 'pj' = plaster jacket; 'C' = Crate. Note 1: not in a numbered box, brought in by Nigel Larkin – continued

object no.	box	spit no.	context no.	facies	size	weathering	iron staining	abrasion	root damage	carnivore gnawing	rodent gnawing	deliberate fracturing	taxon	element
50316	6	61216	20003	B-iii:03	2	5							large mammal	small fragment of long bone
50317	6	61216	20003	B-iii:03	2	3							large mammal	small fragment of long bone
50318	6	60924	20003	B-iii:03	1	5		ü					undetermined	small indeterminate bone fragment
50319	6	60973	20003	B-iii:03	3	2							Mammuthus	small tusk fragment
50320	6	60973	20003	B-iii:03	2	3							Mammuthus	small tusk fragment
50321	6	61169	20003	B-iii:03	2	3							undetermined	small cranial fragment
50322	6	61172	20003	B-iii:03	2	3							Mammuthus	small tusk fragments
50323	6	61172	20003	B-iii:03	2	2							Mammuthus	small tusk fragments
50324	6	61172	20003	B-iii:03	3	3							Mammuthus	small tusk fragment
50325	6	61175	20003	B-iii:03	2	2				ü		ü	Rangifer?	2 conjoining long bone diaphyseal fragments, cf. femoral
50326	6	61113	20003	B-iii:03	2	2						ü	Rangifer?	long bone diaphyseal fragment
50327	6	61113	20003	B-iii:03	2	3							Mammuthus	small cranial fragments
50328	6	61113	20003	B-iii:03	3	3							Mammuthus	multiple small tusk fragments
50329	6	61112	20003	B-iii:03	2	3		ü					Mammuthus	small tusk fragment
50330	6	61112	20003	B-iii:03	1	1							Mammuthus	small tusk fragments
50331a	C3	unstratified	20003	B-iii:03	5	4							Mammuthus	proximal rib and part of midshaft (2 pieces, do not conjoin)
50331b	6	unstratified	20003	B-iii:03	2	4							undetermined	4 small indeterminate bone fragments
50332	6	60973	20003	B-iii:03	5	3							Mammuthus	molar plate
50333	6	61215	20003	B-iii:03	5	3							Mammuthus	large cranial fragment
50334	6	61217	20003	B-iii:03	3	3							Mammuthus	cranial fragment
50335	6	61217	20003	B-iii:03	1	5							undetermined	small indeterminate bone fragment

APPENDIX 4

Table A4.4 Individual vertebrate finds: boxes 1–19 provided directly from Gressenhall; boxes with 'B' after the number came from Bradford; 'Spec.' denotes 'Special Box' built by Bradford; 'pj' = plaster jacket; 'C' = Crate. Note 1: not in a numbered box, brought in by Nigel Larkin – continued

object no.	box	spit no.	context no.	facies	size	weathering	iron staining	abrasion	root damage	carnivore gnawing	rodent gnawing	deliberate fracturing	taxon	element
50336	6	61217	20003	B-iii:03	3	5							*Mammuthus*	cranial fragment
50337	6	61218	20003	B-iii:03	2	3							*Mammuthus*	cranial fragment
50338	6	61218	20003	B-iii:03	2	5							undetermined	small indeterminate bone fragment
50339	6	61218	20003	B-iii:03	2	3							undetermined	small cranial fragment
50340	6	61218+61243	20003	B-iii:03	2	3		ü					undetermined	small cranial fragments
50341	6	61218	20003	B-iii:03	1	5							undetermined	multiple small indeterminate bone fragments
50342	6	60974	20003	B-iii:03	3	2		ü					large mammal	rib fragment
50343	6	61259	20003	B-iii:03	3	3							large mammal	4 conjoining rib fragments
50344	6	unstratified	20245	B-ii:01	2	4				ü			large mammal	rib fragments
50345	6	61171	20003	B-iii:03	2	3							*Mammuthus*	small tusk fragment
50346	6	61174	20003	B-iii:03	2	3							*Mammuthus*	maxillary fragment
50347	6	61453	20003	B-iii:03	1	3							*Mammuthus*	very small cranial fragment
50348	6	61305	20003	B-iii:03	2	3							large mammal	rib fragment
50349	6	61351	20003	B-iii:03	1	3							*Mammuthus*	2 small cranial fragments
50350	6	61351	20003	B-iii:03	1	3							undetermined	indeterminate small cranial fragment
50351	6	61351	20003	B-iii:03	2	3							*Mammuthus*	small cranial fragment
50352	6	61354	20003	B-iii:03	1	3							undetermined	small cranial fragment
50353	6	61352	20003	B-iii:03	1	3							*Mammuthus*	small cranial fragment
50354	6	60975	20003	B-iii:03	2	4							large mammal	small fragment of large long bone
50355	6	61351	20003	B-iii:03	1	2							undetermined	indeterminate small cranial fragment
50356	6	61182	20003	B-iii:03	3	2							*Mammuthus*	tusk fragment

continued ▲

Table A4.4 Individual vertebrate finds: boxes 1–19 provided directly from Gressenhall; boxes with 'B' after the number came from Bradford; 'Spec.' denotes 'Special Box' built by Bradford; 'pj' = plaster jacket; 'C' = Crate. Note 1: not in a numbered box, brought in by Nigel Larkin – continued

object no.	box	spit no.	context no.	facies	size	weathering	iron staining	abrasion	root damage	carnivore gnawing	rodent gnawing	deliberate fracturing	taxon	element
50357	6	61222	20003	B-iii:03	1	5							undetermined	small indeterminate bone fragment
50358	23B	60961	20003	B-iii:03	6	3							Mammuthus	R m2+O65, pair of 51730, poss assoc with 50002–3, fragments of maxilla present between roots
50359	6	61116	20003	B-iii:03	3	3							large mammal	small fragment of large long bone
50360	6	61117	20003	B-iii:03	2	2							Mammuthus	multiple small tusk fragments
50361	6	60976	20003	B-iii:03	6	3							Mammuthus	large tusk fragment
50363	6	60633	20003	B-iii:03	3	4							Mammuthus	cranial fragment
50364	6	60927	20003	B-iii:03	1	3							undetermined	small indeterminate bone fragment
50365	6	60973	20003	B-iii:03	5	2							Mammuthus	tusk fragment
50366	6	61179	20003	B-iii:03	2	3							Mammuthus	cranial fragment
50367	6	60976	20003	B-iii:03	6	3							Mammuthus	large tusk fragment
50368	1B	60977	20003	B-iii:03	4	4							Mammuthus	multiple fragments of large long bone
50369	6	61218+61223	20003	B-iii:03	5	4							Mammuthus	long bone fragments, poss same as 50373
50370	6	61223	20003	B-iii:03	2	5							Mammuthus	small tusk fragments
50371	6	61224	20003	B-iii:03	1	2							undetermined	small bone fragment, probably rib midshaft
50372	6	60930	20003	B-iii:03	1	5			ü				undetermined	small indeterminate bone fragment
50373	6	60981	20003	B-iii:03	6	4							Mammuthus	long bone fragment
50374	6	61360	20003	B-iii:03	1	3							undetermined	small indeterminate bone fragment
50375	6	unknown	20003	B-iii:03	3	5		ü					Mammuthus	cranial fragment
50376a	16B	unknown	20051	B-iii:03	5	4		ü					Rangifer	large unshed male R antler base and large and small beam fragments, probably from same individual as below

APPENDIX 4

Table A4.4 Individual vertebrate finds: boxes 1–19 provided directly from Gressenhall; boxes with 'B' after the number came from Bradford; 'Spec.' denotes 'Special Box' built by Bradford; 'pj' = plaster jacket; 'C' = Crate. Note 1: not in a numbered box, brought in by Nigel Larkin – continued

object no.	box	split no.	context no.	facies	size	weathering	iron staining	abrasion	root damage	carnivore gnawing	rodent gnawing	deliberate fracturing	taxon	element
50376b	6	unstratified	20132	B-iii:04	2	5		ü					Rangifer	fragments of antler, probably from same individual as above
50377	6	61361	20003	B-iii:03	1	5							undetermined	small indeterminate bone fragment, probably cranial
50378	6	61360	20003	B-iii:03	1	2							undetermined	very small cranial fragment
50379	6	61361	20003	B-iii:03	2	3							Mammuthus	cranial fragment
50380	6	61361	20003	B-iii:03	3	3							Mammuthus	cranial fragment
50381	7	61361	20003	B-iii:03	2	3							undetermined	cranial fragment
50382	7	61361	20003	B-iii:03	2	3							undetermined	small indeterminate bone fragment, probably cranial
50383	7	61361	20003	B-iii:03	2	3							undetermined	cranial fragment
50384	7	61352	20003	B-iii:03	2	2							undetermined	cranial fragment
50385	7	unstratified	20131	B-iii:04	5	4							Mammuthus	long bone fragment
50386	7	60977	20003	B-iii:03	3	3							Mammuthus	small fragment of large long bone
50387	7	60977	20003	B-iii:03	4	3							undetermined	cranial fragment
50388	7	61178	20003	B-iii:03	3	4							Mammuthus	tusk fragment
50390	7	61178	20003	B-iii:03	2	5							undetermined	cranial fragment
50391	7	61178	20003	B-iii:03	2	3							Mammuthus	cranial fragment
50392	7	60977	20003	B-iii:03	3	4							Mammuthus	small fragment of large long bone
50393	7	60977	20003	B-iii:03	3	3							Mammuthus	small fragment of large long bone
50394	7	60978	20003	B-iii:03	3	3				ü			Mammuthus	rib fragment
50395	7	61226	20003	B-iii:03	2	3							Mammuthus	2 small fragments of large long bone
50396	7	61226	20003	B-iii:03	1	5							undetermined	small indeterminate bone fragments

continued

Table A4.4 Individual vertebrate finds: boxes 1–19 provided directly from Gressenhall; boxes with 'B' after the number came from Bradford; 'Spec.' denotes 'Special Box' built by Bradford; 'pj' = plaster jacket; 'C' = Crate. Note 1: not in a numbered box, brought in by Nigel Larkin – continued

object no.	box	spit no.	context no.	facies	size	weathering	iron staining	abrasion	root damage	carnivore gnawing	rodent gnawing	deliberate fracturing	taxon	element
50397	7	60978	20003	B-iii03	2	3							Mammuthus	cranial fragment
50398	7	60978	20003	B-iii03	3	2							Mammuthus	molar plate fragment
50399	7	61265	20003	B-iii03	2	3							undetermined	3 small bone fragments, probably vertebral, juvenile
50400	7	61011	20003	B-iii03	1	X							Mammuthus	mostly dirt with a few tiny flakes of tusk
50401	7	60978	20003	B-iii03	3	3							Mammuthus	cranial fragment
50402	7	61266	20003	B-iii03	3	5							Mammuthus	sternal fragment?
50403	spec 1	6109?	20021	B-iii03	6	3							Mammuthus	posterior rib (proximal epiphysis missing, damaged distal end)
50404	27B	6107?	20021	B-iii03	6	3							Mammuthus	juvenile 1st rib (damaged proximal end, missing distal epiphysis)
50405	7	61088	20021	B-iii03	6	3							Mammuthus	anterior fragment of middle rib
50406	7	61088	20021	B-iii03	6	3					ü		undetermined	rib midshaft
50407	15B	61078	20021	B-iii03	6	3				ü			cf. Mammuthus	rib midshaft fragment
50408	7	61189	20003	B-iii03	2	3							undetermined	indeterminate bone fragment
50409	7	60980	20003	B-iii03	2	4							Mammuthus	small fragment of large long bone
50410	7	60980	20003	B-iii03	2	3							Mammuthus	cranial fragment
50411	7	61240+61243	20003+20140	B-iii03	2	3							undetermined	cranial fragment
50412	7	61240+61243	20003+20141	B-iii03	3	5							Mammuthus	small fragment of large long bone
50413	7	61240+61243	20003+20142	B-iii03	1	3							undetermined	very small indeterminate bone fragment
50414	7	61240+61243	20003+20143	B-iii03	2	3							undetermined	small indeterminate bone fragment
50415	7	61240+61243	20003+20144	B-iii03	3	3							Mammuthus	small fragment of large long bone
50416	7	61240+61243	20003+20145	B-iii03	1	3							undetermined	small cranial fragment

APPENDIX 4

Table A4.4 Individual vertebrate finds: boxes 1–19 provided directly from Gressenhall; boxes with 'B' after the number came from Bradford; 'Spec.' denotes 'Special Box' built by Bradford; 'pj' = plaster jacket; 'C' = Crate. Note 1: not in a numbered box, brought in by Nigel Larkin – continued

object no.	box	spit no.	context no.	facies	size	weathering	iron staining	abrasion	root damage	carnivore gnawing	rodent gnawing	deliberate fracturing	taxon	element
50417	7	61240+61243	20003+20146	B-iii03	1	3							undetermined	2 small indeterminate bone fragments
50418	7	61240+61243	20003+20147	B-iii03	2	3							undetermined	small indeterminate bone fragment
50419	7	61240+61243	20003+20148	B-iii03	3	3							Mammuthus	small fragment of large long bone
50420	7	61240+61243	20003+20149	B-iii03	2	5							Mammuthus	small fragment of large long bone
50421	7	61240+61243	20003+20150	B-iii03	3	4							Mammuthus	small fragment of large long bone
50422	7	61240+61243	20003+20151	B-iii03	2	5							undetermined	indeterminate bone fragment
50423	7	61240+61243	20003+20152	B-iii03	3	3							Mammuthus	small fragment of large long bone
50424	7	61240+61243	20003+20153	B-iii03	3	3							undetermined	long bone fragment
50425	7	61240+61243	20003	B-iii03	2	3							Mammuthus	small fragment of large long bone
50426	7	61094	20021	B-iii03	3	3							Mammuthus	stylohyoid
50427	7	61081	20021	B-iii03	3	5							Mammuthus	multiple tusk fragments
50428	7	61093	20021	B-iii03	3	2							undetermined	indeterminate bone fragment
50429	7	61088	20021	B-iii03	3	4							Mammuthus	indeterminate bone fragment
50430	7	61090	20021	B-iii03	3	2							Mammuthus	tusk fragment
50431	7	61191	20003	B-iii03	2	3							Mammuthus	small fragment of large long bone
50432	7	unstratified	20021	B-iii03	3	3							Mammuthus	cranial fragment
50433	7	61239	20003	B-iii03	3	3							Mammuthus	small fragment of large long bone
50434	30B	61316	20003	B-iii03	6	4							Mammuthus	fragment of acetabulum, see 50435 and 50436
50437	7	unstratified	20021	B-iii03	2	2							undetermined	3 small indeterminate bone fragments
50438	7	60974	20003	B-iii03	6	3							Mammuthus	large tusk fragments
50439	7	60975	20003	B-iii03	6	4							Mammuthus	large tusk fragments

continued

Table A4.4 Individual vertebrate finds: boxes 1–19 provided directly from Gressenhall; boxes with 'B' after the number came from Bradford; 'Spec.' denotes 'Special Box' built by Bradford; 'pj' = plaster jacket; 'C' = Crate. Note 1: not in a numbered box, brought in by Nigel Larkin – continued

object no.	box	split no.	context no.	facies	size	weathering	iron staining	abrasion	root damage	carnivore gnawing	rodent gnawing	deliberate fracturing	taxon	element
50440	7	60975	20003	B-iii03	5	3							Mammuthus	large cranial fragment
50441	7	60972	20003	B-iii03	4	3							Mammuthus	large tusk fragments
50442	7	61239	20003	B-iii03	6	4							Mammuthus	large long bone fragment
50443	7	60975	20003	B-iii03	4	3							Mammuthus	tusk fragments
50444	7	60975	20003	B-iii03	5	3							Mammuthus	tusk fragment
50445	7	61093	20021	B-iii03	3	2							undetermined	cranial fragments
50446	7	61270	20003	B-iii03	2	5							Mammuthus	?sternal fragments
50447	7	61464	20003	B-iii03	5	3							Mammuthus	small fragment of large long bone
50448	7	61464	20003	B-iii03	2	3							undetermined	small fragment of long bone
50449	7	60983	20003	B-iii03	4	4							Mammuthus	tusk fragments
50450	7	60983	20003	B-iii03	3	3							undetermined	indeterminate bone fragment, possibly cranial
50451	7	60983	20003	B-iii03	3	3							Mammuthus	tusk fragment
50452	7	61244	20003	B-iii03	4	5							Mammuthus	small fragment of large long bone
50453	7	61244	20003	B-iii03	3	4							large mammal	indeterminate bone fragment
50454	7	61679	20140	B-iii04	2	3							undetermined	3 small indeterminate bone fragments
50455	7	61369	20003	B-iii03	2	3							Mammuthus	small cranial fragment
50456	7	61370	20003	B-iii03	2	2							undetermined	small cranial fragment
50457	7	61371	20003	B-iii03	2	2							undetermined	small cranial fragment
50458	7	61371	20003	B-iii03	2	2							undetermined	small cranial fragment
50459	7	61366	20003	B-iii03	3	4							Mammuthus	cranial fragment
50460	7	61368	20003	B-iii03	2	3							undetermined	small cranial fragment

APPENDIX 4

Table A4.4 Individual vertebrate finds: boxes 1–19 provided directly from Gressenhall; boxes with 'B' after the number came from Bradford; 'Spec.' denotes 'Special Box' built by Bradford; 'pj' = plaster jacket; 'C' = Crate. Note 1: not in a numbered box, brought in by Nigel Larkin – continued

object no.	box	split no.	context no.	facies	size	weathering	iron staining	abrasion	root damage	carnivore gnawing	rodent gnawing	deliberate fracturing	taxon	element
50461	7	61368	20003	B-iii:O3	1	3							undetermined	very small cranial fragment
50462	7	61368	20003	B-iii:O3	1	4							undetermined	very small cranial fragment
50463	7	61363	20003	B-iii:O3	2	4							undetermined	indeterminate bone fragment
50464	7	61363	20003	B-iii:O3	2	4							undetermined	small cranial fragment
50465	7	61365	20003	B-iii:O3	2	3							undetermined	small cranial fragment
50466	7	61369	20003	B-iii:O3	2	3							undetermined	small cranial fragment
50467	7	61369	20003	B-iii:O3	1	3							undetermined	very small cranial fragment
50468	7	61370	20003	B-iii:O3	2	4							Mammuthus	cranial fragment
50469	7	61371	20003	B-iii:O3	2	3							Mammuthus	cranial fragment
50470	7	60983	20003	B-iii:O3	4	4							Mammuthus	large bone fragment, ?cranial
50471	7	60984	20003	B-iii:O3	6	2							Mammuthus	large tusk fragment
50473	7	61245	20003	B-iii:O3	2	3							undetermined	small fragment of large long bone
50474	7	60984	20003	B-iii:O3	3	2							Mammuthus	tusk fragment
50475	7	60985	20003	B-iii:O3	4	2							Mammuthus	tusk fragment
50476	7	61319	20003	B-iii:O3	3	4							Mammuthus	small fragment of large long bone
50477	7	61197	20003	B-iii:O3	2	2							undetermined	cranial fragment
50478	7	61197	20003	B-iii:O3	2	3							undetermined	indeterminate bone fragment
50479	7	61198	20003	B-iii:O3	4	3							Mammuthus	molar plate fragment
50480	7	61199	20003	B-iii:O3	2	3							Mammuthus	small tusk fragments
50481	7	61199	20003	B-iii:O3	2	3							cf. Mammuthus	cranial fragment
50482	7	61602	20003	B-iii:O3	3	3							cf. Mammuthus	cranial fragment
50483	1B	unstratified	20003	B-iii:O3	5	5							cf. Mammuthus	indeterminate long bone fragment

continued ▲

Table A4.4 Individual vertebrate finds: boxes 1–19 provided directly from Gressenhall; boxes with 'B' after the number came from Bradford; 'Spec.' denotes 'Special Box' built by Bradford; 'pj' = plaster jacket; 'C' = Crate. Note 1: not in a numbered box, brought in by Nigel Larkin – continued

object no.	box	split no.	context no.	facies	size	weathering	iron staining	abrasion	root damage	carnivore gnawing	rodent gnawing	deliberate fracturing	taxon	element
50484	7	60936	20003	B-iii:O3	2	3							cf. *Mammuthus*	small cranial fragment
50485	7	61651	20003	B-iii:O3	2	3							cf. *Mammuthus*	small fragment of large long bone
50486	7	61320	20003	B-iii:O3	4	3							*Mammuthus*	fragment of large long bone
50488	51B	60984	20003	B-iii:O3	6	4				ü			*Mammuthus*	large ?humerus midshaft fragment, split longitudinally, and unassociated cranial fragments
50489	7	61370	20003	B-iii:O3	2	3							undetermined	rib fragment
50490	7	61370	20003	B-iii:O3	2	3							undetermined	cranial fragment
50491	7	60985	20003	B-iii:O3	2	1							*Coelodonta*	complete L P3, damaged roots; sampled for isotopes.
50492	7	60987	20003	B-iii:O3	3	2							*Mammuthus*	tusk fragment
50493	7	61322	20003	B-iii:O3	2	2				ü			cf. *Mammuthus*	rib fragment
50494	7	61605	20003	B-iii:O3	2	5							undetermined	indeterminate bone fragments
50495	7	61605	20003	B-iii:O3	2	2							undetermined	cranial fragment
50496	7	61605	20003	B-iii:O3	2	4							*Mammuthus*	molar plate fragment
50497	7	61606	20003	B-iii:O3	2	3							cf. *Mammuthus*	cranial fragment
50498	7	61606	20003	B-iii:O3	2	3							undetermined	indeterminate bone fragment
50499	7	61608	20003	B-iii:O3	2	3							undetermined	indeterminate bone fragment
50500	8	61608	20003	B-iii:O3	2	3							*Mammuthus*	molar talon fragment
50501	8	61608	20003	B-iii:O3	5	3							*Mammuthus*	small fragment of large long bone
50502	8	61608	20003	B-iii:O3	4	4							*Mammuthus*	large bone fragment
50503	8	61609	20003	B-iii:O3	2	3							cf. *Mammuthus*	cranial fragment
50504	8	61609	20003	B-iii:O3	4	3							*Mammuthus*	tusk fragments

APPENDIX 4

Table A.4.4 Individual vertebrate finds: boxes 1–19 provided directly from Gressenhall; boxes with 'B' after the number came from Bradford; 'Spec.' denotes 'Special Box' built by Bradford; 'pj' = plaster jacket; 'C' = Crate. Note 1: not in a numbered box, brought in by Nigel Larkin – continued

object no.	box	spit no.	context no.	facies	size	weathering	iron staining	abrasion	root damage	carnivore gnawing	rodent gnawing	deliberate fracturing	taxon	element
50505	8	61609	20003	B-iii:03	1	3							Mammuthus	tusk fragments
50506	8	61609	20003	B-iii:03	4	3							Mammuthus	tusk fragment
50507	8	61610	20003	B-iii:03	2	3							Mammuthus	tusk fragments
50508	8	61610	20003	B-iii:03	3	5							undetermined	indeterminate bone fragments, probably cranial
50509	8	60937	20003	B-iii:03	3	3							Mammuthus	cranial fragment
50511	8	60987	20003	B-iii:03	3	4							undetermined	indeterminate bone fragment
50512	8	60937–6	20003	B-iii:03	1	4							undetermined	indeterminate bone fragment
50513	8	61323	20003	B-iii:03	2	2							Mammuthus	molar talon fragment
50514	8	61323	20003	B-iii:03	2	2							Mammuthus	tusk fragment
50515	8	61471	20003	B-iii:03	3	4							undetermined	indeterminate bone fragment
50516	8	60888	20003	B-iii:03	3	3							Mammuthus	molar plate fragment
50517	8	60988	20003	B-iii:03	3	3							Mammuthus	tusk fragments
50518	8	61325	20003	B-iii:03	3	3							Mammuthus	tusk fragments
50519	8	61676	20247	B-iii:04	3	5							Mammuthus	small fragment of large long bone
50520	8	61472	20003	B-iii:03	2	3							Mammuthus	tusk fragment
50521	8	60990	20003	B-iii:03	3	4							Mammuthus	tusk fragment
50522	8	61326	20003	B-iii:03	2	2						ü	Coelodonta	incomplete R m2
50523	8	60990	20003	B-iii:03	2	5							Mammuthus	tusk fragment
50524	8	60990	20003	B-iii:03	4	3							Mammuthus	tusk fragment
50525	8	60936	20003	B-iii:03	2	3							undetermined	2 indeterminate bone fragments
50526	8	60936	20003	B-iii:03	1	4							undetermined	small indeterminate bone fragment

continued ▶

Table A4.4 Individual vertebrate finds: boxes 1–19 provided directly from Gressenhall; boxes with 'B' after the number came from Bradford; 'Spec.' denotes 'Special Box' built by Bradford; 'pj' = plaster jacket; 'C' = Crate. Note 1: not in a numbered box, brought in by Nigel Larkin – continued

object no.	box	spit no.	context no.	facies	size	weathering	iron staining	abrasion	root damage	carnivore gnawing	rodent gnawing	deliberate fracturing	taxon	element
50527	8	61124	20003	B-iii03	3	3							Mammuthus	multiple tusk fragments
50528	B	61123	20003	B-iii03									Mammuthus	tusk fragment
50529	8	61123	20003	B-iii03	3	3							Mammuthus	cranial fragment
50530	8	61124	20003	B-iii03	2	2							Mammuthus	fragment of proximal epiphysis of rib
50531	8	61125	20003	B-iii03	2	3							undetermined	indeterminate rib midshaft fragment
50532	8	61125	20003	B-iii03	2	2							Canis	proximal first rib
50533	8	61127	20003	B-iii03	2	3							Mammuthus	cranial fragment
50534	8	61128	20003	B-iii03	1	3							Mammuthus	small tusk fragments
50535	B	60990	20003	B-iii03	6	4							Mammuthus	tusk fragments
50536	8	60990	20003	B-iii03	5	3							Mammuthus	tusk fragment
50537	8	60990	20003	B-iii03	5	3							Mammuthus	tusk fragment
50538	8	60990	20003	B-iii03	3	2							Mammuthus	2 tusk fragments
50539	8	60990	20003	B-iii03	3	2							Mammuthus	2 tusk fragments
50540	8	60990	20003	B-iii03	4	4							Mammuthus	tusk fragment
50541	8	61675	20247	B-iii04	2	4							undetermined	indeterminate small bone fragment
50542	8	61675	20247	B-iii04	4	4							Mammuthus	indeterminate bone fragment
50543	8	61675	20247	B-iii04	3	4							undetermined	indeterminate bone fragment
50544	8	61675	20249	B-iii04	3	3							Mammuthus	indeterminate bone fragment
50545	8	61613	20249	B-iii04	3	3							Mammuthus	cranial fragment
50546	8	61613	20249	B-iii04	2	3							Mammuthus	cranial fragment
50547	8	61605	20003	B-iii03	2	4							Mammuthus	tusk fragment
50548	8	61604	20003	B-iii03	4	4							Mammuthus	cranial fragment, maxillary

APPENDIX 4

Table A4.4 Individual vertebrate finds: boxes 1–19 provided directly from Gressenhall; boxes with 'B' after the number came from Bradford; 'Spec.' denotes 'Special Box' built by Bradford; 'pj' = plaster jacket; 'C' = Crate. Note 1: not in a numbered box, brought in by Nigel Larkin – continued

object no.	box	spit no.	context no.	facies	size	weathering	iron staining	abrasion	root damage	carnivore gnawing	rodent gnawing	deliberate fracturing	taxon	element
50549	8	61604	20003	B-iii:O3	1	3							undetermined	2 small cranial fragments
50550	8	61604	20003	B-iii:O3	3	3							*Mammuthus*	tusk fragment
50551	C2	61473	20003	B-iii:O3	6	3				ü			*Mammuthus*	R ulna in 2 large fragments, proximal damaged, distal missing; sampled for isotopes.
50552	8	60990	20003	B-iii:O3	3	2							*Mammuthus*	tusk fragment
50553	8	60991	20003	B-iii:O3	5	4							*Mammuthus*	large tusk fragments
50554	8	60991	20003	B-iii:O3	3	4							*Mammuthus*	tusk fragments
50555	8	60991	20003	B-iii:O3	5	4							*Mammuthus*	large tusk fragments
50556	8	61473	20003	B-iii:O3	3	3							*Mammuthus*	molar plate fragment
50557a	11B	60911+60920+60928	20003	B-iii:O3	3	5							*Mammuthus*	multiple fragments of indeterminate long bone
50557b	8	60911+60920+60928	20003	B-iii:O3	1	4							cf. *Mammuthus*	multiple small fragments, labelled as coming from 50557
50558	8	61654	20003	B-iii:O3	2	1							*Ursus*	L m2; sampled for isotopes.
50559	8	61376	20003	B-iii:O3	2	2							*Coelodonta*	L m1
50560	8	61376	20003	B-iii:O3	2	3							cf. *Mammuthus*	cranial fragment
50561	8	61377	20003	B-iii:O3	1	3							undetermined	cranial fragment
50562	8	61378	20003	B-iii:O3	2	3							*Mammuthus*	cranial fragment
50563	8	61378	20003	B-iii:O3	4	3							*Mammuthus*	cranial fragment
50564	8	61378	20003	B-iii:O3	3	4							cf. *Mammuthus*	cranial fragment
50565	8	61381	20003	B-iii:O3	4	3							undetermined	indeterminate bone fragment
50566	8	61381	20003	B-iii:O3	2	2							undetermined	indeterminate bone fragment
50567	8	61524	20003	B-iii:O3	2	4							undetermined	multiple indeterminate bone fragments

continued ▲

Table A4.4 Individual vertebrate finds: boxes 1–19 provided directly from Gressenhall; boxes with 'B' after the number came from Bradford; 'Spec.' denotes 'Special Box' built by Bradford; 'pj' = plaster jacket; 'C' = Crate. Note 1: not in a numbered box, brought in by Nigel Larkin – continued

object no.	box	spit no.	context no.	facies	size	weathering	iron staining	abrasion	root damage	carnivore gnawing	rodent gnawing	deliberate fracturing	taxon	element
50568	8	60990	20003	B-iii03	6	2							Mammuthus	tusk fragment
50569	8	60990	20003	B-iii03	3	4							Mammuthus	tusk fragment
50570	8	61123	20003	B-iii03	1	2							Mammuthus	small tusk fragments
50571	8	61125	20003	B-iii03	3	5							Mammuthus	cranial fragment
50572	8	61127	20003	B-iii03	2	4							Mammuthus	cranial fragment
50573	8	61128	20003	B-iii03	2	2							Mammuthus	multiple small tusk fragments
50574	8	61615	20250	B-iii03	2	4							cf. Mammuthus	cranial fragment
50575	8	61264+61270	20003	B-iii03	5	4							Mammuthus	large cranial fragment
50576	8	61378	20003	B-iii03	3	2							cf. Mammuthus	cranial fragment
50577	8	61379	20003	B-iii03	2	4							Mammuthus	cranial fragment
50578	8	61379	20003	B-iii03	2	4							Mammuthus	cranial fragment
50579	8	61379	20003	B-iii03	2	4							Mammuthus	cranial fragment
50580	8	61379	20003	B-iii03	1	4							undetermined	indeterminate bone fragment
50581	8	61379	20003	B-iii03	3	2							Mammuthus	cranial fragment
50582	8	61382	20003	B-iii03	2	3							undetermined	small indeterminate bone fragment
50583	8	61382	20003	B-iii03	2	3							undetermined	small cranial fragment
50584	8	61383	20003	B-iii03	2	3							undetermined	small cranial fragment
50585	8	61234	20248	B-iii03	4	5							Mammuthus	long bone or cranial fragments
50586	8	61234	20248	B-iii03	4	5							Mammuthus	long bone fragment
50587	8	61660	20248	B-iii03	3	5							Mammuthus	long bone fragment
50588	8	61660	20248	B-iii03	2	4							undetermined	small indeterminate bone fragment
50589	8	61617	20251	B-iii04	3	3							large mammal	rib fragment

APPENDIX 4

Table A4.4 Individual vertebrate finds: boxes 1–19 provided directly from Gressenhall; boxes with 'B' after the number came from Bradford; 'Spec.' denotes 'Special Box' built by Bradford; 'pj' = plaster jacket; 'C' = Crate. Note 1: not in a numbered box, brought in by Nigel Larkin – continued

object no.	box	split no.	context no.	facies	size	weathering	iron staining	abrasion	root damage	carnivore gnawing	rodent gnawing	deliberate fracturing	taxon	element
50590	8	61383	20003	B-iii:03	2	3							large mammal	rib fragment
50591	8	61383	20003	B-iii:03	2	2							Mammuthus	small tusk fragment
50592	8	61380	20003	B-iii:03	3	2							cf. Mammuthus	cranial fragment
50593	8	61661	20248	B-iii:04	2	3							Mammuthus	small fragment of large long bone
50594	8	61620	20251	B-iii:04	2	2							Mammuthus	tusk fragment
50595	8	60991	20003	B-iii:03	5	4							Mammuthus	large tusk fragment
50596	8	61332	20003	B-iii:03	3	3							Mammuthus	tusk fragments
50599	8	61476	20003	B-iii:03	2	1						ü	Coelodonta	L p3
50600	8	61379	20003	B-iii:03	1	3							Mammuthus	small cranial fragment
50601	9	61233	20248	B-iii:04	3	4							Mammuthus	2 small conjoining fragments of indeterminate long bone
50602	9	61379	20003	B-iii:03	1	3							undetermined	2 very small bone fragments, possibly cranial
50603	9	61379	20003	B-iii:03	2	3							Mammuthus	cranial fragment
50604	9	61379	20003	B-iii:03	2	3							undetermined	small indeterminate bone fragment, probably cranial
50605	9	61379	20003	B-iii:03	1	3							undetermined	small cranial fragment
50606	9	61379	20003	B-iii:03	3	3							Mammuthus	cranial fragment
50607	9	61379	20003	B-iii:03	1	4							undetermined	small indeterminate bone fragment
50608	9	61379	20003	B-iii:03	1	3							undetermined	small indeterminate bone fragment
50609	9	61475	20003	B-iii:03	4	4		ü					Mammuthus	small fragment of indeterminate long bone
50610	9	61475	20003	B-iii:03	4	4							Mammuthus	tusk fragment
50611	9, 79B	61271	20003	B-iii:03	6	3							Mammuthus	one large and several small cranial fragments (some conjoining)

continued ▶

Table A4.4 Individual vertebrate finds: boxes 1–19 provided directly from Gressenhall; boxes with 'B' after the number came from Bradford; 'Spec.' denotes 'Special Box' built by Bradford; 'pj' = plaster jacket; 'C' = Crate. Note 1: not in a numbered box, brought in by Nigel Larkin – continued

object no.	box	spit no.	context no.	facies	size	weathering	iron staining	abrasion	root damage	carnivore gnawing	rodent gnawing	deliberate fracturing	taxon	element
50612	9	61235	20248	B-iii:04	2	3							undetermined	indeterminate bone fragment
50613	9	61231	20248	B-iii:03	2	2						ü	Rangifer?	femoral diaphyseal fragment
50614	9	61379	20003	B-iii:03	2	3							undetermined	cranial fragment
50615	9	61379	20003	B-iii:03	2	3							Mammuthus	cranial fragment
50616	9	61380	20003	B-iii:03	3	2							Mammuthus	cranial fragment
50617	9	60992	20003	B-iii:03	5	4							Mammuthus	tusk fragment
50618	9	60992	20003	B-iii:03	3	3							Mammuthus	tusk fragment
50619	9	60992	20003	B-iii:03	4	5							Mammuthus	tusk fragment and four indeterminate long bone fragments
50620	9	61333	20003	B-iii:03	3	4							Mammuthus	indeterminate bone fragment, probably cranial
50621	9	61333	20003	B-iii:03	2	3							Mammuthus	2 small cranial fragments
50622	9	61379	20003	B-iii:03	5	3							Rangifer	shed R antler base with broken beam and 1st tine, see 50625; sampled for isotopes
50623	9	61379	20003	B-iii:03	2	4							undetermined	indeterminate bone fragment
50624	9	61379	20003	B-iii:03	2	3							Rangifer	antler fragment
50625	9	61379	20003	B-iii:03	2	3							Rangifer	antler fragment, fits with 50622
50626	9	61379	20003	B-iii:03	5	3							Rangifer	antler fragment, possibly part of 50625
50627	9	61379	20003	B-iii:03	3	3							Rangifer	antler fragment, possibly part of 50625
50628	9	61379	20003	B-iii:03	4	3							Rangifer	antler fragment, possibly part of 50625
50629	9	61379	20003	B-iii:03	3	3							Rangifer	antler fragment, possibly part of 50625
50630	9	61379	20003	B-iii:03	4	3							Rangifer	antler fragment, possibly part of 50625
50631	9	61379	20003	B-iii:03	5	3							Rangifer	antler fragment, probably same as 50634

APPENDIX 4

Table A4.4 Individual vertebrate finds: boxes 1–19 provided directly from Gressenhall; boxes with 'B' after the number came from Bradford; 'Spec.' denotes 'Special Box' built by Bradford; 'pj' = plaster jacket; 'C' = Crate. Note 1: not in a numbered box, brought in by Nigel Larkin – continued

object no.	box	spit no.	context no.	facies	size	weathering	iron staining	abrasion	root damage	carnivore gnawing	rodent gnawing	deliberate fracturing	taxon	element
50632	9	61379	20003	B-iii:03	2	2							Mammuthus	tusk fragment
50633	9	61379	20003	B-iii:03	4	3				ü			Mammuthus	rib fragment
50634	9	61379	20003	B-iii:03	3	3							Rangifer	antler fragment
50635	9	61379	20003	B-iii:03	1	2							undetermined	small indeterminate bone fragment
50636	9	61379	20003	B-iii:03	5	3							Rangifer	tine and part of beam
50637	9	61379	20003	B-iii:03	2	3							Rangifer	antler fragment
50638	9	61379	20003	B-iii:03	2	3							undetermined	small indeterminate bone fragment
50639	9	61382	20003	B-iii:03	2	2							Mammuthus	molar plate fragment
50640	9	60935	20003	B-iii:03	2	4							Mammuthus	small cranial fragment
50641	9	60992	20003	B-iii:03	4	2							Mammuthus	small tusk fragments
50642	9	61333	20003	B-iii:03	3	4							Mammuthus	tusk fragment
50644	9	61333	20003	B-iii:03	4	3							Mammuthus	tusk fragment
50645	9	60997	20003	B-iii:03	5	3							Mammuthus	bone fragment
50647	9	61478	20003	B-iii:03	3	3							Mammuthus	rib fragment
50648	9	61478	20003	B-iii:03	4	3							Mammuthus	rib fragment
50649	9	61266+61272	20003	B-iii:03	3	3							Mammuthus	vertebral fragment, conjoins with 50650
50650	9	61266+61272	20003	B-iii:03	4	3							Mammuthus	vertebral fragment, conjoins with 50649
50651	9	61623	20252	B-iii:03	2	4							Mammuthus	tusk fragment
50652	9	61623	20252	B-iii:03	2	2							Mammuthus	tusk fragment
50653	9	61623	20252	B-iii:03	2	4							Mammuthus	tusk fragment
50654	13B	60991	20003	B-iii:03	6	4							Mammuthus	tusk fragments
50655	9	60991	20003	B-iii:03	4	4							Mammuthus	2 conjoining ?mandibular fragments, one cranial fragment

continued ▶

Table A4.4 Individual vertebrate finds: boxes 1–19 provided directly from Gressenhall; boxes with 'B' after the number came from Bradford; 'Spec.' denotes 'Special Box' built by Bradford; 'pj' = plaster jacket; 'C' = Crate. Note 1: not in a numbered box, brought in by Nigel Larkin – continued

object no.	box	spit no.	context no.	facies	size	weathering	iron staining	abrasion	root damage	carnivore gnawing	rodent gnawing	deliberate fracturing	taxon	element
50656a	24B	61667	20248	B-iii03	6	3							Mammuthus	L m3 with roots, pair of 51953 + 51648 + 51154
50656b	9	61667	20248	B-iii03	1	5							Mammuthus	very small tusk fragments and small bone fragments
50657	9	61334	20003	B-iii03	3	.4							Mammuthus	small fragment of large long bone
50658	9	61334	20003	B-iii03	4	2							Mammuthus	small tusk fragment
50659	9	61334	20003	B-iii03	2	2							Mammuthus	small tusk fragments
50660	9	61334	20003	B-iii03	2	4							undetermined	small indeterminate bone fragment
50661	9	61334	20003	B-iii03	4	3							Mammuthus	tusk fragment
50663	9	60995	20003	B-iii03	2	3							undetermined	indeterminate bone fragment
50664	9	61379	20003	B-iii03	3	3							Mammuthus	cranial fragment
50665	9	61480	20003	B-iii03	3	3							undetermined	indeterminate bone fragment, ?vertebral
50666	9	61379	20003	B-iii03	2	3							undetermined	small indeterminate bone fragment
50667	9	61667	20248	B-iii03	1	4							undetermined	small indeterminate bone fragment
50668	9	61667	20248	B-iii03	1	4							undetermined	small indeterminate bone fragment
50669	9	61667	20248	B-iii03	4	4							Mammuthus	fragment of large long bone
50670	9	61272+61274	20003	B-iii03	6	3							Mammuthus	long bone fragment
50671	1B	60940	20003	B-iii03	4	4							Mammuthus	conjoining fragments of rib
50672	9	61626	20252	B-iii03	2	2						ü	Mammuthus	small bone fragment
50673	9	61627	20252	B-iii03	2	4							Mammuthus	small tusk fragment
50674	9	61480	20003	B-iii03	3	·3							cf. Mammuthus	cranial fragment
50675	9	61480	20003	B-iii03	3	3							undetermined	?cranial fragment
50676	9	61480	20003	B-iii03	2	3							Mammuthus	small fragment of large long bone

APPENDIX 4

Table A4.4 Individual vertebrate finds: boxes 1–19 provided directly from Gressenhall; boxes with 'B' after the number came from Bradford; 'Spec.' denotes 'Special Box' built by Bradford; 'pj' = plaster jacket; 'C' = Crate. Note 1: not in a numbered box, brought in by Nigel Larkin – continued

object no.	box	spit no.	context no.	facies	size	weathering	iron staining	abrasion	root damage	carnivore gnawing	rodent gnawing	deliberate fracturing	taxon	element
50677	9	61480	20003	B-iii:03	3	3							cf. *Mammuthus*	cranial fragment
50678	9	61480	20003	B-iii:03	1	2							*Mammuthus*	internal tusk fragment
50679	9	61532	20003	B-iii:03	4	3							*Mammuthus*	2 conjoining fragments of hyoid bone
50680	9	60995	20003	B-iii:03	3	3							*Mammuthus*	tusk fragment
50681	9	60995	20003	B-iii:03	3	3							*Mammuthus*	tusk fragment
50682	9	60995	20003	B-iii:03	2	3							undetermined	indeterminate small bone fragment
50683	9	60990	20003	B-iii:03	4	4							*Mammuthus*	tusk fragment
50684	spec 3	61730	20245	B-iii:01	6	3							*Mammuthus*	midshaft of rib
50685	spec 1	61732–3	20245	B-iii:01	6	3							*Mammuthus*	proximal part of rib (proximal epiphysis and distal end missing)
50686	20B	61733	20245	B-iii:01	6	3							*Mammuthus*	conjoining fragments of rib midshaft
50687	9	61667	20248	B-iii:03	3	2							*Ursus*	fragment of R dentary showing alveolus for p1, found in association with R lower canine
50688	9	61629	20252	B-iii:03	2	2							*Mammuthus*	molar plate fragment and possible cranial fragment
50689	9	61533	20003	B-iii:03	4	3							undetermined	cranial fragment
50690a	9	61667	20248	B-iii:03	6	3							*Mammuthus*	large cranial fragment
50690b	1B	61667	20248	B-iii:03	1	3							cf. *Rangifer*	comminuted fragments of lower premolar (possibly deciduous)
50691	9 + 14B	60995	20003	B-iii:03	6	4							*Mammuthus*	tusk fragments
50692a	9	60995	20003	B-iii:03	2	3							undetermined	small cranial fragment
50692b	9	60995	20003	B-iii:03	2	3							undetermined	small indeterminate bone fragment
50693	9	61536	20003	B-iii:03	2	3							undetermined	cranial fragments

continued

Table A4.4 Individual vertebrate finds: boxes 1–19 provided directly from Gressenhall; boxes with 'B' after the number came from Bradford; 'Spec.' denotes 'Special Box' built by Bradford; 'pj' = plaster jacket; 'C' = Crate. Note 1: not in a numbered box, brought in by Nigel Larkin – continued

object no.	box	split no.	context no.	facies	size	weathering	iron staining	abrasion	root damage	carnivore gnawing	rodent gnawing	deliberate fracturing	taxon	element
50694	9	61630	20252	B-iii03	2	3							*Mammuthus*	cranial fragment
50695	9	61630	20252	B-iii03	3	3							*Mammuthus*	cranial fragment
50696	9	60996	20003	B-iii03	2	3							undetermined	indeterminate bone fragment
50697	9	60996	20003	B-iii03	3	4							*Mammuthus*	2 small cranial fragments
50698	9	60996	20003	B-iii03	3	3							*Mammuthus*	cranial fragment
50699	9	61666	20248	B-iii03	3	3							cf. *Mammuthus*	small fragments of large long bone
50700	9	61666	20248	B-iii03	3	3							cf. *Mammuthus*	small fragments of large long bone
50701	10	61666	20248	B-iii03	3	3							undetermined	indeterminate bone fragment
50702	10	61666	20248	B-iii03	2	3							undetermined	indeterminate bone fragment
50703	10	61536	20003	B-iii03	4	2							*Rangifer*	detached tine
50704	10	60950	20003	B-iii03	2	3							cf. *Mammuthus*	2 small conjoining cranial fragments
50705	10	60996	20003	B-iii03	2	3							undetermined	rib midshaft fragment
50706	10	61633	20252	B-iii03	4	3							*Mammuthus*	rib midshaft fragment
50707a	10	61276	20003	B-iii03	4	4							*Mammuthus*	cranial fragment
50707b	10	61276	20003	B-iii03	5	4							*Mammuthus*	cranial fragment
50708	1B	61338	20003	B-iii03	3	5							undetermined	indeterminate bone fragment
50709	10	60996	20003	B-iii03	3	2		ü					*Mammuthus*	2 tusk fragments
50710	10	61535	20003	B-iii03	3	4							cf. *Mammuthus*	2 indeterminate long bone fragments
50712	10	61386	20003	B-iii03	1	1							undetermined	small cranial fragment
50713	10	61386	20003	B-iii03	1	3							cf. *Mammuthus*	2 small conjoining cranial fragments
50714	10	61386	20003	B-iii03	2	3							undetermined	very small indeterminate bone fragment
50715	10	61385	20003	B-iii03	1	3							undetermined	small cranial fragment

APPENDIX 4

Table A4.4 Individual vertebrate finds: boxes 1–19 provided directly from Gressenhall; boxes with 'B' after the number came from Bradford; 'Spec.' denotes 'Special Box' built by Bradford; 'pj' = plaster jacket; 'C' = Crate. Note 1: not in a numbered box, brought in by Nigel Larkin – continued

object no.	box	split no.	context no.	facies	size	weathering	iron staining	abrasion	root damage	carnivore gnawing	rodent gnawing	deliberate fracturing	taxon	element
50716	10	61385	20003	B-iii:03	3	3							cf. Mammuthus	cranial fragment
50717	10	61385	20003	B-iii:03	4	3							Mammuthus	cranial fragment
50718	10	61385+61388	20003	B-iii:03	5	3							Mammuthus	large cranial fragment
50719	10	61384	20003	B-iii:03	2	3							Mammuthus	small tusk fragment
50720	10	61384	20003	B-iii:03	2	3							Mammuthus	small tusk fragment
50721	10	61387	20003	B-iii:03	1	3							undetermined	small cranial fragment
50722	10	61387	20003	B-iii:03	2	3							cf. Mammuthus	small bone fragment, possibly cranial
50723	10	61387	20003	B-iii:03	3	3							Mammuthus	tusk fragment
50724	10	61387	20003	B-iii:03	2	2							undetermined	cranial fragment
50725	10	61387	20003	B-iii:03	1	5							undetermined	very small indeterminate bone fragment
50726	10	61387	20003	B-iii:03	2	5							cf. Mammuthus	very small bone fragment, possibly cranial
50727	10	61387	20003	B-iii:03	1	5							cf. Mammuthus	very small bone fragment, possibly cranial
50728	10	61387	20003	B-iii:03	1	3							undetermined	very small indeterminate bone fragment
50729	10	61387	20003	B-iii:03	2	3							cf. Mammuthus	2 small cranial fragments
50730	10	60947	20003	B-iii:03	2	3							cf. Mammuthus	small cranial fragment
50731	10	60947	20003	B-iii:03	1	3							undetermined	small indeterminate bone fragment
50732	10	61482	20003	B-iii:03	3	5							Mammuthus	cranial fragment
50733	10	61484	20003	B-iii:03	2	3				ü			Mammuthus	2nd phalanx (3rd podial)
50734	10	61485	20003	B-iii:03	3	2							Mammuthus	molar plate fragment
50735	10	60947	20003	B-iii:03	1	2							Mammuthus	very small molar plate fragment
50736	10	61547	20003	B-iii:03	3	3							Mammuthus	cranial fragments
50737	10	61635	20252	B-iii:03	2	3							Mammuthus	cranial fragment

continued ▲

Table A4.4 Individual vertebrate finds: boxes 1–19 provided directly from Gressenhall; boxes with 'B' after the number came from Bradford; 'Spec.' denotes 'Special Box' built by Bradford; 'pj' = plaster jacket; 'C' = Crate. Note 1: not in a numbered box, brought in by Nigel Larkin – continued

object no.	box	spit no.	context no.	facies	size	weathering	iron staining	abrasion	root damage	carnivore gnawing	rodent gnawing	deliberate fracturing	taxon	element
50738	10	61635	20252	B-iii:03	1	2							Mammuthus	small tusk fragment
50739	10	61635	20252	B-iii:03	2	3							Mammuthus	small cranial fragments
50740	10	61635	20252	B-iii:03	2	3							undetermined	small cranial fragment
50741	10	61636	20252	B-iii:03	2	3							undetermined	small cranial fragment
50742	10	61636	20252	B-iii:03	3	3							cf. Mammuthus	rib midshaft fragment
50743	10	61852	20003	B-iii:03	5	2							Mammuthus	large cranial fragment
50744	10	61549	20003	B-iii:03	3	2							Mammuthus	auditory bulla
50745	10	61640	20252	B-iii:03	-	-							cf. Crocuta	very comminuted possible coprolite
50746	10	61000	20003	B-iii:03	4	3							Mammuthus	tusk fragment
50747	10	61000	20003	B-iii:03	5	4							Mammuthus	tusk fragments
50748	10	60946	20003	B-iii:03	2	3							Mammuthus	cranial fragment
50749	30B	61338	20003	B-iii:03	6	3				ü			Mammuthus	?femoral shaft, split longitudinally
50750	10	61338	20003	B-iii:03	3	2							Mammuthus	tusk fragment
50751	10	61339	20003	B-iii:03	3	2							Mammuthus	molar plate fragment
50752	10	61640	20252	B-iii:03	2	3							Mammuthus	cranial fragment
50753	10	61639	20252	B-iii:03	3	2							Mammuthus	cranial fragment
50754	10	61639	20252	B-iii:03	3	3							cf. Mammuthus	cranial fragment
50755	10	61488	20003	B-iii:03	3	3							Mammuthus	rib midshaft fragment, probably from same specimen as 50756
50756	10	61488	20003	B-iii:03	4	3				ü			Mammuthus	rib midshaft fragment, probably from same specimen as 50755
50757	10	61488	20003	B-iii:03	3	3							Mammuthus	rib midshaft fragment
50758	10	60946	20003	B-iii:03	2	3				ü			undetermined	small indeterminate bone fragment

APPENDIX 4

Table A4.4 Individual vertebrate finds: boxes 1–19 provided directly from Gressenhall; boxes with 'B' after the number came from Bradford; 'Spec.' denotes 'Special Box' built by Bradford; 'pj' = plaster jacket; 'C' = Crate. Note 1: not in a numbered box, brought in by Nigel Larkin – continued

object no.	box	split no.	context no.	facies	size	weathering	iron staining	abrasion	root damage	carnivore gnawing	rodent gnawing	deliberate fracturing	taxon	element
50759	10	60946	20003	B-iii03	4	3							cf. Mammuthus	rib midshaft fragment
50761	10	60945	20003	B-iii03	1	3							undetermined	very small indeterminate bone fragment
50763	10	60945	20003	B-iii03	1	2							undetermined	indeterminate bone fragment
50764	13B	61765	20003	B-iii03	2	5							Mammuthus	very comminuted tusk fragments
50765	10	61387	20003	B-iii03	1	3							undetermined	2 very small conjoining bone fragments
50767	10	61388	20003	B-iii03	2	2							undetermined	small cranial fragment
50768	10	61388	20003	B-iii03	2	3							Mammuthus	small tusk fragment
50769	10	61389	20003	B-iii03	1	3							undetermined	small cranial fragment
50770	10	61389	20003	B-iii03	1	5							undetermined	small indeterminate bone fragment
50771	10	unstratified	20245	B-iii01	1	3							Rangifer	2nd phalanx, lacks distal
50772	10	61854	20003	B-iii03	2	3							Mammuthus	cranial fragment
50773	10	61854	20003	B-iii03	2	2							Mammuthus	small cranial fragment
50774	10	61854	20003	B-iii03	2	3							undetermined	2 small cranial fragments
50775	10	61389	20003	B-iii03	1	5							cf. Mammuthus	2 small conjoining cranial fragments
50776	10	61389	20003	B-iii03	2	3							undetermined	small indeterminate bone fragment, possibly cranial
50777	10	61389	20003	B-iii03	2	3							Mammuthus	small tusk fragment
50778	10	61389	20003	B-iii03	2	3							Mammuthus	small cranial fragment
50779	10	61389	20003	B-iii03	2	3							undetermined	cranial fragment
50780	10	60945	20003	B-iii03	2	3							undetermined	very small indeterminate bone fragment
50781	10	60945	20003	B-iii03	2	3							undetermined	very small indeterminate bone fragment
50782	10	60945	20003	B-iii03	3	3							Mammuthus	molar talon fragment

continued

Table A4.4 Individual vertebrate finds: boxes 1–19 provided directly from Gressenhall; boxes with 'B' after the number came from Bradford; 'Spec.' denotes 'Special Box' built by Bradford; 'pj' = plaster jacket; 'C' = Crate. Note 1: not in a numbered box, brought in by Nigel Larkin – continued

object no.	box	split no.	context no.	facies	size	weathering	iron staining	abrasion	root damage	carnivore gnawing	rodent gnawing	deliberate fracturing	taxon	element
50783	10	60945	20003	B-iii:03	1	3							Mammuthus	very small molar plate fragment
50784	10	61489	20003	B-iii:03	3	5							Mammuthus	small cranial fragment
50785	10	60945	20003	B-iii:03	2	2							undetermined	2 small cranial fragments
50786	10	60948	20003	B-iii:03	1	5							undetermined	multiple small cranial fragments
50787	10	60948	20003	B-iii:03	2	3							undetermined	3 small indeterminate bone fragments
50788	10	60949	20003	B-iii:03	2	3		ü					?Rangifer	tibia midshaft fragment
50789	10	61135	20003	B-iii:03	1	3							undetermined	small indeterminate bone fragment
50790	10	61133	20003	B-iii:03	2	3							Mammuthus	small cranial fragments
50791	10	61133	20003	B-iii:03	2	2							? Rangifer	? vertebral fragment
50792	10	61133	20003	B-iii:03	2	3							Mammuthus	small tusk fragment
50793	27B	62002	20245	B-iii:01	5	3							Mammuthus	large anterior rib midsection
50794	10	62102	20003	B-iii:03	1	1							Ursus	broken tip of upper canine; sampled for isotopes
50795	10	61642	20258	B-iii:03	1	1				ü			Rangifer	R dp2
50796	10	61243	20258	B-iii:03	2	2							undetermined	vertebral fragment
50797	10	61243	20258	B-iii:03	2	.2							Mammuthus	small tusk fragment
50798	10	61242	20258	B-iii:03	3	3							cf. Mammuthus	cranial fragment
50799	10	61856	20003	B-iii:03	3	3							Mammuthus	multiple cranial fragments
50800	1B	61772	20003	B-iii:03	1	5							undetermined	very small indeterminate bone fragments
50801	11	60949	20003	B-iii:03	1	3							Mammuthus	molar root fragment
50802	11	60949	20003	B-iii:03	1	3							undetermined	very small indeterminate bone fragment
50803	11	60949	20003	B-iii:03	1	3							undetermined	very small indeterminate bone fragments

APPENDIX 4

Table A4.4 Individual vertebrate finds: boxes 1–19 provided directly from Gressenhall; boxes with 'B' after the number came from Bradford; 'Spec.' denotes 'Special Box' built by Bradford; 'pj' = plaster jacket; 'C' = Crate. Note 1: not in a numbered box, brought in by Nigel Larkin – continued

object no.	box	spit no.	context no.	facies	size	weathering	iron staining	abrasion	root damage	carnivore gnawing	rodent gnawing	deliberate fracturing	taxon	element
50804	11	61481	20003	B-iii03	3	4							Mammuthus	small tusk fragment
50805	11	61392	20003	B-iii03	2	3							undetermined	small cranial fragment
50806	11	61343	20003	B-iii03	3	4							undetermined	fragment of flat bone
50807	11	61343	20003	B-iii03	2	2							Mammuthus	small tusk fragment
50808	11	61343	20003	B-iii03	2	3							Mammuthus	small tusk fragment
50809	11	61343	20003	B-iii03	3	3							Mammuthus	small tusk fragment
50810	B		20003	B-iii03									Mammuthus	tusk fragments
50811	B		20003	B-iii03									Mammuthus	tusk fragments
50812	11	61903	20003	B-iii03	3	3							Mammuthus	2 small tusk fragments
50813	11	61641	20258	B-iii03	4	3			ü				cf. Mammuthus	small fragment of indeterminate long bone
50814	11	61644	20258	B-iii03	2	3							undetermined	small cranial fragment
50815	1B	61646	20258	B-iii03	2	3							undetermined	cranial fragment
50816	39B	61648	20252	B-iii03	6	2							Mammuthus	large and small fragments of tusk
50817	1B	61392	20003	B-iii03	2	4							Mammuthus	small tusk fragment
50818	11	61392	20003	B-iii03	2	2							undetermined	small cranial fragment
50819	11	61905	20003	B-iii03	2	3							Mammuthus	small molar plate fragment
50820	11	61344	20003	B-iii03	2	3		ü					undetermined	4 small indeterminate bone fragments
50821	1B	61490	20003	B-iii03	6	3							Mammuthus	cranial fragment
50822	1B	61490	20003	B-iii03	3	3							Mammuthus	cranial fragment
50823	11	61626	20252	B-iii03	2	2						ü	Rangifer	fragmentary proximal R femur
50824	11	61906	20003	B-iii03	6	4							Mammuthus	tusk fragments

continued ▶

Table A4.4 Individual vertebrate finds: boxes 1–19 provided directly from Gressenhall; boxes with 'B' after the number came from Bradford; 'Spec.' denotes 'Special Box' built by Bradford; 'pj' = plaster jacket; 'C' = Crate. Note 1: not in a numbered box, brought in by Nigel Larkin – continued

object no.	box	spit no.	context no.	facies	size	weathering	iron staining	abrasion	root damage	carnivore gnawing	rodent gnawing	deliberate fracturing	taxon	element
50826	11	62153	20003	B-ii03	2	3		ü					Mammuthus	small fragment of indeterminate long bone
50827	11	61649	20003	B-ii03	2	3							Mammuthus	small cranial fragment
50828	14B	61906	20003	B-ii03	6	3							Mammuthus	tusk fragments
50829	11	61392	20003	B-ii03	2	3							undetermined	small cranial fragment
50830	11	61391	20003	B-ii03	2	3							Mammuthus	small cranial fragment
50831	11	62105	20003	B-ii03	2	2							Mammuthus	small tusk fragment
50832	11	61344	20003	B-ii03	1	2							Rangifer	fragment of neural spine with posterior zygapophyses
50833	1B	61497	20003	B-ii03	4	3							Mammuthus	maxilla fragment
50834	13B	61344	20003	B-ii03	6	3							Mammuthus	tusk fragments
50835	11	61344	20003	B-ii03	6	2							Mammuthus	large tusk fragments
50836	11	61344	20003	B-ii03	2	4							cf. Rangifer	3 small antler base fragments, 2 conjoining
50837	11	61344	20003	B-ii03	1	2							undetermined	small bone fragment, ?vertebral
50838	1B	61907	20003	B-ii03	3	3							Mammuthus	sternal fragment
50839	1B	61907	20003	B-ii03	3	4							Mammuthus	sternal fragment
50840	1B	61345	20003	B-ii03	3	2							Mammuthus	small fragment of indeterminate long bone
50841	11	61345	20003	B-ii03	2	3							Mammuthus	small tusk fragment
50842	1B	61650	20258	B-ii03	5	4							Mammuthus	cranial fragment
50843	11	61953	20258	B-ii03	3	3							Mammuthus	small cranial fragment
50844	11	61952	20258	B-ii03	2	3			ü				?Rangifer	?tibia midshaft fragment
50845	11	61647	20003	B-ii03	2	3							Mammuthus	small tusk fragment
50846	1B	61544	20003	B-ii03	3	3							Mammuthus	cranial fragment

APPENDIX 4

Table A4.4 Individual vertebrate finds: boxes 1–19 provided directly from Gressenhall; boxes with 'B' after the number came from Bradford; 'Spec.' denotes 'Special Box' built by Bradford; 'pj' = plaster jacket; 'C' = Crate. Note 1: not in a numbered box, brought in by Nigel Larkin – continued

object no.	box	split no.	context no.	facies	size	weathering	iron staining	abrasion	root damage	carnivore gnawing	rodent gnawing	deliberate fracturing	taxon	element
50847a	28B	61283	20003	B-iii:03	6	4							Mammuthus	cranial fragment with part of tusk alveolus
50847b	11	61283	20003	B-iii:03	5	4							Mammuthus	large cranial fragment
50847c	28B	61283	20003	B-iii:03	6	4							Mammuthus	large cranial fragment with part of jugal
50848	11	61283	20003	B-iii:03	6	3							Mammuthus	large cranial fragment
50849	11	62106	20003	B-iii:03	2	5		ü					undetermined	small bone fragment, probably cranial
50850	11	62106	20003	B-iii:03	2	3							undetermined	indeterminate small bone fragment
50851	11	61908	20003	B-iii:03	2	2							Mammuthus	small tusk fragment
50852	11	61908	20003	B-iii:03	2	3							Mammuthus	small tusk fragment
50853	33B	61953	20258	B-iii:03	5	2							Mammuthus	base of neural spine of thoracic/lumbar vertebra
50854	11	61857	20003	B-iii:03	2	3							undetermined	indeterminate small bone fragment
50855	11	61857	20003	B-iii:03	2	3							undetermined	small cranial fragment
50856	11	61857	20003	B-iii:03	3	3							Mammuthus	large cranial fragment
50857	11	61857	20003	B-iii:03	4	3							Mammuthus	small bone fragment, probably cranial
50858	11	62106	20003	B-iii:03	2	3							undetermined	indeterminate small bone fragment
50859	11	62106	20003	B-iii:03	1	3							undetermined	2 very small indeterminate bone fragments
50860	11	62106	20003	B-iii:03	1	3							undetermined	indeterminate small bone fragment
50861	11	62106	20003	B-iii:03	1	2							undetermined	indeterminate small bone fragment
50862	11	62106	20003	B-iii:03	1	2							Mammuthus	very small tusk fragment
50863	11	61909	20003	B-iii:03	2	3							Mammuthus	small cranial fragment
50864	11	61908	20003	B-iii:03	3	2							Mammuthus	2 small tusk fragments
50865	11	61131	20003	B-iii:03	2	3							Mammuthus	small tusk fragment

continued ▶

Table A4.4 Individual vertebrate finds: boxes 1–19 provided directly from Gressenhall; boxes with 'B' after the number came from Bradford; 'Spec.' denotes 'Special Box' built by Bradford; 'pj' = plaster jacket; 'C' = Crate. Note 1: not in a numbered box, brought in by Nigel Larkin – continued

object no.	box	spit no.	context no.	facies	size	weathering	iron staining	abrasion	root damage	carnivore gnawing	rodent gnawing	deliberate fracturing	taxon	element
50866	11	61131	20003	B-iii:03	2	3							*Mammuthus*	small tusk fragments
50867	11	61132	20003	B-iii:03	1	3							undetermined	very small fragments, probably cranial
50868	11	61134	20003	B-iii:03	2	4							undetermined	small cranial fragment
50869	11	61957	20258	B-iii:03	6	1							*Rangifer*	complete L metacarpal
50870	11	61957	20258	B-iii:03	3	3							*Mammuthus*	small cranial fragment
50871	11	61391	20003	B-iii:03	3	4							undetermined	2 very small indeterminate bone fragments
50872	11	61910	20003	B-iii:03	3	4							*Mammuthus*	small tusk fragment
50873	11	61910	20003	B-iii:03	2	2							*Mammuthus*	small fragment of central core of tusk
50874	11	61910	20003	B-iii:03	2	3							*Mammuthus*	small tusk fragment
50875	11	61904	20003	B-iii:03	3	4							cf. *Mammuthus*	small fragment of indeterminate long bone
50876	11	61130	20003	B-iii:03	1	4							undetermined	small cranial fragment
50877	11	61131e	20003	B-iii:03	1	3							*Mammuthus*	small molar fragment
50878	1B	61956	20258	B-iii:03	2	3							cf. *Mammuthus*	cranial fragment
50879	11	61911	20003	B-iii:03	3	3							*Mammuthus*	small cranial fragment
50880	11	62106	20003	B-iii:03	1	2							*Mammuthus*	2 small tusk fragments
50881	11	62106	20003	B-iii:03	1	3							undetermined	indeterminate small bone fragment
50882	11	62106	20003	B-iii:03	1	3							undetermined	indeterminate small bone fragment
50883	11	61260	20003	B-iii:03	2	3							undetermined	small fragment of ?rib midshaft
50884	11	60383	20003	B-iii:03	2	3							undetermined	2 small indeterminate bone fragments
50885	11	61911	20003	B-iii:03	2	5							*Mammuthus*	small cranial fragment
50886	11	61911	20003	B-iii:03	2	3							cf. *Mammuthus*	small cranial fragment
50887	11	61129	20003	B-iii:03	2	4							cf. *Mammuthus*	small cranial fragment

APPENDIX 4

Table A4.4 Individual vertebrate finds: boxes 1–19 provided directly from Gressenhall; boxes with 'B' after the number came from Bradford; 'Spec.' denotes 'Special Box' built by Bradford; 'pj' = plaster jacket; 'C' = Crate. Note 1: not in a numbered box, brought in by Nigel Larkin – continued

object no.	box	split no.	context no.	facies	size	weathering	iron staining	abrasion	root damage	carnivore gnawing	rodent gnawing	deliberate fracturing	taxon	element
50888	11	62107	20003	B-iii:O3	2	2							Ursus	partial root and enamel fragment of right upper canine
50889	11	62107	20003	B-iii:O3	1	5							undetermined	indeterminate small bone fragment
50890	11	62107	20003	B-iii:O3	2	3							undetermined	small indeterminate bone fragment
50891	11	62107	20003	B-iii:O3	2	4							undetermined	small indeterminate bone fragment
50892	11	62107	20003	B-iii:O3	2	2							undetermined	small indeterminate bone fragment
50894	11	61262	20003	B-iii:O3	1	3							Mammuthus	small tusk fragment
50895	11B	61813	20003	B-iii:O3	4	4							Coelodonta	medial distal articulation of R humerus
50896	11	61913	20003	B-iii:O3	3	2							Mammuthus	tusk fragment
50897	11	61394	20252	B-iii:O3	1	3							undetermined	very small indeterminate bone fragments
50898	11	61394	20252	B-iii:O3	1	3							undetermined	very small cranial fragments
50899	11	61394	20252	B-iii:O3	1	3							undetermined	very small cranial fragment
50900	11	61394	20252	B-iii:O3	1	3							undetermined	very small fragments, probably cranial
50901	11	61394	20252	B-iii:O3	1	3							undetermined	very small indeterminate bone fragments
50902	11	61395	20252	B-iii:O3	1	3							Mammuthus	very small indeterminate bone fragments
50903	11	61395	20252	B-iii:O3	1	3							Mammuthus	very small tusk fragment
50904	11	61395	20252	B-iii:O3	1	2							undetermined	2 small cranial fragments
50905	1B	61395	20252	B-iii:O3	1	4							Mammuthus	very small tusk fragments
50906	11	61395	20252	B-iii:O3	1	2							Rangifer	L m3
50907	11	61395	20252	B-iii:O3	1	3							Mammuthus	small tusk fragment
50908	11	61396	20252	B-iii:O3	2	2							Mammuthus	small tusk fragment
50909	1B	61394	20252	B-iii:O3	2	3							Mammuthus	cranial fragment

continued

Table A4.4 Individual vertebrate finds: boxes 1–19 provided directly from Gressenhall; boxes with 'B' after the number came from Bradford; 'Spec.' denotes 'Special Box' built by Bradford; 'pj' = plaster jacket; 'C' = Crate. Note 1: not in a numbered box, brought in by Nigel Larkin – continued

object no.	box	split no.	context no.	facies	size	weathering	iron staining	abrasion	root damage	carnivore gnawing	rodent gnawing	deliberate fracturing	taxon	element
50910	11	61397	20252	B-iii:03	1	2							undetermined	very small and thin cranial fragment, possible nasal scroll bone
50911	11	61397	20252	B-iii:03	1	3							undetermined	small indeterminate bone fragment
50912	11	61397	20252	B-iii:03	2	3							Mammuthus	small cranial fragment
50913	11	61397	20252	B-iii:03	2	3							Mammuthus	small tusk fragment
50914	spec 2	61397	20252	B-iii:03	6	3							Mammuthus	posterior thoracic vertebra, lacks both central epiphyses
50915	11	61858	20003	B-iii:03	2	4							undetermined	small cranial fragment
50916	11	61858	20003	B-iii:03	2	3							undetermined	small cranial fragments
50918	11	60384	20003	B-iii:03	2	3							Mammuthus	small tusk fragment
50919	11	60384	20003	B-iii:03	1	2							undetermined	small cranial fragment
50920	11	60384	20003	B-iii:03	3	3							large mammal	cranial fragment
50921	11	62107	20003	B-iii:03	1	3							undetermined	very small indeterminate bone fragment
50922	11	62107	20003	B-iii:03	1	2							undetermined	very small indeterminate bone fragment
50923	11	62107	20003	B-iii:03	1	3							undetermined	very small cranial fragment
50925	11	61268	20003	B-iii:03	3	4							Mammuthus	small fragment of indeterminate long bone
50926	11	61267	20003	B-iii:03	2	3							Mammuthus	small fragment of indeterminate long bone
50927	11	61267	20003	B-iii:03	2	3							undetermined	indeterminate bone fragment
50928	11	61266	20003	B-iii:03	2	3							undetermined	indeterminate bone fragment
50929	11	60383	20003	B-iii:03	6	4		ü					Bovini, cf. Bison	posterior part of L metatarsal proximal midshaft
50930	11	61913	20003	B-iii:03	2	3							Rangifer	detached tine
50931	11	62108	20003	B-iii:03	2	3							Mammuthus	small fragment of indeterminate long bone

APPENDIX 4

Table A4.4 Individual vertebrate finds: boxes 1–19 provided directly from Gressenhall; boxes with 'B' after the number came from Bradford; 'Spec.' denotes 'Special Box' built by Bradford; 'pj' = plaster jacket; 'C' = Crate. Note 1: not in a numbered box, brought in by Nigel Larkin – continued

object no.	box	split no.	context no.	facies	size	weathering	iron staining	abrasion	root damage	carnivore gnawing	rodent gnawing	deliberate fracturing	taxon	element
50932	11	62108	20003	B-iii:O3	1	3							undetermined	very small indeterminate bone fragment
50933	11	62108	20003	B-iii:O3	2	3							undetermined	indeterminate bone fragment
50934	11	62108	20003	B-iii:O3	2	3							undetermined	2 small conjoining indeterminate bone fragments
50935	11	62108	20003	B-iii:O3	2	3							cf. Mammuthus	small fragment of indeterminate long bone
50936	11	62108	20003	B-iii:O3	1	3							undetermined	indeterminate bone fragment
50937	11	62108	20003	B-iii:O3	2	3							cf. Mammuthus	small rib midshaft fragment
50938	11	62108	20003	B-iii:O3	2	3							Mammuthus	molar plate fragment
50939	13B	61346	20003	B-iii:O3	4	3							Mammuthus	tusk fragments
50940	11	61346	20003	B-iii:O3	5	4							Mammuthus	tusk fragment
50941	11	61346	20003	B-iii:O3	2	2							Mammuthus	tusk fragment
50942	11	61346	20003	B-iii:O3	4	3							Mammuthus	molar plate fragment
50943	11	61346	20003	B-iii:O3	3	3							undetermined	indeterminate bone fragment
50944	11	62251	20003	B-iii:O3	3	3							Mammuthus	cranial fragment
50945	11	60384	20003	B-iii:O3	2	2							undetermined	cranial fragment
50946	11	60385	20003	B-iii:O3	2	3							cf. Mammuthus	small cranial fragments
50947	11	60385	20003	B-iii:O3	1	3							undetermined	small cranial fragment
50948a	11	60386	20003	B-iii:O3	4	3							undetermined	proximal rib midshaft fragment, posterior rib
50948b	11	60386	20003	B-iii:O3	5	3							Mammuthus	large cranial fragment
50950	1B	62253	20003	B-iii:O3	2	3							Mammuthus	cranial fragments
50951a	72B	61124+61132	20003	B-iii:O3	4	4							Mammuthus	multiple very comminuted tusk fragments
50951b	11	61124+61132	20003	B-iii:O3	5	3							Mammuthus	multiple tusk fragments

continued

Table A4.4 Individual vertebrate finds: boxes 1–19 provided directly from Gressenhall; boxes with 'B' after the number came from Bradford; 'Spec.' denotes 'Special Box' built by Bradford; 'pj' = plaster jacket; 'C' = Crate. Note 1: not in a numbered box, brought in by Nigel Larkin – continued

object no.	box	spit no.	context no.	facies	size	weathering	iron staining	abrasion	root damage	carnivore gnawing	rodent gnawing	deliberate fracturing	taxon	element
50951c	76B	61124+61132	20003	B-iii:03	5	4							Mammuthus	2 fragments, not conjoining, from central part of tusk
50952	1B	61498	20003	B-iii:03	5	4							Mammuthus	2 conjoining cranial fragments
50953	11	61490	20003	B-iii:03	3	3							Mammuthus	small cranial fragment
50954	11	62108	20003	B-iii:03	1	3							Mammuthus	very small molar plate fragment
50955	11	62108	20003	B-iii:03	3	3							cf. Mammuthus	small fragment of indeterminate long bone
50956	11	62108	20003	B-iii:03	3	4							Mammuthus	tusk fragment
50957	11	62108	20003	B-iii:03	2	3							undetermined	small rib midshaft fragment
50958	11	62108	20003	B-iii:03	2	3							Mammuthus	small tusk fragment
50959	11	60385	20003	B-iii:03	2	3							undetermined	3 small cranial fragments
50960	11	60386	20003	B-iii:03	2	3							undetermined	small cranial fragment
50961	11	62253	20003	B-iii:03	2	3							undetermined	small cranial fragment
50962	11	62302	20003	B-iii:03	2	2							Rangifer	fragment of L acetabulum
50963	1B	62302	20003	B-iii:03	2	4							undetermined	cranial fragment
50965	11	61804	20003	B-iii:03	1	3							undetermined	3 small cranial fragments
50966	11	61860	20003	B-iii:03	2	3							undetermined	4 small indeterminate bone fragments
50967	11	61860	20003	B-iii:03	3	4							large mammal	multiple cranial fragments
50968	11	61860	20003	B-iii:03	2	3							Mammuthus	cranial fragment
50969	11	61858	20003	B-iii:03	4	3							Mammuthus	large cranial fragments
50970	11B	61858	20003	B-iii:03	4	4							Mammuthus	cranial fragments
50971	11	61858	20003	B-iii:03	2	3							cf. Mammuthus	small bone fragment, probably cranial
50973	1B	62010	20254	B-iii:01	4	3						ü	undetermined	indeterminate bone fragment

APPENDIX 4

Table A4.4 Individual vertebrate finds: boxes 1–19 provided directly from Gressenhall; boxes with 'B' after the number came from Bradford; 'Spec.' denotes 'Special Box' built by Bradford; 'pj' = plaster jacket; 'C' = Crate. Note 1: not in a numbered box, brought in by Nigel Larkin – continued

object no.	box	spit no.	context no.	facies	size	weathering	iron staining	abrasion	root damage	carnivore gnawing	rodent gnawing	deliberate fracturing	taxon	element
50974	1B	60385	20003	B-iii03	4	4							Mammuthus	cranial fragment
50975	1B	60385	20003	B-iii03	3	3							Mammuthus	2 cranial fragments
50976	1B	61915	20003	B-iii03	4	5							Mammuthus	tusk fragment
50977	spec 3	61854	20003	B-iii03	6	3				ü			Mammuthus	midshaft of middle rib (missing both ends)
50978	11	61398	20252	B-iii03	2	2							undetermined	small cranial fragment
50979	11	61398	20252	B-iii03	2	5							cf. Mammuthus	small cranial fragment
50980	11	61398	20252	B-iii03	3	5							Mammuthus	epiphyseal fragment of vertebral centrum
50981	11	61398	20252	B-iii03	2	5							Mammuthus	epiphyseal fragment of vertebral centrum, conjoins with 50980
50982	11	61398	20252	B-iii03	2	4							undetermined	small cranial fragment
50983	11	61398	20252	B-iii03	2	3							undetermined	indeterminate small bone fragment
50984	11	61398	20252	B-iii03	1	5							undetermined	4 small indeterminate bone fragments
50985	11	61398	20252	B-iii03	3	4							Mammuthus	tusk fragment
50986	11	61398	20252	B-iii03	2	3							Mammuthus	small cranial fragment
50987	11	61398	20252	B-iii03	2	3							Mammuthus	small cranial fragment
50988	11	61399	20252	B-iii03	2	3							undetermined	small cranial fragment
50989	11	61399	20252	B-iii03	2	3							Mammuthus	small tusk fragment
50990	11	61399	20252	B-iii03	3	3							Mammuthus	small cranial fragment
50991	11	61400	20252	B-iii03	2	2							Mammuthus	small tusk fragment
50992	11	62401	20252	B-iii03	2	1							undetermined	small cranial fragment
50993	11	61807	20003	B-iii03	2	5							undetermined	multiple small indeterminate bone fragments
50994	11	62110	20003	B-iii03	2	3							undetermined	4 small indeterminate bone fragments

continued ▶

Table A4.4 Individual vertebrate finds: boxes 1–19 provided directly from Gressenhall; boxes with 'B' after the number came from Bradford; 'Spec.' denotes 'Special Box' built by Bradford; 'pj' = plaster jacket; 'C' = Crate. Note 1: not in a numbered box, brought in by Nigel Larkin – continued

object no.	box	split no.	context no.	facies	size	weathering	iron staining	abrasion	root damage	carnivore gnawing	rodent gnawing	deliberate fracturing	taxon	element
50995	11	61488	20003	B-iii03	1	2							Crocuta	posterior part of very worn L p4
50996	11	61806	20003	B-iii03	3	3						ü	Rangifer	underside of ?R mandibular ramus
50997	11	61281	20003	B-iii03	2	3							Mammuthus	small tusk fragment
50998	11	61398	20252	B-iii03	2	3							cf. Mammuthus	small cranial fragment
50999	11	61398	20252	B-iii03	2	3							Mammuthus	small tusk fragment
51000	12	61399	20252	B-iii03	2	3							undetermined	small indeterminate cranial fragment
51001	12	61400	20252	B-iii03	2	3							undetermined	small indeterminate bone fragment
51002	12	61857	20003	B-iii03	3	5							undetermined	cranial fragment
51003	12	62304	20003	B-iii03	2	3							Mammuthus	molar plate fragment
51004	12	61347	20003	B-iii03	2	4							undetermined	small indeterminate bone fragment
51005	12	61347	20003	B-iii03	2	4							Mammuthus	internal tusk fragment
51006	1B	61347	20003	B-iii03	2	4							Mammuthus	tusk fragment
51007	12	61347	20003	B-iii03	2	4							Mammuthus	tusk fragment
51008	12	61347	20003	B-iii03	3	4							Mammuthus	tusk fragment
51009	1B	61347	20003	B-iii03	4	5							Mammuthus	tusk fragment
51010	12	61347	20003	B-iii03	4	3							Mammuthus	tusk fragment
51011	12	61347	20003	B-iii03	3	4							Mammuthus	tusk fragment
51012	12	61347	20003	B-iii03	2	4							Mammuthus	tusk fragment
51013	12	61347	20003	B-iii03	1	2							Mammuthus	very small tusk fragment
51014	12	62255	20003	B-iii03	3	3							Mammuthus ?	rib midshaft fragment
51015	1B	61285	20003	B-iii03	2	5	ü						undetermined	indeterminate bone fragment
51016	12	61280	20003	B-iii03	2	3							Mammuthus ?	small bone fragment, probably cranial

APPENDIX 4

Table A4.4 Individual vertebrate finds: boxes 1–19 provided directly from Gressenhall; boxes with 'B' after the number came from Bradford; 'Spec.' denotes 'Special Box' built by Bradford; 'pj' = plaster jacket; 'C' = Crate. Note 1: not in a numbered box, brought in by Nigel Larkin – continued

object no.	box	spit no.	context no.	facies	size	weathering	iron staining	abrasion	root damage	carnivore gnawing	rodent gnawing	deliberate fracturing	taxon	element
51017	12	61286	20003	B-iii03	2	4							undetermined	small indeterminate bone fragment
51018	1B	62018	20254	B-iii01	1	5							undetermined	indeterminate small bone fragments
51019	12	62021	20254	B-iii01	3	4							Mammuthus	distal rib fragments
51020	1B	62021	20254	B-iii01	1	4							undetermined	cranial fragments
51021	1B	62017	20254	B-iii01	3	3							Mammuthus	proximal epiphysis of rib
51022	12	unstratified	20003	B-iii03	3	2							Mammuthus	tusk fragments
51023	12	62305	20003	B-iii03	6	2							Rangifer	L acetabulum, incomplete ilium and ischium; sampled for isotopes
51024	18B	62305	20003	B-iii03	6	3					ü		Mammuthus	femoral head, unfused
51025	9B	61285	20003	B-iii03	6	4							Mammuthus	cranial fragment
51026	12	61285	20003	B-iii03	2	3							Cervidae	antler fragment
51027	12	62256	20003	B-iii03	4	3							cf. Mammuthus	cranial fragment
51028	12	unstratified	20247	B-iii04	2	5							undetermined	small indeterminate bone fragment
51029	12	unstratified	20247	B-iii04	1	3		ü					Mammuthus	very small tusk fragment
51030	15B	61682	20247	B-iii04	4	5							Mammuthus	indeterminate fragments of large long bone
51031	12	61682	20247	B-iii04	3	4							Mammuthus	indeterminate fragment of large long bone, probably same as 51032
51032	12	61682	20247	B-iii04	6	4							Mammuthus	indeterminate fragment of large long bone, probably same as 51031
51033	12	62113	20003	B-iii03	2	3							undetermined	indeterminate bone fragment
51034	12	61682	20247	B-iii04	3	4							undetermined	indeterminate bone fragment
51035	12	61683	20247	B-iii04	2	3							undetermined	rib midshaft fragments
51036	12	61280	20003	B-iii03	1	2							Mammuthus	small tusk fragments

continued ▲

Table A4.4 Individual vertebrate finds: boxes 1–19 provided directly from Gressenhall; boxes with 'B' after the number came from Bradford; 'Spec.' denotes 'Special Box' built by Bradford; 'pj' = plaster jacket; 'C' = Crate. Note 1: not in a numbered box, brought in by Nigel Larkin – continued

object no.	box	spit no.	context no.	facies	size	weathering	iron staining	abrasion	root damage	carnivore gnawing	rodent gnawing	deliberate fracturing	taxon	element
51037	12	61288	20003	B-iii03	1	3							undetermined	2 very small indeterminate bone fragments
51038	5B	unstratified	20364	B-iii01	5	4							Mammuthus	cranial fragments, associated with 51619
51039	12	62113	20003	B-iii03	2	3							Mammuthus	1 small tusk fragment and 2 small indeterminate bone fragments
51040	1B	61284	20003	B-iii03	2	4							undetermined	indeterminate bone fragment
51041	12	61284	20003	B-iii03	3	4							Mammuthus	small indeterminate fragment of large long bone
51042	12	62113	20003	B-iii03	2	3							Mammuthus	small fragment of molar plate
51043	12	61282	20003	B-iii03	1	3							undetermined	small cranial fragment
51044	12	61282	20003	B-iii03	2	2							Mammuthus?	small cranial fragment
51045	12	62113	20003	B-iii03	2	5							undetermined	indeterminate small bone fragment
51046	75B	61770+61801	20003	B-iii03	6	3							Mammuthus	R m3, associated with 51047
51047	75B	61770+61801	20003	B-iii03	6	4							Mammuthus	incomplete lower jaw with L m3 in situ and loose R m3
51048	spec 1	61770	20003	B-iii03	6	4				ü			Mammuthus	rib midshaft
51049	12	61287	20003	B-iii03	2	3							undetermined	indeterminate small bone fragment
51050	12	61287	20003	B-iii03	2	3							undetermined	indeterminate small bone fragment
51051	12	60485	20003	B-iii03	2	3							undetermined	small cranial fragment
51052	11B	61346	20003	B-iii03	4	3							Mammuthus	multiple tusk and small bone fragments
51053	12	61347	20003	B-iii03	2	3							Cervidae	small antler beam fragment
51054	1B	61347	20003	B-iii03	2	4							undetermined	indeterminate bone fragment
51055	12	62302	20003	B-iii03	2	3							undetermined	small cranial fragment
51056	12	61347	20003	B-iii03	3	3							Mammuthus	fragment of R maxilla (behind last molar)

APPENDIX 4

Table A4.4 Individual vertebrate finds: boxes 1–19 provided directly from Gressenhall; boxes with 'B' after the number came from Bradford; 'Spec.' denotes 'Special Box' built by Bradford; 'pj' = plaster jacket; 'C' = Crate. Note 1: not in a numbered box, brought in by Nigel Larkin – continued

object no.	box	spit no.	context no.	facies	size	weathering	iron staining	abrasion	root damage	carnivore gnawing	rodent gnawing	deliberate fracturing	taxon	element
51057	12	61347	20003	B-iii:03	2	2							*Mammuthus*	internal tusk fragment
51058	12	61347	20003	B-iii:03	3	2							*Mammuthus*	tusk fragment
51059	12	60482	20003	B-iii:03	2	3							undetermined	indeterminate bone fragment
51060	12	62115	20003	B-iii:03	2	3							undetermined	3 small indeterminate bone fragments
51061	12	62259	20003	B-iii:03	3	3							*Mammuthus*	multiple small cranial fragments
51062	12	62027	20254	B-iii:01	2	5							undetermined	indeterminate bone fragments
51064	C1	62031	20,254	B-iii:01	6	5							?*Mammuthus*	reconstructed fragmentary bone, possibly cervical vertebra fragment
51065	12	62115	20003	B-iii:03	2	2							*Mammuthus*	small tusk fragment
51066	12	62119	20003	B-iii:03	2	3							undetermined	small indeterminate bone fragment
51067	12	62119	20003	B-iii:03	2	3							undetermined	small indeterminate bone fragment
51068	12	62025	20254	B-iii:01	3	3							*Mammuthus*	proximal epiphysis of rib
51069	12	60387	20003	B-iii:03	2	4							*Mammuthus*	small tusk fragment
51070	1B	62301	20003	B-iii:03	4	3							*Mammuthus*	2 conjoining cranial fragments
51071	12	62316	20003	B-iii:03	1	2							undetermined	very small cranial fragment
51072	12	62316	20003	B-iii:03	3	3				ü			*Mammuthus*	fragment of indeterminate long bone
51073	12	62316	20003	B-iii:03	2	3							undetermined	small indeterminate bone fragment
51074a	spec 1	62260	20003	B-iii:03	6	3							*Mammuthus*	anterior rib (missing distal epiphysis)
51074b	12	61288	20003	B-iii:03	2	3							undetermined	small indeterminate bone fragments
51075	12	62115	20003	B-iii:03	2	1						ü	cf. Cervidae	fragment of femoral diaphysis?
51076	12	62516	20003	B-iii:03	2	3							*Mammuthus*	small indeterminate long bone fragment
51077	12	62516	20003	B-iii:03	2	5							*Mammuthus*	small indeterminate long bone fragment

continued ▲

Table A4.4 Individual vertebrate finds: boxes 1–19 provided directly from Gressenhall; boxes with 'B' after the number came from Bradford; 'Spec.' denotes 'Special Box' built by Bradford; 'pj' = plaster jacket; 'C' = Crate. Note 1: not in a numbered box, brought in by Nigel Larkin – continued

object no.	box	spit no.	context no.	facies	size	weathering	iron staining	abrasion	root damage	carnivore gnawing	rodent gnawing	deliberate fracturing	taxon	element
51078	12	62516	20003	B-iii03	2	3							Mammuthus	small indeterminate long bone fragment
51079	12	60389	20003	B-iii03	4	3							undetermined	indeterminate long bone fragment
51080	6B	60389	20003	B-iii03	4	5							Mammuthus	incomplete occipital condyle
51081	12	62117	20003	B-iii03	2	1							Mammuthus	small tusk fragment
51082	12	62116	20003	B-iii03	2	5							undetermined	small indeterminate bone fragment
51083	12	62116	20003	B-iii03	2	3							Mammuthus	small tusk fragment
51084	12	62117	20003	B-iii03	2	3							undetermined	small rib midshaft fragment
51085	12	62117	20003	B-iii03	2	3							undetermined	small indeterminate bone fragment
51086	12	62319	20003	B-iii03	2	4							undetermined	small cranial fragment
51087	12	62319	20003	B-iii03	3	3							undetermined	small indeterminate bone fragment
51088	12	61298	20003	B-iii03	1	2							Mammuthus	very small tusk fragment
51089	12	61298	20003	B-iii03	2	2							Mammuthus	very small tusk fragment
51090	12	62508	20003	B-iii03	2	2							undetermined	multiple small bone fragments, including some rib midshaft
51091a	12	62508	20003	B-iii03	2	4							Rangifer	antler beam fragment; sampled for isotopes
51091b	71B	62508	20003	B-iii03	6	5							Mammuthus	multiple tusk fragments
51092	12	62508	20003	B-iii03	1	2							Mammuthus	2 very small tusk fragments
51094	12	62512	20003	B-iii03	1	3							Mammuthus	very small tusk alveolus/cranial fragment
51095	12	unstratified	20367	B-iii04	2	4							Mammuthus	multiple small tusk fragments
51096	12	unstratified	20366	B-iii04	3	4							Mammuthus	tusk fragment
51097	12	unstratified	20366	B-iii04	2	4							Mammuthus	small tusk fragments
51098	12	61860	20003	B-iii03	2	2							undetermined	small cranial fragment

APPENDIX 4

Table A4.4 Individual vertebrate finds: boxes 1–19 provided directly from Gressenhall; boxes with 'B' after the number came from Bradford; 'Spec.' denotes 'Special Box' built by Bradford; 'pj' = plaster jacket; 'C' = Crate. Note 1: not in a numbered box, brought in by Nigel Larkin – continued

object no.	box	split no.	context no.	facies	size	weathering	iron staining	abrasion	root damage	carnivore gnawing	rodent gnawing	deliberate fracturing	taxon	element
51099	12	61349	20003	B-iii:03	2	4							Cervidae	small antler fragment
51100	13	61349	20003	B-iii:03	2	3							undetermined	small indeterminate bone fragment
51101	13	62201	20003	B-iii:03	2	3							Mammuthus?	indeterminate bone fragment
51102	13	62118	20003	B-iii:03	2	3							undetermined	indeterminate bone fragment
51103	13	60392	20003	B-iii:03	1	3							undetermined	small cranial fragment
51105	57–59B	60723+60732	20003	B-iii:03	6	4							Mammuthus	large tusk fragments and multiple small fragments, one cranial fragment
51106	13	61275–8	20003	B-iii:03	1	3							undetermined	5 small cranial fragments
51107	5B + 9B	61278	20003	B-iii:03	6	3							Mammuthus	3 large cranial fragments and multiple small fragments
51108	9B	61274+61277	20003	B-iii:03	4	3							Mammuthus	one large and multiple small cranial fragments
51109	7B	61278+61280	20003	B-iii:03	6	4							Mammuthus	one large and multiple small cranial fragments
51111	13	62201	20003	B-iii:03	2	3							Mammuthus	6 small tusk fragments
51112	1B	62118	20003	B-iii:03	4	3							Mammuthus	cranial fragment
51113	13	62465	20003	B-iii:03	6	2							Mammuthus	large tusk fragment
51114	13	60392	20003	B-iii:03	2	3							undetermined	small cranial fragment
51115	13	60392	20003	B-iii:03	2	3							undetermined	small indeterminate bone fragment
51116	13	62201	20003	B-iii:03	2	3							undetermined	2 small conjoining cranial fragments
51117	13	62201	20003	B-iii:03	4	4							Mammuthus	tusk fragment
51118	13	62118	20003	B-iii:03	2	3							undetermined	small indeterminate bone fragment
51119	13	62121	20003	B-iii:03	2	1							Coelodonta	fragment of R dp2

continued ▶

Table A4.4 Individual vertebrate finds: boxes 1–19 provided directly from Gressenhall; boxes with 'B' after the number came from Bradford; 'Spec.' denotes 'Special Box' built by Bradford; 'pj' = plaster jacket; 'C' = Crate. Note 1: not in a numbered box, brought in by Nigel Larkin – continued

object no.	box	split no.	context no.	facies	size	weathering	iron staining	abrasion	root damage	carnivore gnawing	rodent gnawing	deliberate fracturing	taxon	element
51120	1B	unstratified	20367	B-iii04	4	4		ü					undetermined	cranial fragment
51121	13	60392	20003	B-iii03	2	3							undetermined	small cranial fragment
51122	13	60392	20003	B-iii03	1	3							undetermined	small cranial fragment
51123	13	unstratified	20367	B-iii04	3	3							Mammuthus	small indeterminate fragment of large long bone
51124	13	62121	20003	B-iii03	2	3							Mammuthus	small tusk fragment
51125	13	62121	20003	B-iii03	2	3							Mammuthus	small tusk fragment
51126	13	62121	20003	B-iii03	2	3							Mammuthus	small tusk fragment
51127	13	62117	20003	B-iii03	3	3							Mammuthus	large molar plate fragment
51128	13	62118	20003	B-iii03	2	3							Mammuthus	small molar plate fragment
51129	13	62202	20003	B-iii03	2	2							Mammuthus	3 small tusk fragments
51130	13	62202	20003	B-iii03	2	3							Mammuthus	small tusk fragment
51131	13	62202	20003	B-iii03	2	5							undetermined	small indeterminate fragment
51132	13	unstratified	20366	B-iii04	2	3							Mammuthus	conjoining rib midshaft fragments
51133	13	62121	20003	B-iii03	2	3							Mammuthus ?	2 small conjoining bone fragments, probably cranial
51134	C6	61281+61283	20003	B-iii03	6	4							Mammuthus	large R tusk alveolus
51135a	18B	61284+61288	20003	B-iii03	6	4							Mammuthus	part of cranium with R jugal, jugal fragments, part of orbit
51135b	13	61284+61288	20003	B-iii03	6	2							Mammuthus	pelvis fragment
51137	13	62503	20003	B-iii03	2	3				ü			Cervidae	small antler fragment
51138	13	61296	20003	B-iii03	3	4							Mammuthus	multiple tusk fragments
51139	13	61296	20003	B-iii03	2	2							Mammuthus	2 small tusk fragments

APPENDIX 4

Table A4.4 Individual vertebrate finds: boxes 1–19 provided directly from Gressenhall; boxes with 'B' after the number came from Bradford; 'Spec.' denotes 'Special Box' built by Bradford; 'pj' = plaster jacket; 'C' = Crate. Note 1: not in a numbered box, brought in by Nigel Larkin – continued

object no.	box	spit no.	context no.	facies	size	weathering	iron staining	abrasion	root damage	carnivore gnawing	rodent gnawing	deliberate fracturing	taxon	element
51140	13B	61287	20003	B-iii03	6	4							Mammuthus	large tusk fragment
51141	13	61287	20003	B-iii03	2	3							Mammuthus	small fragment of molar plate
51142	13	61287	20003	B-iii03	1	4							Mammuthus	small tusk fragment
51143	1B	61287	20003	B-iii03	2	3							cf. Mammuthus	3 cranial fragments
51144	13	62202	20003	B-iii03	1	4		ü					Mammuthus	3 small tusk fragments
51145	13	62202	20003	B-iii03	2	2							Mammuthus	3 small tusk fragments
51146	13	62202	20003	B-iii03	2	2							Mammuthus	small tusk fragment
51147	13	62202	20003	B-iii03	3	2							Mammuthus	internal part of tusk
51148	13	62202	20003	B-iii03	2	3							Mammuthus	small tusk fragment
51149	13	62120	20003	B-iii03	2	2							undetermined	indeterminate bone fragment
51150	13	62202	20003	B-iii03	2	3							Mammuthus	small tusk fragment
51151	13	62202	20003	B-iii03	4	4							Mammuthus	tusk fragments
51152	13	62202	20003	B-iii03	2	3							Mammuthus	small tusk fragment
51153	13	62202	20003	B-iii03	2	3							Mammuthus	small tusk fragment
51154	23B	62202	20003	B-iii03	5	3							Mammuthus	R m3 fragment, see 51953 + 51648
51555	13	62511	20003	B-iii03	2	3							Mammuthus	3 small indeterminate fragment of large long bone
51556	13	62511	20003	B-iii03	3	3							Mammuthus	small indeterminate fragment of large long bone
51557	13	62517	20003	B-iii03	3	5							Mammuthus	small indeterminate fragment of large long bone
51158	33B	60391	20003	B-iii03	6	2							Mammuthus	large cranial fragment and multiple small fragments
51159	13	62264	20003	B-iii03	1	3			ü				undetermined	small indeterminate bone fragment

continued ▶

443

Table A4.4 Individual vertebrate finds: boxes 1–19 provided directly from Gressenhall; boxes with 'B' after the number came from Bradford; 'Spec.' denotes 'Special Box' built by Bradford; 'pj' = plaster jacket; 'C' = Crate. Note 1: not in a numbered box, brought in by Nigel Larkin – continued

object no.	box	split no.	context no.	facies	size	weathering	iron staining	abrasion	root damage	carnivore gnawing	rodent gnawing	deliberate fracturing	taxon	element
51160	C4	62263	20003	B-iii03	1	3							*Mammuthus*	multiple small cranial fragments
51161	13	60391	20003	B-iii03	1	3							undetermined	small indeterminate bone fragment, from sieve
51162	13	60392	20133	B-iii01	1	2							*Mammuthus*	small fragment of molar plate
51163	1B	61385	20003	B-iii03	4	4							*Mammuthus*	cranial fragments
51164	13	61286	20003	B-iii03	2	3							undetermined	multiple small cranial fragments
51165	13	62120	20003	B-iii03	2	3							*Mammuthus*	small indeterminate fragment of large long bone
51166	13	unstratified	20133	B-iii01	2	2							undetermined	cranial fragment
51167	13	62266	20003	B-iii03	2	3							undetermined	small cranial fragment
51168	13	62265	20003	B-iii03	2	3							undetermined	small cranial fragments
51169	13	62123	20003	B-iii03	2	3							undetermined	small cranial fragment
51170	13	62123	20003	B-iii03	2	3							*Mammuthus*	small tusk fragment
51171	26B	60393	20003	B-iii03	6	3							*Mammuthus*	L M1, pair of 51201
51172	13	60393	20003	B-iii03	3	3							*Mammuthus*	one large and multiple small cranial fragments
51173	13	60393	20003	B-iii03	3	3							cf. *Mammuthus*	multiple small cranial fragments
51175	13	60393	20003	B-iii03	4	3							cf. *Mammuthus*	rib midshaft fragment
51176	13	62510	20003	B-iii03	3	2					ü		cf. *Rangifer*	bone splinter, ?ulna
51177	13	62120	20003	B-iii03	2	3							undetermined	small indeterminate bone fragment
51178	C5	62202+62218	20003	B-iii03	6	4							*Mammuthus*	partial L femur midshaft and associated small fragments
51179	38B	62044	20254	B-iii01	6	2							*Mammuthus*	3 conjoining fragments of proximal and mid section of rib

APPENDIX 4

Table A4.4 Individual vertebrate finds: boxes 1–19 provided directly from Gressenhall; boxes with 'B' after the number came from Bradford; 'Spec.' denotes 'Special Box' built by Bradford; 'pj' = plaster jacket; 'C' = Crate. Note 1: not in a numbered box, brought in by Nigel Larkin – continued

object no.	box	spit no.	context no.	facies	size	weathering	iron staining	abrasion	root damage	carnivore gnawing	rodent gnawing	deliberate fracturing	taxon	element
51180	13	62044	20254	B-ii:01	6	4							undetermined	rib midshaft fragment, medium-sized animal (horse)
51181	13	62044	20254	B-ii:01	3	5							Mammuthus?	cranial fragment
51182	13	62271	20003	B-ii:03	4	3							Mammuthus	tusk fragment
51183	13	62044	20254	B-ii:01	2	2							Mammuthus	2 small molar roots
51184	13	62044	20254	B-ii:01	2	3							Mammuthus	small cranial fragment
51185	13	62044	20254	B-ii:01	2	2							Mammuthus	small tusk fragment
51186	13	60393	20003	B-ii:03	2	2							undetermined	multiple small cranial fragments
51187	9B	60393	20003	B-ii:03	4	3							Mammuthus	one large and multiple small cranial fragments
51188	13	60393	20003	B-ii:03	3	2							undetermined	multiple small cranial fragments
51189	13	62125	20003	B-ii:03	3	3							Mammuthus	small molar plate fragment
51190	13	62125	20003	B-ii:03	3	3							undetermined	indeterminate bone fragment
51191	13	62125	20003	B-ii:03	3	3							Mammuthus	molar plate fragment
51192	13	62125	20003	B-ii:03	2	3							Mammuthus	small tusk fragment
51193	13	62125	20003	B-ii:03	2	3							Mammuthus	small tusk fragment
51194	13	62125	20003	B-ii:03	2	3							Mammuthus	small tusk fragment
51195	13	62205	20003	B-ii:03	2	3							Mammuthus	indeterminate bone fragment
51196	13	62122	20003	B-ii:03	2	3							Mammuthus?	small cranial fragment
51197	13	62122	20003	B-ii:03	4	3							Mammuthus	tusk fragments
51198	13	62122	20003	B-ii:03	2	4							Mammuthus	multiple small tusk fragments
51199	13	62122	20003	B-ii:03	4	4							Mammuthus	tusk fragments
51200	14	62272	20003	B-ii:03	2	3							Mammuthus	cranial fragments

continued ▶

Table A4.4 Individual vertebrate finds: boxes 1–19 provided directly from Gressenhall; boxes with 'B' after the number came from Bradford; 'Spec.' denotes 'Special Box' built by Bradford; 'pj' = plaster jacket; 'C' = Crate. Note 1: not in a numbered box, brought in by Nigel Larkin – continued

object no.	box	split no.	context no.	facies	size	weathering	iron staining	abrasion	root damage	carnivore gnawing	rodent gnawing	deliberate fracturing	taxon	element
51201	25B	60396	20003	B-ii:03	6	3							Mammuthus	R M1, pair of 51171
51202	14	62206	20003	B-ii:03	2	3							undetermined	small indeterminate bone fragment
51203	14	62206	20003	B-ii:03	2	3							Mammuthus	tusk fragment
51204	14	62253	20003	B-ii:03	4	3							undetermined	cranial fragments
51205	14	62125	20003	B-ii:03	2	3							undetermined	small indeterminate bone fragment
51206	1B	60395	20003	B-ii:03	1	4							undetermined	comminuted cranial fragments
51207	14	60395	20003	B-ii:03	2	3							undetermined	multiple small cranial fragments
51208	14	60396	20003	B-ii:03	2	3							undetermined	small indeterminate bone fragment
51209	14	62206	20003	B-ii:03	2	3							undetermined	small cranial fragment
51210	14	62206	20003	B-ii:03	1	3							undetermined	small indeterminate bone fragments
51211	14	62124	20003	B-ii:03	2	4							Mammuthus	small cranial fragment
51212	14	62206	20003	B-ii:03	2	1							Ursus	L m1, pair of 51726
51213	14	62124	20003	B-ii:03	2	4							Mammuthus	small tusk fragment
51214	14	62124	20003	B-ii:03	2	3							Mammuthus	small tusk fragment
51215	14	60394	20003	B-ii:03	2	3							undetermined	cf. femoral midshaft fragment
51216	14	62207	20003	B-ii:03	4	3							Mammuthus	2 tusk fragments
51217	14	62124	20003	B-ii:03	2	3			ü				cf. Mammuthus	cranial fragment
51218	14	62124	20003	B-ii:03	3	2							Canis	conjoining underside of mandible 51223; sampled for isotopes
51219	14	62207	20003	B-ii:03	2	3							Mammuthus	small tusk fragment
51220	14	61861	20003	B-ii:03	2	5							undetermined	cranial fragment
51221	14	unstratified	20078	B-ii:03	2	4							undetermined	indeterminate bone fragment, possibly cranial

APPENDIX 4

Table A4.4 Individual vertebrate finds: boxes 1–19 provided directly from Gressenhall; boxes with 'B' after the number came from Bradford; 'Spec.' denotes 'Special Box' built by Bradford; 'pj' = plaster jacket; 'C' = Crate. Note 1: not in a numbered box, brought in by Nigel Larkin – continued

object no.	box	spit no.	context no.	facies	size	weathering	iron staining	abrasion	root damage	carnivore gnawing	rodent gnawing	deliberate fracturing	taxon	element
51222	14	unstratified	20078	B-ii:03	2	4							undetermined	indeterminate bone fragment
51223	14	62124	20003	B-iii:03	3	3							Canis	fragment of R lower jaw with alveolus and fragment of m2
51224	14	62207	20003	B-iii:03	2	3							Mammuthus	small molar plate fragment
51225	14	62207	20003	B-iii:03	2	4							Mammuthus	small tusk fragment
51226	14	62128	20003	B-iii:03	3	3							Mammuthus	small molar plate fragment
51227	14	62128	20003	B-iii:03	4	3				ü			undetermined	fragments of scapula blade?
51228	14	unstratified	20021	B-iii:03	2	2							Mammuthus?	epiphyseal fragment of very large rib, conjoins 51229
51229	14	unstratified	20021	B-iii:03	2	2							Mammuthus?	epiphyseal fragment of very large rib, conjoins 51228
51230	14	62124	20003	B-iii:03	2	2							Mammuthus	small tusk fragment
51231	14	62128	20003	B-iii:03	1	3							Mammuthus	multiple small tusk fragments
51232	14	62128	20003	B-iii:03	2	3							Mammuthus	small cranial fragment
51233	14	60399	20003	B-iii:03	2	4							undetermined	small indeterminate bone fragment
51234	24B	60399	20003	B-iii:03	4	2							Mammuthus	L M1, pair of 51440
51235	7B	60399	20003	B-iii:03	4	5							undetermined	extremely crushed cancellous bone fragments cemented into matrix, possibly vertebral
51236	C4	60399	20003	B-iii:03	5	5							undetermined	shattered and crushed bone shaft, cemeted into matrix
51237	14	62402	20021	B-iii:03	1	3							undetermined	3 very small indeterminate bone fragments
51238	14	62402	20021	B-iii:03	2	2							Mammuthus	small fragment of molar plate
51239	14	62208	20003	B-iii:03	2	2							Mammuthus	small tusk fragment
51240	24B	61865	20003	B-iii:03	5	2							Mammuthus	R M1

continued ▶

Table A4.4 Individual vertebrate finds: boxes 1–19 provided directly from Gressenhall; boxes with 'B' after the number came from Bradford; 'Spec.' denotes 'Special Box' built by Bradford; 'pj' = plaster jacket; 'C' = Crate. Note I: not in a numbered box, brought in by Nigel Larkin – continued

object no.	box	spit no.	context no.	facies	size	weathering	iron staining	abrasion	root damage	carnivore gnawing	rodent gnawing	deliberate fracturing	taxon	element
51241	14	62534	20003	B-iii03	2	3							undetermined	2 small conjoining fragments of indeterminate bone
51242	14	62538	20003	B-iii03	4	3							Mammuthus	indeterminate fragment of long bone
51243	14	62538	20003	B-iii03	3	5							Mammuthus?	multiple small fragments of indeterminate long bone
51244	14	62538	20003	B-iii03	3	3							undetermined	indeterminate bone fragment
51245	14	62208	20003	B-iii03	3	3							Mammuthus	small tusk fragment
51246	13B	62208	20003	B-iii03	3	3							Mammuthus	tusk fragments
51247	14	62216	20003	B-iii03	2	4							undetermined	indeterminate bone fragment
51248	14	62216	20003	B-iii03	2	2							Mammuthus	small cranial fragment
51249	14	62208	20003	B-iii03	3	1							Mammuthus	small tusk fragment
51250	14	62208	20003	B-iii03	1	2							undetermined	small cranial fragment
51251	14	62279	20003	B-iii03	3	3							Mammuthus	cranial fragment
51252	26B	62277	20003+20369	B-iii03	4	3							Mammuthus	middle part of L m2/m3
51253	14	62278	20003	B-iii03	4	4							Mammuthus	tusk fragment
51254	14	62128	20003	B-iii03	1	3							undetermined	small cranial fragment
51255	14	62128	20003	B-iii03	2	3							Mammuthus	small tusk fragment
51256	14	62128	20003	B-iii03	2	3							undetermined	small cranial fragment
51257	14	62216	20003	B-iii03	4	4							Mammuthus	cranial fragment
51258	14	62216	20003	B-iii03	2	3							undetermined	possible cranial fragment
51259	spec 3	61864	20003	B-iii03	6	3							Mammuthus	proximal end of posterior rib, conjoins with 51262
51260	14	61864	20003	B-iii03	2	3							undetermined	small cranial fragment

APPENDIX 4

Table A4.4 Individual vertebrate finds: boxes 1–19 provided directly from Gressenhall; boxes with 'B' after the number came from Bradford; 'Spec.' denotes 'Special Box' built by Bradford; 'pj' = plaster jacket; 'C' = Crate. Note 1: not in a numbered box, brought in by Nigel Larkin – continued

object no.	box	spit no.	context no.	facies	size	weathering	iron staining	abrasion	root damage	carnivore gnawing	rodent gnawing	deliberate fracturing	taxon	element
51261	1B	61864	20003	B-iii:03	5	3							Mammuthus	cranial fragment
51262	spec 3	61866	20003	B-iii:03	6	3							Mammuthus	midshaft and distal end of posterior rib (lacks distal epiphysis), conjoins with 51259
51263	14	62279	20003	B-iii:03	2	2							undetermined	cranial fragment
51264	14	62278	20003	B-iii:03	2	2							undetermined	cranial fragment
51265	14	62208	20003	B-iii:03	5	2							Mammuthus	tusk fragments
51266	14	62208	20003	B-iii:03	1	2							undetermined	very small indeterminate bone fragment
51267	14	62128	20003	B-iii:03	2	3							undetermined	indeterminate bone fragment
51268	14	62128	20003	B-iii:03	2	5							Mammuthus	small cranial fragment
51269	14	62128	20003	B-iii:03	2	3							undetermined	small indeterminate bone fragment
51270	14	62217	20003	B-iii:03	2	3							Mammuthus	tusk fragment
51271	1B	61247+61653	20248	B-iii:03	5	5							Mammuthus	indeterminate long bone fragments
51272	1B	61247+61653	20248	B-iii:03	6	5							Mammuthus	large fragment of indeterminate long bone
51273	14	62606	20003	B-iii:03	3	3							Mammuthus	cranial fragment
51274	14	61867	20003	B-iii:03	3	2						ü	Rangifer?	?tibia midshaft fragment
51275	14	61299	20003	B-iii:03	3	3							Mammuthus	rib midshaft fragment
51276	14	61247	20248	B-iii:03	1	3							Mammuthus	small tusk fragment
51277	14	61247	20248	B-iii:03	1	2							Mammuthus	2 conjoining small tusk fragments
51278	14	61247	20248	B-iii:03	1	2							Mammuthus	small tusk fragment
51279	spec 2	62403	20021	B-iii:03	6	3							Mammuthus	thoracic vertebra with detached distal epiphysis of neural spine; lacks posterior central epiphysis but preserves posterior centrum of vertebra in front
51280	14	62402	20021	B-iii:03	2	3							cf. Mammuthus	small cranial fragment

continued ▲

Table A4.4 Individual vertebrate finds: boxes 1–19 provided directly from Gressenhall; boxes with 'B' after the number came from Bradford; 'Spec.' denotes 'Special Box' built by Bradford; 'pj' = plaster jacket; 'C' = Crate. Note 1: not in a numbered box, brought in by Nigel Larkin – continued

object no.	box	spit no.	context no.	facies	size	weathering	iron staining	abrasion	root damage	carnivore gnawing	rodent gnawing	deliberate fracturing	taxon	element
51281	14	62403	20021	B-iii03	2	2							cf. *Mammuthus*	small cranial fragment
51282	14	62404	20021	B-iii03	1	2							cf. *Mammuthus*	small cranial fragment
51283	14	62404	20021	B-iii03	2	3							cf. *Mammuthus*	small cranial fragment
51284	14	62404	20021	B-iii03	1	3							undetermined	very small cranial fragment
52185	19	62404	20021	B-iii03	2	4							undetermined	small indeterminate bone fragment
52186	19	62404	20021	B-iii03	2	3							undetermined	small cranial fragment
51287	14	62404	20021	B-iii03	2	3							cf. *Mammuthus*	small cranial fragment
51288	14	62405	20021	B-iii03	3	2							*Rangifer*	small antler beam fragment
51289	14	62405	20021	B-iii03	2	2							cf. *Mammuthus*	small cranial fragment
51290	14	62406	20021	B-iii03	2	2							*Rangifer*?	posterior fragment of L ascending ramus
51292	14	62406	20021	B-iii03	1	3							cf. *Mammuthus*	small cranial fragment
51293	14	62406	20021	B-iii03	1	3							*Mammuthus*	very small tusk fragment
51294	14	61869	20003	B-iii03	3	3							*Mammuthus*	cranial fragment
51295	14	61869	20003	B-iii03	2	3							*Mammuthus*	small cranial fragment
51296	14	61869	20003	B-iii03	2	2							*Mammuthus*	small tusk fragment
51297	14	62126	20003	B-iii03	2	3							*Mammuthus*	small cranial fragment
51298	14	62126	20003	B-iii03	2	3							*Mammuthus*	small cranial fragment
51299	14	62126	20003	B-iii03	3	3							undetermined	indeterminate bone fragment, conjoins with 51300
51300	14	62126	20003	B-iii03	2	3							undetermined	indeterminate bone fragment, conjoins with 51299
51301	14	62126	20003	B-iii03	3	3							*Mammuthus*	small bone fragment
51302	2B	62126	20003	B-iii03	2	4							undetermined	cranial fragment

APPENDIX 4

Table A4.4 Individual vertebrate finds: boxes 1–19 provided directly from Gressenhall; boxes with 'B' after the number came from Bradford; 'Spec.' denotes 'Special Box' built by Bradford; 'pj' = plaster jacket; 'C' = Crate. Note 1: not in a numbered box, brought in by Nigel Larkin – continued

object no.	box	split no.	context no.	facies	size	weathering	iron staining	abrasion	root damage	carnivore gnawing	rodent gnawing	deliberate fracturing	taxon	element
51303	11B	62209	20003	B-iii:O3	5	4							Mammuthus	multiple tusk fragments
51304	14	62218	20003	B-iii:O3	5	3							Mammuthus	small tusk fragments
51305	14+14B	62218	20003	B-iii:O3	5	3							Mammuthus	tusk fragments
51307	14	62281	20003	B-iii:O3	3	3							Mammuthus	cranial fragment
51308	14	62278	20003	B-iii:O3	3	3							Mammuthus	small molar plate fragment
51309	9B	62278	20003	B-iii:O3	6	4							undetermined	cranial fragment
51310	2B	62280	20003	B-iii:O3	5	5							Mammuthus	indeterminate long bone fragment
51311	14	61869	20003	B-iii:O3	3	3							Mammuthus	molar plate fragment
51312	14	62126	20003	B-iii:O3	2	2							Mammuthus	molar talon fragment
51313	14	62126	20003	B-iii:O3	1	5							cf. Mammuthus	small indeterminate bone fragment, possibly cranial
51314	14	62126	20003	B-iii:O3	1	3							cf. Mammuthus	very small cranial fragment
51315	14	62209	20003	B-iii:O3	2	2							Mammuthus	small tusk fragment
51316	14	62280	20003	B-iii:O3	3	3							Mammuthus	cranial fragment
51317	14	62280	20003	B-iii:O3	2	3							Mammuthus	cranial fragment
51318	14	62653	20021	B-iii:O3	2	2							Mammuthus	cranial fragment
51319	14	62653	20021	B-iii:O3	2	2							cf. Mammuthus	small cranial fragment
51320	14	62653	20021	B-iii:O3	2	3							Mammuthus	cranial fragment
51321	14	62653	20021	B-iii:O3	3	5							Mammuthus	cranial fragment
51322	14	62653	20021	B-iii:O3	1	2							Rangifer	L p4
51323	2B	61497	20003	B-iii:O3	2	4				ü			undetermined	indeterminate bone fragment
51324	14	62209	20003	B-iii:O3	2	2							Coelodonta	unworn R DP3, lacking roots; sampled for isotopes

continued

Table A4.4 Individual vertebrate finds: boxes 1–19 provided directly from Gressenhall; boxes with 'B' after the number came from Bradford; 'Spec.' denotes 'Special Box' built by Bradford; 'pj' = plaster jacket; 'C' = Crate. Note 1: not in a numbered box, brought in by Nigel Larkin – continued

object no.	box	split no.	context no.	facies	size	weathering	iron staining	abrasion	root damage	carnivore gnawing	rodent gnawing	deliberate fracturing	taxon	element
51325	14	62210	20003	B-iii03	1	3							undetermined	small indeterminate bone fragment
51326	14	62214	20003	B-iii03	2	3							cf. Mammuthus	small cranial fragment
51327	14	62214	20003	B-iii03	2	3							cf. Mammuthus	small cranial fragment
51328	11B+14B	62214	20003	B-iii03	6	3							Mammuthus	tusk fragments
51329	14, 79B, pj	62609-10	20003	B-iii03	6	4							Mammuthus	crushed section of cranium with small fragment of tusk alveolus in plaster jacket, one large (jugal) and multiple small cranial fragments
51330	14	61871	20003	B-iii03	2	2							undetermined	hyoid fragment?
51331	14	62126	20003	B-iii03	1	2							undetermined	very small cranial fragment
51332	14	62548	20003	B-iii03	3	3							Mammuthus	molar talon fragment
51333	14	62704	20003	B-iii03	3	3							Mammuthus	cranial fragment
51334	14	62718	20003	B-iii03	3	3							Mammuthus	cranial fragment
51335	14	62718	20003	B-iii03	3	5							Rangifer	fragment of shed antler base
51336	11B	62210	20003	B-iii03	3	3				ü			cf. Mammuthus	2 cranial fragments
51337	14	62210	20003	B-iii03	1	3							Mammuthus	small tusk fragment
51338	14	62655	20021	B-iii03	2	3							Mammuthus	cranial fragment
51339	14	62287	20003	B-iii03	3	3							Mammuthus	2 cranial fragments
51340	14B	62464	20003	B-iii03	6	3							Mammuthus	tusk fragments
51341	14B	62463	20003	B-iii03	6	3							Mammuthus	tusk fragments
51342	14	62657	20003	B-iii03	1	3							Mammuthus	small cranial fragments
51343	2B	62657	20021	B-iii03	1	5							undetermined	2 small cranial fragments
51344	14	62709	20003	B-iii03	2	3					ü		undetermined	small rib midshaft fragment

APPENDIX 4

Table A4.4 Individual vertebrate finds: boxes 1–19 provided directly from Gressenhall; boxes with 'B' after the number came from Bradford; 'Spec.' denotes 'Special Box' built by Bradford; 'pj' = plaster jacket; 'C' = Crate. Note 1: not in a numbered box, brought in by Nigel Larkin – continued

object no.	box	spit no.	context no.	facies	size	weathering	iron staining	abrasion	root damage	carnivore gnawing	rodent gnawing	deliberate fracturing	taxon	element
51345	2B	61874	20003	B-ii:03	4	4				ü			Rangifer	antler tine fragment
51346	14	61874	20003	B-ii:03	2	3							cf. Mammuthus	small cranial fragment
51347	14	62212	20003	B-ii:03	2	2							Rangifer	rib midshaft fragment
51348	2B	62212	20003	B-ii:03	2	5							undetermined	indeterminate bone fragment
51349	2B	61874	20003	B-ii:03	2	5							undetermined	indeterminate bone fragment
51350	14	61874	20003	B-ii:03	2	3							cf. Mammuthus	2 small cranial fragments
51351	14	62131	20003	B-ii:03	2	3							Mammuthus	fragment of molar plate
51352	6B	62212	20003	B-ii:03	4	5							Mammuthus	centrum of vertebra
51353	14	62212	20003	B-ii:03	3	3							undetermined	small indeterminate bone fragment
51354	14	62135	20003	B-ii:03	2	1							Mammuthus	very small cranial fragment
51355	14	62135	20003	B-ii:03	1	2							cf. Mammuthus	very small cranial fragment
51356	14	62135	20003	B-ii:03	1	2							undetermined	indeterminate bone fragment
51357	14	62212	20003	B-ii:03	3	3							Mammuthus	cranial fragment
51358	14	62658	20021	B-ii:03	2	3							Mammuthus	cranial fragment
51359	14	62658	20021	B-ii:03	3	4							cf. Mammuthus	rib midshaft fragment
51360	30B	62287	20003	B-ii:03	6	3				ü			Equus	distal R femur; sampled for isotopes
51361	14	62287	20003	B-ii:03	2	2							cf. Mammuthus	small cranial fragment
51362	14	62548	20003	B-ii:03	3	4							Mammuthus	small tusk fragments
51363	14	62701	20003	B-ii:03	4	3							Mammuthus	rib midshaft fragment
51364	14	62713	20003	B-ii:03	3	3							cf. Mammuthus	rib midshaft fragment
51365	14	62131	20003	B-ii:03	2	3							Mammuthus	small tusk fragment
51366	2B	62135	20003	B-ii:03	5	4							Mammuthus	cranial fragments

continued

Table A4.4 Individual vertebrate finds: boxes 1–19 provided directly from Gressenhall; boxes with 'B' after the number came from Bradford; 'Spec.' denotes 'Special Box' built by Bradford; 'pj' = plaster jacket; 'C' = Crate. Note 1: not in a numbered box, brought in by Nigel Larkin – continued

object no.	box	split no.	context no.	facies	size	weathering	iron staining	abrasion	root damage	carnivore gnawing	rodent gnawing	deliberate fracturing	taxon	element
51367	14	62135	20003	B-iii:03	3	3							*Mammuthus*	molar talon fragment
51368	14	62135	20003	B-iii:03	3	3							*Mammuthus*	small tusk fragment
51369	14	62658	20021	B-iii:03	2	2							*Mammuthus*	cranial fragment, nasal
51370	14	62658	20021	B-iii:03	2	3							cf. *Mammuthus*	small cranial fragment
51371	14	62658	20021	B-iii:03	2	3							cf. *Mammuthus*	small cranial fragment
51372	14	62131	20003	B-iii:03	1	2							*Mammuthus*	very small molar plate fragment
51373	14	62211	20003	B-iii:03	4	3							*Mammuthus*	cranial fragments
51374	14	62211	20003	B-iii:03	3	4				ü			*Coelodonta*	midshaft of juvenile tibia
51375	14	62409	20021	B-iii:03	2	3							undetermined	indeterminate bone fragment
51376	14	62409	20021	B-iii:03	4	3							cf. *Mammuthus*	rib midshaft fragment
51377	14	62409	20021	B-iii:03	5	3				ü			*Mammuthus*	fragment of epiphysis of vertebral centrum
51378	14	62409	20021	B-iii:03	4	3							*Mammuthus*	fragment of epiphysis of thoracic vertebral centrum, possibly associated with 51377
51379	14	62409	20021	B-iii:03	2	3							cf. *Mammuthus*	cranial fragment
51380	14	62410	20021	B-iii:03	3	3							*Mammuthus*	cranial fragment
51381	14	62411	20021	B-iii:03	2	2							*Equus*	L11
51382	14	62411	20021	B-iii:03	2	3							*Mammuthus*	small tusk fragment
51383	14	62412	20021	B-iii:03	3	3							*Mammuthus*	small tusk fragment
51384	14	62413	20021	B-iii:03	2	2							undetermined	small cranial fragment
51385	14	62413	20021	B-iii:03	2	3							undetermined	small cranial fragments
51387	14	62413	20021	B-iii:03	4	3							*Mammuthus*	cuneiform
51388	14	62413	20021	B-iii:03	1	2							undetermined	very small cranial fragment

APPENDIX 4

Table A4.4 Individual vertebrate finds: boxes 1–19 provided directly from Gressenhall; boxes with 'B' after the number came from Bradford; 'Spec.' denotes 'Special Box' built by Bradford; 'pj' = plaster jacket; 'C' = Crate. Note 1: not in a numbered box, brought in by Nigel Larkin – continued

object no.	box	spit no.	context no.	facies	size	weathering	iron staining	abrasion	root damage	carnivore gnawing	rodent gnawing	deliberate fracturing	taxon	element
51389	14	62135	20003	B-iii03	2	3							undetermined	small indeterminate bone fragment
51390	14	62211	20003	B-iii03	2	3							Mammuthus	small molar plate fragment
51391	2B	60490	20374	B-iii04	2	5		ü					undetermined	indeterminate small bone fragments
51392	38B	62285	20003	B-iii03	6	3							undetermined	neural spine
51393	14	62285	20003	B-iii03	2	3							Mammuthus	indeterminate bone fragment
51394	14	62285	20003	B-iii03	3	3							cf. Mammuthus	small cranial fragment
51395	14	61699	20255	B-iii01	3	3							cf. Mammuthus	indeterminate long bone fragments
51396	14	62721	20003	B-iii03	2	3							undetermined	small indeterminate bone fragments
51397	14	60500	20003	B-iii03	3	3							cf. Mammuthus	multiple small cranial fragments
51399	14	62665	20021	B-iii03	3	3							Mammuthus	cranial fragment
51400	15	62130	20003	B-iii03	4	3							Mammuthus	tusk fragments
51401	15	62130	20003	B-iii03	3	3							Coelodonta	complete R DP4 with roots
51402	15	62136	20003	B-iii03	1	2							undetermined	small indeterminate bone fragment
51403	15	62136	20003	B-iii03	3	3							undetermined	indeterminate bone fragment
51404	15	62136	20003	B-iii03	2	2							Mammuthus?	small bone fragment, probably cranial
51405	15	62288	20003	B-iii03	2	3							undetermined	indeterminate bone fragment
51406	15	62664	20021	B-iii03	3	3							Mammuthus?	bone fragment, probably cranial
51407	15	62665	20021	B-iii03	2	3							undetermined	indeterminate bone fragment
51408	15	62133	20003	B-iii03	1	3							undetermined	indeterminate bone fragment
51409	15	62133	20003	B-iii03	2	2							undetermined	indeterminate bone fragment
51410	15	62133	20003	B-iii03	2	3							Mammuthus	small tusk fragment
51413	15	62133	20003	B-iii03	2	4							undetermined	indeterminate bone fragment

continued

Table A4.4 Individual vertebrate finds: boxes 1–19 provided directly from Gressenhall; boxes with 'B' after the number came from Bradford; 'Spec.' denotes 'Special Box' built by Bradford; 'pj' = plaster jacket; 'C' = Crate. Note 1: not in a numbered box, brought in by Nigel Larkin – continued

object no.	box	spit no.	context no.	facies	size	weathering	iron staining	abrasion	root damage	carnivore gnawing	rodent gnawing	deliberate fracturing	taxon	element
51414	15	62215	20002	B-iii05	2	3							undetermined	indeterminate bone fragment
51415	15	62215	20003	B-iii03	3	4							Mammuthus	small tusk fragment
51416	15	62665	20021	B-iii03	5	3							Mammuthus	cranial fragment
51417	15	62665	20021	B-iii03	2	3							undetermined	indeterminate bone fragment
51418	15	62132	20003	B-iii03	2	3							undetermined	indeterminate bone fragment
51419	15	62667	20021	B-iii03	3	4							Mammuthus	cranial fragment
51420	15	62667	20021	B-iii03	2	2							Mammuthus	small cranial fragment
51421	15	62668	20021	B-iii03	2	3							undetermined	indeterminate bone fragment
51422	15	62668	20021	B-iii03	1	3							undetermined	indeterminate bone fragment
51423	15	62668	20021	B-iii03	2	3							undetermined	indeterminate bone fragment
51424	15	62669	20021	B-iii03	4	3							Mammuthus	rib midshaft fragment
51425	15	62291	20003	B-iii03	3	4							Mammuthus?	cranial fragment
51426	15	62132	20003	B-iii03	1	2							undetermined	indeterminate bone fragment
51427	33B	62132	20003	B-iii03	6	3							Mammuthus	3 scapula blade fragments (2 conjoining)
51428	15	62133	20003	B-iii03	1	3							undetermined	indeterminate bone fragment
51429	15	62133	20003	B-iii03	1	2							undetermined	2 indeterminate bone fragments
51430	15	62133	20003	B-iii03	2	2							undetermined	cranial fragment
51431	15	62133	20003	B-iii03	3	3							cf. Mammuthus	posterior part of palate
51432	15	62669	20021	B-iii03	3	5							undetermined	cranial fragment
51433	15	62669	20021	B-iii03	3	3							cf. Mammuthus	cranial fragment
51434	15	62669	20021	B-iii03	3	3							cf. Mammuthus	cranial fragment
51435	15	62293	20003	B-iii03	2	4							undetermined	indeterminate bone fragment

APPENDIX 4

Table A4.4 Individual vertebrate finds: boxes 1–19 provided directly from Gressenhall; boxes with 'B' after the number came from Bradford; 'Spec.' denotes 'Special Box' built by Bradford; 'pj' = plaster jacket; 'C' = Crate. Note 1: not in a numbered box, brought in by Nigel Larkin – continued

object no.	box	spit no.	context no.	facies	size	weathering	iron staining	abrasion	root damage	carnivore gnawing	rodent gnawing	deliberate fracturing	taxon	element
51436	15	62720	20003	B-iii:03	4	3							undetermined	indeterminate limb bone fragment
51437	C4	62298	20003	B-iii:03	6	3							Rangifer	shed right male antler, with two tine fragments (brow and second) to be attached
51438	15	62672	20021	B-iii:03	2	2							undetermined	indeterminate bone fragment
51439	15	62672	20021	B-iii:03	4	3							Mammuthus	cranial fragment
51440	25B	62298	20003	B-iii:03	5	2							Mammuthus	R M1, pair of 51234
51441	15	62298	20003	B-iii:03	3	2							Mammuthus	fragment of auditory region of cranium
51442	15	62414	20021	B-iii:03	3	3							undetermined	indeterminate bone fragment
51443	15	62414	20021	B-iii:03	2	4							undetermined	3 indeterminate cranial fragments
51444	18B	62414	20021	B-iii:03	6	3							Mammuthus	tusk alveolus, two fragments
51445	15	62414	20021	B-iii:03	3	3							Mammuthus	fragment of tusk alveolus
51446	15	62414	20021	B-iii:03	2	2							Mammuthus	small tusk fragment
51447	15	62414	20021	B-iii:03	3	3							undetermined	indeterminate bone fragment
51448	spec 3	62414	20021	B-iii:03	6	3							Mammuthus	virtually complete posterior rib (missing proximal epiphysis, slight damage to distal end), possibly same individual as 51451
51449	C1	62578	20078	B-i:03	6	3							Mammuthus	2 incomplete, fused caudal vertebrae
51450	15	62673	20021	B-iii:03	3	3							undetermined	indeterminate bone fragment
51451	spec 3	62414	20021	B-iii:03	6	3							Mammuthus	virtually complete posterior rib (missing proximal epiphysis, slight damage to distal end), possibly same individual as 51448
51452	15	62415	20021	B-iii:03	2	2							undetermined	indeterminate bone fragments
51453	15	62415	20021	B-iii:03	3	3							undetermined	indeterminate bone fragment
51454	15	62416	20021	B-iii:03	6	2							Mammuthus	rib midshaft fragment, near proximal end

continued ▶

Table A4.4 Individual vertebrate finds: boxes 1–19 provided directly from Gressenhall; boxes with 'B' after the number came from Bradford; 'Spec.' denotes 'Special Box' built by Bradford; 'pj' = plaster jacket; 'C' = Crate. Note 1: not in a numbered box, brought in by Nigel Larkin – continued

object no.	box	spit no.	context no.	facies	size	weathering	iron staining	abrasion	root damage	carnivore gnawing	rodent gnawing	deliberate fracturing	taxon	element
51455	15	62417	20021	B-iii03	4	2				ü			Mammuthus?	large bone fragment
51456	15	62417	20021	B-iii03	1	2							undetermined	very small indeterminate bone fragment
51457	15	62142	20003	B-iii03	4	4							Mammuthus	tusk fragment
51458	15	62142	20003	B-iii03	2	2							Mammuthus	cranial fragment
51459	15	62142	20003	B-iii03	2	3							undetermined	indeterminate bone fragment
51460	15	62222	20003	B-iii03	6	2							Mammuthus	tusk fragment
51461	15	62545	20003	B-iii03	3	3							Mammuthus	molar plate fragment
51462	15	62545	20003	B-iii03	2	3							undetermined	indeterminate bone fragment
51463	15	62219	20003	B-iii03	3	3							undetermined	indeterminate bone fragment
51464	15	62142	20003	B-iii03	1	2							undetermined	indeterminate bone fragment
51465	15	62140	20003	B-iii03	4	3							Mammuthus	tusk fragment
51466	15	62222	20003+20364	B-iii03	2	3							undetermined	indeterminate bone fragment
51467	15	62674	20021	B-iii03	2	3							cf. Mammuthus	cranial fragment
51468	15	62674	20021	B-iii03	2	4							cf. Mammuthus	cranial fragment
51469	15	62674	20021	B-iii03	2	2							undetermined	indeterminate bone fragment
51470	15	62674	20021	B-iii03	4	3							cf. Mammuthus	juvenile rib fragment
51471	15	62410	20021	B-iii03	3	3							Mammuthus	tusk fragments
51472	15	62418	20021	B-iii03	2	3							cf. Mammuthus	cranial fragments
51473	15	62420	20021	B-iii03	2	3							cf. Mammuthus	cranial fragment
51474	15	62420	20021	B-iii03	1	2							undetermined	cranial fragment
51475	15	62420	20021	B-iii03	2	2							undetermined	cranial fragment
51476	15	62139	20003	B-iii03	1	2							undetermined	indeterminate bone fragment

APPENDIX 4

Table A4.4 Individual vertebrate finds: boxes 1–19 provided directly from Gressenhall; boxes with 'B' after the number came from Bradford; 'Spec.' denotes 'Special Box' built by Bradford; 'pj' = plaster jacket; 'C' = Crate. Note 1: not in a numbered box, brought in by Nigel Larkin – continued

object no.	box	spit no.	context no.	facies	size	weathering	iron staining	abrasion	root damage	carnivore gnawing	rodent gnawing	deliberate fracturing	taxon	element
51477	15	62139	20003	B-iii03	1	4							undetermined	indeterminate bone fragments
51478	15	62141	20003	B-iii03	2	3							undetermined	indeterminate bone fragment
51479	15	62141	20003	B-iii03	2	2							undetermined	indeterminate bone fragment
51480	15	62141	20003	B-iii03	2	3							undetermined	indeterminate bone fragment
51481	15	62141	20003	B-iii03	2	3							Mammuthus	fragment of molar plate
51482	15	62221	20003	B-iii03	2	2							Canis	articular condyle of L dentary
51483	15	62221	20003	B-iii03	2	3							undetermined	indeterminate bone fragment
51484	15	62219	20003	B-iii03	2	3							undetermined	indeterminate bone fragment
51485	15	62219	20003	B-iii03	2	3							Mammuthus	cranial fragment
51486	15	62743	20003	B-iii03	2	3							undetermined	indeterminate bone fragment
51487	15	62744	20003	B-iii03	3	3							Mammuthus?	rib fragment?
51488	15	62141	20003	B-iii03	2	4							undetermined	cranial fragment
51489	15	62141	20003	B-iii03	3	4							cf. Mammuthus	cranial fragment
51490	15	62408	20021	B-iii03	2	3							undetermined	cranial fragment
51491	15	62221	20003	B-iii03	2	3							Mammuthus?	vertebral articular surface?
51492	15	62675	20021	B-iii03	2	2							undetermined	indeterminate bone fragment
51493	15	62675	20021	B-iii03	2	2							undetermined	cranial fragment
51494	15	62675	20021	B-iii03	2	4							undetermined	indeterminate bone fragment
51495	spec 2	62675+62719	20021	B-iii03	6	3							Mammuthus	thoracic vertebra, lacking distal epiphysis, and both central epiphyses
51496	15	62144	20003	B-iii03	2	3							undetermined	indeterminate bone fragment
51497	15	62144	20003	B-iii03	3	3							Mammuthus	tusk fragment

continued ▶

Table A4.4 Individual vertebrate finds: boxes 1–19 provided directly from Gressenhall; boxes with 'B' after the number came from Bradford; 'Spec.' denotes 'Special Box' built by Bradford; 'pj' = plaster jacket; 'C' = Crate. Note 1: not in a numbered box, brought in by Nigel Larkin – continued

object no.	box	spit no.	context no.	facies	size	weathering	iron staining	abrasion	root damage	carnivore gnawing	rodent gnawing	deliberate fracturing	taxon	element
51498	15	62144	20003	B-iii03	2	3							undetermined	indeterminate bone fragment
51499	15	62221	20003	B-iii03	4	3							cf. Mammuthus	rib midshaft fragment
51500	15	62221	20003	B-iii03	2	3							undetermined	cranial fragment
51501	15	62856	20003	B-iii03	3	5							undetermined	indeterminate bone fragment
51502	29B	61299–300	20003	B-iii03	6	3							Mammuthus	R jugal and part of parietal
51503	12B	62461–2	20021	B-iii03	6	3							Mammuthus	tusk fragments
51504	15	62676	20021	B-iii03	1	3							undetermined	indeterminate bone fragment
51505	15	62676	20003	B-iii03	2	3							undetermined	indeterminate bone fragment
51506	15	62234	20003	B-iii03	3	3							undetermined	indeterminate bone fragment
51507	15	62230	20003	B-iii03	2	3							undetermined	2 large indeterminate bone fragments
51508	15	62230	20003	B-iii03	2	3							undetermined	indeterminate bone fragment
51509	27B	62225	20003	B-iii03	6	3							cf. Mammuthus	rib midshaft section
51510	22B	62225	20003	B-iii03	6	4				ü			Mammuthus	tibia midshaft fragment, split longitudinally
51511	15	62224	20003	B-iii03	3	3							Mammuthus	large rib fragment
51512	17B	62223	20003	B-iii03	6	3							Mammuthus	virtually complete fragmentary rib
51513	15	62225	20003	B-iii03	5	3				ü			Mammuthus	basicranium fragment
51514	15	62225	20003	B-iii03	3	2							cf. Mammuthus	fragment of cup-shaped articular surface, possibly acetabulum
51515	52B	62225	20003	B-iii03	2	2							Mammuthus	complete atlas vertebra (see 51537)
51516	plaster	62952	20245	B-iii01	6	4							Mammuthus	long bone fragment, possibly anterior shaft of humerus showing deltoid muscle, cemented into matrix
51517	2B	62952	20245	B-iii01	3	5							undetermined	very fragmentary bone material

APPENDIX 4

Table A4.4 Individual vertebrate finds: boxes 1–19 provided directly from Gressenhall; boxes with 'B' after the number came from Bradford; 'Spec.' denotes 'Special Box' built by Bradford; 'pj' = plaster jacket; 'C' = Crate. Note 1: not in a numbered box, brought in by Nigel Larkin – continued

object no.	box	spit no.	context no.	facies	size	weathering	iron staining	abrasion	root damage	carnivore gnawing	rodent gnawing	deliberate fracturing	taxon	element
51519	15	62859	20003	B-iii:O3	2	3							undetermined	indeterminate bone fragment
51520	15	62859	20003	B-iii:O3	3	3							Mammuthus	rib midshaft fragment
51521	16	62677	20021	B-iii:O3	2	3							undetermined	cranial fragments
51522	16	62677	20021	B-iii:O3	2	3							undetermined	cranial fragment
51523	16	62859	20003	B-iii:O3	2	3							undetermined	indeterminate bone fragment
51524	2B	62424	20021	B-iii:O3	6	4							Mammuthus	cranial fragment
51525	spec 2	62424–5	20021	B-iii:O3	6	3							Mammuthus	thoracic vertebra, lacking both central epiphyses
51526	16	62429	20021	B-iii:O3	3	3							Mammuthus	proximal epiphysis of rib
51527	spec 1	62429	20021	B-iii:O3	6	3							Mammuthus	posterior rib (proximal epiphysis missing, damaged distal end)
51528	2B	62429	20021	B-iii:O3	5	3							Mammuthus	epiphyseal fragment of vertebral centrum
51529	2B	62860	20003	B-iii:O3	2	4							undetermined	indeterminate bone fragment
51530	2B	62229	20003	B-iii:O3	3	4							Mammuthus	small tusk fragments and indeterminate bone fragment
51531	2B	62232	20003	B-iii:O3	2	5							undetermined	indeterminate bone fragment
51532	2B	62232	20003	B-iii:O3	5	3				ü			Mammuthus	rib midshaft fragment
51533	2B	62860	20003	B-iii:O3	4	4							Mammuthus	indeterminate long bone fragment
51534	16	62470	20003	B-iii:O3	3	3							undetermined	cranial fragment
51535	16	62678	20021	B-iii:O3	2	2							undetermined	cranial fragment
51536	C3	62225	20003	B-iii:O3	6	4				ü			Coelodonta	R acetabulum
51537	52B	62225	20003	B-iii:O3	6	4							Mammuthus	complete atlas vertebra (see 51515)
51538	2B	62496	20003	B-iii:O3	2	5							undetermined	indeterminate bone fragment

continued ▶

Table A4.4 Individual vertebrate finds: boxes 1–19 provided directly from Gressenhall; boxes with 'B' after the number came from Bradford; 'Spec.' denotes 'Special Box' built by Bradford; 'pj' = plaster jacket; 'C' = Crate. Note 1: not in a numbered box, brought in by Nigel Larkin – continued

object no.	box	spit no.	context no.	facies	size	weathering	iron staining	abrasion	root damage	carnivore gnawing	rodent gnawing	deliberate fracturing	taxon	element
51539	2B	62496	20003	B-iii03	5	5							Mammuthus	cranial fragment
51541	29B	62864	20003	B-iii03	3	3							Rangifer	small antler fragment
51542	16	63051	20003	B-iii03	5	2				ü			Mammuthus	rib midshaft fragment
51543	16	63051	20003	B-iii03	2	3							undetermined	cranial fragment
51544	2B	62677	20021	B-iii03	4	3							cf. Mammuthus	cranial fragment
51545	9B	62678	20021	B-iii03	6	3							Mammuthus	cranial fragment
51546	2B	62678	20021	B-iii03	2	5							undetermined	indeterminate bone fragment
51547	29B	62678	20021	B-iii03	4	3							Mammuthus	cranial fragment
51548	2B	62679	20021	B-iii03	3	4							Mammuthus	indeterminate long bone fragment
51550	28B	62432	20021	B-iii03	6	4							Mammuthus	partial R jugal
51551	2B	62437	20021	B-iii03	3	3							Mammuthus	fragment of neural spine and posterior zygapophyses
51552	16	62437	20003	B-iii03	3	3							Mammuthus	rib midshaft fragment
51553	16	62865	20003	B-iii03	2	3							undetermined	indeterminate bone fragment
51554	16	62867	20003	B-iii03	3	2							Mammuthus	tusk fragment
51555	2B	62960	20254	B-iii01	4	3							Mammuthus	complete right mesocuneiform
51556	spec 3	62679–80+62424	20021	B-iii03	6	3							Mammuthus	virtually complete middle rib (proximal and distal epiphyses missing), probably from the same individual as 51604
51557	16	62964	20254	B-iii01	2	4							undetermined	multiple small indeterminate bone fragments
51558	47B	62962	20254	B-iii01	6	3							cf. Mammuthus	very fragmentary rib midshaft
51559	C4	62959	20254	B-iii01	4	3							undetermined	small bone fragments, possibly cranial
51560	16	63057	20003	B-iii03	4	4							undetermined	cranial fragment

Table A.4.4 Individual vertebrate finds: boxes 1–19 provided directly from Gressenhall; boxes with 'B' after the number came from Bradford; 'Spec.' denotes 'Special Box' built by Bradford; 'pj' = plaster jacket; 'C' = Crate. Note 1: not in a numbered box, brought in by Nigel Larkin – continued

object no.	box	spit no.	context no.	facies	size	weathering	iron staining	abrasion	root damage	carnivore gnawing	rodent gnawing	deliberate fracturing	taxon	element
51562	2B	63165	20003	B-iii03	5	5							Rangifer	broken antler base (fragment of coronet, part of beam)
51564	76B	unstratified	20254	B-iii01	2	4							undetermined	multiple small rib midshaft fragments
51565	16	63161	20003	B-iii03	3	3							undetermined	indeterminate bone fragment
51566	16	63165	20003	B-iii03	3	2							Rangifer	anterior surface fragment of metatarsal midshaft
51567	2B	63162	20003	B-iii03	4	3							Mammuthus	cranial fragment
51568	30B	62438	20021	B-iii03	6	3							Mammuthus	fragment of tusk alveolus
51569	74B	62438	20021	B-iii03	6	3							Mammuthus	detached epiphysis of iliac blade
51570	16	62464	20021	B-iii03	4	2							Mammuthus	tusk fragment
51571	16	unstratified	20003	B-iii03	4	4							Mammuthus	tusk fragment
51572	16	63125	20371	B-iii02	1	2							undetermined	small cranial fragment
51573	2B	62428	20021	B-iii03	2	4							undetermined	small cranial fragment
51574	2B	62435+62440	20021	B-iii03	3	4							undetermined	cranial fragment
51575	C5	unstratified	20371+20374	B-iii04	6	3					ü		Mammuthus	midshaft of R femur
51576	16	63140	20371	B-iii02	2	3							Mammuthus	small molar plate fragment
51577	16	unstratified	20011	C	2	2							Coelodonta	3 conjoining fragments of L upper molar
51578	16	63172	20003	B-iii03	2	3							undetermined	indeterminate bone fragment
51579	16	63186	20003	B-iii03	3	3							undetermined	indeterminate bone fragment
51580	16	63189	20003	B-iii03	3	3							cf. Rangifer	antler beam fragment
51581	16	62444	20021	B-iii03	3	3							undetermined	indeterminate bone fragment
51582	16	62444	20021	B-iii03	3	2							undetermined	cranial fragment
51583	16	62444	20021	B-iii03	2	3							Mammuthus	tusk fragment

continued ▶

Table A4.4 Individual vertebrate finds: boxes 1–19 provided directly from Gressenhall; boxes with 'B' after the number came from Bradford; 'Spec.' denotes 'Special Box' built by Bradford; 'pj' = plaster jacket; 'C' = Crate. Note 1: not in a numbered box, brought in by Nigel Larkin – continued

object no.	box	spit no.	context no.	facies	size	weathering	iron staining	abrasion	root damage	carnivore gnawing	rodent gnawing	deliberate fracturing	taxon	element
51584	12B+14B	61635	20252	B-iii03	6	4							Mammuthus	tusk fragments
51585	16	63181	20003	B-iii03	3	3							Mammuthus	small tusk fragment
51586	16	63184	20003	B-iii03	3	4							undetermined	indeterminate bone fragment
51587	16	63185	20003	B-iii03	2	3							Mammuthus	tusk fragments
51588	16	63189	20003	B-iii03	3	3							cf. Rangifer	?antler beam fragment
51589	51B	63157–8	20003	B-iii03	6	2				ü			Rangifer	shed L antler (3 parts), pedicle, brow tine and beam
51590	16	63158	20003	B-iii03	3	2							cf. Rangifer	antler beam fragment
51591	2B	62870	20003	B-iii03	5	4							Mammuthus	indeterminate bone fragment
51592	16	61635	20364	B-iii01	3	3							Mammuthus	cranial fragment
51593	16	61635	20364	B-iii01	2	3							Mammuthus	small cranial fragment
51594	16	61635	20364	B-iii01	2	3							Mammuthus	small cranial fragment
51595	16	unstratified	20003	B-iii03	3	3		ü		ü			undetermined	indeterminate bone fragment, probably rib midshaft
51596	16	63177	20003	B-iii03	3	2							Mammuthus	tusk fragment
51597	16	63158	20003	B-iii03	3	2				ü			Rangifer	antler beam fragment
51598	16	62431	20021	B-iii03	3	4							undetermined	cranial fragment
51599	16	62451	20021	B-iii03	4	3							undetermined	indeterminate bone fragment
51600	2B	62871	20003	B-iii03	3	3							Mammuthus	fragment of molar plate
51601	27B	63197	20003	B-iii03	6	3							Mammuthus	proximal posterior rib (proximal epiphysis missing)
51602	2B	63198	20003	B-iii03	2	4							cf. Mammuthus	cranial fragment
51603	27B	61634	20364	B-iii01	5	3							cf. Mammuthus	proximal and midshaft fragments of rib

APPENDIX 4

Table A4.4 Individual vertebrate finds: boxes 1–19 provided directly from Gressenhall; boxes with 'B' after the number came from Bradford; 'Spec.' denotes 'Special Box' built by Bradford; 'pj' = plaster jacket; 'C' = Crate. Note 1: not in a numbered box, brought in by Nigel Larkin – continued

object no.	box	split no.	context no.	facies	size	weathering	iron staining	abrasion	root damage	carnivore gnawing	rodent gnawing	deliberate fracturing	taxon	element
51604	spec 3	62677	20021	B-ii03	6	3							Mammuthus	virtually complete middle rib (missing proximal and distal epiphyses), probably from the same individual as 51556
51605	2B	62876	20003	B-ii03	3	4							Mammuthus	indeterminate long bone fragment
51606	11B	unstratified	20356		6	4							Mammuthus	tusk fragment, near distal end
51607	2B	62436	20021	B-ii03	5	3							Mammuthus	fragment of proximal midshaft of rib, lacking proximal end
51608	16	62449	20021	B-ii03	3	2							Mammuthus	proximal epiphysis of rib
51609	16	62453	20021	B-ii03	4	2							cf. Mammuthus	cranial fragment
51610	2B	62453	20021	B-ii03	5	2							Mammuthus	fragment of neural spine with anterior zygapophyses
51611	16	62872	20003	B-ii03	3	4							undetermined	indeterminate bone fragment
51612	16	62436	20021	B-ii03	3	2							Equus	R lower cheek tooth (p3-m1)
51613	2B	63309	20003	B-ii03	4	3							Mammuthus	rib midshaft fragment
51614	29B	63311	20003	B-ii03	4	2							cf. Mammuthus	cranial fragment
51615	2B	63314	20003	B-ii03	3	5							Mammuthus	tusk fragments
51616	9B	63314	20003	B-ii03	5	4							Mammuthus	cranial fragment
51617	16	63226	20371	B-ii02	3	3							undetermined	indeterminate bone fragment
51618	68B	unstratified	20384	B-ii01	6	4							Mammuthus	tusk alveolus, very poor condition
51619	78B	unstratified	20384	B-ii01	6	4							Mammuthus	R M2 in crushed maxilla, associated with cranial fragments from 51038
51620	C4	unstratified	20384	B-ii01	6	3							Mammuthus	large cranial fragments
51621	6B	64234	20384	B-ii01	6	4							Mammuthus	right ischium fragment and part of acetabulum

continued ▶

Table A4.4 Individual vertebrate finds: boxes 1–19 provided directly from Gressenhall; boxes with 'B' after the number came from Bradford; 'Spec.' denotes 'Special Box' built by Bradford; 'pj' = plaster jacket; 'C' = Crate. Note 1: not in a numbered box, brought in by Nigel Larkin – continued

object no.	box	split no.	context no.	facies	size	weathering	iron staining	abrasion	root damage	carnivore gnawing	rodent gnawing	deliberate fracturing	taxon	element
51622	27B	64234	20384	B-iii01	6	3							Mammuthus	complete rib, comprised of four conjoining fragments
51623	2B	63504	20384	B-iii01	4	3							Mammuthus	cranial fragment
51624	16	62363	20131	B-iii04	2	3							Mammuthus	tusk fragments
51625	16	62363	20131	B-iii04	1	3							Mammuthus	tusk fragment
51627	16	62363	20131	B-iii04	2	2							Mammuthus	tusk fragment
51628	C4	63509	20384	B-iii01	5	3							Mammuthus	R magnum
51629	16	62475	20021	B-iii03	4	3							undetermined	indeterminate bone fragment
51630	16	62363	20131	B-iii04	2	3							Mammuthus	tusk fragment
51631	16	62451	20021	B-iii03	3	2						ü	Equus	R m3; sampled for isotopes
51633	11B	62971	20003	B-iii03	3	5							Mammuthus	multiple tusk fragments
51634	spec 3	64902	20369	B-iii01	6	3							Mammuthus	virtually complete middle rib, broken in 2 (distal end slightly damaged)
51635	50B	65195	20384	B-iii01	6	3							Mammuthus	crushed and damaged rib, almost complete (proximal end present)
51636	13B	62362–3	20131	B-iii04	5	4							Mammuthus	tusk fragments
51637	2B	62880	20003	B-iii03	3	3							Mammuthus	fragments of tusk alveolus
51638	2B	62478	20021	B-iii03	3	4							undetermined	indeterminate bone fragment
51639	16	62483	20021	B-iii03	2	2							Fish	cranial element
51640	16	62978	20003	B-iii03	2	3							undetermined	indeterminate bone fragment
51641	16	62979	20003	B-iii03	2	2							Mammuthus	cranial fragment
51642	16	62979	20003	B-iii03	3	2							undetermined	multiple cranial fragments
51643	16	62982	20003	B-iii03	3	3							Mammuthus	tusk fragment

APPENDIX 4

Table A4.4 Individual vertebrate finds: boxes 1–19 provided directly from Gressenhall; boxes with 'B' after the number came from Bradford; 'Spec.' denotes 'Special Box' built by Bradford; 'pj' = plaster jacket; 'C' = Crate. Note 1: not in a numbered box, brought in by Nigel Larkin – continued

object no.	box	spit no.	context no.	facies	size	weathering	iron staining	abrasion	root damage	carnivore gnawing	rodent gnawing	deliberate fracturing	taxon	element
51644	16	62990	20021	B-iii03	3	3							undetermined	cranial fragments
51645	16	62900–1+62425+625198	20021	B-iii03	3	3							undetermined	bag of multiple cranial fragments
51646	16	62993	20021	B-iii03	3	3							undetermined	indeterminate bone fragment
51647	16	62885	20003	B-iii03	3	3							undetermined	indeterminate bone fragment
51648	26B	62882	20003	B-iii03	5	3							Mammuthus	fragment of Rm3, see 51953 + 51154
51649	16	62883	20021	B-iii03	4	4							undetermined	indeterminate bone fragment, possibly rib
51650	16	62990	20021	B-iii03	5	3							Mammuthus	cranial fragment
51651	29B	62990	20021	B-iii03	5	3							Mammuthus	cranial fragment
51652	16	62990	20021	B-iii03	3	3							cf. Mammuthus	cranial fragment
51653	B	62990	20021	B-iii03									undetermined	cranial fragment
51654	2B	62990	20021	B-iii03	2	3							undetermined	cranial fragments
51655	16	62990	20021	B-iii03	3	4							cf. Mammuthus	cranial fragment
51656	16	62990	20021	B-iii03	3	3							cf. Mammuthus	cranial fragment
51657	16	62990	20021	B-iii03	3	2							cf. Mammuthus	cranial fragment
51658	16	62682	20021	B-iii03	2	3							undetermined	cranial fragment
51659	16	62682	20021	B-iii03	2	3							Mammuthus	tusk fragments
51660	2B	63607	20003	B-iii03	3	4							Mammuthus	multiple indeterminate long bone fragments
51661	16	62990	20021	B-iii03	2	3							undetermined	2 small cranial fragments
51662	16	62990	20021	B-iii03	3	3							undetermined	cranial fragment
51663	16	62990	20021	B-iii03	3	2							undetermined	cranial fragment
51664	33B	63622	20003	B-iii03	6	4							Mammuthus	3 conjoining fragments of indeterminate large limb bone

continued ▲

Table A4.4 Individual vertebrate finds: boxes 1–19 provided directly from Gressenhall; boxes with 'B' after the number came from Bradford; 'Spec.' denotes 'Special Box' built by Bradford; 'pj' = plaster jacket; 'C' = Crate. Note 1: not in a numbered box, brought in by Nigel Larkin – continued

object no.	box	spit no.	context no.	facies	size	weathering	iron staining	abrasion	root damage	carnivore gnawing	rodent gnawing	deliberate fracturing	taxon	element
51665	16	63627	20003	B-iii03	2	3							undetermined	multiple small indeterminate bone fragments
51666	plaster	62990	20021	B-iii03	6	3							Mammuthus	crushed posterior part of cranium and palate in plaster jacket, with occipital condyle and posterior molar plate fragments present
51667	2B	63614	20003	B-iii03	5	4							Mammuthus	fragments of large long bone
51668	16	65651	20003	B-iii03	2	3							Mammuthus	molar root fragment
51669	16	65651	20003	B-iii03	2	4							Mammuthus	multiple small tusk fragments
51670	2B	63622	20003	B-iii03	4	5							Mammuthus	indeterminate bone fragment
51671	16	63617	20003	B-iii03	3	3							Mammuthus	indeterminate bone fragment
51672	16	65652	20003	B-iii03	2	2						ü	Rangifer	fragment of metatarsal midshaft
51673	16	63629	20003	B-iii03	2	5							undetermined	indeterminate bone fragment
51674	16	63629	20003	B-iii03	3	5							undetermined	indeterminate bone fragment
51675	7B	62997	20021	B-iii03	3	3							Mammuthus	small cranial fragments; sampled for isotopes
51676	16	65657	20003	B-iii03	2	3							undetermined	indeterminate bone fragment
51677	16	63640	20003	B-iii03	3	4							undetermined	indeterminate bone fragment
51678	16	63638	20003	B-iii03	3	4							undetermined	indeterminate bone fragment
51679	16	63631	20003	B-iii03	4	4							Mammuthus	indeterminate bone fragment
51680	16	62877	20003	B-iii03	3	3							Mammuthus	molar plate fragment
51681	16	62877	20003	B-iii03	4	4							undetermined	indeterminate bone fragment
51682	16	63634	20003	B-iii03	5	3							Mammuthus	multiple indeterminate long bone fragments
51683	16	63634	20003	B-iii03	3	3							undetermined	indeterminate bone fragment

APPENDIX 4

Table A4.4 Individual vertebrate finds: boxes 1–19 provided directly from Gressenhall; boxes with 'B' after the number came from Bradford; 'Spec.' denotes 'Special Box' built by Bradford; 'pj' = plaster jacket; 'C' = Crate. Note 1: not in a numbered box, brought in by Nigel Larkin – continued

object no.	box	spit no.	context no.	facies	size	weathering	iron staining	abrasion	root damage	carnivore gnawing	rodent gnawing	deliberate fracturing	taxon	element
51684	16	65198	20021	B-iii03	4	3							*Mammuthus*	molar plate fragment
51685	16	62887	20003	B-iii03	2	3							undetermined	indeterminate bone fragment, probably cranial
51686	16	62880	20003	B-iii03	2	3							*Mammuthus*	molar plate fragment
51687	16	62877	20003	B-iii03	3	4							undetermined	indeterminate bone fragment
51588	16	64260	20021	B-iii03	3	3							*Mammuthus*	molar plate fragment
51689	16	62995	20021	B-iii03	2	2							cf. Cervidae	fragment of L dentary
51690	16	62887	20003	B-iii03	3	3							*Mammuthus*	molar talon fragment
51691	16	3D co-ords only	20389	B-iii04	2	2							*Mammuthus*	multiple tusk fragments
51692	16	63419	20003+20384	B-iii03	2	3							undetermined	indeterminate bone fragment
51693	C6	63458	20384	B-iii01	6	3		ü					*Rangifer*	unshed R antler base (pedicle, no brow tine, beam)
51694	6B	63452	20384	B-iii01	6	4							Bison	fragment of proximal end and medial diaphysis of L radius
51695	7B	63457	20384	B-iii01	4	3							cf. *Mammuthus*	crushed and fragmented rib midshaft fragments
51696	29B	63451	20384	B-iii01	2	3							undetermined	3 small indeterminate bone fragments
51697	C5	63638	20003	B-iii03	6	5							*Mammuthus*	shattered long bone midshaft and associated fragments
51698	16	63636	20003	B-iii03	4	5							*Mammuthus*	large limb bone fragment
51699	16	63636	20003	B-iii03	6	4							*Mammuthus*	one large fragment and several small fragments of indeterminate long bone
51700	29B	63636	20003	B-iii03	6	5							*Mammuthus*	indeterminate large limb bone fragment
51701	33B	63636	20003	B-iii03	6	5							*Mammuthus*	large long bone fragment, ?humerus midshaft

continued

Table A4.4 Individual vertebrate finds: boxes 1–19 provided directly from Gressenhall; boxes with 'B' after the number came from Bradford; 'Spec.' denotes 'Special Box' built by Bradford; 'pj' = plaster jacket; 'C' = Crate. Note 1: not in a numbered box, brought in by Nigel Larkin – continued

object no.	box	spit no.	context no.	facies	size	weathering	iron staining	abrasion	root damage	carnivore gnawing	rodent gnawing	deliberate fracturing	taxon	element
51702	17	63635	20003	B-iii03	3	3							undetermined	indeterminate long bone fragments
51703	27B	63633	20003	B-iii03	6	4				ü			Mammuthus	rib midshaft fragment
51704	27B	64762+64765	20254	B-iii01	6	3							Mammuthus	proximal anterior rib and large part of midshaft, multiple fragments
51705	27B	64750+64763	20254	B-iii01	6	3							Mammuthus	multiple fragments of rib midshaft
51706	3B	65680	20003	B-iii03	6	5							Mammuthus	tusk fragments
51707	33B	63644	20003	B-iii03	6	5							Mammuthus	mandibular symphysis, small molar plate fragment found in surrounding matrix
51708	17	63644	20003	B-iii03	2	2							cf. Mammuthus	rib midshaft fragment
51709	20B	63645	20003	B-iii03	5	3							Mammuthus	conjoining fragments of rib midshaft
51710	24B	63721	20003	B-iii03	6	4							Mammuthus	R m2
51711	17	63645	20003	B-iii03	3	4							undetermined	indeterminate long bone fragment
51712	17	63563	20003	B-iii03	4	3							Mammuthus	large indeterminate bone fragment
51713	17	3D co-ords only	20364	B-iii01	3	3							undetermined	indeterminate bone fragment
51714	17	3D co-ords only	20364	B-iii01	3	3							undetermined	indeterminate bone fragment
51715	17	3D co-ords only	20364	B-iii01	4	4							cf. Mammuthus	indeterminate long bone fragment
51716	17	3D co-ords only	20364	B-iii01	3	3							cf. Mammuthus	indeterminate long bone fragment
51717	17	3D co-ords only	20364	B-iii01	3	3							cf. Mammuthus	indeterminate long bone fragment
51718	17	63814	20021	B-iii03	4	3							Mammuthus	multiple tusk fragments
51719	17	63643	20003	B-iii03	2	4							undetermined	indeterminate bone fragment
51720	3B	63643	20003	B-iii03	3	5							undetermined	indeterminate long bone fragment
51721	3B	63650	20003	B-iii03	5	5							cf. Mammuthus	indeterminate bone fragments
51722	17	65682	20003	B-iii03	2	3							cf. Mammuthus	cranial fragment

APPENDIX 4

Table A4.4 Individual vertebrate finds: boxes 1–19 provided directly from Gressenhall; boxes with 'B' after the number came from Bradford; 'Spec.' denotes 'Special Box' built by Bradford; 'pj' = plaster jacket; 'C' = Crate. Note 1: not in a numbered box, brought in by Nigel Larkin – continued

object no.	box	split no.	context no.	facies	size	weathering	iron staining	abrasion	root damage	carnivore gnawing	rodent gnawing	deliberate fracturing	taxon	element
51723	17	63643	20003	B-iii:O3	2	3							cf. Mammuthus	cranial fragment
51724	17	63643	20003	B-iii:O3	3	3							cf. Mammuthus	cranial fragment
51725	17	63565	20003	B-iii:O3	4	3							cf. Mammuthus	rib midshaft fragment
51726	17	63649	20003	B-iii:O3	2	2							Ursus	R m1, pair of 51212
51727	17	63646	20003	B-iii:O3	4	3							Mammuthus	molar plate
51728	3B	63646	20003	B-iii:O3	4	4							Mammuthus	indeterminate bone fragment
51729	17	63646	20003	B-iii:O3	2	3							undetermined	indeterminate bone fragment
51730	24B	62887	20003	B-iii:O3	6	3							Mammuthus	L m2, pair of 50358
51731	6B	62887	20003	B-iii:O3	5	3				ü			Mammuthus	mandibular symphyseal fragments
51732	17	62887	20003	B-iii:O3	3	3							Mammuthus	molar plate fragments
51733	spec 4	62880	20003	B-iii:O3	6	3				ü			Mammuthus	large piece of L pelvis with damaged acetabulum
51734	17	63575	20003	B-iii:O3	4	3							Mammuthus	molar plate fragment
51735	17	63648	20003	B-iii:O3	3	4							undetermined	indeterminate bone fragments
51736	17	63817	20003	B-iii:O3	4	2							cf. Mammuthus	neural spine fragment?
51737	17	63567	20003	B-iii:O3	2	3							Cervidae	antler beam fragment
51738	17	62994	20021	B-iii:O3	3	3							undetermined	indeterminate bone fragment
51739	17	64259	20021	B-iii:O3	4	2							Mammuthus	cranial fragment
51740	17	63755	20003	B-iii:O3	2	4							undetermined	indeterminate bone fragment
51741	17	63755	20003	B-iii:O3	3	4							undetermined	indeterminate bone fragment
51742	33B	63755	20003	B-iii:O3	6	4							Mammuthus	R dentary fragment
51743a	17	63578	20003	B-iii:O3	3	4							Mammuthus	cranial fragment

continued ▶

Table A4.4 Individual vertebrate finds: boxes 1–19 provided directly from Gressenhall; boxes with 'B' after the number came from Bradford; 'Spec.' denotes 'Special Box' built by Bradford; 'pj' = plaster jacket; 'C' = Crate. Note 1: not in a numbered box, brought in by Nigel Larkin – continued

object no.	box	spit no.	context no.	facies	size	weathering	iron staining	abrasion	root damage	carnivore gnawing	rodent gnawing	deliberate fracturing	taxon	element
51743b	3B	63578	20003	B-iii03	4	4							Mammuthus	indeterminate bone fragment
51744	17	62370	20132	B-iii04	4	5							undetermined	indeterminate bone fragment
51746	17	63767	20003	B-iii03	4	3							undetermined	indeterminate bone fragment
51747	27B	63767	20003	B-iii03	6	4							Mammuthus	2 conjoining fragments of rib midshaft
51748	17	62891	20003	B-iii03	2	2							Rangifer	antler beam fragment
51749	17	62370	20132	B-iii04	3	4							Mammuthus	tusk fragment
51750	17	62370	20132	B-iii04	2	3							Mammuthus	tusk fragment
51751	17	62372	20132	B-iii04	4	3							Mammuthus	multiple tusk fragments
51752	17	63766	20003	B-iii03	3	2							Mammuthus	small fragment of large rib
51753	17	63819	20003	B-iii03	5	2							undetermined	indeterminate bone fragment
51754	17	63819	20003	B-iii03	3	2							Rangifer	antler fragment
51755	17	63814	20003	B-iii03	2	2							Mammuthus	proximal epiphysis of rib
51756	3B	63464	20384	B-iii01	1	5							Mammuthus	multiple small tusk fragments
51757	11B	63819	20003	B-iii03	5	3							Mammuthus	cranial fragments
51758	3B	63765	20003	B-iii03	3	4			ü				Mammuthus	assorted fragments, including rib midshaft fragments, 2 small molar plate fragments and small fragment of ?humerus midshaft (non-mammoth)
51759	3B	62890	20003	B-iii03	3	4							cf. Mammuthus	indeterminate bone fragment
51760	17	63734	20003	B-iii03	3	3							Mammuthus	tusk fragment
51761	17	63589	20003	B-iii03	4	3							Mammuthus	tusk fragments
51762	3B	63589	20003	B-iii03	3	3							Mammuthus	cranial fragment
51763	17	63589	20003	B-iii03	2	4							cf. Mammuthus	cranial fragment

APPENDIX 4

Table A4.4 Individual vertebrate finds: boxes 1–19 provided directly from Gressenhall; boxes with 'B' after the number came from Bradford; 'Spec.' denotes 'Special Box' built by Bradford; 'pj' = plaster jacket; 'C' = Crate. Note 1: not in a numbered box, brought in by Nigel Larkin – continued

object no.	box	split no.	context no.	facies	size	weathering	iron staining	abrasion	root damage	carnivore gnawing	rodent gnawing	deliberate fracturing	taxon	element
51764	3B	63769	20003	B-iii:O3	3	5							cf. Mammuthus	cranial fragments
51765	17	62892	20003	B-iii:O3	2	4							undetermined	indeterminate bone fragment
51766	17	63951	20003	B-iii:O3	2	3							Mammuthus	molar root
51767	17	63951	20003	B-iii:O3	2	3							Mammuthus	molar root
51768	17	63748	20003	B-iii:O3	2	3							Mammuthus	molar plate fragment
51769	17	63750	20003	B-iii:O3	5	4				ü			Mammuthus	rib midshaft section
51770	17	63571	20003	B-iii:O3	3	2							Mammuthus	tusk fragment
51771	3B	62899	20003	B-iii:O3	4	4							Mammuthus	indeterminate bone fragment
51772	3B	62899	20003	B-iii:O3	3	2							Mammuthus	cranial fragment
51773	11B	63586	20003	B-iii:O3	2	4							Mammuthus	multiple small tusk and bone fragments
51774	3B	63780	20363	B-iii:O1	3	4							undetermined	indeterminate bone fragment
51775	34–37B	63747	20003	B-iii:O3	6	3							Mammuthus	large tusk fragments and multiple small tusk fragments
51776	17	64102	20003	B-iii:O3	2	2							Mammuthus	tusk fragments
51777	17	64001	20003	B-iii:O3	3	3							Mammuthus	molar plate fragment
51779	17	63574	20003	B-iii:O3	3	3							undetermined	indeterminate bone fragment
51780	17	62384	20364	B-iii:O1	3	2							undetermined	indeterminate bone fragment
51781	17	64002	20003	B-iii:O3	6	2				ü			Rangifer	unshed R antler base (pedicle, part of brow tine and small part of beam)
51782	17	63514	20003	B-iii:O3	5	4							Mammuthus	tusk fragment
51783	3B	63966	20003	B-iii:O3	3	5							undetermined	multiple indeterminate bone fragments
51784	17	63966	20003	B-iii:O3	3	3							undetermined	indeterminate bone fragments
51785	17	63966	20003	B-iii:O3	2	3							Mammuthus	molar talon fragment

continued ▶

473

Table A4.4 Individual vertebrate finds: boxes 1–19 provided directly from Gressenhall; boxes with 'B' after the number came from Bradford; 'Spec.' denotes 'Special Box' built by Bradford; 'pj' = plaster jacket; 'C' = Crate. Note 1: not in a numbered box, brought in by Nigel Larkin – continued

object no.	box	spit no.	context no.	facies	size	weathering	iron staining	abrasion	root damage	carnivore gnawing	rodent gnawing	deliberate fracturing	taxon	element
51786	17	64107	20003	B-iii03	3	2						ü	Rangifer	L humerus midshaft fragment
51787	17	64107	20003	B-iii03	1	3							undetermined	small cranial fragment
51788	3B	63965	20003	B-iii03	2	2							Mammuthus	small cranial fragment
51789	17	64251	20021	B-iii03	2	3							Mammuthus	small tusk fragment
51790	17	64251	20021	B-iii03	3	3							Mammuthus	tusk fragment
51791	17	64251	20021	B-iii03	1	2							undetermined	small indeterminate bone fragment
51792	3B	64251	20021	B-iii03	2	4							undetermined	indeterminate bone fragment
51793	17	64251	20021	B-iii03	4	3							undetermined	indeterminate bone fragment
51794	17	62893	20003	B-iii03	2	3							Mammuthus	molar plate fragments
51795	3B	63964	20003	B-iii03	2	3							cf. Mammuthus	small cranial fragment
51796	3B	63969	20003	B-iii03	4	3				ü			Mammuthus	rib midshaft fragment
51797	3B	63969	20003	B-iii03	3	3							Mammuthus	tusk fragment
51798	3B	63968	20003	B-iii03	2	3							Mammuthus	cranial fragment
51799	17	62389	20364	B-iii01	2	3							undetermined	indeterminate bone fragment
51800	3B	63461	20384	B-iii01	4	5							Rangifer	unshed R antler base (frontal, pedicle and broken beam fragments)
51801	loose	63461	20384	B-iii01	1	3							Mammuthus	small tusk fragments
51802	18	63461	20384	B-iii01	2	3							Mammuthus	molar plate fragment
51803	18	63968	20003	B-iii03	3	3							cf. Mammuthus	cranial fragment
51804	18	64252	20021	B-iii03	2	3							undetermined	cranial fragment
51805	18	64252+64258	20021	B-iii03	5	3							Mammuthus	large cranial fragments
51806	18	64252	20021	B-iii03	1	2							undetermined	small cranial fragment

APPENDIX 4

Table A4.4 Individual vertebrate finds: boxes 1–19 provided directly from Gressenhall; boxes with 'B' after the number came from Bradford; 'Spec.' denotes 'Special Box' built by Bradford; 'pj' = plaster jacket; 'C' = Crate. Note 1: not in a numbered box, brought in by Nigel Larkin – continued

object no.	box	spit no.	context no.	facies	size	weathering	iron staining	abrasion	root damage	carnivore gnawing	rodent gnawing	deliberate fracturing	taxon	element
51807	18	64252+64258	20021	B-iii03	3	3							Mammuthus	tusk fragment
51808	18	64252+64258	20021	B-iii03	4	3				ü			undetermined	indeterminate bone fragment
51809	18	64252	20021	B-iii03	2	3							undetermined	small cranial fragment
51810	18	64252	20021	B-iii03	1	3							undetermined	small cranial fragment
51811	18	64252	20021	B-iii03	2	4							undetermined	small cranial fragments
51812	18	63457	20384	B-iii01	2	3							Mammuthus	molar plate fragment
51813	3B	63968	20003	B-iii03	4	3							Mammuthus	2 small cranial fragments
51814	C1	63333	20004	B-iii03	6	4							Rangifer	base of shed R antler
51815	3B	63597	20003	B-iii03	2	4							Mammuthus	cranial fragments
51816a	B		20254	B-iii01									Mammuthus	proximal rib articulation
51816b	18B		20003	B-iii03	6	4							Mammuthus	part of R acetabulum and ischium (not from same individual as 51733)
51817	Bradford	63325–31	20004	B-iii01									Mammuthus	tusk, jacketed
51818	3B	64309	20003	B-iii03	3	5							undetermined	indeterminate bone fragments
51819	18	63590	20003	B-iii03	4	3							Mammuthus	molar plate
51820	26B	64006	20003	B-iii03	5	3							Mammuthus	R m3, pair of 51997
51821	18	64253	20021	B-iii03	1	3							undetermined	small cranial fragments
51822	18	64253	20021	B-iii03	2	3							undetermined	cranial fragment
51823a	18	63334	20004	B-iii01	2	3							undetermined	small cranial fragment
51823b	3B	63334	20004	B-iii01	3	4							undetermined	indeterminate bone fragment
51824	18	63329	20004	B-iii01	3	4							undetermined	indeterminate bone fragment
51825	18	64125	20003	B-iii03	2	2							undetermined	cranial fragment

continued ▶

Table A4.4 Individual vertebrate finds: boxes 1–19 provided directly from Gressenhall; boxes with 'B' after the number came from Bradford; 'Spec.' denotes 'Special Box' built by Bradford; 'pj' = plaster jacket; 'C' = Crate. Note 1: not in a numbered box, brought in by Nigel Larkin – continued

object no.	box	spit no.	context no.	facies	size	weathering	iron staining	abrasion	root damage	carnivore gnawing	rodent gnawing	deliberate fracturing	taxon	element
51826	18	64125	20003	B-iii03	2	3							Mammuthus	small tusk fragment
51827	18	64125	20003	B-iii03	2	3							undetermined	small cranial fragment
51828	18	64125	20003	B-iii03	2	4							Mammuthus	cranial fragment
51829	18	63970	20003	B-iii03	3	3							cf. Mammuthus	cranial fragments
51830	7B	61287	20003	B-iii03	6	3							Mammuthus	large fragment and multiple small cranial fragments, including auditory bulla
51831	3B	64081	20003	B-iii03	3	3		ü					Equus	complete R astragalus, associated with 51869
51832a	29B	64082	20003	B-iii03	5	3		ü		ü			Mammuthus	jugal and cranial fragment
51832b	29B	64082	20003	B-iii03	3	3							Mammuthus	epiphysis of femoral head
51833	18	64126	20003	B-iii03	2	3							Mammuthus	tusk fragment
51834	18	64126	20003	B-iii03	3	3							Mammuthus	tusk fragment
51835	18	64126	20003	B-iii03	3	2							Mammuthus	tusk fragment
51836	18	64126	20003	B-iii03	2	2							Mammuthus	3rd phalanx
51837	15B	64314	20003	B-iii03	5	3				ü			Mammuthus	rib midshaft fragment
51838	18	64314	20003	B-iii03	3	4							Mammuthus	rib midshaft fragment
51839	18	64314	20003	B-iii03	2	3							undetermined	indeterminate bone fragment
51840	18	64315	20003	B-iii03	2	3							Mammuthus	molar root fragment
51841	18	64315	20003	B-iii03	3	3							Mammuthus	molar talon fragment
51842	3B	64313	20003	B-iii03	6	5							Mammuthus	indeterminate bone fragment
51843	18	63974	20003	B-iii03	5	3							Mammuthus	scapula blade fragment
51844	18	63974	20003	B-iii03	2	3							undetermined	cranial fragment
51845	18	63975	20003	B-iii03	3	3							Mammuthus	molar plate fragment

APPENDIX 4

Table A.4.4 Individual vertebrate finds: boxes 1–19 provided directly from Gressenhall; boxes with 'B' after the number came from Bradford; 'Spec.' denotes 'Special Box' built by Bradford; 'pj' = plaster jacket; 'C' = Crate. Note 1: not in a numbered box, brought in by Nigel Larkin – continued

object no.	box	spit no.	context no.	facies	size	weathering	iron staining	abrasion	root damage	carnivore gnawing	rodent gnawing	deliberate fracturing	taxon	element
51846	3B	64313	20003	B-iii03	3	3							Mammuthus	tusk fragments
51847	3B	64313	20003	B-iii03	2	4							Mammuthus	2 small tusk fragments
51848	18	64313	20003	B-iii03	5	3							Mammuthus	long bone fragment
51849	18	64313	20003	B-iii03	2	3							undetermined	small fragment of long bone
51850	3B	63509	20384	B-iii01	4	5							Mammuthus	fragment of large long bone
51851	3B	63509	20384	B-iii01	4	5							undetermined	cranial fragment
51852	30B	unstratified	20246	B-iii02	4	4		ü					Bison	fragmentary distal L humerus
51853	3B	63512	20384	B-iii01	2	5							Mammuthus	cranial fragment
51854	18	64313	20003	B-iii03	3	2							Mammuthus	rib midshaft fragment
51855	22B	63972	20003	B-iii03	6	3				ü			Mammuthus	part of L pelvis (acetabulum missing)
51856	18	63972	20003	B-iii03	3	3							undetermined	cranial fragment
51857	18	63972	20003	B-iii03	3	4							undetermined	cranial fragment
51858	3B	63972	20003	B-iii03	3	3							Mammuthus	cranial fragment
51859	3B	63972	20003	B-iii03	5	5							Mammuthus	cranial fragment
51860	18	63972	20003	B-iii03	4	3		ü					Canis lupus	R ulna, missing part of proximal, see also 50233; sampled for isotopes
51861	18	64129	20003	B-iii03	2	2							cf. Mammuthus	cranial fragment
51862	18	64129	20003	B-iii03	2	3							cf. Mammuthus	cranial fragment
51864	18	64129	20003	B-iii03	2	4							Mammuthus	tusk fragment
51865	3B	64316	20003	B-iii03	3	4							Mammuthus	tusk fragments
51866	3B	64256	20021	B-iii03	3	4				ü			Mammuthus	incomplete ?magnum
51867	18	64255	20021	B-iii03	3	3							cf. Mammuthus	cranial fragments

continued ▶

477

Table A4.4 Individual vertebrate finds: boxes 1–19 provided directly from Gressenhall; boxes with 'B' after the number came from Bradford; 'Spec.' denotes 'Special Box' built by Bradford; 'pj' = plaster jacket; 'C' = Crate. Note 1: not in a numbered box, brought in by Nigel Larkin – continued

object no.	box	split no.	context no.	facies	size	weathering	iron staining	abrasion	root damage	carnivore gnawing	rodent gnawing	deliberate fracturing	taxon	element
51868	18	64316	20003	B-iii03	4	2							Mammuthus	tusk fragments
51869	18	63975	20003	B-iii03	4	3							Equus	complete R calcaneum, associated with 5183 J; sampled for isotopes
51870	18	64316	20003	B-iii03	1	1							Vulpes cf. vulpes	R C
51871	18	64256	20021	B-iii03	2	4							Mammuthus	tusk fragment
51872	18	64256	20021	B-iii03	2	3					ü		undetermined	small fragment of long bone
51873	15B	63975	20021	B-iii03	6	3							Mammuthus	jugal fragment
51874	18	63975	20003	B-iii03	4	4							Mammuthus	cranial fragment
51875	18	63961	20003	B-iii03	5	3							Mammuthus	large molar plate fragment
51876	18	64364	20003	B-iii03	3	3							Mammuthus	maxillary fragment
51877	18	64133	20003	B-iii03	3	3							undetermined	indeterminate bone fragment
51878	18	64148	20003	B-iii01	4	3							undetermined	fragment of ?cervical vertebra
51879	18	64367	20384	B-iii01	4	3							Mammuthus	tusk fragment
51880	3B	64394	20384	B-iii01	3	5							undetermined	indeterminate bone fragment
51881	15B	64394	20384	B-iii03	4	4							Mammuthus	rib midshaft fragments
51882	18	64213	20003	B-iii03	6	3							Mammuthus	very large molar plate
51883	18	64218	20003	B-iii03	3	4							Mammuthus	tusk fragment
51884	18	64318	20003	B-iii03	3	3							Rangifer	antler fragment
51885	3B	64017	20003	B-iii03	4	5				ü			Mammuthus	distal diaphysis of juvenile L humerus
51886	3B	64321	20003	B-iii03	3	4				ü			cf. Mammuthus	rib midshaft fragment
51887	24B	63962	20003	B-iii03	6	4							Mammuthus	R M3 fragment
51888	3B	63963	20003	B-iii03	5	2							Mammuthus	molar plate

APPENDIX 4

Table A4.4 Individual vertebrate finds: boxes 1–19 provided directly from Gressenhall; boxes with 'B' after the number came from Bradford; 'Spec.' denotes 'Special Box' built by Bradford; 'pj' = plaster jacket; 'C' = Crate. Note 1: not in a numbered box, brought in by Nigel Larkin – continued

object no.	box	spit no.	context no.	facies	size	weathering	iron staining	abrasion	root damage	carnivore gnawing	rodent gnawing	deliberate fracturing	taxon	element
51889	18	63963	20003	B-iii:03	6	4		ü	ü				Bison	distal L humerus
51890	18	64019	20003	B-iii:03	3	3							cf. Mammuthus	cranial fragment
51891a	18	64019	20003	B-iii:03	3	4							Mammuthus	tusk fragments
51891b	3B	64019	20003	B-iii:03	4	4							Mammuthus	cranial fragment
51893	18	64134	20003	B-iii:03	3	4							undetermined	indeterminate bone fragment
51895	18	64143	20003	B-iii:03	2	4							undetermined	small cranial fragment
51898	18	64362	20384	B-iii:01	4	4							undetermined	indeterminate bone fragment
51899	18	64324	20003	B-iii:03	1	2							Rangifer	R p3
51900	18	64144	20003	B-iii:03	3	3							undetermined	cranial fragment
51902	18	64323	20003	B-iii:03	1	1							Ursus	R m3
51903	C5	64384	20384	B-iii:01	6	4							Mammuthus	proximal L radius
51904	4B	63980	20003	B-iii:03	3	3							Mammuthus	cranial fragment
51905	18	64322	20003	B-iii:03	4	3							Mammuthus	molar plate fragment
51906	18	64330	20003	B-iii:03	4	3							Mammuthus	molar plate fragment
51907	4B	64325	20003	B-iii:03	4	4							Mammuthus	indeterminate bone fragment
51908	18	64325	20003	B-iii:03	3	3							undetermined	indeterminate bone fragment
51909	18	64328	20003	B-iii:03	3	4							undetermined	indeterminate bone fragment
51910	18	64333+64336	20003	B-iii:03	5	4							Mammuthus	tusk fragment
51911	18	64226	20003	B-iii:03	2	3							undetermined	indeterminate bone fragment
51912	18	64335	20003	B-iii:03	2	2							Rangifer	fragment of lumbar vertebra
51913	18	64336	20003	B-iii:03	2	3							undetermined	indeterminate bone fragment
51914	18	64336	20003	B-iii:03	2	3							Mammuthus	small tusk fragment

continued

Table A4.4 Individual vertebrate finds: boxes 1–19 provided directly from Gressenhall; boxes with 'B' after the number came from Bradford; 'Spec.' denotes 'Special Box' built by Bradford; 'pj' = plaster jacket; 'C' = Crate. Note 1: not in a numbered box, brought in by Nigel Larkin – continued

object no.	box	spit no.	context no.	facies	size	weathering	iron staining	abrasion	root damage	carnivore gnawing	rodent gnawing	deliberate fracturing	taxon	element
51915	4B	64336	20003	B-iii03	3	4							undetermined	indeterminate bone fragment
51916	18	64335	20003	B-iii03	3	3							Mammuthus	tusk fragment
51917	18	64221	20003	B-iii03	3	3							Mammuthus	tusk fragment
51918	18	63985	20003	B-iii03	3	2							cf. Rangifer	probable femoral midshaft fragment
51919	18	63986	20003	B-iii03	3	3							cf. Mammuthus	cranial fragment
51920	18	64235	20003	B-iii03	2	3							Mammuthus	tusk fragment
51921	4B	64259	20021	B-iii03	2	3							undetermined	cranial fragment
51922	18	64259	20021	B-iii03	3	3							Mammuthus	cranial fragment
51923	spec 2	64259	20021	B-iii03	6	3							Mammuthus	thoracic vertebra with damaged centrum and detached epiphyses
51924			20021	B-iii03	1	4							undetermined	indeterminate bone fragment
51925	18	64529	20021	B-iii03	3	3							undetermined	indeterminate bone fragment
51926	4B	64259	20021	B-iii03	4	2							Mammuthus	cranial fragment
51927	18	64258	20021	B-iii03	3	2							Mammuthus	proximal epiphysis of rib
51928	4B	64259	20021	B-iii03	2	4							undetermined	cranial fragments
51929			20021	B-iii03	1	3							Mammuthus	small cranial fragments
51930	18	64235	20003	B-iii03	4	3							Mammuthus	tusk fragment
51931	18	64235	20003	B-iii03	4	4							undetermined	indeterminate bone fragment
51932	4B	64235	20003	B-iii03	4	5							Mammuthus	large fragments of cancellous bone and indeterminate long bone fragments
51933	15B	64224+64226	20003	B-iii03	6	4							Mammuthus	2 conjoining rib midshaft fragments
51934	18	64264	20021	B-iii03	3	3							undetermined	indeterminate bone fragment
51935	18	64264	20021	B-iii03	4	3							undetermined	rib midshaft fragment

APPENDIX 4

Table A4.4 Individual vertebrate finds: boxes 1–19 provided directly from Gressenhall; boxes with 'B' after the number came from Bradford; 'Spec.' denotes 'Special Box' built by Bradford; 'pj' = plaster jacket; 'C' = Crate. Note 1: not in a numbered box, brought in by Nigel Larkin – continued

object no.	box	spit no.	context no.	facies	size	weathering	iron staining	abrasion	root damage	carnivore gnawing	rodent gnawing	deliberate fracturing	taxon	element
51936	spec 1	63000+64266	20021	B-iii03	6	3							Mammuthus	virtually complete rib (proximal epiphysis missing), fragment of proximal end in Box B4
51937	4B	62999	20021	B-iii03	5	3							Mammuthus	cranial fragment
51938	18	62999+64265	20021	B-iii03	6	3							Mammuthus	rib midshaft fragment
51939	18	64265	20021	B-iii03	2	3							undetermined	cranial fragment
51940	18	64266	20021	B-iii03	3	2							undetermined	indeterminate bone fragment
51941	18	64266	20021	B-iii03	2	2							undetermined	cranial fragment
51942	18	64265	20021	B-iii03	3	2							cf. Mammuthus	cranial fragment
51943	spec 3	62999+64265	20021	B-iii03	6	3							Mammuthus	virtually complete middle rib (detached proximal epiphysis, damaged distal end)
51944	spec 1	64264-6	20021	B-iii03	6	3							Mammuthus	virtually complete middle rib (lacking proximal end, four conjoining distal fragments (3 in Box B27))
51945	4B	64266-7	20021	B-iii03	3	5							cf. Mammuthus	cranial fragments
51946	18	64266	20021	B-iii03	2	2							undetermined	small cranial fragments
51947	4B	64229	20003	B-iii03	4	5							undetermined	thin indeterminate bone fragment, cemented onto matrix
51948	15B	64229	20003	B-iii03	6	3							Mammuthus	proximal rib, lacking epiphysis
51949	20B	64229+64231	20003	B-iii03	6	3							Mammuthus	rib midshaft fragments
51950	14B	64232	20003	B-iii03	5	3							Mammuthus	tusk fragments, from large tusk, jacketed
51951	18	64243	20003	B-iii03	4	3							Mammuthus	proximal rib articular fragment
51952	4B	64557	20371	B-iii02	4	4							Mammuthus	tusk fragments
51953	26B	64345	20003	B-iii03	6	3							Mammuthus	posterior part of R m3, with 51648+51154

continued ▶

Table A4.4 Individual vertebrate finds: boxes 1–19 provided directly from Gressenhall; boxes with 'B' after the number came from Bradford; 'Spec.' denotes 'Special Box' built by Bradford; 'pj' = plaster jacket; 'C' = Crate. Note 1: not in a numbered box, brought in by Nigel Larkin – continued

object no.	box	split no.	context no.	facies	size	weathering	iron staining	abrasion	root damage	carnivore gnawing	rodent gnawing	deliberate fracturing	taxon	element
51955	spec 1	unstratified	20375	B-iii01	6	3							Mammuthus	middle rib, missing proximal end and distal epiphysis
51956	29B	64654	20003	B-iii03	6	3				ü			Mammuthus	incomplete lumbar vertebra (missing proximal epiphysis)
51957	18	64229	20003	B-iii03	2	3							cf. Mammuthus	multiple small rib fragments
51958	19	64265	20021	B-iii03	3	3							cf. Mammuthus	cranial fragment
51959	9B	64651	20003	B-iii03	3	3							Mammuthus	cranial fragment
51960	19	64147	20003	B-iii03	3	3							undetermined	indeterminate bone fragment
51961a	46B	64240	20003	B-iii03	6	3							Mammuthus	multiple tusk fragments
51961b	48B	64240	20003	B-iii03	6	3				ü			Mammuthus	large cranial fragment, multiple small fragments, small fragment of rib
51961c	49B	64240	20003	B-iii03	6	3							Mammuthus	large very crushed tusk fragment on matrix block
51961d	10B	64240	20003	B-iii03	3	4							Mammuthus	cranial and tusk fragments
51962	B	unknown	unknown	unknown									Mammuthus	cranial and alveolus fragments
51963	4B	64658	20384	B-iii01	5	5							Mammuthus	miscellaneous fragments, including tusk, rib and indeterminate bone fragments
51964	19	64656	20384	B-iii01	4	3							Mammuthus	molar plate fragment
51965	23B	64655	20384	B-iii01	6	3							Mammuthus	part of L M3, pair of 52063
51966	26B	64658	20384	B-iii01	6	3							Mammuthus	L M2
51967	21B	64656	20384	B-iii01	6	3				ü			Mammuthus	femoral midshaft
51968	4B	64658	20384	B-iii01	4	4							Mammuthus	cranial fragment
51969	4B	64658	20384	B-iii01	3	5							undetermined	cranial fragment
51970	19	64655	20384	B-iii01	3	3							cf. Mammuthus	multiple cranial fragments

APPENDIX 4

Table A4.4 Individual vertebrate finds: boxes 1–19 provided directly from Gressenhall; boxes with 'B' after the number came from Bradford; 'Spec.' denotes 'Special Box' built by Bradford; 'pj' = plaster jacket; 'C' = Crate. Note 1: not in a numbered box, brought in by Nigel Larkin – continued

object no.	box	spit no.	context no.	facies	size	weathering	iron staining	abrasion	root damage	carnivore gnawing	rodent gnawing	deliberate fracturing	taxon	element
51971	4B	64281	20139	B-iii01	3	5							undetermined	multiple bone fragments, probably rib midshaft
51972	16B	64280	20139	B-iii01	6	3							Mammuthus	proximal rib fragment with articulation, fairly anterior, conjoins with 51999
51973	20B	64273	20139	B-iii01	6	4							Mammuthus	rib midshaft fragments
51974	19	64601	20364	B-iii01	2	3							undetermined	indeterminate bone fragment
51975	4B	64601	20364	B-iii01	3	4							Mammuthus	cranial fragment
51976	C3	unstratified	20003	B-iii03	6	3				ü			Mammuthus	incomplete R ulna (3 large fragments), comprising part of proximal articulation and shaft
51977	4B	64758	20254	B-iii01	2	5							undetermined	thin fragment of indeterminate bone, cemented onto sandy gravel
51978	4B	64712	20003	B-iii03	3	4							undetermined	indeterminate bone fragments
51979	11B	64716	20003	B-iii03	5	4							Mammuthus	multiple tusk fragments
51980	69B	64715+64718+64724+64727	20003	B-iii03	6	4							Mammuthus	multiple bags of tusk fragments
51981	19	64715	20003	B-iii03	2	3							undetermined	small rib midshaft fragment
51982	19	64712	20003	B-iii03	2	3							undetermined	cf. vertebral fragment
51983	19	64712	20003	B-iii03	5	4							Mammuthus	fragment of ?dentary
51984	19	64715	20003	B-iii03	2	3							undetermined	indeterminate bone fragment
51985	19	64715	20003	B-iii03	2	4							undetermined	indeterminate bone fragment
51986	4B	64714	20003	B-iii03	3	4							Mammuthus	?dentary fragment
51987a	4B	64714	20003	B-iii03	4	4							Mammuthus	cranial fragment
51987b	19	64714	20003	B-iii03	2	3							undetermined	indeterminate bone fragment
51988	5B	64711	20003	B-iii03	6	4							Mammuthus	2 large and multiple small bone fragments, dentary?

continued

Table A4.4 Individual vertebrate finds: boxes 1–19 provided directly from Gressenhall; boxes with 'B' after the number came from Bradford; 'Spec.' denotes 'Special Box' built by Bradford; 'pj' = plaster jacket; 'C' = Crate. Note 1: not in a numbered box, brought in by Nigel Larkin – continued

object no.	box	split no.	context no.	facies	size	weathering	iron staining	abrasion	root damage	carnivore gnawing	rodent gnawing	deliberate fracturing	taxon	element
51989	19	64711	20003	B-iii03	2	3							undetermined	indeterminate bone fragment
51990	19	64710	20003	B-iii03	3	3							cf. *Mammuthus*	cranial fragment
51991	19	64717	20003	B-iii03	2	3							*Mammuthus*	2 conjoining rib midshaft fragments
51992	B	64714	20003	B-iii03									*Mammuthus*	cranial or mandibular fragments
51993	19	64714	20003	B-iii03	3	4							*Mammuthus*	tusk fragments
51994	19	64711	20003	B-iii03	2	3							undetermined	indeterminate bone fragment
51995	19	64714	20003	B-iii03	3	3							*Mammuthus*	molar plate fragment
51996	19	64710	20003	B-iii03	3	3							undetermined	indeterminate bone fragment
51997	24B	64710	20003	B-iii03	5	3							*Mammuthus*	L m3, pair of 51820
51998	19	64804	20003	B-iii03	4	2							cf. *Mammuthus*	midshaft of juvenile limb bone fragment, missing epiphysis
51999a	16B	64299	20254	B-iii01	6	4							*Mammuthus*	distal end of large rib, including epiphysis (separate), conjoins with 51972
51999b	28B	64299	20254	B-iii01	6	2							*Mammuthus*	virtually complete axis vertebra
52000	6B	64751	20254	B-iii01	3	5							cf. *Mammuthus*	very fragmentary vertebra
52001	19	64300	20254	B-iii01	2	4							undetermined	indeterminate bone fragment
52002	4B	unstratified	20369	B-iii01	3	5		ü					undetermined	cranial fragments
52003	20B	64805	20369	B-iii01	3	4							*Mammuthus*	conjoining fragments of rib midshaft
52004	17B	64829+64832+64835	20369	B-iii01	6	3							*Mammuthus*	fragmentary incomplete rib
52005	20B	64832+64834+64836-7	20369	B-iii01	6	3							*Mammuthus*	fragmentary rib, virtually complete
52007	15B	64847	20369	B-iii01	6	4							*Mammuthus*	proximal rib, large fragments of proximal midshaft and multiple comminuted midshaft fragments
52008	15B	64848	20369	B-iii01	5	5							*Mammuthus*	indeterminate bone fragment

APPENDIX 4

Table A4.4 Individual vertebrate finds: boxes 1–19 provided directly from Gressenhall; boxes with 'B' after the number came from Bradford; 'Spec.' denotes 'Special Box' built by Bradford; 'pj' = plaster jacket; 'C' = Crate. Note 1: not in a numbered box, brought in by Nigel Larkin – continued

object no.	box	split no.	context no.	facies	size	weathering	iron staining	abrasion	root damage	carnivore gnawing	rodent gnawing	deliberate fracturing	taxon	element
52009	4B	64763–4	20254	B-iii01	2	5		ü					undetermined	multiple indeterminate bone fragments
52010	19	64765	20254	B-iii01	2	3							undetermined	rib midshaft fragment, probably same as 52011-2
52011	19	64765	20254	B-iii01	3	3							undetermined	rib midshaft fragments, probably same as 52010,3
52012	19	64765	20254	B-iii01	3	3				ü			undetermined	rib midshaft fragment, probably same as 52010-1
52013	19	64805	20369	B-iii01	2	3							undetermined	indeterminate bone fragments
52014	19	64805	20369	B-iii01	2	3							undetermined	indeterminate bone fragment
52016	19	64767	20254	B-iii01	3	3							undetermined	rib midshaft fragment
52017	19	64767	20254	B-iii01	3	4				ü			Mammuthus	part of proximal midshaft of rib
52018	10B	64755	20254	B-iii01	2	5		ü					undetermined	multiple comminuted cranial fragments
52019	19	64758	20254	B-iii01	4	3							undetermined	rib midshaft fragment
52020	20B	64822+64826–7	20369	B-iii01	6	4							Mammuthus	fragmented rib midshaft
52021	19	64727	20003	B-iii03	2	3							undetermined	indeterminate bone fragment
52022	19	64724	20003	B-iii03	2	3							undetermined	indeterminate bone fragment
52023	19	64724	20003	B-iii03	3	3							undetermined	indeterminate bone fragment
52024	19	64726	20003	B-iii03	5	3							Mammuthus	tusk fragment
52025	19	64725–6	20003	B-iii03	4	3							undetermined	indeterminate bone fragment
52026	19	64725	20003	B-iii03	3	3							undetermined	indeterminate bone fragment
52027	19	64724	20003	B-iii03	2	3							undetermined	cranial fragment
52028	4B	64723	20003	B-iii03	3	4							Mammuthus	tusk fragments
52029	19	64723	20003	B-iii03	2	3							undetermined	indeterminate bone fragments

continued ▲

485

Table A4.4 Individual vertebrate finds: boxes 1–19 provided directly from Gressenhall; boxes with 'B' after the number came from Bradford; 'Spec.' denotes 'Special Box' built by Bradford; 'pj' = plaster jacket; 'C' = Crate. Note 1: not in a numbered box, brought in by Nigel Larkin – continued

object no.	box	spit no.	context no.	facies	size	weathering	iron staining	abrasion	root damage	carnivore gnawing	rodent gnawing	deliberate fracturing	taxon	element
52030	19	64724	20003	B-iii03	3	3							undetermined	indeterminate bone fragment
52031	19	64723	20003	B-iii03	5	2							Mammuthus	rib midshaft fragment
52032	19	64723	20003	B-iii03	3	4							cf. Mammuthus	?vertebral fragment
52033	27B	64723	20003	B-iii03	6	4					ü		cf. Mammuthus	rib midshaft
52034	19	64720	20003	B-iii03	6	4		ü					Mammuthus	fragment of ?acetabulum
52035	19	64720	20003	B-iii03	1	2							undetermined	small cranial fragment
52036	19	64720	20003	B-iii03	3	3							undetermined	indeterminate bone fragment
52037	19	64719	20003	B-iii03	5	3							Mammuthus	large bone fragments
52038	24B	64772	20254	B-iii01	5	3							Mammuthus	very worn R ?m2 fragment
52039	4B	64772	20254	B-iii01	3	5							undetermined	rib midshaft fragment
52040	29B	64788	20254	B-iii01	6	4							Mammuthus	midsection of scapula
52041	19	64788	20254	B-iii01	2	3							undetermined	indeterminate bone fragments
52042	20B	64828+64835	20369	B-iii03	5	3							Mammuthus	proximal head and rib midshaft fragments
52043	21B	64829+64835	20369	B-iii01	6	4							Mammuthus	large fragment of tibia midshaft
52044	19	64735	20003	B-iii03	2	4							undetermined	indeterminate bone fragment
52045	19	64735	20003	B-iii03	2	3							Mammuthus	small tusk fragment
52046	19	64733	20003	B-iii03	2	2							undetermined	cranial fragment
52047	19	64733	20003	B-iii03	2	3							Mammuthus	small tusk fragment and indeterminate bone fragment
52048	19	64733	20003	B-iii03	3	3							Mammuthus	molar plate fragment
52049	19	64734	20003	B-iii03	3	3							undetermined	indeterminate bone fragment
52050	19	64730	20003	B-iii03	2	1							undetermined	small cranial fragment

APPENDIX 4

Table A4.4 Individual vertebrate finds: boxes 1–19 provided directly from Gressenhall; boxes with 'B' after the number came from Bradford; 'Spec.' denotes 'Special Box' built by Bradford; 'pj' = plaster jacket; 'C' = Crate. Note 1: not in a numbered box, brought in by Nigel Larkin – continued

object no.	box	spit no.	context no.	facies	size	weathering	iron staining	abrasion	root damage	carnivore gnawing	rodent gnawing	deliberate fracturing	taxon	element
52051	19	64731	20003	B-ii:03	2	3							undetermined	indeterminate bone fragment
52052	19	64730	20003	B-ii:03	3	3							Mammuthus	molar plate fragment
52053	19	64730	20003	B-ii:03	3	3							Mammuthus	molar plate fragment
52054	33B	64730	20003	B-ii:03	6	2							Mammuthus	part of neural spine + arch of thoracic/lumbar vertebra
52055	19	64731	20003	B-ii:03	2	3							undetermined	small indeterminate bone fragment
52056	10B	64838–9	20369	B-iii:01	5	5							cf. Mammuthus	fragment of distal condyle of humerus or femur
52057	4B, 10B	64832	20369	B-iii:01	4	5							Mammuthus	cranial fragments
52058	15B	64839+64832	20369	B-iii:01	3	5							Mammuthus	multiple rib midshaft fragments
52059	10B	64842	20369	B-iii:01	3	4		ü					undetermined	2 conjoining cranial fragments
52060	19B	unstratified	20051	B-ii:03	6	5							Mammuthus	2 large conjoining fragments and associated smaller fragments, split longitudinally, cf. femur
52061	19	unstratified	20078	B-ii:03	2	3							undetermined	multiple indeterminate bone fragments
52062	30B	unstratified	20078	B-ii:03	5	3							Mammuthus	caudal vertebra
52063	23B	64816	20369	B-iii:01	6	4							Mammuthus	part of R M3, pair of 51965
52064	41B	unstratified	20078	B-ii:03	3	4							Mammuthus	undetermined epiphyseal fragment
52065	28B	64901–3	20369	B-iii:01	5	4		ü					Mammuthus	proximal head and multiple rib midshaft fragments
52066	41B	64813	20369	B-iii:01	4	5							Mammuthus	occipital condyle
52067	19	64813	20369	B-iii:01	3	3							undetermined	indeterminate bone fragment
52068	19	64957	20369	B-iii:01	4	3							Mammuthus	cranial fragment
52069	19	64957	20369	B-iii:01	3	3							Mammuthus	cranial fragments

continued

Table A4.4 Individual vertebrate finds: boxes 1–19 provided directly from Gressenhall; boxes with 'B' after the number came from Bradford; 'Spec.' denotes 'Special Box' built by Bradford; 'pj' = plaster jacket; 'C' = Crate. Note 1: not in a numbered box, brought in by Nigel Larkin – continued

object no.	box	split no.	context no.	facies	size	weathering	iron staining	abrasion	root damage	carnivore gnawing	rodent gnawing	deliberate fracturing	taxon	element
52070	19	64962	20369	B-iii01	3	4							Mammuthus	cranial fragments
52071	4B	64963	20369	B-iii01	1	4							undetermined	indeterminate bone fragments, probably cranial
52073	19	64962	20369	B-iii01	1	5							undetermined	small indeterminate bone fragments
52074	19	64953	20369	B-iii01	2	3							Coelodonta	incomplete L P3 and miscellaneous bone fragments
52075	76B	64833	20369	B-iii01	3	4							Rangifer	small antler palmation fragment
52076	19	64847	20369	B-iii01	3	3							cf. Mammuthus	rib midshaft fragment
52077	19	64840	20369	B-iii01	2	3							Mammuthus	molar plate fragment
52078	19	64834	20369	B-iii01	2	3							undetermined	cranial fragment
problem numbers														
5072?	76B				5	3							undetermined	cranial fragment
	76B												Mammuthus	small tusk fragment
52100	C1		20003	B-iii03	4	4							Mammuthus	fragments of indeterminate bone, tusk and molar; from "taphonomic spread" (new number assigned by Bradford, NL may know real number)
52102	42B		20003	B-iii03	6	3							Mammuthus	fragmentary glenoid area of R scapula, marked as originally un-numbered
52101	8B		20003	B-iii03	6	3				ü			Mammuthus	several fragments of cranium originally lacking numbers from 'just south of the large pile of tusks', including large fragment from orbital region and large fragment with upper parts of both alveoli, probably from different individuals (former is younger animal)
unnumbered finds														
box 12B					3	4							Mammuthus	bag of tusk fragments

Table A4.4 Individual vertebrate finds: boxes 1–19 provided directly from Gressenhall; boxes with 'B' after the number came from Bradford; 'Spec.' denotes 'Special Box' built by Bradford; 'pj' = plaster jacket; 'C' = Crate. Note 1: not in a numbered box, brought in by Nigel Larkin – continued

object no.	box	spit no.	context no.	facies	size	weathering	iron staining	abrasion	root damage	carnivore gnawing	rodent gnawing	deliberate fracturing	taxon	element
	box 43B	individual bags												
	Central spoil		20048	destroyed/disturbed channel sediments	6	4							Mammuthus	multiple large and small tusk fragments (5 bags)
	Central spoil		20048	destroyed/disturbed channel sediments	5	3							Mammuthus	large cranial and indeterminate long bone fragments (4 bags)
	Central spoil		20048	destroyed/disturbed channel sediments	4	4							Mammuthus	molar plate fragments
	no data				4	4							Mammuthus	tusk fragments
	box 44B	individual bags												
			20135	B-iii03	6	4							undetermined	4 small indeterminate bone fragments
			20365	B-iii04	2	4							undetermined	indeterminate bone fragment (400E, 839N, 6mm sieve)
			20003	B-iii03	3	4							undetermined	indeterminate bone fragments
			20021	B-iii03	4	4							Mammuthus	multiple tusk fragments
			20021	B-iii03	3	4							undetermined	indeterminate small bone fragments
			20021	B-iii03	4	4							Mammuthus	10 indeterminate bone fragments and one molar plate fragment
			20021	B-iii03	3	4							Mammuthus	4 tusk fragments from interior of tusk
			20021	B-iii03	4	4							Mammuthus	tusk fragment
			20021	B-iii03	2	4							Mammuthus	2 small tusk fragments and 2 indeterminate bone fragments
			20044		1	4							undetermined	indeterminate bone fragment
			20044		4	3							Mammuthus	cranial fragments 'from under Russell Coope's detritus'
			20044		2	4							Mammuthus	multiple fragments of tusk, cranium and indeterminate bone

continued ▶

Table A4.4 Individual vertebrate finds: boxes 1–19 provided directly from Gressenhall; boxes with 'B' after the number came from Bradford; 'Spec.' denotes 'Special Box' built by Bradford; 'pj' = plaster jacket; 'C' = Crate. Note 1: not in a numbered box, brought in by Nigel Larkin – continued

object no.	box	spit no.	context no.	facies	size	weathering	iron staining	abrasion	root damage	carnivore gnawing	rodent gnawing	deliberate fracturing	taxon	element
			20044		4	3							Mammuthus	multiple fragment of tusk and cranium
			20044		5	4							Mammuthus	multiple tusk fragments (tusk in trial')
			20044		3	3							Mammuthus	tusk fragment
			20052	destroyed/disturbed channel sediments	6	3							Mammuthus	proximal rib midshaft fragment
			20052	destroyed/disturbed channel sediments	4	5							Mammuthus	tusk fragment
			20052	destroyed/disturbed channel sediments	3	4							Mammuthus	2 indeterminate bone fragments and tusk fragments
			20052	destroyed/disturbed channel sediments	3	4							Mammuthus	molar plate fragment
			20052	destroyed/disturbed channel sediments	4	5							undetermined	indeterminate bone fragment
			20053	B-iii04	3	4							undetermined	indeterminate bone fragment
			20254	B-iii01	2	4							undetermined	4 small indeterminate bone fragments
			20254	B-iii01	1	3							Mammuthus	2 small tusk fragments
			20367	B-iii04	2	4							Mammuthus	tusk fragments
box 45B individual bags														
			20048	destroyed/disturbed channel sediments	5	3							Mammuthus	internal, deformed tusk fragments
			20048	destroyed/disturbed channel sediments	6	3							Mammuthus	distal end of anterior rib (missing distal epiphysis)
			20048	destroyed/disturbed channel sediments	5	3							Mammuthus	13 separate unmarked bags of cranial fragment
			20048	destroyed/disturbed channel sediments	5	3							Mammuthus	tusk alveolus fragment

APPENDIX 4

Table A4.4 Individual vertebrate finds: boxes 1–19 provided directly from Gressenhall; boxes with 'B' after the number came from Bradford; 'Spec.' denotes 'Special Box' built by Bradford; 'pj' = plaster jacket; 'C' = Crate. Note 1: not in a numbered box, brought in by Nigel Larkin – continued

object no.	box	spit no.	context no.	facies	size	weathering	iron staining	abrasion	root damage	carnivore gnawing	rodent gnawing	deliberate fracturing	taxon	element
			20048	destroyed/disturbed channel sediments	4	4							Mammuthus	2 tusk fragments and 1 indeterminate bone fragment
			20048	destroyed/disturbed channel sediments	6	3							Mammuthus	large section of tusk alveolus
			20048	destroyed/disturbed channel sediments	5	3							Mammuthus	8 rib midshaft fragments
			20048	destroyed/disturbed channel sediments	6	3							Mammuthus	6 large cranial fragment and 1 tusk fragment
			20048	destroyed/disturbed channel sediments	6	3							Mammuthus	2 large cranial fragments, jugal region
	box 55B individual bags													
	no data		20048	destroyed/disturbed channel sediments	5	4							Mammuthus	miscellaneous indeterminate large bone and small cranial fragments
	no data		20048	destroyed/disturbed channel sediments	4	4							Mammuthus	cranial fragments
	no data		20048	destroyed/disturbed channel sediments	2	4							Mammuthus	cranial fragments
	no data		20048	destroyed/disturbed channel sediments	6	4							Mammuthus	tusk fragments (4 bags)
	central spoil, black deposit				4	5							Mammuthus	tusk fragments and one indeterminate long bone fragment destroyed/disturbed channel sediments
	central spoil, black deposit		20048	destroyed/disturbed channel sediments	4	5							Mammuthus	tusk fragments
	central spoil		20048	destroyed/disturbed channel sediments	4	4							Mammuthus	indeterminate long bone fragments
	central spoil, 'disturbed material'		20048	destroyed/disturbed channel sediments	6	4							Mammuthus	miscellaneous indeterminate large bone and tusk fragments
				destroyed/disturbed channel sediments										

continued ▲

Table A4.4 Individual vertebrate finds: boxes 1–19 provided directly from Gressenhall; boxes with 'B' after the number came from Bradford; 'Spec.' denotes 'Special Box' built by Bradford; 'pj' = plaster jacket; 'C' = Crate. Note 1: not in a numbered box, brought in by Nigel Larkin – continued

object no.	box	spit no.	context no.	facies	size	weathering	iron staining	abrasion	root damage	carnivore gnawing	rodent gnawing	deliberate fracturing	taxon	element
	box 60B	individual bags												
	no data	62879	20003	B-iii03	6	3							Mammuthus	multiple large and small tusk fragments
	box 81B	individual bags												
	no data				2	3							Mammuthus	tusk fragments
	no data				2	3							Mammuthus	tusk and cranial fragments
	no data				3	4							Mammuthus	2 tusk fragments
	no data				3	4							Mammuthus	rib fragments
	no data				3	5							Mammuthus	rib midshaft fragment and small indeterminate bone fragment (size 1, condition 5)
	no data				3	4							Mammuthus	iron-stained molar fragments
	no data				3	4							Mammuthus	multiple cranial and small tusk fragments
bag of specimens 'found by John Lord with mammoth molars, near original tusk': small cranial fragments, long bone midshaft fragment of Mammuthus				destroyed/disturbed channel sediments										
6mm sieve		61370 + 61382	20003	B-iii03	1	4							Mammuthus	small tusk fragments
6mm sieve		61372–4+61381–3	20003	B-iii03	1	4							Mammuthus	small tusk and cranial fragments
	no data	61354+61370+61382+ 61391+61400	20003+ 20252	B-iii03	2	4							Mammuthus	tusk fragments
	no data	61369+61383	20003	B-iii03	1	4							Mammuthus	4 small tusk fragments
?distal fibula found by John Lord				destroyed/disturbed channel sediments										

492

APPENDIX 5

Table A5.1 Concordance list of context numbers

component	subdivision	context	facies[1]	description	interpretation
B-i	B-i:01	20035		concave-up channel base	base of palaeochannel for B-i and B-ii incised into Association A gravels
		20332	Gh	medium to coarse gravel and pale brown coarse sand with crude horizontal stratification, poorly sorted	gravel bedform (in-channel longitudinal bar)
		20334	Fm	light grey/green sandy silt	low-stage drape (bar top)
	B-i:02	20336		upper contact	erosion surface
		20361	Fm	light grey sandy silt	low-stage drape (bar top)
		20362	Gh	small to medium-coarse gravel and coarse to fine sand with fining-upward normal grading	gravel bedform (in-channel longitudinal bar)
	B-i:03	20051	Gh	medium to coarse gravel, clast supported with fining-upward normal grading	gravel bedform (longitudinal bar element)
		20078	Fm	grey-white/pale brown fine silty sand	low-stage drape (bar top); equivalent to 20400 and 20405
		20129	Gh	small to medium-coarse gravel and grey-white coarse sand with crude horizontal stratification, clast supported, poorly sorted	gravel bedform (longitudinal bar element)
		20130	Gh	small to medium-coarse gravel and pale brown-yellow coarse sand with crude horizontal stratification, clast supported, poorly sorted	gravel bedform (longitudinal bar element)
		20338		upper contact	erosion Surface
		20379	Gh	medium to coarse gravel and orange-brownish orange coarse sand with crude horizontal stratification, clast supported, poorly sorted	gravel bedform (longitudinal bar element)
		20389	Gh	small to medium-coarse gravel and dark yellow medium to coarse sand, poorly sorted, matrix supported	gravel bedform (longitudinal bar element)
		20398	Gh	medium to coarse gravel and pale grey coarse sand with crude horizontal stratification, poorly sorted, matrix supported	gravel bedform (longitudinal bar element)
		20405	Fm	pale brown/light grey sandy clay	low-stage drape (bar top); equivalent to 20078 and 20400
B-ii	B-ii:01	20004	St, Sm	pale brown medium-fine sand with common small-medium gravel and rare flint cobbles (pebbly); partially massive	cross-bedded (trough cross-beds – 3-D dunes) and disturbed sand
		20032		upper contact	erosion surface; equivalent to 20033

continued ▶

Table A5.1 Concordance list of context numbers – *continued*

component	subdivision	context	facies[1]	description	interpretation
		20033		upper contact	erosion surface; equivalent to 20032
		20133	Sm	pale brown fine sand with common small-medium gravel (pebbly); massive	disturbed sand
		20139		mid to dark brown medium to fine sand	organic staining of upper contact below organic sediments of B-ii:03. equivalent to 20255, 20346, 20363 and 20364
		20245	St	pale brown fine sand with occasional small flint gravel; discontinous non-parallel laminae present	cross-bedded sand (trough cross-beds – 3-D dunes)
		20254	St	light grey medium-fine sand with common small-medium gravel and rare flint cobbles (pebbly); rare discontinous non-parallel laminae internally	cross-bedded sand (trough cross-beds – 3-D dunes)
		20255		mid to dark brown medium to fine sand	organic staining of upper contact below organic sediments of B-ii:03. equivalent to 20139, 20346, 20363 and 20364
		20346		mid to dark brown medium to fine sand	organic staining of upper contact below organic sediments of B-ii:03. equivalent to 20139, 20255, 20363 and 20364
		20354	St	pale to yellowish brown medium sand with common small-medium gravel (pebbly); rare discontinous non-parallel laminae present	cross-bedded sand (trough cross-beds – 3-D dunes)
		20363		mid to dark brown medium to fine sand	organic staining of upper contact below organic sediments of B-ii:03. equivalent to 20139, 20255, 20346 and 20364
		20364		mid to dark brown medium to fine sand	organic staining of upper contact below organic sediments of B-ii:03. equivalent to 20139, 20255, 20346 and 20363
		20369	St	pale brown fine sand with sparse small-medium gravel; discontinuous non-parallel laminae present	cross-bedded sand (trough cross-beds – 3-D dunes)
		20375	Sm	pale brownish grey medium sand with sparse mediul-coarse gravel; massive	disturbed sand
		20381	St	pale brown to whitish grey medium sand with common medium-coarse gravel (pebbly); discontinuous non-parallel laminae present	cross-bedded sand (trough cross-beds – 3-D dunes)
		20383	Sm	pale brownish grey medium sand with sparse mediul-coarse gravel; massive	disturbed sand
		20384	Sm	pale brown/grey medium sand with sparse medium-coarse gravel; massive	disturbed sand
		20399	Sm	pale brown/grey medium sand with sparse medium-coarse gravel; massive	disturbed sand
	B-ii:02	20031	Fm	mid brownish-grey organic clayey silt with rare discontinuous lenses of fine sand present	organic silt
		20246	Fm	dark brownish-grey organic clayey silt with sparse medium gravel; massive	organic silt
		20355	Fm	mid grey-brown organic clayey silt with sparse medium grave; massive	organic silt

continued ▶

Table A5.1 Concordance list of context numbers – *continued*

component	subdivision	context	facies[1]	description	interpretation
		20371	Fm	mid grey-brown/greenish-brown organic clayey silt with rare discontinuous lenses of fine-medium sand present	organic silt
		20378	Fm	mid brownish-grey organic clayey silt, massive	organic silt
		20386	Fm	mid brownish-grey organic clayey silt; massive	organic silt
		20387	Fm	dark brownish-grey organic clayey silt with sparse medium gravel; rare discontinuous lenses of fine sand present	organic silt
		20390	Fm	mid brownish-grey organic clayey silt; massive	organic silt
		20400	Fm	dark brownish organic clayey silt with sparse small to medium gravel	organic silt
		20401	Fm	brownish-grey organic clayey silt with lenses of fine and medium gravel present	organic silt
		20403	Fm	brownish-grey organic clayey silt with lenses of fine and medium gravel present	organic silt
	B-ii:03	20003	Fl	dark brown-black fine-grained organic silty sand; predominately massive with fine alternating discontinuous parallel-subparallel laminae of sand and detrital organic matter in upper 0.20m; laterally variable densities of medium to coarse gravel and cobbles and lenses of stony organic sand	organic mud. equivalent to 20021, 20248, 20252, 20253 and 20258. Partially interbedded with debris flow and bank sediments with stony organic sands along southern edge of channel forming part of sediment gravity flow B-ii:04A
		20021	Fl	dark brown-black fine-grained organic silty sand; massive with lenses of stony organic sand	organic mud. equivalent to 20003, 20248, 20252, 20253 and 20258
		20135	Ss	mid grey coarse sand with thin discontinuous lenses of orange-brown sand and fine gravel	small irregular machine truncated thin patch of sand on top of organic sediments
		20248	Fl	dark brown-black fine-grained organic silty sand; massive with sparse small to medium-coarse gravel	organic mud. equivalent to 20003, 20021, 20252, 20253 and 20258
		20250	Fl	dark brown-black fine-grained organic silty sand; massive with rare small to medium gravel	eroded patch of organic sediment within sediment gravity flow B-ii:04C
		20252	Fl	dark brown-black fine-grained organic silty sand with lenses of coarse white sand and stony organic sand	organic mud. equivalent to 20003, 20021`, 20248, 20253 and 20258
		20253	Fl	mid-grey silty sand with discontinuous non-parallel laminae	leached organic mud by groundwater flow. equivalent to 20003, 20021`, 20248, 20252 and 20258
		20258	Fl	dark brown-black fine-grained organic silty sand; massive with rare small gravel	organic mud. equivalent to 20003, 20021`, 20248, 20252 and 20253
	B-ii:04	20053	Gmm	small to medium-coarse gravel and pale orange-yellow coarse sand; massive, poorly sorted and matrix supported	element of sediment gravity flow B-ii:04D
		20055	Gcm	small to medium-coarse gravel and mid grey coarse sand; massive, poorly sorted, clast supported	element of sediment gravity flow B-ii:04A
		20131	Gmm	small to medium-coarse flint gravel and pale grey medium sand; massive, poorly sorted and matrix supported	element of sediment gravity flow B-ii:04B

continued ▶

Table A5.1 Concordance list of context numbers – *continued*

component	subdivision	context	facies[1]	description	interpretation
		20132	Gcm	small to medium-coarse gravel and mid orange coarse sand; massive, poorly sorted and clasr supported	element of sediment gravity flow B-ii:04B
		20134	Gmm	small to medium-coarse gravel and mid orange-yellow coarse sand; massive, poorly sorted and matrix supported	element of sediment gravity flow B-ii:04B
		20137	Gcm	fine to medium-coarse gravel and mid brown-orange coarse sand; massive, poorly sorted and clast supported	element of sediment gravity flow B-ii:04B
		20140	Sm	mid yellow brown silty coarse sand with sparse small to medium gravel; massive	element of sediment gravity flow B-ii:04D
		20243	Gcm	medium-coarse gravel and greyish-brown silty sand; massive, poorly sorted and clast supported	element of sediment gravity flow B-ii:04A
		20247	Gcm	fine to medium-coarse gravel and mid grey medium sand; massive, poorly sorted and clast supported	element of sediment gravity flow B-ii:04D
		20249	Gmm	small to medium gravel and pale brown/grey coarse sand; massive, poorly sorted and matrix supported	element of sediment gravity flow B-ii:04C (gravelly sand)
		20251	Gmm	small to medium gravel and pale brown-orange/grey coarse sand; massive, poorly sorted and matrix supported	element of sediment gravity flow B-ii:04C (gravelly sand)
		20257	Gmm	small to medium-coarse gravel and grey-mid orange coarse sand; massive, poorly sorted and matrix supported	element of sediment gravity flow B-ii:04B
		20347	Gmm	medium-coarse gravel and pale grey medium sand; massive, poorly sorted and matrix supported	element of sediment gravity flow B-ii:04A
		20348	Gmm	small to medium-coarse gravel and mid orange-yellow coarse sand; massive, poorly sorted and matrix supported	element of sediment gravity flow B-ii:04A
		20365	Gmm	small to medium gravel and pale brown/grey coarse sand; massive, poorly sorted and matrix supported	element of sediment gravity flow B-ii:04B
		20366	Gcm	fine to medium-coarse gravel and mid brown-orange coarse sand; massive, poorly sorted and clast supported	element of sediment gravity flow B-ii:04B
		20367	Gmm	small to medium-coarse gravel and pale yellow/white coarse sand; massive, poorly sorted and matrix supported	element of sediment gravity flow B-ii:04B
		20368	Gcm	small to medium-coarse gravel and mid grey-white coarse sand; massive, poorly sorted and clast supported	element of sediment gravity flow B-ii:04B
		20370	Gmm	medium-coarse gravel and pale grey coarse sand; massive, partially imbricated and matrix supported	element of sediment gravity flow B-ii:04B
		20372	Sm	pale grey fine to medium sand with sparse small-medium gravel; massive	element of sediment gravity flow B-ii:04D
		20373	Sm	pale grey-orange fine sand with sparse small-medium gravel; massive	element of sediment gravity flow B-ii:04D
		20374	Gmm	small to medium-coarse gravel and pale grey medium sand; massive, poorly sorted and matrix supported	element of sediment gravity flow B-ii:04A
		20376	Gmm	small to medium-coarse gravel and pale grey coarse sand; massive, poorly sorted and matrix supported	element of sediment gravity flow B-ii:04A

continued ▶

Table A5.1 Concordance list of context numbers – *continued*

component	subdivision	context	facies¹	description	interpretation
		20389	Gmm	medium-coarse gravel and pale grey medium sand; massive, poorly sorted and matrix supported	element of sediment gravity flow B-ii:04A
		20392	Gmm	small to medium gravel and pale yellow coarse sand; massive, poorly sorted and matrix supported	element of sediment gravity flow B-ii:04B
		20408	Sm	pale yellow/brownish grey fine to medium sand with sparse small-medium gravel; massive	element of sediment gravity flow B-ii:04A
	B-ii:05	20002	Sr, Fm	pale grey/brown fine silty sand with discontinuous parallel/non-parallel dark brown-black organic sand/silt laminations; rare medium-coarse gravel	lateral infill sediments
		20005	Sr, Ss	pale to medium grey fine silty sand with discontinuous parallel/non-parallel wavey laminations; pale brown sand with fine-medium grave at base	lateral infill sediments
		20006		erosion surface	scour
		20056	Ss/ Gh	small to medium gravel with light grey to yellow/pale brown coarse sand; poorly sorted	scour fill
		20070	Sr, Flr, Ss	pale grey-brown fine silty sand with dark grey-brown silt and organic laminae (discontinuous parallel/non-parallel) and lenses of small subrounded flint gravel; ripples and clasts of reworked organic sediment present; medium-coarse flint dropstones embedded within sediments	sandy bedform (mid-channel bar elements) and lateral infill sediments; equivalent to 20170
		20071	Sm/Sr	mid grey/pale brown fine silty sand; predominately massive with rare discontinuous parallel/non-parallel wavey laminations (fine greyish-white sand laminae); rare medium-coarse gravel	lateral infill sediments
		20072	Sr	pale grey-brown to greyish-orange fine silty sand with discontinuous parallel/non-parallel wavey laminations	lateral infill sediments
		20116	Sr	mid grey-brown silty sand with discontinuous parallel/non-parallel wavey laminations; rare medium-coarse gravel	lateral infill sediments
		20118/ 20119	Smdef	mid orange-brown fine to medium silty sand	soft sediment deformation due to compaction by overlying B-iii channel base. Some diagenetic colour changes
		20120/ 20136	Sr	pale grey/brown silty sand with discontinuous parallel/non-parallel wavey laminations; rare small-medium gravel	lateral infill sediments
		20122		shallow erosion surface	scour
		20170	Sr, Flr, Ss	pale grey-brown fine silty sand with dark grey-brown silt and organic laminae (discontinuous parallel/non-parallel) and lenses of small subrounded flint gravel; clasts of reworked organic sediment present; medium-coarse flint dropstones embedded within sediments	sandy bedform (mid-channel bar elements) and lateral infill sediments; equivalent to 20070
		20351	Sr, Ss	greyish-brown fine silty sand with discontinuous parallel/non-parallel wavey laminations; fine to medium gravel and pale brown sand at base	lateral infill sediments
		20344		shallow erosion surface	scour

continued ▶

Table A5.1 Concordance list of context numbers – *continued*

component	subdivision	context	facies[1]	description	interpretation
		20345	Sr, Ss	yellow/orange-brown coarse silty sand with discontinuous parallel/non-parallel wavey laminations; fine to medium gravel and pale brown sand at base	lateral infill sediments
		20352		shallow erosion surface	scour
	B-iii	20012	Sp	yellowish orange, mid grey and pale grey medium sand with discontinuous non-parallel laminations and lenses of fine to medium gravel	final infill element; equivalent to 20125/20211
		20016	Fl	dark brown-black organic silty sand and lenses of pale brown/grey medium sand with fine to medium gravel	final infill element
		20015	Sp	pale grey/white medium-coarse sand with discontinuous parallel and non-parallel silty sand laminae	channel infill element (point bar). equivalent to 20018, 20199 and 20213
		20017	Fl	dark brown-black organic silty sand and lenses of pale brown/grey medium sand with fine to medium gravel	final infill element; equivalent to 20066
		20018	Sp	mid grey/white medium-coarse sand with silty sand laminae and small-medium gravel lenses	channel infill element (point bar). equivalent to 20015, 20199 and 20213
		20019		upper contact	erosion surface; equivalent to 20046 and 20198
		20020	Gp	small to medium gravel and pale yellow orange fine sand	channel infill element (point bar)
		20023	Sp	pale brown-pale grey medium sand with mid-grey silty sand laminae	
		20024		upper contact	erosion surface
		20025	Sp	pale orange-brown coarse sand with parallel/non-parallel mid-ple grey silty sand laminae and sparse small-medium gravel	channel infill element (point bar)
		20026	Sp	pale yellow-grey medium to coarse sand with sparse small-medium gravel	channel infill element (point bar)
		20028	Gh	small-medium-coarse gravel and light orange to pale brown coarse sand	channel infill element (point bar). equivalent to 20178
		20065	Fl/Gh	dark brown-black organic sediment with lenses of medium-coarse flint gravel and pale brown-mid orange medium sand	final infill element; equivalent to 20115
		20066	Fl	dark brown-black organic silty sand with occasional discontinuous parallel and non-parallel lenses of pale brown/grey medium sand	final infill element; equivalent to 20017
		20115	Gh	fine to medium-coarse gravel and mid orange coarse sand	final infill element; equivalent to 20065
		20123	Gh	small to medium-coarse gravel and pale yellow/pale brown medium to coarse sand	channel infill element (point bar)
		20124		upper contact	erosion surface; equivalent to 20244
		20125/20211	Sp	pale brown-mid grey fine to medium sand with parallel/non-parallel laminae and medium-coarse gravel at base	final infill element
		20126	Gh	small to medium gravel and yellow coarse sand	channel infill element (point bar)

continued ▶

Table A5.1 Concordance list of context numbers – *continued*

component	subdivision	context	facies[1]	description	interpretation
		20127		concave-up channel base	base of palaeochannel for B-iii; equivalent to 20177
		20142	Gh	small-medium gravel and mid orange coarse sand	channel infill element (point bar)
		20244		upper contact	erosion surface; equivalent to 20124
		20177		concave-up channel base	base of palaeochannel for B-iii; equivalent to 20127
		20178	Gh	small-medium-coarse gravel and light orange to pale brown coarse sand	channel infill element (point bar). equivalent to 20028
		20195	Sp	pale brownish-grey coarse sand with parallel/non-parallel silty sand laminae and small to medium-coarse gravel (pebbly)	final infill element
		20198		upper contact	erosion surface; equivalent to 20019 and 20046
		20199	Sp	pale grey/white fine sand with mid grey parallel/non-parallel silty sand laminae and rare medium gravel	channel infill element (point bar). equivalent to 20015, 20018 and 20213
		20213	Sp	pale brown-brownish orange medium sand with brown-orange parallel silty sand laminae (Fe stained) and sparse small to medium grvel at base	channel infill element (point bar). equivalent to 20015, 20018 and 20199
		20216	Sp	pale brown medium to coarse sand with brown parallel inclined laminae	channel infill element (point bar)
		20394	Sh	pale brown fine to medium to coarse sand	final infill element

GLOSSARY

acetabulum the articular surface where the hip fits into the pelvis

acetolysis decomposition of an organic substance using acetic acid or acetic anhydride

Acheulian a mode of percussive stone tool technology that first appears in Africa c 1.65Ma in which the sharp edges of stone flakes are worked on both sides ('bifacially'), and particularly exemplified by the handaxe

actinomycosis an inflammatory disease of cattle and pigs, and sometimes humans, caused by microorganisms of the genus *Actinomyces* – a type of bacteria causing localised infections

aeolian wind-borne

aliquot a portion of the total amount of a solution in which it is contained an exact number of times

allochthonous originating elsewhere (especially sediments or rocks)

allometric relating to a scalar relationship between two measurements (eg length and width) in which an increase in one is accompanied by an unequal increase (or decrease) in the other

amino-acid racemisation a dating technique that measures the ratio between two different forms of amino acids that occur in living animals in order to determine the time that has elapsed since death

Anglian a cold period of the Middle Pleistocene equivalent to Marine Isotope Stage 12 (MIS 12); dated to between 478,000 and 424,000 years ago

anthropogenic created by hominins

apical occurring at the extremity or apex

aquiclude an impermeable body of rock or stratum of sediment that prevents the passage of water

aragonitic molluscan shells shells of molluscs composed of calcium carbonate $CaCO_3$

arrise a minuscule scar on the cutting edge of a stone tool produced by use, retouch and/or post-depositional processes

arthropathy disease or injury to a skeletal joint, especially resulting from arthritis

asparagine an amino acid, a naturally occurring biochemical substance

association objects found in proximity to one another

Astragalus the family of herbs and shrubs that includes the vetches; alternatively, one of the bones making up the ankle or lower rear leg joint, also known as the talus in humans

atomic absorption spectrophotometric analysis a method of determining the concentration of a chemical element in a sample by measuring the extent to which it reflects or absorbs light

aurochs (*Bos primigenius*) a large Pleistocene member of the bovid (cow) family, now extinct

authochthonous originating in the same place as recovered, especially of a sediment or rock

bar surfaces the surfaces of a bar of sediment deposited by a river

biocenose a group of organisms forming an ecological community in a particular habitat

biostratigraphical correlation the correlation of the mammalian remains found in distinct stratigraphic levels of different sites in order to determine whether they were occupied contemporaneously, and how biogeographies change at a regional and continental scale

bioturbation disturbance of the order of deposition of geological and archaeological materials by living creatures

birefringence (also known as double refraction) the decomposition of a ray of light when it passes through certain materials

boreal belonging to northerly latitudes, especially arctic regions

boreo-montane belonging to northerly latitudes and/or to high altitudes in mountainous areas

bounding surface layer of contact between discrete geometric bodies of different sediments

***bout coupé* handaxe** distinctive Late Middle Palaeolithic handaxe/biface with a relatively flat base, rather than the usual rounded type

braided river shallow river running across gravels in multiple, interwoven streams

buccal the side of the tooth nearest the cheek, ie the outer side of a tooth

bunodont having rounded molar surfaces, generally a characteristic of animals consuming a broad diet

burination the removal of a spall of stone from the very edge of a stone flake, producing a characteristic 'burin spall' that is triangular in cross-section and has a chisel-like edge on the flake from which it was removed; probably used for carving wood or bone

caballine relating to horses (*Equus caballus*)

cal BP calibrated radiocarbon years before the present

calcaneum the heel-bone of a human, or the hock bone of a quadruped mammal

cancellous 'spongy' bone inside long bones in which a matrix of bone mineral is interwoven with soft tissue and blood vessels; also known as trabecular bone

carabid member of the beetle family Carabidae

cephalothorax the frontmost body section, sometimes including the head, of spiders and insects

cervids animals belonging to the deer family

chaîne opératoire the sequence of gestures and material actions by which stone tools and other technologies are made

channel-fill sediments filling a palaeochannel cut by water

Characean a kind of algae

chert a fine-grained, silica-rich sedimentary rock such as flint; highly suitable for the manufacture of stone tools

chronocultural a temporal division of the stone age by cultural/technological practices, eg the Acheulian; the Mousterian

clast fragment of rock

Coleoptera insects

comminuted fragmented

conchoidal fracture the way fine-grained and brittle materials with no or limited internal structural planes of separation (such as chert, flint, obsidian and glass) break apart; unlike non-conchoidal fractures (*see below*), conchoidal fractures are only produced by localised mechanical impact, such as by a hammerstone, and can be recognised by the clear 'ripple' pattern on the surface of the break

condyle parts of arm and leg bones that form hinge joints

consolidant substance used to repair fragmented remains

coprolite fossilised dung

coprophages insects consuming dung

coprophilous dung-loving

cordiform heart-shaped (of a handaxe)

Corg organic Carbon

crista the shearing crest of a molar tooth

crochet referring to teeth, a hook-like branch from a ridge of enamel on the dentine surface of a molar

Dansgaard-Oeschger (D-O) events brief interstadials (*see below*) identified in the Greenland ice cores

de-amination the process by which amino acids (important substances in biochemistry) are broken down

débitage small by-products of stone artefact manufacture, sometimes also known as waste flakes; alternatively, a mode of technology focused on the use of sharp stones flakes produced from cores, rather than on the shaping of the cores themselves (*'façonnage'* – *see below*)

Devensian the last glacial period, dating from 110,000 to 10,000 years ago and including Marine Isotope Stages 5d to 2 (MIS 5d–2)

diagenesis the sum of all processes, but chiefly chemical, that produce changes in a sediment after its deposition, but before it becomes fossilised

diaphyseal relating to the diaphysis or shaft of a bone, rather than to the epiphyses or ends

diapir an intrusion of a more deformable type of material into overlying rocks

distal epiphyses the end of a bone farthest from the body

downwarped a sediment layer bent downwards

dropstones isolated fragments of rock found among finer-grained water-deposited sediments, usually the result of deposition of material picked up by glaciers when the ice they are suspended in melts

dytiscid a family of predaceous diving water beetles

edaphic the geophysical factors affecting the distribution of plants and animals

elytron (also known as shard) a modified, hardened forewing of some orders of insects, especially beetles (Coleoptera) and some true bugs (Heteroptera)

encephalisation evolutionary enlargement of the brain (a distinguishing characteristic of the hominin line relative to other primates)

epiphyseal relating to the epiphyses or ends of long bones, rather than to their diaphyses or shafts

equids members of the equid family: horses

euhedral describes crystals with well-formed, easily recognised faces

eurytopic a widely distributed species, or one able to tolerate a wide range of environmental conditions

eutrophic describes water rich in nutrients, in which overgrowth of plant life such as algae can occur, reducing oxygen levels and hence animal life

facies different assemblages of tools made using similar overall technologies, for example the MTA or La Quina facies of the Mousterian

façonnage a mode of stone tool technology that focuses on the 'fashioning' of a core-tool by the removal of flakes, rather than on the flakes themselves (*'débitage'*)

facultative halophyte a plant that prefers to grow in soils relatively high in salt

felids members of the cat family

Fennoscandia a geologically defined area to the north of the Baltic Sea, comprising the Scandinavian Peninsula, Kola Peninsula, Karelia and Finland

flat-butted cordate a heart-shaped handaxe with a flat base

foraminifera single-celled largely marine life forms with calcium carbonate shells. Vast numbers of these creatures live and die in the oceans, their shells sinking to ocean-floor sediments. Because their shells are formed from the elements available in the ocean at the time they live, they preserve the ratio of stable isotopes of oxygen and carbon, which can be used to reconstruct past climates. The species and concentrations of foraminifera fossils in sedimentary rock such as that used to make raw material can also be used to identify the source of that stone by matching it to an outcrop containing the same fossil 'signature'.

framboid (French for 'raspberry') term used to describe the appearance under a microscope of some types of sedimentary mineral such as pyrites

frass fine, powdery substance (eg of mashed-up bone)

gamma dose rate measure of the accumulation of gamma rays from a source of radiation

geofact an object superficially resembling a stone tool but produced by natural rather than by anthropogenic processes

glaciogenic produced by the action of glaciers

hachoir a type of elongated handaxe with a very narrow point

Heinrich (H) events brief but dramatic declines in sea temperature and climate thought to relate to increased calving of ice bergs from expanded ice caps

heliophilous (of a plant) preferring bright sunlight

heliophyte a plant that flourishes in bright sunlight

herpetofaunal the remains of reptiles and amphibians

Holocene the most recent geological era of unusually stable climatic conditions, which began c 11,600 cal BP

hominid the biological super-family that includes all great apes and humans and our fossil ancestors (**hominins** – *see below*)

hominin the biological family including humans and all our fossil ancestors (including the Neanderthals)

horizonation the formation in soil of horizons, layers forming parallel to the surface, which differ in their physical characteristics to the soil above and below

human the biological species *Homo sapiens*, including all living people and fossils of *Homo sapiens* (excluding *Homo neanderthalensis*)

humified organic matter that has fully broken down into humus, a highly fertile soil

hydraenid one of a family of small aquatic beetles

hydrophilid one of a family of mainly aquatic beetles known as water scavengers

hyoid bone small and fragile bone found in the throat and forming part of the voice box

hypsodont teeth with high crowns

imbricated overlapping like roof tiles

inter-aliquot variability the variability between individual portions ('**aliquots**' – *see above*) of a substance

interdigitated interlocking like the fingers ('digits') of clasped hands

Interglacial a major warm period such as MIS 5e (128–118ka) and the present period of Holocene climate

Interstadial less substantial warm period event occurring during during a predominantly cold phase

introgression (also known as introgressive hybridization) a process by which genes (particularly of plants) of one species are incorporated into the gene pool of another when a hybrid, the product of a cross of both species, goes on to breed with other members of either population

ischium one of the three bones that fuse together in early childhood to make the adult pelvis

isotope different kinds of atoms of the same chemical element with differing numbers of neutrons. Isotopic analysis is widely used archaeologically in a number of different ways – one major use is in analysing the ratio between the oxygen isotopes ^{18}O and ^{16}O in deep-sea cores containing the remains of shells of microscopic marine organisms known as *foraminifera*. When large amounts of seawater are locked up in glaciers during cold periods, denser and more saline oceans contain increased proportions of ^{18}O in seawater, which are absorbed by marine shells. Ratios of these isotopes thus reflect the temperature of seas in the past and, by extension, global climates. Cold and warm periods in the past dated by this method are known as Marine Isotope Stages (*see below*).

ka thousands of years before the present

kink point the point at which the trend line of graphed points changes angle, ie the point at which the relationship between the measured variables changes

kurtosis statistical term describing the extent to which a probability distribution curve has a high central peak around the mean and rapid fall-off to either side or a lower, broader peak with more gradual fall-off

lacustrine relating to lakes

lagomorph belonging to the biological family lagomorphia, including rabbits and hares

lamellar composed of fine layers

laminae layer of a lamellar structure

Last Cold Stage extends from the beginning of MIS 5d (118ka) to the end of MIS 2 (12ka)

Last Glacial Maximum (LGM) extremely cold period of maximum advance of the northern ice-sheets in MIS 2, c 18,000ka

leafpoint stone spear-point finely worked into a shape resembling a leaf, especially characteristic of groups living in southern Europe during the Last Glacial Maximum

lenticular lens- or ellipse-shaped

leptokurtic tail statistical term describing the rapid fall-off of a probability distribution tail with a high central peak

Levallois mode of stone tool technology involving a distinctive way of preparing a stone core before removing a characteristic flake; particularly associated with the Neanderthal Mousterian

lingual the inner side of a tooth, that nearest the tongue

linguoid dunes sand deposits demonstrating asymmetrical ripple marks with tongue-like projections produced by (and that point into) a water current

lithic relating to stone tools

lithofacies a subdivision of a stratigraphic unit distinguished by the macroscopic physical character of its rock

lithological relating to the macroscopic physical character of a rock

lithostratigraphic the study of rock layers, and their correlation across multiple sites to establish contemporaneity of deposition

local pollen zone (LPZ) a subdivision of the last glacial period and Holocene defined by similarities in the kinds of pollen recovered from pollen cores and hence in the kinds of plant communities present at time of deposition across multiple sites in a relatively small area

Ma Millions of years before the present

malacological relating to molluscs

mammoth-steppe a particular community of steppe-plants and large herbivores (including mammoth) that characterised the northern part of Europe during the last ice age

manuports objects (especially stone) introduced to a location by hominins or humans

Marine Isotope Stage *see* MIS

maxilla the upper part of the mouth

mammal assemblage zone (MAZ) a formally defined biostratigraphic unit made up of a distinctive set of mammals

medial diaphysis part of the shaft of a long bone closest to the middle of the body

medifossette on the surface of a molar tooth, an isolated 'islet' of enamel in an area of dentine

medullary bone marrow cavity inside long bones

melanterite hydrated iron sulphate

mesocuneiform one of the small, oddly-shaped bones of the wrist or fore-leg joint

mesostyle the middle point of a tooth along the outside or cheek side of a molar of the upper jaw

metapodial one of the long-bones of the hand (in humans) or lower foreleg in quadrupeds

meteoric phreatic water originating from precipitation collected in the phreatic zone, or zone of saturation of the ground below the water table

Micoquian a late form of Achuelian (*see above*) in which handaxes were made long and thin

micritic limestone formed by the recrystallisation of lime mud and characterised by microscopic calcareous particles

Microtinae members of the mouse family

minerogenic of mineral origin

MIS (Marine Isotope Stage) the division of the stratigraphically continuous chronology of ice cap to ocean volumes (cold:warm climate) as recorded isotopically in the skeletons of marine organisms, and recovered by the deep-sea drilling programmes

MIS 2 A cold period that saw the Last Glacial Maximum when sea levels were at their lowest and ice sheets reached their greatest extent (24–12ka)

MIS 3 A cold period punctuated by interstadials (60–24ka) during which Britain was reoccupied after a long absence (as attested to by the finds at Lynford)

MIS 4 a cold period with major ice advance (71 – 60ka) when Britain and Northwest Europe was abandoned by hominins

MNI Minimum Number of Individuals – the smallest number of animals of any species that could account for the skeletal elements recovered

morphological relating to outward shape

Mousterian a specific kind of Levallois (*see above*) technology practised by Neanderthals; also a distinctively-shaped point it produced

mustelid a member of the family of weasels and stoats

NISP Number of Identified Specimens – raw number of individual finds of bone identified to a particular species

non-conchoidal a fracture in a material with no natural planes of separation, such as chert, flint and obsidian, with no cleavage plains or structure to the fractured surface; unlike conchoidal fractures (*see above*), non-conchoidal fractures usually occur naturally

Norg organic Nitrogen

obligate by necessity rather than by choice

obliquity the angle of tilt of the Earth to the Sun. On a yearly timescale changes in obliquity cause the Earth's seasons; millennial-scale obliquity variation affects climate.

omega point point where the trend lines linking observations together on a graph converge

ontogeny childhood development of an individual (as opposed to phylogeny, evolutionary development of a species)

OSL (Optically Stimulated Luminescence) a dating technique

osteomyelitis infection of bone

osteophyte bone growth in the spine in response to disease, trauma or long-term loading

ovate oval handaxe

overburden soil above the levels of interest

oxbow typically crescent-shaped still-water lakes that are formed when a river bend, or meander, is cut off from the active main channel; also known as palaeochannels (*see* chapter 2.1)

palaeochannel *see* oxbow

palaeodose the ionising radiation dose to which a sample was exposed during burial

palaoecological relating to the ecologies of the Pleistocene

palynology the study of pollen remains to establish the flora of past landscapes

parietal relating to a wall; alternatively, a paired bone forming part of the side of the skull

pedicle attachment of antlers to the skull of a cervid

pedogenic zone layer of the Earth's crust in which soil is forming

pelage fur

perched aquifer an aquifer occurring above the level of the local water table due to the presence of an impermeable stratum of rock or sediment

periosteum covering of living bone

periostitis an infection of the periosteum

perissodactyl single-toed ungulate including equids and rhinoceroses

phytophagous – feeding on plants (especially of insects and other invertebrates plant-eating mammals are usually termed herbivores)

plagiolophodont molar teeth having low, flat ridges running from side to side across the tooth surface

plaquette flat plate, eg in mammoth molars

polyostotic affecting more than one bone

post-carnassial tooth towards the back of the jaw from the carnassials or canine tooth

precession the changing orientation of the axis around which the Earth rotates, which follows a cycle of approximately 26,000 years

proboscidean relating to elephants

protocone a cusp or protruberance on the middle of the inner side (that sitting nearest the tongue in a living animal) of the molars of the upper dentition in vertebrates

radiocarbon dating method of dating organic materials. Plants and animals take up carbon isotope 14 throughout life, and after death the proportion of ^{14}C declines at a steady rate, enabling estimation of the time elapsed since its death.

ramus a branch: often applied to portions of bones, eg the two branching sides of the jawbone or of the pubic bone of the pelvis

redox potential (also known as reduction potential or oxidation) a measure of the tendency of a chemical substance to acquire electrons

refit/refitting studies studies in which the successive flakes taken off a core during the manufacture of a stone tool are fitted back together to determine the process of manufacture

rinderpest an infectious disease of cattle and some other species with a very high mortality rate

rugose having a rugged surface

Saalian the penultimate cold stage of the last ice age of the Middle Pleistocene in northern Europe, roughly equivalent to MIS stages 10 –6, sometimes also known as the Riss in the Alps and the Wolstonian in the UK, ending with the last interglacial (MIS stage 5e)

SediGraph proprietary particle size analyzer

sesquioxide an oxide containing three atoms of oxygen with two atoms of another element

Sodium hexametaphosphate ($NaPO_3$) a chemical often used as a dispersing agent to break down clay and other soil types

sordariaceous belonging to the Sordariaceae, a family of fungi including a number of species that inhabit herbivore dung

spectophotometry measurement of the light-reflective or transmission properties of a material

spherule a miniature sphere or globule

spicules tiny spike-like structures found in many organisms, with a variety of functions

sporulate to produce or form a spore or spores

stenonid an extinct group of equids that was replaced in the Middle Pleistocene by the caballine equids (*Equus caballus*) who survived to the present day

stenotopic species tolerant of only a narrow range of environmental types

strongylocerine from *Cervus strongyloceros*, a now outdated term for the Canadian elk or wapiti *Cervus canadensis*, larger than the European red deer. Early fossil specialists mistook the remains of large deer found at Middle Devensian sites for this species, but they are now regarded simply as much larger forms of the European red deer *Cervus elaphus*.

stylohyoid muscle in the throat that plays a role in chewing and swallowing

sutral lines thin joint lines describing the borders between plates of bone, for example the separate bones of the skull

symphysis a cartilaginous joint between two bones

syncline in geology, a 'u'-shaped fold in multiple layers of sediment (as opposed to an anticline, an inverted 'u'-shaped fold

tabular-lenticular deposit a stratum of rock or sediment that is flat ('table-like'), with convex edges ('lenticular', or shaped like a lentil in being curved on both sides)

taphonomy the study of the processes that occur to archaeologically recovered specimens between their deposition and excavation

tarsometatarsus a bone found in the lower leg of some animals, notably birds; the equivalent of the mammalian ankle and foot bones

taxa biological groups such as species or families

techno-complex group of sites and assemblages belonging to a particular cultural/technological tradition

thar (also known as tahr) a family of Asian ungulates related to the wild goat

thermoluminescence (TL) dating a method of dating archaeologically recovered crystalline materials by heating a sample to release a light signal whose strength is proportional to the length of time since the material was last heated or exposed to light (ie since its deposition or firing in the case of lava or ceramics respectively, and since its burial in the case of other substances)

thermophilous warmth-loving

till mixed sediments deposited by glaciers

trabecular bone see cancellous bone

tranchet flake sometimes removed across the tip of a handaxe to refresh its edge

GLOSSARY

trochanter the diaphysis of a bone forming part of a hinge joint

trophic the position an animal occupies in the food chain

trypanosomiasis disease leaving traces on bones

unabraded unworn

void ratio a measure of how compacted a substance is

xerophilous preferring dry conditions

zygapophyses the protruding parts of the vertebrae of the spine that link to those of the vertebrae above and below to stabilise the spine

REFERENCES

Adam, K-D 1951 'Der waldelefant von Lehringen, eine jagdbeute des diluvialen menschen'. *Quartär* **5**, 72–92

Adam, K-D 1961 'Die bedeutung der pleistozänen Säugetier-Faunen Mitteleuropas für die geschichte des eiszeitalters'. *Stuttgarter Beiträge zur Naturkunde* **78**, 1–34

Adams, A L 1877–81 *Monograph of the British Fossil Elephants*. London: Palaeontographical Society

Adler, D S, Bar-Oz, G, Belfer-Cohen, A and Bar-Yosef, O 2006 'Ahead of the game: Middle and Upper Palaeolithic hunting behaviours in the southern Caucasus'. *Curr Anthropol* **47**, 89–118

Adler, D S and Jöris, O 2009 'Dating the Middle to Upper Palaeolithic boundary across Eurasia'. *Eurasian Prehist* **5**, 5–18

Aiello, L and Dunbar, R 1993 'Neocortex size, group size and the evolution of language'. *Curr Anthropol* **34**, 184–93

Aiello, L C and Wheeler, P 2003 'Neanderthal thermoregulation and the glacial climate', in Van Andel, T and Davies, W (eds) *Neanderthals and Modern Humans in the European Landscape During the Last Glaciation: Archaeological Results of the Stage 3 Project*. Cambridge: McDonald Inst Archaeol Res Monogr, 147–66

Aitken, M J 1998 *An Introduction to Optical Dating: The Dating of Quaternary Sediments by the Use of Photon-stimulated Luminescence*. Oxford: Oxford U P

Aitken, M J 1990 *Science-based Dating in Archaeology*. London: Longman

Aldhouse-Green, S, Scott, K, Schwarcz, H, Grün, R, Housley, R, Rae, A, Bevins, R and Rednap, M 1995 'Coygan Cave, Laugharne, South Wales, a Mousterian site and hyaena den: a report on the University of Cambridge excavations'. *Proc Prehist Soc* **61**, 37–79

Aldhouse-Green, S and Pettitt, P 1998 'Paviland Cave: contextualising the "Red Lady"'. *Antiquity* **72**, 756–72

Allen, M J 1991 'Analysing the landscape: a geographical approach to archaeological problems', in Schofield, A J (ed) *Interpreting Artefact Scatters: Contributions to Ploughzone Archaeology*. Oxford: Oxbow, 39–57

Ambrose, S H 1993 'Isotopic analysis of paleodiets: methodological and interpretive considerations', *in* Sandford, M K (ed) *Investigations of Ancient Human Tissue: Chemical Analyses in Anthropology*. Langhorne, Pennsylvania: Gordon and Breach Science Publishers, 59–130

Ambrose S H and Norr, L 1993 'Experimental evidence for the relationship of the carbon isotope ratios of whole diet and dietary protein to those of bone collagen and carbonate', *in* Lambert, J B and Grupe, G (eds) *Prehistoric Human Bone: Archaeology at the Molecular Level*. Berlin: Springer-Verlag, 1–37

Anderson, R 2005 'An annotated list of the non-marine *mollusca* of Britain and Ireland'. *J Conchology* **38**, 607–37

Andrew, R 1984 *A Practical Pollen Guide to the British Flora*. Cambridge: Quat Res Assoc Techn Guides **1**

Andrews, J E, Greenaway, A M and Dennis, P F 1998 'Combined carbon isotope and C/N ratios as indicators of source and fate of organic matterin a poorly flushed, tropical estuary: Hunts Bay, Kingston Harbour, Jamaica'. *Estuarine, Coastal and Shelf Sci* **46**, 743–56

Andrews, J E, Pedley, H M and Dennis, P F, 1994 'Stable isotope record of palaeoclimate change in a British Holocene tufa'. *The Holocene* **4**, 349–55

Andrews, J E, Riding, R and Dennis, P F 1993 'Stable istopic compositions of recent freshwater cyanobacterial carbonates from the British Isles: local and regional environmental controls'. *Sedimentol* **40**, 303–14

Andrews, J E, Riding, R and Dennis, P F 1997 'The stable isotope record of environmental and climatic signals in modern terrestrial microbial carbonates from Europe'. *Palaeogeogr, Palaeoclimatol, Palaeoecol* **129**, 171–89

Andrews, J E, Samways, G, Dennis, P F and Maher, B A 2000 'Origin, abundance and storage of organic carbon and sulphur in the Holocene Humber estuary: emphasizing human impact on storage changes', *in* Shennan, I and Andrews, J E (eds) *Holocene Land-Ocean Interaction and Environmental Change Around the North Sea*. Geol Soc, London Special Publ 166, 145–70

Andrews, P 1990 *Owls, Caves and Fossils*. London: Natural History Museum Publications

Andrews, P and Cook, J 1985. 'Natural modifications to bones in a temperate setting'. *Man* **20**, 675–91

Antoine, P, Lautridou, J-P, Sommé, J, Auguste, P, Auffret, J-P, Baize, S, Clet-Pellerin, M, Coutard, J-P, Dewolf, Y, Dugué, O, Joly, F, Laignal, B, Laurent, M, Lavollé, M, Lebret, P, Lécolle, F, Lefebvre, D, Limondin-Lozouet, N, Munuat, A-V, Ozouf, J-C, Quesnel, F and Rousseau, D-D 1998 'Les formations quaternaires de la France du Nord-Ouest: limites et correlations'. *Quaternaire* **9**, 227–41

Anzidei, A P, Ruffo, M 1985 'The Pleistocene deposit of Rebbibia – Casal de' Pazzi (Rome-Italy)', in Malone, C and Stoddart, S (eds) *Papers in Italian Archaeology IV. The Human Landscape*. London: Accordia Research Centre, 141–53

Anzidei, A P, Angelelli, F, Arnoldus-Huyzendveld, A, Caloi, L, Palombo, M, Segre, A G 1989 'Le gisement Pléistocène de la Polledrara di Cecanibbio (Rome, Italie)'. *L'Anthropologie* **93**, 749–81

ApSimon, A M 1986 'Picken's Hole, Compton Bishop, Somerset; Early Devensian bear and wolf den, and Middle Devensian Hyaena Den and Palaeolithic Site', *in* Collcutt, S N (ed) *The Palaeolithic of Britain and its Neighbours: Recent Trends*. Sheffield: Depart Archaeol Prehist, U Sheffield, 55–6

Arensburg, B, Duday, H, Tillier, A M, Schepartz, L A and Rak, Y 1989 'A Middle Palaeolithic human hyoid bone'. *Nature* **338**, 758–60

Arnold, E N and Burton, J A 1978. *A Field Guide to the Reptiles and Amphibians of Britain and Europe*. London: Collins

Ashton, N M 1998a 'The taphonomy of the flint assemblages', in Ashton, N M, Lewis S G and Parfitt, S (eds) *Excavations at the Lower Palaeolithic Site at East Farm, Barnham, Suffolk 1989–94*. London: Brit Mus Occas Pap **125**, 183–204

Ashton, N M 1998b 'The technology of the flint assemblages', in Ashton, N M, Lewis S G and Parfitt, S (eds), *Excavations at the Lower Palaeolithic Site at East Farm, Barnham, Suffolk 1989–94*. London: Brit Mus Occas Pap **125**, 205–36

Ashton, N M 1998c 'Appendix VI: Flint analysis methodology', in Ashton, N M, Lewis S G and Parfitt, S (eds), *Excavations at the Lower Palaeolithic Site at East Farm, Barnham, Suffolk 1989–94*. London: Brit Mus Occas Pap **125**, 288–91

Ashton, N M 2002 'Absence of humans in Britain during the last interglacial (oxygen isotope stage 5e)', *in* Roebroeks, W and Tuffreau, A (eds) *Le dernier Interglaciaire et les occupations du Paléolithique moyen*. Lille: Centre Etudes Recherche Préhist **8**, U Sci Technol Lille, 93–103

Ashton, N, Cook, J, Lewis, S G and Rose, R 1992 *High Lodge: Excavations by G de G Sieveking, 1962–8 and J. Cook, 1988*. London: Brit Mus Press

Ashton, N, Dean, P and McNabb J 1991 'Flaked flakes: what, where, when and why?' *Lithics* **12**, 1–11

Ashton, N and Lewis, S G 2002 'Deserted Britain: declining populations in the British Late Middle Pleistocene'. Antiquity 76, 388–96

Ashton, N, Lewis, S G and Parfitt, S 1998 Excavations at the Lower Palaeolithic Site at East Farm, Barnham, Suffolk 1989–97. London: Brit Mus Occas Pap 125

Ashton, N, Lewis, S, Parfitt, S, Candy, I, Keen, D, Kemp, R, Penkman, K, Thomas, G, Whittaker, J and White, M 2005 'Excavations at the Lower Palaeolithic site at Elveden, Suffolk'. *Proc Prehist Soc* **71**, 1–62

Ashton, N M, Jacobi, R and White, M 2003. 'The dating of Levallois sites in West London'. *Quat Newsletter* **99**, 25–32

Ashton, N M and McNabb, J 1996a 'The flint industries from the Waechter excavation', *in* Conway, B, McNabb, J and Ashton, N M (eds) *Excavations at Barnfield Pit, Swanscombe, 1968–72*. Brit Mus Occas Pap **94**), 201–36

Ashton, N M and McNabb, J 1996b 'Appendix 1: Methodology of flint analysis', in: Conway, B, McNabb, J. and Ashton N M (eds), *Excavations at Barnfield Pit, Swanscombe, 1968–72*. Brit Mus Occas Pap **94**, 241–6

Atkinson, T C, Briffa, K R and Coope G R 1987 'Seasonal temperatures in Britain during the past 32,000 years, reconstructed using beetle remains'. *Nature* **325**, 587–92

Austin, L 1997 'Palaeolithic and Mesolithic', *in* Glazebrook, J (ed) *Research and Archaeology: a Framework for the Eastern Counties 1. Resource Assessment*. Hunstanton, Norfolk: East Anglian Archaeol, 5–11

Austin, L 2000 'Palaeolithic and Mesolithic', in Bronw, N and Glazebrook, J (eds) *Research and Archaeology: a Framework for the Eastern Counties 2. Research Agenda and Strategy*. Hunstanton, Norfolk: East Anglian Archaeol, 5–8

Averianov, A O 1996 'Sexual dimorphism in the mammoth skull, teeth and long bones', *in* Shoshani, J and Tassy P (eds) *The Proboscidea: Trends in Evolution and Palaeoecology*. Oxford: Oxford U P, 260–67

Bada, J, Scoeninger, M and Schimmelmann, A 1989 'Isotopic fractionation during peptide bond hydrolysis'. *Geochim et Cosmochim Acta* **53**, 3337–41

Bagyaraj, D J and Varma, A 1995 'Interaction between arbuscular mycorrhizal fungi and plants: their importance in sustainable agriculture in arid and semi arid tropics', *in* Jones, J G (ed) *Advances in Microbial Ecology Vol 14*. New York: Plenum Press, 119–36

Ballantyne, C K and Harris, C 1994 *The Periglaciation of Great Britain*. Cambridge: Cambridge U P

Balter, M 2009 'Better homes and hearths, Neanderthal-style'. *Science* **326**, 1056–7

Bamforth, D 1986 'Technological efficiency and tool curation'. *Amer Antiq* **51**, 38–50

Banfield, A W F 1974 *The Mammals of Canada*. Toronto: U Toronto P

Banks, W E, d'Errico, F, Peterson, A, Kageyama, M, Sima, A and Sánchez-Goñi, M F 2008 'Neanderthal extinction by competitive exclusion'. *PLoS One* **3**(12), e3972

Banerjee, D, Murray, A S, Bøtter-Jensen, L and Lang, A 2001 'Equivalent dose estimation using a single aliquot of polymineral fine grains'. *Radiation Measurements* **33**, 73–94

Barham, L S and Mitchell, P 2008 *The First Africans: African Archaeology from the Earliest Toolmakers to Most Recent Foragers*. Cambridge: Cambridge U P

Bar-Yosef, O 2002 'The Upper Palaeolithic revolution'. *Ann Rev Anthropol* **31**, 363–93

Barron, E, Van Andel, T H and Pollard, D 2003 'Glacial environments II: reconstructing the climate of Europe in the last glaciation', *in* van Andel, T H and Davies, W (eds) *Neanderthals and Modern Humans in the European Landscape During the Last Glaciation: Archaeological Results of the Stage 3 Project*. Cambridge: McDonald Inst Archaeol Res Monagr, 57–78

Barton, R N E 2000 'Mousterian hearths and shellfish: Late Neanderthal activities on Gibraltar', *in* Stringer, C, Barton, R N E and Finlayson, J C (eds) *Neanderthals on the Edge*. Oxford: Oxbow, 211–20

Baumann, W and Mania, D 1983. *Die Paläolithischen Neufunde von Markkleebera bei Leibzig*. Berlin: VEB Deutscher Verlag der Wissenschaften

Baxter, M 2003 *Statistics in Archaeology*. London: Arnold

Behre, K E and van der Plicht, J 1992'. *Vegetation History and Archaeobotany* **1**, 111–17

Behrensmeyer, A K 1975 'The taphonomy and paleoecology of Plio-Pleistocene vertebrate assemblages east of Lake Rudolf, Kenya'. *Bull Mus Comparat Zool* **146**, 473–578

Behrensmeyer, A K 1978 'Taphonomic and ecologic information on bone weathering'. *Paleobiology* **4**, 150–62

Behrensmeyer, A K 1982 'Time resolution in vertebrate assemblages'. *Paleobiol* **8**, 211–28

Behrensmeyer, A K 1987 'Taphonomy and hunting', *in* Nitecki, M H and Nitecki D V (eds) *The Evolution of Human Hunting*. New York: Plenum Press, 423–50

Behrensmeyer, A K 1991 'Terrestrial vertebrate accumulations', *in* Allison, P A and Briggs, D E G *Taphonomy: Releasing the Data Locked in the Fossil Record*. Topics in Geobiol **9**. New York: Plenum Press, 291–335

Behrensmeyer, A K, Gordon, K and Yanogi, G 1986 'Trampling as a cause of bone surface damage and pseudo-cutmarks'. *Nature* **319**, 768–71

Bell, F G 1969 'The occurrence of southern, steppe and halophyte elements in Weichselian (Last Glacial) floras from southern Britain'. *New Phytologist* **68**, 913–22

Bell, F G 1970 'Late Pleistocene floras from Earith, Huntingdonshire'. *Phil Trans Roy Soc London Series B* **256**, 347–78

Bell, M 1983 'Valley sediments as evidence of prehistoric land-use on the South Downs'. *Proc Prehist Soc* **49**, 119–50

Benedict, J B 1970 'Downslope movement in a Colorado alpine region: rates, processes and climatic significance'. *Arctic and Alpine Res* **2**, 165–226

Benner, R, Fogel, M L, Sprague, E K and Hudson, R E 1987 'Depletion of ^{13}C in lignin and its implications for stable carbon isotope studies'. *Nature* **329**, 708–10

Berger, T D and Trinkhaus, E 1995 'Patterns of trauma among the Neanderthals'. *J Archaeol Sci* **22**, 841–52

Best, A 2003 *Regional Variation in the Material Culture of Hunter Gatherers Social and Ecological Approaches to Ethnographic Objects from Queensland, Australia*. BAR Int Ser **1149**. Oxford: Archaeopress

Binford, L R 1973 'Interassemblage variability – the Mousterian and the 'functional' argument', *in* Renfrew, A C (ed) *The Explanation of Culture Change*. London: Duckworth, 227–54

Binford, L R 1978 *Nunamiut Ethnoarchaeology*. New York: Academic Press

Binford, L R 1979 'Organisation and formation processes: looking at curated technologies'. *J Anthropol Res* **35**, 255–73

Binford, L R 1981 *Bones: Ancient Men and Modern Myths*. New York: Academic Press

Binford, L R 1983 *In Pursuit of the Past*. London: Thames and Hudson

Binford L R 1984 *Faunal Remains from Klasies River Mouth*. New York: Academic Press

Binford, L R 1985 'Human ancestors: changing views of their behaviour'. *J Anthropol Archaeol* **4**, 292–327

Binford, L R 1989 'Isolating the transition to cultural adaptations: an organisational approach', *in* Trinkaus, E (ed) *The Emergence of Modern Humans: Biocultural Adaptations in the Later Pleistocene*. Cambridge: Cambridge U P, 18–41

Binford, L R 2001 *Constructing Frames of Reference: an Analytical Method for Archaeological Theory Building Using Ethnographic and Environmental Datasets*. Berkeley: U California P

Binford, L R 2007 'The diet of early hominins: some things we need to know before "reading" the menu from the archaeological record', *in* Roebroeks, W (ed) *Guts and brains: an integrative approach to the hominin record*. Leiden: U Leiden P, 185–222

Birks, C 2000 *Report on an Archaeological Evaluation at Lynford Gravel Pit, Mundford*. Norfolk Archaeol Unit Rep 499

Birks, C 2001 *Report on an Archaeological Watching Brief at Lynford Gravel Pit, Mundford*. Norfolk Archaeol Unit Rep 575

Birks, C and Robertson, D 2005 'Prehistoric settlement at Stanford: excavations at Lynford Quarry, Norfolk 2000–2001'. *Norfolk Archaeol* **44**, 676–701

Bishop, M J 1982 *The Mammal Fauna of the Early Middle Pleistocene Cavern Infill site of Westbury-sub-Mendip, Somerset*. Spec Pap Palaeontol Assoc **26**. London: Palaeontol Assoc

Blasco Sancho, M F 1995 *Hombres, fieras y presas: estudio arqueozoológico y tafonómico del yacimiento del paleolitico medio de la Cueva de Gabasa 1 (Huesca)*. Monogr Arqueol **38**. Zaragoza: U Zaragoza, Depart Cien Antig

Bleed, P 1986 'The optimal design of hunting weapons: maintainability or reliability'. *Amer Antiq* **51**, 737–47

Blalock, H M 1979 *Social Statistics*. London: McGraw-Hill Kogakusha

Blomberg, A, Hogmark S and Jun Lu 1993 'An electron microscope study of worn ceramic surfaces'. *Tribology Internat* **26**, 369–80

Bocherens, H, Billiou, D, Mariotti, A, Patou-Mathis, M, Otte, M, Bonjean, D and Toussainte, M 1999 'Palaeoenvironmental and Palaeodietary Implications of Isotopic Biogeochemistry of Last Interglacial Neanderthal and Mammal Bones in Scladina Cave (Belgium)'. *J Archaeol Sci* **26**, 599–607

Bocherens, H, Billiou, D, Mariotti, M, Toussaint, M, Patou-Mathis, M, Bonjean, D and Otte, M 2001 'New isotopic evidence for dietary habits of Neanderthals from Belgium'. *J Human Evol* **40**, 497–505

Bocherens H, Drucker DG, Billiou D, Patou-Mathis M, Vandermeersch B 2005 'Isotopic evidence for diet and subsistence pattern of the Saint-Césaire I Neanderthal: review and use of a multi-source mixing model'. *J Human Evol* **49**, 71–87

Bocherens H, Fizet, M, Mariotti, A, Gangloff, R A and Burns, J A 1994 'Contribution of isotopic biogeochemistry (^{13}C, ^{15}N, ^{18}O) to the paleoecology of mammoths (*Mammuthus primigenius*)'. *Hist Biol* **7**, 187–202

Bocherens H, Pacaud G, Lazarev PA, Mariotti A 1996 'Stable isotope abundances (^{13}C, ^{15}N) in collagen and soft tissues from Pleistocene mammals from Yakutia: Implications for the palaeobiology of the Mammoth Steppe'. *Palaeogeogr, Palaeoclimatol, Palaeoecol* **126**, 31–44

Boëda, E, Geneste, J M and Meignen, L 1990. 'Identification de chaînes opératoire lithiques du Paléolithique ancien et moyen'. *Paléo* **2**, 43–80

Boëda, E 2001 'Détermination des unités techno-fonctionnelles de pièces bifaciales provenant de la couche acheuléenne C'3 base du site de Barbas I', *in* Cliquet, D (ed) *Les industries à outils bifaciaux du Paléolithique moyen d'Europe occidentale*. Etudes Recherche Archéol U Liège **98**. Liège: ERAUL, 51–76

Boismier, W A 2003 'A Middle Palaeolithic site at Lynford Quarry, Mundford, Norfolk: Interim Statement'. *Proc Prehist Soc* **69**, 315–24

Boismier, W A 2003 'Lynford Quarry, Mundford Norfolk: Project Design for Archaeological Excavation'. Unpub ms, Norfolk Archaeol Unit

Boismier, W A, Schreve, D C, White, M J, Robertson, DA, Stuart, AJ Etienne, S, Andrews, J, Coope, G R, Field, M H, Green, F M, Keen, D H, Lewis, S G, French, C A, Rhodes, E, Schwenninger, J-L, Tovey, K and O'Connor, S 2003 'A Middle Palaeolithic site at Lynford Quarry Mundford, Norfolk: interim statement'. *Proc Prehist Soc* **69**, 315–24

Bond, G C, Broecker, W S, Johnsen, S, McManus, J, Labeyrie, L, Jouzel, J and Bonani, G 1993 'Correlations between climate records from North Atlantic sediments and Greenland ice'. *Nature* **365**, 143–7

Bonifay, M-F 1966 'Les Carnivores', *in* Lavocat, R (ed) *Faunes et flores préhistoriques de l'Europe Occidentale*. Paris: Boubée, 337–96

Bonifay, M-F 1971 'Carnivores Quaternaires du sud-est de la France'. *Mém Mus Hist Naturelle Sér C* **21(2)**, 1–377

Bordes, F 1961 *Typologie du Paléolithique Ancien et Moyen*. Paris: Centre Nat Recherche Scientif

Bordes, F 1972 *A Tale of Two Caves*. New York: Harper and Row

Bordes, F 1984. *Leçons sur le Paléolithique Vol 2: Le Paléolithique en Europe*. Paris: Centre Nat Recherche Scientif

Bordes, F 2002 *Typologie du Paléolithique Ancien et Moyen*, 5 edn. Paris: Centre Nat Recherche Scientif

Bordovsky, O K 1965 'Sources of organic matter in marine basins'. *Marine Geol* **3**, 5–31

Bosinski, G 1967 *Die Mittelpaläolithischen Funde im Westlichen Mitteleuropa*. Fundamenta **A/4**. Cologne: Bohlau

Bottrell, S H, Hannam, J A, Andrews, J E and Maher, B A 1998 'Diagenesis and remobilization of carbon and sulfur in mid-Pleistocene organic-rich freshwater sediment'. *J Sedimentary Res* **68**, 37–42

Bouchud, J 1966a 'Les Rhinocéros', *in* Lavocat, R (ed) *Faunes et Flores Préhistoriques de l'Europe Occidentale*. Paris: Boubée, 174–93

Bouchud, J 1966b 'Les Cervidés', *in* Lavocat, R (ed) *Faunes et Flores Préhistoriques de l'Europe Occidentale*. Paris: Boubée, 244–77

Bowen, D Q 1999 (ed.) *A Revised Correlation of Quaternary Deposits in the British Isles*. London: Geol Soc London Special Rep **23**

Boyle, K 1998 *The Middle Palaeolithic Geography of Southern France*. BAR Int Ser **723**. Oxford: Archaeopress

Brady, N C and Weil, R R 1999. *The Nature and Properties of Soils*. Upper Sadle River, New Jersey: Prentice-Hall Inc

Bradley, B and Sampson, G 1986 'Analysis by replication of two Acheulian artefact assemblages from Caddington, England', *in* Bailey, G N and Callow, P (eds) *Stone Age Prehistory: Studies in Memory of Charles McBurney*. Cambridge: Cambridge U P, 29–46

Bratlund, B 1999a 'Anthropogenic factors in the thanatocoenose of the last interglacial travertines at Taubach, Germany', *in* Gaudzinski, S (ed) *The Role of Early Humans in the Accumulation of Lower and Middle Palaeolithic Bone Assemblages*, Römisch-Germanisches Zentralmuseum Mainz Monogr **42**, 255–62

Bratlund, B 1999b *Taubach Revisited*. Mainz: Jahrb Römisch-Germanisches Zentralmuseum

Brenner, D, Amundson, R, Baisden, W T, Kendall, C and Harden, J 2001 'Soil N and ^{15}N variation with time in California annual grassland ecosystem'. *Geochim et Cosmochim Acta* **65**, 4171–86

Briant, R M 2002 'Fluvial responses to rapid climate change in Eastern England during the last glacial period'. Unpub PhD thesis, U Cambridge

Bridgland, D R 1994 *Quaternary of the Thames*. London: Chapman and Hall

Bridgland, D R and Harding, P 1993 'Middle Pleistocene deposits at Globe Pit, Little Thurrock, and their contained Clactonian industry'. *Proc Geolog Assoc* **104**, 263–83

Briggs, D J and Gilbertson, D D 1973 'The age of the Hanborough Terrace of the River Evenlode, Oxfordshire'. *Proc Geol Assoc* **84(2)**, 155–73

Brimblecombe, P, Dent, D L and McCave, I N 1982 'Chapter 5: Laboratory techniques', *in* Haynes, R M (eds) *Environmental Science Methods*. London: Chapman and Hall, 186–208

Bristow, C R 1990 'Geology of the country around Bury St Edmunds'. *Mem Brit Geol Survey*, Sheet **189** (England and Wales). London: HMSO

British Geological Survey 1991 *East Anglia*. Sheet 52°N-00°, Quaternary Geology. 1:250,000 Series. Swindon: Natural Environment Research Council

British Geological Survey 1999 *Swaffham. England and Wales Sheet 160 Solid and Drift Geology* (1:50,000 Provisional Series). Keyworth: British Geological Survey

Brothwell, D R 1983 'The palaeopathology of Pleistocene and more recent mammals', *in* Brothwell, D and Higgs, E (eds) *Science in Archaeology*. London: Thames and Hudson, 310–14

Brothwell, D R 2008 'Problems of differential diagnosis in Pleistocene mammal pathology'. *Veterinarija Ir Zootechnica* **44**, 88–90

Brown, A G 1996 *Alluvial Geoarchaeology*. Cambridge: Cambridge U P

Brown, T A, Nelson, D E and Southon, J R 1988 'Improved collagen extraction by modified Longin method'. *Radiocarbon* 30, 171–7

Browne, S 1983 'Investigations into the evidence for postcranial variation in *Bos primigenius* (BOJANUS) in England and the problem of its differentiation from *Bison priscus* (BOJANUS)'. *Bull Inst Archaeol London* **20**, 79–92

Brugère, A, Fontana, L and Oliva, M 2009 'Mammoth procurement and exploitation at Milovice (Czech Republic): New data for the Moravian Gravettian', *in* Fontana, L Chauvière, F-X and Bridault, A (eds) *In Search of Total Animal Exploitation: Case Studies from the Upper Palaeolithic and Mesolithic*. BAR Int Ser **2040**. Oxford: Archaeopress, 45–69

Brumm, A and Moore, M W 2005 'Symbolic revolutions and the Australian archaeological record'. *Cambridge Archaeol J* **15**, 157–75

Buckhouse, J C, Skovlin, J M and Knight, R W 1981 'Streambank erosion and ungulate grazing relationships'. *J Range Management* **34**, 339–40

Bullock, P, Fedoroff, N, Jongeruis, A, Stoops, G and Tursina, T 1985 *Handbook for Soil Thin Section Description*. Wolverhampton: Waine Research

Bunn, H, Isaac, G, Kufulu, Z, Kroll, E, Schick, K, Toth, N and Behrensmeyer, A K 1980 'FxJj50: an early Pleistocene site in northern Kenya'. *World Archaeol* **12**, 109–36

Burke, A 2000 'Hunting in the Middle Palaeolithic'. *Internat J Osteoarchaeol* **10**, 281–5

Burroni, D B, Donahue, R E, Mussi, M and Pollard, A M 2002 'The surface alteration feature of flint artefacts as a record of environmental processes'. *J Archaeol Sce* **29**, 1277–87

Butzer, K W 1982 *Archaeology as Human Ecology*. Cambridge: Cambridge U P

Caine, N 1980 'The rainfall intensity-duration control of shallow landslides and debris flows'. *Geografiska Annaler* **62A**, 23–7

Callow, P 1986a 'The stratigraphic sequence: description and problems', *in* Callow, P and Cornford, J M (eds) *La Cotte De St. Brelade 1961–1978. Excavations by C.B.M. McBurney*. Norwich: Geo Books, 55–71

Callow, P 1986b 'The flint tools', *in* Callow, P and Cornford, J M (eds) *La Cotte De St. Brelade 1961–1978. Excavations by C.B.M. McBurney*. Norwich: Geo Books, 251–314

Callow, P and Cornford, J M (eds) 1986 *La Cotte de St. Brelade 1961–1978: Excavations by C.B.M. McBurney*. Norwich: Geo Books

Campbell, J B 1977 *The Upper Palaeolithic of Britain: a Study of Man and Nature in the Late Ice Age*. Oxford: Clarendon Press

Campbell, J B and Sampson, C G 1971 *A New Analysis of Kent's Cavern, Devonshire, England*. Eugene, Oregon: U Oregon P

Campetti S, d'Errico F, Giacobini G, Radmilli A M 1989 'Taphonomie, industrie osseuse et pseudo-instruments en os dans le site du Paléolithique inférieur de Castel di Guido (Rome)', *in* Patou, M (ed) *Outillage peu élaboré en os et en bois de cérvides, III*. Treignes: édition du centre d'etudes et de documentation archéologique, 21–3

Caspers, G and Freund, H 2001 'Vegetation and climate in the Early and Pleni-Weichseian in northern Europe'. *J Quat Sci* **16**, 31–48

Chaline, J 1966 'Les Insectivores', *in* Lavocat, R (ed) *Faunes et Flores Préhistoriques de l'Europe Occidentale*. Paris: Boubée, 442–50

Churchill, S E 1993 'Weapon technology, prey size selection and hunting methods in modern hunter-gatherers: implications for hunting in the Palaeolithic and Mesolithic', in Peterkin, G L, Bricker, H and Mellars, P A (eds) *Hunting and Animal Exploitation in the Later Palaeolithic and Mesolithic of Eurasia*. Washington: Archaeol Pap Amer Antropol Assoc **4**, 11–24

Churchill, S E, Franciscus, R G, McKean-Peraza, H A, Daniel, J A and Warren, B R 2009 'Shanidar 3 Neandertal rib puncture wound and Paleolithic weaponry'. *J Human Evol* **57**, 163–78

Clark, J G D 1969 *World Prehistory: a New Outline*, 2 edn. Cambridge: Cambridge U P

Cliquet, D (ed) 2001 *Les Industries à Outils Bifaciaux du Paléolithique Moyen d'Europe Occidentale*. Etudes Recherche Archéol U Liège 98. Liège: ERAUL

Cliquet, D, Ladjadj, J, Lautridou, J-P, Lereprtier, J, Lorren, P, Michel, D, Pruvost, P, Rivard, J-J and Vilgrain G 2001b 'Le Paléolithique moyen à outils bifaciaux en Normandie: états des connaissances', in Cliquet, D (ed) *Les Industries à Outils Bifaciaux du Paléolithique Moyen d'Europe Occidentale*. Etudes Recherche Archéol U Liège **98**. Liège: ERAUL, 115–27

Cliquet, D, Lautridou, J-P, Rivard, J-J, Alix, P, Gosselin, R and Lorren, P 2001a 'Les industries à outils bifaciaux du Paléolithique moyen en Normandie armoricaine: l'example due site de Saint-Brice-sous-Rânes (Orne, France)', in Cliquet, D (ed) *Les Industries à Outils Bifaciaux du Paléolithique Moyen d'Europe Occidentale*. Etudes Recherche Archéol U Liège **98**. Liège: ERAUL, 93–106

Collcutt, S N 1984 'The sediments', in Stephen Green, H (ed) *Pontnewydd Cave: a Lower Palaeolithic Hominid Cave in Wales. The First Report*. Cardiff: Nat Mus Wales, 31–76

Collcutt, S N 1986 'Contextual archaeology: the example of debris flows in Caves', in Collcutt, S N (ed) *In The Palaeolithic of Britain and its Neighbours: Recent Trends*. Sheffield: Depart Archaeol Prehist, U Sheffield, 57–8

Collina-Girard, J 1998. *Le Feu Avant les Allumettes*. Paris: Editions de la Maison des Sciences de l'Homme

Collins, D M and Collins, A 1970 'Cultural evidence from Oldbury'. *Bull Inst Archaeol London* **8–9**, 151–76

Conard N J 1992 'Tönchesberg and its position in the prehistory of Northern Europe'. *Monogr Römisch-Germanisch Zentralmusuem* **20**. Bonn: Habert

Conard, N J and Adler, D S 1997 'Lithic reduction and hominid behaviour in the Middle Palaeolithic of the Rhineland'. *J Anthropol Res* **53**, 147–76

Conard, N J and Fischer, B 2000 'Are there recognisable cultural entities in the German Middle Palaeolithic?', in Ronen, A and Weinstein-Evron, M (eds) *Towards Modern Humans: Yabrudian and Micoquian, 400–50 Kyears Ago*. BAR Int Ser **850**. Oxford: Archaeopress

Conard, N J and Niven, L 2001 'The Paleolithic finds from Bollschweil and the question of Neanderthal mammoth hunting in the Black Forest', in Cavarretta, G Giola, P, Mussi, M and Palomba, M (eds) *La Terra Degli Elefanti*. Proceedings of the 1st International Congress. Rome: Consiglio Nazionale delle Richerche, 194–200

Conard, N J and Prindiville, T J 2000 'Middle Paeolithic hunting economies in the Rhineland'. *Internat J Osteoarchaeol* **10**, 286–309

Cook, J, Ashton, N, Coope, G R, Hunt, C O, Lewis, S G and Rose, J 1991 'High Lodge, Mildenhall, Suffolk (TL 739754)', in Lewis, S G, Whiteman, C A and Bridgland, D R (eds) *Central East Anglia and the Fen Basin*. London: Quat Res Assoc, 127–30

Cook, J and Jacobi, R 1998 'Discoidal core technology in the Palaeolithic at Oldbury, Kent', in Ashton, N, Healy, F and Pettitt, P (eds) *Stone Age Archaeology. Essays in honour of John Wymer*. Oxbow Monogr **102**/Lithics Stud Soc Occas Pap **6**). Oxford: Oxbow: Books, 124–36

Coope, G R 1968. 'An insect fauna from Mid-Weichselian deposits at Brandon, Warwickshire'. *Philos Trans Roy Soc London Ser B* **254**, 425–56

Coope, G R 1973 'Tibetan Species of Dung Beetle from Late Pleistocene Deposits in England'. *Nature* **245**, 335–6

Coope, G R 1986 'Coleoptera analysis', in Berglund, B E (ed) *Handbook of Holocene Palaeoecology and Palaeohydrology*. Chichester: J. Wiley & Sons, 703–13

Coope G R 2000 'Middle Devensian (Weichselian) coleopteran assemblages from Earth, Cambridgeshire (UK) and their bearing on the interpretation of "Full Glacial" floras and faunas'. *J Quat Sci* **15**, 779–88

Coope, G R 2002 'Changes in the thermal climate in northwestern Europe during Marine Oxygen Isotope Stage 3, estimated from fossil insect assemblages'. *Quat Res* **57**, 401–8

Coope, G R and Angus, R B 1975. 'An ecological study of a temperate interlude in the middle of the last glaciation, based on fossil Coleoptera from Isleworth, Middlesex'. *J Animal Ecol* **44**, 365–91

Coope, G R, Shotton, F W and Strachan, I 1961 'A late Pleistocene fauna and flora from Upton Warren, Worcestershire'. *Philos Trans Roy Soc London Ser B* **244**, 379–421

Coope, R G, Gibbard, P L, Hall, A R, Preece, R C, Robinson, J E and Sutcliffe, A J 1997 'Climatic and environmental reconstruction based on fossil assemblages from Middle Devensian (Weichselian) assemblages of the River Thames at South Kensington, central London, UK'. *Quat Sci Rev* **16**, 1163–95

Corbet, G R 1978. *The Mammals of the Palaearctic Region: a Taxonomic Review*. London and Ithaca: Brit Mus NatHist and Cornell U P

Costa, J E 1984 'Physical geomorphology of debris flows', in Costa, J E and Fleischer (eds) *Developments and Applications of Geomorphology*. Berlin: Springer-Verlag, 268–317

Coulson, S D 1986 'The Bout Coupé handaxe as a typological mistake', in Collcutt, S N (ed) *The Palaeolithic of Britain and its nearest Neighbours: Recent Trends*. Sheffield: Depart Archaeol Prehist, U Sheffield, 53–4

Coulson, S D 1990 *Middle Palaeolithic Industries of Great Britain*. Bonn: Holos

Crowson, R A, Showers, W J, Wright, E K and Hoering, T C 1991 'Preparation of phosphate samples for oxygen isotope analysis'. *Analyt Chemis* **63**, 2397–400

Currant, A P 1999 'A brief review of the Westbury Cave small mammal faunas', in Andrews, P, Cook, J, Currant, A and Stringer, C (eds) *Westbury Cave. The Natural History Museum Excavations 1976–1984*. Bristol: Western Archaeological and Specialist Press, 127–37

Currant A P and Jacobi R M 2001 'A formal mammalian biostratigraphy for the Late Pleistocene of Britain'. *Quat Sci Rev* **20**, 1707–16

Currant, A and Jacobi, R 2002 'Human presence and absence in Britain during the early part of the Late Pleistocene', in Roebroeks, W and Truffreau, A (eds) *Le Dernier Interglaciaire et les Occupations Humaines du Paléolithique Moyen*. Lille: Centre Etudes Recherche Préhist, U Sci Technol Lille, 105–13

Currant, A and Jacobi, R 2004 'A Middle Devensian mammalian assemblage from the Hyaena Den, Wookey, Hole, Somerset', in Schreve, D C (ed) *The Quaternary Mammals of Southern and Eastern England*. London: Quat Res Assoc, 87–92

Cziesla, E, Eickhoff, S, Arts, N and Winter, D 1990 (eds) *The Big Puzzle; International Symposium on Refitting Stone Artefacts*. Bonn: Holos

Dansgaard, W 1964 'Stable isotopes in precipitation'. *Tellus* **16**, 436–68

Davies, W and Gollop, P 2003 'The human presence in Europe during the last glacial period II. Climate tolerance and climate preferences of mid- and late glacial hominids', in van Andel, T and Davies, W (eds) *Neanderthals and Modern Humans in the European Landscape during the Last Glaciation*. Cambridge: McDonald Inst Archaeol Res Monogr, 131–46

Davis, O K 1987 'Spores of the dung fungus *Sporormiella*: increased abundance in historic sediments and before Pleistocene megafaunal extinction'. *Quat Res* **28**, 290–4

Dawkins, W B 1874 *Cave Hunting, Researches on the Evidence of Caves Respecting the Early Inhabitants of Europe*. London: Macmillan

Debruyne, R 2003 'Différenciation morphologique et moléculaire des Elephantinae (Mammalia, Proboscidea)'. Unpub PhD thesis, Mus Nat d'Hist Natur, Paris

Deines, P 1980 'The isotopic composition of reduced organic carbon', in Fritz, P and Fontes, J C (eds) *Handbook of Environmental Isotope Geochemistry, Volume 1*. Amsterdam: Elsevier, 329–406

Delagnes, A and Ropars, A 1996 *Paléolithique Moyen en Pays de Caux (Haute-Normandie)*. Paris: Documents d'Archéologie Française

Delair, J B and Shackley, M L 1978 'The Fisherton Brickpits: their stratigraphy and fossil contents'. *Wilts Nat Hist Soc Mag* **73**, 3–19

De Loecker, D 1994 'On the refitting analysis of Site K: a Middle Palaeolithic findspot at Maastricht-Belvedere (The Netherlands)'. *Ethnogr-archaol Zeitschr* **35**, 107–17

Delpech, F 1983 'Les faunes du Paléolithique Supérieur dans le Sud-Ouest de la France'. *Cahiers Quat* **6**, 1–453

DeNiro, M J 1985 'Post-mortem preservation and alteration of in vivo bone collagen isotope ratios in relation to paleodietary reconstruction'. *Nature* **317**, 806–9

Depaepe, P 2001 'Pour une poignée de biface: les industries pauvres en biface du Paléolithique moyen de la vallée de la Vanne (Yonne-France)', in Cliquet, D (ed) *Les Industries à Outils Bifaciaux du Paléolithique Moyen d'Europe Occidentale*. Etudes Recherche Archéol U Liège **98**. Liège: ERAUL, 135–40

d'Errico, F, Henshilwood, C S, Vanhaeren, M and van Niekerk, K 2005 '*Nassarius kraussianus* shell beads from Blombos Cave: evidence for symbolic behaviour in the Middle Stone Age'. *J Hum Evol* **48**, 3–24

Dibble, H L 1995 'Introduction to site formation', in Dibble, H L and Lenoir, M (eds) *The Middle Paleolithic site of Combe-Capelle Bas (France)*. Philadelphia: U Mus, U Pennsylvania, 175–8

Dibble, H L, Chase, P G, McPherron, S P and Tuffreau, A 1997 'Testing the reality of a "living floor" with archaeological data'. *Amer Antiq* **62**, 629–51

Dibble, H and Roland, N 1992 'Beyond the Bordes-Binford debate: a new synthesis of factors underlying assemblage variability in the Middle Palaeolithic of Western Europe', in Dibble, H and Mellars, P A (eds) *The Middle Paleolithic: Adaptation, Behavior and Variability*. Philadelphia: U Mus, U Pennsylvania, 1–28

Donahue, R E 1986 *Technomorphology, Tool Use and Site Function in the Italian Upper Paleolithic*. Ann Arbor: Microfilms Internat

Donahue, R E 1994 'The current state of lithic microwear research', in Ashton, N and David, A (eds) *Stories in Stone I: Proceedings of Anniversary Conference at St Hilda's College, Oxford, April 1993*. Lithic Stud Soc Occas Pap **4**. Oxford: Lithic Stud Soc, 156–68

Donahue, R E and Burroni, D B 2004 'Lithic microwear analysis and the formation of archaeological assemblages', in Walker, E A, Wenban-Smith, F and Healy, F (eds) *Lithics in Action: Papers for the Conference Lithic Studies in the Year 2000*. Oxford: Oxbow Books, 140–8

Donahue, R E, Murphy, M L and Robbins, L H 2002–04. 'Lithic microwear analysis of Middle Stone Age artifacts from White Paintings Rock Shelter, Botswana'. *J Field Archaeol* **29**, 155–63

Drennan, R D 1996 *Statistics for Archaeologists: a Commonsense Approach*. New York: Plenum Press

Duchadeau-Kervazo, C 1986 'Les sites paléolithiques du bassin de la Dronne (nord de l'Aquitaine): observations sur les modes et emplacements'. *Bull Soc Préhist Française* **83**, 56–64

Dunbar, R I M 2003 'The social brain: mind, language and society in evolutionary perspective'. *Annl Rev Anthropol* **32**, 163–81

Edwards, H G M, Jorge Villar S E, Nik Hassan N F, Arya N, O'Connor S and Charlton D M, 2005 'Ancient biodeterioration: an FT-Raman spectroscopic study of mammoth and elephant ivory'. *Analyt Bioanalyt Chem* **383**, 713–20

Ellerman, J R and Morrison-Scott, T C S 1966 *Checklist of Palaearctic and Indian Mammals 1758–1946*. London: Brit Mus Nat Hist

Ellis, E A 1978 *British Freshwater Bivalve Mollusca*, Synopses of the British Fauna **11**. London: Linnean Soc London

Eltringham, S K 1979 *The Ecology and Conservation of Large African Mammmals*. London: Macmillan

English Heritage 1998 *Identifying and Protecting Palaeolithic Remains: Archaeological Guidance for Planning Authorities and Developers*. London: English Heritage

English Heritage 1999 *Research Frameworks for the Palaeolithic and Mesolithic of Britain and Ireland*. London: English Heritage

Enos, P 1977 'Flow regimes in debris flows'. *Sedimentol* **24**, 133–42

Faegri, K and Iversen, J 1975 *Textbook of Pollen Analysis*, 3 edn. Oxford: Blackwell Scientific Publications

Farizy, C 1994 'Spatial patterning of Middle Paleolithic sites'. *J Anthropol Archaeol* **13**, 153–60

Farizy, C and David, F 1989 'Chasse et alimentation carnée au Paléolithique moyen, l'apport des gisements de plein air', in Otte, M (ed) *L'Homme de Neandertal Vol. 6 La Subsistance*. Liège: Etudes Recherche Archéol U Liège, 59–62

Farizy, C and David, F 1992 'Subsistence and behavioral patterns of some Middle Paléolithic local groups', in Dibble, H and Mellars, P A (eds) *The Middle Paleolithic: Adaptation, Behavior and Variability*. Philadelphia: U Mus, U Pennsylvania, 87–96

Farizy, C, David, F and Jaubert, J 1994 *Hommes et Bisons du Paléolithique Moyen à Mauran (Haute-Garonne)*. Paris: Centre Nat Recherche Scientif

Féblot-Augustins, J 1993 'Mobility strategies in the Late Middle Palaeolithic of Central Europe and Western Europe: elements of stability and variability'. *J Anthropol Archaeol* **12**, 211–65

Féblot-Augustins, J 1997 *La Circulation des Matières Premières au Paléolithique*. Etudes Recherche Archéol U Liège **75**. Liège: ERAUL

Féblot-Augustins, J 1999 'Raw material transport patterns and settlement systems in the European Lower and Middle Palaeolithic: continuity, change and variability', in Roebroeks, W and Gamble, C (eds) *The Middle Palaeolithic Occupation of Europe*. Leiden: U Leiden P, 193–214

Fischer, T E, Zhu, Z, Kim, H and Shin, D S 2000 'Genesis and role of wear debris in sliding wear of ceramics'. *Wear* **245**, 53–60

Fitter, R, Fitter, A and Blamey, M 1985 *The Wild Flowers of Britain and Northern Europe*, 4 edn. London: Collins

Foley, R and C Gamble 2009 'The ecology of social transitions in human evolution'. *Philos Trans Roy Soc London Ser B* **364**, 3267–79

Foley, R and Lahr, M M 1997 'Mode 3 technologies and the evolution of modern humans'. *Cambridge Archaeol J* **7**, 3–36

Folk, R 1974 *Petrology of Sedimentary Rocks*. Austin, Texas: Hemphill Publishing Company

Forstén, A 1991 'Size decrease in Pleistocene-Holocene true or caballoid horses of Europe'. *Mammalia* **55**, 407–19

Fowler, M E and Mikota, S K 2006 *The Biology, Medicine and Surgery of Elephants*. Oxford: Blackwell

Frechen, M 1991 'Thermolumineszenz-Datierungen an Lössen des Mittelrheingebiets'. *Sonderveröffentlichungen, Geol Inst U Köln* **79**, 1–137

Frechen, M 1994 'Thermolumineszenz-Datierungen an Lössen des Tönchesberges aus der Osteifel'. *Eiszeitalter und Gegenwart* **44**, 79–93

French, C 2003 *Geoarchaeology in Action: Studies in Soil Micromorphology and Landscape Evolution*. London: Routledge

French, H M 1976 *The Periglacial Environment*. Longman: London

Fricke, H C, Clyde, W C and O'Neil, J R 1998 'Intra-tooth variations in delta O-18 (PO4) of mammalian tooth enamel as a record of seasonal variations in continental climate variables'. *Geochim et Cosmoch Acta* **62**, 1839–50

Frison, G 1989 'Experimental use of Clovis weaponry and tools on African elephants'. *Amer Antiq* **54**, 766–84

Frison, G C 1991 *Prehistoric Hunters of the High Plains*, 2 edn. San Diego: Academic Press

Fritz, W J and Moore, J N 1988 *Basics of Physical Stratigraphy and Sedimentology*. Chichester: John Wiley

Frostrick, L E and Reid, I 1983 'Taphonomic significance of sub-aerial transport of vertebrate fossils on steep semi-arid slopes'. *Lethaia* **16**, 157–64

Gamble, C S 1979 'Hunting strategies in the central European Palaeolithic'. *Proc Prehist Soc* **45**, 35–52

Gamble, C 1983 'Caves and fauna from Last Glacial Europe', in Clutton-Brock, J and Grigson, C (eds) *Animals and Archaeology: 1. Hunters and Their Prey*. BAR Int Ser **163**. Oxford: Archaeopress, 163–72

Gamble, C 1986 *The Palaeolithic Settlement of Europe*. Cambridge: Cambridge U P

Gamble, C 1995 'The earliest occupation of Europe: the environmental background', in Roebroeks, W and van Kolfschoten, T (eds) *The Earliest Occupation of Europe*. Leiden: U Leiden P, 279–95

Gamble, C 1999. *The Palaeolithic Societies of Europe*. Cambridge: Cambridge U P

Gamble, C 2009 'Human display and dispersal: a case study from biotidal Britain in the Middle and Upper Pleistocene'. *Evol Anthropol* **18**, 144–56

Gamble, C 2010 'Technologies of separation and the evolution of social extension', in Dunbar, R, Gamble, C and Gowlett, J A J (eds) *Social Brain, Distributed Mind*. Oxford: Oxford U P, 17–42

Gamble, C and Roebroeks, W 1999 'The Middle Palaeolithic: a point of inflection', in Roebroeks, W and Gamble, C (eds) *The Middle Palaeolithic Occupation of Europe*. Leiden: U Leiden P, 3–21

Garrutt, V Y 1964 *Das Mammut Mammuthus primigenius (Blumenbach)*. *Die Neue Brehm-Bücherei* **331**. Wittenberg: A Ziemsen Verlag

Gaudzinski, S 1992. 'Wisentjäger in Wallertheim: zur taphonomie einer mittelpaläolithischen Freilandfundstelle in Rheinhessen'. *Jahrb Römisch-Germanischen Zentralmus Mainz* **39**, 245–423

Gaudzinski, S 1996 'On bovid assemblages and their consequences for the knowledge of subsistence patterns in the Middle Palaeolithic'. *Proc Prehist Soc* **62**, 19–39

Gaudzinski, S 1999a 'The faunal record of the Lower and Middle Palaeolithic of Europe: remarks on human interference', in Roebroeks, W and Gamble, C (eds) *The Middle Palaeolithic Occupation of Europe*. Leiden: U Leiden P, 215–33

Gaudzinksi, S 1999b 'Middle Palaeolithic bone tools from the open-air site Salzgitter-Lebenstedt (Germany)'. *J Archaeol Sci* **25**, 125–41

Gaudzinski, S and Roebroeks, W 2000 'Adults only: reindeer hunting at the Palaeolithic site Salzgitter-Lebenstedt, northern Germany'. *J Hum Evol* **38**, 497–521

Gaudzinski, S and Turner, E 1999 'Summarising the role of early humans in the accumulation of European Lower and Middle Palaeolithic bone assemblages', in Gaudzinski, S and Turner, E (eds) *The Role of Early Humans in the Accumulation of European Lower and Middle Palaeolithic Bone Assemblages*. Mainz: Römisch-Germanischen Zentralmus, 381–93

Gedda, B 2001 *Environmental and Climatic Aspects of the Early to Mid Holocene Calcareous Tufa and Land Mollusc Fauna in Southern Sweden*. LundQua Thesis **45**. Lund U, Sweden

Gee, H 1993 'The distinction between postcranial bones of *Bos primigenius* Bojanus, 1827 and *Bison priscus* Bojanus, 1827 from the British Pleistocene and the taxonomic status of *Bos and Bison*'. *J Quat Sci* **8**, 79–92

Gehre, M 2001 'High temperature pyrolysis: a new system for isotopic and elemental analysis – new approaches for stable isotope ratio measurements'. *IAEA TecDoc* **1247**, 33–8

Geneste, J-M 1985 'Analyse lithique des industries Moustériennes du Périgord: une approche technologique du comportement des groups au Paléolithique moyen'. Unpub PhD thesis, U Bordeaux

Geneste, J-M 1989 'Economie des ressources lithiques dans le Moustérien du Sud-Ouest de la France', in Otte, M (ed) *L'Homme de Neandertal Vol. 6 La Subsistance*. Liège: Etudes Recherche Archéol U Liège, 75–97

Gentry, A W 1999 'Fossil ruminants (Mammalia: Artiodactyla) from Westbury Cave', in Andrews, P, Cook, J, Currant, A and Stringer, C (eds) *Westbury Cave. The Natural History Museum Excavations 1976–1984*. Bristol: Western Archaeol Specialist Press, 139–74

Gentry, A, Clutton-Brock, J and Groves, C P 1996 'Proposed conservation of usage of 15 mammal specific names based on wild species which are antedated by or contemporary with those based on domestic animals'. *Bull Zool Nomenclature* **53**, 28–37

Gibbard, P L, Coope, G R, Hall, A R, Preece, R C and Robinson, J E 1982 'Middle Devensian deposits beneath the "Upper Floodplain" terrace of the River Thames at Kempton Park, Sunbury, England'. *Proc Geol Assoc* **93**(3), 275–89

Gifford, D P and Behrensmeyer, A K 1977 'Observed formation and burial of a recent human occupation site in Kenya'. *Quat Res* **8**, 245–66

Gil, E and Slupik, J 1972 'Hydroclimatic conditions of slope wash during snow melt in the Flysch Carpathians', in Maca, P and Pissart, A (eds) *Processus Periglaciaires: Etudies sur le Terrain*. Les Congrès et Colloques U Liège **67**, 75–90

Gilmour, M, Currant, A, Jacobi, R and Stringer, C 2007 'Recent TIMS dating results from British Late Pleistocene vertebrate faunal localities: context and interpretation'. *J Quat Sci* **22**, 793–800

Gleed-Owen, C P 1998 'Quaternary Herpetofaunas of the British Isles: taxonomic descriptions, palaeoenvironmental reconstructions and biostratigraphic implications'. Unpub PhD thesis, Coventry U

Gleed-Owen, C P 2003 'Holocene herpetofaunas from Scania and Halland, southern Sweden'. *Quat Newsletter* **99**, 33–41

Godwin, H 1975 *The History of the British Flora*, 2 edn. Cambridge: Cambridge U P

Goldberg, P and Macphail, R I 2006 *Practical and Theoretical Geoarchaeology*. Oxford: Blackwell

Gowlett, J A J 2010 'Firing up the social brain', *in* Dunbar, R, Gamble, C and Gowlett, J A J (eds) *Social Brain, Distributed Mind*. Oxford: Oxford U P, 345–70

Gowlett, J A J and Crompton, R H 1994 'Kariandusi: Acheulean morphology and the question of allometry'. *African Archaeol Rev* **12**, 1–40

Gowlett, J A and Hallos, J 2000 'Beeches Pit: overview of the archaeology', *in* Lewis, S G, Whiteman, C A and Preece, R C (eds) *The Quaternary of Norfolk and Suffolk: Field Guide*. London: Quat Res Assoc, 197–206

Griffiths, B M 1927 'Studies in the phytoplankton of the lowland waters of Great Britain. No. V. The phytoplankton of some Norfolk Broads'. *J Linnean Soc – Botany*, **47**, 595–612

Grimm, E C, 1987 'CONISS: a Fortran 77 program for stratigraphically constrained cluster analysis by the method of incremental sum of squares'. *Computer Geosci* **13**, 3–55

Grimm, E 2005 TILIA and TILA Graph Software Packages. Springfield: Illinois State Mus

Grootes P M, Stuiver M, White J W C, Johnsen S J and Jouzel J 1993 'Comparison of oxygen isotope records from the GISP2 and GRIP Greenland ice cores'. *Nature* **366**, 552–4

Grün, R 1994 'Estimation de l'âge de Mauran par resonance paramagnétique électronique', *in* Farizy, C, David, F and Jaubert, J (eds) *Hommes et Bisons du Paléolithique Moyen à Mauran (Haute-Garonne)*. Paris: Centre Nat Recherche Scientif, 65–7

Guérin, C 1980 'Les Rhinocéros (Mammalia, Perissodactyla) du Miocène Terminal au Pléistocène Supérieur en Europe Occidentale'. *Doc Laboratoires Géol Lyon* **79**, 1–3

Guliksen, S and Scott, M 1995 'Report of the TIRI workshop: Saturday 13th August 1994'. *Radiocarbon* **37**, 820–1

Guthrie, R D 1982 'Mammals of the mammoth steppe as paleoenvironmental indicators', *in* Hopkins, J V, Matthews, C E, Schweger, C E and Young, S B (eds) *Paleoecology of Beringia*. London: Academic Press, 307–26

Guthrie, R D 1984 'Mosaics, allelochemics and nutrients: an ecological theory of Late Pleistocene magafaunal extinctions', *in* Martin, P S and Klein, R G (eds) *Quaternary Extinctions: a Prehistoric Revolution*. Tucson, Arizona: U Arizona P, 259–98

Guthrie, R D 1990. *Frozen Fauna of the Mammoth Steppe: the Story of Blue Babe*. Chicago: U Chicago P

Guthrie, R D, 2001. 'Origin and causes of the mammoth steppe: a story of cloud cover, woolly mammal tooth pits and inside-out Beringia'. *Quat Sci Rev* **20**, 549–74

Guthrie, R D and Van Kolfschoten, T 2000 'Neither warm and moist, nor cold and arid: the ecology of the Mid Upper Palaeolithic', *in* Roebroeks, W, Mussi, M, Svoboda, J and Fennema, K (eds) *Hunters of the Golden Age: the Mid Upper Palaeolithic of Eurasia 30,000–20,000 BP*. Leiden: U Leiden P, 13–20

Hahn, J, Müller-Beck, H and Taute, W 1985 *Eiszeithöhlen im Lonental*. Tübingen: Konrad Theiss

Hall, A R 1980 'Late Pleistocene deposits at Wing, Rutland'. *Philos Trans Roy Soc London Ser B* **289**, 135–64

Halternorth, T and Diller, H 1980. *A Field Guide to the Mammals of Africa, Including Madagascar*. London: Collins

Hannus, L A 1990 'Mammoth hunting in the New World', *in* Davis, L B and Reeves, B O K (eds) *Hunters of the Recent Past*. London: Unwin Hyman, 47–67

Hansen, M 1987 'The Hydrophiloidea (Coleoptera) of Fennoscandia and Denmark'. *Fauna Entomol Scandin* **18**, 1–254

Harding, P, Bridgland, D R, Madgett, P A and Rose, J 1991 'Recent investigations of Pleistocene sediments near Maidenhead, Berkshire and their archaeological content'. *Proc Geol Assoc* **102**, 25–53

Harding, P, Gibbard, P L, Lewin, J, Macklin, M G and Moss E H 1987 'The transport and abrasion of handaxes in a gravel bed', *in* de Sieveking, G and Newcomer, M H (eds) *The Human Uses of Flint and Chert*. Cambridge: Cambridge U P, 115–26

Harris, E 1979 *Principles of Archaeological Stratigraphy*. London: Academic Press

Harris, E 1989 *Principles of Archaeological Stratigraphy*, 2 edn. London: Academic Press

Harrison, B 1892 'Report of the committee appointed to carry on excavations at Oldbury Hill near Ightham. Report of the Sixty-First Meeting of the British Association for the Advancement of Science, Cardiff 1891. Cardiff: BAAS, 353–4

Harrison, R A 1977 'The Uphill Quarry Caves, Weston-Super-Mare, a reappraisal'. *Proc U Bristol Spelaeol Soc* **14**, 233–54

Hartwig, F and B E Dearing 1979 *Exploratory Data Analysis*. Beverly Hill: Sage

Harvey, H, Tuttle, J and Bell, J 1995 'Kinetics of phytoplankton decay during simulated sedimentation: changes in biochemical composition and microbial activity under oxic and anoxic conditions'. *Geochem et Cosmochim Acta* **59**, 3367–77

Hayden, B (ed) 1979 *Lithic Use-Wear Analysis*. New York: Academic Press

Haynes, G 1980 'Evidence of carnivore gnawing on Pleistocene and Recent mammalian bones'. *Palaeobiol* **6**, 341–51

Haynes, G 1985 'On watering holes, mineral licks, death and predation', *in* Meltzer, D and Mead, J I (eds) *Environments and Extinctions in Late Glacial North America*. Orono, Maine: Center for the Study of Early Man, 53–71

Haynes, G 1988a 'Longitudinal studies of African elephant death and bone deposits'. *J Archaeol Sci* **15**, 131–57

Haynes, G 1988b 'Mass deaths and serial predation: comparative taphonomic studies of large mammal death sites'. *J Archaeol Sci* **15**, 219–35

Haynes, G 1991 *Mammoths, Mastodonts and Elephants: Biology, Behaviour and the Fossil Record*, 1 edn. Cambridge: Cambridge U P

Haynes, G 1993 *Mammoths, Mastodonts and Elephants: Biology, Behaviour and the Fossil Record*, 2 edn. Cambridge: Cambridge U P

Haynes, G 1999 *Mammoths, Mastodonts and Elephants* (reprint of 2 edn). Cambridge: Cambridge U P

Haynes, G 2002 *The Early Settlement of North America.: the Clovis Era*. Cambridge: Cambridge U P

Heaton, T H E, Vogel, J C, von la Chevallerie, G and Collett, G 1986 'Climatic influence on the isotopic composition of bone nitrogen'. *Nature* **322**, 822–3

Hedges, J I, Clark, W and Cowie, G 1988 'Fluxes and reactivitries of organic matter in a coastal marine bay'. *Limnol Oceanogr* **33**, 1137–52

Hedges, R E M, Housley, R A, Law, I and Perry, C 1988 'Radiocarbon dates from the Oxford AMS system: archaeometry datelist 7'. *Archaeometry* **30**, 155–64

Hedges, R E M, Housely, R A, Law, I and Bronk, C R 1989 'Radiocarbon dates from the Oxford AMS system: Archaeometry datelist 9'. *Archaeometry* **31**, 207–34

Hedges, R E M, Pettitt, P B, Bronk Ramsay, C and van Klinken, G J 1996 'Radiocarbon dates from the Oxford AMS system: Archaeometry datelist 22' *Archaeometry* **38**, 391–415

Hedges, R E M, Pettitt, P B, Bronk Ramsay, C and van Klinken, G J 1998 'Radiocarbon dates from the Oxford AMS system: Archaeometry datelist 26'. *Archaeometry*, **40**, 437–55

Hedges, R E M and van Klinken, G J 1992 'A review of current approaches in the pretreatment of bone for radiocarbon dating by AMS'. *Radiocarbon* **34**, 279–91

Henry, D 1992 'Transhumance during the late Levantine Mousterian', in Dibble, H and Mellars, P A (eds) *The Middle Paleolithic: Adaptation, Behavior and Variability*. Philadelphia: U Mus, U Pennsylvania, 143–62

Henshilwood, C S, d'Errico, F, Yates, R, Jacobs, Z, Tribolo, C, Duller, G, Mercier, N, Sealy, J, Valladas, H, Watts, I and Wintle, A G 2002 'Emergence of modern human behaviour: Middle Stone Age engravings from South Africa'. *Science* **295**, 1278–80

Hill, A 1979 'Disarticulation and scattering of mammal skeletons'. *Paleobiol* **5**, 261–74

Hill, A 1980 'Early postmortem damage to the remains of some contemporary east African mammals', in Behrensmeyer, A K and Hill, A P (eds) *Fossils in the Making*. Chicago: U Chicago P, 131–52

Hill, R L 1965 'Hydrolysis of proteins'. *Advances in Protein Chemistry* **20**, 37–107

Hinton, M A C 1923 'Diagnoses of species of *Pitymys* and *Microtus* occurring in the Upper Freshwater Bed of West Runton, Norfolk'. *Ann Mag Nat Hist* **9**, 541–2

Hiscock, K M 1993 'The influence of pre-Devensian glacial deposits on the hydrogeochemistry of the Chalk aquifer system of north Norfolk, UK'. *J Hydrol* **144**, 335–69

Hodge, C A H, Burton, R G O, Corbett, W M, Evans, E and Seale, R S 1984 *Soils and Their use in Eastern England*. Whitstable: Harpend

Holdaway, S 1989 'Were there hafted projectile points in the Mousterian?' *J Field Archaeol* **16**, 79–85

Holdhaus, K and Lindroth, C H 1939 'Die europäischen Koleopteren mit boreoalpiner Verbreitung'. *Sonder-abdruck aus dem 50 Band Annal Naturhis Mus Wein*, 123–292

Holmen, M 1987 'The aquatic Adaphaga (Coleoptera) of Fennoscandia and Denmark'. *Fauna Entomol Scandin* **20**, 1–168

Holyoak, D T 1982 'Non-marine Mollusca of the Last Glacial Period (Devensian) in Britain'. *Malacol* **22**, 727–30

Howell, F C 1965 *Early Man*. London: Time Life Books

Howell, F C 1966 'Observations of the earlier phases of the European Lower Palaeolithic'. *Amer Anthropol* **68**, 88–201

Hultén, E and Fries, M 1986 *Atlas of North European Vascular Plants North of the Tropic of Cancer (3 vols)*. Königstein: Koeltz Scientific Books

Iacumin P, Nikolaev V, Ramigni M 2000 'C and N stable isotope measurements on Eurasian fossil mammals, 40,000 to 10,000 years BP: Herbivore physiologies and palaeoenvironmental reconstruction'. *Palaeogeogr Palaeoclimatol Palaeoecol* **163**, 33–47

Iacumin, P, Nikolaev, V, Ramigni, M and Longinelli, A 2004 'Oxygen isotope analyses of mammal bone remains from Holocene sites in European Russia: palaeoclimatic implications'. *Global and Planetary Change* **40**, 169–76

Ingold, T 1983 'The significance of storage in hunting societies'. *Man* **18**, 553–71

Innes, J L 1983 'Debris Flows'. *Prog Physical Geogr* **7**, 469–501

Isaac, G 1989 *The Archaeology of Human Origins: Papers by Glynn Isaac Edited by Barbara Isaac*. Cambridge: Cambridge U P

Isarin, R F B and Bohncke, S J P 1998 'Summer temperatures during the Younger Dryas in north-western Europe inferred from climate indicator species'. *Quat Res* **51**, 158–73

Iversen J 1954 'The Late–glacial flora of Denmark and its relation to climate and soil'. *Danmarks Geolog Undersogel* **2**, 38

Isaac, G 1967 'Towards the interpretation of occupation debris: some experiments and observations'. *Kroeber Anthropol Soc Pap* **5**, 31–57

Jachmann, H 1988 'Estimating age in African elephants: a revision of Laws' molar evaluation technique'. *African J Ecol* **26**, 51–6

Jacobi, R 2004 'Some observations on the non-flint lithics from Creswell Crags'. *Lithics* **25**. 39–64

Jacobi, R and Grün, R 2003 'ESR dates from Robin Hood Cave, Creswell Crags, Derbyshire and the age of its early human occupation'. *Quat Newslet* **100**, 1–12

Jacobi, R and Hawkes, C J 1993 'Work at the Hyaena Den, Wookey Hole'. *Proc U Bristol Spelaeol Soc* **19**, 369–71

Jacobi, R M and Higham, T F G 2008 'The "Red Lady" ages gracefully: new ultrafiltration AMS determinations from Paviland'. *J Hum Evol* **55**, 898–907

Jacobi, R M, Higham, T F G and Bronk Ramsey, C 2006 'AMS radiocarbon dating of Middle and Upper Palaeolithic bone in the British Isles: improved reliability using ultrafiltration'. *J Quat Sc* **21**, 557–73

Jacobi, R M, Rowe, P J, Gilmour, M A, Grün, R and Atkinson, T C 1998 'Radiometric dating of the Middle Palaeolithic tool industry and associated fauna of Pin Hole Cave, Creswell Crags, England'. *J Quat Sci* **13**, 29–42

Jalas, J and Suominen, J (eds) 1972 *Atlas Florae Europaeae. Pteridophyta (Volume 1)*. Helsinki: The Committee for mapping the flora of Europe and Societas Biologica Fennica Vanamo

Jaubert, J and Brugal, J 1990 'Contribution à l'étude du mode de vie au Paléolithique moyen: les chasseurs d'aurochs de la Borde', in Jaubert, J. Lorblanchet, M. Laville, H, Slott-Moller, R. Truro, A and Brugal, J P (eds) *Les Chasseurs d'Aurochs de La Borde*. Paris: Ed Maison Sci Homme, 128–45

Jaubert, J, Lorblanchet, M, Laville, H, Slot-Moller, R, Turq, A and Brugal, J-P 1990 *Les Chasseurs d'Aurochs de La Borde.: un Site du Paléolithique Moyen (Livernon, Lot)*. Doc d'Archeol Française **27**. Paris: Maison Sci Homme

Jenkinson, R D S 1984 *Creswell Crags: Late Pleistocene Sites in the East Midlands*. BAR Brit Ser **122**. Oxford: Archaeopress

John, D M, Whitton, B A and Brook, A J (eds.) 2002 *The Freshwater Algal Flora of the British Isles*. Cambridge: Cambridge U P

Jones A M, O'Connell T C, Young E D, Scott K, Buckingham C M, Iacumin P, Brasier M D 2001 'Biogeochemical data from well preserved 200 ka collagen and skeletal remains'. *Earth Sci Planetary Lett* **193**, 143–9

Jones, A P 1999 'Background to sedimentary facies', in Jones, A P, Tucker, M E and Hart, J K (eds.) *The Description and Analysis of Quaternary Stratigraphic Field Sections*. London: Quat Res Assoc Tech Guide **7**, 5–26

Jones, A P, Tucker, M E and Hart, J K 1999 'Guidelines and recommendations', in Jones, A P, Tucker, M E and Hart, J K (eds) *The Description and Analysis of Quaternary Stratigraphic Field Sections*. London: Quate Res Assoc Tech Guide **7**, 27–62

Jones, R L and Keen, D 1993 *Pleistocene Environments in the British Isles*. London: Chapman and Hall

Jones, R L, Keen, D H and Robinson, J E 2000 'Devensian Lateglacial and early Holocene floral and faunal records from NE Northumberland'. *Proc Yorks Geol Soc* **53**, 97–110

Jöris, O 2006 'Bifacially backed knives (Keilmesser) in the Central European Middle Palaeolithic', in Goren-Inbar, N and Sharon, G (eds) *The Axe Age: Acheulean Toolmaking from Quarry to Discard*. London: Equinox, 287–310

Kahlke, R D 1999 *The History of the Origin, Evolution and Dispersal of the Late Pleistocene Mammuthus-Coelodonta Faunal Complex in Eurasia (Large Mammals)*. Hot Sprigs, SD: Mammoth Site

Kahlke, R-D and Lacombat, F 2008 'The earliest immigration of woolly rhinoceros (*Coelodonta tologoijensis*, Rhinocerotidae, Mammalia) into Europe and its adaptive evolution in Palaearctic cold stage mammal faunas'. *Quat Sci Rev* **27**, 1951–61

Kaplan, I 1983 'Stable isotopes of sulfer, nitrogen and deuterium in recent marine environments', in Arthur, M A, Anderson, T F, Kaplan, I R, Veizer, J and Land, L S (eds) *Stable Isotopes in Sedimentary Geology*. Dallas: Soc Econ Paleontol Mineral, 2–108

Kaufman D S and Manley W F 1998 'A new procedure for determining DL amino acid ratios in fossils using Reverse Phase Liquid Chromatography'. *Quat Sci Rev* **17**, 987–1000

Keeley, L H 1980 *Experimental Determination of Stone Tool Uses: a Microwear Analysis*. Chicago: U Chicago P

Keen, D H 1987 'Non-marine molluscan faunas of periglacial deposits in Britain', in Boardman, J (ed.) *Periglacial Processes and Landforms in Britain and Ireland*. Cambridge: Cambridge U P 257–63

Keen, D H 2001 'Towards a late Middle Pleistocene non-marine molluscan biostratigraphy for the British Isles'. *Quat Sci Rev* **20**, 1657–65

Keen, D H, Bateman, M D, Coope, G R, Field, M H, Langford, H E, Merry, J S and Mighall, T M 1999 'Sedimentology, palaeoecology and geochronology of Last Interglacial deposits from Deeping St James, Lincolnshire, England'. *J Quat Sci* **14**, 411–16

Kelly, R 1995 *The Foraging Spectrum: Diversity in Hunter-gatherer Lifeways*. Washington and London: Smithsonian Inst P

Kendall, C 1998 'Tracing nitrogen sources and cycling catchments', in Kendall, C and McDonnell, J J (eds) *Isotope tracers in catchment hydrology*. Amsterdam: Elsevier, 519–76

Kennard, A S 1944 'The Crayford Brickearths'. *Proc Geol Assoc* **55**, 121–69

Kerney, M P 1963 'Late-glacial deposits on the Chalk of south-east England'. *Philos Trans Roy Soc London Ser B* **246**, 203–54

Kerney, M P 1971 'A Middle Weichselian Deposit at Halling, Kent'. *Proc Geol Assoc* **82**, 1–11

Kerney, M P 1977 'British Quaternary non-marine Mollusca: a brief review', in Shotton, F W (ed) *British Quaternary Studies – Recent Advances*. Oxford: Clarendon, 32–42

Kerney, M P 1999 *Atlas of the Land and Freshwater Molluscs of Britain and Ireland*. Colchester: Harley Books

Kerney, M P and Cameron, R A D 1979 *A Field Guide to the Land Snails of Britain and North-west Europe*. London: Collins

Kerney, M P, Gibbard, P L, Hall, A R and Robinson, J E 1982 'Middle Devensian river deposits beneath the "Upper Floodplain" terrace of the River Thames at Isleworth, West London'. *Proc Geol Assoc* **93**, 385–93

Kintigh, K W 1990 'Intrasite spatial analysis: a commentary on major methods', in Voorips, A (ed) *Mathematics and Information Science in Archaeology: a Flexible Framework*. Bonn: Holos-Verlag, 165–200

Kintigh, K W 1992 *Tools for Quantitative Archaeology: Programs for Quantitative Analysis in Archaeology*. Software package available from http://tfqa.com

Kintigh, K W and Ammerman, A J 1982 'Heuristic approaches to spatial analysis'. *Amer Antiq* **47**, 31–63

Klein, R G 1975 'Paleoanthropological implications of the nonarcheological bone assemblage from Swartklip 1, South-Western Cape Province, S. Africa'. *Quat Res* **5**, 275–88

Kluskens, S L 1995 'Archaeological taphonomy of Combe-Capelle Bas from artefact orientation and density analysis', in Dibble, H L and Lenoir, M (eds) *The Middle Paleolithic site of Combe-Capelle Bas (France)*. Philadelphia: U Mus, U Pennsylvania, 199–243

Knighton, D 1998 *Fluvial Forms and Processes*. London: Arnold

Koch K1989 and 1992 *Die Käfer Mitteleuropas – Ökologie*, parts 1, 2 and 3. Krefeld: Goecke & Evers

Koetje, T A 1987 *Spatial Patterns in Magdalenian Open Air Sites from the Isle Valley, Southwestern France*. BAR Int Ser **346**. Oxford: Archaeopress

Koetje, T A 1991 'Simulated archaeological levels and the analysis of Le Flageolet II, the Dordogne, France'. *J Field Archaeol* **18**, 187–98

Kolen, J 1999 'Hominids without homes: on the nature of Middle Palaeolithic settlement in Europe', in Roebroeks, W and Gamble, C (eds) *The Middle Palaeolithic Occupation of Europe*. Leiden: U Leiden and Eur Sci Foundation, 139–75

Kolen, J, De Loecker, D, Groenendijk, A J and de Warriment J-P 1999 'Middle Palaeolithic surface scatters: how informative? A case study from southern Limberg (The Netherlands)', in Roebroeks, W and Gamble, C (eds) *The Middle Palaeolithic Occupation of Europe*. Leiden: U Leiden P, 177–91

Kolstrop E 1980 'Climate and stratigraphy of Northwestern Europe between 30,000 and 13,000 BP, with special reference to the Netherlands'. *Mededelingen Rijks Geolog Dienst* **32**, 181–253

Kolstrop, E 1990 'The puzzle of Weichselian vegetation poor in trees'. *Geol en Mijnbouw* **69**, 253–62

Kos, A M 2003 'Pre-burial taphonomic characterisation of a vertebrate assemblage from a pitfall cave fossil deposit in southeastern Australia'. *J Archaeol Sci* **30**, 769–79

Krasinska, M 1971 'Hybridization of European bison with domestic cattle. Part VI' *Acta Theriol* **16**, 413–22

Krause, J, Lalueza-Fox, C, Orlando, L, Enard, W, Green, R E, Burbano, H A, Hublin, J-J, Hänni, C, Fortea, J, de la Rasilla, M, Bertranpetit, J, Rosas, A and Pääbo, S 2007 'The derived FOXP2 variant of modern humans was shared with Neanderthals'. *Current Biol* **17**, 1908–12

Kruuk, H 1972 *The Spotted Hyaena: a Study of Predation and Social Behaviour*. Chicago: U Chicago P

Kubiak, H 1982 'Morphological adaptations of the mammoth: an adaptation to the arctic-steppe environment', *in* Hopkins, D M, Matthews, J V, Schweger, C E and Young, S B (eds) *Paleoecology of Beringia*. New York: Academic Press, 281–9

Kuhn, S J 1995 *Mousterian Lithic Technology*. Princeton: Princeton U P

Kuiper, J G J, Økland, K A, Knudsen, J, Koli, L, von Proschwitz, T and Valovirta, I 1989 'Geographical distribution of the small mussels (Sphaeriidae) in North Europe (Denmark, Faroes, Finland, Iceland, Norway and Sweden)'. *Annal Zool Fennici* **26**, 73–101

Kurtén, B 1959 'On the bears of the Holsteinian Interglacial'. *Acta U Stockholmiensis, Stockholm Contrib Geol* **2**, 73–102

Kurtén, B 1968 *Pleistocene Mammals of Europe*. London: Weidenfeld and Nicholson

Kurtén, B and Poulianos, N A 1977 'New stratigraphic amd faunal material from Petralona Cave with special reference to the Carnivora'. *Anthropos* **4**, 47–130

Lambert, C A, Pearson, R G and Sparks, B W 1963 'A flora and fauna from Late Pleistocene deposits at Sidgwick Avenue, Cambridge'. *Proc Linnean Soc London* **174**, 13–29

Larkin, N and Makridou, E 1999 'Comparing gap-fillers used in conserving sub-fossil material'. *Geol Curator* **7**, 81–90

Larsson, S 1982 'Geomorphological effects on the slopes of Longyear Valley, Spitzbergen, after a heavy rainstorm in July 1972'. *Geogr Annaler* **64A**, 105–26

Laws, R M 1966 'Age criteria for the African elephant' *East African Wildlife J* **4**, 1–37

Laws, R M, Parker, I S and Johnstone, R C 1975 *Elephants and Their Habitats*. Oxford: Clarendon

Lawson, A J 1978 'A hand-axe from Little Cressingham'. *East Anglian Archaeol* **8**, 1–8

Layard, N F 1912 'Animal remains from the railway cutting at Ipswich'. *Proc Suffolk Inst Archaeol* **14**, 59–68

Layard, N F 1920 'The Stoke Bone Bed'. *Proc Prehist Soc of East Anglia* **3**, 210–19

Lehmann, M F, Bernasconi, S, Barbieri, A and McKenzie, J A 2002 'Preservation of organic matter and alteration of its carbon and nitrogen isotope composition during simulated and in situ early diagenesis'. *Geochem et Cosmochim Acta* **66**, 3573–84

Lepneva, S G 1971 *Trichoptera of the U.S.S.R; Trichoptera vol. 2* (English translation of 1966 Russian original). Jerusalem: Israel Program for Scientific Translations, 1–638

Lewis, S G 1991 'Shouldham Thorpe, Norfolk', *in* Lewis, S G, Whiteman, C A and Bridgland, D R (eds) *Central East Anglia and the Fen Basin: Field Guide*. London: Quat Res Assoc, 127–30

Lewis, S G 1993 'The status of the Wolstonian glaciation in the English Midlands and East Anglia'. Unpub PhD thesis, U London

Lewis, S G 1999 'Eastern England', *in* Bowen, D Q (ed.) *A Revised Correlation of Quaternary Deposits in the British Isles*. Geol Soc London Special Rep **23**, 10–27

Lewis, S G and Maddy, D 1999 'Description and analysis of Quaternary fluvial sediments: a case study from the upper River Thames', *in* Jones, A P, Tucker, M E and Hart, J K (eds) *The Description and Analysis of Quaternary Stratigraphic Field Sections*. London: Quat Res Assoc Tech Guide 7, 111–35

Lewis, S G, Maddy, D and Scaife, R G 2001 'The fluvial system response to abrupt climate change during the last cold stage: the Upper Pleistocene River Thames fluvial succession at Ashton Keynes, UK'. *Global and Planetary Change* **28**, 341–59

L'homme, V and Connet, N 2001 'Observations sur les pieces bifaciales et les chaîne opératoire de façonnage du Pléistocène moyen du Soucy (Yonne)', *in* Cliquet, D (ed) *Les Industries à Outils Bifaciaux du Paléolithique Moyen d'Europe Occidentale*. Etudes Recherche Archéol U Liège **98**. Liège: ERAUL, 43–50

Limbrey, S 1975 *Soil Science and Archaeology*. London: Academic Press

Lindroth, C H 1992 *Ground Beetles (Carabidae) of Fennoscandia* – a Zoogeographical Study tl 1 (English Translation of 1945 German original). Andover: Intercept, 1–630

Lister, A M 1981 'Evolutionary studies on Pleistocene deer. Unpub PhD thesis: U Cambridge

Lister, A M 1989 'Mammalian faunas and the Wolstonian debate', *in* Keen, D H (ed) *West Midlands: Field Guide*. Cambridge: Quat Res Assoc, 5–12

Lister, A M 1993 'Patterns of evolution in Quaternary mammal lineages', *in* Edwards, D (ed) *Patterns and Processes of Evolution*. London: Academic Press, 72–9

Lister, A M 1994 'Skeletal associations and bone maturation in the Hot Springs mammoths', *in* Agenbroad, L D and Mead, J I (eds) *The Hot Springs Mammoth Site: a Decade of Field and Laboratory Research in Paleontology, Geology and Paleoecology*. Hot Springs, SD: Mammoth Site, 253–68

Lister, A M 1996a 'Evolution and taxonomy of Eurasian mammoths', *in* Shoshani J and Tassy P (eds) *The Proboscidea: Trends in Evolution and Paleoecology*. Oxford: Oxford U P, 203–13

Lister, A M 1996b 'Sexual dimorphism in the mammoth pelvis: an aid to gender determination', *in* Shoshani J and Tassy P (eds) *The Proboscidea: Trends in Evolution and Paleoecology*. Oxford: Oxford U P, 254–9

Lister, A M 1999 'Epiphyseal fusion and postcranial age determination in the woolly mammoth, *Mammuthus primigenius* (Blum.)'. *Deinsea* **6**, 79–88

Lister, A M 2001 'Age profile of mammoths in a Late Pleistocene hyaena den at Kent's Cavern, Devon, England'. *Anthropol Pap U Kansas*. **22**, 35–43

Lister, A M 2009 'Late-glacial mammoth skeletons (*Mammuthus primigenius*) from Condover (Shropshire, UK): anatomy, pathology, taphonomy and chronological significance'. *Geol J* **44**, 447–79

Lister, A M and Agenbroad, L D 1994 'Gender determination of the Hot Springs mammoths', *in* Agenbroad, L D and Mead, J I (eds) *The Hot Springs Mammoth Site: a Decade of Field and Laboratory Research in Paleontology, Geology and Paleoecology*. Hot Springs, SD: Mammoth Site, 208–14

Lister, A and Bahn, P 2007 *Mammoths: Giants of the Ice Age*, 3 edn. London: Marshall Editions

Lister, A M and Brandon, A 1991 'A pre–Ipswichian cold stage mammalian fauna from the Balderton Sand and Gravel, Lincolnshire, England'. *J Quat Sci* **6**, 139–57

Lister, A M and Joysey, K A 1992 'Scaling effects in elephant dental evolution: the example of Eurasian *Mammuthus*', in Smith, P and Tchernov, E (eds) *Structure, Function and Evolution of Teeth*. Jerusalem: Freund, 185–213

Lister, A M and Sher, A V 2001 'The origin and evolution of the woolly mammoth'. *Science* **294**, 1094–7

Lister, A M and van Essen, H 2003 'Mammuthus rumanus (Stefanescu), the earliest mammoth in Europe', *in* Petulescu, A and Stiuca, E (eds) *Advances in Vertebrae Palaeontology 'Hen to Panta'*. Bucharest: Romanian Academy, 'Emil Racovita' Inst Speleol, 47–52

Lister, A M, Sher, A V, van Essen, H and Wei, G 2005 'The pattern and process of mammoth evolution in Eurasia'. *Quat Internat* **126–8**, 49–64

Locht, J-L and Antoine, P 2001 'Caractérisation techo-typologique et position chronostratigraphique de plusiers industries à rares bifaces ou amincissements bifaciaux du nord de la France', *in* Cliquet, D (ed) *Les industries à Outils Bifaciaux du Paléolithique Moyen d'Europe Occidentale*. Etudes Recherche Archéol U Liège **98**. Liège: ERAUL, 129–34

Lockwood, J G 1979 'Water balance of Britain 50 000 to the present day'. *Quat Res* **12**, 297–310

Longinelli, A 1984 'Oxygen isotopes in mammal bone phosphate: a new tool for paleohydrological and paleoclimatological research?' *Geochim et Cosmochim Acta* **48**, 385–90

Lord, J unpublished manuscript 'Report on the examination of some worked flint from Lynford, Norfolk'. Unpub ms obtained from author

Lord, J 2002 'A flint knapper's foreword to Lynford'. *Lithics* **23**, 60–70

Lucht, W L 1987. *Die Käfer Mitteleuropas – Katalog*. Krefeld: Goecke and Evers, 1–342

Luz, B, Cormie, A B and Schwarcz, H P 1990 'Oxygen isotope variations in phosphate of deer bones'. *Geochim et Cosmochim Acta* **54**, 1723–8

Luz, B and Kolodny, Y 1989 'Oxygen isotope variation in bone phosphate'. *Applied Geochem* **4**, 317–23

Lyman, R L 1994a *Vertebrate Taphonomy*. Cambridge: Cambridge U P

Lyman, R L 1994b 'Quantitative units and terminology in zooarchaeology'. *Amer Antiq* **59**, 36–71

MacDonald, D W and Barrett, P 1993 *Collins Field Guide, Mammals of Britain and Europe*. London: HarperCollins

Macko, S E and Estep, M L F 1984 'Microbial alteration of stable nitrogen and carbon isotopic compositions of organic matter'. *Organic Geochem* **6**, 787–90

MacRae, R J and Moloney, N 1988 'Note on Cresswell Crags', in MacRae, R J and Moloney, N (eds) *Non-Flint Stone Tools and the Palaeolithic Occupation of Britain*. BAR Brit Ser **189**. Oxford: Archaeopress, 233

Maddy, D, Lewis, S G, Scaife, R G, Bowen, D Q, Coope G R, Green, C P, Hardaker, T, Keen, D H, Rees-Jones, J, Parfitt, S A and Scott, K 1998 'The Upper Pleistocene deposits at Cassington, near Oxford, England'. *J Quat Sci* **13**, 205–31

Maddy, D, Passmore, D G and Lewis, S G 2003 'Fluvial morphology and sediments: archives of past fluvial system response to global change', *in* Gregory, K J and Benito, G (eds) *Palaeohydroloy: Understanding Global Change*. Chichester: John Wiley and Sons, 274–89

Maglio, V J 1973 'Origin and evolution of the Elephantidae'. *Trans Amer Philos Soc* **63**, 1–149

Mania, U 1995 'The utilisation of large mammal bones in Bilzingsleben – a special variant of Middle Pleistocene man's relationship to his environment', *in* Ullrich, H (ed) *Man and Environment in the Palaeolithic*. Etudes Recherche Archaeol U Liège. Liège: ERAUL, 239–46

Mania, D, Thomae, M, Litt, T and Weber, T 1990 (eds) *Neumark-Gröbern: Beiträge zur Jagd des Mittelpaläolithischen Menhen*. Publication of the Landesmuseum für Halle **42**. Berlin: Deutscher Vrlag der Wissenschaft

Marean, C W, Bar-Matthews, M, Bernatchez, J, Fisher, E, Goldberg, P, Herries, A I R, Jacobs, Z, Jerardino, A, Karkanas, P, Minichillo, T, Nilssen, P J, Thompson, E, Watts, I and Williams, H M 2007 'Early human use of marine resources and pigment in South Africa during the Middle Pleistocene'. *Nature* **449**, 905–8

Marks, A 1988 'The curation of stone tools during the Upper Pleistocene: a view from the central Negev, Israel', *in* Dibble, H and Montet-White, A (eds) *Upper Pleistocene Prehistory of Western Europe*. Philadelphia: U Mus, U Pennsylvania, 275–85

Mashchenko, E N 2002 'Individual development, biology and evolution of the woolly mammoth'. *Cranium* **19**, 4–120

Matthews, L H 1960 *British Mammals*, 2 edn. London: Collins

McBryde, I 1988 'Goods from another country: exchange networks and the people of the Lake Eyre basin', *in* Mulvaney, J and White, P *Archaeology to 1788*. Sydney: Waddon Associates, 253–73

McManus, J 1988 'Grain size determination and interpretation', *in* Tucker, M (ed) *Techniques in Sedimentology*. Oxford: Blackwell Scientific Publications, 63–85

McManus, J, Bond, G C, Broecker, W S, Johnsen, S, Labeyrie, L and Higgins, S 1994 'High resolution climate records from the North Atlantic during the last interglacial'. *Nature* **371**, 326–9

McNabb, J 2007 *The British Lower Palaeolithic: Stones in Contention*. London: Routledge

Melentis, J 1963 'Die Osteologie der Pleistozaner Proboscidier des Beckens von Megalopolis in Peloponnes (Griechenland)'. *Annal Geol Pays Helleniques* **14** Ser **1**, 1–107

Mellars, P A 1974 'The Palaeolithic and Mesolithic', *in* Renfrew, C (ed) *British Prehistory: a New Outline*. London: Duckworth, 41–99

Mellars, P A 1996 *The Neanderthal Legacy*. Princeton: Princeton U P

Mellars, P 2005 'The impossible coincidence: a single-species model for the origins of modern human behaviour in Europe'. *Evolut Anthropol* **14**, 12–27

Mellars, P, Bar-Yosef, C, Stringer, C and Boyle, K V (eds) 2007 *Rethinking the Human Revolution*. Cambridge: McDonald Inst Archaeol Res Monogr

Meusel, H and Jäger, E J 1965 *Vergleichende Chorologie der Zentaleuropäischen Flora. Volume 1*. Jena: Gustav Fischer Verlag

Meusel, H and Jäger, E J 1978 *Vergleichende Chorologie der Zentaleuropäischen Flora. Volume 2*. Jena: Gustav Fischer Verlag

Miall, A D 1985 'Architectural-element analysis: a new method of facies analysis applied to fluvial deposits'. *Earth Sci Rev* **22**, 261–308

Miall, A D 2006 *The Geology of Fluvial Deposits*, 4 edn. Berlin: Springer-Verlag

Miller, G S 1912 *Catalogue of the Mammals of Western Europe*. London: Brit Mus Nat Hist

Moir, J R 1931 'Ancient man in the Gipping-Orwell Valley, Suffolk'. *Proc Prehist Soc East Anglia* **6**, 182–221

Molines, N, Hinguant, S and Monnier, J-L 2001 'Le Paléolithique moyen à outils bifaciaux dans l'ouest de la France; synthèse des données anciennes et récentes', *in* Cliquet, D (ed) *Les Industries à Outils Bifaciaux du Paléolithique Moyen d'Europe Occidentale*. Etudes Recherche Archaeol U Liège **98**. Liège: ERAUL, 107–14

Monnier, G 2003 'The spatial distribution of lithic artefacts at Stranska skala IIIc and IIId: 1997–199 Excavations', *in* Svoboda, J A and Bar-Yosef, O (eds) *Stranska Skala: Origins of the Upper Palaeolithic in the Brno Basin, Moravia, Czech Republic*. Cambridge, MA: Peabody Mus Archaeol Ethnol, 45–57

Mook, W G and Streurman, H J 1983 'Physical and chemical aspects of radiocarbon dating', *in* Mook, W G and Waterbolk. H T (eds) *Proceedings of the Groningen Conference on 14C and Archaeology*. PACT Publication **8**. Strasbourg: Council of Europe, 517–25

Moore, M W and Brumm, A 2007 'Stone artifacts and hominins in island Southeast Asia: new insights from Flores, eastern Indonesia'. *J Human Evol* **52**, 85–102

Moore, P D, Webb, J A and Collinson, M E 1991 *Pollen Analysis*, 2 edn. Oxford: Blackwell Scientific Publications

Morrison, D A 1997 *Caribou Hunters in the Western Arctic. Zooarchaeology of the Rita-Claire and Bison Skull Sites*. Mercury Ser Archeol Survey Canada Pap **157**. Hull (Quebec): Canadian Mus Civilisation

Morton, A G T 2004 *Archaeological Site Formation: Understanding Lake Margin Contexts*. BAR Int Ser **1211**. Oxford: Archaeopress

Murphy, C P 1986 *Thin Section Preparation of Soils and Sediments*. Berkhamsted: AB Academic

Murray, A S and Wintle, A G 2000 'Luminescence dating of quartz using an improved single-aliquot regenerative-dose protocol'. *Radiation Measurements* **32**, 57–73

Musil, R 1968 'Die Mammutmolaren von Předmostí (CSSR)'. *Paläontol Abhandlungen, Abt. A (Paläozool)* **3**, 1–192

Mussi, M 1999 'The Neanderthals in Italy: a tale of many caves', in Roebroeks, W and Gamble, C (eds) *The Middle Palaeolithic Occupation of Europe*. Leiden: U Leiden P, 49–80

Muus, B J and Dahlstrøm, P 1971 *Collins Guide to the Freshwater Fishes of Britain and Europe*. London: Collins

Nash, S E 1996 'Is curation a useful heuristic?', in Odell, G (ed) *Stone Tools: Theoretical Insights into Human Prehistory*. London: Plenum, 81–99

Nelson, M 1991 'The study of technological organisation' *Archaeol Method Theory* **3**, 57–100

Newcomer, M 1971 'Some quantitative experiments in handaxe manufacture'. *World Archaeol* **3**, 85–94

Newton, E T 1882 'On the occurrence of *Spermophilus* beneath the glacial till of Norfolk'. *Geol Mag* ns 2 **9**, 51–4

Nilsson, A N and Holmen, M 1995 'The aquatic adephaga (Coleoptera) of Fennoscandia and Denmark. II Dytiscidae'. *Fauna Entomol Scandin* **32**, 1–192

Niven, L 2006 *The Palaeolithic Occupation of Vogelherd Cave: Implications for the Subsistence Behavior of Late Neanderthals and Early Modern Humans*. Tübingen: Kerns Verlag

Odell, G H 1996 'Economizing behavior and the concept of curation', in Odell, G (ed) *Stone Tools: Theoretical Insights into Human Prehistory*. London: Plenum, 51–80

Ohel, M Y 1987 'The Acheulean handaxe: a maintainable multi-functional tool?' *Lithic Technol* **16**, 54–5

Økland, J 1990 *Lakes and Snails: Environment and Gastropoda in 1,500 Norwegian Lakes, Ponds and Rivers*. Oegstgeest, Universal Book Services/Dr W. Backhuys

Olsen, S J 1960 'Post-cranial skeletal characters of *Bison* and *Bos*'. *Pap Peabody Mus Archaeol Ethnol* **35(4)**. Cambridge, MA: Peabody Mus Archaeol Ethnol

Olsen, S J 1972 'Osteology for the archaeologist, no. 3: the American mastodon and the woolly mammoth'. *Pap Peabody Mus Archaeol Ethnol* **56**. Cambridge, MA: Peabody Mus Archaeol Ethnol, 1–45

Olsen, S L and Shipman, P 1988 'Surface modification on bone: trampling versus butchery'. *J Archaeol Sci* **15**, 535–53

O'Neil, J R, Roe, L J Reinhard, E and Blake, R E 1994 'A rapid and precise method of oxygen isotope analysis of biogenic phosphate'. *Israel J Earth Sci* **43**, 203–12

Orton, C 1980 *Mathematics in Archaeology*. London: Collins

Osborn, H F 1942 *Proboscidea: a Monograph of the Discovery, Evolution, Migration and Extinction of the Mastodonts and Elephants of the World. Volume II: Stegodontoidea, Elephantoidea*. New York: Amer Mus Nat Hist

Owen, L 1991 'Mass movement deposits in the Karakoram Mountains: their sedimentary characteristics, recognition and role in Karakoram landform evolution'. *Zeitschr Geomorphol* **35**, 410–24

Owen-Smith, R N 1992 *Megaherbivores*. Cambridge: Cambridge U P

Pals, J P, van Geel, B and Delfos, A 1980 'Palaeoecological studies in the Klokkeweel bog near Hoogkarspel (Noord Holland)'. *Rev Palaeobot Palynol* **30**, 371–418

Pardoe, C 1990 'The demographic basis of human evolution in southeastern Australia', in Meehan, B and White, N (eds) *Hunter-gatherer Demography: Past and Present, Oceania Monographs*. Sydney: U Sydney, 59–70

Parkin R A, Rowley-Conwy P and Serjeantson D 1986 'Late Palaeolithic exploitation of horse and red deer at Gough's Cave, Cheddar, Somerset'. *Proc U Bristol Spelaeol Soc* **17**, 311–30

Paterson, T T and Tebbutt, C F 1947 'Studies in the Palaeolithic succession in England No. III. palaeoliths from St. Neots, Huntingdonshire'. *Proc Prehist Soc* **13**, 37–46

Patou, M 1989 'Subsistance et approvisionnement au Paleolithique moyen', in Otte, M (ed) *L'Homme de Neandertal Vol. 6 La Subsistance*. Liège: Etudes Recherche Archéol U Liège, 11–18

Patou-Mathis, M 2000 'Neanderthal subsistence behaviours in Europe'. *Internat J Osteoachaeol* **10**, 379–95

Pelegrin, J 1990 'Prehistoric lithic technology: some aspects of research'. *Archaeol Rev Cambridge* **9.1**, 116–25

Penkman K E H 2005 'Amino acid geochronology: a closed system approach to test and refine the UK model'. Unpub PhD thesis, U Newcastle

Penkman K E H, Preece R C, Keen D H, Maddy D, Schreve D S, Collins M J, 2007 'Testing the aminostratigraphy of fluvial archives: the evidence from intra-crystalline proteins within freshwater shells'. *Quat Sci Rev* **26**, 2958–69

Penkman, K E H, Kaufman, D S, Maddy, D, Collins, M J 2008 'Closed-system behaviour of the intra-crystalline fraction of amino acids in mollusc shells'. *Quat Geochronol* **3**, 2–25

Perlès, C 1977. *Préhistoire du Feu*. Paris: Masson

Perrin, R M S, Rose, J and Davies, H 1979 'The distribution, variation and origins of pre-Devensian tills in eastern England'. *Philos Trans Roy Soc London Ser B* **287**, 535–70

Pettitt, P B 2003 'The Mousterian in action: chronology, mobility and Middle Palaeolithic variability', in Moloney, N and Shott, M (eds) *Lithic Analysis at the Millennium*. London: Inst Archaeol, 29–44

Pettitt, P B 2008 'The British Upper Palaeolithic', in Pollard, J (ed) *Prehistoric Britain*. Blackwell: Oxford, 18–57

Petraglia, M D 1993 'The genesis and alteration of archaeological patterns at the Abri Dufaure: an Upper Paleolithic rockshelter and slope site in southwestern France', in Goldberg, P, Nash, D T and Petraglia, M D (eds) *Formation Processes in Archaeological Context*. Madison, Wisconisn: Prehistory Press, 97–112

Pettitt, P B 1997 'High resolution Neanderthals? Interpreting Middle Palaeolithic intrasite spatial data'. *World Archaeol* **29**, 208–24

Pierson, T 1981 'Dominant particle support mechanisms in debris flows at Mount Thomas, New Zealand and implications for flow mobility'. *Sedimentol* **28**, 49–60

Plisson, H and Beyries, S 1998 'Pointes ou outils triangulaires? Données Fonctionnelles dans le Moustérien Levantin. *Paléorient* **24**, 5–24

Prat, F 1966 'Les Equidés', in Lavocat, R (ed) *Faunes et Flores Préhistoriques de l'Europe Occidentale*. Paris: Boubée, 194–215

Preece, R C, Lewis, S G, Wymer, J J, Bridgland, D R and Parfitt, S A 1991 'Beeches Pit, West Stow, Suffolk', in Lewis, S G, Whiteman, C A and Bridgland, D R (eds) *Central East Anglia and the Fen Basin*. London: Quat Res Assoc, 94–104

Preece, R C, Penkman, K E H, 2005 'New faunal analyses and amino acid dating of the Lower Palaeolithic site at East Farm, Barnham, Suffolk'. *Proc Geol Assoc* **116**, 363–77

Prescott, J R and Hutton, J T 1994 'Cosmic ray contributions to dose rates for luminescence and ESR dating: large depths and long term time variations'. *Radiation Measurements* **23**, 497–500

Preston, C D 1995 *Pondweeds of Great Britain and Ireland*. London: Botanical Soc Brit Isles

Proctor, C J, Collcutt, S N, Currant, A P, Hawkes, C J, Roe, D A and Smart, P L 1996 'A report on the excavations at Rhinoceros Hole, Wookey'. *Proc U Bristol Spelaeol Soc* **20**, 237–62

Rădulescu, C and Samson, P 1985 'Pliocene and Pleistocene mammalian biostratigraphy in southeastern Transylvania (Romania)'. *Trav Inst Spéol «Emil Racovitza»* **24**, 85–95

Reading, 1986. *Sedimentary Environments and Facies*, 2 edn. Oxford: Blackwell

Reimer, P J, Baillie, M G L, Bard, E, Beck, J W, Bertrand, C J H, Blackwell, P G, Buck, C E, Burr, G S, Cutler, K B, Damon, P E, Edwards, R L, Fairbanks, R G, Friedrich, M, Guilderson, T P, Hogg, A G, Hughen, K A, Kromer, B, McCormac, G, Manning, S, Ramsey, C B, Reimer, R W, Remmele, S, Southon, J R, Stuiver, M, Talamo, S, Taylor, F W, van der Plicht, J, Weyhenmeyer, C E 2004 'IntCal04 terrestrial radiocarbon age calibration, 0–26 cal kyr BP'. *Radiocarbon* **46** (3), 1029–59

Reineck, H and Singh, I 1980 *Depositional Sedimentary Environments*, 2 edn. New York: Springer-Verlag

Rendell, H, Worsley, P, Green, F and Parks D 1991 'Thermoluminescence dating of the Chelford Interstadial'. *Earth Sci Planetary Lett* **103**, 182–9

Reynolds, S H 1906 *A Monograph of the British Pleistocene Mammalia. Vol. II, Part II. The Bears*. London: Palaeontographical Society

Reynolds, S H 1939 *A Monograph of the British Pleistocene Mammalia. Vol. III, Part VI. The Bovidae*. London: Palaeontograph Soc

Richards, M, Harvati, K, Grimes, V, Smith, C, Smith, T, Hublin, J-J, Karkanas, P and Panagopolou, E 2008 'Strontium isotope evidence of Neanderthal mobility at the site of Lakonis Greece using laser ablation PIMMS'. *J Archaeol Sci* **35**, 1251–6

Richards, M and Trinkaus, E 2009 'Isotopic evidence for the diets of European Neanderthals and early modern humans'. *Proc Nat Acad Sci USA* **106**, 16034–9

Rick, J W 1976 'Downslope movement and intrasite spatial analysis'. *Amer Antiq* **41**, 133–44

Rigaud, J-P and Simek, J F 1987 '"Arms to short to box with God": Problems and Prospects for Paleolithic prehistory in Dordogne, France', in Soffer, O (ed) *The Pleistocene Old World: Regional Perspectives*. New York: Plenum, 47–61

Rightmire, P 2004 'Brain size and encephalization in Early to Mid-Pleistocene *Homo*'. *Amer J Phys Anthropol* **124**, 109–23

Ringrose, T J 1993 'Bone counts and statistics: a critique'. *J Archaeol Sci*, **20**, 121–57

Rivers, C, Barrett, M, Hiscock, K, Dennis, P, Feast, N and Lerner, D 1996 'Use of nitrogen isotopes to identify nitrogen contamination of the Sherwood Sandstone aquifer beneath the city of Nottingham, United Kingdom'. *Hydrogeol J* **4**, 90–102

Roberts, A 1996 'Evidence for Late Pleistocene and Early Holocene human activity and environmental change from the Torbryan Valley, south Devon', in Charman, D J, Newnham, R M and Croot, D G (eds) *Devon and East Cornwall: Field Guide*. London: Quat Res Assoc, 168–204

Roberts, M B and Parfitt, S A 1999 *Boxgrove: a Middle Palaeolithic Pleistocene Hominid Site at Eartham Quarry, Boxgrove, West Sussex*. London: English Heritage

Roe, D A 1964 'The British Lower and Middle Palaeolithic: some problems, method of study and preliminary results'. *Proc Prehist Soc* **30**, 245–67

Roe, D A 1968a *A Gazetter of British Lower and Middle Palaeolithic Sites*. London: CBA

Roe, D A 1968b 'British Lower and Middle Palaeolithic handaxe groups'. *Proc Prehist Soc* **34**, 1–82

Roe, D A 1981 *The Lower and Middle Palaeolithic Periods in Britain*. London: Routledge and Kegan Paul

Roebroeks, W 1988 'From find scatters to early hominid behaviour: a study of Middle Palaeolithic riverside settlements at Maastricht-Belvédère (The Netherlands)'. *Anal Praehist Leidensia* **21**. Leiden: U Leiden

Roebroeks, W, Hublin, J-J and MacDonald, K 2010 'Continuities and discontinuities in Neandertal presence: a closer look at Northwestern Europe', in Ashton, N, Lewis, S and Stringer, C (eds) *The Ancient Human Occupation of Britain*. Amsterdam: Elsevier

Roebroeks, W, Kolen, J and Rensink, E 1988 'Planning depth, anticipation and the organisation of Middle Palaeolithic technology: the "archaic natives" meet Eve's descendants'. *Helinium* **27**, 17–34

Roebroeks, W and Hennekens, P 1990 'Transport of lithics in the Middle Palaeolithic: conjoining evidence from Maastricht-Belvedere (NL)', in Cziesla, E. Eickhoff, S, Arts, N and Winter, D (eds) *The Big Puzzle: International Symposium on Refitting Stone Artefacts*. Bonn: Holos, 284–91

Roebroeks, W, Kolen, J, Van Poecke, M and Van Gijn, A 1997 'Site J: an early Weichselian (Middle Palaeolithic) flint scatter at Maastricht-Belvedere, The Netherlands'. *Paleo* **9**, 143–72

Roebroeks, W, de Loecker, D, Hennekens, P and van Ieperen, M 1992 '"A veil of stones": on the interpretation of an early Middle Palaeolithic low density scatter site at Maastricht-Belvédère (The Netherlands). *Anal Praehist Leidensia* **25**, 1–16

Roebroeks, W and Tuffreau, A 1999 'Palaeoenvironment and settlement patterns of the Northwest European middle Palaeolithic', in Roebroeks, W and Gamble, C (eds) *The Middle Palaeolithic Occupation of Europe*. Leiden: U Leiden P, 121–38

Rolland, N and Dibble, H 1990 'A new synthesis of Middle Palaeolithic assemblage variability'. *Amer Antiq* **55**, 480–99

Rose, J. 1987 'The status of the Wolstonian glaciation in the British Quaternary'. *Quat Newslett* **53**, 1–9

Rose, J 1994 'Major river systems of central and southern Britain during the Early and Middle Pleistocene'. *Terra Nova* **6**, 435–43

Rose, J, Moorlock, B S P and Hamblin, R J O 2001 'Pre-Anglian fluvial and coastal deposits in Eastern England: lithostratigraphy and palaeoenvironments'. *Quat Internat* **79**, 5–22

Roskams, S 2001 *Excavation*. Cambridge: Cambridge U P

Roth, V L 1982 'Dwarf mammoths from the Santa Barbara, California Channel Islands: size, shape, development and evolution'. Unpub DPhil thesis, Yale U

Roth, V L 1984 'How elephants grow: heterochrony and the calibration of developmental stages in some living and fossil species'. *J Vertebrate Palaeontol* **4**, 126–45

Rozanski, K, Sticher, W, Gonfiantini, R, Scott, E M, Beukens, K P, Kromer, B and van der Plicht, J 1992 'The IAEA ^{14}C intercomparison exercise 1990'. *Radiocarbon* **34**, 506–19

Sackett, J R 1981 'From de Mortillet to Bordes: a century of French Palaeolithic research', in Daniel, G E (ed) *Towards a History of Archaeology*. London: Thames and Hudson, 85–99

Sampson, C G 1978 *Paleoecology and Archaeology of an Acheulian site at Caddington, England*. Dallas: Southern Methodist U

Sánchez-Goñi, M F, Landais, A, Fletcher, W J, Naughton, F, Desprat, S and Duprat, J 2008 'Contrasting impacts of Dansgaard-Oeschger events over a western European latitudinal transect modulated by orbital parameters'. **Quat Sci Rev 27**, 1136–51

Santonja, M (ed) 2005. *Esperando el Diluvio: Ambrona y Torralba hace 400,000 Años*. Madrid: Mus Arqueol Reg

Santonja, M and Villa, P 1990 'The Lower Palaeolithic of Spain and Portugal'. *J World Prehist* **4**, 45–93

Schmid, E 1972 *Atlas of Animal Bones/Knochenatlas*. Amsterdam: Elsevier

Schertz, E 1936 'Zur Unterscheidung von *Bison priscus* Boj, und *Bos primigenius* Boj, an Metapodien und Astragalus'. *Senckenbergiana* **18**, 37–71

Schick, K 1986 *Stone Age Sites in the Making: Experiments in the Formation and Transformation of Archaeological Occurrences*. BAR Int Ser **314**. Oxford: Archaeopress

Schild, R 2005 'Lithostratigraphy and chronology, a synopis', in Schild, R (ed) *The Killing Fields of Zwolen: a Middle Paleolithic Kill-Butchery-Site in Central Poland*. Warsaw: Inst Archaeol Ethnol, Polish Acad Sci, 35–64

Schofield, A N and Wroth, C P 1968 *Critical State Soil Mechanics*. London: McGraw-Hill

Schreve, D C 1997 'Mammalian biostratigraphy of the later Middle Pleistocene in Britain'. Unpub PhD thesis, U London

Schreve, D C 2001a 'Differentiation of the British late Middle Pleistocene interglacials: the evidence from mammalian biostratigraphy'. *Quat Sci Rev* **20**, 1693–705

Schreve, D C 2001b 'Mammalian evidence from fluvial sequences for complex environmental change at the oxygen isotope substage level'. *Quat Internat* **79**, 65–74

Schreve, D C 2006 'The taphonomy of a Middle Devensian (MIS3) vertebrate assemblage from Lynford, Norfolk, UK and its implications for Middle Palaeolithic subsistence strategies'. *J Quat Sci* **21**, 543–57

Schreve, D C and Bridgland, D R 2002 'Correlation of English and German Middle Pleistocene fluvial sequences based on mammalian biostratigraphy'. *Netherlands J Geosci* **81**, 357–73

Schreve, D C, Bridgland, D R, Allen, P, Blackford, J J, Gleed-Owen, C P, Griffiths, H I, Keen, D H and White, M J 2002 'Sedimentology, palaeontology and archaeology of late Middle Pleistocene River Thames terrace deposits at Purfleet, Essex, UK'. *Quat Sci Rev* **21**, 1423–64

Schreve, D C and Currant, A P 2003 'The Pleistocene history of the Brown Bear (*Ursus arctos* L.) in the western Palaearctic: a review', in Kryštufek, B, Flajšman, B and Griffiths, H I (eds) *Living with Bears: a Large European Carnivore in a Shrinking World*. Ljubljana, Ekološki forum LDS, 27–39

Schreve, D C, Harding, P, White, M J, Bridgland, D R, Allen, P, Clayton, F and Keen, D H 2006 'A Levallois knapping site at West Thurrock, Lower Thames, UK: its Quaternary context, environment and age'. *Proc Prehist Assoc* **72**, 21–52

Schwenninger, J-L and Rhodes, E J R 2005 *Optically Stimulated Luminescence (OSL) Dating of Sediments from a Middle Palaeolithic Site at Lynford Quarry, Norfolk*. English Heritage: Centre Archaeol Rep **25/2005**

Scott, K 1980 'Two hunting episodes of Middle Palaeolithic age at La Cotte de St Brelade, Jersey'. *World Archaeol* **12**, 137–52

Scott, K 1986 'The large mammal fauna', in Callow, P and Cornford, J M (eds) *La Cotte de St Brelade, Jersey: Excavations by C B M. McBurney 1961–1978*. Norwich: Geo Books, 109–38

Scott, R 2006 'The Early Middle Palaeolithic in Britain'. Unpub PhD thesis, U Durham

Segre, A and Ascenzi, A 1984 'Fontana Ranuccio: Italy's earliest Middle Pleistocene hominin site'. *Curr Anthropol* **25**, 230–3

Sher, A V and Garutt, V E 1987 'New data on the morphology of elephant molars'. *Trans USSR Acad Sci, Earth Sci Sections* **285**, 195–9

Shackley, M L 1973 'A contextual study of the Mousterian industry from Great Pan Farm, Isle of Wright'. *Proc Isle of Wright Nat His Archaeol* **6**, 542–54

Shackley, M 1974 'Stream abrasion of flint implements'. *Nature* **248**, 501–2

Shackley, M L 1977 'The *bout coupé* handaxe as a typological marker for the British Mousterian Industries', in Wright, R S V (ed) *Stone Tools as Cultural Markers: Change, Evolution and Complexity*. Canberra: Australian Inst Aborig Stud, 332–9

Shea, J J 1988 'Spear points from the Middle Palaeolithic of the Levant'. *J Field Archaeol* **15**, 441–56

Shennan, S 1985 *Experiments in the Collection and Analysis of Archaeological Survey Data: the East Hampshire Survey*. Sheffield: Dept Archaeol Prehist, U Sheffield

Shennan, S 1988 *Quantifying Archaeology*. Edinburgh: Edinburgh U P

Sher A V 1997 'Late-Quaternary extinction of large mammals in northern Eurasia: a new look at the Siberian contribution', in Huntley, B, Cramer, W, Morgan, A V, Prentice, H C, Allen, J R M (eds) *Past and Future Rapid Environmental Changes: the Spatial and Evolutionary Responses of Terrestrial Biota*. Berlin-Heidelberg-New York: Springer-Verlag, 319–39

Sher, A V and Garutt, V E 1987 'New data on the morphology of elephant molars'. *Trans USSR Acad Sci, Earth Sci Sections* **285**, 195–9

Shipman, P 1977 'Paleoecology, taphonomic history and population dynamics of the vertebrate assemblage from the middle Miocene of Fort Ternan, Kenya'. Unpub PhD thesis, New York U

Shipman, P 1981 *Life History of a Fossil: an Introduction to Taphonomy and Paleoecology*. Cambridge, MA: Harvard U P

Shotton, F W 1953 'Pleistocene deposits of the area between Coventry, Rugby and Leamington and their bearing on the topographic development of the Midlands'. *Philos Trans Roy Soc London Ser B* **237**, 209–60

Shotton, F W, Keen, D H, Coope, G R, Currant, A P, Gibbard, P L, Aalto, M, Peglar, S M and Robinson, J E 1993 'The Middle Pleistocene deposits of Waverley Wood Pit, Warwickshire, England'. *J Quat Sci* **8**, 293–325

Silfer, J, Engel, M and Macko, S 1992 'Kinetic fractionation of stable carbon and nitrogen isotopes during peptide bond hydrolysis: experimental evidence and geochemical implications', in Macko, S and Engel, M (eds) *Isotope Fractionations in Organic Matter; Biosynthetic and Diagenetic Processes*. Amsterdam: Elsevier, 211–21

Simek, J F 1984 *A K-means Approach to the Analysis of Spatial Structure in Upper Palaeolithic Habitation Sites: Le Flageolet I and Pincevent section 36*. BAR Int Ser **S205**. Oxford: Archaeopress

Simonet, P 1992 'Les associations de grands mammifères du gisement de la grotte Scladina à Sclayn (Namur, Belgique)', *in* Otte, M, Bastin, B, Gautier, A and Haesaerts, P (eds) *Recherches aux Grottes de Sclayn Vol. 1, Le Contexte*. Etudes Recherche Archéol U Liège **27**, 127–51

Singer, R and Wymer, J 1982 *The Middle Stone Age at Klasies River Mouth in South Africa*. Chicago: U Chicago P

Skertchly, S J B 1879 *On the Manufacture of Gun Flints, the Methods of Excavating for Flint, the Age of Palaeolithic Man and the Connexion between Neolithic Art and the Gun-flint Trade*. London: Mem Geol Survey Great Brit

Slimak, L and Giraud, Y 2007 'Circulations sur plusiers centaines de kilomètres durant le Paléolithique moyen: contribution à la connaissance des sociétés néanderthaliennes'. *Comptes Rendus Palevol* **6**, 359–68

Smith, R A 1911 'A Palaeolithic industry at Northfleet, Kent'. *Archaeolog* **62**, 515–32

Soares, P, Achilli, A, Semino, O, Davies, W, Macaulay, V, Bandelt, H-J, Torroni, A and Richards, M B 2010 'The archaeogenetics of Europe'. *Current Biol* **20**, 174–83

Soffer, O 1985. *The Upper Palaeolithic of the Central Russian Plain*. New York: Academic Press

Soffer, O 1991 'Storage, sedentism and the Eurasian Palaeolithic record'. *Antiquity* **63**, 719–32

Soffer, O 1992 'Social transformations at the Middle to Upper Palaeolithic transition: the implications of the European record', in Bräuer, G and Smith, F H (eds) *Continuity or Replacement: Controversies in Homo sapiens Evolution*. Rotterdam: Balkema, 247–59

Sorensen, M V and Leonard, W R 2001 'Neanderthal energetic and foraging efficiency'. *J Human Evol* **40**, 483–95

Soressi, M and Hays, M A 2003 'Manufacture, transport and use of Mousterian bifaces: a case study from the Perigord (France)', in Soressi, M and Dibble, H (eds) *Multiple Approaches to the Study of Bifacial Technologies*. Pennsylvania: U Pennsylvania Mus P, 125–48

Sparks, B W 1961 'The ecological interpretation of Quaternary non-marine Mollusca'. *Proc Linnaean Soc London* **172**, 71–80

Sparks, B W and West, R G 1970 'Late Pleistocene deposits at Wretton, Norfolk. I. Ipswichian interglacial deposits'. *Philos Trans Roy Soc London Ser B* **258**, 1–30

Speth, J D 1983 *Bison kills and Bone Counts: Decision-Making by Ancient Hunters*. Chicago: U Chicago P

Speth, J D 1987 'Early hominid subsistence strategies in seasonal habitats'. *J Archaeol Sci* **14**, 13–29

Spiker, E C and Hatcher, P 1987 'The effects of early diagenesis on the chemical and stable carbon isotopic composition of wood'. *Geochem et Cosmochim Acta* **51**, 1385–91

Spurrell, F C J 1880a 'On the discovery of the place where Palaeolithic implements were made at Crayford'. *Quart J Geol Soc London* **36**, 544–8

Spurrell, F C J 1880b 'On implements and chips from the floor of a Palaeolithic workshop'. *Archaeol J* **37**, 294–9

Stace, C 1997 *New Flora of the British Isles*, 2 edn. Cambridge: Cambridge U P

Stanford, D, Bonnischen, R and Morlan, R E 1981 'The Ginsberg experiment: modern and prehistoric evidence of a bone flaking technology'. *Science* **212**, 438–40

Stapert, D 1976 'Middle Palaeolithic finds from the northern Netherlands'. *Palaeohist* **18**, 44–73

Stapert, D 1979 'The handaxe from Drouwen (Province of Drenthe, The Netherlands) and the Upper Acheulian'. *Palaeohist* **21**, 128–42

Steegmann, A T, Cerny, F J and Holliday T W 2002 'Neanderthal cold adaptation: physiology and energetic factors'. *Amer J Human Biol* **14**, 566–83

Steele, T 2003 'Using mortality profiles to infer behaviour in the fossil record'. *J Mammal* **84**, 418–30

Stenton, D R 1991 'The adaptive significance of Caribou winter clothing for arctic hunter-gatherers'. *Inuit Stud* **15**, 3–28

Stephan, E 2000 'Oxygen isotope analysis of animal bone phosphate: method refinement, influence of consolidants and reconstruction of palaeotemperatures for Holocene sites'. *J Archaeol Sci* **27**, 523–35

Stewart, D A, Walker, A, Dickson, J 1984 'Pollen diagrams from Dubh Lochan, near Loch Lommond'. *New Phytologist* **98**, 531–49

Stuiver, M and Kra, R S 1986 'Editorial comment' *Radiocarbon* **28**, ii

Stuiver, M and Polach, H A 1977 'Reporting of ^{14}C data'. *Radiocarbon* **19**, 355–63

Stiner, M C 1994 *Honor Among Thieves: a Zooarchaeological Study of Neandertal Ecology*. Princeton: Princeton U P

Stiner, M C, Barkai R and Gopher A 2009 'Cooperative hunting and meat sharing 400–200 kya at Qesem Cave, Israel'. *Proc Nat Acad Sci USA* **106**, 13207–12

Stiner, M and Kuhn, S 1992 'Subsistence, technology and adaptive variation in Middle Palaeolithic Italy'. *Amer Anthropol* **94**, 12–46

Stiner, M C, Munro, N D and Surovell, T A 2000 'The tortoise and the hare: small-game use, the broad spectrum revolution and Palaeolithic demography'. *Curr Anthropol* **41**, 39–73

Straus, L G 1982 'Carnivores and cave sites in Cantabrian Spain'. *J Anthropol Res* 38, 75–96

Street, M 2002 *Plaidter Hummerich: an Early Weichselian Middle Palaeolithic Site in the Central Rhineland*. Bonn: Römisch-Germanischen Zentralmus

Stringer, C 2006 *Homo britannicus: the Incredible Story of Human Life in Britain*. London: Penguin

Stringer, C B, Andrews, P and Currant, A P 1996 'Palaeoclimatic significance of mammalian faunas from Westbury Cave, Somerset, England', *in* Turner, C (ed) *The Early Middle Pleistocene in Europe*. Rotterdam: Balkema, 135–43

Stringer, C and Gamble, C 1993 *In Search of the Neanderthals: Solving the Puzzle of Human Origins*. London: Thames and Hudson

Stuart, A J 1977 'The vertebrates of the Last Cold Stage in Britain and Ireland'. *Philos Trans Royl Soc London Ser B* **280**, 295–312

Stuart, A J 1982 *Pleistocene Vertebrates in the British Isles*. London and New York: Longman

Stuart, A J 1991 'Mammalian extinctions in the late Pleistocene of northern Eurasia and North America'. *Biol Rev* **66**, 453–562

Stuart, A J 1996 'Vertebrate faunas from the early Middle Pleistocene of East Anglia', *in* Turner, C (ed) *The Early Middle Pleistocene in Europe*. Rotterdam: Balkema, 9–24

Stuart, A J 2004 'The extinction of woolly mammoth (*Mammuthus primigenius*) and straight-tusked elephant (*Palaeoloxodon antiquus*) in Europe'. *Quat Internat* **126–8**, 171–7

Stuart, A J and Lister, A M 2007 'Patterns of Late Quaternary megafaunal extinctions in Europe and northern Asia'. *Courier Forschunginstitut Senckenberg* **25**, 289–99

Stuart, A J, Sulerzhitsky, L D, Orlova, L A, Kuzmin, Y V and Lister, A M 2002 'The latest woolly mammoths (*Mammuthus primigenius*) in Europe and Asia: a review of the current evidence'. *Quat Sci Rev* **21**, 1559–69

Sukumar, R 1992 *The Asian Elephant: Ecology and Management*. Cambridge: Cambridge U P

Sukumar, R 2003 *The Living Elephants*. Oxford: Oxford U P

Sulerzhitsky L D 1997 'Patterns of the radiocarbon chronology of mammoths in Siberia and northern Eastern Europe (as sub-stratum for human dispersal)', *in* Velichko, A A and Soffer, O (eds) *Humans Settle the Planet Earth*. Moscow: Inst Geogr, 184–202 (in Russian)

Sutcliffe, A J 1995 'Insularity of the British Isles 250,000–30,000 years ago: the mammalian, including human, evidence', *in* Preece, R C (ed) *Island Britain: a Quaternary Perspective*. Geol Soc Special Pub **96**. Bath: Geol Soc, 127–40

Sutcliffe, A J and Kowalski, K 1976 'Pleistocene Rodents of the British Isles'. *Bull Brit Mus Nat Hist* **27/2**

Sykes, G A, Collins, M J and Walton, D I, 1995 'The significance of a geochemically isolated intracrystalline organic fraction within biominerals'. *Organic Geochem* **23**, 1039–65

Thieme, H 2005 'The Lower Palaeolithic art of hunting: the case of Schöningen 13 II–4, Lower Saxony, Germany', *in* Gamble, C and Porr, M (eds) *The Individual Hominid in Context:Archaeological Investigations of Lower and Middle Palaeolithic Landscapes, Locales and Artefacts*. London: Routledge, 115–32

Thieme, H and Veil, S 1985 'Neue untersuchungen zum eemzeitlichen elefanten-jagdplatz Lehringen, Lkr. Verden'. *Die Kunde* **36**, 11–58

Thorne, C R 1982 'Processes and mechanism of river bank erosion', *in* Hey, R D, Bathurst, J C and Thorne, C R (eds.) *Gravel Bed Rivers*. Chichester: Wiley, 227–59

Thornton, S F and McManus, J 1994 'Application of organic carbon and nitrogen stable isotope and C/N ratios as source indicators of organic matter provenance in estuarine systems: evidence from the Tay Estuary, Scotland'. *Estuarine Coastal Shelf Sci* **38**, 219–33

Torrence, R 1986 'Time budgeting and technology', *in* Bailey, G (ed) Hunter Gatherer Economy in Prehistory: a European Perspective. Cambridge: Cambridge U P, 11–23

Torrence, R 1989 'Retooling: towards a behavioural theory of stone tools', in Torrence, R (ed) *Time, Energy and Stone Tools*. Cambridge: Cambridge U P, 57–67

Tovey, N K and Paul, M A 2002 'Modelling self-weight consolidation in Holocene sediments'. *Bull Engineering Geol Environ* **61**, 21–33

Tratman, E K 1964 'Picken's Hole, Crook Peak, Somerset: a Pleistocene site. Preliminary note'. *Proc U Bristol Spelaeol Soc* **10**, 112–15

Tratman, E K, Donovan, D T and Campbell, J B 1971 'The Hyaena Den (Wookey Hole), Mendip Hills, Somerset'. *Proc U Bristol Spelaeol Soc* **12**, 245–79

Trimble, S W 1994 'Erosional effects of cattle on streambanks in Tennessee, USA'. *Earth Processes and Landforms* **19**, 451–64

Trinkaus, E 1983 *The Shanidar Neanderthals*. New York: Academic Press

Trinkaus, E 2003 'An early modern human from the Peçstera cu Oase, Romania'. *Proc Nat Acad Sci USA* **100**, 11231–6

Tuffreau, A, Révillion, S, Sommé, J, Van Vliet-Lanoë, B 1994 'Les gisements paléolithique moyens de Seclin (Nord)'. *Bull Soc Préhist Française* **91**, 23–46

Tukey, J W 1977 *Exploratory Data Analysis*. London: Addison Wesley

Turner, A 1981 'Ipswichian mammal faunas, cave deposits and hyaena activity'. *Quat Newslett* **33**, 17–22

Turner, E 1990 'Middle and Late Pleistocene Macrofaunas of the Neuwied Basin Region (Rhineland-Palatinate) of West Germany'. *Jahrb Römisch-Germanischen Zentralmus Mainz*, 133–403

Turner, G, Bergersen, F and Tantala, H 1983 'Natural enrichment of ^{15}N during decomposition of plant material in soils'. *Soil Biol Biochem* **15**, 495–7

Turner, H, Kuiper, J G J, Thew, N, Bernasconi, R, Rüetschi, J, Wüthrich, M and Gosteli, M. 1998 *Atlas der Mollusken der Schweiz und Liechtensteins*. Neuchâtel: Centre Suisse de cartographie de la faune

Turner-Walker, G 1998 'The West Runton Fossil Elephant: A pre-conservation evaluation of its condition, chemistry and burial environment'. *The Conservator* **22**, 26–35

Turq, A 1988 'Le Paléolithique inférieur et moyen en Haute-Agenais: état des recherches'. *Rev l'Argenais* **115**, 83–112

Turq, A 1989 'Exploitation des matères primières lithiques et occupation du sol: l'exemple du Moustérien entre Dordogne et Lot', *in* Laville, H (ed) *Variations des Paléomilieux et Peuplement Préhistorique*. Paris: Centre Nat Reserche Scientif, 179–204

Turq, A 2000 *Paléolithique Inférieur et Moyen entre Dordogne et Lot* (Paléo Supplement 2). Les Eyzies: Société Amis Mus Nat Préhist

Turq, A 2001 'Rèflexions sur les biface dans quelques sites du Paléolithique ancien-moyen en grotte ou abri du nord-est basin Aquitain', *in* Cliquet, D (ed) *Les Industries à Outils Bifaciaux du Moyen d'Europe Occidentale*. Etudes Recherche Archéol U Liège **98**. Liège: ERAUL, 141–9

Tyldesley J A 1987 *The Bout Coupé Handaxe: a Typological Problem*. BAR Brit Ser **170**. Oxford: Archaeopress

Tyrberg, T 1998 'Pleistocene birds of the Palearctic: a catalogue'. *Pub Nuttall Ornithol Club* **27**

Ukraintseva, V V 1993 *Vegetation Cover and Environment of the "Mammoth Epoch" in Siberia*. Hot Springs, SD: Mammoth Site

van Andel, T H 2003 'Glacial Environments I: the Weichselian Climate in Europe between the end of the OIS-5 Interglacial and the Last Glacial Maximum', *in* van Andel, T H and Davies, W (eds) *Neanderthals and Modern Humans in the European Landscape during the Last Glaciation: Archaeological Results of the Stage 3 Project*. Cambridge: McDonald Inst Archaeol Res Monogr, 9–19

van Andel, T H and Davies, W (eds) 2003 *Neanderthals and Modern Humans in the European Landscape during the Last Glaciation: Archaeological Results of the Stage 3 Project*. Cambridge: McDonald Inst Archaeol Res Monogr

van Andel, T H and P C Tzedakis, 1996 'Palaeolithic landscapes of Europe and Environs, 150,000–25,000 years ago'. *Quat Sci Rev* **15**, 481–500

Van Geel, B, 1976 *A Palaeoecological Study of Holocene Peat Bog Sections Based on the Analysis of Pollen, Spores and Macro and Microscopic Remains of Fungi, Algae, Cormophytes and Animals*. Amsterdam: U Amsterdam Acad proefschrift, Hugo de Vries laboratorium

Van Geel, B 1978 'A palaeoecological study of Holocene peat bog sections in Germany and the Netherlands based on the analysis of pollen, spores and macro and microscopic remains of fungi, cormophytes and animals'. *Rev Palaeobot Palynol* **22**, 237–344

Van Geel, B, Coope, R G and Van der Hammen, T 1989 'Palaeoecology and stratigraphy of the Late-Glacial type section at Usselo (The Netherlands)'. *Rev Palaeobot Palynol* **60**, 25–129

van Gijn, A L 1990 *The Wear and Tear of Flint*. Anal Praehist Leidensia **22**. Leiden: U Leiden P

Van Hoeve, M L and Hendrikse, M (eds) 1998. 'A study of non-pollen objects in pollen slides: the types as described by Dr Bas van Geel and colleagues'. Unpub compilation, U Utrecht

Van Huissteden, J, Gibbard, P L and Briant, R M 2001 'Periglacial river systems in northwest Europe during marine isotope stages 4 and 3'. *Quat Internat* **79**, 75–88

van Kolfschoten, T 1990 'The evolution of the mammal fauna in the Netherlands and the middle Rhine Area (Western Germany) during the late Middle Pleistocene'. *Mededelingen Rijks Geol Dienst* **43/3**, 1–69

van Kolfschoten, T and Roebroeks, W 1985 'Maastricht-Belvédère: stratigraphy, Palaeoenvironment and archaeology of the Middle and Upper Pleistocene deposits'. *Mededelingen Rijks Geol Dienst* **39/1**, 1–32

Van Steijn, H and Coutard, J-P 1989 'Laboratory experiments with small debris flows: physical properties related to sedimentary characteristics'. *Earth Surface Processes and Landforms* **14**, 587–96

Van Steijn, H, de Ruig, J and Hoozemans, H 1988a 'Morphological and mechanical aspects of debris flows in parts of the French Alps'. *Zeitschr Geomorphol* **32**, 143–61

Van Steijn, H, Coutard, J-P, Filppo, H and Mandersloot, C 1988b 'Simulation experimentale de laves de ruissellement: mouvement et sedimentation'. *Bull Assoc Géogr Français* **1**, 33–40

Vaquero, M 1999 'Intrasite spatial organization of lithic production in the Middle Palaeolithic: the evidence of the Abríc, Romani (Capelledes, Spain)'. *Antiquity* **73**, 493–504

Vaquero, M 2005 'Les stratégies de transport d'outils dans un contexte résidentiel: un exemple du Paléolithique moyen', in Vialou, D, Renault-Miskovsky, J and Patou-Mathis, M (eds) *Comportements des Hommes du Paléolithique Moyen et Supérieur en Europe: Territoires et Milleux*. Liège: Etudes Recherche Archéol U Liège, 121–32

Vartanyan, S L, Garrut, V E, Sher, A V 1993 'Holocene dwarf mammoths from Wrangel Island in the Siberian Arctic'. *Nature* **382**, 337–40

Vartanyan, S L, Arslanov, K A, Tertychynaya, T V, Chernov, S 1995 'Radiocarbon evidence for mammoths on Wrangel Island, Arctic Ocean until 2,000 BC'. *Radiocarbon* **37**, 7–10

Vasil'chuk Y, Punning J M, Vasil'chuk A 1997 'Radiocarbon ages of mammoths in Northern Eurasia: Implications for population development and Late Quaternary environment'. *Radiocarbon* **39**, 1–18

Vereshchagin, N K and Baryshnikov, G F 1982 'Palaeoecology of the mammoth fauna in the Eurasian Arctic', in Hopikins, D M, Matthews, J V, Schweger, C E and Young, S B (eds) *Palaeoecology of Beringia*. New York: Academic Press, 267–80

Vereshchagin, N K and Tichonov, A N 1986 'A study of mammoth tusks', in Vereshchagin, N K and Kuzmina, I E (eds) *Mammals of the Quaternary Fauna of the USSR. Proc Zool Inst Leningrad* **149**, 3–14 (in Russian)

Villa, P 1982 'Conjoinable pieces and site formation processes'. *Amer Antiq* **47**, 276–90

Villa, P 1983 *Terra Amata and the Middle Pleistocene Archaeological Record of Southern France*. Berkeley: U California P

Villa, P 1990 'Torralba and Aridos: elephant exploitation in Middle Pleistocene Spain'. *J Human Evol* **19**, 299–309

Vitousek, P, Shearer, G and Khol, D 1989 'Foliar ^{15}N natural abundances in Hawaiian rainforest: patterns and possible mechanisms'. *Oecologia* **78**, 383–8

von den Driesch, A 1976 *A Guide to the Measurement of Animal Bones from Archaeological Sites* (Peabody Museum Bulletin 1). Cambridge, MA: Harvard U P

Voorhies, M R 1969 *Taphonomy and population dynamics of the early Pliocene vertebrate fauna, Knox County, Nebraska*. Contributions to Geology Special Paper **1**. Laramie: U Wyoming

Walkling, A 1997 'Kaferkundliche Untersuchungen an weichselzeitlichen Ablagerungen der Bohrung Gros Todtshorn (Kr Harburg: Neidersachsen)'. *Schriftenreihe der Deutschen Geol Gesellsch* **4**, 87–102

Warren, S H 1920 'A natural eolith factory beneath the Thanet Sand'. *Quart J Geol Soc London* **76**, 238–53

Warren, S H 1923 'The sub-soil flint flaking sites at Grays'. *Proc Geol Assoc* **34**, 38–42

Watson, E 1977 'The periglacial environment of Great Britain during the Devensian'. *Philos Trans Roy Soc London Ser B* **280**, 183–98

Wenban-Smith, F F 1995 'The Ebbsfleet Valley, Northfleet (Baker's Hole) (TQ 615 735)', *in* Bridgland, D R, Allen, P and Haggert, B A (eds) *The Quaternary of the Lower Reaches of the Thames: Field Guide*. Durham: Quat Res Assoc, 147–64

Wenban-Smith, F F 1999 'Knapping technology', *in* Roberts, M B and Parfitt, S A (eds) *Boxgrove: a Middle Palaeolithic Pleistocene Hominid Site at Eartham Quarry, Boxgrove, West Sussex*. London: English Heritage, 384–95

Wenban-Smith, F, Gamble, C G and Apsimon, A 2000 'The Lower Palaeolithic site at Red Barns, Porchester, Hampshire: bifacial technology, raw material quality and the organisation of archaic behaviour'. *Proc Prehist Soc* **66**, 209–55

West, R G 1979. *Pleistocene Geology and Biology*, 2 edn. London: Longman

West, R G 2000 *Plant Life of the Quaternary Cold Stages: Evidence from the British Isles*. Cambridge: Cambridge U P

West, R.G, Dickson, CA, Catt, J A, Weir, A H and Sparks, BW 1974. 'Late Pleistocene deposits at Wretton, Norfolk II: Devensian deposits'. *Philos Trans Roy Soc London Ser B* **267**, 337–420

White, M J 1996 'Biface variability and human behaviour: a study from South-eastern England'. Unpub Ph.D thesis, U Cambridge

White, M J 1998 'On the significance of Acheulean biface variability in Southern Britain'. *Proc Prehist Soc* **64**, 15–44

White, M J 2006 'Things to do in Doggerland when you're dead: surviving OIS3 at the northwestern-most fringe of Middle Palaeolithic Europe'. *World Archaeol* **38**, 547–75

White, M J and Ashton, N M 2003 'Lower Palaeolithic core technology and the origins of the Levallois method in NW Europe'. *Curr Anthropol* **44**, 598–609

White, M J and Jacobi, R M 2002 'Two sides to every story: bout coupé handaxes revisited'. *Oxford J Archaeol* **21**, 109–33

White, M J and Pettitt, P B 1995 'Technology of early Palaeolithic Western Europe: innovation, variability and a unified framework'. *Lithics* **16**, 27–40

White, M J, Scott, R and Ashton, N M 2006 'The Early Middle Palaeolithic in Britain: archaeology, settlement history and human behaviour'. *J Quat Sci* **21**, 525–41

Wiessner, P 1982 'Risk, reciprocity and social influences on !Kung San economics', *in* Leacock, E and Lee, R (eds) *Politics and History in Band Societies*. Cambridge: Cambridge U P, 61–84

Wiltshire, P E J, Edwards, K J and Bond, S 1994 'Microbially-derived metallic sulphide spherules, pollen and waterlogging of archaeological sites', *in* Davies, O K (ed) *Aspects of Archaeological Palynology: Methodology and Applications*. Amer Assoc Stratigraphic Palynolo Contrib Ser **29**, 207–21

Wobst, H M 1990 'Minitime and megaspace in the Palaeolithic at 18K and otherwise', *in* Soffer, O and Gamble, C (eds) *The World at 18 000 BP, Volume 2: High Latitudes*. London: Unwin Hyman, 331–43

Woillard, G and Mook, W G 1982 'Carbon dates at Grande Pile: correlation of land and sea chronologies'. *Science* 215, 150–61

Wood, W R and Johnson, D L 1978 'A survey of disturbance processes in archaeological site formation', *in* Schiffer, M B (ed) *Advances in Archaeological Method and Theory* **1**, 315–81

Woodburn, J 1980 'Hunters and gatherers today and reconstruction of the past', *in* Gellner, E (ed) *Soviet and Western Anthropology*. London: Duckworth, 95–117

Woodburn, J 1991 'African hunter-gatherer social organization: is it best understood as a product of encapsulation?', *in* Ingold, T, Riches, D and Woodburn, J (eds) *Hunters and Gatherers 1: History, Evolution and Social Change*. New York: Berg, 31–64

Wrangham, R W 1980 'An ecological model of female-bonded primate groups'. *Behaviour* **75**, 262–99

Wymer, J J 1968 *Lower Palaeolithic Archaeology in Britain as Represented by the Thames Valley*. London: John Baker

Wymer, J J 1985 *The Palaeolithic Sites of East Anglia*. Norwich: Geo Books

Wymer, J J 1988 'Palaeolithic archaeology and the British Quaternary sequence'. *Quat Sci Rev* **7**, 79–98

Wymer, J J 1996 *The Great Ouse Drainage and the Yorkshire and Lincolnshire Wolds*. The English Rivers Palaeolithic Project Report **2**, 1995–1996. Salisbury: Trust for Wessex Archaeol and English Heritage

Wymer, J J 1999 *The Lower Palaeolithic Occupation of Britain*. Salisbury: Wessex Archaeology and English Heritage

Wymer, J J 2001 'Palaeoliths in a lost pre-Anglian landscape', *in* Milliken, S and Cook, J (eds) *A Very Remote Period Indeed: Papers on the Palaeolithic Presented to Derek Roe*. Oxford: Oxbow, 174–9

Wymer, J J 2008a *The J J Wymer Archive*, L Mepham (ed) Volume 7: 1978–1996, Archaeological Data Service (http://ads.ahds.ac.uk/catalogue/resources.html?wymer_ed_2008)

Wymer, J J 2008b *The J J Wymer Archive*, L Mepham (ed) Volume 8: 1996–2004. Archaeological Data Service (http://ads.ahds.ac.uk/catalogue/resources.html?wymer_ed_2008)

Wymer, J J, Bridgland, D R and Lewis, S G 1991 'Warren Hill, Mildenhall, Suffolk (TL 744743)', *in* Lewis, S G, Whiteman, C A and Bridgland, D R (eds) *Central East Anglia and the Fen Basin: Field Guide*. London: Quat Res Assoc, 50–8

Yeatman, S, Spokes, L, Dennis, P and Jickells, T 2001 'Comparisons of aerosol nitrogen isotopic composition at two coastal polluted sites'. *Atmospheric Environ* **35**, 1307–20

Zilhão, J, Angelucci, D E, Badal-Garcia, E, d'Errico, F, Daniel, F, Dayet, L, Douka, K, Higham, T F G, Martinez-Sánchez, M J, Montes-Bernárdez, R, Murcia-Mascarós, S, Pérez-Sirvent, C, Roldán-Garcia, C, Vanhaeren, M, Villaverde, V, Wood, R and Zapata, J 2010 'Symbolic use of marine shells and mineral pigments by Iberian Neandertals'. *Proc Nat Acad Sci USA* Early Edition 10.1073/pnas.0914088107

INDEX

Index
(Page numbers in **bold** are references to entries in figures and tables.)

A

Aggregates Levy Sustainability Fund xv, 1, 3, 70
Allerød 130; *see also* Marine Isotope Stage, MIS 2
Ambrona 197, 258, 285
America
  North 93, 109, 129–33, 176, 285
  American bison, *see Bison bison*
amino-acid racemisation 17, 71–2, 97, 101, 284, 500
amphibian 129, 133, 214–216, 285; *see also Anura*, herpetofauna, *Rana*
AMS, *see* radiocarbon dating
Anglian (and Elsterian) 1 7–19, 166, 171, 173–4, 176, 500
animal, *see* fauna (living) or bone (faunal remains)
Anura sp. 165, 215
Arctic 92, 94, 95, 99–100, 101, 125, 128, 130–3, 166, 216, 291–3
  fauna, *see* fauna
  fox, *see Alopex lagopus*
  lemming, *see Dicrostonyx torquatus*
  Palearctic, *see* habitat
  subarctic 99–100, 131, 133–4
  tundra, *see* tundra
Aridos 197, 258
Asia 94, 131, 171–2
  central 91, 131–3, 203
  eastern 213
  northern 70, 130, 132, 203
  southern 132
Association A *19*, *22–3*, 25, 27–8, 30–1, 33, *36*–37, 40, 69
Association B xv, 17, *19*, *22–3*, 25–*37*, 44, 69, 73, 75–6, *78*, 100, 160
B-i xv, 25, 27, 32–3, *35*, 37–8, 44–7, 220, *223*, *493*
  B-i:01 33–*6*, *493*
  B-i:02 34–*6*, *220–1*, *493*
  B-i:03 34–*6*, 44–5, 160, 176, 188, *220–1*, *225*, *250*, *266*, 270–2, *401*, *493*, *446–7*
B-ii xv, 17, 25–7, 32–3, 35–*8*, *43*–7, 53, 62–3, 69–70, 73, 77, 95, 102–3, 110–11, 118–20, 123–5, 135, *139*, 141–5, 155–6, 160, 165, 176, 219, 220–5, 227–*8*, *230–1*, *234–5*, *238*–42, 245, *247*, 249, *250*–2, 274, *493*
  B-ii:01 26–7, *34–6*, 38–9, 45–*52*, *57–60*, *78–83*, *83–9*, *97–8*, 103, *106–8*, 110, 135–6, 143–4, 160–2, 165, 184, *189*, 219–*21*, *223*, *225*, *235*, *237*–*42*, *245*, *250–1*, *265–6*, 270, 312, *389*, *392*, *405–6*, *421*, *425–6*, *434*, *437–9*, *444–5*, *455*, *460*, *462–6*, *469–70*, *472–5*, *477–9*, *482–8*, *490*, *493*
  B-ii:02 26–7, *34–6*, 38, 39, *83–9*, *96*, *98–9*, 119, *104*, 111–*12*, *114–17*, 119, *127*, 143, *161*, *163*, 164, 219, *220–1*, *223*, *238–9*, *250–1*, *265*, 274, *49–95*, *463*, *465*, *477*
  B-ii:03 26–7, *34–6*, 38–40, *43*, 45–52, 56–63, 69–72, 77–*89*, *96–8*, 103–*8*, 110–*16*, 119, 121, 124, *127*, 135–7, 143–4, 152, 155, 160–*2*, 164–5, 184, 187–8, 219–*21*, *223*, *225*, 227–8, *230*, *235*, 237–*8*, 240–2, *245*, 249–*51*, *263*, 270–2, 274, 311, *388–489*, *492*, *495*
  B-ii:04 *34–5*, 39–40, *42*, 45, 135, *163*, 165, *189*, 219–*21*, *238–9*, *250*, *263*, *495–7*, *389*, *392*, *407*, *410*, *413–14*, *416–18*, *437*, *440*, *442*, *455*, *463*, *466*, *469*, *472*, *489–90*
  B-ii:04A *40–2*, 112, 136, 144, 153
  B-ii:04B *34*, *40–1*, 136–7, 144
  B-ii:04C *34*, *40*, *42*, 136–37, 144
  B-ii:04D *40*, 136, 144, 153
  B-ii: 05 26–*7*, *35*, 39–40, *43*, *46*–9, 56–63, 69, 77, *96*, *98*, 103–6, 111–*14*, 125, *127*, *163*, *165*, 188–*9*, 219–*21*, 311, *391*, *393*, *456*
  B-ii:05 *497–8*, *396*
  B-iii xv, 25–8, 32, *35*, 37, 38, *40*, 43–7, 69, 73, 102, 120, *122*–5, *164*–5, 176, *220–21*, *263*, *391*, *396–7*, *498*
  B-iii:05 *36*
Association C *19*, *22–3*, *27*–8, 30–2, *36*, 38, 40, 43, 69, 103–*4*, *164*, 220, *263*, *388*, *463*
Association D *19*, *23*, 28–32, 70–1,
Association E *19*, *23*, *28*–32, 70–1
Australia 284, 292–3
Aveley 192, 254
Ayton Asphalte xv, 1, 3

B

Balderton 174, *209*, 214
Banwell Bone Cave mammal assemblage zone 203, 204
bear, *see Ursus*
Beeches Pit 3, 290
beetle, *see* coleoptera
biface, *see* handaxe
biome, *see* habitat
bird 32–3, 158, 181, 258, 283, 285, 504
Porzana sp./crake 133, 165, 181
Bison 7, 95, 132–34, *139*, 147–8, 176, 180, 201, 203–4, 254, 259, 285, 288–9, 294, *432*, *469*, *477*, *479*
  B. bison 130, 176
  B. bonasus 130, 176
  plains, *see Bison bison*
  steppe, *see Bison priscus*
  B. priscus 129, 130, 166, 174–5, *176*, 177
  B. schotensacki 176
bovid 166, 174–5, 181, 197, 205, 208, 259, *332*, *336*
bone, faunal remains 4, 11–*12*, 15, 17, 21, 25, 30–2, 38, 46–7, 57, 67, 73, 75, 92, 111, 129, 138–9, 148–9, 157–219, 226, 261–2, 280, 285–6, *388–492*
ageing 210–13, 215
association with lithics xv, 5, 197, 157, 254, 285
bird, *see* bird
bovid, *see Bison*
chemistry 63, 216–19, 286, 297, 300
conjoins, *see* refit
dating of 70–7
elephant, *see* elephant
fish, *see* fish
fragments, splinters 147, 148, 158, *160*, 179–81, 186, *188*, 191–2, 197, 277, 280, 282
herpetofaunal, *see* herpetofauna
horse, *see Equus*
mammoth, *see Mammuthus*
microvertebrates 158, 180, 184
modification by animals
  carnivore gnawing/consumption xv, 131, *148*, 150–1, *153*, 169, 182, 184, 186–7, *190–1*, 200, 215, *286*, *388–492*
  rodent gnawing *148*, 182, 190–1
  trampling 143, 150, 177, 180, 182, 184, 186–7, 196, 200, 299; *see also* fauna, bioturbation
modification by hominins/Neanderthals 151, 165, 184, 195, 199
  breakage, marrow extraction xv, 151, 182, 195, 196–7, 199–201, 254, 286
  cutmarks xv, 8, 182, 186, 196–7, 200, 202, 254, *286*, 290; *see also* butchery
  selective removal of elements xv, 200–2, *286*, 294
  working of, artefacts 62, *151*, 165, 195, 196, 200, 260, 290
pathology 191–5, 199–200, 286, 301, 304–5, 500, 503–5
reindeer, *see* reindeer

refits, *see* refit
reindeer, *see* Rangifer
root damage, etching **148**, 150, 182, 187, 189, ***388–492***
sex determination, *see* sex, determination
size 11, **139**, 140–3, 148, 158, 182, **186**
small vertebrates and mammals 180–1, 187–8, 191, 316–42; *see also* herpetofauna, bird, fish, *Microtus*
spatial patterning/orientation of 138–56, **182–3**, **185**
water transport of 138, 142–3, 147, 155, 164–5, 181–6, 188–9, 200, 216
    Voorhies group 182, **184**, 200
weathering, preservation and condition of 8, 14–15, 45, 62–3, 129, **148**, 150–3, 157, 176, 182, 187–91, 197, 215–17, 254, 286, 297–310, ***388–492***, 501
    conservation of 14–15, 297–310
Bordes, François 8, 237–38, **250**, 253
Bos primigenius 175, 176, 285, 500
bovid, *see* Bison
Bramford Road 5, **6**, 219
butchery 4, 9, 196–7, 259, 274, 301
    evidence of, *see* bone, modification by hominins/ Neanderthals

C

Canis
    C. arnensis 167
    C. familiaris 191
    C. lupus 133, 135, 148, **155**, 165, **167**, 184, 191, 203, 204–5, 283, ***328, 334, 399, 414, 446–7, 459, 477***
    C. (lupus) mosbachensis 167
carnivore 8, 91, 131, 134, **139**, **145, 147–51, 153**, 176, 179–80, 182–3, **185**, 191–2, 196–7, 199, 203, 255, 258, 285, 287, 289, 292, 294
    accumulations 8, 202, 283, **286**–7
    bone modification by, *see* bone, modification by animals
Cervus, cervidae, cervids ***437–9, 441–2, 469, 471***, 501, 503
Cervus elaphus 204, 326
Chaîne opératoire 8, 9, 219, 256–7, 501

Chelford interstadial 126
chert *21*, 23, 501; *see also* flint
Church Hole Cave 5, **6**, 204
Coelodonta 158, 173, 202, 321
C. antiquitatis 4, 7, 95, 129–31, 134, **139**, 147–**8, 151**, 166, 172–4, 177, **191**, 197, 202–5, 254, 288, 291, 294, **329, 389, 391, 412–13, 415, 417, 431, 441, 451, 454–5, 461, 463, 488**
    C. tologoijensis 172
Merck's rhinoceros, *see* Stephanorhinus
coleoptera 45–6, 75–**89**, 93–4, 188, 254, 284, 287, 291, 501–2
Condover 192–4, **211**, 213
Coygan Cave 5, **6**, 204, 252
Crayford 166, 253–4
Creswell Crags 204, 252, 261
    see also Pin Hole Cave
Crocuta
    C. crocuta 29, 131–2, 134, **159**–65, **169**, 182, 190–1, 197, 203, 205, 215, 283, ***349, 424, 436***
    C. sivalensis 169
Cromerian 169, 171, 176
cutmarks, *see* bone modification by hominins

D

Dansgaard-Oeschger events (D-O) xv, 17, **73**, 252, 284, 294–5, 501
débitage, *see* lithics
deer
    giant, *see* Megaloceros giganteus
    red, *see* Cervus elaphus
    reindeer, *see* Rangifer tarandus
Dent 214
desert, *see* biome
Devensian (and Weichselian; Last Glacial) 5, 73, 94, 125–6, 166, 169, 171, 173–5, 204, 209, 216, 252–3, 501
    deposits 103, 126
    Early 30, 169, 174, 176, 203
    fauna 203–4; *see also* fauna
    Late 5, 17, 30, 103, 167
    Middle 4, 6, 9, 94, 123, 126, 174, 190, 202–4, 216, 238, 252
Dicrostonyx torquatus 134

E

Electron Spin Resonance (ESR) 7, 203
scanning electron microscope (SEM) 67, 196, 268, 276

Elephantidae 192, 195–7, 199–201, 208–10, 212–14, 217, 258–9, 285, 504
    African elephant, *see* Loxodonta
    mammoth, *see* Mammuthus
Elsterian, *see* Anglian
Equus, equid 501, 504
    E. caballus 171, 501, 504
    E. ferus 131, **139**, 147–**8, 151**, 155, 165, **171–2**, 184, 192, 197, 199, **200**, 202–5, 208, 254, 283, 288, 294, **339–40, 453–4, 465–6**
    E. hydruntinus 204
Eurasia(n) 129, 131, 208, 284, 290, 295
    northern 129–33

F

Fennoscandia 109, 130–3, 204, 501
fauna, faunal 48, 52, 129, 203–5, 260, 283, 285–7, 289–90, 293–4
    arctic 33
    assemblage, *see* bone
    bioturbation, faunal mixing, trampling xv, 39, 40, 46–8, 52, 77, 128, 135–6, 138, 143, 150, 155, 225, 311–12; *see also* bone, modification by animals
    dating 202–5
    faunal change 176, 181, 203
    coleopteran, *see* coleoptera
    cold-stage 132–3, 174, 204–5
    conservation, *see* bone
    Devensian, *see* Devensian
    exploitation, *see* hunting
    faunal remains, bones, *see* bone
    insect, *see* coleoptera
    Last Cold Stage 205
    mammal(ian) 75, 92–3, 125, 132–4, 176, 195, 202–4, 284, 287, 291, 294
        marine mammal 291
        small mammal 32, 285
    material, *see* bone
    megafauna xv, 46, 94, 109, 129, 203, 225, 258, 291
        extinction of 70, 131
    microfauna, *see* microfauna
    molluscan, *see* mollusc
    Pin Hole, *see* Pin Hole
    Pleistocene 131
    remains, *see* bone
    temperate, interglacial 32, 203–4
    type 4, 6; *see also* Mammal Assemblage Zone (MAZ)
    vertebrate 95, 133, 204
fire xvi, 48–9, 53, 157, 260, 268, 282–3, 286, 290; *see also* hearth

fish 132, 165, 283, 285, ***316–42, 466, 476***
    bone/remains of 129, 133, 158, 180–1
    Cyprinidae 165, 180, ***319***
    Esox lucius/pike 133, 165, 180, ***316–42***
    fishing 291
    Gasterosteus aculeatus/ stickleback 4, 7, 133, 165, 180, ***316–42***
    Perca fluviatilis/perch 133, 165, 180, 316–42
    scales 180, 184
    shellfish 285
Fisherton Brick Pit 5–6
flake, *see* lithic, flake
Flandrian, *see* Holocene
flint 18, *21*, 23, 28, 31, **104, 112**, 157, 224, 227–8, 230, 243, 260, 262, 268, 282, 501, 503
    clasts 20, 23, 27, 68
    cobbles **54, 55, 56**
    gravel 33, **35**–6, 38–**40**, 42–4, *47*–8, 52, *55, 57*, 103, 120, 160, 287
    nodules 21, 32, 256
    pebbles **47**–9, 51–2, *57*, 311–12
    plaquette/tabular 242, 246
    use by hominins/Neanderthals 225, 227–8, 230, 287
    procurement, selection and transport 8–9, 157, 254–8, 287, 294
    quality 18, 32, 227, 287
    rage 247
    source and availability 8, 32, 196, 225, 227–8, 232, 254, 255, 259, 287, 294
    strategies of use 254–8
    tools/artefacts, *see* lithics
forest, *see* habitat
fox
    arctic, *see* Alopex lagopus
    red, *see* Vulpes vulpes
France 168, 197, 201, **211**, 253, 258, 276, 282
    northern 5, 237, 250, 252–3, 252, 294
    north-west 5
    southern 131
    south-west 129, 219, 240, 253–4
frog, *see* Rana spp.

G

Germany 73, 173–4, 176, 195–7, 200–1, 204, 209, 211, 214, 253, 258, 282, 288, 290
glacial 17, 75, 93–4, 100, 125
    cycle 31, 259
    deposits 18–**19**, 62, 93, 108, 227

interglacial, *see* interglacial
Late Glacial 108, 133, 200
Last Glacial Maximum, *see* Last Glacial Maximum
gnawing, *see* bone modification, gnawing
grassland, *see* habitat
Great Pan Farm 5–*6*, 242

H

habitat xv–xvi, 5, 8, 75, 77, 90–1, 93–4, 99–101, 103, 108–10, 126, 128, 132, 93–4, 288, 291, *295*, 504
  desert
    semi-desert 132–3
  forest 20, 130–3, 170, 284
    boreal, *see* biome, taiga
    rainforest 293
    steppe 91
  grassland 4, 7, 99–100, 103, 109, 111, 118–20, 124–8, 131, 133
    calcareous 53, 108, 110–11, 118–19, 124–5, ***287–8***
    damp/wet 90, 101, 108–9, 111, 118, 120, 128, 287
    dry 99, 102–8
    steppic 174, 254
  heath, heathland 91, 254, 287
  hilly, montane 100, 109, 285
    boreo-montane 93
  marsh, fen, swamp, wetland, bog xv, 18–*19*, 31, 90, 100–1, 109–11, 118–20, 123–4, 133, 195, 199, 283, 286–***8***
  meadow 90–1, 99
  Palearctic 133, 166
  steppe 9, 125, 132, 174, 203
    bison, *see* Bison priscus
    mammoth- 4, 7–8, 94, 129–30, 133, 203, 205, 258, 503
      -mammoth, *see* Mammuthus trogontherii
    -tundra 130–3, 170, 205
  taiga, boreal forest/woodland 131–2, 134, 203; *see also* forest
  tundra 73, 91, 94, 131–4, 203, 260
    steppe-, *see* steppe-tundra
    vole, *see* Microtus gregalis
  woodland *12*, 91, 125, ***127***, 131–3, 204
    boreal, *see* taiga
hammer, *see* lithics
handaxe xv, 3–5, 141, ***145–6, 149–52, 154–5***, 220–*1*, ***226–7***, 237, ***243–4, 246***, 251–61, ***263–7, 269***–70, 273, 284, 287, 292, 294
  bone 195–6
  manufacture 4, 157, 224, 228–8, 242–8, 254–5, 257
    cortex percentage 230–***4***, 243, ***245***
    débitage, debris 220, 247, 255–6, 501
    size distribution 223–4, 229
    finishing 140, 151, 228–9, 233–4, 242, 255–6
    perform ***145, 149–52, 154, 221, 226***, 248, 256, ***265***
    reduction 223, 229–30, 232–6, 244, 251, 254
    roughout 3, 220–*1*, ***228***–9, 235, 237, 248, 255, 257
    scar count 228–9, ***231***–5, 242, ***245***
    scar pattern 228, ***231***–5
    shaping (flake) ***145–7, 149–52, 154–5, 226***, 228–9, 242, 256
    thinning 228–9, 234, 242, ***251***, 255–6, ***264–6***, 270
  modification ***225***, 227–8, ***231***, 233–4, 236, 251, 256–7
    reworking, re-cycling 202, ***225***, 237, 245–7, 255, 256
    resharpening 202, 245, 247, 256, 259
    tranchet flake 228, ***245, 247***, 504
  preservation and condition 222–*3*
    broken, fragments xv, ***145***–*6, 149–50, 154–5, 225–6, 228***–9, ***231***, 237, 244–7, 254, 256–8
    fresh, unrolled 4, 202, 220, 222–*3*, 225, 227–9, 234–5, 237, ***238***
    rolled 220, 222–3, ***228***, 234–5, ***238***
  raw material, *see* flint
  refit, *see* refit
  shape, form 157, ***238, 240–2***, 253
    bout coupé xv, 3–5, 8, 157, ***237***–8, 252–3, 267, ***288***, 500
    cleaver ***238–9***
    cordate 3, 501
    sub-cordate ***238***
    cordiform xv, 220, ***237–8***, 246, 252–3
    ovate, ovoid xv, 3, 220, ***238–9***, 241–2, 244, 246, 253, 503
    point ***238–9***, 241–2
    Roe type ***239***–42
    triangular 252
    subtriangular xv, 3, 220, 238
    Wymer type 238–*9*
  size 221, 240, 247–8
  spatial arrangement 138–56, 224–7, 256
    transport by water 138, 142–3, 155, 221
  use, function 4, 219, 227, 238, 243–4, 246–8, 249, 251, 254, 256–9
    curation 247, 257, 258, 260
    damage 197, 238, 244, 247, 256
    wear, microwear xv, 242, 244, 246–7, 260–74
hare, *see* Lepus
hearth 8, 259, 286, 288, 290; *see also* fire
Heinrich event 285, 295, 502
herpetofauna 159, 165, 180–1, 214–16, 316–42, 502
Holocene (and Flandrian) 14, 19, 21, 28–9, 31–2, 67, 70–3, 95, 108, 130, 132–3, 502–3
Holsteinian, *see* Hoxnian
hominin 501–3; *see also* Homo neanderthalensis
Homo
  H. erectus 284
  H. floresiensis 284
  H. heidelbergensis 289
  H. neanderthalensis xv–xvi, 4–5, 7, 17, 74–5, 95, 131, 135, 151, 156–7, 165, 182, 184, 199–200, 204, 221–2, 225, 254–5, 258–9, 283–7, 289–96, 502–3
    group(s) 5, 7, 75, 288–9, 290, 294
    activities 25, 32, 45–6, 48, 53, 65, 143, 184
    behaviour xv, 4, 9, 135, 138, 143, 153, 156, 259
    diet 195–7, 285–7, 289–90
    hunting/exploitation of/ interaction with animals, *see* hunting
    mobility patterns, *see* mobility
    occupation, settlement, *see* settlement
    site use 9, 44, 290
  H. sapiens xvi, 25, 91, 132, 192, 201, 214, 257, 260, 284–6, 290–6, 502–3
horse, *see* Equus
Hot Springs, South Dakota 201, 214
Hoxnian (and Holsteinian) 167–9
human, *see* Homo sapiens
hunter-gatherers 195, 291–3
hunting, faunal exploitation
  by animals 89, 131–2
  by hominins/Neanderthals 8, 157, 192, 195–203, 205, 214–15, 252, 255, 258–61, 284, 285, 286, 287, 289, 290, 295, 296; *see also* bone, modification by hominins/Neanderthals; *Mammuthus*, hominin interaction with
hyaena, *see* Crocuta crocuta
Hyaena Den 5–*6*, 73, 204

I

Iberia 130, 292; *see also* Spain
ibex, *see* Capra
ice cores 17, *73*, 101, 204, 501
Ilford 171, **209**
insect 4, 13, 14, 61, 75–7, 89, 92, 94–5, 101, 132–3, 184, 190, 302
  fossil 59, 61, 73, 75, 77
interglacial 53, 75, 100–1, 131–2, 169, 171, 174, 200, 203–4, 252, 258, 502
  Last Interglacial, *see* Ipswichian
interstadial 17, 73, 94, 101, 175, 200, 203, 205, 284, 294, 501–2; *see also* Dansgaard-Oeschger events
Ipswichian 5, 30, 32, *73*, 131, 169, 502, 504
Ireland 130–1, 133
  Northern, *see* Northern Ireland
isotope analysis *55*, 71, 285–6, 291, 502
  carbon isotope ratio analysis 53–63, 216–19
  oxygen
    istotope ratio analysis 53–63, 216–19
    marine oxygen isotope record 9, 17, 203, 502
    stage, *see* Marine Isotope Stage (MIS)
  nitrogen isotope ratio analysis 53–63, 216–19
Italy 130–1, 196, 219, 259–60, 285

J

Japan **66**, 92

K

Kent's Cavern 5–*6*, 191, 204, 214, 252, 261, 285

L

La Borde 201, 253, 259
lagomorph 132, *286*, 502; *see also* Lepus sp.
La Cotte de St. Brelade 197–8, 213, 259, 288

Last Glacial, *see* Devensian
Last Glacial Maximum (LGM) 30, 131–2, 502–3; *see also* Marine Isotope Stage, MIS 2
Lea Valley **209**, **210**
leafpoints, *see* lithics
Lehringen 197, 258–9, 286
lemming, *see Dicrostonyx torquatus*
Lepus sp. 203, 285, 502; *see also* lagomorph
Levallois 3–5, 8, 220, 235, 252–5, 260, 502–3
  core 3, 220, 222, 234, 254, 264
Lillington 173–4
limacid slugs 62, 97, 100
lithics, stone tools xv, 8–9, 11, 15, 31, **151**, 165, 186, 196–7, 219–74, 285, 287, 290–1, 302, 501, 503–4
  blank 232, 234, 236, 242–3, 245, 254–7, 259
  core **145–6**, **150–1**, 219–**21**, 226, **228**–9, 234–**6**, 247, 254–5, 256–60, 264, 501, 504
  Prepared Core Technology 253, 254, 284
  flake 25, 28, 219, **221**, 224, 228–37, 245, 247, 249–51, 256, 259, 261, **263–7**, 268, 270, 272, 274, 501
    refit, conjoin *see* refit, lithic
    soft/hard hammer, *see* lithic, hammer
  handaxe, *see* handaxe
  tools xv, 151, 220–**1**, 225, 237, **250**
    tranchet, *see* handaxe
    unretouched 141, **145**, **149–52**, **154**, 220, **226**, 261, 270–1, 273
  hachoir **145**, **151**, **226**, 249, **250**, 251, 502
  hammer 280
    hard 228–**32**, **234**, **238**, 246–8, 251, 255–6
    soft 228–**32**, **234**, 236, 248, 255
    stone 221, 251, 501
  handaxe, *see* handaxe
  leafpoints 253, 502
  Levallois, *see* Levallois
  Mousterian, *see* Mousterian
  notch 8, **145**, **150**–2, 220, 225–**6**, **228**, 247, 249, **250**–1, **263–7**, **269**, 274
  raw material, *see flint*
  scraper 8, **145–6**, **149–52**, **154**, 200, **221**, **226**, **228**, 237, 247, **249**, 253, 255–7, **263–6**, **269**
    retouch 242, 245, 24–**48**, **250–1**, 255
  spear-point, stone-tipped spear 157, 270, 285

technology, tradition 284
Little Cressingham 5–**6**, 252
Little Paxton 5–**6**, 252
lion, *see Panthera leo*
Lough Neagh 99, 100
Lord, John 3, 4, 157, 256
Loxodonta africana 208, 217; *see also* Elephantidae

M

Maastricht-Belvédèr 253–4, 288
mammal assemblage zone (MAZ) 503
  Banwell Bone Cave, *see* Banwell Bone Cave
  Pin Hole, *see* Pin Hole
mammoth
  Mammuthus sp., *see mammuthus*
  -steppe, *see* habitat, mammoth-steppe
Mammuthus
  in art 129
  M. meridionalis 171
  M. primigenius/woolly mammoth xv, 4, 7, 75, 109, 126, 129, 130–2, 134, 157–8, **161**–**4**, 197–8, 203–5, 254, 288, 290–1, 294
    bone, skeletal remains xv, 1, 4, **15**, 45, 63, 70, 75, 95, **139**, 141, **145–50**, **152**, **154–5**, 157, **159–60**, 166, 169–71, 176–81, **183–6**, **189–90**, 196–7, 199–214, 254, 283, 286, 299–**300**, 302, 304–8, **316–42**, **388–492**
    bone chemistry 216–19
    working of 260
    channel, *see* Association B
    hominin interaction with 157, 195–202, 213–14, 254–5, 258–61, 285–6, 295–6
    tusk 3–4, 10, 14–15, 129, **136**, 141, 144, 157–60, 169, 177, **179**, 180–1, 196, 213–14, **217**–**18**, **286**, 295, **298**–301, **316–42**, **389–492**
  M. rumanus 171
  M. trogontherii 130, 171, 208–9, 213
Marine Isotope Stage 17, **73**, 502
  MIS 1, *see* Holocene
  MIS 2 30–1, **73**, 130, 502–3; *see also* Allerød, Last Glacial Maximum
  MIS 3 xv, 17, 30–1, 72–4, 130, 284–5, 287–9, 291, 294–6, 503

MIS 4 xv–xvi, 17, 30, 73–4, 130, 252, 290–1, 294–5, 503
MIS 5 30, **73**
MIS 5d **73**, 130, 502
MIS 5e, *see* Ipswichian
MIS 6, 7, 8, 9, 10 *see* Wolstonian
MIS 11, *see* Hoxnian
MIS 12, *see* Anglian
Mauran 201, 253, 259
MCR, *see* mutual climatic range
megafauna, *see* fauna
Megaloceros giganteus 204–5
Micoquian 246, 253, 503
microfauna 13–14
microfossil 57, 110
microwear, *see* lithics
Microtus sp., Microtinae 165, 166, 180–1, 316–42, 503
  M. gregalis 132, 134, 165, 166, **167**, 191, 330
  M. gregaloides 166
  M. oeconomicus 203
mobility 8, 9, 143, 251, 255, 258–9, 261, 286–8, 294
mollusca 4, 13–14, 59, 62–3, 71, 75–6, **78–89**, **95**–101, 124, 180–1, **316–19**
  shell 59, 71–2, 76, 500
moose, *see Alces alces*
Mosbach 176, 214
Mousterian technology xv, 1, 5, 205, 235, 252–4, **295**, 501–3
  biface, *see* handaxe, Mousterian
  site 282, 205
  of Acheulean tradition (MTA) 4–5, 252, 501
Mustela sp. 203

N

Natural History Museum 158, 181
Neanderthal, *see Homo neanderthalensis*
Neolithic 32, 294
Neumark-Gröbern 197, 259
Northern Ireland 99–100
Norway 93, 131
notch, *see* lithics, notch

O

Oldbury Rock Shelter 5–**6**, 219, 242
optically stimulated luminescence (OSL) dating xv, 17, 30–1, 44, **68**–74, 205, 252, 284, 503
ostracod 58–9

P

Palaeoloxodon antiquus/Elephas (Palaeoloxodon) antiquus 192

Panthera leo 132, 134, 203, 205
pathology, *see Mammuthus primigenius*, pathology
patination, *see* lithics, condition/weathering
Paviland Cave 290
Picken's Hole 5–**6**, 204
pike, *see Esox lucius*
Pin Hole
  cave 5–**6**, 73–4, 203–4
  mammal assemblage zone/-type fauna 4, **6**–7, 203
  plants xv, 53, 59, 287–91, 302, 311–12, 502–3
    fibre 268, 282
    macrofossils 4, 13–14, 29, **47**, 48, **49**, **51**, 52, 70, 75, 95, 124, 126–9, 133
polecat, *see Mustela putorius*
pollen 7, 14, 57, 59, 70, 75, 101–26, 133, 158, 282, 502–3; *see also* plant
  data 45–6, 73, 284, 286, 291
Pontnewydd Cave 166
Purfleet 168, 254

Q

quartz 19, **21**, 23, 68, 251, 277–**8**, 279–80, 282
  sand 48–9, 51–2, 311–12
quartzite 19, **21**, 23, 221, 251, 259

R

radiocarbon dating 7, 14, 17, 28–31, 70, 72–3, 94–5, 100, 130, 203–5, 252, 284–5, 501, 504
  AMS 7, **70**, 72, 73
Rana spp. 4, 133, 165, 214–16, 388
Rangifer tarandus 7, 95, 130–4, **139**, 166, 174, 201–5, 254, 260, 283–4, 288, 290, 294, **326**, **332**, **336**, **341**, **359**, **388–9**, **393**, **396–8**, **404**, **406–7**, **418–19**, **421–2**, **425–8**, **430–2**, **434**, **436–7**, **440**, **444**, **449–53**, **457**, **462–4**, **468–9**, **472–5**, **478–80**, **488**
  antler 4, 130, 134, 141, 143, 148, **155**, **159**, **174**, 179, 203, **217**, 289, 300, 302, 303, 306, **388**, **393**, **406–7**, **418**, **419**, **428**, **440**, **450**, **452–3**, **457**, **462–4**, **469**, **471–5**, **478**, **488**
  refits, *see* refits, antler
  bone and tooth 146, **148**, **151**, 174–5, 177, 179, 189, **190–1**, **198–9**, 203, 254, 260

raw material, *see* flint
refitting 44, 138, 143, 152–3, *155*–6, 164, 504
   antler 143, 153
   bone, antler 44–5, 138, 153, *155*, 184–*5*, *389*, *397–401*, *404–5*, *417*, *419–22*, *425*, *428*, *433–5*, *439*, *441–2*, *444*, *446–50*, *456*, *463*, *466–7*, *470*, *472*, *480–1*, *483–4*, *487*
   distance 138, 143, *155*, 184, *225*
   handaxe *225*, 244, 248
   lithic 44, 152–3, *155*, 184, 220–1, 223, *225*–7, 229, 240, 247, 251, 254–6
reindeer, *see Rangifer tarandus*
rhinoceros 504
   Hole (cave) 5, *6*
   African white, *see Ceratotherium simum*
   woolly, *see Coelodonta antiquitatis* 4, 7
   see also Stephanorhinus hemitoechus
Robin Hood's Cave 5–*6*, 73–4, 204
rodent xv, 132, 164, 166, ***286***
   gnawing, *see* bone modification/gnawing
roe deer, *see Capreolus capreolus*
Romania 173, 285
Russia 93, *211*, 212–14
   Siberia 92–4, 100, 129–33, 192, 202, 212–13

S

Saalian, *see* Wolstonian
Salzgitter Lebenstedt 195, 201, 253, 260, 282

Scandinavia 99, 103, 108, 123, 125, 128, 133, 216
Schöningen 288, 290
Sciurus sp. 166
scraper, *see* lithics, scraper
sea
   Atlantic 100–1, 203
   journey 292
   -level 5, 17, 252
   North *16*, 134, 252, 288, 289
season, seasonal, seasonality 7, 125, 134, 201–2, 216, 259–60, 283, 286–91, 293–94; *see also* temperature
   migration 201
   rainfall, precipitation 7, 43, 136, 283
   resources 131, 132, 134, 283, 286–7, 288–9, 293
   water level 99, 101, 111, 120, 124, 125, 126, 221–2
Seclin 253
settlement, occupation 4, 5, 7, 8–9, 73–4, 219, 251–2, 288–91, 294
Sevsk 213–14
sex(es) 289, 294
   determination 158, 174–5, 200, 202, 205, *211*, 213–15
   female 131, 201–2, *211*–15, 284, 286, 289, *292*–4, 296
   male 131, 134, 157, 192, 201–2, *211*–15, 284, *292*–6
Siberia, *see* Russia
skeletal element, skeleton, *see* bone
Spain 131, 197, 219, 259, 295; *see also* Iberia
spear 195, 197, 258–9, 270, 285–6

point, *see* lithic
thrower 286, 291
Spermophilus sp. 132–4, 165–*6*, 181
   S. parryi 133
   S. undulates 133
squirrel, *see Spermophilus*
Star Carr 282
Stephanorhinus sp.
   S. hemitoechus 204
   S. kirchbergensis (Merck's rhinoceros) 201
steppe, *see* habitat

T

taiga, *see* habitat
temperature xv, 58, 75, 94, 125–6, 132, 134, 218, 284, 291, ***295***
   change 187, 262, 268
   cool, cold, low 53, 73, 132, 268, 283, 291, 294
   Effective Temperature (ET) 291–2
   summer 7, 75, 187, 254, 291
   warm, hot, high 73, 94, 100, 126, 218, 252, 262, 291, 297
   winter 7, 75, 94, 109, 126, 187, 192, 254, 291, ***295***
toad, *see Anura* sp.
Torralba 197, 258, 285
tranchet flake, *see* handaxe
tundra, *see* habitat

U

Uphill Quarry Cave 8 5–*6*
Upton Warren
   interstadial 73, 101, 126, 216, 284

site xv, 73, 75, 94–5, 101, 126, 216, 284–5
Uranium series dating 7, 203
Ursus
   U. arctos 132, 134, 148, 165, ***168***, 191, 203, 205, ***388***, ***415***, ***421***, ***426***, ***431***, ***446***, ***471***, ***479***
   U. spelaeus 168–9, 205

V

Villafranchian 167, 169
Vogelherd Cave 205, 282
vole, *see Microtus*
Vulpes vulpes 132, 134, 148, ***159–60***, 165, 167, 205, ***478***

W

weathering, *see* bone
Westbury-sub-Mendip 166–7, 169, 174, 176
West Runton 166, 168, 171
wisent, *see Bison bonasus*
Wolstonian 30, 73, 171, 173–4, 253, 504
Wookey Hole, *see* Hyaena Den
Würm, *see* Devensian
Wymer, John 3, 238, ***239***